Editor in Chief	**EDWARD HUMPHREY**
Executive Editor	**JAMES E. CHURCHILL, JR.**
Senior Editor	**HALLBERG HALLMUNDSSON**
Art Director	**FRANKLIN N. SAYLES**
Editors	**JAMES W. CARROLL**
	DONALD R. YOUNG
Special Editor, Mexico and Latin America	**PEDRO LÓPEZ CORTEZO**
Indexer	**VITRUDE DeSPAIN**
Proofreader	**CHARLES PAUL MAY**
Layout Artist	**ROBERT REDDY**
Production Supervisor	**HARRIET L. SMITH**
Picture Researchers	**NATALIE GOLDSTEIN**
	MARGARET L. SKAGGS
Editorial Assistants	**NILSA JIMENEZ**
	JEAN KIRSHNER

GROLIER INCORPORATED

HOWARD B. GRAHAM
Senior Vice-President, Publishing

WALLACE S. MURRAY
Vice-President and Editorial Director

CONTENTS

THE ALPHABETICAL SECTION

Articles listed below are in the Review of the Year section, which begins on page 67, and are grouped in broad subject categories. Separate entries on the continents, the major nations of the world, U. S. states, Canadian provinces, and chief cities will be found under their own alphabetically arranged headings.

ECONOMICS AND INDUSTRY

GOVERNMENT, HUMAN WELFARE, LAW, AND POLITICS

HUMANITIES, ARTS, AND HOBBIES

SCIENCE AND TECHNOLOGY

MISCELLANEOUS

SPECIAL REPORTS

"No one could have ever conceived that the president of the biggest Arab state, which bears the heaviest burden and the main responsibility pertaining to the cause of war and peace in the Middle East, should declare his readiness to go to the land of the adversary while we were still in a state of war."

"Yet today I tell you, and I declare it to the whole world, that we accept to live with you in permanent peace based on justice. We do not want to encircle you or be encircled...."

"I have announced on more than one occasion that Israel has become a fait accompli, recognized by the world, and that the two superpowers have undertaken the responsibility for its security.... We really and truly welcome you to live among us in peace and security."

"In all sincerity I tell you that there can be no peace without the Palestinians. It is a grave error of unpredictable consequences to overlook or brush aside this cause."

"Ring the bells for your sons. Tell them that those wars were the last of wars and the end of sorrows. Tell them that we are entering upon a new beginning, a new life...."

ANWAR EL-SADAT, PRESIDENT OF EGYPT

"The time of the flight between Cairo and Jerusalem is short. But the distance between them was, until yesterday, quite large. President Sadat passed this great distance with courage, heartfelt courage. We, the Jews, know how to appreciate this courage...."

"We do not believe in might. We believe in right—only in right. And, therefore, our hope ... is for peace."

"Let us continue a dialogue and negotiations, Mr. President, on a treaty of peace...."

"Israel does not wish to rule and does not want to disturb or divide."

"We wish to establish normal relations between us."

"Let us develop our countries. Let us abolish poverty ... and let the world not call us developing countries."

"And also the legitimate spokesmen of the Arabs of Israel, I invite them to come and meet with us for discussions on our joint policies, on justice, ... on joint mutual respect."

"Everything is given to negotiation. No side can say the reverse."

"And let us conduct the negotiations as equals. There are no victors, there are no losers."

MENAHEM BEGIN, PRIME MINISTER OF ISRAEL

WILLIAM KAREL/SYGMA

The diplomatic coup of the year was scored jointly by President Anwar el-Sadat of Egypt (*center*) and Prime Minister Menahem Begin of Israel (*left*), when the former visited Jerusalem and addressed the Israeli Knesset. Prime Minister Begin responded to the president's address. It was a truly historic moment.

CHRONOLOGY 1977

JANUARY

DEATH PENALTY REVIVED IN U.S.

CARTER, MONDALE INAUGURATED

VIETNAM DRAFT EVADERS PARDONED

S	M	T	W	T	F	S
						1
2	3	4	5	6	7	8
9	10	11	12	13	14	15
16	17	18	19	20	21	22
23	24	25	26	27	28	29
30	31					

UPI

Jimmy Carter, in his first official act as president of the United States, signs document nominating the "following named persons to the positions indicated:"

Cyrus Vance, of New York, to be secretary of state.

W. Michael Blumenthal, of Michigan, to be secretary of the treasury.

Harold Brown, of California, to be secretary of defense.

Griffin B. Bell, of Georgia, to be attorney general.

Cecil D. Andrus, of Idaho, to be secretary of the interior.

Bob S. Bergland, of Minnesota, to be secretary of agriculture.

Juanita M. Kreps, of North Carolina, to be secretary of commerce.

Ray Marshall, of Texas, to be secretary of labor.

Joseph A. Califano, Jr., of the District of Columbia, to be secretary of health, education, and welfare.

Patricia Roberts Harris, of the District of Columbia, to be secretary of housing and urban development.

Brockman Adams, of Washington, to be secretary of transportation.

3 The International Monetary Fund gives final approval for a $3,900,000,000 loan to Great Britain.

4 The first session of the 95th Congress convenes; Sen. Robert C. Byrd (D-W. Va.) and Sen. Howard H. Baker, Jr. (R-Tenn.) are chosen as Senate majority and minority leaders respectively.

9 The Oakland Raiders win the National Football League Super Bowl game, defeating the Minnesota Vikings, 32–14.

11 A French court in Paris releases Abu Daoud, a Palestinian militant arrested by police on suspicion of having plotted the terror attack at the 1972 Summer Olympics in Munich. The action is criticized in Israel, West Germany, and other Western nations.

12 U. S. President Gerald Ford delivers his third State of the Union message.

14 Lord Avon (Sir Anthony Eden), former prime minister of Great Britain, dies at the age of 79. ● Former Sen. William E. Brock 3d is elected chairman of the Republican National Committee.

17 Gary Mark Gilmore, 36-year-old convicted murderer, is executed by a firing squad at Utah State Prison. The action ends a 10-year moratorium on capital punishment in the United States.

18 India's Prime Minister Indira Gandhi announces that parliamentary elections will be held in March, the first such elections since a state of emergency was declared in June 1975.

20 Jimmy Carter is sworn in as the 39th president of the United States; Walter F. Mondale takes the oath as vice president.

21 President Carter grants an unconditional pardon to almost all military draft evaders of the Vietnam war era. ● Kenneth M. Curtis, former governor of Maine, is elected chairman of the Democratic National Committee.

24 Rhodesia's Prime Minister Ian Smith rejects a British proposal to reconvene the Geneva Conference on Rhodesia and move toward black majority rule in Rhodesia.

28 As the United States is experiencing an unusually severe winter, a major blizzard begins to sweep across the Midwestern section of the nation. ● Following a week of political violence in which several persons are killed in Spain, Prime Minister Adolfo Suarez issues a decree suspending for 30 days the constitutional protection against unreasonable searches and the right of a suspect to be charged within 72 hours of arrest.

FEBRUARY

S	M	T	W	T	F	S
		1	2	3	4	5
6	7	8	9	10	11	12
13	14	15	16	17	18	19
20	21	22	23	24	25	26
27	28					

U.S. ENACTS EMERGENCY GAS BILL

MISSIONARIES SHOT IN RHODESIA

CANADA'S TRUDEAU VISITS U.S.

1 Concluding a ten-day tour of Western Europe and Japan, Vice President Mondale reports that U.S. relations with its "friends are on the finest possible, most hopeful basis."

2 President Carter delivers his first report to the nation. ● President Carter signs the emergency natural gas bill, authorizing the relocation of natural gas supplies from areas of surplus to communities experiencing shortages.

3 Factional fighting breaks out among members of Ethiopia's ruling military council. Chief of State, Brig. Gen. Tafari Banti, and six other members of the council are reported killed.

6 In Rhodesia, seven white Roman Catholic missionaries are shot to death by black nationalist guerrillas 37 miles (59 km) northwest of Salisbury.

9 Spain and the Soviet Union announce the resumption of diplomatic relations, suspended since the end of the Spanish Civil War. ● Queen Alia of Jordan is killed in the crash of a military helicopter in southern Jordan.

10 In a nationwide plebiscite in Egypt, President Anwar Sadat's decree limiting national political activity is approved.

14 President Carter and Mexico's President José López Portillo confer at the White House.

15 In Denmark, the Social Democrats, who have governed as a minority since January 1975, gain 12 seats in parliamentary elections. ● A state of emergency imposed in 1971 ends in Sri Lanka.

18 *The Washington Post* publishes a report stating that the U. S. Central Intelligence Agency has made secret annual payments to Jordan's King Hussein since 1957.

21 Britain's Prime Minister James Callaghan names David Owen to succeed the late Anthony Crosland as foreign secretary. ● U.S. Secretary of State Cyrus Vance completes a tour of the Middle East.

22 In a speech to a joint session of the U. S. Congress, Canada's Prime Minister Pierre Elliott Trudeau declares that Canada may have to revise some aspects of its constitution "so that the Canadian federation can be seen by six and a half million French-speaking Canadians to be the strongest bulwark against submersion by some 220 million English-speaking North Americans."

24 Foreign ministers of the five-nation Association of Southeast Asian Nations (ASEAN) sign an agreement to increase mutual trade.

25 Following 18 days in orbit, Soviet spacecraft Soyuz 24, with Col. Viktor V. Gorbatko and Lt. Col. Yuri Glazkov aboard, lands safely in Soviet Central Asia.

UPI

Concluding a ten-day tour of Western Europe and Japan, February 1, Walter Mondale, the new U. S. vice president, meets with Takeo Fukuda at the prime minister's official residence in Tokyo.

MARCH

CARTER EMPHASIZES HUMAN RIGHTS

DESAI SUCCEEDS GANDHI IN INDIA

TWO 747s COLLIDE IN CANARIES

S	M	T	W	T	F	S
		1	2	3	4	5
6	7	8	9	10	11	12
13	14	15	16	17	18	19
20	21	22	23	24	25	26
27	28	29	30	31		

1 In Uganda, President Idi Amin drops his demand that the more than 200 Americans in Uganda meet with him before leaving the country.

4 A devastating earthquake strikes Rumania. ● The foreign ministers of Thailand and Malaysia sign a joint border agreement.

7 As delegates from 59 nations attend opening of the Arab-African conference in Cairo, Saudi Arabia announces the allocation of $1,000,000,000 for assistance to black Africa. ● The ruling Pakistan People's Party wins a heavy majority in parliamentary elections.

9 The U.S. Senate confirms the appointment of Paul C. Warnke as the nation's chief arms negotiator. ● Adm. Stansfield Turner is sworn in as director of the Central Intelligence Agency. ● President Carter announces the lifting of all travel bans on Americans to Cuba, Vietnam, North Korea, and Cambodia effective March 18.

11 In Washington, D. C., 134 hostages held for nearly two days by a small group of Hanafi Muslim gunmen are released unharmed; the gunmen are arrested. ● A U.S. State Department report criticizing Brazil's alleged violations of human rights leads Brazil to cancel its 25-year-old military assistance agreement with the United States.

14 The United Nations Conference on Water opens in Mar del Plata, Argentina.

15 The United States announces that it has approved a request from Zaire for military equipment to help counteract invading forces from Angola.

16 Kemal Jumblat, a Muslim leader in Lebanon, is assassinated in Beirut.

17 In an address to the United Nations, President Carter states that "there is much that can be done to strengthen" the organization's human rights machinery.

23 President Carter receives a report from a special commission he sent to Vietnam and Laos to discuss Americans missing since the Indochina War.

24 Morarji R. Desai, head of India's Janata Party, is sworn in as the nation's fourth prime minister. (Earlier, Prime Minister Gandhi had resigned following the defeat of her Congress Party in national elections.)

27 More than 570 persons are killed as two Boeing 747 jets collide and burst into flames on an airport runway in the Canary Islands.

30 As U.S. Secretary of State Vance meets with Soviet Party Secretary Brezhnev for a third consecutive day, the USSR rejects U.S. arms limitation proposals.

31 The Soviet Union and Mozambique sign a treaty of friendship.

PHOTOS UPI

As a result of March 16–20 parliamentary elections in India, Morarji R. Desai (*right*) succeeded Indira Gandhi as prime minister.

APRIL

S	M	T	W	T	F	S
					1	2
3	4	5	6	7	8	9
10	11	12	13	14	15	16
17	18	19	20	21	22	23
24	25	26	27	28	29	30

CASTRO ENDS AFRICAN TOUR

ISRAEL'S RABIN RESIGNS

U.S. OUTLINES NEW ENERGY PLAN

1 Brazil's President Ernesto Geisel dissolves Congress for an indefinite period after the legislative opposition blocked passage of a judicial reform bill.

2 Cuba's President Fidel Castro ends a month-long tour of Africa.

3 Col. Joachim Yombi Opango is named president of the Congo, succeeding Marien Ngouabi who was assassinated March 18.

4 At the White House, President Carter discusses the Arab-Israeli dispute with Egypt's President Sadat. ● President Carter names Esther Peterson as special assistant to the president for consumer affairs.

5 Los Angeles Mayor Thomas Bradley is elected to a second term.

6 President Carter signs into law a government reorganization bill.

8 Israel's Prime Minister Rabin resigns as the ruling Labor Party's candidate for a second term. (Earlier, Israel's newspapers had charged that Rabin and his wife had lied about the amount of money they illegally kept in U. S. banks.)

9 The Communist Party is legalized in Spain.

10 Tom Watson wins the Master's golf tournament.

12 In Lebanon, heavy fighting that had broken out between Christian militiamen and a combined force of Palestinian guerrillas and Lebanese Muslims virtually ceases.

15 At a news conference, President Carter outlines his administration's program to reduce inflation to about 4% by the end of 1979.

17 In Belgium's parliamentary elections, the Christian Social Party of Prime Minister Leo Tindemans scores significant gains.

19 The U. S. Supreme Court rules that the Constitution does not prohibit the spanking of school-children by teachers or other school officials.

20 President Carter outlines a national energy policy, designed to discourage excessive consumption.

21 Following weeks of political rioting in Pakistan, Prime Minister Zulfikar Ali Bhutto assumes emergency powers and imposes martial law in the cities of Karachi, Lahore, and Hyderabad. ● Gen. Ziaur Rahman becomes the fifth president of Bangladesh following the resignation of Abu Sadat Mohammed Sayem due to ill health.

22 A pipe on an oil well in the North Sea blows out causing a major oil slick.

28 The United States and Cuba sign two fishing agreements.

UPI

Leonid Brezhnev greets Fidel Castro as the Cuban president arrives in Moscow April 4 to brief Soviet leaders on his tour of Africa.

MAY

S	M	T	W	T	F	S
1	2	3	4	5	6	7
8	9	10	11	12	13	14
15	16	17	18	19	20	21
22	23	24	25	26	27	28
29	30	31				

U.S., VIETNAM TALKS BEGIN

WESTERN LEADERS MEET IN LONDON

ISRAEL'S LABOR PARTY DEFEATED

1 A May Day rally in Istanbul, Turkey, turns into a gun battle between ultraleftists and police and trade unionists. ● It is disclosed in Washington that negotiations to settle financial claims between China and the United States have been occurring for the last several weeks.

3 In Paris, the United States and Vietnam open formal discussions "looking toward normalizing relations."

4 During the first of a series of televised conversations between Richard Nixon and interviewer David Frost, the former president denies that he committed any crime in connection with Watergate but admits that he "let the American people down."

5 President Carter arrives in London for an economic summit conference with the leaders of five Western nations and Japan.

6 The U. S. Department of Labor announces that the nation's unemployment rate fell to 7% in April—the lowest level since November 1974. ● Ethiopia and the Soviet Union sign a protocol on economic and technical cooperation and a declaration of friendship.

9 Syria's President Hafez al-Assad and President Carter discuss the Middle East in Geneva.

11 Peter Jay, 40-year-old British journalist and son-in-law of Prime Minister Callaghan, is named British ambassador to Washington.

15 In Finland, Kalevi Sorsa and a new coalition government take the oath of office.

17 Israel's Labor Party is defeated in national elections by the Likud, led by Menahem Begin.

21 Maj. Gen. John K. Singlaub, who as chief of staff of U. S. forces in South Korea publicly criticized President Carter's plan to withdraw U. S. troops from South Korea, is ordered home for reassignment.

23 President Carter signs into law the Tax Reduction and Simplification Bill of 1977. ● Robert A. Frosch, 49-year-old physicist-oceanographer, is nominated as administrator of the National Aeronautics and Space Administration.

26 Andrew J. Young, U. S. ambassador to the UN, returns to Washington after a headline-making trip to Africa and Britain.

27 Canada's Prime Minister Trudeau and his wife, Margaret, announce that they have separated.

28 At least 160 persons are killed in a nightclub fire in Southgate, Ky.

29 A. J. Foyt wins the Indianapolis 500.

UPI

Israel's Likud Party leader Menahem Begin, who won an upset victory in May 17 elections, returns the applause of his supporters.

JUNE

S	M	T	W	T	F	S
			1	2	3	4
5	6	7	8	9	10	11
12	13	14	15	16	17	18
19	20	21	22	23	24	25
26	27	28	29	30		

SEATTLE SLEW WINS TRIPLE CROWN

ELECTIONS HELD IN SPAIN

BREZHNEV BECOMES PRESIDENT

3 The Conference on International Economic Co-operation (the so-called North-South talks of rich and poor nations) ends inconclusively in Paris.

4 The Soviet Union publishes the draft of a new constitution.

5 In the Seychelles, the government of President James R. M. Mancham is overthrown in a coup led by leftist Prime Minister F. Albert René. ● The Portland Trail Blazers win the National Basketball Association championships. ● In general elections in Turkey, the party of former Prime Minister Bulent Ecevit wins 213 out of a possible 450 parliamentary seats.

7 The 25th anniversary of the reign of Queen Elizabeth II is officially celebrated in London.

11 The Dutch armed forces storm a hijacked train and a school to release 55 hostages held by South Moluccan guerrillas since May 23. Two hostages and six kidnappers are killed in the raid. (The Moluccans want the Dutch government to press Indonesia to give independence to their homeland.) ● Seattle Slew captures the Belmont Stakes and becomes the tenth horse to win racing's Triple Crown.

12 U. S. First Lady Rosalynn Carter returns to Washington following a 13-day, 7-nation tour of the Caribbean and Latin America.

13 James Earl Ray, convicted murderer of Dr. Martin Luther King, Jr., is captured in eastern Tennessee 54 hours after he escaped from a maximum-security prison.

15 Approximately 80% of Spain's electorate vote in the nation's first free elections since 1936; the rightist coalition of Prime Minister Adolfo Suárez gains a clear-cut victory.

16 Leonid Brezhnev is given the additional post of chairman of the presidium of the Supreme Soviet (president). ● In elections in Ireland, the Fianna Fail Party defeats the ruling coalition government of the Fine Gael and Labor parties.

21 Menahem Begin becomes the sixth prime minister of Israel.

27 The former French Territory of the Afars and the Issas becomes the independent Republic of Djibouti.

30 President Carter announces that the B-1 strategic bomber is "a very expensive weapons system basically conceived in the absence of the cruise missile factor (and) is not necessary." ● The UN Security Council votes to ask UN members to give "material" aid to Mozambique to counter border attacks by Rhodesia's government. ● The Southeast Asia Treaty Organization (SEATO) is formally dissolved.

UPI

The widow of Generalissimo Francisco Franco registers to vote as Spain holds its first free national elections in 41 years, June 15.

13

JULY

ARMY TAKES OVER IN PAKISTAN

JAPAN, SRI LANKA HOLD ELECTIONS

EGYPT AND LIBYA CLASH AT BORDER

S	M	T	W	T	F	S
					1	2
3	4	5	6	7	8	9
10	11	12	13	14	15	16
17	18	19	20	21	22	23
24	25	26	27	28	29	30
31						

In late July, areas surrounding drought-stricken Santa Barbara, Calif., were hit by an explosive brush fire.

UPI

1 Gen. Carlos Humberto Romero is installed as president of El Salvador.

5 In Pakistan, the Army seizes control of the nation in a bloodless coup, imposes martial law, and promises new elections in October. ● The 14th annual summit conference of the Organization of African Unity (OAU) ends in Libreville, Gabon.

10 In elections for Japan's upper house of Parliament, the ruling Liberal-Democratic Party loses its majority but gains the support of 3 conservative independents for a total of 127 of the 252 seats in the House of Councillors.

13 A U.S. Army helicopter is shot down by North Koreans, after it had mistakenly strayed into North Korean airspace; three U.S. crewmen are killed and one is injured. ● Leaders of Britain's labor movement announce that they will no longer be bound by the voluntary standards regulating wages and prices since July 1975. ● German Chancellor Helmut Schmidt arrives at the White House for talks with President Carter.

13–14 A vast electrical power failure cripples New York City and Westchester County; some 3,700 persons are arrested as massive looting occurs in certain areas of the city.

17 The Begin government in Israel announces a major program to curb inflation, including an immediate 25% increase in prices of consumer goods.

19 Opening two days of White House meetings, President Carter and Israel's Prime Minister Begin agree that the convening of a new Geneva conference on the Middle East is highest priority.

20 Leon A. Jaworski is named special counsel to the U.S. House of Representatives Ethics Committee's investigation of influence-buying by South Korea.

21 A major border clash occurs between Egypt and Libya.

22 China officially announces that Teng Hsiao-ping, who was purged in April 1976, has been restored to his posts as a party deputy chairman and deputy prime minister.

23 Junius Richard Jayewardene, leader of Sri Lanka's United National Party, is sworn in as prime minister, following the overwhelming defeat of Prime Minister Sirimavo Bandaranaike's Freedom Party in July 21 general elections.

26 Israel's Prime Minister Begin approves the legalization of three existing Israeli settlements on the occupied lands of the West Bank of the Jordan River.

AUGUST

S	M	T	W	T	F	S
	1	2	3	4	5	6
7	8	9	10	11	12	13
14	15	16	17	18	19	20
21	22	23	24	25	26	27
28	29	30	31			

MAKARIOS OF CYPRUS IS DEAD

U.S. ENERGY DEPARTMENT FORMED

U.S., PANAMA FRAME NEW ACCORD

3 President Carter signs into law a bill establishing federal controls on strip mining.

4 President Carter signs into law a bill creating the Department of Energy; James R. Schlesinger is nominated to be the new cabinet secretary. ● Tanzania's President Julius K. Nyerere discusses the Rhodesia situation with President Carter at the White House.

5 A two-day summit conference of the leaders of the Association of Southeast Asian nations ends in Kuala Lumpur, Malaysia.

6 The Carter administration unveils a comprehensive welfare reform program.

10 The United States and Panama announce that they have reached "agreement in principle" on "the basic elements" of new treaties that will effect the transfer of the Panama Canal and the Canal Zone to Panamanian control by the year 2000, and assure the canal's neutrality. ● In Yonkers, N.Y., police arrest a suspect (David Berkowitz, a 24-year-old postal worker) in the "Son of Sam" murder case. During a 12-month period in New York City, six young persons were killed and seven others were wounded by one .44 caliber revolver. ● The Canadian Parliament enacts emergency legislation, ending a three-day strike by air-traffic controllers.

12 The U.S. space shuttle Enterprise successfully completes its first solo flight test.

17 The USSR announces that its nuclear icebreaker *Arktika* reached the North Pole on August 16, becoming the first surface vessel to break through the Arctic ice pack. ● Frank M. Johnson, Jr., of Alabama, a 58-year-old Federal District Court judge, is named director of the Federal Bureau of Investigation.

18 A report by the comptroller of the currency states that no evidence has been found on which to prosecute Bert Lance, director of the U.S. Office of Management and Budget, but criticizes as "unsound and unsafe" certain banking practices of Lance as an executive of a Georgia bank.

20 Communist China announces the completion of the 11th National Party Congress. A new central committee was elected at the Congress.

22 U.S. Secretary of State Cyrus R. Vance arrives in Peking, China.

23 Gov. Marvin Mandel of Maryland and five friends are convicted of mail fraud and racketeering.

26 The Quebec Assembly approves legislation establishing French as the province's principal language.

31 In elections in Rhodesia, the Rhodesian Front Party of Prime Minister Ian Smith wins an overwhelming victory. ● Spyros Achilles Kyprianou takes over as president of Cyprus, succeeding Archbishop Makarios, who died August 3.

UPI

Panama's Romulo Escobar Betancourt, left, Ellsworth Bunker and Sol Linowitz of the U.S., and Panama's Aristides Royo announce that agreement in principle has been reached concerning new Panama Canal treaties.

SEPTEMBER

PANAMA CANAL TREATIES SIGNED

VIETNAM AND DJIBOUTI JOIN UN

BUDGET DIRECTOR LANCE RESIGNS

S	M	T	W	T	F	S
				1	2	3
4	5	6	7	8	9	10
11	12	13	14	15	16	17
18	19	20	21	22	23	24
25	26	27	28	29	30	

1 The United States and Cuba establish "interest sections" in Havana and Washington. The move is considered a step closer to full diplomatic relations, suspended in January 1961, between the two nations.

3 Zulfikar Ali Bhutto, former prime minister of Pakistan, is arrested in Karachi and charged with conspiracy to murder.

6 U. S. Attorney General Griffin Bell announces that Park Tong Sun (also known as Tongsun Park), a central figure in the Korean lobbying scandal, has been indicted by a federal grand jury.

7 At the Organization of American States headquarters in Washington, President Carter and Brig. Gen. Omar Torrijos Herrera of Panama sign the Panama Canal treaties.

8 Canada and the United States agree in principle on a joint proposal to construct a natural gas pipeline through Canada to the lower 48 states.

11 In its annual report, the International Monetary Fund states that because of increasing unemployment and "subnormal growth" the state of the world's economy is "unsatisfactory." ● Guillermo Vilas defeats Jimmy Connors to win the men's singles tennis title of the U. S. Open. Earlier, Chris Evert retained the women's singles crown.

12 In Norway, the ruling Labor Party wins a one-seat majority in parliament elections.

13 Symphonic conductor Leopold Stokowski dies at the age of 95.

14 At least 14 persons are killed in a violent general strike in Colombia.

16 Canada's Prime Minister Pierre Elliott Trudeau reshuffles his 32-member cabinet.

18 The United States defends the America's Cup as the U. S. yacht *Courageous* defeats the *Australia* in the fourth straight race.

20 At the opening of the 32d General Assembly of the United Nations, Vietnam and the new nation of Djibouti are admitted as UN members.

21 Bert Lance resigns as director of the U. S. Office of Management and Budget. The resignation follows weeks of controversy and hearings regarding Lance's past business and banking policies.

26 The Israeli Defense Ministry announces that a cease-fire, arranged by the United States, has gone into effect in the Israeli-Lebanese border area, scene of recent heavy fighting between Palestinian guerrillas and Lebanese Christians, supported by Israel.

28 Pol Pot, recently identified as Cambodia's highest ranking government official, arrives in Peking.

30 Vietnam returns to U. S. officials the remains of 21 U. S. servicemen who died during the Vietnam war and of a civilian who died in Saigon in 1976.

UPI

Residents of Calhoun, Ga., welcome home Bert and Labelle Lance. He resigned under pressure as OMB director on September 21.

OCTOBER

S	M	T	W	T	F	S
						1
2	3	4	5	6	7	8
9	10	11	12	13	14	15
16	17	18	19	20	21	22
23	24	25	26	27	28	29
30	31					

QUEEN ELIZABETH VISITS CANADA

TERRORISTS STRIKE W. GERMANY

SANCTIONS v. S. AFRICA VETOED

1 A US-USSR declaration states that a Geneva conference on the Middle East should "guarantee the legitimate rights of the Palestinian people."

4 In an address to the UN General Assembly, President Carter emphasizes the issue of arms control. ● The prison sentences of John Mitchell, H. R. Haldeman, and John D. Ehrlichman—convicted in the Watergate case—are reduced by Judge John J. Sirica. ● A 35-nation conference, organized to review progress on European security, human rights, and economic cooperation, opens in Belgrade, Yugoslavia.

5 President Carter signs two UN covenants on human rights.

10 Mairead Corrigan and Betty Williams, both active in peace movements in Northern Ireland, are named winners of the 1976 Nobel Peace Prize; Amnesty International, a London-based human-rights organization, is the recipient of the 1977 prize. ● An unexplained docking failure halts a Soviet manned space mission.

14 Meeting in Washington, President Carter and Panama's Brig. Gen. Omar Torrijos Herrera issue a "statement of understanding" on the new Panama Canal treaties. ● Entertainer Bing Crosby, 73, dies in Madrid. ● Queen Elizabeth II begins six-day Silver Jubilee visit to Canada.

18 In Mogadishu, Somalia, West German troops storm a hijacked Lufthansa airliner, freeing 86 unharmed hostages and ending a five-day episode.

19 The body of West German industrialist Hanns-Martin Schleyer who was kidnapped on September 5 is found in a car trunk in Mulhouse, France. ● The government of South Africa bans black protest groups, closes the nation's principal black newspaper, and arrests its editor.

20 Thailand's civilian government, installed by the military in 1976, is deposed in a coup.

23 In a plebiscite, Panamanians vote in favor of ratification of the new Panama Canal treaties.

28 With the United States and six other nations abstaining, the UN General Assembly censures Israel for establishing settlements in occupied Arab territory.

31 In the UN Security Council, the United States, Britain, and France veto three African-sponsored resolutions that would have placed severe economic restrictions on South Africa. ● Richard Helms, former director of the CIA, pleads no contest to criminal information charging him with two misdemeanor counts of not testifying "fully, completely, and accurately" before a U.S. Senate committee.

UPI

A London newspaper reveals Nobel Peace Prize winners. Reggie Jackson led N. Y. to World Series victory.

UPI

NOVEMBER

U.S. WITHDRAWS FROM THE ILO

RENÉ LÉVESQUE VISITS FRANCE

SADAT ADDRESSES KNESSET

S	M	T	W	T	F	S
		1	2	3	4	5
6	7	8	9	10	11	12
13	14	15	16	17	18	19
20	21	22	23	24	25	26
27	28	29	30			

1 The United States withdraws from the International Labor Organization (ILO). ● President Carter signs legislation increasing the minimum wage.

4 The UN Security Council votes unanimously to impose a mandatory embargo of arms shipments to South Africa. ● Quebec's Premier René Lévesque concludes a visit to France, during which he was made a Grand Officer of the Legion of Honor.

7 The Soviet Union concludes week-long celebrations marking the 60th anniversary of the Bolshevik Revolution.

8 In U.S. elections, Brendan Byrne (D) wins a second term as governor of New Jersey; John Dalton (R) defeats Henry Howell for the governorship of Virginia; and Edward Koch (D) and Dennis J. Kucinich (D), 31, are elected mayors of New York City and Cleveland, respectively.

9 Israeli jets stage massive attacks against Palestinian guerrilla strongholds in southern Lebanon. The attacks were "purely against terrorist bases" from which the Israeli town of Nahariya had been shelled, November 6 and 8.

12 Ernest N. Morial, a black, is elected mayor of New Orleans, La.

13 Somalia orders all Soviet advisers to leave the country, terminates a 1974 Somalia-Soviet treaty of friendship and cooperation, and breaks diplomatic relations with Cuba.

15 Demonstrations for and against the Shah of Iran, Mohammed Riza Pahlavi, occur near the White House, as the Shah arrives for talks with President Carter. ● Representatives of Canada and the United States sign an agreement governing U. S. sales of Canadian uranium.

19 Egypt's President Anwar el-Sadat arrives in Jerusalem, the first Arab national leader to visit the Jewish state since its establishment in 1948. ● A devastating cyclone sweeps the coast of Andhra Pradesh, India.

20 In parliamentary elections in Greece, the opposition Panhellenic Socialist Movement, led by Andreas Papandreou, scores major gains. ● U. S. Secretary of State Vance begins a three-day trip to Argentina, Brazil, and Venezuela.

21 After adopting a platform of action to produce women's equality, the National Women's Conference ends in Houston.

27 Sen. John L. McClellan (D-Ark.), chairman of the Senate Appropriations Committee, dies at the age of 81.

28 The Rhodesian government announces that during the week of November 20 it had carried its fight against black nationalist guerrillas deep inside Mozambique, killing at least 1,200 persons.

29 U. S. Federal District Judge Frank M. Johnson, Jr., asks that his name be withdrawn from nomination to be director of the FBI.

UPI

Election night, New York City, Rep. Edward Koch, mayor-elect, Bess Myerson, Koch's campaign cochairman, and Carol Bellamy, president-elect of the City Council, enjoy their victories.

DECEMBER

S	M	T	W	T	F	S
					1	2	3
4	5	6	7	8	9	10
11	12	13	14	15	16	17
18	19	20	21	22	23	24
25	26	27	28	29	30	31

RIOTING BREAKS OUT IN BERMUDA

ISRAEL, EGYPT CONTINUE TALKS

MILLER NAMED TO SUCCEED BURNS

2–4 Following the hanging of two convicted murderers, outbreaks of rioting and arson stun Bermuda; a curfew is imposed, a state of emergency is declared, and British troops are sent to the island.

4 Jean-Bedel Bokassa crowns himself Bokassa I, emperor of the Central African Empire.

5 Egypt severs diplomatic relations with Syria, Iraq, Libya, Algeria, and Southern Yemen in retaliation for efforts by the Arab hard-liners to halt new Egyptian peace efforts toward Israel.

8 Negotiations aimed at a new government begin in Portugal, after Prime Minister Mário Soares is defeated on a motion of confidence.

9 The United States and Mexico carry out the first phase of a prisoner exchange, agreed to by treaty.

14 Egyptian and Israeli negotiators open a conference in Cairo.

16 Israel's Prime Minister Menahem Begin confers with President Carter in Washington.

18 The kidnapped son of the president of Cyprus is released unharmed.

21 After adopting a budget of $986 million for the next two years, the UN General Assembly adjourns. ● The Organization of Petroleum Exporting Countries (OPEC) announces that it will not increase crude oil prices in the immediate future.

25 Charlie Chaplin, 88, dies in Switzerland.

26 Egypt's President Sadat and Israel's Prime Minister Begin conclude two days of talks in Ismailia, Egypt, without agreement on the issues of a Palestinian state and Israel's withdrawal from the Sinai, the West Bank of the Jordan, and the Gaza Strip.

27 James T. McIntyre, Jr., is named director of the Office of Management and Budget.

31 Accusing Vietnam of "ferocious and barbarous aggression," Cambodia breaks diplomatic relations with its neighbor.

PHOTOS UPI

G. William Miller, president of Textron, addresses reporters after being named to succeed Arthur Burns, left, as chairman of the Federal Reserve System. Mrs. Miller is at right.

Jimmy Carter ended 1977 on a world tour. In Teheran, the President discussed the Middle East situation with Jordan's King Hussein and the Shah of Iran, right.

HUMAN RIGHTS

BY CARL Q. CHRISTOL
Professor of International Law and Political Science
University of Southern California

In the past few years "human rights" has become a subject suddenly on the lips of almost everyone. Why is this so, and what does it mean?

Human rights are an ancient concern, but present interest stems from the atrocities of World War II, the cruelties of recent wars in Asia, the Middle East, and Africa, the inhumane treatment by some governments of their own citizens, and a general recognition that there are enormous differences between the conditions of life in the relatively affluent societies and in the most impoverished of the less developed countries. The world has grown smaller. Its peoples and countries have become more interdependent. Matters once considered wholly within a nation's domestic jurisdiction have become legitimate concerns of the entire world community. Intimidated and poverty-stricken peoples, having acquired awareness of a better life, have given notice that they expect to share in new-found opportunities. Basic human yearnings for a meaningful existence are being perceived as achievable. Growing dissatisfaction with the past, a swelling momentum of human expectations, and a wider public manifestation of moral commitment have found expression in the term human rights. The result has been a human rights movement of universal dimensions.

The interdependence of peoples and nations is the totem of our times. It has produced an awareness of the need for an optimum world order, and this has focused attention on the identification and clarification of fundamental human values. Such values, in a philosophical context, are identified both abstractly and specifically—dignity, respect, and well-being on the one hand, and the right to travel, produce income, and transmit it across national boundaries, on the other.

The problem is for human beings to identify their rights with particularity, so that governments can be required to respect and protect them. The process of identification serves to impress such inherent rights with governmental acceptance, thereby providing individuals and governments suitable guidance for interpretation. Governments require such guidance since the claims of individuals are frequently opposed. Moreover, the rights claimed by individuals and governments often clash. For example, one person's claim to freedom may be in opposition to a government's view of law and order. One government's perspective may be at variance with world community expectations.

The Substance of Human Rights. The terms of international declarations and agreements provide guidance in identifying the substance and quality of human rights, the most fundamental and important of which are set out in the 1948 UN Universal Declaration of Human Rights

(UDHR). These rights are essentially two in number, even though the declaration contains 30 articles, each with many ramifications. First, there is the personal right to physical and mental well-being, including access to goods and opportunities to maximize such well-being. Included under this heading are protection against physical harm by private malefactors and protection against torture, cruel and inhuman punishment, and assorted misdeeds by governments. Such considerations focus on the protection of individuals against the wrongs of others. More recently, this has been modified to emphasize the affirmative right of individuals to enjoy material benefits and basic freedoms. Included is the opportunity to obtain food, shelter, health care, and education. Procedures to restrict governmental excesses are also stressed.

Second, there is the essential right of the individual to share in the operation of a humane system of government. This calls for civil and political rights and liberties of the kind guaranteed in the U. S. Bill of Rights, including especially such First Amendment guarantees as those of free speech, press, religion, petition, assembly, and association, and the right to privacy, and movement within and out of one's home country. History has demonstrated that the enjoyment of both sets of rights depends in fact on the economic and political maturity of a state.

One can assess the substance of human rights by counting the concepts that have achieved protection in existing legal systems, both national and international. Such an appraisal might be refined by assigning higher values to those rights that are designed to extend special benefits to mankind. Another approach is to look at the fundamental but unfulfilled needs of people and to assert that all basic needs and freedoms must be included within the orbit of human rights, whether or not they are supported within existing legal systems. From this second approach arises the possibility that new principles may be identified, and specific assurances will then take on legal qualities. In the long run, this will afford more detailed protections and larger opportunities.

The basic principles set forth in the UDHR have been reconsidered and restated in a number of later international agreements. Illustrative are the 1966 International Covenant on Civil and Political Rights and the 1966 International Covenant on Economic, Social, and Cultural Rights. The former emphasizes the integrity of the person, the right to equality of treatment under law, the right to participation in public affairs, and the First Amendment freedoms. The latter deals with working conditions, family rights, entitlement to high health standards, social security, and much more. This covenant, unlike the first, was formulated as a statement of goals to be achieved progressively rather than immediately.

The civil rights and liberties guaranteed in the U. S. Constitution compose an important part of the active inventory of human rights. The link between constitutional and human rights is forged by the common purpose of maximizing human well-being. Both stem from so-called "inherent rights" of individuals. Such rights can be traced back in history to the philosophical underpinnings of natural law, which posits that "right reason" supports the inherent dignity of the human being—that God, having given us life, is also the source of rights and liberties.

In a narrower, more technical sense, civil rights and liberties have been assured by such historic documents as Magna Carta, the Declaration of Independence, the U. S. Constitution, and the Civil Rights Acts dating from 1866, 1870, 1875, and the period from 1957 to the present. Under Magna Carta, Englishmen obtained due process guarantees. The Declaration of Independence stated: "We hold these truths to be self-evident, that all men are created equal, that they are endowed by their Creator with certain unalienable Rights, that among these are Life, Liberty and the pursuit of Happiness." An understanding of American rights was enunciated by Justice Samuel Chase in the case of *Calder* v. *Bull,* 1798. Following the premise of the inherent rights of individuals, he observed that, "There are certain vital principles in our free republican governments which will determine and overrule an apparent and flagrant abuse of legislative power [such] as to authorize manifest injustice by positive law or to take away that security for personal liberty, or private property, for the protection whereof the government was established." Justice Chase said that "an act of the legislature (for I cannot call it a law), contrary to the great first principles of the social compact, cannot be considered a rightful exercise of legislative authority." U. S. civil rights statutes mandate affirmative benefits. These involve elections, voting, housing, travel, and equal accommodations in inns, theaters, and public conveyances.

The Legal Bases for Human Rights. Civil rights and liberties can be claimed specifically because they have found their way into the formal sources of law, namely, constitutions, statutes, and judicial decisions. They have also been received into human rights documents of international status in the form of declarations, treaties, covenants, conventions, and judicial holdings. These rights are, moreover, assumed by pragmatic international practice or custom. The presence of such guarantees in national constitutions means that they are general principles of law, recognized by civilized nations. As such, the principles constitute international law. Like all explicit agreements, they impose important duties on sovereign states.

At the world level, the more formal processes, but not necessarily the most real bases, for human rights include the UN Charter, the UDHR as it has emerged in the actual practice of states, the 1966 international

MARGOT GRANITSAS, PHOTO RESEARCHERS

...freedom of religion

"...a basic standard of material existence"

F. A. O. PHOTO

covenants, and numerous other UN and specialized agency conventions, such as the International Labor Organization conventions relating to working conditions, the Genocide Convention, and the Treaty for the Elimination of All Forms of Racial Discrimination. Additionally, there have been regional declarations and agreements, such as the 1948 American Declaration of the Rights and Duties of Man by the Organization of American States (OAS), the 1950 European Convention on Human Rights, and the 1969 American Convention on Human Rights.

Both the concepts and the means for their implementation have expanded during the years. While the UDHR at its inception was not considered binding international law, this soon changed. Professor Louis B. Sohn noted in 1968 that, "In a relatively short period, the Universal Declaration of Human Rights has thus become a part of the constitutional law of the world community; and, together with the Charter of the United Nations, it has achieved the character of a world law superior to all other international instruments and to domestic laws."

A further example of the development of human rights can be drawn from the Western Hemisphere. In 1960, the OAS Council approved a Statute for the Inter-American Commission on Human Rights. Its functions were revised and enlarged in 1965 and 1970. Thus, in 1965 it was authorized to investigate individual complaints and to make specific recommendations. This was a daring step at the time, for it threatened the

EPA NEWSPHOTO

JAN LUKAS, RAPHO/PHOTO RESEARCHERS

... the right to an education

"... the freedom of speech ...
or the right of the people
peaceably to assemble"

sovereign prerogatives of states that did not wish to have their misdeeds scrutinized or criticized. In 1970 the commission was given the status of an OAS organ.

In Europe, as early as 1950, a convention was adopted that went beyond the assurances contained in the UDHR. The agreement established advanced procedures for the resolution of disputes. When the OAS drafted the American Convention on Human Rights in 1969, it borrowed heavily from the European experience.

The presence of such rights in explicit and implicit sources of law contributes to their identification and to their enforceability. In an ultimate sense, however, these rights depend upon man's inherent qualities because they continue to flow from his very nature. In this respect, his rights do not depend upon the formality with which they have been conferred. Rather, they are inalienable rights, proper to man simply because he is man. Nonetheless, there is a need for such rights to be recognized in a formal way. Then they can be protected by on-going, man-operated legal processes. The right to such processes provides protection and extension of fundamental freedoms. In this way, living human rights become part of both the substance and the process of law.

President Carter and Human Rights. President Carter has committed himself to human rights and has made that commitment a fundamental part of his foreign policy. He has informed the UN of his acceptance of the Genocide Convention and the Treaty for the Elimination of All Forms of Racial Discrimination. On June 1, 1977, he signed the American Convention on Human Rights, stating that it constituted a "noble commitment and endeavor," and on October 5 he signed the two 1966 international covenants as well.

President Carter's first pronouncements on the subject stressed the view that the well-being of individuals and nations could best be served by respect for human equality and the enlargement of freedom. By September 1977, the focus had changed. Carter wrote: "Human rights cannot be the only goal of our foreign policy, not in a world in which peace is literally a matter of survival." His administration, while searching for a definition of human rights, has acknowledged that many desirable goals may not be a part of this concept. The Department of State has said that a human rights policy has not become a "be-all and end-all" of the president's thinking.

His position has been variously analyzed. It was first suggested that he had embarked on a new evangelism likely to lead the United States into grievous foreign policy mistakes. Specific criticisms have been numerous: First, an even-handed, human-rights-based foreign policy would be difficult to implement, since in practical situations the United States will be obliged to give some preferences to countries that disregard human rights. Second, the view that individuals prefer freedom over material benefits is invalid. Third, totalitarian leaders see a human rights policy as a threat to their power and their internal political structures. Fourth, U. S. policy will interfere with the constitutional functions of international organizations, such as the World Bank. Fifth, U. S. allies in western Europe have perceived the unilateral initiatives as producing an additional disequilibrium in areas now experiencing uncertainty and instability. Sixth, preaching, particularly when it touches sensitive foreign nerves, produces irritation. Possibly, U. S. strategic and economic interests could be put in jeopardy. (Former Secretary of State Henry Kissinger has suggested that the universal implementation of a wide-ranging, ill-defined policy might require the United States to become the world's policeman. In his view, neither the objective nor the means would receive the support of the American people.) Finally, some human rights supporters feel that the Carter initiative could weaken even more basic foreign policy commitments, such as (to quote Sen. Daniel Moynihan), "the central political struggle of our time—that between liberal democracy and totalitarian Communism."

The responses of the Carter administration are, first, that the U. S. commitment to human rights is a restatement of time-proven democratic principles. Such principles serve the basic needs of mankind. They have a life and force of their own. Second, the time is ripe to reassert the Jeffersonian tradition and establish affirmative policies rather than react to foreign initiatives. Third, there is a relationship between human rights at home and in the world at large. If the United States were to blink violations beyond its borders, valid doubts would be established about its domestic commitments. While criticism of violations abroad may produce some political turbulence, the wide-ranging demands for the protection of human rights have removed this subject from the wholly domestic authority of all states. World interdependence has terminated the obsolete view that national sovereignty allows human rights to fall under the exclusive control of states. Fourth, basket three of the 1975 Helsinki Conference on Security and Cooperation in Europe linked human rights to the need for world order, but it did not intend to impede détente. In July 1977, President Carter said, "There are no hidden meanings in our commitment to human rights. We stand on what we have said on this subject before. Our policy is exactly what it appears to be: the positive and sincere expression of our deepest beliefs as a people. It is addressed not to any particular people or area of the world, but to all countries equally, including our own. And it is specifically *not* designed to heat up the arms race or bring back the Cold War." Fifth, if the United States and the less developed countries are to reduce their mutual suspicions, the United States must remain committed to its goal of implementing strong human rights policies. Finally, the Carter initiative must be considered as an invitation to the entire world to give thoughtful attention to a movement compatible with interdependence. Such interdependence can only be beneficial if states apply the human rights standards set out in international agreements to their own nationals. The Carter policy has already led to a wider application of such standards in several non-democratic states.

An Assessment of the Carter Initiative. Since it is a basic tenet of human rights that governments must respect the opinions of their peoples, the Carter initiative must gain the approval of Americans. Congressmen now seek substantially greater authority in the formulation of foreign policy than heretofore. In the past, they have not given human rights much attention. Individual congressmen have given some lip service to basic principles, but the United States has not in fact become a party to any of the major human rights treaties. As members of Congress attempt to be informed about the public's views on human rights, they may hear a variety of sounds, some of them discordant. Dissatisfaction with human rights violations in South Korea has induced some members to deny military aid to that country, even though such aid might allow U. S. troops to be withdrawn. Members of Congress opposed to autocratic regimes

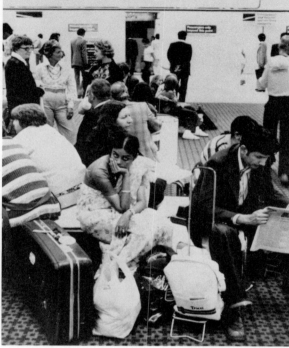

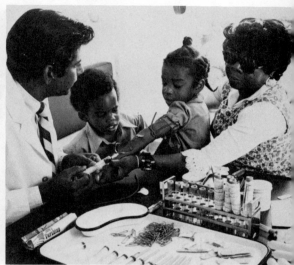

. . . the right to travel and emigrate

" . . . the provision of good health."

UPI   BRUCE ANSPACH/EPA NEWSPHOTO

in Panama and Cuba cite them as a reason for opposition to the proposed Panama Canal treaty and the resumption of normal relations with Cuba, even though human rights might be enlarged in these areas following the contemplated steps. Dr. Kissinger has observed in this connection that "if the conservatives succeed in unraveling ties with nations of the Left and liberals block relations with nations on the Right, we could find ourselves with no constructive foreign relations at all."

The possibility of double human rights standards at home will be quickly noted by an observant world. The gravity of this situation will require optimum cooperation on the part of Congress and the president. Until the ratification process for the two 1966 covenants has been completed, the Carter initiative will lack the world credibility essential to an effective U. S. human rights foreign policy.

Enforcement of Human Rights Principles. Within nations, human rights principles can be mandated under domestic law. States and their nationals can, by example, heighten public consciousness. Preferred rights can be identified, and public demands that they be respected can be voiced. Publicity, both domestic and international, can be given to nonconformity, with the expectation that it would be sufficiently embarrassing to oppressors to make them humanize their policies.

Vigorous demands that human rights be respected have produced a new element in the condition of statehood. In the past it had been assumed that territory, people, sovereignty, and a viable government allowed a political entity to assert that it was a state, with all of the rights and duties of such a legal person. It is now being suggested that a new requirement exists, namely, that a state accord a decent respect to the rights of human beings. If this comes about, all of the human rights initiatives of the past will have served a valuable purpose.

Egypt's President Nasser, *left*, India's Prime Minister Nehru, and Yugoslavia's President Tito met on Brioni Island, Yugoslavia, in July 1956. The nonaligned Third World movement had its beginnings in this historic conference.

EASTFOTO

THE THIRD WORLD

By Richard C. Hottelet
United Nations Correspondent, CBS

The Third World has grown over the past 25 years from an unclear concept to an important, though still ill-defined, political reality. It embraces the poor or industrially undeveloped countries that after World War II wanted to remain outside the East-West struggle and today see their interests as different from those of the two super powers and the industrial Northern Hemisphere.

Beginnings. U. S. Secretary of State John Foster Dulles implicitly accepted the category in the early 1950's when he rebuked those who sought refuge in neutrality. Russia's Nikita Khrushchev, on the other hand, looking for a way out of the isolation of the Stalin period, saw the neutrals as a third sector distinct from the "capitalist" camp, with whom the communist bloc could create "a vast zone of peace."

In April 1955, 29 countries of Africa and Asia met at Bandung, Indonesia, to launch nonalignment as a political force. China, incidentally, helped to exclude the Soviet Union which was seeking participation as an Asian state.

In July 1956, Nasser of Egypt, Nehru of India, and Tito of Yugoslavia met on Brioni Island, Yugoslavia, to turn the regional beginnings of Bandung into a worldwide nonaligned movement. It was then swept forward by the wave of national independence. At the 15th General Assembly in 1960, 17 new nations were admitted to the UN, and the Assembly demanded an end to all colonialism without regard for the political, economic, social, or educational preparedness of the subject peoples. By late 1977, UN membership had risen to 149 states. The prolifera-

tion of new countries ushered in an age of coalition politics. The Third World, diverse as it was, became the UN majority and easily rallied against anything labeled racist, imperialist, or neocolonialist.

Into the 1970's the primary target of the Third World was Portugal's African empire. Scores of UN resolutions piled up a massive public record approving the various national liberation movements and condemning Portugal and its supporters. This helped to create a political burden under which Portugal's empire collapsed. The same process is now being directed against the remaining white regimes of southern Africa in Rhodesia, Namibia (South West Africa), and South Africa itself.

Composition and Significance. Power of a new kind obviously resides in this Third World grouping when it can be activated as a bloc. It is not real power in the traditional sense but the aggregate strength of feeble individuals. The UN's assessment scale for its regular budget is designed to reflect the members' economic conditions. It shows that 101 of the members, more than two thirds needed to adopt important resolutions, together pay 3.90% of the total cost of the UN. The United States alone pays 25%.

While there is something platonic about the paper majorities that characterize the UN, there is nothing unreal about their factual weight. A study prepared by the U. S. Library of Congress declares, "the economic security of the United States and its allies depends increasingly upon raw material resources imported from abroad, some having strategic value and many short in supply and great in demand. The main sources of these

The Conference on International Economic Cooperation (known as the North-South talks) held its final session in Paris in June 1977. During 18 months of talks, representatives of the industrial and developing nations failed to agree on world economic reform.

materials are located in the Third World." Oil is the most striking example, but it holds true for a dozen or more important minerals. For instance, U. S. industry is almost wholly dependent on foreign sources of cobalt, chromium, bauxite, manganese, and tin; it draws between 40% and 95% of these commodities from the Third World.

Geopoliticians will note what the Library of Congress report says about strategic importance: "Third World nations border on most of the world's important strategic straits, described in naval terminology as 'choke-points.'" It cites the Strait of Malacca, connecting the Pacific and the Indian Ocean, as well as the Strait of Hormuz at the mouth of the Persian Gulf, and Bab el Mandeb, the southern access to the Red Sea.

Third World countries absorb about one third of U. S. exports. They are in debt to international credit agencies, dominated by the Western industrial countries, including Japan, as well as to individual states and Western private banks in an amount approaching $200,000,000,000. The Third World comprises 70% of the human race and covers more than 40% of the globe's total land area, excluding Antarctica, but earns only 30% of the world's income.

The great physical problems confronting mankind—environment, population, and food—cannot be solved without the Third World's effective cooperation. On today's shrunken, interdependent planet, political unrest, economic collapse, or social upheaval in that quarter have direct implications for the well-being of the United States and the Western camp.

Economic Focus. The Third World acquired its political strength in the early 1960's when the many newly independent nations, under the influence of the nonaligned movement, swelled its membership, but its main thrust has been in the economic field, although the two lines of interests have become more and more interwoven, as they, indeed, must be; the most important economic questions are inevitably political.

The UN members proclaim "the current decade as the United Nations Development Decade, in which member states will intensify their efforts . . . to attain in each underdeveloped country a substantial increase in the rate of growth."
Resolution UN General Assembly Dec. 19, 1961

From the very beginning the newly independent countries, barely able, if at all, to stand on their own feet, looked for help to build viable economies. In 1961, the UN General Assembly declared the 1960's a "Decade of Development." It set a goal of 5% annual increase in the gross national product but said nothing about how to achieve it. The idea of an economic dialogue between industrial and developing countries was not yet ripe. Problems were dealt with piecemeal, bilaterally, or through the established international credit agencies, like the World Bank. The developing countries, importers of manufactured goods and exporters of raw materials, felt increasing anger at what they saw as a permanent position of disadvantage. They argued that the price of what they bought and sold was set by others, subjecting them to unpredictable and ruinous market fluctuations.

UNCTAD, the UN Conference on Trade and Development, embracing the full UN membership, was formed in 1964. The representatives of the then 77 developing countries decided, during the first session, that they could not singly assert themselves against the industrial nations. They united to establish the Group of 77, which has kept that name even though it now numbers 112. The Group of 77 is the Third World's economic lobby, and the nonaligned apply political pressure. The nonaligned now comprise 82 UN member states. The two groups overlap—and so, increasingly, do their operations. The age of colonalism is obviously over. Rhodesia and Namibia are the only territories of any consequence left to liberate. The operational focus of the 77 and the nonaligned has swung to the "neocolonialism" of economic dependency.

UNITED NATIONS

Uniting Issues and Dividing Policies.
Some issues are still capable of drawing broad instantaneous support. Racism, as exemplified by South Africa's apartheid policy, is a prime example. Others require the politics of coalition—the classic parliamentary backscratching—to build up a head of steam. The Arab world can easily summon the larger Islamic community and the Communist camp for votes against Israel; it has tried, but with pyrrhic success, to enlist African votes as well with the flimsy proposition that Zionism is a form of racism. Mutual support for particular causes, like the Panama Canal and the Falkland Islands, weaves a more conventional web of interest.

While the Third World has seemed on occasion to vote like a bloc or to stampede at the drop of a code word like "colonialism," it is an immensely varied bag which spills easily when there is no containing discipline. Collisions of policy inside Africa and Asia show that unanimity is directed chiefly against outside forces. One need only recall the divisive passions aroused in Africa by the Angolan civil war or the invasion of Shaba province in Zaire. The absorption of the Spanish Sahara by Morocco and Mauritania split the Arab camp. Indonesia's annexation of Timor divided the Third World. The reversal of alliances affecting Sudan, Ethiopia, and Somalia suggests that old-fashioned power politics can also beguile small new powers.

U. S. Reactions.
The United States was not quick to understand the new game. When Daniel Patrick Moynihan, then U. S. ambassador to the UN, did battle against a world of enemies at UN headquarters in 1975,

The UN Conference on Trade and Development (UNCTAD) held its fourth session in Kenya in May 1976, and launched a new program to restructure global commodity trade to stabilize and increase the earnings of the developing nations.

FAO PHOTO BY G. DE SABATINO

HILDA BIJUR FOR WORLD BANK

A sugar processing plant in the Philippines and a government coconut research station in the Ivory Coast. The Third World seeks a new deal for its chief exports, raw materials.

he was to some extent tilting with windmills. His exuberance may have done more good than harm in warning the Third World rank and file that extremists among them were leading them into impermissible attacks on U. S. national interests, including Puerto Rico and Guam. Moynihan may also have pleased an American public grown weary of being whipped by highly dubious critics in the world community. But he did not differentiate; and in lumping opponent states together, he created a unity which was otherwise not there. In his famous denunciation of Ugandan President Idi Amin as a "racist murderer," Moynihan alienated Africans, who agreed with him on this point, by adding that it was no accident that Amin was then president of the Organization of African Unity. It was precisely the accident of rotation that had put Amin in the post for one year.

After a period of psychological normalization under William Scranton, the Carter administration sent Andrew Young to the UN. Young's mission was deliberate cultivation of a new relationship with the Third World. In the UN politics of coalition, Africa with nearly 50 votes is a major factor. Southern Africa is also one of the global flash points to which the United States cannot remain indifferent. President Carter adopted a policy of full support for racial equality as the only way of preserving strategic stability in this area; his predecessor, Gerald Ford, and Secretary of State Kissinger had pursued that stability with more conventional means. Young plunged into African affairs wearing his heart on his sleeve, and gained considerable sympathy among Africans.

Demand for New Economic Order. Underlying the political hurly-burly, economic considerations are likely to direct the behavior of the Third World and its relationship with the industrial Western camp. That relationship is characterized now by what is called the North-South struggle and the drive by the developing countries for nothing less than a New International Economic Order.

This idea is highly charged with emotion. It reflects, in part, a desire to redistribute the world's wealth and to force a new deal for the benefit of raw material producers who have arrived so late and with such handicaps on the economic scene. Some of the corrective means envisaged are —to label them most baldly—confiscation, cartelization, and indexation. Confiscation is implicit in the claim of right to nationalize foreign holdings without compensation. Cartelization is the establishment of raw material associations to push up prices. The success of OPEC (Organization of Petroleum Exporting Countries) in quadrupling the price of oil stirred even those developing countries most severely affected by this inflationary shock to hope they could do the same with copper, tin, bauxite, bananas, and the rest. Indexation is the mechanical linkage of raw material prices to the cost of manufactured goods.

The economic dialogue with the Third World has been carried on by the 24 industrial nations of the OECD (Organization for Economic Cooperation and Development). The communist bloc—irrelevant as a market force or as a source of economic aid—has been literally outside the discussion, devoting itself to cheering from the sidelines every Third World move to punish the industrial camp.

The industrial powers, the United States among them, have tried to cope with this new phenomenon but, it must be said, awkwardly at best. Habit, perhaps, has led them, until recently, to approach the problem mainly in technical terms: exchange rates, "economic aid," trade concessions, and such. In fact, it is deeply political. Manifesting itself as economic trouble, it affects the stability of governments and the security of nations going through the social storms of poverty, frustration, and overpopulation. Alleviating these ills requires concerted national and international action, that is, political effort even though it is expressed in words like credit, price, and production.

The North-South Colloquy. As the industrial nations floundered under the impact of the oil embargo, Algeria seized the initiative by summoning the Sixth Special Session of the UN General Assembly in April 1974. It mobilized the Third World under the banner of the New International Economic Order to "redress existing injustices" and "make it possible to eliminate the widening gap between the developed and the developing countries." The powerful urge behind all this also found expression in political radicalism launched by the "new majority" in the assembly as well as other organs and agencies of the UN. In September 1975, the United States succeeded in reining in this tumultuous force by addressing itself seriously and sympathetically to the basic problem and promising a serious search for remedy.

Since then, several international conferences have been fruitless. While there has been no new world crisis, the confrontation between the industrial and the developing nations is no less ominous. Not only has conventional economics failed utterly to find a solution; it seems also that the two sides have failed to agree even on a diagnosis. The North-South colloquy has many aspects of a dialogue of the deaf and all the indignation of those who shout too loudly to hear the others.

The Third World, varied as its members are, has not yet come to a common clear view of its interests. The industrial nations for their part are still groping for a new functional balance between the two camps which need each other but do not yet know how to mesh. Until this equilibrium is found, the underlying tension can break out at any moment of crisis or confusion, compounding the trouble which sometimes seems to be the only thing the modern world possesses in abundance.

"We, the members of the United Nations, . . . solemnly proclaim our united determination to work urgently for the establishment of a New International Economic Order based on equity, sovereign equality, interdependence, common interest, and cooperation among all states. . . ."

*Declaration
UN General Assembly
May 1, 1974*

Slum housing in Rio de Janeiro, Brazil. Improved housing remains a principal objective of the Third World.

LISL STEINER

THE THIRD WORLD

A kaleidoscope of high objectives, stunning achievements, ambitious programs, and mountainous problems.

Outdoor vegetable markets are common not only in Mexico, below, but throughout the world.

JANE LATTA

Although Venezuela is classified as a developing nation, Caracas, its capital, is modern.

CARL FRANK

With India's population still growing at a high rate, the government emphasizes family planning programs.

Pipeline construction in Algeria. Earnings from oil account for c. 90% of Algeria's export revenues.

National University, Kinshasa, Zaire. Improved education raises the hopes of the Third World.

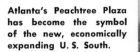

Atlanta's Peachtree Plaza has become the symbol of the new, economically expanding U. S. South.

Coming of Age

THE POST-ADOLESCENT U. S. SOUTH

By H. Brandt Ayers, *Editor and Publisher,* "The Anniston Star"

Listening to a description of the U. S. South in the language of sun belt statistics is like overhearing middle-class mothers detailing with mock dismay the fabulous sproutings of their offspring. "That child of mine," one inevitably says, "is growing just like a WEED!"

Psychological Growth. It is of more than mild interest, how many pounds and inches have been added to the region's population and economy. Even more notable are the signs of psychological growth. But what makes the American South so fascinating today is that it is growing both ways. It has passed through adolescence into a surer sense of emotional maturity and yet, physically, it is still growing—just like a WEED!

The end of adolescence is a bitter-sweet moment; the child is gone before the adult is really noticed. A new person inhabits the skin of old behavior and creed, and no one can recall exactly when it happened. Was it the passage of the Voting Rights Act in 1965? Was it the election of the class of 1970 Southern governors, Jimmy Carter's own class? Or, did the change happen sometime during the early morning hours of Nov. 3, 1976, when it became apparent that the nation had elected a president from the Deep South for the first time in well over a century?

Who can say and, in a sense, who cares? What really matters is that coming of age in a family decisively and permanently alters past relationships. Among the South's relationships with the rest of the American family those with the industrial North, and particularly the East, were most important because they affected the region's assumptions about itself.

How smart and successful and cocksure the East had always seemed to the scorned and "backward" South, consoled only by the inferior quality of Ivy League football. The East spoke down from a great, moral height, rendering the cruel but almost casual judgments of someone who had never been tested by frustration, defeat, prolonged hard times, or even temptation.

Born of the same Revolution at the same time, these contending regional siblings had to be able to see the same truth about each other, and about themselves, before a degree of peace and mature communication could develop within the family. The slow process of recognizing the truth can end in the stabbing realization that, as a character says in a Tom Stoppard play: "All your life you live so close to the truth, it becomes a permanent blur in the corner of your eye, and when something nudges it into outline, it is like being ambushed by a grotesque."

The unattended refuse heap of the central cities in the industrial North burst into spontaneous combustion in 1965 that coincided with a violent prelude in the South to the passage of the Voting Rights Act. Both regions were forced to confront unpleasant truths about themselves that they had seen only peripherally before. Since then, the psychological trade has changed. The North no longer exports barge loads of moral preachments stamped "Made in Boston," to get in return a chorus of "Dixie," the musical equivalent of a punch in the nose.

A New Political Breed. By 1970, the networks in New York were beaming different images of Southerners, pictures more to the South's liking. The nation had discovered the latest version of "the New South." Part of that discovery was the class of 1970 governors who represented the end of racial politics in the South. Three members of that class hit the national limelight almost immediately: Reubin Askew of Florida, Dale Bumpers of Arkansas, now a U. S. senator, and Jimmy Carter of Georgia, who became the first president from the Deep South since Zachary Taylor.

Florida Gov. Reubin Askew (*top*) and Sen. Dale Bumpers of Arkansas personify the end of racial politics in the South.

PHOTOS WIDE WORLD

LEROY WOODSON, EPA-DOCUMERICA

Blacks prepare to vote in a Birmingham, Ala., primary election. The number of Southern blacks registered to vote almost doubled between enactment of the Voting Rights Act of 1965 and the 1976 presidential elections.

A Gibson, La., family stands in front of its mobile home. As the population of the South increases, adequate housing is a crucial problem.

JOHN MESSINA, EPA-DOCUMERICA

When a new set of self-confident assumptions develops among people who previously felt themselves to be scorned, they are likely to put away some of the emotional symbols of the past. What people project to the world is what they think of themselves, and Southerners are feeling differently about who they are and where they are going.

It is likely that the people of the South will send some young men, many in their 30's, to the U. S. Senate in 1978. This could seriously alter the seniority structure of that body. Thus, 1978 may be the last year for the "Golden Age Club" of Southern senators. John Sparkman of Alabama will then be 79, John McClellan of Arkansas, 82, James Eastland of Mississippi, 74, and Strom Thurmond of South Carolina, 75, and they are all up for reelection.

Symbolic of the new breed of Southern politician is Charles R. (Pug) Ravenel of Charleston, S. C. As a 35-year-old unknown in the 1974 governor's race, he turned the state's legislative oligarchy upside down. After Ravenel's victory in the Democratic primary, the legislatively appointed state Supreme Court ruled that he was ineligible for the governorship because he did not meet a five-year residence requirement. However in 1978, Ravenel is expected to have a good shot at toppling one of the monuments to Old South politics, Strom Thurmond.

What is happening is not a total rejection of the past, a pulling down of the statues in the courthouse squares. Those monuments, like some Southern senators, have represented powerful feelings: that people can bear scorn and ruin without admitting the final defeat—the destruction of the human spirit. But few in the South today want to raise money to erect new Confederate memorials or to send those statues in the square to the U. S. Senate.

The entry of men like Pug Ravenel into Congress will not revive the Southern Caucus because the anti-civil rights issue, which was its organizing motive, is dead; rather, it will accelerate the break-up of the coalition of

In spite of economic advancement, rural poverty, particularly in Negro areas, persists.

Republicans and Southern Democrats. But neither are there, among the new breed, many likely recruits for the Democratic left, old New Dealers, or Americans for Democratic Action. These younger Southern politicians are likely to be independent because they have been conditioned by different experiences of life. They were born in a segregated society, first became politically aware when racial politics was being challenged and discarded, and today are representatives of a newly emerged region— economically, culturally, and spiritually.

A farmer cultivates his corn field on St. Helena Island, S. C. Agricultural employment in the South is now stabilizing.

The port of Charleston, S. C., currently being expanded, is the number one port of the U. S. southern Atlantic shore in terms of container ships and cargo value.

SOUTH CAROLINA STATE PORT AUTHORITY

A Louisiana chemical plant and a South Carolina garment factory are among the energy-intensive, low-wage manufacturing industries that are dominant factors in the economic life of today's South.

MARC ST. GIL, EPA-DOCUMERICA   BRUCE ROBERTS, RAPHO/PHOTO RESEARCHERS

Economic Growth. Dark suspicions may be harbored in some quarters that the South's economic good fortune is the result of Dixie chamber of commerce cavalry-raids on Eastern and Midwestern manufacturing towns. However, only 1.2% of the region's economic growth was caused by companies moving to the South and 64.3% of that growth came from expansion of existing firms.

What caused the yeasting of the Southern economy may be no more mysterious than the development of economically feasible air conditioning. But the growth is indisputable. Between 1970 and 1975, all Southeastern states grew at rates faster than the national average. Particularly impressive was the gain in higher-income, service industry employment. While the South was still behind the nation in every economic category, its personal income was growing at a much faster rate than the rest of the country, and average per-capita income in 1975 was 89.1% of the average throughout the United States.

But the breaching of the Mason-Dixon line by the twin gods of Yankee material progress, cities and factories, is neither all-pervasive nor a total blessing. Vast areas within some states are stagnating or worse. "There's still plenty of shade in the sun belt," says A. J. (Jay) Cooper, Jr., the brilliant, young black mayor of Prichard, Ala. And Atlanta's black mayor, Maynard Jackson, looks with dismay at the great crabgrass stampede to suburbia and exurbia which one day could leave his central city looking much like Newark, N. J.

Urban problems are understood by many young Southern politicians, including Wyche F. Fowler, Jr., former president of the Atlanta City Council, who won Ambassador Andrew Young's seat in the U. S. House of Representatives. Fowler believes that the source of urban problems lies in the flight of poor blacks and whites from the blighted rural areas. But the question remains, can the new Congressman convince his colleagues to fund an attack on the problem at its source?

Bill Monroe and his Blue Grass Boys entertain a packed house at the Grand Ole Opry in Nashville, Tenn., the fountainhead of country music.

WSM PHOTO BY LES LEVERETT

Social, Cultural, and Educational Advancement. Other questions and possibilities are raised by the growing urbanization, wealth, and self-esteem of the South. Among them are the possibility of creating a network of social and educational leadership to rival the Ivy League connection and the development of an establishment of cultural philanthropy.

Outside of a few major cities, Southern businessmen have not considered support for the performing arts as worthy as capital campaigns for YMCAs, boys' clubs, and the Salvation Army. There are a few exceptions. The county seat of Calhoun County, Ala., Anniston, hosted the sixth season of the Alabama Shakespeare Festival in 1977. A professional repertory company, the festival has drawn favorable national attention. Also, in 1977, High Point, N. C., unveiled its own Shakespeare Festival. American editor and satirist H. L. Mencken referred to the South as "the Sahara of the Bozarts." It will take time to lift that slur but the trends are favorable.

Until Jimmy Carter established a Georgia White House and appointed a few conspicuous Southerners to cabinet and sub-cabinet posts, U. S. government leaders were likely to come from the same source—the Northeast, particularly such Ivy League establishments as Harvard and Yale. The South failed to develop institutions to train potential policymakers because it did not have the money. Again, however, new assumptions and money are generating new trends. Duke University's Institute of Policy Sciences and Public Affairs became seven years old in 1977, and former U. S. Secretary of State Dean Rusk helped midwife the birth of the region's most comprehensive foreign-policy institution, the Southern Center on International Studies in Atlanta.

For children born of the South in 1977, one century after the end of the first reconstruction, there will be great opportunities, challenges, and problems. But their parents can view the events and trends of the little-noted centennial only with disbelief. As much as there is yet to do, few among them were optimistic enough in their own youth to believe that half of what has happened would come to pass. Incredibly enough, the second reconstruction promises to be permanent.

LEROY WOODSON, EPA-DOCUMERICA

The Sixth Avenue Baptist Church in Birmingham is representative of the vigorous evangelical spirit of many southern congregations.

HORACE MCDONALD, ''THE ANNISTON STAR''

At the Alabama Shakespeare Festival in Anniston, Charles Antalosky, Philip Pleasants, and Marlene Egan perform Hamlet. The festival, a professional repertory company, marked its sixth year in 1977.

FESTAC '77

By Andrew Young

*United States Ambassador
to the United Nations*

PHOTOS BRENT JONES

Some 17,000 singers, dancers, artists, musicians, and black cultural representatives from 55 nations, including the traditional Tutsi dancer (*right*), participated in the Second World Black and African Festival of Arts and Culture early in 1977. U. S. Ambassador to the UN Andrew Young (*above*) attends a FESTAC reception.

In our past, we can find a sense of our destiny. To me, the lasting value of the Second World Black and African Festival of Arts and Culture (FESTAC '77), held in Lagos, Nigeria, early in 1977, was that it afforded black people a unique opportunity to examine our history and seriously discuss our future. FESTAC was a celebration, at once joyous and solemn, of a richly varied culture, formed and nurtured in suffering and struggle and love. The scholars and artists from all parts of the world who participated in FESTAC were reaffirming and strengthening a majestic heritage— a heritage that has given humanity much of its moral, intellectual, and artistic leadership. FESTAC also had an immediate purpose: it fostered a recommitment to the ongoing movements of black and other oppressed people for liberation and justice. And finally, the participants in FESTAC, as well as the people they reached afterward, were stimulated by a spirit of reunion, brotherhood, and solidarity which will be so important to the continued quest for global freedom and equality among all peoples.

Liberation fighters from Southern Africa parade in the 60,000-seat National Stadium, one of six sites used for the celebrations. Nigeria, the host nation, spent considerable sums preparing for the 29-day festival.

FESTAC '77

The incredible performances of the Nigerian stilt walkers brought ovations from the spectators.

The Nigerian delegation and some of the youngest performers prepare for the close. North African musicians demonstrate their skills.

Heads of state and other dignitaries follow events from the reviewing stand.

THE CITIES

A Continuing Crisis

By Charles L. Leven

*Professor of Economics and Director
of the Institute for Urban and Regional Studies
Washington University*

Beginning some time in the 1950's, manufacturing employment in the cities of America began first to grow more slowly and then to decline. To some degree, this was a consequence of a general shift in the American economy from the production of goods to services; in large measure, though, it was part of the process of the American city spilling out into its suburbs. This reduced the demand for central-city living, resulting in decay and demolition of residential property, mainly in the early 1960's, and finally, in the larger and older cities, to actual abandonment of commercial as well as residential housing before the decade was over. Paralleling this trend, as the more affluent moved to suburbia, was a steady fall in the central-city tax base, coupled with rapidly rising needs of the remaining central-city population for increased public services, mainly health and welfare.

Population Shifts. In the early 1970's, population loss in the central city had become more typical than exceptional; between 1970 and 1975, no less than 93 of the 162 U. S. cities with 100,000 or more inhabitants lost population. Even the metropolitan area as a whole began to lose; between 1970 and 1975, loss occurred in 10 of the 36 Standard Metropolitan Statistical Areas (SMSA) with population of more than 1,000,000. (Between 1960 and 1970, only one such area—Pittsburgh—had lost population.) The median census projection of U. S. population for the year 2000 now stands at 262 million, compared with a projection of 304 million made in 1969.

Both economic and demographic forces influence urban and metropolitan trends. The economic factors actually are related to the emergence of the modern metropolis in the 19th century, as a consequence of the rise of the factory system which made large-scale production so efficient. During the 19th and into the 20th century, the steam engine and the intercity railroad made it both possible and profitable to initiate large-scale manufacturing, with a substantial concentration of many kinds of producers

efficiently located at, or between, raw materials and markets and near each other. Compared to the present, however, industrial technology of the past used a vast bulk of raw material. Considering the fact that intra-city movement of goods was very expensive compared to the cost of moving people, and considering the relatively high cost of utilizing steam, or even electric power, very far from its source, the early industrial metropolis became, by necessity, compact as well as large.

As the 20th century progressed, a variety of developments produced sprawl and eventually stagnation in U. S. metropolitan areas. One of these developments was the passenger car, but perhaps even more important was the motor truck. Compared with the horse-drawn wagon that it replaced, it vastly reduced the cost of internal movement of goods and permitted work places to spread out. When car ownership became common, residences and work places were no longer bound to locations along fixed routes. This permitted still more spread which, in turn, allowed even greater scale of production. These basic forces were enhanced by two government policies after World War II: the building of high-speed urban expressways wherever projected traffic demand seemed sufficient, and the availability of mortgage credit at attractive terms for new, single-family, detached suburban housing.

Business Moves to Suburbia. More recently, locating production units near the core of an urban area, or even within an SMSA at all, has become less important. In large measure, this stems from reduction in the bulk of materials associated with most workers' occupations. At present, about two thirds of U. S. workers are not involved with any raw materials at all, and even for the rest, there has been a steady drop in the weight of raw materials processed. At the same time, since the extent of scale economies at the establishment level is more limited for services than for goods, the need for large production units has been reduced. Finally, advances in information storage, retrieval, and transmission have reduced

U. S. cities spend approximately 13% of their annual budgets for public welfare and hospitals.

The construction of massive urban expressways after World War II helped produce stagnation in the U. S. metropolitan areas.

the need for closely related activities to be located near each other. Some other contributing factors can be identified. Air-conditioning has led to more dispersal of economic activities regionally, though not necessarily away from cities. On the other hand, such amenities as television, quick-food chains, and standardized shopping facilities have reduced the cultural isolation of small towns and rural areas, adding to the feasibility of economic activities escaping the higher public service and congestion costs of the metropolis.

Declining Birth Rate. Demographic trends associated with metropolitan change reveal clearly, however, that the economic shifts indicated above have been neither so abrupt nor so recent a phenomenon as is popularly supposed. In fact, the number of people moving away from SMSA's has been greater than the number moving to them at least since the early 1960's. This relative trend away from the metropolis was not generally noticed until recently, however, because up until about 1970 the excess of births over deaths was greater than the net outmigration, and the combined SMSA's continued to show absolute growth in population. The great natural increase in the SMSA's was partly due to high, if dwindling, birth rates and partly to the large representation in metropolitan populations of women in their child-bearing years.

The long-term trend directing economic activities progressively away from the metropolis was revealed by the precipitous drop in the birth rate since 1970. It is this factor more than any other which has caused the unprecedented phenomenon of absolute decline of metropolitan population and an even sharper loss of central-city population since 1970. Thus, the decline is not a reflection of some sudden change in the economic viability of the metropolis. If anything "sudden" has occurred, it is the drop in the birth rate, which in the mid-1970's stood at 1.8 per female—below the equilibrium replacement rate of 2.1—compared with a rate of about 3.7 as recently as the late 1950's.

Leapfrogging Metropolis. In part, the apparent population loss in the metropolis reflects the spread of, rather than a turning away from, the metropolis, that is, the sprawl of population beyond the official boundaries of SMSA's, with some time lag to be expected before the boundaries are adjusted outward. From that, however, it should not be concluded that little of real consequence has happened. First, counties well beyond metropolitan hinterlands are growing in significant numbers for the first time in this century; and such growth is occurring in almost all sections of the country. Second, even to the extent that it represents a "spreading out" of existing metro areas, the more recent pattern of sprawl is producing an organization of urban life which may be as different in kind as it is in degree. It has been found, for example, that job growth is not following a course of continuous suburbanization but one of leapfrogging to outlying, previously nonurban sites. Thus, it is not so much that metropolitan life is being forsaken for a return to a small-town or rural existence, but rather that the metropolis is moving to the countryside. Increasingly, individuals and families can be participants in economic, informational, and even cultural and social aspects of metropolitan life without actually having to live in the city or even the suburbs.

Urban Amenities—Rural Setting. For individual families, it is obvious that proximity to an urban area or its center still brings certain advantages of access to many specialized facilities. Distance from the metropolis provides fewer of these things but greater assurance of space, privacy, and safety. Recently, it has also become less necessary to go to the metropolis to find nonrural work. The communications revolution has diminished the cultural and informational disadvantage of smaller communities, while the "safety" advantage of distance from the metropolis may have increased substantially. Lower crime rates outside the city may allow the nonmetropolitan resident greater participation in cultural life and entertainment outside the home than the city resident. Thus, it may be concluded that strong and widespread forces are working to disperse what are thought of as *urban activities* far beyond what are considered *urban areas*.

As population shrinks, and as service activities increasingly replace manufacturing as the major employment, the physical dimensions of urban regions will also shift. In large metropolitan areas, the number of commuters from the suburbs to the central city has grown slowly in recent years, while the number commuting from the city out to the suburbs—though still smaller—has grown at a much more rapid rate. Workers who both live and work in the suburbs have increased sharply, and those who both live and work in the central city have similarly decreased. On top of that, the number of workers commuting from residences inside to working places outside the SMSA has risen quite rapidly.

Shape of the New Metropolis. These trends indicate little likelihood of a continuation of historic urban development patterns, that is, creeping suburbanization with dispersal of population and employment in a regular and continuous fashion. Neither is there much likelihood of substantial reconcentration of population within older urban areas along existing, or even new, public transport routes. The most likely development is that of truly multicentered metropolitan areas in which there are relatively few, large, secondary employment centers, drawing most of their labor from nearby densely settled areas. The future metropolis is likely to consist of a loose federation of smaller and fairly compact residential-employment centers. While the system itself may be very large—perhaps even a few hundred miles across—very few people are likely to engage in regular long-distance commuting, and much or most of the land in an individual region may still be used for nonmetropolitan pursuits, such as agriculture or mining.

The shape of the metropolis will also be molded by changes in demography. The average size of a household will decline so that even though overall population is likely to fall in most urban areas, there may still be need for more housing units. These will most likely be smaller units, typically in multifamily dwellings. Some obvious economies are possible if these units are built at fairly high density. This, along with a desire for privacy, the possibility for work-place dispersal (which new information technology may permit), and higher fuel cost, points to a future metropolis with a number of fairly dense but spatially separated nodes.

Throughout the 1950's, and even more in the 1960's, one of the fastest growing sectors in the American economy was local government. In fact, until recently, substantial increases in public-service employment masked the decline of industrial jobs in urban areas. Unfortunately, the prospects for continued expansion in public employment are weak indeed, due to growing fiscal pressures, such as those of New York City. Increased business investment in any metropolitan economy depends upon the profitability of growing output or the substitution of a superior technology in the activities now concentrated in urban areas. These are mainly services catering to a national or large-scale regional market—such activities as research and development, maintenance of central offices, large-scale record and information processing, and specializations in cultural, educational, and tourist facilities.

Mismatch of Needs and Skills. Ultimately, the future of the mature metropolis may rest upon the quality of its human resources. And if there is anything special about the human resources of major U. S. cities, it is that their training, experience, and skills are badly matched to the needs of emerging economic opportunities. Indeed, as metropolitan activities spread to the "new metropolis" of the countryside, a residue of the economically disadvantaged, who cannot compete effectively, is left behind in the "old" metropolis. Thus, especially in the older cities and urban areas, growing proportions of minority and female-headed households may be noticed. These particular groups are the most likely to be in poverty and to have low confidence in their prospective success.

To some extent, the problems caused by this mismatch will be self-adjusting. As the more routine industrial and construction jobs, which can use unskilled labor, leave the declining areas, some of the less skilled work force may follow, while those seeking such opportunity are less likely than before to come to the mature metropolis. Nor will those seeking im-

Inadequate housing and public transportation as well as dirty streets are common urban problems.

Many suburbanites now live, work, and seek entertainment in the home community. This development has increased the financial problems of U. S. cities.

proved health and welfare services find the traditional big-city destinations as attractive as in the past, because support levels are likely to be lower than before. (This, however, may depend on the federal government's role.) Also, at some stage, vacant land and empty factories and warehouses may become sufficiently available in the central city to foster rebirth of activities with low labor-skill requirements. But there is little reason to believe that this self-adjustment will occur rapidly or to forget the human losses and forsaken business opportunities that will continue until it takes place. In order to match their human resources to their developmental opportunities before they "hit bottom," the cities will have to seek more imaginative ways of utilizing human beings and more effective techniques for giving the disadvantaged what they need to compete.

Of course, overreacting to very recent trends should be avoided. In the days of the "exploding metropolis" many spoke and planned as if growth would go on forever; and that was less than 20 years ago. Now, in the era of "urban maturity," it seems equally foolhardy to expect decline to be with us forever. This caution notwithstanding, there is substantial reason to believe that decline in cities and urban areas will continue at least for the next decade and likely to the end of the century.

WATER

By M. Gordon Wolman, *Professor of Geography*
The Johns Hopkins University

In March 1977, the United Nations Conference on Water in Mar Del Plata, Argentina, highlighted once again the unique importance of water in meeting the fundamental needs and aspirations of the peoples of the world. Representatives of all nations, from the poorest to the richest, recognized that for each of them adequate water supplies are essential to improving health, increasing production of food, developing industry, reducing pollution, and protecting the environment.

Why, one might ask, were the nations of the world compelled to affirm the obvious importance of water? There were two reasons. First, the recurrence of drought in parts of Africa, the United States, Europe, and Asia; and second, the important global facts on water and people. The world supply of water is constant but unevenly distributed in space and time. In contrast, the world's population is doubling every 20–30 years. Some live where land is plentiful but water scarce, others are flocking to cities, or to marginal lands to produce food for hungry mouths. Where water is normally abundant, periodic droughts are reminders that the local supply is variable and that unchecked use may at times deplete the supply. For those whose water is perennially limited, drought, even for a modest period of time, reduces subsistence living to a battle for survival. Water-supply problems, then, are continuous, not episodic. The vagaries of weather and climate serve to shock people into thinking about these problems.

The Water Budget. While the worldwide problems of water supply are complicated, the framework for looking at them is a simple budget, relating the quantity, quality, and distribution of natural supply to the demands of man. The globe has a fixed quantity of water. Of this, 97% is salt water in the sea; only 3% is fresh. And three fourths of the fresh water are tied up in glaciers and ice caps, leaving less than 1% in rivers, lakes, groundwater, soil, and atmosphere. Virtually all of this 1% is groundwater; rivers account for only a tiny fraction. It is this fresh water, 1% of the earth's total, which provides the basis for supplying the global needs of mankind.

The hydrologic cycle describes the constant movement of water from the ocean and the land to the atmosphere, its transport in the atmosphere, precipitation as rain or snow, evaporation or infiltration into the ground, runoff into rivers, and return to lakes or to the ocean. On a global scale, most of the water evaporated from the ocean falls over the ocean. Of that which moves over and precipitates on land, two thirds evaporate; one third runs to rivers, either over the surface or through the ground. These fractions differ from place to place. The annual

UPI

budget is a simple equation: Precipitation (P), minus Evaporation (E) (from water, land, and plants), equals Runoff (R), plus or minus any change in Storage (S), or $P - E = R \pm \triangle S$. What is available from nature for continuous use in any given place is the renewable supply provided each year by precipitation, minus the amount evaporated from land or water or by plant life. Water can be drawn from storage—groundwater or lakes—but the "reservoir" will be depleted unless replenished in the cycle.

The timing and distribution of the annual fresh-water supply vary enormously over the surface of the globe. The circulation of the atmosphere and the ocean, determined by the differential heating of the globe at the equator and the poles and the rotation of the earth on its axis, govern the climate and the pattern of the transport of water vapor in the atmosphere. In a few areas, such as around Portland, Oreg., precipitation is plentiful (60 inches, or 152 cm) and evenly distributed throughout the year. In contrast, 900 inches (2,286 cm) of rain may fall in one year in Assam, India, all during the seasonal monsoons. Rainfall in Yuma, Ariz., is about 5 inches (12.7 cm) and evaporation much greater, resulting in virtually no average runoff and the need to irrigate to make up the difference between the natural supply and what agriculture requires. The great deserts of Africa, central Asia, and Australia often receive only a trace of rain in a year, sometimes none.

These facts, the fixed quantity of water at the surface of the earth, its cycle, and irregular distribution in time and place, define the opportunities and dilemmas faced by mankind when trying to manage water to meet its needs. Global figures are averages. Regions or drainage basins provide the most realistic scale for matching demand and supply.

Water Use in Selected Places

[in gallons (liters) a day per person]

New York.........276 (1,045)
Moscow..........159 (600)
Paris.............132 (500)
London...........69 (263)
Brussels..........35 (132)
São Paulo.........53 (200)[1]
Nairobi...........36 (135)
Bombay...........32 (121)[2]
Addis Ababa.......8 (30)[3]
Tanzania Village....8 (30)[4]

[1] 54% of population served by house connection. [2] 23% of population served by house connection. [3] 65% house, 18% standpipe. [4] Planned; actual use one tenth or less.

Figures include all uses: industrial and domestic.

Figure showing the present state of the water balance of the world's land area. The numbers stand for cubic kilometers, the equivalent of 1,308,000,000 cubic yards.

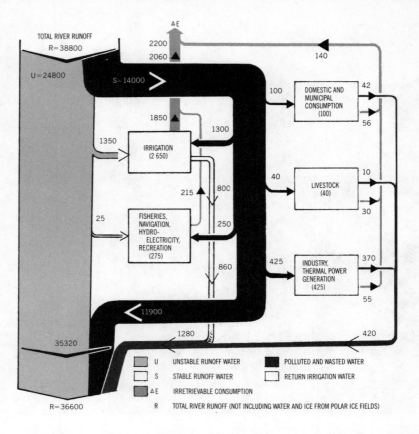

Uses of Water.

Some clear definitions are vital to the effort to relate demand for water to available supply. Simply put, need is a desire, use is an activity, and demand is an economic term relating a quantity supplied for a price. They are *not* synonymous. Water withdrawn for use means water taken from a source—river, lake, or well—and put to some use by man. Water withdrawn for production of hydroelectric power simply drops from a higher to a lower elevation through a turbine. Immense quantities flow through the system, but consumptive use—water actually consumed or lost by evaporation or seepage—is less than 0.5% of the total withdrawn. In contrast, of the water withdrawn to irrigate crops, some 60% or more may be consumed (lost to the system). The plants require (use) water to grow, and some evaporates and seeps from unlined canals on its way to the fields. Water not consumed returns to water courses after passing through the soil. Thus, quantity withdrawn equals the consumptive use, plus the return flow.

In the world as a whole, the quantity of water for domestic, municipal, industrial, and thermal power generation is considerably less than that withdrawn for irrigation agriculture (see figure). Similarly, the amount consumed in irrigation (approximately 60%) far exceeds that of municipal and industrial uses (5–20%). Because most of the water withdrawn returns to the system, water can be "reused" many times. A deficit exists when consumptive use exceeds available supply. Water quality may be degraded by use, requiring treatment by reusers.

Different parts of the world and different activities use very different quantities of water (see table). A New Yorker uses about 276 gallons 1,045 1) a day, while a resident of Bombay, if he has public water supply, uses 32 (121 1). A Tanzanian villager uses no more than 8 gallons (30 1) per day and generally no more than 2–3 quarts (2–3 1).

Similarly, water withdrawn for use in making a ton of steel may range from the average 65,000 gallons (2,460 hl) to as little as 1,400 (53 hl) in dry California. Some 650,000 gallons per acre (60,800 hl/ha) are used annually in some areas to irrigate wheat; sophisticated trickle irrigation of orange groves in Israel draws roughly one third the water of more common furrow methods.

Projections of Future Uses. The need to feed burgeoning populations and rising expectations for a better life spur demands for more water throughout the world. More water use goes together with higher living standards, especially near the bottom of the economic ladder. Both withdrawals and consumptive use of water in the United States and elsewhere climbed rapidly from the 1950's to 1975. Some project continued per-capita growth of withdrawals, but it is likely that increasing costs will slow demand in the industrialized nations. In contrast, the World Health Organization estimates that only 22% of the (U. S.) 1½ billion people living in rural areas in the developing world have reasonably adequate community water supplies, essential to drinking and simple hygiene, and only 15% have similar sanitation services. While large cities throughout the world are better served with water, many urban centers, such as Calcutta, India, and Cairo, Egypt, are growing explosively. Expansion of supplies to metropolitan areas requires not only development of sources, but elaborate systems of treatment and distribution. Some expect these demands to treble or more than treble by the year 2000.

Much of the arable land in climates with good growing seasons must be irrigated to be made productive. Between 1967 and 2000 it is estimated that fresh water required for irrigation will double from 18,300 to 36,600 trillion (U. S.) cubic yards (14,000–28,000 trillion m³) per year. China is expanding irrigated land by 2.5–5 million acres (1–2 million ha) per year, and from 1950 to 1970 irrigated land in India grew by 50%, much of it watered from wells. Crop yields can increase much more—conceivably as much as ten-fold on alluvial soils in India.

Ethiopians gather available water near Mersa. Only one fifth of rural people in underdeveloped countries have adequate water supply systems.

UPI

Father and son used to fish in the Snake River near Blackfoot, Idaho; it dried up in the 1977 drought. In California, the Folsom Lake reservoir (*right*) receded more than 40 ft (12 m) below normal level.

Available quantities of water alone do not tell the whole story. Waters polluted by industrial and urban wastes, or by accelerated erosion from the land, degrade water quality. Expansion of rural populations to marginal lands on steep hillsides in Nepal, Indonesia, Latin America, and elsewhere result in rapid runoff of water and erosion of soil which clogs downstream river channels, reservoirs, and lakes.

Rising demands, particularly those associated with growing food production and economic development, place ever increasing pressure on the world's available fresh-water supplies. Global generalizations and projections are at best a warning that the world's population faces a myriad of problems in providing an adequate quantity of water of satisfactory quality to meet human needs. Matching supply and demand requires realistic appraisal of the unique problems and opportunities of specific areas. Virtually no region will have sufficient water supply for projected uses unless it has adequate plans for development and management.

Increasing Water Supplies. Storage in reservoirs, lakes, or in the ground to even out high and low river flow is the most common method of augmenting supply. Worldwide, it is estimated that regulation of runoff by reservoirs might increase stable supplies by 15%. Not all areas provide good reservoir sites, nor are reservoirs without both hydrological and ecological problems. In dry regions, they create large surface areas from which water evaporates. Additional reservoirs may not make more water available because evaporation may exceed the amount provided by additional regulation—a condition currently reached on the lower Colorado River. Over much of the world, however, as major projects on the Indus, Ganges, Volga, Mekong, and Yellow rivers testify, reservoirs will continue to provide much needed water. Ecological changes, including the spread of water-borne diseases such as schistosomiasis, the growth of water plants, changes in downstream habitats, and water and salt logging of irrigated lands pose additional problems.

In many regions, groundwater provides an immense potential source of fresh water, much larger than rivers or lakes. But while the stored supply may be large, the rate of replenishment is exceedingly slow and sometimes zero. In very dry regions, continuous removal of large quantities of groundwater, as in parts of California or the High Plains of Texas, has reduced the supply and lowered the water table to such depths that the cost of pumping has become prohibitive for some uses. In coastal areas, excessive removal of fresh water can result in the intrusion of adjacent salt water from estuaries and contamination of the overlying fresh water.

Many more modest opportunities are available for augmenting water supplies. These include drainage or channelization of swamps (such as the Sudd on the White Nile) to reduce evaporation from wetland surfaces, although wetlands in other areas have storage and wildlife values which may transcend that of the water supply. Reduction of vegetation that draws water from great depths may also increase supplies. In some areas, brackish water can be obtained from surface or underground sources and used for purposes to which high mineral content is not important. By use of special techniques even irrigation is sometimes possible with rather saline water. Various techniques are also available for desalting not only brackish but sea water. It is price, not technology, which limits desalinization.

Floods devastated Johnstown, Pa., in July. The jungle-like scene was previously Cooper Avenue.

UPI

While drought scorched some regions of the earth, torrential rains lashed others. Drivers in southwest France found the going slow through floodwaters in May. School-girls in Manila were similarly hampered in August.

PHOTOS, UPI

Conserving Water. Perhaps the largest "additional" supplies may be secured by more careful and appropriate use of available water, that is, by conservation and reuse. Although both industrial and agricultural uses may degrade its quality, water today is continuously withdrawn from major water courses in populated areas, then returned and reused, perhaps 2–5 times.

Water savings, occasionally as high as 100%, can also be brought about by less profligate application of irrigation water. Low prices for water may encourage waste, and so may fears that water rights will be lost if all that is legally allocated is not used.

Possibilities for recycling vary greatly among industries and from one plant to another. For example, since 1950, there has been a five-fold reduction in the amount of water used to process a ton of oil, and similar reductions have been achieved in many other cases. The wide range, noted earlier, in the quantity used by various industries suggests many opportunities to reduce water use in the making of specific products —opportunities increasingly being sought both to conserve water and reduce polluting discharges.

Eliminating leakage in water systems and replacing unlined with lined canals in some large irrigation projects may also reduce waste. Seepage losses in canals can be exceedingly large. A variety of other conservation opportunities has been proposed, ranging from reducing the quantity of water used to flush toilets, or to take a shower, to complete elimination of water transmission systems for sewers to be replaced by so-called modern organic disposal systems. Each of these possibilities may be appropriate in some areas, but it is unlikely that large quantities of water will be saved by such measures alone.

Incentives to Altering Demand. While the mix of opportunities both to augment supply and to reduce demand is large, what incentives are needed to induce desired changes? Memories of recurrent shortages are usually short-lived and projected imbalances between perceived needs and available supplies often unpersuasive.

In some regions, there is good evidence that what is termed a "water shortage" is in fact only shortage of water for specific uses at the low prices to which people have become accustomed. Because of federal subsidies in the United States, irrigators may pay one fourth the price charged to cities and industry. And since cities and industries pay the full price, less water is likely, in the long run, to be used for irrigation

PERKIN-ELMER

With water rationing in effect in northern California in early 1977, a Marin County resident (*below right*) used a pump, plastic container, and a large barrel to collect water from the roof of his home. Water vending machines, selling reprocessed city water, were a popular convenience in the area.

A lab director in Suffolk County, N.Y., uses an atomic absorption spectrophotometer to analyze water quality.

UPI

UPI

(particularly in view of the high consumptive loss) and more for municipal and industrial purposes—a change in life style resulting in the "conservation" of water.

Higher water prices may reduce water use, and in communities where water meters have been installed households may use 10–20% less water as they realize the high cost of waste. Because peak demands for a given hour may be five times the average daily use, higher prices during such times could reduce not only the use, but also the need for excessive capacity in the water-supply system. While pricing schemes have been most used in the industrialized countries, evidence from many other nations indicates that even the poorest citizens are willing to save pennies and pay for wholesome fresh-water supplies—evidence of the vital importance of water to health and human well-being.

Since antiquity, legal and administrative institutions have developed in the dry regions of the world to regulate or allocate water among competing users. Local, regional, national, and international institutions have been organized to apportion limited supplies equitably and to encourage efficient application, conservation, and reuse of water. Irrigation districts, organized to assure delivery of stated quantities of water at stated times, even predate the pharaohs. They remain essential to water management.

Water rationing during dry spells is a form of allocation more familiar to urban dwellers. Most such measures—designated times for specific water uses, restrictions on car washing or on the number of glasses of water volunteered in restaurants, and fines for unauthorized uses—are temporary. While they cannot alone replace long-term plans to provide enough water of adequate quality for diverse uses, they can be a part of efficient management, where it is recognized that bearing some risk of drought may be less costly than continuously augmenting supplies.

Conclusion. Current local shortages as well as worldwide evidence of significant fluctuations in climate, producing long dry spells in most parts of the world, demand the most thoughtful management of the earth's fixed quantity of water. While the technical difficulties are formidable, the social problems of management are probably more so. It may be possible to calculate and to build a series of reservoirs on a river system that will provide the maximum yield of water for the greatest number of people and the greatest variety of uses. However, even in a single country or region it is by no means easy to establish the political and social institutions which make it possible to plan and to execute such a development and to share the costs and the benefits of such an integrated system. The 52 largest rivers in the world, with drainage areas greater than 38,600 square miles (100,000 km²) are international, flowing through 2–8 countries. For the people of the world as a whole, the political and social systems required to develop and manage the available water on the surface of the globe will in all likelihood prove to be more complex and difficult to establish than the engineering, scientific, and technical know-how needed to bring about the desired result. Many of the major rivers of the world, such as the Nile, Ganges, Jordan, and the Tigris-Euphrates, illustrate, from earliest antiquity, the problems involved in matching the needs of people in one area with the water sources located in another. A growing world population and higher aspirations among people of all nations for a better life—in which water plays a fundamental part—place one more demand upon the ingenuity and good will of statesman and citizen alike.

Las Vegas, Nev., a gambler's mecca.

GAMBLING

A Review of an Inherent Principle

By Charles F. Phillips, Jr.
Professor of Economics, Washington and Lee University

Speaking before the House of Commons, Feb. 11, 1780, British states-man Edmund Burke referred to the practice of gambling as a "principle inherent in human nature." The statement is true today, just as it was at that time. In fact, the inevitability of gambling is at the base of the change in public policy that has been taking place, both in the United States and abroad, in relation to this complex social phenomenon. And it was with this in mind that the 15-member Commission on the Review of the National Policy Toward Gambling, established by the Organized Crime Control Act of 1970, completed its three-year comprehensive analysis of gambling with the issuance of a 413-page report in late 1976.

Current Attitudes. According to studies made for the commission, the following findings are pertinent to an assessment of current attitudes toward gambling:

> Some 61% of the adult U. S. population—about 88 million people—participated in some form of gambling in 1974. Of these, 48% (about 69 million people) patronized some form of legal or illegal commercial gambling. The remaining wagered only with friends in a social setting.

TED THAI

Although the stereotypical bingo player is the older woman, surveys show that the game appeals to both sexes, all ages, and persons of mixed incomes and educational attainment.

Almost 80% of those responding to a comprehensive, nationwide survey favored legalization of some form of gambling, though there was considerable disagreement on which forms should be legalized. The strongest opposition was to legalization of numbers games and betting on sport events, particularly on high school and college levels.

Most local police departments cannot deal effectively with large gambling operations. This is due to a lack of resources, inadequate legal tools, noncooperation by the courts, interjurisdictional problems, and corruption. Law enforcement efforts, consequently, are commonly directed against low-level gambling violators, while high-level operators remain untouched. The trend toward legalization further complicates the law enforcement problems.

Given these findings, the growth of legal gambling is not surprising. Americans wagered more than $17,000,000,000 through legal commercial channels in 1974, compared with about $5,000,000,000 in 1960, and more than $5,000,000,000 through illegal channels. During the period 1960–1974, six states established pari-mutuel horse racing (bringing the total to 32); 13 states, beginning with New Hampshire in 1964, established state-operated lotteries; New York legalized the nation's first pari-mutuel off-track betting system in 1971; and New Jersey established the first legal numbers game in 1974. Subsequently New Jersey voters approved the establishment of casinos in Atlantic City, and Rhode Island joined Connecticut, Florida, and Nevada in legalizing jai alai. Existing legal gambling industries, moreover, have undergone substantial expansion since 1960; gross taxable revenue from Nevada's casino industry increased from less than $200 million in 1960 to more than $1,000,000,000 in 1974.

Trend Toward Legalized Gambling. A similar trend toward legalization of gambling is evident in many foreign countries. In 1968, for example, Great Britain legalized casino gaming, though its rules and regulations differ significantly from those found in Nevada. In Great Britain, an organization conducting commercial casino gaming must do so as a member-

ABOVE: PHOTO RESEARCHERS; BELOW: JAN LUKAS, PHOTO RESEARCHERS

NANCY M. HAMILTON, PHOTO RESEARCHERS   WIDE WORLD

Comfort and elegance are important elements for the successful casino. In 1971, New York State introduced the nation's first pari-mutuel off-track betting system.

In recent years, Rhode Island joined Connecticut in legalizing jai alai (*below, left*). Several states hold elaborate, theatrical productions to announce their lottery winners.

PRESS BUREAU, CITY OF ATLANTIC CITY

In Atlantic City, N. J., the introduction of casino gambling, approved by the electorate in 1976, is expected to revive the deteriorated resort, once one of the most popular.

ship club; gaming is restricted to the hours between 2 P. M. and 4 A. M.; and live entertainment on the casino premises, credit to players, and advertising are prohibited. Not long ago Spain reintroduced gambling.

The trend toward legalization is predicated upon two dominant and incompatible goals. On the one hand, state governments view legalization as a means of raising needed revenues, either for general purposes or for specifically designated programs (for instance, education, property-tax relief). On the other hand, many view legalization as a means of dealing with illegal gambling, and especially that part of it controlled by organized crime. The incompatibility of these two goals is obvious. To achieve maximum state revenues, the necessary taxation may make it impossible for the legal entrepreneur to compete with his illegal counterpart, who is not so burdened. To control crime, the legal entrepreneur may have to offer both competitive odds and payoffs and the state may have to eliminate taxes on the bettor and the operator—which again would eliminate the likelihood of substantial revenue. At a minimum, a state must decide upon which goal it wishes to pursue in formulating a policy toward legalization.

At the same time, there are other factors which must be considered in the debate over legalization. Legal gambling, often portrayed as a painless, voluntary form of taxation, is both a regressive and an expensive form of taxation. The legalization of gambling creates new gamblers (and additional compulsive gamblers), intrudes into areas of sincerely held theological and ethical convictions, may encourage citizens to seek a profit through chance rather than through work, and presents complex regulatory problems for the states. Nor have government revenues from new forms of legal gambling been so high as initial estimates, and extensive advertising appears necessary to maintain interest.

(continued on page 66)

Gambling — A Losing Proposition

BY REV. MSGR. JOSEPH A. DUNNE
President and Executive Director
The National Council on Compulsive Gambling

The history of the United States reveals that gambling, though popular at different times and locations until repressed by federal legislation at the time of the Civil War, has always been accompanied by vice and lawlessness. Thus, lotteries were run in the colonies to support public projects *until fraudulent practices were detected.* Casino gambling flourished in Western mining towns and later in the larger cities *until crime and corruption stimulated public opposition,* particularly by fundamentalist Protestants and reform groups such as the Woman's Christian Temperance Union.

Today, in view of the general trend toward the acceptance of legalized gambling, anti-gambling forces are again becoming active and vocal. Though pro-gambling statutes and referenda have been approved in many states, successful campaigns have also been mounted to defeat proposals for casinos in Detroit, dog racing in California, and slot machines in Delaware. Since 1968, moreover, church groups in Texas have succeeded in having three propositions for pari-mutuel betting defeated in statewide referenda.

In the words of Sen. John L. McClellan (D.-Ark.), the basic premise of the opposition forces is that traditional American work values "will not tolerate elevating gambling activities to an advantageous position over income earned by honest endeavor." In addition, anti-gamblers believe that gambling is strictly a losing proposition, that limited gambling only leads to more and more of the same and possibly to pathologically compulsive gambling, and that it encourages organized crime.

To counteract the trend toward legalization, those opposed to gambling suggest massive public education campaigns to demonstrate the economic limitations of the activity, a blitz of letter writing to state legislators in order to halt pro-gambling legislation, increased activity to publicize the dangers of compulsive gambling, and greater effort by state and federal agencies to fight illegal operations.

The strongest and most effective resistance to gambling is in the South and Southwest, the so-called Bible belt. In these areas, fundamentalist religious principles prevail, and the Protestant work ethic remains strong. Testifying before the Commission on the Review of the National Policy Toward Gambling, many Protestant and Jewish leaders voiced keen opposition to, and outright condemnation of, legalized gambling; Roman Catholic leaders generally expressed the view that gambling is an indifferent act until it interferes with the discharge of duty and obligations.

The National Council on Compulsive Gambling, Inc., was organized in New York City in 1972. Its purpose is to educate the public to understand that compulsive gambling is an illness and a public health problem. It refers compulsive gamblers to Gamblers Anonymous and their families to Gam-Anon and Gamateen.

Commission Recommendations and Studies. In its final report, the national gambling commission made the following major policy recommendations:

> The states should have the primary responsibility for determining what forms of gambling may legally take place within their borders.
>
> The federal government should take care not to interfere with state efforts to compete with illegal gambling operations. Toward this end, the winnings from legal gambling entities should be excluded from gross income for federal income tax purposes, and the federal wagering excise and occupational stamp taxes should be repealed.
>
> State and local law enforcement agencies, in conjunction with prosecutors, should direct their efforts against high-level gambling offenses, particularly bookmaking and numbers operations, through the creation of specialized gambling units in state and large urban police departments.

The commission also studied the five principal forms of legal gambling—casinos in Nevada, pari-mutuel horse racing and dog racing, off-track betting, lotteries, and bingo.

> "With respect to casinos, the commission has concluded that Nevada state gambling regulations are on the whole sufficiently stringent and that enforcement of the regulations is sound. It has also found that the influence of organized crime in Nevada casinos has been significantly reduced during the past 10 years. Nevertheless, it has determined that some aspects of Nevada casino gambling should not be reproduced elsewhere.
> "In the area of pari-mutuel racing, the commission found that, in most states, the takeout—money not returned to bettors—is too high. It also found that a serious potential for conflict of interest exists when racing commissioners are permitted to hold financial interests in racetracks they regulate. On the issue of off-track betting, the commission has concluded that the passage of a federal law banning all interstate off-track betting would interfere with each state's ability to determine its own gambling policies and that such interference undermines the national policy toward gambling recommended by the commission. Regarding lotteries (and off-track betting), the commission has found that the active publicity given these forms of gambling by the states induces citizen participation contrary to the public's best interest. Finally, the commission has found that commercial bingo operators running games for the benefit of charitable groups often retain most of the profits for themselves."

While the trend toward legalization of gambling is clear, an early resolution of the complex issues raised by gambling is unlikely and perhaps impossible. These issues will continue to be widely debated, as each state seeks to formulate a policy toward gambling.

A thanksgiving service is held in St. Paul's Cathedral to mark the 25th anniversary of Queen Elizabeth's coronation.

REVIEW
OF THE YEAR

ACCIDENTS AND DISASTERS

UPI

A young child stands in bewilderment amid the ruins of her home, destroyed by the cyclone that swept the coast of Andhra Pradesh state, India, in November.

AVIATION

Jan. 13—Soviet TU-104 airliner explodes and crashes in Alma-Ata, USSR, killing at least 90.

Feb. 9—Queen Alia of Jordan and three other persons die when helicopter crashes in rain on flight to Amman.

March 27—KLM and Pan American Boeing 747s collide on runway on the Canary island of Tenerife, killing 581 persons in the world's worst aviation disaster.

April 4—Southern Airways jet crashes in New Hope, Ga., after its engines ingest hail, killing 62 on plane and 8 on the ground.

April 5—Alexander Guterma, a coal company executive, five members of his family, and a pilot die when their private plane crashes near New York City's La Guardia Airport; one son survives.

May 10—Israeli helicopter crash during military exercise is fatal to all 54 paratroopers and crewmen aboard.

May 16—Helicopter tips over after landing atop New York City's Pan Am Building, killing four on roof and one on ground after rotors snap off.

May 27—Soviet jet en route from Moscow crashes on approach to Havana, Cuba, airport, killing 66.

Sept. 5—Ecuadorian airliner crashes into a mountain north of Cuenca, Ecuador, killing all 33 persons aboard.

Sept. 27—Japan Air Lines DC-8 crashes short of runway in Kuala Lumpur, Malaysia, killing 34 of 79 aboard.

Nov. 19—TAP-Portuguese Airways Boeing 727 crashes in rain on resort island of Madeira, killing 130.

Dec. 4—Malaysian jetliner hijacked by Japanese terrorists explodes and crashes in southern Malaysia, killing 100.

Dec. 13—University of Evansville basketball team among 29 killed when chartered DC-3 crashes near Evansville, Ind., after takeoff.

Dec. 18—Thirty-six tourists are killed when a Swiss Caravelle crashes near Funchal, Madeira.

EARTHQUAKES

March 4—Some 1,500 are dead, 11,000 injured, and 80,000 homeless after a quake hit Bucharest and other Rumanian cities.

March 22–23 and April 6—Two quakes in Iran kill more than 500 persons.

March 25—Earthquake in Turkey's mountainous Elazig Province kills 30 and damages homes, schools, and mosques.

Aug. 19—One of the strongest quakes ever recorded, measuring 8.9 on the Richter Scale, leaves more than 100 dead on islands in Indonesia.

Nov. 23—Quake in San Juan Province, Argentina, claims 80 to 100 lives, leaves 10,000 homeless.

Dec. 20—At least 519 die as earthquake devastates three villages in Iran.

FIRES AND EXPLOSIONS

Feb. 25—Forty-five persons reportedly die when fire sweeps Moscow's *Rossiya* hotel, the world's largest.

May 11—Gas explosion 800 feet (240 m) underground kills 25 miners in Hokkaido, Japan.

May 28—Flames and smoke kill 164 persons at the Beverly Hills Supper Club in Southgate, Ky.

June 9—Fire in a club in Abidjan, Ivory Coast, kills 41, mostly French nationals.

June 26—Fire attributed to the lighting of padded material with a cigarette kills 42 persons in a jail in Maury County, Tennessee.

July–August—In drought-parched California, fires of various origins destroy millions of acres of timber, valuable watershed foliage, and expensive homes.

Aug. 2—Explosion in coal mine in Mozambique kills about 70 miners and results in rioting in which nine officials die.

Nov. 14—Fire ignited by a candle during a power outage caused by a typhoon kills at least 47 persons in a Manila hotel.

Dec. 16—At least 32 mental patients die when fire destroys a wing of a crowded hospital in Manila.

LAND AND SEA TRANSPORTATION

Jan. 11—Following a search off Cape Cod, U. S. and Canadian coast guards report loss of Panamanian tanker and all 38 aboard.

Jan. 17—At least 46 U. S. servicemen die when launch returning them from weekend shore leave collides with a Spanish freighter in Barcelona harbor.

Jan. 18—At least 82 die when a commuter train derails outside Sydney, Australia, and smashes supports of an overhead bridge, which collapses on train.

May 31—Indian express train crashes into flood-swollen river in Assam, killing at least 44.

June 27—Express passenger train and freight train crash head-on near Lebus, East Germany, killing 29.

Oct. 10—Sixty-one die as passenger express train crashes into the rear of a stationary freight train near Allahabad in northern India.

Nov. 11—Train loaded with dynamite explodes in a railway station in Iri, South Korea, killing 57 and injuring 1,348.

STORMS AND FLOODS

January–March—Unusually severe blizzards in northern parts of the United States leave many dead and disrupt economy.

April 1—Tornado strikes two regions of Bangladesh, killing 900 and leaving thousands homeless.

April 3–6—Tornadoes, rains, and flooding kill at least 40 and cause $275 million in damage in southeastern United States.

July 11—Floods and landslides kill at least 111 persons in and near Seoul, South Korea.

July 20—Nightlong rainfall causes flash flood fatal to at least 68 in Johnstown, Pa., and leaves 2,000 persons homeless.

July 25–30—Two typhoons hit Taiwan, killing 39 persons and destroying more than 200,000 homes.

Sept. 12—Heavy rains in the vicinity of Kansas City, Mo., cause severe flash flooding that kills 28 persons.

Nov. 2–3—Unprecedented torrential rains fall on Athens and Piraeus, Greece, causing the death of 25 persons and millions of dollars in damage.

Nov. 6—Earthen dam collapses in Georgia following heavy rains, and the subsequent flooding kills 39 persons on the campus of Toccoa Falls Bible College.

Nov. 10—Genoa, Venice, and other areas of northern Italy are hit by rains, floods, and landslides that kill at least 15 persons and cause millions of dollars of damage.

Nov. 12—Tropical storm in Tamil Nadu state, in India, kills at least 400 persons.

Nov. 19—Cyclone sweeps coast of Andhra Pradesh state, in India, killing some 15,000 persons in villages battered by 100 mph (150 km/h) winds and 18-foot (5.5-m) wave.

ADVERTISING

Following the surge of 1976, spending for advertisements in 1977 grew 12%, ahead of most economic indicators. After a decade of slower growth, the trend reflected new reliance on advertising, as competition for consumer markets intensified and personal selling declined. Backed by large budgets, record numbers of new products were introduced, ranging from diesel cars to lower-priced coffee beverages. Soaring media costs and mounting television clutter, however, led advertisers to reevaluate strategies and stress alternate methods of marketing, such as product sampling and telephone selling. The industry stepped up self-regulation, bracing for more government intervention.

Law and Regulation. Advertising by lawyers was cleared by the Supreme Court, and the Federal Trade Commission (FTC) challenged codes restricting doctors' ads. An FTC test case attacked discounts for high-volume newspaper advertisers. Comparative advertising attracted the spotlight when pain-reliever claims wound up in court and a halt to a current campaign was ordered for the first time. Ad portrayals of women, the elderly, and minorities and advertisements aimed at children also came under government scrutiny.

Copy. Use of spokespeople, from Billy Carter to sports stars, proliferated as advertisers sought to personalize their messages. Long-copy ads

UPI

An unusual approach to finding a wife: a N. Y. C. advertising executive took billboard space in subway locales.

Large advertising budgets promoted a record number of new products—including a ground and instant beverage.

© GENERAL FOODS CORPORATION 1977

also extolled such features as energy economy. For beer and beauty aids alike, claims stressed lightness, natural ingredients, and therapeutic benefits, reflecting consumer concern with health, weight control, and self-improvement.

Media. Sex replaced violence as the key television issue, with pressure groups opposing prime-time airing of the "adult" comedy series *Soap*. The televised version of the bestseller *Roots* won larger audiences than ever before. Advertisers sought relief from high television prices by syndication of their own shows and support for a fourth network. They also eyed other options: cable television, now eligible to compete with the networks for top shows, sporting events, and paid ads; two-way cable, which had its first test in Columbus, Ohio; and home video recording equipment, now marketed by major manufacturers.

Consumer magazines flourished, and publications responded to demand for space by increasing the frequency of issue. Dozens of new special-interest periodicals were launched, while newspapers fought declining circulation with emphasis on gossip and regional editions.

Agencies. Major agencies had a banner year, increasing billings, profits, and their share of total volume. International operations were expanded. In their attempt to broaden regional coverage and solve the problem of handling competing accounts, some big shops acquired smaller ones. Several publicly held agencies took steps to go private. Controversy erupted over the role of consultants in the agency search by Datsun automobiles; at $35 million, it was the year's largest account switch.

Volume. Spending rose by 12.1%, to $37.5 billion (U. S.) from $33.5 billion in 1976. Newspaper ads were up to $10.9 billion and television commercials to $7.6 billion, a 15% rise due entirely to higher costs. Direct mail advertising expanded to $5.3 billion, radio to $2.5 billion. Magazines nearly matched the spurt of 1976 with a 20% gain to $2.1 billion. Business publications edged to $1.1 billion, farm books to nearly $1 billion, and outdoor ads were $413 million. All other media—from bus shelters to skywriting—totaled $7.4 billion.

Canada. Instability amid economic stagflation, wage-and-price controls, several major retailer failures, and tough government regulations enacted the previous year characterized Canadian advertising in 1977. Quebec imposed a 2% broadcast-ad tax and legislated French language for all ads, promotion, and packaging in the province. Spending in measured media grew 12.5% to $687 million, pushing total outlays for all media well above $700 million. Television's growth slowed, but it still increased its share to 55% and $385 million. Magazines gained most, reaching $62 million (up 26%). Newspapers captured $151 million (up 15%) and farm books more than $8 million (up 22%), while radio held its own—$59.5 million.

EDWARD H. MEYER, *Grey Advertising, Inc.*

AFGHANISTAN

While political agitation and turmoil changed the governments of neighboring Pakistan and India, Afghanistan continued the tradition from kingdom to republic amid complete calm.

Politics. The fourth year of the republic was greeted by the announcement in January that the long-awaited new constitution would be presented for ratification to a *loya jirgah* (Grand tribal assembly) in February. Representatives were selected in national elections rather than chosen in the traditional manner by local elites. The constitution, written by a committee of experts and reviewed by a separate group representing various occupational and social groups, was the subject of considerable free debate at the *loya jirgah* proceedings. In the end the draft was approved substantially as written. Minor modifications were made concerning the rights of women (who were among *loya jirgah* members) and the language issue. The latter, a potentially explosive problem in this multilingual, multiethnic country, was cleverly defused by the floor managers with an evasive and emollient compromise. This did not suit the Pushtun extremists but pleased the majority. It clearly recognized the linguistic realities of the country.

The ratification of the constitution by the *loya jirgah* greatly strengthened President Daud's position by legitimizing the de facto rule he has exercised since he overthrew the government of King Zahir. The constitution provides for a long transitional period during which Daud's rule will in effect be absolute. In spite of some underground dissatisfaction with the Daud authoritarian regime, political opposition has diminished to the vanishing point. Early in 1977, an attempted coup was swiftly disposed of amid considerable government-sponsored publicity. The leader turned out to be an elderly and ineffectual army general who resented his recent retirement. Most knowledgeable Afghans are convinced that it was nothing more than grumbling with no teeth behind it.

Economics. In 1977, stagnation was the word for the private sector. The government subjected it to mild harassment mostly through taxes but on the whole it ignored rather than persecuted private business. In the public sector, Afghanistan continued its major development plans largely financed by foreign aid. It continued to diversify its sources of aid, drawing especially from Arab countries and Iran as well as from such world economic institutions as the World Bank and the Asian Development Bank. The USSR maintained its dominant position as an aid donor while the United States continued a modest but important effort to fill in gaps left by other donors.

A new Seven-Year development plan was published. Early analysis showed that this was the first time the Afghan government gave agriculture the emphasis it should have.

Foreign Relations. In 1977, Afghanistan maintained its position of "positive neutrality," pursued an essentially conservative foreign policy, and took stands corresponding with other Third World countries. As a result, it enjoyed friendly but arms-length relations with almost every country on the globe. Progress on its principal foreign policy problem, "Pushtunistan," its dispute with Pakistan regarding the status of the Pushtun tribes which straddle the Pakistan-Afghanistan border, came to a standstill after promising developments in 1976.

LEON B. POULLADA
Professor of Political Science
Northern Arizona University

——— AFGHANISTAN · Information Highlights ———

Official Name: Republic of Afghanistan.
Location: Central Asia.
Area: 250,000 square miles (647,500 km²).
Population (1977 est.): 20,000,000.
Chief Cities (1975 est.): Kabul, the capital, 749,000 (met. area); Kandahar, 209,000; Herat, 157,000.
Government: *Head of state and government*, Mohammed Daud Khan, president and prime minister (took office July 1973). *Legislature*—Shura (dissolved July 1973).
Monetary Unit: Afghani (45 afghanis equal U. S.$1, Aug. 1977).
Manufacturing (major products): Textiles, cement, processed fruit, carpets, furniture.
Major Agricultural Products: Wheat, cotton, fruit and nuts, karakul pelts.

AFRICA

Africa in 1977 became an ever more controversial center of international attention, as traumatic changes began to affect every corner of the continent. Violence reached a new pitch in battles between and within various countries. The involvement of the great powers in African disputes became a continuous factor, as the presidents of the Soviet Union, the United States, France, and many other nations made forays into Africa and the contorted politics of the continent. Political and military issues pushed aside the persisting problems of poverty and disease, except for the systematic efforts of West Africans to create a viable Economic Community of West African States (ECOWAS). In sum, the role of force assumed primacy in African affairs to a degree unprecedented in the post-independence era.

THE UNITED STATES IN AFRICA

American Leadership. The most dramatic change in the American attitude toward Africa could be seen in the installation of Jimmy Carter of Georgia as president and his appointment of Andrew Young, the articulate black Congressman from Georgia, as ambassador to the United Nations with responsibility for the new administration's African policies. The immediate policy statements of the new U. S. team repudiated the white Africa "tilt" of former Secretary of State Henry Kissinger, and attempted to install a new policy of giving primacy to relations with the leading black African states, particularly Nigeria, Tanzania, and Zambia.

The rationale for the new policy became clear in many statements of Ambassador Young and President Carter. The primary tenets were: (1) the influence of the Soviet Union could best be restricted by the United States' cultivating relations with those African states with the greatest political clout; (2) the United States had a naturally advantageous position on the continent by virtue of the economic interdependence of African producers and American consumers; (3) the United States should focus more on north-south economic problems and less on east-west political conflicts; (4) the first goal of the president's emphasis on international human rights should be the removal of racial discrimination in southern Africa, based on the precedent of the peaceful transformation of the American South since the early 1950's.

Such an outline of policies required new initiatives by the United States, a task assumed early in the year by Ambassador Young in repeated trips through the major African states. The deliberate cultivation of relations with Nigeria's General Olusegun Obasanjo and Tanzania's President Julius Nyerere resulted in both leaders traveling to Washington during 1977. Both indicated their gratification with the reno-

UPI

President Carter met with Tanzania's President Julius Nyerere in August. The Carter administration promised open, not secret, diplomacy with the African states.

vated policy emanating from the Carter administration. At the same time, the gap between the South African government and the U. S. leadership grew until South African Prime Minister John Vorster would say in public, defending his October crackdown on black organizations, that whatever was said by the American leadership was "totally irrelevant to South Africa."

The Expanding Dialogue. The United States undertook a policy of consultation with the parties to all disputes, in an effort to hasten the nonviolent solutions to various African conflicts. In the Namibian case, not only were active talks begun with the South African government, also involving the major European powers, but there was an effort to reach an understanding with Sam Nujoma, leader of Namibia's guerrilla force, the South West African People's Organization (SWAPO). Talks were thus initiated with the variety of forces at work in African politics— and the talks were open. The change from Kissinger's "secret diplomacy" to the open style of Carter and Young provided a much greater public awareness of the progress, or lack thereof, toward political solutions of African disputes. Ambassador Young utilized the United Nations as a forum for intensive consultation with the African delegates, in an effort to break up the North-South confrontation that had plagued U. S. diplomacy for some years.

Not all of Africa is enchanted with the attentions of the Soviet Union, which seeks an active role in African affairs. An anti-Cuba/USSR rally was held at a Kinshasa, Zaire, stadium in April 1977.

UPI

Material Efforts. At the same time, the magnitude of United States aid did not increase. And the interest of the United States in providing aid to the guerrilla nationalist forces did not rise, as the Carter administration used every opportunity to advocate nonviolence. Indeed, the Carter interest in cutting back arms transfers to the Third World meant that such sales decreased in some parts of Africa, such as Ethiopia. American economic aid remained at a low level, as the United States and its developed allies attempted to work out a coherent approach to the problem of African debt mounting in the wake of oil price rises. Until such a solution was developed, it was felt, an increase in economic aid would be missing the main problem facing the impoverished African states.

THE USSR IN AFRICA

Residue of the Angolan Civil War. The Soviet Union and Cuba, confident that they had safely installed the MPLA as the government of Angola during the civil war of 1975–1976, began to withdraw forces from the area in early 1977, only to find that the opposition forces of Jonas Savimbi (UNITA) were alive and fighting in the southeastern part of the country. As a result, the level of Soviet/Cuban forces began to rise again during the year, reaching record levels of nearly 20,000 men by the end of the year. The importance of Angola as a Soviet staging base grew during the year as aid to the Rhodesian guerrilla forces increased dramatically. The roads eastward from Luanda into Zambia and the training bases of Joshua Nkomo's nationalist forces became clogged with Cuban military convoys shipping arms eastward for the Rhodesian battle. Many of the Cuban forces, too, were tied down by the internal Angolan battle with the UNITA forces.

Soviet Diplomacy. The highly publicized trip by Soviet President Nikolai Podgorny in February garnered much attention for the Soviet efforts in a number of African countries. The Soviet leader, who made the trip just weeks before his unexpected ouster from his high position in the Soviet hierarchy, projected an image of a permanent Soviet interest in the growth and security of east and southern Africa. Podgorny led a delegation of over 120 people to the pivotal countries of Tanzania, Zambia, and Mozambique. In each country he had talks both with the government and resident guerrilla leaders. The intense Soviet involvement on both sides of the war in the Horn of Africa, between Somalia and Ethiopia, also led to heavy diplomatic efforts to heal the conflict. At one point in March, Cuban President Fidel Castro was enlisted in an effort of "shuttle diplomacy" among Addis Ababa, Mogadishu, San'a, and Aden to bring about a new political alignment and thereby an end to the state of undeclared war between the Soviet clients in the area. By the end of 1977, the Soviet Union had obtained a far more satisfactory diplomatic position in southern Africa, compared to the beginning of the year, but had clearly suffered a setback in the Horn of Africa.

Soviet Strategic Planning. The increase in Soviet projection of power in the African region had continued in 1977. In Mali, the USSR finished a large military base with jet-capacity runways, thereby completing the overland link from Algeria to Guinea and the air-support link to Soviet activities farther south. At the same time, Soviet access to its bases in Somalia was considerably restricted by the Somali government, in retribution for Soviet support of Ethiopian forces in the war in the Horn of Africa. The ejection of Soviet personnel from Somalia was rapid during 1977. In fact, in mid-November, all Soviet civilian and military advisers remaining in Somalia were ordered to leave within seven days and all Soviet military facilities in that country were closed. At the same time, Somalia broke diplomatic relations with Cuba. While the efforts of the USSR to obtain hard bases in Angola and Mozambique were rebuffed, it was understood that agreements between the former Portuguese colonies and the USSR did provide for unlimited access to existing facilities, both air and naval, in the two countries. The increasing involvement of the Soviet Union in conventional military terms,

U. S. Secretary of State Cyrus Vance and Britain's Foreign Secretary David Owen, right, made joint attempts to find a southern Africa peace settlement. In London, in August, they met with South Africa's Foreign Minister Roelof Botha.

UPI

then, was at the root of the Soviet alarm over the possible nuclear weapon test of South Africa in August. The USSR notified the United States that satellite information indicated an imminent test of a nuclear device in the Kalahari Desert. Following substantial public pressure from the United States, Britain, and France, the South African government indicated that it would not test such a device (and that it had never planned such a test), and in the process granted the Soviet Union a substantially increased voice in the security of Southern Africa. Clearly, the Soviet Union had a major stake in the outcome; it was the only possible target of South African use of nuclear weapons.

PURSUIT OF PEACE IN RHODESIA

Great Power Involvement. The level of intense international interest in Rhodesian developments remained high during 1977, with the USSR, Britain, and the United States taking leading roles. The Soviet Union continued its active support of the nationalist guerrilla forces, the so-called Patriotic Front, under the leadership of Joshua Nkomo and Robert Mugabe.

Joshua Nkomo, leader of the Zimbabwe African Peoples Union, is a key figure in the struggle for Rhodesia.

UPI

The Soviets' interest in a violent solution of the Rhodesian crisis was clear from their shipping of highly sophisticated weaponry to the guerrilla forces, as well as providing training at rear bases in Tanzania, Zambia, and Mozambique. The British and Americans, through U. S. Ambassador to the UN Andrew Young and British Foreign Secretary David Owen, attempted to pursue a negotiated path to a transfer of power in Rhodesia. Young and Owen made repeated trips throughout the continent in order to keep all parties on a talking basis. Rhodesian Prime Minister Ian Smith continued to negotiate with the Anglo-American team while disagreeing with their proposals for the security of Rhodesia during the transition of power. He did agree, however, to the speedy transition of power to a multiracial government, an important issue of principle not granted in the past. On the other side, Owen and Young attempted to bring along the leaders of the front-line states (Zambia, Botswana, Tanzania, and Mozambique) in order to ensure their cooperation and their willingness to place pressure on the guerrilla leaders. The latter remained uncertain. So that the backup parties would also be involved, Nigeria and South Africa were consulted by Owen and Young, with considerably less success in the case of South Africa. The alienation of South Africa from the United States and Britain on other issues meant that the South African government drew back from exerting pressure on Rhodesia for a diplomatic settlement, as it had done repeatedly in the past.

African Efforts. The leaders of the front-line states found that there were few initiatives they could take in the evolution of Rhodesia. Their marginal control over the guerrilla forces of the Patriotic Front meant that the front-line leaders only hoped to regulate the flow of arms from outside suppliers such as the Soviet Union to the Patriotic Front forces. The African states, however, were acutely sensitive to the split between the Patriotic Front forces, that is, the Mugabe forces versus the Nkomo forces. At one point in October, Zambian President Kenneth Kaunda flew Ian Smith to Lusaka for talks with Joshua Nkomo, in an effort to arrange a political settlement without Robert Mugabe. The effort did not appear to succeed, but did serve to highlight once again the deep-seated split between the nationalist movements of Rhodesia. The African leaders of the front-line states were concerned about the spillover of the Rhodesian war into their countries. The ability of the Rhodesian forces to range at will in Mozambique and Botswana suggested that they might begin to do the same in Tanzania and Zambia. The possibility of a wider war without respect for national boundaries was not attractive to the leaders with fragile political bases.

CIVIL/INTERNATIONAL WAR IN ZAIRE

Shaba (Katanga) Erupts. On March 8, a force of about 2,000 former Katangese gendarmes moved across the border from Angola into Shaba province, formerly known as Katanga. The gendarmes, who had been in exile from Zaire for over ten years in opposition to the government of Mobutu Sese Seko, appeared to have been trained and motivated to go home by the Angolan government, after consultation with the Soviet Union. The MPLA, which had been opposed by Mobutu, saw an opportunity to destabilize the government of Zaire, and equipped the Katangan gendarmes for their "invasion" and return home.

The International Response. The clear threat to the stability of Zaire, most of whose revenue comes from the copper mines of Shaba, generated concern in the United States and Western Europe. With congressional sentiment in the United States quite opposed to any substantial involvement, the Carter administration decided to send only $13 million of "nonlethal aid"— a C-130 transport plane, medical supplies, and

some support equipment. Since the threat to Mobutu's government continued, however, the French government leaped into the fray, organizing a relief effort for the Zairian forces that combined French air transport with 1,500 Moroccan troops. The Moroccan European forces turned back the invading Katangans after several weeks of intermittent fighting. International opinion split drastically on the issue of the wisdom of the intervention, largely along the same lines as the divisions previously formed over the Angolan civil war.

WAR IN THE HORN OF AFRICA

Djibouti—A Spark for War. The decolonization of the former French Territory of the Afars and Issas (FTAI) took place as scheduled, with independence granted in June. Little changed in the desolate harbor on the lower Red Sea, as the new government signed a treaty of protection with the French, and most forces remained. The formality of independence, however, set in motion a series of incidents in the region, which gradually emerged as a full-scale war between Somalia and Ethiopia. The Western Somali Liberation Front (WSLF), which had eagerly awaited the independence of Djibouti as an opportunity to expand the territory of Somalia, found its ambitions frustrated, and turned its energies on the weakening Ethiopian regime instead. Knowing that the Ethiopians were fighting a losing battle in Eritrea, the WSLF solicited the support of the Somali government in undertaking an invasion of the Ogaden region of Ethiopia. The war became increasingly visible throughout 1977, as the Somalis occupied most of the Ogaden desert region, facing stiff Ethiopian resistance only when they reached the key cities of Jijiga, Harar,

UPI

With support from Moroccan troops, Zairian forces, some wearing camouflage uniforms, fought off a rebel invasion force in Shaba Province in May.

INFORMATION HIGHLIGHTS ON THE COUNTRIES OF AFRICA

Nation	1977 Population in millions	Capital	Area in sq mi (km²)	Head of State and/or Government (as of Dec. 1, 1977)
Algeria	17.8	Algiers	919,662 (2,381,925)	Houari Boumédienne, president
Angola	6.3	Luanda	481,351 (1,246,700)	Agostinho Neto, president
Benin (Dahomey)	3.3	Porto-Novo	43,541 (112,770)	Mathieu Kerekou, president
Botswana	.72	Gaborone	231,822 (600,420)	Sir Seretse Khama, president
Burundi	3.9	Bujumbura	10,748 (27,834)	Jean-Baptiste Bagaza, president
Cameroon	6.7	Yaoundé	183,583 (475,480)	Ahmadou Ahidjo, president
Cape Verde	.31	Praia	1,559 (4,033)	Aristides Pereira, president
Central African Empire	1.9	Bangui	240,553 (623,030)	Jean-Bedel Bokassa, emperor
Chad	4.2	N'Djamena	495,791 (1,284,100)	Felix Malloum, president
Comoro Islands	.32	Moroni	838 (2,171)	Ali Soilih, president
Congo	1.4	Brazzaville	132,057 (342,028)	Joachim Yombi Opango, president
Djibouti	.11	Djibouti	8,495 (22,000)	Hassan Gouled, president
Egypt	38.9	Cairo	386,660 (1,001,449)	Anwar el-Sadat, president
Equatorial Guinea	.32	Malabo	10,831 (28,051)	Francisco Macías Nguema, president
Ethiopia	29.4	Addis Ababa	471,777 (1,221,900)	Mengistu Haile Mariam, chairman, Provisional Military Administration Committee
Gabon	.54	Libreville	103,354 (267,687)	Albert-Bernard Bongo, president
Gambia, The	.55	Banjul	4,361 (11,295)	Sir Dawda K. Jawara, president
Ghana	10.4	Accra	92,099 (238,537)	Ignatius K. Acheampong, head, National Redemption Council
Guinea	4.7	Conakry	94,971 (245,975)	Ahmed Sékou Touré, president
Guinea-Bissau	.54	Bissau	13,949 (36,125)	Luíz de Almeida Cabral, president
Ivory Coast	7.0	Abidjan	124,512 (322,485)	Félix Houphouët-Boigny, president
Kenya	14.4	Nairobi	244,959 (634,444)	Jomo Kenyatta, president
Lesotho	1.1	Maseru	11,721 (30,355)	Moshoeshoe II, king Chief Leabua Jonathan, premier
Liberia	1.7	Monrovia	43,003 (111,378)	William R. Tolbert, president
Libya	2.7	Tripoli	679,360 (1,759,540)	Muammar el-Qaddafi, secretary general, General People's Congress
Madagascar	7.9	Antananarivo	266,674 (690,686)	Didier Ratsiraka, president
Malawi	5.3	Lilongwe	45,750 (118,494)	H. Kamuzu Banda, president
Mali	5.9	Bamako	478,800 (1,240,000)	Moussa Traoré, president
Mauritania	1.4	Nouakchott	397,984 (1,030,780)	Mokhtar Ould Daddah, president
Mauritius	.91	Port Louis	790 (2,045)	Sir Raman Osman, governor general Sir Seewoosagur Ramgoolam, premier
Morocco	18.3	Rabat	172,413 (446,550)	Hassan II, king
Mozambique	9.5	Maputo	302,328 (783,029)	Samora M. Machel, president
Niger	4.9	Niamey	489,227 (1,267,100)	Seyni Kountché, president
Nigeria	66.6	Lagos	356,668 (923,768)	Olusegun Obasanjo, head of government
Rhodesia	6.8	Salisbury	150,803 (390,580)	John Wrathall, president Ian D. Smith, prime minister
Rwanda	4.5	Kigali	10,170 (26,338)	Juvénal Habyalimana, president
São Tomé and Príncipe	.08	São Tomé	372 (964)	Mañuel Pinto da Costa, president
Senegal	5.3	Dakar	75,756 (196,208)	Léopold S. Senghor, president
Seychelles	.06	Victoria	108 (280)	F. Albert René, president
Sierra Leone	3.2	Freetown	27,700 (71,740)	Siaka P. Stevens, president
Somalia	3.4	Mogadishu	246,219 (637,707)	Mohammed Siad Barre, president
South Africa, Rep. of	26.1	Pretoria and Cape Town	471,444 (1,221,037)	Nicolaas Diederichs, president B. J. Vorster, prime minister
Sudan	16.3	Khartoum	967,497 (2,505,813)	Jaafar al-Numeiry, president
Swaziland	.52	Mbabane	6,704 (17,363)	Sobhuza II, king
Tanzania	16.0	Dar es Salaam	364,899 (945,087)	Julius K. Nyerere, president
Togo	2.3	Lomé	21,623 (56,000)	Gnassingbe Eyadéma, president
Tunisia	6.0	Tunis	63,170 (163,600)	Habib Bourguiba, president
Uganda	12.4	Kampala	91,134 (236,036)	Idi Amin, president
Upper Volta	6.4	Ouagadougou	105,877 (274,200)	Sangoulé Lamizana, president
Zaire	26.3	Kinshasa	905,565 (2,345,409)	Mobutu Sese Seko, president
Zambia	5.2	Lusaka	290,607 (752,670)	Kenneth D. Kaunda, president

UPI

With a club in hand and a child on her back, an Ethiopian woman prepares to welcome guerrillas from Somalia.

The Somalis turned to the United States for military aid, through the assistance of the Saudis, and the Carter administration initially responded positively. After consultation with Britain and France, however, the United States decided that they would jointly avoid involvement in the war. The Somalis then began receiving clandestine shipments of weapons from Iraq, paid for by Saudi Arabia, since Iraq could provide parts and supplies that were compatible with Soviet-made weapons that dominated the military stocks of Somalia.

With so many governments changing sides, then, the alignments of countries in the war in the Horn took on a surprising character. Actively aiding the Ethiopians were the Soviet Union, Cuba, Israel, and Libya. On the Somali side with active contributions were Iraq, Saudi Arabia, Egypt, and China. Attempting to stay out of the conflict were the United States and the Western European allies. Some states, including most of the Organization of African Unity, were confused: opposed to the use of armed force as instigated by Somalia, but quite unsympathetic to the socialist government of Ethiopia. Many of the OAU members feared, for instance, that the war would spill over into the Somali-inhabited region of Kenya.

AFRICAN REGIONAL GROUPINGS

OAU. The Organization of African Unity (OAU) displayed even less unity than in 1976. A number of issues, the continuing civil war in Angola, the war in the Horn of Africa, and the attitudes of governments toward factions of the Rhodesian Patriotic Front, served to split the organization into several groups. Each problem reduced the effectiveness of the OAU, especially since the organization's headquarters were located in Addis Ababa, a city under siege.

ECOWAS. A bright spot in African regional planning was the emergence of the Economic Community of West African States. Sixteen states got together in July in Lagos, Nigeria, and Lomé, Togo, to establish a group of institutions committed to healing the age-old breach between anglophone and francophone states in West Africa. The headquarters of the ECOWAS Secretariat was established in Lagos, and the headquarters of the Fund for Cooperation, Compensation, and Development was established in Lomé. The institutions are not limited to economic purposes, however, as the Council of Ministers also undertook the final drafting of a treaty of non-aggression, in an effort to reduce some of the friction between politically insecure governments in West Africa. In the economic realm, some of the areas outlined for initial focus were the coordination of airline services, development of the iron and steel industry, integration of the fishing industry, and unity in negotiations with the developed countries.

and Diredawa. When the Somali government threw its MiG airplanes into the successful battle for Jijiga, it became clear that the government was wholeheartedly involved with the WSLF.

International Reaction. The United States had undertaken its withdrawal from Ethiopia long before the battle of the Ogaden began. With the clear disintegration of the Ethiopian government, and its publicly expressed preference for an alliance with the socialist states, the United States had seen little gain in remaining involved with the Ethiopian military government. Military aid was terminated, and economic aid suspended until the U. S.-Ethiopian relationship was clarified.

The Soviet Union, on the other hand, possessed a long-standing relationship with Somalia that provided for important Soviet air and naval bases on the Indian Ocean. The Somali military machine could not operate without supplies of Soviet spare parts and fuel. In early 1977, however, the Soviet Union decided to respond to the overtures of the Ethiopian regime, and gave its approval for the shipment of small arms and advisers to Addis Ababa to aid the Ethiopians in their battle for survival. Soviet and Cuban leaders became involved in a complex plan to create a federation of "socialist" states in the lower Red Sea area, a scheme that came to nought as the Somali-Ethiopian war intensified. In addition, the irritation of the Somali government with the Soviet aid to Ethiopia reached a crisis point and led to the November break.

RICHARD E. BISSELL
Foreign Policy Research Institute

AGRICULTURE

The most important variable in world agricultural production is the weather. And in 1977, the weather was mostly "average," meaning that other things being equal, farm output should have increased by 2% to 3%—about in line with the growth of world population.

Late in the year, however, the weather turned sour in the midst of harvest—or just before harvest—particularly in the Soviet Union. This led the UN Food and Agriculture Organization (FAO) and the U. S. Department of Agriculture (USDA) to revise estimates downward.

WORLD TRENDS

The key index to world food production is grain yield. If there is plenty of grain, not only will there be bread, but surplus grain boosts output of livestock and livestock products—meat and milk.

In May 1977, assumptions were that the world grain crops were large but not quite so large as the previous year's record high. It was further conjectured that the 1977 large output would exceed consumption and result in an additional accumulation of reserve grain stocks. But because of the subpar weather late in 1977, and perhaps political factors, experts later concluded that there would be no buildup of stocks —indeed, there would be a decline.

The 1977 total world wheat, coarse grains and rice production was estimated late in the year at 1,426,000,000 metric tons, almost 19 million tons below mid-October estimates and 1% less than the 1,444,000,000 tons initially projected in July. This grain production, if realized, would be about 1% less than the record of 1,447,000,000 tons achieved in 1976.

The early estimates of grain output suggested an aggregate stocks buildup of about 35 million metric tons, including about 10 of wheat and 25 of coarse grains (corn, oats, barley, rye). At year-end, experts revised these figures to show a buildup, still, in coarse grains of nearly 9 million tons, but a drawdown of wheat stocks by 13 million tons. This would be a net grain-stocks decline of about 4 million tons.

"The single most significant recent crop development," the USDA's Foreign Agricultural Service reported, "has been the change in the anticipated grain production in the USSR. It appears that weather and problems associated with completion of harvesting operations were worse than had been reported or expected . . . .

"The latest estimates of USSR grain production for 1977 show wheat and coarse grain outturn of 90 million tons each, down 5 million tons for wheat and 15 million tons for coarse grain from the previous estimate. Total grain production—including miscellaneous grains, rice, and pulses—is now placed at 194 million tons, down 21 million from the estimates of mid-October."

And there was more trouble. "With the start of the wheat harvesting season in the Southern Hemisphere," the USDA reported, "it also appears that final grain production in Australia and Argentina will be far below forecasts made earlier and even below mid-October estimates."

This outlook contrasted sharply with the huge outturn in 1976 that resulted in a very large buildup of about 58 million metric tons of grain reserves. The size of this reserve depressed prices and the lower prices encouraged farmers to increase their feeding of grains to animals, which in turn led to increased meat and milk production. Therefore, meat production in the world's principal meat-consuming regions held near the record 1976 levels, with larger pork and poultry output offsetting declines in beef. Net imports into these regions changed little from the previous year. With herd liquidations in process, low world producer prices were in prospect.

World milk production in the major producing lands was expected to increase about 2% to record highs in 1977, with the USSR, Europe, and the United States primarily responsible. Troublesome milk surpluses in the developed lands are causing policymakers to consider painful remedies aimed at restoring the balance between consumption and demand.

World sugar output was of record size at about 91 million metric tons, about 3.5 million larger than in 1976. After 1974, larger crops

U. S. trainee inspectors examine grain prior to export. Drought caused world's grain supply to be below forecast.

UPI

in Europe, the USSR, and South America contributed to the steady growth in sugar output.

The new International Sugar Agreement, scheduled to be implemented on about Jan. 1, 1978, established export quotas in an effort to reduce the quantity of sugar available in the world market and thereby raise depressed world sugar prices to the 11–21 cents a pound range provided in the agreement. A reserve stock of 2.5 million tons will be accumulated during the first three years of the agreement and is to be administered so as to keep prices between 15 and 19 cents a pound. When world prices average around 11 cents, duty, freight, and insurance costs would result in a domestic price of about 13.5 cents for raw sugar.

Production records in 1977 were set also in cotton production. World cotton output was about 64.8 million bales, 12% more than in the previous year and 1% larger than the previous high in 1974. Cotton plantings at 32.6 million hectares were 6% larger than in 1976. Excellent weather in most producing countries probably resulted in record yield of more than 430 kilograms per hectare.

Estimated world rice production in 1977 was record large at 362 million tons because of increases in India, Bangladesh, Japan, Korea, and several other countries.

WORLD FARM OUTPUT

U. S. Agriculture. The United States' incomparable agricultural sector demonstrated again in 1977 its fantastic ability to perform ever larger production feats. Nearly ideal weather accounted for record high crop yield. Lower prices for grain led livestock producers to continue to expand production, also to record highs. Total farm output rose more than 3% over 1976. Record production was achieved in such major commodities as corn and other animal feeds, soybeans and other oilseeds, livestock and livestock products, particularly broilers and pork.

Production. In 1977, U. S. farm output of crops and livestock reached an index number of 121 (1967 = 100), up from the revised 1976 index level of 117, the previous record high. Plantings for harvest of major crops totaled about the same as in 1976—about 335 million acres (134 million hectares). Yields per acre rose for most major crops.

August rains in the key crop production areas of the Corn Belt and the Great Plains erased fears that drought would deal U. S. production severe setbacks. Instead, corn production was a record of about 6.4 billion bushels, 2% larger than in the previous year. Total output of corn and other feed grains (grain sorghums, oats, and barley) was 201 million metric tons, 5% more than in 1976.

But soybeans, the so-called glamor commodity, set the world agricultural picture on its ear. U. S. output was nearly 1.7 billion bushels, 9% larger than the previous record in 1973

—and a whopping 30% larger than in 1976. Agricultural economists assume the reason for this large expansion of production is that farmers were lured to the crop by recent higher prices for vegetable oils, while grain prices, particularly for wheat and corn, were trending down.

Oilseed output (soybeans, cottonseed, peanuts and flaxseed combined) was about 53 million metric tons, 32% more than in 1976, with most of the increase in soybeans. Other crop output was large, but among major field crops, production of wheat, rice, sugar, and tobacco was smaller than in previous years. Crop output was placed at an index figure of 128 (1967 = 100), up from the record of 122 in 1976.

The livestock industry continued to expand, encouraged by lower grain prices. Large supplies of red meat, poultry, and dairy products continued to hold retail food prices to slower increases than in previous years. Livestock output was placed at an index figure of 108, up from the previous record of 106 in 1976.

New Farm Legislation. For the first time in four years, major new U. S. agricultural legislation was enacted. However, the Food and Agriculture Act of 1977 departed only in minor ways from past practice and policy. The new four-year act provides the framework for U. S. farm policy beginning in 1978. The measure continues the dual target price and loan-rate system to provide price and income support to farmers. This legislation also boosted target prices for wheat and feed grains. Loan rates for 1977 crop feed grains were increased earlier. Direct government payments to wheat producers could total more than $1 billion in 1977, and the higher loan rates for feed grains will help bolster market prices. Government-backed loans are part of the complex U. S. system of farm subsidies.

Income and Consumption. Reduced crop and livestock prices continued to weaken farm income, while production expenses continued to rise persistently. Despite large commitments of government price-propping cash, 1977 realized farm income was down significantly from the 1976 level of $22 billion, and far below the record $32.2 billion of 1973. Reacting to the low prices, a farmer protest movement organized a nationwide strike in December.

Per capita consumption was down slightly from the 1976 record high, largely due to a 1% decline in such foods as coffee, fresh and processed fruits, and fresh vegetables. Prices of these commodities were well above normal early in 1977.

Other Developed Countries. Despite adverse weather conditions in many sections of Western Europe, the region's crop prospects for 1977 were favorable. Total grain production rebounded from the 1976 drought-related slump. Coarse grain output was about 13 million tons larger than in the previous year, reaching about 86 million tons, mainly because of higher yields

UPI

A young Missouri farmer holds a soybean stalk. U. S. soybean production neared 1.7 billion bushels, a record.

per hectare. Wheat production was about 50 million tons, down a bit from 1976. Heavy summer rains in France and elsewhere reduced the protein content of the wheat crop.

Poor spring weather hurt the European Economic Community's fruit crop. The apple harvest, for example, was the poorest since 1964. July storms devastated tobacco fields in France and Spain. In Australia, favorable planting conditions led to record wheat seedings, but drought conditions late in 1977 hurt the crop severely. Canada's wheat harvest declined by nearly 26% from the 1976 record, to about 17.3 million tons. The corn crop was smaller than in 1976. Barley output was at about the 1976 level. A switch to rapeseed and flaxseed occurred.

The livestock performance in the developed countries was mixed and uneven. In the EEC, the struggle centered on how to reduce dairy surpluses, especially in West Germany. The EEC plan encourages increased slaughterings of dairy cows. Even so, output of beef and veal dipped by around 4% to about 6.2 million tons. Pork and poultry output was up by 3%. Egg production rose slightly. Australian beef and veal output rose by 4%. Mutton and lamb output was down 10% partly because of larger exports of live sheep. Increases in Canada's pork and poultry production were offset by a decline in beef. In Japan, increases occurred for all types of meat and combined output reached 2.3 million metric tons.

Soviet Union. The USSR had its second relatively favorable growing season in a row. But adverse weather, presumably, late in 1977, cut the key grain crops sharply. Russian grain stocks seemed adequate to support the livestock industry. There were gains in output of meat and dairy products. Meat and milk output rose about 12% above 1976 levels.

East Europe. The northern countries were plagued by rains and flooding, especially Poland, East Germany, and Czechoslovakia. Yugoslavia and Rumania expanded sunflower and soybean plantings. Increased forage crops in this region helped rebuild herds slaughtered for lack of feed from drought-stricken crops in 1976.

China and Asia. Prospects for significant boosts in China's grain output dimmed under pressure from severe drought in the winter from 1976 to early spring 1977 in the North China Plain and South China. An analysis of provincial reports suggested that winter wheat suffered a loss which even a much improved spring wheat crop did not offset. The early rice crop was a bumper one.

With above-average monsoon rains and adequate fertilizer supplies, Pakistan increased its rice output. Afghanistan's wheat crop was hurt by lack of rain. In India, lack of water in late August hurt crops. Food-grain output in 1977 was up from the 1976 harvest but well below the 1975 peak. The food situation was stable in Bangladesh. Burma's rice crop increased over 1976. Thailand's corn crop was hurt by drought. Malaysia boosted palm oil output sharply. Drought and pest problems troubled Indonesia's rice crop for the third consecutive year. The Philippines enjoyed a third consecutive year of good weather and record rice and corn crops.

Syria's farm output was generally reduced by dry weather. Iran's wheat production was down 9% from the 1976 record. In Turkey, excellent weather, combined with improved cultural practices, particularly greater use of fertilizer, produced the country's third record wheat crop. In Israel, wheat output was up 13% over 1976, but Jordan's wheat crop was devastated by drought.

Africa. An unusually dry spell cut wheat and barley production in Morocco, Algeria, and Tunisia. Agricultural output in Egypt rose. The Sahel (Chad, Niger, Upper Volta, Mali, Mauritania, Senegal, and The Gambia) continued to suffer food shortages in some areas. In South Africa, both production and export of farm goods were slightly above average, but the wheat crop was off sharply.

Latin America. Wheat output was down in Argentina and Mexico, and rice harvests were reduced by dry weather in Brazil and Colombia. However, coffee, cotton, and feed grains recovered. Oilseeds, sugar, and other food crops expanded. Latin America's total agricultural production exceeded the 1976 record by about 5%.

JOE WESTERN, *Free-lance Writer*

ALABAMA

Politics and the weather seemed to dominate the scene in Alabama during 1977.

The Weather. The year began in Alabama with an especially hard winter, and some schools were closed as a fuel conservation measure. But such problems were less severe in Alabama than in other areas, for natural gas supplies were generally adequate. Later, a summer drought caused considerable agricultural damage across the state.

Governmental Developments. The legislature met in regular session on February 1, under a schedule adopted in 1976. Except for a new code of laws to replace the 1940 code and a revised criminal code, little significant legislation was enacted at the regular session, which adjourned on May 16. On that same day, the governor called a special session, to convene on the day after, in order to deal with a package of controversial measures that he had proposed for the regulation of public utilities. Only one of these measures, a minor item regarding auditing, was subsequently enacted into law. A second special session was called for June 28 to consolidate referenda on proposed amendments to the state Constitution. Thirteen such proposals were submitted to the voters on September 13. Of these, only one, defining the jurisdiction of probate courts, was of statewide application; the remainder dealt with local matters. Seven amendments were adopted, including a measure relating to probate courts. This added Amendment No. 370 to Alabama's repeatedly patched Constitution of 1901. Toward the end of the year it seemed that a third special session to revise the state's unemployment compensation laws could be avoided by deferring action on the matter until the 1978 regular session. Problems concerning adequate financial support for highways, prisons, Medicaid, and judicial functions continued throughout the year, although relief for the courts was provided in September by an attorney general's opinion that invalidated a legislative restriction on the judiciary's authority to spend its full appropriation.

FBI Nomination. On August 17, U. S. Attorney General Griffin Bell announced President Carter's nomination of U. S. District Judge Frank M. Johnson, Jr., of Montgomery, Ala., to succeed Clarence M. Kelley as director of the Federal Bureau of Investigation. Because of Johnson's decisions in important civil rights cases, he was expected to gain Senate confirmation with little difficulty. On August 26, however, Judge Johnson underwent surgery for the repair of an aneurysm discovered during a routine physical examination. As his recuperation proceeded more slowly than expected, Judge Johnson, in late November, requested that his nomination for the post be withdrawn.

Bombing Investigation. In September, indictments were returned by a Jefferson County grand jury for bombings in the Birmingham area during the late 1950's and early 1960's. One indictment was for a 1963 church bombing in which four black children lost their lives; a conviction in this case was obtained on November 18. The indictments were pursued by the state attorney general's office, which had reopened its investigation of the cases in February, 1976. On October 18, George Wallace approved rewards totaling $100,000 for information regarding ten bombing incidents.

JAMES D. THOMAS
The University of Alabama

ALABAMA · Information Highlights

Area: 51,609 square miles (133,667 km²).
Population (1976 est.): 3,665,000.
Chief Cities (1970 census): Montgomery, the capital, 133,386; Birmingham, 300,910; Mobile, 190,026.
Government (1977): *Chief Officers*—governor, George C. Wallace (D); lt. gov., Jere L. Beasley (D). *Legislature*—Senate, 35 members; House of Representatives, 105 members.
Education (1976–77): *Enrollment*—public elementary schools, 380,042 pupils; public secondary, 372,465; nonpublic, 56,400; colleges and universities, 146,653. *Public school expenditures*, $912,406,000 ($1,109 per pupil).
State Finances (fiscal year 1976): *Revenues*, $2,826,853,000; *expenditures*, $2,844,643,000.
Personal Income (1976): $18,714,000,000; per capita, $5,106.
Labor Force (July 1977): *Nonagricultural wage and salary earners*, 1,268,000; *unemployed*, 96,900 (6.3% of total force).

In Washington for the winter meeting of the National Governors' Conference, Alabama Gov. George Wallace chats with Sen. Howard Baker (Tenn.), Gov. George Busbee (Ga.), and Gov. Ella Grasso (Conn.).

ALASKA

Environmental issues continued to figure prominently in the news from Alaska.

The Wilderness Controversy. Alaskans were divided by the D–2 lands issue. The Alaskan Wilderness bill, proposed by Rep. Morris Udall, (D–Ariz.), would commit 114 million acres (46 million hectares) of land to national parks, national wildlife refuges, and wild and scenic rivers. Hearings on the Udall bill were conducted during July and August around the state. Hundreds of Alaskans participated. Many were concerned that Udall's bill would prevent the state of Alaska from exercising control over development of much of its natural resources. On the other hand, many Alaskans supported federal efforts to preserve the wilderness. Alaskans also expressed concern that the subsistence lifestyle of bush Alaskans be respected. Gov. Jay Hammond and Alaska's congressional delegation continued to urge joint federal-state management of Alaskan lands.

Some North Slope Eskimos reacted strongly when the International Whaling Commission decided to propose an end to the hunting of bowhead whales. Eskimo spokesmen urged the government to press for an exception to the ban for subsistence hunting. They argued that bowhead whale hunting is essential to their way of life and diet. The whale ranges in the Beaufort and Chuckchi Seas.

The Pipeline. On June 20 the first oil moved into the Trans-Alaska Pipeline System (TAPS) at Prudhoe Bay and arrived at Valdez on July 28. The *ARCO Juneau* was the first tanker to carry Alaskan crude oil to Cherry Point, Wash. Incidents during the first few weeks of operation included an explosion and fire fatal to one worker, oil spills at various points along the pipeline, and at least one deliberate attempt to dynamite the line a few miles from Fairbanks. All but the last incident seemed to result from a combination of mechanical defects.

Reflecting completion of TAPS, unemployment reached 15.5% in the spring, the highest rate in 20 years. A study of the TAPS project,

UPI

Oil executive William Darch poses with the first barrel of Prudhoe Bay crude oil transported via the pipeline.

commissioned by the Alaska Pipeline Commission, accused the consortium responsible for construction of condoning waste to the amount of $1.5 billion.

Alaskan response was mixed to President Carter's endorsement of a natural gas pipeline route from Prudhoe Bay along the oil pipeline to Fairbanks and then through Canada along the Alcan Highway to Fort Nelson, B. C., where it would divide to carry gas to the West and Middle West. Estimated cost of the Alcan gas pipeline is $6.7 billion. Those hoping to minimize the impact of resource development on the environment would have preferred an alternate route that would have been almost entirely within Canada. Such a route would be less desirable than an all-Alaska line to those favoring economic development.

University. Dr. Neil Humphrey, formerly chancellor of the University of Nevada system, became president of the University of Alaska.

Fisheries. The 200-mile limit opened up a new bottom fishery industry in Alaska. Previously pollock and other bottom fish off Alaska were exploited almost exclusively by Japan. The commercial pink salmon run was the biggest odd-year run since 1949. Almost 2.5 million pounds (1.1 million kg) of pink salmon were shipped out-of-state after Alaska canneries were filled to capacity.

ANDREA R. C. HELMS
University of Alaska

ALASKA · Information Highlights

Area: 586,412 square miles (1,518,807 km²).
Population (1976 est.): 382,000.
Chief Cities (1970 census): Juneau, the capital, 6,050; Anchorage, 48,081; Fairbanks, 14,771.
Government (1977): *Chief Officers*—governor, Jay S. Hammond (R); lt. gov., Lowell Thomas, Jr. (R). *Legislature*—Senate, 20 members; House of Representatives, 40 members.
Education (1976–77): *Enrollment*—public elementary schools, 51,590 pupils; public secondary, 39,600; nonpublic, 1,900; colleges and universities, 13,831. *Public school expenditures*, $308,629,000 ($2,780 per pupil).
State Finances (fiscal year 1976): *Revenues*, $1,188,-279,000; *expenditures*, $1,032,889,000.
Personal Income (1976): $3,979,000,000; per capita, $10,415.
Labor Force (June 1977): *Nonagricultural wage and salary earners*, 159,000; *unemployed*, 17,200 (11.1% of total force).

ALBANIA

Albania's determination during 1977 to persist in hard-line domestic and foreign policies appeared to be paving the way for an ideological break with its most important ally, the People's Republic of China.

Foreign Relations. In July, an editorial in the Albanian party daily accused the Chinese of betraying the world revolutionary movement by developing too close a relationship with the United States and non-Communist regimes in the Third World. China and Albania also began publicly to compete for the support of pro-Peking "Marxist-Leninist" parties. In addition, the Albanians appeared to be irritated by the decision of the new Chinese regime to pursue a more moderate line at home.

Despite the widening Sino-Albanian ideological rift, neither Peking nor Tiranë seemed inclined to sever the diplomatic and economic ties between the two countries. Albania also remained opposed to a reconciliation with the Soviet Union.

Political Developments. The new Albanian constitution, promulgated in December 1976, seems intended to enhance the dominant position of the Communist party in all phases of the nation's life and to ensure that the Stalinist policies of party leader Enver Hoxha will be continued after his death.

On June 20–23, the United Trade Unions of Albania held its congress and reelected President Rita Marko to his post. Lumturi Rexha was reelected first secretary of the Union of Albanian Labor Youth at the organization's congress in late September.

The purge of the top-level economic leadership was completed in February when Kristaq Dollaku replaced Myqerem Fuga as minister of light and food industries.

Economy. Albania failed to achieve the economic goals for the first year of the 1976–80 plan period. Industrial production in 1977 was scheduled to rise by 9.3% and agricultural output by 13.8%.

NICHOLAS C. PANO
Professor of History
Western Illinois University

ALBERTA

Alberta's boom atmosphere of recent years continued in 1977 despite continuing inflation. Unemployment remained below 5%.

Agriculture. Scant snowfall for a second year and a dry spring raised the specter of drought conditions. Except in the extreme southwest corner of the province, the threat was negated by abundant summer rains, but poor fall weather hindered harvesting of a bountiful crop. Grain and beef prices were disappointing.

Energy. Alberta's first significant oil discoveries in several years were made west of Edmonton. Newly developed natural gas resources proved larger than expected. Completion neared for the Syncrude oil sand project, with production forecast within a year. Work also began on a large coal strip-mining project to generate thermal electricity.

Construction. At year's end, building permits promised to exceed previous records. Major projects included new airport facilities in Calgary, a major health center and facilities for the 1978 Commonwealth Games in Edmonton, and the Syncrude plant near Fort McMurray.

Labor. Labor unrest continued, especially in the public sector. The legislature rescinded the right to strike of employees of provincial institutions. The government outlawed a work stoppage by nurses in nonprovincial hospitals after five days, imposing compulsory arbitration. Nevertheless, employers refused to accept the arbitration award, which was subsequently disallowed by the Anti-Inflation Board.

Recreation. The Alberta government continued work on new urban provincial parks within Edmonton and Calgary, and announced a new park and wilderness area west of Calgary in the Rockies.

Government and Politics. With the defection of Jack Horner to the Liberal party and appointment as industry, trade, and commerce minister, Alberta gained its first federal government member and first cabinet member in many years.

JOHN W. CHALMERS, *University of Alberta*

In Algiers in August, Algeria's President Houari Boumédienne and Cuba's Vice President Raul Castro discuss relations between their two nations.

UPI

ALGERIA

Still mainly reliant on oil revenues, from dwindling reserves, Algeria accelerated its rush to build a natural gas industry by 1980, but conceded it would not meet the schedule. Diplomatic rapprochement formalized strong economic ties with the United States.

Economy. Using American technology for the liquefaction of natural gas and the construction of cryogenic (extremely low temperature) tankers for shipping liquefied natural gas (LNG), Algeria had hoped to begin exporting 2.5 trillion cubic feet (71 billion m³) of LNG in 1980, 50% to the United States and 50% to Western Europe. But government officials admitted the program was 18 months behind schedule. The state-owned gas and oil company, Sonatrach, blamed the U. S. government for some of the delay. The U. S. Federal Power Commission in 1977 approved only a few of the many Algerian contracts with U. S. importers, totaling 1.2 trillion cubic feet (34 billion m³) of LNG a year.

Oil continued to be Algeria's major source of revenue, accounting for 90% of foreign exchange earnings and for 35% of its gross national product. The biggest customer was the United States, which bought 55% of the daily production of 1.1 million barrels. Total 1977 revenues from gas and oil production were expected to be about $6 billion (U. S.), a 20% increase over 1976.

───── ALGERIA · Information Highlights ─────

Official Name: Democratic and Popular Republic of Algeria.
Location: North Africa.
Area: 919,662 square miles (2,381,925 km²).
Population (1977 est.): 17,800,000.
Chief Cities (1974): Algiers, the capital, 1,000,000; Oran, 330,000; Constantine, 254,000.
Government: *Head of state and government,* Houari Boumédienne, president (took office June 1965).
Monetary Unit: Dinar (4.15 dinars equal U. S.$1, Aug. 1977).
Manufacturing (major products): Processed foods, textiles, leather goods, liquefied natural gas, cement, petroleum products.
Major Agricultural Products: Wheat, citrus fruits, wine grapes, cork, olives, dates, figs, tobacco, livestock.

The four-year industrial development plan that ended in 1977 cost almost double the projected price of $14 billion. Besides the natural gas industry, the money was spent on power generation, a huge steel complex, several cement plants, mines, the metal working industry, and factories. The major share of the 1977 budget was devoted to industry, 60% of the total $7 billion. Resources were also allocated for building homes, 22 new secondary schools, more than 1,800 miles (3,000 km) of new roads, and a major plan to end distribution bottlenecks that clog the ports and create artificial shortages of food supplies and consumer goods.

Foreign Affairs. Growing economic ties between Algeria and the United States, which replaced France as Algeria's biggest trading partner, led to an exchange of ambassadors in 1977. With American imports of Algerian oil leaping from $215 million in 1973 to $2.2 billion in 1976, the balance of trade remained in Algeria's favor.

Relations with France, the top exporter to Algeria, were not so rosy. Algeria was bitter about French support of Morocco and Mauritania in their war against insurgents, backed by Algeria, in the annexed Western Sahara territory. Algeria reacted sharply in November to French threats of military intervention to free French civilian technicians captured by Polisario Front insurgents in raids on Mauritania. (They were released in December.) Morocco was also criticized after King Hassan said he would exercise the right of pursuit into Algeria if Polisario insurgents crossed his frontiers again. Algiers replied that any violation of its frontiers would be considered a declaration of war.

Politics. Algeria elected a one-party national assembly in February, the first parliament since President Houari Boumédienne seized power in a 1965 military coup. Boumédienne will be impervious to censure by the national assembly, whose members all belong to the only legal party, the National Liberation Front, which the president heads.

JOSEPH MARGOLIS, *"African Update"*
African-American Institute

UPI

Angola President Agostinho Neto and President Tito leave the summer residence of the Yugoslav leader on Brioni.

ANGOLA

The woes besetting Angola since its birth in 1975 persisted in 1977.

Insurgency and Politics. Angola's independence from Portugal in 1975 after more than a decade of conflict was accompanied by a three-sided struggle for control. The Movimento Popular de Libertação de Angola (MPLA) emerged as the victor. However, its rapid supremacy over the União Nacional para Independência Total de Angola (UNITA) and the Frente Nacional de Libertação de Angola (FNLA) was made possible by large-scale Soviet and Cuban intervention. Bailed out and propped up by Soviet-bloc advisors and Cuban soldiers, the MPLA government has faced widening guerrilla warfare from its two rivals since early in 1976. Operating in the vast southern region, UNITA has been particularly successful in rallying the population to its banner of nationalism, anticommunism, and anti-MPLA rule. It has withstood repeated Cuban and MPLA counterinsurgency drives.

In the northeast the FNLA made harassment raids, some from sanctuaries in neighboring Zaire. In the oil-wealthy Cabinda enclave, the MPLA met local opposition by the Front de Liberation de l'Enclave de Cabinda (FLEC).

As the year closed, fighting increased within Angola, various anti-MPLA groups sought an alliance, and UNITA promised the declaration of an independent state in the southern lands it dominates.

After achieving power, the MPLA seemingly stood united within its own ranks until late May, when an abortive coup took place. Headed by former Interior Minister Nito Alves, the rebels temporarily seized government installations and the radio station in the seaside capital. Alves preached a populist and racialist message against the MPLA hierarchy, which is comprised of many *mestiços* and a few Europeans. Alves was also militantly pro-Soviet, although he had no assistance from foreign governments according to the MPLA. His followers came from the African poor in the Luanda slums and army clements. Cuban troops played a prominent role in suppressing the rebellion, which cost the lives of seven high-ranking MPLA leaders.

Foreign Affairs. Angola's relations with Zaire and South Africa, which controls the neighboring territory of Namibia, have persisted in the same hostile pattern that was formed in the civil war. Relations with Zambia have steadily improved. On the other hand, Luanda charged South Africa with actively aiding UNITA by making attacks from Namibia.

Angola maintained its active role in the five "front-line" states opposed to white rule in Rhodesia, and it stayed aligned closely to the Soviet Union while remaining hostile to China. It made overtures to some Western businesses.

Economy. The economy remained precarious in 1977 as the flight of 400,000 Portuguese settlers stripped the country of skilled workers and capital. Technicians from the Soviet bloc and Cuba have not compensated for the dislocation. Ongoing war also impaired development. Crop production was well below pre-independence peaks. UNITA regularly cut the Benguela railway across the country to Zambia, depriving Angola of transit revenue. War-damaged trucks and lack of mechanics made transportation a crucial problem. An estimated 300,000 refugees in Zaire, Zambia, and Namibia disrupted planting and harvesting. For replacements, the MPLA turned to town dwellers. Despite well-endowed resources, oil is the only major earner of foreign currency.

THOMAS H. HENRIKSEN
State University of New York, Plattsburgh

ANGOLA · Information Highlights

Official Name: People's Republic of Angola.
Location: Southwestern Africa.
Area: 481,351 square miles (1,246,700 km²).
Population (1977 est.): 6,300,000.
Chief Cities (1973): Luanda, the capital, 540,000; Huambo, 89,000; Lobito, 74,000.
Government: *Head of state,* Agostinho Neto, president (took office Nov. 1975). *Head of government,* Lopo do Nascimento, prime minister (took office Nov. 1975).
Monetary Unit: Kwanza (38.71 kwanzas equal U. S.$1, April 1977).
Manufacturing: Chemicals, foodstuffs, tobacco products, cotton textiles, petroleum products.
Major Agricultural Products: Coffee, cotton, sisal, corn, sugar, palm oil.

ANTHROPOLOGY

The year 1977 was marked by the establishment of the Margaret Mead Fund for the Advancement of Anthropology in honor of her 75th birthday, the opening in Kenya of a major new center for research on early man, and the discovery of *Homo erectus* fossils in Europe.

Fund to Honor Mead. The American Museum of Natural History, on the occasion of Margaret Mead's 75th birthday in December 1976, established the Margaret Mead Fund for the Advancement of Anthropology. A Margaret Mead chair of anthropology will be endowed. The museum also organized a Margaret Mead Film Festival in September 1977 as part of a year-long tribute to Dr. Mead for her pioneering work in film ethnography.

Leakey Center. Kenya formally opened a major new center for research on early man in Africa. The International Louis Leakey Memorial Institute for African Prehistory is located on the grounds of the National Museum of Kenya (directed by Leakey's son, Richard) in Nairobi. The new center is a three-story, $1.1-million complex of fossil storage facilities, laboratories, and offices.

Conference on Prehistory. At a conference on prehistory and paleoanthropology in Africa, leading scientists in the study of human evolution agreed that there was disagreement on most of the basic questions about the origins of the human species. There was agreement, however, that the evidence for the emergence of human beings is stronger in Africa than anywhere else in the world. Most of the controversy centers on the time when the genus *Homo* is believed to have appeared. Drs. Donald Johanson of Case Western Reserve University and Mary Leakey both claim that the fossils they have found indicate the time was about 3.3–3.8 million years ago. Dr. Philip V. Tobias of the University of Witwatersrand, South Africa, has disputed this, holding that both Johanson's and Leakey's fossils are not really different from *Australopithecus,* a fossil form which he believes to be ancestral to *Homo.* The latter fossils have been dated at about 2 million years. Dr. Tobias' views, however, were distinctly in the minority.

Homo Erectus Fossils in Europe. Dr. Aris N. Poulianos, a New York-trained Greek anthropologist, announced the finding of fossils, identified as *Archanthropus europaeus petraloniensis,* a form belonging to the same species as *Homo erectus,* in a cave at Petralona, northern Greece. Preliminary dating seems to indicate that they are older, by some 500,000–700,000 years, than the famed Heidelberg jaw. Dr. Poulianos believes that southeastern Europe must now be included in the zone of hominization where the modern human species evolved.

Aztec Cannibalism? Dr. Michael Harner of the New School of Social Research, New York, claimed in the journal *American Ethnologist* (February 1977) that before contact with Europeans in the 15th century the Aztecs of Mexico had a cannibalistic culture. The number of people sacrificed by the Aztecs has been recently revised upward to as many as 250,000 a year. Dr. Harner's theory of nutritional need, based on this revision, contends that while there were various vegetable foods available, the Aztecs had no domesticated animals, such as pigs or cattle, and consequently lacked protein in their diet. Thus, sacrifices of prisoners captured in battle were not simply for religious purposes but also for consumption; the Aztecs had to eat human flesh in order to obtain the needed protein. Harner feels that "the evidence of Aztec cannibalism has largely been ignored and consciously or unconsciously covered up." His theory has been sharply disputed by many anthropologists who are authorities on Aztec culture and history. They explain that the very sources used by Harner also show that supplies of game and other foods were more than adequate and that cannibalism had only a religious significance.

Death. Loren C. Eiseley, the widely acclaimed anthropologist and writer, died in July. He was Benjamin Franklin and University Professor of Anthropology and History of Science at the University of Pennsylvania (see OBITUARIES).

HERMAN J. JAFFE
Brooklyn College, City University of New York

ARCHAEOLOGY

A pattern begun several years ago flourished during 1977. The adaptation and application to archaeological research of instruments and technologies from chemistry, physics, zoology, botany, and geology, continued in mind-boggling fashion; mathematical modeling and scientific methodologies contributed greatly to what Albert C. Spaulding called "liberated archaeology." Advances were made in thermoluminescent dating and in photon and neutron activation analyses. Radiocarbon dating was enhanced when the University of Rochester, the University of Toronto, and the General Ionex Corporation announced the development of a process using very small samples and yet theoretically capable of giving dates up to 100,000 years old.

The Americas

Archaeoastronomy was the focus of a number of investigations in 1977. At Cahokia, Ill., further work was done at the so-called woodhenge feature. It consists of a series of posts set in alignments with a large central post and mounds on the nearby bluffs of the Mississippi River Valley. The alignments mark such celestial events as summer and winter solstices as well as equinoxes. The famed Wyoming medicine wheel and similar structures in Alberta and Saskatchewan, Canada, were attributed to solar and stellar observatories built by prehistoric

Indians. A considerable debate arose over a comparable interpretation for building alignments at Pueblo Bonito, Chaco Canyon, N. Mex.

Texas. The George C. Davis site, a prehistoric Caddoan settlement in east-central Texas, is a landmark in North American archaeology. The original work was accomplished before the advent of radiocarbon dating, and the age of the site has long been argued. The results of 79 radiocarbon determinations have now convincingly established the life span of the site as 780–1260 A. D.

Washington. The Ozette site, a Makah Indian whaling village in northwest Washington, has produced a find unprecedented in the area. The village was buried in a mud slide some 300–500 years ago, and preservation of organic materials is nearly perfect. Bone and wooden artifacts remain as solid as the day they were covered. The Makah Tribal Council and Washington State University are doing the work, and a $1.9-million museum is being built on the reservation for housing the recovered materials.

Ontario. Through the bitter winter of 1976–77, the Royal Ontario Museum struggled to complete the excavation of the Grimsby site. The dig is a mortuary center of the Neutrals, the shadowy occupants of the middle ground between the Iroquois and Huron. Controversy between archaeologists and Indians forced the excavation to close for two months. The resolution of the dispute will be in the courts, with potentially far-reaching effects on archaeological research.

Illinois. No summary of North American archaeology would be complete without mention of the ongoing work at the Koster site in west-central Illinois. Hundreds of students, professors, and interested laypersons devoted thousands of hours in 1977 to the excavation and analysis of this cultural layer cake. It extends in time from approximately 1200 A. D. back to nearly 7000 B. C. Enormous amounts of floral, faunal, and cultural debris have been recovered since the work began in 1969.

Guatemala. Abaj Takalik, an early classic Maya site on the piedmont of the south coast of Guatemala, has been under investigation since February 1976 by the University of California. Workers believe the site refutes the thesis that classic Maya art styles were derived from the widespread Izapa style. In addition, for the first time, Olmec and Maya monuments were found within the same ruin.

Ecuador. A University of Illinois expedition continued excavation of Real Alto, a large Valdivian site near the coast of Ecuador. The work extended a long investigation of eary Formative culture in that region. Of particular significance was the interpretation of Real Alto as a ceremonial center organized around a rectangular plaza. The dates, set at about 2300 B. C. for the well-developed Valdivian III phase and at 3100 B. C. for the initial occupation, make this the earliest known such site. The excavators, however, are quick to suggest that still earlier examples probably exist in the Guayas Basin and the lower flood plain of the Magdalena River in Colombia.

Peru. Heretofore, it has been almost axiomatic that civilization cannot appear until a well-developed agricultural system provides a base.

A 12,000-year-old Indian site at Washington Depot, Conn., yielded a 2¼-inch (6-cm) fluted point, used to kill or butcher game, and a smaller one, perhaps a toy. The find was the first *in situ* in the state.

AMERICAN INDIAN ARCHAEOLOGICAL INSTITUTE

FOREST SERVICE, USDA PHOTO

Prehistoric Indians made use of the medicine wheel of Bighorn National Forest in their astronomical observations.

At Aspero, on the central Peruvian coast, evidences of trade, large public structures, extensive textile manufacturing, and a large socially stratified population have been found. These clearly point to a Formative culture on its way to civilization, even though the site dates to 2500 B.C. and is pre-ceramic. The most significant feature is the apparent reliance of the site's occupants on seafoods and marine estuary resources, not agriculture.

Colombia. The Indiana University Museum reported the excavation of the El Abra Rockshelters, some 50 km (30 mi) north of Bogotá. Evidence of human occupation in the shelters was dated to 10500 B.C. Less reliable were some indications of even earlier human activity.

JOHN T DORWIN, *Soil Systems Inc.*

The Old World

Although chance finds continued to play a role in archaeological discoveries, the most significant results in 1977 came from persevering long-term projects.

Africa. Human fossil remains are seldom found associated with hand-axes, the most common tool from the latter half of the Lower Palaeolithic period, but at Ndutu, Tanzania, a skull and long bones have been found with such implements. Accompanying these remains were flake tools and bones of other mammals, eaten as food. The find is estimated to date back at least to the end of the Mindel (third last) glaciation.

Collaborating archaeologists and paleolinguists have found that the earliest Bantu-speaking peoples came from the territory around the central African lakes, essentially in what is now Uganda, with a western leg into Zaire. This is the land of the Urewe Iron Age culture, which about 500 B.C. crystallized around a mixed farming-and-herding economy, with a material complex of point-butted iron axes, tagged spears and barbed arrow-heads, x-shaped copper ingots, and distinctive twisted copper neck rings. This metal work is accompanied by round-bottom pottery, often decorated with incised lines on the rim and upper shoulder.

The occurrence of such pottery farther south in Africa coincides with the present distribution of Bantu languages. Similar remains, dating to the fourth century A.D., have just been found south of the Zambesi at Enkwanezi in Zululand, South Africa.

Near East. On a rise near the Yarkon River, Israel, investigation is progressing of city ruins dating from 3000 B.C., the time of the oldest civilization in the Near East, until the days of the Turkish Empire. A Roman road crosses the site. Work was done in the summer of 1977 on a Canaanite palace dating from 1200 B.C.

Radially oriented rock-cut chamber tombs from the early Bronze Age, about 3000 B.C., have been systematically excavated by archaeologists at Bab-edh-Dhra in Jordan. Some metal daggers and spearheads have been found in these collective burial chambers, which contain the burials of apparently closely related individuals, but pottery vessels and beads are the most frequent archaeological finds.

The Karnak temples at Thebes, the capital of the Egyptian pharaohs of the New Empire, have been studied by French archaeologists since 1798. The Aswan Dam, which halted the Nile's

El Abra Rockshelters, north of Bogotá, Colombia, may have been ancient "luxury apartment buildings."

INDIANA UNIVERSITY MUSEUM

flooding, has permitted excavation of the deeper levels of the Middle Empire. The main work is concentrated on dismantling Pylon IX, the work of King Horemheb, to get at the inscribed, decorated "talatat" blocks, which came originally from the temples of Amenhotep IV (Akhenaton), at the end of the 18th dynasty. Nearly 6,000 of these blocks with inscriptions have been systematically excavated and photographed for study. Together, some of them represent scenes more than 200 m (600 feet) long, providing comic-strip-like depictions of Egyptian life.

The Mediterranean. Another Minoan Bronze-Age city has been discovered at Komos on the south coast of Crete, where little has been found before. The trading port's location helps explain how the innumerable Egyptian and North African products got to north Cretan cities such as Knossos. An important industrial area for grinding grain supplemented the entrepot facilities of this city. Farther north in the Aegean, discoveries continue at the contemporary site of Thera, destroyed by a volcanic eruption about 1500 B.C. The African contacts are manifested by a battle scene showing armored Therans fighting dark-skinned adversaries.

Perhaps the most exciting discovery of the year was that of the tomb of Philip of Macedon, father of Alexander the Great, at Vergina, near Salonika, Greece. The tomb was intact and contained a painting depicting a royal hunt, a wealth of gold, silver, and bronze objects, and a white marble sarcophagus. Also found were a gold diadem worn by Macedonian kings and ivory heads of King Philip, his parents, his first wife, Olympias, and Alexander.

Archaeologists attribute the stone tablet found in northern Italy to the practice of a "dog cult" around 4000 B.C.

UPI

Yugoslavia. Excavation at ancient Stobi in Yugoslav Macedonia has cleared the remains of a synagogue, complete with the names of philanthropists and an inscribed seven-branched candlestick. The structure had been converted into a Christian church after the conversion of the region. Underneath were Roman and pre-Roman remains of a Greek-speaking population. Just under the inscription of a philanthropist was a small pit with two vessels containing more than 500 coins dating from 300 to 150 B.C. A nearly intact theater abandoned in the 4th century, when Gothic newcomers changed the residential patterns, was also brought to light.

Denmark. Tollund Bog on Jutland, Denmark, which yielded the most famous of the bog bodies, has now produced a woman to accompany the Tollund Man. She is not so well-preserved as the male. New radiocarbon dating of the Tollund Man himself places him at about 220 B.C.

Danish finds from the later Iron Age, after the time of Christ, have been marked by unusual frequency of gold. On Zealand, near Copenhagen, there is a grave containing a gold ring bracelet and ruby-red drinking horn, apparently an import from Frankish tribes neighboring the Romans on the Rhine. Zealand also produced the second largest gold find in Denmark, with the discovery of a 30-cm (12-inch), 2-kg (4.5-lb) massive gold neck ring from the Viking times, about 900 A.D.

At Illerup Bog, a gold armlet, belt buckle, and numerous weapons were found with wooden shields made of fir. Since fir did not grow in Denmark during Roman times, this indicates that the arms were those of raiders from Norway or Sweden.

Germany. Lignite mining near Leipzig, East Germany, has revealed the site of wild horse hunters from the interglacial period after the Mindel. Cutting tools and hammer stones (for flaking tools) were the most numerous artifacts among the horse bones.

Luxembourg. Inflation and recycling were 4th-century concerns in the Celtic hill-fort town of Titelberg in Luxembourg. Although Titelberg has produced more coins than most other sites in Europe, archaeologists have found a 4th-century bronze foundry which seems to have specialized in the smelting down of old coins, either those of discredited emperors, or coins debased as a consequence of inflation. Perhaps not coincidentally, this smelter was the only structure ever built over the floors of an old mint dating back to La Tène Iron Age.

China. In the passageway of a Han tomb, archaeologists came upon a 2,000-year-old bronze horse and chariot, 1.37 m (4.5 ft) long and .9 m (3 ft) tall. The find, in the southeastern Kweichow province, resembles similar tombs in the north and west; the chariot directly explains how the close communication behind such similarity was maintained in the far-flung Han Empire.

RALPH M. ROWLETT, *University of Missouri*

Paris' Pompidou center, designed by Renzo Piano and Richard Rogers, was one of the year's most talked about buildings.

ARCHITECTURE

There were some new directions in architectural activity in 1977, both in terms of increased construction and stylistic trends.

After adjusting for inflation, housing expenditures were up some 30% over 1976, although experts said spending on nonresidential structures rose very little or not at all. Inflation drove construction costs higher by 5% to 10%, leading many homeowners to remodel rather than build new houses. (*See also* HOUSING.)

Architectural design appeared to confirm its turn away from the "cigar box" glass skin construction that has dominated urban office buildings throughout the United States. Increased interest was shown in styles intended to be more responsive to the needs of sites and the needs and wants of users. This trend was particularly evident in two areas traditionally considered harbingers of architectural change: publications and education.

Perhaps the most important book focusing on an architecture more responsive to people's needs was *The Language of Post Modern Architecture* by architectural critic and historian Charles Jencks. It attacked modern architecture, favoring "inclusive architecture . . . [that] brings much more of our personality and behavior into focus."

Schools of architecture placed increased emphasis on the cultural aspects of design: how the built environment affects those who use it. Many schools gave new emphasis to drawing (as distinct from engineering, although concentration on engineering did not necessarily decrease as a result). The "inclusivist" theory of relating new structures to their surroundings became more prevalent in most schools, with a corresponding drop in support for the "exclusivist" theory wherein structures are viewed as units largely independent of the surrounding architectural and cultural environment.

An outstanding example of this emerging architectural philosophy is the 23-story apartment under construction on 5th Avenue across from the Metropolitan Museum of Art in New York City. Architects Philip Johnson and John Burgee, who designed the building's 5th Avenue façade, eschewed traditional skyscraper architecture in favor of a sedate grey limestone and glass structure divided horizontally by shallow moldings and vertically by unusual, continuous bay windows. The design fits comfortably with neighboring structures.

Restoration and preservation figured prominently in the year's architectural activities.

Landmark status for New York City's Grand Central Terminal was upheld by the state's Court of Appeals (the state's highest court) in a dramatic chapter in the five-year court battle by preservationists to block construction of a 55-

story office tower atop the 64-year-old Beaux Arts style terminal. A city "should not be forced to choose between witnessing the demolition of its glorious past and mortgaging its hopes for the future," the court declared in its unanimous decision.

Four firms were selected to design the U. S. $16-million restoration of Washington, D.C.'s 78-year-old Romanesque revival post office. The General Services Administration chose McGaughy, Marshall & McMillan of Norfolk, Va.; Associated Space Design, Inc., of Atlanta, Ga.; Arthur Cotton Moore/Associates and Stewart Daniel Hoban/Associates, both of Washington, D. C., for the major job.

Important progress was made on what is probably the biggest single ongoing restoration project in the United States: Boston's Faneuil Hall Marketplace. Architects Benjamin Thompson & Associates, Inc., of Cambridge, Mass., designed the master plan.

Neighborhood restoration was initiated or continued in such diverse cities as Worcester, Mass., Columbus, Ohio, Indianapolis, Ind., Dallas, Tex., Chicago, Ill., and Denver, Colo.

Madison, Ind., Hot Springs, S. D., and Galesburg, Ill., were selected by the National Trust for Historic Preservation as demonstration towns for downtown rehabilitation. Each city will be provided a new downtown master plan as part of the National Trust's "Main Street Project," designed to "encourage small municipalities to restore the economic, social, and aesthetic integrity of their central business districts."

Undoubtedly, the year's most widely recognized and controversial building was the Centre National d'Art et de Culture Georges Pompidou in Paris, France. Superstructure, pipes, conduits, and other traditional architectural innards are exposed on the outside of the two-block-long Pompidou center, leaving five levels of uninterrupted floorspace. Oversized escalators encased in transparent tubes bring people up and down the government-financed structure that has the look of being built by a sophisticated giant with an oversized Erector set. (*See also* ART.)

Among widely noted structures completed in the United States in 1977 were the elegant, aluminum-skinned Bronx (N. Y.) Developmental Center (winner of an American Institute of Architects Honor Award) by Richard Meier & Associates; the gracious, highly refined Yale Center for British Art in New Haven, Conn., by Louis I. Kahn; the hotel tower and office segment of Detroit's 32-acre (13-ha) Renaissance Center by John Portman & Associates; and the symbolically ornamented addition and renovation at the Allen Memorial Art Museum on the Oberlin College campus in Oberlin, Ohio, by Venturi and Rauch, Architects and Planners.

Among the nation's most important new commissions was the addition to the Museum of Modern Art in New York. Cesar Pelli, newly appointed dean at Yale School of Architecture, is designing the addition in collaboration with Gruen Associates. Plans for the museum expansion initiated one of the year's major architectural controversies, not only because of aesthetic questions involved with doubling the facility's gallery space in six stories beneath a new 42-floor apartment and condominium tower (the interior designed by J. Robertson), but also due to the tax free museum's ability to derive income from real estate on its property. That advantage was made possible by special state legislation effectively useful only to the museum.

Alternative energy sources became an area of increased architectural activity and interest, particularly the "passive" use of solar energy, wherein a structure makes use of the sun through insulation, orientation, building materials, and other nonelectronic and nonmechanical means. Interest in "active" solar energy use, through such devices as solar collectors, also increased.

The federal government, through the Energy Research and Development Administration of the new Department of Energy, continued its active support of solar and other energy-saving systems.

Using information gained from evaluating energy needs of 3,000 randomly selected buildings, the American Institute of Architects Research Corp. developed a data base for U. S. energy standards for architectural structures. In 1979 the Department of Housing and Urban Development is scheduled to recommend implementation of such standards to Congress. The AIA Research Corp. also organized a consortium of 19 schools to do research on projects of national scope with regional variables.

Architectural exhibitions were noteworthy for quality and quantity. New York's Cooper-Hewitt Museum led the way with five shows, including an excellent exhibition of work by the influential 16th-century Italian architect Andrea Palladio. Among other noted shows were "Women in American Architecture," sponsored by the Architectural League of New York at the Brooklyn Museum; "A View of California Architecture: 1960–1976," at the San Francisco Museum of Modern Art; and "Drawing Toward a More Modern Architecture," which explored numerous kinds of architectural drawing in concurrent shows at the Cooper-Hewitt and The Drawing Center in New York.

The death of Eliot Noyes, 66, on July 17 in New Canaan, Conn., cost the United States an architect who had major impact on American design. From 1940 to 1945 he was the Museum of Modern Art's first director of its Department of Industrial Design. Shortly thereafter he opened his own office. Noyes, an award-winning architect, was better known as a designer for such corporations as IBM, Westinghouse, Cummins, and Mobil. At his death, he was consultant design director for IBM and Mobil.

JOHN DREYFUSS
Architecture and Design Writer
"Los Angeles Times"

A 23-story apartment building, to stand opposite the Metropolitan Museum of Art in New York City, fits in perfectly with the surrounding structures. Philip Johnson and John Burgee are the architects.

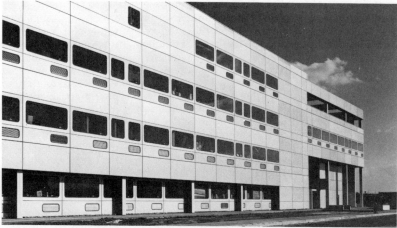

The aluminum-skinned Bronx (N. Y.) Developmental Center (*above*) and the Yale Center for British Art in New Haven, Conn., are among major architectural works completed during 1977.

ARGENTINA

As the antiguerrilla campaign subsided, the dichotomy between hard-liners and moderates within Argentina's ruling military junta became more obvious. Army Gen. Jorge Videla, presiding over the three-man junta, preferred moderate policies with a gradual return to democratic rule and encouraged further development of manufacturing. Fellow junta members Orlando R. Agosti, head of the air force, and Emilio Massera, navy commander, favored a continuation of military rule and the economic predominance of the agrarian sector.

Scandal. While Videla was attempting the first steps toward civilian rule, the hard-liners in his administration were expanding the investigation of a financial scandal. It also had the earmarks of a crusade against Argentine Jews. The late David Graiver had been accused of managing U. S.$12 million in ransom money obtained by the Montonero guerrilla forces. In its investigation of the case, the army implicated the late José Bel Gelbard, a naturalized Argentine Jew and former Peronist minister of the economy, under whom Graiver had served. Former President Lanusse, who had dealt with Gelbard, was held for 41 days. In all, 100 persons were detained, including members of the Graiver family. Twenty-nine of those interrogated were held for trial in the nation's military courts.

Human Rights. Even though the regime told its critics that the human rights issue was an entirely domestic one, there was widespread concern over human rights violations. Amnesty International issued a report in March, decrying torture and summary executions in Argentina and claiming that the military government held as many as 6,000 political prisoners, while up to 5,000 were unaccounted for.

After the U. S. State Department was rebuked for its assessment of the rights situation in Argentina, the department's coordinator for human rights, Mrs. Patricia Derian, observed the situation in March and August. President Videla received a delegation of ten U. S. congressmen in August. The congressional trip was motivated by the rights matter.

The Argentine Assembly for Human Rights pleaded for the release of all prisoners against whom the government had no charges. Some 500 detainees were released by midyear, but many new arrests were made. Abuses of human rights, occurring in the government campaign against leftist terrorists, were strongly denounced in May by Roman Catholic bishops. The governing junta announced in August that it would fully investigate the unexplained disappearance of several thousand persons. The regime recognized that disappearances were on the increase as a result of the struggle against terrorism. Relatives of the missing persons staged silent protests near the executive mansion.

Economic Policies. Growing public dissatisfaction with the current economic situation, specifically a recession produced by rigid wage controls and by reduced purchasing power, provoked a full-scale review of the controversial economic recovery plan, prepared by Minister of Economy José Martínez de Hoz. The military leadership expressed support for Martínez and his plan, but recommended salary readjustments not contemplated by the minister. Under the anti-inflationary plan, wages were frozen, while prices were allowed to rise, but the minister of economy did request in March a voluntary price freeze for a 120-day period. Inflation was projected at 120% in 1977, as opposed to a 347.5% rate in 1976. An increase of 4.5% in the gross national product was anticipated for 1977. Martínez was unable to hold the budget deficit to 3% of the GNP, in accordance with an International Monetary Fund (IMF) demand; a 6% deficit was expected. Crucial to the economic plan was the heavy borrowing of funds from outside sources. Loans of U. S.$1.2 billion were negotiated by Martínez during the first year of the Videla regime. Credits and loans amounting to about $500 million were obtained during the first five months of 1977. In June, the World Bank extended a $100 million loan for financing industrial development. A $174 million contingency credit was obtained from the IMF.

While manufacturing was off slightly, 1977 proved to be a banner year for agriculture. Wheat production rose to a record 12 million metric tons; cotton production reached 90,000 metric tons; and soybeans topped 1.2 million metric tons, also a record yield. A trade surplus for 1977 of $1 billion was expected, surpassing the 1976 surplus of nearly $900 million.

Labor Activity Curtailed. The plan of General Videla to turn over the labor unions to elected leaders received a setback in October, when the military junta announced that the ban on union activity, in effect since March 1976, would be extended for another year. Earlier, Labor Minister Horacio Tomás Liendo had initiated a revision of the basic law on professional organizations which, once approved, would normalize labor activities. Attempts by Liendo to hold

---

ARGENTINA • Information Highlights

Official Name: Argentine Republic.
Location: Southern South America.
Area: 1,072,158 square miles (2,776,889 km²).
Population (1977 est.): 26,100,000.
Chief Cities (1970 census, met. areas): Buenos Aires, the capital (1974), 8,925,000; Rosario, 810,840; Cordoba, 798,663.
Government: *Head of state and government,* Jorge Videla, president (assumed office March 1976). *Legislature*—Congress: Senate and Chamber of Deputies.
Monetary Unit: Peso (437.50 pesos equal U. S.$1, Aug. 1977).
Manufacturing (major products): Iron and steel, automobiles, machinery, processed foods, chemicals, petroleum products, packed meat.
Major Agricultural Products: Wheat, corn, grapes, sugarcane, oats, sunflower seeds, sorghum.

President Jorge Videla inspects one of Argentina's locally-made, medium-size tanks during a visit to a garrison near Buenos Aires.

UPI

talks with independent (non-Peronist) unions, regarding the election of laborers to joint labor-government commissions, were frustrated. The commissions would replace the military interveners now controlling the labor unions. Illegal strikes, slowdowns, and sabotage were abetted by governmental economic recovery strategies that reduced real wage levels of workers to 50% of what they had been in 1975, increased the work week from 35 to 42 hours, pared social benefits, and forced reductions in the work force of publicly-owned enterprises.

Foreign Relations. Videla visited Venezuela in May, Uruguay in June, and the United States in September. General Agosti, a junta member, paid an official visit to Peru in June.

Relations with the United States cooled, following an Argentine charge in February of U. S. interference in its internal affairs. The allegation was based on criticism by the Carter administration of Argentine practices regarding human rights, which caused a reduction in U. S. military aid. Terence Todman, U. S. assistant secretary of state for inter-American affairs, traveled to Buenos Aires in August. In their conversation in Washington in September, Videla and Carter considered human rights and also nonproliferation of nuclear explosives.

A transport pact was signed with Brazil in August. Under the accord, Brazilian commerce would have access to Argentine highways and the Río de la Plata. Argentina joined Brazil and Paraguay in seeking a treaty to cover rival hydroelectric projects on the Paraná river.

LARRY L. PIPPIN, *Elbert Covell College*
University of the Pacific

ARIZONA

Issues receiving the most attention in Arizona during 1977 included the continuing water supply problem, the battle against organized crime, and the resignation of the governor. The state's economy continued to show indications of strength. Arizona also continued to lead the nation in population growth.

State Government. Top priorities on the agenda of the 33rd Legislature were proposed groundwater legislation and tax reform. A compromise groundwater bill passed after a protracted struggle involving the competing interests of mining, agriculture, and urban-related water uses.

A coalition between rural-based Democrats and Republicans defeated most proposed liberal legislation. The Equal Rights Amendment was again rejected; a bottle-recycling bill was defeated; and a bill calling for the repeal of the Medicaid program in Arizona was enacted. Arizona is the only state in the nation not participating in the Medicaid program.

Gov. Raul Castro's budget called for significantly higher state expenditures and lower taxes. However, an increase in revenues and income was forecast. In October, Secretary of State Wesley Bolin became governor. Castro had resigned to become U. S. ambassador to Argentina.

Crime. The existence of organized criminal elements in the state became the issue demanding most attention in 1977. A number of court cases relating to land fraud charges resulted in several convictions, some of which involved prominent Arizona business figures.

The murder of *The Arizona Republic* reporter Don Bolles in June 1976 resulted in several indictments and a lengthy trial. John Adamson, who pleaded guilty to second-degree murder and then testified, under immunity, implicated three businessmen in a murder conspiracy against Bolles and others. In November,

---

ARIZONA • Information Highlights

Area: 113,909 square miles (295,024 km²).
Population (1976 est.): 2,270,000.
Chief Cities (1970 census): Phoenix, the capital, 581,-562; Tucson, 262,933; Scottsdale, 67,823.
Government (1977): *Chief Officers*—governor, Wesley Bolin (D). *Legislature*—Senate, 30 members; House of Representatives, 60 members.
Education (1976–77): *Enrollment*—public elementary schools, 354,281 pupils; public secondary, 148,536; nonpublic, 56,200; colleges and universities, 139,631 students. *Public school expenditures*, $788,146,000 ($1,356 per pupil).
State Finances (fiscal year 1976): *Revenues*, $1,864,-083,000; *expenditures*, $1,838,885,000.
Personal Income (1976): $13,166,000,000; per capita, $5,799.
Labor Force (July 1977): *Nonagricultural wage and salary earners*, 769,300; *unemployed*, 65,800 (7.0% of total force).

Max Dunlap and James Robinson were found guilty of murder and conspiracy in the case.

Also in response to the Bolles killing, a nationwide group of reporters formed Investigative Reporters and Editors (IRE) to look into organized crime in Arizona. The group produced a controversial 23-part series of articles, in which they alleged that there exists widespread corruption in the political and economic life of the state. The group implicated several of the state's most prominent politicians. IRE was accused of making some unsubstantiated charges, and as a result *The Arizona Republic* refused to print the series. The IRE series also resulted in several lawsuits.

Water. Arizona's water shortage continued to worsen as a result of droughts and increased consumption. Overdraft of underground aquifers has increased 14% since 1970, and Arizonans are now annually using 2.2 million acre-feet (2.7 billion m³) more water than can be replenished. U. S. Rep. Morris Udall and other Arizonans renewed their support for the federally-funded Central Arizona Project which is to divert Colorado River water to the cities of Phoenix and Tucson. President Carter supported the project, asking only that some dams be eliminated.

Illegal Aliens. The entry of thousands of Mexican nationals into Arizona became an increasing problem as illegal arrivals continued to rise. President Carter proposed granting amnesty for Mexican aliens already residing in the United States. The problem remains acute in Arizona, where an estimated 50,000 aliens live.

JEANNE NIENABER
University of Arizona

In front of the Capitol in Phoenix, marchers express their views against Arizona's capital punishment law.

UPI

ARKANSAS

Turbulence marked relationships between Arkansas' persistent and aggressive Gov. David H. Pryor and an obstreperous, locally oriented legislature. In many counties, traditionally dominant county judges sparred with quorum courts, recently empowered to act as county legislatures, for control of county funds and policies.

The Legislature. In its 71st biennial session, the General Assembly rejected Governor Pryor's highly publicized, but unpopular, Arkansas plan to offset a proposed reduction in state aid to local government with a local option income tax, and so changed his constitutional convention bill that he vetoed it. Another convention bill, acceptable to the governor, was later passed in a special session. Among other enacted laws were a revised code to adapt county law to the new county government system, an addition of a consumer representative to state regulatory boards, and a sunset bill requiring periodic legislative review to determine whether state agencies should be continued or terminated.

The Executive. Thirty-four bills were vetoed by Governor Pryor, including expansion of the regulatory powers of the Board of Optometry, creation of a West Memphis community college, and partial repeal of the 1971 state government reorganization act. The Highway Department faced fiscal problems as the legislature refused to increase state road taxes. The Department of Education began setting educational goals for all public schools.

The Judiciary. Identical district lines were drawn for the chancery (equity) and the circuit (trial) courts, facilitating future consolidation of the two court systems. A Judicial Qualification Committee was created to investigate complaints of misconduct and disability of minor court judges. Even a legislative committee, acting under a legislative address system permitting removal of judges for "good cause," censured a circuit judge for improprieties.

WILLIAM C. NOLAN
Southern Arkansas University

——— ARKANSAS • Information Highlights ———

Area: 53,104 square miles (137,539 km²).
Population (1976 est.): 2,109,000.
Chief Cities (1970 census): Little Rock, the capital, 132,483; Fort Smith, 62,802.
Government (1977): *Chief Officers*—governor, David Pryor (D); lt. gov., Joe Purcell (D). *General Assembly*—Senate, 35 members; House of Representatives, 100 members.
Education (1976–77): *Enrollment*—public elementary schools, 240,004 pupils; public secondary, 220,589; nonpublic, 20,800; colleges and universities, 61,977 students. *Public school expenditures,* $517,757,000 ($1,056 per pupil).
State Finances (fiscal year 1976): *Revenues,* $1,492,-345,000; *expenditures,* $1,482,793,000.
Personal Income (1976): $10,408,000,000; per capita, $4,934.
Labor Force (June 1977): *Nonagricultural wage and salary earners,* 700,700; *unemployed,* 51,300 (5.6% of total force).

ARMS CONTROL AND DISARMAMENT

The cause of arms control and disarmament suffered two setbacks in 1977, but these were partially offset by two encouraging developments.

Disappointments. The first setback occurred in March when Secretary of State Cyrus Vance flew to Moscow carrying a set of proposals from the new Carter administration for reducing the numbers of strategic nuclear weapons possessed by the USSR and the United States. The initial, or "deep cut," proposal called for substantial reductions beyond the number agreed to in principle by President Ford and Soviet leader Leonid Brezhnev at Vladivostok in 1974. The United States suggested reducing missiles and heavy bombers from the earlier figure of 2,400 to something under 2,000. Vance also suggested cutting the number of missiles equipped with multiple warheads (MIRVs) from 1,320 to 1,100, and banning the modernization or the development of new intercontinental ballistic missiles (ICBMs). The United States offered to ban cruise missiles with an intercontinental range but to permit shorter range models.

After the Soviet Union rejected the "deep cut" proposal the United States switched to its "fallback" position. This was to suggest acceptance of the higher number of weapons contained in the Vladivostok figures. The Soviet Union also rejected this proposal.

The second setback for US–USSR arms control and disarmament occurred on October 3 when the Interim Agreement on the Limitation of Strategic Arms expired. For five years this accord had established numerical ceilings on the numbers of ICBMs and submarine-launched ballistic missiles that would be possessed by the two super-powers.

Later in the autumn President Carter said that a new strategic arms agreement was "in sight." It was generally understood that the new proposal included the following provisions: an 8–10 year accord containing a ceiling on overall numbers of ballistic missiles and long-range bombers, and a ceiling on the numbers of ballistic missiles equipped with MIRVs. A separate three-year protocol was thought to contain a temporary range limitation on cruise missiles, and a limitation on the Soviet deployment of heavy ICBMs, the SS–18, to approximately 300. There was conjecture the Soviets would agree to limit the production of Backfire bombers to two or three a month.

Successes. Brezhnev communicated to Carter his suspicion that the Republic of South Africa was planning to test a nuclear bomb in the Kalahari desert. American intelligence confirmed the Soviet fear. The Carter administration then engaged in intensive diplomatic activity, which included the British, French, and West German governments, as well as the Soviet Union, to discourage the suspected nuclear test from taking place.

UPI

Paul C. Warnke was nominated as chief U.S. arms negotiator and director of the U.S. Arms Control and Disarmament Agency. Following Senate hearings, the appointment was confirmed by a Senate vote of 58–40. Born Jan. 31, 1920, in Webster, Mass., the Washington, D.C., lawyer was educated at Yale and Columbia universities. Warnke served in the Coast Guard (1942–46) and in the Defense Department during the Johnson administration.

The South African government of Prime Minister John Vorster branded as unfounded rumor the fears expressed concerning an impending nuclear bomb test. Nevertheless, on August 23 President Carter announced at a news conference that the South African government had promised Washington that no nuclear explosive test would be made. Arms controllers hailed the outcome of the diplomatic pressure on Pretoria as evidence that such leverage could be used to prevent the further proliferation of nuclear weapons.

The other example of successful arms control efforts involved India and the United States. The former agreed not to conduct a second nuclear explosion for peaceful purposes. (The first Indian test occurred in 1974.) Diplomatic pressure had been applied to the government of Prime Minister Morarji Desai by Washington because of the American fear that so-called peaceful nuclear explosive tests can lead to the development of military nuclear devices. In return for India's concession, the United States agreed to furnish 12 metric tons of enriched uranium, which had previously been withheld, for use by India as fuel in the Tarapur nuclear power plant, which produces electricity.

ROBERT M. LAWRENCE
Colorado State University

ART

The 400th anniversary of the birth of Flemish painter Peter Paul Rubens was celebrated throughout 1977. A self-portrait, right, was completed about 1630.

RÉUNION DES MUSÉES NATIONAUX, PARIS

The Art Market. In terms of sales totals and record prices, 1977 surpassed all previous years. Sotheby's reported the highest net sales ever achieved by an art auction house. Worldwide sales of Sotheby Parke Bernet rose about 25% over the year before and those of Christie, Manson & Woods by about 35%. The third largest auction house, Phillips Son & Neale, also announced sales up 37%. During the year, this house joined the other two in maintaining permanent offices and in holding auctions in New York, which continues to be the major sales center. It was Sotheby's London office, however, that actually had the highest sales total in 1977: a record $98.9 million. Much of this was due to the sale for $10.3 million of the contents of Mentmore Towers, a record for a single collection.

High prices during the year were paid not so much for old masters, as was formerly the case, but for such items as Lafayette's sword ($145,000), a Heriz carpet ($200,000), a clock ($119,000), an American postage stamp ($90,000), a Hopper painting ($200,000), and a copy of Audubon's four-volume "The Birds of America" ($320,000). There is no doubt that art and antiques are valued as appreciating investments, and the auction houses themselves also attract investors. In July, when Sotheby offered 38.5 million shares, representing one third of its capital, applications for more than 99 million shares were received.

The Mentmore sale publicized once more the sad plight of England's stately homes. The Earl of Roseberry decided in 1976 to offer one of his ancestral homes, Mentmore Towers in Buckinghamshire, and its contents to the British government in lieu of inheritance taxes ($6.84 million). Never opened to the public and almost unknown, Mentmore had been built by Joseph Paxton for Mayer de Rothschild in the 1850's in neo-Jacobean style. It was filled with furniture, art objects, and curiosities. While the artistic quality of the single pieces varied, the aggregate represented an unparalleled example of Victorian taste. The Victoria and Albert Museum would have liked to add it to its holdings, but the government refused the offer. The price realized through auction was eventually much higher than the tax debt, and the house itself is yet to be sold. The failure to keep the collection intact and in Britain was a great disappointment to preservationists, and it bodes ill for the fate of many more stately homes in the near future. Confiscatory taxes and rising maintenance costs will make it almost impossible for most private owners to keep their houses and estates. The country itself is having difficulty in maintaining the collections and museums it already owns, and the public, which has been very generous in subscribing to buy individual works of art in the recent past, cannot be counted on indefinitely.

The proposed sale of the Palazzo Serristori and its contents in Florence was somewhat reminiscent of the Mentmore situation, but the outcome was fortunately different. The palace, built during the Renaissance and filled with treasures, had also become a liability to the descendants of the original owners. Again in order to pay taxes, the heirs commissioned the Florentine branch of Sotheby to sell, and permission was granted by a municipal functionary. But when publicity for the sale brought it to the attention of the public, indignation flared. Mainly through the efforts of Rodolfo Siviero, known for his successful recovery of art works stolen or illegally exported from Italy during and after the last war, the sale was stopped.

Rubens' triptych—the "Visitation," left, "Deposition from the Cross," and the "Presentation in the Temple"—was painted for the Cathedral of Antwerp between 1611 and 1614.

Finally, by means of rare cooperation among city, regional, and state officials in procuring funds, the city was able to buy the palace and its contents. Siviero hopes to establish in it an international center for the recovery of works of art. While this story had a happy ending, Italy faces the same potential loss of an important part of its heritage as England does.

Another item of good news in the field of preservation came from Paris: the recovery of a large group of fragments, including 21 heads, from the cathedral of Notre Dame. Originally on the kings' gallery of the west façade and the southern portal, they were pulled down and broken by a mob in 1793; since 1796, they have been buried in the cellar of a nearby house. A recent examination of the house, just bought by a bank, revealed the extraordinary find concealed behind a cellar wall.

Hoving at the Met. Nineteen seventy-seven marked the end of the ten-year reign of Thomas Hoving as director of the Metropolitan Museum of Art in New York—a period of enormous activity, much controversy, and many fundamental changes. The appearance of the building itself was changed by the redesigning of the sidewalk to include fountains and plantings that interrupt the unified Fifth Avenue pattern, and by modernizing the façade, staircase, and entrance hall in a manner incompatible with the original Beaux-Arts design. Moreover, physical expansion—the Lehman wing, the housing for the Temple of Dendur, and the Michael Rockefeller and American wings (some projects not yet begun)—not only conflicted with other interests of the city, especially the inviolability of Central Park, but threatens to achieve the ultimate in labyrinthine groundplans.

Under Hoving, the Met often made headlines with spectacular acquisitions; regrettably, secret decisions to "deaccession" paintings from the permanent collection also caused a great deal of publicity. In this case, adverse criticism may well lead to the loss of future donations. The number and variety of special exhibitions mounted during these years, and never before did the museum enjoy such popularity. Many of the shows were designed as educational instruments, following a trend, now current, that gives museums a direct role in bringing culture to the masses, a trend encouraged in the United States by the availability of federal funds for this very purpose. Exhibitions of 1977 included the newly installed Islamic and Egyptian collections; a loan from Bulgaria of Thracian treasures, notable for exquisite gold jewelry; two exhibitions from the Soviet Union, one of Russian costumes, very successful because of the beauty of the sumptuous materials and colors, and the other of Russian paintings that ranged from wonderful 14th-century icons to contemporary official art, mediocre propaganda works questionable both for their politics and taste; also, a show of Celtic art that displayed the fabled Book of Kells, and a survey of early Christian art from all over the world.

What was meant to be a final year of glory for the outgoing director was marred by an

97

The Yale Center for British Art, completed in 1977, houses the Paul Mellon collection of English paintings, drawings, prints, rare books, and sculpture. Natural light illuminates the main exhibit area.

event that led to Hoving's premature departure and rekindled criticisms periodically raised against him. This was the proposal by the millionaire publisher Walter Annenberg to establish the Fine Arts Center of the Annenberg School of Communications in one wing of the Met. Hoving was to be the director. However, the press questioned the propriety of several aspects of the proposal: the use of parkland, the combination of a partly commercial enterprise with the museum, the utilization of art objects and museum personnel, and the manipulation of the Board of Trustees. Annenberg subsequently decided to move his project.

American Art. The year was a good one for re-viewing American art. At the Whitney Museum in New York the popular summer exhibition presented "Turn-of-the-century America," later shown also in St. Louis, Mo., Seattle, Wash., and Oakland, Calif. It covered a wide range of subject matter, reflecting the social and cultural history of the period between 1893 and 1917. Major painters like Eakins, Cassatt, Homer, Sloan, and Sargent were included, as well as illustrators and photographers. Winslow Homer was also the subject of a comprehensive exhibition at the Boston Museum of Fine Arts, consisting entirely of watercolors, drawings, and prints. "20th-Century American Art from Friends' Collection" at the Whitney afforded a cross section of unfamiliar works by established painters. The 10th anniversary of Edward Hopper's death was the occasion for a show of his paintings at the Kennedy Galleries in New York.

Two contemporary artists, Richard Diebenkorn and Robert Rauschenberg, were subjects of important retrospective exhibitions, the former at the Whitney Museum, the latter in a show that had opened at the National Collection of Fine Arts in Washington in 1976 and was subsequently seen in New York, San Francisco, and Buffalo, N. Y. In the field of photography two veteran American photographers were also given comprehensive surveys: Willard Van Dyke at the Witkin Gallery and Ansel Adams at the Light Gallery, both in New York.

Yale Center for British Art. Paul Mellon began seriously collecting English paintings only in the 1950's. But because of his English mother and the happy summers he spent in her country he had long had a predilection for all things English. During his student days at Cambridge he particularly enjoyed hunting, and this interest led to his first acquisitions of rare illustrated books on sports. His first painting, bought in 1939, was a George Stubbs racehorse. Ultimately, he had about 20,000 books, more than 2,000 paintings, 5,000 prints, and 7,000 drawings. This collection, which he donated to Yale University, ranges from the Elizabethan period to the mid-19th century, but it is especially strong in the 18th and early 19th centuries. Yale already possesses a notable library of English manuscripts and rare books; with the Mellon addition it becomes the foremost American center for English and 18th-century studies. Mellon also gave a building designed by the late Louis Kahn especially to house the collection. The

J. M. W. Turner's "Dort or Dordrecht: The Dort Packet-boat from Rotterdam Becalmed," 1818, at Yale.

main exhibition area is on the top floor and is provided with natural skylighting. Here is the permanent collection, including the great English painters like Constable, Reynolds, and Gainsborough, and the foreigners like Van Dyck, Canaletto, and Rubens who played important roles in the development of English painting. The inaugural shows on the lower floors were "The Pursuit of Happiness: A View of Life in Georgian England," and "English Landscape from 1630 to 1850."

Venice Biennale. Formerly one of the main international attractions, the Venice Biennale seemed to be losing stature in recent years, but in 1977 its theme drew a great deal of attention. The director, Carlo Ripa di Meana, felt that, after several exhibitions critical of official and governmental attitudes toward art in the western countries, it was time to focus on the situation in the East and to devote the biennale entirely to what he called the "problem of 'dissent' in the art and culture of those European countries currently defined as socialist." The biennale, in which the United States officially participates, is financed almost entirely by Italy, and its parliament must provide funds each year. Last year this process was delayed by the official protests of the Soviet Foreign Ministry, and by debate on possible repercussions also in other iron-curtain countries. For this reason it had to be postponed, first from its usual September date to November 15–December 15 and finally, after the director had resigned in protest over the pressure put on the Italian

government by the Soviet ambassador, to 1978 —which could mean forever. If held, however, the biennale will include not only works of art but also a cinema program and a book exhibition, together with symposia. Dissident artists from the Communist countries, as well as artists from the West, will be invited to participate in the exhibitions and discussions.

Beaubourg. The government-subsidized Centre National d'Art et de Culture Georges Pompidou, popularly known as Beaubourg, was inaugurated in Paris in 1977 and promises to remain a subject of controversy for a long time to come. Its huge modernistic building has glass walls that expose heating pipes and ducts, electric systems, escalators, and freight elevators. Set in the midst of historic Paris, it antagonized many, who saw it as an esthetic affront, especially since its rise coincided with the destruction of the highly regarded, historically important 19th-century cast-iron architecture of Les Halles on an adjacent site. But it has been extremely successful in attracting crowds of visitors and tourists—more than 2 million of them in the first four months of its existence. Most of these are not the usual museum goers. Many come only to see the spectacular view of Paris from the roof. Others come to enjoy the fringe entertainment provided far into the night by street performers and peddlers who are drawn to the large open square in front of the museum; this area is now attracting life and excitement when most city streets are deserted. Some of the exhibits them-

Fukae Roshu's "The Ivy Lane," above, was one of 37 Japanese screens exhibited at the Cleveland Museum of Art. "La Negresse" was featured at "Henri Matisse: Paper Cut-Outs" display at Washington's National Gallery.

A mask of King Tutankhamen, from an Egyptian exhibit which toured the U. S.

selves contribute to the carnival atmosphere. One such is the Crocrodrome in the lobby, a fantasy contraption designed by a group of artists, including Nicky de Saint Phalle and Jean Tinguely. More than 100 feet (30 m) long and 33 feet (10 m) high, it is made of moving parts, and one of its paws consists of a two-ton block of chocolate, at which children are permitted to chip with small hammers.

However, there is more to Beaubourg. It includes a museum of modern art, a public library, the Centre de Création Industrielle (which examines man in his environment), the Institut de Recherche et de Coordination Acoustique-musique (directed by Pierre Boulez), a ciné-mathèque, a theater, a children's workshop, and various shops. The opening exhibits included a retrospective of Marcel Duchamp and a show called "Paris–New York" which surveyed a half century of painting in the two cities. True to its controversial image, the center opened just at the time when indignation with France for releasing a suspected Palestinian terrorist was at its height. As a result, American artists and dealers boycotted the inauguration and withdrew promised contributions. It will be interesting to see whether this kind of museum, combining culture and a popular fair, will set a trend for the future. (See also special report on p. 101.)

ISA RAGUSA, *Princeton University*

The Georges Pompidou Center

The Georges Pompidou National Center for Art and Culture (Centre National d'Art et de Culture), which officially opened in Paris, France, in January 1977, is in its conception and its architectural design a unique and original attempt to bring together the different elements of modern culture and to make them accessible to the public in one place. The center goes beyond the static structures of the past. It greatly increases our opportunity to explore the elements that link and separate the different disciplines, and makes possible collaborative projects on a much larger scale than those to which traditional cultural institutions have accustomed us. It enables new connections to develop between painting and music, cinema and sculpture, literature and ballet. The memory of a visit to the new center will not be simply the impression left by some particular work—a painting, book, or exhibition—but rather an interplay of reflections among experience, contradictions, and sparks of inspiration moving from recent works. At the center, we look at the past through modern eyes, and we need to look at the great innovations of this century to understand the present. If it is true that all history is the present's interpretation of the past, the consciousness of today's art must underlie the history of art.

In the past, only the elite was able to pursue an interest in artistic creation; today, large numbers of people will continue to move toward disciplines of which they used to know nothing. Museums must answer this new need; the Pompidou Center was developed specifically to answer it.

The National Museum of Modern Art at the Georges Pompidou Center is concerned with painting, sculpture, drawing, graphic art, and photography. The museum's three sections have three different functions. The collections section deals with what is permanent—preservation, the presentation of works, acquisitions, gifts. The exhibitions section is concerned with everything that is temporary—exhibitions, series of displays. The documentation section provides the tools of research and study, and houses all the writings concerned with the plastic arts.

In addition, the center contains a public library with works covering all fields of knowledge, the Industrial Design Center, and the Institute of Acoustical-Musical Research and Coordination.

PONTUS HULTEN

With its unique design—a transparent escalator, glass walls, and visible heating and electrical systems—Paris' new Pompidou Center was the focus of much attention. A portrait of the late French president is dominant.

GIANCARLO BOTTI, SYGMA   P. VAUTHEY, SYGMA

The New Museum of London

The new Museum of London tells the story of Britain's capital and its people from the mists of prehistory to the present time. It is a story that unfolds dramatically as visitors stroll through exhibits of various periods.

Built around, and overlooking, what remains of the city's Roman and medieval walls, the museum is believed to be the first in the world designed specifically to display the history of a capital city. It is intended both as a center for serious, scholarly study and as a place for enjoyment and entertainment. It is a welcome addition to London's tourist attractions.

The building, opened by Queen Elizabeth in December 1976, was designed by architects Powell and Moya. They brilliantly exploited an awkward, multiangular site. Elevated above street level to connect with a series of overhead pedestrian walkways, it guards the western end of London Wall like a modern, urban fortress.

Pincerlike, the two story museum, with its bold exterior of white tiles, encircles the old Ironmonger's Hall, one of the few buildings in the area to escape the German blitz of World War II. In addition to 41,000 square feet (3,809 m²) of exhibition area, the museum contains a lecture hall, library, school wing with refectory, administration area, research laboratory, café, souvenir shop, and space for a restaurant and bars. A 14-story office block completes the £11-million complex.

The exhibition areas are arranged in two galleries, one above the other, which enclose a central garden courtyard. Entering at the upper level, visitors walk into the prehistoric section, then on into the Roman occupation, Saxon London, and the Middle Ages. Tudor and early Stuart periods complete the upper gallery.

A vaulted ramp, overlooking the garden courtyard, leads down to the elegant Georgian era, the gin palaces, music hall and imperial splendor of Victorian London, and finally the continuing story of the 20th century.

Low-key lighting, appropriate music, eye-catching floor and wall finishes, and the clever transition from historic period to historic period add to the museum's enjoyment. Every turn in the walk through time seems to signify a turning point in London's history. There are short cuts between different eras. Everywhere there is a sense of unhurried enjoyment.

The 7,500 exhibits—ranging from a 200,000-year-old flint axe found in the Thames to a pair of elegant, bronze elevators taken from an Oxford Street department store—are imaginatively displayed in realistic settings. There are glimpses into a Roman kitchen, a Victorian grocer's shop, a cell from the forbidding Newgate Prison, and a Georgian street scene. But perhaps the most spectacular attraction is a 12-foot square (13.4 m²) model depicting the Great Fire of London, so real that the crackling of the burning timbers is audible.

The new museum has a staff of 150 under the directorship of Max Hebditch. Two archeological units work full-time on excavations in the London area.

Two great London collections were the basis for the new museum. They came from the Guildhall Museum and the old London Museum. The new institution is funded equally by the central government, the Greater London Council, and the city. Each body appoints six representatives to the controlling board of governors.

DAVID NORRIS

An early Roman kitchen and the Lord Mayor's 1757 gilded State Coach are typical of the broad sweep of the exhibits at the new Museum of London, which recreates the complete history of the British capital.

Following years of war, reconstruction continues in Vietnam. Bomb craters, near Hue, and a broken bridge are only two of the endless repair jobs needed.

ASIA

Asia, as a continent, was relatively peaceful in 1977, but it also was marked by more political changes than in many of the preceding years in which there was so much shedding of blood on the battlefield and elsewhere.

The two largest nation-states in the world, China and India, experienced major realignments of political power, while another big Asian country, Pakistan, underwent yet another transition. Sri Lanka also changed governments by democratic means, a dramatic political shift from the left to the right.

The continuing instability of several of the states of the region was reflected in the second thwarted assassination plot in a year against Burmese strongman Ne Win and a new military coup in Thailand in October.

Interstate Relations. Several states of the sprawling Asian region—particularly the Communist countries of China, Vietnam, Laos, and Kampuchea (Cambodia)—witnessed the increased consolidation of the political authority of their ruling elites in 1977, and this tended to stabilize interstate relations. However, relations among governments in general remained tentative and fragile, and it appeared that Asia would have to wait still another year (and possibly longer) for a new and more durable post-Vietnam and post-Mao pattern of international relationships to send down roots. Some foreign relations, indeed, especially the complicated competition and conflict between China and the Soviet Union, seemed just as distant from peaceful resolution as ever.

The United States was a source of the persisting international instability. The Carter administration signalled its intention to withdraw the 33,000 American servicemen from South Korea, but it also seemed to want to retain the largest U. S. overseas air facility (Clark Air Field) and the smaller but still strategic Subic Bay naval base in the Philippines. Washington appeared to be still deciding its post-Vietnam strategic role in Asia, and there were many states, particularly in Southeast Asia (but probably also China), which did not want the "Yankees" to "go home." Negotiations between the Philippines and the United States over the bases dragged on—without resolution.

Regional Cooperation. The governments still most concerned over the shape of post-Vietnam Asia were those of Southeast Asia. Many of them possessed serious internal ethnic, religious, and cultural divisions as well as domestic Communist movements that posed persisting threats to their ruling elites. Five of the Southeast Asian countries which had joined together to form the Association of Southeast Asian Nations (ASEAN) in 1967—Indonesia, the Philippines, Thailand, Malaysia, and Singapore—continued their efforts to forge new bonds of unity among themselves. A second heads of state meeting was held in the Malaysian capital of Kuala Lumpur in August.

Japan, Asia's major economic power, drew closer to the ASEAN countries. Various ASEAN leaders travelled to Tokyo in pursuit of expanded economic aid and ties, and Japanese Premier Takeo Fukuda made a very successful tour of the ASEAN countries. In August, Japan pledged U. S.$5 billion in new economic assistance to the ASEAN states. The United States, hitherto seemingly somewhat indifferent to the efforts of these key Southeast Asian states to stabilize their subregion in the wake of the Indochina wars, held high-level economic talks with the ASEAN governments but made no lavish promises. Protectionist Australia and New Zealand, Southeast Asia's neighbors in the Southwest Pacific, also indicated their intention to help the resource-rich but underdeveloped ASEAN states.

Perhaps most encouraging to the ASEAN leaders, however, were the positive public remarks made about the regional grouping by Vietnam, which had hitherto labelled the association an American creation and puppet.

New Regimes. Three of the four largest South Asian countries—India, Pakistan, and Sri Lanka —experienced major political shifts to the right, India and Sri Lanka by democratic means. Most startling was the March electoral defeat of India's Prime Minister Indira Gandhi and her Congress Party—which had ruled the nation since independence in 1947. Mrs. Gandhi's fall from political power was more the result of a strong public reaction against the authoritarian drift of her government than a mass preference for the policies of successor Morarji Desai.

Desai, more favorably disposed toward the United States than Mrs. Gandhi, sought to reduce his country's dependence on the USSR, but Indian-Soviet ties were sufficiently close and cordial that the effect of the government change was not felt in 1977.

In Sri Lanka, India's smaller island-neighbor to the immediate south, 71-year-old J. R. Jayewardene displaced Mrs. Sirimavo Bandaranaike as the country's leader. Following Jayewardene's victory, the national legislature amended the constitution to replace the country's prime ministerial form of government with a presidential one.

Pakistan held a national election in March —which Prime Minister Zulfikar Ali Bhutto won amid charges of large-scale fraud and corruption. Bhutto was ousted in July by Gen. Mohammed Zia ul-Haq—who first promised new elections and then cancelled them.

Another coup was attempted in October by junior officers in Bangladesh, South Asia's other major country, but was crushed by military strongman Ziaur Rahman.

China and Asia. China did not experience a change of governments in 1977, but the change of policies that began after Mao Tse-tung's death in 1976 continued. "Radicals" were purged, moreover, from party central committee and other important posts. Teng Hsiao-p'ing, rehabilitated for a second time, emerged as vice premier, and Wang Tung-hsing, internal security chief, became vice chairman. Chairman Hua Kuo-feng and his allies felt confident enough by August to hold a full Communist Party Congress.

TERZANI, SYGMA

Bicycles remain the most available means of transportation in the city of Hanoi, capital of united Vietnam.

The Chinese were correct hosts to visiting U. S. Secretary of State Cyrus Vance, but Mao's successors were visibly disappointed that Washington did not make any concessions.

Peking—which also sought to improve relations with Japan, the Southeast Asian states, and West European countries—openly declared that for all practical purposes the Sino-Soviet treaty of friendship had ceased to exist.

Continuing Conflict. Despite the absence of major military conflict, the consolidation of the political position of several regimes, and the largely peaceful changes of government in India and Sri Lanka, the clash of arms continued unabated, albeit on a fairly contained basis, on several Asian fronts.

At least one third of Burma was in the hands of various types of insurgents. Plots against strongman Gen. Ne Win continued to be uncovered among hitherto loyal military and civilian elements. Fighting also flared along the frontier between the Indochinese Communist states of Vietnam and Kampuchea as well as between Kampuchea and its non-Communist neighbor Thailand.

Perhaps most threatening of the continuing conflicts was the resumption of warfare in late 1977 between Muslim secessionists and the government of dictator Ferdinand E. Marcos in the

———————————————————— **ASIA*** • **Information Highlights** ————————————————————

Nation	1977 Population in millions	Capital	Area in sq mi (km²)	Head of state and/or government
Bahrain	.26	Manama	231 (598)	Isa ibn Salman, emir Khalifa ibn Salman, prime minister
Bhutan	1.2	Punakha	18,110 (46,900)	Jigme Singhye Wangchuk, king
Kuwait	1.0	Kuwait	6,178 (16,000)	Jabir al-Ahmad al-Sabah, emir and prime minister
Maldives	.12	Male	111 (288)	Ibrahim Nasir, president
Mongolia	1.5	Ulan Bator	684,294 (1,772,320)	Yumjaagin Tsedenbal, president Jambyn Batmönh, prime minister
Nepal	13.2	Katmandu	54,366 (140,807)	Birendra Bir Bikram, king Kirtinidhi Bista, prime minister
Oman	.8	Muscat	82,036 (212,473)	Qabus ibn Said, sultan
Qatar	.10	Doha	8,500 (22,014)	Khalifa bin Hamad al-Thani, emir
United Arab Emirates	.23	Abu Dhabi	32,280 (83,600)	Zaid ibn al-Nuhayan, president Maktum ibn Rashid al-Maktum, prime minister
Yemen	5.6	Sana	75,257 (195,000)	Abdul Hussein al-Ghashmi, chairman, Military Command Council Abdul Aziz Abdul Ghani, prime minister
Yemen, Democratic	1.8	Madinet al-Shaab	111,083 (287,704)	Salim Rubayi Ali, chairman, presidential Council Ali Nasir Muhammad Hasani, prime minister

* Excepting major nations, which see.

Philippines. The persisting interest of interventionist Muslim governments outside the region in the fate of their religious brethren threatened stability in the area.

See also articles on individual countries of Asia.

RICHARD BUTWELL, *State University of New York, College at Fredonia*

ASTRONOMY

During 1977 impressive progress was made in solar system studies, cosmology, and X-ray astronomy.

Uranus' Rings. For a long time Saturn's rings have been regarded as a unique wonder of the solar system. Consequently, a great deal of excitement was produced over the discovery of the rings of Uranus in 1977. Airborne astronomers observed the occultation of the star SAO 158687 on March 10, 1977. Before the star disappeared behind the disk of Uranus and after it had reappeared, brief diminutions of its light occurred. This indicated that the star had passed behind absorbing material spread in five thin rings 40,000 to 51,000 kilometers (24,800–31,700 mi) from the center of Uranus.

The occultations started suddenly, were very brief, and did not totally hide the star. This showed that the rings have sharp boundaries, widths less than a few kilometers, and are composed of bodies less than 4 kilometers (2.5 mi) in diameter. The rings have not yet been seen optically in spite of diligent, scientific searches, suggesting that they may be composed of dark material.

Venus. Further analyses of the data from the Russian Venera landers confirmed that the surface temperature of Venus is 450° C (842° F). At one landing site a gamma-ray spectrometer found concentrations of potassium, uranium, and thorium resembling terrestrial basalts, while at another site the rocky terrain resembled granite. The clouds of Venus probably are composed mostly of sulfuric acid droplets. The atmosphere seems to be transparent.

Radar observations from earth have identified regions of high and low reflectivity on the Venusian surface. Much of the surface seems flat, possibly cratered or covered with lava.

Asteroids. A significant achievement in celestial mechanics in 1977 was the rediscovery of the asteroid Adonis, which was originally discovered on Feb. 12, 1936. At that time it passed the earth at about four times the distance of the moon.

Advances in photometry and infrared measurements have made it possible to determine the diameters of the asteroids. The largest, Ceres, has a diameter of 1,000 kilometers (620 mi). More than one hundred asteroids are known to have diameters greater than 100 kilometers (62 mi). Most of them are very dark objects akin to a class of meteorites called carbonaceous chondrites, but some have reflectivities that suggest silicate or even metallic surfaces.

Cosmology. Additional evidence now supports the idea that the universe is open—that it will go on expanding forever. The present abundance of deuterium indicates that the density of matter must have been too low in the original Big Bang to ensure closure of the universe—it will go on expanding forever. The present low value of the predicted density, 5×10^{-31} g/cm³, is in excellent agreement with the value found from an analysis of the dynamics of galaxies.

The age of the universe, as deduced from its expansion, is between 8 and 20 billion years. From data on the oldest stars, astronomers deduce ages of the universe between 9 and 18 billion years. If one assumes that the rare metal rhenium is formed in explosions of massive stars and that the produced amounts of radioactive Rh-187 and stable Rh-185 are predictable, then the age of the universe can be estimated from the present ratio of Rh-187 to Rh-185. As deduced in this way, the age of the universe is between 10 and 20 billion years. It is presumed that our galaxy was formed a mere ten to one hundred million years after the original Big Bang gave birth to the universe.

X-Ray Astronomy. X-ray astronomy has catapulted into prime importance since 1970. Satellites in orbit by 1977 permitted X-ray observations to be made with a millisecond resolution, a 10″ angular resolution, and over an energy range from 1 to 1,000 keV.

Supernova remnants produce X-rays under shock conditions as their ejecta plow into the interstellar medium. Other galactic X-ray sources seem to involve the infall of matter into compact objects such as white dwarfs, neutron stars, or black holes.

Attention has been paid to variable X-ray sources called bursters. Although some show intervals of hours or even days between activity, one object—MXB 1730-335 shows thousands of outbursts in a day. Bursts rise to peak intensity in less than one second and persist for intervals of a few seconds to two minutes. High peaks tend to be followed by long intervals, but bursts tend to follow regular patterns. These bursters seem to be concentrated toward the galactic center. The peak X-ray luminosities of these objects may be a million times that of the sun.

The general picture of a point source with a continuous X-ray emission entails a binary system with a normal or evolved star that feeds material into a compact object possessing an enormous gravitational field. The infalling gas may attain velocities approaching that of light. As it is accelerated downward or decelerated as it jams into dense material, the gas may be heated to a billion degrees and radiate X rays. Bursters require some inhibiting mechanism that restrains the infalling material—holding it back now, and letting it cascade later. White dwarf and neutron stars, which have strong magnetic fields with magnetospheres, apparently trap hot gas in their magnetopause. When the gas cools, it falls into the white dwarf or neutron star and produces an X-ray outburst.

The compact source in an X-ray binary may be a white dwarf, a neutron star, or a black hole. The binaries Vela X-1 and Hercules X-1 seem to have neutron stars with masses somewhat in excess of the sun and densities of 10^{15} g/cm³. AM Herculis, the most intensely observed low-mass X-ray binary, has a normal-sized star of possibly one-half a solar mass revolving in 3.1 hours about a white dwarf of apparently one solar mass and terrestrial radius. A stream of gas feeding onto the highly magnetized white dwarf produces complex polarization, X rays, and spectroscopic variations. Cygnus X-1 is a compact, massive X-ray source associated with a normal star HDE 226868. Cygnus X-1, which has a mass equal to five solar masses, must be a black hole because no extremely small star with a mass equal to five solar masses can exist.

LAWRENCE H. ALLER, *University of California*

AUSTRALIA

Prime Minister Malcolm Fraser and his Liberal-National Party coalition followed the orthodox approach in holding down inflationary pressures and killing off inflationary expectations. Thanks to productivity gains, the gross national product (GNP) rose 3% and for the first time since 1972 the inflation rate came below 10%. More than 5% of the work force was unemployed, the highest rate since the 1930's.

Leading financiers diagnosed Australia's basic economic slackness as stemming from a continuing lack of consumer and investor confidence, which led to "too many industries operating below capacity." Nevertheless, they said, on balance the government's measures of restraint were essential for the improvement of the economic fabric and future prospects. On the other hand, the high level of unemployment brought condemnation from union leaders and the parliamentary opposition.

The Australian Labor Party did its best to build the state of the economy into the major political issue, but the persistence of unions in pressing for higher wages and causing disruptive strikes gave Fraser an issue on which to call an election for December 10, a full year ahead of time.

As the campaign developed, unemployment and economic management became the key issues, and although Fraser refused to match the ALP's promises for immediate measures to stimulate employment, and Liberal-National Party coalition was reelected. The coalition won a handsome majority in the House of Representatives and maintained control of the Senate. Donald Chipp, a dissident Liberal, won a Senate seat, as his new Australian Democrats received about 10% of the vote. Following the ALP's defeat, Edward Gough Whitlam, 61, announced that he was stepping down as party leader.

Economy. Prior to the election, the Fraser government's main policy thrust was to hold the line on wages in order to halt the wages-prices spiral to which Australians had been conditioned throughout the 1970's. To reinforce

---

AUSTRALIA · Information Highlights

Official Name: Commonwealth of Australia.
Location: Southwestern Pacific Ocean.
Area: 2,967,900 square miles (7,686,861 km²).
Population (1977 est.): 13,900,000.
Chief Cities (1975 est., met. areas): Canberra, the capital, 210,600; Sydney, 2,923,000; Melbourne, 2,661,000.
Government: *Head of state,* Elizabeth II, queen; represented by Sir Zelman Cowen, governor general (took office December 1977). *Head of government,* Malcolm Fraser, prime minister (took office Dec. 1975). *Legislature*—Parliament: Senate and House of Representatives.
Monetary Unit: Australian dollar (0.90 A. dollar equals U. S.$1, Aug. 1977).
Manufacturing (major products): Petroleum products, steel, machinery, chemicals, automobiles, meat products.
Major Agricultural Products: Wool, sugarcane, barley, fruit, tobacco, dairy products, sheep.

On Jan. 18, 1977, more than 80 persons were killed in the worst train disaster in Australian history when a commuter train, bound for Sydney, jumped the tracks and toppled a rail traffic bridge.

UPI

other austerity measures, the government reduced the number of federal employees by not filling vacancies as they occurred. A move in March to institute a three-month wages-and-prices freeze failed when unions refused to accept total wage restraint. Subsequently the government pressed the wage-determining Arbitration Commission to forgo quarterly cost-of-living increases, and succeeded in cutting these below the official price index rises. As a counter to the pressure for higher pay, the government eased income tax by restructuring the tax scale.

Treasurer Phillip Lynch's budget provided for total expenditure of (U. S.) $29,321,000,000 and receipts of $26,882,000,000. The budget deficit of $2,439,000,000 compared with a total deficit of $3,014,000,000 in fiscal 1977. The budget outlays showed a 10.4% increase on the actual expenditure in fiscal 1977. Social security and welfare outlays at $7,975,000,000 were up 13% and education expenditures, at $2,608,000,000, were up 10%. Other major items were more or less steady in real terms. The heaviest cuts were in housing and urban development projects. The money supply increase was set at 10%, and the inflation rate was down to about 9%.

The year's migrant intake was held at the existing level of about 70,000.

Industrial Discipline. Industrial law and its enforcement became a dominant issue in national affairs as unions showed an increasing proclivity for strike action in support of political issues. Union pressure was evident in such key policy matters as wage restraint and the government's approval of uranium mining (a decision long in abeyance pending the outcome of a searching inquiry into what should be done about the continent's uranium deposits), but most clearly at issue was the role of unions and union leadership in industrial disruption.

In October the government introduced new industrial legislation enlarging the Industrial Relations Bureau's power to investigate breaches of awards and seek corrective action through the Arbitration Court. Most newspapers welcomed the promise of a toughened stance.

Foreign Relations. The Fraser cabinet expressed basic agreement with the foreign policy initiatives of the new Carter administration. The change of government in India, leading to renunciation of former pro-Soviet leanings, came as Foreign Affairs Minister Andrew Peacock was expressing complete accord on policies lowering U. S. and Soviet military strength in the Indian Ocean.

With the changes in American power and influence in Asia, Australia's interest in the South Pacific was strengthened. In 1977 Australia pledged increased financial support for Papua New Guinea and nine English-speaking nations of Oceania.

In parliament, Peacock indicated that Australia would hold firm against challenges that its extensive Antarctic territory was "the common heritage of mankind." Meanwhile Australia worked with its treaty partners on a convention which would safeguard the ecological balance of Antarctic marine life.

Events and Change. With record exports (up 21% in fiscal 1977) and record imports (up 31%), the government was concerned at limited access to certain markets. In midyear a minister for Special Trade Negotiations with the European Economic Community was appointed. The move was part of a concerted effort to ease Europe's exclusion of Australian agricultural products and the EEC's "disruption of Australia's traditional markets in Third World countries by subsidizing exports of food supplies."

On a jubilee visit to Australia, Queen Elizabeth II was greeted by enthusiastic crowds.

UPI

Australia's Prime Minister Fraser and Britain's Chancellor of the Exchequer Healey, right, meet in London.

Prime Minister Fraser said the enthusiasm shown was confirmation of Australians' deep loyalty to the monarch and commitment to monarchy.

In December, Sir Zelman Cowen, a constitutional lawyer and university administrator, succeeded Sir John Kerr as governor general.

R. M. YOUNGER, *Australian Author*

AUSTRIA

Steady growth prevailed in Austria's economy in 1977. Industrial output expanded, exports and imports increased, employment improved, and the inflation rate declined.

Political Events. In January, the Austrian press disclosed that in December 1976 customs officials had held up a consignment of 600 Austrian-made rifles and 400,000 rounds of ammunition being sent to Syria as sporting equipment. The sale had been arranged by a private dealer, an old friend of Defense Minister Karl Lütgendorf, and the arms came from military stocks. Despite the customs interception, the shipment shortly reached Syria via a Yugoslavian port. The conservative opposition parties held that the sale was illegal under Austria's Neutrality Law of 1955 and another law barring shipment of arms to war zones. Two motions of no confidence were defeated in the National Council but led to the appointment of a commission of inquiry. The commission found that Lütgendorf, who had sought to aid Austria's arms industry and made no personal gains, was inaccurate in his dealings with Chancellor Bruno Kreisky, leading the latter to make erroneous statements to parliament. Lütgendorf, faced with dismissal, resigned May 30. On June 8, Otto Rösch, previously minister of the interior, became defense minister; Erwin Lanc moved from the ministry of transport to that of the interior; Under-Secretary of State Karl Lau-

secker succeeded Lanc, and Franz Löschnak became the new under-secretary of state.

Economic Developments. The gross national product grew at a rate of 5.2% in 1976, and similar growth was estimated for 1977. The inflation rate was expected to decline from 7.3% to about 6%. On May 31, 1977, unemployment stood at 1.3%. The number of foreigners employed in Austria rose again, to 199,635 in May. With 1971 equaling 100, the price index of exports stood at 129.8 in 1976 and the volume index at 145.9, while the price index for imports was 131.5 and the volume index 149.2.

The progressive elimination of tariffs on industrial goods between Austria and the European Economic Community was completed on July 1, 1977. Austria's most important trading partner is the Federal Republic of Germany, followed by Italy and Switzerland.

Foreign Affairs. On January 10, Austria became a non-regional member of the Inter-American Development Bank. An agreement signed on January 19 in Geneva with 13 other European countries provides for the establishment of stations to monitor air pollution. From May 2 to 13, an International Conference on Nuclear Power and Fuel Cycle was held in Salzburg; more than 60 nations attended.

Chancellor Kreisky visited Tel Aviv on February 23 to speak to the Israeli Labor party convention; he stated that the Palestinians had as much right as the Israelis to recognition of their national entity. The chancellor also discussed the Middle East with President Carter when he visited the United States in March. On that occasion, Kreisky also turned over to the University of Minnesota and Stanford University a bicentennial gift to the United States in gratitude for aid given to Austria after World War II.

Early in the year, Ambassador Karl H. Schober presented his credentials to President Carter; on June 22, the Senate confirmed Milton A. Wolf, an Ohio businessman, as the new U. S. ambassador to Austria.

ERNST C. HELMREICH
Bowdoin College

AUSTRIA • Information Highlights

Official Name: Republic of Austria.
Location: Central Europe.
Area: 32,374 square miles (83,849 km²).
Population (1977 est.): 7,500,000.
Chief Cities (1975 est.): Vienna, the capital, 1,650,000; Graz, 253,000; Linz, 207,000; Salzburg, 132,000.
Government: *Head of state,* Rudolf Kirchschläger, president (took office July 1974). *Head of government,* Bruno Kreisky, chancellor (took office April 1970). *Legislature*—Federal Assembly: Federal Council and National Council.
Monetary Unit: Schilling (16.16 schillings equal U. S.$1, Aug. 1977).
Manufacturing (major products): Processed foods, chemicals, textiles, iron, steel, electrical goods.
Major Agricultural Products: Rye, wheat, barley, potatoes, sugar beets, oats, forest products.

Ford's new compact, the Fairmont, is much shorter and lighter than the Maverick which it replaced.

UPI

AUTOMOBILES

Automobile production in the United States rose to nearly 9 million units in the 1977-model run, the second highest volume ever.

Output and Sales. The 1977-model total of 8,845,012 through August 31 was 9% ahead of the 1976-model count of 8,114,376. Only the record output of 9,915,802 cars in the 1973-model run surpassed 1977-model production.

Contributing to the surge in 1977-model sales and production were substantial gains for cars in the higher-priced segments of the market. General Motors, dominating regular-sized and intermediate-sized car sales, raised its share of domestic-car production to 58.6% from 56.6% in the previous model run. GM's five car divisions all brought out drastically "downsized" full-sized models for 1977. GM's top-selling intermediates had enjoyed brisk demand in the 1976-model year and remained strong in 1977. But the restyled regular-size Chevrolet Caprice, Buick Electra, Pontiac Bonneville, Oldsmobile 88/98, and Cadillac lines also scored impressive sales increases in 1977.

GM built 5,181,006 cars in the 1977-model run through Aug. 31; Ford Motor Co., 2,175,-315; Chrysler Corp., 1,311,122; and American Motors, 177,569. For the 1976-model run, GM accounted for 4,593,892; Ford, 2,148,270; Chrysler, 1,088,637, and AMC, 283,577. Chrysler had the largest year-to-year increase, 20.4%. GM rose 12.8% and Ford, 0.1%; AMC fell 37.4%.

New production records were chalked up by three GM divisions—Chevrolet, Oldsmobile, and Cadillac. Chevrolet built 2,056,917 cars, compared with 1,943,532 in 1976; Oldsmobile, 1,-100,927, against 874,618, and Cadillac, 352,199, vs. 309,139. Chevrolet's restyled regular-size Caprice/Impala series barely edged out Olds' midsize Cutlass for top production honors.

Station-wagon leadership for its compact Volare and Aspen models and introduction of new LeBaron and Diplomat intermediates were prime factors in Chrysler's advance. Chrysler also excelled in the growing van production segment. Ford lagged in its smaller-size entries but made gains in full-size models, unchanged for 1977, and in its restyled Thunderbird and Cougar intermediates. AMC stumbled as its unrestyled Hornet compact and Gremlin and Pacer subcompacts met increasing competition from the Big Three and imports. The 1977-model upswing for the Big Three was achieved despite price increases averaging 5%–6% and concern about gas prices and fuel economy averages.

The 1978 Models. The weight-shrinkage and size-reduction movement continued when GM introduced a fleet of redesigned intermediate cars, Ford brought out two new compacts, and Chrysler entered production of two new subcompacts. The Big Three counted on their smaller new models to ensure compliance with a Federal Energy Act requirement that every automaker's Corporate Average Fuel Energy (CAFE) on 1978 models be no less than 18 miles (29 km) per U. S. gallon. The CAFE rises to 19 miles per gallon on 1979 models and 20 miles per gallon on 1980 cars.

WORLD MOTOR VEHICLE DATA, 1976

	Passenger car production	Truck/bus production	Motor vehicle registrations
Argentina	142,072	51,445	3,101,014
Australia	360,927	86,289	6,065,400
Austria	...	8,739	1,874,717
Belgium	296,677	30,301	2,935,937
Brazil	526,943	458,526	6,700,000
Canada	1,137,313	502,799	11,028,111
Czechoslovakia	179,094	36,736	1,765,000
France	2,979,559	423,156	17,932,000
East Germany	168,000	37,000	2,413,000
West Germany	3,546,900*	321,189	19,453,073
Hungary	...	12,900	704,410
India	38,297	46,761	1,420,598
Italy	1,471,308	119,369	16,253,642
Japan	5,027,792	2,813,655	28,090,558
Mexico	212,549	112,430	3,339,604
Netherlands	74,223	12,338	3,757,000
Poland	228,900	81,500	1,554,800
Portugal	...	683	911,500
Rumania	60,700	46,000	138,000
Spain	753,125	113,115	5,860,117
Sweden	317,126	50,654	2,930,978
Switzerland	...	954	1,973,726
United Kingdom	1,333,449	372,057	15,995,821
United States	8,497,893	2,999,498	132,950,410**
USSR	1,239,000	786,000	9,895,000
Yugoslavia	192,801	23,270	1,694,570
TOTAL	28,793,648****	9,547,364****	327,900,635***

*Includes 245,548 microbuses.

**U. S. total includes 106,712,551 cars and 26,237,859 trucks, excluding Puerto Rico (648,806 and 114,730, respectively); Canal Zone (17,600 and 9,000); and U. S. Virgin Islands (32,500 and 6,250).

***Registration total includes all countries, of which nonproducing countries exceeding 1 million registrations are: Venezuela, 1,324,515; South Africa, 2,994,194; Denmark, 1,528,606; Finland, 1,139,967; Norway, 1,100,834; and New Zealand, 1,366,652. Total includes 260,207,459 cars and 67,693,176 trucks and buses.

****Excludes 1,778,837 car and 641,619 truck and bus assemblies, principally in Belgium (742,824 car/67,483 truck); South Africa (185,132 car/115,116 truck); Iran (105,000 car/35,000 truck); Taiwan (98,923 car/36,043 truck); and Venezuela (96,446 car/67,003 truck).

Source: Motor Vehicle Manufacturers Association of the United States, Inc.

AMERICAN HONDA MOTOR CO.

VOLKSWAGEN OF AMERICA, INC.

The new Honda Civic (above) and the Volkswagen Rabbit, with a diesel engine, were expected to be extremely popular. It was a banner year for imported cars.

Tests of 1978 models completed in September 1977 by the Environmental Protection Agency revealed a strong showing by diesel-powered cars. The Volkswagen Rabbit, a diesel car, led all cars tested by averaging 45 miles (72 km) per gallon. Other division leaders included Oldsmobile Delta 88 (full-size), Ford Fairmont (compact), and Peugeot 504 (compact).

Looking ahead to the 18-MPG average deadline, GM had drastically "downsized" its full-size models for the 1977-model year. For 1978, GM reduced the wheelbase of its Buick, Chevrolet, Oldsmobile, and Pontiac intermediates to 108 inches (274 cm). Lighter-weight plastics and aluminum materials were used to pare car weights by 500 to 900 pounds (227 to 408 kg). "Fastback" sedans were added to the notchback models in the Buick and Olds lines.

GM divisions introduced more efficient engines for 1978 to improve fuel economy. A diesel V-8 engine made its debut on Oldsmobile regular-size cars. Buick pioneered among domestic automakers with a turbocharger for its V-6 engine. Chevrolet introduced a new smaller V-6 on subcompact and intermediate models.

The new Ford compacts—the Ford Fairmont and Mercury Zephyr—were substantially lighter and shorter in overall length than the Maverick and Comet models that they replaced. Ford's basic four-cylinder engine was offered on the Fairmont and Zephyr for the first time. Ford deferred scaling-down its full-size models until the 1979-model year, when GM planned to extend its own reduction operation to compacts.

Front-wheel drive was pioneered among smaller domestic cars in the Plymouth Horizon and Dodge Omni subcompacts from Chrysler. The Horizon and Omni were four-door sedans with a "fifth door" hatchback. Chrysler dropped its full-size Plymouth and Dodge models and added station wagons to its intermediate Chrysler LeBaron and Dodge Diplomat series. AMC's 1978 change was to rename its Hornet compact the Concord, with new grille styling featured.

Prices of 1978 models rose by an average of nearly 6%. The "average" regular-sized model, such as a Chevrolet Caprice four-door sedan with automatic transmission and air conditioning, sold for about $7,000.

Imported Cars. Imports boomed in 1977, breaking all U. S. sales records. Nearly 1.5 million imports were sold in the January-August period, compared with only 978,000 in the comparable span of 1976. Japanese makes paced the upsurge, with Toyota and Datsun ahead of Volkswagen. A strong gainer was Japan's Honda, whose minicompacts doubled in volume from 1976. Ford introduced its European mini—the Fiesta—in August 1977.

MAYNARD M. GORDON, *"Motor News Analysis"*

BANGLADESH

Except for an abortive coup in October, Bangladesh was relatively quiet in 1977. Major General Ziaur Rahman became president in April and retained the position of martial law administrator.

Domestic Affairs. Originally General Ziaur had promised to return Bangladesh to "civilian" rule in February but he canceled the scheduled elections because, in his words, they would bring political chaos. However in April, he again promised such elections, this time by the end of 1978. In February, former President Moshtaque Ahmed, who was overthrown by Ziaur in November 1975, was convicted of corruption and abuse of power and sentenced to five years in prison. In late April, the ailing president of Bangladesh, Abu Sadat Mohammad Sayem, resigned. In accordance with the constitution, General Ziaur was named as his successor.

Ziaur thus became the seventh president in the six years of Bangladesh's independence. In accepting the presidency, he asked the nation to appraise him in a referendum to be held in May 1977. He also proclaimed that one of the constitutional "ideals," secularism, should be replaced by Islam. General Ziaur asked that his record be approved. In the approximately 18 months that he had been Bangladesh's ruler, he had maintained unusual stability and order, cut down traditional corruption, controlled inflation at least to an extent, and generally had given the nation the best government it had had in its short history. In May, the voters not unexpectedly approved Ziaur and his record by a 99% majority. Some of his political critics were skeptical of the honesty of the election results, but they were generally accepted in Bangladesh as legitimate.

Yet in early October, dissident members of the armed forces attempted a coup against Ziaur's regime. The armed attack involved several hours of fighting in Dacca, and nearly 100 soldiers and airmen were reported killed. The abortive coup coincided with a five-day hijacking of a Japanese airliner to Dacca.

Foreign Affairs. Relations with other nations were generally good during a year of no great diplomatic crises. Bangladesh pursued a wary policy regarding the new Indian government. In October, Bangladesh and India reached an agreement on the sharing of the Ganges River waters. It was an important diplomatic accomplishment.

Tornado. Some 900 persons were killed by a devastating tornado which struck two areas of Bangladesh in April. The Madaripur district, southwest of Dacca, was particularly hard hit.

CARL LEIDEN
Professor of Government
The University of Texas at Austin

BANKING

Banking in the United States was marked by a tone of conservatism in 1977, partly as a result of revelations about the activities of Bert Lance, who resigned as director of the Office of Management and Budget. Furthermore, bankers were still retrenching from the excesses of diversification and aggressive leading of earlier years, and they devoted much effort to working out bad loans still on the books. Also, a poor bank-stock market made it difficult for banks to raise new capital to back growth. This gave even more incentive for conservative lending and growth policies.

Meanwhile, a battle went on between commercial banks and thrift institutions, both of which wanted a bigger share of consumer deposits.

Thrift Institutions. The thrift institutions—savings banks, savings and loan associations, and credit unions—pushed forward with plans for expanded power in 1977, all of which involved encroachment on commercial banking's traditional markets. The thrift institutions traditionally had relied on savings deposits as their basic source of funds. But now many thrift institutions felt they must obtain new fund sources. For there was a real question as to how long people would continue to save when inflation was 6% or 7% while savings rates were only 5%. In addition, many people began to feel that with growing social security and social services provided by the government, there was less need to save for a rainy day.

As a result, thrift institutions began to push for checking account privileges in the states where this was legal in order to gain money that was left in financial institutions for convenience as well as for rate of return. In addition, many thrift institutions also added payments features to savings accounts through development of electronic means of funds transfer. For example, they allow people to move money into and out of their savings accounts at a point-of-sale electronic terminal in a grocery store.

In New England, thrift institutions had already achieved full banking privileges through the NOW account, or Negotiable Order of Withdrawal, which is virtually the privilege of writing a check on a savings account. Also, credit unions were actively developing share draft programs

---

—— **BANGLADESH · Information Highlights** ——

Official Name: People's Republic of Bangladesh.
Location: South Asia.
Area: 55,126 square miles (142,776 km²).
Population (1977 est.): 83,300,000.
Chief Cities (1974 census): Dacca, the capital, 1,320,000; Chittagong, 458,000; Khulna, 436,000.
Government: *Head of state,* Ziaur Rahman, president (took office April 1977). *Head of military junta,* Ziaur Rahman (took office Nov. 1975).
Monetary Unit: Taka (15.32 takas equal U.S.$1, Aug. 1977).
Manufacturing (major products): Jute products, cotton textiles, processed foods, wood products.
Major Agricultural Products: Rice, jute, sugarcane, tea, oilseeds, pulses, forest products.

that allowed their members to write checklike drafts on their savings balances to pay bills. In addition, some thrift institutions inaugurated telephonic transfer services. These are similar to the European giro system in that the account holder instructs the institution to pay the person who is to receive money. Only instead of having to come into the bank or provide written notice, as is frequently the case in European giros, the saver instructs the institution by telephone whom to pay and how much. In all these ways, the powers of thrift institutions were becoming more and more like those of commercial banks in the United States.

Commercial Bank Activities. The bankers' reaction was to push for similar power of electronic fund transfer in many instances. In addition, bankers started an intense political campaign to reduce the regulatory advantages that they felt thrift institutions held over banks in the United States. For instance, the banks have tried to win elimination of the "differential" under the interest-rate ceiling laws that allow thrift institutions to pay savers more than banks are allowed to pay. The commercial banks also have tried to make thrift institutions subject to certain regulations on reserve requirements and tax payments.

Toward the end of the year the banks' political activities were blunted both by internal disagreement as to goals and by the crisis in the Carter administration over budget director Bert Lance's activities as a banker before going to Washington. Before Lance was forced to resign, it was revealed that he had taken huge overdrafts from banks he ran, had moved bank funds from place to place to serve as deposit compensation for personal loans that benefited him, and

had taken other actions that made many people question banking practices and demand greater governmental regulation of the entire banking industry.

As the year drew to a close, it looked as if basic regulatory change would be slowed by controversy over issues such as the Lance affair and by uncertainty as to what bankers themselves wanted in the way of new powers.

But one point was clear—the aggressive use of new electronic equipment by thrift institutions and banks was providing the customer more convenience in obtaining banking service than ever before, with people able to tap their accounts 24 hours a day from convenient locations like supermarkets and free-standing automatic teller machines.

The intensity of the competition for savings and checking deposits thus had speeded up. And in the search for earnings to pay for the new services, banks and thrift institutions also had started to fight for each other's lending business, thereby intensifying competition, too.

International Expansion. One area of diversification in 1977 was the continued effort of many major banks to open branches in other nations. This developed despite the worries some bankers had about the repayment of loans previously made to less developed countries. Many bankers continued to look at international expansion as a means of gaining new fund sources and new lending outlets whose potential for profit, hopefully, will be greater than that available under the intensely competitive banking conditions at home.

PAUL S. NADLER
Professor of Business Administration
Rutgers—The State University of New Jersey

CITIBANK, N.A.

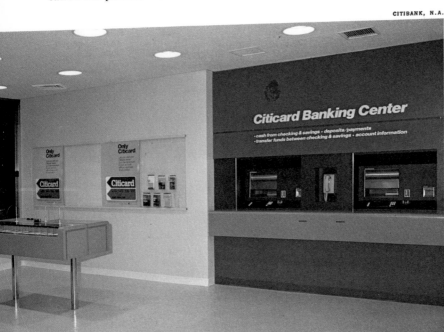

Electronic banking systems, offering customers 24-hours-a-day service, were introduced on a wide scale.

BELGIUM

Major developments in Belgium in 1977 concerned the spring elections, with the resulting prospects of a constitutional change to a federal state, and the maladies of an economy with stagflation and high unemployment.

Politics. The linguistic quarrels between the country's French and Dutch speakers have been the central element of Belgian politics since the modern state's creation in 1830. In March 1977, this issue again destroyed a ministry, when a minority coalition party, the Rassemblement Walloon, failed to support a budget vote. Prime Minister Leo Tindemans recreated a coalition which attempted to reconcile not only the sometimes diametrically opposed ideas and aspirations of Walloons and Flemings, but also to solve the sensitive dispute over the status of the capital, Brussels.

The mixed ministry announced in May was unique in that it brought together the right-of-center Christian Social party and the Socialist party, and also embraced two extreme and rather militant language parties, Volksunie and the Front Démocratique des Francophones.

The Tindemans plan aimed at major constitutional change. It would divide the nation into three regions, with the insistent *Bruxellois* receiving a separate status, parallel to Wallonia and Flanders but with less sweeping powers. If given legislative approval, the plan would virtually dissolve the country into constituent regions and create three devolved assemblies and governments. The crux of the reform controversy was Brussels, which is the capital of the "New Europe," headquarters of the European Community, NATO, and numerous international and multinational private organizations. In a nation where the Flemings are a clear majority and Brussels a geographical enclave in a Flemish area, there was much opposition to a tripartite compromise settlement. Flemings, questioning the concept of Brussels as a neutral district, feared the three-way split would quickly slip the city into the francophone camp. Clearly, the decentralization plan would give regional assemblies the greater part of the present national government's authority on domestic issues like

UPI

Leo Tindemans votes in Belgium's general elections. The prime minister's party gained additional strength.

taxation, commercial and industrial policy, and even social programs, and thus leave the central government little more than defense and foreign policy.

The Economy. Continued recession and unemployment, and particularly the accentuated squeeze on living standards, have all exacerbated the language war. Striking economic disparities, such as depressed Liège, with its nearly 15% unemployment rate, and affluent Antwerp, benefiting from its busy port, commerce, and dynamic new industrial base, have only aggravated the ethnolinguistic differences.

Austerity measures, imposed in February, failed to get much public sympathy and achieved only moderate results; at year's end, the economic prospects were still on the bleak side. The upward trend in consumer prices was stronger than in 1976, unemployment had increased, and industrial investments remained sluggish. The selective government package of public investments, early retirements, tax incentives, traineeships for the young, and increased value-added tax did significantly stimulate economic growth and recovery. It was apparent that the nation was suffering through the longest and severest economic crisis since the 1930's.

Belgian Nobelist. Ilya Prigogine of the Free University of Brussels, received the Nobel Prize for Chemistry (see PRIZES AND AWARDS).

PIERRE-HENRI LAURENT, *Tufts University*

BELGIUM • Information Highlights

Official Name: Kingdom of Belgium.
Location: Northwestern Europe.
Area: 11,781 square miles (30,513 km²).
Population (1977 est.): 9,900,000.
Chief Cities (1975 est.): Brussels, the capital, 1,100,-000; Antwerp, 670,000; Liège, 440,000.
Government: *Head of state*, Baudouin I, king (acceded 1951). *Head of government*, Leo Tindemans, prime minister (took office 1974). *Legislature*—Parliament: Senate and Chamber of Representatives.
Monetary Unit: Franc (35.72 francs equal U. S.$1, Aug. 1977).
Manufacturing (major products): Steel, metals, textiles, cut diamonds, chemicals, glass.
Major Agricultural Products: Sugar beets, potatoes, wheat, oats, barley, flax, hay.

BIOCHEMISTRY

The year 1977 was an active one for the field of biochemistry as advances were made in genetic manipulation, gene sequencing, and other areas.

Biochemical Markers. Although detection of cancer has improved considerably in the last two decades, half of all cancers spread before they are first detected. It is generally believed that if early warning signs could be found, 90% rather than the current 35% of cancers could be cured.

Many see biochemical markers in the blood and urine as a useful basis for early cancer detection. Efforts toward developing such marker systems have increased dramatically.

In 1977 investigators found tiny quantities of an abnormal enzyme called acid phosphotase in the blood of patients with prostate tumors. They also found minute quantities of melanin-pigment by-products in the urine of melanoma skin-cancer patients. They also found a unique sugar-protein complex in human breast tumors, and it is hoped that it will show up in blood analyses. Also, several other carbohydrates, hormones, and polyamines that seem to be linked with various cancers were found.

It is hoped that further development of assay systems to detect tiny amounts of these biochemicals can help physicians find and cure cancers before they spread.

Enzymes. X-ray diffraction studies nearly a decade ago began to reveal the detailed structure of certain enzymes and thus to lay a groundwork for understanding the highly important catalytic function that all enzymes perform in living organisms. These studies centered mainly on hydrolytic enzymes (those in which water is split during the decomposition of another molecule). However, many nonhydrolytic enzymes such as the so-called acid proteases are biologically significant. Acid proteases such as pepsin and gastricsin function in digestion; renin is an important agent in the control of blood pressure; and acid proteases are used in the preparation of fermented rice and soybean products and, experimentally, for cheese production.

In 1977 four Canadian biochemists determined the amino acid sequence and the three-dimensional structure of an acid protease called penicillopepsin, which is derived from a species of Penicillium fungus. They found the enzyme has two lobes with a pronounced cleft between them in which the important catalytic sites are believed to reside—a structure quite similar to hydrolytic enzymes. This work should serve as a model for studying other acid protease enzymes, and help biochemists determine the precise action of all enzymes—the catalysts for life processes—at the molecular level.

Genetic Manipulation. In the debates on safety that have ensued since genetic manipulation or "recombinant DNA" techniques were first developed about 1972, one potential application for the new technology has received perhaps greatest attention—the insertion of human insulin genes into bacterial chromosomes and the subsequent broad-scale manufacture of human insulin for use by diabetics.

A first major step toward that goal was taken in 1977. Researchers at the University of California at San Francisco successfully cloned a mammalian insulin gene, isolated from rat pancreas, into a common bacterium. The researchers predict that they can coax the cells to produce rat insulin. Cloning of the human insulin gene would then follow.

After that work was reported, an investigation revealed that the California research team had broken the guidelines issued in 1976 by the National Institutes of Health to govern the safety of recombinant DNA experiments. The investigators concluded that the breach did not pose a health hazard and was probably inadvertent. However, the incident points up the difficulties inherent in the self-policing effort scientists have undertaken in this field.

Gene Sequencing. An offshoot of these genetic manipulation studies is the sophisticated gene sequencing technique developed in 1977 by A. Maxam and W. Gilbert of Harvard University. The technique uses restriction enzymes to break up long strands of DNA into a complex mixture of different-size fragments. Four parallel preparations are analyzed by gel electrophoresis and the differences between the pieces are compared. After that the specific nucleotide order can be read off the gel in the sequence in which it appears on the DNA molecule.

This technique has already been used to study the human gene sequences that code for two hemoglobin proteins and a hormone produced by the placenta.

A related but slightly less streamlined technique developed in 1975 by British researcher F. Sanger was used in 1977 to determine the complete nucleotide sequence in the nine genes of a bacterial virus called PhiXl74. It thus became the largest living organism for which the entire sequence is known.

Such sequencing has revealed some startling information about the way genes are structured and seem to operate. It is widely believed that the long DNA molecule is stable and that genes are situated end to end on the DNA strands. However, new work made possible by sequencing strongly suggests that gene sequences overlap and that one gene can begin or end entirely within another gene; that functioning genes can have long intervening sequences that do not seem to contain useful information; and that genes actually jump from place to place on the molecule. While the meaning of these phenomena is uncertain, it is clear that gene sequencing techniques will unveil important information about the way genes work.

JANET L. HOPSON
Contributing Editor, "Science News"

BIOGRAPHY

A selection of profiles of persons prominent in the news during 1977 appears on pages 115–127. The affiliation of the contributor is listed on pages 589–92. Included are sketches of:

AMIN DADA, Idi

In 1977, there was increasing resistance to President Idi Amin Dada of Uganda and his brutal regime. Amin himself admitted that there had been two conspiracies against him during the year, and after one of them, which included an attempt on his life, Amin disappeared for a time. He claimed to be on a belated honeymoon with his latest wife, Sarah.

Throughout the year, Amin kept to the forefront of world attention, after a quiescent period following his humiliation during the Israeli raid on Entebbe Airport to free hijacked hostages in July 1976. The Ugandan leader kept the British guessing in June 1977 when he asserted he would attend the Commonwealth Conference in London. The Ugandan media claimed he had left for London but Amin never arrived. (The British government had barred Amin but not the Ugandan nation from the meeting.) The hulking Amin played another hoax in September when he was said to be in a coma after a minor operation. The "coma" was a trick to thwart opposition from fellow Muslims after Amin ordered 15 political opponents executed during the Muslim holy month of Ramadan. Such flouting of the Islamic code earned Amin more enemies in the Arab world. But with Uganda's economy strong as a result of the high world price for coffee, Amin appeared as firmly in power as ever.

Background. Idi Amin Dada was born in January 1928 at Arua in Uganda's West Nile district, a member of a small, predominately Muslim Kakwa tribe. In his teens, he joined the King's African Rifles where his physique made him an ideal recruit for this tough corps. As a sergeant, Amin campaigned with his unit in Kenya against the Mau Mau revolt. An excellent sportsman, he was Uganda's heavyweight boxing champion (1951–60). He was later commissioned an officer and by independence in 1962 held the rank of captain. He took an advanced paratrooper course in Israel, earning warm praise from his instructors. He rose fast, and by 1967 was in command of his country's armed forces.

His relationship with President Milton Obote was increasingly tense until January 1971 when soldiers from Amin's home district killed their officers and carried Amin to power. In 1972, Amin expelled the country's 40,000 Asians and was accused of the murder of many thousands of Langi and Acholi tribesmen. During and after the Entebbe hijacking and the killing of Mrs. Dora Bloch, a passenger on the hijacked plane, he was widely considered mad. Since then, his behavior has been increasingly contemptuous of international moral structures. In February 1977, Uganda's leading Anglican, Archbishop Janani Luwum, died in suspicious circumstances. By late 1977, Amin's name had become a byword for terror throughout Africa and the world.

JAMES PRINGLE

BEGIN, Menahem

For the new prime minister of Israel, Menahem Begin, the road to power was far from smooth. In eight general elections before those of May 17, which catapulted him into the prime minister's chair, he had lost his bid for leadership of his country. Even on the home stretch, during the election campaign, it was touch and go when he suffered a heart attack. After the surprise victory, however, he recovered sufficiently to assume office on June 20 and subsequently go on a tiring visit to the United States, where he conferred with President Carter. While the two leaders did not see eye to eye—the prime minister being an eloquent believer in *Erez Israel*, the tenet that Israel is entitled to all the area that belonged to ancient Israel, including the West Bank—the meeting was nevertheless friendly. In November, Begin held a historic meeting with Egypt's President Sadat.

Background. Menahem Begin was born on Aug. 16, 1913, in Brest-Litovsk, which was in Poland between the wars but in 1913, as now, within the Russian frontiers. He grew up in Poland and was graduated in law from the University of Warsaw. Early active in politics, he became a member of the leadership of Betar, a Zionist youth movement, in 1931, and its head in 1938. He had been briefly imprisoned in 1936 in Warsaw for organizing a demonstration at the British legation against the policy of the mandatory power in Palestine.

The German invasion of Poland in 1939 led to the murder of Begin's brother and their parents in a German concentration camp. Begin fled to Wilno, occupied by the Russians, who soon arrested him. In 1942 he was allowed to enlist in a Polish army being formed in the USSR, and he arrived in Palestine as a corporal with this force in May 1942. He deserted and joined Irgun Zvai Leumi, the extreme Zionist group. Becoming its commander, he conducted a vigorous underground "armed warfare" against the mandatory government by methods which have since become popular among the Arab opponents of Israel. The British vainly offered £10,000 for his capture. Irgun blew up a wing of the King David Hotel in Jerusalem, causing 90 deaths (British, Jewish, and Arab), massacred 250 people in a raid on Deir Yassin, an Arab village, and perpetrated other atrocities.

In June 1948, when Israel had just become independent, Begin had a confrontation with Prime Minister Ben-Gurion, when the latter refused to permit the gun-running Irgun ship *Altalena* to discharge its cargo at Tel Aviv. Worsted in that showdown, Begin briefly went underground but, reconsidering, founded his own political group, the Herut (Freedom) party, and won a seat in the Knesset. Later (1967), the Herut joined with several other parties to form the rightist Likud, now in power. Begin held office from 1967 to 1970 as minister without portfolio but was chiefly a stinging critic of the ruling Labor coalition. He opposed the German reparations agreement of 1952. He left office in 1970 protesting the "softness" of Golda Meir's government.

Begin's manners exhibit an old-fashioned courtesy and his dress also tends to the formal. His personal life is above reproach. He and his wife Aliza, 57, live in a small Tel Aviv apartment which they have occupied since 1946. They have three grown children.

ARTHUR CAMPBELL TURNER

UPI

Michael A. Bilandic, a Daley protégé, was not only elected mayor of Chicago but was also married in 1977.

BILANDIC, Michael A.

In a few short months in 1977, Michael A. Bilandic, 54, was elected mayor of Chicago, Ill., was married for the first time, and jogged nonstop for 26 miles (41.6 km) around the city. After 21 years of rule by Mayor Richard J. Daley, who died Dec. 20, 1976, Chicagoans gave Bilandic an overwhelming mandate to head the city in a special June mayoral election.

Bilandic's manner in office and his political astuteness mirrored those of his mentor, Richard J. Daley. The new mayor retained ironhanded control over Chicago's City Council and, like Daley, won confidence from the city's big labor and big business. And he avoided sensitive issues that could become a political liability. When school busing started in Chicago in the fall, Bilandic remained silent, saying that busing was a problem for the educators, not for him.

Yet the life-style of Bilandic and his June bride, socialite Heather Morgan, contrasted with the pomp and circumstance and private home life Chicagoans remember of Daley. The Bilandics could be seen regularly at restaurants and nightclubs, ball games, cultural events, or jogging in the city parks.

Background. Bilandic, of Croatian heritage, was born in Chicago, Feb. 13, 1923. He served in the Marines in World War II, and attended St. Mary's College, Winona, Minn. In 1948, he received a law degree from DePaul University in Chicago, the alma mater of many Chicago politicians and judges.

Bilandic maintained a successful corporate law practice in Chicago for 20 years before entering politics in 1969 as Daley's handpicked candidate for alderman of the 11th ward. It was Daley's ward and the same one that has given Chicago its mayors for 44 years.

After only three years on the City Council, Bilandic was selected by Daley to head the council's powerful finance committee when the former chairman, another Daley protégé, went to prison for graft. In his many years in office, Daley never talked publicly of a successor. But if he had, most political observers in the city believe he would have tapped Bilandic.

When Daley died, a black alderman, Wilson Frost, who was president pro tem of the council, proclaimed himself the new mayor. However, the Daley machine aldermen in the council said no and appointed Bilandic as the interim mayor.

ROBERT ENSTAD

BIRD, Rose Elizabeth

On Feb. 12, 1977, Gov. Edmund G. Brown, Jr., of California appointed Rose Bird to be chief justice of the California Supreme Court—the first woman ever to serve on that judicial body. Her appointment (in effect, for life) generated considerable controversy, perhaps because she is a woman, certainly because of her youth, lack of judicial experience, and strong stand in favor of agricultural workers (cases concerning whom will come before the court), but the Commission on Judicial Appointments approved her by a 2–1 vote.

Generally described as a "liberal" and a "populist," Bird is credited with getting the State Supreme Court to accept the doctrine of "independent state grounds" in one of her appearances before the court as an appellate lawyer. She successfully argued that the state can have a different interpretation of a state constitutional provision from that of the federal constitution, even though the wording is identical, because the two constitutions serve different purposes. This interpretation has been welcomed by liberals as the U. S. Supreme Court has become more conservative.

Background. Rose Elizabeth Bird was born on Nov. 2, 1936, in Tucson, Ariz. She was reared in upstate New York and on Long Island and was graduated *magna cum laude* from Long Island University. She later attended Boalt Hall Law School of the University of California, Berkeley, where she won the moot court competition and was graduated in 1965.

Bird served first as a legislative intern in Sacramento and then became law clerk to the chief justice of the Nevada Supreme Court. A year later she joined the staff of the Santa Clara County public defender in San Jose. She rose to the position of senior trial deputy and also handled appeals. At the same time, she lectured on criminal and consumer-protection law at Stanford University.

When Edmund G. Brown, Jr., successfully ran for secretary of state in 1970 and then for governor in 1974, Bird served as a volunteer worker. Subsequently, Brown appointed her secretary of agriculture and services, the head of a conglomerate agency with 11 subdivisions. In that position, she helped to work out the complex and controversial Agricultural Labor Relations Act and became one of the governor's most important advisers.

CHARLES R. ADRIAN

BYRD, Robert C.

Few men have ever worked harder to earn a leadership post in the U. S. Senate, or planned more carefully to get one, than Robert C. Byrd (D-W. Va.), who was selected as majority leader in January 1977.

Picked in 1967 for the obscure post of secretary of the Democratic Conference, Byrd used the job to do thousands of tiny favors for his colleagues. He did the routine business that kept the Senate moving. When an auto accident at Chappaquiddick affected Sen. Edward M. Kennedy's concentration and reduced his popularity, Byrd challenged Kennedy for the job of majority whip and got it in January 1971.

The new whip did the same work he had done in his previous post, scheduling Senate business efficiently but according to colleagues' wishes. When Mike Mansfield (D-Mont.) retired as majority leader, Byrd was the man to beat. Even the much respected Sen. Hubert H. Humphrey of Minnesota had to acknowledge defeat, and Byrd won the job without opposition.

Background. Robert Carlyle Byrd was born Nov. 20, 1917, in North Wilkesboro, N. C. His name at birth was

UPI

Robert C. Byrd, U.S. senator from West Virginia since 1959, became Senate majority leader in January 1977.

Cornelius Calvin Sale, Jr., but he was orphaned at age one and was reared by relatives in West Virginia. He later adopted his guardian's name.

Byrd attended high school and four different colleges in West Virginia, but did not obtain an undergraduate degree. (While serving in the Senate in 1963, he received a law degree from American University in Washington, D. C.)

Byrd's early adult years were not easy. He worked as a butcher. He also made one of his few political misjudgments, joining the Ku Klux Klan. The issue has hounded him throughout his Senate career, but he has called it a mistake and it has never hurt him politically in West Virginia.

Once Byrd was elected to the West Virginia House of Delegates in 1946, he moved quickly. He was chosen for the state Senate in 1950, the U. S. House in 1952, and the Senate in 1958.

Byrd came to the Senate with a reputation as a rigid conservative, and he kept that reputation through the 1960's. He filibustered against the Civil Rights Act of 1964, opposed the Voting Rights Act of 1965, and supported the Johnson administration in Vietnam.

But Byrd's election as whip coincided with a move to the center on key issues. He voted for some antiwar amendments in 1971, supported extension of the Voting Rights Act, and won national attention for his intense questioning of Nixon administration witnesses before the Senate Judiciary Committee.

Byrd's outspoken concern about civil liberties abuses by the FBI helped change liberal attitudes toward him in the Senate and establish the centrist reputation that made his election as majority leader possible.

ALAN EHRENHALT

CAREW, Rod

Rodney Cline Carew was born Oct. 1, 1945, on a train rolling through the Panama Canal Zone. His mother, en route to a hospital, named the infant after Dr. Rodney Cline, who aided in the delivery. Rod Carew, now a major-league baseball star, is still on the move.

The day after his 32nd birthday, the lean, swift left-handed batter completed the 1977 American League season with a .388 average for the Minnesota Twins. That was the highest mark in the major leagues since Ted Williams batted .388 for the Boston Red Sox in 1957. Carew's 239 hits were the most in the majors since Bill Terry had 254 for the New York Giants in 1930. Carew was later named the league's most valuable player.

During the regular season, the intriguing question was: could Carew become baseball's first .400 hitter since Williams hit .406 in 1941? Carew carried a .400 average into midseason, then slipped a bit before finishing with a rush.

Growing up in Panama, Carew played with baseballs made of rags and tape. He became an outstanding player in local Little Leagues, once winning a Ted Williams model bat, a prize he treasured.

At 14, Rod was hospitalized for six weeks with rheumatic fever, leaving him weak and a target of scorn from his father, who considered him a "sissy." A year later, Olga Carew took her children to live in New York where, although Rod was walloping sandlot shots in the shadow of Yankee Stadium, he was signed by Twins scout Herbie Stein, a railroad detective.

In 1967, Carew became the Twins' second baseman and was named Rookie of the Year. He has been voted to the All-Star game starting lineup in each of his 11 AL seasons. Only four players have won more batting titles than Carew's six—Ty Cobb (12), Honus Wagner (8), Rogers Hornsby (7), and Stan Musial (7).

Carew is at home in the batter's box. The home run does not interest him—his preference is spraying line drives around the field, interspersing an occasional bunt. Unlike most hitters, he varies his stance often. He also stands deep in the box to get the longest possible look at the ball. Carew is also a multifaceted player. One year, he stole home a record-tying seven times. Since switching from second base in 1975, he has become a defensive master at first base. But Carew's ability to hit is what awes his fellow players.

In 1970, Carew, black and Hispanic, married Marilynn Levy, white and Jewish. The couple had to endure cranks' racial slurs and even death threats.

BOB BROEG

CARTER, Rosalynn Smith

When Rosalynn Smith Carter moved into the White House in January 1977, it became clear immediately that the nation had a new First Lady of a sort not seen for many years—not since the days of Eleanor Roosevelt, who Mrs. Carter has said is indeed her model.

The slight, brown-haired Mrs. Carter, 50, made it evident that she was not interested in being merely a decorative First Lady, that such traditional preoccupations as fashion, entertaining, or redecorating the White House were not enough. "There is so much you can do and there are things I want to do," she said. To help accomplish her objectives the new First Lady appointed a staff of 18.

In February, President Carter, at her urging, set up the Presidential Commission on Mental Health. The First Lady was first appointed chairman, and when it was pointed out that members of a president's family are barred from such appointments, made honorary chairman. As such, she has flown to cities around the country for hearings.

Another area of substantive interest has been the problems of the elderly; a round table on the aging was held at the White House in the spring under Mrs. Carter's aegis. Still another arena where she has chosen to speak out is the equal rights amendment; she lobbied for its passage in several states, with mixed results.

Her most visible venture was a trip at the end of May, a 12-day visit to 7 Latin American countries. During the trip, she officially represented her husband. To the questions—and they came thick and fast—about

UPI

The official portrait of First Lady Rosalynn Carter was taken in the Vermeil Room of the White House.

the appropriateness of a president's wife engaging in diplomacy Mrs. Carter replied flatly: "I think that I am the person closest to the President of the United States."

All this has had her husband's enthusiastic assent. Mr. Carter has called her his "political partner," and there is no doubt that she has been and remains one of his most influential advisers. One luncheon a week is set aside for President and Mrs. Carter to talk over, alone, the matters she thinks should be brought to his attention.

Born in Plains, Ga., Aug. 18, 1927, Rosalynn Smith was a painfully shy 19-year-old when she married Jimmy Carter. After seven years of Navy life, they returned to Plains and in the hardworking years that followed, she became his partner in everything. His entry into politics forced her to overcome her shyness; by 1976, she was an indefatigable campaigner.

She has devoted her life to her husband's ambitions, but says: "I feel that I have always had my own identity. I have never felt submerged." As for life in the White House, she told an interviewer: "Jimmy's at home more than he ever was."

LINDA CHARLTON

DESAI, Morarji Ranchhodji

One of the first opposition leaders to be arrested when Prime Minister Indira Gandhi proclaimed a national emergency on June 26, 1975, Morarji Desai was released only in January 1977, when Mrs. Gandhi suddenly decided to permit the sixth national elections to be held. On March 24, after the surprising electoral defeat of Mrs. Gandhi and the Congress party, Desai became prime minister of India at the head of a Janata party government. Twice earlier denied the post of prime minister—after the death of Jawaharlal Nehru in May 1964 and again after the death of Lal Bahadur Shastri in January 1966—he had joined his Old Congress party with three other opposition groups to

form the Janata, of which he was chosen leader. For a man of 81, he was remarkably buoyant during the rigorous two-month campaign, and victory in the March elections was overwhelming.

Noted for his rigidity, autocratic tendencies, and asceticism in food, dress, and manners, Morarjibhai, as he is generally called, has been described as "perhaps the most controversial leader in modern India." He is widely respected, if not beloved, for his experience, ability, dedication, and integrity.

Background. Morarji Ranchhodji Desai was born into a Brahmin family in Bhaddi, a village in what is now the state of Gujarat, on Feb. 29, 1896, and brought up in a religiously orthodox village environment. Educated at Wilson College in Bombay, he joined the Bombay Provincial Service in 1918. During the 1920's he came under the influence of Mahatma Gandhi, and in 1930 he resigned from the administrative service and joined the nationalist movement. He became a member of the Bombay Legislative Assembly in 1937 and was minister in charge of revenue in the first Congress government of the province. In 1946 he was placed in charge of home affairs and revenue in the Bombay government.

From 1952 to 1956 Desai was chief minister of Bombay State. He won a considerable reputation for his progressive legislation but lost support because of his opposition to the division of Bombay into the two states of Maharashtra and Gujarat in 1956. Nevertheless, he continued to have a solid political base in Gujarat. After 1956 he was active mainly at the national level. He was minister of commerce and industry in the central government from 1956 to 1958 and minister of finance from 1958 to 1963. In 1966–67 he served as chairman of the Administrative Reforms Commission. He joined Mrs. Gandhi's cabinet as deputy prime minister and minister of finance in 1967. Two years later, when she dismissed him as finance minister, he resigned as deputy premier as well. A leader of the Old Congress after the Congress party split in 1969, he was a prominent opponent of Mrs. Gandhi and her policies. As such, he demonstrated his political influence in the spring of 1975 by resorting to a "fast unto death" to force Mrs. Gandhi to agree to hold elections in his native state, Gujarat.

NORMAN D. PALMER

FASSBINDER, Rainer Werner

The 31-year-old German writer, director, and actor Rainer Werner Fassbinder has won international acclaim as one of the most creative and innovative contemporary filmmakers. Working on a low budget, with a close-knit group of talented performers, he has made some 30 full-length motion pictures. In his films he presents an irreverent view of West German society, equally castigating bourgeois philistinism and pretentious leftism, and he deals frankly with homosexuality, the inferior status of women, and the oppression of foreign laborers.

In the spring of 1977, a dozen Fassbinder films were included in a retrospective at a New York City theater. Current projects include his first high-budget, English-language film, based on Nabokov's novel *Despair*, about a man who in middle age changes his identity.

Background. Fassbinder was born in Bad Wörishofen, Bavaria, on May 31, 1946. He left school at 16, worked at various jobs, and made his first short films in 1965. He then founded the Munich "Antitheater" and staged irreverent adaptations of classic dramas. In 1969 he wrote and directed his first full-length film, *Love Is Colder Than Death,* inspired by American gangster movies. Other early films include *Katzelmacher* (1969), about the persecution of an immigrant worker, and the partly autobiographical *Beware of a Holy Whore* (1970). For West German television, Fassbinder made several films later shown in theaters, including *Jailbait* (1972), about an ill-fated teen-age love affair.

In *The Bitter Tears of Petra von Kant* (1972) Fassbinder explored lesbian relationships. *Effi Briest* (1974) is about a young girl married off to an older nobleman. *Ali* (1974) tells of a May–December romance.

Fassbinder became director of the Theater am Turm in Frankfurt in 1974 but resigned after government censors called one of his plays anti-Semitic, a charge he denied. He plans to settle in the United States, where he hopes to find greater artistic freedom.

HENRY S. SLOAN

FROST, David

Among the top "media events" of 1977 were David Frost's historic televised interviews with former President Richard Nixon, presented in four 90-minute segments at weekly intervals beginning on May 4, at least one of which was viewed by as many as 45 million people. (A fifth interview by Frost with the former chief executive was televised in early September.)

The British-born producer, writer, and television personality had been well-known to Americans for his popular *David Frost Show* of talk and entertainment, which brought him Emmy awards in 1970 and 1971, and for his incisive satirical program *That Was the Week That Was* (or *TW3*), first presented by BBC television in the early 1960's.

The Nixon interviews were taped at the former president's home in San Clemente, Calif., in March and April, with the understanding that Frost was to have a completely free hand. While the talks uncovered little that had not already been known, they gave audiences a review of the Nixon years, and they enabled Frost to elicit revealing comments from Nixon—including his view that a president's action could under certain circumstances transcend the law. The former president continued to deny any willful wrongdoing in the Watergate affair, although he admitted that he "let the American people down." A critic for *The New York Times* observed that Frost, in his conduct of the interviews, was "persistent without being abrasive, clear-headed without being vicious, and compassionate without being sentimental," and that he "scored his points neatly and efficiently."

During 1977, Frost also began working on a book

Television personality David Frost made news himself by conducting a series of interviews with Richard Nixon.

UPI

about the Nixon interviews, did an historical series about the Persian Empire, and produced a series of programs for British independent television about former British prime ministers.

Background. The son of a Methodist minister, David Paradine Frost was born in Beccles, Suffolk, on April 7, 1939. He was educated in private schools and at Cambridge University, where he edited a student magazine, acted in satirical revues, and earned a masters degree, with honors. After some London cabaret appearances, he joined the BBC, where he won instant acclaim with his irreverent *TW3* program (1962–63) and presented such other shows as *The Frost Report* (1966–67) and *The Frost Programme* (1966–68). He formed his own company, David Paradine Productions, in 1966. In the United States, where his *David Frost Show* (1969–72) made his name a household term, he also produced television specials. His many and varied activities also include theatrical appearances and film production. He has written several books, including *To England With Love* (1967).

A bachelor, Frost is often seen in the company of glamorous women. He was created an officer of the Order of the British Empire (OBE) in 1970.

HENRY S. SLOAN

FUKUDA, Takeo

On Dec. 24, 1976, just three weeks before his 72nd birthday, Takeo Fukuda, a tenacious politician and economic expert, was elected Japan's 13th postwar prime minister. Despite his campaign promise to eliminate the powerful factions within the Liberal-Democratic party (LDP), his selection of a cabinet necessarily reflected a delicate balancing of factional demands and debts. On March 21, 1977, Prime Minister Fukuda called on President Carter in Washington for two days of conversations on joint security problems, Japan's exports, and U. S. supply of nuclear energy. He invited President and Mrs. Carter, along with Miss Lillian and Amy, to visit Japan. The president accepted, but no date was set. In London, on May 7–8, Fukuda represented Japan at an economic summit attended by representatives of seven large industrial democracies (Japan, Britain, the United States, West Germany, France, Italy, and Canada).

Background. Takeo Fukuda was born in Gumma prefecture on Jan. 14, 1905. Having achieved the highest academic average in his middle school, he attended the First National High School and then Tokyo Imperial University, two of Japan's most prestigious educational institutions. In 1928 he passed the rigorous civil service examination, and the year after, having graduated *cum laude,* he joined the finance ministry. Over the next two decades he enjoyed a brilliant career, but in 1950 he was suspended on a charge of involvement in a bribery scandal. After a long trial, he was acquitted in 1958.

In the meantime, Fukuda turned to politics and in 1952 won the first of nine consecutive elections to the (lower) House of Representatives. He gained prominence under the tutelage of premiers Kishi and Sato and in 1959 became secretary general of the majority LDP. In the 1960's he headed various ministries—agriculture, finance, foreign affairs, and economic planning—and in 1974 became deputy premier under Prime Minister Takeo Miki. In October 1975 Fukuda served as head of suite for the emperor and empress during their U. S. visit. On Dec. 23, 1976, he succeeded Miki as president of the LDP and the next day was elected prime minister on the first ballot by a two-vote margin in the lower house and by one vote in the (upper) House of Councillors.

Fukuda and Mitsui Arai arranged their own marriage, a rare occurrence in prewar Japan. They have three sons, two daughters, and 10 grandchildren. Son-in-law Michi Ochi serves in the lower house alongside the prime minister.

ARDATH W. BURKS

The Henning, Tenn., boyhood home of Alex Haley, author of the best-seller *Roots*, was declared an historic site.

HALEY, Alex

On April 18, 1977, a Pulitzer Prize jury presented a special award to author and historian Alex Haley for his monumental, best-selling *Roots: The Saga of an American Family* (1976). The product of 12 years of meticulous research, *Roots* is the first work by an American descendant of African slaves that systematically traces a family's history back to its African origins. Inspired by family stories told to him during his childhood by his maternal grandmother, Haley embarked on a search that involved travel totaling 500,000 miles (800,000 km). The expenditures of $80,000 were advanced by Doubleday & Co. and by the *Reader's Digest*. After he had traced his maternal bloodline back through seven generations in the United States by means of archive records, his research took him to the village of Juffure in what is now the Republic of the Gambia, West Africa. There, with the help of the tribal oral historian (*griot*), Haley traced his ancestry back to Kunta Kinte, born in 1750 and captured by slave traders in 1767. Further research in England and the United States pinpointed the slave ship in which Kunta Kinte was sent across the Atlantic to America. Haley also took a freighter trip from West Africa to the United States on which he tried to duplicate some of the harrowing conditions experienced by his ancestor.

Published in condensed form by *Reader's Digest* in 1974 and in book form by Doubleday in 1976, *Roots* was presented on ABC-TV early in 1977 (*see* TELEVISION). Since the lack of concrete data in some instances compelled Haley to rely on his imagination —a fact that had caused the Pulitzer committee to decline to classify *Roots* as either history or fiction— his sources and facts were challenged by some scholars. More serious were charges of plagiarism leveled against Haley by two authors in April and May 1977. Haley denied the charges, and asserted that the symbolic truth of *Roots* is more important than its literal accuracy.

Background. Alex Palmer Haley was born in Ithaca, N. Y., on Aug. 11, 1921. He spent his early years in Henning, Tenn., where his father—later a college teacher—managed the family lumber business. In 1939, after two years at Elizabeth City (N. C.) Teachers College, he joined the Coast Guard, serving as a messman,

cook, and journalist, a rating created for him. After his retirement from the service in 1959, he wrote stories for *Reader's Digest* and other publications, and conducted interviews for *Playboy*. Haley assisted one of his interview subjects, the late black nationalist leader Malcolm X, in writing his memoirs, *The Autobiography of Malcolm X* (1965). It sold several million copies and is a major document of black literature.

HENRY S. SLOAN

HOOKS, Benjamin L.

Benjamin L. Hooks, a Memphis lawyer, businessman, clergyman, former judge, and civil rights crusader, took office on Aug. 1, 1977, as executive director of the National Association for the Advancement of Colored People, succeeding Roy Wilkins, who retired after 22 years of service. Hooks had been serving as the first black commissioner on the Federal Communications Commission.

Hooks hopes to alleviate discord among the NAACP staff; to quadruple the organization's membership, which has dwindled to less than half a million in 1977; to replenish its treasury, which had been depleted partly as a result of an unfavorable court judgment in Mississippi, where white merchants had sued for damages resulting from a black boycott; and to cement ties with such traditional allies as Jewish groups and organized labor, which had become strained.

An activist, Hooks nevertheless intends to adhere to such peaceful means of combating discrimination as litigation and lobbying. Although the NAACP's overriding concern is high unemployment among blacks, Hooks also expects to deal with education, health care, urban problems, the criminal justice system, and welfare reform.

Background. The fifth of seven children, Hooks was born in Memphis, Tenn., on Jan. 31, 1925. He attended LeMoyne College in Memphis, served in the army, and graduated from DePaul University with a J. D. degree in 1948. After practicing law and serving as assistant public defender, he was appointed the first black judge of Shelby County (Tenn.) Criminal Court in 1964. Ordained as a Baptist minister in 1955, he has served as a pastor in Memphis and Detroit.

A life member of the NAACP and ex-director of the Southern Christian Leadership Conference, Hooks took part with the Rev. Martin Luther King, Jr., in some civil rights struggles. As FCC commissioner, he backed the interests of minorities and the right of free expression. The NAACP board elected him on Nov. 6, 1976, to succeed Wilkins.

HENRY S. SLOAN

JORDAN, Hamilton

At the age of 32, Hamilton Jordan came to the White House in 1977 as a close adviser to President Jimmy Carter. There is no official "chief of staff" in the Carter administration, but Jordan comes as close to filling that role as anyone. He and other youthful men around Carter, such as Press Secretary Jody Powell, surprised Washington with their informality, brashness, and unorthodox ways of conducting official business.

Although Jordan can reach the president's ear whenever he chooses, Carter listens to many other persons too, and Jordan is not regarded as greatly influential in formulating policy. He is regarded more as a political strategist whose greatest achievement was devising the successful strategy used by Carter to capture the presidency in 1976. As for issues, Jordan says that he is better at "conceptualizing the process by which goals are met" rather than giving advice on the details of carrying out a program. Nonetheless he controls most of the flow of paper work to and from the president and has shown growing interest in major national issues with which the president is concerned.

Jordan also functions as a troubleshooter and image-builder for Carter who can move quickly to avert a developing political crisis.

Background. William Hamilton McWhorter Jordan was born in Charlotte, N. Car., on Sept. 21, 1944, while his father was serving in World War II. After the war his parents returned to their home in Georgia. Jordan studied political science at the University of Georgia. An indifferent student, he needed 5½ years to earn his degree. In 1967 and 1968, he spent 10 months in Vietnam as a social worker with International Voluntary Services, a private organization.

On returning to Georgia, he became active in Carter's campaign to win the governorship in 1970. Jordan, who had been impressed with Carter during the latter's unsuccessful bid for the office in 1966, managed the successful 1970 campaign. Jordan then served as executive secretary to the new governor.

In 1972, Jordan took the lead among Carter's aides in developing a plan for a presidential campaign in 1976. His 72-page memo on strategy was followed almost exactly. His blueprint included techniques for exploiting the national disenchantment with Washington after Vietnam and Watergate. He also devised means by which the little known Georgia governor could develop important political contacts around the country. Carter's election clinched a key place in the White House for Jordan.

DONALD R. YOUNG

KOCH, Edward I.

Though no newcomer to elective politics, Ed Koch could hardly be blamed if he was tired after his victory in the New York mayoralty race. In order to secure "the second toughest job in the country," he had to win no less than three elections. Having entered the Democratic primary race against six rivals, among them incumbent Mayor Abe Beame, former Rep. Bella Abzug, and N. Y. Secretary of State Mario Cuomo, he won a 20% plurality on September 8 and then faced a runoff against Cuomo 11 days later—which he also won by an easy 54%. After the bitter primary contest, the actual election campaign was almost a let-down, and Koch defeated his three rivals—Liberal, Republican, and Conservative—on November 8. The newly elected mayor promised a no-frills, effective government.

Background. Edward Irving Koch was born in The Bronx, N. Y., on Dec. 12, 1924, the second of three

Hamilton Jordan, 32-year-old political strategist, was a principal member of the White House staff in 1977.

children of Louis and Joyce Koch, Polish immigrants. During the Depression, in 1931, the family moved to Newark, N. J., where their son attended Southside High School. In 1941, the Koch family moved back to New York City (Ocean Parkway, Brooklyn), and young Edward began attending the City College of New York. Two years later, the Army called, and as a combat infantryman, the future mayor earned two battle stars and was promoted to sergeant.

After the war, Koch attended New York University Law School. He was graduated in 1948 and admitted to the bar in 1949. He then began a legal career which terminated in 1962, when he ran unsuccessfully to represent Greenwich Village in the N. Y. Assembly; he had moved into the district in 1956. As a candidate of the Village Independent Democrats, he lost to Tammany leader Carmine DeSapio's candidate, but did obtain the support of Eleanor Roosevelt. A year later, in 1963, he defeated DeSapio as the Village Democratic district leader and did so again in two successive elections.

Known as a hard-working reform independent, he was elected to the City Council in 1966 and in 1968 won his race for Congress, representing the 17th district. This victory was repeated three more times.

Respected and well liked as an effective New York congressman, Koch worked hard for his constituents. He supported home-health care for the aged, wider subsidies for mass transit, and decriminalization of pot. For the latter, he received conservative support to establish the National Commission on Marijuana and Drug Abuse. He actively supported individual privacy. Koch considers himself to be a "liberal with sanity."

LEO HERSHKOWITZ

LEFEBVRE, Marcel

In 1969, with the opening of a seminary in Econe, Switzerland, and the formation of the Society of St. Pius X, Archbishop Marcel Lefebvre, C. S. Sp., former archbishop of Dakar, Senegal, and former superior general of the Holy Ghost Fathers, launched what has become the foremost threat to unity within the Roman Catholic Church in this century. The 72-year-old French prelate's crusade against Vatican Council II reforms has

UPI

French traditionalist Archbishop Marcel Lefebvre continued to challenge reforms of the Catholic Church.

raised the possibility of a major schism and made him a rallying point for dissident traditionalist Catholics in Europe and the Americas. The confrontation between the archbishop and the Vatican came to a head in July 1976, after he defied Pope Paul VI by ordaining 13 priests of his society. He was suspended from his priestly faculties by the Pope. During 1977, Archbishop Lefebvre ignored the suspension and continued to celebrate the outdated Tridentine Mass (the Latin form authorized by the Council of Trent), to speak out against Church renewal, and illicitly to ordain priests and deacons. On the verge of excommunication from the church, he maintains that he and his followers—not Pope Paul and the bishops—are in continuity with true Catholic tradition. Over the past few years, he has rebuffed several calls to reconciliation made by Pope Paul. In June 1977, the archbishop ordained 14 priests and 16 subdeacons and promised to ordain more in 1978.

Background. Born in Tourcoing, France, Nov. 29, 1905, Archbishop Lefebvre was ordained a priest in 1929. He entered the Holy Ghost Fathers and was sent to Gabon in Africa, where he remained for 13 years. He was appointed Vicar Apostolic of Dakar, Senegal, in 1947, and became Apostolic Delegate for all French Africa a year later. From 1955 to 1962, he was archbishop of Dakar and served as a member of the Preparatory Commission for Vatican II. He was named bishop of Tulle, France, in 1962, but resigned after a few months to become superior general of his order. Although named to a 12-year term, he resigned after six years following a disagreement with the majority of his order who voted for the implementation of Vatican II reforms. A year later, he opened the traditionalist seminary at Econe.

ROBERT L. JOHNSTON

LÉVESQUE, René

For the slight, voluble, hyperactive, and brilliant premier of Quebec, a man of fierce temper, still fiercer devotion to French Quebec, and maddening honesty,

the year began with some much publicized events. In January, two months after he achieved the feat, unique in the modern developed world, of winning provincial elections, on a platform of sovereignty and mildly social-democratic policies, René Lévesque went on a week-long trip to New York. His stay there was highlighted by a speech in which he told prospective U. S. investors that independence for Quebec was "inevitable." Two weeks later he was back in the news, this time because, driving home late one night, he accidentally hit a derelict lying on the road, with fatal consequences. Though the premier was completely cleared of responsibility, it was deplorable publicity for a man in his position.

Baggy-eyed, chain-smoking, and bristling with new ideas, Premier Lévesque is endowed with a rare talent for making the obvious more obvious and the complex understandable to the common man. Having been the main spark of the "Quiet Revolution," he now aims for a "Quiet Separation."

Background. René Lévesque was born in New Carlisle, Quebec, on Aug. 24, 1922. A brilliant student, he acquired his early education under Jesuit tutelage and later yawned through law school. In 1944 he went to Europe to cover the last phase of World War II as a reporter, and he also reported from Korea. By 1960, he had become a star among television commentators. At that point he plunged into provincial politics with Jean Lesage, then leader of the Quebec Liberal party. He subsequently became one of the prime movers of the "Quiet Revolution" (1960–66), which nationalized hydroelectric facilities, established boards (*sociétés*) for industrial investment and mineral exploration, and overhauled the social security system. This led to confrontations with the federal government and his old friends, Pierre Elliott Trudeau, Gérard Pelletier, and Jean Marchand, then rising to power in Ottawa.

Lévesque evolved "naturally" and gradually toward the idea of sovereign Quebec, which he envisioned in an economic association (customs union and common monetary policy) with the rest of Canada. His proposal, however, was quashed by the Liberal party, and in late 1967 he quit the Liberals to form the *Souveraineté-Association* movement, which the following year became the Parti Québécois. The progress to power was slow, painful, and costly. The party contested two elections (in 1970, when it received 23.1% of the vote but only 7 seats, and in 1973, when it got 30%, yet merely 6 seats) before the victory of Nov. 15, 1976. Many attribute that triumph mostly to Lévesque's renown and hard work, but the poor performance of the Liberal government also worked in his favor.

The premier is married and has three children, but he has been separated from his wife since 1971.

JEAN-PIERRE WALLOT

O'NEILL, Thomas P. ("Tip"), Jr.

It took Thomas P. ("Tip") O'Neill, Jr., of Massachusetts nearly 20 years in the U. S. House of Representatives to become part of its Democratic leadership—as majority whip in 1971. But it took him only six years to move from whip to speaker. His selection as majority leader in 1973 made him heir apparent to the speakership, and when Carl Albert (D-Okla.) retired, O'Neill became speaker without opposition.

O'Neill has been called the "ultimate Boston Irish politician" so often he winces at the description. But it fits. Big and beefy, with a fondness for a good story and a friendly slap on the back, Tip O'Neill has his roots in the "last hurrah" generation of Boston politics. But as an ally of the Kennedy family and an early opponent of the Vietnam war, he has a rapport with the left wing of his party that few legislators of his generation can match.

Background. Thomas P. O'Neill, Jr., was born in Cambridge, Mass., on Dec. 9, 1912. He was elected to the Massachusetts House during his senior year at Boston College, and has held legislative office without interruption ever since. In 1947, O'Neill became minority leader of the state House, and when Democrats took control of that body two years later, breaking a century of Republican dominance, O'Neill was chosen speaker. He took John F. Kennedy's seat in the U.S. House in 1953, when Kennedy became a senator.

O'Neill has always preferred the tactical side of the legislative process to the detailed drafting of bills. He served 20 years on the House Rules Committee, which guides the procedural flow of legislation but rarely writes any. Rules is the place to learn the politics and personalities of the House, and it was there that O'Neill developed his reputation as a nose-counter par excellence.

Despite his skills and popularity, O'Neill needed considerable luck to make it into the Democratic leadership. Hale Boggs of Louisiana, the incoming majority leader in 1971, nearly chose Dan Rostenkowski of Illinois as whip. But Speaker Albert wanted someone with more solid liberal credentials, and prevailed upon Boggs to appoint O'Neill. Two years later, Boggs was dead, the victim of an October 1972 air crash in Alaska, and O'Neill was chosen majority leader unanimously. That made his eventual promotion to speaker almost automatic.

O'Neill's first months in the speakership showed him to be more forceful than many observers had predicted. He set an August deadline for House approval of President Carter's energy program, and then rammed it through—demonstrating a control over the House that has been rare since Speaker Sam Rayburn (D-Tex.) died in November 1961.

ALAN EHRENHALT

UPI

House Majority Leader Tip O'Neill believes strongly in the necessity of a powerful congressional branch.

OWEN, David

At the age of only 38, David Owen was marked out in February 1977 as Britain's fastest rising young political leader when he was appointed foreign secretary. He was the youngest man to win the post since Sir Anthony Eden, who went on to become prime minister, was appointed 42 years ago.

David Owen, Britain's foreign secretary, is known to be "firm on principle, flexible on details."

UPI

Owen had been the deputy to his predecessor, Anthony Crosland, another brilliant political leader of social democratic views who died suddenly after a massive heart attack. Owen was appointed over the heads of many other aspirants who might well have felt better qualified through age and experience, though his appointment won substantial public approval.

Since his appointment, Owen's main task has been to seek a settlement of the Rhodesia problem, a job that he has undertaken with his U.S. opposite number, Cyrus Vance, and Andrew Young. His evident willingness to start afresh and to tell the truth as he saw it rapidly won him the respect of political leaders in southern Africa. However, as the year wore on, the signs were that this respect was waning as the problems remained.

In British political terms, Owen's chief mistake in 1977 was to recommend the appointment of his personal friend, journalist, and television interviewer Peter Jay, as the British ambassador to the United States. Jay is also the son-in-law of Prime Minister James Callaghan, and in a political atmosphere suspicious of any hint of corruption, the appointment smacked unpleasantly of nepotism.

Background. Born in 1938, Owen was educated at Cambridge University, and went on to become a hospital intern. He won election to the House of Commons in 1966, and within two years became minister for the Royal Navy—the beginning of his rapid rise. He is a right-winger in Labour party terms, though his easy, engaging manner and obvious candor have enabled him to avoid some of the unpleasantly bruising political battles which characterize that party.

SIMON HOGGART

PRESS, Frank

On March 18, 1977, President Carter announced his nomination of Dr. Frank Press as presidential science and technology adviser and as director of the new Office of Science and Technology Policy, created to draft federal science policies. A world-renowned earth scientist and an expert on nuclear test detection and earthquake prediction, Press is on leave from the Massachusetts Institute of Technology, where he had been a professor of geophysics and head of the department of earth and planetary science since 1965.

As White House science adviser, Press is expected to counsel the president on such diverse problems as aid to underdeveloped countries, development of new sources of energy, the drafting of a comprehensive nuclear test-ban treaty, protection of the environment, and promotion of industrial research and development.

Background. Press was born in Brooklyn, N. Y., on Dec. 4, 1924. He graduated *magna cum laude* with a B. S. degree in physics from the City College of New York in 1944 and joined the Columbia University faculty after obtaining his Ph. D. in geophysics there is 1949. From 1955 to 1965 he was a professor of geophysics at the California Institute of Technology, serving also, from 1957, as head of its seismological laboratory.

A member of the U. S. delegations to nuclear test ban conferences in the late 1950's and early 1960's, Press has also served on the President's Science Advisory Committee and the National Science Board, and he has been a consultant to the National Aeronautics and Space Administration, the U. S. Geological Survey, the State and Defense departments, and other agencies.

Press collaborated with Dr. Maurice Ewing on the development of the Press-Ewing long-period seismograph, now a standard tool of earth scientists, and he designed the seismographs installed by astronauts at various locations on the moon. Among the honors he has received is the medal of the British Royal Astronomical Society.

HENRY S. SLOAN

RHODES, John J.

It has not been the fate of John J. Rhodes of Arizona to lead the Republicans in the U. S. House of Representatives in prosperous times. Elected minority leader when Gerald R. Ford left the job to become vice president in December 1973, Rhodes immediately had to steer his way between the demands of a beleaguered Nixon administration for support and the refusal of most House Republicans to give it much.

Less than a year after he took over, Republicans lost 42 House seats, slipping into a one-third minority status. Rhodes launched an intensive campaign to

Arizona's John J. Rhodes has been a member of the U. S. House since 1953 and its minority leader since 1973.

UPI

regain most of the seats in 1976, only to see the GOP fail to hold its 1974 strength and lose its one piece of legislative leverage, a Republican White House.

But the minority leader has persevered, seeking throughout 1977 to convince his fellow House Republicans that unity is essential in the face of a Democratic Congress and a Democratic presidency.

Background. John Jacob Rhodes was born in Council Grove, Kans., on Sept. 18, 1916. After attending Kansas State College and Harvard Law School, he moved to Arizona to practice law. He was elected to the U. S. House in 1952, and has been reelected every two years since, usually by comfortable margins.

Rhodes spent his early House years on the Appropriations Committee, where he specialized in defense. He helped Rep. Gerald Ford oust Charles A. Halleck of Indiana as GOP leader in 1965, in part because he felt Halleck was too negative. But the role that made Rhodes the logical contender for Ford's position in 1973 was that of chairman of the House Republican Policy Committee. He held it from 1965 to 1973, using it first to develop policy alternatives to Johnson administration bills and then to support Nixon objectives. It made him a key member of Ford's House leadership group.

Rhodes is a conservative Republican—a believer in limited government, sound money, and heavy commitment to national defense. He has been a crusader for right-to-work laws and a frequent critic of organized labor.

His foreign policy has generally been hawkish. He opposed the limited war concept in Southeast Asia, favoring an all-out military effort, and was outspoken throughout the 1960's in his belief that the United States should maintain its policy of nonrecognition toward the People's Republic of China.

ALAN EHRENHALT

STABLER, Ken

Ken Stabler, told that he was an excellent quarterback, an opinion that he shared, said that the only way to prove it was to win in the Super Bowl. This he did on Jan. 9, 1977, guiding the Oakland Raiders to a 32–14 victory over the Minnesota Vikings. In directing the Raiders to a record-breaking Super Bowl offense of 429 yards, Stabler again dimmed the performance of Fran Tarkenton, considered the top signal-caller in the National Football League.

The conquest also gave Stabler a psychological boost. He throws left-handed and for years he had been told that southpaw quarterbacks could not make it big in pro football. He had been disproving that for years. Now he had shattered anything that remained of the assumption by working his way to the top of the active passers in the American Football Conference (AFC). He showed diversity in alternating Oakland's running and passing game, hitting Cliff Branch with long bombs and taking full advantage of the intricate patterns of Fred Biletnikoff and Dave Casper. Stabler had broken Joe Namath's passing records at Alabama before joining the pros. He led the Crimson Tide to the national title in 1965. He went to Alabama after playing high school ball in Foley, Ala., where he was born Dec. 25, 1945.

His early years with Oakland were far from successful. Drafted in 1968, he spent a year with the taxi squad. He missed the next season because of injuries and played in only three games in 1970. He was running third to Daryl Lamonica and George Blanda and was so discouraged he signed with Birmingham of the World Football League, which folded before he joined the new team.

Then in 1973, John Madden, the Oakland coach, gave the 6-foot-3-inch (1.8 m) player the call over Lamonica early in the season and the quarterback job was his through the following seasons leading to the 1977 Super Bowl. In 1974 he was named the AFC's

Sylvester Stallone, left, and Burt Young were both nominated for Oscars for their acting in *Rocky*. Some critics consider Stallone to be Hollywood's new rising star.

UPI

most valuable player and *The Sporting News* chose him over Bert Jones of Baltimore as the top quarterback in the conference in 1976. However, his finest accolades as a leader were given him by his teammates who twice voted him "the player who best exemplifies the pride and spirit of the Oakland Raiders."

BILL BRADDOCK

STALLONE, Sylvester

Sylvester Stallone, the star and scenarist of *Rocky* —designated the best motion picture of 1976 at the 49th Academy Award ceremonies on March 28, 1977— is perhaps the most promising newcomer on the Hollywood scene today. In the film—which brought him Oscar nominations as the best actor and screenwriter and earned an Academy Award for its director, John G. Avildsen—Stallone portrays Rocky Balboa, an amiable small-time boxer and reluctant muscleman for a loan shark, who gets a chance at the title and simultaneously finds true love. Stallone, who has been called the next Marlon Brando, had previously appeared in a featured role as a teen-age hood in *The Lords of Flatbush* (1974) and had small parts in other films, including *Capone, Prisoner of Second Avenue, Death Race 2000,* and Woody Allen's *Bananas*.

Stallone wrote *Rocky* in three and a half days in 1975, and, although he was financially down and out, he reportedly turned down offers of as much as $265,-000 for the film rights because producers rejected his demand that he be permitted to play the lead. In the end he accepted from United Artists a much less lucrative offer that met his conditions. Stallone attributes the film's success to the fact that it represents a triumph of the human spirit. In the film *F. I. S. T.,* scheduled for release in 1978, Stallone portrays a powerful labor leader. Stallone's novel, *Paradise Alley,* was published in 1977.

The son of a Sicilian immigrant, Michael Sylvester ("Sly") Stallone was born in New York's tough Hell's Kitchen area on July 6, 1946. A rebel from childhood, he was expelled from about a dozen schools by the time he was 15. His parents, who for a time owned beauty shops in Silver Spring, Md., were divorced when he was 11, and he went to live with his mother in Philadelphia, where he played on the high school football team. As a student at the American College in Switzerland he had his first acting experience— playing Biff in a production of *Death of a Salesman.* Later he studied drama at the University of Miami but dropped out before graduation. In 1969 he returned to New York, where he appeared in occasional Off-Off-Broadway plays, worked at such jobs as cleaning the lions' cages in the Central Park Zoo, and wrote.

Sly Stallone spends much of his free time keeping physically fit. He makes his home in California's Coldwater Canyon with his wife, Sasha, their son, Sage Moonblood, and their bull mastiff, Butkus, who was also featured in *Rocky*.

HENRY S. SLOAN

TENG Hsiao-p'ing

Few political figures of the modern world have demonstrated such durability in adversity as Teng Hsiao-p'ing, the tough, intelligent, and often arrogant senior deputy prime minister of the People's Republic of China. Brought back from political exile for the second time in 1977, he promptly became one of the country's three most powerful leaders, after Chairman Hua Kuo-feng and Defense Minister Yeh Chien-ying. His titles, which also include those of vice chairman of the Central Committee of the Communist party and of its Military Commission, as well as chief of the General Staff of the armed forces, were reconfirmed during the 11th party congress in August. With his extensive personal connections in the party, army, and vast bureaucracy, his proven administrative ability, organizational talents, and forceful personality, Teng is already considered China's real chief administrator.

Background. Teng Hsiao-p'ing was born into a family of landlords in Chia-ting, Szechwan, in 1904. He went to France as a student in 1924 and soon began to participate in Communist activities there, working closely with Chou En-lai. Back in China, Teng took part in the historic Long March, 1934–35, when the Communist army, pursued by the Nationalist forces of Chiang Kai-shek, moved from its base in central China to Yenan in the northwest, and he played an important role in the final defeat of the Nationalist forces in 1948–49. After 1949, Teng rose rapidly through the party hierarchy, becoming general secretary of the party and deputy prime minister in 1956. He fell victim to the Cultural Revolution, 1966–69, when he was purged for his "revisionist" policies, but was rehabilitated in 1973 and to all appearances groomed to succeed Prime Minister Chou En-lai, who was already in frail health. However, shortly after Chou's death, in January 1976, Teng came under bitter attack from Chiang Ch'ing, Chairman Mao's wife, and her radical faction, later known as the "Gang of Four." Branded as a "capitalist roader," Teng was dismissed from all his party and government posts in April 1976 and sent into political exile for the second time. Only after the "Gang of Four" was purged and disgraced, following Mao's death in September 1976, did he again gradually emerge as a powerful figure.

Contrary to Mao, Teng is known for pragmatism

rather than ideology. His policy stresses stability, unity, production, economic modernization, and growth, together with a strong anti-Soviet line and progress toward normalization of relations with the United States. His realistic approach to China's economic problems, his stance on law and order, and his emphasis on higher wages and other incentives for workers and for a rise in the living standard have won him wide support among his countrymen.

WINSTON L. Y. YANG

TOMLIN, Lily

On June 5, 1977, actress-comedienne Lily Tomlin was presented with a special Tony Award for her one-woman comedy revue, *Appearing Nitely.* One of the most creative and imaginative performers, with a genius for facial expression and pantomime, Miss Tomlin is noted for her knack of poking good-natured fun at human foibles through a colorful array of madcap characters of her own creation—Tess, the Shopping Bag Lady; Sister Boogie Woman, a 77-year-old Southern evangelist; Fortune, the singles-bar habitué; and Crystal, the Terrible Tumbleweed, a wheelchair-bound quadriplegic with ambitions to go hang-gliding off Big Sur. A veteran of NBC-TV's popular *Rowan and Martin's Laugh-In,* where her most famous characterizations were those of Ernestine, the crusty, power-mad telephone operator, and Edith Ann, a diabolically precocious five-year-old, Lily Tomlin—true to Charlie Chaplin's dictum that "comedy must be real and true to life"—invests her characters with the appropriate combination of humor and pathos to give them credibility.

Lily Tomlin's motion picture debut, in Robert Altman's epic *Nashville* (1975), brought her an Oscar nomination for her performance in the noncomedy role of a matron who has an adulterous affair with a rock star. She also won plaudits for her second film appearance, the comedy thriller *The Late Show* (1977). In the latter, she is Margo, a Hollywood oddball, who gets involved in solving a murder case with an aging private eye, portrayed by Art Carney. In July 1977, Universal Pictures signed Miss Tomlin to write, produce, and star in two pictures.

Actress-comedienne Lily Tomlin received a special 1977 Tony Award for her comedy revue, *Appearing Nitely.*

UPI

Background. Lily Tomlin (originally named Mary Jean Tomlin) was born in 1939 in Detroit, Mich., to rural Kentuckians who had moved north during the depression. As a child she was close to her father who encouraged her budding talent for singing and dancing. A premedical student at Wayne State University, she was so successful in college productions that she decided to pursue a show-business career and dropped out after her sophomore year. After performing in Detroit and New York nightclubs, doing some television commercials, and appearing on the Garry Moore show and on other television programs, Lily Tomlin was hired in 1969 by producer George Schlatter as one of the regulars on *Laugh-In.* She later starred in four comedy-variety television specials and made three best-selling recordings. She is the recipient of three Emmy Awards and a Grammy Award.

Miss Tomlin, a staunch feminist and a political liberal, is single and lives near Hollywood's Sunset Strip.

HENRY S. SLOAN

TURNER, Robert Edward, 3d

Robert Edward (Ted) Turner 3d, a flamboyant millionaire who believes strongly in the value of hard work, skippered *Courageous,* the defender of the 1974 America's Cup, to victory in the cup races that began off Newport, R. I., on September 13. The *Courageous* defeated the 12-meter *Australia* in four straight races.

During the summer-long U. S. trials, Turner mounted such a winning streak that the New York Yacht Club was left with no choice but to name him defender of the "auld mug." By August 30, Turner's yacht had defeated the American contenders *Independence* in 12 of 14 races and the *Enterprise* in 12 of 18 races. The austere yachting fraternity winced throughout the summer at Turner shenanigans. His behavior had earned the Atlanta-based businessman such nicknames as "Mouth of the South" and "Captain Outrageous." But few could deny his mastery at the helm of a 12-meter yacht, or the loyalty he drew from his 10-man crew.

Background. Ted Turner was born in Cincinnati, Ohio, on Nov. 19, 1938. His father, Robert Edward Turner 2d, was a billboard advertising executive. While studying the classics at Brown University, Turner began sailing competitively, and became a champion dinghy sailor. At age 24, he moved to Atlanta to take over the family business affairs after the death of his father. Expanding the company into a million-dollar advertising and communications empire, Turner bought several TV and radio stations. In sailing, he stockpiled wins in one-design racing and ocean circuits. He was named yachtsman of the year in 1970, and in 1974 he skippered the ill-fated 12-meter *Mariner* in the early America's Cup trials, but was replaced as skipper before the yacht was eliminated as a contender. In 1977, he won the Congressional Cup and placed second in the Southern Ocean Racing Circuit.

Turner bought the Atlanta Braves baseball team in January 1976 and the Atlanta Hawks basketball team in 1977. A dispute with baseball commissioner Bowie Kuhn resulted in Turner being suspended from baseball for one year after he allegedly tampered with player contracts. But the row did not dampen his enthusiasm for the Braves, a team with one of the poorest records in 1977.

BARBARA LLOYD

TURNER, Stansfield

After 31 years as a naval officer, Adm. Stansfield Turner began a new "watch" on March 9, 1977, as Director of Central Intelligence for the United States.

Turner's nomination to the top CIA post came after President Carter's first choice, Theodore Sorensen, ran into a fusillade of criticism in the Senate. Sorensen asked Carter to withdraw his name.

Turner inherited an intelligence community troubled by low morale, damaged by leaks of sensitive informa-

UPI

"With a sense of relief ... and confidence," President Carter appointed Adm. Stansfield Turner CIA director.

tion, and peppered with charges of illegal activities. Evidence had linked the CIA to domestic spying, foreign assassination plots, and a wide range of drug experiments on unsuspecting U. S. citizens. Turner set out to put the CIA's house in order and cleanse the image of the entire intelligence community.

The White House increased Turner's overall authority. It gave him control of the budget for the entire intelligence apparatus, including the supersecret agencies in the Defense Department. It allowed Turner to set goals and priorities for the whole intelligence structure.

Background. Turner was born Dec. 1, 1923, in Highland Park, Ill. In 1941, he entered Amherst College, and two years later was appointed to the U. S. Naval Academy at Annapolis, Md. Jimmy Carter was one of his classmates. After sea duty in 1946, Turner spent three years as a Rhodes Scholar, studying philosophy, economics, and politics, at Oxford University.

Returning to sea in 1950, Turner commanded a mine-sweeper, a destroyer, and a guided missile frigate. Shore assignments were with the Politico-Military Policy Division of the Office of Chief of Naval Operations and the office of the Assistant Secretary of Defense for Systems Analysis. Turner also served as executive assistant and naval aide to the Secretary of the Navy, and studied management at Harvard University.

Turner won promotion to rear admiral in 1970 and was given command of a carrier task group in the Sixth Fleet. In 1972 he became the 36th president of the Naval War College at Newport, R. I. He left that post in 1974 to command the U. S. Second Fleet. Turner was made full admiral in 1975, when he became commander in chief of the Allied Forces in Southern Europe.

JOHN DILLIN

YOUNG, Andrew

Nominated U. S. ambassador to the United Nations on Dec. 16, 1976, by President-elect Carter, Andrew Young, a black congressman from Georgia, was unanimously endorsed by the Senate Foreign Relations Committee in Jan. 25, 1977, and quickly approved by the Senate. He immediately set about giving the U. S. mission a new image by appointing women and members of minority groups to it and bringing in his own staff. Frank and outspoken on world affairs, Young frequently appeared to express views which did not

coincide with those of the State Department or the president and which he later had to defend at news conferences. Typical of such comments was his remark in a BBC interview on April 5 that Britain had "invented racism" and his April 11 comments on U. S. policy in Africa, which he called "paranoid" on Communist activities. A further remark on May 25 about racism in Russia, Sweden, and Queens, N. Y., caused a new furor, and so did an interview in *Playboy* magazine where he referred to former presidents Nixon and Ford as racists. Having made his meaning clear, however, Young secured the "full authority and ... support" of President Carter, who declared there was "no incompatibility" between them.

After his second tour of Africa in May, the peripatetic Young agreed with President Carter that he should broaden his range to include the Western Hemisphere and perhaps Asia, too. Accordingly, he concluded a 10-nation Caribbean trip in August.

Background. Andrew Young, the son of a dentist, was born in New Orleans, La., on March 12, 1932. Intending to be a dentist himself, he attended Dillard and Howard universities but, influenced by a dedicated clergyman, then entered the Hartford Theological Seminary. After graduation in 1955 and ordination in the United Church of Christ, he accepted pastorates in Marion, Ala., and Thomaston and Beachton, Ga. From 1957 to 1961 he worked in New York City for the National Council of Churches, in the course of which he met Dr. Martin Luther King, Jr. Joining the Southern Christian Leadership Conference in late 1961, he became its executive director in 1964.

Young helped draft the Civil Rights Act of 1964 and the Voting Rights Act of 1965, and he was in charge of the demonstration in Birmingham, Ala., on May 3, 1963, when Police Commissioner Eugene ("Bull") O'Connor used dogs and firehoses to repulse the marchers. After running unsuccessfully in 1970, Young was elected to represent Georgia's fifth congressional district in 1972, the state's first black representative in a century. His record in Congress was liberal and, at times, surprisingly independent. Young first met President Carter when the latter was seeking the governorship of Georgia in 1970. He delivered one of the seconding speeches at the New York convention in July 1976. During the presidential campaign, he initiated a massive voter registration drive in the inner cities, which many credit with Carter's victory.

RICHARD E. WEBB

The remarks of Andrew Young, the first black to serve as U. S. ambassador to the UN, frequently made headlines.

UPI

A large Bolivian tin mine: the mineral gained on the world market and helped the nation's balance of trade during 1977.

CARL FRANK, PHOTO RESEARCHERS

BOLIVIA

International issues and activities spilled over from the previous year and dominated Bolivian politics in 1977, while Gen. Hugo Banzer Suárez moved uncertainly toward reinstallment of constitutional government.

Population and Territory. It was announced in late 1976 that the population had been over-estimated and was only 4.6 million; it later emerged, coincidentally, that the government planned to open consulates in Namibia (South West Africa) and Rhodesia, with a view to attracting 30,000 families of white settlers. However, the last months of 1976 were dominated by the discussion of a Chilean offer of a corridor to the sea in return for a portion of Bolivian territory; the proposal aroused almost unanimous opposition, and Banzer's apparent willingness to negotiate provoked a crisis, leading to several dismissals of high-ranking officials and the reorganization of the army. The crisis was resolved by the rejection of the proposals in December.

Human Rights. Apparently with an eye to U. S. President Carter's stance on human rights, Banzer suggested in January 1977 that trade-union rights might be restored; he subsequently modified his position substantially, as pressure from Washington failed to materialize. His policy, however, remained under national and international scrutiny. First, a "Permanent Assembly for Human Rights," headed by former President Siles Salinas called in June for the restoration of democratic and trade-union rights. Then, a visit by a British delegation from the National Union of Mineworkers led to a report critical of working conditions in Bolivian mines and to the cancellation of a $33-million loan previously promised to the state mining corporation COMIBOL by the British government. In July, troops were withdrawn from the major mines, Siglo XX and Catavi, and in the same month Banzer, seeking domestic and international support for planned reinstallment of constitutional government, declared official the Indian languages Quechua and Aymara, and accepted an invitation to visit Venezuela.

Economy. International problems recurred after Banzer's August visit to Brazil to discuss terms of a sale of 240 million cubic feet (6.8 million m³) of natural gas. Details of the Bolivian proposal were not announced. Concern over the contract reflected the relatively disappointing performance of the hydrocarbon sector, which received nearly a fifth of government investment in 1976, but showed low returns. Production, at 35,000 barrels (4,700 metric tons) per day, was still far short of the 1980 target of 180,000 barrels (24,000 tons), and new deposits were difficult to find. The steady improvement of tin on the world market, however, helped the balance of trade, and prospects in 1977 were bright as tin continued to prosper; in negotiations over the International Tin Agreement Bolivia held out for increased floor and ceiling prices, and signed the June 1977 agreement only at the last moment.

Cabinet. In October, Banzer reorganized his cabinet, replacing Finance Minister Carlos Calvo with David Blanco Zabala, Transport and Communications Minister Maj. Julio Trigo Ramírez with civilian Fradique Muñoz Reyes, Energy and Fuels Minister Gen. Guillermo Jiménez Gallo with Lt. Col. Luis Cordero Montellano, and Housing Minister Comm. Santiago Maese Roca with Comm. Fernando Guillen Monje. There was speculation that these changes were preparing for elections, scheduled by the military government for July 1978.

PAUL CAMMACK, *St. Anthony's College, Oxford*

─────── **BOLIVIA · Information Highlights** ───────

Official Name: Republic of Bolivia.
Location: West-central South America.
Area: 424,163 square miles (1,098,581 km²).
Population (1977 est.): 4,800,000.
Chief Cities (1974 est.): Sucre, the legal capital, 90,000; La Paz, the actual capital, 700,000; Cochabamba, 245,000.
Government: *Head of state and government,* Gen. Hugo Banzer Suárez, president (took office Aug. 1971). *Legislature*—Congress (suspended Sept. 1969): Senate and Chamber of Deputies.
Monetary Unit: Peso (20 pesos equal U. S.$1, Aug. 1977).
Manufacturing (major products): Processed foods, textiles, leather goods, cement.
Major Agricultural Products: Sugar, cotton, corn, potatoes, wheat, rice, coffee, bananas.
Major Export Commodities: Tin, petroleum.

BOSTON

Schools. Boston's public schools, opened during the period of September 7–12, entered the fourth year of desegregation ordered by federal courts. In sharp contrast to previous years, when disturbances inside the schools and antibusing demonstrations outside them required police intervention and forced the closing of a few schools, the opening days were, on the whole, quiet. The city's school officials were cautiously optimistic that the orderly opening would persuade the federal court to return full control of the school system to the city.

Taxes. Boston property owners breathed a sigh of relief when no increase in the city's property tax rate was announced. A 28% increase in 1976 had led many to expect another such rise in 1977. Budgetary austerity and an aggressive program to collect millions of dollars in back taxes were cited as major reasons for the stable tax rate.

Urban Renewal. August saw the opening of the latest project in a downtown urban renewal program that has been under way for almost two decades. The Quincy Market area, located behind historic Faneuil Hall, was restored and the early 19th-century buildings converted to a variety of specialty shops and business offices. Boston Mayor Kevin H. White, speaking at the opening ceremony, hailed the new facilities, which he said would attract more people to the downtown area.

Jordan Marsh Company, one of the city's oldest and largest department stores, opened a newly refurbished, block-long building in September 1977. Earlier in the year, federal funds were received to study the feasibility of tearing down the Central Artery, a 30-year-old elevated highway that runs through the city's downtown area, and reconstructing it underground. The road, which carries nearly double the volume of traffic for which it was originally designed, has been widely viewed as a major eyesore in the center of the city.

Elections. Municipal elections in 1977 involved only the City Council and School Committee. Louise Day Hicks, a leader of the city's antibusing movement, was defeated in her bid for reelection to the City Council.

New Police Commissioner. Robert Jordan, a career Boston police officer, was selected by Mayor White in July to head the 1,900-member department. Jordan replaced Robert DiGrazia, whose five-year tenure as police commissioner had often sparked controversy.

A federal court ordered the 135-year-old Charles Street Jail, Boston's main detention facility, to close by November 1. The prison was declared unsafe and unhealthful by the court. City and state officials, as well as those of Suffolk County, which operates the jail, were unable to agree on a plan for a new prison.

HARVEY BOULAY, *Boston University*

BOTANY

Botanists and other plant scientists have become concerned that the genetic diversity of the 15 major crops that stand between mankind and starvation is threatened.

Best-Fed Nation. At no time in the history of civilization has a nation been so well fed with such a variety of foods as the United States. However, only a relatively small number of these foods are indigenous to the country. Most of the important food crops, such as wheat, soybeans, tomatoes, citrus, and others, are native to other parts of the world. Dependent on native plants alone, Americans would have to live on a diet of such crops as sunflower seeds, Jerusalem artichokes, and blueberries. The abundance of foods in the United States is due not only to good crop land but also to plants that have been bred scientifically for high yields. These high yields would not have been possible had not plant breeders had access to diverse gene pools, but genetic diversity is in some danger of disappearing.

Garrison Wilkes, plant geneticist at the University of Massachusetts, has reported that 15 plants account for three quarters of all plant calories consumed in the world. They include five grasses: rice, wheat, corn, barley, and sorghum; three legumes: soybean, common bean, and peanut; two sources of sugar: cane and beet; two tropical tree crops: coconut and banana; and three starchy root crops: potato, sweet potato, and cassava. This is an amazingly small number. Even more sobering is the fact that genetic variation, the basis for developing new varieties, is becoming smaller.

Genetic Change. Many crop plants, during the process of domestication, have become so genetically altered that they cannot compete in the wild. In most cases, the wild plant from which the domesticated type was derived is extinct. The varieties that most nearly resemble the wild type are those derived in regions where the plant was originally domesticated.

According to N. I. Vavilov, the Russian plant breeder, each of the basic food plants now grown originated in a relatively confined region which in many cases has remained the area of greatest genetic diversity. He counts nine major centers of origin and in some cases secondary centers where the plant has undergone rapid evolution.

Since primitive varieties are the major repositories for genetic variety, it is important for the welfare of mankind that they be preserved. Varieties grown in the United States and other areas where plants have been bred for high yields have such a narrow gene base that the risks of crop failure are much greater. More important, perhaps, is the fact that because they are so genetically pure they are much more susceptible to new plant pathogens.

DONALD W. NEWSOM
Louisiana State University

In June, President Ernesto Geisel presents visiting Mrs. Rosalynn Carter with a portrait of the first family of Brazil.

UPI

BRAZIL

While Brazil made significant economic progress in 1977, students took to the streets in their first mass demonstrations in nearly a decade, and business, professional, and even some military voices joined the chorus of those demanding a return to political democracy.

Economy. The government's greatest success was in reducing the rate of inflation and improving Brazil's balance of payments. The rate of increase in the cost of living, around 4% a month at the beginning of the year, was down to about 2% a month toward the year's end; this cut the annual rate to less than 35% for the first time since 1973, when Brazil was caught in the world energy crunch. An international balance-of-payments deficit at the beginning of the year was transformed into a surplus as the government decreed stringent fuel conservation measures and domestic oil wells produced an increasing proportion of the petroleum consumed in the country.

Also, the value of Brazilian exports rose, as prices for coffee remained high and foreign sales of Brazilian-manufactured goods continued to increase. The balance-of-payments situation was further helped by high interest rates imposed to fight domestic inflation, which also served to attract foreign "hot money."

While bankers, exporters, and big manufacturing concerns (often multinational companies) had a good year, smaller Brazilian industries, producing mostly consumer goods for the domestic market, were severely squeezed by the high interest rates. Feeling that the government of President Ernesto Geisel was unsympathetic to them, more and more Brazilian businessmen began calling for an end to the military-dominated regime and a return to full political democracy. One member of Geisel's cabinet, Industry Minister Severo Gomes, was forced to resign when he refused to dissociate himself from a pro-democracy speech made by the president of the São Paulo Chamber of Commerce.

U. S.–Brazilian Relations. A conflict soon developed with the new U. S. administration of President Jimmy Carter, which President Geisel exaggerated and used to distract attention from the Severo Gomes affair. A U. S. State Department report, moderately critical of Brazil's handling of human rights, was sent to the Brazilian government as a "courtesy" before being released. Geisel immediately denounced the report as an "insult" to Brazil, and rejected a proffered $50 million in U. S. military aid. Even the opposition party, the Brazilian Democratic Movement (MDB), which had criticized the government for failing to respect human rights, denounced U. S. "interference" in Brazilian affairs. In March, Brazil canceled its 1952 Military Assistance Pact with the United States.

Mrs. Carter was sent to mend fences in Brazil in June. But the human rights issue could not be avoided. Student protesters, a women's amnesty group, and some political prisoners managed to deliver statements to Mrs. Carter denouncing Brazilian transgressions against human rights. President Carter scheduled, but then postponed, a visit to Brasília, and relations between the U. S. and Brazil remained cool.

─────── **BRAZIL · Information Highlights** ───────

Official Name: Federative Republic of Brazil.
Location: Eastern South America.
Area: 3,286,478 square miles (8,511,965 km²).
Population (1977 est.): 112,000,000.
Chief Cities (1975 est.): Brasília, the capital (1974), 545,000; São Paulo, 7,200,000; Rio de Janeiro, 4,860,000; Belo Horizonte, 1,560,000.
Government: Head of state and government, Ernesto Geisel, president (took office March 1974). Legislature—National Congress: Federal Senate and Chamber of Deputies.
Monetary Unit: Cruzeiro (14.74 cruzeiros equal U. S.$1, Aug. 1977).
Manufacturing (major products): Processed foods, chemicals, textiles, automobiles, metals, petroleum products, paper, fertilizers.
Major Agricultural Products: Coffee, soybeans, rice, corn, sugarcane, wheat, oranges, cacao.

Political Developments. Faced with the probability that elections scheduled for 1978 would give the MDB the governorships of Brazil's four most important states and control of the federal Senate, President Geisel sought to change the electoral system to ensure the continued dominance of the government party, ARENA. Constitutional amendments were proposed providing for the indirect election of governors and of one third of the senators. The amendments failed in Congress because ARENA lacked the necessary two-thirds majority to pass them. In April, Geisel resorted to emergency powers: he suspended Congress for 15 days and, by presidential decree, promulgated the amendments he desired, including one permitting Congress to amend the constitution by a simple majority.

The president's actions set off widespread protests. The Brazilian Bar Association denounced Geisel's decrees as illegal and called for a constituent assembly to write a new constitution for Brazil. Fifty-six army and air force colonels signed a letter to Geisel, calling for a return to democracy. In São Paulo, 10,000 students demonstrated for free elections, amnesty, and an end to repression, while smaller student protests were staged in other Brazilian cities. Government reaction to the protests was low-key; it left to local police the job of suppressing the nationwide student demonstrations. This was done on May 19 with considerable violence, though no fatalities were recorded. The campus of the University of Brasília was invaded by 3,000 police, who made 800 arrests, though most of those arrested were soon released. The subsequent expulsion of 16 students involved in the protest led to a student strike at Brasília and sympathy demonstrations on other campuses in June. An MDB congressman, who met with the striking students, was soon removed from office—allegedly for voicing Communist sentiments.

The leaders of the MDB addressed the situation in a nationwide television broadcast in June, the first since 1974. They denounced the political repression and deplored the government's lack of respect for human rights and its indifference to the "starvation" wages paid to Brazilian labor. The government reacted by removing from office the MDB leader in the federal Chamber of Deputies and banning further political broadcasts. At a national convention of the party in August a resolution was adopted, calling for the convocation of a constitutional convention and the installation of a regime of full political freedom.

Chances for political reform seemed slim as leading military figures, prospective candidates for the presidency in 1978, began jockeying for position. In October, Geisel reminded them that he was still in charge by firing Army Minister Sylvio Frota, a leading contender.

Divorce Law. Apparently annoyed by the support given to the opposition by leading Roman Catholic churchmen, President Geisel facilitated the enactment by Congress of a constitutional amendment permitting divorce in Brazil. ARENA congressmen were freed to vote their consciences on the matter, assuring the necessary simple majority. Previous attempts to legalize divorce had failed as proponents were unable to muster the two-thirds majority formerly needed for enacting a constitutional amendment. In June, Brazil, the world's largest Catholic country, made divorce legal. Pope Paul VI expressed his displeasure and, in July, publicly criticized Brazil's record on human rights.

NEILL MACAULAY, *University of Florida*

John Crimmins, U. S. ambassador to Brazil, leaves the U. S. Embassy in Brasília after learning that Brazil had canceled the 1952 Military Assistance Pact with the United States.

BRITISH COLUMBIA

Politically, 1977 was marked by some 11 investigations into various aspects of provincial and municipal administration and the conduct of public officials. These included a judicial inquiry into the Grizzly Valley pipeline stock trading and an examination by a royal commission of the British Columbia Railway Company. An investigation of the province's food industry was also begun.

Legislation. The provincial legislature sat for a record 133 days between January and September. Major items of legislation provided for financial aid to independent schools, new rules for the certification of labor unions, a revised system of property assessment, the establishment of a B. C. Resources Investment Corporation, new appeal procedures for the Land Commission, a new Ombudsman Act, and acquisition of Notre Dame University. The abolition of the Vancouver Resources Board was also approved after a record 15½-hour filibuster. Following a strike by ferry workers, the legislature was recalled for three days in October to secure passage of an Essential Services Disputes Act.

Budget. Government expenditure proposals for 1977–78 amounted to $3,830 million, a 5.9% increase over the previous year's budget. The balanced budget omitted succession duties and gift taxes, and reduced the taxation of mobile homes and sales of propane gas for home heating. A universal "pharmacare" program was announced and increases made in the homeowner grant to senior citizens. A new revenue-sharing formula was introduced to assist the municipalities. Actual budgetary revenues and expenditures for 1976–77 were reported at $3,530 million and $3,491 million, respectively.

Economy. Due primarily to increased U. S. demands for forest products, some recovery was made from the slow growth of the previous two years. Long-term capital investment projects were announced by the forest industry, and final approval was given for B. C. Hydro to proceed with a $1,200-million hydroelectric dam near Revelstoke.

NORMAN J. RUFF, *University of Victoria*

BULGARIA

Domestic Affairs. An earthquake shook both northern and southern Bulgaria in March, but did relatively little damage. There were more upheavals when the Fatherland Front held its Eighth Congress in June. More than 1,960 delegates, representing 4 million members, took part in the proceedings amid indications that Todor Zhivkov, the highest official of both party and state, was continuing to consolidate his personal power. Boris Velchev, for years considered Zhivkov's successor, was removed from the Politburo and the party's Central Committee; the Politburo membership was reduced from 12 to 8. Several local party leaders were replaced and four cabinet members and 20 ambassadors (out of 64) were dismissed.

Numerous changes also took place in the Komsomol (young Communist) leadership. Tighter party control over all mass organizations and institutions was officially announced, and 28,000 secretaries of basic party groupings were given new responsibilities.

The Third Congress of Bulgarian Culture starred Lyudmila Zhivkova, Todor's daughter.

Economy. The report on the 1976 socio-economic plan was published in February. Most of the plan's targets, such as that for national income, as well as gains in various branches of industry, agriculture, construction, retail goods, and services, fell short of predicted government expectations.

Foreign Affairs. A Bulgarian-Soviet Protocol on trade was signed in January, providing for reciprocal deliveries totaling nearly $6.4 billion (U. S.) in value, an 11% increase over 1976. In June, Zhivkov paid an official visit to the USSR, his ninth since 1972, and was decorated a Hero of the Soviet Union. In August, he went to see Soviet President Brezhnev again "privately."

A new Bulgarian-East German treaty of friendship and mutual assistance was signed in September. Several high government officials visited OPEC (Organization of Petroleum Exporting Countries) members to negotiate oil imports. Iran granted Bulgaria a $150-million credit.

JAN KARSKI
Georgetown University

Insurgent groups remained active in Burma. Above, young guerrillas guard their camp.

BURMA

During 1977, the regime in Burma sought to counter both domestic and external challenges.

Politics. The struggle to succeed aging military strongman President Ne Win accelerated despite the January sentencing to death of the leader of a 1976 coup attempt. Five ethnic secessionists, one a member of the government party, were arrested in September in the second would-be assassination plot in a year. Two ministers dropped from the cabinet in August were also arrested in September as "threats" to "presidential authority," while 50 other high officials —many of them soldiers or former military officers—were also dismissed and detained.

In February, the third congress of the ruling Burma Socialist Program Party had blamed Premier U Sein Win and his chief deputy for the country's economic woes, and they subsequently resigned. The late 1977 shakeup and detentions, however, appeared to involve partisans of number two strongman Gen. San Yu, who had not been engaged in anti-Ne Win activity.

Insurgency. The Communists, one of several insurgent groups, struck deeper into government-controlled territory. For the first time, they continued their fighting into the rainy season.

------------ **BURMA · Information Highlights** ------------

Official Name: Socialist Republic of the Union of Burma.
Location: Southeast Asia.
Area: 261,789 square miles (678,033 km²).
Population (1977 est.): 31,800,000.
Chief Cities (1975 est.): Rangoon, the capital, 2,100,000; Mandalay, 417,000; Moulmein, 202,000.
Government: *Head of state,* U Ne Win, president (took office March 1974). *Head of government,* U Maung Kha, prime minister (took office March 1977). *Legislature* (unicameral)—People's Assembly.
Monetary Unit: Kyat (7.32 kyats equal U. S.$1, July 1977).
Manufacturing (major products): Processed foods, textiles, tobacco products, wood products.
Major Agricultural Products: Rice, groundnuts, sesame, tobacco, sugarcane, millet, cotton, forest products.

Economy. A good rice harvest, the second in a row, combined with new foreign credits, lent modest stimulation to Burma's otherwise stagnant economy. Rising food prices leveled off by the year-end to about 20%, compared with 40% 12 months earlier. About 65% of foreign trade was probably conducted illegally.

Foreign Affairs. Gen. Ne Win's second trip of the year to Peking—his third in two years— underscored the importance he placed on Sino-Burmese relations in general and his concern over Chinese aid to Communist and other rebels. Ne Win also visited North Korea and Cambodia and received important official visitors from China, the Soviet Union, Japan, Cambodia, and Thailand. Burma sought improved ties with Cambodia and, with Soviet help, Vietnam.

RICHARD BUTWELL
State University of New York College at Fredonia

CALIFORNIA

The year was a relatively quiet one in California, although there were conflicts. Among economic matters, the state's continuing drought was a major concern.

Legislation. The legislature passed fewer bills in 1977 than in 1976 and fewer major pieces of legislation than in most recent years. The budget reached $14.52 billion (U. S.), a 13% increase over 1976. In all, 1,360 bills were sent to Gov. Edmund G. Brown, Jr. He vetoed about 9% of them, somewhat less than the average in recent decades, and 60 fewer than in 1976. One of his 124 vetoes—and easily the most controversial one—concerned the restoration of the death penalty. This veto was the only one overridden, and only the fourth veto not sustained in California since 1945.

Of other legislation becoming law, perhaps the most important was a basic revision of the state's method of financing education, from kindergarten through 12th grade. The new law, worked out between the governor and legislative leaders, seeks to make more even the financial backing per child, regardless of district, in compliance with a 1972 state supreme court decision. Other major pieces of legislation prohibit lending institutions from refusing to grant mortgages simply because of the area in which property is located ("redlining"); require prison sentences for crimes of violence committed while the perpetrator is on parole, or against the aged, blind, or disabled; establish a pilot program for zero-based budgeting for fiscal 1979; prohibit forced retirement in public or private employment solely because of age; and increase the annual salary of legislators by 10% to $25,555, effective at the end of 1978.

Government. Gov. Brown continued to be popular. His most controversial appointment of the year was that of Rose Elizabeth Bird as chief justice (*see* BIOGRAPHY). In early October, according to the California Poll, 80% of the respondents in a sample thought the governor was doing a fair or good job, down only 4% from two years earlier. There were signs of increasing dissatisfaction, however. Two sample questions indicated a belief growing during Brown's tenure, that he is not really "getting things done," and 60% agreed that all of his actions were designed to prepare for a try for the presidential nomination in 1980.

The California Health and Welfare Agency was plagued throughout the year with administrative and other problems. These included legislative dissatisfaction with the performance of some administrators, the influence of the "Mexican Mafia"—a prison gang that has spread its influence into some ghettoes—in at least one state-funded drug-use rehabilitation organization, violence and numerous murders in prisons, a projected $200-million medicaid deficit, and poor care standards in some state mental institutions and in nursing homes.

Drought. The state suffered its second year of drought caused by lack of precipitation in the High Sierra, which normally supplies many large cities and most of the agriculture in the Sacramento and San Joaquin valleys. The fire season consequently began two months earlier than usual, in July. Many destructive fires damaged watershed foliage as well as homes.

Bakke Case. In higher education, the case of *Bakke* v. *The University of California* went to the U.S. Supreme Court. The case involved university "affirmative action" policies to encourage enrollments by women and certain minority groups. Bakke claimed "reverse discrimination" in that he was rejected although he had higher qualifications than some accepted minority-group members. Advocates of the policy said it was necessary in order to advance certain minority groups in the professions. The regents of the university, in another controversial matter, voted 13–12 to accept a Faculty Senate recommendation that would raise admissions standards slightly. Critics said this would work hardship on minority-group applicants.

Faster Permits. Early in the year, a large chemical company announced that it was aban-

---

CALIFORNIA • Information Highlights

Area: 158,693 square miles (411,015 km²).
Population (1977 est.): 21,520,000.
Chief Cities (1970 census): Sacramento, the capital, 257,105; Los Angeles, 2,809,596; San Francisco, 715,674.
Government (1977): *Chief Officer*—governor, Edmund G. Brown, Jr. (D); lt. gov., Mervyn M. Dymally (D). *Legislature*—Senate, 40 members; Assembly, 80 members.
Education (1976–77): *Enrollment*—public elementary schools, 2,606,200 pupils; public secondary, 1,774,-100; nonpublic, 437,800; colleges and universities, 1,404,866 students. *Public school expenditures,* $8,-114,784,000 ($1,571 per pupil).
State Finances (fiscal year 1976): *Revenues,* $22,124,-617,000; *expenditures,* $20,533,635,000.
Personal Income (1976): $153,892,000,000; per capita, $7,151.
Labor Force (July 1977): *Nonagricultural wage and salary earners,* 8,515,500; *unemployed,* 767,300 (7.6% of total force).

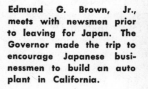

Edmund G. Brown, Jr., meets with newsmen prior to leaving for Japan. The Governor made the trip to encourage Japanese businessmen to build an auto plant in California.

doning plans to build a $500-million petrochemical plant in the northern part of the state because it was having too much difficulty in getting the necessary 65 permits. The resulting loss of jobs for the area prodded the Brown administration to seek and obtain from the legislature a simpler, speedier review process for environmental and other permits.

CHARLES R. ADRIAN
University of California, Riverside

CAMBODIA

Communist Cambodia, now known officially as Kampuchea, took a substantial step out of its almost total isolation in 1977—a reflection in part of the apparent resolution of an internal power struggle and the effective establishment of a truly national administration two years after the fall of the previous pro-American Lon Nol regime.

Politics. Prime Minister Pol Pot was officially noted as secretary general, top leader, of *Angka* (Organization)—the ruling political body. *Angka* was, in turn, identified as the Kampuchean Communist Party. These two related announcements were generally interpreted as reflecting the completion of the consolidation of its political power by Kampuchea's new political elite, which came to power in April 1975.

Other top party leaders identified in 1977 included Deputy Party Secretary Nuon Chea, Ieng Sary, Son Sen, and Von Vet. Nuon Chea was also chairman of Kampuchea's People's Congress. Ieng Sary, Son Sen, and Von Vet were deputy premiers of foreign affairs, defense, and economic affairs, respectively. Pol Pot himself was believed to be the former school teacher and radical agitator Saloth Sar, while Nuon Chea and Von Vet were also widely thought to be pseudonyms of other longtime Communist revolutionaries.

Political executions were reported to have continued in 1977, although declining considerably in number as the year progressed. There was also apparently a major discouragement of the historic Buddhist religious faith of the country, priests being the primary victims of the action. In another antitraditional move, the regime reportedly required all men to wear trousers in place of the conventional sarong worn by both sexes.

The size of Kampuchea's army may have increased to 60,000 regulars—with the target of a force twice this size by the end of 1978.

Economy. There were reports of crop failures at the year's start, but by the end of 1977 Kampuchea was claiming to have exported 100,000 tons of rice as well as some rubber, teak, black pepper, and soybeans. Despite such exports, however, there were still widespread malnutrition and probably more deaths due to starvation than execution. Premier Pol Pot claimed a per capita consumption of 686.4 pounds (308.9 kg)

GAMMA/LIAISON
Pol Pot was photographed as Kampuchea's leader for the first time during a September visit to Peking, China.

of rice a year, but refugees reported that most people ate only two bowls of rice gruel every day.

According to the government, most of the country's claimed rural population of eight million was organized into cooperatives of 100 to 1,000 households. Forced labor was apparently still very widespread.

Foreign Relations. China remained Kampuchea's only major ally, and Premier Pol Pot made two visits to Peking in as many months in 1977—his first announced trips outside the country and a significant break from a pattern of two years of almost complete isolation. It was also revealed that Pol Pot had made a secret visit to Peking in 1975, in the wake of the Communist takeover.

Ne Win of Burma visited Kampuchea in November. The trip was interpreted as another attempt by Kampuchea to end its isolation.

Border wars with its two Communist neighbors, Vietnam and Laos, and anti-Communist Thailand reflected Kampuchea's strongly assertive posture that its badly demarcated "reduced frontiers" were being violated by adjacent peoples.

RICHARD BUTWELL
State University of New York College at Fredonia

———— CAMBODIA · Information Highlights ————

Official Name: Democratic Kampuchea.
Location: Southeast Asia.
Area: 69,898 square miles (181,035 km²).
Population (1977 est.): 8,000,000.
Chief Cities (1976 est.): Phnom Penh, the capital, 100,000.
Government: *Head of state,* Khieu Samphan, president (took office April 1976). *Head of government and secretary of the Communist party,* Pol Pot, prime minister. *Legislature* (unicameral)—People's Representative Assembly.
Monetary Unit: Riel (1,111.11 riels equal U. S.$1, Dec. 1976).
Manufacturing (major products): Paper, textiles, tobacco products, sawnwood.
Major Agricultural Products: Rice, corn, rubber, beans, sweet potatoes and yams.

In Ottawa in March, Prime Minister Pierre Elliott Trudeau and British Prime Minister James Callaghan exchanged views on a wide variety of national and international issues.

CANADA

During 1977, Canada confronted two main issues: the survival of the nation as a unit in the face of possible future separation of the Province of Quebec; and the maintenance of a vital economy, strained now by worldwide inflationary trends, slumping markets, and rising unemployment at home.

DOMESTIC AFFAIRS

National Unity. With a declared separatist government having been elected in the Province of Quebec on Nov. 15, 1976, the federal government's policies were directed toward maintaining the nation state. René Lévesque's Parti Québécois announced, shortly after election to power, that a provincial referendum would be held, perhaps in 1980, in order that the Québécois could voice their opinions on the great issue. Prime Minister Pierre Elliott Trudeau's Liberal government in Ottawa strongly opposed the separatists and announced that Canada would hold its own nationwide referendum on keeping the country together. The issue sparked provincial and regional responses and heightened discontent with Ottawa elsewhere.

Trudeau opened a two-day debate on national unity in the House of Commons on July 5 by urging English Canadians to be more accommodating to the French-speaking minority. Trudeau claimed that French Canadians should share more power in business, professions, and private organizations. The use of French should be expanded countrywide. Canadian confederation would break up, he said, if Canada drifted into two entities—Quebec speaking only French and the remainder of Canada speaking only English. He then announced that a special Task Force on Canadian Unity, headed by Jean Luc Pépin and John Robarts, would investigate this critical issue, gather information from the country, and report to the government.

The leader of the opposition, Joe Clark, responded to the prime minister's urgings by saying that the government placed too much emphasis on the language issue; national disunity also arises from regional disparities, high unemployment and Western alienations.

Quebec's government introduced legislation designed to make the French language supreme in the province, prevent all new residents from attending English-language schools, and force businesses to conduct operations in French. The federal government's language policy, announced in June, did not challenge Quebec's legislation and urged that French be more widely adopted across the nation. Ottawa's declared policy is "to preserve and strengthen" identities of minorities.

Energy Issues. The ongoing energy crisis in North America had ramifications in Canada. Under pressure from the United States to export more natural gas to American consumers,

---

CANADA • Information Highlights

Official Name: Canada.
Location: Northern North America.
Area: 3,851,809 square miles (9,976,185 km²).
Population (1977 est.): 23,500,000.
Chief Cities (1976 met. census): Ottawa, the capital, 669,000; Montreal, 2,759,000; Toronto, 2,753,000.
Government: *Head of state,* Elizabeth II, queen; represented by Jules Léger, governor general (took office Jan. 1974). *Head of government,* Pierre Elliott Trudeau, prime minister (took office April 1968). *Legislature*—Parliament: Senate and House of Commons.
Monetary Unit: Canadian dollar (1.07 C. dollars equal U. S.$1, Aug. 1977).
Manufacturing (major products): Pulp and paper, petroleum products, iron and steel, motor vehicles.
Major Agricultural Products: Wheat, barley, oats, rye, potatoes, forest products, livestock, furs.

Canada sold extra emergency crude oil and natural gas supplies to alleviate widespread shortages brought about by the unusually severe winter of 1976–77. Canadian utility companies sold thousands of kilowatts of surplus electric power to neighboring U. S. utilities. Canada became more self-dependent with the flow of crude through the Interprovincial Pipeline from Edmonton to Montreal via the newly completed extension from Sarnia, Ont., to Montreal. Fuel prices, however, continued to rise because of increased costs, tariffs, and inflation.

On May 9, Mr. Justice Thomas Berger recommended that no pipeline be built along the Mackenzie River Valley for ten years and that there should be a permanent ban on any pipeline from Alaska crossing the environmentally-sensitive northern Yukon. He said he felt it would take a decade to settle and implement native land claims. Moreover, time was needed to solve technical and environmental problems involved in building the line.

Berger's report to Ottawa came after two years of exhaustive travels through the North and countless meetings with northerners—white, Indian, Métis, and Eskimo. Native people are pushing for a greater share in future northern development. Berger said the government must "honor the legitimate claims and aspirations of the native people." Noel Starblanket, president of the 300,000-member National Indian Brotherhood, said that Berger had done his job and that the government now had to do its share. Some Indians, including George Erasmus of the Indian Brotherhood of the Northwest Territories, said that ten years were insufficient. Rich Hardy of the Northwest Indian Métis Association reported that the delay "dooms the valley . . . to a welfare economy." The Métis differ from the Indians in supporting pipeline construction. The Indians are more concerned with native rights and the environment.

Meanwhile, Ottawa had made no firm decision on the Mackenzie natural gas line. Canadian Arctic Gas Pipeline Ltd. and Foothills Pipeline Ltd. vied for government approval and the former's proposal was rejected. At the same time Kitimat Pipeline Ltd. proposed building an oil line from that west coast port to Edmonton, a project worrying to environmentalists, who fear a North Pacific oil spill. Polar Gas suggested a pipeline from the Arctic islands to central Canada.

The United States and Canada finally reached an agreement on a gas pipeline through the Yukon, along the Alaska Highway, and the choice was supported by the Canadian Parliament and the U. S. Congress in November.

Mounted Police Scandal. During 1977 news broke that the Royal Canadian Mounted Police Special Security Service had engaged in illegal and undercover operations, most notably a 1972 break in at the headquarters of left-wing *L'Agence de Presse Libre du Québec.* The Province of Quebec immediately launched its own inquiry into police wrongdoing in Quebec. Solicitor-General Francis Fox and a federal royal commission of inquiry also began investigations. As the inquiries progressed it became apparent that the Mounties had concealed their activities

Work continued on North America's most powerful hydroelectric generating plant, located in La Grande, Que.

UPI

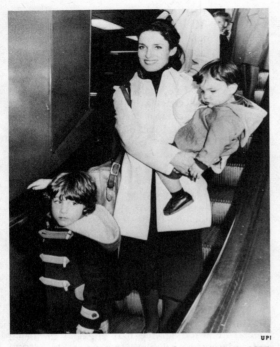

Margaret and Pierre Trudeau agreed to separate in 1977. The prime minister gained custody of their children—Dustin, 5, Michel, 1, and Sacha, 3 (not in photograph).

government information. They are charged, along with intelligence officers in the Canadian Armed Forces and Post Office, with having been trained in the United States by the Central Intelligence Agency in covert mail-interception techniques.

Margaret Trudeau. In May, Margaret Trudeau separated from her husband. "I felt my role as the prime minister's wife, a political life," she told a reporter in November, "was limited and very thankless; an old fashioned role, where the new breed of woman—a category I put myself in—doesn't really fit." At age 29 she is pursuing a career as a photojournalist and learning to be an actress for a forthcoming movie role.

FOREIGN AFFAIRS

Canada took several steps to encourage international cooperation. In January the government welcomed André Rossi, the French trade minister, to promote economic relations between the two countries. The mission reflected France's growing interest in Quebec's mining, paper, and petrochemical industries. During the year Canada began promoting the formation of a commonwealth of French-speaking nations. Canada signed protocols with Brazil for technical and financial cooperation. Also, External Affairs Minister Donald Jamieson conducted a trade mission to Colombia, Brazil, and Peru to expand Latin American trade and reduce Canada's dependence on the United States.

Visitors to Canada. Canada received James Callaghan in March, and Trudeau and his British counterpart discussed South Africa's apartheid, the Soviet arms buildup, Quebec's proposed separation, and the threatened African boycott of the 1978 Commonwealth Games in Edmonton. On the question of Canadian unity, Callaghan told reporters that Trudeau was "perfectly capable of handling the issue with a deep

from the government. The Commons justice committee revealed a long list of illegal operations. These included the burning of a barn, breaking in, stealing dynamite, opening private mail, and (in 1973) stealing Parti Québécois membership lists. The Mounties also obtained a secret agreement with the federal revenue department to get income tax information. It is alleged that they conducted Operation Feather Bed, the surveillance of the prime minister and other public officials with access to classified

Don Jamieson, Canada's secretary of state for external affairs, met informally with his U. S. counterpart, Cyrus Vance, in New York in September.

understanding of English- and French-speaking Canadians."

National leaders visiting Canada in 1977 also included the Italian premier, Giulio Andreotti, who in November discussed with Trudeau matters affecting Italian immigration and citizenship. They agreed to permit reciprocal transfer of old-age pension and family allowances to Canadians in Italy and Italians living in Canada.

Conferences in London. In May in London Trudeau joined President Carter and leaders of Britain, France, West Germany, Italy, and Japan in pledging to fight protectionism and to contain the spread of nuclear war technology while helping those who need more energy. Trudeau applauded his colleagues for going beyond the study of inflation and unemployment and into the question of social peace that might be disrupted by failure to solve economic problems. On Canada's role in NATO, he supported policies encouraging standardization of military equipment and reducing expenditures. Trudeau suggested to the leaders of NATO countries, meeting in London in May, that member states should look at the world in more than East-West context. He drew attention to a North-South axis—the developed versus the developing world. The organization must, the prime minister said, relate to each of these "if we are to continue to play a role which will be regarded as relevant

UPI

U. S. & Canadian officials sign agreement regarding allegations of illicit acts in sales by the Boeing Co. to Canada.

by our youth, as much as it is regarded as credible by our adversaries."

U. S. Relations. Though Canadian external policies reflected a trend toward new links with Europe, Latin America, and the developing world, the bulk of its international activities was with its neighbor, the United States. In answer to pressure from Ottawa, President Carter stopped funds for building the Garrison diversion project in North Dakota, a project that might have polluted the Red and Souris rivers of Manitoba and introduced undesirable species of aquatic life into provincial waterways. During the year Canadian and U. S. representatives continued to negotiate a reciprocal fisheries agreement to enable fishermen from each country to fish within agreed limits of each other's new 200-mile zones.

On February 22, Trudeau reassured the U. S. Congress that Canada would survive Quebec's threatened separation. His speech was the first to Congress by a Canadian prime minister. The speech, a response to Quebec Premier René Lévesque's address in January to the Economic Club of New York, stressed that Canadians knew that their country's division would be "a crime against the history of mankind." Canada, Trudeau said, might have to alter its constitution to ensure that Confederation can be seen by 6.5 million French-speaking Canadians "to be the strongest bulwark against submersion by 220 million English-speaking North Americans." The speech pledged continuing Canadian–U. S. friendship. At a press conference, Trudeau said Quebec's separation would have greater consequences for the United States than the 1962 Soviet attempt to place missiles on Cuban soil. But he told U. S. businessmen that they would fan separatists' fires if they withdrew economic investments from Quebec.

BARRY GOUGH, *Wilfrid Laurier University*

THE CANADIAN MINISTRY

(According to precedence, December 1977)

Pierre Elliott Trudeau, Prime Minister
Allan Joseph MacEachen, Deputy Prime Minister, President of the Queen's Privy Council for Canada and House Leader
Jean Chrétien, Minister of Finance
John Carr Munro, Minister of Labour
Stanley Ronald Basford, Minister of Justice and Attorney General of Canada
Donald Campbell Jamieson, Secretary of State for External Affairs
Robert Knight Andras, President of the Treasury Board
Otto Emil Lang, Minister of Transport
Jean-Pierre Goyer, Minister of Supply and Services
Alastair William Gillespie, Minister of Energy, Mines and Resources
Eugene Francis Whelan, Minister of Agriculture
W. Warren Allmand, Minister of Consumer and Corporate Affairs
James Hugh Faulkner, Minister of Indian Affairs and Northern Development
André Ouellet, Minister of State for Urban Affairs
Daniel Joseph MacDonald, Minister of Veterans Affairs
Marc Lalonde, Minister of State for Federal-Provincial Relations and Status of Women
Jeanne Sauvé, Minister of Communications
Raymond Joseph Perrault, Leader of the Government in the Senate
Barnett Jerome Danson, Minister of National Defence
J. Judd Buchanan, Minister of Public Works and Minister of State for Science and Technology
Roméo LeBlanc, Minister of Fisheries and the Environment
Marcel Lessard, Minister of Regional Economic Expansion
Jack Sydney Cullen, Minister of Employment and Immigration
Leonard S. Marchand, Minister of State (Environment)
John Roberts, Secretary of State
Monique Bégin, Minister of National Health and Welfare
Jean-Jacques Blais, Postmaster General and Deputy House Leader
Francis Fox, Solicitor General of Canada
Anthony C. Abbott, Minister of State (Small Business)
Iona Campagnolo, Minister of State (Fitness and Sport)
Joseph-Philippe Guay, Minister of National Revenue
Jack H. Horner, Minister of Industry, Trade and Commerce
Norman Cafik, Minister of State (Multiculturalism)

THE ECONOMY

The Canadian economy continued in a depressed condition throughout 1977, showing signs of returning to its pre-World War II characteristics. Manufacturing continued its decline as a portion of the total economy and experienced growing excess capacity. The resource sector, after years of relative strength, entered a period of difficulty, which included massive layoffs in the nickle industry and a world glut of copper. Oil, gas, and cereals continued fairly strong and created a regional distribution of prosperity different from the traditional.

In the economy as a whole, real gross national product advanced between 0.0% and 2.0%. The Consumer Price Index rose 8% and the jobless rate by the end of the year was also 8%. The labor force grew by 3%, contributing to an increase of total labor income of 9.3%. Pre-tax profits rose about 2%. The Long-Term Canada Bond Average stayed at about 8.75%, although the 91-day Treasury Bill Rate fell from above 8% to just about 7%. The money supply (M2) rose 18% over the year. The federal deficit, a record $C6 billion in fiscal 1977, was forecast at over $8 billion for fiscal 1978. Stock prices, which should have risen or stayed constant, given the behavior of interest rates, fell. The decline affected industrials, financial services, communications, and, most dramatically, metals and minerals. The general decline was partially offset by dramatic rises in golds and pipelines and a moderate rise in oil and gas.

The nation was also experiencing an unfavorable trade balance, typical of periods of depression in Canada. Merchandise trade was in surplus but the current account was in deficit due to interest and dividend payments and, particularly, a $2 billion deficit in travel. Public and private borrowing covered the total deficit of about $4 billion but confidence in the value of the Canadian dollar sank by 25–30% in terms of the German mark and the Japanese yen and by 7–10% in terms of the U. S. dollar.

The new structure of regional disparities was evident in unemployment rates which peaked at over 15% in Newfoundland, remained fairly steadily at about 4.5% in Alberta, and rose to almost 9% in British Columbia.

Federal government policy foundered as a result of the situation. Wage and price controls were ineffective in the face of changes in the economy and of international pressures. Their removal was announced late in 1977 after several provinces had withdrawn support. The date of termination was set well into 1978 and in the interim allowable increases in wages and salaries were reduced from 8% to 6%. This reflected the opinion that higher wages in Canada were destroying international competitiveness. The economic conservatism introduced in 1975–76—reduced government spending, slower growth of the bureaucracy, and tighter control of the money supply—evaporated. Deficits increased, despite minimal reductions in taxes, and the money supply grew at a rate well beyond the rate of nominal growth in GNP.

The economy was depressed. The federal government seemed impotent. A surge of effort at the provincial level, typical of such periods in Canada, lacked direction and contributed heavily to the general uncertainty.

R. F. NEILL
Department of Economics
Carleton University

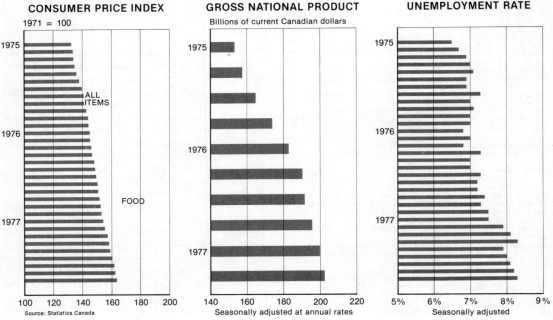

CONSUMER PRICE INDEX
1971 = 100
ALL ITEMS
FOOD
100 120 140 160 180 200
Source: Statistics Canada

GROSS NATIONAL PRODUCT
Billions of current Canadian dollars
140 160 180 200 220
Seasonally adjusted at annual rates

UNEMPLOYMENT RATE
5%   6%   7%   8%   9%
Seasonally adjusted

CULTURE

Throughout 1977 the "French fact" tended to overshadow many aspects of the total Canadian experience and in the cultural area it was somewhat dismaying. The Quebec provincial election of 1976 had had the stunning effect of placing in power the Parti Québécois, a party officially committed to a struggle for the province's independence from Canada. The new government embarked upon a broad, aggressive program of "pro-French" measures which were interpreted as "anti-English" by most Canadians. The new ministry made it clear that Quebec artists will have to choose between being Canadians or being Québécois; there would be no in-between option. Following a decree that French-Canadian content must be stepped up notably in all cultural programs, massive sums were budgeted for the support of Quebec artists and organizations.

Aside from the Canada-Quebec controversy the cultural scene was calm and successful.

Dance. If continuous attention from the mass media and excellent box-office support are indicators of a healthy condition, the dance was definitely Canada's most vigorous cultural area in 1977. Both at home and abroad Canadian dancers were happy with their efforts. The Royal Winnipeg Ballet's annual report showed a substantial net cash balance, following five years of accumulating deficits. Les Grands Ballets Canadiens enjoyed a successful Latin American tour, involving 41 performances in 19 cities in 10 countries. Toronto's National Ballet Company reported record box-office receipts exceeding $1.25 million. The company's U. S. tour was their most successful in years.

A number of foreign dance groups toured Canada in 1977. Spain's National Festival Ballet and the Shanghai Ballet of the People's Republic of China delighted sellout houses.

A Dance in Canada Conference, held in Winnipeg in August, brought together two of the big companies, numerous small modern dance groups, choreographers, critics, producers, and executives for several days of performances and discussions.

Theater. The 1977 theater season was marked by massive publicity relating to the Stratford Festival's 25th anniversary, by an outstanding offering of plays, and by unprecedented financial success. By mid-April, long before the Stratford season's opening, the advance ticket sale had exceeded $2 million. The house was 95% sold for the season's productions, which included *Midsummer Night's Dream, All's Well, Richard III, Much Ado,* and *As You Like It.*

Despite a generally good season, there was much grumbling by theater executives because fund-granting agencies refused to relax the belt-tightening conditions laid down in 1975. The well-established companies, such as Shaw Festival, Centaur, Neptune, Royal Alex, Vancouver Centre, Citadel, Nouveau Monde, and the National Arts Centre, enjoyed artistic success and, somehow, managed to avoid slipping further into deficit.

A newsworthy theater event was a nasty row between the unions and the producers over the issue of non-Canadian (especially British) actors being permitted to play leading roles in stage, television, and radio productions. Strikes were threatened, and compromises were made, but it seemed evident that the simmering unrest would surface again in the near future. A significant

ROBERT C. RAGSDALE, STRATFORD FESTIVAL

During its 25th anniversary year, the Stratford Festival presented *Miss Julie* with Douglas Rain as Jean and Pamela Hyatt as Kristin.

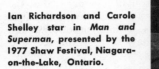

Ian Richardson and Carole Shelley star in *Man and Superman*, presented by the 1977 Shaw Festival, Niagara-on-the-Lake, Ontario.

ROBERT C. RAGSDALE, SHAW FESTIVAL

development which underlines one growth aspect of Canadian theater was the organizing, in Toronto, of the Canadian Playwrights Guild.

Music. There was bad news and good news from the Canadian musical scene. The prestigious, long-established Montreal Symphony Orchestra was a "no show" for its announced 1977/78 season, following a walkout by its 90 unionized musicians. Both basic and trivial disagreements were behind the move which deprived Montrealers of a cherished annual musical treat. The problems will, in all likelihood, be solved before the 1978/79 season arrives, but a matter of great worry was the planned exodus of important instrumentalists.

The good news included continued nationwide support and encouragement for every form of musical endeavor. But the year's most important Canadian musical happening did not happen in Canada. MUSICANADA, the first Canadian musical festival in Europe, occurred in London and in Paris in November. Five major ensembles performed works by 32 Canadian composers. The participating groups were: Canadian Brass, Festival Singers, Orford String Quartette, Quintette à Vent, and Société de Musique Contemporaine. The concerts were heard in St. John's, Smith Square (London) and in Salle Caveau (Paris). Icing for these two cakes included a BBC Symphony concert, conducted by Mario Barnhardi of Canada's National Arts Centre, and a concert by the Nouvel Orchestre Philharmonique of Paris, conducted by Pierre Hétu of Montreal. Most of the chief cultural agencies of Canada pooled their financial and expert resources to make MUSICANADA a memorable event.

The venerable Canadian Opera Company sprang the biggest musical surprise of the year when it reported to its annual meeting that the whopping 1976 deficit of $477,000 had been retired and that the new season was starting with cash in the bank. A fund raising drive by friends of the opera brought in $770,000. The company's artistic season included full-scale performances of Verdi's *Don Carlos*, Mozart's *The Magic Flute*, and Berg's *Wozzeck*.

Visual Arts. It was a calm and productive time for the nation's painters, sculptors, fine craftsmen, and filmmakers. However, two special events, one at home and one abroad, gave the visual arts people much pleasure. In August, a notable exhibition of Canada's Group of Seven (1920–1940) opened in Moscow's Pushkin Museum of Fine Arts. This was in exchange for a show of contemporary Soviet paintings which toured Canada in 1976. In September, the Art Gallery of Ontario opened its long-awaited Canadian Wing. The new area cost close to $8.4 million. For 50 years the gallery has been a dedicated collector of Canadian works and now, for the first time, it is able to exhibit its collection appropriately

People. The important Molson Prizes, awarded annually by the Canada Council and carrying a cash grant of $20,000 each, were awarded to John Hirsch, head of television drama for the Canadian Broadcasting Corporation; Jean-Louis Roux, director of Montreal's Théâtre du Nouveau Monde; and Bill Reid, Haida Indian wood-carver and jeweler. The chief of the National Library's music division, Helmut Kallman, received the Canadian Music Council medal for 1977. Jean Trudel, 36, formerly with the National Gallery, was named director of the Montreal Museum of Fine Arts. He is the first French-Canadian to hold the post in 117 years.

After directing the Shaw Festival Company with notable success since 1973, Paxton Whitehead retired and was succeeded by Richard Kirschner, formerly with the Annenberg Center in Philadelphia. The National Arts Centre in Ottawa saw important personnel changes. Jean Roberts, one of Canada's most admired theater managers, retired and was succeeded by the two-man team of Jean Gascon and John Wood. In Halifax, a distinguished English theater man, John Neville, took over direction of the Neptune Theatre. A big surprise was the appointment of Dr. Hsio-Yen Shih as director of the National Gallery following the resignation of Dr. Jean Boggs.

WALTER B. HERBERT
Consultant on Canadian Cultural Affairs

CARIBBEAN

The Caribbean received a number of distinguished visitors in 1977, and each of them served to focus attention on the problems of a neglected region. Undoubtedly, the two most important visitors were women: Rosalynn Carter visited Jamaica at the end of May, and Queen Elizabeth II, escorted by her husband, Prince Philip, toured the British Virgin Islands, Antigua, and Barbados at the end of October. Other visitors included U. S. Sen. Frank Church, who flew to Cuba in August; U. S. Assistant Secretary of State for Inter-American Affairs Terence Todman, a native of the Virgin Islands, who went to a number of Caribbean states, including Cuba and Puerto Rico; Secretary of State Cyrus Vance, who in June led the U. S. delegation to the Organization of American States meeting on the island of Grenada; a four-man UN commission, which visited the U. S. Virgin Islands in April; and last, but not least, the peripatetic U. S. Ambassador to the United Nations, Andrew Young, who in August toured no less than 10 nations in the wider Caribbean region.

While no concrete effects of these visits on the serious economic problems of the region were immediately apparent, they brought visual evidence of a change in the attitude of the United States (or at least its new political leaders) toward the Caribbean. The United States and Cuba reached agreement on fishing boundaries between the two nations and also exchanged low-level diplomatic missions. Cuban President Fidel Castro, moreover, gave permission for some 80 American citizens to return to the United States. In response to some not-so-subtle pressure from Andrew Young, Jean-Claude Duvalier, president of Haiti, freed more than 100 political prisoners.

Jamaica. Nowhere in the Caribbean was an overture by the United States more necessary than in Jamaica. Relations in 1976 had been strained because of the leftist leanings of the ruling party and Prime Minister Michael Manley's open friendship with Fidel Castro. In the elections of December 1976, however, Manley's incumbent People's National party won a resounding endorsement of its socialist policies by sweeping back into power with the greatest majority of any party since independence—47 out of 60 seats. Rosalynn Carter's visit, therefore, was timely, and all Jamaicans responded warmly. (For the death of former Prime Minister Sir Alexander Bustamante, see OBITUARIES.)

The Jamaican economy has been exceptionally hard hit by the world-wide recession. Tourism, which once flourished on the north coast, has virtually disappeared as an economic activity. The droughts, which have recurred with yearly regularity in the Caribbean, have dealt Jamaican agriculture heavy blows. Sugar production dropped to a 30-year low in 1977, when the total was merely about 290,000 tons, some 30,000 less than predicted. The bauxite industry, a major source of income for the government, experienced a change of ownership, when the government acquired 51% of the shares of all major producers on the island. In view of the serious economic deterioration the government devalued the Jamaican dollar and imposed severe restrictions on imports, the movement of capital, and use of foreign exchange.

Haiti. The drought that hampered Jamaican agriculture was even more seriously felt in Haiti, where outright famine and starvation led both Canada and the United States to rush in emergency supplies. The situation was so critical that lack of water in the Péligre hydroelectric complex, which produces 99% of Haiti's power, forced the suspension of electricity in the capital, Port-au-Prince.

The Antilles. The Lesser Antilles had similar problems caused by adverse weather and economic conditions. Grenada, however, in marked contrast to the rest of the Caribbean, has doubled its exports of spices (mace and nutmeg) since 1975, bringing some economic prosperity to the small population. In Dominica, the legislature in March voted overwhelmingly (18 to 3) to request independence from Great Britain. However, the movement toward freedom was halted, at least temporarily, because one party favored a republican-style government while the other wanted independence under the symbolic sovereignty of the queen. The government of St. Kitts, already truncated by the successful breakaway of Anguilla, in 1977 also faced secession by the island of Nevis. In an official referendum held on Aug. 19, 1977, 99.4% of the 4,220 votes cast (out of some 6,000 eligible voters) approved of the separation. The secessionist move has successfully stalled the drive for independence which Prime Minister Robert Bradshaw had carried to Great Britain. A similar attempt to separate the small island of Barbuda from Antigua was successfully checked by Prime Minister Vere Bird, who agreed to grant the off-lying island a greater degree of local autonomy.

CARIBBEAN · Information Highlights

Nation	Population (in millions)	Area sq mi (km²)	Capital	Head of state and/or government
Bahamas	.21	4,408 (11,405)	Nassau	Lynden O. Pindling, prime minister
Barbados	.25	166 (430)	Bridgetown	John M. G. Adams, prime minister
Cuba	9.6	44,221 (114,524)	Havana	Fidel Castro, president
Dominican Republic	5.0	18,818 (48,734)	Santo Domingo	Joaquín Balaguer, president
Grenada	.10	133 (344)	St. George's	Eric M. Gairy, prime minister
Haiti	5.3	10,715 (27,750)	Port-au-Prince	Jean-Claude Duvalier, president
Jamaica	2.1	4,233 (10,962)	Kingston	Michael Manley, prime minister
Netherlands Antilles	.24	371 (961)	Willemstad	Juan M. G. Evertsz, minister president
Trinidad and Tobago	1.0	1,980 (5,128)	Port-of-Spain	Eric E. Williams, prime minister

Prime Minister Lynden Pindling is jubilant following his party's victory in the Bahamas' first elections since independence.

UPI

Aruba Strike. The most important step toward breaking up existing island confederation governments did not occur in the English-speaking islands but in the Netherlands Antilles. The Dutch government had taken definite measures to prepare the six islands of the group for complete independence. This orderly preparation was interrupted in 1977 by secessionist sentiments among the people of Aruba, who resent the hegemony exercised by the neighboring island of Curaçao. In mid-August the Arubans called a general strike to stress the sincerity of a previous referendum, which had demanded immediate independence from the Netherlands Antilles government.

To sum up, the Caribbean is witnessing a strong centrifugal movement, aggravated by adverse economic conditions. The best illustration of this is the weakening of the Caribbean Common Market, or CARICOM, whose out-going director, shortly before his resignation, stated: "With all the optimism in the world, the Caribbean region will be in deep trouble throughout 1977 . . . . I don't know how we are going to survive."

THOMAS G. MATHEWS
University of Puerto Rico

CENSORSHIP

The number of countries enjoying a free press dwindled in 1977, continuing the worldwide trend toward censorship that has been burgeoning for a decade. Few countries are free, and most of these are concentrated in western Europe and North America. A continuing study by Freedom House found that at the end of 1976 close to half the world's population lived in "not free" countries, more than a third in "partly free," and only about one fifth in "free" countries. In 1973, about a third of mankind lived in free nations.

The Press. Amnesty International reported a 50% increase, from May 1976 to May 1977, in the number of journalists suffering repressive actions by governments of 25 countries. Foreign correspondents find it more difficult to gain entry to various countries and meet countless restrictions of their movements when they succeed in entering.

UNESCO (United Nations Educational, Scientific, and Cultural Organization) shelved until its 1979 meeting an action on a resolution by Russia—strongly resisted by Western democracies —that governments be made responsible for all foreign and domestic operations of mass media within their borders. A projected Third World news agency, which supporters in UNESCO councils claim to be necessary to offset the "cultural and economic imperialism" of Western wire services, is in the planning stage. Since any Third World news agency will be underwritten by a consortium of governments, Western observers see it as a certain instrument of censorship.

Censorship at the Source. The amended U. S. Freedom of Information Act continues to free records held by government, despite complaints by executive agencies of the burden of retrieving information and by businesses concerned that trade secrets they supply government are imperiled under provisions of the act. With the passage of the "Sunshine Act" (effective March 12, 1977), about 50 executive agencies were required to open their meetings to the public.

President Carter has proposed to shorten the time during which documents classified in the interest of national security are withheld from inspection. An often revised criminal code, which some critics in the news media feel is potentially restrictive to the free flow of information, is still pending in Congress.

Censorship by the Courts. Florida leads the few states which have eased their rules on camera coverage of criminal trials. Unique to that state is the allowance of cameras despite objections from either prosecution or defense.

Courts preparing to hear cases that are certain to invite wide coverage have continued to impose orders infringing on the freedom of reporters. With rare exceptions, appellate courts have found such orders unconstitutional.

Censorship and Community Standards. In recent years, the U. S. Supreme Court has favored local control of publications that offend community standards of morality. Consequently, there has been a rapid increase in local prosecution of allegedly obscene materials. The court has ruled, however, that an individual may be prosecuted under federal statutes in states that have abolished laws regulating obscenity for adults.

PAUL FISHER
Director, Freedom of Information Center

CENTRAL AMERICA

In 1977, Central Americans were most concerned with violations of human rights, the implications of new Panama Canal treaties, terrorism and assassinations, and attempts to reduce the long-standing reliance on single crop economies.

In April, U. S. President Jimmy Carter announced his policy toward Latin America. One element of this policy—reiterated support of human rights in the Americas—met with varied response in Central America, and, in fact, caused El Salvador and Honduras to renounce U. S. military aid. The Panama Canal treaties were supported by all of the Central American governments initially, and representatives from each of the states went to Washington in September to observe the formal signing ceremonies and to express personally some of their concerns to the Carter administration. Violence and terrorism, especially in El Salvador and Guatemala, were frequent, and at times activities in one of the states seemed to be tied to those in another. The ever-present questions of plant disease and the instability of the markets of certain Central American crops led to new agricultural developments.

Costa Rica. President Daniel Oduber Quirós declared that he strongly supported President Carter's human rights proposals, especially since they seemed to be the same as those offered by Costa Rica to the United Nations some years before. President and Mrs. Oduber were hosts to Mrs. Carter during her May visit to San José. The U. S. First Lady addressed some 1,500 Costa Ricans on the matter of human rights. Whether the visit was used to put pressure on Oduber to solve the Robert Vesco question is not known. However, a few days later, the president

appeared on television and urged the former associate of Richard Nixon to leave the country because he was hurting the nation's prestige. Former President José Figueres Ferrer added to the government's embarrassment by alleging corruption and interference by Vesco in Costa Rican affairs. Oduber's policy toward Vesco seemed to vacillate throughout the year.

In September, Oduber visited Great Britain and reportedly discussed with Prime Minister James Callaghan matters of common concern, including Belize (British Honduras—"the last mainland colony in America"), and some form of British aid for Costa Rica.

The increased use of copper-based fungicides appeared to have saved the rich coffee crop from blight, but the economy was threatened by the report that United Brands might break away from its heavy reliance on the banana and, in switching to other crops, cause the loss of thousands of jobs. Late 1977 figures indicated that Costa Rica had exported more than 53 million 40-pound (18-kg) boxes of bananas in 1976, placing the republic first in the sale of that commodity.

El Salvador. On February 20, in a violent election, Gen. Carlos Humberto Romero defeated Col. Ernesto Claramount Rozeville for the presidency of El Salvador. Romero's National Conciliation Party (PCN) had previously captured control of the Congress and all of the municipalities. Colonel Claramount's charges of fraud, accompanied by mass demonstrations, brought out the troops in the capital and led to a declaration of a state of siege by the incumbent, Col. Arturo Armando Molina. There were many casualties and Claramount fled.

The leadership opposing the administration largely rests in the hands of the clergy, which has strongly supported land reform measures and other aid to the peasantry. In May, the nation's seven bishops broadcast over the radio their allegation that President Molina persecuted the church and falsely accused the priesthood of being the dupes of communists. Molina denied this; nevertheless, several Jesuits were expelled.

The inauguration of President Romero in July brought little change. Right and left wing groups vied with one another in promoting terror, and in September, the rector of the University of El Salvador was murdered. No peaceful settlement seemed imminent.

On a brighter note, however, relations with Honduras appeared slightly more friendly, although full diplomatic ties were not restored.

CENTRAL AMERICA · Information Highlights

Nation	Population (in millions)	Area in sq mi (km²)	Capital	Head of State and Government
Costa Rica	2.1	19,575 (50,705)	San José	Daniel Oduber Quirós, president
El Salvador	4.3	8,260 (21,392)	San Salvador	Carlos Humberto Romero, president
Guatemala	6.4	42,042 (108,880)	Guatemala City	Gen. Kjell Laugerud García, president
Honduras	3.3	43,277 (112,079)	Tegucigalpa	Col. Juan Melgar Castro, president
Nicaragua	2.3	50,193 (129,990)	Managua	Anastasio Somoza, president
Panama	1.8	29,209 (75,650)	Panama City	Demetrio Lakas Bahas, president
				Omar Torrijos Herrera, chief executive

Guatemala. Important progress was made to rebuild what had been destroyed by the tragic earthquake of February 1976, which took some 25,000 lives in Guatemala. International agencies provided many millions of dollars for roads, schools, and homes. Ingenious new materials were introduced to accelerate home construction at costs far lower than ever before, but complete renewal is years away.

In May, Guatemala broke relations with Panama because of General Omar Torrijos' support of Belize in the Guatemala boundary dispute. Guatemala's President Kjell Laugerud García insisted upon the reestablishment of the 1856 boundary with Belize, which would reduce Belize's size by about one third or some 8,000 square kilometers (3,000 mi²). While talks on the question continued, Britain retained a small military force in its former colony.

Violence in Guatemala diminished during 1977. Laugerud claimed he never jailed or exiled a journalist for his views. However, in September terrorists assassinated a former minister of defense, and Salvadorian guerrillas alleged that the two governments jointly supported repressive measures against the poor.

Honduras. To lessen the nation's dependence upon the banana, the government, the Inter American Development Bank, and private sources are combining efforts in a vast development program for northern Honduras. There, more than three million acres (1.2 million hectares) of timber comprise the largest undeveloped pine forest in Latin America. Roads, houses, and a paper mill are planned, leading to a basic transformation in the entire Honduran economy. Much of the crop will go initially to Europe but the long-range plan is to manufacture paper and boxes for the shipment of bananas.

During the Panama Canal treaty signing ceremonies, the chief executives of Honduras and El Salvador held informal talks about their border question. Meanwhile, a number of Hondurans visited El Salvador where they were addressed by President Romero on the need for peace.

Amid charges that Honduras' social reform program had slowed down, a large union called for a workers' assembly to accelerate land reform. In response, a coalition of land owners warned that if necessary they would use arms to defend themselves against leftist guerrillas.

Nicaragua. In 1966, the fungus *roya,* a coffee blight, first appeared in Nicaragua. It slowly spread through that nation and began to threaten the entire Central America coffee crop. The fungus, which stains the leaf and prevents photosynthesis, reached epidemic proportions in 1976, causing the coffee growers of all five states to combine their efforts to protect an investment which brought $1.5 billion in revenue to the region in 1976. By the end of 1977, it appeared that the expenditures and labors had succeeded.

President Carter's human rights plans were put to serious test in Nicaragua where church bishops alleged that the government of Anastasio Somoza had committed summary executions and large-scale tortures in order to combat guerrillas. The bishops declared that hundreds of peasants had vanished or had been found dead in two northern provinces. Late in September, President Somoza lifted the state of siege which had lasted almost three years. He suffered a heart attack in July and, in October, was reported working only on a very limited schedule. Peasant groups, called "Sandinistas," and the opposition party, Unión Democrática, called for Somoza's resignation.

See also LATIN AMERICA; PANAMA; UNITED STATES—*Foreign Affairs.*

THOMAS L. KARNES
Arizona State University

UPI

In October, Nicaraguan helicopters searching for guerrillas along the Frio River attacked three Costa Rican boats. Mario Charpentier, Costa Rica's minister of security, and an Army major were aboard one of the boats and were forced to seek shelter.

CHEMISTRY

Carcinogens and other toxic chemicals were prominent in the news during 1977. Among the topics highlighted were saccharin, an artificial sweetener; carcinogens in cosmetics and plastic soft-drink bottles; and a soil fumigant.

Saccharin. In March a proposal by the U.S. Food and Drug Administration (FDA) to ban saccharin because it caused bladder cancer in rats raised a public furor. Opponents of the ban said that consumption of refined sugar by Americans, already dangerously high at 102 pounds (46.3 kg) per person per year, would increase and constitute a hazard far greater than that caused by saccharin. More importantly, they said that the test data were not valid for human beings and that the rats were fed doses far larger than those people consumed. (*See also* page 322.)

But in June a Canadian study showed a much higher incidence of bladder cancer among men users of saccharin than in nonusers. The more saccharin used, the more cancers were found in men. No increase in cancer was found among women saccharin users.

Cosmetics. Items such as hand and body lotions and shampoos were found to contain N-nitrosodiethanolamines, which are chemicals known to cause cancer in animals. According to the announcement at the meeting of the American Chemical Society in March, the chemicals probably resulted from a reaction of diethanolamine or triethanolamine with a nitrite impurity, the source of which was unknown. Although carcinogenic activity was tested by feeding the chemicals to animals, the possibility that the chemicals are absorbed through the skin is likely. The FDA said it would study the problem.

Soft-Drink Bottles. Plastic soft-drink bottles made of acrylonitrile were finally banned by the FDA in 1977 after an 18-month battle. This development began with the finding that acrylonitrile is toxic to animals. Later, a high incidence of cancer was found among workers in manufacturing plants making or processing the material. The FDA claimed that unreacted acrylonitrile can dissolve into beverages.

Monsanto, the maker of the bottles, said that tests conducted to reach that conclusion were unrealistic and that if the ban were enforced, its total losses in sales and bottle-making facilities would amount to about $90 million. Coca Cola was the main user of the acrylonitrile bottles.

Soil Fumigant. In 1973 dibromochloropropane (DBCP) was shown to be a potent carcinogen for animals. It was used as a soil fumigant to control nematodes, which are small worms that destroy the roots of crops.

By 1977 tests began to show a high incidence of sterility among male workers in plants either making or processing the chemical. Also, a Canadian study showed traces of the chemical in radishes and carrots. DBCP was withdrawn from the market without the usual controversy, and manufacturers asked that existing stocks be returned.

Pest Control. To avoid using toxic synthetic pesticides, two interesting approaches were suggested. One was the use of Dimilin (diflubenzuron) to inhibit the synthesis of chitin, a main component of the tough outer shell of insects. In this way, insects could not reach maturity and reproduce.

The chemical seems to be relatively nontoxic for higher animals, but it could prevent synthesis of chitin by beneficial insects and crustaceans such as lobsters, crabs, and shrimp. Also, it would not prevent damage by those insects that are destructive in their larval stage.

The second approach to pest control involved an inquiry at the molecular level into the natural resistance of plants to pests and disease. This required isolating and identifying the chemicals responsible for the resistance and determining how they operate in nature. For example, in sunflowers, two diterpene acids that are toxic to sunflower moths have been identified. Also, certain polyphenols protect corn from earworms. All of the chemicals identified as pest-resistant had low toxicity and were quite selective in their targets.

To control plant disease, a process similar to immunization was proposed. For example, experiments with watermelons, muskmelons, and cucumbers showed that inoculating just one leaf with a pathogenic fungus caused that leaf to die, but a protective response was stimulated throughout the plant. If pathogenic factors of this and other diseases could be isolated and identified, a variety of food plants could be inoculated.

The Atmosphere. Two more threats to the stratospheric ozone layer that prevents lethal ultraviolet rays from reaching earth were reported. One was the depletion of the hydroxyl radical (OH) in the troposphere above the Northern Hemisphere. This was found to be only 0.1 of the amount previously estimated. But above the Southern Hemisphere the OH radical content was 60% to 300% greater than above the Northern Hemisphere. The OH radical reacts with several air pollutants, and its depletion means that more air pollutants can reach the stratosphere and destroy the ozone.

Nitrogen fertilizers, on which adequate world food supplies depend, also were linked with ozone destruction. In the soil, they release nitrous oxide (N_2O), which can reach the stratosphere and react with ozone. If use of such fertilizers continues to increase from about 2 megatons in 1950 to an estimated 120 to 300 megatons by the year 2000, the predictions are that 15% of the stratospheric ozone would be destroyed in a little more than a century.

EUGENIA KELLER
Senior Editor, "Chemistry"

UPI

Claes Oldenburg inspects the Chicago skyline as his $100,000 sculpture, "Batcolumn," designed after a baseball bat, is set in place in front of a Social Security center.

CHICAGO

Chicago, which some have called the most segregated city in the nation, resolved some nagging racial problems in 1977. A new city administration, as well as the realization that the city was fighting a losing battle, brought a resolution to a number of legal disputes.

Early in the year the new administration of Mayor Michael A. Bilandic abandoned a six-year fight in U. S. District Court over alleged discrimination in the hiring and promoting of minorities in the Chicago Police Department. It had been a losing battle for the city. Federal Judge Prentice H. Marshall ordered quota hiring for Chicago police officers, new procedures for promotion, and, for a time, froze $114 million in federal revenue-sharing funds to force the city to comply. Even then, the late Mayor Richard J. Daley borrowed money to make up for the lost revenues so the city could continue its court fight.

The last portion of the federal funds was released by Judge Marshall in June when he said he believed the city was finally attempting to correct the discrimination in the Police Department.

In the city's Fire Department, another predominantly white organization, the city agreed to hire 208 black and Latino firemen and 66 white firemen. They were the first city firemen hired since 1973, when 152 white firemen and 10 black firemen were hired.

In September, the Board of Education instituted a voluntary busing program whereby 1,004 pupils from overcrowded schools were bused to 13 less-crowded schools. There were scattered protests from white parents, but for the most part school officials were satisfied with the voluntary busing program. The Board of Education also reached agreement, in October, with the U. S. Department of Health, Education, and Welfare on integration of faculties in the city's 578 public schools. The agreement avoided a threatened cutoff of $150 million in federal funds for city schools.

In local politics, Bilandic won a four-way Democratic primary in March and then a special mayoral election in June to fill the term of Daley, who died in 1976. Bilandic captured 77.4% of the vote; his Republican opponent, Alderman Dennis Block had 22.6%. Three months after the election, Block, the only Republican in the City Council, resigned his seat and moved to the more Republican suburbs.

Tragedy struck Chicago in February when a Chicago Transit Authority elevated train rammed the end of another train during a Friday evening rush hour, leaving 11 persons dead and 180 injured. It was the worst elevated train wreck in Chicago's history.

See also BIOGRAPHY: Bilandic, Michael A.

ROBERT ENSTAD, *Chicago Tribune*

CHILE

The most significant 1977 events in Chile were Gen. Augusto Pinochet Ugarte's unexpected announcement of a provisional timetable for the return of constitutional government, an improved economy, and human-rights matters.

Election Timetable. Speaking before a youth group on July 9, President Pinochet disclosed several dates relative to the transfer of power to a civilian regime by 1985. "Leftist groups" will not be allowed to participate in the transfer. The plan includes the appointment of a unicameral legislature in 1980, elections (between 1981 and 1985) to replace the appointed legislators, and the selection of a president by the elected legislature in 1985.

Political Parties Dissolved. On January 28, the government indefinitely closed Radio Balmaceda, the Christian Democratic station that had criticized government handling of various unofficial private lending groups which had gone bankrupt. On March 11, Gen. Hernán Bejares, secretary general of the government, announced the seizure of antigovernment documents drafted by Christian Democratic leaders Andres Zaldivar and Tomas Reyes Vicuna. The next day, the government dissolved the Christian Democratic Party, the conservative National Party, and two minor conservative parties, all of which had been "in recess" since the military ousted the

Santiago's ultramodern subway ("Metro") runs on rubber wheels. Cleanliness is particularly apparent.

UPI

government of Salvador Allende Gossens in 1973. President Pinochet said the four parties had to be eliminated "to keep them from returning Chile to chaos, misery, and demagoguery."

Intelligence. In August, the Directorate of National Intelligence (DINA) was reorganized into a new National Intelligence Center (CNI). Col. Manuel Contreras, DINA's head, was not part of the new civilian agency, which reportedly would not have DINA's police powers.

Human Rights. Small groups of Chileans organized hunger strikes in Santiago, Paris, Geneva, and Mexico City in June to pressure the government to release information on 504 persons whose disappearance since September 1973 was verified by Amnesty International. The demonstration at the Santiago headquarters of the UN's Economic Commission for Latin America ended after Chile promised UN Secretary General Kurt Waldheim to supply the information and that it would not take reprisals against the strikers who claimed to be relatives of persons, many of whom it was feared had been summarily executed or tortured to death.

On June 18, Jorge Montes, a former Communist senator jailed in 1974, was flown to Frankfurt, Germany, in return for 11 West German prisoners being released from East German jails. This exchange came after the Soviet Union released Vladimir K. Bukovsky, one of the most prominent Soviet dissidents, in December 1976 in exchange for Chile's release of Luís Corvalán Lepe, head of the Chilean Communist Party.

--------- **CHILE · Information Highlights** ---------

Official Name: Republic of Chile.
Location: Southwestern coast of South America.
Area: 292,257 square miles (756,945 km²).
Population (1977 est.): 11,000,000.
Chief Cities (1975 met. est.): Santiago, the capital, 3,-263,000; Valparaiso, 592,000.
Government: *Head of state and government,* Gen. Augusto Pinochet Ugarte, president (took power Sept. 1973). *Legislature*—Congress (dissolved Sept. 1973).
Monetary Unit: Peso (19.82 pesos equal U. S.$1, May 1977).
Manufacturing (major products): Iron and steel, petroleum products, pulp and paper, chemicals.
Major Agricultural Products: Wheat, sugar beets, potatoes, corn, grapes, citrus fruits, rapeseed.

Economic Affairs. Foreign reserves grew to more than $700 million in late September after several years of deficits and government measures to make exports more competitive in the world market. The foreign debt—which reached U. S.$5.2 billion in September, with yearly principal and interest payments of $1.2 billion—proved difficult to reduce as world copper prices fell in late August to an 18-month low of $.51 a pound.

After the government further cut public welfare budgets and agricultural and industrial subsidies, the National Statistics Institute estimated that inflation would be reduced to 70% in 1977 compared with 174.3% in 1976.

In January, the State Oil Company said it found petroleum deposits in the Strait of Magellan. Commercial production was expected to begin in about two years.

On May 1, the government announced a series of measures designed to "speed up Chile's socioeconomic recovery." The program included a 4% wage boost for government employees, a 4% increase in the minimum wage, allocation of 350 million pesos ($17.5 million) to revive the stagnant housing industry, and reductions in income, property, and import taxes.

Foreign Relations. Chile withdrew its delegation from the UN Human Rights Commission in late March. The commission had approved, and the United States had co-signed, a resolution condemning Chile. On June 28, Chile rejected a $27.5 million U. S. loan to help Chilean farmers. The loan was refused because of U. S. "interference in its [Chile's] internal affairs" on human rights questions. President Pinochet, in Washington for the signing of the Panama Canal treaties, discussed these questions with President Carter on September 6.

Between June 27 and August 9, Chile and Argentina exchanged seven bitter diplomatic notes, charging violations of air and maritime space. On May 2, British arbitrators had rendered a judgment favorable to Chile over disputed boundaries and islands in the Beagle Channel in the extreme south. Earlier in the year, border tensions with Peru were eased.

NEALE J. PEARSON, *Texas Tech University*

隆重纪念伟大的领袖和导师毛主席逝世一周年及毛主席纪念堂落成典礼大会

UPI

The Mao Tse-tung Memorial Hall was opened in Peking on Sept. 9, 1977, the first anniversary of Chairman Mao's death. The opening was the occasion for a mass rally.

CHINA

China, the world's most populous nation, remains divided between two opposing regimes: the People's Republic of China (Communist China) on the mainland, and the Republic of China (Nationalist China) on the island of Taiwan.

PEOPLE'S REPUBLIC OF CHINA

Hua Kuo-feng was confirmed as chairman of the Chinese Communist party by the 11th party congress in August 1977, but the return of Teng Hsiao-p'ing, formerly a senior deputy premier, turned the leadership into a collective one. The congress elected a new Central Committee and its Politbureau. Both of these powerful bodies were dominated by party veterans and pragmatic bureaucrats, with a large representation of the military.

Rapid development of China into a modern and powerful socialist country was the new leadership's prime objective. Departing from Mao Tse-tung's radical revolutionary line, Peking now referred to the past decade as the "ten lost years." American efforts to normalize relations with Peking met with little success. Sino-Soviet relations showed no improvement in 1977.

Leadership of Hua Kuo-feng. Hua Kuo–feng became the top leader of Communist China in 1976, when he purged Mao Tse-tung's widow, Chiang Ch'ing, and three other leftist leaders. These radicals had been the favorites of the late Chairman Mao and under his patronage had dominated the political scene since the Cultural Revolution of 1966. With Mao's death, in Sep-

tember 1976, the leftists lost the prop that was indispensable to their power. The moderates and bureaucrats, who had long been subject to pressure and persecution by the leftist group, were quick to seize the opportunity to overthrow them. Thus, in October 1976, Hua Kuo-feng was elected chairman of the Chinese Communist party to succeed Mao Tse-tung.

With a somewhat obscure background—a mere minister of public safety—Hua had been named acting prime minister after the death of Premier Chou En-lai in January 1976. It was not clear whether his patron was the pragmatic Chou En-lai or the revolutionary Mao Tse-tung. Shrewd, courteous, thorough, and well balanced, he was responsive to his superiors and modest toward his colleagues. He apparently had won the confidence of both Mao and Chou.

The sudden arrest of Chiang Ch'ing's group, referred to as the "Gang of Four," in October 1976, showed Hua's alertness and his ability to decide and act swiftly. He moved quickly to consolidate his power, but he was beset with difficulties. Members of Chiang Ch'ing's group were well entrenched in the various provinces, and Hua lacked extensive relationship with party veterans and military leaders. As a result, unrest spread throughout the country; there were serious disturbances in the provinces of Szechwan, Kiangsi, and Fukien, as well as the cities of Wuhan, Hangchow, and even Paoting, only 90 miles (145 km) south of Peking. Troops were sent into these areas to prevent the seizure of power by supporters of the Gang of Four, and changes in military and administrative leadership were ordered in Heilungkiang, Chekiang, Kiangsu, Kweichow, and four other provinces.

The speedy rise of military power was significant. Suppression of factional disturbances was much dependent upon the cooperation of regional and provincial military leaders.

Return of Teng Hsiao-p'ing. Demands for the return to power of Teng Hsiao-p'ing added to the unrest. Teng was first purged as a rightist during the 1966 Cultural Revolution. With the assistance of Premier Chou En-lai, he was later rehabilitated and in 1975 named first deputy premier. He was expected to succeed Premier Chou, who was in poor health, and to arrest the trend to radicalism by means of moderate pragmatism and economic development. Considering him a menace to their continuing revolution, the leftists purged him for the second time in April 1976. With the arrest of the Gang of Four, however, the tide again turned in his favor. Early in 1977, wall posters appeared in Peking calling for his return, and demonstrations were held to stress similar demands.

Teng was backed by a powerful force, represented in the capital by Yeh Chien-ying and in the south by influential generals, such as Hsu Shih-yu and Wei Kuo-ch'ing. In July, the Central Committee of the party finally restored Teng Hsiao-p'ing to his posts as member of the Politbureau and its Standing Committee, vice chairman of the Central Committee, vice chairman of the Military Commission of the party, deputy premier, and chief of the General Staff of the army. Tough and blunt, he was regarded as one of the most capable administrators in Communist China. He seemed likely to dominate the party center and deviate further from Mao's radical party line.

The 11th Congress. In August, the 11th congress of the Chinese Communist party met in Peking. It confirmed the party leadership, composed of Chairman Hua Kuo-feng, Minister of Defense Yeh Chien-ying, and Deputy Premier Teng Hsiao-p'ing. The congress elected a new Central Committee of 201 regular members and 132 alternate members. A number of these members had been victims of the Cultural Revolution; their rehabilitation confirmed the end of leftist radicalism.

The new Central Committee met on August 21 and elected 23 members to the Politbureau, to be headed by Hua Kuo-feng. The Standing Committee of the Politbureau was composed of Chairman Hua and four deputy chairmen: Yeh Chien-ying, Teng Hsiao-p'ing, Li Hsien-nien, and Wang Tung-hsiang. Of the Politbureau members, 11 had military background, reflecting Peking's stress on order and discipline.

The 11th congress adopted a new party constitution which allows more discussion within the party. The Communist party, states the constitution, should create a situation in which there would be "both unity of will and personal ease of mind and liveliness." Party members should have the right to criticize party organizations and officials and carry their appeals to the highest authority. On the other hand, party agencies should be responsible for checking up on the observance of discipline.

Principles and Policies. Under the new leadership, Mao's rigorous revolutionary line was replaced by a set of liberal policies that were to promote "political liveliness and economic prosperity." In January 1977, official newspapers revived the liberal slogan of the 1950's that called for the contention of a hundred schools of thought and the blooming of a hundred flowers in science and culture. Peking now stressed the importance of a "revolutionary united front" that would include not only workers and peasants but also intellectuals and "patriotic democratic parties." The new leadership declared that it would continue to "raise high" the thought of Mao Tse-tung, but subtly cited from

Defense Minister Yeh Chien-ying emerged in 1977 as the second most powerful man in Communist China.

Deputy Premier Teng Hsiao-p'ing delivered the closing speech at the 11th congress of the Communist party.

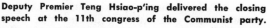

UPI

President Tito of Yugoslavia, second from left, visited China in August and held talks with Chairman Hua Kuo-feng, second from right, and other prominent Chinese leaders.

Mao only those statements that lent support to the new policies.

Education and Science. Education underwent a major change under Peking's new leadership. To provide a basis for China's rapid modernization, it was found necessary to reverse Mao's educational policies, which were oriented toward class struggle rather than technical learning. Emphasis was put on quality rather than the political background of the students. Examinations were reinstituted, and authority to discipline students was restored. High school graduates, particularly those in natural science, could enter college directly, without having to spend years working in the countryside.

Special attention was given to science and technology. Large funds were promised to universities and technical institutes for scientific research. Scientists were given more time and freedom to do their work.

National Defense. In February 1977, Peking convened four national conferences on military affairs to discuss modernization of the defense establishment, especially air defense and arms production. There was a keen recognition by military leaders of the need for modern, sophisticated weapons, which were deemed absolutely necessary to deal with a possible surprise attack by the Soviet Union.

Parallel to the emphasis on advanced weapons was the demand for a smaller, efficient army, trained to use modern weapons. The large army of three million men, backed by an armed militia of several millions, was the pride of Mao Tse-tung, who believed in the "human sea" of troops that would "drown" foreign invaders. Peking now backed away from Mao's precept that "men are more important than weapons." The new leadership was prepared to import foreign arms if necessary.

Economy. In 1977, economic development was given high priority by Peking, not only because it was indispensable to making China a modern, powerful nation, but also because of the slow economic growth, attributable to political strife, in the previous year. At the beginning of the year, a series of conferences was held to discuss various economic problems. In a major economic review, issued in September, Peking called for centralized control of industry, higher production and profits, and introduction of foreign technology. "Revolution," the leadership declared, "can never be substituted for production."

In October, the State Planning Commission announced that industrial production was on the increase after a period of stagnation. The grain harvest was "fairly good," in spite of a drought in the spring. Petroleum output for the first six months of 1977 rose 10.6% over the same period a year earlier. The increase, however, represented a sharp decline when compared with the annual rise of about 20% in the past decade.

In line with the policy of fostering economic prosperity, Peking announced, in October, wage raises for factory workers at the bottom levels and for low-paid teachers and government officials. About 50–60% of the urban work force would be covered by the increases. In addition, the government would offer urban residents bet-

─ **COMMUNIST CHINA · Information Highlights** ─

Official Name: People's Republic of China.
Location: Central part of eastern Asia.
Area: 3,705,396 square miles (9,596,976 km²).
Population (1977 est.): 850,000,000.
Chief Cities (1974 est.): Peking, the capital, 7,600,000; Shanghai, 10,800,000; Tientsin, 4,000,000.
Government: *Chairman of the Chinese Communist Party:* Hua Kuo-feng (took office Oct. 1976). *Head of government,* Hua Kuo-feng, premier (took office April 1976). *Legislature* (unicameral)—National People's Congress.
Monetary Unit: Yüan (2.04 yüan equal U. S.$1, 1977).
Manufacturing (major products): Iron and steel, machinery, cotton textiles, fertilizers, electronics, pharmaceuticals, instruments, transportation equipment.
Major Agricultural Products: Rice, wheat, sweet potatoes, sorghum, corn, cotton, tobacco, soybeans, barley, tea.

ter housing, food, and welfare benefits, while peasants were to receive higher incomes and more consumer goods.

To ensure sufficient food supply, Peking increased its purchases of foreign grain in 1977. The total purchase of wheat for the year added up to more than 5 million tons, the largest since 1973.

Foreign Relations—United States. When President Richard Nixon visited Peking in 1972, he expressed his intention to normalize relations with China. He was soon thereafter driven out of office by the Watergate scandal, and Sino-American relations had shown no progress since.

The new administration of Jimmy Carter reaffirmed its interest in normalizing ties. But because of public opposition to abandoning Taiwan, President Carter had to look for a formula that would improve relations without "the appearance" of foreseaking Taiwan. In pursuit of this policy, Secretary of State Cyrus R. Vance visited Peking during August 22–26. He was received at the airport by Huang Hua, Chinese minister of foreign affairs, but the Chinese reception was notably less enthusiastic than that accorded former Secretary of State Henry A. Kissinger during his several visits to China.

For two days, Secretary Vance talked with Huang Hua. Finally, on August 25, he had a long discussion with Teng Hsiao-p'ing. The talks were cordial, but there was no progress on the improvement of relations; Vance was unable to find a formula to satisfy Peking. The Communist conditions for normalization remained unchanged, namely, that the United States withdraw its remaining military personnel from Taiwan, that diplomatic relations with Nationalist China be severed, and the 1954 security treaty with it be abrogated. Peking was not interested in any formula that would enable the United States to give Taiwan some form of guarantee in place of the security treaty. Nor would Peking consider the possibility that upon severing diplomatic relations with the Nationalist regime, the United States might establish a liaison office in Taipei. More important, Peking rejected any suggestion that it would not use force against Taiwan.

On August 27, upon the return of Secretary Vance, President Carter lauded his China trip as a "major step" toward normalizing relations with Peking. But the Chinese Communists disagreed. On September 6, in a manner unusual in diplomatic circles, the redoubtable Deputy Premier Teng Hsiao-p'ing told the executives of The Associated Press that China's efforts to establish diplomatic relations with the United States had "suffered a setback" during the visit of Secretary Vance. He called Vance's discussions in Peking a retreat from proposals made by former President Gerald R. Ford and former Secretary of State Henry Kissinger. According to Teng, President Ford in December 1975 had promised that if he was reelected he would sever diplo-

UPI

Chairman Hua led the officials who greeted President Ne Win of Burma on his arrival on a state visit in April.

matic ties with Taiwan and establish relations with Peking.

Soviet Union. The purge of the Chiang Ch'ing group did not result in any change in Peking's anti-Soviet policy. In an interview with a visiting West German delegation on September 25, Deputy Premier Teng Hsiao-p'ing said that the "warming up" of Sino-Soviet relations was out of the question not only for this generation, but even for the next.

On October 7, a limited agreement was concluded between China and the Soviet Union concerning navigation on the Ussuri River on their disputed border. It was provided that at times of low water Chinese ships could use a channel near Khabarovsk, at the junction of the Amur and Ussuri rivers. The agreement had no impact on the dispute over regions along the border.

Europe. There were increasing contacts between China and Western Europe. A Chinese delegation was sent to France to visit defense industries for possible armaments purchases. In April, Margaret Thatcher, the British Conservative party leader, was invited to visit China. She was given a banquet by Deputy Premier Li Hsien-nien, who did not miss the opportunity to discuss the menace of Soviet power.

In Eastern Europe, Peking continued its efforts to isolate the Soviet Union, whenever possible. When President Tito of Yugoslavia visited China on August 30, he was given a regal reception—in sharp contrast to the time when Mao Tse-tung considered him among the worst of renegades.

Asia and Africa. Peking constantly reminded Japan that the Soviet troops stationed in eastern Siberia were directed not only against China, but more against the United States and Japan. To divert Tokyo from helping develop oil and gas resources in Soviet Siberia, China was willing to increase its oil exports to Japan.

Friendly relations were maintained with North Korea, which had adopted a detached at-

Premier Chiang Ching-kuo of Nationalist China tested the first electric automobile to come off the assembly line in Taipei. Afterward, the premier praised the vehicle.

UPI

titude toward the Soviet Union. Peking pledged support for North Korea's struggle for an "independent and peaceful unification" of Korea.

Sino-Indian relations improved after the exchange of ambassadors in 1976. Indian ships were admitted to Chinese ports and trade ties revived. But the Tibetan question continued to be a thorny issue between the two countries. Peking accused India of supporting refugees for Tibet's secession from China.

Many heads of state visited Peking in 1977, including President Ne Win of Burma, President Francisco Macías Nguema of Equatorial Guinea, President Ahmadou Ahidjo of Cameroon, and Lt.-Col. Seyni Kountché, the chief of state of Niger. Peking granted small amounts of aid to Equatorial Guinea and Niger during the visits of their chief executives.

REPUBLIC OF CHINA

Continued political stability in Taiwan made it possible to allow more civil liberties to the people. Many Taiwanese were brought into the government, particularly at the local levels.

The six-year economic plan was pushed forward to turn Taiwan into a developed country. Emphasis was laid on development of heavy and chemical industries, expansion of foreign trade, and improvement of transportation.

Efforts by the United States to normalize relations with Peking caused Taiwan grave concern. The Nationalists were opposed to any deal with Peking.

Domestic Affairs. After five years in his office, Premier Chiang Ching-kuo had won the confidence and support of the people on Taiwan. He had led the country through difficult times, including the worldwide economic recession and unfavorable international changes. A man of popular touch, he often toured the countryside and talked to people of various walks of life, especially the peasants.

By subtle control of the political apparatus, Premier Chiang provided Taiwan with the continued stability essential to economic prosperity. A vigorous man, he saw to it that his administration carried out his policies efficiently. He brought into the government many Taiwanese, who assumed all the offices of county magistrates and mayors and several at the cabinet and deputy-minister levels.

Taiwan gave much attention to the question of human rights, partly in response to President Carter's emphasis, and partly because political stability with prosperity and educational expansion made it practical for Taiwan to become an open society. Measures taken by the government to allow more civil liberties included a cautious liberalization of press censorship and a greater tolerance of dissenting opinions.

On July 25, southern Taiwan was struck by a powerful typhoon. It left 28 persons killed and 20,000 homes destroyed. The damaged area covered 2,000 square miles (5,200 km²). Kaohsiung, a major port and industrial city, suffered the most.

Economic Development. The six-year economic development plan, which began in 1976, aimed at modernizing the economy and turning

— NATIONALIST CHINA • Information Highlights —

Official Name: Republic of China.
Location: Taiwan, island off the southeastern coast of mainland China.
Area: 13,885 square miles (35,961 km²).
Population (1977 est.): 16,600,000.
Chief Cities (1975 est.): Taipei, the capital, 2,000,000; Kaohsiung, 975,000; Taichung, 530,000.
Government: *Head of state,* Yen Chia-kan, president (installed April 1975). *Head of government,* Chiang Ching-kuo, premier (took office May 1972). *Legislature* (unicameral)—Legislative Yüan.
Monetary Unit: New Taiwan dollar (37.04 NT dollars equal U. S.$1, Nov. 1977).
Manufacturing (major products): Petroleum products, processed foods, textiles, electrical machinery, electronics, chemicals, apparel.
Major Agricultural Products: Sugarcane, bananas, mushrooms, pineapples, rice, tea, vegetables.

Taiwan into a developed country. The major targets were the development of heavy and chemical industries, expansion of foreign trade, and mechanization of agriculture. Special attention was given to such pivotal industries as electronics, steel, machinery, and transportation equipment.

The gross national product of Taiwan reached $9.3 billion (U. S.) in the first eight months of 1977, an increase of 13.1% over the corresponding period of 1976. For the first half of the year, industrial production increased 12.1% and agricultural production 5.9% over the same period of the preceding year.

The ten major construction projects, which began in the early 1970's to expand heavy industry and to improve communications and transportation, were proceeding smoothly despite the worldwide economic slump. When completed, the projects were expected to stimulate industrial production and divert economic stagnation. Among those whose first phase was completed in 1977 were the integrated steel mill, the huge shipyard designed to build supertankers, and the Taichung Harbor.

Taiwan's two-way trade in the first nine months of 1977 amounted to $12,822.6 million, an increase of 12.2% over the corresponding period of 1976. Exports reached $6,637.3 million and imports $6,185.3 million, resulting in a favorable balance of $452 million.

Taiwan's rapidly increasing exports of shoes to the United States caused Washington considerable concern. Manufactured at a much lower cost, shoes from Taiwan drove a large number of American shoe companies out of business. The Carter administration, which rejected any move toward protectionism, sought an orderly market agreement with Taiwan. On June 14, the two sides reached an accord, limiting Taiwan's export of nonrubber shoes to the United States to 122 million pairs for the following year.

Foreign Relations. Taiwan expressed grave concern when Secretary of State Cyrus Vance, in July, announced his intention to pursue normalization of relations with Peking. Though Vance's visit to Communist China made no progress toward that goal, Taiwan's worries over possible U. S. ties with Peking remained undiminished.

In his oral report to the Legislative Yüan on September 23, Premier Chiang Ching-kuo poignantly expressed his government's anxiety and its opposition to the United States' change of course. "Any deal between the United States and the Peking regime," he said, "is bound to lead straight to a new war in Asia." As he saw it, the Communists only sought to lead Washington into diplomatic blunders that would "cost America credibility among its allies and destroy its leadership of the free world." He urged Washington to "desist from its flirtation" with Peking. The Republic of China, he added, would never waver from its determined, anti-Communist position.

With only 23 nations still recognizing Nationalist China, Taiwan had developed an ingenious policy that made it possible to have trade and other nondiplomatic ties with about 140 nations. Through such agencies as Interchange Association, Anglo-Taiwan Trade Committee, and others, numerous countries unofficially handled matters of trade or relations with Taiwan. Nationalist China joined in technical projects with more than 50 developing countries. Agricultural and technical demonstration teams were sent to countries in Asia, the Middle East, Africa, and Latin America. President Yen Chia-kan's visit to Saudi Arabia in July further strengthened the relations between the two countries.

CHESTER C. TAN, *New York University*

UPI

MiG pilot Fan Yuan-yen, who defected from the mainland to Taiwan in June, at a subsequent press conference displayed the gun he carried.

Civil-rights groups in Norfolk, Va., protest Anita Bryant's anti-gay rights campaign. The issue of homosexual rights came to the forefront in 1977.

UPI

CIVIL LIBERTIES AND CIVIL RIGHTS

Although the United States had a new president, committed to racial justice, human rights, open government, and fairness in the courts, 1977 was a year in which civil liberties and minority rights lost more than they gained at the hands of the federal government. The nationwide drift to the political right saw erstwhile liberals in Congress become leading opponents of busing and abortion, saving their political hides at the expense of their professed principles. The new head of the Office for Civil Rights in the Department of Health, Education, and Welfare (HEW) admitted, "Almost everything we're doing now is defensive." Amid the defeats, however, there were a number of victories.

Defendants' Rights. While Gary Gilmore finally got his wish to have his Utah death sentence carried out, the U. S. Supreme Court was still grappling with the whys and wheres of execution. In a Louisiana case it interpreted the constitutional prohibition against cruel and unusual punishment as banning a mandatory sentence of death for killing a policeman. And in its last decision before the summer recess, the tribunal struck down the nation's only remaining state law that imposed capital punishment for the crime of rape. (Though the defendant in this particular case was white, the court was not unmindful that 405 of the 455 men put to death for rape since 1930 were black.)

Law-and-order zealots attacked but civil libertarians praised the court for determining, in a Missouri case, that the police had denied a child-murder suspect his right to counsel by not allowing his attorney to accompany him on an intercity police car journey during which incriminating information was cajoled from him. In still another case that distressed law-enforcement authorities, the court ruled that police and federal agents, under most circumstances, could not search a person's locked luggage for suspected contraband without first obtaining a warrant for the specific purpose.

Women's Rights. The stonewalled status of the Equal Rights Amendment was indicative of the difficulties encountered by the women's rights movement in 1977. It was one step forward, one step back. The Supreme Court struck down height and weight restrictions that prevented women from becoming Alabama prison guards, but then turned around and condoned the exclusion of women from positions in male prisons because of the jungle conditions found there. Although the high court in 1976 had refused to compel private industry to equalize treatment of male and female employees under disability protection plans, in 1977 it struck down part of the Social Security law as discriminating between the sexes with respect to eligibility for survivor's benefits.

Right-to-Lifers scored victories over Right-to-Choicers in Congress and the courts. The Supreme Court ruled that neither the Constitution nor federal Medicaid law required states to pay for abortions when the lives of mothers are not endangered. This stand was endorsed by President Carter and HEW Secretary Califano. Welfare and women's rights groups argued that indigent women would be the victims of such a cutoff of funds, but Congress, which had passed the so-called Hyde amendment, barring the use of federal funds to pay for or promote abortion, extended the ban after lower court judges had lifted the order against enforcement of the amendment. The Supreme Court did rule, however, that states may not prohibit the sale of contraceptives to children nor advertising of birth control materials.

School Desegregation. Perhaps the good news on this front for civil rights attorneys was what the Supreme Court did not do: it did not curtail the power of federal courts to impose city-wide desegregation plans. Though it invalidated a Dayton, Ohio, proposal as too broad for the effects of discrimination that had been found, it upheld a Detroit arrangement which mandated compensatory education programs to help children recover from the disadvantages of having attended illegally segregated schools. Congress, on the other hand, sought to prohibit the executive branch from withholding federal aid to districts that refuse to merge black and white schools.

The spotlight was again on the Supreme Court as it grappled with the case of *Allan Bakke* v. *The Regents of the University of California.* Bakke, a white man, sued the university when the medical school at Davis denied him admission while reserving places for applicants of racial and ethnic minorities whose admissions scores were lower. The state, the associations of medical and law schools, and the civil rights groups that entered briefs on the side of the university argued that without such special admissions programs the number of non-white students would drop dramatically. Others attacked racial quotas as producing their own victims of discrimination. (*See also* ETHNIC GROUPS.)

Children's Rights. The conservative pattern of decision-making by the high court was exemplified in three cases dealing with the rights of children. By a 5–4 vote, in the most publicized case, the court decided that the Constitution does not bar even severe spanking of pupils by school officials. A second case found the court declining to decide whether children, whose parents seek to commit them to mental institutions, are entitled to lawyers and other legal protections. In a third ruling, the court said that a child may ordinarily be removed from its foster family without a hearing. This overturned a three-judge federal court decision that a child had a constitutional right to a hearing "before being compelled to suffer grievous loss" by such removal.

Gay Rights. Nationwide attention was attracted to Dade County, Fla., when a campaign led by Anita Bryant, a singer and orange juice promoter, succeeded in repealing an ordinance that had banned discrimination because of a person's sexual orientation. A national Gallup poll, taken after the referendum, found that a slim majority of Americans approved of equal job rights for homosexuals but a large majority of those sampled disapproved of homosexuals in specific professions, such as the clergy and elementary education.

Religion. There are many chinks in the "wall of separation" between church and state. Once more, the Supreme Court considered whether state aid to parochial school pupils violated the Constitution's prohibition of any establishment of religion. The court held the use of public funds to buy or lend standard texts and scoring services and to provide therapeutic services to be constitutional, while rejecting as unconstitutional the financing of field trips or the lending of equipment to parochial schools.

Freedom of Speech and Press. Obscenity convictions in Cincinnati, Ohio, Memphis, Tenn., and Wichita, Kan., caused even such majoritarian publications as *TV Guide* and the New York *Daily News* to be alarmed at the repercussions of the 1973 *Miller* v. *California* decision, which permitted local "community standards" to rule on what is obscene.

MARTIN GRUBERG
University of Wisconsin, Oshkosh

COINS AND COIN COLLECTING

The year 1977 was an eventful one in numismatics. Designs for the U. S. quarter, half dollar, and dollar reverted to those used before the special 1776–1976 bicentennial issues. About 4 million proof sets were struck in San Francisco and were sold for $9 each. President Carter named Stella Hackel Director of the Mint and Azie Taylor Morton U. S. Treasurer.

Treasury officials recommended the elimination of the one-cent piece because of its negligible purchasing power and high production costs. They also proposed that the half dollar, rarely seen in circulation, be discontinued, and that the dollar coin be reduced in diameter to a size between the quarter and half dollar to facilitate its use in vending machines.

Currency was in the limelight in 1977. Use of a new automated printing process resulted in a number of errors. Most spectacular were overprinted signatures caused when the sheets of notes were printed on the first press run without signatures and then were misaligned on the second press so that the signatures were printed upside down. Thousands of these were released into circulation, creating a sensation. Values for error notes ranged from about $100 to several hundred dollars.

The $2 bills, introduced in 1976, continued

The Hong Kong government issued a snake coin, left, valued at $195 Canadian, to mark the year of the snake. A rare U. S. trade dollar, minted in 1885, sold for a six-figure sum.

to cause a problem for the Treasury. It had been expected that use of the $2 note in transactions would sharply reduce the need for $1 notes, thereby effecting savings. However, the public remained apathetic.

Some 14,000 persons attended the American Numismatic Association (ANA) convention in Atlanta in August. Grover Criswell was elected president for the 1977–79 term. The ANA announced that its official ANA grading guide was scheduled for release in November. This guide proposes a system of grading coins based on a scale ranging from 0 to 70 points, the 70 designation reserved for an absolutely perfect coin.

The American Numismatic Society, in New York City, announced the acquisition by bequest of 1,155 Byzantine and Greek coins, valued at $500,000, from the Robert F. Kelley Estate. The Smithsonian Institution announced that it expected to acquire the Chase Manhattan Bank's "Moneys of the World" collection valued in excess of $1 million.

Israel released a 100-pound banknote, the largest in the country's history. Canada produced a $100 gold coin in commemorating the silver jubilee of Queen Elizabeth II. In January 1978, Canada will issue a smaller one-cent piece in an effort to fight rising production costs for the small denomination. Mexico announced a new 100-peso silver coin, the largest silver denomination in Mexican history.

> Q. DAVID BOWERS,
> *Columnist, "Coin World"*

COLOMBIA

The Colombian economy and political system were both badly shaken in 1977. Nevertheless, the country's political elite—traditionally divided between the Liberal and Conservative parties—continued to approach politics with the same repressive formulas they have used for the past 30 years.

Politics. Major candidates of the two old-line political parties spent most of the year jockeying for position in the presidential elections of 1978. The Liberal party was split down the middle between former President Carlos Lleras Restrepo and former Foreign Minister Julio Cesar Turbay Ayala, who was apparently backed by incumbent Liberal President Adolfo López Michelsen. The so-called "Consensus of San Carlos" (the name of the presidential palace in Bogotá) called for the congressional and municipal elections in February 1978—prior to the presidential ones—to be a sort of primary for the Liberal party. The idea was to allow Liberal voters to express their presidential preference by voting for lesser candidates identified with the major presidential contenders, thus providing the badly split Liberal party with a single candidate to run against the Conservatives. By mid-year, all parties began backing off from the idea. Unlike the Liberals, the Conservatives seemed united behind the candidacy of Belisario Betancur, and at one point Betancur offered himself as the candidate of national union for both parties. The Liberals, predictably, rejected this offer. Betancur, a proven vote-getter, remained out of the country most of the year, allowing the Liberals to continue their feuding.

Crippling Strike. The air of unreality surrounding the political infighting was thickened during the second week in September, when the nation's first general strike was carried out by the major labor unions. Colombian labor is only about 20% unionized, and economic conditions for much of the working class had become quite intolerable. The strike paralyzed Bogotá and many other cities, and the violence that erupted—at least 23 people were killed, and all major cities reported serious disturbances—indicated that discontent with the economic conditions, particularly inflation, was widespread. The government used force to quell the disturbances, and mass arrests were made. The demands of the striking unions were not met.

Economy. The Colombian economy grew at a rate of more than 7% during 1977, continuing trends of recent years (the 1976 figure was 6–7%). Only a prolonged drought and a lack of growth in the agricultural sector (excepting coffee) kept the growth figure from soaring much higher. At the same time, world coffee prices of more than $3.00 a pound caused a substantial increase in export earnings. This, coupled with the inability of the Colombian economy to absorb enough additional imports to offset these earnings, led to a further increase in the money supply and greater inflation. During the first three months of 1977, prices increased by 10.7%, and the annual inflation rate exceeded 30%.

In a major move to reduce foreign control over the Colombian economy, the Congress passed a bank Colombianization bill, under which new foreign investment in the financial and insurance sectors was prohibited and existing branches were required to sell down to a 49% position over three years. The initial stages of this reform were accomplished smoothly.

> ERNEST A. DUFF
> *Randolph-Macon Woman's College*

───── **COLOMBIA · Information Highlights** ─────

Official Name: Republic of Colombia.
Location: Northwest South America.
Area: 439,736 square miles (1,138,914 km²).
Population (1977 est.): 25,200,000.
Chief Cities (1975 est.): Bogotá, the capital, 2,850,000; Medellín, 1,100,000; Cali, 920,000.
Government: *Head of state and government,* Alfonso López Michelsen, president (took office Aug. 1974). *Legislature*—Congress: Senate and Chamber of Representatives.
Monetary Unit: Peso (36.65 pesos equal U. S.$1, June 1977).
Manufacturing (major products): Textiles, beverages, iron and steel, petroleum products.
Major Agricultural Products: Coffee, bananas, rice, cotton, sugarcane, tobacco, potatoes, corn, cattle, plantain, yucca.

During 1977, a total of 3,800 acres (1,520 hectares) of the White River National Forest in northwest Colorado burned. A lightning storm, left, was cited as the cause of the Brook Creek fire.

UPI

COLORADO

Energy development kindled a boom in the Colorado economy in 1977, renewing old debates about the merits or ills of swift growth.

Booming Business. While not a large energy producer itself, Colorado has become the administrative hub for energy exploration and development throughout the west. That status was reinforced by the federal government's decision to locate the Solar Energy Research Institute in Golden, near Denver.

In Denver itself the boom triggered a series of major new office buildings. The city budget, perennially tight, suddenly showed a $20-million surplus. Metropolitan sales-tax collections at the summer's end had jumped 22% over 1976.

Canadian investors, wary of the political climate in some of that nation's provinces, also poured money into Denver real estate. Phillips and Amerada Hess announced major expansions in Denver, joining a host of energy companies that have located in the city.

Voter Reaction. But while businessmen smiled, some voters used local elections to put crimps on growth. Boulder passed a citizen-initiated measure limiting growth in that city to about 2% annually for five years. Wheat Ridge voters ousted a popular mayor, viewed as favoring too swift a growth in that suburban community.

Water. The growth controversy spilled over to the Denver Water Board's attempt to build a new water treatment facility. While most regional governmental units backed the plan—already delayed four years by environmental protests—opponents argued it would only spawn more growth.

A drought which depleted the usual winter snowpacks led to water rationing among the approximately one million people on the Denver system. Later, the board announced that 88,000 homes still on flat-rate plans would have to adopt water meters as a conservation step.

State political leaders reacted angrily when President Carter proposed eliminating or reducing seven federally funded water projects in the state. After an intensive congressional fight, three of the projects were killed.

Strikes and Lockouts. Nationwide discontent over farm prices gave rise to a Colorado-based American Agriculture Movement, which urged farmers to strike for higher prices. While many agriculturalists were skeptical about the effect of such a strike, they warned that falling prices endangered many family farms.

About 500 workers at the Adolph Coors Co. went on strike, and labor leaders launched a boycott of the popular beer when the brewery maintained production with nonstriking workers.

The Denver Symphony also had labor troubles. The management, citing financial problems, locked out musicians when a new contract could not be agreed upon. The dispute was resolved when symphony backers collected a $500,-000 "survival fund" to raise the musicians' pay. But the summer concerts had to be canceled.

Other Events. A Denver minister, the Rev. James O. Mote, was named bishop of a breakaway Episcopalian group after the mother church voted to ordain women priests.

The Auraria Higher Education Complex opened in Denver, finally bringing the state's largest city a full range of educational services right in its midst.

A major expansion of Denver's Mile High Stadium was completed, with novel movable stands expanding capacity to about 75,000 fans.

BOB EWEGEN
Staff Writer, The Denver "Post"

––––––– **COLORADO · Information Highlights** –––––––

Area: 104,247 square miles (270,000 km²).
Population (1976 est.): 2,583,000.
Chief Cities (1970 census): Denver, the capital, 514,678; Colorado Springs, 135,060; Pueblo, 97,453.
Government (1977): *Chief Officers*—governor, Richard D. Lamm (D); lt. gov., George L. Brown (D). *General Assembly*—Senate, 35 members; House of Representatives, 65 members.
Education (1976–77): *Enrollment*—public elementary schools, 300,750 pupils; public secondary, 269,250; nonpublic, 40,600; colleges and universities, 130,275 students. *Public school expenditures,* $970,500,000 ($1,476 per pupil).
State Finances (fiscal year 1976): *Revenues,* $2,167,-903,000; *expenditures,* $1,996,742,000.
Personal Income (1976): $16,633,000,000; per capita, $6,440.
Labor Force (June 1977): *Nonagricultural wage and salary earners,* 1,007,400; *unemployed,* 76,800 (July 1976), 6.1% of total force.

CONNECTICUT

Consolidation of more than 200 state government units into 22 superagencies, effective Jan. 1, 1979, was the major achievement of the 1977 General Assembly. It adopted a $1.9 billion budget, up 11%, with no general tax increases. A 1921 law requiring a minimum temperature of 68° F (20° C) in buildings was amended, with the minimum temperature lowered three degrees to 65° F (18.3° C). The praying mantis was made the state insect.

Pay increases totaling $43 million went to 40,000 state employees. Elected state officials and judges also were voted increased pay. Members of Connecticut's next legislature will receive $17,000 for a two-year term. In the November elections, Republicans gained nine towns, controlling 74 to the Democrats' 83.

Economy. The state ended its fiscal year with a surplus of $76 million, the second of Gov. Ella Grasso's administration. The per capita income ranked the state third in the nation, behind Alaska and Illinois. Environmental problems stalled much of the state's highway building program, with projects totaling $1.7 billion awaiting final authorization. The state's single dog track and three jai alai frontons in 12 months attracted 5 million bets totaling $373 million, of which the state received $24 million, cities $2.1 million, and the facilities $41 million.

Education. The state's public school financing method, relying heavily on uneven local property taxes, was held unconstitutional by the state Supreme Court. School equalization grants were doubled to $20 million, and a legislative panel is studying substitute methods of school financing, including a state income tax. Public school enrollment dropped for the fifth consecutive year. The state per pupil cost was sixth highest in the nation. State support of 32% to 34% of public school costs, compared with a national average of 41%, ranked Connecticut 38th nationally.

Labor. The state's unemployment rate dropped to 6.7% in August. Non-farm workers totaled 1,273,300. A grave-diggers' strike against 26 Roman Catholic cemeteries lasted six weeks, postponing more than 400 burials. The strikers won an increase of 45 cents an hour over a 20-month period.

Religion. The Rt. Rev. Morgan Porteus, 60, succeeded 66-year-old Bishop J. Warren Hutchens on September 1 as leader of the 107,000-member Episcopal Diocese of Connecticut, the oldest and third largest in the United States. Bishop Porteus advocates female priests.

Weather. The latest measurable snowfall on May 9 deposited nine inches in the northwest part of the state. On April 9, the temperature fell to a record 23° F (−5° C). Five days later, it rose to a record 86° F (30° C).

People. The nation's oldest twins, Edith Northrup and Edda Northrup Gibney, born on a Windsor farm in 1876, observed their 101st birthday anniversary on February 22. John T. Downey, a CIA agent who spent 20 years as a prisoner of Red China and became a lawyer after his release in 1973, is serving as a member of the state Personnel Appeal Board.

The fate of Peter A. Reilly, accused at 17 of the 1973 slaying of his mother, continued to attract national attention. Tried, convicted, retried, and cleared, Reilly is a free man. A second police report again named him as the killer, but the state's attorney refused to prosecute.

CHARLES L. TOWNE, *Former Associate Editor*
"The Hartford Courant"

—— CONNECTICUT • Information Highlights ——

Area: 5,009 square miles (12,973 km²).
Population (1976 est.): 3,117,000.
Chief Cities (1970 census): Hartford, the capital, 158,-017; Bridgeport, 156,542; New Haven, 137,707.
Government (1977): *Chief Officers*—governor, Ella T. Grasso (D); lt. gov., Robert K. Killian (D). *General Assembly*—Senate, 36 members; House of Representatives, 151 members.
Education (1976–77): *Enrollment*—public elementary schools, 388,233 pupils; public secondary, 246,767; nonpublic, 98,900; colleges and universities, 145,-053 students. *Public school expenditures,* $1,189,-762,000 ($1,770 per pupil).
State Finances (fiscal year 1976): *Revenues,* $2,678,-703,000; *expenditures,* $2,651,232,000.
Personal Income (1976): $22,929,000,000; per capita, $7,356.
Labor Force (June 1977): *Nonagricultural wage and salary earners,* 1,273,300; *unemployed,* 110,800 (7.5% of total force).

UPI

Gov. Ella Grasso is first to go before the cameras as a new regulation requiring photographs on Connecticut drivers' licenses goes into effect.

CONSUMERISM

Consumers in the United States watched with interest as power was transferred from a Republican to a Democratic president. Jimmy Carter promised during his presidential campaign that he would challenge Ralph Nader for the role of top consumer advocate in the country. On taking office the president began to fulfill his promise in a number of ways. He appointed Esther Peterson his special assistant for consummer affairs. She had been the first person ever appointed to this position, having served with distinction as special assistant for consumer affairs to President Lyndon Johnson.

Other significant consumer appointments were: Michael Pertschuk, former general counsel to the Senate Commerce Committee, as chairman of the Federal Trade Commission; Carol Tucker Foreman, former executive director of the Consumer Federation of America, as assistant secretary of agriculture; Peter Schuck, former head of Consumers Union's Washington office, as deputy assistant secretary, Department of Health, Education, and Welfare; and Joan Claybrook, former director of Congress Watch —a Nader organization—as administrator of the National Highway Traffic Safety Administration.

The president's major effort in the consumer's interest was his support of an Agency for Consumer Protection. In 1976, a bill creating such an agency had been passed with large majorities in both the House and Senate, but it never reached President Ford's desk because he had said that he would veto it. With the election of Carter and the continuation of a Democratic House and Senate it was thought that the bill would pass both the House and Senate with ease, and be signed by the president early in 1977. But opposition to the bill, particularly from the business community, was persuasive enough that many congressmen who had voted for it in previous sessions were reluctant to do so. The bill did not come to the floor for a vote in either the House or Senate during 1977. Supporters, realizing that they did not have the votes, countered with a trimmed-down bill for an Office of Consumer Representation rather than an Agency for Consumer Protection. This bill, too, died because the congressional votes to pass it were just not there.

The first important consumer bill passed during Carter's first year as president was the Fair Debt Collection Practices Act. It seeks to eliminate abusive and unfair debt collection practices. It prohibits debt collectors from making threats of financial ruin and loss of jobs and reputation, and it also prohibits harassing tactics such as late night telephone calls.

Airbags. Under the authority granted to him by Congress, Secretary of Transportation Brock Adams mandated that beginning with the model year 1982, all full-size automobiles must have front seat automatic crash protection, either airbags or passive seat belts. A passive seat belt is a combination lap and shoulder harness that automatically goes into place when the car door is closed. Intermediate and compact cars (in 1983) and sub-compact and mini-cars (in 1984) must have the same equipment. The Department of Transportation estimates that passive restraint systems will save 9,000 lives a year, and will reduce the severity of injuries for tens of thousands of persons.

Food and Drug Administration. The FDA continued in the middle of the battle over what chemical additives should and should not be allowed in foods. It banned the use of Red Dye No. 4, a food coloring used in a variety of products. Its banning of the sugar substitute, saccharin, created such a public outcry that Congress passed legislation extending for 18 months its use to allow for further studies. Both of these chemical additives were banned because tests showed them to produce cancer in test animals.

The FDA established labeling requirements for "hypoallergenic" cosmetics. The regulation specifies the conditions under which a cosmetic may be labeled hypoallergenic. For example, it requires that dermatological testing be done before such claims can be made. In addition the FDA now requires cosmetics manufacturers to list the ingredients on the labels of beauty and cleansing products.

"Consumerism at the Crossroads." A national opinion survey conducted by Marketing Sciences Institute and Louis Harris and Associates found broad public support for the consumer movement and the job being done by consumer activists, as well as considerable public disenchantment with the business community's response to meeting consumers' needs. By a majority of 52% to 34%, the public favors a new federal agency for consumer protection, while 92% of the public believes that consumer affairs should be a compulsory subject in all high schools.

Canada. A significant step taken to aid Canadian consumers was the announcement by the minister of consumer and corporate affairs that a grant of $100,000 would be made to support its program of presenting consumer interests before regulatory boards and agencies. In making the grant the minister stated, "It is highly important that the rights of consumers be effectively represented before boards, commissions, and quasi-judicial agencies responsible for approving rate hikes or other decisions made by industries governed by federal regulations."

Great Britain. In a major decision by the British Department of Prices and Consumer Protection that should have broad implications for British consumers, it was announced that priority will be given to dealing with uncompetitive pricing arising from the concentration of industry.

STEWART M. LEE
Geneva College

CRIME

"Treat them tougher" has become the prevailing public sentiment in regard to criminals, both in the United States and abroad. Harsher sentences, mandatory imprisonment for certain kinds of crimes, and more punitive attitudes toward juvenile offenders are some of the measures that mark this mood.

At the same time, both professional and popular views of prison suggest that incarceration of offenders is not likely to produce any benefit, that it is costly, and that it often results in a more embittered individual returning to more serious criminal acts after release. Resolution of the debate involved in these views represents at the moment the most perplexing issue in the area of crime control.

Crime Statistics. Paradoxically, as public and professional attitudes toward criminals stiffen, statistics indicate a decrease in the rate of criminal activity in the United States. Year-end figures showed that murders had dropped by 8% in 1976 and robberies by 10%. The rate for all crimes covered by the report issued by the Federal Bureau of Investigation rose a little less than 1%. This compared with a 10% increase for the previous year. Larceny accounted for 55% of all reported criminal offenses; its 5% increase was the largest contributory factor in the slight rise in reported crime for the year.

The optimistic results for 1976 were followed by an even rosier statement covering the first quarter of 1977. This showed a 9% slide in crime rates, the steepest drop since the FBI began issuing quarterly crime reports in 1958. A later survey by the *Wall Street Journal* indicated further good news. In the twenty major cities examined, it was found that crime dropped an average of 8% for the second three months of the year. The declines were stunning in some cities. Boston showed a first quarter drop of 26% in its crime index, followed by a 14% drop in the second quarter. Indianapolis and Oklahoma City also reported crime declines of well over 15% for the first half of 1977.

These figures ignore white-collar crimes, of course, such as embezzlement and corporate violations, about which no accurate count is maintained. But public concern is largely focused on the "street" rather than the "suite" crimes, on mugging, burglary, rape, and various forms of assault—and it was these offenses that were becoming less common.

A particularly harsh winter was partially responsible for the decline in the number of street crimes, according to some experts. Criminals, like all citizens, prefer to stay at home when temperatures are low. Besides, there are fewer people moving about for them to prey upon in cold weather.

The major explanation for the drop in crime rates, however, involves changes in the age structure of the country's population. Street crime is principally a youthful activity. Of every 100 persons arrested for burglary or auto theft, 85 are under 25 years of age. So are 77 of every 100 persons arrested for robbery, and 58 of every 100 persons arrested for rape. As the country's teen-age population began to decline in 1977, an inevitable impact was reflected in the FBI reports on the amount of crime. The matter was summarized by James Q. Wilson, a Harvard University criminal justice expert: "The babies born in the baby boom of the '50s are starting to age," Wilson noted. "Some of the young men who helped produce the crime wave of the '60s are getting too old for that nonsense."

Murder and Manslaughter. Figures for homicide, which include murder and manslaughter, are regarded as good barometers of criminal activity, because it is believed that most killings—unlike other crimes—come to the attention of the police and can be accurately reflected in numerical tallies by enforcement agencies.

This makes homicide a particularly valuable offense for study, and a number of researchers concentrated last year on gathering detailed information on the characteristics of death-dealing crimes. A particularly grim conclusion by a panel of doctors from Case Western Reserve University was reported in the *New England Journal of Medicine*. The doctors found that the leading cause of death among young black men in the United States was neither accident nor any single disease; rather, they concluded, it was

UPI

A member of the Organized Crime Bureau inspects sculpture and negotiable bonds recovered in a raid on a Long Island clearing house for stolen items.

violent, intentional killing. Surveying homicides in Cleveland, they found that during the past two decades about 15 nonwhites died of homicide in the city for every white. "The homicide trends reported in this study shock us," the researchers noted. Dr. Amassa D. Ford, a member of the investigative team, said that the results should convince doctors to take up gun control as a medical issue.

Another study found that half of all victims of homicide had prior arrest records. The investigation also showed that almost 50% of the murder victims had "detectable levels of alcohol, narcotics, or both in their blood at the time of death." And more than half of the victims were killed by friends or acquaintances during a dispute.

Reforming Data Sources. A far-reaching measure to centralize and improve information available about the extent and nature of crime was proposed by U. S. Attorney General Griffin B. Bell in 1977. Currently, 17 federal units produce 54 sets of statistics dealing with crime, the courts, prosecutors, prisons, and other aspects of the criminal justice system. A new statistical bureau in the Department of Justice will begin coordinating operations early in 1978. Its aim is to produce a more reliable "crime indicator," a measure similar to statistics on gross national product, consumer prices, and unemployment. The new national crime data agency would also compile information regarding the manner in which charges are disposed of by the police and courts. At present, there are no cohesive data on convictions, sentences, time served in prison, or repetition of criminal acts available for the nation as a whole.

Crimes Against the Elderly. Intensive efforts are being made throughout the nation to provide special kinds of protection to older persons. Often living on low incomes, forced to reside in high-crime areas, and physically weak, such persons are particularly vulnerable to criminal activity. The new approach is one of the responses to the conclusion that older persons have too long been shamefully neglected in American society.

Among other things, law enforcement agencies are warning older persons not to be alone when they go on banking errands. In some localities, volunteers help escort the elderly on trips to the bank. In addition, older persons are advised to have their Social Security checks mailed to the bank rather than to their residence. If they do receive such checks by mail, they are told to try to avoid the streets around the first and the fifteenth of the month because muggers are aware that these are the times when government payments come to the elderly.

In California, Gov. Jerry Brown signed a measure in October that provides mandatory prison terms for persons who commit crimes against elderly individuals, or against blind or handicapped persons. Gov. Hugh Carey of New York vetoed a similar bill earlier in the year because he did not believe it "would be effective in achieving its stated goals."

Advocates of such measures point out that they follow other laws that single out specific kinds of victims for special protection. Congress made assassination of government officials a federal offense following the killing of President John F. Kennedy, and crimes against foreign diplomats are regarded by law as more serious than similar crimes against other people. There are also statutes that decree the death penalty for the murder of law enforcement officers or prison guards. Opponents say such measures are "class" legislation, and therefore are unsuitable in a democratic society where all persons are entitled to equal protection before the law. They emphasize that "special victim" laws represent a return to earlier, less satisfactory conditions under which crimes against the nobility in England were regarded as more heinous than crimes against ordinary persons. They also insist that the present laws are perfectly adequate, if only they were enforced swiftly and surely.

Homosexuality and the Law. Considerable change had marked earlier years in regard to decriminalization of "victimless crimes," or, more precisely, crimes in which there are no complaining witnesses. Abortion in the first trimester had been declared legal, penalties for marijuana use had declined, and state lotteries had been made legal. This movement received a rebuff, however, on June 7 when residents of Dade County, Florida—which includes the city of Miami—voted to repeal a county ordinance that banned discrimination in employment and housing based on a person's "affectional or sexual preference." More than 40 cities, including San Francisco, Detroit, and Minneapolis, had enacted similar legislation, though no state legislature had passed a comparable measure. The fight for repeal was led by Anita Bryant, a television performer and mother of four school children.

Organized Crime. Debate continued during the year about the entity known as the Mafia or as the Cosa Nostra, a group said to run organized crime in the United States. Some criminal justice authorities insist that Mafia control reaches deep into government circles, with one report during the year maintaining that the Mafia had infiltrated the FBI. Other persons say that members of most ethnic groups, not only Italians, are involved in organized crime. Richard D. Alba and Dwight C. Smith, Jr., supported the latter view during the year in an article claiming that the idea of the Mafia was "a journalist's cliché," and that organized crime was not very organized, but rather was "an endlessly shifting alliance among men who are endangered on all sides, by the police and by each other." Alba and Smith said that organized crime represents "the extension of entrepreneurial behavior into areas normally proscribed, for the pursuit of profit."

Crime in the News. The activities of a man who called himself "Son of Sam" received much publicity in 1977. This individual killed six young persons and wounded seven others with a .44-caliber revolver in New York City. After an extensive manhunt, police arrested David Berkowitz, a 24-year-old post office employee, for the crimes. Berkowitz was a loner, an innocuous-appearing, unexceptional person who could blend in with the city's millions. The suspect was quoted as saying that he had killed on command, that he had a sign and had followed it, and that he had to do what he did. Berkowitz

was declared by the court legally competent to stand trial.

The escape of James Earl Ray from the Brushy Mountain State Prison in Tennessee held the nation's attention for the 54-hour period during which the convicted killer of the Rev. Martin Luther King remained at large. Ray was recaptured eight miles from the prison.

In October, Joan Little escaped from the North Carolina Correctional Center for Women. In 1975, Miss Little, who is black, was acquitted of killing a white jailer. She was arrested in New York City on Dec. 7, 1977.

GILBERT GEIS
University of California, Irvine

Cory Moore surrendered to authorities in Ohio on March 9 after holding two hostages for many hours. The former marine had demanded that President Carter apologize to blacks for past mistreatment by whites. Extensive looting and vandalism during New York City's electricity blackout in July led to the arrest of some 3,700 persons.

PHOTOS UPI

Following the arrest of David Berkowitz (*right*), the alleged "Son of Sam," in Yonkers, N. Y., in August, the arresting officer displayed for the press the .44-caliber revolver found with the suspect. During a 12-month period, the "Son of Sam" had murdered six young persons and wounded seven others.

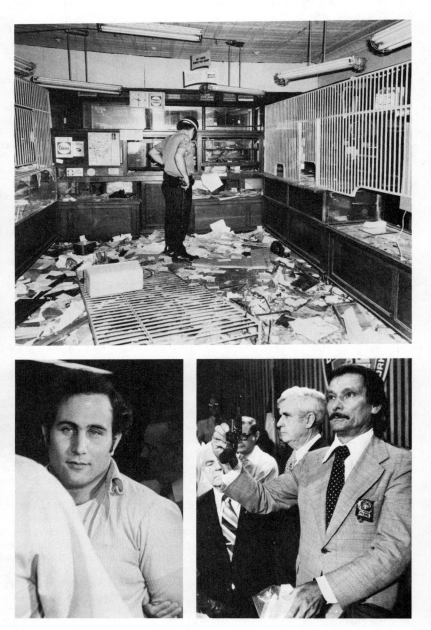

Capital Punishment

On Jan. 17, 1977, the state of Utah ended a decade long hiatus in the United States in the imposition of the death penalty by strapping Gary Gilmore to a wooden chair, placing a black hood over his head and a target over his heart, and ordering a rifle squad to take his life. Unlike other death row prisoners, the 36-year-old Gilmore had admitted robbing and killing a young hotel clerk and had declared: "I want to be executed. I don't want anybody to do anything for me." Gilmore fired his attorneys but, against his wishes, they filed appeals on his behalf and stays of execution were granted by various courts. Gilmore doggedly insisted, however, upon his execution—even attempting suicide at one point—and his wish was finally granted.

Gary Gilmore's death was a sharp reminder that a series of U. S. Supreme Court decisions during the summer of 1976 meant the resumption of executions in the United States. On July 2, 1976, nine years to the day after the nation's last legal execution, the Supreme Court held, in *Gregg* v. *Georgia* and four companion cases, that capital punishment did *not* violate the eighth amendment's ban on "cruel and unusual punishments." This was the first time the high court had ever directly faced this issue. Analysis of the Georgia, Texas, and Florida statutes approved by the court points to the following three criteria as significant: (1) a bifurcated trial, i.e., a finding of guilt separated from the penalty decision; (2) consideration by the sentencing authority (whether judge or jury) of both aggravating and mitigating circumstances; and (3) appellate review. Typical aggravating circumstances, found in various state capital punishment provisions, are that the offender have a prior felony conviction, be an inmate serving a life sentence, or have committed the crime for remuneration; that the offense have been committed during the course of some other felony; or that the victim have been a police officer, prison guard, or fire fighter.

In 1972, in *Furman* v. *Georgia,* the Supreme Court had voided most then-existing capital punishment statutes owing to their capricious and discriminatory application. The *Gregg* decision took note of public support for the death penalty, declaring that the "most marked indication of society's endorsement of the death penalty for murder is the legislative response to *Furman.*" The legislatures of at least 35 states had enacted new statutes that provide for the death penalty for at least some crimes that result in the death of another person. The court might also have observed that, at the time of the *Gregg* decision, 611 prisoners nationwide were under sentence of death, and that national public opinion polls have also expressed widespread public approval of capital punishment. In fact, a Harris Survey, based on a poll of 1,459 adults and reported in February 1977, showed that U. S. citizens favored capital punishment by a margin of 67–25. A similar survey, taken in 1965, had reported support at a margin of 47–38.

The political power of the capital punishment issue is such that no candidate for office has been able to straddle the issue; indeed, even though the mayor of New York City has no authority whatsoever with regard to the death penalty, analysts cite it as the *major* issue in the September 1977 primary elections for that office. Moreover, following *Gregg* itself, 36 states enacted new provisions modeled on the three approved death penalty statutes.

Internationally also, there has been a turnabout. In the early 1900's, for example, the death penalty was virtually abolished throughout Latin America, but it has been reinstated recently, particularly as military regimes have resumed power. In Communist countries, in Africa, and in the Far East, capital punishment has widespread support. While most West European nations, including Britain, Italy, and West Germany, have abolished capital punishment, public opinion polls consistently register majority sentiment in favor of it. Even French President Valéry Giscard d'Estaing, in one highly publicized incident early in 1977, felt forced to set aside his personal opposition to capital punishment and bow to public opinion by condemning to the guillotine the kidnap killer of an 8-year-old. After considerable debate, Canada abolished the death penalty in 1976.

The two principal reasons for the resurgence of capital punishment relate to its philosophical underpinnings. First, as the belief grew in recent decades that the treatment of criminals should stress rehabilitation rather than retribution, the obviously punitive death penalty declined in significance. But the pendulum has recently swung back to retribution (now usually referred to as "just deserts") as critics have deplored the pragmatic failure of the rehabilitative ideal.

Second, as the *Gregg* decision noted, capital punishment is "an expression of society's moral outrage at particularly offensive conduct. [This] may be unappealing to many, but it is essential in an ordered society that asks its citizens to rely on legal processes rather than self-help to vindicate their wrongs." Increased public support for capital punishment might be seen, then, as a symbolic reaction by a citizenry frustrated at constantly rising crime rates.

JACK M. KRESS
State University of New York at Albany

During a six-day, much-publicized visit to Jamaica, Cuba's President Castro met with sugarcane workers.

CUBA

Even though 1977 was officially named by the Havana government "The Year of Institutionalization," foreign affairs took precedence over domestic concerns. Some 30 high-level foreign delegations met in Havana with top leaders of the Communist party and the government. The Cuban capital was also the site of several international gatherings.

African Relations. Havana had supported black anticolonial movements in Mozambique, Guinea-Bissau, and Angola that later took over the government in their respective countries. In 1975, Cuba sent as many as 15,000 Cuban soldiers, supported logistically by the Soviet Union, to fight in the Angolan civil war and help the pro-Marxist movement defeat two pro-Western, nationalist groups. Late in 1976, Cuba began to withdraw its troops from Angola, but stopped doing so early in 1977, apparently because the government of President Agostinho Neto continued to battle antigovernment guerrillas.

Late in 1977, Cuban troops in Angola increased to 19,000, according to the White House, which saw in the buildup a serious obstacle to improving ties with Havana. At the same time, the State Department placed at 2,700 the number of Cuban military advisers in 13 other African countries, including Ethiopia.

Zaire, charging that Cuba was involved in the invasion of the Shaba province by Angola-based rebels in March, broke off relations with Cuba, which denied any role in the military operations. In his July 26, 1977, speech, President Fidel Castro said that, military personnel excluded, about 6,000 Cuban civilians were serving abroad on "internationalist missions," 90% of them in Africa.

In March and April, Castro visited seven African countries (Libya, Somalia, Ethiopia, Tanzania, Mozambique, Angola, and Algeria),

in addition to the Soviet Union, East Germany, and Southern Yemen. His African tour preceded a trip to Africa by Nikolai Podgorny, chairman of the Presidium of the Supreme Soviet of the USSR. According to some Western observers, Havana and Moscow, working in tandem, were trying to eliminate American and Chinese influence in Africa.

During his African visit, Castro tried to reconcile Ethiopia and Somalia by urging Somali President Mohammed Siad Barre to moderate his demands on Ethiopia's Ogaden region. Castro's diplomacy failed to defuse the animosity between the two allies of the Soviet Union. His preference for Ethiopia soon became apparent, and Cuban experts began arriving in Addis Ababa to train local forces in the use of Soviet military equipment, simultaneously shipped there by Moscow. As a result, in November, Somalia expelled Soviet military advisers and broke diplomatic relations with Cuba.

Another result of Castro's trip was Cuba's support for Colonel Muammar al-Qaddafi in the ongoing Libyan-Egyptian dispute. In July, the Egyptian ambassador in Havana was told his country must "stop actions it has undertaken against Libya." Also, during a visit to Uganda, the Cuban Deputy Defense Minister Gen. Francisco Cabrera joined President Idi Amin in affirming that the goal of both countries "has always been the fight against colonialism, Zionism, and racism."

Explaining Cuba's growing interest in Africa, Castro said, "We are not only a Latin-American nation, we are also a Latin African nation." Commenting on reports that the Carter administration considered Cuban military presence in Africa a major obstacle to rapprochement between Cuba and the United States, Castro said

Direct Cuban-U. S. communications reopen: Ramon Sanchez Parodi is the chief of Cuba's interest section, Washington.

Cuban tanks were displayed during a full-scale military parade, Plaza de la Revolution, Havana.

UPI

in July that he would never withdraw his troops from Angola as a quid pro quo for Washington's lifting of the economic blockade against his country, because Cuba's solidarity with Angola and other African countries was not negotiable. Castro denied Cuba had sent troops to Ethiopia.

U. S. and Caribbean Relations. During 1977, Cuba and the United States moved toward resuming normal diplomatic relations, in what both sides realized would be a long and complex process. Shortly after entering the White House, President Carter ended American surveillance flights over Cuba. In March, the Carter administration allowed U. S. visitors to spend dollars in Cuba, a move that facilitated American tourism in that country. In April, after the first direct talks (in New York and Havana) between U. S. and Cuba officials since 1961, when the relations were broken, the two countries signed a fishing agreement. Under the accord, Cuban vessels were permitted to fish in the U. S. fishing zone.

On its part, Cuba indicated that even though it allowed a 1973 bilateral antihijacking agreement to lapse, it would abide by its provisions. On September 1, Cuba in Washington and the United States in Havana opened the offices of their missions, called "interest sections," to carry out some diplomatic and consular functions. A growing number of U. S. political figures and businessmen visited Cuba to explore trade possibilities with Havana.

Cultural exchanges also began. In 1978 the Ballet Nacional de Cuba was scheduled to perform in Washington and New York. But many issues remained to be discussed, among them that of political prisoners in Cuba, who according to Castro total between 2,000 and 3,000; the settlement of American claims to expropriated property in Cuba; and the lifting of the U. S. trade embargo on Cuban goods.

Castro's six-day state visit to Jamaica in October was one of several signs of Cuba's interest in the neighboring Caribbean area. In moderate speeches, Castro assured Jamaicans that Cuba did not intend to interfere in their domestic affairs and promised material assistance. A

number of Caribbean political leaders and intellectuals traveled to Havana, invited by the Castro government, as did Caribbean Communist leaders.

Domestic Affairs. The Cuban economy showed no appreciable change. The sugar harvest, the mainstay of the economy, totaled about 5.6 million tons, according to foreign estimates. As in the last several years, the 1977 sugar output and other meaningful economic data were not made public by Havana. Cuba's export earnings declined as the price of sugar fell on the world market. This has forced the government to reduce purchases in western countries, affecting the chances for an early economic recovery. In discussions with American businessmen and other visitors to Cuba, Castro and other Cuban leaders spoke frankly of the country's economic plight. The Cubans indicated that the end of the country's present dependence on Soviet aid was not in sight. The Soviet subsidy was estimated by western economists at between 3 million and 4 million dollars a day.

The country's institutionalization—adjustment to new juridical, political, and economic structures established in 1975 and 1976—proceded slowly, especially the introduction of monetary-mercantile relationships between Cuba's state-owned producing, consumer, and importing enterprises.

GEORGE VOLSKY
University of Miami

CUBA · Information Highlights

Official Name: Republic of Cuba.
Location: Caribbean Sea.
Area: 44,218 square miles (114,524 km²).
Population (1977 est.): 9,600,000.
Chief Cities (1970 census): Havana, the capital, 1,755,400; Santiago de Cuba, 276,000; Camaguey, 196,900.
Government: *Head of state and government,* Fidel Castro Ruz, president (took office under a new constitution Dec. 1976). *Legislature* (unicameral)—National Assembly of People's Power.
Monetary Unit: Peso (0.83 peso equals U. S.$1, 1977).
Manufacturing (major products): Sugar products, tobacco products.
Major Agricultural Products: Sugarcane, tobacco, rice, oranges and tangerines, sweet potatoes and yams, cattle, poultry.

CYPRUS

The death of the president, Archbishop Makarios III, and the continued Turkish occupation of the northern part of the island dominated the news in Cyprus during 1977.

President's Last Months. Archbishop Makarios suffered a heart attack on April 3, while officiating at Palm Sunday services. He soon resumed a busy schedule, including a visit to London where he was present, on June 7, at St. Paul's Cathedral for the thanksgiving service marking the silver jubilee of Queen Elizabeth II. While in England, he also attended the conference of Commonwealth leaders. That same month, he met with Greek Premier Constantine Caramanlis and other Greek officials at Athens, who emphasized the solidarity of the Greek government with the Greek Cypriots against the Turkish occupation. Back on Cyprus, Makarios made a stirring address to a huge crowd at Nicosia on July 20, the third anniversary of the Turkish invasion of 1974, which forcibly split the island in two. This turned out to be the last spectacular appearance of his public life. He died on August 3, following his second heart attack.

Successors. Makarios' secular and religious functions were split upon his death. Metropolitan Chrysostomos of Paphos became acting archbishop until he was elected to the office and

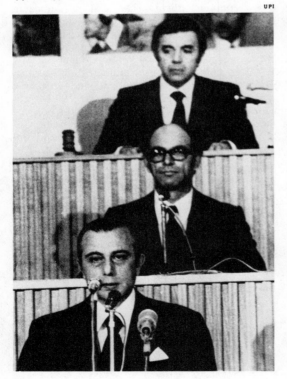

Leaders of the Cypriot House of Representatives listen as Spyros Kyprianou takes the oath as president, Sept. 3.

UPI

formally enthroned in November; and Spyros Kyprianou, speaker of the Cyprus House of Representatives and former foreign minister, immediately became acting president. A special presidential election that would have been held in September was averted when the four leading Greek Cypriot political parties—including the far left and right—agreed that Kyprianou should be the single candidate. He was sworn in on September 3 to finish Makarios' term (expiration, February 1978).

The Turkish Occupation. Both Makarios and Kyprianou faced a critical problem: how to find a formula that would end the Turkish hold on northern Cyprus, an area unilaterally proclaimed the "Turkish Federated State of Cyprus," with Rauf Denktaş, as president. Early in 1977, U. S. President Jimmy Carter appointed Clark M. Clifford to help mediate the dispute. Clifford traveled to Athens, Ankara, and Nicosia in February. But although he was well received by all parties then, he seemed to irritate the Turks and Turkish Cypriots when, attending Makarios' funeral in August, he voiced support for American recognition of the new president as ruler of the whole island. Denktaş flatly said that Kyprianou had no jurisdiction over the north. Intercommunal talks between the Greek and Turkish Cypriots broke down even before the death of Makarios. These had been sponsored by Secretary General Kurt Waldheim of the United Nations, which maintained a peace-keeping force on Cyprus throughout the year.

Kyprianou went to New York in October to address the UN General Assembly and stress the gravity of the Cyprus situation. During the visit, he met with President Carter, Clark Clifford, and Secretary of State Cyrus Vance. Foreign Minister John Christophides also worked for a solution through the United Nations.

The Demographic Issue. Some 200,000 Greek Cypriot refugees, displaced from the north in 1974, remained in the south, deterred by the Turks from returning to their homes. The Cypriot government strongly condemned this situation, as well as Turkish efforts to bring in mainland Turks to repopulate the north, particularly around the port city of Famagusta.

See also OBITUARIES.

GEORGE J. MARCOPOULOS, *Tufts University*

─────── **CYPRUS · Information Highlights** ───────

Official Name: Cyprus.
Location: Eastern Mediterranean.
Area: 3,572 square miles (9,251 km²).
Population (1977 est.): 645,000.
Chief Cities (1973 est.): Nicosia, the capital, 112,000; Limassol, 80,000.
Government: *Head of state and government,* Spyros Kyprianou, president (took office Aug. 1977). *Legislature*—House of Representatives.
Monetary Unit: Pound (0.41 pound equals U. S.$1, July 1977).
Manufacturing: Food and beverage processing, nonmetallic mineral products.
Major Agricultural Products: Potatoes, grapes, citrus fruits, wheat, barley, carobs, sheep, goats, pigs.

CZECHOSLOVAKIA

The event that in 1977 attracted worldwide attention to Czechoslovakia was the "Charter 77" and the vitriolic campaign of denunciations and reprisals unleashed against its signatories by the regime of Gustav Husák.

Charter 77. On Jan. 1, 1977, a group of 242 citizens of various convictions and walks of life signed a declaration called Charter 77, in which they accused Husák's regime of gross violations of the human rights Czechoslovakia had committed itself to respect by the Final Act of the Helsinki Conference in 1975. When the delivery of the charter to the Czechoslovak Federal Assembly, the chairman of the Council of Ministers (premier), and the Czechoslovak News Agency was prevented by the arrest of the signatories deputed to do so, the charter was made available to correspondents of the foreign press. Thus, the Czechoslovak public learned about it by word of mouth and from foreign broadcasts. In the ensuing months the charter was signed by several hundred more persons, and numbers of additional statements were issued, further detailing the regime's disregard of human rights.

Afraid that these activities could lead to a revival of the reform movement of 1968, the regime resorted to repressive measures against the charter's signatories. Many were harassed by the police, others dismissed from their jobs, or arrested; some of the leaders were forced into exile. In addition, various groups were pressured by threats of dismissals to sign declarations condemning the charter.

Economy. The following economic results were achieved in the first half of 1977, the figures denoting increases over the corresponding period in 1976: industrial production, 5.6%; construction, 4.2%; labor productivity, 4.7% (industry) and 4.2% (construction); retail trade, 3.6%; foreign trade, 13.7%; average wage, 3.2%; and monetary income of the population, 4.8%. Freight transport was down 0.5%.

While the overall results were considered satisfactory, 11% of industrial enterprises and 42% of construction enterprises failed to fulfill the economic plan. Fault was also found with the quality of industrial products. Export to non-socialist countries fell below the planned target, and only 38.5% of the apartments scheduled to be built in 1977 were completed by midyear. Prices were raised in July for a number of consumer goods, such as coffee (50%), chocolate products (33%), and woolen and cotton textiles (35%). Conversely, prices for some products were lowered: synthetic fabrics (28%), television sets (26%), and refrigerators (16%). Prospects of a 10-million-ton crop of grain were somewhat dimmed by exceptionally inclement weather at harvest time.

Foreign Affairs. During an official visit, in early July, of a Polish party and government delegation, headed by Edward Gierek, the two countries agreed to intensify the exchange of experience and cooperation in every field. Similar agreements with Rumania and Hungary were reached during visits to these countries by a Czechoslovak delegation, headed by President Husák, in June and September. In August, Husák received the Shah of Iran in Prague, and an agreement on economic, scientific, and technical cooperation was signed on that occasion. A new Czechoslovak-East German treaty of friendship, cooperation, and mutual assistance, to be valid for 25 years, was signed in October.

EDWARD TABORSKY
University of Texas at Austin

— CZECHOSLOVAKIA • Information Highlights —

Official Name: Czechoslovak Socialist Republic.
Location: East-central Europe.
Area: 49,370 square miles (127,869 km²).
Population (1977 est.): 15,000,000.
Chief Cities (1975 est.): Prague, the capital, 1,165,000; Brno, 355,000; Bratislava, 335,000.
Government: *Head of state,* Gustav Husák, president (took office 1975). *Head of government,* Lubomir Strougal, premier (took office 1970). *Communist party secretary general,* Gustav Husák (took office 1969). *Legislature*—Federal Assembly: Chamber of Nations and Chamber of the People.
Monetary Unit: Koruna (5.97 koruny equal U. S.$1, 1977).
Manufacturing (major products): Machinery, chemicals, petroleum products, glass, textiles, iron, steel.
Major Agricultural Products: Sugar beets, wheat, potatoes.

DANCE

For the first time since the American dance boom began a decade ago, the 1977 dance season was marked by an unusually high number of cancelled engagements. The reasons were financial and administrative, or rooted in labor disputes.

Artistically, however, performance standards in both ballet and modern dance remained at the lofty level of recent years. It was also a dance season that relied heavily upon revivals and star vehicles rather than creativity.

Nonetheless the revivals included Martha Graham's 1931 "Primitive Mysteries," a masterpiece that was inspired by the Spanish-Indian rituals of the American Southwest and which remains the epitome of the stark, spare style of Graham's modern dance in the 1930's.

Two popular premieres in New York City, both big on spectacle, were Mikhail Baryshnikov's version of "The Nutcracker" for American Ballet Theater and George Balanchine's new "Vienna Waltzes" for the New York City Ballet. Baryshnikov, Natalia Makarova, and Rudolf Nureyev were again the top superstars.

Three superstars from another generation—the bygone Age of the Ballerina—also made rare appearances to the delight of their followers. The ballerinas included Alicia Alonso, the 55-year-old Cuban star, who returned to American Ballet Theater to dance her first full-evening "Giselle" in the United States in almost 20 years. Maya Plisetskaya, the 51-year-old Prima

MARTHA SWOPE

George Balanchine's new "Vienna Waltzes" for the New York City Ballet was particularly favored by the public.

Ballerina of Moscow's Bolshoi Ballet, was seen in Maurice Béjart's contemporary works with Belgium's Ballet of the 20th Century. Margot Fonteyn, 58, of Britain, appeared at a benefit for Martha Graham's company in a solo from Frederick Ashton's ballet, "The Wise Virgins."

The less glamorous side of the dance world's concerns surfaced at the beginning of the year with an orchestra strike that shut down the New York City Ballet for six weeks. Shortly afterward, the Joffrey Ballet announced cancellation of its four-week New York spring season in order to keep down its projected deficit. A similar reason was given for the cancellation of the Dance Theater of Harlem's New York season. After its spring season at the City Center, the Alvin Ailey American Dance Theater decided to cancel its usual summer season at the State Theater in Lincoln Center. The Dance Umbrella series lost some scheduled performances in an administrative-financial dispute with the Roundabout Theater and moved its fall season to the Entermedia on Second Avenue.

It was the Minskoff Theater that was the site of Merce Cunningham's first independent Broadway season. The company's week-long engagement, sold out, introduced Cunningham's modernist ideas to a broader audience. "Travelogue," a Cunningham premiere in collaboration with artist Robert Rauschenberg, used a sound score with Australian bird calls by John Cage. There was a gentle retrospective tone to a season that brought back Cunningham's serene 1958 "pointillist" ballet, "Summerspace," and underscored the master-student relationship between the 57-year-old Cunningham and his young dancers. Yet the local premiere of "Sounddance," with Cunningham in the lead, brought the audience to its feet.

Other dancers also appeared on Broadway. Among them was the innovative group of former Dartmouth students known as Pilobolus. At the Uris Theater, Béjart's company brought on the usual debate about the French-born choreographer. The compromise verdict from the critics suggested that although Béjart was a poor choreographer, he should be viewed as a man of the theater. Béjart himself performed in "Notre Faust." "Isadora," his vehicle for Plisetskaya, made camp out of Isadora Duncan's legend.

Plisetskaya was at her most compelling in "Bolero," also danced by another guest star, Suzanne Farrell of the New York City Ballet.

Also at the Uris, Rudolf Nureyev presented himself and three members of the Royal Danish Ballet, Vivi Flindt, Johnny Eliasen, and Anne Marie Vessel. The program of three ballets was grim but allowed Nureyev to perform in new U. S. roles, such as the psychopathic dancing teacher in Flemming Flindt's "The Lesson," Pierrot in Glen Tetley's "Pierrot Lunaire," and in Béjart's "Songs of a Wayfarer." Nureyev also danced for a week with Martha Graham's company on Broadway, continuing his exploration of modern dance. The first week's programming was built around his appearances in "El Penitente" and "Appalachian Spring."

It was Graham's own dancers, however, who had the strongest impact. Elisa Monte and Tim Wengerd gave true power to Graham's erotic and sophisticated new duet, "O Thou Desire Who Art About to Sing." A more romantic tone, of love recalled, was set in the other Graham priemere, "Shadows." Yet it was "Primitive Mysteries" that became one of the season's most talked-about events.

Mikhail Baryshnikov and Marianna Tcherkassky starred in "The Nutcracker," also for the ABT.

Cuban star Alicia Alonso returned to the American Ballet Theater to dance "Giselle."

PHOTOS MARTHA SWOPE

A very different kind of revival was the New York City Ballet's "Bournonville Divertissements," a series of excerpts from ballets by Denmark's famous 19th-century choreographer, August Bournonville. A mild sensation was caused by this staging from a foreign ballet tradition and for a company established especially to create new works. Yet the City Ballet had the advantage of a cast of several Danish-trained dancers (Peter Martins, Adam Luders, Helgi Tomasson) and the production, staged by former Royal Danish Ballet soloist Stanley Williams, soon became an audience favorite.

Tomasson and Peter Schaufuss, another Dane in the City Ballet, also made memorable debuts as Albrecht in "Giselle" on separate occasions as guest stars with American Ballet Theater during the City Ballet strike. Schaufuss later joined the National Ballet of Canada.

This was the Toronto company's first season in New York without Nureyev. Fernando Bujones and Schaufuss were invited as guests to bolster the troupe's weak male contingent. Yet with the novelty of a new ballet, based on a Canadian story, Ann Ditchburn's "Mad Shadows," and an admirable production of Ashton's "La Fille Mal Gardée," the company held its own. The Stuttgart Ballet was the other major foreign ballet company to visit the United States in 1977. The new ballets were Kenneth MacMillan's "Requiem," William Forsythe's "Daphne," and a version of "The Sleeping Beauty" that relied upon production values more than first-rate classical dancing. The Metropolitan Opera House, where these companies performed, also became the new "home" of American Ballet Theater, which revived the Royal Ballet production of Michel Fokine's "Firebird" for Makarova and introduced into the repertory Glen Tetley's tribute to John Cranko, "Voluntaries." Among the guest stars in addition to Alonso were Eva Evdokimova, who made her U. S. debut in "Swan Lake." Earlier, important debuts came from the troupe's own dancers—Martine van Hamel in "Giselle" and Gelsey Kirkland in "Swan Lake."

Although the year was low on creativity, there were exceptions. Paul Taylor's new "Images," "Dust," and "Polaris" showed the modern-dance choreographer still riding the crest of originality. Taylor's dancers appeared to be at their peak and it was hard to recall that the company was on the verge of dissolution in 1976. Balanchine's "Vienna Waltzes" for the City Ballet was also inventive although it was not considered one of his deeper works. Spectacle and even a Hollywood-style ballroom finale set the mood for this five-part exploration of waltz rhythms to music by Johann Strauss II, Franz Lehar, and Richard Strauss, all framed by Rouben Ter-Arutunian's elaborate decor. Two new ballets were produced by Eliot Feld for his company. Baryshnikov, as guest, and Christine Sarray performed a mock-bicentennial pas de deux to music by Charles Ives called "Variations on 'America'." Feld himself appeared as a fumbling Scottish swordsman in a group work inspired by Beethoven's arrangement of Scottish and Irish folk songs, "A Footstep of Air."

The Joffrey Ballet returned to New York in the autumn with company premieres of·Ashton's "Les Patineurs" and "Jazz Calendar." The hope of Robert Joffrey, the troupe's director, of having his company become the American repository of the British choreographer's ballets, seemed closer to fulfillment. For the first time, the Joffrey Ballet presented a full-evening ballet, albeit an untraditional one. "Romeo and Juliet," by the Argentine choreographer Oscar Araiz, was greeted more warmly by the public than the critics who appeared jarred by Araiz's abstract approach to the Prokofiev score. Gerald Arpino created a solo to gospel music for Christian Holder, "Touch Me." A pleasant novelty was "La Vivandière," a 19th-century excerpt by Arthur Saint-Léon that was "reconstructed" especially for the Joffrey.

In modern dance, there were seasons by the José Limon company and companies headed by Alwin Nikolais, Murray Louis, Twyla Tharp, Paul Sanasardo, Pearl Lang, and Louis Falco.

Two new international festivals—both outside New York—were born: the "Spoleto Festival, USA" in Charleston, S. C., and the First Chicago International Dance Festival.

ANNA KISSELGOFF
Chief Dance Critic, "The New York Times"

DELAWARE

Delaware was confronted by two burdensome problems in 1977. One was the state's poor finances; the other was the ruling by federal courts that public-school pupils be bused between the suburbs and the city of Wilmington.

State Finances. Delaware's financial plight comes from a long history of meeting legislative expenditures by bond issue rather than taxation. When Gov. Pierre duPont came to office in 1977, he moved to bring the state into fiscal balance. But the inability of the governor and the General Assembly to agree resulted in the legislature's enactment of a $453-million state budget over the governor's veto. Toward the end of the year the financial picture brightened somewhat. Leading banks made short-term money available, and the state's credit rating improved.

Busing. Desegregation in public education has long been a thorny issue in Delaware. In 1968, the public schools underwent complete redistricting. Wilmington, whose pupils are more than 90% black, was retained as a separate district, while the surrounding new suburban districts were left close to 90% white. In 1976, the U. S. District Court declared this unconstitutional and ordered the creation of a new composite district that included both suburban and urban areas; busing within this large district was also ordered, beginning in 1978. The U. S. Supreme Court upheld this ruling in late 1977. Opposition by suburban residents has been intense.

Legislation. The General Assembly enacted a new capital punishment statute; decreed licensing of adult book stores to prevent the spread of so-called "porn shops"; permitted production of Laetrile; adopted the concept of zero-based budgeting; extended unemployment insurance to migrant farm workers; and made the Wilmington wage tax permanent.

Corrections. In early 1977, the U. S. District Court reduced the number of inmates in state prisons to 600 because of overcrowding. The resultant furloughing of some dangerous convicts caused a public uproar.

PAUL DOLAN, *University of Delaware*

DELAWARE · Information Highlights

Area: 2,057 square miles (5,328 km²).
Population (1976 est.): 582,000.
Chief Cities (1970 census): Dover, the capital, 17,488; Wilmington, 80,386; Newark, 21,078.
Government (1977): *Chief Officers*—governor, Pierre S. duPont IV (R); lt. gov., James D. McGinnis (D). *General Assembly*—Senate, 21; House of Representatives, 41 members.
Education (1976–77): *Enrollment*—public elementary schools, 60,747; public secondary, 61,526; nonpublic, 18,700; colleges and universities, 29,956 students. *Public school expenditures,* $233,000,000 ($1,739 per pupil).
State Finances (fiscal year 1976): *Revenues,* $661,580,-000; *expenditures,* $702,412,000.
Personal Income (1976): $4,092,000,000; per capita, $7,030.
Labor Force (July 1977): *Nonagricultural wage and salary earners,* 237,600; *unemployed,* 19,400 (7.3% of total force).

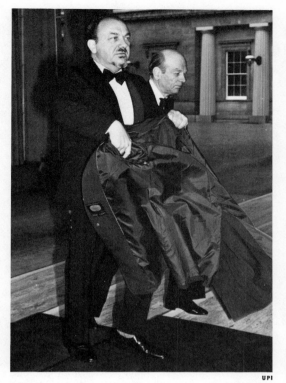

UPI

Following election gains by his party, Danish Prime Minister Jørgensen formed a new minority government.

DENMARK

The election of a new Parliament and the naming of a minority cabinet, followed by an economic compromise in September and a devaluation of the currency, were not very effective in curing the economic ills of Denmark.

Political Affairs. Due to the deteriorating economic situation and a political deadlock regarding employment and related policies, Social Democratic Prime Minister Anker Jørgensen dissolved Parliament and announced new elections for February 15. Held at a time favorable to the Social Democrats, the election returned 65 members of that party to Parliament (a gain of 12), while the Liberals, led by Poul Hartling, suffered a severe loss, electing only 21 representatives. By gaining two seats (from 24 to 26), the Progressive Party assumed the position of Opposition Party to the Social Democrats.

Unwilling to form another majority coalition cabinet, Jørgensen decided to go it alone with a Social Democratic minority government. There were a number of reshufflings and new faces in the cabinet. K. B. Andersen retained the foreign ministry and also assumed the post of minister of foreign economic affairs vacated by Ivar Nørgaard, who became minister of trade.

Economic Affairs. The weak Danish economy did not improve during 1977. The year started with a payments deficit of 11.5 billion (U. S.)

kroner and the foreign debt exceeded 38 billion kroner. Unemployment stood at about 7%, and strikes and other labor disputes served to aggravate the situation. One of the more serious conflicts, involving the biggest Danish newspaper, *Berlingske Tidende,* and its tabloid edition, *B. T.,* ended on June 21 after a strike lasting five months, the longest in Danish newspaper history.

A main effort to improve the national economy was initiated in September following protracted negotiations among four parties (Social Democrats, Liberals, Conservatives, and Radical Liberals) and the cabinet. This so-called "Midway" Compromise introduced new and heavier consumer taxes, the hope being that they would yield $1 billion yearly over three years. This was the twelfth major "crisis package" adopted since February 1974.

While the Midway Compromise was being debated, it was announced that the Danish krone would be devaluated by 5%. The devaluation was explained as an adjustment necessitated by the 10% devaluation of the Swedish krona. Since September 1976, the Danish krone has been devalued 14%.

Cultural Affairs. In August the spotlight was turned to the relationship between government and cultural life. Mrs. Ritt Bjerregaard, the minister of education, published a book containing an exchange of letters with the well-known author Klaus Rifbjerg. Mrs. Bjerregaard maintained that the Social Democratic Party supported art and cultural activities which are unrelated to the politics of the party and working-class values. Her book raised a storm of protest, even within her own party.

Christiania. The commune of Christiania, consisting of about 80 adherents of a "new life style" who had settled illegally in military barracks in Copenhagen, seemed to be nearing its end. The commune had gained status as a social experiment when the Parliament in 1973 approved its tenure on government property for three years. In February the Court of Appeals of the city of Copenhagen decided that the so-called "Free City" would have to be evacuated. The ruling was immediately appealed to the Supreme Court.

ERIK J. FRIIS
Editor, "The Scandinavian-American Bulletin"

──────── **DENMARK · Information Highlights** ────────

Official Name: Kingdom of Denmark.
Location: Northwest Europe.
Area: 16,629 square miles (43,069 km²).
Population (1977 est.): 5,100,000.
Chief Cities (1975 est.): Copenhagen, the capital, 1,300,-000; Aarhus, 246,000; Odense, 169,000.
Government: *Head of state,* Margrethe II, queen (acceded Jan. 1972). *Head of government,* Anker Jørgensen, prime minister (took office Feb. 1975). *Legislature* (unicameral)—Folketing.
Monetary Unit: Krone (6.20 kroner equal U. S.$1, Aug. 1977).
Manufacturing (major products): Beverages, processed foods, machinery, ships, chemicals, furniture.
Major Agricultural Products: Barley, oats, sugar beets, dairy products, cattle, hogs.

A Vaccine Against Tooth Decay

The dream of a life free from tooth decay is a reality for few—in America, for example, only one in 2,000. Research efforts are progressing in the United States and elsewhere to extend this reality to everyone by developing a safe and effective vaccine against the disease, which scientists call dental caries. In this age, when smallpox and polio have been almost eradicated and open-heart and kidney-transplant surgery are common, why must people suffer fear of dental treatment or the pain of neglect?

The problem of effective prevention of caries is many-sided. As in all disease, there are three basic components: 1) the host, the teeth and supporting structures; 2) the agent, a complex combination of different micro-organisms referred to as oral flora; and 3) the environment, the mouth, with its normal saliva plus the food people eat. In the past, preventive measures have sought to increase "host resistance," that is, to strengthen the teeth, by counseling mothers-to-be to maintain adequate nutritional intake of proteins and the minerals calcium and phosphorus during pregnancy, and to feed their children properly once they are born. This includes fluoride supplements from birth through age 10, wherever the water supply is deficient in this natural mineral ion that increases decay resistance.

Each mouth contains thousands of millions of microbes. These exist in a dynamic balance between different organisms that are generally harmless and do not cause disease in their human host. In fact, this oral flora usually prevents harmful organisms from taking up disease-causing residence. Research indicates that caries is caused by combinations of different bacteria which adhere to the teeth and gingivae (gums), metabolize some of the foods eaten, and produce acids, or bacterial toxins, strong enough to dissolve the mineral-like enamel coating of the teeth. Once the enamel has been pierced, decay spreads more rapidly through the softer dentine layer into the pulp, which contains the nerves and blood vessels. The same toxins attack the gingivae, inducing bone loss and loosening the teeth, a process called periodontal disease, or pyorrhea. Effective brushing, flossing, and irrigation of the teeth pry loose the colonies referred to as dental plaque. Limiting the dietary intake of sugar and refined starches deprives the bacteria of the raw materials they utilize most readily to produce both demineralizing acid and sticky polysaccharides that help them adhere to tooth surfaces.

Can we expect a vaccine against caries-producing bacteria? The answer is a qualified yes. There are, however, some complex stumbling blocks. To produce a vaccine, the caries-causing microbe or microbes have to be identified and a way found to induce immunity in human beings that could attack the bacteria in the oral environment.

Research into the cause of caries dates back to W. D. Miller and A. S. Underwood, two American dentists in the last quarter of the 19th century. They showed that bacteria from the mouth can produce enamel-dissolving acid. The Englishman J. K. Clarke, in the 1920's, found a bacterium which he suspected caused decay and called it Streptococcus mutans (meaning chains of bacteria that change from spherical to rod-like shapes). Further research in Scandinavia, England, Canada, and the United States during the past 50 years has shown that S. mutans can produce decay in test animals, but there is also evidence that other members of the oral flora cause caries in man.

Vaccines stimulate the production of antibodies which circulate in the blood and can attack a specific organism. Dr. Thomas Lehner, working with animals at Guys Hospital in London, is investigating the immunological basis for some test vaccines against decay. Some antibodies called IgG and IgM, may pass from the blood into the mouth in the minute amounts of fluid that normally seep out of the crevices where the gingivae meet the teeth. These crevicular antibodies adhere to bacteria and enhance the action of certain white blood cells, which engulf and destroy S. mutans. IgA antibodies, secreted in saliva, may prevent bacteria from adhering to teeth.

Inducing antibody production can be done in several ways. Dr. Morris Wagner at Notre Dame, Ind., has studied injection of dead S. mutans in rats. Dr. William H. Bowen, who inoculated monkeys with the live bacteria while working at the Royal College of Surgeons in London, is currently researching an oral vaccine at the National Institute for Dental Research in Bethesda, Md. At the Forsyth Dental Center in Boston, Mass., Dr. Martin Taubman is investigating the use of a Streptococcus enzyme preparation claimed to have few side effects.

As with all drugs, once a vaccine for use in human beings is developed, suitable testing must proceed to ensure it is both safe and effective. The experience of the German-manufactured tranquilizer thalidomide, used in the 1950's, and the more recent controversies over side effects of the swine flu vaccine dramatize the need for exhaustive testing.

In summary, the problem of caries is complicated by the intricate nature of the causative agents in a complex oral environment. But research is proceeding at the early stages of animal experimentation on approaches to a safe and effective vaccine against tooth decay.

SIMON W. ROSENBERG, D. M. D.

DJIBOUTI

Djibouti, the former French Territory of Afars and Issas, became Africa's 49th independent state on June 27, 1977, and was admitted into the UN in September.

A hot, barren land without resources, its importance is its location at the entrance to the Red Sea and its position as Ethiopia's sole rail link to the outside world. The population is divided between Issas (akin to the Somali) and Afars, related to Ethiopian peoples, and some "foreigners" (Europeans, Arabs, and other Africans). The Afars and Issas are bitter rivals for power in the poverty-stricken country, reflecting the tension between the neighboring states of Somalia and Ethiopia.

Government and Politics. Djibouti is a parliamentary state with a president, prime minister, and a popularly elected 65-member National Assembly. Since both Somalia and Ethiopia flooded the territory with their nationals to influence the result of the pre-independence voting, a major problem exists in determining who is a legal inhabitant and voter.

The ruling party is the "African Peoples' League for Independence," led by President Hassan Gouled Aptidon, an Issa. The party holds all 65 legislative seats (33 members are Issas, 30 Afars, and 2 Arabs). Two Afar parties, the "National Union for Independence" and the "Popular Liberation Movement," are the (legal) Opposition. The first prime minister, Ahmed Dini Ahmed, resigned on December 17.

Economy. Djibouti is totally without significant resources or hope of economic development, relying on continued French aid and Afro-Arab assistance for survival. The annual budget is only $40 million, and imports exceed exports by more than 6 to 1. Most Europeans left at independence. The unemployment rate is 85%.

ROBERT GARFIELD, *DePaul University*

DRUG ADDICTION AND ABUSE

Two related 1977 research findings promised to open up new advances in the control of pain and in dealing with some of the problems of narcotic addiction.

Opiate Receptors and Internal Narcotics. During 1977 it became known that human beings, as well as all other vertebrates, have built-in chemicals that relieve pain, and that both the naturally-occurring substances and the drugs called narcotics fit into the same receptor sites on the synapse of nerve cells. The synapse is the junction of two nerve cells where a chemical reaction transmits an electrical impulse from one cell to another.

The narcotic drugs are those that relieve pain, produce pleasurable feelings (euphoria), and reduce various drives, such as drives for food or sex. The classical narcotics are either

---

DJIBOUTI · Information Highlights

Official Name: Republic of Djibouti.
Location: Eastern Africa.
Area: 8,495 square miles (22,000 km²).
Population (1977 est.): 110,000.
Chief City (1976 est.): Djibouti, the capital, 102,000.
Government: *Head of state,* Hassan Gouled Aptidon, president (took office June 1977). *Legislature* (unicameral)—National Assembly.
Monetary Unit: Djibouti franc (166.67 D. francs equal U.S.$1, Nov. 1977).

---

opium or active principles derived from opium, such as morphine or codeine. Heroin is included because it is made by treating morphine with strong acetic acid. In addition, a series of synthetic compounds—methadone, Demerol, and others—also produce narcotic effects. After it became evident that drugs like morphine acted in specific parts of the brain by fitting onto specific receptor molecules, scientists wondered why such receptors existed in vertebrates. It now seems clear that certain chains of amino acids (the building blocks of protein) also set down on these receptors and also reduce the sensation of pain. These particular amino acid chains are called endorphins (from endogenous morphine-like compounds). They vary from chains of 5 to chains of 91 amino acids. One linkage is a short chain consisting of tyrosine-glycine-glycine-phenylalanine-methionine.

Interestingly, just as the narcotic antagonist drugs are able to eliminate the effects of all narcotic agents, so do they also cancel out the effect of the endorphins. This they accomplish by moving both the narcotics and the endorphins off the receptor site and occupying it themselves. The endorphins modulate the sensation of pain and the emotional reaction to it. They do not completely eliminate the pain which is useful as a signal when something goes wrong.

Although it will take time before the application of these scientific developments can help with the problem of narcotic abuse, the new knowledge opens up potentially rewarding investigatory approaches:

1. It now seems feasible to assume that one day a nonaddicting narcotic drug can be developed for the treatment of severe pain. The development would be a boon to medicine and would make the cultivation of opium and the manufacture of synthetic narcotics superfluous.

2. The current treatments of narcotic addiction may be improved by developing a specially designed molecule that would occupy the narcotic receptor for long periods of time. This would eliminate the effect of a drug like heroin.

3. Alternatively, the possibility of inactivating the receptor site could be studied. Without a binding site to occupy, the effects of injected narcotics would be negligible.

LAAM. The long-acting methadone, LAAM (levo-alpha-acetyl-methadol), reached the final field testing phase in 1977 and may have a much more direct impact on the treatment of heroin addicts. This narcotic, intended for the maintenance of patients dependent on heroin, has certain advantages over methadone for maintaining those who are unable to benefit from or who are unwilling to try drug-free treatment programs. Its duration of action is 48–72 hours in contrast to methadone which must be swallowed daily. This not only saves patient and staff time, but it can eliminate all take-home medication from maintenance clinics. The diversion of take-home methadone onto the black market has been a major problem in the past, with hundreds of deaths in the United States yearly from illicit-methadone overdoses. A further advantage of LAAM is that it reduces from daily to 2–3 times a week the drug-dependent person's preoccupation with drug taking.

SIDNEY COHEN, M. D.
Neuropsychiatric Institute
University of California

ECUADOR

Politics. The year was marked by continuous maneuvering in connection with the military regime's announced plan for reestablishing constitutional government. The plan called for submission to the electorate of two alternative proposals for a constitution and then general elections for president and Congress. By March, regulations for the proposed referendum were approved, and an electoral court was established to supervise the process.

The original plan called for full return to constitutional government by January 1978, but in April the government postponed that date.

Quito riot police prepare to quell students protesting the Ecuador visit of U. S. First Lady Rosalynn Carter.

UPI

The referendum was later set for January 1978 and the general elections for some time after that.

Early in May, the "first commission," named to draw up an entirely new constitution, decided to extend the franchise to all citizens over 21, remove the clause which has traditionally barred anyone whose parents had not been born in Ecuador from running for president, and drop the ban that former presidents run again. These moves made possible the candidacies of Assad Bucaram, former mayor of Guayaquil and head of the Concentracion de Fuerzas Populares party (whose parents were born in Lebanon) and a number of former presidents. The "second commission," which proposed amendments to the 1945 constitution, kept the literacy franchise.

Assad Bucaram openly proclaimed his candidacy for president. It appeared likely that there would be at least two other candidates.

Behind the maneuvers of civilian politicians were those of the military. Adm. Alfredo Poveda, head of the junta, was generally regarded as most committed to the program for constitutional government, while army commander Guillermo Duran Arcentales was widely reported to be plotting a coup to end such efforts.

Strikes. Serious labor problems complicated the political situation. On May Day, the country's three labor confederations held a joint demonstration. On May 18, they organized a partially successful nationwide general strike. That same day, the Unión Nacional de Educadores (UNE) called a general teachers' strike which lasted a month. The government in reprisal outlawed UNE and arrested its leaders.

In October, the 1,800 workers of the Aztra sugar plantation near Guayaquil struck and seized the mill, whereupon some 1,500 police attacked them, killing at least 25. Several labor leaders were subsequently arrested. These events precipitated widespread protests.

Economy. Ecuador continued to enjoy the effects of its oil prosperity. On Dec. 31, 1976, the Gulf Oil Co. had been expropriated, and on May 31 it received the first payment of $82 million for its property. During the year, plans were announced for a large cement plant and a brewery. Several loans were received, the largest being $70 million from private foreign banks.

ROBERT J. ALEXANDER, *Rutgers University*

─────── **ECUADOR · Information Highlights** ───────

Official Name: Republic of Ecuador.
Location: Northwest South America.
Area: 109,483 square miles (283,561 km²).
Population (1977 est.): 7,500,000.
Chief Cities (1974 est.): Quito, the capital, 557,000; Guayaquil, 814,000.
Government: *Head of state and government,* Alfredo Poveda Burbano, president of military junta (took office Jan. 1976). *Legislature*—Congress (dissolved Feb. 1972).
Monetary Unit: Sucre (25 sucres equal U. S.$1, Aug. 1977).
Manufacturing (major products): Processed foods, textiles, petroleum products.
Major Agricultural Products: Bananas, coffee, cacao, rice, potatoes, sugarcane, cotton, forest products.

EDUCATION

In U. S. educational circles in 1977, concern and interest centered on national test scores, high school competency, and a California case involving affirmative action (reverse discrimination). In Canada, the province of Quebec enacted legislation making French the mandatory language in schools and other agencies. Elsewhere, universities in Italy experienced extreme overcrowding, and rioting by South African black students was again widespread.

United States

Scholastic Aptitude Tests (SAT). An advisory panel investigating the reasons for the decline in Scholastic Aptitude Test scores since 1963 issued its report in August. The panel was chaired by former U. S. Secretary of Labor Willard Wirtz and was sponsored by the College Entrance Examination Board and the Educational Testing Service. The report pointed out that the decline was partially due to the fact that many previously excluded youths—the poor, minorities, women—were now taking the tests for college entrance. Generally schools have been unable to meet the special needs of these youths. Other possible causes were more electives which did not require student exertion in reading and writing, lower standards, higher rate of absenteeism, grade inflation, automatic promotions, undue TV watching instead of homework, more students from broken homes, decline in student motivation, and the traumas of Vietnam, Watergate, and the assassinations of national heroes. The report said that there is, in school and society, "observable evidence of diminished seriousness of purpose and attention to mastery of skills and knowledge." It emphasized the "central importance of restoring the traditions of critical reading and careful writing."

Minimum Competency. The back-to-basics movement and test score declines have led 24 states to adopt minimum competency tests for high school diplomas. New York State will have compulsory reading and mathematics tests in 1979 and civics, health, and writing tests in 1980 (some districts use them optionally now). California's 1,042 school districts will set their own standards and tests. A widely watched Greensville County, Virginia, experiment has replaced automatic promotion with achievement promotion. Chicago, attempting to reform schooling from the bottom up, does not put students in grade levels but assigns each pupil at his or her competency level in every subject, allowing the bright to progress quickly and the slow to get special tutoring. Newly appointed U. S. Commissioner of Education Ernest L. Boyer wants to see a "network of basic skills centers around the country." Critics charge that minimum proficiency requirements are window dressing, that minimum standards are set too

UPI

A severe winter and a shortage of natural gas closed many schools. The Columbus (O.) *Dispatch* printed supplements to help children keep up with classroom work.

low, that politicians and testing organizations hastened the pendulum swing, that competency testing narrows educational goals by prompting teachers to teach to the tests, and that competency testing hampers creativity of excellent students and teachers.

Desegregation and the U. S. Supreme Court. Important Supreme Court desegregation rulings issued in late June held that no more desegregation was required under the Constitution than was necessary to redress or balance intentional segregation policies. When Dayton, Ohio, officials challenged as too sweeping federal orders to bus students until integration matched the city's racial composition, the court responded by returning the busing plan to the lower court for reexamination but also affirmed court-ordered busing as an appropriate way to desegregate. When Michigan officials balked at paying for remedial courses for Detroit students (already being bused) who had suffered in segregated classes, the court held that federal judges may go beyond busing to correct segregation wrongs. This Detroit decision marked a new approval by the court of compensatory remedies to offset specific segregation violations.

Chicago schools opened tensely under a voluntary desegregation plan that bused about 900 blacks to less crowded white schools. A white antibusing rally led to some injuries and arrests.

In Boston, where a Parent Advisory Council defused racial tension, school authorities worried about low SAT scores, particularly for blacks.

Allan Bakke filed a suit charging reverse discrimination. As the case, upheld in California, came up before the U. S. Supreme Court in October, an anti-Bakke protest was held.

PHOTOS UPI

Louisville, Ky., schools, scene of past racial turmoil, opened without incident. The main concerns were student discipline (14,611 suspensions in 1976–77) and white flight to the suburbs to escape integration (large drop in enrollment).

Significant white flight also affected the Dallas school integration plan begun in 1976.

A boycott by blacks marked school opening in Amite County, Miss. Since 1969, the district has had separate schools for boys and girls. White authorities claim that the sex segregation was started by a white-and-black parent committee with court approval as a way to ease racial integration. Blacks claim that sex segregation is retained to keep black boys from contact with white girls. After years of protest, blacks began the school boycott and took the case to federal court.

New York City Teacher Integration. Having found disproportionate numbers of white teachers in white schools and black teachers in black schools, civil rights officials threatened to withhold federal funds from impoverished New York City unless its teachers were integrated. In September, the compromise teacher integration plan, reluctantly initiated by Education Chancellor Irving Anker and American Federation of Teachers (AFT) President Albert Shanker, assigned on a racial basis the 3,500 teachers rehired in 1977 from among the 17,000 teachers laid off in 1975 and 1976. The plan avoided forced transfer of the city's 51,000 teachers, as occurred in Chicago and Los Angeles. The intent is to have by 1980 the same racial ratio of teachers as students. New York City now has 67% black and Hispanic students and 17% black and Hispanic teachers.

The Handicapped. A new civil rights movement emerged when various handicapped persons held sit-ins at the federal and regional offices of the Department of Health, Education, and Welfare in April. Subsequently, a White House Conference on Handicapped Individuals was held in May. Advocates won their demands for implementing recent laws barring discrimination against handicapped persons. Under the All Handicapped Children Act, schools must offer free public education to all the handicapped who, including the unreached, may total up to 35 million. Only 40% of the 8 million handicapped children in public schools now receive adequate special education at an average cost of $2,800 per pupil per year (compared with $1,400 for a normal child). Controversy has arisen over "mainstreaming," educating the handicapped with normal children; over the cost to local schools, since federal aid per handicapped child will rise from only 5% in 1978 to 40% in 1982; and over including drug addicts and alcoholics as handicapped.

Winter School Closings. A record freeze combined with natural gas shortages to close many schools for up to one month in January and February. Hard-hit Pennsylvania declared a state of emergency. In Ohio, declared a disaster area, commercial TV and radio carried lessons in Columbus, and makeshift classes met in available heated public places.

Corporal Punishment. On April 19, the U. S. Supreme Court upheld the decision that the 1970 paddling of 2 Dade County, Florida, junior high school students did not violate the Constitution's ban on cruel and unusual punishment. Some groups objected to the approval of corporal punishment in school. But the close ruling (5–4) was praised by the AFT.

Bakke Case. The U. S. Supreme Court heard evidence in October in the case of Allan Paul Bakke, 37, denied admission to the University of California Medical School at Davis in 1973 and 1974. His suit, upheld by the California Supreme Court in 1976, charged reverse discrimination since his admission scores were higher than those of 16 minority students (out of 100) admitted annually under the school's special minorities' affirmative action admissions program. Of the record 58 briefs submitted to the court, that of the U. S. Justice Department was important. The first Justice Department draft allegedly sided with Bakke against the medical school's minority quota policy. But this threat to the government's affirmative action policy (i.e., preference to compensate for past discrimination) was modified in a September 19 statement which stressed that race should be one among other factors in minority hiring and admissions and intimated that, since lower courts had not examined the school's admission policy carefully, the case should be reexamined by the California court. The Bakke case is important in loudly raising the charge of reverse discrimination against the majority as inevitable under affirmative action for minorities. It has split the Jewish-black axis which originally worked for affirmative action. Jews oppose quotas, which historically limited their entry to medical schools. Blacks see quotas as the only way to make up for long-time discrimination. The smaller labor-oriented AFT opposes quotas; the 1.8 million-member National Education Association (NEA) backs quotas. The split is cited as a reason for the breakdown of AFT-NEA merger talks. A Supreme Court ruling is expected in 1978.

Medical Schools. The Association of American Medical Colleges (AAMC) opposed a 1976 federal health education law requiring the 119 U. S. medical schools to accept as third-year transfer students in 1978 some 1,500 Americans studying in medical schools abroad. Nineteen of the more famous medical schools said they would refuse federal funds rather than comply, claiming that they would have no voice in selecting such transfers, stating that they were already filled to capacity, and charging that many Americans studying in medical schools abroad had been rejected by U. S. medical schools. The disputed law was being reconsidered by Congress.

In 1976, U. S. medical schools admitted 15,-613 first-year medical students (8.9% from minority groups) out of 42,000 applicants. A 1977 report listed a national average of 1 white doctor per 538 white persons and 1 black doctor per 4,100 blacks.

Kent State. On July 12, police arrested 194 persons protesting construction of a $6 million gymnasium annex on Blanket Hill, Kent State University. The protesters refused a court order to vacate the site they had occupied for 62 days. Instead of a gym, they wanted a memorial to the four students slain there in 1970.

Enrollments, Costs, Graduates. The Health, Education, and Welfare Department's National Center for Education Statistics issued the following 1977–78 estimates (1976–77 comparisons in parentheses):

Enrollments, kindergarten through grade 8: 33.3 million pupils (33.8 million, —1.5%); high school: 15.7 million (15.8 million, decline of under 1%); colleges and universities: 11.3 million (11 million, +2.5%; slow rise expected until early 1980's); total: 60.3 million students (60.6 million, —.5%).

Number of teachers, elementary and secondary, 2.4 million (2.5 million, small decrease); colleges and universities, 700,000 (680,000, + nearly 3%). Graduates, high school, 3,150,-000+ (3.1 million+); bachelor's degrees, 969,-000 (918,000); first professional degrees, 64,000 (60,000); master's, 356,000 (338,000); doctorates, 35,000 (37,000).

Education directly involved 63.7 million people (63.6 million), or 3 out of 10 Americans; at a total expenditure for public schools and colleges of about $117 billion, plus $27 billion for private institutions from all sources, constituting 8% of the 1976 gross national product, and divided among state governments, $50.8 billion, or 35.3% ($45 billion, 34.5%); local, $41.2 billion, or 28.6% ($38.2 billion, 29.3%); Federal, $15.2 billion, or 10.55% ($13.4 billion, 10.3%); and all other sources, $36.8 billion, or 25.55% ($33.7 billion, 25.9%).

Kent State University students protest the construction of a gymnasium near the site where four students were killed by National Guardsmen in 1970.

On June 16–17, 1977, the anniversary of black student-led riots in Soweto, South Africa, in which more than 600 blacks died, defiant youths assembled in illegal groups to mark the day.

UPI

International

Quebec's French Language Schools. Long conflict over substituting French for English as Quebec's language of instruction reached a climax on August 26 when the Assembly passed a law making French mandatory in schools, courts, government, and other agencies. English-speaking schools were limited to their present level. If one parent living in Quebec received a primary education in English, his or her child may attend an English-language school. Children of families entering Quebec from other provinces and foreign countries will attend French language schools. Some English-language schools are defying the law. Although pressed to do so, the federal government has not challenged the law's constitutionality, presumably because of the backing of Quebec's French-speaking majority. Still, there is concern among French Quebeckers because of their declining birth rate and because most immigrants to Canada prefer English-speaking areas.

Observers believe the new law will help create a sovereign French-speaking nation within Canada. Francophiles say economic survival is behind the new law. Just as English Canada is more powerful economically and politically than French Canada, so the 900,000 English-speaking Quebec minority has been politically and economically more powerful than the 5 million Francophones, 75% of whom speak only French. Quebec separatists suspect that Canada's bilingual policy is not designed for unity but to continue English-speaking economic dominance. Hence, observers explain, as English-speaking Canadians have moved more toward bilingualism, Quebec separatists' fears have forced them to raise to primacy the French language and culture, particularly in schools. (*See also* QUEBEC.)

Italy. Italian universities, all under state control, were pressured in 1968 by student radical protests to accept, for political reasons, an open admissions policy for any secondary school graduate. Since then, mounting enrollments have caused intense overcrowding. Total university enrollment of 255,000 in 1962 rose to 731,000 in 1975, without a corresponding increase in professors or facilities.

Rome University, built originally for 40,000 students, enrolled over 88,000 in 1970–71 and about 150,000 in 1977. Student riots, which closed Rome University for short periods in 1976 and 1977, occurred less for political reasons than because too few jobs awaited university graduates. In 1977, only 30% of the 72,000 new graduates expected to find jobs. The rest joined the estimated 240,000 to 350,000 jobless degree holders, out of Italy's 1 million unemployed youths.

University saturation led the minister of education to announce on June 28 a two-year ban on foreign students, evoking complaints from many of the estimated 14,000–20,000 foreign students who annually attend Italian universities. The announced ban, lifted in September, hit Greek students hardest. An estimated 14,000 Greeks are in Italian universities, and 1,500 more planned to enter in 1977. About 450 U. S. students were expected in 1977, 75% of them to enter Italian medical schools. Even before the announcement that the ban had been lifted, one group of 105 U. S. students under the auspices of the Italo-American Medical Foundation, flew to Perugia, Italy, in July to study Italian, hoping to be assigned to medical schools. Most had been rejected by at least a dozen U. S. medical schools. Many are Italian-Americans. Most hoped to transfer to U. S. medical schools after two years of study in an Italian medical school (annual tuition cost to students, $70; estimated annual cost to Italian Government, $1,235).

South Africa. Quietly defying the Republic of South Africa's school segregation laws, the Roman Catholic bishops of that country endorsed school integration. In March 1976, a dozen blacks, Asians, and mixed-race Coloreds were admitted to three formerly all-white, Catholic schools. In November 1976, 50 more nonwhites were admitted. Six formerly all-white, Catholic schools are now integrated, despite warnings from the government that the action is "contrary to established policy." Government officials in the Transvaal and Cape provinces

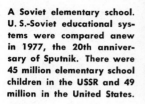

A Soviet elementary school. U. S.-Soviet educational systems were compared anew in 1977, the 20th anniversary of Sputnik. There were 45 million elementary school children in the USSR and 49 million in the United States.

threatened to close the offending schools and to prosecute offending parents. But Catholic authorities stood firm; 85% of Catholic white parents and most white pupils supported desegregation. All of South Africa's church-related schools enroll only 5% of the nation's white students; the other 95% (some 900,000) attend free compulsory white-only state schools. South Africa's 3.7 million black students attend less adequate all-black schools where tuition costs are $50 annually. The government spends 10 times as much for white students as for black students. The student-to-teacher ratio is 20–1 for whites and 60–1 for blacks. The Catholic church's breaking of the segregation barrier had important symbolic significance, since it induced the Anglican church to announce in January its intent to integrate 20 schools and the Methodist church to integrate 4 schools. The South African government has been loathe to do more than to censure the Roman Catholic authorities, particularly since the international uproar that followed the repression of student-initiated rioting in the ghetto township of Soweto.

Student Unrest. Black student-led riots on June 16–17, 1976, in the sprawling black township of Soweto (acronym for Southwest Township), 10 miles (16 km) southwest of Johannesburg, triggered a six-month wave of violence in South Africa in which over 600 blacks died. On the June 16–17, 1977, anniversary, police used tear gas to break up illegal gatherings of youths. Also in June, Soweto students led an unprecedented black march on police headquarters in white Johannesburg.

Black students, who observers noted had studied little during the last year, demanded the resignation of black school board members of Soweto's eight high schools, charging that they were not independent but were agents of the government (board members appoint teachers and supervise funds). Students also said that they would ask for the resignations of the eight high school principals. Observers feared that such forced resignations would lead to the collapse of the high schools. The government announced plans to build six new schools in So-

weto, to upgrade the township's 2,300 teachers, and to expand the recently established five adult training centers. A private organization was also working to upgrade the abilities of Soweto's high school students.

Widely scattered black-student riots erupted again on October 5–6. Soweto students had been on strike for weeks. Secondary schools in a black homeland were closed. Some 400 students from a nearby township marched in protest to the center of Grahamstown, 500 miles (800 km) south of Johannesburg (96 youths arrested). Students at a school in Whittlesea, Cape Province, smashed windows (62 arrested). Bookshelves were burned in a Transvaal high school.

Observers say that black students have become adamant about politicizing their schools and that it is the increased job shortage that has obsessed them with politics. No matter what favorable action white officials announce, blacks see the national government's Bantu (i.e., black) education as deliberately segregated and hence an inferior system.

USSR. The year 1977 marked the 20th anniversary of the launching of Sputnik, which began the U. S.–USSR space-education race. As a direct result of Sputnik, the U. S. National Defense Education Act was passed in 1958. U. S. federal aid to education has increased significantly since. Commenting on the Sputnik anniversary, *Newsweek* magazine noted the following: 49 million U. S. elementary and secondary school students (45 million in the USSR), 11.3 million U. S. university and technical school students (5 million, USSR); 26.7% U. S. youths aged 18–24 in higher education institutions (10%, USSR); 36.2% U. S. adults over age 25 completed high school (18.7%, USSR); 26.5% U. S. adults over age 25 with some higher education (5.5%, USSR); 3,047 U. S. institutions of higher education (861, USSR); $144 billion U. S. annual education budget ($27.6 billion, USSR), 3.2 million U. S. teachers and professors (2.9 million, USSR), 99% U. S. literacy rate (99.7%, USSR).

FRANKLIN PARKER, *West Virginia University*

During their historic meeting in November, Egypt's President Anwar el-Sadat and Israel's Prime Minister Menahem Begin held a "working dinner" at the King David Hotel in Jerusalem.

UPI

EGYPT

Dramatic events related to Egypt's dispute with Israel were dominant in 1977.

Relations with Israel. Throughout 1977, Egypt's primary concern continued to be Israel's ten-year-old occupation of its territory in the Sinai, taken in the Six-Day War of 1967. Egyptian policy was chiefly affected by two factors: a major U. S. effort to reconvene the Geneva conference on the Middle East, stalled since 1973, and the emergence of Menahem Begin as prime minister of Israel. Sadat seemed to become more conciliatory as the year progressed. In April, he expressed willingness to assume "full relations" with Israel five years after the signing of a Geneva accord, although he reiterated the necessity of some Palestinian presence at Geneva—a stance that Israel rejected. Until November, however, little was accomplished toward breaking the stalemate.

Then, taking Sadat's word that he would go to the Knesset for peace, Prime Minister Begin invited him to Israel for talks. Sadat accepted and, on November 19 (the feast of their biblical ancestor, Abraham), became the first Arab head of state to make a visit to the Jewish state. While in Israel, Sadat met with Begin and other Israeli leaders, addressed the Knesset (parliament), and visited Jerusalem's holy places and Israel's monument to the victims of the holocaust. In his parliamentary address, Sadat made it clear that he had "not come to sign a separate peace [or] to arrange a third disengagement agreement." He repeatedly called for a Palestinian entity and for the Israeli withdrawal from all occupied Arab lands, including Old Jerusalem. But he did recognize Israel's right to exist.

Although few details were made known of the Sadat-Begin meeting, it was clear at once that the trip was an opportunity for leaders of two nations, technically at war, to become personally acquainted. After the Jerusalem visit, Sadat arranged a follow-up Israeli-Egyptian summit in Cairo; other Arab states, the United States, and the USSR were invited. Only the United States accepted. Begin made a reciprocal visit to Egypt on Christmas Day.

While Sadat's diplomatic ventures were welcomed by the United States and the Egyptian and Israeli peoples, reaction in the Arab world was mixed. Sudan, Morocco, Oman, and Somalia supported Sadat outright. Jordan, Tunisia, and Saudi Arabia viewed the moves with caution. But representatives of hard-line Arab nations—Algeria, Southern Yemen, Libya, Iraq, and Syria, as well as the Palestine Liberation Organization—met in Tripoli, Libya, and sought measures to "freeze" political and diplomatic relations with Egypt for what they regarded as treasonable behavior. Iraq, believing the Tripoli conference was too soft on Egypt, withdrew. Sadat's retaliation was swift and dramatic: he broke off diplomatic relations with the five on December 5. (*See also* MIDDLE EAST.)

Other Foreign Relations. Early in the year, Kuwait and Saudi Arabia (with the United States) pledged renewed economic support for

---

EGYPT • Information Highlights

Official Name: Arab Republic of Egypt.
Location: Northeastern Africa.
Area: 386,660 square miles (1,001,449 km²).
Population (1976 census): 39 million.
Chief Cities (1975 est.): Cairo, the capital, 8,400,000; Alexandria, 2,500,000.
Government: *Head of state,* Anwar el-Sadat, president (took office Oct. 1970). *Head of government,* Mamdouh Muhammad Salem, prime minister (took office April 1975). *Legislature* (unicameral)—People's Assembly.
Monetary Unit: Pound (0.39 pound equals U. S.$1, Aug. 1977).
Manufacturing (major products): Cotton textiles, processed foods, fertilizer, iron and steel.
Major Agricultural Products: Cotton, forage plants (berseem), rice, wheat, sugarcane, millet, corn.

Sadat's troubled government. In July, open warfare broke out on the Libyan-Egyptian frontier. After several days of fighting, Arab mediators were successful in ending the incidents.

In October, the parliaments of Egypt and Sudan met jointly for a week, proclaiming their desire for eventual unification of the two nations.

President Sadat visited the United States in April. He requested military as well as economic aid (amounting to roughly $1 billion). It was later announced that American firms would help Egypt repair its Russian-built MiG fighters.

In May, Egypt announced its intention of sending air force units to Zaire to help put down a rebellion there.

Domestic Affairs. President Sadat's removal of subsidies from a number of basic foods and other items led to rioting early in the year. The removal had been urged by the International Monetary Fund, the United States, and the Arab financial backers of Sadat's government, Saudi Arabia and Kuwait. The immediate reaction was to rescind the price increases but the basic problems remained. The first complete census since 1960 was completed in late 1976; it counted 39 million Egyptians and predicted nearly 80 million by 2007. In view of this population increase, not enough foodstuffs are produced and Egyptian industry remains underdeveloped. Sadat's various measures to rescind Nasserite controls have contributed to the economic chaos of the country as has the continued need to arm militarily.

After easing prices, Sadat issued a strongly repressive decree emphasizing law and order. The decree was then submitted to the voting public as a referendum. Not surprisingly, it was approved by a 99.4% vote, a result viewed skeptically by many Egyptians. Sadat tended to blame leftists and Communists for inciting the riots. Arrests were made.

In July, a former cabinet member, Mohammed Hussein el-Zahabi, was murdered by a terrorist belonging to a clandestine extremist religious group. By late August, about 80 members of the group, including its leader Ahmed Mustapha Shukri, had been arrested. Several death sentences resulted. This was an acute problem for Sadat because of his need to court religious support. In mid-August, Ramadan—the Muslim month of fasting—began and there were several violent incidents. One Coptic (Christian) church was burned and pictures of the Virgin Mary were smashed. At this time the government announced its intention to introduce "strict Islamic law" into Egypt. Of particular concern to the nation's Copts (about 10% of the population) was the proposal of the death penalty for apostasy. After strong appeals to Sadat, the government announced that the proposed decrees would be modified or abandoned.

CARL LEIDEN
University of Texas at Austin

ELECTIONS, U. S.

In the "off-year" elections of 1977, the political spotlight was focused on local issues and candidates. Republicans, hoping to recover from the loss of the White House in 1976, claimed to find signs of a GOP resurgence in their victories in three out of four special elections for congressional seats held during the year. But 1977's various other election contests offered little evidence of a national trend toward either major party.

Governorships. The major parties split the year's two gubernatorial races, on Nov. 8, the Democrats holding on to New Jersey while the Republicans retained Virginia. These results left the Democrats with 37 governorships and the Republicans with 12. One state, Maine, has an independent for governor.

The outcome in New Jersey was surprising, given the expectations of political leaders in both parties. Incumbent Democratic Gov. Brendan Byrne, a political novice when he was first elected in 1973, appeared to be in serious difficulty early in the year. He had lost the backing of many leaders in his own party and alienated much of the electorate largely because of his support for a state income tax, the first in New Jersey's history. Byrne's position seemed to be so weak that nine other candidates entered the Democratic primary in June against him. But the opposition splintered among the challengers and Governor Byrne won renomination.

His Republican opponent, State Sen. Raymond Bateman, was generally considered the favorite to defeat Byrne in November. Bateman made the income tax the main issue, vowing to oppose its extension when it came up for renewal in 1978. But as unpopular as the tax was among voters, Bateman had trouble convincing the electorate that the state could get along without it or some alternative revenue measure. As a result his overall credibility suf-

The Charles Robbs prepare to vote. President Johnson's son-in-law won Virginia's lieutenant governorship.

UPI

fered. Byrne campaigned vigorously, defending the tax and using the powers of his incumbency to full advantage to gain publicity. He won a second term with 57 percent of the vote.

The Virginia governorship had long been considered exclusive Democratic property. But then Republicans Linwood Holton and Mills Godwin captured that office in 1969 and 1973, respectively. In 1977, with Godwin ineligible to succeed himself, the Republicans chose as candidate the lieutenant governor, John Dalton.

Democratic hopes in the state initially were bolstered by the presence of Jimmy Carter in the White House. Party leaders thought that the president could transfer some of his popularity in the South to the Democratic gubernatorial candidate, Henry Howell. But Carter's hold on Virginia was tenuous; it was the only Southern state that did not support him for president. And Howell, in two previous efforts to win the governorship, alienated many voters in the conservative Old Dominion by his populist rhetoric and style. Howell tried to present a more subdued image to the electorate in the 1977 campaign, but memories of his controversial past lingered on, and Dalton swept to an easy victory. In a bright spot for Democrats, Charles S. Robb, son-in-law of the late President Johnson, was elected lieutenant governor.

Mayoralties. Contests in the nation's three largest cities highlighted municipal elections in 1977. In New York, incumbent Mayor Abe Beame, discredited by the city's financial troubles, lost the Democratic nomination to Manhattan Congressman Ed Koch. Koch capitalized on New Yorkers' concern about crime by supporting capital punishment in his campaign for the nomination. In the general election Koch defeated Liberal Party candidate Mario Cuomo, who had originally been the choice of Gov. Hugh Carey, Republican Roy Goodman, and Barry Farber, a Conservative.

In Chicago, the death in 1976 of Richard Daley, the city's longtime mayor and boss, set the stage for a special election in 1977. Democrat Michael Bilandic won and inherited control of Daley's party machine.

Los Angeles' first black mayor, Thomas Bradley, won a second four-year term with 59 percent of the vote against 11 challengers. Mayor Bradley is a Democrat; the municipal election is nonpartisan.

Blacks, who make up an increasing proportion of the nation's urban population, won other victories in municipal contests. Ernest Morial, a state appeals judge, was elected the first black mayor of New Orleans. And City Councilman Henry L. Marsh was chosen the first black mayor of Richmond, once the capital of the Confederacy. Detroit's black Mayor Coleman Young won reelection to a second term. In Buffalo, however, Conservative James Griffin defeated Democrat Arthur Eve, a black.

Congress. In special elections to the House of Representatives, Democrats suffered a net loss of three seats. In Minnesota's seventh district, Republican Arlan Stangeland captured the seat vacated by Democratic Rep. Bob Bergland, who had been named secretary of agriculture. In Washington's seventh congressional district Republican Jack Cunningham won the seat left vacant by Democrat Brock Adams, who quit to become secretary of transportation. In Louisiana Robert Livingston became the first Republican to represent the first congressional district since Reconstruction. The vacancy was created by the resignation of Democrat Richard Tonry, who was convicted of campaign fraud. In Georgia's fifth district Democrat Wyche Fowler won the seat vacated by Democrat Andrew Young when he became United Nations Ambassador.

ROBERT SHOGAN
Washington Bureau, "Los Angeles Times"

Off-year elections: Ernest Morial (*left*), a Louisiana appeals judge, was the first black to be elected mayor of New Orleans. Dennis Kucinich, 31, took over the mayor's desk in Cleveland.

PHOTOS UPI

A sign in front of the District Building, Washington, D. C., publicizes the need for energy conservation.

ENERGY

The cold winter of 1977, massive oil imports, and the vigorous proposals for energy reform introduced by President Jimmy Carter made 1977 a year which may be remembered as the turning point in U. S. energy policy.

Despite exhortations to conserve and past talk of energy independence, U. S. oil consumption continued to rise, and in the course of 1977 Americans imported almost half of the petroleum they used. The continued existence of the Organization of Petroleum Exporting Countries (OPEC) and worldwide oil demand kept oil prices high. Partly due to high oil prices, the United States again suffered a balance of payments deficit. Foreign oil availability was not a problem, as the continued slowdown in the world economy and OPEC desires for increased economic growth among its members kept supply up with demand.

A combination of a very cold winter, declining U. S. gas supplies, gas utility unpreparedness, and insufficient transmission capacity led to a severe natural gas shortage, especially in the Eastern and Midwestern states where factory and school closures created economic and social disruptions.

The price of electricity continued to go up as fuel costs rose, a drought in the Western states reduced cheap hydroelectric supplies, and the cost of building new power plants continued to increase faster than inflation. The decline in demand for electricity, which had begun with the economic decline and the 1973 OPEC embargo, reversed, and demand for electricity grew slightly, despite higher electricity prices.

As a result of these trends and their impact on the American public and economy, Congress followed President Carter's proposals and reorganized the energy agencies of the government. The president also made a major effort to formulate a national energy policy that would promote energy conservation and shift dependence away from declining and expensive supplies of oil and natural gas to increased use of coal and renewable energy sources, as well as increased use of nuclear energy.

Energy Reorganization. During October 1977, the Department of Energy was formally established. This was the first new cabinet-level department to be set up since the Department of Transportation in 1966. The Department of Energy brings together into a single organization functions that had been widely scattered. The Energy Research and Development Administration (ERDA), the Federal Energy Administration (FEA), and the Federal Power Commission (FPC), are among the most important divisions of the new cabinet department. The Energy Research and Development Administration was established in 1974 when the Atomic Energy Commission was abolished. At that time, the research functions of the AEC were transferred to ERDA and the commission's regulatory functions to the Nuclear Regulatory Commission (NRC). The NRC was not affected by the new department.

The Federal Energy Administration was established at about the time of the oil embargo of 1973 to centralize regulatory functions relating to oil. Most of the FEA functions are concentrated in the Department of Energy under an Economic Regulatory Administration.

The Federal Power Commission functions are largely included in the Department of Energy's Federal Energy Regulatory Commission

Energy adviser James R. Schlesinger looks on attentively as President Jimmy Carter briefs a Congressional committee on his national energy plan.

UPI

(FERC). President Carter appointed James R. Schlesinger, who had served in various capacities in the Nixon and Ford administrations, secretary of the new department.

At year-end it was too early to tell how effective the Department of Energy would be in promoting and administering a coherent national energy policy. Several features of the department are important in understanding how it will operate. The department includes both research and development (R&D) functions as well as regulatory functions. These functions may come into conflict with each other in the Department of Energy just as they did within the AEC. The Department of Energy has an assistant secretary for the environment with responsibility to assure that environmental considerations are fully addressed before technologies or national policies are implemented. It remains to be seen whether the assistant secretary for the environment will be able to muster the power to say "no" to policies which are environmentally unsound.

In the transition from the Atomic Energy Commission to the Energy Research and Development Administration and subsequently to the Department of Energy the enchantment with nuclear energy has significantly diminished. The prospect of nuclear power gave rise to the Atomic Energy Commission. In more recent times, disenchantment with nuclear power has set in. Even the once powerful Joint Committee on Atomic Energy of the U. S. Congress was abolished, and there is no assistant secretary for nuclear energy within the new department. Nuclear energy is simply one of the many technologies being explored by the department.

The National Energy Plan. Energy became a major theme of the new Carter administration. Its National Energy Plan proposed striking changes in our use of energy. The plan was presented to the American people and to Congress in three steps, each on nationwide television. On Monday, April 18, the President addressed the nation on energy problems. With the exception of war, the President called the energy situation the "greatest challenge that our country will face during our lifetime." On Wednesday, April 20, the plan was formally presented to the Congress in joint session, and on Friday, April 22, the details of the plan were discussed in a presidential news conference. The main features of the administration's proposals were:

"to reduce the annual growth rate in energy consumption by more than 2%;

"to reduce gasoline consumption by 10%;

"to cut imports of foreign oil to less than 6 million barrels a day, less than half the amount that we would be importing if we do not conserve;

"to establish strategic petroleum reserve supply of at least a billion barrels, which will meet our needs for about 10 months;

"to increase our coal production by more than two thirds, to over a billion tons a year;

"to insulate 90% of American homes and all new buildings; and

"to use solar energy in more than 2.5 million American homes."

The goals were to be accomplished by 1985.

Some of the items called for under President Carter's plan were to be carried out by administrative directive. A large number required Congressional approval, however. The Congress did not respond to the president's proposals with enthusiasm. Major differences of opinion between the Congress and the administration came to light during Congressional hearings on the energy package. The House passed legislation generally supportive of the President's goals. The Senate was much more resistant. The approach of the House was generally to introduce taxes on energy at the point of end use, thereby driving up the cost of energy to consumers but not passing these higher costs to energy producers. The Senate took the view that energy problems can best be addressed by providing incentives to energy producers to develop more resources. Among many areas of disagreement, deregulation of natural gas stands out as particularly significant. At year-end the House and Senate had failed even to come close to a compromise, and no energy legislation emerged. The fate of nuclear breeder reactor development was also uncertain. Energy issues awaited the second session of the 95th Congress.

Citizen Awareness. Despite the importance of energy as a major presidential theme, most Americans did not appear to consider energy issues critical. Several polls taken during the year showed that a sizeable proportion of Americans did not even know that the United States imports a large portion of its oil. Many Americans also believed that the energy problems were related not to impending oil shortages at all, but were due to the machinations of the energy industry. Energy has thus declined substantially in perceived importance as compared to the time of the oil embargo, for example.

Yet there are important energy related matters of which citizens are highly aware. The cost of gasoline is an example. The major theme of automobile advertising during 1977 was fuel economy. The estimated miles per gallon figures were almost the first information given out by car salesmen. The exceptionally cold winter led to astronomical electricity bills in some parts of the nation. Monthly electric bills above $400 were reported for some all-electric homes. On balance, the single aspect of the energy problem of which most people were aware related to the increasing cost of energy. All signs point toward even greater energy prices in the future.

One particularly positive indication was insulation sales, which rose dramatically. Citizens recognized that investment in insulation would lower future fuel consumption. Shortages of insulation resulted, but these were of short duration. Insulation manufacturers generally sought to meet growing demands.

During 1977, the Organization of Petroleum Exporting Countries (OPEC) continued to control international oil prices. There were no signs to suggest that this international cartel might collapse. OPEC did not, however, raise oil prices at rates significantly faster than normal inflation. The vast revenues being accumulated by the OPEC nations continued to concern all oil importing nations. As recently as 1973, the United States had spent only $8.4 billion for oil imports. This rose to $34.6 billion in 1976, and increased even further in 1977 as the imported fraction of all oil used approached 50% for the first time in history.

Several studies of international oil lead to the conclusion that major problems lie ahead. Sometime within the 1980's it appears likely that the demand for oil will exceed the supply capability of the oil exporting countries. When this occurs major dislocations are considered likely; these could take the form of oil shortages, rapid fluctuations in oil costs leading to very large increases in oil prices, or possibly even wars over oil. The agreement of many energy analysts over the likelihood of such difficulties in the mid 1980's is becoming a major stimulus to more prudent planning, and especially to the implementation of energy conservation within the United States.

The most positive aspect of U. S. oil supply during 1977 was the start-up of the Trans-

Oil ministers from 13 member-states of the Organization of Petroleum Exporting Countries (OPEC) met in Stockholm in July. Existing differences in oil prices charged by OPEC members were discussed.

UPI

Alaska Pipeline System (TAPS). This pipeline, first proposed in 1965, suffered major delays due to environmental litigations and construction difficulties, and dramatic cost overruns. The final estimated cost of the TAPS was about $8 billion, making this one of the most expensive construction projects ever undertaken. The start-up of oil transport through TAPS precipitated extensive debate over how best to handle this oil. The capacity of the pipeline is 2 million barrels per day, substantially more oil than can be utilized by the West Coast, to which it will be delivered for transshipment to the East. Furthermore, the West Coast does not have sufficient refining capacity to process this oil. Thus, the United States is in the position of having a short term regional surplus of oil from TAPS at the same time that there is excessive reliance upon imported oil.

Natural Gas. For a number of years, natural gas has been supplying about one third of the United States' energy needs. Proved U. S. natural gas reserves have been declining since 1967, however, while demand for gas has continued to grow. In the winter of 1977, the severest in decades, a crisis stage was reached and natural gas supplies were unable to meet the heating demand. This resulted in the closing of factories and schools in Eastern and Midwestern states, with resulting economic and social disruption. It also stimulated a harder look at U. S. natural gas policy.

U. S. demand for natural gas began to grow in the 1940's and 1950's as what was originally considered to be merely a by-product of oil production began to be valued as a clean-burning, inexpensive energy source. Federal government action led to the existence of two natural gas markets—an interstate market regulated by the Federal Power Commission and an unregulated intrastate market. New gas finds flowed to the unregulated market, resulting in declining supplies to interstate pipelines. Thus while natural gas is still used for electricity generation in gas-rich states like Texas, Louisiana, and Oklahoma, gas supplies have been curtailed for "low priority" users (large industry, electricity generation) in states served by interstate pipelines. The major issues with respect to gas supply have thus revolved around the wisdom of price regulation (v. market pricing) and whether higher prices will stimulate new supply and end the unequal distribution of gas between regulated and unregulated markets.

President Carter urged that price rises resultant from deregulation would result in economic dislocations and hardship for existing customers. He proposed regulation of both the interstate and intrastate gas markets, with phased price increases for new gas and a combination of tax and regulatory measures to induce industry and electric utilities to stop using gas, making it more available for smaller users. Others argued that gas is a valuable fuel, that

regulation has led to shortages, and that high prices from price deregulation will cause price-based conservation and stimulate the search for new and harder-to-find supplies of gas. At year-end, the House favored the president's plan while the Senate supported deregulation; no legislation resulted.

Another major event related to gas was the decision to transport substantial amounts of natural gas found on the north slope of Alaska to the lower 48 states. President Carter and Canada's Prime Minister Pierre Elliott Trudeau signed a natural gas pipeline agreement in September. The U. S. Congress subsequently enacted the required legislation.

The largest known new supplies of natural gas available to the United States are in Alaska. This gas is produced in association with Alaskan oil. Extensive debates were underway in 1977 relating to the best way to make this Alaskan gas available to the United States. The major options (all in the $8–10 billion range) were two gas pipeline routes extending from Alaska through Canada to the lower 48 states, one along the Alcan (Alaska/Canada) Highway and the other following a more direct route, or a transportation scheme whereby the gas would be liquefied in Alaska to reduce its volume and taken to California in cryogenic tankers. Environmentalists in California and Alaska had expressed major reservation about the safety of liquefied natural gas, as any spills could cause major moving fire hazards if ignited while vaporizing.

At the same time, concern, including native Indian resistance and questions about environmental issues, was expressed about transportation through Canada. President Carter, with Congressional approval, chose the Alcan system.

Nuclear Energy. The year 1977 proved extremely trying for advocates of nuclear energy. President Carter stated that nuclear energy was to be the technology of last resort for meeting the nation's electrical energy needs. He expressed his concern about nuclear proliferation, which could become a major international problem if reactor systems based on plutonium were used throughout the world. To decrease the dangers of proliferation Carter announced a U. S. policy discouraging plutonium-fueled breeder reactors (reactors which produce more fissionable material than they consume), and deferring the reprocessing and recycling of plutonium from conventional reactors.

Congress disagreed with the president on slowing down research into breeder reactor technology, and authorized $150 million for continued work on the controversial Clinch River Breeder Reactor (CRBR). President Carter vetoed the appropriation bill when it reached him in November.

While the president opposed plutonium-based systems, he also recognized a need for speeding up the licensing of conventional re-

A natural gas pipeline control and dispatching center. The flow of natural gas was of vital concern in 1977.

actors in the hope of decreasing the very long delay between the planning for a reactor and the time it becomes operational. These delays now exceed 10 years, of which only about five are devoted to manufacture, the remainder being used for such procedures as siting approval and safety analysis.

Conventional light-water reactors experienced such major cost increases in 1977 that new orders for them dropped to almost zero. Projections of the contribution to U. S. electricity needs which might be made by reactors have been dropping for several years. In 1977 there were 65 reactors in operation in the U. S., providing about 10% of the nation's electricity. By 1985 this could double, according to current government estimates—a growth rate of about 9% per year, less than half the growth rate projected only a few years ago.

The availability of uranium to fuel light-water reactors was another concern. Each 1,000 megawatt-capacity light-water reactor requires about 5,000 tons of uranium oxide over its lifetime. The total U. S. resource base of uranium has been estimated by various groups to be somewhere in the range of less than two million tons to more than five million tons. The lower number would mean that only about 400 reactors could ever be built, because of fuel limitations. Should this lower resource limit be confirmed as more exploration takes place, the total possible contribution of light-water reactors to U. S. energy needs will be severely limited.

The major safety-related issues discussed during 1977 bore on the long term storage of nuclear wastes. There is at present no facility for long term storage (thousands of years) for the high-level wastes which are an inevitable concomitant of reactor operation. While nu-merous studies have suggested that the problem may be technically solvable, the fact that it has not been solved has led to major public outcry. Within the state of California, for example, legislation now prohibits the siting of new reactors until a satisfactory means of waste disposal is demonstrated. Whether or not waste disposal actually prevents nuclear expansion remains to be seen.

Citizen concern over nuclear reactors continued to be significant. The "Clamshell Alliance," a broad-spectrum citizen action group based in New England, drew attention nationwide when it objected to construction of a reactor in Seabrook, N. H., and the concern thus generated may well extend to other reactor projects. Divergences of opinion within the administration came to light as the Department of Energy endeavored to speed licensing of reactors at the same time that the Council on Environmental Quality wrote the president recommending delay of increased reliance on reactors until a number of safety and storage-related issues could be addressed and satisfactorily resolved.

Economics. The relationship between growth in the gross national product (GNP) of the United States and the use of energy has been debated by economists and energy analysts for many years. Historically, many analysts have tended to believe that GNP and energy vary together. That is, they believe that energy is critically linked to the productive capability of the nation, and that the only way in which GNP can increase is through increased energy use. This viewpoint has led such analysts to argue that the potential for energy conservation is extremely limited, and that vigorous energy conservation can be accomplished only at the expense of decrease in the economic well-being of the country. Analyses carried out for the past several years, especially since the 1973 OPEC embargo, have challenged these ideas. During 1977 a major energy study carried on under the auspices of the National Academy of Science made it clear that productivity and economic growth are affected by energy, but only indirectly. The prices charged for energy, and regulations governing the use of energy, are key determinants of the relationships between energy and economic growth. If, as energy prices go up, regulations are developed to limit wasteful use of energy, then growth in energy use will slow down while GNP will continue to grow.

New Technologies. Interest in the potential of new energy technologies increased perceptibly in 1977. Surveys showed that several thousand solar houses have been built in the nation, compared to only a handful a few years ago. A National Solar Energy Research Institute was established in Golden, Col., with responsibility to carry out extensive research in all aspects of solar energy. Solar demonstration units are being put into operation across the country, ranging from simple collectors, to solar-equipped public buildings, to a major solar system test center located at Albuquerque, N. Mex.

The price of solar cells to produce electricity photovoltaically continued to drop, with Department of Energy officials holding out the promise that by the mid-1980's solar cells may be cost-competitive with other means of generating electricity.

Progress was reported on new techniques for using lasers to separate particular isotopes of uranium for use in reactors far more efficiently than had previously been possible.

Funding for energy research continued to be strongly skewed toward nuclear energy, with solar energy and energy conservation receiving only a small fraction of the total federal research budget. Extensive criticism was leveled by Congress at President Carter's proposed staffing of the research and development part of the Department of Energy on the grounds of overcommitment to nuclear energy relative to solar.

Conservation. There is enormous opportunity to save energy in the United States. This can be inferred from comparing the nations of the world. No other nation uses as much energy per capita as the United States, despite the fact that there are several other nations (Switzerland, Sweden, for example) which have higher per capita income than does the United States. As it is increasingly recognized that economic growth does not require corresponding growth in energy use, it should become more acceptable to encourage energy conservation.

From a technical point of view, it is clear that extensive energy conservation is feasible. For example, improved energy management in buildings can often cut energy use in half. Typical measures include improvements in insulation, decrease in lighting levels, management of building heating and air conditioning systems, and arranging windows so that they can be conveniently opened. New buildings designed with attention to energy management can also make use of passive solar energy, leading to overall energy consumption that is a fraction of that of older buildings. The National Academy of Sciences demonstrated in 1977 that by the year 2010 economic output of the United States could double with essentially no increase in the per capita energy requirements.

The rate at which energy conservation measures take effect will depend on the price of energy and on government regulations. Several laws passed at both the federal and state level encourage such conservation. Among the most important of these are the Energy Conservation and Production Act (PL 94-385) and the Energy Policy and Conservation Act (PL 94-163). These laws provide for the establishment of in-

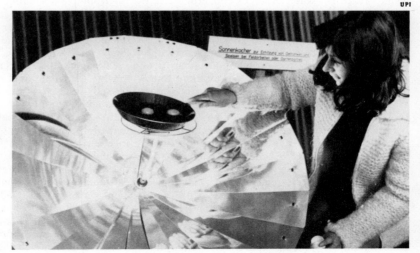

UPI

A solar stove, weighing about 13 pounds (6 kg) and costing $100, is demonstrated in West Germany. With sun power, the stove can cook a meal in ten minutes.

A massive blackout left some 9 million New Yorkers and Westchester County residents without electricity for between 4½ and 25 hours, July 13–14. Although looting and vandalism were widespread, many citizens performed acts of public service, including directing traffic.

sulation standards and standards for the performance of the most important building appliances. In the transportation sector regulations require automobile manufacturers to obtain a fleet-weighted average fuel economy of 27.5 miles per gallon by 1985. These and other laws under consideration can be expected to have a significant dampening effect on the demand for energy. Nevertheless, the United States will import large amounts of energy for many years to come.

Alternate Energy Strategies. In the decade of the 1960's, concern over environmental issues reached a high level, culminating in passage of the National Environmental Quality Act, the Clean Air Act, etc. Simultaneously, massive objection was voiced to nuclear energy systems. What has generally been lacking in criticisms of conventional energy systems has been a carefully thought-out alternative strategy. During 1977, substantial progress was made in the development and characterization of such alternatives. E. F. Schumacher, in his book *Small Is Beautiful,* made interesting proposals. At the policy level, discussion over alternative energy futures for the United States was stimulated by A. Lovins, the British representative of Friends of the Earth. His book, *Soft Energy Paths,* explores problems which conventional energy dependence encounters and proposes specific ways in which alternative energy futures may be implemented. The thrust of his argument is that the economic costs and the adverse environmental effects associated with conventional energy forms, especially nuclear systems and large-scale coal systems, are becoming too great for industrial societies to bear. These problems, combined with the global depletion of oil and natural gas, mandate detailed exploration of alternatives. Lovins sees our future dominated by solar energy systems, especially relatively small-scale systems used to provide heat and refrigeration. Electricity is de-emphasized. The objective of his proposals is to show the feasibility of a rapid transition to a society based upon renewable resources. These proposals aroused debate, but it remained to be seen whether they would produce new strategies.

BARBARA R. BARKOVICH
California Public Utilities Commission
PAUL P. CRAIG
University of California, Davis

ENGINEERING, CIVIL

Many significant civil engineering projects were either completed, still under construction, or in the planning stage during 1977.

BRIDGES

United States. Traffic bypassing Baltimore, Md., was eased with the opening of the Francis Scott Key Bridge across the Patapsco River near its mouth at Chesapeake Bay. This new bridge route on Interstate 695 provides an alternate to the tunnel passage. The $50-million, 8,636-foot (2,632-m) crossing includes a three-span continuous steel truss, 2,644 feet (806 m) long. The truss consists of a 1,200-foot (366-m) main span, flanked by 722-foot (220-m) anchor arms that provide a 180-foot (55-m) vertical clearance. Its 66-foot (20-m) width has four traffic lanes. Steel-girder approach spans are from 150 to 300 feet (46–91 m) long.

The Betsy Ross Bridge, opened to traffic in 1977, is the eighth crossing of the Delaware River built in this century. Connecting Philadelphia, Pa., and Pensauken, N.J., the $105-million, 8,481-foot (2,585-m), three-span continuous steel truss bridge carries eight lanes of traffic. The 728-foot (222-m) main span has two 446-foot (136-m) anchor spans. Vertical clearance is 135 feet (41 m). Approach-span trusses are 308 feet (94 m) long.

A twin parallel steel structure is being constructed over the Hudson River next to the Newburgh-Beacon Bridge in upstate New York. On completion, in 1980, the $107-million span will eliminate a bottleneck on the existing bridge, built in 1963 at a cost of $55 million. The 7,000-foot (2,134-m) bridge includes a 1,000-foot (305 m) through truss span over the navigation channel, and two 602-foot (184-m) deck truss spans. Its three traffic lanes will eventually carry easterly traffic on Interstate 84, from New York across Connecticut to Massachusetts. The older two-lane span will be widened to three lanes for west-bound traffic.

Argentina. At a cost of about $350 million, Argentina in 1977 completed twin stayed-box girder steel bridges over two branches of the Paraná River that are separated by a 15-mile (25-km) wide island. Connecting Zárate and Braza Largo, the four-lane bridges also carry a rail track. Each structure is 1,804 feet (550 m) long, comprising a 1,082-foot (330-m) main span and 361-foot (110-m) side spans. Each bridge has two main towers of prestressed concrete, 396 feet (121 m) high. Vertical clearance is 164 feet (50 m). The total length of each bridge is 2.5 and 2.2 miles (4 and 3.5 km), including river crossings and trestle approach spans of prestressed concrete. The new route eliminates a 10-hour ferry trip.

France. A cable-stayed bridge over the Seine at Caudebec, Normandy, was finished in 1977. Named Pont de Brotonne, it is built of pre-stressed concrete, employing both precast and cast-in-place box girders. Its total length of 4,193 feet (1 278 m) incorporates 15 spans, the main span being 1,050 feet (320 m). Two central towers rise 395 feet (120 m) above the water and provide vertical clearance of 164 feet (50 m). The four-lane structure replaces a time-consuming ferry service.

CANALS

France. A 5.6-mile (9-km) canal was completed in 1977 to supply water for the new Péage de Roussillon hydroelectric station on the Rhône River, south of Lyon. Water is tapped from the Rhône into the 164-foot (50-m) wide waterway, which parallels the river. Another 0.9-mile (1.5-km) section of canal returns the water downstream. Some 18,000,000 cubic yards (14 000 000 m³) of mixed material were moved during the two-year project.

Egypt. A 50-mile (80-km) long channel is being considered by Egypt to move water from the Mediterranean Sea to the Qattara Depression, an immense desert valley with a low point of about 440 feet (134 m) below sea level. The intake of the 750-foot (229-m) wide canal would be about 125 miles (201 km) west of Alexandria, and about 130 feet (40 m) below sea level for its full length. At its south end, water from the canal would drop through penstocks to a proposed hydroelectric power plant. Nuclear blasts have been suggested to excavate the channel, but ban treaties on such detonations might prevent their use. The cost of conventional excavation could be prohibitive.

DAMS

United States. In 1978 the U.S. Army Corps of Engineers will complete R. D. Bailey Dam on the Guyandot River 100 miles (160 km) south of Huntington, W. Va. The $160-million project will reduce flooding along the Guyandot River and offer recreational facilities on its 630-acre (255-ha) lake. The 6,500,000-cubic-yard (4 970 000-m³) rockfill dam, with concrete facing, is 310 feet (94 m) high, with a crest 1,400 feet (427 m) long. The facing is 12 inches (30 cm) thick at the crest, increasing to 23 inches (50 cm) at the base of the dam.

Another Corps of Engineers project, Lost Creek Dam, was completed in 1977. The $150-million rockfill embankment, with impervious earth core, is on the Rogue River 30 miles (48 km) east of Medford, Oreg. It is 344 feet (105 m) high, extends 3,642 feet (1 110 m) between abutments, and contains 11,000,000 cubic yards (8 400 000 m³) of material. The dam was planned to control flooding, improve low-water flows, and generate electric power from two 24.5 Mw turbines.

Scheduled for a 1979 completion is the $308-million New Melones Dam on the Stanislaus River near Sonora, Calif. Built by the Army Engineers, the 16,000,000-cubic-yard (12 000 000-m³)

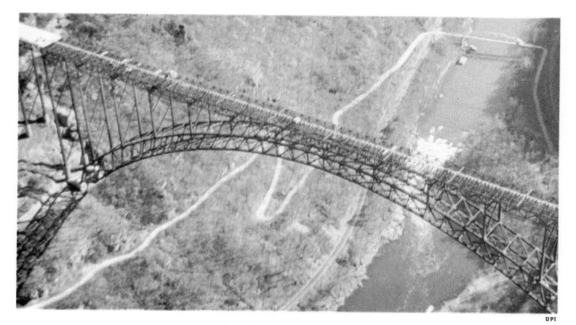

New bridge construction: the River Gorge Bridge, connecting Fayette Station and South Fayette, W. Va., is the world's longest steel arch span.

embankment will have a crest length of 1,560 feet (475 m), a base width of 2,630 feet (800 m), and a height of 625 feet (190 m). Its purposes include flood control, water supply, recreation, and power. Electric capacity will be 300 Mw.

Austria. Kölnbrein Dam is a double-curved concrete arch, the tallest dam in Austria. Completed in 1977 at a cost of $81 million, the 656-foot (200-m) high dam is 135 feet (41 m) thick at the base and 26 feet (8 m) at the crest. Its length is 2,033 feet (620 m).

England. Kielder Dam is rising on the north Tyne River, west of Newcastle, forming a reservoir to provide water for communities along the North Sea coast. Costing $170 million, the 170-foot (52-m) high earthfill dam will be 3,740 feet (1 140 m) long when finished in 1979.

Mexico. The Federal Electricity Commission is constructing the highest rockfill dam in Latin America and one of the highest in the world. Chicoasén Dam on the Grijalva River, near Tuxtla Gutiérrez in southern Mexico, will be 820 feet (250 m) high and 1,378 feet (420 m) long and contain 21,000,000 cubic yards (19 000 000 m³) of material. An eight-generator power house will produce 2,400 Mw of electricity. Costing $640 million, the dam will form a 15-mile (25-km) long reservoir.

TUNNELS

United States. Chicago has started construction on one of the largest tunnel projects in the country. The ten-year program, which may cost as much as $2.5 billion (U. S.), involves nearly 125 miles (201 km) of hardrock storm and sanitary sewers, up to 35 feet (11 m) in diameter and bored as deep as 300 feet (91 m). The plan also includes underground reservoir caverns to control overflow and runoffs.

In 1977 the U. S. Bureau of Reclamation completed a 1.5-mile (2.4-km) irrigation tunnel in New Mexico, part of the Navajo Irrigation Project. The 11.5-foot (3.5-m) diameter water tunnel was driven by a boring machine or mole, and later lined with one foot (30 cm) of concrete. It conducts water from the Navajo Reservoir on the San Juan River, near Blanco, for delivery to an Indian reservation.

Water for irrigational, industrial, and municipal use will flow through a 23.5-foot (7.2-m) diameter, concrete-lined tunnel that the Bureau of Reclamation is boring through Bucksin Mountain in western Arizona. Originating in Lake Havasu, behind Parker Dam, the water will be pumped 800 feet (244 m) up to the inlet portal of a 6.5-mile (10.5-km) tunnel. From the outlet portal the water will flow through an aqueduct to serve Phoenix. The tunnel will cost $58 million.

Hong Kong. One of the world's most densely populated areas, Hong Kong, is getting a new subway. Now in its first phase, the twin-tube transit line is scheduled to open in 1980. The initial 10-mile (16-km), 15-station route is expected to cost $1 billion. Its twin 16-foot (4.9-m) diameter bores are being driven at depths of 82 to 115 feet (25 to 35 m). The line includes a 4,592-foot (1 400-m) sunken tube segment under Victoria harbor, connecting Hong Kong Island and Kowloon on the mainland.

WILLIAM H. QUIRK
"Construction Industry International" Magazine

ENVIRONMENT

During 1977, national governments repeated their performance of recent years: international and domestic forums rubber-stamped generalized policy statements, pledging a commitment to a cleaner environment. There was more cause for optimism in the United States, where the new administration of Jimmy Carter appeared to be sympathetic to the pleas of environmentalists.

INTERNATIONAL

The year produced its quota of international parleys and reunions. As usual, the meetings generated few concrete proposals.

Lackluster Conferences. The first worldwide conference on deserts was held in Nairobi, Kenya. Conferees agreed that a recognizable problem exists: in the next 25 years, one third of the world's current arable land could be lost. Solutions were more elusive. A conference sponsored by the United Nations Environment Programme (UNEP) on threats to the ozone layer reached similar conclusions. Fluorocarbons were identified as a menace to the earth's ozone, but no attempt was made to regulate their use. The latest round in the UN Law of the Sea Conference again failed to find solid ground for a treaty on seabed mining. The meeting was polarized yet another time between the interests of industrialized and developing nations. Disgruntled over Third World countries' last-minute attempts to adopt a statement antagonistic to the views of industrialized nations, chief U. S. representative Elliot Richardson threatened a withdrawal from future negotiations.

Energy. The hazards of oil drilling were demonstrated when an oil rig in the North Sea exploded. Efforts to cap the well and contain the slick were hampered by gale-force winds. After eight days, when the well was finally capped, 7.5 million gallons (24,000 metric tons) of oil had been spilled over an estimated 175–250 sq mi (450–650 km²).

Concern about the dangers of nuclear power brought 30,000 protesters to the construction site of a French breeder reactor. Similar efforts in West Germany, Britain, and other European countries indicated growing grass-root forces determined to stem the nuclear tide.

Defenders and opponents of nuclear power met separately in Salzburg, Austria. The pronuclear forces sought practical solutions to the problems of atomic energy. West Germany took the first concrete step to create a nuclear-wastes repository, announcing plans to construct a "fuel cycle park." The Salzburg Conference for a Non-Nuclear Future resolved to step up activity against conventional nuclear power plants and to end the use of plutonium as reactor fuel. (*See also* ENERGY.)

Family Planning. Population planning continued to be a problem. In Latin America and the Caribbean, where population is still dramat-ically increasing, family-planning programs have met with some success, particularly in Costa Rica, Chile, and Jamaica. Mexico, which has one of the highest growth rates in the world, ceased its long-standing opposition to outside intervention in national population policy, expressing interest in World Bank funds to establish family planning programs.

Wildlife. The need for wildlife protection is about the only issue on which both the Third World and industrialized nations agree. Multilateral environmental accords, such as the UN Man and the Biosphere program, encouraged member nations to set aside large self-regulating habitats to encourage natural, unhindered evolution. Independently, several nations initiated wildlife and habitat protection programs. Colombia created 21 new national parks covering 5.5 million acres (22,260 km²), and Sweden established a new nature reserve of 1,186,000 acres (4,800 km²), which more than doubled the total area of its reserves. Ireland, the USSR, and Kenya also initiated significant wildlife preservation efforts.

U. S. ENVIRONMENT

In the United States, 1977 brought new evidence of deterioration in the nation's environment. Among the most ominous signs were confirmations of the deleterious effects that pesticides and other toxic substances are having on human health.

Sympathetic Administration. Although a pessimistic outlook was inevitable, granted the continuing pollution of air and water, a note of optimism was generated by the change of administration. Impressed by President Carter's choices for key environmental posts, preservationists rallied to his support. While he did not introduce any major new programs, Carter sent a wide-ranging environmental policy statement to Congress and followed it by concrete legislative proposals addressing air and water pollution control, strip-mining, wilderness preservation, and energy.

Air Pollution. Although no major inroads were made on air pollution, clean-air proponents demonstrated great perseverance against a powerful industry-labor coalition. Under threat of an auto industry shutdown, Congress amended the Clean Air Act, granting automakers a respite until model-year 1980 to comply with its emission standards. More stringent standards were to become effective with the 1978 models, but automobile manufacturers persuaded Congress to grant the industry its fourth extension since the original 1975 deadline. Amendments to the Clean Air Act cover other sources of air pollution as well. Industry and municipalities were granted waivers of up to a decade for compliance with standards scheduled to take effect in 1977. Environmentalists, however, prevailed against efforts to weaken existing legislation that protects the air quality of pristine areas.

In May 1977, the government of Kenya banned all game hunting in that nation. The action was intended to preserve the world's dwindling wildlife.

KENYA TOURIST BOARD

The federal Environmental Protection Agency (EPA) acknowledged its inability to mandate effective transportation controls. Faced with a bewildering array of lawsuits challenging its authority to regulate the flow of automobile traffic, EPA will, instead, seek voluntary cooperation of states and localities. Inspection of automobile pollution control devices, however, will be mandatory. A U. S. district court decision strengthened EPA's hand in dealing with industrial polluters by ruling that the agency has authority to penalize violators by prohibiting them from receiving federal contracts.

The Ozone Layer. Scientific studies continued to confirm that industrial and consumer practices are damaging the earth's delicate shield of ozone. Acting on its mandate, the federal Food and Drug Administration ordered that all aerosol containers using fluorocarbon propellants carry a warning that they pose a demonstrable threat to the earth's ozone layer. The labeling requirement represents a first step toward a total ban of fluorocarbons. The Federal Aviation Administration released new laboratory findings indicating that no existing aircraft, including SST's, pose any imminent threat to the ozone layer.

Water Pollution. Legislation and court decisions in 1977 strengthened the regulatory ability of the federal government to deal with industrial water polluters. In accordance with the provisions of the 1974 Safe Drinking Water Act, some 240,000 water systems were placed under federal supervision. Previously the domain of state governments, the nation's drinking water supply had showed signs of deterioration caused by chemicals and other pollutants. Although states will still shoulder the primary responsibility for safety, drinking water will have to meet minimum federal standards.

The authority of EPA over the dumping of sewage sludge in the ocean was reaffirmed by a federal court; marine life is threatened with extinction from the daily dumping. Encouraged by the finding, EPA ruled that the influx of inadequately treated sewage into the nation's waterways must cease by 1981. DuPont and seven other chemical companies contested EPA's authority to limit industrial effluence. The companies argued that the agency was empowered only to issue guidelines. The U. S. Supreme Court ruled in favor of EPA, thus establishing a clear precedent for its current practice of setting effluence limitations for classes of plants.

The Great Lakes. In its efforts to clean up the Great Lakes, EPA was able to report at least limited progress. It revealed that more than 80% of industrial polluters are currently meeting federal regulations. (Local governments, however, are not so compliant: only 40% of municipal sewage systems meet federal standards.) The agency's success was enhanced by a number of favorable court decisions. In a case involving U. S. Steel Corp., the U. S. Court of Appeals ordered the company to install $84.7-million worth of wastewater recycling equipment in its Gary, Ind., plant, and thus cut its discharge by 90%. EPA officials called it "the single, biggest clean-water victory to date."

Energy. Record cold during the winter of 1976–77 and a shortage of natural gas underlined U. S. dependence on ever-dwindling energy supplies. In the summer, New York City residents suffered through a second major blackout in the last 12 years.

As the year ended, attention shifted from personal discomfort to potential solutions. On October 1, the new U. S. Department of Energy came into existence, merging three giant agencies: the Energy Research and Development Administration, the Federal Energy Administration, and the Federal Power Commission. President Carter introduced a comprehensive national energy plan, emphasizing conservation of the nation's fossil fuel reserves. The House of Representatives acted swiftly and passed the plan with few major changes; the Senate proceeded to dismantle it. At year's end, the legislation was locked in a House-Senate conference committee.

The Alaska Pipeline finally began operations, but not without problems. Shortly after the opening on June 20, a crack forced a temporary halt in the oil flow. In July, an explosion and fire ripped a pumping station, causing a second shutdown. Meanwhile, U. S. and Canadian officials agreed on a trans-Canada pipeline to transport natural gas from Alaska's Prudhoe Bay to the lower 48 states.

Nuclear power continued to arouse public opposition. More than 2,000 demonstrators occupied the construction site of a major nuclear generating facility in Seabrook, N. H. The protesters remained until New Hampshire's Gov. Meldrim Thompson (R) ordered them removed. A major concern of nuclear opponents is radioactive waste disposal. Radioactive wastes must be interred in an undisturbed environment for as long as a quarter of a million years.

Population. Studies indicate that the birth rate is once again tending upward. In the first four months of 1977, the rate was 6% higher than in the same period of 1976. Population experts, however, are not disturbed by the rise, viewing it as a leveling off after the historic low reached in 1976. Of greater concern to advocates of zero population growth is the fight over federal funding for abortions. Early in the summer, the U. S. Supreme Court ruled that public funds need not be expended on abortions, and a provision in existing legislation, prohibiting federal funding for abortions, went into effect. By fall, 14 states or jurisdictions had rescinded all state funding, and 28 were planning similar action. Only 11 states decided to continue using public funds for abortions.

Toxic Substances. An alarming number of potentially cancer-causing agents have infiltrated the environment. In a study of work environments, the Occupational Safety and Health Administration found that one out of every four workers is exposed to hazardous conditions or substances, some believed to be cancer-causing. More specific studies tended to prove the agency's claims. DBCP (dibromochloropropane), a pesticide, caused sterility in 14 workers at the Occidental Chemical Company in California, and more than 250,000 workers exposed to nickel dust in a variety of industrial processes were found to risk nasal and lung cancer. Nor is the general public immune to chemical hazards. For example, the ingestion of PBB's (polybrominated biphenyls) as a result of the accidental substitution of a fire retardant for magnesium oxide in cattle feed has produced serious immunological defects in Michigan residents who ate products from these animals.

EPA tests on 1,400 women have furthermore revealed the presence beyond safe levels of dangerous chemicals, such as DDT and PCB's (polychlorinated biphenyls), in breast milk. EPA also reported that a major laboratory for testing pesticides before they are marketed may be using faulty testing and reporting procedures.

The threat to public health prompted Congress to pass the Toxic Substance Control Act which, it is hoped, will provide the framework for control of industrial chemicals and other hazardous substances.

Noise Pollution. The controversy over landing rights for the Concorde at Kennedy Airport was legally ended in October, when the U. S. Supreme Court removed the last obstacle to the SST flights into New York. Trial runs to test noise-standard compliance began immediately.

Land Use. After repeated failures to enact strip-mining legislation, Congress finally passed and President Carter signed a bill that establishes federal control over strip-mined land. The bill stipulates that strip-mine operators must restore mined land to its original state. Environ-

SUSAN SZASZ, EPA-DOCUMERICA

The increasing number of intown flower and vegetable gardens attests to an on-going interest in the environment, but also to the gratification that derives from making things grow.

Oil poured into the North Sea for eight days in early 1977 following a blowout in Norway's Ekofish well. The spill's proximity to mackerel spawning grounds caused particular concern.

mentalists, however, were disappointed with a number of provisions in the legislation. Among these was an 18-month delay for small-mine owners—who account for approximately 80% of the country's total strip-mining operations—to comply with the law.

To ensure that the Yukon wilderness does not suffer the same fate as the Appalachians, Secretary of the Interior Cecil Andrus asked Congress to preserve 92.8 million acres (375,550 km²) of land in Alaska. The request is expected to ignite a heated battle between mineral developers and conservationists.

Wildlife. The cornerstone of wildlife protection, the Endangered Species Act, was again put to the test. Work on the Tennessee Valley Authority's Tellico Dam Project was curtailed when it was learned the project would destroy the spawning ground of an endangered species of perch. On Long Island, a man was brought to trial for killing a bald eagle—one of few instances when killing or maiming wildlife threatened with extinction has come to trial.

JAMES G. KOLLEGGER
Environment Information Center, Inc.

ETHIOPIA

Internal and external conflicts engaged the Ethiopian military government in 1977. It continued its battle against Eritrean secessionists, fought a war with Somalia over the Ogaden region, and established a strong political relationship with the Soviet Union, breaking almost totally with the United States.

Domestic Conflict. The ideological feud between factions of the military junta culminated in the execution on February 3 of the chief of state, Brig. Gen. Tafari Banti, and six other leaders of the ruling military council. Lt. Col. Mengistu Haile Mariam, the strongman of the junta, was named head of state on February 11 and took control of all political institutions re-

sponsible for carrying out Ethiopia's Marxist revolution.

Faced with continuous opposition from students, labor, and civil servants, connected with the old Haile Selassie regime, the junta cracked down on its opponents. This was met by counterviolence and created a situation in which Marxists and non-Marxists executed one another in the streets of Addis Ababa. A reign of terror swept Ethiopian cities. On April 29, some 2,000 students were summarily executed by the regime; the *London Daily Telegraph* claimed on July 3 that more than 30,000 Ethiopians had been killed as a result of the revolutionary situation in the country.

Civil War. Throughout 1977, Ethiopia fought to maintain its geographical integrity, confronting separatist movements in Eritrea and Ogaden. In the province of Eritrea, after more than 15 years of fighting, separatists gained control of more than 85% of the territory, while government forces held only the major cities. The junta, fearing a devastating defeat, created a peasant army to support its military. Some 50 Cuban military advisers were brought to Ethiopia in August to train this army. The Eritreans had all but closed the government's access to the ports of Assab and Massawa.

───────**ETHIOPIA · Information Highlights**───────

Official Name: Ethiopia.
Location: Eastern Africa.
Area: 471,777 square miles (1,221,900 km²).
Population (1977 est.): 29,400,000.
Chief Cities (1975): Addis Ababa, the capital, 1,161,000; Asmara, 318,000.
Government: *Head of state and government,* Mengistu Haile Mariam, chairman of the Provisional Military Administrative Committee (took office Feb. 1977).
Monetary Unit: Birr (2.04 birrs equal U.S.$1, Sept. 1977).
Manufacturing (major products): Processed foods, textiles, cement, leather and shoes.
Major Agricultural Products: Coffee, cotton, sugarcane, corn, millet and sorghum, oilseeds, pulses, cattle, sheep.

The Ogaden region, which is claimed by Somalia as part of its own territory, was the scene of fierce fighting. Conquered by Ethiopia in the 19th century, the Ogaden was almost totally occupied by the Western Somali Liberation Front in 1977; only Harar and Diredawa remained under Ethiopian control. Occupied with the war in Eritrea and battling its internal opponents, the government was unable to stem the insurgency in the Ogaden.

Foreign Affairs. U. S. President Jimmy Carter condemned the Ethiopian junta on February 24 for violating the human rights of its citizens. As a result, a $6-million military-aid program was eliminated. Ethiopia responded by ordering the closing on April 23 of all U. S. civilian and military offices in Ethiopia, with the sole exception of the U. S. embassy. Americans were given four days to leave the country. At the same time, the junta initiated a military-economic relationship with the USSR, and the Soviets signed a $400-million military accord with Ethiopia after Col. Mengistu visited Moscow in May. The military equipment, along with the Cuban advisers, was an attempt to shore up the Ethiopian armed forces; the once-powerful American presence in Ethiopia was replaced by a Soviet one.

The French Territory of the Afars and the Issas received its independence on June 26. Djibouti, as the new country is known, is also at the center of an Ethiopian-Somalian controversy, since the former uses the port at Djibouti and the latter claims it as part of "Greater Somalia." Both have said they would go to war over Djibouti if either attempted military action to secure its interests in the country.

PETER SCHWAB
State University of New York at Purchase

ETHNIC GROUPS

The question of affirmative action, President Carter's policies toward minority groups, general urban problems, and a series of land claims by American Indians were of prime concern to American ethnic groups during 1977.

The Bakke Case. On a crisp October morning in Washington, D. C., hundreds of people lined up outside the U. S. Supreme Court building as if they were awaiting the opening game of a World Series. But the spectacle they hoped to see was far more important than any athletic contest. That morning, the nine high court justices heard oral arguments in the case of *Allan Bakke* v. *the Regents of the University of California*—a legal battle widely thought to be the most important civil-rights case since the court outlawed racial segregation in *Brown* v. *the Board of Education of Topeka* in 1954.

The central issue seemed fairly simple: Bakke claimed he had been denied admission to the University of California at Davis Medical School because he is white—while less-qualified minority-group students were accepted instead. In fact, the university had set aside 16 of 100 places for "disadvantaged" students in an affirmative-action program designed to admit more minority students. After he was rejected in 1973 Bakke sued, charging that the school's special-admissions program constituted a violation of his 14th Amendment right to equal protection under the law regardless of race. The California Supreme Court ruled in Bakke's favor but the university elected to appeal—touching off a legal controversy that ripples through every segment of American life.

The question of affirmative action has been hotly debated for years. Supporters argue that, in education and employment, such special consideration is necessary for minorities—and women—to overcome the discrimination of the past. Opponents, charging "reverse discrimination," insist that white men should not suffer arbitrarily for the sins of history. Many on both sides, moreover, are uncomfortable with racial quotas as a means of achieving integration. It has been an issue begging for a Supreme Court ruling—and Bakke has given it that chance.

A decision that ruled broadly against affirmative action could have immediate, specific consequences. Scores of federal programs are based already on the concept of special help for minorities, and educators agree that the number of minority students in professional schools, which has been going up in recent years, would decline sharply if admissions were based simply on traditional criteria like test scores. The pervasive nature of the issue was indicated by the record number of friends-of-the-court briefs—nearly 60—filed on behalf of one side or the other. Old liberal alliances were broken; the NAACP lined up squarely against Bakke, while several Jewish groups—recalling old discriminatory quotas against Jews—supported his case.

The Carter administration, through the Justice Department—after much-publicized internal debate—strongly supported the affirmative action concept. The court was expected to rule in the first half of 1978.

Wilkins-Hooks. Even as the NAACP was accepting the challenge of the Bakke case, it was remembering past victories in a sentimental tribute to Roy Wilkins, who retired after 32 years as the organization's chief executive. Wilkins stepped down at the annual convention in his hometown of St. Louis. Benjamin Hooks, a former judge, minister, businessman, and Federal Communications Commissioner from Memphis, was installed as the new executive director of the NAACP.

That convention reflected not only nostalgia over past civil rights achievements but also unrest over current difficulties. Striving to become more aggressive after losing influence in recent years, the association lashed out against President Carter, Congress, and organized labor for unfavorable positions on school integration

UPI

In Ignacio, Colo., July 27, elders of the Comanche tribes and the Ute nations formally ended a 200-year-old disagreement over hunting rights. More than 2,000 persons attended the ceremonies.

and affirmative action in employment. Recalling the heavy black vote widely held to have provided Carter's margin of election victory, the association, in effect, warned the President not to take the concerns of black America for granted.

Carter Administration Attacked. That same theme was taken up in midsummer by National Urban League Director Vernon Jordan—a long-time supporter of Carter. Jordan's attack was the most bitter and publicized statement to date of black disaffection with Carter. He chided the President for stressing "balanced budgets instead of balanced lives" and giving slight attention to the country's social ills. Carter replied with thinly veiled anger that he was doing just fine and that, in any event, black leaders like Jordan should not criticize him because he was the best hope for black people. That terse exchange left a noticeable strain on Carter's bond with black America that only began to loosen later in the year when the President addressed himself more often to matters of unemployment and housing in the cities. He also offered a plan to revise the nation's scrambled welfare system, although the proposal met with some opposition from both conservative congressmen and civil rights groups.

Urban Problems. It was not just the plaintive cries of black leaders, however, that brought urban problems back into the news. Shortly after dark on a sweltering July night in New York City the lights went out—and the city

suffered the worst display of man-made destruction since the riots of the 1960's. Twelve years before, the entire Northeast had been plunged into darkness in a similar electrical power failure, and people rallied round each other as if in time of war. In most of the city that pattern was repeated. But in several poor neighborhoods, mostly black and Puerto Rican, the sudden blackout (which lasted for 24 hours in some areas) instantly became an opportunity for plunder. Within minutes people poured into the streets and began ransacking stores. Working by flashlight, they walked off with the entire inventory of several businesses, many of them small and minority-owned. In all, 2,000 businesses were sacked and an estimated $1 billion in property was lost. Although police made only minimal efforts to halt the looting, they arrested nearly 4,000 people. New Yorkers reacted to the wanton lawlessness with a mixture of dismay and anger.

Illegal Aliens. Earlier in the year, a more national problem took center stage as President Carter formulated his position on illegal aliens in the United States. By most estimates, there were at least six million such persons in the United States in 1977, more than half of them Mexicans who had crossed the border to find jobs, often as migrant laborers. During the summer, Carter proposed a series of potential remedies. He recommended civil fines for employers who knowingly hired illegal aliens and amnesty for those who had been living in the

UPI

Benjamin Hooks, 52-year-old lawyer and Baptist clergyman, became executive director of the NAACP in August.

country illegally but continuously since before 1970. New Immigration and Naturalization Service Director Leonel Castillo, a Chicano, estimated that half a million aliens fit that description; under Carter's plan, they would be eligible to apply for "permanent resident" status. Aliens who entered the country between 1970 and 1977 would be eligible for a new "nondeportable" classification, allowing them to remain and work but not receive public assistance. Finally, Carter proposed a 40% increase in the hopelessly outmanned Border Patrol force to help stem the flow of immigrants who slip in daily.

Carter's proposals received mixed reviews. Businessmen contended the penalties to be leveled against employers were too severe, since illegal aliens could easily be hired by mistake. The AFL-CIO, on the other hand, thought those same penalties should be even tougher to discourage employers from exploiting a cheap labor force. And some Mexican-Americans claimed that the fines would give employers a license to discriminate against all Chicanoes, even legal aliens or U. S. citizens. Still others simply likened the plan to surrendering to a foreign invasion. Those hard-liners would prefer to solve the problem by mass deportation.

American Indians. Land claims were a dominant issue for American Indians. In February, the U. S. Department of Justice filed a memorandum in federal district court in Portland, Maine, supporting the Passamaquoddy and Penobscot Indians in their suit against Maine over land. Other states where Indians were pressing land claims included Massachusetts, Rhode Island, Connecticut, New York, and South Carolina.

Forrest J. Gerard, a Blackfoot Indian from Montana, took over as assistant secretary of the Interior for Indian Affairs. He said that he wanted his office to be seen by Indian tribes as an "advocate rather than an adversary."

DENNIS A. WILLIAMS, *"Newsweek"*

EUROPE

Europe's economic recovery in 1977 was disappointingly slow; inflation and unemployment increased the political difficulties of all West European governments. Further strains were imposed by festering social or regional disputes.

Slow Economic Recovery. Many European governments imposed austerity programs in 1976 to limit inflation, but the result was to restrict expansion in 1977. Reduction of expenditure on social services and attempts to hold down wage demands, were made by Britain and Italy, in part to justify requests for large loans from the International Monetary Fund to cover balance-of-payments deficits. Britain expected to cut its inflation from 25% in 1976 to 12% in 1977; but union demands remained an inflationary threat and a danger to the large trade surplus achieved during the summer. In Italy, the minority government of Christian Democrat Giulio Andreotti required abstention by the large Communist party in parliament to push through increased utility and gasoline prices and proposals for wage restraint; but opposition within the Communist party to the leadership's policy, and violent public demonstrations by workers and left-wing students, made imposition of further austerity measures impossible.

South European countries experienced great economic problems, indicating the continuing division of non-Communist Europe between a few economically strong countries and a large number with great structural difficulties. Greece, Turkey, Italy, Spain, and Portugal, with their large rural populations and insufficient industrial capital, lacked the newly exploited resources of gas and oil of countries bordering the North Sea. Moreover, unemployment among migrant workers in Western Europe reduced their ability to transmit foreign exchange to their home countries. The new democratic regimes of Spain and Portugal were particularly challenged. Although Spain had undergone an economic boom in the 1960's, progress had slowed in the 1970's. In 1977, with unemployment at 8% and inflation at 30%, discontent was widespread. Portugal, with a similar inflation rate, suffered unemployment up to 15%. Although the European Community (EEC) continued to consider applications for membership from Spain, Portugal, and Greece, opposition from farm groups in France and Italy, as well as industrial fears of competition from low-paid workers in Spain, seemed likely to block any enlargement of the EEC for several years.

Political Strains. The economic difficulties tested fragile governments in many West European countries. In Britain, James Callaghan's Labour government was able to maintain a slim majority only by winning Liberal support with promises of concessions on devolution of power to Wales and Scotland. Italy's Andreotti was

Portugal's Prime Minister Mário Soares, second from right, and Spain's Prime Minister Adolfo Suárez hold a joint press conference in Madrid. The two Iberian nations applied for full EEC membership during 1977.

UPI

compelled to make a package of agreements on local taxes and government spending with the Communists and Socialists, thus giving them a direct voice in governmental policy. Even West Germany, with the highest living standard in Europe and the lowest rate of inflation, faced political unrest. The Social Democratic party of Chancellor Helmut Schmidt was divided internally, its left wing demanding more rapid social change, while its coalition partners, the Free Democrats, were pressing for a reduction in social programs. In Portugal, Socialist Premier Mário Soares, was able to hold together his coalition of moderate centrist and leftist parties only by playing one group off against another; and although Premier Adolfo Suárez' coalition, the Democratic Center Union, won Spain's first national elections since 1936, it was severely challenged by separatist demands from Basque and Catalán groups. Other governments were rejected in elections dominated by economic issues. In Ireland, for example, the shaky coalition of Liam Cosgrave was trounced by Jack Lynch's Fianna Fáil party, whose economic program appeared to offer greater promise of reducing Ireland's 10% unemployment rate.

Eurocommunism. The only political groups to profit from the economic unrest were the

In London for a May economic conference, Japan's Fukuda, Britain's Callaghan, France's Giscard, Carter of the U. S., Italy's Andreotti, and Germany's Schmidt dined with Queen Elizabeth.

UPI

UPI

Western European leaders mark the 20th anniversary of the signings of the treaties of Rome, which established the European Economic Community and the European Atomic Energy Community.

Communist parties of Western Europe, which emphasized their claim to be democratic reformist parties, independent of Soviet control. The most persuasive spokesmen for the doctrine of Eurocommunism were Spain's Santiago Carrillo, whose party was legalized in April, Italy's Enrico Berlinguer, and, to a lesser degree, France's Georges Marchais. Although the Spanish Communists obtained only 9% of the votes in the national elections, both the French and Italian Communists had real hopes of gaining power in the near future. The French, in a somewhat troubled alliance with the Socialists, were preparing for the national elections in 1978, when they hoped to defeat the quarreling alliance of President Valéry Giscard d'Estaing's Independent Republicans and the Gaullists. In municipal elections in the spring, the Communist-Socialist alliance won 53% of the vote, gaining control of many provincial cities.

West European Communists were particularly concerned to establish their independence of Soviet control in view of the increasing evidence in 1977 of repression of political dissent in the USSR and Eastern Europe. Official censure of such dissenters as Andrei Sakharov in Russia, the expulsion to the West of dissenters from East Germany, and the harassment in Czechoslovakia of the signers of Charter 77 (a demand for greater respect for human rights), were regarded by many Europeans as violation of the Helsinki agreements of 1975.

Increase in Terrorism. Europeans were most disturbed, however, by the increase in violence. In Italy, kidnapping of businessmen for ransom continued. In Spain, kidnapping and murder by left-wing extremists provoked retaliatory assassinations by right-wingers. Terrorism by the Catholic Irish Republican Army in Northern Ireland continued to provoke counter-measures by Protestants, though there were favorable signs of a slackening in the hostilities between the groups. The society most shaken by terrorism was West Germany. Extraordinary security measures were unable to prevent the kidnapping and/or murder of some of the country's most prominent business and legal leaders, including Hanns-Martin Schleyer, president of the West German employers' association. What most disturbed the German public was the strong support for the well-armed terrorist groups among radical university students.

Thus, a sense of economic and political, and even personal, insecurity gave to European life in 1977 an unease that the slow economic revival could hardly dissipate.

F. ROY WILLIS
University of California, Davis

EUROPE—SPECIAL REPORT:

The EEC at 20

The European Economic Community celebrated the twentieth anniversary of its founding Treaty of Rome early in 1977, and then sagged ever more deeply into gloomy paralysis. At year-end, hopes to restore progress through the daily haggling which had become its custom were so low that Commission President Roy Jenkins and Energy Commissioner Guido Brunner launched bold proposals. The effort at least to provoke a debate on how to get the European ideal moving again met with a resounding silence. Jenkins' arguments in favor of another try at monetary union and Brunner's appeal for treaty amendments and reform while new applications are considered were brushed aside.

Warnings had been multiplying for years that the Community must regain momentum or crash. Neither had happened, nor seemed a realistic prospect. Not only was the Community still there, still arguing bitterly about such things as standardizing regulations for truck drivers, three eager new members were knocking at the door. The requests of Greece, Spain, and Portugal to be allowed to join were received both as a symbol of the Community's continuing magnetism and painful proof of its disarray. Member states welcomed the evidence that the existence of their club formed an important incentive and a desired support for democracy. But they were also deeply worried and divided about the practical and institutional effects of larger union. With agreement on anything beyond technicalities so difficult among nine, how could twelve avoid deteriorating into a mere free trade area with loose political consultations?

There were some 1977 achievements: establishment of a 200-mile offshore economic zone which the Russians were obliged to recognize, an agreement after years of bickering on where to put a joint research facility to make energy from nuclear fusion (in England), an increased habit of consultation and occasional joint positions on foreign policy. But nobody involved pretended that any of this would be enough to rally a new generation of Europeans to support the immediate sacrifices which longer term Community needs would require.

Even the uncompleted plans for direct elections of a European parliament in 1978 had lost their galvanizing sheen. The elections would probably take place, but once again niggling and the primacy of domestic politics had worn away the hopes of a fresh European vision.

In its early years, just after the treaty was signed, the Community raced ahead of the deadlines set for trade integration. After all, people were eager to work and live in a larger, multinational grouping. The surge slowed down in the Gaullist years, and by the time the road began to be unblocked, attitudes had changed. It was the ravage of war and the challenge of reconstruction and cold war which had pressed the original six together in the first place. All flourished, though at different rates, as the benefits of cooperation took hold. But the creeping crisis of the 1970's diverted attention to the home front and revived the ideas that protection is the point of national borders.

The initial dream of a United States of Europe—equal with the superpowers in population, economic capacity, and vitality—had faded. Britain, Ireland, and Denmark had joined in 1973 but they brought new demands and new bureaucrats, not new spirit.

And yet, in capital after capital, the local issues were the same—inflation, unemployment, energy, environment, disgruntled youth, a sense of aimlessness. Still, summit and experts' meetings failed to find the way to confront these common concerns. The major failure had been the Community's inability and unwillingness to redistribute the wealth of its richer members for the benefit of the poorer ones, to create vested interests in its creative capacity.

The divergence among members had become so great and their wants from the Community so dissynchronized that no magic formula seemed a credible cure. In the large sense, the similarities had become far greater than the differences. War among West Europeans, who had fought each other for a thousand years, was rendered inconceivable. Members and applicants shared a dedication to the principles of democracy and at least a desire for greater social justice.

What Europa lacked at 20 was not an assured existence but confidence and identity. The grand hopes for a union that would drive a battered world forward had not survived.

FLORA LEWIS

Roy Jenkins is president of the European Commission.

UPI

The 1977 fashion message: softness. Challis, peasant look, and shawls were fabric, design, and accessory in the forefront.

FASHION

Fashion for 1977 had more than a touch of class. Women turned to the frankly feminine; for day through evening, clothes and accessories were graceful, elegant, and pretty. Men preferred a conservative look, after years of flamboyance.

WOMEN'S CLOTHES

Totally Feminine. Fashion was characterized by fine fabrics, distinctive detailing, delicate touches, and a genteel quality. The soft dirndl skirt was one of the most important items. In fabrics that were pleasingly drapable, such as lightweight flannel, crepes, and especially challis, it seemed to epitomize the mood of designers, retailers and customers alike. Detailing of the softened, gathered skirts included button fronts, slash pockets and hem ruffles. Other skirt styles included some that were gathered from wide hip yokes or tiered in rows of two or three ruffles, in fabrics suitable either for day or for evening wear.

The Slouch. With this total immersion in skirts, pants were hardly to be seen. The only new pants silhouette was "The Slouch"—pants that were narrowed through the leg, pegged at the ankle, and cut long to buckle and drape or "slouch" over boots or heavy shoes. Designed for casualness, they were most often shown with down or quilted jackets, shearling coats, bulky sweaters, and walking or hiking boots. This look was the only remnant of past years' trends toward the outdoors look.

The dress, after two years of competing with sportswear, made it big in many ways. For designers, and at the retail level for stores and customers alike, it was a winner in all price categories. The loose fitting sundress, tentdress or chemise, in challis or floral prints of various fabrics, became almost a uniform for women who had grown tired of putting themselves together from separates. Most of the dresses were romantic in feeling and decidedly feminine, with nostalgic Victorian touches such as bib fronts, neck or pinafore ruffles, or lace and eyelet trims.

The separates that were still around had their points of femininity. The classic sportswear look was softened in details. Blazers were shorter and more fitted. Often a lace handkerchief was tucked into the pocket to help soften the severity. Other jackets were short and boxy, often unlined, and in yielding fabrics such as mohair or wool jersey.

A graceful sensuousness was achieved by combining blouson top with dirndl skirt, left. Mixed textures were the rule. Above, printed challis is worn with ruffled-collar velvet jacket.

A fitted fur coat under a sleeveless woolen jacket is topped by a cloud-soft scarf, left. Real fur was back. Full-length raccoon contrasts with muted knit separates and matching ski-type head band.

Mollie Parnis ruffled the neck, cuffs, and hemline of her lace evening dress with red taffeta overskirt.

UPI

The blouson was another popular style for jackets, blouses, dresses and even coats. This "bubble" effect, achieved with a drawstring, was the new silhouette and the blouson was seen tied at the waist, the hip, and in some cases, even at the thigh. Again, it was always done in soft fabrics to keep it controlled and graceful.

Coats, while utilitarian, also had refined detailings. The double-coat was a clear favorite. It consisted of a classic raincoat with button-in plaid lining that could be worn as a coat and often was. Other linings were quilted and sleeveless. These were incorporated in the layered look as separates and sometimes were worn over the coat itself, having the appearance of a sort of long, sleeveless vest.

The layered look was still strong. However, because the fabrics used were lighter in weight and had more elegance—silks, cashmere, mohair and the like—the look was much less bulky and more wearable for many women than the look of prior years.

Fur Again. A most important trend was the return of fur. Because of ecologists' and conservationists' protests, the use of fur in fashion had for several years been restricted to fakes or so-called fun-furs. This year, however, fur coats were the most sought-after, and even cloth coats were lavish with fur collars, linings, and trims. Fur boas and hats and muffs were luxe accessories and the furs in demand included nutria, sable, lynx, and fox.

Sweaters in cashmere, mohair or angora blends were everywhere, and the deep cowl-necked style was still the most popular. Other sweaters were cobwebby floats of openwork lace knits or crochets. The bulky sweater became the sweater-coat, but of last year's strong ethnic influence only the Fair Isle patterned shetland remained a popular item.

Shirts became blouses, largely because of the fabrics and detailing. Crepe de chine, handkerchief linen, and soft cotton broadcloths and lawns were tucked, gathered, shirred, smocked, lace-yoked, bowed, or ruffled at the neck and wrists, or given demure collars of lace or lace trim. The gently gathered peasant blouse was also popular, with soft ties and delicate embroidery touches. Worn with last year's blazer and skirt, it gave an updated look of refined co-ordinates.

The most popular fabric was challis, with cashmere a close second. Expensive fabrics, both were in such demand that suppliers were hard put to fill orders and synthetic blends were concocted to meet the need. They also accounted for the "look" in lower priced lines. However, any soft and drapable fabric was part of the new refinement. Broadcloths, crepe de chine, whisper-weight flannels and delicate light tweeds, mohair, chiffons, and velvets, as well as jersey, conveyed the mood of femininity, delicacy, and taste. Colors were powdery and muted—celadon, peach, stone, mauve and honey were the popular tones. Even the earth tones used as accents were greyed and the summer brights were pure but softened with black grounds. Typical challis prints of florals and paisley were the only meaningful patterns and the few stripings or plaids that were much esteemed were ombre or lightly shaded.

Everywhere, quality detailing defined fashion. In addition to the gathers, ruffles, tucking, and bows already mentioned, there was the "Pier-

Fedora-style hats, footwear that included ghillies, ballet slippers, and boots, and narrow tie belts suspending tiny porcelain vases in the shape of boots, were captivating details of the great new look.

rot" collar, a large pleated or gathered ruching around the neck of a dress or blouse that framed the face as petals would a flower. Separate collars were sold at accessory counters for instant updating of last year's blouse, dress, or sweater. There were also jabot cascades, scalloping on hems and jacket edges, and ribbon trim on skirts and peasant blouses.

Accessories. Shawls were the number one accessory item, especially in challis prints that coordinated or contrasted with prints in skirts and dresses. Other shawls of soft wools, jerseys or cashmere were tied or draped around the shoulders, waist or hip. Knit mufflers of pale colored hairpin-like lace were twisted, knotted or wrapped around the throat. Combs held hair in romantic coifs, baring the nape for neck ruffles, and flowers were everywhere. Real or silk, shell or porcelain, they were worn on lapels, waists, wrists, dangling from cords as belts or necklaces, or used as chokers or to tie a topknot.

Neck bags were a form of jewelry. Small pouches hung from silk cord and dangled at the neck to carry precious little, and even mittens, on a string, were used as necklaces and belts, when not warming hands.

With skirts giving emphasis to the leg, textured stockings in fine mesh patterns in grey, brown and burgundy were worn with flattish ghillies and oxfords of shiny, fine leathers. Boots were still popular, especially when worn with their own accessory, the leg warmer, a heavy-knit sock with a wide cuff that was folded down over the boot top.

Belts were narrow cord or leather, or obi sashes embroidered or embossed. The bag was still the clutch refined in elegant smooth leathers for day, or a small envelope of snakeskin or brocade for evening.

Lace hankies, fur boas, pearls or antique jewelry with a Victorian spirit were also part of the accessory picture lending an air of gentility to the clothes. Small skull caps or narrow-brimmed fedoras alternated with rolled-brimmed knit caps for headcoverings. Matching mufflers or challis scarves were tied at the neck, as were soft silk squares often worn two at a time in contrasting colors or patterns and tied loosely to form a deep cowl in the back.

Evening fashions provided a choice: to be luxuriously demure or tastefully sexy. Ruffled blouses of soft chenille or lacy mohair sweaters were worn with floor-length, full-gathered skirts of velvet or satin for the innocent. The more world weary wore slinky, bared-shoulder gowns of draped satin, lamé, or matelassé. Glitter was everywhere for evening. Fabrics were shot with gold or silver, woven or printed; chiffon, lace, and even velvet were quilted with gold. Gold or silver sandals or flat ballet shoes in dark satin were worn with sheer, dark stockings, often with clocking. Long velvet capes lined in fur complemented either look for the ultimate in understated luxury and elegance.

MEN'S WEAR

In men's wear, the look was "Country Squire." It was casual but classy, coordinated but unstudied and polished, stressing fine tailoring and quality. The fabrics had much to do with this traditional look. Natural fibers in such classic fabric as Harris and birdsye tweeds, corduroy, flannel, and twill were most often used. Luxury cashmere and camel hair were back. Real cotton shirtings of oxford cloth and broadcloth in patterns of tattersall and classic stripes were strong, and silk and challis in small traditional patterns were the fabrics for the newly narrowed ties.

The city suit was double-breasted in pinstripes, glen plaids or herringbones. More casual suits had single breasted styling, often with vests. Jackets offered softer shoulders, narrower lapels and double vents. They often featured such country touches as leather buttons, suede elbow patches, and collars with wind tabs. In husky Harris tweeds or corduroy, the jacket was worn with other trousers for a sporty look. For the most part, trousers were straightlegged and uncuffed, with plain or one-pleat fronts. The classic camel hair polo coat came back. And other coat styles were equally traditional—trench, balmacaan, storm, and top coat. In tweeds and poplins, they were often lined in wool or alpaca.

Shirts were no longer tapered or fitted and their collars were smaller and buttoned down or pinned. They were most often worn with sweaters or sweater vests of shetland or cashmere with cable detailing. Under the country jacket they epitomized a look that was relaxed but discreetly dashing. The shawl-collared cardigan and poplin parka were other sporty jacket types for country dressing.

Accessories were neat and trim, in keeping with the general air of polished understatement. Little jewelry was worn. A watch, an I. D. bracelet, and perhaps an unglittery ring were all that were seen. The collar pin was the new accessory, and the classic attaché case in elegant leather was back. Driving gloves in pigskin were cuffed in wool knit or crochet.

Soft tweed hats or caps were the headgear and scarves or mufflers of cashmere or wool plaids were given a contemporary look when worn under the collar of a tweed jacket. Knit ties were other revivals.

Belts were narrow, in soft leathers and suedes with tastefully detailed hardware and buckles. In burgundy and navy, accent colors for the wool tweeds and flannels, they were often the only accessory a man wore.

Shoes were highly polished and detailed with wing-tips, tassels and stitching and of soft and handsome leathers. Moccasins, loafers, oxfords and short boots were the prevalent styles in warm browns, russets and black.

ANN M. ELKINS
Senior Editor, "Good Housekeeping"

UPI

Soviet Premier Kosygin and President Kekkonen dine in the Presidential Palace in Helsinki in March. Two months later, Finland and the USSR signed an economic pact.

FINLAND

A new cabinet, based on majority representation in Parliament, strove valiantly, and with some success, during 1977 to improve the Finnish economic situation. The celebration of the 60th anniversary of Finnish independence and a new economic agreement with the USSR were also among the highlights of the year.

Political Affairs. By the beginning of the year, it had become evident that Premier Martti Miettunen's nonsocialist three-party minority cabinet (appointed in September 1976) was unable to act effectively and to solve such economic problems as inflation and unemployment. Miettunen's cabinet (his third) was backed by the conservatives in Parliament and had strained relations with the socialist parties. To make matters worse, a number of serious strikes was ineptly handled by the cabinet.

In the deteriorating situation, it was felt that a majority cabinet would serve the nation better. Following negotiations between the center and leftist parties, a new cabinet took office on May 15. The 60th cabinet in the 60-year history of the republic, it was headed by Kalevi Sorsa, a former premier and minister of foreign affairs, who is chairman of the Social Democratic Party, Finland's biggest. The new minister for foreign affairs was Paavo Väyrynen, who at 31 was the youngest man ever to hold that office. In the cabinet were five ministers from the Center Party, four from the Social Democrats, three from the People's Democratic League (Communists), one from the Swedish Party, one from the Liberal Party, and a nonsocialist "expert" minister. The fact that three Communists accepted cabinet positions aggravated a split within the Communist Party.

At year-end, Finland was preparing for a presidential election, scheduled for February 1978. Five candidates had been nominated for the office.

Relations with the USSR. The spring of 1977 also saw important Finnish-Soviet developments. In March, Soviet Premier Kosygin paid an official visit to Finland, and in May President Urho K. Kekkonen made his fourth state visit to the Soviet Union. During the visit, President Kekkonen and Secretary General Brezhnev signed a Finnish-Soviet economic cooperation agreement to last until 1990. Another agreement concerned the building, on the Russian side of the border, of a new mining city, to be called Kostamus, in which Finnish engineers and no less than 10,000–20,000 Finnish workers would be employed. The enterprise will cost about four billion Finnish marks.

Economic Affairs. Inflation represented an ever-present problem. Since the real income of trade union members was decreasing rapidly—and unemployment stood at a new high, 13,000—the unions resorted to strikes.

Anniversary. The 60th anniversary of Finnish independence was celebrated throughout Finland on December 6. More modest in scope than the 50th anniversary commemoration, the festivities included a solemn service in Helsinki Cathedral, a festival concert in Finlandia Hall in Helsinki, and a gala reception at the Presidential Palace.

Cultural Affairs. In the cultural sector, the most noteworthy development was the heightened prominence of the Finnish basso Martti Talvela. His singing of the title role in *Boris Godunov* at the fall opening of the Metropolitan Opera in New York was characterized as peerless by the critics.

ERIK J. FRIIS
Editor, The Scandinavian-American Bulletin

——— **FINLAND · Information Highlights** ———

Official Name: Republic of Finland.
Location: Northern Europe.
Area: 130,120 square miles (337,011 km²).
Population (1977 est.): 4,800,000.
Chief Cities (1975 est.): Helsinki, the capital, 502,400; Tampere, 165,300; Turku, 163,200.
Government: *Head of state,* Urho Kaleva Kekkonen, president (took office March 1974 for 4th term). *Head of government,* Kalevi Sorsa, prime minister (took office May 1977). *Legislature* (unicameral)—Eduskunta.
Monetary Unit: Markka, or Finnish mark (4.04 markkas, equal U.S.$1, Aug. 1977).
Manufacturing (major products): Wood and paper products, ships, machinery, chemicals, metals, textiles, cement.
Major Agricultural Products: Oats, potatoes, sugar beets, barley, rye, wheat, forest products.

FLORIDA

While the national media seemed fascinated by the gay-rights issue in Miami, Floridians in 1977 were more concerned about taxes, the economy, and government in the sunshine.

The Legislature. Even before the legislature convened, it was obvious that new taxes would be needed to fund rising state expenditures, but there was disagreement over the type and amount. In a heated session, followed by a special session lasting into June, some $130 million in new taxes were levied, primarily on cigarettes and alcohol. Ironically, the added tax on cigarettes stimulated smuggling and created fears about loss of revenue.

Several important pieces of legislation were passed. A "sunset act" requires a periodic review of state agencies, and the Florida Crime Compensation Act initiated a program to compensate up to $10,000 the victims of violent crime. The largest legislative package reformed the state election laws and eliminated the loophole which had allowed officeholders to give testimonial dinners in order to raise large sums of money for unrestricted use. The most liberal reform was the Human Rights Act, which not only prohibits discrimination on the basis of sex, race, and religion, but also because of age, handicap, or marital status.

Women's liberation groups showed little joy over the Human Rights Act, however, because the legislature again refused to ratify the Equal Rights Amendment (ERA). The rejection came in spite of an intensive campaign by the pro-ERA group. Anti-ERA women also mobilized their forces for the largest, most intensive lobbying campaign ever seen in the state. Pro-ERA threats of a boycott of Florida failed to intimidate the tourist-conscious lawmakers.

The Governor. Reubin Askew, nearing the end of his second and final term as governor, began to have problems maintaining his consensus. His influence was diminished partly because of a sales-tax increase and because he supported Henry Jackson in the 1976 primaries rather than Jimmy Carter. Common Cause also criticized him for his veto of the strong financial-disclosure law passed by the legislature. Governor Askew justified the veto by saying the law invaded the privacy of officials and would lead to mass resignations of local officials. He then provoked new opposition by urging the Constitutional Revision Commission to strengthen the governor's office by removing the two-term limit and by replacing the elected cabinet with one appointed by the governor.

The Economy. Florida's agriculture, second only to tourism as an income producer, suffered severely from the drought in the southeastern states. Thirty counties in north Florida were declared disaster areas after sustaining damage estimated at $133 million. The impact in central Florida was less serious, but the 1977–78 orange crop was expected to be unusually small. Fortunately, tourism increased from 1976, and the construction industry began to emerge from a long slump. In the first three quarters of 1977, Florida's unemployment rate was slightly below the national average.

Miscellaneous. National attention was focused on the state, when Anita Bryant, a television personality and Florida resident, joined the struggle to rescind a Dade County (Miami) ordinance which specifically protected the rights of homosexuals. The residents of Dade County repealed the ordinance by a margin of 70%.

J. LARRY DURRENCE, *Florida Southern College*

FLORIDA · Information Highlights

Area: 58,560 square miles (151,670 km²).
Population (1976 est.): 8,421,000.
Chief Cities (1970 census): Tallahassee, the capital, 72,586; Jacksonville, 528,865; Miami, 334,859.
Government (1977): *Chief Officers*—governor, Reubin O'D. Askew (D); lt. gov., J. H. Williams (D). *Legislature*—Senate, 40 members; House of Representatives, 120.
Education (1976–77): *Enrollment*—public elementary schools, 777,168; public secondary, 760,168; nonpublic, 147,600; colleges and universities, 295,703 students. *Public school expenditures,* $2,341,173,000 ($1,364 per pupil).
State Finances (fiscal year 1976): *Revenues,* $5,178,-835,000; *expenditures,* $5,157,603,000.
Personal Income (1976): $50,690,000,000; per capita, $6,020.
Labor Force (July 1977): *Nonagricultural wage and salary earners,* 2,831,100; *unemployed,* 245,800 (7.1% of total force).

UPI

Anita Bryant comments on her successful campaign to have a Dade County ordinance, protecting the rights of homosexuals, rescinded.

FOOD

The world's food supply can be generally compared with a ride on a roller coaster. In 1977 the general trend for the harvest of grain was upward. Because grain is the world's basic foodstuff, much of what happens to world grain production, supplies, prices, and distribution is of great importance to both producer and consumer nations. Two years ago the world supply picture was grim, whereas today it is much brighter. Nonetheless, certain areas or countries still have problems in supply, price, and quality.

WORLD FOOD SUPPLY

With world population still on the increase, food production is a critical factor, especially in those countries that are both unable to produce enough to feed their people, and not supplied with enough money to pay for imported foods. In a good harvest year prices drop, enabling the poorer nations to buy at a price that does not cripple their economies. In 1975–76, the total world grain harvest was 1.216 billion (U. S.) metric tons, or 30 million tons above the poor harvest years of 1974–75. However, this harvest was below that of the record 1973–74 harvest. Estimated world production of 1.330 billion metric tons of grain in 1976–77 will represent an increase of 115 million tons over 1975–76, and if achieved will constitute an all-time record.

However, this increase would only maintain world output at about 2.5% above the long-term production trend. Other trends show that production per capita in the developing countries in 1976–77 would be only 2.3% above the 1969–71 level, while the centrally planned economies (Russia, China) would be over 12% above the base period and in the developed countries some 10% higher. The Protein Advisory Group of the United Nations System has pointed out that such figures mask differences between regions and countries. In 1975–76, per capita grain production was at or below levels achieved in the 1969–71 base period for 46 out of 81 developing market economies. It was expected that this figure would increase in 1976–77 to 49 out of 81 developing market economies in which the per capita production was below the 1969–71 level. A like trend was anticipated among the low-income countries or countries designated by the UN as "most seriously affected areas." In general, there is faster growth in grain production per capita in advanced countries, and more dependence on them for grains by the slower-developing countries.

Europe. As in the past, weather played a strong role in the production of all foodstuffs. In Europe, where drought seriously reduced output of most crops (except wheat) and lowered pasture yields, with some forced slaughterings, in 1976, the outlook for 1977 was much brighter. Increased harvests were forecast for wheat, barley, corn, potatoes, sugarbeets, and fruit. Only

UPI

Severe drought caused U. S. corn production to fall below normal in some areas. Many farmers did not harvest.

beef production was expected to be lower, largely because of fewer slaughterings. While U. S. farm exports to Western Europe rose 10% in 1976, mostly because of feed demand, it was expected that the increase in 1977 would be smaller.

Asia and Oceania. Total agricultural production was virtually unchanged during 1976, although there was considerable change in some countries in this region. Renewed growth in total agricultural production was forecast for 1977. When population is considered, the current situation is somewhat different. On a per capita basis, the 1976 output was down, because of lowered yields in Japan and Australia. The forecast for Asia and Oceania in 1977 was brighter, with increased production of rice, wheat, and other crops anticipated. However, price increases and decreases for trade products such as coffee, tea, spices, rubber, and grain made the 1977 outlook variable. Overall, the 1977 expectation for Asia and Oceania was for renewed growth in total agricultural production and continued strong growth by individual economies.

Canada and Latin America. In the Western Hemisphere (excluding the United States) there was a moderate economic recovery in 1976. The recovery continued in 1977 at a diminished rate. Canada, the largest agricultural producer other than the United States, expected a decline in net farm income, and a reduction in total wheat production because of wheat stock holdings and lower world wheat prices.

Within the Western Hemisphere, the coffee situation in South America gathered headlines because of small harvests in 1976. Brazil was particularly hard hit by a freeze in the coffee-producing areas that resulted in the smallest Latin American coffee harvest since 1970. This shortage led to sharply higher coffee prices early in 1977, but prices declined in the third quarter. Overall, agricultural production grew in the Western Hemisphere in 1977, despite soft spots for certain crops such as sugars.

The Soviet Bloc and China. In the USSR, other Soviet-bloc countries, and China the picture was less clear. Demand for imported grains from the large Western producing nations fell. In the Soviet Union, a record wheat crop had been expected, barring late weather problems, but the reported figures fell 10% below the 1976 record. Accurate information on China's crops is difficult to find, but it was expected that the Chinese will share in increased harvests.

United States. In the United States, the 1977 harvest results were mixed. Parts of the Northwest, Midwest, and central California were stricken by one of the worst droughts in years, while the Great Plains and central areas were producing at a record rate. U. S. yield estimates were about 2 billion (U. S.) bushels of wheat (third largest in history), 6.2 billion bushels of corn (second largest), and a record 1.8 billion bushels of soybeans.

In two years, the world has gone from a shortage of grain and fears of hunger and famine to a world concern over grain surpluses. Normally, the United States exports about 35% of its grain (1977 estimates—89 million metric tons of grain and soybeans), but with surpluses throughout the world this figure could be expected to drop some 10–15% in 1978. The world-record crops of 1977, combined with stocks held over from 1976, totaled 190 to 200 million metric tons (USDA estimate) in 1978, or the largest reserve ever. But the biggest surpluses are in the United States, Canada, USSR, Australia, and Argentina, while areas in North Africa and the Near East have little or no reserve. The presence of surpluses in one area does not solve shortages in another area. In consequence, major exporting and importing nations have discussed ways to establish grain reserves to provide for areas in need.

U. S. FOOD INDUSTRY

All segments of the U. S. food industry, along with the American consumer, faced similar problems in 1977. Rising costs, energy supplies, effect of governmental regulations, and food safety were paramount topics whenever food was discussed. Although food shortages or soaring prices did affect consumer buying, the food supply was abundant, varied, and safe when compared with the rest of the world.

Food Costs. The record harvest yields were welcome news for consumers, who faced modest food price hikes of 4% to 6% in 1977. In the wholesale markets, wheat sold at about $2.60 a bushel compared with $3 in 1976 and $12 in 1973. Corn was down about $1 per bushel over 1976, and soybeans had dropped nearly $5. While these price drops were not entirely reflected at the retail level, they tended to prevent high increases. Other consumer foods rose to very high price levels, especially such products as coffee, cocoa, tea, and other imported foods that were either in short supply or in great demand. With food taking about 17% of the

UPI

With coffee prices skyrocketing, Elinor Guggenheimer, New York City's commissioner of consumer affairs, urged the public to boycott the beverage.

UPI
Florida's citrus industry suffered from a winter cold wave.

consumer's income after taxes, it is well to note that the American consumer prefers to buy food that is partially or fully prepared. A study of food consumption revealed that in 1975 ready-to-eat foods had a 46.6% share and ready-to-cook foods had a 50.3% share. Foods requiring preparation accounted for only 3.1%. Although further processing usually results in higher prices at the retail level, it is evident that the American consumer tends to emphasize convenience.

Regulatory Actions. Of the many regulatory actions affecting the food industry, none had a greater impact than the proposal to ban or remove saccharin, an artificial sweetener, from the market. All previous artificial sweeteners except saccharin have been removed from the market place or delisted by the Food and Drug Administration (FDA) for use in food, leaving only saccharin for use by consumers and food processors to control calories and for use by diabetics. In March of 1977, the FDA announced that saccharin would be removed from the market as of Oct. 1, 1977, because 1976–77 studies using rats showed a link between saccharin and bladder cancer. Consumers and members of Congress began to defend the "unsafe" chemical. As of November, the ban had not taken effect. Congress, meanwhile, was enacting legislation that would suspend the ban for 18 months.

Other areas of regulation drawing attention from governmental agencies and consumer groups include ingredient listing, nutrition labeling, sanitary standards for fresh foods, and food safety. Regulatory control of food currently involves 14 governmental agencies and more than 2,000 regulations. Inevitably, the additional costs for compliance will be passed on to the consumer.

Retort Pouches. In May, the FDA and the USDA approved the use of retort pouches for heat processed foods. Widely used in Japan and Europe, the retort pouch was subjected to arduous approval tests in the United States. Basically, it is a laminated flexible pouch of three or more layers of plastic and foil filled with food which, after sealing, is processed under steam pressure. After processing, the single serving can be stored at room temperature until heated in boiling water for serving. The pouch flexibility, the relatively short heat treatment when compared with a can or jar, and easy stacking are expected to make the retort pouch a useful item because of convenience and quality.

The use of nitrites and nitrates in meat and poultry products was studied intensely by both the FDA and the USDA to determine if nitrosamines are formed when the products are heated, and whether the amounts so formed could be linked to cancer. The initial inquiry placed responsibility on the users to provide information to these agencies as to whether nitrites are harmful.

Nutrition. Although a number of proposals and changes in school lunch programs and other USDA support programs in the nutrition area were proposed, the issuance of the dietary recommendations by a U. S. Senate committee made the biggest news. The Senate Select Committee on Nutrition and Human Needs published *Dietary Goals for the United States,* which called for six basic changes in the national diet, included guides to help consumers, and made recommendations for action by government and industry to improve nutritional health. The changes or goals were to increase carbohydrate consumption, to reduce overall fat consumption to about 30% of energy (caloric) intake, to reduce saturated fat consumption to 10%, and balance the rest equally between poly- and mono-unsaturated fats, reduce cholesterol levels to 300 mg. per day, reduce sugar consumption by 40%, and reduce salt consumption per day by 50–85% or to about 3 grams. Consumption of fruits, vegetables, and whole grains would be increased along with poultry and fish, while meat, butter fat, eggs, sugar and high sugar content foods, and salt and high salt foods would be decreased. Nonfat milk would be substituted for whole milk, and foods high in fat would be decreased and unsaturated fats substituted.

The report met with both praise and condemnation. To achieve such a drastic change in the American diet will require an intensive and massive nutrition education program, which will encounter the opposition of many commodity-oriented groups. Regardless of the outcome, it will be a number of years before the results will be known.

See also AGRICULTURE; MEDICINE AND HEALTH.

KIRBY M. HAYES
University of Massachusetts

UPI

Former Prime Minister Jacques Chirac signs the oath of office as the first mayor of Paris in more than a century.

FRANCE

Instability within stability was the prevailing theme in French public life during 1977. Nearly everything was conducted with an eye on the elections of 1978. The odds changed constantly. Optimism and pessimism flowed from camp to camp. Toward the end of the year it was impossible to predict whether it was the close of one more *ancien régime* or merely the 19th year of the conservative Fifth Republic.

DOMESTIC AFFAIRS

President Valéry Giscard d'Estaing's fortunes waned and waxed. Nineteen seventy-six had not been a vintage year for him. Nineteen seventy-seven opened with profound divisions in his ruling coalition. His authority was robustly challenged by Gaullist former Prime Minister Jacques Chirac. For much of the year Giscard kept a low profile; his mood was melancholy as he opened the brilliantly controversial Georges Pompidou National Center of Arts and Culture in February, though he vowed to serve out his full term. The polls indicated his falling popularity. The municipal council elections in March confirmed a leftist tide. On March 30, he asked Prime Minister Raymond Barre to form a new government, dropping his close friend and adviser, Minister of the Interior Michel Poniatowski, Minister of Regional Development and Planning Jean Lacanuet, and Minister of Justice

Olivier Guichard, all casualties of the struggle with Chirac. This was Giscard's attempt to bind up the wounds of 1976 and confront the left with a restored governing unity. And with the breakdown of the leftist coalition in the summer, the presidential strategy appeared successful. Giscard's personal standing rose in the polls; he seemed more confident; Chirac's abrasive, exaggerated ambition was less obtrusive. As winter came on, the outcome for Giscard in 1978 was evidently far from determined.

Nonetheless, Chirac's flamboyant transformation of the old Union of Democrats for the Republic into the Rassemblement pour la République (RPR) in December 1976 struck a fresh, personal, and aggressive note. On January 19 he announced he would seek the prestigious, renascent office of mayor of Paris, against the left and Giscard's candidate, Minister of Industry and Research Michel d'Ornano. Giscard denounced the challenge, but could not prevent Chirac's besting his man in the March 13 first round. In the second, on March 20, Chirac and d'Ornano withdrew in one another's favor in whichever district they trailed, thus assuring a united conservative vote which secured the mayoralty for Chirac. Thereupon, the new RPR leader proclaimed his crusade against "the collectivist challenge to our society."

The challenge was tangible in the overall outcome of the municipal elections, held in 36,000 cities, towns, and villages. In the first round, 52.5% of the vote went to the Communist-Socialist bloc, 45.5% to the ruling coalition (RPR, Independent Republicans, Radical Socialists, Centrists), and 2% to the growing Environmental Movement. The second round confirmed the left's victory. The stock market dropped. "It's a veritable tidal wave!" said Socialist leader François Mitterrand. "It's crazy. I haven't seen a landslide like this for the left since the war." In all, the left controlled two thirds of France's largest municipalities and was widely assumed to be the winner in the 1978 National Assembly election. Giscard called for "frank and loyal" cooperation between his own Independent Republicans (renamed the Republican party, in May) and Chirac's RPR, but the future of the troubled gov-

——— FRANCE · Information Highlights ———

Official Name: French Republic.
Location: Western Europe.
Area: 211,207 square miles (547,026 km²).
Population (1977 est.): 53,400,000.
Chief Cities (1975 census): Paris, the capital, 2,291,000; Marseille, 908,000; Lyon, 457,000; Toulouse, 383,000.
Government: *Head of state,* Valéry Giscard d'Estaing, president (took office May 1974). *Chief minister,* Raymond Barre, prime minister (took office Aug. 1976). *Legislature*—Parliament: Senate and National Assembly.
Monetary Unit: Franc (4.91 francs equal U. S.$1, Aug. 1977).
Manufacturing (major products): Steel, machinery, metals, chemicals, automobiles, airplanes, processed foods, beverages, clothing, textiles.
Major Agricultural Products: Wheat, barley, oats, sugar beets, vegetables, apples, grapes, cattle.

erning coalition depended at least as much on how well or ill the always delicate state of the Union of the Left survived personal and programmatic disputes. The results of the partial, indirect elections to the Senate (115 of 295 seats at stake) on September 25 reflected this weakness: the left gained 10 seats (for 106) but the center-right gained 2 (for 189). A minor cabinet shuffle ensued, as three ministers had won seats in the Senate.

The Giscard-Chirac quarrel was less shrill in the second half of the year, and attention concentrated on the Union of the Left. Basically a coalition of Mitterrand's Socialists, Georges Marchais' Communists, and Robert Fabre's small Left Radical party, its history since 1972 has been marked by recurrent difficulties, mutual reservations, and the electrifying rise to primacy of the Socialists; their share of the popular vote increased from 5% to 32% as the Communists' fell from 25% to 20%. By May 1977, the Communists were demanding increased nationalizations and more radical social reform. Both Mitterrand and Fabre resisted. Between June and September, the polls registered a turnaround, with the odds for 1978 no longer on the Union of the Left but on the ruling coalition. When the three leaders met, September 14, to revise their program, disagreement boiled over. Fabre walked out, declaring he would never support measures to bring about a collectivist society. Controlling no more than 3% or 4% of the national vote, the Left Radicals were nevertheless a gauge of the union's health. If they could not be reconciled to a common program, Mitterrand's chances of becoming prime minister and Marchais' of being the first Communist cabinet minister in more than 30 years were slim.

Their differences seemed intractable. In 1972, they agreed on nationalization of the arms, aerospace, nuclear, pharmaceutical, electronics, minerals, chemical, and computer industries. The Communists now wanted to include all the subsidiary companies, plus oil, steel, and Peu-geot-Citroën. Mitterrand and Fabre objected in principle; they also thought the cash indemnities would be ruinous. Moreover, such a program would terrify their small-business supporters, and the rigid control of salaries proposed by Marchais would alienate the Socialist and Left Radical voters. In addition, the Communists suddenly proclaimed support for France's nuclear striking force (provided it was directed against the United States as well as the USSR), while Mitterrand was fundamentally opposed and wished to put its future to a referendum.

Possibly, the Communists were simply maneuvering to avoid having to take office as the junior partner in Mitterrand's cabinet; should the Union of the Left obtain a majority in the assembly, the Communists might merely support a leftist government, without participating in it. But the early "provisional breakdown" (as Mitterrand called it), though it seemed certain to be made good before the election, did not bode well for the left. In the meantime, the country prepared for a possible change of government. High-level civil servants made approving noises about the Socialists; large amounts of money illegally left the country. But whatever the election outcome, the balance of forces was such that no profoundly disturbing changes seemed likely.

Reforms and Scandals. The quest for social justice made no great progress. Some 4% of the nation continued to belong to "the sub-proletariat." Giscard showed concern, but it was left to a welter of public and private agencies to deal piecemeal with the problem. Reform of industrial relations remained pending. The 1975 Sudreau report had brought new safety measures and managerial reforms, but a degree of worker participation in management continued to be difficult to achieve. The *patronat* was largely hostile, the unions suspicious. Only a few hundred companies yet had supervisory boards (Peugeot-Citroën was the largest).

A rising sense of general insecurity because of increased social violence was reported in the

UPI

Parisian taxi drivers tied up traffic in front of the Ministry of Finance on March 15, protesting high gasoline prices and high taxes.

President Valéry Giscard d'Estaing, on a state visit to Saudi Arabia in January, is escorted by Crown Prince Fahd (*left*) and aides.

UPI

summer by the government's Committee to Study Violence, Delinquency, and Crime. By U. S. standards, the incidence of urban violence was low. Significantly, however, it had risen markedly in the past decade and disproportionately among youth and resident foreigners. There was no evident solution to the underlying problem of cultural alienation, exploitation, and poverty.

A scandal which briefly titillated the public was the murder on Christmas eve 1976 of Prince Jean de Broglie, a deputy and a former Gaullist minister, an early supporter of Giscard. He was struck down in the street by a pimp allegedly hired by business associates who owed him money. Characteristically, the trail led toward other prominent persons and was quickly closed off. The case was one in an endless series of crimes involving the *haut monde*'s money, politics, and sexual proclivities, which governments, through manipulation of the judicial system, consign to oblivion.

Strikes and Protests. The first general strike since 1968 took place on May 24, with the participation of all four major unions. Protesting Prime Minister Barre's ceiling on wage increases (6.5%, with inflation running around 10%), some 8–10 million people participated for 24 hours. Police action was, by French standards, minimal. Other strikes during the year occurred in the transport, garbage-disposal, customs, post-office, and newspaper sectors of the economy. The most violent clash between security forces and demonstrators came in the Rhône Valley on August 1, when some 30,000 supporters of the Environmental Movement protested construction of a giant plutonium breeder reactor at Malville, about 28 miles (45 km) east of Lyon. A young chemistry teacher was killed by a concussion grenade; more than 100 other demonstrators and 10 policemen were injured.

This did not halt the nuclear energy program which is designed to cut oil imports by 75% as of 1985.

Economy. There were no victories in the battle against inflation. Barre's moderately austere program had wide support, despite labor's formal protests. The business community was cooperative, leery of Chirac's politics of polarization, ready to believe that Barre's approach was the best hope of avoiding a possible leap in the dark with the Union of the Left. The realities were an immense trade deficit—nearly $7 billion (U. S.) in 1976—one million unemployed, illegal flight of funds, and the enormous appeal of imported goods and foreign vacations. The Common Market meant that the "Buy French" slogan could not be backed by protectionism. Money was allocated to public works and a youth employment program, but the situation was, at best, barely satisfactory.

Defense and Europe. No substantial defense changes were in the offing. The contradictions of the left committed it to the status quo. The Socialists might hanker after dismantling of both NATO and the Warsaw Pact, but on August 8 even Mitterrand admitted the value of the French nuclear deterrent. And given the Communists' about-face this year in support of it, it was perhaps true, as the party theoretician Jean Kanapa said in July, that "We're not very different from the Gaullists on Europe and defense."

A representative European parliament came one step closer, so far as France was concerned, when a bill authorizing direct elections was put through the National Assembly on June 16.

FOREIGN POLICY

Relations with most nations remained good. If France could not get the British to construct a Channel tunnel, at least it obtained an award by an international tribunal of a larger share of the western approaches, some 3,360 square miles (8,700 km²) of potentially oil-rich seabed. The usual fruit and vegetable wars with the Italians marked the passing of summer; this time, battalions of Italian mushroom pickers were accused of rising early to plunder French fields close to the frontier.

Relations with the USSR were more cordial, characterized by long-term economic agreements and Russian attempts to refurbish détente. President Leonid Brezhnev visited France June 20–22, calling for disarmament efforts and accepting personal gifts of two automobiles. The visit permitted Giscard to play the broker between the Soviets and the Americans, whose recent moralizing and intervention in Soviet human-rights cases had annoyed the Russians. To Giscard's displeasure, Brezhnev met Chirac, but he did not see Marchais, who had no reason to see him, having criticized Soviet and East European intolerance and seeking to establish his own Eurocommunist image.

Visiting Riyadh, January 22–25, Giscard continued courting Saudi Arabia and negotiated an oil-for-arms deal. The price of keeping oil suppliers friendly, however, was clear in January, when the Palestinian terrorist Abu Daoud, said to have planned the 1972 Munich Olympics massacre of Israeli athletes, entered France under an assumed name as a member of a Palestine Liberation Organization delegation. Someone tipped off the police. Abu Daoud was arrested, while headlines shrieked; the Germans moved indifferently, and the Israelis ineffectively, to extradite him. Determined not to incur Arab wrath and reprisal, Giscard and his prime minister had Daoud swiftly and secretly brought before a tribunal, which found that neither Germany nor Israel had properly made its case and packed him off by air to Algeria. It was an exemplary lesson in *realpolitik,* accompanied by routine official obfuscation.

In Africa, France demonstrated its active presence. Though the government tried to avoid deeper involvement in the struggle for the former Spanish Sahara between Algerian-backed rebels and Morocco and Mauritania, irate public opinion finally pushed it to act in November to free French citizens held by the Polisario rebels. In April, Chirac and the right pushed the government to action in Zaire on behalf of President Mobutu against rebel forces. Foreign Minister Louis de Guiringaud showed the flag in a round of African visits in July and August, staging a haughty demonstration of outrage when confronted by hostile pickets in Tanzania on August 18; he flew home next day, assailed by scathing attacks from Tanzanian President Julius Nyerere and Zambian President Kenneth Kaunda among others. On June 27, France withdrew formally from its Red Sea colony of Djibouti (French Territory of the Afars and the Issas).

Relations with the United States were cordial, punctuated by threats to take some nameless reprisal, should the Anglo-French Concorde aircraft not obtain firm landing rights at New York. Clearly, President Carter perplexed Giscard as he did everyone else. In an interview in July, Giscard finally rapped Carter's knuckles for violating the code of noninterference in other nations' domestic affairs, heightening ideological warfare with the USSR, and generally playing the amateur in the professional game of world politics.

With Canada, France continued its cynical policy of official nonintervention, while publicly supporting Quebec's separatist government. It accorded Premier René Lévesque the honors of a head of state on November 2–4, in flagrant violation of both protocol and Canadian sensibilities, thus pursuing the francophone Gaullist policy of abetting the breakup of Canada.

JOHN C. CAIRNS
University of Toronto

For a week in May, Parisian artists painted in the Métro (subway) to the delight of commuters.

UPI

DEREK FELL

The *Zinnia Cherry Ruffles* is a new color in the Ruffles class of hybrid zinnias, bred for display and cutting.

GARDENING AND HORTICULTURE

Home vegetable gardening in the United States increased dramatically in 1977. As several factors combined to bring about shortages and high prices for commercially grown vegetables, many consumers reacted by growing their own. The severe drought in California and the disastrous weather in other parts, which reduced water supplies in some places and caused flooding in others, delayed planting and harvesting and even prevented commercial growers from planting at all. Prices for fresh fruit and vegetables were considerably higher in 1977 because of higher prices paid by growers for energy and labor. Heating costs for greenhouses, in which seedlings are started, doubled in some areas.

All-America Selections. There were two award-winning roses for 1978. William Warriner gained his fourth award for Color Magic, a very fine hybrid tea, which produces an intriguing series of color changes during its cycle from bud to mature flower. Beginning as creamy, apricot-pink buds, the blossoms unfold to six-to-seven-inch (15–18-cm) blooms that are a delicate ivory pink in the center but shade into deep pink and finally deep rose-red on the outer petals. Sometimes, particularly in the fall, the flowers turn bright cherry red at maturity.

The name Color Magic was well chosen and suggests the greatest problem with this rose: presenting a color illustration that adequately depicts the flower.

Plants of Color Magic are vigorous and produce an abundance of very large, 30-petal blooms, usually on a single 18–20-inch (46–51-cm) stem which gives an excellent cut flower. The plants grow tall and should be used accordingly in the garden. The foliage is dark, glossy green and covers the plant well.

Color Magic is described as similar to, but better than, the cultivar Spellbinder, having a lighter, more pleasing color. The blossoms have a light, sweet fragrance and, as an added asset, possess what is known as a good flower finish: the petals fall cleanly when the blooms reach the peak of maturity.

With its huge blooms, vigorous growth, many flower stems, clean green foliage, and attractive fragrance, Color Magic should find a ready place in all gardens. It is expected that it will also do well on the show tables.

Charisma, the other award winner, is a floribunda of intense coloration and excellent, bushy mound-like growth habit. The blooms are a flaming blend of brilliant scarlet and bright golden yellow. The plants, in full flower, covered with clusters of vivid blooms, will most certainly attract attention from as far away as they can be seen. As the blooms mature, the scarlet deepens, gradually sweeping over the golden yellow until the entire flowers become an intense, deep, fiery red. This bright color holds up well until the petals drop.

The dainty buds of Charisma are nicely shaped and develop into attractive, small-to-medium-sized, high-centered blooms; there are several to a cluster, and the many clusters blanket the plant throughout the growing season. There is a slight fading of the flowers during the extreme heat of summer.

The blossom petals are tough and weather-resistant, allowing the cultivar to preserve an attractive appearance during rainy weather, when the flowers of most others take on a distinctly bedraggled look. Because of its masses of brilliant blossoms, Charisma will serve well in any part of the home grounds and add beauty and color to any garden. It is definitely an eye-catching rose in any location.

The blooms of Charisma have good lasting quality, both as cut flowers and on the plants.

Charisma plants are attractive and do not grow wildly out of bounds as do some floribundas. This characteristic is a most desirable asset because it allows use in mass plantings for a concentration of intense color, or in borders where the plants should remain within reasonable growth bounds.

Charisma is as disease-resistant as most modern roses. It was developed by Robert Telly of Richmond, Ind., and is his first All-America award winner.

DONALD W. NEWSOM
Louisiana State University

GENETICS

Molecular genetics made great progress in 1977. Specifically, the relationship between DNA (deoxyribonucleic acid) and proteins was shown to be more complex than anyone had thought. First, Dr. Frederick Sanger and his colleagues in Cambridge, England, reported the entire nucleotide sequence of the DNA of the bacterial virus φX 174. DNA is the material of which genes are made; it is, in turn, composed of linear chains of the four nucleotides, containing the bases adenine, guanine, cytosine, and thymine (A, G, C, and T). It is the *order* of A, G, C, and T that specifies the nature of any particular gene or group of genes. This order, or sequence, is transferred to molecules called RNA's (ribonucleic acids), which are also long chains and also contain A, G, and C, but instead of T have uracil (U) in them. (For our purposes, U is the same as T. Thus, if in the DNA there is a sequence AACCTG, the corresponding RNA will have the sequence AACCUG.) The function of most RNA's is to direct the synthesis of proteins.

Basically, whether a cell is to be a bacterium, part of the human eye, or an egg is determined by its proteins. It is known that the machinery of the cell which makes proteins does so by reading the order of the four nucleotides and interpreting it to a chain of amino acids. Thus, we know that UUU spells out phenylalanine, and AAA spells out lysine; UUU.AAA would mean phenylalanine-lysine, hooked together. The protein-making machinery reads three bases of an RNA sequence at a time: thus, UUU.AAA.UUU will specify phenylalanine-lysine-phenylalanine—but only if the machinery starts reading at the first U. If it starts with the second U, it will see this sequence as UUA.AAU.UU, which means it will make leucine-asparagine as the first two hooked-together amino acids, and go on to make an entirely different protein. In other words, any sequence of nucleotides, when read in groups of three, is able to form three entirely different proteins.

Now it is also known that the RNA contains *signals*—sequences that tell the protein-making machinery where to start, so that, normally, only one of the three possible proteins is actually made. What Sanger and his coworkers found is that in the DNA of φX 174 there are sometimes two "start here" signals close to one another, so that the same piece of RNA will actually code for two completely different functions. An example will illustrate this. Consider the sequence AUG.AAA.GUG.AUU.GAU.GCU.CUA.UUC.CG.

... and take the arrows to mean "start here." The first sequence, then, will spell out methionine-lysine-valine-isoleucine-aspartic acid-alanine-leucine-phenylalanine, and so forth, while the second will read methionine-leucine-tyrosine-serine, and so forth. The two proteins made will be completely different, and will probably have different functions, as in the case of φX 174. Indeed, from the genetic point of view, the two proteins are the products of two different genes; what happens is that more than one gene is packed into one piece of DNA.

While theory did not exclude such a result, few scientists thought they would ever see it in a living organism. Such a genetic organization brings with it certain problems: if one base in the region coding for two proteins changes by mutation, it may affect two proteins. But the demonstration is clear, and the possibility that two genes will be encoded on the same piece of DNA will have to be considered in all detailed genetic analysis.

The second major finding of 1977 was that RNA transcribed from DNA may have adjacent sequences which were not adjacent in the DNA that served as the template. DNA molecules are, in general, very large and may possibly extend to tens of millions of connected nucleotides. RNA molecules, while chemically very similar, are usually much shorter—on the order of tens of thousands of nucleotides. Previously, it had been thought that RNA molecules came from a single, connected region of DNA, as in the illustration below.

```
   a     b     c     d     e     f     g     h
 --|--|--|--|--|--|--|--|--|--|--|--|--|--|--|--
    RNA₁       RNA₂       RNA₃    RNA₄ RNA₅
 --|--|--|--|--|--|--|--|--|--|--|--|--|--|--|--
   a     b     c     d     e     f     g     h
```

Here, several RNA molecules are made from one DNA molecule, but any parts that are connected in the RNA were also connected in its DNA template. Thus, the end of "a" is still joined to the beginning of "b," the end of "c" to the beginning of "d," and so forth.

What has been clearly shown for at least one DNA-RNA system (the genome of the adenovirus and its product RNA) and indicated for a number of other systems is that an RNA can be found which does *not* correspond to the simple model above. Instead, a DNA-to-RNA pattern of the sort shown below has been observed:

```
   a    b    c   d   e   f      g
 --|----|----|---|---|---|------|--
   a    d    e        f   ↓   RNA₁
 --|----|----|--------|------------
   a    d    e        g      RNA₂
 --|----|----|--------|------------
```

Here, sections which were *not* adjacent in the DNA are joined in the RNA. In RNA₁, it appears as though segments "b" and "c" have been removed and in RNA₂ as though "f" has been dropped as well. Thus, the order of nucleotide blocks in the RNA need not reflect their order in the DNA. Since the RNA is read by the protein-making machinery, this means that information for two closely spaced regions in a protein may have come from stretches in the DNA which are very far apart.

PETER MODEL
Rockefeller University

An active year for volcanoes: Day and night views of Sicily's Mount Etna which erupted in July, hurling volcanic rock 2,000 feet (600 m) into the air.

GEOLOGY

Geologists were faced with a number of problems in 1977, including radioactive waste disposal, long-term climatic change, and development of geothermal energy. Meanwhile, the state of geological science was changing.

Radioactive Waste. A pressing current problem for geologists is the disposal of radioactive wastes. West Germany has pioneered in this field. Since 1967, it has been depositing material of low- and medium-level radioactivity in an unused salt mine nearly one-half mile (0.8 km) below the surface near Remlingen. The United States also has vast unused salt mines and salt deposits in which cavities could be opened miles below the surface.

Although salt beds appear to be the best containers for long-lived radioactive wastes, geologists are being very cautious about any positive guarantees about their use. Salt is self-healing with respect to fractures and is watertight when dry, but it is extremely soluble in the presence of water. The danger in storing radioactive waste underground, even when it is embedded in glass and encased in steel, is that it may escape, enter underground water, and reach the surface, perhaps thousands of years in the future. A recent seemingly far-fetched suggestion is that certain tracts in the great open fracture zones of the ocean floors may be ideal for the disposal of dangerous material.

Climatic Change. Climatic changes of the past and future received much attention in 1977. Geologists James D. Hall, John Imbrie, and Nickolas J. Shackelton made the unequivocal claim that they have established the cause of the recent ice age and associated climatic oscillations. Cyclic changes in the astronomical relations of the earth are held responsible by them, including the earth's nearness to the sun, the inclination of its axis, and the shape of its orbit. These effects, known from mathematical calculations, were found to coincide with changes of climate as recorded in sediment cores from the ocean. Another outcome of this study is evidence that temperatures must have risen from full glacial to full interglacial levels between 13,000 and 11,000 years ago.

Borings into the Greenland ice cap have revealed the curious fact that climatic changes happen in Greenland long before they do elsewhere in the Northern Hemisphere. The lag seems to be 100 to 150 years for Iceland and 250 years for England. It is anticipated that a climatic record extending back 100,000 years can be obtained by drilling in Greenland.

Although all evidence points to ominous future events, authorities differ in their predictions as to when a full-scale glacial period might commence. Short-term present changes made evident in erratic weather and creeping deserts are extremely serious. Looking backward, geologists especially note the effects of rising sea level due to the melting of ice sheets. For instance, San Francisco Bay did not exist 15,000 years ago. Sea water entered the area gradually and began to spread inland 10,000 years ago. Specimens of fossil cedar and redwood, dated at 23,000 years old, are found in place 20 feet (6 meters) below present sea level.

Geothermal Energy. Geologists have assumed a major role in the development of geothermal power. Areas of past and present hot springs and geysers are being studied on a global scale. The emergence of steam and hot water indicates only a few of the areas where geothermal energy might be tapped. For instance, the heat of hot but dry rock can be utilized by introducing surface water so as to create a circulating system that delivers energy back to the surface.

The geysers area near San Francisco, which is marked by numerous natural steam vents, is being drilled and developed as a major geothermal resource. It is estimated that by 1990 California could receive 25% of its electrical power from clean, cheap geothermal energy.

Earthquakes. The true devastation of the Tangshan quakes in China in July 1976 was re-

UPI

Edward Olsen examines a 900-pound (408 kg) meteorite, discovered in Antarctica in January. The geologist estimates that there are less than 2,000 meteorites worldwide.

Looking forward, geologists will be almost compelled to assume a leading role in earthquake studies and prediction. The United States Geological Survey Office of Earthquake Studies is charged with coping with a problem of gargantuan proportions. Concerned officials are trying to imagine the various situations that could arise from earthquakes and are trying to devise strategies to deal with them. There are problems for engineers, sociologists, economists, political leaders, government officials, the news media, and even the individual citizen.

Volcanoes. Volcanoes also acted up in 1977. On January 10, 70 persons were killed by being incinerated in a lava flow from the Nyiragongo volcano in Zaire. The most spectacular eruption of the year was that of Mt. Usu, on the island of Hokkaido, Japan, early in August. More than 1,000 light earthquakes preceded the eruption, thousands of tourists and residents fled the area, and destructive dust settled over a wide region.

State of Geological Science. After the exhilaration from explorations of the moon and the nearby planets, geologists are turning earthward to deal with the growing emergencies and perils of terrestrial existence. A recent survey shows 340 geology-oriented societies operating in various parts of the world. The vast majority are of regional scope, but there are numerous specialized associations such as the Glaciological Society, Society of Vertebrate Paleontology, and National Water Well Association.

Another indication of the state of geological science is a list of 177 conferences, conventions, and field trips scheduled to take place between Aug. 22, 1977, and Aug. 28, 1978. Of these, 82 deal with applied or practical matters such as energy, water, mineral exploration, coal, highway geology, mining law, remote sensing, and land subsidence. Only two clearly deal with extraterrestrial subjects.

Literary output is another index of heightened activity. A diversity of new journals has appeared over the past few years, particularly in environment-related fields. Editors of older established journals argue that such new outlets are unnecessary and they urge their readers to support existing organizations and their established publications.

There is also a great outpouring of maps. It is estimated that the U. S. government distributes about 50 million copies of its 40,000 topographic maps each year and a large number of geologic maps also. Citizens are learning to read and use maps as they take to the road, fly over the land, cruise the coasts and inland lakes, or hike in the wilderness. The fact that geologic maps of China, Australia, Mexico, and the Pacific Ocean went on sale during 1977 indicates that knowledge of these vast areas has reached a mature stage.

vealed by the figure of about 655,000 deaths given out by Chinese officials early in 1977. Although they missed predicting this big one, the Chinese claim to have successfully predicted three other major quakes—those of about 7 on the Richter scale—during 1976. The basis for their predictions appears to have been the detection of foreshocks. Six earthquakes of magnitude 7 or greater shook China in 1976. Such activity is rare in China's history.

During 1977 other parts of the earth experienced earthquakes. The Tonga Island region had a severe quake on April 2 (7.5 Richter, no damage) and again in June (7.2 Richter, no deaths). On April 6, central Iran was shaken (6.0 Richter, 348 deaths). The Solomon Islands had three quakes on April 20 (6.7, 7.4, and 7.6 Richter). On August 19, a major quake—8.9 Richter—originating 323 miles (520 km) southeast of Bali shook Indonesia and Australia. This generated a tidal wave and landslides that took at least 100 lives on the islands of Lombok and Sumbawa.

A quake of magnitude 6.6 Richter jolted northwestern Colombia on August 30, killing 3 persons in Apatado. A swarm of earthquakes, the two strongest of which were 4.9 and 6.6 on the Richter scale, were recorded on September 4 with the epicenter about 10 miles (16 km) southwest of Amchitka Island in the Aleutians. Citizens fled their homes on September 16 when a quake of magnitude 5.1 Richter shook the Italian Alps, but no casualties were recorded.

Looking backward, 1976 was a year of killer quakes. The first half of 1977 produced less than one tenth the number of deaths and one half the number of significant quakes compared with the corresponding period of 1976.

W. LEE STOKES
Department of Geology and Geophysics
University of Utah

GEORGIA

With the election of President Jimmy Carter, Georgians became prominent on the national scene and tourists flocked to the state.

Politics. Many Georgians joined Carter in Washington as White House staff members. Known as the "Georgia Mafia," the group included Jody Powell, the press secretary, and special assistants Hamilton Jordan and Stuart Eisenstat.

The appointments of two other Georgians were surrounded by controversy. Opposition to Griffin Bell's appointment as attorney general was based on his role in the desegregation of Georgia's schools and his membership in an exclusive, all-white private club.

Bert Lance, director of the Office of Management and Budget, resigned and returned to Georgia after a U. S. Senate committee and several governmental investigatory agencies opened inquiries into Lance's banking practices while he was president of the National Bank of Georgia.

Former Georgia Congressman Andrew Young made headlines as the outspoken U. S. ambassador to the United Nations. Atlanta City Council President Wyche Fowler was elected to Young's congressional seat. Maynard Jackson, Atlanta's first black mayor, was reelected by an overwhelming majority of 63.7%.

Economy. Georgia's economy showed only small gains early in 1977, primarily because of weaknesses in the agricultural and corporate sectors. But large increases in construction activity and changes in mortgage financing encouraged forecasts of healthy growth in the economy.

The two million tourists who visited the president's hometown of Plains and the fact that Atlanta has become the third largest U. S. convention city have made the tourist industry a major factor in the economy.

Legislation. The General Assembly failed to approve the equal rights amendment to the U. S. Constitution or any new gun control legislation but it did approve Gov. George Busbee's education plan, which included teacher salary raises, increases in the state kindergarten program, and increased funding for compensatory education.

Boundary Dispute. A border dispute arose when Georgia officers tried to arrest a South Carolina shrimper for fishing in waters claimed by both states. Basing its position on a 1787 treaty, Georgia has claimed all islands in the Savannah River and the southern half of the riverbed. Due to improvements for navigation purposes made in the river by the U. S. Corps of Engineers, the islands have become affixed to the South Carolina mainland, on which basis South Carolina claims ownership. These sites are prime industrial and port development areas.

The seaward boundary from the city of Savannah to the ocean is also in dispute. Both South Carolina and Georgia are seeking the fishing, mineral, and oil rights in this area. The U. S. Supreme Court will decide whether to accept original jurisdiction in the case.

Other Events. Georgia experienced the second coldest winter on record, and a severe summer drought. Weather also caused the first air crash there in 35 years. Near New Hope on April 4 a Southern Airways DC-9 crashed in a thunderstorm, killing 70 people.

After days of heavy rains had soaked northern Georgia, a 30-foot-high dam of earth and rock on Toccoa creek collapsed Nov. 6. Tons of released water boiled through tiny Toccoa Falls Bible College. In their wake lay 39 dead and flinders where there had been a community.

KAY BECK, *Georgia State University*

Following an overwhelming reelection victory, Atlanta Mayor Maynard Jackson married Valerie Richardson.

UPI

GEORGIA · Information Highlights

Area: 58,876 square miles (152,489 km²).
Population (1976 est.): 4,970,000.
Chief Cities (1970 census): Atlanta, the capital, 497,421; Columbus, 155,028; Macon, 122,423.
Government (1977): *Chief Officers*—governor, George D. Busbee (D); lt. gov., Zell Miller (D). *General Assembly*—Senate, 56 members; House of Representatives, 180 members.
Education (1976–77): *Enrollment*—public elementary schools, 672,816 pupils; public secondary, 422,326; nonpublic, 71,200; colleges and universities, 165,595 students. *Public school expenditures*, $1,283,701,000 ($1,117 per pupil).
State Finances (fiscal year 1976): *Revenues*, $3,357,513,000; *expenditures*, $3,324,401,000.
Personal Income (1976): $27,576,000,000; per capita, $5,548.
Labor Force (July 1977): *Nonagricultural wage and salary earners*, 1,918,500; *unemployed*, 148,700 (6.7% of total force).

Chancellor Helmut Schmidt, left, and British Prime Minister James Callaghan met in Bonn in October for discussions of their two countries' common problems.

UPI

GERMANY

Germany, now only a geographical area, is divided into two separate states. One is the Federal Republic of Germany (West Germany), a parliamentary democracy allied with other Western nations in the North Atlantic Treaty Organization (NATO) and the European Community. The other is the German Democratic Republic (East Germany, or DDR from its German-language initials), which is, in effect, a Communist one-party state. It is a member of the Warsaw Pact and the Council for Mutual Economic Assistance (COMECON).

Between these two states, West Berlin, a Western outpost within East Germany, maintains a precarious existence. Economically and culturally, it is closely tied to West Germany, but politically and militarily, it has a separate status.

FEDERAL REPUBLIC OF GERMANY
(West Germany)

Throughout the year, West Germany was, economically, considerably better off than most Western countries. Its inflation rate stayed at 4%, slightly below its growth rate of 4.5%; its unemployment rate remained stable at 4.1%. Yet the country was ill at ease. Public opinion polls indicated that people were disenchanted with their work, their way of life, and their government. They regarded the comparatively low inflation and unemployment rates as serious threats.

The government, a coalition of Social Democrats and right-of-center Free Democrats, headed by Chancellor Helmut Schmidt, had a precarious 10-vote majority in the *Bundestag* and was un-able to agree on a major reform program. Its prestige suffered also as a result of its inability to check the increasingly brazen activities of small terrorist groups. Even the skillfully organized rescue of a Lufthansa plane and its 86 passengers and crew, hijacked over France by four Arab-speaking terrorists, seemed to improve its popular standing only moderately, since this success was followed by the killing of a kidnapped industrialist, Hanns-Martin Schleyer, by his West German captors. Nor did the success of the terrorists in eluding a police dragnet enhance the government's image.

A bugging scandal was a further embarrassment. Many Social Democrats also objected to the government's pro-business priorities at the expense of social objectives. What helped to keep Schmidt in office was the ineptness of the opposition parties, the Christian Democratic Union and its Bavarian offshoot, the Christian Social Union. Embroiled in internal squabbles, they did not present any plausible alternative policies.

—— WEST GERMANY • Information Highlights ——

Official Name: Federal Republic of Germany.
Location: North-central Europe.
Area: 95,790 square miles (248,096 km²). West Berlin, 186 square miles (481 km²).
Population (1977 est.): 61,200,000.
Chief Cities (1975): Bonn, the capital, 285,000; Hamburg, 1,735,000; Munich, 1,325,000.
Government: *Head of state,* Walter Scheel, president (took office July 1974). *Head of government,* Helmut Schmidt, federal chancellor (took office May 1974). *Legislature*—Parliament: Bundesrat and Bundestag.
Monetary Unit: Deutsche Mark (2.32 D. Marks equal U.S.$1, Aug. 1977).
Manufacturing (major products): Mechanical engineering products, automobiles, chemicals, iron and steel.
Major Agricultural Products: Rye, oats, wheat, barley, potatoes, sugar beets, hops, forest products.

Terrorism. In April, urban guerrillas assassinated West German Solicitor General Siegfried Buback. Three months later they killed a prominent banker, Jürgen Ponto, in a bungled kidnap attempt. In September, industrialist Schleyer was kidnapped and his driver and bodyguards murdered. While the German government drew out negotiations about Schleyer's release in return for the freedom of 11 imprisoned terrorists, among them three members of the notorious Baader-Meinhof band, the Lufthansa plane was hijacked. The captors threatened to kill all aboard unless the 11 West German prisoners and two Palestinians jailed in Turkey were freed. They also demanded a ransom of $15 million. The plane was rescued in Mogadishu, Somalia, East Africa, by West German commandos; shortly afterward, however, the three Baader-Meinhof members killed themselves under rather puzzling circumstances in their maximum-security cells in Stuttgart, and Schleyer was "executed" in retaliation. His body was left in the trunk of an abandoned automobile in Mulhouse, France.

The terrorists have never stated their specific objectives. In general terms, they have expressed their disgust with West Germany's materialistic concerns and have attacked U. S. and West German "imperialism." Most likely, their number is very small, but they seem to have sympathizers willing to help them. However, without any major popular following they cannot expect to attain their goals, whatever they are. But they may well succeed in bringing about a more repressive society.

Security measures were greatly increased and new checks and controls introduced. They included an extensive screening system of civil servants, especially teachers. These moves led to impassioned debates on how far the state may lawfully go without unduly curbing individual rights. Some fears were voiced concerning the ability of the Bonn regime to preserve its democratic institutions.

Economy. West German exports continue to grow, but the production facilities required for this increase were obtained by improved efficiency rather than plant expansion. Manufacturers have been reluctant to increase their domestic investments because high costs of production and the strength of the *Deutschmark* threaten the competitiveness of future exports. To avoid these problems, West German firms are building plants in other countries rather than expanding domestic production.

There were widespread complaints that because of generous relief payments many of the unemployed did not want to work. In 60,000 cases (out of 900,000) support payments were temporarily suspended for refusal to accept an available job. On the whole, however, it was lack of adequate training, inability to take full-time positions (in the case of housewives), or medical reasons that kept people from accepting jobs offered to them. In case of need, the Bonn government now provides moving subsidies to those who find jobs in other cities.

Citizens' Initiatives. Popular disenchantment with government and political parties has led many persons to join "citizens' initiatives" (*Bürgerinitiativen*)—action groups that promote environmental causes, oppose the building of nuclear reactors, and call for action on other matters of public concern. This they do by means of meetings, demonstrations, pickets, and sit-downs. They also distribute a large number of publications. Some 950 such groups exist, with about 340,000 members. In addition, there are local bodies involved in urban planning, senior-citizen problems, playgrounds, and other such issues. Altogether, these groups have had the support of some two million nonmembers in their various activities. Determinedly nonviolent, they have been embarrassed at times by attempts of extremists to turn their demonstrations into violent confrontations with the police. They have been successful in many of their efforts. In the summer of 1977, the anti-nuclear groups forced the government to suspend its reactor construction program for the time being.

Social Conditions. On July 1, a new marriage and family law went into effect. It establishes the full legal equality of wives and leaves the responsibility for taking care of the household to individual arrangements. Newlyweds may adopt either the husband's or the wife's family name. The law also provides for "no-fault" divorces. Alimony will depend on the need of one side and the ability to pay of the other.

Foreign Relations. West Germany's foreign relations were troubled. The government refused to yield to Western demands that it accept a higher inflation rate and increase its imports in order to enable other countries to reduce their unemployment. Having invested heavily in nuclear technology, Bonn also insisted on exporting a nuclear plant to Brazil over the objections of the United States which feared that the plant might be used to produce atomic bombs. In July, however, Chancellor Schmidt announced an embargo on future exports of nuclear equipment with which bombs can be built. The Bonn government in turn had misgivings about U. S. President Jimmy Carter's human-rights campaign and its impact on Western-Soviet relations. West Germans also expressed strong reservations about the neutron bomb, which is being developed specifically for a possible war in Europe. They were not convinced that its effects would be as limited as has been claimed.

The Federal Republic was worried, too, about growing anti-German sentiments in Western Europe. Such feelings expressed themselves in warnings of a new German military and economic hegemony. There were also charges of police-state methods and witch-hunts, of a new "Hitler wave" and a resurgence of anti-Semitism. West Germans attributed such attacks to envy

West Germans were shocked and dismayed by the scope and coordination of terrorist acts in 1977. The murder of kidnapped industrialist Hanns-Martin Schleyer in October brought on a large-scale manhunt—without success. The picture shows a police search on the Bremen-Vahr Autobahn.

PHOTOS UPI

The passengers of the Lufthansa jetliner, hijacked by terrorists, leave the plane in Frankfurt am Main, having been freed from their five-day captivity by West German antiterrorist commandos in Mogadishu, Somalia.

Commando leader Ulrich Wegener, second from left, and his men were decorated in Bonn after their successful raid on the Lufthansa jet in Somalia. Chancellor Schmidt, CDU leader Helmut Kohl, right, and Interior Minister Werner Maierhofer, left, look on.

over the country's relative prosperity and its emergence as Western Europe's chief military power, and to over-reactions to minor incidents, but they did not take them lightly.

GERMAN DEMOCRATIC REPUBLIC
(East Germany)

In the DDR, too, there were signs of discontent. The expulsion of the dissident singer-poet Wolf Biermann, who was deprived of his citizenship while on a concert-and-lecture tour in West Germany, touched off a wave of protests from East German authors, artists, and actors. Some of the protesters were jailed, several were forced into exile. Many others were publicly reprimanded, but allowed to continue to publish in West Germany. As a result, the debate between dissidents and hardliners often was carried on in West German journals and newspapers.

Emigration. A great many East Germans were reported to have applied for permission to emigrate. They based their pleas on family ties with West Germans, which give them the right to leave according to East-West German agreements, or on the Helsinki Agreements of 1975, which include the right to emigration (somewhat modified, though, by the obligation to fulfill one's duties as a citizen). Apparently, the number was such that, after some initial flexibility, virtually all applications were denied. To deter others, applicants were dismissed from their jobs and subjected to other hardships. Later, however, these penalties were no more invoked—probably because of their disrupting economic effect.

Anxious to avoid a merely negative stance, the government encouraged citizens to file complaints concerning deficiencies, bureaucratic ineptness, and other personal problems. A special committee of the East German parliament was set up to deal with such matters. According to the committee chairman, about 75% of all presentations are resolved in favor of the complainant. The State Council, the highest government body, introduced special "office hours" during which citizens are counseled. Over 500 persons per month are reported to make use of this opportunity.

Foreign Minister Oskar Fischer of the German Democratic Republic addressed the UN General Assembly.

Economy. The East German economy was seriously affected by rising prices for foodstuffs, raw materials, and imported industrial products. To cope with the growing trade deficit, East German firms resorted to barter agreements with Western exporters. Matters were complicated by the fact that since 1974 East Germans may accept gifts of 500 *Deutschmarks* (about $200) a year from West German relatives. While this created a source of additional hard currency for the government, it also enabled the recipients to buy scarce imported goods and East German products reserved for export at so-called Intershops, which accept only foreign currency. Moreover, those without access to *Deutschmarks* were resentful of these arrangements.

Despite increased import costs, the government, through subsidies, maintains the stability of retail prices for bread, meat, and milk, gas and electricity, and public transportation. These prices have not risen in 20 years. Expenditures for this and for social services amount to one third of the state's total budget.

WEST BERLIN

In May, the city elected a new mayor, Dietrich Stobbe, a Social Democrat, after his party colleague, Klaus Schütz, resigned in the wake of a series of corruption and mismanagement scandals. Stobbe promised to concentrate his efforts on the city's economic rehabilitation and cultural development, but also spoke of West Berlin, in a somewhat mangled metaphor, as "that rock that keeps open the German question [of national unity] and assures its continued discussion." This remark was made partly in reference to new Soviet attempts to curtail the Western right to send military patrols into East Berlin. But West Berlin was a source of East-West friction in other ways, too. In September, quarrels arose over the question of whether the city had the right to send delegates to the new European parliament within the contingent assigned to West Germany.

West Berlin's economy continued to decline, despite subsidies, tax incentives, and other assistance from the Federal Republic (46% of the city budget is financed by Bonn, $500 million more than the city remits to Bonn in taxes). New efforts were made to attract business orders to local firms, especially for electronics equipment, the city's most important industry. West Berlin also hopes to expand its convention business with the help of an International Congress Center that is to open in April 1979.

EAST-WEST GERMAN RELATIONS

Throughout the year, relations between the two Germanys remained tense. East Germany continued to demand recognition by West Germany of the DDR as a foreign country and Bonn's acceptance of a separate East German citizenship, which West Germany has so far refused. The Federal Republic, on its part, complained about the increasing exclusions of West Germans wishing to visit the DDR. The introduction of higher fees for visits to East Berlin—apparently to discourage Westerners from buying up scarce low-priced goods—was another irritant. In turn, the rather lenient treatment by a West German court of an East German, who had killed two DDR border guards while escaping to the West, led to sharp protests from East Berlin.

Trade between the two states, on the other hand, continued without serious difficulties. It has become fairly evenly balanced, unlike earlier years, when DDR imports from West Germany were far larger than its exports to the Federal Republic. Some 1,400 West German engineers, technicians, and specialized workers are scheduled to go to the DDR for several years to build a new chemical plant. They will have separate apartment houses, and a Western-style school will also be opened for the children of the West German team.

ANDREAS DORPALEN
The Ohio State University

GHANA

A stagnant economy dominated Ghanaian affairs in 1977, producing unrest and suggestions for major reforms in the military government.

Politics. Gen. Ignatius K. Acheampong, the head of state, suggested the creation of a "union government" to deal with the growing economic crisis in Ghana. The proposal would mix military and civilian rule but would still prohibit political parties and would not include a functioning parliament. General Acheampong made the proposal late in 1976, hoping that civilian expertise could succeed where the military had failed. Most civilian leaders opposed the plan as a sham and called for a return to genuine civilian government by the end of 1978.

Economy. Despite a temporarily favorable trade balance, Ghana's economy went from bad to worse in 1977. Inflation averaged 63% annually, and import restrictions (to conserve badly needed foreign exchange) stifled the economy by keeping materials from Ghanaian factories and businesses. Strikes and boycotts were commonplace, and a vast smuggling network grew up to evade the trade regulations. Although the new cedi is officially worth $0.87, black marketers were reportedly selling cedis for 25 cents, and the government all but admitted that the trade controls were hurting far more than they were helping the stagnant economy. However, no basic changes were proposed in a system that everyone in Ghana concedes is ineffective and harmful to the country.

The major effort made by General Acheampong to solve the country's economic dilemma was "Operation Feed Yourself" and "Operation Feed Your Factories," both designed to encourage local production of food and raw materials and hold down the demand for imports that was bleeding the economy.

Among the few economic bright spots was the grant to Ghana by the World Bank and a consortium of nations of a $300-million, 50-year, no-interest loan to build the new Kpong hydroelectric complex. On the strength of this, General Acheampong announced a five-year plan calling for the investment of about $7 billion to make the country agriculturally self-sufficient. The success of this plan depends on the world price of cocoa remaining at its current high level.

Foreign Relations. Strained relations with the United States, symbolized by a refusal to receive Secretary of State Henry Kissinger in April 1976, were eased by the visit of Ambassador Andrew Young to Ghana in May 1977.

ROBERT GARFIELD, *DePaul University*

GHANA · Information Highlights

Official Name: Republic of Ghana.
Location: West Africa.
Area: 92,099 square miles (238,537 km²).
Population (1977 est.): 10,400,000.
Chief Cities (1973 est.): Accra, the capital, 848,800; Kumasi, 249,000.
Government: *Head of state,* Gen. I. K. Acheampong, chairman of the National Redemption Council (took office Jan. 1972). *Legislature*—National Assembly (dissolved Jan. 1972).
Monetary Unit: New cedi (1.15 new cedis equal U.S.$1, Aug. 1977).
Manufacturing (major products): Processed agricultural products, wood products, cement.
Major Agricultural Products: Cocoa, corn, cassava, groundnuts, sweet potatoes, forest products.

The year of the silver jubilee was an active one for the British royal family. Queen Elizabeth and Prince Philip visited many Commonwealth lands, including Canada (above). Prince Charles turned 29 and assumed more duties.

GREAT BRITAIN

In 1977 Britain had, at last, something like a good year. There were signs that the country was really beginning to move out of its long and painfull economic turmoil, and the nation which had seemed one of the weakest in the Western world was moving toward recovery. The pound was strengthening, the trade balance was in surplus, and the inflation rate was moving steadily downward. Unhappily, unemployment still stood at a record figure of over 1.5 million, and industrial production was lower than it had been four years before, but the essential conditions for recovery had been met.

The Jubilee and Royal Family. It was also the year of the silver jubilee, the 25th year since Queen Elizabeth II ascended the throne, and the occasion was marked by long national festivities. The Queen herself attended scores of ceremonies, lighting the first of a chain of bonfires, driving in ceremonial state to a thanksgiving service in St. Paul's Cathedral, going on frequent "walk-abouts" to meet the people. Perhaps most important were the innumerable hometown festivities all over the country.

The Jubilee was also the occasion for much national soul-searching about the monarchy in a modern democracy. In a curious way, the British monarchy has survived better than in other nations by abnegating all its real power while preserving its regal distance. Though the Royal Family has cultivated a more relaxed and informal image in recent years, they have carefully kept alive the mystique of monarchy, perhaps realizing this is what the British people want and expect. The country seems to take satisfaction in observing all the glittering trappings of power, while knowing that the reality is the opposite.

It was a good year all round for royalty. The Queen and her husband, Prince Philip, visited Canada, Australia, New Zealand, and most other areas of the British Commonwealth; their second son, Andrew, went to school happily and successfully in Canada; and the heir to the throne, Prince Charles, assumed more public duties. He was the subject of almost endless speculation about his love-life and possible bride. A number of reports said he was to have married the beautiful Princess Marie-Astrid of Luxembourg, but that this had fallen through because she is a Roman Catholic—still, apparently, an insuperable barrier for a future king who will be nominal head of the episcopal Church of England. Best of all for the Royal Family was the birth in November of the Queen's first grandchild. A son was born to Princess Anne and her husband, Mark Phillips.

Economic Recovery. The economic recovery was gained in part through an extraordinary act of national self-denial over two years, by which workers and employers agreed that wage rises would be lower than the prevailing rate of inflation. This meant that for the first time since World War II most people found their standard of living falling at a noticeable rate.

The pressure for wage rises after two unpleasant years rapidly became too strong and the government and labor unions were unable to reach an agreement for a third year. This time the government fixed its own 10% limit on wage increases without union support and announced that it would do whatever it could to enforce the limit. The policy was successful until the coal miners, crucial to Britain's energy supplies, announced a whole-hearted rejection of the limit. By November, not only was the wage policy in danger, but the whole economic recovery was imperiled by the miners' decision.

In the later months of the year, inflation was falling toward the long-promised "single figures," and with Britain's oil supplies (due to fill 90% of the country's needs in the 1980's) coming along, ministers allowed themselves a burst of something like euphoria. It was too early to say if this was justified, but the public opinion polls showed the government and Conservative opposition tied for support.

Politics. Labour's revival was in startling contrast to the series of shattering blows the government had received in parliamentary by-elections, often in working class constituencies whose electors had never before chosen a Conservative candidate, and did so for the first time in revolt against high prices, low wages, and high unemployment. All British governments expect midterm unpopularity, but this seemed to go further and suggested to some observers that the Labour Party might be destroyed as an important political force. At the end of the year, though, the volatility of the British electorate had restored Labour as marginal favorite to win the next general election.

New support of Labour was largely due to the help of the smallest of Britain's three main parties, the Liberals. A party with a proud history stretching back to the 18th century, the Liberals had gone into a rapid decline in the 20th century. It survived with a handful of parliamentary members, sent from the slow-to-change outlying areas of Britain. In the 1970's, however, it achieved an important revival under the dynamic leadership of a young lawyer, Jeremy Thorpe, and in the two elections of 1974 gained about one fifth of the popular vote. Under the British electoral system, however, it was left with only 13 parliamentary seats, about one tenth the number its votes would justify.

In March 1977, the new Liberal leader, David Steel, saw the opportunity of suddenly giving his party a real part in political power. Thanks to the by-election defeats, defections, and tactics of the other minor parties, the Labour government faced likely defeat in a "confidence" vote in the House of Commons. This would have meant an immediate general election, with the near certainty of a Conservative victory, and the government was desperate for help. It found willing listeners in the Liberals.

After a series of late-night meetings, ended only hours before the crucial vote, the two parties agreed to terms that pleased them both. The government gave away only the promise to consult the Liberals on all important decisions, and for this they would have the full voting support of the smaller party. In exchange, the Liberals had won precious influence and the power of veto over any decision they did not like. Labour's active left-wing, unhappy at the compromise with the political center, accepted the inevitable with hardly a murmur. The Conservatives were enraged and denounced the "Lib-Lab" pact throughout the country.

The pact was also unpopular with most voters at first, and the Liberals suffered stinging defeats in by-elections. But as the economic situation seemed to improve, so did the popularity of the pact. It won much-needed support from the Liberal grass roots, who voted overwhelmingly in favor of it at their conference.

But the Liberals had other problems, and found themselves again at the center of a traditional British political sex scandal. The row dated back several years, and concerned an unemployed male model, called Norman Scott, who claimed he had had a homosexual relationship with Jeremy Thorpe, the former Liberal leader. The allegation would have gotten scant attention, except that Scott's dog had been shot dead by a man who was evidently trying to murder Scott himself, and the ramifications had forced Thorpe to give up the leadership in 1976.

During a strike at Ford's Dagenham plant, pickets hand out leaflets to workers entering the factory. The British economy moved toward recovery in 1977.

"Black flag" marchers, protesting the visit of the Queen to Northern Ireland, confronted a very heavy police and troop security.

UPI

In October 1977, the man who shot the dog was released from jail, and made a series of allegations linking friends of Thorpe with the shooting and the attempted murder. After days of speculation, Thorpe was forced into a unique position for a British politician—he held a press conference at which he flatly denied both the homosexual affair and any knowledge of the shooting. He emphatically refused to resign his parliamentary seat.

Scotland and Wales. In February, there was a setback in the plans to give a measure of home rule to Scotland and Wales, countries that are part of the United Kingdom but have their own separate identity. The rise of Scottish nationalism, partly the result of the discovery of huge oil reserves off its coast, had convinced the Labour Party that without concessions to national feeling it stood to lose millions of votes. However, in November, advocates of home-rule won a major victory. A bill granting partial self-government to Scotland and Wales passed its most important stage. Under the legislation, the Scottish assembly would have the right

to enact and administer laws dealing with various domestic matters, including health, education, housing, and transportation. On the other hand, the Welsh assembly would have no legislative power, only administrative jurisdiction over laws passed in London. In the cases of both Scotland and Wales, taxation authority remains in the hands of the British Parliament. Before the bill, considered a victory for Prime Minister Callaghan, could become law three steps remained: 1) final approval by the House of Commons; 2) assent by the House of Lords; and 3) ratification by the citizens of Wales and Scotland.

Race Relations. It was a worrying year for race relations in Britain. Never particularly good, they had nonetheless been largely free of violence. However, 1977 showed that an increasing number of people were actively trying to fan racial hatred in the working class areas of some big cities. There was much concern about the growth of the National Front, a right-wing, racist and populist party that blamed immigration for most of England's misfortunes. It supported the compulsory repatriation of immigrants and, to rub the point home, held a series of deliberately provocative marches through areas with high colored populations.

As left-wingers and liberals began counter-marches the chances of violence increased, erupting in the southeast London borough of Lewisham in August. Scores of policemen and demonstrators were injured in the fighting. Days later there was more fighting in Birmingham where the National Front was holding an election meeting. The violence was condemned on all sides, but there was an uneasy feeling that the publicity would help the National Front, already scoring heavily in local elections.

GREAT BRITAIN • Information Highlights

Official Name: United Kingdom of Great Britain and Northern Ireland.
Area: 94,226 square miles (244,046 km²).
Population (1977 est.): 56,000,000.
Chief Cities (1973 est.): London, the capital, 7,281,000; Birmingham, 1,004,000; Glasgow, 836,000; Liverpool, 575,000.
Government: *Head of state,* Elizabeth II, queen (acceded Feb. 1952). *Head of government,* James Callaghan, prime minister (took office April 1976). *Legislature*—Parliament: House of Lords and House of Commons.
Monetary Unit: Pound (0.57 pound equals U. S.$1, Aug. 1977).
Manufacturing (major products): Iron and steel, motor vehicles, aircraft, textiles, chemicals.
Major Agricultural Products: Barley, oats, sugar beets, potatoes, wheat.

The Rev. Ian Paisley led militant Protestants (loyalists) in an unsuccessful general strike in Northern Ireland.

Northern Ireland. By contrast, it was a better year for trouble-wracked Northern Ireland, which in 1978 marks the tenth year of its present "troubles." The province's murder rate dropped very sharply, partly because of military successes by the Army and detection work by the police and partly because of growing dislike of the violence among the population supposedly protected by the various illegal paramilitary groups.

Two "peace women," Mairead Corrigan and Betty Williams, won the Nobel Peace Prize for their work in the province. They were honored for promoting the belief that peace in itself is more important than any one political philosophy. However, their international acclaim was matched by some cynicism at home where the people living in the troubled areas felt that the peace women had lost touch and were interested chiefly in glamorous globe-trotting.

The most significant event of the year in Ulster was probably the Protestant strike in May, called in imitation of a 1974 strike that had brought down the power-sharing government of the province and destroyed a real hope of Catholic-Protestant reconciliation. Learning the lessons of its earlier failure, the British government decided to tough this strike out, preventing intimidation of workers, keeping roads open, and generally offering full support to the normal work of the province. Day by day the strike, led by the fiery, obstinate Rev. Ian Paisley, petered out, ending in humiliation for the loyalists (militant Protestants). The affair added considerably to the standing and authority of the new British minister for Ulster, Roy Mason, a pugnacious former coal miner.

Foreign Affairs, Miscellaneous. Another successful minister was Dr. David Owen (*see* BI-

OGRAPHY), the young up-and-coming Labour MP appointed foreign secretary in February. He succeeded Anthony Crosland, a brilliant intellectual, who died suddenly of a heart attack. Southern Africa became an area of particular concern to Dr. Owen.

Two of Britain's national obsessions, cricket and animals, featured in the news. Cricket, that lengthy, fascinating but often tedious game, has had something of a revival in Britain in recent years. The revival was helped along by the recent success of the England team, which in 1977 resoundingly beat the old enemy, Australia. But into this decorous and gentlemanly world of peaceful green lawns, there burst the figure of Kerry Packer, an aggressive Australian businessman who had, in complete secrecy, managed to sign up more than four dozen of the world's very finest players to play in private matches on his behalf. The contracts offered were substantial, far higher than the miserable wages paid usually to even the best cricketers. The cricket authorities moved swiftly, banning all Packer's players from domestic matches and challenging him in the courts. The result was unclear at year-end.

In September, the nation thought about only one thing. A giraffe named Victor, a resident of a small zoo in southern England, was preparing to mate when he slipped and fell to the ground with his legs splayed apart. The problem of raising Victor turned out to be almost unsolvable. Several days later he was hoisted by a huge, specially built, canvas sling and then, at the moment of triumph, Victor expired. The nation went into mourning. Victor's brave but fruitless struggle was seen by some as a metaphor for the national condition.

SIMON HOGGART, *"The Guardian," Manchester*

The appointment of Peter Jay, 40-year-old journalist and son-in-law of Prime Minister Callaghan, as ambassador to the United States stirred initial controversy.

Celebrating her silver jubilee, June 7, 1977, Queen Elizabeth II chats with a delighted crowd during a walk-about in St. Paul's Churchyard.

UPI

GREAT BRITAIN—SPECIAL REPORT:

Queen Elizabeth's Silver Jubilee

In true Elizabethan style, Britain celebrated the silver jubilee of its reigning queen in 1977. There were bonfires, pageants, street parties, and royal visits to over 100 towns and cities.

Wherever the royal family went the people turned out in thousands. Streets were submerged beneath seas of red, white, and blue union jacks; teenagers sported jubilee T-shirts; older, more staid folk drank their afternoon tea from jubilee cups; and many quaffed their ale from jubilee pint pots. Throughout the nation, pictures of Her Majesty and Prince Philip appeared in houses, shops, offices, and pubs.

The message seemed clear: though the Queen's role within the mainly unwritten British constitution is vague and though some argue that the monarchy is an anachronism, most British people are proud of the royal family. It is not certain whether this pride emanates from the color and breathtaking splendor royalty brings to state occasions or from a sense of history—a living reminder of when Britain was the richest, most powerful nation in the world. Whatever the reason, jubilee year brought a much needed fillip to a Britain dogged by economic crises and political uncertainty.

Her Majesty's hectic year began with state visits to the South Pacific, Australia, and New Zealand. She also toured Scotland in May, Northern Ireland in August, and the Caribbean in October.

Perhaps the most impressive event of all came on June 7, when the entire royal family took part in a huge procession from Buckingham Palace to St. Paul's Cathedral for a thanksgiving service, and then to Guildhall for a luncheon. The Queen and Prince Philip rode together in the magnificent Gold State Coach and walked the half mile (.8 km) between the cathedral and Guildhall, chatting and shaking hands with delighted spectators.

The young Princess Elizabeth acceded to the throne in February 1952 on the death of her father, King George VI. But it was not until June 2, 1953, that Queen Elizabeth II was crowned in Westminster Abbey. She was 27.

One of her first actions as Queen was to abolish a system under which debutantes, the young daughters of wealthy society members, were presented to the monarch at court. It was a well-judged and popular move, which was seen at the time as heralding a period of equal opportunity.

Though Her Majesty has never sought a political role, she has shown an acute awareness of domestic and international problems, and has commanded the respect of the seven prime ministers who have served during her 25-year reign. She has traveled widely, and not only to Commonwealth nations. In 1965 she became the first British monarch since 1913 to visit Germany.

It was the resignation in 1963 of Prime Minister Harold Macmillan for reasons of health that focused public attention, some of it hostile, on the Queen's role as a constitutional monarch. When the Conservative Party, which was still in power, failed to announce a successor, the Queen, after consultations with Macmillan, sent for Lord Home. He became prime minister, after renouncing his peerage. Such a situation is unlikely to arise again. Both the Conservative and Labour parties have adopted more efficient methods of selecting their leaders.

DAVID NORRIS

GREECE

Foreign Affairs. Greek-Turkish relations continued to be strained, as they have been since the summer of 1974, when Turkey occupied a part of Cyprus. The Greek government of Premier Constantine Caramanlis gave full support to the Cypriot government in seeking a solution to that problem. In addition, Greece and Turkey were involved in a dispute over international airspace and continental shelf rights around the thousands of Greek islands in the Aegean Sea, some located right off the coast of Turkey. Though the two governments arranged talks during the year about Aegean matters, no basis for any accord was reached.

The Greek government welcomed U. S. President Jimmy Carter's initiative in appointing Clark M. Clifford as his special representative on the Cyprus dispute. Clifford visited Athens in February. But there was Greek criticism of the American president when, in his first months of office, he supported legislation to give the Turkish government up to $175 million in military sales credits, an increase of the $125 million that the Ford administration had secured for the Turks in each of the two preceding fiscal years (1976, 1977). Greek sensibilities were assuaged, however, when pro-Greek forces in the U. S. Congress blocked a further plan of President Carter's to allow the Turks $50-million worth of extra purchases of F–4 Phantom jets. The president also did not press for passage of a $1-billion (U. S.) aid pact which Henry Kissinger had negotiated in March, 1976. Although Caramanlis publicly chided the United States in October for not being more forceful in pressing the Turkish government to reach an accord on Cyprus, he remained in favor of a U. S.-Greek alignment. When attending a NATO meeting in London in May, Caramanlis met with President Carter, Secretary of State Cyrus Vance, and Clark Clifford. Conversely, a caustic anti-American stand was taken by former U. S. citizen Andreas Papandreou, head of the Panhellenic Socialist Movement, who became the chief opposition leader after the parliamentary elections in November.

A furor developed in Greece during July,

KAREL, SYGMA

Election fever captures Greece as voters prepare to select a new parliament, November 20. The ruling party of Premier Constantine Caramanlis suffered a setback.

when it was disclosed that the newly-named U. S. ambassador, William E. Schaufele, Jr., in testifying before the Senate Foreign Relations Committee had used the word "unusual" to describe the geographical location of the Greek islands near Turkey. The testimony was seen as an indication of a pro-Turkish bias. Schaufele's appointment was not immediately rescinded, but in December it was revealed that Robert J. McCloskey, a former ambassador to Cyprus, would be named in his place.

Internal Affairs. Premier Caramanlis governed in a parliamentary way, though there were criticisms of his policies from the opposition and even from his own party. One persistent comment was that he was not properly preparing a successor for his New Democracy party; he is 70 years old. In September, Caramanlis revealed that parliamentary elections would be held on November 20, a year before the constitution required. The election results, however, reduced the premier's majority in parliament from 215 to 173 seats, while the Panhellenic Socialist Movement won 92 places.

Disaster. Unusual torrential rains, causing rivers to overflow their banks, left 25 people dead in Athens and Piraeus in early November. Similar floods hit northern Athens in December, with a further loss of lives.

GEORGE J. MARCOPOULOS, *Tufts University*

GREECE · Information Highlights

Official Name: Hellenic Republic.
Location: Southeastern Europe.
Area: 50,944 square miles (131,944 km²).
Population (1977 est.): 9,100,000.
Chief Cities (1971 census): Athens, the capital, 867,023; Salonika, 345,799; Piraeus, 187,458.
Government: *Head of state,* Constantine Tsatsos, president (took office June 1975). *Head of government,* Constantine Caramanlis, premier (took office July 1974). *Legislature*—Parliament.
Monetary Unit: Drachma (37.01 drachmas equal U. S.$1, June 1977).
Manufacturing (major products): Construction materials, textiles, chemicals, petroleum products, processed foods, metals, ships.
Major Agricultural Products: Tobacco, grapes, cotton, wheat, olives, citrus fruits, tomatoes, raisins.

233

GUYANA

Failure of overtures by the major opposition party to the governing Peoples National Congress (PNC), a sugar strike, and increase in foreign aid were among the important events of 1977.

Coalition Rejected. On the eve of the biennial congress of the PNC in August, Cheddi Jagan, former premier and head of the Peoples Progressive party (PPP), urged establishment of a coalition between the PNC and PPP. He suggested that after new elections they agree that the majority party take the prime ministership and the minority take the largely ceremonial presidency. However, Prime Minister Forbes Burnham rejected this notion. He said that the PNC, as a "vanguard" party, needed no such coalition and would continue to govern alone. Shortly before Burnham spoke, the country's military, the Guyana Defense Force, had taken an oath of loyalty to the PNC.

Strike-Breaking Power. The political situation became more critical when, on August 22, the Guyana Agricultural and General Workers Union, representing workers in the country's largest industry, sugar, and controlled by the PPP, declared a general strike over the issue of profit sharing. On August 30, the government used the military and "volunteers" to help strikebreakers go to work, a move which brought strong protests from the independent Clerical and Commercial Workers Union, representing most of the country's commercial employees. On September 1, the National Assembly passed emergency legislation, giving the government wide powers of search and arrest and authorizing the imposition, if need be, of a curfew.

Foreign Aid. Chinese Communist textile experts worked on building a large textile plant just outside Georgetown. The plant will make the country self-sufficient in everyday clothing. In July, a technical cooperation agreement with the USSR was signed, providing help in developing the timber and mineral industries; East Germany agreed to help expand bauxite mining. After the visit of Ambassador Andrew Young in August, it was announced that U. S. aid would be reestablished after a hiatus of several years. It would amount to about $12.3 million a year over a three-year period.

ROBERT J. ALEXANDER, *Rutgers University*

GUYANA · Information Highlights

Official Name: Cooperative Republic of Guyana.
Location: Northeast coast of South America.
Area: 83,000 square miles (214,970 km²).
Population (1977 est.): 825,000.
Chief City (1976 est.): Georgetown, the capital, 205,000 (met. area).
Government: *Head of state,* Arthur Chung, president (took office March 1970). *Head of government,* Forbes Burnham, prime minister (took office Dec. 1964). *Legislature* (unicameral)—National Assembly.
Monetary Unit: Guyana dollar (2.55 G. dollars equal U. S.$1, Aug. 1977).
Major Agricultural Products: Sugarcane, rice, corn.

HAWAII

Hawaii in 1977 continued to show great concern for the environment. The increasing population was viewed as a problem by many, including Gov. George Ariyoshi (D), who proposed federal and state legislation to control its growth.

State Plan. The state plan, mandated by the legislature, appeared in draft form for public discussion. The intent is to have the 1978 legislature officially adopt the plan as a guide to orderly development. If and when this is accomplished, Hawaii will be among the first states to have a comprehensive plan to chart its growth.

Politics. The legislature adoped a "sunset law" providing for a review of 39 regulatory boards and commissions over a six-year period.

HAWAII · Information Highlights

Area: 6,450 square miles (16,706 km²).
Population (1976 est.): 887,000.
Chief Cities (1970 census): Honolulu, the capital, 324,-871; Kailua, 33,783; Kaneohe, 29,903; Hilo, 26,353; Waipahu, 22,798.
Government (1977): *Chief Officers*—governor, George R. Ariyoshi (D); lt. gov., Nelson K. Doi (D). *Legislature* —Senate, 25 members; House of Representatives, 51 members.
Education (1976–77): *Enrollment*—public elementary schools, 91,956; public secondary, 82,987; nonpublic, 34,300; colleges and universities, 37,677 students. *Public school expenditures,* $310,791,000 ($1,543 per pupil).
State Finances (fiscal year 1976): *Revenues,* $1,330,-484,000; *expenditures,* $1,381,535,000.
Personal Income (1976): $6,198,000,000; per capita, $7,080.
Labor Force (July 1977): *Nonagricultural wage and salary earners,* 354,700; *unemployed,* 30,800 (7.5% of total force).

Hawaiian officials comb a sugarcane field in a "search and destroy" mission against the state's marijuana crop.

UPI

Legislation was also passed to enable election of 102 delegates to a constitutional convention, commencing on July 5, 1978.

Bribery charges were brought against Mayor Frank Fasi (D) of Honolulu by the state administration. Pretrial maneuvering and jury selection took a great deal of time, and all knew that the political stakes were high; Mayor Fasi had announced his intention to enter the gubernatorial race in 1978.

Economy. Tourism continued to be the mainstay of the economy; more than 3 million visitors came to the islands. But the increase was less than that of 1976, and residents still hoped to develop other means of support. Sugar prices were low, but there were signs of renewed federal support by the end of the year.

Native Hawaiian Claims. Native Hawaiians asserted their claims for reparations against the U. S. government. The most dramatic gesture was the repeated occupancy by a few persons of the uninhabited island of Kahoolawe which is used by the U. S. military as a practice target. Some of the activists were arrested and found guilty of trespassing, and Kahoolawe became a rallying symbol.

Eruption. Kilauea volcano erupted in September. The lava flow threatened the village of Kalapana, but stopped half a mile (800 m) short of evacuated homes and churches.

RICHARD H. KOSAKI, *University of Hawaii*

HONG KONG

The dual system of summer and winter time was in 1977 replaced by one standard time—Greenwich mean time plus eight hours. The governor's term of office was extended for a year until November 1978.

Economy. Hong Kong's economic prospects remained strong. In the first half of 1977 exports increased 6.6%, re-exports 8.2%, and imports 13.7% compared with the same period in 1976. Hong Kong has become the third largest container port, after New York and Rotterdam, handling 1.03 million TEU's (20-foot equivalent units) in 1976. The first H. K. Commodity Exchange opened for trading in May 1977. Foreign investments at midyear amounted to some $437 million, of which 51% came from the United States, 13% from Japan, and 8% from Great Britain.

Water Rationing. By May, four fifths of the 24 (U. S.) billion gallons (908.5 million hl) of water purchased from China had been consumed, and the level of Hong Kong's 17 reservoirs had dropped to half their 67-billion-gallon (2.5-billion-hl) capacity. This led to rationing throughout the summer. The situation was somewhat alleviated when China sold an additional 2.4 billion gallons (90.9 million hl), the Castle Peak desalting plant became fully operative, and High Island Reservoir, still under construction, began impounding water.

UPI

In jammed, bustling Hong Kong jinrikishas and pedestrians are dwarfed by masses of motorized vehicles.

Transport. Construction of the Aberdeen Tunnel, linking Aberdeen and Happy Valley, began in May. The double-tracking of the Kowloon-Canton Railway was completed from Hunghom to Shatin; it will continue to Tai Po Market. The second Lion Rock Tunnel was also completed and will open to traffic in 1978. Beginning in March, holders of driving licenses issued in the United States, Canada, Britain, Japan, and some other countries were granted a Hong Kong license without a test.

Housing. Government-planned construction of 7,200 housing units for lower-middle income groups began in the autumn. Each unit will have a floor area of 400–600 square feet (37–56 m²) and be sold at $17,200–28,000.

Education. Because of the decreasing number of children of primary-school age, some 650 superfluous teachers have been given three years to find other jobs or retire.

CHUEN-YAN DAVID LAI
University of Victoria, British Columbia

———— **HONG KONG · Information Highlights** ————

Location: Southeastern coast of China.
Area: 398 square miles (1,034 km²).
Population (1977 est.): 4,500,000.
Chief City (1976 est.): Victoria, the capital, 1,100,000.
Government: *Head of state,* Elizabeth II, queen (acceded Feb. 1952). *Head of government,* Sir Murray MacLehose, governor (took office 1971).
Monetary Unit: Hong Kong dollar (4.69 H. K. dollars equal U. S.$1, Sept. 1977).
Manufacturing (major products): Textiles, clothing, furniture, jewelry, electronic components.

The second segment of a modular "raised ranch" is put into place in 16 minutes. Modular housing is considered one way of fighting high construction costs.

HOUSING

A renewed confidence in the U. S. economy played an important part in making 1977 a good year for the nation's housing industry. Internationally, the housing policies of many of the developing countries were being influenced by urbanization.

THE UNITED STATES

Housing production played a major part in the economic recovery of 1977. A renewed confidence in the economy encouraged consumers to make the long-term commitment of a home purchase. Total housing starts reached an annual rate of 2 million, a considerable improvement over the annual rate of 1.5 million starts in 1976.

Single-family home construction dominated the housing picture with starts approximating 1.5 million, the largest number of single-family starts since 1972. Interest rates for single-family dwellings were generally in the 8¼–9¼% range. Ten years ago, home buyers would have thought these interest rates prohibitive; however, in 1977, consumers regarded a home as a good investment in spite of high interest rates, particularly when increasing inflation was considered. Even

though interest rates were relatively high, mortgage money was fairly plentiful. The availability of a mortgage was conducive to an active housing market.

Outlook for 1978. Housing production was expected to continue at a high level throughout most of 1978. Total housing starts should be at an annual rate of about 2.2 million in January 1978 and will probably remain at that pace. The economy is in fairly good shape and does not show the signs of expanding too rapidly. There will probably be a moderate rise in interest rates which will keep housing production from increasing beyond its current rate.

Multifamily Housing. Construction remained somewhat sluggish in 1977, although there seemed to be an abundance of investors with ready capital. The occupancy rates of apartments in the major metropolitan areas were slowly climbing back to a respectable level of about 95%. Even though occupancy was up, total rents were not. Most investors seemed to feel that under current conditions, apartments did not provide an adequate return on their investment dollars. In spite of generally low rates of return, some investors felt the long-range prospects of apartments were good and production reached about 400,000 units.

Demographic factors play a major role in determining housing needs. Young families, products of the post-World War II baby boom, are still entering the housing market; they consider a home their most important investment. Typically, these families have lived in apartments for several years and are now ready to purchase their first home. Just as the formation of new families adds to the demand for housing, family separation and divorce also create demand for housing. The number of one-adult families is increasing, and with the decline in the birth rate, adult-oriented households are also increasing. All these demographic factors influence housing needs. In addition, there continues to be a long-term trend of migration from the Northeast and Midwest to the West and South. Florida was one of the fastest growing states in 1977, and the cities of Houston, Denver, Santa Barbara, and Seattle showed very strong housing markets.

Supply Restrictions. In some areas of the country, notably California, there were more buyers than available new homes. Some developers even resorted to lotteries to select who would be "allowed" to purchase available units. The low supply of new units can be traced partly to the environmental protection legislation enacted in the mid-1970's. Many projects, which formerly had required several months to a year to plan and get into the market, now require several years and a much larger capital investment to meet more stringent environmental laws and to comply with the rules of increased numbers of local planning commissions and agencies. Many of these developments reached the market in 1977, and evidence now indicates that production is coming closer to demand.

Housing Costs. Planners, sociologists, and other housing experts have been forecasting the decline of the single-family home. However, despite this prediction, the single-family home is still the most important type of housing in the United States. The continued demand for traditional housing has caused a steady rise in the price of both new and existing homes at a rate of increase several percent greater than the general rate of inflation.

According to the Harvard-MIT Joint Center for Urban Studies, the median price of existing housing was up 65% from 1970 to 1976, an annual increase of almost 9%. New construction was up even more, over 11%. The average price of a new home built in 1977 was between $50,-000 and $55,000. In some urban areas it was difficult to find any new housing for less than $60,000 to $70,000. Many homeowners, who were surprised at the price they could get for their home, were shocked by the cost of their next home.

Rising heating costs, property taxes, maintenance expenses, and interest rates raised the monthly cost of home ownership. Property taxes have increased over 75% since 1970. This increase in property taxes is especially felt by the fixed-income elderly whose homes may be their most valuable asset. Rising costs for all types of home heating fuels caused many people to lower the thermostat and bundle up while inside their own home. President Carter recognized the importance of efficient home heating in his national energy policy. He proposed and Congress enacted a tax credit for homeowners who increase the energy efficiency of their home (for example, by insulating, adding storm windows, or installing solar energy devices). This was an important step, but it will take years to improve the efficiency of most existing housing.

In an effort to hold down rising costs, the Department of Housing and Urban Development announced the appointment of a 40-member task force to study the problem of rising costs and develop new approaches to the problem. Several plans have been proposed to make homes more affordable. One of the more innovative is the graduated payment mortgage. This was designed to help the young family and entails reduced mortgage payments during the early years of the loan and higher mortgage payments later.

OTHER COUNTRIES

The factors which caused urbanization in the United States are now influencing the developing countries. Unfortunately, most of these countries are not equipped to cope with the large number of people moving into the cities.

Canada. Disposable income in Canada was up around 10% and as the U. S. economy improved, so did Canadian exports. Canada also experienced a renewed optimism and a lessening of antibusiness feeling.

The housing market remained one of the strong sectors of the economy. Total starts were at a high level in 1976 and ended 1977 at a level of about 235,000 units a year. The housing market seemed fairly stable and 1978 was expected to be a strong year. Total starts for 1978 were forecast as a little over 250,000 units.

Arab States. The Arab states are experiencing a boom in housing demand. Vast amounts of capital are flowing into these countries, and they are experiencing a modern-day industrial revolution. (Saudi Arabia expects $30 billion a year in oil revenues over the next decade.) Large numbers of the rural population are moving to the cities in order to obtain higher-paying jobs. Housing is in great demand, but scarce resources constrain production. Some of the governments are attempting to raise the standard of housing by ensuring that new construction be at a higher level of quality. While production is slow now, it is increasing and should be strong for many years to come.

Israel. In contrast, Israel is in a housing recession. Building starts were down to around 25,000 a year, barely above the annual rate of immigration of 20,000. The reduced level of production is evidenced by fewer contractors. In one area, the number of builders dropped from around 200 to 40.

South America. Many of the developing nations in South America are experiencing a large scale migration to the large cities. Part of the migration can be attributed to better job opportunities in the cities. However, a large part of the migration may be from unemployment caused by large-scale agribusiness replacing the peasant farmers. The South American countries lack the capital of the Arab states and are having many problems in providing enough housing. The overall quality of housing is decreasing as dwellings are constructed of scrap material and are not connected to municipal sanitary systems.

EDGAR McDOUGALL
The University of Connecticut

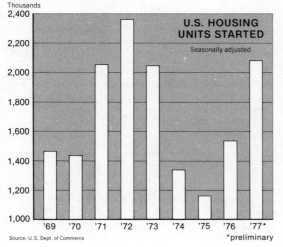

Thousands

U.S. HOUSING UNITS STARTED

Seasonally adjusted

2,400 — 2,200 — 2,000 — 1,800 — 1,600 — 1,400 — 1,200 — 1,000

'69 '70 '71 '72 '73 '74 '75 '76 '77*

Source: U.S. Dept. of Commerce   *preliminary

HOUSTON

As one of the fastest growing cities in the United States, Houston had its share of growing pains during 1977.

City Hall. Amidst charges of police brutality against minority groups, Capt. B. G. ("Pappy") Bond, head of the city police force, resigned in June. He was succeeded by Harry Caldwell. A grand jury, after a lengthy investigation, in August failed to return an indictment against Mayor Fred Hofheinz, thereby ending false rumors of a drug-abuse arrest that had been covered up. Earlier, Hofheinz had indicated that he would not be a candidate for reelection, presaging a spirited race for the office. Jim McConn, a former city councilman, was elected mayor on November 22, defeating Frank Briscoe.

Politics. Donald Yarborough, a Houston attorney, was elected to the Texas Supreme Court, though many voters may have felt they were casting a ballot for former Sen. Ralph Yarborough. Shortly afterward, charges of financial irregularities and plotting the murder of a business associate surfaced against Yarborough. Facing disbarment proceedings and criminal charges, Yarborough resigned his office.

Urban Problems. Houston, the nation's fifth largest city, anticipates continued growth because of its favorable employment opportunities. The city's mild climate is also expected to serve as a lure for many northerners who suffered through the severe winter of 1976–77. However, growth has been accompanied by a continued rise in crime, and the rate of inflation is slightly ahead of the rest of the nation. Also, Houston ranks third among major cities in traffic accidents and fatalities.

Education. A still undecided court battle raged during the year to determine if the proposed Westheimer School District, an all-white enclave, can break away from the Houston Independent School District. Basically, opposition to integration is at the root of the Westheimer action. On a higher level, the University of Houston, founded in 1927, has attained recognition as one of the leading state universities in the South.

STANLEY E. SIEGEL, *University of Houston*

HUNGARY

Domestic Affairs. Thirty-four prominent intellectuals in January publicly expressed solidarity with the signers of the Czechoslovak Charter 77. Philosophers György Markus, Mihály Vaida, Vilmos Sos, and János Kis, sociologists Judith Haber and Maria Markus, and scientist Ferenc Donath, as well as writers Miklós Haraszti and Istvan Eorsi were among the 34. Tibor Dery, the writer widely admired for his role in the 1956 uprising, died in August at the age of 82.

The Central Committee of the Hungarian Socialist Workers' party (HSWP) decided to

In U. S. custody since 1945, the Crown of St. Stephen was returned to the Hungarian capital in January 1978.

issue new membership cards in order to purge the 766,000-member organization of undesirable elements.

In a series of decrees, the government raised the minimum wage level and increased salaries for teachers and health-service employees by 4–20%. It imposed stricter controls over professional qualifications and offered more opportunities for private artisans and shopkeepers.

Housing shortages persisted, and some 1,500,000 people were looking for homes; the current five-year plan provides for no more than 440,000 new apartments.

The Third Congress of Agricultural Cooperatives took place in December 1976, with some 500 delegates participating. New measures aiming at more efficient production were recommended, including subsidies for private farmers. According to official data, the 1,500 cooperatives, which farm 67% of Hungary's arable land, performed below the expected 7–8% increase. In April 1977, the annual agricultural exhibition was held in Budapest. Some 160 Hungarian and foreign exhibitors displayed more than 2,000 agricultural and food-industry machines. Sixty-seven Western firms were represented. More than 130,000 visitors attended.

HUNGARY · Information Highlights

Official Name: Hungarian People's Republic.
Location: East-central Europe.
Area: 35,919 square miles (93,030 km²).
Population (1977 est.): 10,700,000.
Chief Cities (1975 est.): Budapest, the capital, 2,039,000; Miskolc, 190,000; Debrecen, 173,000.
Government: *Head of state,* Pál Losonczi, chairman of the presidential council (took office April 1967). *Head of government,* György Lázár, premier (took office 1975). *First secretary of the Hungarian Socialist Workers' party,* János Kádár (took office 1956). *Legislature* (unicameral)—Parliament.
Monetary Unit: Forint (8.51 forints equal U. S.$1, 1977).
Manufacturing (major products): Machinery and tools, vehicles, chemicals, pharmaceuticals.
Major Agricultural Products: Corn, wheat, potatoes.

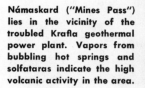

Námaskard ("Mines Pass") lies in the vicinity of the troubled Krafla geothermal power plant. Vapors from bubbling hot springs and solfataras indicate the high volcanic activity in the area.

ICELANDIC NATIONAL TOURIST OFFICE

Foreign Affairs. In June, First Secretary of the Central Committee of the HSWP János Kádár, accompanied by high government officials, paid a highly publicized visit to Italy, traditionally one of the principal importers of Hungarian agricultural products. Increase of trade between the countries was discussed. Italian imports from Hungary markedly decreased after 1974, when the Common Market put an embargo on Hungarian slaughter cattle. Kádár was received by the Pope. While the Vatican emphasized the importance of the audience, the Hungarian party press warned the public against "excessive" expectations of change in state-church relations. The government would not ignore the "presence of religious outlook in Hungarian social life," the press noted, but Communist attitude toward religion would not change. In July, Kádár visited the Federal Republic of Germany at the invitation of Chancellor Helmut Schmidt. Both leaders agreed to cooperate, particularly in the economic, cultural, and scientific fields.

Hungarian foreign trade deteriorated in 1977; by the end of June the export-import balance showed a deficit of $459 million. Hungary's debt to the non-Communist countries grew to more than $2,200 million. The export of agricultural products, which represents 25% of all exports and more than 50% of those going to the West, showed a decreasing tendency.

The Hungarian National Bank opened a New York branch and negotiated a $200 million credit, accorded by a group of American banks.

JAN KARSKI, *Georgetown University*

ICELAND

A troubled economy and worsening finances left their mark on Iceland in 1977.

Fisheries Policies. The 200-mile fisheries zone went unchallenged, though the European Economic Community showed interest in concessions. The Icelandic government, however, ruled out any new quotas for foreign fleets, declaring that West German trawlers would be barred upon expiration of the two-nation accord from 1975. Domestically, conservation was stressed; one of the measures taken was the diversion of effort from cod to less threatened species.

The Economy. Export prices for fish products were generally favorable, and excellent in the United States. The capelin catch was much larger than in 1976. The take of bottom fish—perhaps some 315,000 metric tons—exceeded the recommendations of marine biologists. The output of aluminum went up significantly.

Finances, nonetheless, took a turn for the worse. By late summer, the freezing plants faced serious operational deficits from steeply rising labor costs. General wage contracts were agreed on in June, without major work stoppages, but in October both state and municipal employees went on strike for the first time ever, leaving Iceland virtually cut off from the rest of the world for two weeks. While the government had depressed inflation to less than 30%, a new wage-price spiral was forecast. Credit remained tight, and the banks took steps to safeguard deposits from shrinkage caused by inflation. Debt service on foreign loans continued to be a heavy burden.

Energy Projects. Drilling for geothermal water for space heating was considered a high priority. The Krafla geothermal power plant in northern

--- **ICELAND · Information Highlights** ---

Official Name: Republic of Iceland.
Location: North Atlantic Ocean.
Area: 39,768 square miles (103,000 km²).
Population (1977 est.): 225,000.
Chief City (1977 est.): Reykjavík, the capital, 85,000.
Government: *Head of state,* Kristján Eldjárn, president (took office for 3d 4-year term Aug. 1976). *Head of government,* Geir Hallgrimsson, prime minister (took office Aug. 1974). *Legislature*—Althing: Upper House and Lower House.
Monetary Unit: Króna (204.85 krónur equal U. S.$1, Aug. 1977).
Manufacturing (major products): Fish products, aluminum, cement, fertilizers, clothing.
Major Agricultural Products: Hay, potatoes, dairy products, sheep.

239

Sen. Frank Church of Idaho (end of table) visited Cuba in August. Guitar music was provided with his lunch at La Bodeguita restaurant near Havana's waterfront.

UPI

Iceland was successfully test-run under no load, but it was uncertain when enough steam would be on hand for generation; two small eruptions occurred in the vicinity during the year, and there was quake damage to installations in the nearby Lake Mývatn community, most particularly to the facilities of the diatomite plant. Renewed outbreaks were feared.

Despite the Krafla setbacks, adequate electric power for the northern region was assured, thanks to the completion of a supply-grid hookup in southwestern Iceland. The now operative Sigalda hydro station in the south has also been linked to the ferro-silicon smelter that is under construction some distance north of Reykjavík.

HAUKUR BÖDVARSSON
Coeditor, "News From Iceland"

IDAHO

In January 1977, Gov. Cecil D. Andrus took office as U. S. Secretary of the Interior and moved to Washington, D. C. Lt. Gov. John V. Evans assumed the governorship.

Dry Year. The state received only half the normal rainfall for its 1977 crops. The northern and southeastern portions, which are not irrigated, suffered heavily. As a result, the U. S. government allowed "deficiency payments" to help make up losses. Wheat farmers were to receive a total of $40.8 million. Irrigated sections had sufficient water from prior years stored in their large reservoirs to make most crops nearly normal. The potato harvest hit a record high. But the reservoirs were emptied and, unless refilled by more than normal winter snow in the mountains, farmers who irrigate face disaster in 1978. The northern portion of the state received unusually heavy rainfall in late August and September. This supplied sufficient moisture to renew range grass and germinate the fall wheat. In spite of the dry weather, damages from forest fires were held to normal.

Compensation. The U. S. government has paid more than $200 million to people who suffered losses from the collapse of the Teton Dam in 1976.

Endangered Wilderness. Sen. Frank Church arranged for the creation of a task force of lumbermen, environmentalists, and businessmen to negotiate the boundary lines between harvestable timber and wilderness in the Gospel Hump area of northern Idaho. He and Sen. James McClure introduced the compromise as an amendment to the Endangered Wilderness Bill. It is said to be the first time that local people have participated in the search for a workable solution to a problem that concerns the lands of the National Forest.

Legislation. The legislature passed bills to rescind ratification of the Equal Rights Amendment (the Senate ignored its rule requiring a two-thirds vote to declare it passed); define the duties of landlords and tenants; provide low-interest financing for housing to help low-income people; require cities and counties to provide for initiative and referendum; void actions taken in meetings not open to the public; require legislative approval of a state water plan 13 years in the making; and make men criminally liable for soliciting prostitutes. It failed to pass bills providing for the right to work; repealing land-use planning and compulsory education laws; introducing no-fault insurance; and locating power plants.

CLIFFORD DOBLER
University of Idaho

----------IDAHO · Information Highlights----------

Area: 83,557 square miles (216,413 km²).
Population (1976 est.): 831,000.
Chief Cities (1970 census): Boise, the capital, 74,990; Pocatello, 40,036; Idaho Falls, 35,776.
Government (1977): *Chief Officers*—governor, John V. Evans (D); lt. gov., William J. Murphy (D). *Legislature*—Senate, 35 members; House of Representatives, 70 members.
Education (1976–77): *Enrollment*—public elementary schools, 103,368; public secondary, 96,637; nonpublic, 4,800; colleges and universities, 35,347 students. *Public school expenditures,* $288,974,000 ($1,158 per pupil).
State Finances (fiscal year 1976): *Revenues,* $711,110,000; *expenditures,* $708,116,000.
Personal Income (1976): $4,684,000,000; per capita, $5,640.
Labor Force (July 1977): *Nonagricultural wage and salary earners,* 312,000; *unemployed,* 18,300 (4.6% of total force).

ILLINOIS

Politics dominated state government as Republican James R. Thompson, a former crusading U. S. attorney in Chicago, took office for a two-year term. Vowing not to raise taxes and to hold the line on state spending, Thompson had a close eye on his political future—reelection in 1978 and a possible campaign for president in 1980.

The Legislature. Thompson was generally successful with the Democratic-controlled Illinois General Assembly in holding down state spending, at least once the Senate got going. It took the senators five weeks of political infighting and 186 ballots, the most ever cast on a single issue, to elect a Senate president.

The lawmakers reinstituted the death penalty for certain types of murder. But they rejected the governor's proposal to fix mandatory prison sentences for certain types of crimes—crimes which Thompson calls "Class X" felonies.

The proposed equal rights amendment to the U. S. Constitution suffered a setback when it failed to win approval from the Illinois House.

The Economy. Industrial production in the state continued to expand and the agricultural economy remained strong. Illinois farmers led the nation in corn and soybean production for the third consecutive year. Corn production of 1.21 billion (U. S.) bushels was down from 1.25 billion bushels in 1976, but still ahead of Iowa, for years the nation's top corn producer.

The 1977 soybean harvest was projected at 319 million bushels, according to U. S. Department of Agriculture figures. Livestock and dairy cattle showed cash receipts of $1.063 billion in the first seven months of the year, a slight decrease from a year before.

Unemployment remained well below national averages and declined steadily during most of the year. From a 6% rate in January the statewide unemployment dipped to 4.9% by fall, or 251,000 persons. Employment was strongest in industrial Chicago, where unemployment was only 4.5% in the fall, a drop of 2.2% from a year earlier. The highest unemployment was in the East St. Louis area, which had a 6.5% rate in September—still below the national rate for the month of 6.9% unemployment.

Transportation. The on-again off-again metropolitan St. Louis airport for Waterloo and Columbia, Ill., became off again when Transportation Secretary Brock Adams canceled federal funds for the proposed airport. Adams' predecessor, William Coleman, had authorized the site and the first $100,000 for land acquisition in Illinois.

The 15-year controversy over building Chicago's Crosstown Expressway—a north-south superhighway to run near the western edge of the city—apparently was resolved when Gov. Thompson and Mayor Michael Bilandic of Chicago agreed to build one half of the roadway, the south leg. It was an about-face for Thompson, who had earlier pledged that "so long as I am governor of Illinois we're not going to build the Crosstown."

For Bilandic, the $1.5-billion artery will mean as many as 40,000 new jobs in the city. For Thompson, abandonment of the north leg of the highway means release of about $500 million in federal monies. About $200 million of that can be used for other road improvements in metropolitan Chicago. Thus, Thompson will not be forced to raise state gasoline taxes to pay for the much-needed repairs.

ROBERT ENSTAD
Reporter, "Chicago Tribune"

ILLINOIS • Information Highlights

Area: 56,400 square miles (146,076 km²).

Population (1976 est.): 11,229,000.

Chief Cities (1970 census): Springfield, the capital, 91,753; Chicago, 3,369,359; Rockford, 147,370.

Government (1977): *Chief Officers*—governor, James R. Thompson (R); lt. gov., Dave O'Neal (R). *General Assembly*—Senate, 59 members; House of Representatives, 177 members.

Education (1976–77): *Enrollment*—public elementary schools, 1,506,052 pupils; public secondary, 732,077; nonpublic, 412,400; colleges and universities, 481,260 students. *Public school expenditures*, $4,616,331,000 ($1,733 per pupil).

State Finances (fiscal year 1976): *Revenues*, $9,148,441,000; *expenditures*, $9,477,017,000.

Personal Income (1976): $82,503,000,000; per capita, $7,347.

Labor Force (July 1977): *Nonagricultural wage and salary earners*, 4,603,800; *unemployed*, 267,600 (5.1% of total force).

James R. Thompson, newly inaugurated governor of Illinois, delivers his first address to the state.

The Sixth General Elections

The political scene in India was abruptly and fundamentally changed as a result of Prime Minister Indira Gandhi's unexpected decision, announced on January 18, to go ahead with the sixth general elections, already twice postponed. The balloting, held in March, was a decisive repudiation of Mrs. Gandhi and the Congress party by the Indian voters.

At the beginning of 1977, the emergency proclaimed on June 26, 1975, had been in effect for 18 months, and the position of Mrs. Gandhi and the Congress government seemed to be unchallangeable. Yet, within a month, she was on the defensive, and her continuance in office was clearly threatened. The immediate cause was her decision to permit the sixth general elections to take place—a reversal of a negative decision in the previous November.

With the announcement of the elections, the emergency was partially lifted but not completely ended. Most of the political prisoners were released, and many joined the newly-formed Janata (People's) party, which was in reality a coalition of four major opposition parties—the Old Congress, the Jana Sangh, the Socialist party, and the Bharatriya Lok Dal (BLD). Morarji Desai, an 81-year-old veteran Congress politician and deputy prime minister under Mrs. Gandhi in 1966–69, who had been a leader of the Old Congress, was chosen as head of the Janata party. The opposition was greatly strengthened in early February when Jagjivan Ram, India's leading "untouchable," who had been a senior member of Mrs. Gandhi's cabinet and a minister in virtually every Congress government since independence, unexpectedly resigned from the Congress, with a strong criticism of Mrs. Gandhi's authoritarian policies. Ram formed a new group called the Congress for Democracy (CFD), which cooperated with the Janata party without merging with it.

Mrs. Gandhi and other Congress politicians insisted that the central issue was "stability versus chaos." The opposition leaders centered their attacks on the alleged excesses of the emergency and proclaimed that the main issue was "democracy versus dictatorship." Seeking to capitalize on the strong anti-Congress wave (*hawa*) that swept over the northern part of the country, they exploited the resentment of the program of forced sterilization and the ruthless clearance of slums and slum-dwellers in several north Indian cities. They also benefited from the growing unpopularity of Sanjay Gandhi, Mrs.

Raj Narain campaigns in New Delhi. The Socialist leader defeated Indira Gandhi in her home constituency.
UPI

A New Delhi newspaper billboard informs the public of the election results.

Gandhi's imperious son, who was seeking political office for the first time.

Mrs. Gandhi was the dominant figure in the Congress campaign, as she had been in Indian politics for many years. The most prominent opposition leaders were Morarji Desai, Jagjivan Ram, and Jayaprakash Narayan, the ailing 74-year-old Gandhian who, while not a candidate for office, served as a kind of super-leader of the opposition.

Between March 16 and 20 nearly 194 million Indians—60.54% of the eligible voters—went to the polls in the 22 states and 9 union territories. Except in a few constituencies in West Bengal and Bihar, the voting was peaceful.

When the results were known, it was apparent that a real "revolution by ballot" had occurred. The Congress got only 34.54% of the votes (as compared with 43.68% in 1971) and only 153 of the 540 seats in the Lok Sabha (polling for two seats was held later). It won not a single seat from Bihar, Delhi, Haryana, and Uttar Pradesh, and only one each from Madhya Pradesh and Rajasthan. (In 1971 it won 161 seats from these states.) Mrs. Gandhi, Sanjay, and most members of the Congress cabinet were defeated. The Janata party and the CFD won 297 seats, with 43.57% of the votes.

The election results created an extraordinary division between north and south; the Congress party was almost wiped out in the north, while the Janata-CFD gained only 6 out of 132 seats in the four southern states. In West Bengal the Communist party of India (Marxist) won more seats than the Janata-CFD or the Congress, and regional parties won a plurality of seats in two states—the Anna Dravida Munnetra Kazhagam in Tamil Nadu and the Akali Dal in the Punjab.

Immediately after the elections Mrs. Gandhi officially terminated the emergency and resigned her office. On March 24, Morarji Desai was sworn in as prime minister at the head of a Janata-CFD government.

NORMAN D. PALMER

Morarji Desai, who was sworn in as prime minister, March 24, meets with Lord Thompson, envoy of British Prime Minister Callaghan.

INDIA

In March 1977, Mrs. Indira Gandhi's tenure of more than 11 years as prime minister and the internal emergency, which she had proclaimed on June 26, 1975, came to an abrupt and unexpected end as a result of the country's sixth general elections. The new Janata party government promised to restore the freedoms that had been curtailed during the emergency and to effect decentralization of authority on both the political and economic fronts. By August 15, the 30th anniversary of India's independence, some disillusionment with the new regime was already becoming manifest. The economic picture was a mixed one, but the chronic problems of poverty and unemployment remained. In foreign policy there was little basic change, although the new government pledged that it would follow a more "genuinely nonaligned" course.

The Sixth General Elections. From Mrs. Gandhi's unexpected announcement, on January 18, that general elections would be held in March, until the elections (on March 16–20), with their surprising results, the political scene in India was dominated by the election campaign. The basic issues that were raised were those of the country's political future, and some saw in the elections an even larger stake—that of the future of democracy in the Third World. The unexpected end of the emergency and of Mrs. Gandhi's long rule, as a result of the decision by the Indian voters, produced a new political climate in India, very different from what had been during the emergency. Moreover, it was quite different from the climate that had existed during India's experiment with democratic rule, from independence in 1947 to the imposition of the emergency in 1975. For the first time, a non-Congress government came into power at the center, dedicated to a new orientation featuring emphasis on Gandhian models and decentralization, and pledged to a restoration and strengthening of basic freedoms. But most of the leaders of the new regime were veterans of Indian politics, mainly former members of the Congress party, and their capacity to lead India into a new and more promising future remained to be tested. (*See also* Special Report on the sixth general elections.)

The Post-Election Scene. As soon as the election results were known, the acting president of India, on Mrs. Gandhi's recommendation, issued a proclamation ending the internal emergency. (On March 27, the external emergency that had been in existence since December 1971 was also ended.) On March 22, Mrs. Gandhi resigned, and two days later, after a brief struggle for leadership of the new government between Morarji R. Desai and Jagjivan Ram was resolved by reference to Jayaprakash Narayan and Acharya Kripalani, two other veteran political leaders, Desai was sworn in as the new prime minister. After some hesitation, Ram agreed to join the cabinet as minister of defense, although Charan Singh, who became minister of home affairs, was given the second ranking post. Other prominent members of the new cabinet were H. M. Patel (finance), Atal Behari Vaypayee (external affairs), H. N. Bahugana (chemicals, fertilizers, and petroleum), George Fernandes (communications), and Raj Narain (health and family planning, soon renamed health and family welfare).

The new government took prompt steps to remove the curbs on freedoms and civil rights that had been imposed during the emergency, although it was not able to devise immediate means to remove amendments to the Constitution that had, in effect, institutionalized in fundamental law some of the restrictions on freedom. It appointed a former chief justice of the Supreme Court as a one-man commission to investigate the excesses committed during the emergency, and took other steps to look into alleged offenses committed by leaders of the Congress government during the emergency period.

On May 1, the four constituent parties that had joined together under the name of the Janata party to fight the election formally merged; on May 3, Chandra Sekhar was elected president of the party. Two days later, the Congress for Democracy also formally merged with the Janata. At about the same time, the Congress chose a new president, Brahamananda Reddy. Just after the elections, Y. B. Chavan, minister of external affairs in the outgoing government, was chosen leader of the Congress parliamentary party.

On April 30, in a very controversial move, the new government compelled the acting president of India, against his will, to dissolve the legislative assemblies and proclaim president's rule (direct rule by the central government) in nine states—Bihar, Haryana, Himachal Pradesh, Madhya Pradesh, Orissa, the Punjab, Rajasthan, Uttar Pradesh, and West Bengal. All of these states still had Congress governments and Congress majorities in the state assemblies. In all of them, the Congress had fared very badly in the March general elections.

--------- **INDIA · Information Highlights** ---------

Official Name: Republic of India.
Location: South Asia.
Area: 1.269,438 square miles (3,287,844 km²).
Population (1977 est.): 622,700,000.
Chief Cities (1973 est.): New Delhi, the capital, 3,600,-000; Bombay, 6,000,000; Madras, 2,500,000.
Government: *Head of state,* Neelam Sanjiva Reddy, president (took office July 1977). *Head of government,* Morarji R. Desai, prime minister (took office March 1977). *Legislature*—Parliament: Rajya Sabha (Council of States) and Lok Sabha (House of the People).
Monetary Unit: Rupee (8.72 rupees equal U. S.$1, July 1977).
Manufacturing (major products): Iron and steel, industrial machinery and equipment, chemicals.
Major Agricultural Products: Rice, wheat, groundnuts, barley, sesame, sugarcane, corn, rubber.

A large crowd in Allahabad, India, observes the Hindu festival of Kumbh Mela. The woman in the litter was carried to the River Ganges for purification bathing.

UPI

Between June 10 and 14, elections were held in these nine states, as well as Tamil Nadu and the union territories of Delhi and Pondicherry The Janata won decisive majorities in all but three of the states: the Punjab, where the Akali Dal was the victor; Tamil Nadu, where the All-India Anna Dravida Munnetra Kazhagam scored heavily; and West Bengal, where the Communist party of India (Marxist) won 178 of the 294 seats. New non-Congress (mostly Janata) governments were installed in all of these states. In July elections in Jammu and Kashmir, which had been under president's rule since March 27, the National Conference, led by the aging and ailing Sheikh Abdullah, won a decisive victory over both the Janata and the Congress.

One of the reasons for the ousting of the Congress governments in the northern states was that if they had remained in power, the Congress party might have been able to select the next president of India, in succession to Fakhruddin Ali Ahmed, who had suddenly died of a heart attack on February 11. After the state elections, the Congress was in no position to do more than impede the complicated process of presidential election, and it decided no to do so. As a result, on July 21, Neelam Sanjiva Reddy, speaker of the Lok Sabha (House of the People), was declared to be unanimously elected sixth president of the Indian Republic.

When India commemorated the 30th anniversary of its independence on August 15, there was some evidence of erosion of popular support for the Janata government. This could be attributed to growing economic difficulties and the apparent inability of the government, after five months in office, to implement as rapidly and effectively as had been expected its promises of basic improvements and sweeping changes.

On independence day, P. C. Sethi, a former union minister, together with Mrs. Gandhi's former personal assistant, her former private secretary, and seven others were arrested on a variety of charges relating to their actions during the emergency. On August 23, Bansi Lal, former defense minister and one of Mrs. Gandhi's chief advisers, was added to the group. Mrs. Gandhi, who then began to emerge from semi-seclusion, became involved in efforts to regain her hold on the Congress party and to appeal to the people as a victim of a political vendetta. As she moved around the country, she attracted large crowds and, apparently, growing sympathy and support. (This in spite of violent mass demonstrations against her in and around Madras, where two people were killed and more than 40 injured in late October during her visit to the state of Tamil Nadu.) On October 3, the government, as she had predicted, ordered her arrest. After 16 hours' confinement, however, she was given an "unconditional" release (which the government promptly appealed) on the ground that the charges against her, relatively minor ones, were unsubstantiated. Mrs. Gandhi denounced her arrest as a political move, designed "to prevent me from going to the people" and "to discredit me in their eyes."

The Economy. Favorable trends in the nation's external payments position during 1977 were more than offset by many unfavorable trends in the internal economic situation. It was a year of uneven growth, with some serious setbacks. The gross national product (GNP) increased by less than 2%, compared with 8.5% the previous year; agricultural production declined by 5–6%, compared with an increase of 15.6% in 1975–76; prices rose by 11.6%; and money supply increased by 17.1%, thus adding to inflationary pressures. Unemployment remained one of the nation's most intractable problems. The monsoon in 1977 was not so good as in the two previous years, with consequent adverse effects on food production; but food reserves reached a record level of some 20 million tons.

The first budget of the new government, presented to parliament by the finance minister on June 17, was designed to reflect the philosophy, programs, and priorities of the new regime. It sought to accelerate the pace of economic development, to place greater emphasis on agricultural and rural development, to improve the lot of the "weaker" sections of the population, to reduce unemployment, and to expand social welfare programs. Total expenditures were estimated at $17.85 billion (U. S.), including $6.97

billion for capital expenditures, $3.47 billion for agriculture and allied services, and $3.16 billion for defense. The overall deficit was estimated at $232 million.

The external payments position was much more favorable. Exports increased in value by 23.8%, while imports declined, leaving a trade surplus of $82.57 million, as compared with a deficit of approximately $1.87 billion in the previous year. Foreign exchange reserves increased spectacularly both in 1976 and 1977, reaching a record level of nearly $5.73 billion by the end of 1977.

Net external assistance for fiscal 1977–78 was estimated at approximately $1.21 billion. Additional amounts would be needed for debt servicing (interest and other repayments). The prospects on the foreign-aid front seemed to be brighter than in 1976–77, when the amount of the aid made available declined substantially. In mid-July, the Aid-India Consortium increased its assistance pledge to $2.1 billion, as compared with $1.67 billion promised during the previous year.

In spite of its promises to accelerate the pace of economic development and to distribute the fruits of increased development more equitably, the Janata government made little progress in dealing with the country's economic problems. The Planning Commission was reorganized, but largely along technical lines. It was unable to give much direction to the economic effort. The fifth Five-Year Plan was ended in 1977, and it was announced that the sixth plan, to begin in 1978, would be a "rolling" one.

Foreign Policy. In his first press conference as prime minister, Morarji Desai said that his government's foreign policy would be a "properly nonaligned one," with friendship based on reciprocity with all nations and no special relationships. This was widely interpreted as presaging a shift in India's foreign policy from a pro-Soviet to a pro-Western, and especially pro-U. S., orientation. Regarding the Indo-Soviet treaty of August 1971, which he and other Janata leaders had often criticized in the past, Desai said that if it interfered with his government's efforts to avoid special relationships and to establish good relations with all countries, it would be ended. Apparently, the Soviet Union was concerned about the abrupt change in India's political leadership and direction; but at the end of a two-day visit to India in late April by Soviet Foreign Minister Andrei Gromyko, the two governments agreed that they would continue and strengthen their "time-tested friendship." Agreements were signed for economic and technical cooperation, the establishment of a telecommunications link, and an increase in trade. In October, Desai was warmly received in the Soviet Union on his first state visit after becoming prime minister.

With the advent of new governments in both India and the United States in 1977, the prospects for improvement in Indo-U. S. relations seemed to be brighter than they had been in many years. Some evidences of improvement were apparent even before the change of government in India. President Carter's gesture in naming his mother, "Miss Lillian," who had been a Peace Corps volunteer in India, to head the official American delegation to the funeral of President Fakhruddin Ali Ahmed in February was widely appreciated, and widely publicized, in India. In May, Robert Goheen, former president of Princeton University, who had been born in India, presented his credentials as U. S. ambassador, and in September, Nani A. Palkhivala, a prominent lawyer and industrialist, who had been a leading and courageous critic of Mrs. Gandhi's efforts to emasculate the constitution and the judicial system, became India's ambassador to the United States. Two prominent Indian leaders went to the United States in 1977 for major medical treatment—Jayaprakash Narayan in May and President N. Sanjiva Reddy in September.

In 1977, the United States and India opened negotiations on a possible resumption of U. S. aid, which had been cut off in 1971. Demonstrating a special interest in India, President Carter planned to visit the country in late November. U. S. domestic matters, however, forced the trip's postponement.

Disagreements between the United States and India in the nuclear field continued. Desai repeatedly stated that India would never build nuclear weapons, but he insisted on its right to develop nuclear energy for peaceful purposes. He endorsed India's refusal to adhere to the nuclear nonproliferation treaty, and he criticized the nuclear powers for not reducing their nuclear arsenals, while asking non-nuclear states to pledge never to build nuclear weapons.

Relations with Pakistan showed little improvement, although the two countries did agree on some liberalization of policies regarding air flights and telecommunications. Prime Minister Bhutto of Pakistan irritated Indians by claiming that his decision to hold general elections in Pakistan in March was a major factor in influencing Mrs. Gandhi to make a similar decision two weeks later. Bangladesh continued to be suspicious of Indian moves and intentions, but relations improved considerably with the advent of the new regime in India. In particular, the thorny Farakka Barrage issue, involving use of the waters of the Ganges River by the two countries, was at last resolved by a comprehensive agreement signed on November 5.

Cyclone Disaster. The worst cyclone in more than a century struck Andhra Pradesh November 19. Winds of 100 miles per hour (160 km/h) drove a wall of water 10 miles (16 km) inland, killing some 8,000 and drowning the land that produces 40% of India's food grains.

NORMAN D. PALMER
University of Pennsylvania

INDIANA

Legislation enacted by the 1977 Indiana General Assembly provided for substantial changes in the lives of most Hoosiers. Weather also made news in the state during the year.

Legislation. For the first time since 1965 it was necessary to call the General Assembly into special session in order to pass the state's annual budget and tax control bills. The record total of 1,770 bills to be considered, and a lengthy debate of controversial measures prevented the legislators from completing work during the regular session. New legislation included a comprehensive "sunshine," or open door, law requiring most state government agencies to conduct their business in public sessions except in certain specified instances, and a package of "sunset" laws that will reduce the number of state agencies, commissions, and boards, and eliminate them when no longer needed.

The General Assembly authorized over Gov. Otis Bowen's veto the use of Laetrile, a substance banned by the U. S. Food and Drug Administration, for treatment of cancer patients. Also passed over the governor's veto was a bill allowing pari-mutuel betting at horse tracks in counties where approved by the county council and by a referendum of county voters. This law's constitutionality has been questioned, and its future is now pending in the courts. Forwarded to the U. S. Congress was a joint resolution ratifying the Equal Rights Amendment to the U. S. Constitution.

A proposed repeal of Indiana's two-year-old direct primary law, giving choice of governor, lieutenant governor, and U. S. senator to the voters instead of a political convention, failed to pass by only a two-vote margin. Also defeated were measures increasing the gasoline tax and tightening laws on child abuse and on landlord-tenant relations.

Budget. In a one-day special session the General Assembly provided for 1977–79 operating, construction, and highway budgets totaling $7.74 billion. Included in this amount was $1.7 billion for public schools, although Bowen

UPI

Some 400 Indianapolis policemen, demonstrating their disapproval of the city's latest contract offer, park their cars with sirens blasting around city buildings.

vetoed a distribution formula that would have amounted to a 6% increase each year in state support for schools. Mental health facilities benefited under the terms of the budget. Earmarked for the Norman Beatty Memorial Hospital in Indianapolis, a mental health institution being converted into a correctional center, were $7 million in construction funds and $8.5 million for operation. The legislature designated $3.1 million for a mental health center at Bloomington and $1.5 million and $300,000 for community mental retardation centers at Columbus and New Albany, respectively. About $5 million were scheduled for Patoka Reservoir, Williams Dam near Bedford, and Hardy Lake near Austin. As designed, the budget could leave a General Fund surplus of $100 million in 1979.

Weather. Along with most of the nation, Indiana experienced during 1977 one of the coldest winters on record. Record low temperatures were felt throughout the state. A shortage of natural gas forced many plants to reduce production and lay off employees temporarily. Emergency legislation bypassed antipollution laws and allowed factories to burn coal. All schools were closed on January 28, and many school corporations shut down for longer periods of time.

LORNA LUTES SYLVESTER
Indiana University

--- **INDIANA • Information Highlights** ---

Area: 36,291 square miles (93,994 km²).
Population (1976 est.): 5,302,000.
Chief Cities (1970 census): Indianapolis, the capital, 744,743; Fort Wayne, 178,021; Gary, 175,415; Evansville, 138,764.
Government (1977): *Chief Officers*—governor, Otis R. Bowen (R); lt. gov., Robert D. Orr (R). *General Assembly*—Senate, 50 members; House of Representatives, 100 members.
Education (1976–77): *Enrollment*—public elementary schools, 595,938 pupils; public secondary, 567,241; nonpublic, 102,700; colleges and universities, 198,964 students. *Public school expenditures*, $1,676,000,000 ($1,218 per pupil).
State Finances (fiscal year 1976): *Revenues*, $3,493,933,000; *expenditures*, $3,522,701,000.
Personal Income (1976): $32,990,000,000; per capita, $6,222.
Labor Force (July 1977): *Nonagricultural wage and salary earners*, 2,086,700; *unemployed*, 120,300 (4.8% of total force).

An oil exploration site in Sumatra. Current oil production in Indonesia is running at just about capacity.

INDONESIA

The year was marked by significant recovery from the financial shocks of 1976, by the successful conclusion of national elections, and by continuing good relations with most of Indonesia's neighbors.

Economy. The crash in 1976 of Pertamina, the overextended state oil corporation, dimmed economic prospects, and Indonesia seemed on the brink of bankruptcy. By mid-1977 the picture looked much brighter. Technocrats had regained control of economic planning, and petroleum multinationals, reassured by the technocrats, had adjusted to the new demands imposed on them.

Foreign exchange reserves stood at U. S.$2.4 billion in July 1977 (up one billion in a year and about $1.8 billion in 18 months). Smuggling was better policed and import receipts jumped more than 50%. Inflation was, for Indonesia, a modest 14% in 1976 and showed signs of dropping to less than 10% in 1977.

Many areas of concern remain, however. Oil production, accounting for 55% of Indonesia's revenues and 73% of its foreign exchange earnings, cannot expand much more; foreign assistance continues to contribute about a third to the development budget. Pressures related to population, population growth, and maldistribution of population, resources, and rewards continue.

Politics. General elections were held on May 2, and the new assembly was installed on October 1. As expected, the government party, Golkar, did well, but not so well as officials had hoped and predicted. Golkar took 62% of the vote; Partai Persatuan Pembangunang, its Muslim opposition, 29%; and a coalition of five parties, Partai Demokrasi Indonesia, dominated by the old National Party, about 9%. Golkar did worst in the capital, Jakarta, where it got 39%. Golkar support was up in East Java but down in the west. In general it also lost support in most traditional Muslim areas of the country. Golkar's impressive showing was aided by the fact that the field of parties permitted to contest the 1977 elections had been "simplified" by government order, candidates were pre-screened by the government, and the ground rules for political discussions were imposed and enforced by the government.

Two important personnel changes took place in 1977: the colorful and controversial governor of Jakarta for 11 years, Ali Sadikin, "retired," and Adam Malik was "promoted" from foreign minister to chairman of the legislature.

Foreign Affairs. Relations with Malaysia were close and cordial as the two countries exchanged teachers and many distinguished visitors, continued to standardize their common language, undertook a joint naval exercise in the Malacca Straits and joint patrols on their common Bornean border, and began an ambitious process of surveying and marking the border itself. Indonesian relations with Singapore have recovered almost fully from the days of "confrontation," and the two are now cooperating in suppressing a lucrative smuggling trade.

Australia is the one neighbor with which Indonesia had serious problems in 1977, mostly stemming from Australia's opposition to Indonesian incorporation of East Timor into its territory. It had been hinted that relations with China might resume after the elections, but Chinese attention to the outlawed Indonesian Communist party and the low priority of the recognition issue served as delays.

See also ASIA.

ROBERT O. TILMAN
North Carolina State University

INDONESIA • Information Highlights

Official Name: Republic of Indonesia.
Location: Southeast Asia.
Area: 735,269 square miles (1,904,345 km²).
Population (1977 est.): 136,900,000.
Chief Cities (1974 est.): Jakarta, the capital, 5,000,000; Surabaja, 2,000,000; Bandung, 2,000,000; Medan, 1,000,000.
Government: *Head of state and government,* Suharto, president (took office for second 5-year term March 1973). *Legislature* (unicameral)—Dewan Perwakilan Rakyat (House of Representatives).
Monetary Unit: Rupiah (415 rupiahs equal U. S.$1, Aug. 1977).
Manufacturing (major products): Processed agricultural products, petroleum products, mineral products, cotton textiles, tires, cement.
Major Agricultural Products: Rice, rubber, sweet potatoes, cassava, copra, sugarcane, coffee.

INDUSTRIAL REVIEW

World industrial production again presented a mixed picture in 1977. Output in the United States advanced by a modest amount, but other major industrial nations fell behind that.

The United States. Industrial production in the United States increased 6% in 1977. The Federal Reserve Board's index of total industrial production registered 138 (1967 = 100) for the year, according to preliminary estimates. Production increase in manufacturing matched the overall increase. Production growth in mining was just a little above 5% and utilities expanded their output by a shade under 5%.

The industrial production index measures the physical volume of production of U.S. factories, mines, and utilities. It accounted for 43% of the nation's total output of goods and services in 1977.

In manufacturing, durables producers expanded production by nearly 7%. Business equipment production led the way with a 10% gain. Output of trucks, buses, and trailers jumped about 23%, while machinery production gained 8% and that of fixtures and office furniture advanced 10%. Producers of business equipment owed much of their production increase to a nearly 14% increase in business expenditures on plant and equipment. According to the Bureau of Economic Analysis of the U.S. Department of Commerce, the total for 1977 came to $137 billion.

Capital spending by manufacturers totaled $61 billion, 16% above 1976. Durables producers increased plant and equipment spending by 19%, with the largest increase—64%—in motor vehicles. Electrical machinery producers increased capital spending by 26%, nonelectrical machinery producers by 17%, and the stone-clay-glass industries by 19%. Iron and steel producers decreased their capital spending by 6%.

But there were plenty of weak spots in durables manufacturing. The overall increase of over 3% in primary metals was registered on the strength of a 10% increase in the output of iron and steel foundries and in nonferrous metals, masking a nearly 3% decline in basic steel.

The production of consumer goods increased about 5.5%, spurred by a strong performance by some durables producers. Household appliance production grew almost 19%, reflecting the strength in home construction. Auto output increased 14%, and the production of tires rolled up an impressive 38% gain. The production of television and radio sets increased barely 2%, and the output of household furniture expanded by a modest 3%. The production of mobile homes gained just about 7½%. Food and food products output increased almost 6%. Output of drugs and medicine grew 11%, while the production of soaps and toiletries came close to a 5% gain. Apparel production turned in a disappointing performance, showing a fractional decrease for the year.

Nondurables producers as a group increased output by just about 5½%. The rubber and plastics products group registered a 16½% gain. Petroleum products output increased nearly 8%. The chemicals and chemical products group showed a 7½% increase. Printing and publishing output rose only 3½%. Paper and paper products production increased by 4%. Textile mill output was practically unchanged.

U.S. automakers produced a little under 9.2 million cars in 1977, an 8.4% gain from 1976. That makes 1977 the third best year for auto production. Car production in Canada, too, had its third best year, totaling 1,169,063 vehicles, for a 2% increase over 1976.

U.S. truckmakers pushed their output to a record 3,482,405 units in 1977, a 16% increase from the preceding year. Some 90% of the production was in light trucks having a gross vehicle weight of less than 14,000 pounds. Much of their popularity is traceable to consumer fascination with vans and pickup trucks. Manufacturers have made all kinds of accessories, comforts, and options available, from swiveling captain's chairs to lush carpeting. On top of that was the powerful lure of space and zippy engines; the fuel economy standards will not be applied to most light trucks until 1979.

The aircraft industry production index rose 3% in 1977. General aviation—corporate and private aircraft—output increased about 14% while transport aircraft production amounted to 180 units, a 17% decline from 1976.

Energy production increased less than energy consumption. Production of crude petroleum increased less than 1% in 1977, to 3.7 trillion barrels. Domestic production provided for only 48% of the U.S. oil consumption.

Faced with a strike that began in December, idling half of the nation's mines, coal producers stepped up production, especially in September, October, and November, to accommodate the stockpiling demand from steel companies and electric utilities. Coal production amounted to 673 million tons in 1977, a gain of a little more than 1% over 1976.

The energy situation helped producers of home insulation to a record year. Memories of the coldest winter in 200 years and the concern with high energy prices sparked a boom in fiberglass insulation, boosting production by more than 50%, and in such competing materials as cellulosic fiber, rock wool, and Styrofoam. Because cellulosic fiber insulation can be produced fairly simply and cheaply, about 100 new producers rushed into the field in 1977. While cellulosic fiber insulation production is expected

The energy-saving, geodesic dome home is offered in an easy-to-assemble kit.

SINCLAIR RADIONICS

The first pocket-size TV sold at a retail price of c. $300.

UPI

INDUSTRIAL PRODUCTS—THE NEW, THE PROFITABLE, THE EXPERIMENTAL

MITS

With some 100 companies manufacturing computer products, computers for home use are now readily available.

MAGNAVOX

Television video games enjoyed new levels of popularity and excellent sales, particularly at Christmastime.

to surpass fiberglass production in a year, the product is getting a bad reputation from operators who take shortcuts in flameproofing the material. Short supply of boric acid—used in fireproofing the macerated newsprint—was a limiting factor in expanding production of high quality cellulosic fiber insulation in 1977.

Consumers' quests for the latest in gadgets continued unabated. Nearly 20 different kinds of food processors made their way into an estimated 750,000 households in 1977. Microwave ovens racked up a record 2 million sales, up from 1.5 million in 1976. One of the hottest electronic items was the home smoke alarm, with production estimated at 10 million units. That compares with a production volume of only 50,000 units in 1972. Perhaps the ultimate

in consumer electronics is about to be reached: about 100 manufacturers are now producing personal computing devices. Microcomputers for home use now come in kit form or assembled.

Another big-ticket item for gadget lovers is the TV recorder. Although sold under American nameplates, all these machines are manufactured in Japan. Betting on the public's addiction to television, manufacturers were planning for a 250,000-unit market in 1977.

The electronic glamor product of 1976—citizens' band radio—fell upon relatively hard times in 1977. Sales dropped about 30% from the 10 million of 1976. With prices discounted by as much as 50%, only half a dozen firms were weathering the industry's shakeout that came in the wake of overproduction and the

FORD

Vans were a growing segment of the auto industry. They were sought for their power, individuality, and promise of adventure.

Exxon Enterprises unveiled an electric-powered experimental auto at the International Vehicle Exposition in Chicago.

UPI

rush to clear the shelves that followed the Federal Communications Commission's ruling that 23-channel models could not be sold after Dec. 31, 1977. But CB radios have a brighter future in Europe. Compared with the 30 million units that already exist in the United States, the European CB radio ownership numbers just about 3 million, with half of them purchased in 1977. Because the technology used to manufacture CB radios is the same as that used in the manufacture of handheld calculators, the prices have been coming down rapidly. The Japanese manufacturers dominate the CB radio supply.

Manufacturing industries employed 17.2 million workers in recession-ridden 1975, 1.5 million fewer than in 1974, according to the 1975 Annual Survey of Manufacturers released by the Census Bureau in June 1977. Manufacturing payrolls totaled $191 billion.

Value added by manufacture reached $442 billion in 1975, a 2% decline from 1974. Value added is the difference between the value of shipments and the value of materials, supplies, containers, and fuel consumed in the production process. The five giants in U. S. manufacturing in 1975 were machinery (except electrical), with $51 billion in value added; food, with $48 billion; transportation equipment, with $45 billion; chemicals, with $45 billion; and electrical machinery and electronic equipment, with $35 billion.

World Production. Internationally, industrial production increased very slowly. The six major

The boutique offers the latest fashion, usually in an elaborate setting.

A Berkeley poster shop emphasizes variety at a relatively low price.

The Specialty Shop

Recently, the specialty shop, a store selling one particular type of item, has again become a major force in U.S. retailing circles. It is now almost a law that every shopping mall in the nation have at least a fashion boutique, a cheese shop, and a health food store. In fact, a late 1977 issue of Business Week pointed out that some economic analysts expect the small shop "to continue to be an area of above-average growth" in the industry.

CHRISTA ARMSTRONG, RAPHO/PHOTO RESEARCHERS

With questions raised concerning food quality, health food stores enjoy excellent sales.

BRUCE ROBERTS, RAPHO/PHOTO RESEARCHERS

At the cheese shop—the greater the variety, the longer the customer line.

UPI

T-shirts have become such an "in" item that some stores sell nothing else.

foreign industrial countries saw their combined production index advance by only 1%.

Among the major noncommunist developed countries, the highest rate of growth in industrial production was registered in the United States—6%. Japan saw its production index rise less than 3%. Canada and West Germany both had an industrial production growth rate of about 2½%. There was no growth in industrial production in France. Two major countries had declined in industrial output: Italy, down 2%, and Britain, down 1%.

Among developing countries, industrial production grew fastest in South Korea, nearly 15% in 1977. Available data suggest that production increased about 10% in Brazil, about 9% in both India and Nigeria, about 2½% in Mexico and a little over 1% in Taiwan.

The fastest growth in South Korea's industrial production was spurred by an ambitious export program that had a $10 billion target in 1977. Although better known for its textile products, Korea also exported 1 million tons of steel to the United States in 1977. The Korean steel industry boasts an annual capacity of 3 million tons a year, much of its coming from what is reputed to be the most modern integrated steel mill in the world. The country has increased its auto production capacity to 150,000 units a year, aiming its marketing efforts at southeast Asia. Actual production reached about 50,000 units in 1976, and the gain in 1977 was about 40%. Korean shoes, textiles, and television sets faced rising world-market protectionism.

Industrial competition grew more intense internationally, especially in basics. A case in point is steel. The world's production capacity is clearly in excess of market needs. Capable of pouring 153 million tons of raw steel in 1977, United States steelmakers produced 124 million tons, utilizing only 81% of plant capacity. The American steel industry laid off 24,000 employees in just the last half of the year and closed many plants and production facilities, trimming its annual raw steel production capacity by about 6 million tons.

While the American steel industry's problems have been present to some degree for the past three decades, the layoffs and plant closings created a crisis atmosphere in 1977. Many American plants are outmoded and inefficient. According to one study, production per employee is considerably higher in a Japanese steel plant than in an American one. While some 80% of the Japanese steel is produced in efficient basic oxygen furnaces, only 63% of the American steel production flows from such facilities. The Japanese steel industry, like that of much of the rest of the world, is relatively new and fully integrated. In contrast, the American steel industry is old and quite dispersed.

With imported steel claiming nearly 18% of total U. S. steel consumption, the industry pushed hard for protective measures. The government announced in early December a plan to bar foreign steelmakers from selling their products below cost in the United States.

Japanese steelmakers operated at 70% of capacity in 1977, producing just about 100 million tons—7% less than in 1976. To them, access to export markets is a matter of survival. And it is against them that protection efforts are aimed by both the United States and the European Economic Community. What makes the Japanese steel exports so noticeable is the fact that they go for particular products: they have captured 40% of some markets in the United States. About half of the nearly 20 million tons of U. S.-imported steel came from Japan.

But even the Japanese were being undersold in the U. S. steel market. While Japanese steel prices were 5–10% less than those for U. S. domestic steel, metal from such countries as South Korea, Taiwan, Australia, New Zealand, and the Philippines was being sold for 10% below the Japanese prices.

Textile and apparel industries in the United States and Europe continued to face severe competition from more than 30 developing countries. Clothing manufacturers were especially vulnerable to low-priced imports. Clothing manufacturing is a low-skill, labor-intensive industry, and it is one of the easiest operations to start in a developing country. Faced with tough competition and severe cutbacks in domestic production, textile and apparel industries in the United States and Europe are seeking a toughened Multifiber Arrangement, initially negotiated in 1973 under the auspices of the General Agreement on Tariffs and Trade, to stem the flow of imports. Imports accounted for more than one third of the sport coats and shirts, a fifth of all pants, and more than one tenth of all suits sold in the United States.

Even the U. S. semiconductor industry, so far the world leader in technological advances, kept a wary eye on its foreign competitors. While U. S. firms accounted for about two thirds of all semiconductors sold worldwide, they noted with concern the growing presence of the Japanese, who had captured about 25% of the world's market for transistors, integrated circuits, and other solid-state electronic components. American producers view their product as basic to industrial technology in general. Leadership in semiconductor technology is of vital importance to the manufacturers of data processing equipment, industrial controls, and telecommunications equipment. Texas Instruments recently announced the so-called bubble memory that contains 100,000 bits of information on a one-inch-square memory chip. Future developments should increase this density to 250,000 bits per chip. Such memory packages could make handheld computers a reality.

See also UNITED STATES: THE ECONOMY.

AGO AMBRE, *Bureau of Economic Analysis*
U. S. Department of Commerce

B. BRUKOFF INTERIORS, INC.; PHOTO BY JEREMIAH O. BRAGSTAD

INTERIOR DESIGN

Blue is an everlasting source of delight.
John Ruskin

There is a basic human need for color. In the words of Herbert Holt, dean of the Westchester Institute of Psychology, Rye, N. Y., "Color and comfort, physical as well as psychological, are closely related. We cannot say beforehand how one person or another will react to a specific color, but we do know that how he actually responds to color gives some light on the personality.

"Monochromatic colors may first appear enormously liberating, but with the passage of time that sense of freedom and release changes to oppression because man needs color—different colors in varying quantity—in order to organize and define his world" (*House & Garden,* March 1977).

The 1970's are witnessing a new emphasis on the psychological reaction to color and on the controlled and contrived use of it. Back in the 1940's, it was considered a daring psychological breakthrough when hospitals changed their color scheme to pale green (opposite of red) from the age-old tradition of clinical white. It rested the eyes and provided a psychological uplift.

As modest as that change might appear today, the fact is that it showed a stirring new awareness that color could be manipulated for specific results other than mere pleasure. We are now reaching the age of maturity, and we find not only that the use of color has become more sophisticated, but also that the useful palette has been extended with colors that never existed before. Chemistry is producing tertiary colors for both paints and dyes, which blend with and extend the standard spectrum.

Color is currently being emphasized anew. At the San Francisco Erhard Seminar Training (EST) headquarters (above), each floor is decorated in a different color. Each bay of the cafeteria of the U. S. Automobile Association building complex in San Antonio, Tex., is defined by a change in the colors of a geometric carpet.

COURTESY USAA, SAN ANTONIO; BENHAM, BLAIR ASSOCIATES ARCHITECTS

In *House & Garden* (March 1977) a young Californian artist, Michael Balog, dramatized the psychological reaction to color by setting up three rooms: one painted all white, one all red, and one half black and half white. Reacting to the all-white room, Robert Scull, an art collector, felt that, "the incredible white took away every known association or feeling I remembered about a normal room—I felt a stranger to myself." About the red one, Robert Bray, an interior designer, said, "the red was shocking and somewhat morbid—most of all I remember urgently wanting to leave." Renee Gladstein, a color-analysis instructor at the Fashion Institute of Technology, moving from the white to black side of the divided room, commented, "the idea that colors could manipulate my feelings, which they certainly did, struck me as very funny."

Homes. "The eye and mind, in order to function at their best, need moderation—shades, textures, lights and darks—a range to stimulate, not a flat one-dimensional environment," Dr. Melvin Schrier, former president of the New York Center of Learning, has remarked. Residential interior designers have long striven to create just that—contrast, color, texture. Theirs has been a response to an innate sense of "right," refined by an education in what colors "relate" to each other in harmony. But fashion, indeed fad, still is a positive force in their successful decoration of the home.

The public and work environment require a different approach. The architect and contract designer see color as a tool, a solution to a design problem, and a means to create cheerful, stimulating, or interesting surroundings.

Offices. In offices, color has an even farther-ranging function. Designers have found that the open office plan may create psychological upheaval, since personal territory is not visually explicit. There are no walls or obvious definitions of each worker's personal area. The solution, now becoming standard, is to change the color of each work station, or that of the carpet within each "private" territory, thereby marking the public walkway and the individual's "pad." In the case of the San Francisco EST (Erhard Seminar Training) headquarters, designed by Barry Brukoff, each floor was decorated in a different color, and although individual open-plan work stations were composed of the same furniture system throughout, variations in color and placement gave each staff member a sense of personal territory.

Hospitals and Nursing Homes. In the Southampton (N. Y.) Hospital, designed by Stephanie Mallis, color has a different, yet distinct, function. Since all floors are basically identical, colors in the "pure" sense should also be the same. But variance gives a sense of order. Strong, formal reds identify the entrance, quiet blue the intensive care area. Orange seems appropriate for the active pace of the pediatric section, cheerful yellow for patients' rooms.

Architects Rogers, Butler and Burgun also used color to code areas of the Farrand Building of the Misericordia Hospital, Bronx, N. Y. Narrow corridors were colored red to "symbolize activity and movement," stairways and doors were painted green, and doors to lecture halls were identified by yellow.

Commercial Complex. Color and graphics play an important role throughout the United States Automobile Association building complex in the foothills of San Antonio, Texas. Interior architects Neuhaus & Taylor used color in subtle, sophisticated ways, such as in directional arrows woven into the carpeted sides of escalators to indicate "up" or "down." Because of the size of the complex, coded colors on hanging banners were used to relate to each clerical area. One can look back to any part of the building for orientation.

JEANNE WEEKS
Associate, American Society of Interior Designers

ROGERS, BUTLER & BURGUN ARCHITECTS

Symbolic colors were carefully selected to code areas of the Farrand Building of the Misericordia Hospital, Bronx, N. Y.

INTERNATIONAL TRADE AND FINANCE

In mid-1977 economic and financial conditions were better than they were one or two years previously, but a great number of countries were still attempting to recover from disturbances of 1973–75. These disturbances included a rapid increase in prices and costs, a prolonged recession, and an international oil crisis. By past standards the economic picture in 1977 was still unsatisfactory with subnormal growth rates, high unemployment, excess plant capacity, and lagging investment. Inflation continued on a wide scale, and in a number of countries was coupled with weakness of the external position. Economic policies in most countries placed primary emphasis on medium-term objectives of combatting inflation and strengthening the external position; these would ostensibly yield the best results for economic growth and employment in the longer run.

TRADE AND PAYMENTS

World trade at the beginning of the year seemed to be settling into a sustainable pace of moderate expansion, but with volume growing less rapidly than in 1976. Foreign trade prices rose a bit faster than in 1976, partly because of the increase in primary commodity prices from early 1976 through April 1977. The volume of world trade increased by 11.5% starting in 1975 and continuing through 1976, but the rise in the latter year was unevenly distributed among groups of importing countries. There was strong import demand from industrial countries and oil exporters, while imports of non-oil primary producing countries remained somewhat depressed. Import volume of trade for industrial countries was 14.5% higher in 1976 than in 1975; other developed countries' volume was 3.5% higher; major oil exporters' volume was 18.5% more; other developing countries' imports were 1.5% higher. Export volume over the same broad groups ranged within 10.5–13%; the 1977 rates of export expansion were estimated at about 7%. Imports of industrial countries rose less rapidly in real terms in 1977 while those of non-oil developing countries were expected to show a stronger rise.

In 1976, the value of goods traded internationally amounted to nearly $1 trillion, exceeding the 1975 total by 11% after allowing for inflation. By mid-1977 the year-to-year gains had averaged only about 7%, amid prospects that the gains would continue to fall. Without oil it was estimated that world trade would have risen by only 4%. U.S. imports, led by oil, were nearly 20% higher than in 1976, but the major factor underlying the trade slowdown overall appears to be protectionism. The International Monetary Fund (IMF) reported in midsummer on the increase in protectionism among industrialized nations as measured by the proportion of world trade being subject to increasingly restrictive nontariff barriers, such as quotas and "negotiated" export restraint agreements. It is feared that these restrictions may lead to retaliation and escalate into a "trade war" reminiscent of the depression of the 1930's.

Both in 1976 and in the first half of 1977, the main impetus for higher foreign trade unit values came from increases in prices of primary commodities. In the case of oil, there was a 10% increase in Organization of Petroleum Exporting Countries (OPEC) "marker crude" in October 1975, and further increases of 5% for two members of OPEC and 10% for others on Jan. 1, 1977. Rising prices for coffee, cocoa, and tea, in addition to vegetable oils and oilseeds, contributed disproportionately to the rise. Prices for several important food products, including grains and sugar, went down throughout 1976 and the first half of 1977. Differences in supply situations explain the price pattern—e.g., frost damage adversely affected coffee production in Brazil while there were abundant harvests of food grains elsewhere. Price increases of metals and agricultural materials during 1977 were moderate. The upward influence of unit labor costs on export unit values for manufactured goods was considerably stronger from mid-1976 to mid-1977 than it had been during the preceding year. Differentials in export unit value movements during that period had a marked impact on the terms of trade. For non-oil developing countries there was a 4% improvement in 1976, with the prospect for a larger gain in 1977. The terms of trade of more developed primary producers continued to deteriorate, with a 2% decrease in 1976 and the same prospect for 1977. Industrial countries experienced a 1% decline, while the major oil exporters realized a 5% improvement in 1976.

ADJUSTMENT PROCESS AND INTERNATIONAL FINANCE

Between 1973 and 1976 the combined current account surplus in the balance of payments of major oil exporting countries increased from $6 billion (U. S.) to more than $40 billion and was concentrated in a small number of countries which had little potential to increase imports. Over the same period, the United States, West Germany, and Japan acted against inflationary pressures, and the impact on their current account balances was significant. In the aggregate the current account balances of oil importing countries other than these three shifted from a deficit of $8 billion in 1973 to deficits of $6 billion in 1974 and about $55 billion in both 1975 and 1976. This shift in the global structure of current account balances reflects the emergence of oil exporting countries as the

With floating exchange rate systems continuing, the world money markets, including those in Frankfurt, *above*, and London, remained active.

principal surplus group, and also the disappearance of the once large surplus of the industrial countries. Non-oil developing countries, as well as the more developed primary producing group, are large scale net recipients of capital and foreign aid since they are not importers of goods and services. The projected global structure of current account balances for 1977 is:

(in billions of U. S. dollars)

Major oil exporting countries	37
Industrial countries	−1
Other non-oil countries:	
More developed	−12
Less developed	−25

Source: IMF, Annual Report 1977.

Industrial countries as a group are no longer net suppliers of *real* resources or financing needed to cover current account deficits of non-oil primary producing countries, but they are still the direct *source* of the financing mainly via the "recycling" process. (Industrial lenders obtain the funds directly or indirectly from placement of surplus funds by major oil exporting countries.)

Major Oil Exporting Countries. In 1976 there was a $6 billion increase—to $41 billion—in the surplus of major oil exporters. This surplus tends to shrink gradually as imports rise; as shown above it is less in 1977 but will remain large for some years to come.

Information on investments of the surplus indicates a trend toward diversification and shifts into less liquid forms. Slightly more than one fourth of the funds went into bank deposits and short-term government securities in 1976, as compared with about two thirds in 1974. The proportion going into other investments in developed countries rose from about one fifth to one half. Grants and loans to developing countries were one seventh of the total in 1976, substantially larger than in 1974.

At the end of 1977 members of OPEC held an estimated $205 billion in investments and assets abroad. After adjusting for some $50 billion in external debt the net external assets totalled $155 billion. Of this estimated $155 billion, 95% is held by five of the thirteen cartel members:

(in billions of dollars)

Saudi Arabia	68
Kuwait	31
Iran	22
United Arab Emirates	16
Venezuela	10

(Algeria, Equador, Gabon, and Indonesia were in deficit at year-end.)

During the first half of 1977, about three fourths of identifiable investments by OPEC went into dollar-denominated assets though not necessarily into the United States. About 18% of OPEC's surplus was placed in the United States, as compared with almost 30% in 1976. Net purchases of stock during the first nine months were a third below 1976; holdings at midyear amounted to a relatively small $4.3 billion. Deposits in U. S. banks declined by $500 million as differences between interest rates on Eurodollar deposits and U. S. deposit rates widened. Net new purchases of U. S. Treasury securities in the third quarter amounted to about $50 million after rising by $3 billion during the first half. Total investments by OPEC in the United States for the first eight months of 1977 amounted to $5.7 billion. It was estimated that some $31 billion of the OPEC 1977 current account surplus of approximately $37 billion would be available for net investment abroad.

Industrial Countries. The current account positions that were strongest in 1975 and 1976 remained strong through 1977. West Germany's export strength continued despite the loss in price competitiveness in the early 1970's. The persistent current account surplus of the Netherlands reflects in large part the increasing importance of exports of natural gas. Recession in Switzerland combined with the strong export orientation of several industries explains the Swiss current account surplus. Japan's current account surplus was in substantial deficit after the oil price rise in 1974 but by the first half of 1977 was quite large. The large shrinkage in the current account surplus of the United States reflected the fact that its economic recovery was occurring at a faster rate than was true for its trading partners. Net capital outflows from the United States exceeded the small current account surplus in 1976, illustrating the role of the U. S. money and capital markets as intermediaries on an international scale. A further downward movement in the U. S. current account balance occurred in the first half of 1977, carrying it into substantial deficit. In addition to strong domestic demand, other influences bringing about this deficit include increases in prices of many imported primary commodities and the impact of an exceptionally severe winter on requirements for imported oil.

More Developed Primary Producing Countries. These countries were still in the backwash of the international recession in 1976 and their external deficit on current account was still at approximately the high level reached in 1974 and 1975. Since these countries are predominantly net importers of capital their current accounts are generally in substantial deficit. Financing of these deficits is enhanced via ready access to international financial markets. The cumulative deterioration of the terms of trade since 1973 has been greater for this group than any other. The estimated $12 billion deficit in current account for this group will remain about twice as large as the average deficit of the same

group over the period 1967–72 after allowing for the effects of growth and inflation.

Less Developed Primary Producing Countries. The current account deficit of these countries rose to unprecedented size in 1974 and 1975 but showed a substantial reduction in 1976 with no change expected for 1977. The estimated $25 billion 1977 deficit is some $12–13 billion below the 1975 peak. These countries have long been major net importers of goods and services, and, as a group, make domestic developmental investments in excess of domestic savings via persistent net inflow of capital and aid from abroad. The overhang of external indebtedness built up to finance the 1974 and 1975 deficits is a problem in some countries. A major feature of this debt was the heavy reliance on borrowing in international financial markets, especially from commercial banks, and there is concern as to the sustainability of flows of funds to these countries from these sources. Through mid-1977 such concern did not prove justified for the countries as a group, and some slackening of external borrowing, especially from commercial banks, seemed likely for all of 1977. Yet nearly 30% of an estimated total outstanding debt of $150 billion is owed to commercial banks. For 1977, the aggregate deficit for non-oil developing countries as a group was virtually unchanged but there were regional changes: an appreciable reduction in Latin America and the Caribbean, a small reduction in Africa, largely offset by changes in the Middle East, and a minor upturn in the current account deficit of countries in Asia.

INTERNATIONAL MONETARY SYSTEM

Since the adoption of floating exchange rate systems by major industrial countries in 1973 there has been a growing heterogeneity of exchange rate practices in the international monetary system. These practices range from independent floating with little attempt to influence market forces to the maintenance of a fixed peg against a single intervention currency. For ex-

UPI

South Korea agreed in May to restrict its shipment of shoes to the United States. The intention was to help U. S. shoe manufacturers compete with low-cost imports. Increased protectionism by industrialized nations characterized international trade during the year.

ample, Canada, the United States, and members of the European Common Market arrangement (the snake) taken as a group generally refrain from influencing rates except to smooth out short-term disturbances or to counter disorderly market conditions. In the case of other countries which consider their rates to be floating there has been a greater disposition to use intervention.

Among these countries that formally pursue a policy of fixing their exchange rates several differing pegging techniques are used, with the most common being the unitary peg (to a single currency). As of Oct. 31, 1977, a total of 44 countries were pegged to the U. S. dollar; 5 were pegged to the pound sterling; 14 to the French franc; 4 to some other single currency; 15 to Special Drawing Rights (SDR); 18 to currency composites other than SDR, and 6 to other currencies in a group. (Belgium, Denmark, West Germany, Luxembourg, the Netherlands, and Norway maintain the "snake"—margins of 2.25% for transactions between their currencies and those of other countries in the group.) On the same date, there were 46 countries which described their exchange rate regions as floating independently and/or those who adjust rates according to a set of indicators. All regimes imply varying degrees of intervention in the exchange markets and during the third period of 1977 (August through October) intervention by major central banks was a record $30 billion, up from $22 billion in the preceding quarter, and $20 billion in the February–April period. Much of the intervention is done by central banks of West Germany and other European countries whose currencies are linked together. In addition, there were heavy purchases of dollars by the Bank of England in an effort to stop the rise of the pound. From the adoption of floating rate in March 1973 through July 1977, gross interventions by central banks were more than $215 billion.

"Snake" Problems. Effective Aug. 29, 1977, Sweden discontinued its membership in the European common margins agreement and devalued the krona by 10% vis-à-vis a trade-weighted basket of 15 currencies, to which the krona is now pegged. In related moves Denmark and Norway devalued their kroner 5% under the "snake" arrangement; Iceland depreciated the krona by 2.5% vis-à-vis the U. S. dollar on August 30; a day later Finland devalued the markka by 3.1% against a basket of currencies.

In unrelated earlier developments, the Portuguese government on August 25 announced that it was allowing the exchange rate for the escudo to undergo small and successive adjustments in line with price developments in Portugal and its major trading partners. Also, the Spanish peseta was devalued in mid-July by 20% (25% relative to the U. S. dollar); this was the second devaluation since early 1976. (*See also* individual country articles.)

Pound Problems. In January 1977, there was a $3.9 billion IMF loan to Britain to help support the exchange rate of the pound in the face of balance of payments deficits and domestic economic problems. Additional aid involved a $3-billion line of credit established at the Bank of International Settlements (BIS) by seven governments in Europe and the United States. The BIS aid was to help Britain achieve an orderly liquidation of the last remnants of the reserve-currency role of the pound sterling. A private loan of $1.5 billion was extended by a syndicate of major U. S., West German, Canadian, and British banks, temporarily to boost official reserves which could be used in pound support. During 1977, Britain's external accounts began to show improvement as a "cheaper" pound increased exports and as the North Sea oil began to replace oil imports. By the third quarter, the United Kingdom recorded a current account surplus of $900 million, the largest quarterly surplus on record. In October 1976, the pound low was $1.56; a year later it was $1.84 as the British government "unpegged" the floating pound after several months of heavy intervention designed to moderate the upward pressure on the currency and keep British goods competitive in world markets. Britain's foreign currency reserves exceeded $20 billion and were the third highest in the world after Saudi Arabia and West Germany. The Israeli pound was also set afloat in late October along with other actions designed to reduce the inflation rate and improve its trade deficit.

U. S. Developments. During the first six months of 1977 the U. S. trade deficit was $12,587,300,000, as compared with a deficit of $790,600,000 over the same period in 1976. In July the cumulative deficit was $14.92 billion; in August $17.58 billion. The deficits continued to grow, cumulating to $19.3 billion for the first three quarters. Then in October the trade deficit was at a record $3.1 billion. This was the 17th consecutive deficit month. The cumulative deficit for the year up to October was $22.4 billion. An East-Gulf Coast dock strike, which brought container shipping to a halt, was singled out as the main factor in the October deterioration. For the year as a whole, slower economic growth in other countries and rising consumption of imported oil were cited as chief factors. The total trade deficit for 1977 was upward of $30 billion.

The United States participated in a London summit conference in May, along with Canada, France, West Germany, Italy, Japan, and Britain. The meeting was called to emphasize the Western nations' commitment to economic cooperation. A joint communiqué focused on creation of jobs and reducing unemployment, attaining stated economic growth targets, improving international financial resources, expanding trade and resisting protectionism, increasing the flow of aid to developing countries, and con-

PHOTOS UPI

In Washington, Canada's Finance Minister Jean Chrétien addresses joint annual meeting of the IMF and the World Bank.

serving energy and diversifying energy sources to reduce dependence on petroleum. Some progress was made in the trade area as countries reached negotiating agreement on tariff cuts under the Tokyo Round of GATT (General Agreements on Tariffs and Trade). Also, agreement was reached on increasing the financial resources of the IMF. The summit conference foresaw a coordinated effort to reduce unemployment by achieving a 5% annual average rate of growth by 1980 in the United States and the 23 countries in the Organization for Economic Cooperation and Development (OECD). By late November, the OECD forecast rising unemployment in 1978, with growth rates below the London target. Based on current national policies, OECD stated that the average growth rate of its members would rise slightly from 3.5% during the last half of 1977 to about 4% in the first six months of 1978 and then perhaps slip back to 3% during the second half. The United States, West Germany, and Japan were to provide the leadership for growth; the OECD indicated the target growth rate cannot be achieved unless West Germany and Japan adopt more expansionary policies. The United States in turn, brought pressure to bear on these two countries to expand, as their balance of payments surpluses and appreciated currencies are the counterparts of the U.S. trade deficit and depreciating dollar.

During 1977, some currencies gained sharply against the dollar. The German mark was up 8.4%, the Swiss franc 13.3%, the Japanese yen 23.2%, and the British pound 10.5%. The Canadian dollar declined 10.4% and the U.S. dollar firmed or held about even against most other currencies. With respect to oil imports, the dollar's decline had no immediate impact since oil in international trade is priced and generally paid in U.S. dollars. Yet a depreciation of the U.S. dollar internationally reflects the U.S. trade deficit and could make the overall balance of payments worse if speculative pressures elicited capital outflows from the United States and/or sale of dollars by foreign holders. In an effort to keep markets orderly, the Federal Reserve Board intervened by making gross purchases and sales of foreign currencies equivalent to $365 million during the August–October period. This was up sharply from nearly $300 million in the preceding three months. In October alone federal intervention came to about $200 million. Toward year-end there were indications, based on evidence of U.S. economic expansion, a relatively low inflation rate, and rising interest rates, that the dollar would experience an upturn in exchange markets. In addition, Japan, whose 1977 trade surplus with the United States totaled about $8 billion, was taking steps to reduce this surplus.

International Monetary Fund. Important activities during 1977 included the following:

1. Agreement on principles for guidance of members relative to their exchange policies and on procedures for Fund surveillance over those policies.
2. Initiation of the Seventh General Review of Quotas, which was to be completed in February 1978. Quotas determine drawing rights.
3. Consideration of whether a further allocation of Special Drawing Rights would be advisable at present.
4. Provision for balance of payments assistance for members with extensive drawings and enlargement of the General Arrangements to Borrow relative to drawing by industrial countries.
5. Initiation of gold sales to the market through auctions and for distribution to members.

Initiation of the Trust Fund providing assistance to developing countries; the resources of the Trust Fund consist of profits from gold sales.

Originally gold auctions were scheduled every six weeks, but starting in March 1977 auctions on the first Wednesday of each month were initiated. Therefore, during 1977, 11 auctions occurred, the last on December 7. Up through the December auction, $964 million had accrued to the Trust Fund to be distributed for the benefit of developing countries. The first of these Trust Fund disbursements, amounting to SDR 31.6 million, was made in January 1977 to 12 members. The second disbursements were made in July to 24 members and amounted to SDR 121.3 million. Further loan disbursements are planned at six-month intervals.

The first phase of restitution (sales of Fund gold to members in proportion to their quotas on Aug. 31, 1975) was carried out from Jan. 10 to Feb. 23, 1977. Gold was restituted to 112 members and the amount of gold actually sold was nearly 6 million fine ounces, amounting to SDR 209.95 million. The Fund made the second of these sales of gold to members in December 1977. Amount sold was 6.25 million ounces at a price of SDR 35 per fine ounce. The restitution and auctioning programs result from an agreement reached in 1975 that the role of gold in the international monetary system should be reduced.

From September 1976 through November 1977, the market price of gold bullion rose from a low of $102 to $163 an ounce. As of Jan. 2, 1975, U. S. citizens could legally own bullion for the first time since February 1934. On Oct. 28, 1977, President Carter signed the Helms Bill—a measure reestablishing the gold clause. So for the first time since 1934 Americans are permitted to lend money with repayment tied to the fluctuations in the value of gold. Today, however, the best market for gold is the oil-rich Middle East, which in 1976 absorbed almost 16 million ounces, or one third of total mine output.

JOHN R. MATTHEWS, *Professor of Economics College of William & Mary*

IOWA

Economy. The 1977 Iowa corn harvest totaled some 1,037 million bushels (365 million hl), about 10% below the 1976 crop. The soybean yield was estimated at 33 bushels per acre (29 hl/ha), some 3 bushels per acre (2.6 hl/ha) less than the record of 1972. However, the total soybean crop of 237.6 million bushels (83.7 million hl) was 27% larger than 1976 because of increased acreage. The state's corn harvest was reduced because of extreme drought in central Iowa during late June and July. August weather reversed the trend with the greatest rains in more than 105 years.

Unemployment remained 3.5% of the work force, about half of the national average.

Education. Enrollment in Iowa's three state-supported universities continued to increase. The 1977–78 school year found Iowa State University's student body larger than that of the University of Iowa for the first time. Northern Iowa enrollment rose nearly 10% to top the 10,000-student mark.

Legislation. The 1977 Iowa General Assembly was under Democratic control, with a narrow margin of 26 to 24 in the Senate but a working majority of 61 to 39 in the House. The legislature enacted 166 laws. Gov. Robert D. Ray (R) vetoed three bills in their entirety and sections of two other statutes. One of the vetoes erased a 2% liquor price increase at state liquor stores, while eliminating a 15% surtax paid by tavern operators. Another salvaged a requirement that county governments accept the "lowest responsible bid" for contracts of supplies, materials, or services.

Urban residents were upset that the legislature changed the basis of appraising farm land, which now will be based entirely upon productivity rather than 50% land value and 50% productivity. Also, farm corporations were required to pay corporation income tax, even if they sell all their produce outside Iowa, a practice heretofore given tax exemption.

All state employees were granted about 8% salary increases. Key executive officers, however, were given much greater raises. The governor's salary was increased from $40,000 to $55,000 and the state attorney general's from $29,000 to $40,000; lesser increases were given to other state elective and appointive officials and all state judges.

The legislature allotted a record $47 million for aid to families with dependent children and $82 million to pay health-care costs for the indigent, elderly, blind, or disabled.

Employers will pay higher unemployment insurance taxes in 1978 because of a new statute designed to keep the state jobless benefits fund in the black.

RUSSELL M. ROSS, *University of Iowa*

─────── **IOWA • Information Highlights** ───────

Area: 56,290 square miles (145,791 km²).
Population (1976 est.): 2,870,000.
Chief Cities (1970 census): Des Moines, the capital, 201,404; Cedar Rapids, 110,642; Davenport, 98,469.
Government (1977): *Chief Officers*—governor, Robert D. Ray (R); lt. gov., Arthur A. Neu (R). *General Assembly*—Senate, 50 members; House of Representatives, 100 members.
Education (1976–77): *Enrollment*—public elementary schools, 315,985 pupils; public secondary, 289,142; nonpublic, 66,700; colleges and universities, 106,458 students. *Public school expenditures*, $1,054,355,000 ($1,550 per pupil).
State Finances (fiscal year 1976): *Revenues*, $2,314,349,000; *expenditures*, $2,346,284,000.
Personal Income (1976): $17,923,000,000; per capita, $6,245.
Labor Force (June 1977): *Nonagricultural wage and salary earners*, 1,039,400; *unemployed*, 43,800 (3.1% of total force).

Shah Mohammed Reza Pahlavi receives top delegates to the Central Treaty Organization at the Niavaran Palace, Teheran. From left: CENTO Secretary General Umit Bayulken, U. S. Secretary of State Cyrus Vance, British Foreign Secretary, David Owen, and Turkish Foreign Minister Ihsan Caglayangil.

UPI

IRAN

There was a change in the premiership of Iran in 1977, the first in 12 years, but in basic policies no more than modifications. The prime minister, after all, is but the executant of a policy determined by the Shah.

Aims of the Shah. Shah Mohammed Reza Pahlavi has been pursuing for many years a course of enlightened autocracy, in which the main emphasis has been on rapid economic development, made possible by oil revenues. The Shah sees an economically developed Iran as fulfilling a role of regional leadership and as providing a core of stability and strength in an area much subject to political unrest. Iran seems well cast for such a role, with its large population, immense natural resources, and ample size.

Oil Revenues. For the moment, though a broader industrial base is being energetically developed, almost everything turns on the oil revenues, and these had their ups and downs during the year. Toward the end of 1976, in anticipation of an oil price increase, world demand was running extremely high, and Iranian oil sales were at a level of about 6 million barrels (810,000 metric tons) per day. Iran and 10 other members of the Organization of Petroleum Exporting Countries (OPEC), agreed in December 1976 to raise oil prices by an average of 10%, effective Jan. 1, 1977. Saudi Arabia, however, the Middle East's largest producer, and the United Arab Emirates (UAE) limited their price increase to 5%. This had an immediate adverse impact on Iranian sales. By January, total petroleum exports had dropped 38%.

However, unusually cold weather in Western Europe, as well as other factors, led to another sharp reversal. Iranian sales and production rose again as the year advanced, and on July 3, Saudi and UAE prices were raised 5% to equal those of Iran and other OPEC members.

The Iranian budget for fiscal 1977–78, announced on February 20, embodied a comparatively modest increase of 10%, totaling $49.5 billion (U. S.), but it provided for a $2.26 bil-

lion reduction in military expenditures, compared with 1976.

Growing Pains. The rapid pace of economic development has produced all kinds of dislocations, both social and economic. These reached a new level of intensity in the early summer of 1977, when the oil-rich nation, paradoxically, suffered an energy crisis. Electric power was lacking in Teheran several hours each day. Conditions were worst in the southern part of the country, where plans for boosting the energy output of the Reza Shah Kebir Dam had fallen behind schedule. Many industrial plants were working at only two thirds of capacity.

Changes in Government. It was apparently because the Shah shared the public's discontent with the running of affairs that the premiership abruptly changed hands on August 6, when Amir Abbas Hoveida was replaced by Dr. Jamshid Amouzegar. Hoveida was let down lightly, however, becoming minister of court. Dr. Amouzegar had previously been secretary general of Rastakhiz, the only legal party. He enjoyed a reputation as a precise and efficient administrator, and in particular as a sharp negotiator in oil matters. Of his new cabinet of 23, eleven had been members of Hoveida's government.

New Policies. The key word under the new administration was "coordination." In his first half-year in office, Amouzegar attacked such

——— IRAN · Information Highlights ———
Official Name: Empire of Iran.
Location: Southwest Asia.
Area: 636,294 square miles (1,648,000 km²).
Population (1977 est.): 34,800,000.
Chief Cities (1975 est.): Teheran, the capital, 4,170,000 (met. area); Isfahan, 620,000; Meshed, 585,000; Tabriz, 570,000.
Government: *Head of state*, Mohammed Reza Pahlavi, shah (acceded Sept. 1941; crowned Oct. 1967). *Head of government*, Jamshid Amouzegar, prime minister (took office Aug. 1977). *Legislature*—Parliament: Senate and Majlis (Lower House).
Monetary Unit: Rial (70.62 rials equal U. S.$1, Aug. 1977).
Manufacturing (major products): Petroleum products, iron, steel, textiles, carpets, food products, caviar.
Major Agricultural Products: Wheat, rice, barley, cotton, tobacco, almonds, fruits.

evils as the swollen bureaucracy and inflation, reduced from early 1976 but still serious. On August 18, the premier announced a $35-million annual cutback in the industrial development program. He also enunciated his preference for encouraging private enterprise rather than relying on nationalized industries.

The month of August also saw continued easing of the Shah's tight political controls, possibly in response to pressures of opinion. Some 500 prisoners, mostly political, were amnestied, and press censorship was lightened.

Foreign Relations. There were no great changes in foreign affairs. U. S. arms, however, may not be so readily available to the Shah as before. This was indicated by President Carter's reluctance to sell AWAC (airborne command) planes to Iran; sale of some modified planes was allowed, however. The empress visited several U. S. cities in July (8–12), and in November the Shah made his first visit to Washington under the Carter regime. Normal relations with Iraq, established in 1975, after long hostility, continued. Withdrawal of Iranian forces from Oman, where they had been assisting Sultan Qabus against guerrillas for four years, was announced in January. The Treaty of Izmir, with Pakistan and Turkey, signed in Teheran on March 12, sought to revitalize the three-nation Regional Council for Development.

ARTHUR CAMPBELL TURNER
University of California, Riverside

IRAQ

Iraq in 1977 continued to be ruled by a Ba'ath party government, its top stratum organized in the Revolutionary Command Council (RCC). In charge of the government since 1968, Field Marshal Ahmed Hassan al-Bakr held the triple title of president, prime minister, and minister of defense.

Rising Star. Regarding so tightly controlled and secretive a regime, any interpretation must be speculative, but some rivalry seemed to be emerging between the president and Saddam Husain Takriti, deputy chairman of the RCC and second man in the state. Takriti was certainly becoming more visible and active as the government's representative.

An Extremist Regime. The nature of the

─────── **IRAQ · Information Highlights** ───────

Official Name: Republic of Iraq.
Location: Southwest Asia.
Area: 167,925 square miles (434,924 km²).
Population (1977 est.): 11,800,000.
Chief Cities (1970 est.): Baghdad, the capital, 2,183,800 (met. area); Basra, 370,900; Mosul, 293,100.
Government: *Head of state and government,* Ahmed Hassan al-Bakr, president (took office July 1968).
Monetary Unit: Dinar (0.30 dinar equals U. S.$1, Aug. 1977).
Manufacturing (major products): Petroleum products, processed foods, textiles, cigarettes, cement.
Major Agricultural Products: Barley, wheat, dates, rice, cotton, tobacco.

regime did not change or moderate. Iraq is by far the most radical and revolutionary of important Arab states. An uneasy and dangerous neighbor, it is (paradoxically) on the worst of terms with the other Ba'ath regime, in neighboring Syria, and has border disputes with Kuwait, but (since 1975) is reasonably friendly with its eastern neighbor—imperial, non-Arab, non-Socialist Iran. The Iraqi regime is a virulent critic of all who think in terms of any conceivable accommodation with Israel. The United States is denounced as the patron of Israel, and normal diplomatic relations have not existed since 1967. Nevertheless, U. S trade with Iraq is soaring.

Support for Terrorists. The Iraqi regime is widely recognized to be the organizer and sustainer of terrorist activity in many countries. Sen. Jacob Javits of New York in May unearthed U. S. State Department documents, making this specific charge. Abu Daoud, the terrorist whose arrest and then release by France was a *cause célèbre* in January, was traveling on an Iraqi passport.

Domestic Affairs. The first session since 1974 of the Iraqi Regional Congress of the Ba'ath party was held on January 10. On January 23, six ministries changed hands and 11 new men were brought into the government. Two newcomers were appointed on April 5; this was interpreted by *Le Monde* as an accession of strength for Takriti. A presidential decree on September 4 substantially enlarged the RCC.

The Kurds. Kurdish desire for autonomy, supposedly crushed in March 1975, was a specter that still haunted Baghdad. Four Polish technicians working in north-eastern Iraq were captured by Kurdish guerrillas early in January, and fighting broke out again and continued at least through April. Concessions were made by the government: 40,000 Kurds in enforced exile in central and southern Iraq were allowed to return home. On April 2, it was announced that the Kurdish language would be the official tongue in the internal administration of the region.

Oil. Iraq's oil exports fell in 1977 to about 1.7 million barrels (230,000 metric tons) a day from a 1976 average of about 2 million (270,000 tons). The new oil pipeline from Iraq through Turkey was formally opened in January. It replaces the former route through Syria, for political reasons unused since April 1976. On July 5, Iraq fell into line with OPEC and announced it would not impose the 5% oil price hike scheduled for July 1.

The Economy. The value of Iraq's five-year (1975–80) development plan is to be $49 billion (U. S.), 13 times more than its predecessor. The plan is to concentrate on industry and agriculture. Among foreign contracts arranged in 1977 was a $414 million order to Mitsubishi (Japan) for construction of a power plant.

ARTHUR CAMPBELL TURNER
University of California, Riverside

Outgoing Prime Minister Liam Cosgrave (*left*) and his successor, Jack Lynch, cast their ballots in the parliamentary elections held on June 16.

UPI

IRELAND

After four and a half years in office, Liam Cosgrave's coalition government suffered a major defeat at the polls on June 16. During the election campaign, the opposition party, Fianna Fáil, had stressed the need to raise employment and lower taxes, and this appeal to "bread-and-butter" issues damaged the cause of the incumbent Fine Gael-Labour coalition. Resentful of spiraling prices and hopeful that a change of government might improve their purchasing power, Irish voters returned 84 Fianna Fáil members to the 148-seat Dáil (parliament). In the new (21st) Dáil, Fine Gael's strength declined from 53 to 43 seats, and Labour fell from 20 to 17. Independents won the remaining 4 seats.

Jack Lynch, the leader of Fianna Fáil, returned to the premiership which he had occupied from 1966 to 1973. His cabinet included such party stalwarts as George Colley (minister of finance and deputy premier), Charles Haughey (health and social welfare), Desmond O'Malley (industry and commerce), and Michael O'Kennedy (foreign affairs). Lynch followed up his campaign pledge to stimulate the economy by appointing Professor Martin O'Donoghue to the new position of minister in charge of economic planning and development.

In the aftermath of its crushing defeat, Fine Gael chose a new leader to replace Cosgrave. The successor, Dr. Garret FitzGerald, had served as foreign secretary in the coalition government. The Labour party chose Frank Cluskey to succeed Brendan Corish. Two prominent Labour deputies and former ministers in the Cosgrave cabinet, Dr. Conor Cruise O'Brien and Justin Keating, lost their seats in the election; but both men found a political home in the Senate, where Fianna Fáil secured 31 of the 49 available seats.

Economy. The Irish economy continued its disappointing performance, owing in part to the country's heavy dependence on oil imports. According to an OECD (Organization for Economic Cooperation and Development) estimate, Ireland could expect a $1-billion (U.S.) oil deficit by the end of 1977. In January, Irish trade-union leaders reluctantly accepted an agreement restricting wages until 1979. Their consent helped to lower the rate of inflation to approximately 17% during the spring. The unemployment rate showed a modest improvement over the 18% rate for 1976. But increases in the value of exported goods were again offset by the rising cost of imports.

Political Extremism. The gradual decline in sectarian violence in Northern Ireland and the application of more stringent security measures led to a sharp reduction in shootings and bombings in the republic. In Port Laoise jail, some 20 Irish Republican Army members staged a hunger strike in protest against prison conditions. Fourteen of them continued to fast for 47 days, while public sympathy with their cause steadily mounted. After lengthy negotiations, the hunger strikers agreed to end their protest on April 22. On August 30, U.S. President Carter delivered a statement expressing his hope that Northern Ireland could achieve "a peaceful and just society" by nonviolent means. His defense of the democratic process in Anglo-Irish relations was well-received by moderates.

Appointments. On June 20, President Carter named William V. Shannon, an editor of *The New York Times,* U.S. ambassador to Ireland. And on August 22, Pope Paul VI appointed Msgr. Tomás Ó Fiaich archbishop of Armagh and Catholic primate of all Ireland.

L. PERRY CURTIS, JR., *Brown University*

------ **IRELAND · Information Highlights** ------

Official Name: Ireland.
Location: Island in the eastern North Atlantic Ocean.
Area: 27,136 square miles (70,283 km²).
Population (1977 est.): 3,200,000.
Chief Cities (1973 est.): Dublin, the capital, 680,000; Cork, 224,000; Limerick, 140,000.
Government: *Head of state,* Patrick J. Hillery, president (took office Nov. 1976). *Head of government,* John Lynch, prime minister (taoiseach, took office June 1977). *Legislature*—Parliament; House of Representatives (Dáil Éireann) and Senate (Seanad Éireann).
Monetary Unit: Pound (0.57 pound equals U.S.$1, Aug. 1977).
Manufacturing (major products): Processed foods, clothing, textiles, paper products.
Major Agricultural Products: Wheat, potatoes, sugar beets.

Prime Minister Menahem Begin (*left*) held his first cabinet meeting on June 26. Initially shaky, his coalition government acquired additional support later in the year.

ISRAEL

The year was one of substantial changes for Israel. A general election produced an upset of startling dimensions, as the long power monopoly of the Labor party was broken. The new Begin government had policies apparently different in foreign affairs and certainly different in domestic affairs.

Another election, which in the long run might make even more impact on Israel, was the one that produced Carter as U. S. president. There were ambiguities and fumblings in the new U. S. administration's Middle East policies, but they did seem less favorable to Israel.

Before the Election. The long reign of the Labor party and its allies ended in a rather dingy morass of illegality, suicide, and scandal. The parliamentary crisis of December 1976, which turned on a theological issue of a kind peculiar to Israel (did or did not Prime Minister Rabin violate the Sabbath on December 10?), soon led to Rabin's resignation; President Katzir requested him to continue in a caretaker capacity. On January 5, 1977, the Knesset passed a bill mandating an election on May 17.

Housing Minister Abraham Ofer committed suicide on January 3. He was under investigation for possible financial irregularities prior to his joining the government in 1974. The investigation was a byproduct of the arrest of Ofer's close friend, Asher Yadlin, shortly after he was nominated as governor of the Bank of Israel.

In February, Yadlin was found guilty on five charges of conspiracy, accepting bribes, fraud, and tax evasion. During the trial, he implicated several officials of the Labor party in channeling illegally obtained public funds into the party's coffers.

The Rabin Bank Accounts. A fresh storm then broke over the head of Prime Minister Rabin. A newspaper reported on March 15 that his wife, Leah, still had a bank account in Washington, D. C., contrary to the stringent currency regulations. (Though illegal, this was common among Israelis, naturally reluctant to hold their assets in a chronically diminishing currency. Such accounts became legal before the year's end—by action of Rabin's political opponents.) The account dated from Rabin's tour of duty as ambassador in Washington, and Mrs. Rabin immediately confirmed its existence. On April 7 it was revealed that there were two accounts, and that the amounts in them (about $10,000) were much larger than previously mentioned.

Rabin, who on February 23 had been chosen Labor's candidate for prime minister (narrowly defeating Defense Minister Shimon Peres) resigned as candidate the next day. Peres was easily elected to replace him. A fine equivalent to $1,500 was levied on Rabin by the Finance Ministry on April 11, and on April 17 Mrs. Rabin was fined $27,000 in a district court in Tel Aviv. The real punishment, however, was the apparent end of Rabin's political career. He tried to resign the premiership, but since this was legally impossible, he began an "extended holiday," turning over the reins to Peres.

Further Scandals. The fall of Rabin was not the end of embarrassments to the Labor-Mapam government. On April 23 it was announced that the Finance Ministry was inquiring into the legality of U. S. accounts held by former Foreign Minister Abba Eban. But this affair fizzled out because Eban had a permit for his foreign holdings. More serious was the annual report, published at the end of April by the state comptroller, Dr. Isaac Nebenzahl, which strongly criticized the income-tax collection procedures and indicated gross waste, widespread theft, and incompetent maintenance in the defense services. The last-named point appeared to be justified on May 10, when a military transport helicopter crashed north of Jericho, killing all 54 aboard. It was the worst

--- **ISRAEL · Information Highlights** ---

Official Name: State of Israel.
Location: Southwest Asia.
Area: 7,992 square miles (20,700 km²).
Population (1977 est.): 3,600,000.
Chief Cities (1976 est.): Jerusalem, the capital, 356,-000; Tel Aviv-Jaffa, 354,000; Haifa, 227,000.
Government: *Head of state,* Ephraim Katzir, president (took office May 1973). *Head of government,* Menahem Begin, premier (took office June 1977). *Legislature* (unicameral)—Knesset.
Monetary Unit: Pound (15.30 pounds equal U. S.$1, Dec. 1977).
Manufacturing (major products): Polished diamonds, processed foods, chemicals, petroleum products, aircraft, electric and electronic equipment, textiles.
Major Agricultural Products: Citrus fruits, vegetables, cotton, eggs.

peacetime military disaster in Israel since a submarine explosion in 1968.

The General Election. The incredible complexities of Israeli politics led to a contest in the May 17 election of 22 parties. Official results were not available until May 26. It had been widely reported that the mood in Israel was one of pessimism and cynicism, as it was assumed that, whatever the scandals, the Labor alignment would win as usual. But the results afforded no ground for this cynicism; the democratic processes worked. The Labor alignment was swept out of power, the right-wing Likud group replacing it as the largest party in the Knesset. The Likud leader, Menahem Begin (*see* BIOGRAPHY), was able to form a center-right coalition cabinet which commanded at least 61 seats in the 120-seat house. The coalition was made possible by concessions to two minor religious parties as the price of their adherence. Begin's most controversial cabinet nomination was that of Moshe Dayan, former Labor defense minister, as foreign minister.

New Foreign Policies. Likud supported unrestricted Jewish settlement throughout the historic land of Israel, including the Arab-populated West Bank captured from Jordan in the 1967 war. Since the Labor alignment's policy had been more flexible or at least more ambiguous, it was widely feared abroad that Begin's victory would make a peace settlement with the Arabs less likely. These fears tended to wane as Begin's attitudes and statements during the rest of the year suggested that they might be ill-founded. The pressures of coalition government and the necessity of getting on with the United States obviously influenced Begin's postelection statements in the direction of moderation. Begin met Carter in Washington, July 19–20, and Dayan was there in October. That Begin was genuinely concerned with a search for peace was shown in his unprecedented invitation to President Sadat to visit Israel in November and the follow-up meeting of the two in Egypt on Christmas Day (*see* MIDDLE EAST).

New Domestic Policies. The real novelties of Likud's policies are probably to be found in domestic affairs; there, a passionate devotion to the benefits of free enterprise brought changes that were like a cold shower on the cosy, union-dominated welfare-state mentality that had slowed down the economy in the last decade.

Year-End Developments. Implementation of this policy came rather suddenly late in the year, along with a series of important events in other areas. Begin emerged from a hospital near the end of October to score an elegant political coup: he added the 15-seat Dash party (Democratic Movement for Change) to his coalition, assuring it a comfortable majority. Strengthened by this move, the government, on October 28, issued a kind of emancipation proclamation for economic activity: almost all foreign-exchange controls were abolished, and the Israeli pound was allowed to float. It immediately declined by about 30%. There was a predictable rash of strikes protesting higher prices, but most Israelis philosophically faced the daring experiment in economic freedom. Food subsidies were much reduced at the same time. The Begin government believed the new economic climate would stimulate growth and encourage foreign investment.

In foreign relations, Israel was appalled by the joint U. S.-Soviet démarche of October 1 on behalf of "the legitimate rights of the Palestinian people," and by the failure of the United States to do more than abstain on the UN assembly vote of October 29, which condemned Israel, 131 to 1, for establishing new Jewish settlements in occupied Arab-inhabited territory. The old "special relationship" with the United States, vital to Israel's survival, appeared less dependable than hitherto.

Immigration. The number of Soviet Jews permitted to emigrate to Israel, which had been low for some three years, markedly increased again during 1977.

ARTHUR CAMPBELL TURNER
University of California, Riverside

Trilingual signs in shop windows, as well as enthusiastic crowds, welcomed Egyptian President Anwar el-Sadat to Israel in late November.

ITALY

Italy continued to be afflicted in 1977 by high unemployment and terrorism, but the economy registered some improvement. A more formalized political link between the Communists and the ruling Christian Democrats also emerged.

ECONOMY

Italy started the year with an inflation rate of about 22%, an annual balance-of-payments deficit of $4-billion (U. S.), and 7% unemployment (1.4 million in a work force of 20 million).

Austerity Measures. In January, the government, under pressure from the International Monetary Fund (IMF) to institute tough austerity measures as collateral for a loan, sought agreements with the powerful trade unions to curb wage increases for about 1 million workers. The unions at first refused, but in March, at the urging of the Communist party, they reluctantly consented to modest adjustments of the wage "escalator" agreements that are tied to the cost-of-living index. They also accepted the elimination of five public holidays and higher prices for electricity and municipal transportation. Thereafter, the IMF formally granted Italy a $500-million credit. The U. S. share of this was $110 million. EEC (Common Market) countries promised an additional $530 million in standby credit.

Lower Inflation. Meanwhile, the government met with partial success in persuading citizens to "buy Italian" in order to cut the balance-of-payments deficit. By mid-summer, inflation had been cut to 13%, while the growth rate was holding steady at 2.5%. The number of income-tax payers continued to rise (from 4 to 21 million in two years) as a result of the drive against tax evasion. The government also reported that more Italian workers were returning from than going to foreign labor markets.

Budget Deficit. The second and third quarters of the year, however, brought a slump in industrial production and a modest rise in unemployment. It seemed unlikely that the budget deficit

UPI

Premier Giulio Andreotti, a Christian Democrat, chats with Rome Mayor Giulio Argan, left, a Communist.

could be held to the $22-billion ceiling set by the IMF. The government also faced new difficulties in carrying out the painful austerity measures. Confronted by parliamentary opposition, it withdrew in October a proposed money-saving reform of the state pension system. On the other hand, it reaffirmed its determination to curb expansion of the huge state sector of the economy, much of which is run as fiefdoms by Christian Democratic bosses.

POLITICS

Andreotti Government and the Communists. The weak, single-party Christian Democratic government of Premier Giulio Andreotti depended on the tacit support in Parliament of other moderate parties and at least the benevolent abstention on key votes by the powerful Communists. In June, the Christian Democrats, in a move to push through Parliament the unpopular austerity measures demanded by the IMF, agreed to a limited legislative program

UPI

Unemployment and overcrowding at Italy's universities led to massive student unrest in 1977. A large force of national policemen assemble opposite Rome's Unknown Soldier Memorial following the April shooting of a policeman.

and formalized consultations with the Communists and four other parties. The official beginning of this policy took place on July 15, when the Communists added their support to a key vote (421 to 50) in the Chamber of Deputies. Communist party leader Enrico Berlinguer praised these moves as a further step toward possible entry of his party into the government —an arrangement that has not been tried since 1947. Some believe, however, that the Communists would prefer to stay out of the cabinet because of the economy. If the austerity program fails, they can hope to avoid blame.

Eurocommunism. The Italian Communist party, which has strongly advocated a pluralistic Eurocommunist policy, continued to experience tense relations with the Kremlin over the issue of party independence. It also expressed disagreement with the French Communist party in mid-summer, when the latter broke its pact with the other leftist parties. In contrast, Italian Eurocommunists sought to achieve closer ties with Western Europe's Socialist parties.

Neo-Fascism. In January, Giorgio Almirante's neo-Fascist party (the Italian Social Movement-National Right Wing) suffered a serious schism. Ernesto De Marzio led a break-away group and took with him 17 of the 35 neo-Fascist deputies in the Chamber and 9 of the 15 senators. De Marzio called for more moderation. Alleged links between the neo-Fascists and the Secret Service and the Italian army came to the fore in June, when 78 persons, including Gen. Vito Miceli, a former head of the Secret Service and now a neo-Fascist deputy, went on trial for plotting attempted coups in 1970 and 1974.

Abortion. In January, the Chamber of Deputies approved by 310 to 296 a bill that would give Italy one of the most liberal abortion laws in western Europe. It would permit women over 16 to decide, with or without a doctor's authorization, to terminate pregnancies during the first 90 days. To the surprise of many, the Christian Democrats, with crucial Vatican support, defeated the bill in the Senate by two votes in June. No similar measure can be introduced until six months have elapsed. Supporters of abortion considered seeking a national referendum on the subject.

Lockheed Scandals. A long-simmering scandal of alleged payoffs in 1970 to high Italian officials by the Lockheed Corporation came to a head in January. A legislative committee recommended to Parliament that former Defense Minister Luigi Gui, a Christian Democrat, and Mario Tanassi, secretary of the Social Democratic party, stand trial. Former Premier Mariano Rumor escaped indictment, thanks to a tie-breaking vote by a fellow Christian Democrat. On March 10, Parliament voted to lift the immunity of Gui and Tanassi and send them to trial before a special court. The scandal had been a major issue in the 1976 regional elections.

Violence. Italy's universities, especially those in Rome and Bologna, were repeatedly disrupted by waves of student violence. Several people were killed and hundreds injured in clashes with the police. Most of the trouble was triggered by the ultraleftist Red Brigades and the Workers' Autonomy, organizations that draw many of their recruits from youths who are alienated by the Communist party's alleged sell-out to the "capitalists." Chronic unemployment and overcrowding of the universities were other important causes of the unrest.

During September 23–25, some 50,000 teenage extremists from all parts of the country converged on Bologna, waving anarchist banners to emphasize their hostility to the Communist party's collaboration with the "enemy." They chose Bologna because it has been a showpiece of Communist rule.

After learning that three West German terrorist leaders of the Baader-Meinhof gang had committed suicide in prison on October 19, following the storming by German commandos of a hijacked Lufthansa plane in Somalia, Italian urban guerrilla groups rioted in many cities for several days, setting off firebombs at German consulates and businesses.

Kidnapping was also endemic. In the first six months a record number of 45 had taken

UPI

Rome taxi drivers, demanding more police protection, block traffic in the city's Piazza Venezia.

place. In the face of such violence, the government sought to tighten up "law and order." On April 30, it suspended the automatic right of prisoners to be freed pending trial, if their case was not brought up within a maximum time limit. Terrorists had been taking advantage of this provision by shooting and intimidating lawyers and witnesses in order to delay the trials. In June, the government proposed that police be allowed to question suspects without the presence of their lawyers. It also asked for power to make "preventive arrests," so that police could stop anyone they believed to be planning a crime against the state and hold him incommunicado for 48 hours. Parliament would have to approve such a measure.

FOREIGN AFFAIRS

United States. The new administration of President Carter quickly dispatched Vice President Walter Mondale to Europe to reaffirm American ties. He visited Rome on January 26. Richard N. Gardner, former professor of international law at Columbia University, was named U. S. ambassador to Italy. The new administration was more flexible toward the Italian Communist party than the previous ones had been. It gave permission to the Communist party newspaper *L'Unità* to open a news bureau in the United States and granted visas to certain Communist officials.

Engineers investigate the soil under the Roman Colosseum, part of a campaign to protect the ancient edifice.

UPI

On July 26–27, Premier Andreotti went to Washington to discuss Italy's economic and political problems with President Carter. The latter expressed pleasure at the achievements of the Andreotti government and promised to help Italy cope with its energy needs by making funds available from the Export-Import Bank to finance eight more nuclear power plants. He also promised help in finding needed uranium.

At U. S. request, Italy in late summer rescinded a previous ban on admission of new foreign students to Italian universities during the 1977–78 academic year. About 1,600 Americans are enrolled in Italian medical schools.

West Germany. Italy's relations with West Germany were strained in late summer, when that country declined to extradite Herbert Kappler, a convicted Nazi war criminal. The 70-year-old prisoner, suffering from terminal cancer, had been spirited out of a Rome military hospital in a suitcase on August 15 by his wife. Kappler had personally commanded an SS execution squad that massacred 335 Italian civilians in March 1944 in reprisal for an Italian resistance bomb blast that had killed 33 German soldiers. West Germany's constitution forbids extradition of a citizen accused of a crime abroad. Kappler's escape triggered a storm of criticism in Italy.

Soviet Union. In March, the Soviet ambassador put pressure on the Italian government to dissuade the director of the Venice Biennale arts festival from featuring an exhibition on the theme of political dissent in Eastern Europe. After the resignation of the festival director in protest, the festival was put off until 1978.

Yugoslavia. On April 3, Italy and Yugoslavia formally ended their long dispute over the status of Trieste and surrounding areas.

The Vatican. In November, Italian and Vatican negotiators reached agreement on the final version of a new text to replace the Lateran Concordat that has governed relations between the Roman Catholic Church and Italy since 1929. Parliament is expected to ratify the agreement. Under it, Catholicism will no longer be the official state religion in Italy, and the Vatican's influence in matters of education and marriage will be sharply reduced.

CHARLES F. DELZELL, *Vanderbilt University*

───── **ITALY • Information Highlights** ─────

Official Name: Italian Republic.
Location: Southern Europe.
Area: 116,303 square miles (301,225 km²).
Population (1977 est.): 56,500,000.
Chief Cities (1975 est.): Rome, the capital, 2,868,000; Milan, 1,731,000; Naples, 1,224,000; Turin, 1,202,000.
Government: *Head of state,* Giovanni Leone, president (took office Dec. 1971). *Head of government,* Giulio Andreotti, premier (took office July 1976). *Legislature*—Parliament: Senate and Chamber of Deputies.
Monetary Unit: Lira (882.00 lire equal U. S.$1, Aug. 1977).
Manufacturing (major products): Automobiles, petroleum products, machinery, processed foods, chemicals.
Major Agricultural Products: Wheat, grapes, tomatoes, citrus fruits, rice, vegetables, olives, nuts.

JAPAN

At the end of March 1977, the Home Affairs Ministry estimated Japan's total population at 113,226,000. Just over half of that number (50.5%) had been born after World War II. While the postwar "miracle" of economic growth had begun to fade, Japan was, nonetheless, still regarded as one of the "three engine countries" (with the United States and West Germany) leading the Western industrialized world. As a result of elections held late in 1976 and during 1977, the majority Liberal-Democratic party (LDP), for the first time in 21 years, lost its near-monopoly of power and faced the problems of leadership in an environment of coalition politics.

INTERNATIONAL AFFAIRS

In January, at the resumption of the 80th regular Diet session, the new premier, Takeo Fukuda, stressed the need for continued close cooperation among Japan, the United States, and Western Europe. However, Japan's foreign-exchange reserves, which exceeded $17 billion (U. S.) in April, were causing increasing friction with its principal partners.

Relations with the United States. In the very first contact between the six-weeks-old Fukuda government and the 11-day-old Carter administration, the problem of Japan's large trade surplus in relation to the United States was raised. On February 1, Vice President Walter Mondale in Tokyo asked for voluntary restraints on Japanese exports. Following his summit meeting with President Carter in Washington, March 21–22, Premier Fukuda assumed the burden of persuading domestic manufacturers (particularly producers of television sets) to exercise self-control of exports.

On June 11, former Sen. Mike Mansfield went by horse-drawn carriage to present his credentials as the new U. S. ambassador to the emperor. In a more practical vein, at his first press conference in Tokyo, Ambassador Mansfield stated that U. S.-Japan relations must be based on "mutual understanding and tolerance." In his first public speech, delivered June 7, he warned that Japan's $5-billion trade surplus with the United States was an extremely sensitive political issue. His prediction was borne out in late September, when American steel companies filed a complaint with the U. S. Treasury Department that Japanese steel was being dumped (sold below costs) on the American market. On October 3, the Treasury decided to proceed with an investigation, but Tokyo announced that it would curb steel exports if Washington would withdraw the formal complaint.

The premier's concern over Japan's relations with the United States was clearly shown in his reshuffling of his cabinet on November 28. The reorganization created a new Ministry for Ex-

UPI

Carrying flags and large placards, thousands in Tokyo participate in the annual May Day parade.

ternal Economic Affairs, and a former ambassador to the United States, Nobuhiko Ushiba, was appointed to head it.

Another major issue discussed between Tokyo and Washington related to Carter's campaign promise of a gradual withdrawal of American troops from the Korean peninsula. The security of the Republic of (South) Korea is of prime concern to Japan. Early in the year in Tokyo, Vice President Mondale tried to reassure the Japanese that the phased withdrawal would occur only within the context of cooperation among the United States, South Korea, and Japan. Such assurances were repeated later in the year by American security officials to Defense Director Asao Mihara, as the former shuttled, via Tokyo, from Seoul to Washington. Meanwhile, the Japanese were as embarrassed as the Americans by successive revelations of clandestine Korean activities overseas. For example, testimony before the U. S. Congress on July 1 seemed to indicate that the Korean CIA (Central Intelligence Agency) in 1973 had been directly involved in the abduction from Tokyo of Kim Dae-jung, a political opponent of Korean President Park Chung Hee.

A third problem that occupied the attention of officials in Tokyo and in Washington related

Japan sends an engineering test satellite into orbit, becoming the third nation to launch a stationary satellite.

UPI

to the export of nuclear technology. A firm supporter of nuclear nonproliferation, Japan was nonetheless the most vulnerable of the industrialized countries in terms of access to energy. At his summit discussion with President Carter in March, Premier Fukuda appealed for special consideration but admitted that negotiations on Japanese plans for reprocessing nuclear fuel were difficult. The issue remained unresolved after the industrialized nations' conference in London in May. Following three rounds of discussions in Tokyo and in Washington, the two governments on September 12 announced agreement on a two-year demonstration period for Japanese reprocessing of spent nuclear fuel in a facility at Tokai.

Relations with the USSR. Contacts with the Soviet Union, with which diplomacy was normalized in 1956, remained strained. On June 15, USSR leader Leonid Brezhnev proposed talks to lead to a bilateral treaty of friendship and cooperation. In Tokyo, Premier Fukuda firmly declined, because the USSR had refused to discuss Japan's claims to the southern Kurils, occupied by Soviet troops since the war. Difficult negotiations over fishing operations within respective 200-mile coastal zones did not enhance the Soviet image in Japanese eyes.

Relations with China. In somewhat similar fashion, Tokyo had normalized relations with Peking by means of a Sino-Japanese communiqué of 1972. On January 22 in Peking, however, Chairman Hua Kuo-feng told visiting Komeito Chairman Yoshikatsu Takeiri that Premier Fukuda had not accomplished enough toward conclusion of a treaty of peace and amity. On August 9, former Deputy Foreign Minister Fu Hao arrived in Tokyo as China's second envoy to Japan. In an interview with Fukuda, on the occasion of the fifth anniversary of normalization, September 26, Ambassador Fu reaffirmed the two nations' intentions to develop a permanent peace treaty.

Relations with Southeast Asia. Premier Fukuda left Tokyo on August 6 to attend a conference of the Association of Southeast Asian Nations (ASEAN), held in Kuala Lumpur. After calling on ASEAN to coexist with Communist countries in Indochina, August 8, he paid visits to Burma, Indonesia, Singapore, Thailand, and the Philippines. On August 18 in Manila, he announced Japan's intentions to extend assistance to ASEAN for joint industrial projects, as part of the so-called Fukuda Doctrine.

Japan and the UN. On October 3, when he returned from the UN General Assembly in New York, Foreign Minister Iichiro Hatoyama called attention to the special assembly on disarmament scheduled for May 1978. He said that Japan would call for a drive against the arms race, for nuclear disarmament, and for a nuclear test ban.

Meanwhile, the government had decided on a law to expand Japan's territorial waters from the current 3 to 12 miles, and another to establish a 200-mile fishing zone, effective July 1. The traditional 3-mile limit was frozen for international straits shared with Korea and the USSR, and for the Tsugaru Strait.

DOMESTIC AFFAIRS

In late December, 1976, after a general election for the (lower) House of Representatives, the Diet elected Takeo Fukuda, president of the LDP, to be Japan's 13th postwar prime minister. A subsequent election for half the seats in the (upper) House of Councillors clearly showed that the LDP's long near-monopoly of power was steadily eroding. Public opinion polls conducted by Kyodo news service in May and in October revealed that, although the popularity of the LDP had increased slightly, more than 50% of those polled did not support the Fukuda cabinet. A persistent recession and failure in economic management were most often cited as reasons for lack of confidence.

The Lockheed Scandal. Another reason for public distrust of the LDP was the continuation of the Lockheed affair. In late January, the Tokyo public prosecutor brought in an indictment of the shadowy figure Yoshio Kodama on charges of tax evasion, violation of foreign ex-

UPI

Prime Minister Takeo Fukuda jokes with newsmen prior to speaking about the recent upper house elections.

change laws, and bribery. Thus the long investigation, begun in 1976, made the transition to equally long trial procedures. Shortly after, former Prime Minister Kakuei Tanaka, the first Japanese head of government indicted for acts in office, faced his first trial hearing and denied having received funds from the Lockheed corporation in return for favorable consideration of the L-1011 TriStar. On February 22, the Tokyo District Court denied motion to dismiss made by defense counsels of Tanaka, his secretary, and three other defendants (all former executives of Marubeni, a trading company which represented Lockheed in Japan). On June 2, the parallel trial of Kodama began after months of delay and excused absences because of his illness. The long, drawn-out procedures undoubtedly affected the political fate of the LDP.

Party Politics and Elections. In the election for the lower house, held in December 1976, the LDP had won only 249 out of a new total of 511 seats. The remainder was divided among the Japanese Socialists (JSP, 123), the Komeito (55), the Democratic Socialists (DSP, 29), the Communists (JCP), and a group split off from the majority, the New Liberals (17). Only the support of nine independents allowed the LDP to form a new cabinet led by Takeo Fukuda. Iichiro Hatoyama became foreign minister, and Hideo Bo took the important post of finance minister. In the Diet, for the first time in postwar history, committee assignments were shared among the LDP and opposition parties. Almost immediately, all political parties began to prepare for the next critical election, for half the upper house seats, scheduled for July 10.

On June 17, a total of 309 persons regis-

tered their candidacies for the 126 seats, among them representatives of two new splinter groups. In national constituencies, intellectuals formed the United Progressive Liberal (UPL) party; disgruntled opposition members formed the Socialist Citizens League (SCL). As a result of the election, the LDP was again able to maintain a bare majority in the House of Councillors only by the support of three independents; the LDP held 124 seats, with the remainder distributed among the JSP (55), the Komeito (28), the JCP (15), the DSP (11), and the New Liberals (4). The UPL and SCL won one seat each.

The Diet. Although the 80th regular Diet session approved more than 85% of government-sponsored measures, it nonetheless witnessed a dramatic change from LDP dominance and confrontation with the opposition to compromise among factions. A 12-day extension of the 150-day session on May 28 allowed Diet approval of the controversial Japanese-South Korean agreement on joint development of the continental shelf, as well as a Japanese-Soviet fisheries pact. LDP compromise with opposition parties also allowed a personal income-tax cut of some $1.1 billion for fiscal 1977 and special welfare grants of $230 million. On June 9, the lower house adjourned without acting on fare increases for the national rail system. The upper house on August 1 elected Ken Yasui of the LDP to be its president, while Kan Kase became the first JSP vice president in 24 years.

Economy. The government's plan for growth of the gross national product (GNP) in fiscal 1976–77 visualized a 5.7% increase. Thanks to a vigorous last quarter (January–March), the GNP exceeded the previous year by 5.8% for a total of about $329 billion. Per capita income was at about $5,117, however, ranking Japan 16th in the world. At the London summit in May, Premier Fukuda promised an effort to achieve a 6.7% growth rate for 1977–78. Spurred on by a stimulus package announced by the government in September, GNP growth in the second quarter had achieved an annual rate of 7.6%.

These gains were, of course, largely absorbed by parallel inflation. The nationwide consumer price index (CPI) in July registered

─────── **JAPAN • Information Highlights** ───────

Official Name: Japan.
Location: East Asia.
Area: 143,689 square miles (372,154 km²).
Population (1977 est.): 113,226,000.
Chief Cities (1975): Tokyo, the capital, 8,500,000 (1977 est.); Osaka, 2,780,000; Yokohama, 2,620,000; Nagoya, 2,080,000.
Government: *Head of state,* Hirohito, emperor (acceded Dec. 1926). *Head of government,* Takeo Fukuda, premier (took office Dec. 1976). *Legislature*—Diet: House of Councillors and House of Representatives.
Monetary Unit: Yen (267.30 yen equal U. S.$1, Aug. 1977).
Manufacturing (major products): Ships, automobiles, electronic components, textiles, iron, steel, petrochemicals, machinery, electrical appliances, processed foods.
Major Agricultural Products: Rice, wheat, barley, potatoes, vegetables, fruits, tobacco, tea.

PHOTOS UPI

A clerk updates currency exchange quotations. The yen closed at a record high against the dollar in October.

a 7.7% increase over the same month the previous year. In August, the CPI for the ward areas of Tokyo had increased 9.7% over the year before. The unemployment rate was 2.4% of the labor force, the highest recorded level since 1959. Consumption standards at home were not keeping pace with the "strong" yen abroad.

In a report released by the Economic Planning Agency in October, the Japanese economy was described as in process of "inventory adjustment." Exports had risen at the slowest annual rate in almost two years, but imports also declined in September. Private domestic demand remained inactive.

Terrorism. Like other industrially advanced nations (the Netherlands, United States, West Germany), Japan found itself vulnerable to assaults by skillful, dedicated terrorists. They ranged in ideology from extreme right to extreme left. On March 3, four armed men occupied the offices of the powerful Economic Federation (the Keidanren), holding a number of hostages for 11 hours. Led by Yoshio Itoh, 31, these right-wing activists were former members of the Shield Society, a private army organized by novelist Yukio Mishima. Mishima committed ritual suicide in 1970. His widow played a key role in persuading the four to surrender, after their denunciation of the "Yalta-Potsdam structure" had been aired in the media.

In April 1971, the government had planned to open a new Tokyo International Airport at Narita, Chiba Prefecture. Construction of the first phase, including 13,000-foot (4,000-m) runways, was virtually completed in 1973. Local farmers, however, supported by left-wing students, had effectively delayed the opening by construction of steel towers in flight paths. When airport authorities on May 6 dismantled the towers in sudden tactical action, violence erupted between armed police and protestors.

A number of police were severely burned and one protestor, Kaoru Higashiyama, 27, was killed. By August 10, airport authorities were conducting noise-level tests on landings and takeoffs, in preparation for opening the airport in late 1977 or early 1978.

A Japan Air Lines (JAL) DC-8 on a flight from France to Japan was hijacked on September 28 and forced to land in Bangladesh. Five Japan Red Army members demanded $6 million in ransom and release of comrades in Japanese jails. In a tense 6-day odyssey, punctuated by step-by-step release of the 151 passenger-hostages in return for fuel and food, the JAL plane flew from Dacca to Kuwait to Damascus and finally to Algiers. There, on October 4, the five terrorists, their six released comrades, 12 remaining hostages, and seven crew members left the plane. In the face of protests in Japan, the government paid the full ransom. Algerian authorities subsequently refused to surrender the Red Army band or to return the ransom.

ARDATH W. BURKS
Rutgers University

More than 30 persons were killed in northern Japan in February, as the result of a blizzard from Siberia.

JORDAN

During the 25th year of his reign, Jordan's King Hussein continued his traditionally moderate role in Arab efforts to reconvene the Geneva Middle East Peace Conference in 1977. In a year marred by the tragic death of his wife, Queen Alia, in February, and the publication of compromising reports about his relationship with the U. S. Central Intelligence Agency, the Jordanian monarch maintained a position of cautious optimism, tempered by a realistic appraisal of the consequences of an impasse at Geneva.

Arab-Israeli Conflict. Stressing in May that the Arabs "cannot go to Geneva and fail," King Hussein sought to remind his allies of the disparity in the military capacities of Israel and the Arab "confrontation" states. Fearing that a failure at Geneva might prompt some Arab leaders to take hasty action, which would lead to a military disaster and the formal annexation of the occupied West Bank, Hussein emphasized that the Arabs must rebuild their military strength to negotiate on an equal basis with Israel. To this end, he led the way in seeking more financial aid from the Arab oil-producing states. In January, Prime Minister Mudar Badran, who also handles foreign affairs, formally requested, at a meeting of foreign ministers of the confrontation and oil-producing states, some $200 million for Jordan. On May 17, King Hussein raised the request to $261 million from Saudi Arabia alone.

On the delicate issue of the future control of the West Bank, King Hussein's relations with the Palestine Liberation Organization (PLO) appeared to be improving, but events during the summer tended to undermine that trend and raise old doubts. In June, Prime Minister Badran momentarily resuscitated the ill-fated 1972 United-Arab-Kingdom proposal on the future of the West Bank, despite the king's consistent public position that only the PLO could negotiate and determine the future of the Palestinian people. However, reports of a secret August meeting in London with Israeli Foreign Minister Moshe Dayan indicated that Hussein had not limited his options. While not denying the reports, King Hussein reiterated his endorsement

UPI

Jordan's King Hussein and French President Valéry Giscard d'Estaing reviewed the Middle East situation in Paris.

of the PLO's sole right to represent the Palestinians. He stayed aloof of both the Tripoli meeting of "rejectionist states" and the Egyptian-Israeli conference in Cairo, held subsequent to the visit by President Sadat of Egypt to Israel in November. (*See also* MIDDLE EAST.)

Internal Affairs. In January, Hussein promised that the full parliament, suspended since 1974, would be reconvened as soon as practical. A $45-million budget deficit was announced in the same month, but projections of foreign assistance, in the form of grants and loans, promised to provide some relief from the increasing burden of inflation and decreased agricultural production due to drought.

F. NICHOLAS WILLARD, *Georgetown University*

——— JORDAN · Information Highlights ———

Official Name: Hashemite Kingdom of Jordan.
Location: Southwest Asia.
Area: 37,738 square miles (97,740 km²).
Population (1977 est.): 2,900,000.
Chief Cities (1976 est.): Amman, the capital, 750,000; Zarqa, 235,000; Irbid, 120,000.
Government: *Head of state,* Hussein ibn Talal, king (acceded Aug. 1952). *Head of government,* Mudar Badran, prime minister (took office July 1976). *Legislature*—National Assembly: Senate and House of Representatives (dissolved Nov. 1974).
Monetary Unit: Dinar (0.33 dinar equals U. S.$1, Aug. 1977).
Manufacturing (major products): Cement, petroleum products, cigarettes, vegetable oil, flour.
Major Agricultural Products: Wheat, tomatoes, barley, fruits, corn, olives, sorghum, grapes, tobacco.

KANSAS

Despite problems with agricultural prices, the general economic outlook in Kansas was good during 1977. Income was $6,469 per capita, higher than the national average, and the state ranked 15th in the Union in terms of personal income. At a time when the national unemployment was over 6%, Kansas showed only 3.8%.

As 1977 began, 133 new plants were in production and 81 had completed major expansions. Exploration for oil and natural gas was at a record high, and exploratory drilling in the first half of 1977 was more than double that of the same period in 1976.

Agriculture. Wheat production in 1977 was 350.5 million bushels (123.5 million hl), 23 million (8.1 million hl) more than in 1976. The corn crop was estimated at 166.6 million bushels (58.7 million hl), up four million (1.4 million hl) from 1976. The sorghum grain harvest added up to 229.14 million bushels (81.2 million hl), an increase of 72 million (25 million hl), and the soybean production of 25.74 million bushels (9 million hl) was larger by eight million (2.8 million hl) than in 1976. Cattle held steady at 6.4 million head, sheep at 173,000, and hog production was 1.8 million head. The hog market was the most profitable.

Kansas farmers generally faced depressed grain prices and were caught in a cash-flow squeeze as production costs soared above crop values. There was loss on every crop except soybeans. (*See also* AGRICULTURE.)

Weather. Some sections of the state experienced drought conditions during portions of 1977, but moisture came at the right time for most crops. Some areas had flooding during the fall, though urban property damage was minimal. There were severe periods of blowing dust in western Kansas, but no major storms.

Legislation. The 1977 legislature opened with Democrats controlling the House and Republicans barely holding the Senate, a situation that had not existed for 64 years. When the session closed, changes had been made in the tax structure: prescription drugs were exempted from sales tax, liquor taxes increased, and income taxes adjusted upward in the higher brackets. The bingo law was strengthened to prevent illegal gambling, but increased funds for enforcement were not provided. A new cabinet-level Department of Aging was created to consolidate services for the elderly. Child-abuse laws were strengthened by increasing the number of professions required to report suspected cases and by allowing the Department of Social and Rehabilitation Services and peace officers to take a child into protective custody.

Three commissions were established to promote farm products, procedures for mediation between teachers and local school districts were outlined, stringent permit requirements for water use were created, public television was expanded, funding for fuel-saving measures at state institutions was alloted, vocational education was broadened, and a minimum-wage law was passed. The governor's programs to enlarge the state energy office and to build a medium-security prison were unsuccessful.

ROBERT W. RICHMOND
Kansas State Historical Society

——— KANSAS • Information Highlights ———

Area: 82,264 square miles (213,064 km²).
Population (1976 est.): 2,310,000.
Chief Cities (1970 census): Topeka, the capital, 125,011; Wichita, 276,554; Kansas City, 168,213; Overland Park, 79,034.
Government (1977): *Chief Officers*—governor, Robert F. Bennett (R); lt. gov., Shelby Smith (R). *Legislature*—Senate, 40 members; House of Representatives, 125 members.
Education (1976–77): *Enrollment*—public elementary schools, 289,969 pupils; public secondary, 146,557; nonpublic, 32,800; colleges and universities, 115,266 students. *Public school expenditures*, $707,833,000 ($1,434 per pupil).
State Finances (fiscal year 1976): *Revenues*, $1,644,976,000; *expenditures*, $1,596,955,000.
Personal Income (1976): $14,945,000,000; per capita, $6,469.
Labor Force (July 1977): *Nonagricultural wage and salary earners*, 854,100; *unemployed*, 42,200 (3.8% of total force).

KENTUCKY

The most newsworthy events in Kentucky during 1977 were disasters, particularly a tragic nightclub fire in May and record-breaking floods in eastern Kentucky in April.

The Fire. On the night of May 28 a fire swept through the Beverly Hills Supper Club in Southgate, Ky., on the outskirts of Cincinnati. The fire, which apparently started in electrical wiring, spread rapidly through the club, which was crowded for a performance by the singer John Davidson. A total of 164 persons died in the fire, and almost as many were injured.

Extensive investigations by various state officials led to charges of improper construction and lax enforcement of building codes and fire prevention regulations. Conflicts over responsibility for these failures developed and remained unsettled at the end of the year. A number of lawsuits were filed.

Floods. Early in April eastern Kentucky counties were hit by extensive flooding of the Big Sandy, Cumberland, and Kentucky rivers. Particularly hard hit were the cities of Pikeville, Hazard, and Harlan. President Carter declared 15 counties in eastern Kentucky to be disaster areas. Floods in this region of the state are not uncommon, but these were unusually widespread and severe, in many areas the most serious floods in a generation. In the aftermath of the floods, federal and state governments moved to assist in reconstruction and to provide housing for the homeless, but many residents complained that governmental action was too slow and ineffective.

Contamination. Louisville was afflicted with an unusual water problem in March and April. A huge quantity of toxic chemicals, estimated at six tons, which had been dumped into the sewer system, contaminated one of Louisville's major waste treatment plants. The plant had to be closed for several weeks, while workers struggled with the difficult and dangerous task of cleaning out the treatment plant and sewer lines. During this period the city had to dump huge amounts of untreated sewage directly into the Ohio River.

——— KENTUCKY • Information Highlights ———

Area: 40,395 square miles (104,623 km²).
Population (1976 est.): 3,428,000.
Chief Cities (1970 census): Frankfort, the capital, 21,902; Louisville, 361,958; Lexington, 108,137; Covington, 52,535.
Government (1977): *Chief Officers*—governor, Julian M. Carroll (D); lt. gov., Thelma Stovall (D). *General Assembly*—Senate, 38 members; House of Representatives, 100 members.
Education (1976–77): *Enrollment*—public elementary schools, 430,280 pupils; public secondary, 263,720; nonpublic, 71,400; colleges and universities, 113,629 students. *Public school expenditures*, $810,140,000 ($1,074 per pupil).
State Finances (fiscal year 1976): *Revenues*, $2,746,691,000; *expenditures*, $2,641,107,000.
Personal Income (1976): $18,439,000,000; per capita, $5,379.
Labor Force (June 1977): *Nonagricultural wage and salary earners*, 1,151,100; *unemployed*, 70,900 (4.7% of total force).

A devastating fire at a supper club in Southgate, Ky., the night of May 28, took a total of 164 lives.

UPI

Coal Mining. Although the state continued to benefit from the national demands for coal, the mining industry in the state was beset by labor problems. During the summer, miners engaged in wildcat strikes to protest a decision to reduce sharply the medical benefits provided by the health and retirement fund of the bituminous coal industry. One consequence of the cutbacks was financial difficulties for hospitals in coal-mining counties.

Throughout the year there was tension, and occasional gunfire and violence, at the Stearns coal mine in McCreary County, where a strike that had started in 1976 continued throughout 1977. In October state police arrested large numbers of miners and charged them with violating a court order that strictly limited picketing at the mine.

Politics. In the absence of any major elections or a session of the legislature, the state was unusually quiet politically, although preliminary skirmishing for the 1979 gubernatorial election began. The voters once again rejected a proposal to call a state constitutional convention. In the largest metropolitan center, voters once more elected a Democrat to the top position of mayor of Louisville, but chose a Republican as county judge of Jefferson County.

MALCOLM E. JEWELL
University of Kentucky

KENYA

While difficulties with Uganda eased in 1977, new political and diplomatic crises dominated Kenyan affairs.

Tanzanian Border. In February 1977 the close cooperation of Kenya and Tanzania came to an end with the Tanzanian closing of the common border. There also was a breakup of the East African Community, which had provided rail, air, postal, educational, and other common services for Kenya, Tanzania, and Uganda. The alleged reason for the breakup was the inability of the members to agree on cost-sharing, but in fact socialist Tanzania wished to isolate itself from pro-Western Kenya. Talks to end the border dispute failed.

Presidential Succession. Kenya cracked down on even the discussion of a successor to 85-year-old President Jomo Kenyatta, fearing that the stability of the country and the ruling Kenya African National Union (KANU) party would suffer in the jockeying for personal and constitutional advantage. Kenya has come to rely so strongly on Kenyatta's ability to smooth over tribal and political conflicts that fears of a succession dispute led to the cancelling of KANU party elections in April. Vice President Daniel Moi, Educational Minister Taita Towett, Defense Minister James Gichuru, and Finance Minister Mwai Kibaki were each seeking to establish himself as Kenyatta's heir.

Rhodesia and Somalia. Kenya was consulted frequently about possible settlements of the Rhodesian crisis, due to President Kenyatta's prestige in Africa and because of Kenya's example as an African state where black and white live in apparent harmony despite past conflict.

A possible conflict with Somalia was caused by Somali irregulars moving across Kenyan territory into Ethiopia in June, when they killed six guards. The two nations agreed to minimize the incident.

Hunting Ban. To preserve its big game herds on which its huge tourist industry depends, Kenya banned all hunting in May 1977 and cracked down on poachers. It now permits only photographic safaris to move through the game preserves.

ROBERT GARFIELD
DePaul University

─────── **KENYA · Information Highlights** ───────

Official Name: Republic of Kenya.
Location: East coast of Africa.
Area: 244,959 square miles (634,444 km²).
Population (1977 est.): 14,400,000.
Chief Cities (1976 est.): Nairobi, the capital, 645,000; Mombasa, 310,000.
Government: *Head of state and government,* Jomo Kenyatta, president (took office Dec. 1964). *Legislature* (unicameral)—National Assembly.
Monetary Unit: Kenya shilling (8.32 shillings equal U. S.$1, Aug. 1977).
Manufacturing (major products): Construction materials, processed agricultural products, petroleum products.
Major Agricultural Products: Coffee, tea, sugarcane, sisal, corn, cassava, pyrethrum, fruits, livestock.

South Korea's President Park Chung Hee uses a telescope to inspect North Korean equipment during a June visit to the demarcation line.

UPI

KOREA

Inter-Korean relations remained volatile, with no sign of early rapprochement, as Seoul and Pyongyang were both preoccupied with more pressing matters. South Korea intensified its arms buildup, relentlessly pushed its "export-or-perish" drive, and went all-out to downgrade its influence-buying scandals in the United States. North Korea was low-keyed in foreign affairs and continued its belt-tightening measures but with an added emphasis on economic pragmatism.

SOUTH KOREA

Economic and Social Conditions. Major economic targets for 1977 were achieved. The real growth rate was 10%; inflation was held to 10.3%; the trade deficit was all but erased; and per capita GNP rose to $864. Record crops created surplus rice for the first time in recent decades. The country faced a shortage of skilled construction workers; this may blunt Seoul's previous competitive edge—the abundance of skilled labor for low wages—in its profitable construction activity in the Middle East. In October, it was reported in Seoul that as many as 14 countries were considering measures to curb imports from South Korea.

SOUTH KOREA • Information Highlights

Official Name: Republic of Korea.
Location: Northeastern Asia.
Area: 38,022 square miles (98,477 km²).
Population (1977 est.): 35,900,000.
Chief Cities (1977 est.): Seoul, the capital, 7,634,000; Pusan, 2,600,000.
Government: *Head of state,* Park Chung Hee, president (since December 1963). *Head of government,* Choi Kyu Hah, prime minister (took office December 1975). *Legislature* (unicameral)—National Assembly.
Monetary Unit: Won (485 won equal U. S.$1, Dec. 1977).
Manufacturing (major products): Textiles, electronic equipment, petrochemicals, clothing, plywood, hair products, processed foods, metal products, furniture, ships.
Major Agricultural Products: Rice, barley, wheat, soybeans, sweet potatoes and fish.

The phenomenal economic boom was belied by widening gaps between the urban-rural sectors and the rich-poor groups. In November, government sources showed that 51.5% of people with taxable incomes during 1976 were concentrated in Seoul, accounting for 62.7% of total taxable incomes (up from 48.6% and 60.5%, respectively, during 1975). Per capita income in Seoul was 53.6% higher than in the rest of the country. With the minimum monthly cost of living for a city family estimated at $190, 60% of the nation's urbanites earned less than $61 a month; another 20% earned $62 to $100 a month.

In February, President Park Chung Hee announced plans to build a new capital some 60 miles (96 km) south of Seoul. This step was said to be necessary partly because of Seoul's proximity to North Korean guns—only 25 miles (40 km) away—and partly because of Seoul's overpopulation.

Politics and Repression. Park showed no sign of relaxing his autocratic rule. Fear and silence were pervasive in the shadow of the Korean Central Intelligence Agency. In March, the Supreme Court upheld the jail terms of 18 dissidents convicted in 1976; nine subsequently had their sentences commuted or suspended. Among the nine under incarceration was former opposition leader Kim Dae Jung, who was in declining health. After the court ruling, some 200 leading dissidents called on Park to restore political freedoms and revoke his dictatorial 1972 constitution. More crackdowns followed in April. In July and August, it was announced that 31 political prisoners had been released, having "repented" for their crimes. There were still 250 political detainees. In October and November, thousands of students demonstrated against the regime.

Defense and Foreign Relations. In December, the government allocated U. S. $25.8 billion, or 35.6% of the 1978 budget, for defense, an increase of 27.2% over 1977. This underscored Seoul's effort to bolster defense posture in the light of President Jimmy Carter's decision to withdraw U. S. ground troops from South Korea within 4 to 5 years. On July 26, the United States and South Korea announced agreement on a troop-withdrawal plan. The first 6,000 men will be removed in 1978, an undetermined number in 1980, and the last 8,000 in 1981 or 1982. The accord also contained a U. S. pledge to provide a nuclear umbrella for South Korea, even after the American departure, and to furnish, subject to congressional approval, a compensatory aid package totaling $1.9 billion in gifts and military sales credits.

Korean-U. S. relations were strained because of Seoul's refusal to have Tongsun Park, a central figure in its bribery scandal, cross-examined by U. S. officials. In December, an accord was reached, by the terms of which he can be questioned and called to testify in Washington. Seoul remained uneasy, lest President Park himself be implicated in the influence-buying, of which he is said to have known nothing.

NORTH KOREA

Economy. In January, President Kim Il Sung declared 1977 "a year of adjustment," an indication of continued economic tensions. He also said that the cement and steel targets of the 6-year plan (1971-76) were achieved in 1976. In April, he let it be known that a new 7-year plan would be launched in 1978 and that North Korea would welcome advanced foreign technology, but not foreign capital, to help modernize its industry. Signs of stress abounded in the transport sector, and electricity was apparently in short supply. North Korea continued to default on debt repayments to foreign creditors.

Politics. The sense of urgency about the economy led to a cabinet reshuffle in December. Li Jong-ok, perhaps the best known technocrat and long-time advocate of economic priority, was named premier. Technocrats in key public positions also increased. In February, it was reported in Tokyo that President Kim's son, Chong Il, had been named his successor. In November, elections were held for a new Supreme People's Assembly.

——— NORTH KOREA • Information Highlights ———

Official Name: Democratic People's Republic of Korea.
Location: Northeastern Asia.
Area: 46,540 square miles (120,533 km²).
Population (1977 est.): 16,700,000.
Chief Cities (1977 est.): Pyongyang, the capital, 1,339,-000; Chongjin, 332,500.
Government: *Head of state,* Kim Il Sung, president (nominally since December 1972; actually in power since May 1948). *Head of government,* Li Jong-ok, premier (took office December 1977). *Legislature* (unicameral)—Supreme People's Assembly. *The Korean Workers (Communist) Party:* General secretary, Kim Il Sung (since May 1948).
Monetary Unit: Won (2.15 won equal U. S.$1, Dec. 1977).
Manufacturing (major products): Cement, metallurgicals, coke, pig iron, ferroalloys, textiles.
Major Agricultural Products: Rice, corn, sweet potatoes, barley, soybeans, livestock, apples, fish.

Defense and Foreign Relations. In April, $940 million (15.4% of the 1978 budget) was earmarked for defense, a slight decrease from the previous year. Declassified U. S. Defense Department figures showed North Korea to have received a total of $325 million in military aid from the Soviet Union and China during the 1974–77 period as compared with $770 million received by South Korea from the United States.

As of December, Pyongyang had diplomatic ties with 90 countries (Seoul, 101). In January, North Korea, rejecting Seoul's overture for a nonaggression pact, proposed direct north-south talks on mutual force reduction. In March, the United States lifted its travel ban to North Korea. A 200-mile economic sea zone and a military security zone, extending 50 miles offshore in the Sea of Japan and to the limit of the economic zone in the Yellow Sea, became effective on August 1. Foreign ships and planes are banned from the military zone without prior clearances.

Also in August, President Tito of Yugoslavia visited Kim Il Sung, and they jointly appealed for an early removal of foreign troops from South Korea. President Carter reportedly sent a message through Tito to President Kim that the United States was ready to talk with North Korea if South Korea could also participate.

In August, a returning Japanese visitor revealed that ranking officials in Pyongyang expressed interest in trading with, and gaining access to technology from, the United States. Soviet and Chinese economic assistance was said to have been all but terminated. In December, North Korea signed a preliminary agreement with a Singapore-based firm to seek Western help in offshore oil exploration.

RINN-SUP SHINN, *Foreign Area Studies*
The American University

North Korean Corporal Lee Youngsun explains the reasons for his defection to the South during a news conference.

UPI

New York's waterfront was quiet in April as the International Longshoremen's Association, headed by Thomas W. Gleason (*above*) went on strike. The walkout, affecting seven steamship companies, lasted four days.

LABOR

For labor, the economic picture in the United States and most industrialized nations was flawed in 1977. Unemployment and inflation persisted at relatively high levels, despite efforts by governments to reverse the trend.

U. S. Developments. Joblessness in the United States hovered around the 7% rate. That was about 1% below a year earlier, but still above the government's targeted goal of 6% by year's end. Inflation, as measured by the Consumer Price Index, likewise came close to 7%, up about 1.5% from the previous year.

These figures were better than those of most western countries, but not good enough to satisfy either the Carter administration or the labor movement. The administration secured appropriations from Congress designed to create several million temporary jobs among the hard-core unemployed, mainly in the public service sector.

Organized labor kept pressing for full employment legislation. It contended that real unemployment, counting those who would only find part-time work, was close to 10%.

Strikes. For the first nine months, idleness attributed to strikes stood at 0.17% of total working time put in, down from 0.19% in the comparable 1976 period.

The year was marked by wildcat strikes in the Appalachian coal mines in the summer, by a strike of longshoremen on the East and Gulf coasts in the fall, by extended stoppages in such aerospace plants as Boeing and Lockheed, and by a strike of North Central iron ore workers.

Settlements. Union-management contracts in industries with more than 1,000 workers yielded lower average wage and benefit rises than in 1976. Such contracts during the first nine months carried wage increases averaging 7.8% for the first year of the agreements, down from 8.4% in the 1976 period. For the life of these agreements, the wage boost averaged 5.8% a year, down from a 6.4% average a year earlier.

The Labor Department reported that in the economy as a whole weekly wages rose about 6.9% during 1977.

Among significant union-management settlements of the year were those in the telephone, steel, aluminum, and can manufacturing industries. Most of these big settlements provided for roughly 30% in wage and benefit improvements over a three-year period.

Unions involved claimed major breakthroughs in job security clauses. In the steel and aluminum industries, for example, existing earnings guarantees geared to years of service were expanded. They range up to 90 and 95% of normal pay for workers with more than 20 years of service, when laid off, with such pay guarantees continuing for up to two years, double the period in the previous contracts. Also the agreements included improved supplemental pensions for workers facing loss of jobs because of technological changes. The longshoremen likewise won improved year-round job guarantees.

In the depressed construction industry, unions in various localities settled for small or no wage increases, relaxed their working rules and fringe benefits, and made other concessions in order to maintain employment. In a few cases, local unions agreed to pay cuts.

Union Membership. A Labor Department report, issued in September, showed that American unions lost 767,000 members, or 3.9%, in the previous two years, the first drop in 15 years. The declines were laid to after-effects of the 1974–75 recession, softness in construction, and shifts in employment from manufacturing, which is largely unionized, to service occupations, which are lightly unionized.

Plant Shutdowns. There were shock waves in the economy when steel companies announced closing of some of their older plants and layoffs of thousands of employees. Zenith Radio Corporation began laying off 5,500 employees and transferring large portions of its assembly operations to foreign, low-wage countries. Other electronics firms did the same earlier, as have many apparel companies. These moves intensified a clamor by the unions and industry for stiffer curbs on imports from abroad.

Military Unionization. By a four to one margin in a referendum, members of the American Federation of Government Employees rejected a proposal by the union's executive council for a drive to unionize military personnel. Nonetheless, the U. S. Senate approved a bill prohibiting such unionization.

Legislation. Organized labor suffered a sharp setback in Congress on a long-sought "site picketing" bill that would expand the picketing rights of building trades workers at multi-employer construction sites. Later, however, labor triumphed with enactment of a law increasing the federally-mandated minimum wage from $2.65 to $2.90 an hour on January 1, 1978, with further annual increases that would bring the minimum to $3.35 by Jan. 1, 1981. Also, the union movement, backed by many other groups, won House passage of a major "labor reform" bill that would expedite procedures under the National Labor Relations Act and increase penalties for employer violations of the Act. A Senate vote on the bill was delayed.

A bill forbidding employers from imposing mandatory retirement before age 70, except in certain occupations and classifications, passed the Senate and House. The measure also eliminates an existing 70-year-old compulsory retirement rule in federal service.

Union Mergers. The 33,000-member Boot & Shoe Workers union merged into the 700,000-member Retail Clerks International Union. The latter conducted merger talks with other unions. The Allied Industrial Union, with 100,000 members, and the Molders, with 50,000, neared completion of negotiations for a merger.

Public Sector. A drop was reported in strikes among local and state government employees, and among teachers. Some strikes by municipal workers ended in failure as local governments, claiming lack of funds, resisted demands.

International Developments. Most industrial nations faced the pressures of inflation and the threats of recession.

Canada. Labor pressed for a quick end to wage-price controls, instituted in 1975, but the government in October announced continuation of the controls, with provision for phasing them down after April 14, 1978. Previously, the Canadian Labour Congress (CLC) rejected a government offer to end the controls earlier, subject to a commitment by labor to restrain wage demands. The controls in the final year will lower the ceiling on wage increases from 8 to 6%, and limit dividend increases to 6%.

Unions whose contracts expire before April 14, and companies whose fiscal years expire before that date, are to remain under controls until Dec. 31, 1978. Where contracts or fiscal years terminate after April 14, the controls will be lifted on the expiration dates.

Although the government claimed that the controls curbed inflation, the CLC termed them a failure, citing an 8.4% rise in the consumer price index between September 1976 and September 1977, well above the 6% target set by the government when it instituted controls. Also, the CLC pointed to an 8.3% unemployment rate, the highest since the depression of the 1930's, and to declines in the gross national product as well as the value of the Canadian dollar.

Strikes were fewer in 1977 than in 1976. In the first six months time lost from strikes and lockouts dropped 63%. A major strike of the year was that of more than 2,000 air traffic controllers in early August. It was ended after four days by legislation pushed through Parliament, which carried 8% wage increases.

Los Angeles Mayor Tom Bradley, right, congratulates Douglas A. Fraser who in May succeeded Leonard Woodcock, left, as president of the United Auto Workers.

UPI

Forced Retirement

Forced retirement is one of the ironies of progress.

It was not many generations ago that men and women were forced to work until their bodies gave out, a condition prevalent for most of the existence of *Homo sapiens*. This necessity to work was the product of the demands of agrarian economics which pressed into service all strong backs, young and old, and of callous disregard for human needs that continued after the capacity to produce gave out.

A combination of the industrial revolution, urbanization, technological change, resulting economic growth, and public and private pension plans ushered in an era when it became possible to cease working in the regular economy and still have food, clothing, and shelter. While the arrangements for economic security in the latter period of life are incomplete, the basic structure is now in place. As these events unfolded, they proved a blessing and worked to eliminate endless toil as the lot of man. People began to ease their activity in the paid labor force at ever earlier ages.

Increasingly recognizable, however, is a new stage of development, overlapping the stage of removing toil from those too frail for it, and providing economic security in the absence of it. For a large proportion of those who work, the situation today is one of prospective forced retirement, either through what has come to be called "mandatory" retirement or forced "early" retirement. Technological change and its resulting increased productivity, and periodic slowdowns of industrial growth due to business cycles, have reduced the need for labor. Employment institutions have tended to adjust to these developments by establishing a fixed age at which all workers must retire (mandatory retirement) or providing for forced early retirement, in advance of such standard retirement ages, under specified conditions.

A survey of all those newly entitled to Social Security in the period 1968–70 found that 36% of men and 23% of women had been subject to some form of required retirement in their last job. A longitudinal study, begun in 1965 of a national sample of men age 45–59, disclosed that 45% of whites and 43% of blacks encounter compulsory retirement. A 1977 study by the U. S. Bureau of Labor Statistics of pension plans existing in 1974 reveals that over 40% of workers covered by these plans are subject to mandatory retirement at age 65 or later; 10% are in plans in which they are subject to forced early retirement, at the employer's demand, before age 65.

Workers in pension plans established by collective bargaining agreements are somewhat less likely to be subject to mandatory retirement than are those in nonnegotiated plans. Such provisions are also somewhat more frequent in manufacturing than in nonmanufacturing industries. Age 65 is by far the most common age of required retirement.

In the study of men age 45–59 subject to forced retirement, almost two out of five whites and one out of two blacks required to retire at age 65 indicate that they would have wanted to work longer if it had been possible.

Several decades of research, much of it carried out by the Bureau of Labor Statistics in the 1950's, have established that workers' capacity to perform their jobs varies enormously at any specific age level, and that the aging process proceeds quite differently among different people. Yet the trend has been toward arbitrarily set retirement ages, without regard to individual capacities of workers—because of the convenience in administering a uniform rule, the need to reduce employees as productivity advances, preference for younger workers, and the desire to provide opportunities for advancement among young workers. The reasons are complex and interrelated with broad societal and economic developments.

The Age Discrimination in Employment Act of 1967 protects against discrimination in hiring because of age (until age 65) but affords only limited protection against mandatory retirement. The A.D.E.A. directs the secretary of labor to make a study of forced retirement, and make his findings and recommendations available to the president and the Congress. That study has not been made.

While there have not yet been any substantial changes in the forced retirement policy, significant discussion is currently developing of a number of possible courses of action, including extending the protections of the A.D.E.A., gradual or phased retirement, new developments in volunteer work, and educational sabbaticals to permit "second careers." In fact, throughout 1977 the U. S. Congress and some state legislatures were considering various legislative proposals prohibiting mandatory retirement at age 65. Similar federal bills had been discussed in past sessions, but without final action by the Congress.

It was perhaps the greatest social advance of the first part of the 20th century that it came to be recognized that tired people cannot be thrown away like worn-out machines. The prospect for the future is that the ways will be worked out to provide not only security but continued occupational opportunity to those older people who want it and can make good use of it.

WILLARD WIRTZ

Demanding a 30% wage increase, British firemen went on strike in November.

Japan. A softening economy was reflected in moderate wage settlements by unions and employers. After the spring "shunto," or wage offensive—which was marked as usual by brief strikes, parades, and demonstrations—the settlements yielded wage increases in the 9% range.

Japan's seniority-oriented pay system, under which wages automatically increase with length of service, took some batterings. Many firms halted the automatic raises at ages between 35 and 45, or persuaded employees to take early retirement with such incentives as higher severance pay or aid in training for new careers. In more industries, unions secured agreements raising the compulsory retirement age above the traditional 55 years—generally to 60 years.

The official jobless rate climbed to 2.2% of the labor force, almost double the rate of a year earlier, and that understated the true rate. Many employers, under a combination of government pressures and subsidies, retained redundant employees. By western yardsticks, the real unemployment rate was about 6%.

Japan's so-called "Lifetime employment" system did not prevent layoffs. The lifetime guarantee generally applied only to a specified "basic" staff, usually about two thirds of a company's peak force.

Western Europe. Most of the countries of Western Europe suffered a combination of high unemployment and inflationary pressures.

In Great Britain, the British Trades Union Congress, after internal controversy, voted to continue a policy of wage restraint, as urged by the Labour government, which has been trying to keep pay increases at 10% or less. However, in late 1977 there was a rash of strikes as workers in various industries sought to break the wage restraint barrier in the face of an inflation rate of nearly 15%. A strike of air traffic control assistants, which began in August, continued for months, forcing delay or cancelation of many flights. Most serious of the strikes was that of over 30,000 firefighters, which began on November 14. Meantime, the government had some success in reducing the unemployment rate, which has risen to nearly 7%.

In France, beset by an inflation rate of nearly 10%, a stagnant economy, and a 23% rise in the number of unemployed, the government took steps to reverse course. These included expenditures to spur economic growth and appeals to business and labor to exercise price and wage restraint. A price freeze was imposed on some basic foods late in the year.

West Germany remained in better shape than its neighbors, but the government did propose a series of economic stimulation measures in September. At that time, the unemployment rate stood at 4% and so did the inflation rate.

Italy remained in ferment on the economic front. Strikes flared during the year in many industries and in civil service, despite an indexing arrangement under which wages kept abreast or ahead of the cost of living. The government strove to cut the inflation rate, which reached a high of 18% in September; to reduce unemployment, which stood at nearly 10%; and to reverse a drop in industrial production.

Latin America. There was economic strife in many Latin lands during the year.

In Argentina, despite a ban on strikes, there was an outburst of work stoppages in October. Workers pushed demands for pay increases of 70 to 100% as the inflation rate neared 150% (down from over 300% last year). Earlier in the year pay raises totaling 36% were authorized. The government sought to break the strikes by ordering discharges of strikers.

Chile's military regime cut public welfare budgets, eliminated price subsidies, and took austere measures in efforts to reduce the inflation to 70% by year's end. It was 174% in 1976. Two 18% pay increases were authorized during the year, partially offsetting inflation. Unemployment was an estimated 13%.

In Colombia in September, unions staged a 24-hour strike, which turned violent and was accompanied by looting. Troops and police were called in to put down the unrest. The melees ended with an estimated total of 23 dead, 500 wounded, and 4,000 arrests. Strikers had demanded wage increases to offset inflation.

In Peru, where strikes are illegal, a 24-hour stoppage occurred during July in protest against price increases. Violence followed, police attacked, and some demonstrators were killed or injured. The military regime also arrested hundreds of unionists and ordered the discharge of strike instigators.

In Brazil, threats of strikes mounted in a union drive for wage increases to catch up with an estimated 45% inflation rate. The military rulers said they would repress them.

The Mexican government won support from labor leaders for a ceiling of 10% on wage increases as part of its effort to slash a 20% inflation rate. Strikes erupted in protest against the 10% ceiling, but generally wage increases were held at that level. The government secured a pledge from major business organizations to hold down consumer prices until the end of the year, and to give workers a special bonus of 15 days' pay. Unemployment and underemployment were estimated at 40% of the labor force.

RUBEN LEVIN
Editor and Manager, "Labor"

LAOS

Laos experienced its most difficult year since the Communists came to power in 1975. Specifically, the nation suffered the most serious food shortage in Southeast Asia in 25 years, resulting in an emergency appeal for international assistance. Unlike neighboring Kampuchea (Cambodia), Laos is not rich agriculturally and has not been self-sufficient in food in modern times. Also, its new Communist rulers have probably been less ruthless than the counterpart regimes in adjacent Vietnam and Cambodia, especially with respect to national agricultural policies.

Politics. The political transition from the old to the new proceeded slowly as well as awkwardly. The threat of force remained a very important influence. Former King Savang Vatthana, who had abdicated in December 1975, was arrested in March following alleged involvement of his brother Sisouphanh Tharangsi and himself in an unsuccessful (and very small) uprising in the former royal capital city of Luang Prabang. The former king, 69, was subsequently sent to a "re-education center" in the north. The arrest was not announced publicly for fear of offending nationalist sentiments.

Probably influenced by this sequence of events, Prime Minister Kaysone Phoumvihan, leader of the ruling Communist Lao People's Revolutionary Party since December 1975, made his first public appearance as premier in April. The prime minister, whose father was a Vietnamese, is a longtime protégé of the Vietnamese Communists and has lived much of his adult life in adjacent Vietnam.

Antiguerrilla activity continued in traditional Meo tribal areas, but the rebels probably numbered no more than 2,000. Some 30,000 partisans of the pre-1975 pro-American regime were believed to be in re-education or other detention centers. More than 100,000 non-Communists probably have fled the country since 1975.

Economy. Many of Laos' three million inhabitants face starvation in 1978 as a result of a severe drought in 1977 (which followed a small harvest a year earlier). Failure of rice and other crops could be as high as 95%. The rains, which ordinarily begin in May, did not start until August—and, even then, were not sufficient or long enough. Laos' needs were estimated to be 367,500 tons of food for March–November 1978. Food shortages had a severe inflationary effect and led to an officially tolerated black market. Meat and fish were luxury items, and gasoline was rationed.

Foreign Affairs. Neighboring Vietnam continued to increase its influence over Laos, probably exceeding that of the USSR. Vietnamese Premier Pham Van Dong visited Vientiane in July, and a 25-year treaty of friendship and cooperation, a three-year economic aid pact, and a border agreement were signed. In addition, thousands of Vietnamese troops were believed to be still in the country.

Vientiane was on good terms with China but clearly was more friendly with the Soviet Union. Ties with ideologically similar Kampuchea (Cambodia) were almost nonexistent. Border incidents continued to mar the complicated relationship with ethnically close Thailand.

A U. S. presidential mission visited Laos to inquire about U. S. servicemen missing in action in the Indochina wars, but the Kaysone government tied cooperation to future reconstruction aid from Washington.

RICHARD BUTWELL
*State University of
New York at Fredonia*

LAOS · Information Highlights

Official Name: People's Democratic Republic of Laos.
Location: Southeast Asia.
Area: 91,429 square miles (236,800 km²).
Population (1977 est.): 3,500,000.
Chief Cities (1973 census): Vientiane, the capital, 177,-000; Savannakhet, 51,000.
Government: *Head of state,* Prince Souphanouvong, president. *Head of government,* Kaysone Phoumvihan, prime minister. *Legislature* (unicameral)—National Assembly.
Monetary Unit: Kip (198 kips equal U. S.$1, Nov. 1977).
Manufacturing (major products): Cigarettes, textiles.
Major Agricultural Products: Rice, corn, coffee, cotton, tobacco, cardamom, vegetables, forest products.

RESULTADO EXTRAOFICIAL del PLEBISCITO

PROVINCIA	TOTAL MESAS ESCRUTADAS	VOTOS SI	VOTOS NO	VOTOS ANULADOS	TOTAL

As ballots were counted in Panama's plebiscite on the canal treaties, the figures were put on a blackboard in the Legislative Palace. The treaties were approved by a margin of 2–1.

UPI

LATIN AMERICA

The ceremonial signing in Washington, D. C., of two treaties dealing with the Panama Canal was the occasion for an unprecedented gathering of Latin American chiefs of state in 1977. Lines of communication were opened between former enemies or adversaries, contributing to an evolving stability in inter-American relations. Stability was also evident in the internal order of most nations of Latin America: there were no successful revolts, coups d'etat, or major opposition electoral victories in the region during the year, although serious civil disturbances occurred in several countries. The new administration in the United States was both praised and denounced in Latin America for its international stand in favor of human rights, but received nearly unanimous applause for its willingness to relinquish U. S. sovereignty over the Panama Canal.

Economic Developments. Local drought conditions, together with continued low world sugar prices, exacerbated the economic troubles of Jamaica, Barbados, and some of the smaller Caribbean islands. A growing trade imbalance between the primarily sugar-producing members of the Caribbean Common Market (CARICOM) and their oil-rich partner, Trinidad and Tobago, threatened the break-up of the organization. Hardest hit by the drought was Haiti, already a virtual economic basket case, which sank even deeper into abject poverty in 1977.

With coffee and petroleum prices remaining high, economic gains were registered by countries that produced significant quantities of either or both of these commodities—for example, Mexico. Beginning to feel the salutary effects of the 1976 devaluation of the peso, Mexico could look forward to increased revenues from the export of petroleum products. In 1977 work was begun on a pipeline to carry natural gas from Mexico's southern oil fields to markets in the United States. High-value coffee exports contributed to modest economic gains in Brazil and in some Central American and Andean countries. In Colombia, however, high coffee prices also fueled inflation, which led to considerable social unrest. While inflation accelerated in Colombia and a few other countries, and remained a problem almost everywhere in Latin America, the overall rate of increase in the cost of living in 1977 was not so great as in previous years, and some countries made significant progress in reducing inflation.

Relations with the United States. Soon after the inauguration in January of U. S. President Jimmy Carter, spokesmen for the new administration indicated that it would carry its campaign in favor of human rights into Latin America. In February, Robert White, U. S. representative to the Inter-American Council on Education, Science, and Culture, meeting in Uruguay, declared that "culture cannot enrich lives unless the state protects certain rights," including those of "assembly, freedom of expression, [and] protection against arbitrary arrest and punishment." Shortly afterwards, U. S. Secretary of State Cyrus Vance announced plans to reduce military aid to Uruguay and Argentina, because of a lack of respect for human rights on the part of the governments of those countries. In March, a State Department report critical of the human-rights situation in certain countries was circulated to U. S. congressmen reviewing foreign military aid programs. The governments of six Latin American nations named—Argentina, Brazil, Chile, Uruguay, Guatemala, and El Salvador—found the report so offensive that they announced that they would no longer accept any military aid from Washington. In a speech to Organization of American States (OAS) representatives in Washington in April, President Carter persisted in linking U. S. aid to respect for human rights in recipient countries. At the annual General Assembly of the OAS, held in Grenada in June, the U. S. reiterated its concern.

Some Latin American countries—generally, the minority with elected, civilian governments —applauded the U. S. emphasis on human rights. For its part, the Carter administration made clear its preference for "democratic" countries like Mexico, Jamaica, Costa Rica, Colombia, and, especially, Venezuela. The latter seemed to emerge as Washington's favorite in Latin America, replacing military-dominated Brazil, which had enjoyed the favor of the two previous U. S. administrations. But after Brazilian President Ernesto Geisel declined to go to Washington for the Panama Canal treaty signing in September, President Carter took steps to avoid further deterioration of relations between the United States and Brazil; he scheduled a visit to Brasília in November, though it had to be postponed "indefinitely." By the end of the year, Carter had met personally with every Latin American head of state, except Castro and Geisel. Mexican President José López Portillo visited Carter in Washington in February, and others conferred privately with the U. S. president in September, when they were in Washington to attend the canal ceremony.

Panama Canal Treaties. After 12 years of negotiations, the U. S. and Panamanian governments reached an agreement on new treaties defining the status of the Panama Canal. The treaties, signed in Washington in September by President Carter and Panamanian "Supreme Leader" Omar Torrijos, are considered inseparable; one provides for a period of transition until the year 2000, when full control of the Canal Zone passes to Panama; the other declares the permanent neutrality of the canal and the joint responsibility of the United States and Panama, beyond the year 2000, for its defense. Despite protests by Panamanians who felt that the arrangement left their country open indefinitely to U. S. armed intervention, the treaties were declared ratified by Panama after a nationwide plebiscite in October. Ratification by the U. S. Senate was still pending as the year ended.

The chiefs of state of all members of the OAS (which excludes Cuba) were invited to Washington to witness the treaty signing at OAS headquarters. Most national leaders endorsed the treaties by their presence at the ceremony; conspicuously absent were the president of Mexico, who had misgivings about the treaties' apparent extension of the U. S. "right to intervene" in Panama, and the president of Brazil, who resented U. S. criticism of his government's record of human rights.

Unlike Geisel of Brazil, the leaders of other countries accused of human rights violations seized the opportunity to visit Washington, where, under most other circumstances, they would not have been welcome. Chiefs of state with conflicting ideological or national commitments took advantage of the unprecedented gathering for personal meetings with one another and with President Carter, which otherwise might have been impossible. The presidents of Chile and Argentina exchanged views on human rights with Carter, while the leaders of Honduras and El Salvador met to discuss their border conflict. For the first time in 100 years, the chiefs of state of Bolivia, Peru, and Chile got together to discuss Bolivia's lack of an outlet to the sea. President Augusto Pinochet of Chile, heretofore a virtual outcast due to the notoriously repressive nature of his regime, came away from Washington with new international respectability. He had prepared for the meeting by announcing the disbanding of DINA, the dreaded Chilean intelligence service.

Other International Relations. Cuba, though barred from the Washington affair, moved closer to normal relations with its neighbors in 1977. In a long-expected move, Cuba and Costa Rica exchanged ambassadors in February, bringing to 12 the number of OAS members with full diplomatic representation in Havana. The United States established partial diplomatic relations with Cuba after a visit to the island by Terence Todman, U. S. assistant secretary of state for inter-American affairs, who in April became the first U. S. diplomat to set foot in Havana since 1961. In September, a U. S. diplomatic mission was permanently stationed in Havana as a section of the Swiss embassy, while a Cuban mission took up residence in Washington as part of the Czechoslovak embassy.

Mexico ended nearly four decades of estrangement from Spain in March by reestablishing full diplomatic relations, which had been broken at the end of the Spanish Civil War. In October, President López Portillo became the first Mexican president ever to make a state visit to Spain. Spanish King Juan Carlos in September made a highly successful Latin American tour, his second in two years, visiting Central America and Venezuela, reinforcing sentimental ties of *hispanidad.*

The Permanent Court of International Justice at The Hague ruled against Argentine territorial claims in an arbitration decision, handed down in April, which awarded Chile three islands in the Beagle Channel. Chile thus gained status as an Atlantic power, with a claim to offshore oil-drilling rights in waters that had been considered exclusively Argentine.

Internal Political Developments. Presidential decrees in Brazil in April changed the rules for the 1978 federal and state elections, precluding any major opposition victories. The decrees set off a wave of student protest demonstrations, which, when suppressed by the police, led to more protests and student strikes.

Peruvian workers in July temporarily walked off their jobs in a general strike, protesting government austerity measures. While police rounded up the leaders of the illegal strike,

Prime Minister Eric Gairy of Grenada (*above*) played host to the General Assembly of the Organization of American States in June. In El Salvador (*top right*), troops were called out to maintain order following presidential elections in February; opponents charged the elections were rigged. President José López Portillo of Mexico (*right*) addressed the Spanish Cortes (parliament) during his state visit in October.

PHOTOS UPI

government forces sought to avoid confrontation with the masses. President Francisco Morales Bermúdez promised to ease the economic austerity program and pledged a complete return to political democracy by 1980. In August he lifted the state of siege (modified martial law) that had been in effect since 1976.

A 24-hour general strike in Colombia in September, by unions demanding an immediate 50% wage increase, led to street battles between strikers and government forces in Bogotá and other cities, in which at least two dozen people were killed and thousands were arrested. President Alfonso López Michelsen moved to defuse the situation by appointing a judicial commission to investigate the deaths and by accepting the resignation of his interior minister, who had been in charge of dealing with the strike. López promised that his government would negotiate in good faith with the unions on wage increases.

Presidential elections were staged in February in two tightly controlled countries, Paraguay and El Salvador. General Alfredo Stroessner, who has ruled Paraguay since 1954, won another presidential term in an uncontested election. Col. Arturo Armando Molina turned over the presidency of El Salvador to his chosen successor, Gen. Carlos Humberto Romero. The Salvadorean changeover was accompanied by widespread strikes and protests by opponents of the regime, who charged that the elections had been rigged.

In Nicaragua the Sandinista National Liberation Front, a leftist guerrilla organization founded in 1962 but believed virtually extinct at the beginning of 1977, reemerged in October to attack government forces in the Managua-Masaya area, as well as in remote mountain and frontier regions.

NEILL MACAULAY
University of Florida

UPI

The U. S. Supreme Court Building, Washington, D. C., autumn 1977.

LAW

Legal developments in the United States during 1977 continued to reflect the conservative character of the present Supreme Court. On the international scene, the failure by still another session of a UN conference to reach an agreement on a comprehensive law of the sea tended to obscure some real achievements toward that end. A sensitive legal problem is reviewed in a special report on page 292.

U. S. Supreme Court

The decisions of the Supreme Court during the 1976–77 term were curiously mixed. The court generally supported First Amendment rights but also big labor and big business. It declared mandatory death sentences unconstitutional and upheld defendants' claims in several other important criminal prosecutions. But it ruled against women in an important equal-protection case and rejected Medicaid payment for abortions. Remedies for racial discrimination in housing, schools, and employment, as well as access to federal courts in civil rights cases, were seriously limited.

With Chief Justice Warren Burger and Justice William Rehnquist on the right, and Justices William Brennan and Thurgood Marshall on the left, the balance of power rested with the five center members. Justices Lewis Powell, Harry Blackmun, and Byron White were most often in the majority, with 14, 19, and 21 dissents respectively. Justices Potter Stewart and John Paul Stevens showed somewhat more independence (26 and 34 dissents). The court's rulings were rejected by the chief justice in 29 cases and

by Rehnquist in 31. On the left, Brennan registered 55 dissents and Marshall 52. The court handed down 127 signed opinions, of which 41 (32%) were unanimous. This compares with 138 opinions (36% unanimous) in the preceding term. The court also issued 39 per curiam opinions, 21 of them unanimous.

Criminal Prosecutions. In a controversial ruling, *Brewer* v. *Williams,* the court held (5–4) that a man convicted of a brutal child murder must be retried because police had induced him, in the absence of counsel, to lead them to the victim's body. The chief justice attacked the decision as "intolerable." But the *Miranda* rule, which was not at issue in *Brewer,* was narrowed in *Oregon* v. *Mathiason;* here, the court ruled that a suspect who voluntarily went to the police station and was not under arrest could be questioned without receiving the *Miranda* warning on his right to silence and to have a lawyer.

The case of Gary Gilmore, condemned to death in Utah, was carried to the Supreme Court against his wishes, and the claim that he had not made a knowing waiver of his right to appeal was rejected. A second effort to secure a stay of execution from the court failed. The sentence was carried out on Jan. 17, 1977—the first execution in the United States since 1967.

Contrary to expectations, there were no subsequent executions, in part because of Supreme Court intervention. Thus, it held (5–4), in *Roberts* v. *Louisiana,* that the death penalty cannot be made mandatory, because this does not allow jurors to consider possible mitigating circumstances. In *Coker* v. *Georgia* it ruled (6–3) that execution for rape where no death occurs is unconstitutional. The court's decision in *Gardner* v. *Florida* voided a death sentence because the judge based his sentence on an investigative report not disclosed to the defendant's lawyer. And in *Davis* v. *Georgia* it found that exclusion of a potential juror in a capital case because of his scruples against the death penalty would invalidate any death sentence subsequently imposed by the jury.

Inadvertent failure of prison officials to provide medical treatment to an inmate did not violate his rights, the court concluded (*Estelle* v. *Gamble*), but deliberate indifference to serious medical needs would be cruel and unusual punishment. On the other hand, prison officials are obligated to assist prisoners in preparing legal claims, either by providing adequate law libraries or outside assistance (*Bounds* v. *Smith*). But organizations of inmates need not be allowed to meet and solicit members inside prison (*Jones* v. *Prisoners' Labor Union*).

In the case of *United States* v. *Donovan* the court held that, after a court-authorized wiretap is completed, the government must furnish the judge with a list of all identifiable persons overheard; nevertheless, the government may use evidence obtained against persons overheard but not notified.

Customs inspectors may open letters entering the country without search warrants, if there is reasonable cause to suspect that they contain narcotics or smuggled goods (*United States* v. *Ramsey*), but police must obtain warrants before opening suspicious luggage (*United States* v. *Chadwick*).

First Amendment Rights. Since Justice Stevens has joined Brennan, Stewart, and Marshall, the court again has four members who consistently vote against obscenity convictions. This applied to *Smith* v. *United States,* in which a conviction in Iowa for violation of the federal obscenity law was upheld. Materials, mailed in Iowa to two law officers on their request, had been found obscene by the jury, although Iowa law prohibited only distribution of obscene materials to minors. The majority held that the jury, not state law, should decide what is obscene by local community standards. But *Marks* v. *United States,* concerning a federal conviction for transporting obscene materials, was sent back for retrial, because the 1973 *Miller* case standards were applied although the defendant's activities occurred prior to 1973.

Oklahoma Publishing Co. v. *District Court* held that a state judge violated the First Amendment when he ordered the media not to publish the name or photograph of a juvenile in a delinquency proceeding, although reporters had been in the courtroom and learned the juvenile's name there.

In a potentially far-reaching decision, *Bates* v. *State Bar of Arizona,* the court ruled (5–4) that the First Amendment protects lawyers who truthfully advertise their fees for routine legal services. The ruling appears to cover other professional services as well.

Town officials may not forbid owners to post "For Sale" signs on real estate (*Linmark Associates* v. *Willingboro*). In the case of *Wooley* v. *Maynard* the right of auto owners to cover a motto on their license plates conflicting with their religious or moral beliefs was upheld.

Interpreting the provision in the Civil Rights Act that requires employers to make "reasonable accommodations" for employees' religious observances unless it involves "undue hardship," the court ruled, in *TWA* v. *Hardison,* that employers need not grant workers Saturday off for religious reasons if the action discriminates against or burdens other workers. It slightly relaxed its position on "entanglement" of church and state, concluding that public funds may be spent to provide students in parochial schools with textbooks, educational testing, and a variety of health services, but not instructional equipment or field trips (*Wolman* v. *Walter*).

Equal Protection. In the Dayton school case (*Dayton* v. *Brinkman*) the court reaffirmed its 1973 Denver decision that federal judges have power to order widespread busing to combat racial discrimination in northern cities, but warned that orders must be limited to correction of proven past discrimination. In *Milliken* v. *Bradley* (Detroit), it was found that desegregation remedies do not have to be limited to pupil reassignment through busing but may include academic program improvements to benefit children victimized by past discrimination, with financial support from the state. Desegregation orders for Indianapolis, Austin, Omaha, and Milwaukee were returned to the lower courts for review, but the Supreme Court refused to review a Louisville desegregation order and Judge W. Arthur Garrity's assumption of control over the South Boston high school.

The court heard argument in the major case of *Board of Regents* v. *Bakke,* in which the California Supreme Court had declared unconstitutional an affirmative action racial quota system in a state medical school, but decision was put off to next court term (*see also* EDUCATION; ETHNIC GROUPS).

United Jewish Organizations v. *Carey* upheld the use of racial quotas in reapportioning New York legislative districts where the purpose was to increase the voting strength of nonwhites as required by the Voting Rights Act. The redistricting had divided a community of Hasidic Jews between two districts to assure blacks and Puerto Ricans a 65% majority.

Arlington Heights v. *Metropolitan Housing Development Corp.* was resolved in favor of a Chicago suburb that refused to rezone a parcel of land to allow construction of racially integrated housing for low-income families. *International Brotherhood of Teamsters* v. *United States* held that minority truck drivers, though victims of discrimination before passage of the Civil Rights Act in 1964, were not entitled to retroactive job seniority.

Women's rights suffered a serious setback in *General Electric Co. v. Gilbert,* when the court found that failure of an employer's disability benefits plan to cover pregnancy-related disabilities did not violate Title VII of the Civil Rights Act. In *Craig v. Boren* it ruled unconstitutional an Oklahoma law allowing women to buy beer at age 18 while men had to wait until 21. Provisions of the Social Security Act, treating widowers and the husbands of retired wives differently from widows and wives of retired husbands, were found invalid (*Califano v. Goldfarb, Califano v. Silbowitz*). The court decided (5–4) that states may deny welfare aid to families of striking workers without violating the Social Security law (*Batterton v. Francis*).

Privacy and Due Process. The ruling in *Beal v. Doe* was (6–3) that neither the Constitution nor federal law requires states to pay for abortions that are not medically necessary. In the preceding year some 300,000 abortions had been paid for by Medicaid funds. *Carey v. Population Services* held that states may not prohibit the sale of contraceptives to minors under 16 or bar advertising or display of the devices.

Whalen v. Roe affirmed a New York law requiring doctors to report names and addresses of persons for whom they prescribed dangerous drugs. *Moore v. East Cleveland* held invalid an ordinance limiting occupancy in dwelling units to members of an immediate family.

Corporal punishment of students by school authorities is not cruel and unusual, the court concluded (5–4) in *Ingraham v. Wright,* nor is a hearing required before punishment is inflicted. It also found hearings unnecessary before removal of children from foster homes (*Smith v. Organization of Foster Families*).

Watergate. The 1974 law giving the government control over Richard Nixon's presidential papers and tapes was upheld (7–2) in *Nixon v. Administrator of General Services.* But the decision whether tapes used as evidence in the Watergate coverup trial could be broadcast and sold to the public was put off. The court refused to review the Watergate convictions of John Mitchell, H. R. Haldeman, and John D. Ehrlichman. An unusual leak to the press revealed that the chief justice and two other Nixon-appointed justices had voted to grant review, and that Burger had held up announcing the refusal while trying to secure the necessary fourth vote.

Federalism Issues. The court continued to limit the power of federal judges to intervene in state-court proceedings. *Juidice v. Vail* reversed a federal court which had halted contempt-of-court actions in New York against debtors resisting the demands of creditors for financial information.

Jones v. Rath Packing Co. ruled that federal food laws preempted state laws enforcing stricter weight-labeling requirements than federal standards. Also, federal law preempts state laws denying out-of-state vessels the right to fish in state waters on the same terms as state residents (*Douglas v. Seacoast Products*). But *Oregon v. Corvallis Sand & Gravel Co.,* overruling a 1973 decision, found that state rather than federal law governs disputes over the extent of a state's ownership of riverbeds within its boundaries. State taxes were upheld in three cases against charges that they burdened commerce.

Labor and Business. *Abood v. Detroit Board of Education* upheld an "agency shop" for public employees under a Michigan law that permits a school board to reach agreement with a teachers' union requiring all teachers to pay a fee to the union as a condition of employment. *Ohio v. Hodory* ruled that states may deny unemployment compensation to workers laid off because of strikes in other plants.

In an opinion on the almost forgotten contract clause, the court struck down (4–3) a law that had altered the terms of bonds of the New York Port Authority long after they had been sold (*United States Trust Co. v. New Jersey*).

E. I. DuPont v. Train supported the authority of the Environmental Protection Agency to issue uniform industry-wide regulations limiting the amount of pollutants that plants may dump into rivers.

Several decisions weakened the anti-trust laws. Thus, indirect purchasers were denied the right to collect damages from businesses that illegally increase prices (*Illinois Brick Co. v. Illinois*), and a manufacturer's restrictions on the number and location of franchised retail outlets for its products were found not necessarily illegal (*Continental TV v. GTE Sylvania*). The court further held, in *U. S. Steel Corp. v. Fortner Enterprises,* that the steel company had not violated anti-trust laws by "tying" its financing of a housing development to the developer's agreement to purchase the company's prefabricated homes.

C. HERMAN PRITCHETT
University of California, Santa Barbara

International Law

The international legal system, lacking such formal law-generating mechanisms as legislatures and courts, depends on two main sources for its rules: (1) custom, as evidenced by the practice of nations in their dealings with each other; and (2) international agreements, including bilateral and multilateral treaties.

Law of the Sea. Recent trends in the international Law of the Sea demonstrate both sources at work. The 200-mile limit, as an allowable extension of coastal-nation jurisdiction for resource-related purposes (especially fisheries), has become a customary international law through the recent practice of nations. This practice consisted of unilateral claims to 200-mile jurisdiction and acquiescence in the claims by other nations. In 1977 several important 200-mile claims went into effect: those of the United States, the Soviet Union, Japan, Canada, and

U. S. observes 200-mile limit: A Coast Guard officer gives instructions to crew members of a Soviet trawler, caught hake fishing 180 miles southeast of Cape Cod.

UPI

the European Community. Several other nations have followed suit.

Acquiescence in the new standard also demonstrates the operation of the other major source of international law, international agreements. For example, in 1977 several nations formally agreed to recognize the extended U. S. fisheries jurisdiction and to abide by U. S. fisheries regulations within the new limits. These agreements themselves provide legal rules to be applied between the contracting nations. Similar agreements were concluded between other nations in 1977. International agreements establishing boundaries for 200-mile zones—such as the U. S.–Cuban accord signed in April, 1977—were also concluded.

The most ambitious attempt ever made to establish a comprehensive set of international laws by agreement continues to occupy the nearly 150 nations participating in the UN Law of the Sea Conference. Begun in 1973, the conference aims at a treaty that will be a "constitution" for all uses of the sea and seafloor. A successful conclusion of this complex task is not yet in sight. The sixth session, held at UN headquarters in the spring and summer, produced yet another revision of the conference's working document. Termed the Informal Composite Negotiating Text (ICNT), the document reflects substantial consensus on most of the 90-odd items on the conference agenda. The most crucial of the issues still dividing the participants concerns the complicated management rules for mining the deep seabed. Although progress was apparently made in the negotiations on this question, the ICNT still presents a set of management rules unacceptable to the seabed mining nations, including the United States.

Panama Canal Treaties. Normally, treaty-made rules will not be binding unless ratified by the nation parties. This may take different forms in different nations. The U. S. ratification procedure, an important factor in the Law of the Sea negotiations, was in 1977 publicly spotlighted in the controversy over the Panama Canal treaties. The Carter administration negotiated two treaties—one to turn over control of the canal to Panama by the year 2000, the other to establish the future security of the canal —and submitted them to the U. S. Senate. Under the U. S. constitution, the president can ratify treaties only after receiving the affirmative vote of two thirds of the senators present. The Senate's approval was by no means certain. A vote in 1978 was expected.

Human Rights. The Carter administration also took steps toward achieving adherence to apparently emerging rules of international law on human rights and freedoms. These rules, developing largely through UN impetus since World War II, assert that national governments must respect certain fundamental individual rights and freedoms. Human rights were further underscored by the award of the 1977 Nobel Prize for peace to Amnesty International, a nongovernmental group whose mission is to seek worldwide compliance with human rights guarantees on behalf of imprisoned persons. Such pressures, exerted by both government and private groups, are attempts to fill a gap in the international legal system: the lack of effective sanctions against "breaking" international laws.

See also HUMAN RIGHTS (pages 20–27); UNITED NATIONS; UNITED STATES.

JON L. JACOBSON
University of Oregon

The Federal Papers Issue

The question of who owns a departed president's papers is one among many questions that grew out of the resignation of President Richard M. Nixon in August 1974. Until then, it was usual and unquestioned for departing chief executives just to take their papers with them—usually to become the basis of a presidential library. But Mr. Nixon's papers—a term which for the first time covers tapes as well—had a special significance after Watergate.

The former president claimed that everything —some 42 million pages of documents and 800 reels of White House tapes—was his personal property, Watergate or no. At first his successor, Gerald Ford, agreed. Then, in a storm of protest, Congress passed and Ford signed legislation canceling that agreement and giving control of papers and tapes to the General Services Administration. At the same time, a commission was set up to produce a definitive answer to the wider question of what rights all public officials, not just presidents, have over their "job-related" papers and tapes, when they leave office.

The commission, called the National Study Commission on Records and Documents of Federal Officials, was chaired by Herbert Brownell, Jr., who served as attorney general during part of the Eisenhower administration. Other members of the panel included Ernest R. May, chairman of the department of history at Harvard; Lucius D. Battle, senior vice president for corporate affairs at the Communications Satellite Corporation; and Michael M. Uhlmann, a former assistant attorney general. The commission submitted its report to President Carter and to Congress in April 1977.

The commission's general conclusion was firm and unequivocal: All "job-related" papers of presidents, members of Congress, and the federal judiciary should become public property, under closely defined outlines and conditions.

Presidential papers, defined as all documentary materials made or received by the president and his immediate staff "in connection with the president's constitutional or statutory duties," were included in the category of public papers. Similar materials in "all units of the executive office of the president" directly related to the president and in office files of members of Congress, their staffs, and the federal judiciary were also classified as public papers. Access to all such public papers, the commission report recommended, should be restricted for a period not to exceed 15 years, after which there should be "general access" restricted only by privacy or national security.

A second category, federal records, should be set up for papers such as those produced or received by units of the executive office not related to the president and the institutional records of Congress and of the judiciary. These records, the report proposed, should be accessible immediately after one leaves office, under the terms of the Freedom of Information Act (FOI). Presidential papers should be placed in the archivist's custody; congressmen and judges could "designate a depository."

The commission also recommended that the FOI be amended to allow access to federal agency records after 30 years, rather than 50.

The restrictions on access to "public papers" —which might, for example, include conference notes of Supreme Court justices or confidential memos from an official to his staff—were recommended to avoid the possible "chilling effect" of immediate and full public access; to guarantee, the report said, "full and frank advice," and to encourage the president and his associates to keep adequate records. Otherwise, the report surmised, "both the keeping of records and the candor of advisers" might well be inhibited.

Left unresolved—and perhaps not susceptible of resolution—was the "difficult and sometimes impossible" question of defining those presidential papers that do not deal with public matters—diaries, letters to family or friends, and "other papers" of personal use not connected with official duties. And the report conceded that it is often very difficult to separate personal from public, but expressed the feeling that these private papers, however defined, should be a president's personal property, to do with as he likes when he leaves the White House.

The basic principle on which the commission based its conclusions was that "responsible government requires an informed citizenry," and "a necessary basis of responsible government" is for the people to "eventually have access to all governmental documents." For these purposes, "all records and documents accumulated by all federal officials in the discharge of their official duties should be recognized by Congress to be the property of the United States."

The Nixon papers, whose controversial nature stirred the first challenge to a tradition that the commission feels it is time to end, are in a GSA storage area in a Washington suburb. Some 1,800 boxes, those containing the most sensitive of the papers and tapes related to the Watergate scandal, remained in the Old Executive Office Building, next door to the White House, until Aug. 9, 1977, three years to the day after Mr. Nixon resigned. At that time, the GSA finally took them to the National Archives.

LINDA CHARLTON
Washington Bureau, "The New York Times"

Lebanon's Fuad Butros addresses the UN on the fighting in his homeland. (*Right*) Palestinian guerrillas man Soviet-made military equipment.

PHOTOS UPI

LEBANON

Despite the presence of a 30,000-member Syrian peace-keeping force and diplomatic efforts of the Arab League, Lebanon remains a country divided. The bitter civil war and the loss of more than 60,000 lives caused a political and social rift between the Christian right and the Palestinian-allied Muslim left, which not only shows no sign of narrowing but has also moved Lebanon into the middle of the Arab-Israeli conflict. Nearly continuous fighting in the south between Lebanese Christians and Palestinians increased tensions and was responsible in part for the assassination in March of leftist leader Kemal Jumblat, as well as a Christian-Israeli alliance, and a delay in Lebanon's much needed foreign aid.

Sectarian Nationalism. The regulation of Palestinian activities in Lebanon was the primary goal of the Christians. On January 23, the rightist Lebanese Front, led by former president Camille Chamoun and Falangist party leader Pierre Gemayal, issued a proclamation calling for the deportation of Lebanon's Palestinian population to the member states of the Arab League. This absolute position complicated the efforts of the Arab League's Four-Power Committee. Composed of Syrian, Saudi, Egyptian, and Kuwaiti delegates and charged with the responsibility of finding a formula for ending civil disorder, the committee had in January declared that the 1969 Cairo Agreement, which defined relations between the Lebanese and the Palestinian guerrillas, was to serve as a basis for future relations between all parties.

However, at the urging of the right, President Elias Sarkis presented a Lebanese interpretation of the 1969 agreement. According to this view, the 1969 provisions were to be strictly enforced, but also, the number of Palestinians allowed in Lebanon was to be limited to those who had arrived by 1969. Inflexibility on the Palestinian side led to a stalemate that culminated with the lapse of the Four-Power Committee's mandate on May 26. On the following day, the right added further problems by announcing that since the 1969 agreement had never been implemented, it was null and void.

Fighting in the South. In March, Defense Minister Fuad Butros admitted that the hostilities in the south were out of the government's control. The fighting had begun, following the October 1976 ceasefire, when Palestinian units tried to return to the bases they had occupied prior to the civil war. The right, fearing that a return of the guerrillas to the south would again invite Israeli reprisals against civilians, opposed the Syrian-backed Palestinians. While the government attempted to reorganize its badly shattered army to fill the security vacuum in the south, the right, in an unprecedented move, concluded a working alliance with Israel. The Israelis, believing it in their interest to keep the Palestinians away from their border, openly offered artillery support for rightist operations and, by July, were committing armor and troops in tactical roles.

The Israeli incursions added to the tension in the area and compelled the parties in Lebanon

——— **LEBANON · Information Highlights** ———

Official Name: Republic of Lebanon.
Location: Southwest Asia.
Area: 4,015 square miles (10,400 km²).
Population (1977 est.): 2,800,000.
Chief Cities (1974 est.): Beirut, the capital, 1,000,000; Tripoli, 128,000.
Government: *Head of state,* Elias Sarkis, president (took office Sept. 1976). *Head of government,* Selim al-Hoss, premier (took office Dec. 1976). *Legislature* (unicameral)—Chamber of Deputies.
Monetary Unit: Lebanese pound (3.13 pounds equal U. S.$1, Aug. 1977).
Manufacturing (major products): Processed foods, textiles, petroleum products, cement, tobacco products.
Major Agricultural Products: Cereals, fruits, vegetables, tobacco, wheat.

to reach an agreement at Shtura in late July. However, subsequent Israeli initiatives torpedoed the agreement until September 26, when a tripartite committee of Lebanese, Syrian, and Palestinian representatives was formed to regulate the situation in the south and to implement some of the critical provisions of the 1969 Cairo Agreement.

Civil Disorder and Foreign Aid. On June 18, Premier Selim al-Hoss announced that initial war losses in private property, public installations, and national income amounted to $10.8 billion (U. S.). Earlier, Hoss had said that Lebanese appeals for Arab aid for reconstruction had elicited only a "limited" response, but Saudi and Kuwaiti spokesmen maintained that Arab assistance should be linked to better security and a more stable political situation within the country.

The absence of security was underscored by the assassination of Druze and Progressive Socialist party leader Kemal Jumblat on March 16. The death of Jumblat, who had been known as one of Lebanon's kingmakers, left the Muslim left without a responsible voice of authority and contributed to the problem of reforming Lebanon's troubled political system.

F. NICHOLAS WILLARD
Georgetown University

LIBRARIES

Four developments, all national in scope, dominated the American library scene during 1977. At the Library of Congress, there appeared an extraordinary report on goals; the Librarian of Congress proposed a Center for the Book; and the Advisory Group of Libraries offered the first formal recommendations to the Library of Congress by outside librarians in 35 years. In late spring, a three-year schedule was established for the White House Conference on Library and Information Services. Throughout the year, librarians prepared for the Jan. 1, 1978, implementation of An Act for the General Revision of the Copyright Law.

Library of Congress. On January 28, Daniel Boorstin, the Librarian of Congress, received the report of the Library's Task Force on Goals, Organization, and Planning, a panel composed of 11 staff members. The report called for the conversion of the Library of Congress "from a baffling palace of mirrors that researchers have sometimes warned each other against" to "a thriving center of research without parallel." The performance of the library could be improved, argued the task force, by (1) increasing the availability of research materials and delivering them more rapidly to users; (2) seeking "the growth of a system of compatible, coordinated, computerized loan networks that cover without overlap every part of the nation and the world"; (3) documenting American civilization more completely through recording and filming;

(4) coordinating more thoroughly the work of catalogers and reference librarians; and (5) establishing an Office of Planning and Development and a Research Office. The library's ultimate goal, according to the report, should be "to achieve the researcher's dream of a coordinated, comprehensive, international, machine-readable data base covering materials in all formats—books, films, sound recording, periodical literature, and unpublished material—fully indexed."

Boorstin responded to the report by creating the Office of Planning and Development and by instructing it to investigate means of implementing the 87 projects proposed in the report. As champion of the printed word and skeptic concerning the televised image, Boorstin also suggested that a Center for the Book be established at the Library of Congress to provide "a program for the investigation of the transmission of human knowledge and to heighten public interest in the role of books and printing in the diffusion of knowledge." On July 12, the Senate passed the bill to create such a center and House action followed in the fall.

On February 11, Boorstin considered the report of the 12-member Advisory Group of Libraries chaired by Robert Wedgeworth, the executive director of the American Library Association. These outside librarians recommended the development of a permanent "advisory mechanism" by which the thoughts and interests of the national community of librarians could be made known to the Library of Congress on a regular basis.

White House Conference. On May 4, President Jimmy Carter signed a bill providing $3.5 million for the White House Conference on Library and Information Services and for the partial funding of 56 preliminary conferences to be held in the states and territories. The National Commission on Libraries and Information Science announced on June 13 that the state and territorial conferences, two thirds of the delegates to which must be lay persons, would convene between Sept. 15, 1977, and April 30, 1979. The White House Conference, scheduled for September 1979, will consider recommendations from the state and territorial conferences. The Advisory Committee on the White House Conference, which consists of educators, politicians, and other citizens, as well as librarians, is determined that the conference not simply "rubber stamp" the thinking of the national commission and that it produce, even in the absence of built-in support from a large federal agency, recommendations that will be favorably received by Congress and the president.

Copyright. An Act for the General Revision of the Copyright Law, amending the Copyright Act of 1909, was enacted in 1976 and became effective on Jan. 1, 1978. Librarians spent much time in 1977 pondering what the legislation means for them. The new legislation affords statutory protection to all works subject to copyright, whether published or unpublished; extends the duration of copyright to the life of the author plus 50 years; and gives statutory recognition to the heretofore judicial doctrine of "fair use" which allows a limited amount of copying without the permission of the copyright owner. In general, libraries are limited to making a single copy of a copyrighted work provided that the copying does not harm the holder of copyright and is not pursued for commercial gain. Because such activity might substitute for purchases or subscriptions, the new law does not permit libraries to engage in the "related or concerted reproduction or distribution of multiple copies" or in the "systematic reproduction or distribution of single or multiple copies." Copying for interlibrary loan is permitted so long as the copyright owner is not adversely affected. Guidelines were being developed by the National Commission on New Technological Uses of Copyrighted Works. The commission suggested that copyright infringement occurs when a library during one calendar year requests six or more copies of any article or articles from a periodical published within five years of the request date. The Register of Copyrights will review the new law in 1982 to determine whether it has promoted a balance between the rights of copyright proprietors and the needs of users of copyrighted materials.

National Commission on Libraries and Information Science. During 1977, Eric Moon of the American Library Association was critical of what he perceived as an attempt by a politically impotent National Commission on Libraries and Information Science to assume the policymaking role rightfully belonging to the ALA. Moon saw the NCLIS as elitist and essentially dedicated to the construction of an information network serving researchers, an arrangement that does not address the more basic library and information requirements of most Americans. Meanwhile, Alphonse Trezza, executive director of the NCLIS, urged a national network of libraries and information services, embracing public and private institutions, which would respond to the "grass roots" needs of all Americans.

ALA. The 96th annual conference of the American Library Association was held in Detroit, June 17–23, 1977. Eric Moon, president of the Scarecrow Press, became president of the Association and Russell Shank, university librarian at the University of California at Los Angeles, was elected vice president and president-elect. Prominent topics of discussion were racism and sexism as well as the relative merits of tax-supported libraries and those libraries which one must pay directly to use.

The association sponsored National Library Week, April 17–23. Its theme, "Use Your Library," could be applied year round to any kind of library and library materials.

Education. The number of graduate programs in librarianship accredited by the ALA dropped to 64 in 1977 when the School of Library Science, University of Oklahoma, and the Graduate Library School, University of Rhode Island, were denied accreditation under the 1972 standards. The School of Library Science, University of Wisconsin at Milwaukee, was newly accredited and the Faculty of Library Science, University of Alberta, assumed temporary nonaccredited status while its program underwent revision. The University of Oregon made a tentative decision to close its accredited School of Librarianship during the summer of 1978.

International Activities. The International Federation of Library Associations, renamed the International Federation of Library Associations and Institutions to reflect the increased involvement of individual libraries in its affairs, held its 50th anniversary meeting in Brussels, Belgium, Sept. 3–10, 1977. The theme of the congress was "Libraries for All: One World of Information, Culture, and Learning." The Librarian of Congress, Daniel Boorstin, C. P. Snow of the United Kingdom, President Léopold Senghor of Senegal, and Professor Robert Escarpit of France addressed the meeting.

With some 3,600 members, the Canadian Library Association held its annual conference in Montreal in June. Paul Kitchen continued as the association's executive director.

DAN BERGEN, *Graduate Library School*
University of Rhode Island

Major Library Awards of 1977

Beta Phi Mu Award for distinguished service to education for librarianship: Russell E. Bidlack, dean, School of Library Science, University of Michigan

Randolph J. Caldecott Medal for distinction in picture book illustration: Leo and Diane Dillon, *Ashanti to Zulu*

Melvil Dewey Medal for creative professional achievement of a high order: Seymour Lubetzky, former professor, Graduate School of Library and Information Science, University of California at Los Angeles

Grolier Award for stimulating the reading interests of young people: Elizabeth T. Fast, director of media services, Groton (Conn.) Schools (posthumously)

Joseph W. Lippincott Award for distinguished service in the library profession: Virginia Lacy Jones, dean, School of Library Service, Atlanta University

Margaret Mann Citation for outstanding professional contribution in cataloging and classification: Phyllis A. Richmond, professor, School of Library Science, Case Western Reserve University

Isadore Gilbert Mudge Citation for distinguished contributions to reference librarianship: Bohdan S. Wynar, president, Libraries Unlimited, Inc.

John Newbery Medal for the most distinguished contribution to children's literature: Mildred T. Taylor, *Roll of Thunder, Hear My Cry*

During ceremonies commemorating the eighth anniversary of his regime, Muammar Qaddafi meets with Libyan troops in Tripoli.

WIDE WORLD

LIBYA

A reorganization of the Libyan government took place in 1977, but the country's major political figures remained in control. The Revolutionary Command Council (RCC), which had ruled since the 1969 coup that overthrew King Idris, was dissolved, as was the Council of Ministers. In their stead, a General People's Congress, composed of 1,000 representatives of government, trade unions, and professional organizations, exercised power. Former President Muammar Qaddafi became secretary general of the congress and was joined on its executive board by many former members of the RCC.

Foreign Relations. As has been true in recent years, Libya's foreign relations, particularly with its neighbors, were of great importance. A dispute with Tunisia over oil rights in the Gulf of Gabès threatened to become violent until both countries agreed to submit the issue to the World Court. Conflicting territorial claims also arose in the south when Chad accused Libya of attempting to annex parts of its land.

Of far greater importance, however, was the continuing problem with Egypt. Major philosophical differences between presidents Qaddafi and Sadat, especially regarding their views on the proper settlement of the Arab-Israeli confrontation, had led to a barrage of propaganda early in the year. Qaddafi accused Sadat of adopting too moderate a policy toward Israel and of becoming too closely linked with the United States. These verbal attacks spurred incidents in both countries. Libyan and Egyptian consulates were burned, and citizens of each country were harassed while visiting or working in the other. Over the Cairo and Tripoli radios, each regime accused the other of promoting espionage, sabotage, and plots to subvert the government. Thousands of Egyptian workers were expelled from Libya amid charges by Qaddafi that Egypt was seeking to acquire control over Libya's rich oil fields. Warfare between the two countries broke out in late July. For several days, bloody fighting raged along the Egyptian-Libyan frontier, resulting in many casualties on both sides and the destruction of several villages. Air raids also damaged important Libyan military installations near the border. Each side blamed the other for provoking the engagements; cease-fire was arranged by other Arab heads of state, but tension continued. After Sadat's peace mission to Israel in November, Qaddafi hosted a conference of the "rejectionist front" in Tripoli to denounce his overtures (*see also* MIDDLE EAST).

The Economy. In spite of these difficulties, Libya prospered in 1977 from its oil revenues. It was one of only two nations urging the Organization of Petroleum Exporting Countries (OPEC) to implement a proposed 5% price rise, arguing that the additional revenues could be pooled in a development fund for African and Asian countries. Libya's petroleum exports reached 2.4 million barrels (324,000 metric tons) a day in 1977, and statistics indicated that its output was rising at a more rapid rate than that of other OPEC members.

Expenditures on long-range economic plans also rose, stimulating domestic production in most sectors of the economy. At the same time, Libya expended substantial sums on foreign assistance, while arranging numerous technical and commercial agreements with a variety of countries, both Communist and capitalist, to further its own development and growth.

KENNETH J. PERKINS
University of South Carolina

LIBYA • Information Highlights

Official Name: Socialist People's Libyan Arab *Jamahiriya* ("state of the masses").
Location: North Africa.
Area: 679,360 square miles (1,759,540 km²).
Population (1977 est.): 2,700,000.
Chief Cities (1975 est.): Tripoli, the capital, 295,000; Benghazi, 190,000.
Government: *Head of state*, Muammar el-Qaddafi, secretary general of the General People's Congress (took office 1969). *Head of government*, Abdullah Obeidi, chairman of the General People's Congress Committee (took office March 1977).
Monetary Unit: Dinar (0.30 dinar equals U.S.$1, Aug. 1977).
Manufacturing (major products): Petroleum products, processed foods.
Major Agricultural Products: Wheat, barley, tomatoes, dates, olives, peanuts, vegetables.

LITERATURE

American Literature

The deaths in 1977 of Vladimir Nabokov, Robert Lowell, James Jones, and Anaïs Nin deprived America of four of its most distinctive voices (see OBITUARIES).

Awards. U. S. book awards continue to breed controversy. National Book Award winners were: History, Irving Howe's *The World of Our Fathers;* Fiction, Wallace Stegner's *The Spectator Bird;* Biography, W. A. Swanberg's *Norman Thomas: The Last Idealist;* Poetry, Richard Eberhart's *Collected Poems 1930–1976;* Contemporary Thought, Bruno Bettelheim's *The Uses of Enchantment;* Translation, Li-Li Chen's *Master Tung's Western Chamber Romance;* and Children's Literature, Katherine W. Paterson's *The Master Puppeteer.* Special recognition was given to Alex Haley's *Roots.*

But critics and publishers felt that the American Academy and Institute of Arts and Letters, which in 1975 agreed to administer the awards, favored older writers. The Association of American Publishers resumed control.

For the 10th time in its history, the Pulitzer Prize was not awarded for fiction. The awards were: History, David M. Potter's *The Impending Crisis;* Biography, John E. Mack's *A Prince of Our Disorder;* Poetry, James Merrill's *Divine Comedies;* General Nonfiction, William W. Warner's *Beautiful Swimmers: Watermen, Crabs and the Chesapeake Bay;* Drama, Michael Cristofer's *The Shadow Box.*

The National Book Critics Circle Awards for the year were: Fiction, John Gardner's *October Light;* Poetry, Elizabeth Bishop's *Geography III;* Nonfiction, Maxine Hong Kingston's *The Woman Warrior: Memoirs of a Girlhood among Ghosts;* Criticism, Bruno Bettelheim's *The Uses of Enchantment.*

Renata Adler's praised *Speedboat* would have received no major recognition had it not been for the second Ernest Hemingway Foundation award for the best first novel by an American.

The American Academy of Poets' Copernicus Award honored Muriel Rukeyser for her life's work. The American Academy and Institute of Arts and Letters gave Robert Lowell the National Medal for Literature and Saul Bellow the Gold Medal for the Novel. David Ignatow won the Bollingen Prize in Poetry for his "excellent poetry not suitably recognized up to this time."

Novels. For a time the novel seemed exclusively devoted to the problems of the individual. Books would focus on the pains, reflections, and anguish of an isolated person. But introspection seems to have given way to cultural inquiry. Novels which focus on individuals tend to pose them not as rebellious heroes or doomed antiheroes but rather as symptoms or products of their civilization. Writers are energetically seeking unexplored areas and unusual situations. Although it is often said that no one reads serious fiction besides critics and literary students, 1977 saw several fine novels.

John Cheever, highly regarded for his dissections of suburbia, in *Falconer* brilliantly recreated life in a penitentiary as seen through the eyes of a drug addict and fratricide. The real horrors of prison life and the surreal events in the man's life create profound ironies and a curious humor.

While Cheever was praised for exploring new themes, Philip Roth took the risk of staying with old ones. Though its protagonist is akin to previous characters, *The Professor of Desire* is a fresh and vigorous work, a witty academic novel, a comment on modern literature, and a biographical portrait of David Alan Kepesh, the unfortunate victim of the peculiar metamorphosis of Roth's *The Breast* (1972).

The emotional life of literary men was the

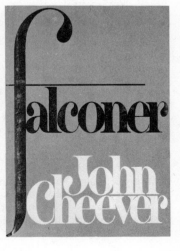

John Cheever's new novel, *Falconer,* is the story of an upper-middle-class man whose excessive passion for life and beauty leads him to crime and then to imprisonment.

center of Robert Penn Warren's 10th novel, *A Place to Come To,* about a southern boy who becomes an internationally renowned Dante scholar, and Curt Leviant's well received story of a writer, *The Yemenite Girl.*

Walker Percy continued his inquiry into our moral collapse in *Lancelot,* the study of a man whose discovery of his wife's infidelity leads him from indulgent alcoholism to a complicated and absurd revenge. Disgusted as he is by contemporary permissiveness, he has no tenable bases for his apocalyptic chivalry, and, in fact, tells the entire story from an insane asylum.

In *A Book of Common Prayer,* Joan Didion tells her story through an ironic, analytical, elderly woman who sees how people do not recognize their history, their culture, or themselves. Specifically, it is the story of a California woman who has drifted through two marriages and is searching for her terrorist daughter.

Toni Morrison's widely praised *Song of Solomon,* a sensitive study of black life in America, focuses on a man's journey toward racial and spiritual identity.

The problems of domestic life continue to be explored, but writers are moving to new strategies. Judith Rossner's *Attachments* posits friends married to male Siamese twins. Anne Roiphe's *Torch Song* has a girl wed a man she knows is impotent unless she grotesquely abases herself. The wife in Anne Tyler's *Earthly Possessions* is kidnapped by an incompetent bank robber. Caroline Slaughter's *Relations* deals with incest. John Casey's *An American Romance* tells of a man seeking total spiritual possession of his wife. Janet Burroway's well written *Raw Silk* interweaves textile design and a disintegrating marriage.

Some fine, relatively unknown writers are receiving the public notice they deserve. Robert Coover attracted attention and controversy with *The Public Burning,* a ferociously satirical fantasy based on the execution of Julius and Ethel Rosenberg. Joseph McElroy's *Plus* is a difficult but worthwhile speculation about a brain orbiting in space. Steven Milhauser's *Portrait of a Romantic* focuses on adolescence. Don DeLillo in *Players* tells of a couple who, in order to give their lives meaning, get involved in a plan to blow up the New York Stock Exchange.

Robert Kotlowitz' *The Boardwalk,* about growing up in Atlantic City, and John Sayles' *Union Dues,* about a runaway son and a searching father in Boston, were both well received. Wright Morris' *The Fork River Space Project* and Joyce Carol Oates' *Childwold* were reviewed with interest, but Louis Auchincloss' *The Dark Lady,* Herbert Gold's *Waiting for Cordelia,* and John Hersey's *The Walnut Door* did little for their reputations. Paul Goodman, whose social criticism generally received more attention than his many works of fiction, is the author of the posthumously published *Don Juan or The Continuum of the Libido.*

Thomas Berger's *Who Is Teddy Villanova?* was well reviewed, but the detective novel and thriller proved deficient as take-off points for Richard Brautigan's *Dreaming of Babylon,* William Kotzwinkle's *Fata Morgana,* and Jerzy Kosinski's ugly *Blind Date.*

Several fine first novels utilized original subjects: John Gregory Dunne's *True Confessions* deals with the Irish of Los Angeles; Jonathan Penner's *Going Blind* tells of friendship and love in a darkening world; Leslie Marmon Silko's *Ceremony* is about Pueblo Indian life after World War II; and Thomas Gavin's *Kingkill* is based on a 19th-century hoax involving a chess-playing robot. Cyra McFadden's sharply satirical picture story of brand-name-saturated, young, wealthy Californians, *The Serial: A Year in the Life of Marin County,* is likely to be widely imitated for its innovative format as well as its distinctive style.

Popular writers were active. Erich Segal's *Oliver's Story,* Richard Bach's *Illusions: The Adventures of a Reluctant Messiah,* Irwin Shaw's *Beggarman, Thief,* and Erica Jong's *How To Save Your Own Life* are all continuations or variations of their previous best sellers.

Short Stories. Short-story collections rarely sell well. Consequently, few are published unless they have special appeal, or are by established writers. Anaïs Nin's *Delta of Venus,* a group of erotic writings done in the 1940's, was both a critical and commercial success. Paul Theroux's *The Consul's File* wittily and perceptively tells of Americans in Malaysia. America's most literate humorist, S. J. Perelman, collected his travel pieces in *Eastward Ha!*

In *Pieces of Life,* Mark Schorer intersperses short stories with autobiographical pieces. Joyce Carol Oates deals with the supernatural in *Night-Side.* Peter Taylor's *In the Miro District* continues his tales of American southerners. The much-admired William Maxwell brings together fine stories in *Over By the River.* Donald Barthelme's peculiar genius is again demonstrated in *Amateurs.* William S. Wilson's *Why I Don't Write Like Franz Kafka* blends literary and scientific wit. The short story seems to be taking on new life as it absorbs the lessons of experimentalism and expands its subject matter.

Poetry. The year was a quiet one for poetry. Few important books appeared, and no new voices generated great excitement. Robert Lowell continued his effective use of lyric poetry for autobiographical purposes. In *Day by Day,* he distills the images, feelings, and thoughts which accompany a deteriorating marriage. John Berryman's *Henry's Fate,* a posthumous collection of 45 more remarkable "Dream Songs," as well as other poems and fragments from 1967 to 1972, supports his growing importance.

Kenneth Koch not only added to his own reputation for spirited and accomplished poetry with *The Duplications,* but also movingly advanced his argument that writing poetry is a

At Random: The Reminiscences of Bennett Cerf is a first-hand account of a major U. S. publishing company. The Dragons of Eden is an exploration of human nature by Carl Sagan.

RANDOM HOUSE, PHOTOGRAPH BY GORDON PARKS

RANDOM HOUSE, PAINTING BY DON DAVIS

wonderful experience for all sorts of people. In *I Never Told Anybody,* he tells of teaching the poet's craft to the elderly in a nursing home.

Muriel Rukeyser's *The Gates,* Philip Levine's *The Names of the Lost,* W. S. Merwin's *The Compass Flower,* John Ashbery's *Houseboat Days,* and James Dickey's *God's Images* added to the canon of these well-known poets.

The works of two relatively neglected but original poets are assembled in *The Collected Poems of Howard Nemerov* and *The Complete Poems of Charles Reznikoff.*

The novelist Larry Woiwode produced his first books of poems, *Even Tide,* and Olga Broumas published her first volume, *Beginning with O.*

Literary History and Criticism. Ann Douglas' *The Feminization of American Culture* effectively argues that the sentimentalism and anti-intellectualism of American mass culture grew out of various reform movements and alliances between women and the clergy in the 19th century. Richard Gray studies the preoccupation of post-World-War-II Southern writing with the idea of history in *The Literature of Memory.* Robert Pinsky emphasizes the continuity with tradition in *The Situation of Poetry.*

Gore Vidal gathers his recent essays in *Matters of Fact and Fiction. Essays of E. B. White* and *The Collected Essays of J. V. Cunningham* are admirable collections by fine writers.

In *Wallace Stevens: The Poems of Our Climate* the provocative critic Harold Bloom directs attention to Stevens' neglected late works. Marjorie Perloff's *Frank O'Hara: Poet Among Painters* argues persuasively for his distinction.

Important collections of private papers also appeared. By interspersing early poetry, letters, and notes with the journal Wallace Stevens kept from 1898 to 1914, Holly Stevens has made *Souvenirs and Prophecies* particularly valuable. Joseph Blotner edited *The Selected Letters of William Faulkner.* Linda Gray Sexton and Lois

Ames assembled *Anne Sexton: A Self Portrait in Letters.* Sally Fitzgerald brought together Flannery O'Connor's letters in *The Habit of Being.* We learn much about the man and our culture in Elena Wilson's huge selection of Edmund Wilson's *Letters on Literature and Politics.* Allen Ginsberg published his early journals, *Early Fifties—Early Sixties.*

Richard Wright's celebrated autobiography, *Black Boy* (1945), had a second part which remained unpublished until now. *American Hunger* is especially interesting for Wright's recounting of his attempts to live with meaning and dignity in America and his painful experiences with the Communist Party. Jessica Mitford sharply recalls her English and American years in *A Fine Old Conflict.* Publishers' views of the literary scene are engagingly stated in Bennett Cerf's *At Random* and Dorothea Straus' *Palaces and Prisons.*

History and Biography. The year was unusually rich in important biographies of writers. Bell Gale Chevigny's *The Woman and the Myth* examined the life and writings of the 19th-century feminist critic Margaret Fuller. Cynthia Griffin Wolff's *A Feast of Words* is an important book on Edith Wharton.

Robert Frost: The Later Years ends the revealing three-volume biography finished by R. H. Winnick after Lawrance Thompson's death. The poet's personal failings should not blind us to his poetic achievement, however, argues Richard Poirier's *Robert Frost: The Work of Knowing.* Two extremely gifted poets whose lives were cut tragically short are studied in James Atlas' *Delmore Schwartz: The Life of an American Poet* and Paul Ferris' *Dylan Thomas.*

Andrew Field's *Nabokov: His Life in Part* is the first major biography of one of the 20th century's most dazzling writers. Jack London's life is reexamined in Andrew Sinclair's *Jack.* Jonathan Yardley's *Ring* gives special attention to Ring Lardner's involvement with baseball. Edna Ferber's life is told in Julie Goldsmith's *Ferber.*

Two fascinating figures, who are remembered more for the writers they knew than for their own work, are the subjects of Linda Simon's *The Biography of Alice B. Toklas* and Emily Hahn's *Mabel: The Biography of Mabel Dodge Luhan.* Two men who have become myths in American history are unsparingly examined in Stephen B. Oates' extremely thorough and objective life of Abraham Lincoln, *With Malice Toward None,* and in Thomas L. Connelly's study, *The Marble Man: Robert E. Lee and His Image in American Society.*

David McCullough's timely *The Path Between the Seas* tells not only of the building of the Panama Canal but also illuminates a crucial era in American history.

Other Nonfiction. Annie Dillard's well received *Holy the Firm* is a personal inquiry and spiritual statement. Her meditation on the world led to an eloquent celebration of life and God.

Human nature is explored by Carl Sagan's *The Dragons of Eden,* which both traces the history and speculates on the evolution of human intelligence. Desmond Morris's *Man-Watching* uses a profusion of pictures to emphasize the animal basis of human behavior. Particularly interesting is Stephen Jay Gould's examination of a rejected biological concept, *Ontogeny and Phylogeny.*

Attempts to understand our culture were made from a variety of viewpoints. Diana Trilling's essays on the 1950's and 1960's, *We Must March My Darlings,* precipitated a controversy with Lillian Hellman over their respective stances on McCarthyism. Morris Dickstein's *Gates of Eden* attempts to describe the literature, music, politics, and people of America in the 1960's. Sara Davidson's *Loose Change* concentrates on the lives of three women who went to college in that decade. Philip Caputo's *A Rumor of War* is his moving account of his years in Vietnam.

Earlier years come vividly to life in Studs Terkel's *Talking to Myself* in which the indefatigable interviewer lets himself talk about his career and Chicago. Luigi Barzini looks back with nostalgia in *O America: When You and I Were Young.* Roger Angell proves again that sportswriting can be evocative and literate with his account of baseball's last several years, *Five Seasons.*

JEROME H. STERN, *Florida State University*

Children's Literature

The major awards presented in 1977 for children's books published the previous year were: the American Library Association's (ALA) John Newbery Medal for the most distinguished contribution to American literature for children to Mildred Taylor for *Roll of Thunder, Hear My Cry,* a novel of black pride set in Mississippi during the Depression; the ALA's Randolph Caldecott Medal for the most distinguished picture book to Leo and Diane Dillon for their illustrations in Margaret Musgrove's *Ashanti to Zulu,* depicting 26 African tribes and their customs; the National Book Award for children's books to Milton Meltzer for *Never to Forget,* first-person accounts of European Jewry under Hitler; the Child Study Association of America award for dealing realistically with young people's problems to Roberta Silman for *Somebody Else's Child,* a novel about adoption. A new award for excellence in poetry for children was given to David McCord by the National Council of Teachers of English.

Trends. The number of individual children's books produced matched the previous year's total of approximately 1,500 titles. There was a trend toward using more black and white and less lavish color in art work. Despite economies achieved, production costs continued to rise, forcing more publishers to turn toward paperbacks. Several publishers introduced new paperback lines, and virtually all of the major houses indicated their intentions for vigorous paperback programs in 1978.

Other trends noted during the year were a preponderance of reissues of the classics, retold or reillustrated, including many from that perennial source, the Brothers Grimm; a new emphasis on publishing individual "easy-to-read" books; innumerable biographies of sports figures; stories of young people's survival under the Nazi regime; hundreds of volumes devoted to hobbies, arts, and crafts.

Leo and Diane Dillon received the Caldecott Medal for *Ashanti to Zulu.* They had also won the prize in 1976.

REPRINTED BY PERMISSION OF THE DIAL PRESS

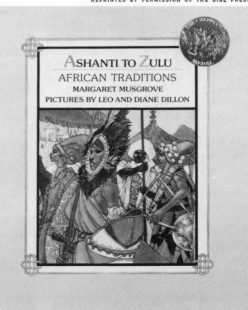

For *Roll of Thunder, Hear My Cry*, a story of black pride in Mississippi during the Depression, Mildred Taylor was awarded the Newbery Medal in 1977.

Also noted was adult dissatisfaction over the outpouring in recent years of novels and nonfiction dealing with divorce, alcoholism, runaways, child molestation, and other sexual deviations. The charge was that such concentration was presenting a distorted view of life. Indeed, the most controversial book of the year was Morton Hunt's *Gay*, which thoroughly surveyed the subject of homosexuality for readers 12 years and older.

The best selling children's books during 1977 were Shel Silverstein's *The Giving Tree*, Richard Scarry's *Best Word Book Ever*, E. B. White's *Charlotte's Web*, *Charlie Brown's Super Book of Questions and Answers* by Charles Schulz, and individual volumes in the Hardy Boys and Nancy Drew series.

For Young Readers. Among the books published during the year these were noteworthy: for the picture book audience (ages 3 to 7) there were *Anno's Counting Book* by Mitsumasa Anno, superbly beautiful, with gentle watercolors showing a town's growth through the seasons and years; Mary Rayner's *Garth Pig and the Ice Cream Lady*, in which a wolf is no match for 10 piglets; Peter Spier's *Noah's Ark*, with its cameo portraits of life within the Biblical ship; William Steig's *Caleb and Kate*, wherein a witch turns a man into a dog; Margot Zemach's retelling of a Yiddish folktale, *It Could Always Be Worse;* Arnold's Lobel's *How the Rooster Saved the Day*, illustrated by Anita Lobel, in which a fowl outwits a robber with a series of ruses; and Philippe Dumas' *The Story of Edward*, about a dapper donkey passing himself off as human.

For those 6 to 10 the best books were Arnold Lobel's *Mouse Soup*, in which a mouse outsmarts a hungry weasel by spinning adventure tales; Mollie Hunter's *A Furl of Fairy Wind*, offering four stories about brownies, changelings, and enchantments; and Bernard Waber's *Good-bye, Funny Dumpy-Lumpy*, five vignettes of an Edwardian cat family.

In the 9-to-12-year-old category the most outstanding books were Laurence Yep's *Child of the Owl,* in which an American-born Chinese girl comes to understand her heritage while living in San Francisco's Chinatown; Natalie Babbitt's *The Eyes of the Amaryllis,* a stark and chilling love and sea story; Russell Baker's hilarious spoof on the Frankenstein tale, *The Upside-Down Man;* and Julia Cunningham's Gothic parable, *Come to the Edge,* about an orphan boy traveling in search of love.

Teen-Age Literature. For teen-agers, the outstanding novels were Robert Cormier's taut, sophisticated suspense tale, *I Am the Cheese;* Vera and Bill Cleaver's *Trial Valley*, with the gutsy Appalachian heroine first introduced in the authors' *Where the Lilies Bloom;* Susan Cooper's *Silver on the Tree,* which completes her five-volume sequence on the struggle between good and evil; M. E. Kerr's *I'll Love You When You're More Like Me,* about a teen-age soap opera star and her boyfriend, who wants to avoid inheriting his father's mortuary business; Robert Lipsyte's *One Fat Summer,* in which a roly-poly boy becomes the target of a small-town roughneck but finds a way to become his own man; and Richard Peck's *Ghosts I Have Been,* featuring a young heroine who has supernatural powers.

Outstanding works of nonfiction for teenagers were Elizabeth Levy's and Tad Richards's *Struggle and Lose, Struggle and Win* on the history of the United Mine Workers; Burton Supree's and Ann Ross' *Bear's Heart*, a 100-year-old record of a Cheyenne Indian's life—leading from the Great Plains to an army prison in Florida—illustrated in delicate pastels and primitive style by the subject, Bear's Heart himself; and David Macaulay's *Castle*, with precisely drawn illustrations and plans of the building of an imaginary 13th-century Welsh castle.

GEORGE A. WOODS
Children's Book Editor, "The New York Times"

Canadian Literature: English

Concern over the possible separation of Quebec from the rest of the country prompted some Canadian writers to look closely at the Quebec question, at the nature of Canadian unity, and at Canadian political leaders, past and present.

Nonfiction. In *Three Scales of Inequality: Perspectives on French-English Relations,* Raymond N. Morris and C. Michael Lanphier discuss the relationship of inequality to cultural distinctiveness. John Saywell's *The Rise of the Parti Québécois* traces the shifting fortunes of the separatist party in Quebec.

Anthony Westell's *The New Society* suggests Canada is moving toward a collective society. *Powertown: Democracy Discarded* by Doris Shackleton claims that federal civil servants in Ottawa, who used to serve the public, are turning into secretive bureaucrats who want to manage, not serve.

Viva Chairman Pierre by Lubor J. Zink is highly critical of Canada's present government, especially Prime Minister Pierre Elliott Trudeau. Also strongly critical of Trudeau and his Liberal government is *The Liberal Idea of Canada* by James Laxer and Robert Laxer.

Former Prime Minister John G. Diefenbaker continues his lively memoirs in the third volume of *One Canada.* Grattan O'Leary tells of a long career as editor and politician in *Recollections of People, Press and Politics.* J. L. Granatstein's *Mackenzie King* is the second in a series, under the editorship of Dr. Kaye Lamb, on Canadian prime ministers. Conrad Black's *Duplessis* exhaustively records the life of the colorful former Quebec premier.

Pierre Berton's 24th book, *The Dionne Years: A Thirties Melodrama,* tells the sad story of the once-famed Dionne quintuplets, born May 28, 1934. Carolyn Gossage's *A Question of Privilege* traces the history of Canada's private schools, with their "persistent image of aristocracy." Warner Troyer's *No Safe Place* is a painstakingly researched record of mercury pollution in northwestern Ontario. It is a disturbing book, suggesting government apathy toward a serious health hazard.

Patricia Morley's *The Comedians* examines the fiction of Hugh Hood and Ruby Wiebe. Jill Vickers' *But Can You Type?*, with statistical material by June Adam, discusses the role women play in Canadian universities and strongly suggests it is an unequal one. *If Teaching Is Important,* edited by Christopher J. Knapper, George L. Geis, Charles E. Pascal, and Bruce M. Shore, discusses the rationale and method of evaluation of university teachers.

Poetry. Leonard Cohen's *Death of a Lady's Man,* his first volume of poetry in five years, is a collection of both traditional and experimental verse. Irving Layton's *The Uncollected Poems: 1936–1959* brings together 130 of his earlier works. *The Selected Poems of Irving Layton,*

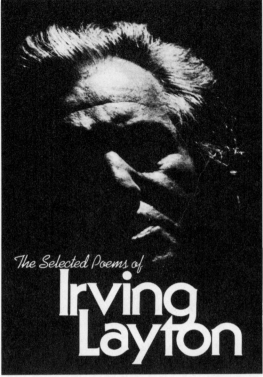

NEW DIRECTIONS

With an introduction by Hugh Kenner, *The Selected Poems of Irving Layton* is a retrospective collection.

edited by Eli Mandel, is a small collection of Layton's best.

Hugh and Ion contains an unfinished narrative poem by 19th-century Canadian poetess Isabella Valancy Crawford, edited by Glenn Clever and published for the first time.

In *Smoked Glass,* his 10th volume of poetry, Alden Nowlan writes with humor and seeming simplicity about life's complexities. Milton Acorn's *Jackpine Sonnets* expresses his love for his country and its people in unexpectedly traditional forms. *A Stone Diary* by Pat Lowther, published more than a year after her death at 40, is her third and best volume. In *The Price of Gold,* Miriam Waddington uses homely images and words to good effect. Robin Skelton's *Because of Love* describes the course of love from the first meeting to final parting. Robert Currie's *Diving Into Fire* tells of boyhood on the edge of a prairie town.

Canadian Poetry—the Modern Era, edited by John Newlove, displays works by 30 writers prominent in Canadian poetry since 1945. *the end uv th world speshul* brings together poems by P. K. Page, Dorothy Livesay, F. R. Scott, and others. *Many Voices,* edited by Marilyn Bowering and David Day, is an anthology of contemporary Indian poetry.

Fiction. Charles Templeton's *Act of God* describes what happens when someone discovers the skeleton of Christ in an old tomb. Morley Callaghan's *Too Close to the Sun* tells of a navy man who decided his head would rule his heart and on his deathbed realizes his mistake. Margaret Atwood's *Dancing Girls and Other Stories* is a collection that explores the human condition in 14 different settings. Jack Hodgins' *The Invention of the World* tells how 115 years ago in Ireland a young woman mates with a black bull-god and gives birth to a son, who emigrates to Canada and founds a settlement off the British Columbia coast called the Revelations Colony of Truth, which eventually breaks up and becomes the Revelation Trailer Park.

Lightly, a first novel by Chipman Hall, convincingly reveals the mind of an 11-year-old boy. Jamie Brown's *Shrewsbury* is the final volume in his trilogy about the powerful Moncrieff family. Carol Shields' second novel, *The Box Garden,* is about a deserted wife in Vancouver. Written in lean, clean prose, Douglas Day's *Journey of the Wolf* deals with a Spanish Civil War veteran's return to modern-day Spain. James Houston's *Ghost Fox* is an exciting story of a white girl's captivity by Indians two centuries ago.

Canadian Short Fiction Anthology, edited by Cathy Ford, and *Toronto Short Stories,* edited by Morris Wolfe and Douglas Daymond, are representative collections of short stories, mostly by well-known Canadian writers.

DAVID SAVAGE
Simon Fraser University

Canadian Literature: Quebec

Three major events marked the past literary season. First, the election victory by the Parti Québécois on Nov. 15, 1976, was not only the end result, that is, the realization—if only partial—of the great dream of independence that has haunted Quebec literature since the beginning of the 1960's, but also a new challenge to writers of every stamp, who henceforth will have to restate their positions in terms of the new-found power and to rethink the nationalist ideology that has inspired them for the past 15 years. It is still too early to say what this readjustment will bring, but one thing is certain: it will happen.

The second important event was the establishment of the Quebec Writers' Union (*Union des écrivains québécois,* or UNEQ) under the presidency of novelist Jacques Godbout. Solely devoted to the professional interests of its 120 members, the union has already launched vigorous campaigns on such issues as authors' rights, the writer and the media, literature and education, and reproduction.

Finally, the suicide on March 15 of novelist Hubert Aquin came as a shock and robbed Quebec literature of one of its most original writers.

Fiction. While the production was abundant, few new novelists appeared. The exceptions were Jean-Yves Soucy who wrote a beautiful woodland tale entitled *Un dieu chasseur* and Lise Lacasse, author of some stirring and cruel short stories collected in *Au défaut de la cuirasse.* Two writers who had not published anything in ten years made notable come-backs: Wilfrid Lemoine, whose *Le Déroulement* is a long interior monologue, and Diane Giguère who in her *Dans les ailes du vent* explores the painful world of a forty-year-old woman.

The best novels, however, were those of well-known authors: Louis-Philippe Hébert, whose *Les Manufactures de machines* is a masterpiece of style and imagination; Yves Thériault who has given us one of the most beautiful books of his mature years, *Moi Pierre Huneau;* Roch Carrier who in his sixth novel, *Il n'y a pas de pays sans grand-père,* has created a character similar to those of Louis Hémon and F.-A. Savard; and Hélène Ouvrard, whose *L'Herbe et le varech* examines the difficulties that writing poses to a conscious woman. One discovery must also be proclaimed: that of forty-year-old Jacques Brossard who by his splendid Kafkaesque novel, *Le Sang du souvenir,* shows himself to be a writer of the first rank.

Poetry. Most memorable were some volumes that confirmed the talents of already well-established poets: *Ici, ailleurs, la lumière* by the "incandescent" Fernand Ouellette; *Gélivures* by Pierre Perrault, a singer of the country and the snows; *Le Prince de sexamour* by Paul Chamberland, who is always attuned to currents of new culture; and *Poèmes 1946–1968,* which won the governor general's prize for Alphonse Piché, the charming disciple of Villon. Among the books of less known though important poets, mention must be made of *Episodes* by Pierre Nepveu, one of the finest of young Quebec writers, and *L'Eau ronde* by Guy Lafond who has been influenced by Maurice Blanchot and Oriental mysticism.

Essays. Three titles deserve attention above all others: *Blocs erratiques 1948–1977* by Hubert Aquin, containing political, literary, and philosophical essays that made a profound impression on intellectual life in Quebec between 1960 and 1970; *Le Roman à l'imparfait* by Gilles Marchotte, which examines the disintegration of traditional forms in the works of four of the most important Quebec novelists of recent years— Gérard Bessette, Réjean Ducharme, Marie-Claire Blais, and Jacques Godbout; and *Rabelais tel quel* by Georges-André Vachon, a penetrating and very personal study of the great Renaissance author's works.

Theater. The number of published plays has much diminished. Notable was the publication of *Sainte Carmen de la Main* and *Damnée Manon sacrée Sandra* by Michel Tremblay which by the author's own acknowledgment conclude the popular *Belles-soeurs* cycle he began nearly ten years ago.

FRANÇOIS RICARD, *McGill University*

English Literature

The silver jubilee of the accession of Elizabeth II caused a number of books on royalty and the British people to be published in Britain. Books on Ireland and various people associated with its struggle for independence were plentiful. Books of poetry burgeoned. The appearance of John Fowles's fourth novel was a major publishing event.

Nonfiction. Three of the best books prompted by the jubilee were John Colville's *The New Elizabethans 1952–1977,* Daniel Counihan's *Royal Progress,* and Robert Lacey's *Majesty: Elizabeth II and the House of Windsor.* Colville recounted the aspirations, troubles, and achievements of Britons during the first quarter-century of Elizabeth's reign. Counihan described the monarch's role and reactions of the public to Elizabeth and her family. Lacey considered the influence on the queen of George V, Edward VIII, and her parents, described her personality, and evaluated her performance.

Two biographies of Charles S. Parnell were among the most important of the books on Irish affairs. R. F. Foster examined the effect on the Irish leader of his forebears and his life in Wicklow. F. S. L. Lyons wrote a definitive biography of Parnell. Ruth Dudley Edward's *Patrick Pearse* is a life of an Anglo-Irish leader of the Easter rebellion, who was executed in 1916. Andrew Boyle's *The Riddle of Erskine Childers* is about another Anglo-Irishman, executed in the troubles of 1922. J. C. Beckett provided a more general study, *The Anglo-Irish Tradition.*

There were several editions of diaries and letters from the earlier part of this century. Anne Olivier Bell began her edition of *The Diary of Virginia Woolf* with Volume I, 1915–1919. Nigel Nicolson and Joanne Trautmann edited the third volume of Woolf's letters, 1923–1928, and C. K. Stead edited *The Letters and Journals of Katherine Mansfield.* Edward David provided glimpses of the inner working of the British government from 1911 to 1915 in *Inside Asquith's Cabinet: the Diaries of Charles Hobhouse.*

Among autobiographies were Peter Ustinov's *Dear Me,* Daphne du Maurier's *Growing Pains: the Shaping of a Writer,* and J. B. Priestley's *Instead of the Trees: A Final Chapter of Autobiography.* The poetess Kathleen Raine concluded her three-volume autobiography with *The Lion's Mouth,* and the philosopher A. J. Ayer wrote of the first 35 years of his life in *Part of My Life. Towards Tomorrow* is the autobiography of Fenner Brockway, a Labour politician. In *A Life of Contrasts,* Diana Mosley (née Mitford) describes her privileged early life, her marriage to Oswald Mosley, leader of the British Fascists, and her imprisonment and exile with him. Max Mallowan's *Mallowan's Memoirs* is about his work as an archaeologist, his experiences in World War II, and his married life of 45 years with Agatha Christie. With the publication of *The Green, Green Grass,* the 24th volume of *The Sensual World,* Rupert Croft-Brooke concluded his autobiography.

Important new studies of famous figures of the past were John Pollock's biography of William Wilberforce, leader of the movement to abolish slavery, Richard B. Fisher's life of Joseph Lister, the originator of antiseptic surgery, and Ruth Hall's life of Marie Stopes, the founder of the first birth-control clinic in Britain. David Marquand's *Ramsay MacDonald* is a biography of the first Labour prime minister and Carolyn Scott's *Dick Sheppard* a life of a popular preacher who was the founder of the Peace Pledge Union in the 1930's. Norman and Jeanne MacKenzie's *The First Fabians* is an account of the founders of the Fabian Society and their contributions to social reform.

Three major biographies of recently deceased writers appeared: Victoria Glendinning's *Elizabeth Bowen,* Humphrey Carpenter's *J. R. R. Tolkien,* and the first volume of P. N. Furbank's *E. M. Forster.* In *Miss Ethel Sands and Her Circle,* Wendy Baron produced a thorough study of Ethel Sand's friendship with many famous writers and artists of the first half of this century. Richard Ingrams described Hugh Kingsmill, Hesketh Pearson, and Malcolm Muggeridge in *God's Apology.*

Among other biographies were John Adlard's *Owen Seaman,* a life of an editor of *Punch;* William Hayter's *Spooner,* a biography of the warden of New College, Oxford, some of whose utterances caused the word "spoonerism" to be added to the English language; Penelope Dell's *Nettie and Sissy,* a description of the unusual life and household of Ethel M. Dell, a successful author of popular romances; David Pryce-Jones's life of Unity Mitford, sister of Diana Mosley, who visited Adolf Hitler with her; John Lehmann's *Edward Lear and His World;* and Mark Holloway's *Norman Douglas.*

Interesting works of social history were Harvey Pitcher's *When Miss Emmie Was in Russia,* an account of the services of English governesses in that country; Alan Lloyd's *The Great Prize Fight,* a description of a 42-round battle in 1860 between the English and American champions; Roger Longrigg's *The English Squire and His Sport;* and David C. Itzkowitz's *Peculiar Privilege: A Social History of English Fox-Hunting.*

Among books of literary history and criticism were A. T. Tolley's *The Poetry of the Thirties,* Derek Stanford's *Inside the Forties,* William H. Pritchard's *Seeing Through Everything: English Writers 1918–1940,* Raymond Williams's *Marxism and Literature,* T. B. Tomlinson's *The English Middle-Class Novel,* and Jina Politi's *The Novel and Its Presuppositions.*

Three books that strongly conveyed the individuality of their authors were Geoffrey Grigson's *The Goddess of Love,* a celebration of

Popular new works by English authors included John Le Carré's *The Honourable Schoolboy* and John Fowles' *Daniel Martin.*

ANDREAS HEUMANN

JACOB SUTTON

woman and heterosexual love; Lawrence Durrell's *Sicilian Carousel,* a description of a bus tour of Sicily undertaken by Durrell in memory of a deceased friend; and Francis Huxley's *The Raven and the Writing Desk,* a book of witty nonsense, logic, riddles, and puns.

Fiction. Daniel Martin, in John Fowles's novel of that name, returns to Oxford from Hollywood, where he has become a successful filmscript writer, to reencounter his past and his divorced wife's sister, whom he has believed he should have married. He travels with her to Egypt in search of material for a script, while considering also a novel that he wants to write, and examining himself. In the process, problems of the relationship of life and fiction are posed.

John Le Carré's *The Honourable Schoolboy* is another long, ambitious novel. A spy story with a complex plot, it is set in England and the Orient. Le Carré's main characters feel that Britain, as well as its secret service, needs to be restored.

Margaret Drabble examines her country's condition in *The Ice Age* through 12, generally unhappy, characters of the 1970's. Caroline Blackwood describes the declining energies of a family in *Great Granny Webster* and hints that her story has a wider significance.

Paul Scott's *Staying On* is the story of a British colonel who chose to remain in India after that country gained its independence. Olivia Manning's characters in *The Danger Tree* are stationed in Egypt during World War II. Benedict Kiely's *Proxopera,* Francis Stuart's *A Hole in the Head,* Jennifer Johnston's *Shadows on Our Skin,* and David Martin's *The Ceremony of Innocence* are set in the troubled Ulster of today.

Other notable novels were J. R. R. Tolkien's *The Silmarillion,* edited by Christopher Tolkien from his father's manuscripts, Richard Adams's *The Plague of Dogs,* Barbara Pym's *Quartet in Autumn,* Keith Aldritt's *The Lover Next Door,* Beryl Bainbridge's *Injury Time,* P. H. Newby's *Kith,* Stanley Middleton's *Ends and Means,* Gordon Giles's *Enemies,* Eva Figes's *Nelly's Vision,* and Penelope Shuttle's *Rainsplitter in the Zodiac Garden.*

Poetry. Ted Hughes published a long narrative poem, *Gaudete.* Originally intended as a film script, it is about a village where the vicar has been supernaturally replaced by a diabolic double, who persuades the women of his flock to assist him in the procreation of a savior. Village and villagers are memorably portrayed as the story is told.

Another narrative poem was Anthony Burgess's *Moses,* a blank verse rendition of the biblical story. F. T. Prince's *Afterword on Rupert Brooke* is a consideration, written in the free verse syllabics of Robert Bridges, of Brooke's career.

Edward Morgan's *The New Divan* is in part a tribute to the medieval Persian poet Hafiz. It is also a modern work of concrete and, at times, surrealistic poetry. Kathleen Raine's *The Oval Portrait* commemorates her mother in poems that describe milieu and states of mind impressionistically. Anthony Thwaite's *A Portion for Foxes* is an entertaining collection of verse by a poet who has traveled and read very widely.

Among books published by newer poets, Peter Redgrove's *Ten Poems* is distinguished by its imagery and its concern for individuals, Neil Powell's *At the Edge* by careful craftsmanship, Robert Well's *The Winter's Task* by the intensity of its landscapes, and John Holloway's *Planet of the Winds* by wit and variety.

Good poetry was again produced in Ireland, notably Paul Muldoon's *Mules,* poems of landscape, strife, and love; Andrew Waterman's *From the Other Country,* filled with details that are often unpleasant; and Tom Paulin's *A State of Justice,* stoical poems about Ulster.

Among books by Scottish poets were Norman MacCaig's *Tree of Strings,* a collection distinguished by accurate observation and quiet humor, and George MacKay Brown's *Selected Poems,* about the Orkney Islands.

J. K. JOHNSTONE
University of Saskatchewan

Two French literary celebrities: Patrick Grainville, winner of the coveted Prix Goncourt, and Raphaèle Billetdoux, recipient of the Prix Interallié.

French Literature

The Novel. Once again there was evidence in 1977 of the generally healthy state of the novel —that which tells a good story and can have romantic overtones. Among the best sellers of that nature were some by well-known authors. Michel Déon continued, in the vein of *Un Taxi mauve* and *Le Jeune homme vert,* the adventures of his hero under the title *Les Vingt ans du jeune homme vert.* Maurice Denuzière wrote *Louisiane,* a well documented, lively, popular novel which has 19th-century America as a background. Lucien Bodard published *La Vallée des roses,* a romanticized reconstruction of pre-Mao China. Françoise Sagan contributed *Le Lit défait,* the bitter-sweet love story of an author and an actress. Mention must also be made of Romain Gary's *Clair de femme.*

Literary Prizes. The Prix Goncourt was awarded to Patrick Grainville's *Les Flamboyants,* the colorful story of a mad African king. Raphaèle Billetdoux won the Prix Interallié for her *Prends garde à la douceur des choses,* a psychological novel about three sisters and their loves. Michel Henry's *L'Amour les yeux fermés* (Renaudot Prize) is a piece of political, apocalyptic, anti-Marxist fiction. Marc Cholodenko's *Les Etats du désert* (Prix Médicis) is a long, ambitious novel within a novel. Marie-Louise Haumont's *Le Trajet* (Femina Prize) is an intelligent, well-written, traditional novel about a day in the life of a 36-year-old woman.

New Writers. Among new novelists who attracted attention was Serge Doubrovsky, a well-known professor and critic, who wrote a long introspective book entitled *Fils.* Noëlle Loriot's *Un Père singulier* treats homosexuality as seen and lived by a young girl. Gérard Guégan's *Père et fils* is a Flaubertian "Tour de France" by a Bouvard-type father and his Pécuchet-type son.

Short Stories. The best collections of short stories were Goncourt laureate Jacques Chessex' *Le Séjour des morts,* Roger Grenier's *La Salle de rédaction* (nostalgic but somewhat bitter portrayal of a journalist's life), Henri Thomas' *Les Tours de Notre-Dame* and Daniel Boulanger's *L'Autre rive.*

Nonfiction. A number of works were devoted to personal reminiscences and memoirs. The most popular of these was *Le Temps des amours* by the late Marcel Pagnol, a book filled with the nostalgic flavor of Provence; three members of the acting profession, Michèle Morgan (*Avec ces yeux-là*), Daniel Gélin (*Deux ou trois rues qui sont les miennes*), and Edwige Feuillère (*Les Feux de la mémoire*), all spoke of their years in the theater and the motion pictures. In a class by itself is Marguerite Yourcenar's *Archives du Nord,* the beautifully written saga of the author's family. André Malraux, the late novelist, critic, art historian, and statesman, had left a kind of literary testament which was published posthumously under the title *L'Homme précaire et la littérature.*

The runaway best-seller of the year was *Le Mal français* by essayist and statesman Alain Peyrefitte. It is essentially a criticism of centralization as practiced in France since Louis XIV. Peyrefitte analyzes its defects and proposes certain well-considered remedies. Other political essays were *Made in France,* by humorist Pierre Daninos, *Le Bonheur est dans le pré* by Pierre Bonte, and *La France et ses mensonges,* in which François de Closets attacks the taboos which, in his opinion, block French society: money, drink, dogmatism, and corporatism. Roland

Barthes, high priest of the new criticism in France, wrote *Fragment d'un discours amoureux,* an essay bearing the stamp of his concerns with structuralism and linguistics.

Poetry. Three well-known poets and a less known one published collections of verse worthy of notice. They were André Du Bouchet, author of *Air,* a tightly-woven crystalline work; Philippe Jaccottet (*A la Lumière d'hiver*); Yves Bonnefoy (*Rue Traversière*); and Tristan Cabral (*Du Pain et des pierres*).

PIERRE BRODIN, *Lycée Français de New York*

German Literature

The rift between the two German literatures was greatly widened in 1977 by the expatriation of prominent authors from East Germany.

West German Fiction. The interesting narratives of 1977 often elucidated the past of German Jewry and the fate of nonconformists under Nazi rule. Novels by Wolfgang Koeppen (*Jugend*), Matthias Schröder (*Der Krähenbaum*), and Jurek Becker (*Das Opfer*) dealt with specific cases, while Hans Sahl's reedited book of 1959, *Die Wenigen und die Vielen,* endeavored to portray a whole generation.

Günter Grass' artful novel, *Der Butt,* belonged to a different category. But its plea for the abolition of discredited patriarchy sounded unconvincing. New books by Gabriele Wohmann, Peter Handke, and Peter Härtlin were not particularly impressive. Two Austrian authors, Gernot Wolfgruber (*Herrenjahre*) and Michael Scharang (*Sohn eines Landarbeiters*) offered debatable accounts of working-class problems. More ambitious were their compatriot Brigitte Schwaiger (*Wie kommt das Salz ins Meer?*) and the Swiss novelist Herman Burger (*Schilten*), who tried to fathom the whole riddle of existence.

Wolf Biermann (*left*), shown here with Heinrich Böll, won for his songs an enthusiastic audience among the young.

GERMAN INFORMATION CENTER

GERMAN INFORMATION CENTER

A book from the pen of Günter Grass is always a publishing event, but his new novel received mixed reviews.

Nonfiction. Kurt Tucholsky's posthumous *Briefe aus dem Schweigen, 1932–1935* and Fritz Molden's *Fepolinski und Waschlapski auf dem berstenden Stern* contributed significantly to the history of the German resistance. Werner Maser, in *Nürnberg, Tribunal der Sieger,* approached the anti-Nazi trial as an objective historian. Female aspirations were critically examined in Marieluise Janssen-Jurreit's study, *Sexismus,* while Julius Hackethal's shocker, *Auf des Messers Schneide,* sensationally attacked German surgery. Elias Canetti's autobiography, *Die gerettete Zunge,* should also be considered and not forgotten.

Drama. Among the many new plays, only Botho Strauss' *Trilogie des Wiedersehens,* a take-off on the diffuse character of reality, appeared destined to last.

Poetry. With the exception of Ernst Meister's *Im Zeitspalt,* the only poetry of consequence was written by East German authors, among whom Sarah Kirsch (*Rückenwind*), Karl Mickel, Paul Wühr, and Wolf Wondraschek tried to come to grips with Communist reality. Of the production of prominent expatriates, Wolf Biermann's songs found enthusiastic reception among the young generation, and Reiner Kunze's prose sketches, *Die wunderbaren Jahre,* achieved bestseller status in West Germany. Thomas Brasch wrote *Vor den Vätern sterben die Söhne,* a pitiless account of the lives of Communist workingmen.

East German Fiction. Hermann Kant's novel, *Der Aufenthalt,* inadequately tried to describe his development from a bourgeois into a convinced Communist. Equally retrospective was Christina Wolf's *Kindheitsmuster*.

ERNST ROSE
Author of "A History of German Literature"

Italian Literature

As in every literary community whose social basis shows conflicting signs of crisis and fruitful transition, literature in Italy in 1977 moved gingerly between the poles of political and social agitation on the one side and cultivation of interiority and tradition on the other.

Renewal of Literary Language. The movements of social protest, which exploded with a force unknown since the late 1960's, left behind them a plethora of new slogans and epigrammatic statements revealing a need for renovation of the literary language. A partial attempt to answer this need was the successful development of the *Interviste* formula by the Laterza publishing house: a series of slim books, each containing a monographic interview in depth with a leading political or social figure. But, as the stylistic grayness of these and similar books shows, literary expression of these matters tends to be unexciting.

On the other hand, there was a resurgence of interest in works of an occultist, astrological, or religious-spiritualistic character and a renewed approach to the literary tradition, exemplified for instance by the debate on the authenticity of a 1586 play, *Intrichi d'Amore*, attributed to the great Italian poet Torquato Tasso. The cultivation of tradition is also the idea behind projects such as the new 13-volume *Storia d'Italia* (by the U.T.E.T. publishing house), whose first volume has just appeared. This comes on the heels of the completed *Storia d'Italia* by Einaudi, which in turn heralded (with perhaps too great a fanfare) his new *Enciclopedia,* planned in 12 volumes. In the meantime, 16 volumes have already appeared (and the whole collection will probably be completed in a couple of years) of what is probably the most thorough and scholarly edition of Nietzsche's works in any language—including German— edited by Giorgio Colli and Mazzino Montinari.

Belles Lettres. On the more specifically literary scene, there still is felt what can be termed a nostalgia for Pier Paolo Pasolini, whose death in 1975 made people realize that there is no major, intellectually nonconformist novelist or poet working in Italy at this point. Six volumes of Pasolini's *Opere* were issued, and collections of letters (*Lettere agli amici, 1941–1945; Lettere luterane*) and articles (*Le belle bandiere*) also appeared.

Some 1977 novels to be mentioned are Guido Morselli's posthumous *Dissipatio H.G.,* Cesare Zavattini's *La notte che ho dato uno schiaffo a Mussolini*, Leonardo Sciascia's *I pugnalatori*, Toni Maraini's *Anno 1424*, Mario Lu-

netta's *I Ratti D'Europa*, and the dramatic monologue *Edipus* by Giovanni Testori. More traditional are Davide Lajolo's *Vedere l'erba dalla parte delle radici*, Fulvio Tomizza's *La miglior vita*, Carlo Sgorlon's *Gli dei torneranno*, Bruno Modugno's *Re di macchia*, and Piero Chiara's short stories, *Le corna del diavolo*.

Poetry was represented by several collections: *Il tradimento* by Tommaso Landolfi, *Il mondo dei creditori* by Giovanni Giudici, and *Marzo e le sue idi* by Bartolo Cattafi. Luca Canale's *Intenzione d'amore,* and Maria Luisa Spaziani's *Transito con catene* should also be mentioned.

PAOLO VALESIO, *Yale University*

Japanese Literature

Fiction. In 1976, some newcomers in their early twenties won prestigious prizes and rang up phenomenal sales with their starkly original novelettes. Hidetoshi Sotooka's *Hokkikō (Northbound)* remained a best seller until April 1977. Kenji Nakagami, the most original of the group, won praise for his first full-length novel, *Kareki Nada (The Sea of Kareki)* early in 1977. Ryū Murakami attracted attention with a graphic fantasy fiction, *Umi no Mukō de Sensō ga Hajimaru (War Begins on the Other Side of the Sea)*. Another newcomer, Masahiro Mita, joined their ranks by winning one of the two Akutagawa prizes for his novelette, *Bokutte Nani (What Am I?)*. These writers are read with interest because they represent fresh ideas by a generation reared on a steady diet of American movies, rock music, and postwar literature. The Naoki Prize was awarded to another relative newcomer to fiction, Kyōzo Miyoshi, for *Kosodate Gokko (A Child-Rearing Game)*.

Nonfiction. The works that won critical acclaim were chiefly biographies, literary histories, and social commentaries. Among the first, Hotta Yoshie's outstanding biography of the Spanish painter Goya won the Osaragi Prize. A life of a 16th-century warrior, Yukinaga Konishi, by Endo Shūsaku, also won high praise. The most notable literary histories were Shinichirō Nakamura's *Taishō Sakka Ron (On Taishō Period Writers)* and Ken Hirano's *Shōwa Bungaku Shiron (On Shōwa Literature)*. Masao Maruyama's perceptive essays on political thought, *Senchū to Sengo no Aida (During and After the War)* won the Osaragi Prize.

Poetry. Both tanka and haiku continued to be enormously popular. Half a million tanka were submitted (1976) by 48,000 persons for an anthology to be published in 1978. A notable event of 1977 was the publication of *Haiku Jiten Kinsei (Dictionary of Haiku, Pre-Modern Period)* by Seishū Matsuo. A debate concerning the nature of modern haiku and the rules of its composition continued, with no agreement in sight. In "modern" free verse, little change was noted from previous years.

EMIKO SAKURAI, *University of Hawaii*

Soviet Literature

In literature, as in all other spheres of life in the Soviet Union, 1977 was a year strongly marked by the 60th anniversary of the October Revolution. As in 1967, the anniversary was the occasion of numerous debates and official appeals to those in the world of creative arts to realize and propagate the achievements of the revolution.

It is natural that publishing activities in this commemorative year were to a large extent retrospective and that the first place was taken by Soviet classics, which often were published in editions reaching 1.5 million copies. Analysis of the figures, however, shows great variations, depending on the ideological significance of the author and of the particular work.

Beginning with the "father of Soviet literature," Maxim Gorky, his *Mother* and *The Life of Klim Samgin* were published in large editions, while printings afforded such once controversial or banned writers as Boris Pilnyak (*Selected Works*) and Ivan Bunin (*The Village*) varied from 4 to 40 thousand. In the case of such works as Dmitri Furmanov's *Chapayev* or Aleksei Tolstoy's *Road to Calgary* the pressrun was from 500,000 to 1.5 million. Special attention was lavished on one of the veterans of Soviet literature, Aleksandr Fadeyev. His novel, *The Young Guard*, glorifying the partisan movement during the last war, was again printed in 400,000 copies. To commemorate his 75th anniversary, the Institute of World Literature of the Soviet Academy prepared a volume, *A. A. Fadeyev*, which contains hitherto unpublished speeches, letters, essays on his writings, and a chronology of his works. Considering that Fadeyev, perhaps longer than any other writer, played a key role in the activities of the powerful Association of Soviet Writers, the volume is an important document in Soviet literary history. Another veteran writer and literary "statesman," Konstantin Fedin, who earlier in the year celebrated his 85th birthday, died suddenly in July. He was honored in many speeches and articles.

Georgi Markov, Yuri Bondarev, and Valentin Rasputin are the writers most often mentioned and discussed in recent literary journals and public debates. Rasputin's story, *Parting with Maria*, in particular, has been the object of lively discussions on the subject of "private" and "public" feelings of literary heroes. The same is true of Sergei Voronin, winner of the Gorky Literary Prize for his volume of stories, *Maria's Stone*. The works of these writers are printed in millions of copies.

In the field of poetry, mention should be made of two volumes by Yevgeni Yevtushenko (*In Full Flight* and *Windy People*) and books by Yevgeni Vinokurov (*Home and World*) and Andrei Voznesensky (*Master of Glass Painting*). Among the older poets, Pavel Antokolsky, who turned 75 in 1977, enjoyed a renaissance. Boris

TASS FROM SOVFOTO

Valentin Rasputin, 40-year-old winner of the Soviet State Prize, is one of the USSR's most talked-about novelists.

Pasternak's *Verses and Poems* was published in a small edition. Eduard Bagritsky's *Verses and Poems* also recalled that forgotten fine poet.

Not only written poetry but also poetry readings have always played an important role in Russia and other Slavic countries. Westerners invited to private parties are often surprised how easily these gatherings can turn into poetry readings (or rather recitals of poems learned by heart). The works recited are frequently poems that would not be allowed to be published, and this gives the gatherings a double significance. Perhaps against this background, the Moscow television in October 1976 decided to introduce a special program of poetry. The readings and discussions were initiated with the appearance of Pavel Antokolsky and have since been a regular part of the program. Interestingly, though not surprisingly, considering the poetic profile of Antokolsky, he emphasized the importance of Vladimir Mayakovsky and Aleksandr Blok as the true source of inspiration to civic poetry in the Soviet Union.

ZBIGNIEW FOLEJEWSKI
University of Ottawa

Spanish and Spanish-American Literature

The year 1977 must be counted a positive one for Hispanic literature. For the highlight of the year was the awarding of the Nobel Prize in Literature to Vicente Aleixandre of Spain. The 79-year-old surrealist poet, little known outside Spain, was cited for his "creative poetic writing, which, with roots in the traditions of Spanish lyric verse and in modern currents, illuminates

UPI

Vicente Aleixandre, a 79-year-old Spanish surrealist poet, was awarded the 1977 Nobel Prize in Literature.

man's condition in the cosmos and in present-day society." In addition, Latin America's most prestigious award, the Rómulo Gallegos Prize, went to Mexico's Carlos Fuentes for his *Terra Nostra*. Important works by internationally recognized masters also appeared.

Fiction. The lucrative Planeta Prize went to Jesús Torbado's *En el día de hoy*, which interestingly reverses the results of the Spanish Civil War, and introduces Ernest Hemingway as a central character. The Ateneo de Sevilla Prize was awarded to Carlos Rojas' *Memorias inéditas de José Antonio Primo de Rivera*, the simulated memoirs of Spain's mythified Fascist leader. The Crítica Prize was received by Rosa Chacel, the long-exiled Spanish novelist, for her *Barrio de maravillas*. Other prizes went to lesser known writers: the Nadal Prize to Raúl Guerra Garrido's *Lectura insólita de el capital;* the Central American Award to Panama's Gloria Guarda for her *El último juego;* and the Casa de las Américas Prize to Cuba's Manlio Argueta's *Caperucita en la zona roja*.

Major novelists publishing during the year included the Argentinian Julio Cortázar, *Alguien anda por ahí;* and the Spaniards Juan Benet, *En el estado,* and Gonzalo Torrente Ballester, *Fragmentos de Apocalípsis*. Among well-known writers with novels in 1977 were the Peruvian Luis Alberto Sánchez, *El pecado de Olazábal;* the Colombian Eduardo Caballero Calderón, *Historia de dos hermanos;* the Argentinian Héctor Bicenciotti, *Detrás del rostro que nos mira;* and the Spaniards Francisco García Pavón, *Los nacionales,* Javier del Amo, *Del cielo cuelgan ciudades,* and Luis Mateo Díez with his novels *Blasón de muérdago* and *Apócrifo del clavel y*

la espina. Younger novelists with well-received books included the Dominican Carlos Federico Pérez, *La ciudad herida;* the Argentinian Aristíbulo Echegaray, *El holocausto;* and the Spaniards Salvador García Jiménez, *Odio sobre cenizas,* and Ana María Badell, *¡Hasta mañana, dolor!*

Significant shorter fiction appearing in 1977 included several prize-winning pieces: the Spaniard Antonio Segundo del Olmo's *Largo trayecto* (Gabriel Miró Prize); the Uruguayan Cristina Peri Rossi's *Ulva lactuca y cotras* (Pérez Galdós Award); and the Mexican Guillermo Samperio's *Miedo ambiente* (Casa de las Américas Prize). Important collections of stories include Juan Benet's *Cuentos completos;* Alfonso Martínez Mena's *Anti-figuraciones;* and the Argentinian Syria Poletti's *Taller de imaginería*.

Nonfiction. Important contributions in literary criticism were Francisco Márquez Villanueva's *Relección de literatura medieval;* Carlos Alvar's *La poesía trovadoresca en España y Portugal;* José Luis Tejada's *Rafael Alberti, entre la tradición y la vanguardia;* and Tomás Yerro's *Aspectos técnicos y estructurales de la novela española actual*. Significant essays published were Jorge Luis Borges' *Gente y la actualidad;* Marta Portal's *Proceso narrativo de la revolución mexicana;* Enrique Gil Calvo's *La novela de este mundo,* which was awarded the Anagram Prize; and the Chilean Alejandro Wither Velázquez' *Los trabajos y los días Recabarren,* which received the Casa de las Américas Prize.

Poetry. Major prizes for poetry were awarded as follows: the Adonais Prize, to Jorge G. Aranguren's *De fuegos, tigres, ríos;* the Angaro Prize, to Walter González Peneles' *Bosque de espejos;* the Aldebarán Award, to José Antonio Moreno's *Razón de la presencia;* the Leopoldo Panero Prize, to Angel García López' *Mester andalusí;* the Francisco de Quevedo Prize, to Salvador Pérez Valiente's *Con odio, con temor, con ira;* the Crítica Award, to the Mexican Octavio Paz' *Vuelta;* and the prestigious Cervantes Prize, to Jorge Guillen's *Aire nuestro*.

Major poets who published during the year were Claudio Rodríguez, *El vuelo de la ceremonia;* Juan Rejano, the long-exiled poet, *Antología de urgencia;* and Francisco Brines' celebrated *Insistencias de Luzbel*. Impressive first incursions into poetry were made by the novelist Juan García Hortelano, *Echarse las pecas a la espalda,* and the dramatist Alfonso Sastre, *Balada de Carabanchel y otros poemas celulares*. Other poets with well-received books included José Antonio Gabriel y Galán, *Descartes mentía;* the Chilean Lidia Alfaro Rojas, *Tiempo de Corriones;* the Venezuelan Alberto José Pérez, *Los gestos tardíos;* the Mexican Bertha María Díaz Olmo, *El agua insomne;* and the Spaniards Eugenio Bueno, *De mar a mar,* Antonio Rubio, *Parentesco,* and Javier Salvago, *Canciones de amor amargo.*

ALFRED RODRIGUEZ
The University of New Mexico

LONDON

Almost everything was reversed in London in 1977, the year of Queen Elizabeth's silver jubilee. Things that underwent major change included the weather, political control of the Greater London Council, the fortunes of the Stock Exchange, and even the policy of dispersing office jobs to the provinces.

Politics. The city's socialist administration was defeated by the Conservatives. The new council immediately cancelled plans to build new suburb housing and resolved to concentrate resources on the neglected inner city areas. At the same time, the central government, which is controlled by the Labour Party, reversed previous policy of the last decade and ordered the Location of Offices Bureau to attempt to attract office jobs into central London rather than disperse them to the provinces. The bureau was told to concentrate on getting multinational and overseas companies to establish major administration centers in the capital. Meanwhile, a glut of offices was rapidly being rented and financial institutions began taking on new development projects. Trammell Crow, a U. S. development group, began preliminary work on a £300 million ($540 million) trade mart complex in a derelict docklands area.

Labor Relations. A strike at film processing works over union recognition entered its second year. Mass picketing frequently led to violent confrontations with police, but despite the recommendations of a Court of Enquiry and the boycott of the factory by other unions, the factory owner refused to recognize the strikers' union.

Royal Silver Jubilee. Despite one of the wettest summers on record, which followed the drought of 1976, the celebrations in honor of the Queen's jubilee brought another big influx of foreign tourists. Londoners themselves took to the streets to hold open air parties to celebrate in a fashion not seen since Queen Elizabeth was crowned in 1953.

See also ART—SPECIAL REPORT: THE NEW MUSEUM OF LONDON; GREAT BRITAIN.

DAVID BREWERTON
Formerly, "The Daily Telegraph," London

LOS ANGELES

Elections, educational policies, urban redevelopment, and a drought dominated Los Angeles public affairs in 1977.

Elections. Mayor Thomas Bradley was elected to a second four-year term with little more than token opposition. Predictions of a vigorous campaign centering on public transportation, urban redevelopment, and the tax rate were wrong. Voter turnout was low. In council races, an incumbent was unseated in one district and a young liberal replaced a retiring older conservative in another, but issues were parochial or general.

In Board of Education races, which took place in the midst of an effort to find a racial integration plan acceptable to the courts, two incumbents were reelected, one an opponent of busing, the other a moderate. The board's strongest advocate of busing for integration was badly defeated in a contest that was a virtual referendum on the issue.

Government and Politics. For the first time, Los Angeles had a municipal budget in excess of $1 billion (U. S.). Property tax rates were increased, but there were fewer organized tax protests than in the previous year. City political issues, in general, were less intense.

After months of effort, the Board of Education sent to the Superior Court a proposed plan for the integration of schools, but Judge Paul Egly rejected it as inadequate and instructed the board to try further. The board also approved a desegregation plan for the teachers to replace the highly unpopular lottery assignment system used last year. The new plan is based on seniority. High school reading-test scores continued their long downward slide. Elementary scores remained basically unchanged.

Drought. A serious drought in northern California resulted in political pressure to reduce water used in the south, which normally draws a large amount of Sierra Nevada runoff. A Los Angeles rationing plan easily met a 10% savings goal.

Urban Renewal. The city's Community Redevelopment Agency finally announced a 1986 completion date for the controversial Bunker Hill project, begun in 1959. The 1,500-room Bonaventure Hotel was completed, and the area is expected to yield greatly increased tax revenues. It is located between the Civic Center and the financial district. A downtown redevelopment project, immediately to the south, was begun.

Los Angeles Philharmonic. The Los Angeles Philharmonic Orchestra announced the appointment, beginning in the fall of 1978, of Carlo Maria Giulini as its new music director. He replaces Zubin Mehta, who will move to New York.

Death of Powers. Francis Gary Powers, who gained notoriety as the pilot of a U-2 spy plane downed over the USSR in 1960, was killed, along with his cameraman, in a helicopter crash on August 11. He had served KNBC-TV as a pilot-reporter for local weather and freeway conditions.

Sports. In March, for the first time since 1967, UCLA failed to win the NCAA West Regional basketball title. The Lakers won the Pacific division of the National Basketball Association for the first time in three years, but lost to the Portland Trail Blazers in the Western Conference finals. The U. S. Olympics Committee in September selected Los Angeles as the site of the 1984 summer games.

CHARLES R. ADRIAN
University of California, Riverside

UPI

Richard Tonry (D-La.), left, and an aide smile in spite of the former congressman's defeat in a special primary.

LOUISIANA

Louisiana was torn by political scandals in 1977. Investments in new industries were up, although unemployment also increased.

Scandals. Former Congressman Richard Tonry was sentenced to 12 months in federal prison after he pleaded guilty to accepting illegal campaign contributions and promising federal jobs in exchange for political support. Tonry's 1976 opponent, New Orleans City Councilman James Moreau, had claimed fraud after Tonry's narrow victory, and in 1977 Tonry resigned to run for reelection as a House committee was about to recommend his removal. Tonry was defeated in the Democratic primary. Republican Robert Livingston won the general election.

Gov. Edwin Edwards was named as having received funds from Korean influence peddler Tongsun Park, who was later indicted by a U. S. grand jury. Edwards, a former congressman, admitted that his wife had received $10,000 from Park. It was later revealed that Edwards' brother had accepted $10,000 from a Park associate for Edwards' 1971 gubernatorial campaign. Former Congressman Otto Passman

--- **LOUISIANA · Information Highlights** ---

Area: 48,523 square miles (125,675 km²).
Population (1976 est.): 3,841,000.
Chief Cities (1970 census): Baton Rouge, the capital, 165,963; New Orleans, 593,471; Shreveport, 182,064.
Government (1977): *Chief Officers*—governor, Edwin W. Edwards (D); lt. gov., James E. Fitzmorris, Jr. (D). *Legislature*—Senate, 39 members; House of Representatives, 105 members.
Education (1976–77): *Enrollment*—public elementary schools, 581,588 pupils; public secondary, 257,911; nonpublic, 165,900; colleges and universities, 148,-335 students. *Public school expenditures*, $1,063,-700,000 ($1,153 per pupil).
State Finances (fiscal year 1976): *Revenues*, $3,497,-916,000; *expenditures*, $3,412,868,000.
Personal Income (1976): $20,762,000,000; per capita, $5,405.
Labor Force (July 1977): *Nonagricultural wage and salary earners*, 1,303,900; *unemployed*, 115,400 (7.6% of total force).

denied a published report that Park had given him $190,000.

Finally, U. S. Attorney Gerald Gallinghouse began to investigate alleged corruption in Jefferson Parish, New Orleans' bedroom community.

Economic Developments. New plants and expansions for the first half of 1977 almost equaled the total investments in 1976. By mid-1977, capital investments, as reflected in tax exemptions and bonds granted, totaled $1.088 billion, compared with $1.108 billion for all of 1976. However, nonagricultural employment fell from 1.59 million to 1.31 million, raising unemployment from 7.3% to 7.6%.

Several hotel chains, including Hilton, Marriott, and Hyatt, expanded or built new facilities in New Orleans, prompting officials to say that the city, with its new hotels and the Superdome, is ready for a national political convention. The Hyatt Corporation, which built its huge luxury hotel next to the dome, took over management of the state-owned facility, which had irregularities in its operations.

Government and Politics. The legislature granted a teachers' pay raise and passed tougher criminal penalties and a "bill of rights" for mental patients. The Equal Rights Amendment to the U. S. Constitution failed in committee.

A black man was elected mayor of New Orleans for the first time when Judge Ernest Morial, the first black to be elected to the state House in the 20th century, defeated Joseph DiRosa in a runoff.

JOSEPH W. DARBY III
The Times-Picayune, New Orleans

LUXEMBOURG

The government's campaign to counteract the slump in the European steel industry, which so sharply depressed Luxembourg's gross national product (GNP) in 1975, is showing positive results. The slippage in steel production, which still accounts for a quarter of the GNP, was compensated for by growth in the banking, tourism, and services sectors. The last now provides 48% of the duchy's employment, surpassing industry's 46%. The GNP increased by 7.1% in 1976 (3% at constant 1970 prices), and the 2–3% growth rate anticipated for 1977 was expected to return it to the 1974 level. The steel and synthetic fiber industries, however, will remain troubled. The inflation rate fell from 9.7% in 1976 to 7.6% in 1977.

Economic Planning. In an effort to support full-employment policies, representatives of the government, labor unions, and employers met to construct a three-year plan for economic stimulus. A National Society for Credit and Investment has been formed to recruit foreign investments and to encourage expansion by resident firms. Overtime work is banned, as is additional immigration of foreign labor. Year-round tourism will be stimulated by construction of a

—— LUXEMBOURG · Information Highlights ——
Official Name: Grand Duchy of Luxembourg.
Area: 999 square miles (2,586 km²).
Population (1977 est.): 362,000.
Chief Cities (1975 est.): Luxembourg, the capital, 78,-800; Esch-sur-Alzette, 27,700; Differdange, 18,300.
Government: *Head of state,* Jean, grand duke (acceded 1964). *Head of government,* Gaston Thorn, prime minister (took office June 18, 1974). *Legislature* (unicameral)—Chamber of Deputies.
Monetary Unit: Franc (35.72 francs equal U. S.$1, Aug. 1977).
Manufacturing (major products): Iron and steel, chemicals, fertilizers, textiles, nonferrous metals.
Major Agricultural Products: Barley, wheat, oats, grapes, potatoes.

combined casino and conference center. The government will further increase its high investment level, especially in public housing.

Affluence and Stability. The country remains one of the most affluent in Europe, although its economy is highly dependent upon those of its neighbors. The Democratic-Socialist Workers' party coalition cabinet of Gaston Thorn has proved stable. When Deputy Prime Minister Raymond Vouel accepted a post with the European Economic Community in July 1976, he was succeeded by Benny Berg, while the former editor-in-chief of the daily *Tageblatt,* Jacques Poos, was appointed minister of finance.

Death. Prince Charles, younger brother of Grand Duke Jean, died suddenly in July. He was 49 years old.

JONATHAN E. HELMREICH
Allegheny College

MAINE

Indian Land Claim. More important than any other affair during 1977 was the claim of the Penobscot and Passamaquoddy Indian tribes to 12,000,000 acres (4,850,000 ha) of land and $300,000,000 in damages. The claim is based on an alleged violation by Massachusetts of a provision of the Trade and Intercourse acts of 1793 and 1796, which forbade land acquisitions from Indians by states without congressional approval. Since Maine was part of Massachusetts until 1820, Maine, it is contended, inherited any liability of Massachusetts.

In January, the U. S. Department of Justice revealed its intention to sue Maine on behalf of the tribes and to seek ejectment of 350,000 Maine citizens from the claim area. In March, President Carter appointed retired Georgia Supreme Court Justice William Gunter as a fact finder to recommend a plan for an out-of-court settlement. In July, Gunter recommended the tribes be awarded $25,000,000, if they dropped their claim to private lands, and that the State of Maine grant them 100,000 acres (40,400 ha) of public land, or, if the state chose to reject the plan, that the state and the tribes be allowed to try the case in court on its merits, with 500,000 acres (202,000 ha) of public land as the prize. Both Gov. James B. Longley and Att. Gen.

UPI
Indian leaders urge Maine not to reduce funding for the Dept. of Indian Affairs because of Indian land claims.

Joseph E. Brennan have consistently maintained that provisions of the laws of 1793 and 1796 exempt from their terms Indians under the jurisdiction of a state, and that the tribes lost their lands in 1759–1763 in the war that ended the French empire in North America. Both want the validity of the claim to be determined in court, while the tribes and the federal government have urged an out-of-court settlement.

Federal-State Relations. Maine continued to pressure the U. S. Defense Department not to close the B–52 air base at Limestone, citing its defensive and economic value. The Dickey-Lincoln hydroelectric project on the St. John River also continued to cause controversy. Environmentalists as well as Maine's two congressmen have urged its rejection, while the state's two U. S. senators and some federal officials have spoken in its favor.

Economy. The economy improved. Unemployment dropped below 7% for the first time in three years. Personal income rose more than 12%. The agricultural sector showed strong gains.

RONALD F. BANKS, *University of Maine*

——— MAINE · Information Highlights ———
Area: 33,215 square miles (86,027 km²).
Population (1976 est.): 1,070,000.
Chief Cities (1970 census): Augusta, the capital, 21,945; Portland, 65,116; Lewiston, 41,779; Bangor, 33,168.
Government (1977): *Chief Officers*—governor, James B. Longley (I). *Legislature*—Senate, 33; House of Representatives, 151 members.
Education (1976–77): *Enrollment*—public elementary schools, 170,531 pupils; public secondary, 78,291; nonpublic, 16,800; colleges and universities, 37,516 students. *Public school expenditures,* $338,300,000 ($1,254 per pupil).
State Finances (fiscal year 1976): *Revenues,* $1,051,-158,000; *expenditures,* $1,036,176,000.
Personal Income (1976): $5,741,000,000; per capita, $5,366.
Labor Force (July 1977): *Nonagricultural wage and salary earners,* 394,500; *unemployed,* 49,400 (9.7% of total force).

In Bangkok, Thailand, in March, Malaysia's Foreign Minister Ahmad Rithaudeen, left, and Thailand's Foreign Minister Uppadit Panchariyangkun sign a border agreement, permitting both countries to cross the other's borders in "hot pursuit" of terrorists.

UPI

MALAYSIA

When Hussein Onn became prime minister in 1976, he had to contend with intra-party squabbles, a slipping economy, and growing urban terrorism by Malaysia's indigenous Communists. Today, Malaysia's future looks brighter.

Economy. On balance, Malaysia's 1977 economic performance reinforced the favorable image the country has deservedly enjoyed abroad. The balance-of-payments situation improved dramatically; the gross national product grew 11.3% in 1976, and 9% was forecast for 1977; and inflation (2.6% in 1976) remained a manageable problem.

On the negative side, unemployment persisted in the 6.5–7.0% range; multinational investors distrust the Industrial Coordination Act and the Petroleum Development (Amendment) Act; indigenous investors are hesitant while banks are suffering from surplus liquidity; and many of the goals of the initial year of the third five-year development plan were missed.

Politics. Malaysia continues to be governed by the National Front, a broad coalition dominated by the United Malays National Organization (UMNO) headed by the prime minister. Onn emerged as the undisputed leader at the July UMNO assembly, but his larger coalition was showing its fragility by year's end. General elections were likely for the spring of 1978.

Internal Security. The security situation, serious in 1975 and of continued concern in 1976, improved considerably in 1977. In fact, no incidents of ambush or sabotage have been reported in the peninsula since 1975, and the field forces have broken up most terrorist concentrations. For their part, the Communists have waged internecine warfare and remain divided into three mutually hostile factions. A new Thai-Malaysian agreement again permits "hot pursuit" of terrorists into Thai sanctuaries, and two joint Thai-Malaysian antiguerrilla operations were conducted successfully in the border area during the year.

Foreign Relations. A change of regime in Thailand permitted the new border agreement. Confessions broadcast over Singapore television involving alleged interference by Malaysians in Singapore's domestic affairs created strains. The Philippine promise to drop all claims to Sabah (made at the Malaysian-hosted summit meeting of the Association of Southeast Asian Nations in August) improved the political climate within ASEAN.

Relations with China remained correct, despite China's continued unofficial support of the Communist guerrillas.

The United States named Robert H. Miller as its new ambassador to Malaysia. Miller, 49, had served as deputy assistant secretary of state for East Asian and Pacific affairs. He succeeded Francis T. Underhill.

ROBERT O. TILMAN
JO H. TILMAN

MALAYSIA • Information Highlights

Official Name: Malaysia.
Location: Southeast Asia.
Area: 127,316 square miles (329,749 km²).
Population (1977 est.): 12,600,000.
Chief Cities (1975 est.): Kuala Lumpur, the capital, 500,000; Pinang, 280,000; Ipoh, 255,000.
Government: *Head of state*, Sultan Yahya Putra (took office Sept. 1975). *Head of government*, Hussein bin Onn, prime minister (took office Jan. 1976). *Legislature*—Parliament: Dewan Negara (Senate) and Dewan Ra'ayat (House of Representatives).
Monetary Unit: Malaysian dollar (2.46 M. dollars equal U. S.$1, Aug. 1977).
Manufacturing (major products): Petroleum products, refined sugar, rubber goods, steel, lumber.
Major Agricultural Products: Rubber, rice, palm oil and kernels, tea, pepper, coconuts, spices.

MANITOBA

Political surprises abounded in 1977, a year that began with a drought, followed by one of the wettest and coolest summers on record.

Politics. The provincial elections on October 11 produced a result no one had foreseen. Premier Edward Schreyer's New Democratic party (NDP), in power since 1969, went down to defeat, winning only 23 of the 57 seats in the legislature. The Progressive Conservative party, led by Sterling Lyon, won 33 seats. The Liberal party ended up with only one. With 49% of the popular vote the Progressive Conservatives won the widest public support in Manitoba's history. The cabinet took office October 24.

Legislation. The 1977 legislature sat for 88 days and passed 52 bills. The NDP government's budget initially amounted to $1,158 million, but $17 million more was added for summer job programs. The most controversial legislation was in the field of family law. The Marital Property Act and the Family Maintenance Act together provide for equal sharing between spouses of property acquired from the time of marriage and mutual financial accountability while a marriage continues.

Winnipeg. Canada's longest-serving and most entrenched civic politician was Steven Juba, mayor of Winnipeg continuously since 1957. On October 7, Mayor Juba pulled one of his biggest political surprises by withdrawing from the mayoralty campaign after nominations had closed. His candidacy had scared off his principal rivals and enemies, who now found themselves maneuvered out of any possibility of election. Alderman Robert Steen was elected mayor.

Garrison Project. Relief and satisfaction were felt by the government and farmers of Manitoba on April 18, when the White House announced that it would abandon most of the remaining work on the Garrison diversion project in North Dakota, which would have diverted polluted waters northward into Manitoba streams. The International Joint Commission later reported that no part of the scheme affecting Canada ought to be completed.

JOHN A. BOVEY
Provincial Archivist of Manitoba

──────── **MANITOBA · Information Highlights** ────────

Area: 251,000 square miles (650,090 km²).
Population (1976 census): 1,021,506.
Chief City (1976 census): Winnipeg, the capital, 560,874.
Government (1977): *Chief Officers*—lt. gov., Francis L. Jobin; premier, Sterling R. Lyon (Progressive Conservative party); chief justice, Samuel Freedman. *Legislature*—Legislative Assembly, 57 members.
Education (1976–77): *Enrollment:* public elementary and secondary schools, 216,050; private schools, 1,480; Indian (federal) schools, 5,910; post-secondary, 22,-230 students. *Total expenditures,* $409,215,000.
Public Finance (1977–78): *Revenues,* $1,071,000,000; *expenditures,* $1,153,000,000.
Personal Income (average weekly salary, July 1977): $230.05.
Unemployment Rate (August 1977, seasonally adjusted): 5.6%.
(All monetary figures given in Canadian dollars.)

MARINE BIOLOGY

Marine biologists have been increasingly concerned with drugs and medicines that can be obtained from marine plants and animals. Many marine animals produce toxic substances which are unpalatable or poisonous to predacious animals. Sponges in tropical marine waters have been found to be more toxic to fish than those from cooler, temperate areas. This toxicity precludes reef-dwelling tropical fish from grazing on sponges, thus protecting them from possible extinction.

It has also been observed that certain deep-water or abyssal sponges can produce substances which allow them to bore holes into hard substrates, such as mollusk shells and certain rock. In addition, reports indicate that some sponges may have bored into steel containers used to dispose of radioactive wastes in the deep sea. If such devices are to be used to discard toxic waste matter, scientists must develop methods to prevent the growth of sponges and other organisms on their surfaces.

Many marine animals prevent other organisms from settling and growing on their surfaces. Small shrimp and other decapod crustaceans have appendages they use to preen themselves. By frequent wiping of their bodies, especially the sensory structures, such as antennae and eyes, these crustaceans keep animals such as barnacles, as well as sediments and bacteria, off their bodies. The electron microscope is used to study details of such activities.

"Red Tides." Marine microbiologists have found a substance, "aponin," which is produced by certain blue-green algae and seems to inhibit growth of the species of phytoplankton called dinoflagellates. These often reproduce in such large numbers that they form plankton blooms called "red tides." Such blooms are toxic to fish and affect people swimming in infested waters. Understanding the interactions between different microorganisms may allow scientists to predict and, perhaps, eliminate such events which often culminate in great economic losses.

Food Chains. Research continued on food and food chains in the sea. Reports indicate that organic detritus may form 40% of the organic matter used as food by zooplankton. The detritus, or fine particulate matter, comes from grasses and sea plants growing in estuaries and coastal waters. Bacteria become associated with the particles and take dissolved organic matter from the water, thus increasing the nutritive value of the complexes formed by particles of organic matter and bacteria. Scientists are also interested in how this detrital material is carried from estuaries to the open sea. Understanding the movements and distribution of foods is extremely important in the management of marine resources.

JOHN B. PEARCE
Sandy Hook Marine Laboratory

MARYLAND

Events in Maryland in 1977 were dominated by the second trial of Gov. Marvin Mandel. His first trial had ended in a mistrial in 1976.

Mandel Convicted. On August 23, a federal court jury in Baltimore found Mandel and five friends guilty of conspiring to defraud the people of Maryland of honest state government. They convicted Mandel of accepting bribes—clothes, jewelry, trips, and financial interests in lucrative business ventures—in exchange for influencing legislation beneficial to his friends' secret ownership of a race track.

Mandel, 57, was sentenced to four years in prison but was not fined because he told the judge his legal defense and divorce from his first wife had left him financially ruined. Appeals were expected to delay the start of his sentence many months. The governorship passed to Lt. Gov. Blair Lee III, who had formally assumed the powers of the office on June 4. Lee, a member of a wealthy family, is a descendant of two signers of the Declaration of Independence.

Mandel's conviction was the result of a federal investigation in Maryland that has been going on for five years. The investigation toppled a number of locally powerful office-holders and forced Spiro Agnew to resign from the vice presidency. A similar investigation resulted in the indictment on August 1 of former Rep. Edward Garmatz, who is charged with taking bribes from shipping firms for swinging legislation in their favor when he was head of the House Maritime Committee.

Other Developments. The 1977 General Assembly had a conservative air. Lawmakers adopted a death penalty bill that was then vetoed by Gov. Mandel in the light of recent U. S. Supreme Court decisions. A law requiring that minor females get parental permission before undergoing abortions was accepted. But a bill that would have prevented punishment of phy-

─── MARYLAND • Information Highlights ───

Area: 10,577 square miles (27,394 km²).
Population (1976 est.): 4,144,000.
Chief Cities (1970 census): Annapolis, the capital, 30,-095; Baltimore, 905,759; Dundalk, 85,377; Towson, 77,799.
Government (1977): *Chief Officers—governor,* Marvin Mandel (D), suspended; lt. gov., Blair Lee III (D). *General Assembly—*Senate, 47 members; House of Delegates, 141 members.
Education (1976–77): *Enrollment—*public elementary schools, 441,006 pupils; public secondary, 419,923; nonpublic, 133,600; colleges and universities, 175,-622 students. *Public school expenditures,* $1,485,-947,000 ($1,505 per pupil).
State Finances (fiscal year 1976): *Revenues,* $3,590,-346,000; *expenditures,* $3,861,429,000.
Personal Income (1976): $28,514,000,000; per capita, $6,880.
Labor Force (July 1977): *Nonagricultural wage and salary earners,* 1,547,200; *unemployed,* 109,400 (5.6% of total force).

sicians prescribing Laetrile, the controversial cancer drug, died in a conference committee.

In Baltimore, excavation started on the first leg of a subway system. The system's future was in doubt because of rising costs and the threat of withdrawal of federal support. At the city's Inner Harbor, the focus of massive urban renewal efforts, a World Trade Center building was completed in September. The 30-story pentagon is 423 feet tall. First steps were taken to initiate "shopsteading," turning over tax-delinquent shops to small businessmen at little cost and with the support of low-interest loans. A "homesteading" program to renovate abandoned houses has been successful.

PEGGY CUNNINGHAM
"The News American," Baltimore

MASSACHUSETTS

Court Reform. Among the dominant issues in Massachusetts during 1977 was reform of the state court system. The reform proposals were initially made public in December 1976 by a select committee appointed by Gov. Michael S. Dukakis. The chairman of the committee was

With his wife at his side, Marvin Mandel answers reporters' questions. The governor had just been convicted of conspiring to defraud Marylanders of honest state government.

Citizens of Nantucket Island, concerned about a redistricting plan, threaten to secede from Massachusetts.

UPI

Harvard Law School Professor Archibald Cox, best known as the special prosecutor in the Watergate affair fired by President Nixon. The "Cox Plan" proposed a sweeping consolidation of the present 72 separate district trial courts into one overall structure, under the direction of seven chief judges. The new court system would be financed through a single annual budget, and the state would gradually assume the costs, now borne by county governments. The plan also proposed the sharing of non-judicial court personnel between courts with light loads and those with heavier ones. Although controversial, the plan won wide support and was eventually approved by the legislature after months of debate and some substantive changes by the Senate and House.

Sacco-Vanzetti Case Reviewed. On July 19, in an unusual action, Governor Dukakis issued a proclamation declaring that Niccolo Sacco and Bartolomeo Vanzetti had not been fairly tried and that doubt existed about their guilt. Aug. 23, 1977, was the 50th anniversary of the execution of the two Italian immigrants, whose conviction for bank robbery and murder sparked world-wide protests. The governor acted on the recommendation of lawyers and historians who had examined new evidence in the case.

Antiabortion Proposals. A more contemporary controversy was prominent throughout the year, as the legislature wrestled with several measures that would outlaw state funds for therapeutic abortions. Partly because of the governor's pledge to veto any such bill sent to him, none of the proposals became law. Opponents of abortion, however, vowed to keep trying for enactment of such laws.

Indians Sue for Land. Though overshadowed by the much larger dispute in the state of Maine, an important similar case continued to develop in Massachusetts, where representatives of the Wampanoag Indian tribe were claiming ownership of nearly 16,000 acres (6,475 ha) of undeveloped land in the Cape Cod town of Mashpee. A personal representative of President Carter, retired Georgia Judge William B. Gunter, was sent to adjudicate the conflict. Among the legal issues in the complex and emotional dispute was the question whether the Indian community constituted a "tribe" in the legal sense. This issue was to be decided in the courts.

Economic Trends. Major economic indicators for Massachusetts were largely positive during the year. At mid-year, unemployment was down to 6.0%, a drop of 3.3% from 1976. While construction and production of nondurable goods were slightly down, the output of durable goods rose, engendering some optimism in both business and government circles that the state's stagnant economy was improving.

HARVEY BOULAY, *Boston University*

MASSACHUSETTS • Information Highlights

Area: 8,257 square miles (21,386 km²).
Population (1976 est.): 5,809,000.
Chief Cities (1970 census): Boston, the capital, 641,-071; Worcester, 176,572; Springfield, 163,905.
Government (1977): *Chief Officers*—governor, Michael S. Dukakis (D); lt. gov., Thomas P. O'Neill III (D). *General Court*—Senate, 40 members; House of Representatives, 240 members.
Education (1975–76): *Enrollment*—public elementary schools, 813,410 pupils; public secondary, 385,000; nonpublic, 175,600; colleges and universities, 356,-362 students. *Public school expenditures*, $2,313,-296,000 ($1,792 per pupil).
State Finances (fiscal year 1976): *Revenues*, $5,727,-697,000; *expenditures*, $5,531,537,000.
Personal Income (1976): $38,272,000,000; per capita, $6,588.
Labor Force (July 1977): *Nonagricultural wage and salary earners*, 2,365,500; *unemployed*, 177,400 (6.4% of total force).

317

MEDICINE AND HEALTH

Infectious diseases made medical headlines in 1977. Perhaps the most important development was the failure of the predicted epidemic of swine influenza to occur. The virus was isolated in Fort Dix, N. J., in February 1976 and affected some 500 soldiers at that military post. After that it never returned as a cause of any major outbreak, although there were a few cases, always affecting persons in contact with swine, reported across the United States. None of these reported cases was fatal.

However, by December 1976, health officials had found a definite association between the swine-flu vaccine, developed and administered in 1976, and a rare neurologic disorder, Guillain-Barre syndrome. By February, more than 680 cases of Guillain-Barre syndrome had been reported, about half occurring in patients who had been immunized against swine influenza.

At the insistence of pharmaceutical manufacturers, a law had been passed under which the federal government assumed liability for untoward reactions to the swine influenza vaccine. So as 1977 ended, there were hundreds of damage suits of claims for millions of dollars pending investigation and settlement. Nevertheless, government agencies continued in 1977 to encourage the use of usual influenza vaccines for selected groups including the very old and the very young.

"Legionnaires' Disease." The so-called "legionnaires' disease" continued to appear sporadically across the country throughout the year. It originally affected a group of persons who attended the American Legion Convention in Philadelphia in August 1976. Twenty-nine of those infected died. At the time, the cause of the disease was obscure. By the early months of 1977, coccoid bacteria were found in blood smears from experimental animals injected with lung tissue from two victims of the disease. Gradually, the characteristics of the disease became somewhat sharper. Fever, cough, shortness of breath, and pneumonia are symptoms of the illness, which most commonly attacks patients debilitated from other causes. The bacterium that causes the disease is small and rod-shaped. It induces in patients an antibody which can be detected by usual laboratory techniques. Erythromycin appears to be effective against it. During 1977, at least 29 persons in 22 states died of legionnaires' disease. There was an outbreak of more than 50 cases in Burlington, Vt., alone in August. In spite of the publicity, one thing is certain about the disease: it has been around for some time, certainly by the time of the Legion Convention of 1976.

Unexplained Fever. Attention was called to yet another unusual infection in 1977. A new cause for unexplained fever may have been discovered. The sickness is caused by a parasite, Babesia microti, which lives inside the red blood cells. The sickness has as its hallmark unexplained fever, sometimes with chills, general feeling of debility, and loss of appetite and weight. Laboratory data are not helpful but some findings suggest liver or kidney disease. Babesiosis was first recognized as a cause of infection in animals in the 19th century but the first human case was not reported until 1957. Since then, a total of 13 cases, 3 of them fatal, has been cited in medical journals. In 1977, there were about 25 cases on Martha's Vineyard and Nantucket, Mass., and a few cases on the eastern end of Long Island, N. Y.

Babesia are fairly common in nature. The germ itself lives in rodents, such as field mice, but any animal, including hamsters and most of the usual household pets, can harbor the organisms. The germ is transmitted from a host by tick bite and finds its way into the blood stream of the victim where it grows within the red blood cells.

Diagnosis of babesiosis can be made by microscopic examination of the red blood cells in which the parasites can be found. These red cells often break down under the stress of the organisms within them, producing waste substances which may obstruct the liver and kidneys, leading to abnormal findings in urine and liver tests. There have been too few human cases identified thus far for the efficacy of any treatment to have been established, but chloroquine, a medicine used for treatment of malaria, may be definitely helpful.

Rocky Mountain Spotted Fever; Bubonic Plague; Sleeping Sickness. With more Americans than ever vacationing outdoors, the incidence of Rocky Mountain spotted fever increased almost 30% in 1977. Surprisingly, most of the reports of this disease came from the eastern part of the country, particularly the Southeast and also several of the northeastern states. The disease is caused by a rickettsia and is transmitted from animal hosts to people by tick bite. Mortality is now between 5% and 10% but could be reduced to almost zero with prompt diagnosis and treatment. This is due to the fact that the causative organism can be successfully treated with an antibiotic if the treatment is begun during the early stages.

Still another disease transmitted by insect continued to be reported in small numbers in the Southwest. Bubonic plague, carried by small animals and transmitted by fleas, had claimed 11 victims and caused 2 deaths by early fall. The number of cases of the illness reported annually remains quite small and the possibility of epidemic continues to be unlikely. The plague bacillus Yersinia pestis responds to antibacterial medicines if the treatment is begun very promptly.

"POOR FOOLS — UNWILLING TO ACCEPT SCIENTIFIC EVIDENCE"

WE WANT LAETRILE

We want our SACCHARIN foods and drinks!

FOOD AND DRUG ADMINISTRATION

Hell with the FDA

©1977 HERBLOCK

COPYRIGHT 1977 BY HERBLOCK IN "THE WASHINGTON POST"

The FDA ban on saccharin and refusal to legalize Laetrile concerned various segments of the American public.

Treatment of virus infections jumped forward with the report of the first successful attempt to use a drug to treat a highly fatal viral disease, and, for the first time, an antiviral agent, ara-A, was available in adequate supply. Ara-A was isolated 20 years ago from a Caribbean sponge and was first used against corneal infection with herpes virus. It proved successful when applied directly to the cornea. In 1977, ara-A was given intravenously to a group of patients with encephalitis caused by herpes simplex virus. The disease, known as brain fever or sleeping sickness, begins with unusual behavior and progresses to fever, lethargy, and coma over a period of about a week. Ara-A improved the condition in about half the patients to whom it was administered. Ara-A is now being tested as possible treatment for chicken pox and cancer sores. The drug, developed by Parke-Davis, can be made in quantity by a fermentation process and, provided that tests continue to reflect its safety, could be readily available in the near future.

SIDS. Sudden infant death syndrome (SIDS) from which infants in the first few months of life die suddenly, often in their sleep, has been attributed to hidden botulism infection. Colstridium botulinum organisms produce a poison that causes a paralysis in adults that may be fatal. This germ has been identified in stools of infants who had illnesses consistent with botulism. Medical findings show constipation, weak sucking and crying ability, pooling oral secretion, nerve paralyses, weakness, and occasionally sudden breathing cessations to be symptoms of the disease. Accordingly, it is possible that infant botulism is a cause of at least some of the cases of sudden infant death syndrome.

Trace Elements and Saccharin. Trace elements, chemical elements present in small amounts in the normal human body, stirred some interest. Selenium is one; it is needed for adequate nutrition in animals and human beings, but is unevenly distributed geographically. Some doctors have suggested that the lack of selenium may be linked to differences in incidence of certain diseases in the various geographic areas. A committee of the National Research Council reported that the 150 micrograms per day of selenium furnished by the average American diet is sufficient. The best sources of the element are organ and muscle meats and seafoods. Garlic, mushrooms, and asparagus contain moderate amounts of selenium but other fruits and vegetables are poor sources. Supplements with selenium are not recommended since persons who live in areas where the soil has a high selenium content have been observed to suffer from loss of hair, brittleness of fingernails, fatigue, and irritability.

According to another study, zinc, another trace element, may be useful in the treatment of sickle cell disease. Zinc deficiency has been implicated previously as the cause for some cases of dwarfism and hypogonadism (inadequate sexual development). When researchers found sickle cell patients with retarded growth and less than normal amounts of zinc in the body, treatment with zinc was begun. After using zinc by mouth, growth increased and body hair seemed to improve. In addition, the anemia, pain crises, and organ damage of sickle cell anemia seemed to be reduced.

Saccharin, an artificial sweetener used for more than 50 years, was removed from the approved list by the Food and Drug Administration (*see* special report, page 322). Safety of the sweetener was questioned as a result of tests on experimental animals. However, pro-saccharin clamor from diabetics, dietitians, soft drink manufacturers, and some doctors stayed the government's decision. Instead of being removed from the market, the sweetener was to be tested extensively and more carefully evaluated before a final decision.

Cancer. There were many developments in cancer research. The risks of X-ray examination of the breast to detect cancer were evaluated. The possibility was considered that the amount of X ray used in the examination to find cancer might itself be enough to cause cancer after repeated examinations. Guidelines were published suggesting that any woman, regardless of age, with signs or symptoms that indicate breast cancer should have the X-ray examination, called a mammogram. A woman who has a high risk for breast cancer should have periodic screening examinations, including mammography. Periodic screening of women over the age of 50 should be continued but women who are not considered high cancer risks and are under the age of 50 should not undergo routine mammography.

Two potential diagnostic tests for prostate cancer were being investigated. The incidence of prostate cancer has increased more than 20% in the last 25 years and was expected to cause 20,000 deaths in 1977. The two tests involve identifying the prostatic fraction of acid phosphatase, an enzyme known to increase in amount in the blood of men with prostatic cancer. A new tumor-associated glycoprotein was identified in the urine of a patient with cancer of the colon. It is immunologically distinct from any other recognized normal human plasma protein. Of low molecular weight, this protein has not been found in the urine of healthy or sick people, only in cancer patients. This is the fourth such tumor-specific glycoprotein discovered and one which seems readily detectable in the urine by usual immunologic techniques.

Nitrosamines have been investigated since 1956 as a cause of human cancer. About 75% of the 100 or more of these compounds investigated so far seem to cause cancer in animals. The stool of normal men on diets typical in the industrial nations seems to contain one or more of these compounds which may cause cancer. Addition of vitamin C to the diet of men with

Automatic machines to take blood pressure were seen more and more in pharmacies across the United States.

nitrosamines in the stool reduced the amount by about half. In general, N-nitroso compounds are formed by normal processes within the body. The precursor compounds are everywhere in nature, but are also plentiful in the nitrites used for preserving foods and in tobacco smoke, drugs, flavoring agents, pesticides, herbicides, and even drinking water.

Estrogen drugs as a possible cause of cancer was again considered. Some studies seem to indicate more likelihood of the development of cancer of the uterus or breast in women who use estrogen drugs after the menopause. Other studies do not confirm these findings. In prescribing estrogen drugs for women who have severe post-menopausal symptoms, the risk of possible development of cancer must be weighed against the need for treatment.

Platinum is being used in the treatment of cancers of the head and neck, lungs, and bones; it has previously been used in the treatment of genitourinary tumors. Platinum is introduced into the body, as cis-diamine-dichloroplatinum (cis-DDP). About half the patients treated for specific testicular germ cancers with cis-DDP and other medicines had done remarkably well despite the virulence of this particular cancer. But the drug is highly toxic to the kidney and may cause hearing loss, so it must be used most carefully and only in highly selected patients.

The use of Laetrile—also known as amygdalin, vitamin-B17, and nitriloside—for cancer treatment stirred considerable controversy in the United States. Although the drug continued to be banned by the federal government and to be looked down on by most U. S. medical authorities, various state legislatures considered and some enacted legislation allowing the use of Laetrile. Part of the Laetrile controversy is the fact that many cancer victims are willing to try any possible cure and to accept any pain reliever. Medical experts, on the other hand, are not convinced of Laetrile's effectiveness.

In the meantime, thousands of Americans suffering from cancer traveled across the border to Tijuana, Mexico, to obtain the amber-colored extract of apricot pits. Some cancer researchers suggested administering Laetrile in extremely controlled trial tests so that the efficacy of the substance can be established.

Alcohol and Pregnancy. Alcohol may cause problems for babies born to mothers who are no more than social drinkers. Nine of seventy babies born to women who drank two alcoholic drinks a day during pregnancy showed signs of fetal alcohol syndrome. Such signs include narrow eyes, microcephaly, small size, and ill-formed features. Another study showed neurologic difficulties in babies born to mothers who drink moderately. Alcohol probably causes fetal damage far more often than doctors were aware of in the past.

IRWIN J. POLK, M. D.
St. Luke's Hospital, New York City

GENERAL ELECTRIC

A radiologist analyzes a body scan. Based on computerized tomography (a diagnostic technique using X rays), the scanners have been successful in pinpointing medical problems.

TOMOGRAPHY

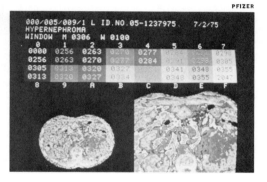

PFIZER

A scan of a chest cavity shows a tumorous mass on the right lung. The abdominal scan, including the enlarged view, below right, was made at kidney level.

PFIZER

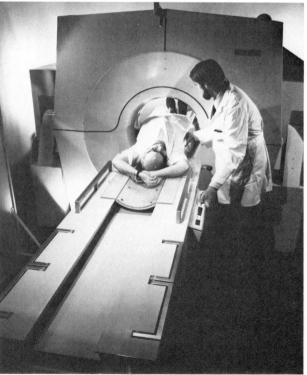

PHOTOS GENERAL ELECTRIC

The tomography scanner, right, takes detailed cross-section X-ray photos, below, in less than five seconds. The scanner also permits radiologists to emphasize details of a single scan.

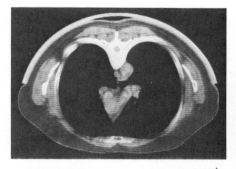

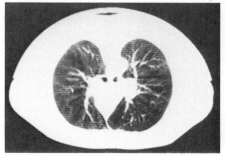

U. S. Food Laws

Although the average American consumer is generally satisfied with the quality of food, questions regarding saccharin and food coloring as well as various outbreaks of food poisoning have recently made headlines.

The Food and Drug Administration (FDA) is charged with carrying out the provisions of the Food, Drug, and Cosmetic Act. This act, with certain amendments, is the key legislation controlling the safety and quality of foods. Embodied in this act is the Delaney Clause, the so-called "cancer clause," which has created much of the recent controversy about food safety and food additives. In addition to controlling food ingredients and additives, FDA has jurisdiction in such areas as standards of identification, packages and packaging materials, nutritional labeling, pesticides, good manufacturing practice guidelines, processing equipment and processes, and recalls of contaminated foods. FDA has a staff of roughly 8,000 and a budget of slightly over $252 million. The 1,000 FDA inspectors monitor 50,000 food plants and 2,000 drug companies.

The Animal and Plant Health Inspection Service of the U. S. Department of Agriculture is responsible for the federal-state inspection of all meat and poultry products as well as plant construction and sanitation. In a consumer service area, USDA's Agricultural Marketing Service provides, for a fee, the quality grading of meat, poultry, vegetables, fruits, and dairy products. For other consumers, the Food and Nutrition Service administers the federal school lunch, school breakfast, commodity distribution, and other child nutrition programs. The National Marine Fisheries Service, on a fee-for-service basis, provides quality assurance in fish processing. These services complement FDA which has regulatory jurisdiction over seafood products.

Unfortunately, scarce headlines and controversy overshadow the many efficient activities of these regulatory agencies. However safe the food supply, advances in science and technology have proliferated to a point where controversy abounds. Simultaneously, rules and regulations have multiplied to the extent that overlapping among agencies has occurred. A third ingredient —an informed and more vocal consumer, supported by various media and pressure groups— is also active in the food law area. In today's setting, food laws must attempt to satisfy government, industry, and consumer.

Food laws are designed to protect the consumer from risk that might cause harm to the user or consumer in any manner. Basically, this concept is incorporated in the Delaney Clause of the 1958 Food Additives Amendment which states "That no additive shall be deemed to be safe if it is found to induce cancer when ingested by man or animal or if it is found, after tests which are appropriate for the evaluation of the safety of food additives, to induce cancer in man or animal." Thus, the act states that no carcinogen shall be added to the food supply, and by implication no scientific judgment is permitted, only a yes or no answer. Further, it takes away from the consumer the possibility of assuming a risk/benefit choice. In recent years, additives such as diethylstilbesterol (DES), Violet No. 1, Red No. 2, cyclamate, saccharin, and nitrite have been or are in question from a food safety viewpoint.

Each of the three major amendments to the Food, Drug and Cosmetic Act of 1938—Pesticides (1954), Food Additives (1958) and Color Additives (1960)—regulated or controlled use of the named group in or on foods. Under the Food Additives Amendment, additives are separated into two groups: GRAS (generally recognized as safe) and regulated additives which are toxic at some level and may be used in specified amounts in specific products. Prior to 1958, most dietetic foods incorporating artificial sweeteners were only available in drug stores. After the passage of the Food Additives Amendment, cyclamate and saccharin were placed on the GRAS list. This led to the wide development of dietetic products for supermarket sale. In 1969, FDA delisted cyclamate, based on tests linking it to cancer. By delisting, and avoiding use of the Delaney Clause, cyclamates could be reapproved for future use via the petition route. Following the cyclamate decision, saccharin became a regulated additive, and FDA initiated a reevaluation of all GRAS compounds. In 1976–77, when studies showed saccharin to be linked with cancer, the situation changed drastically. FDA announced in March 1977 that saccharin would be withdrawn from the market on Oct. 1, 1977. Since this would remove the last nonnutritive sweetener available in the United States, the outcry in defense of an "unsafe chemical" was unusual. Late in 1977, Congress passed a bill suspending the ban for 18 months with strict limitations on use, labeling, and advertising during the control period.

The saccharin controversy emphasizes how advances in scientific diagnosis and testing have outrun the ability of specialists to evaluate or predict effects of a given substance on the population or the overall result when a popularly accepted substance for which there is no substitute is banned. It is also evident that future interpretation of food and drug laws must be tempered by scientific judgment that will include risk/benefit factors and economic impact.

KIRBY M. HAYES

PHOTOS NASA

To improve weather predictions in the Western Pacific, Japan's first weather satellite was launched by a U. S. Delta rocket in July.

METEOROLOGY

Worldwide Weather Observations. The year 1977 was one of intense preparation for the "Global Weather Experiment," organized by the World Meteorological Organization for 1978. The tropics are one of the areas to be studied in depth. Pledges of participation have come from some 80 countries and several international organizations. Worldwide operations are scheduled to begin in September 1978. One of the major innovations will be extensive coverage of the oceans by unmanned drifting weather buoys, reporting by radio. Several geosynchronous (that is, "stationary," or hovering over the same place on earth) satellites have already been launched. These weather eyes are placed over the equator. They watch the cloud cover from about 60° N to 60° S latitude. The U. S. satellite covering the Atlantic, stationed at 75° W longitude, was placed in position on June 16. The Japanese weather satellite at 140° E longitude reached orbit on July 16, and the European satellite was launched on November 22 in a position at 0° longitude. Two more, for complete world coverage, will be launched in 1978.

Aviation Meteorology. Clear air turbulence (CAT) at altitudes where sonic and subsonic aircraft now travel, between 9,000 and 20,000 m (30,000–65,000 ft), causes passenger discomfort and occasionally forces undesirable flight maneuvers. The cause of the wave-like motions in the atmosphere are instabilities induced at the boundary of differently stratified air masses, accompanied by considerable wind shear. There are also notable temperature fluctuations. Attempts to observe this at a distance by infrared sensors aboard aircraft have been only moderately successful. The discovery that there are also anomalies in the moisture concentration in CAT areas has now been used for infrared radiometer measurements of water vapor. Observations from transport aircraft have shown that the water-vapor radiometer can detect changes associated with CAT up to 100 km (62 miles) ahead of the plane. Warnings 4–12 minutes before an encounter will enable pilots to take evasive action. Tests on scheduled airliners are planned by government agencies.

Pilots are also being aided by a new color radar system. Weather radar, which can look up to 300 km (186 miles) ahead on the flight path, used to show cloud and rain reflections on black-and-white picture tubes in the cockpit. Now, heavy rainfall will appear in red, lesser rain in yellow, and light rain in green. The gradations will make clearer which areas to avoid. Crashes of transport planes in thunderstorms in 1972–76 resulted in 250 fatalities.

Satellite Meteorology. Infrared observations from geosynchronous satellites are transmitted now about every 20 minutes. This high frequency permits assessment of the growth and decay rates of clouds. Thunderclouds grow rapidly in vertical direction. Clouds with cold tops produce more rain than those with warmer tops. When two thunderheads merge, rainfall becomes copious. Collapsing clouds produce little or no rainfall. Observations of this type permit quantitative rainfall estimates in ocean areas or regions with sparse rain-gauge networks.

Surveillance from satellites has also cleared up the question of how solar energy received by the earth is partitioned. Actually, more of it reaches the surface than earlier work on radiation income had indicated. A total of 52% is absorbed by the solid earth and the ocean, 29% is reflected back to space, and 19% is absorbed by atmospheric gases and suspensions.

Anthropogenic Effects. Considerable concern continues about man-made changes in the atmosphere. The potential reduction of the ozone layer at 25,000 m (82,000 ft) altitude, though accepted as real by many atmospheric scientists, remains quantitatively unclear. Discovery that the combination of nitric oxide, produced by high-flying aircraft, and hydroperoxyl radical (HO_2) is 10–40 times faster than heretofore assumed considerably lessens the danger to ozone from supersonic transports. At the same time it increases the potential destructiveness of fluorocarbons used in sprays. The United Nations Environmental Program has called for an immediate, three-pronged action: continuous monitoring of ozone concentrations, further studies on stratospheric chemistry, and research on the impact of ozone depletion on human beings and the biosphere.

A committee of the National Academy of Sciences raised the long-range specter of drastic climatic changes by the continuous increase of carbon dioxide (CO_2) in the atmosphere. This is caused by increasing use of fossil fuels. Although immediate consequences are not expected, the global temperature rise after 2050 could exceed 1° C (1.8° F) and increase in later years. Such a change in temperature would lead to the melting of the north polar sea ice and shift the climatic belts, with radical consequences for agriculture.

A four-year study of the effects of the St. Louis metropolitan area on weather has been completed. It found 10% more cloudiness and up to 30% more rainfall than there should be, downwind from the city. There was also a suggestion of more thunderstorms to the east. These changes affect 4,000 km² (1,545 square miles). The increase in water has helped crops, but there have also been more hail damages. A study of Great Plains precipitation has shown around 20–30% increase in rainfall in large irrigated areas.

World Climate. A reevaluation of global temperature trends has revealed a cooling of 0.6° C (1.1° F) between 1959 and 1965. Since then, the southern hemisphere has warmed, but annual values in the northern hemisphere have oscillated without a discernible trend.

Tree-ring analyses have been used to mark the total U. S. area subject to drought. Since 1700, this area has expanded and contracted in a cycle of about 20 years and has shown strong coherence with the cycle of solar magnetic activity, which is about 22 years in length. The evidence for solar radiation changes as one of the principal causes of climatic fluctuations has been strengthened by geological evidence. The radiation effect on climate is also well established from the geochemistry of deep sea cores. These reveal that the position and orbital changes of the earth have been at work for the past 400,000 years, controlling the planet's exposure to solar radiation.

Thunderstorms. Intensive investigations of the frequent Florida thunderstorms have shown that during the active phases of the storms about half of the lightning strokes are from cloud to ground. In midsummer, the density of strokes is about 6 per km² (15 per square mile) per month. The electric fields are 2–4 kilovolts per meter (or yard). The charge centers in the clouds are at levels where the temperatures are between −10° and −25° C (14° and −13° F). Both observations and theory indicate that electric charges and fields, present in incipient and ongoing thunderstorms, considerably increase the collision efficiency of cloud drops, particularly that of very small drops.

Some rare but spectacular lightning bolts have been observed from satellites. They are 100 times as bright as ordinary lightning. Their optical energy has been estimated to range from 1 to 3 billion (U. S.) joules. Although they occur worldwide, they seem to be most frequent in the northern Pacific Ocean just east of Japan, particularly during winter.

Weather Modification. Dispersal of fogs below freezing temperature by creating ice crystals is a well-proven technique. In recent years the necessary cooling has generally been produced by sudden expansion of liquid propane gas from cylinders. It has now been shown that release of highly compressed air will produce the same effect at considerably lower cost. Certain bacteria, present in the air and on plants, have been shown to be highly efficient freezing nuclei. They can induce freezing in supercooled water at −1.3° C (29.7° F), which is considerably above the level at which silver iodide, the favorite cloud-seeding agent, acts.

The Florida area Cumulus Experiment has evaluated seeding results of a five-year period. A 20–70% enhancement in rainfall from the seeding of rising cumulus towers is reported. The heat of fusion, by conversion to ice of the supercooled water in the clouds, adds notably to the buoyancy of the clouds; they become taller, last longer, and rain more than unseeded clouds.

Numerical Weather Prediction. European research aimed at extending the period of forecasting by numerical models continues to show usable information content restricted to about three days. But some forecasts at the substratospheric levels, at 7,000–11,000 m (23,000–36,000 ft), may have a range of more than five days.

H. E. LANDSBERG
University of Maryland

THE WEATHER IN 1977

Too Little or Too Much

The weather in the headlines in 1977 was a mixture of cold, drought, and floods.

December 1976–February 1977. A very anomalous atmospheric circulation pattern caused bitter cold in the eastern part of the country and relatively mild, but very dry, conditions in the West. The core of the cold was just south of the Great Lakes, where temperatures were more than 8° F (4.4° C) below average. In contrast, central Alaska was up to 15° F (8.3° C) warmer than usual; it enjoyed the mildest winter since 1928–29. Montana, western Washington, California, and Arizona were 4–6° F (2.2–3.3° C) warmer than average.

December was the third consecutive cold month east of the Rockies, but January broke cold records in Illinois, Ohio, western Pennsylvania, and West Virginia, where the monthly values were 16–18° F (8.9–10° C) below average. A notable cold wave on January 18–20 brought subfreezing temperatures to Florida, where snow fell as far south as Miami. Another intense cold wave in late January hit the whole eastern United States from the Midwest to the Atlantic coast. Chill factors down to −60° F (−51° C) brought the death toll by freezing to 75. The Buffalo area of New York experienced record-breaking snowfalls. The cold eased in the second week of February.

Anomalous precipitation patterns also prevailed. While the Northeast had heavy snows, the Great Plains and the West suffered drought; west of the Rockies, less than half the average precipitation fell. Severe shortages also extended from New Mexico to the western Great Lakes. In the Pacific Northwest, rain and snow finally fell at the end of February, but Marin County, Calif., had to ration water.

In other parts of the world, the warmth over the whole north polar region was notable. Catastrophic events included the destruction of two fishing villages in Australia by 120-mph (190-km/h) winds in December and the flooding of Jakarta, Indonesia, in January.

March–May. In the spring, contrary to the preceding season, the whole U. S. area east of the Rockies was warm. In the northern Midwest and Great Plains, temperatures were 6–8° F (3.3–4.4° C) above average. Only some parts of California, Nevada, Arizona, and New Mexico were about 2° F (1.1° C) cooler than average. But the departure of winter was unusually violent. On March 11–15, a severe storm, with winds reaching more than 100 mph (160 km/h), moved from California to the Great Plains, where it whipped up a terrific blizzard. It caused 25-foot (7.5-m) snowdrifts in Colorado and left 18 dead in its wake. New England had a very late snowstorm on May 11; it blacked out Boston, parts of Cape Cod, and Rhode Island.

Some precipitation relieved the drought in the Pacific Northwest and the Great Plains. Sudden thaws brought floods to other areas. The Housatonic Valley, Mass., had the worst spring floods since 1936. The Dallas-Fort Worth area, after a 6-inch (15-cm) rainfall late in March, had the highest flood in 20 years. A savage spring storm in Appalachia caused disaster in the first and second weeks of April. A commercial airliner, pelted by hail, crashed in Georgia, killing 70 people. Flash floods in Virginia, West Virginia, Tennessee, and eastern Kentucky were the worst in more than 40 years, causing a total of 103 deaths. Drought continued in California, and Oregon was declared a drought disaster area. Wind erosion in the western Great Plains was the most destructive since 1957.

Elsewhere in the world, central Sweden's rich farmlands were inundated by floods caused by the sudden melting of abundant winter snows. Drought was severe in China and North Korea during the early spring, but copious rains at the end of April brought relief. A tropical storm hit Bangladesh in April, killing 600.

June–August. Summer was not very far from average temperatures in the United States. Few areas had departures of more than 2° F (1.1° C), though interior Alaska was 4° F (2.2° C) warmer than average; a few pockets in Arizona, New Mexico, Nevada, and California had similar temperature excesses. There were some notable heat waves in July and August in the East. But the most important fact was that the Great Plains and the Midwest had not only adequate rainfall but in spots well over the average. This broke the drought conditions in many of the country's most important agricultural regions. Some areas, however, continued to suffer from drought; several counties of Virginia and North Carolina were declared disaster areas.

Catastrophes abounded during the season. In June, there were floods in Soviet Khirgizia and a severe drought in Hungary and the Balkan Peninsula. A heat wave hit the same area and Turkey early in July. In Seoul, Korea, early July brought more than 17 inches (43 cm), of rainfall, exacting a toll of 188 lives.

On July 13, severe thunderstorms in the New York City area caused a partly lightning-induced blackout. Less than a week later, July 19–20, Johnstown, Pa., had its third disastrous flood in a century, when the Conemaugh River system rose precipitously after 8 inches (20 cm) of rain. There were 76 confirmed deaths. At the end of July, a typhoon roared over Taiwan, causing scores of deaths, followed by another at the end of August, with torrential rains and more casualties. The Pacific hurricane Doreen brought the first substantial rain in months to southern California, causing floods in Imperial County. Drought in northern California enabled lightning-induced forest fires in early August to claim more than 200,000 acres (81,000 ha) near the Oregon border. Severe drought developed again in subsaharan Africa. Late tornadoes in Neoga, Ill., and flash floods in southern Oklahoma caused casualties and much damage.

September–November. Autumn did not stray much from average temperatures. September was warm in most of the United States. October was warm in the West but cool in the East; in November, the West cooled off. Rainfall was well above average in many places and the vestiges of drought were wiped out in the Great Plains and Midwest. Along the Pacific Coast, the long lack of rain was ended by a series of vigorous storms from the Pacific. At the end of the season, considerable snow had accumulated in the Cascades, Sierras, and Rocky Mountains. Early in November, intense rainfall led to flash floods in Georgia, the Carolinas, and southern Virginia. In Georgia, the rains broke a dam at Toccoa, drowning 39 persons. In the third week of the month, the northern states assumed a wintry garb, with a snow cover up to a foot (30 cm) deep.

In Asia, the monsoon was good, but some areas, including Vietnam, reported poor crops. The harvest season in the western Soviet Union was also hampered by bad weather, but a record cotton crop was raised in Soviet Asia. Continued foul weather ruined the French wine crop. Australia had incipient drought. In eastern Indonesia, drought impaired the rice crop.

The Caribbean-Atlantic hurricane season had its average quota of storms but there were no serious consequences on land. In contrast, Pacific typhoons were active and spread misery. Kim struck Manila, the Philippines, leaving some 8 million people in the area without electricity and 48,000 without homes. But the worst tragedy was caused by a series of cyclones hitting the southeast coast of India. The third in a row, on November 20, struck with 100-mph (160-km/h) winds and 18-foot (5.5-m) storm surges. It was the worst in a century with a death toll of more than 10,000.

H. E. LANDSBERG

An extremely cold January slowed traffic on New York's generally busy Hudson River.

AND NOW FOR THE WEATHER—
unusual (as usual)

The actually remote Arctic seemed to have moved closer, as even the "sunny south" could attest.

And then it was suddenly tropical. The thermometer proved it, but urbanites had their own evidence.

MARTIN ADLER LEVICK, BLACK STAR   PASCARELO, LIAISON

Snow was excessive in many U. S. locales early in 1977. An "unmerciful" storm struck parts of Pennsylvania (*left*). A series of blizzards isolated Buffalo, N. Y. The city shipped box cars of snow southward to be rid of it.

BILL PIERCE, SYGMA

Some city dwellers were willing to adopt any possible relief from July heat wave.

MEXICO

President José López Portillo, who assumed office in December 1976, immediately took steps to conciliate political groups, streamline the government, stimulate economic recovery, and reassure domestic and foreign investors. On the diplomatic front, Mexico continued its neutralist stance while becoming warmer toward the United States.

Administrative Reorganization. Faced with a recession, a sprawling bureaucracy, and the necessity to restore confidence in Mexico, President López reorganized the executive branch to facilitate national planning and the economic recovery effort. All public-sector activities were put under the new Secretariat of Budget and Programming, replacing the Secretariat of the Presidency. The former secretariats of Agriculture and Water Resources were consolidated into a single agency. The Secretariat of Commerce, given greater power over trade, relinquished industrial development to the new Secretariat of Natural Resources and Industry. All decentralized and state-participation agencies were brought under the cabinet. Work hours and assignments were shifted. Compacts with each state decentralized some public expenditures, and promises to move some federal agencies out of Mexico City were renewed.

Fiscal Policy. As part of a medium-range stabilization policy to readjust the economy gradually, budgetary goals for the year included the curbing of inflation; stimulation of production, employment, private investment, and domestic savings; and reduction of public borrowing to cover deficits. The budget deficit—9% of the gross national product in 1976—was to be cut to 6% in 1977 and down to 2.5% by 1979. Government expenditures were forecast at nearly $30 billion (U. S.), of which $7.4 billion would go to investment. Industry was to receive the largest stimulation (nearly $4 billion), but sizable increases were mandated to other key sectors of the economy: energy (135%), petrochemicals (262%), agriculture (50%), fishing (60%), fertilizers (183%), and mining (300%). Current and capital income were expected to cover 64% of the budget, the remainder coming from borrowing. Taxes were increased on excess profits, luxury items, motor vehicles, and monthly incomes above $230, while price controls were extended on basic foods and many drug prices were decreased by 60%.

Politics. Late in the year, the president proposed constitutional amendments to Congress, followed by implementation bills, which promised to alter the political system and give more visibility to opposition parties. The government party, the Partido Revolucionario Institucional (PRI), in power since the 1920's, was certain to pass them. The move reflected a growing dissatisfaction with the political leadership and an attempt to forestall further violence. Scattered incidents during the year included shoot-outs between police and members of the 23rd of September League in June and bombings in Mexico City, Oaxaca, and Guadalajara in September. President López also promised to make his anti-corruption campaign effective, regardless of scandals that might ensue.

Under the proposed political reforms, the PRI would retain control, while giving minority parties more representation, visibility, and opportunity to participate in state and municipal elections. These parties would receive permanent access to the communications media, financial aid, and a guarantee of 100 seats in the Chamber of Deputies, elected from five super-districts in the country. Membership in the chamber, however, would be raised to 400, three quarters of whom would be elected in single-member congressional districts. Electoral disputes would be judged by an electoral college of 60 majority and 40 minority party members, selected by the chamber. Significant was the decision to grant the Supreme Court the right to hear political cases, a long-term goal of the National Action party. States will be allowed to create their own minority deputy systems, and municipalities of more than 300,000 inhabitants will be able to use proportional representation in creating city councils.

A new party registration scheme will allow more parties to participate. Definitive registration will be given to parties with 65,000 total members spread through at least half the states or 100 congressional districts. Conditional registration will be granted to a smaller group until it receives 1.5% of the national votes. Any party falling below that percentage in two elections will lose its registration. Although more parties, including the Communists, will participate in elections, the dominance of the PRI is carefully preserved.

Economic Performance. The sluggish economy grew less than 2% in 1977 instead of the usual 6% increases of the past; per-capita income fell for the second consecutive year. By mid-year, the inflation rate had dropped to 15% from a high of 30% the year before. Industrial production increased 3.7%, and similar gains were expected in agriculture as a result of higher

---

MEXICO • Information Highlights

Official Name: United Mexican States.
Location: Southern North America.
Area: 761,602 square miles (1,972,546 km²).
Population (1977 est.): 64,400,000.
Chief Cities (1976 est.): Mexico City, the capital, 8,-630,000; Guadalajara, 1,640,000; Monterrey, 1,090,-000.
Government: *Head of state and government,* José López Portillo, president (took office Dec. 1976). *Legislature*—Congress: Senate and Chamber of Deputies.
Monetary Unit: Peso (22.87 pesos equal U. S.$1, Aug. 1977).
Manufacturing (major products): Petroleum products, iron, steel, chemicals, transport equipment, aluminum, pharmaceuticals, cement.
Major Agricultural Products: Corn, cotton, sugarcane, wheat, vegetables, citrus fruits.

UPI

José López Portillo and Jimmy Carter held two days of discussions at the White House in February. The two presidents reconfirmed the "special importance each places on close and friendly relations between the two nations."

price supports. Production targets in millions of metric tons were: corn, 10; wheat, 2; sorghum, 4.2; beans, 1; and rice, ½. Sales of consumer goods lagged.

Good economic news was also available. Tourism, in a slump since 1975, increased as a result of the peso devaluations of 1976 and was expected to earn $830 million. The international monetary reserve of almost $3 billion in August, decreased in the commercial balance-of-payments deficit, and reduction of the growth rate of the external public debt encouraged capital investment from domestic and foreign sources. Higher interest rates, new three-year bonds (Petrobonos) based on the international price of oil at maturity, and new dollar-deposit, peso-credit accounts further enticed capital to Mexico. Organized labor agreed to hold wage-increase demands to 10%, a figure used to raise incomes of government workers, the armed forces, and pensioners in September.

Through the Alliance for Production, the government and more than 140 private enterprises agreed to increase production and employment, reduce imports, and expand exports; such overt cooperation reversed the tone of the previous Echeverría administration. The consolidation of three government steel industries under a single agency (SIDERMEX), with a capital value of $3.1 billion and a yearly output of 4.5 million tons, paved the way for an expansion of production to 10 million tons, sufficient to make Mexico an exporter.

Foreign Affairs. The most significant event of the year was Mexico's decision to break diplomatic relations with the Spanish Republic in exile and to begin ties with the Spanish monarchy. In April, Spanish Prime Minister Adolfo Suárez, paid a three-day visit to Mexico, and in October, President López went to Spain; closer economic and diplomatic ties followed. In their February meeting, Presidents Carter and López stressed their nations' special relationship, emphasized by Mexico's receiving the first invitation for a state visit. President López announced Mexican support of the Panamanian position on the Canal Zone and stressed that the issue of Mexicans illegally entering the United States was an American problem, which would be solved by more U. S. trade with and investment in Mexico. In an August meeting in Bogotá, the heads of state of Costa Rica, Colombia, Jamaica, Mexico, Panama, and Venezuela reaffirmed support of Panama and called for the denuclearization of Latin America, a new international economic order favoring developing countries, and concerted efforts to support coffee prices. The presidents of Costa Rica and the Federal Republic of Germany visited Mexico in 1977 to discuss common economic interests.

DONALD J. MABRY
Mississippi State University

MICHIGAN

The chemical contamination of farm products and attempts to curb the power of the state's largest medical insurance company attracted major public attention in Michigan during 1977.

"Cattlegate." After four years, interest flared anew in the effects of a poisonous chemical, polybrominated biphenyl (PBB), which was accidentally mixed with cattle feed at a Michigan elevator in 1973. The first lawsuit arising from the incident reached trial in Lansing. The suit, expected to set precedents for damage payments in the millions of dollars, was expected to continue into 1978. B. Dale Ball, director of the state Agriculture Department, was accused by several state legislators of masterminding a "Cattlegate" coverup to minimize the problem. Gov. William Milliken originally supported Ball. In the face of public pressure, however, he made a dramatic turnabout and endorsed a law which he had previously opposed, restricting the sale of PBB-contaminated products. Contradictory health claims prompted the state to hire Dr. Irving J. Selikoff, a specialist in environmental diseases, to study the effects of PBB on human health.

Arrogant "Blues." The state attorney general's office pressed a lawsuit to limit the power of the nonprofit Blue Cross-Blue Shield, the state's largest health insurance company, which has 5.4 million subscribers. The company added to the public furor by giving its president a major pay raise a few days after obtaining a large rate increase, by ousting a director who had revealed some company decisions, and by declaring in court that it had the authority, without state interference, to "hire a circus with a herd of white elephants" and pass the cost along to health subscribers if it so desired. The suit was filed in 1974 when the state insurance commissioner slashed $47 million from a requested rate increase after the "Blues" refused to adopt measures the commissioners said would save that much in health costs. Losing in a lower court, the "Blues" appealed to the state Supreme Court, where no decision was expected until 1978.

UPI

U. S. Sen. Robert P. Griffin (R-Mich.) was unsuccessful in his bid to capture the post of minority leader. He was defeated by Sen. Howard Baker of Tennessee.

Double Tanker Controversy. A rash of accidents involving trucks that each pull two fuel tankers caused several deaths and injuries and prompted demands that the giant combinations, illegal in many states, be outlawed in Michigan. The legislature hesitated to act, however, when oil-company spokesmen argued that the ban would increase fuel costs and hamper distribution during the winter of 1977–78. But the governor ordered the state police to begin strict enforcement of safety measures, and on-the-road inspections resulted in half the tankers checked being condemned for violations.

Elections. Detroit Mayor Coleman A. Young, the city's first black mayor, sought and won re-election to a second term in November. Young defeated Ernest C. Browne, a city councilman. It was the nation's first mayoralty race between two black candidates. In Dearborn, Mayor Orville Hubbard, 74 and paralyzed from a stroke, retired after 36 years in office, one of the longest mayoral tenures in the nation.

Other Events. The $337-million, 73-story Plaza Hotel opened in Detroit's riverfront Renaissance Center on March 1.

The Detroit City Council on September 1 approved a 30-year lease of the city's Cobo Arena and a new $23.5-million riverfront arena to the Detroit Red Wings, the city's National Hockey League team. The Red Wings had threatened to leave Detroit for quarters in suburban Oakland County.

CHARLES W. THEISEN
The Detroit "News"

MICHIGAN · Information Highlights

Area: 58,216 square miles (150,779 km²).
Population (1976 est.): 9,104,000.
Chief Cities (1970 census): Lansing, the capital, 131,-546; Detroit, 1,513,601.
Government (1977): *Chief Officers*—governor, William G. Milliken (R); lt. gov., James J. Damman (R). *Legislature*—Senate, 38 members; House of Representatives, 110 members.
Education (1976–77): *Enrollment*—public elementary schools, 1,064,312 pupils; public secondary, 971,-391; nonpublic, 220,100; colleges and universities, 414,450 students. *Public school expenditures,* $3,858,736,000.
State Finances (fiscal year 1976): *Revenues,* $8,803,-753,000; *expenditures,* $8,711,398,000.
Personal Income (1976): $61,485,000,000; per capita, $6,754.
Labor Force (June 1977): *Nonagricultural wage and salary earners,* 3,443,200; *unemployed,* 283,700 (6.9% of total force).

MICROBIOLOGY

Much important work continued to be done in microbiology during 1977.

Microbial Genetics. Confidence is growing that recombinant DNA (deoxyribonucleic acid, the essential genetic material) experiments and genetic engineering can be conducted with more safety than once thought. An important disclosure in this field during 1977 was the announcement that bacteria had been engineered to make insulin. Scientists succeeded in transplanting into bacteria a gene from rat cells carrying the instructions to synthesize insulin. Much work remains to be done to determine if such insulin will function in human diabetics, and if the bacteria can be implanted in the human intestine and continue to produce the hormone.

Scientists also broke the genetic information code of a DNA-containing bacterial virus. By arranging more than 100 DNA fragments in various combinations they identified the sequence of the 5,375 nucleotides that make up the chromosomal strand of the virus. The technique will now be used to determine the nucleotide sequences of other viruses.

Microbial Detection of Carcinogens. A useful laboratory test was perfected to detect chemicals that are possibly cancer-producing. The substances are added to petri plates containing bacteria, which are sensitive indicators of DNA damage, and mammalian liver cells that convert the chemicals to their active mutagenic forms. In tests of 300 chemicals, a high correlation was found between carcinogens and mutagenic compounds.

Soil Microbes. Extensive research continues on nitrogen-fixing root-nodule bacteria because of their great significance to agriculture and food production. The capsule of the root-nodule bacteria (rhizobia) has an affinity for specific root hairs; for example, capsular material from *Rhizobium meliloti* binds only to alfalfa, and that of *R. trifolii* attaches specifically to clover roots.

Selenium in the soil is of considerable biological interest because it is both required for and toxic to various forms of life. Certain soil corynebacteria were shown to metabolize various selenium compounds, and it was postulated that a selenium cycle similar to the sulfur cycle exists in nature.

Marine Microbes. Important studies were made on microbial activities in the oceans. These included observations on the growth rates of bacteria that had been isolated from sea water at a depth of 2,000 m (6,500 ft); determination of the percentages of microorganisms that make up the biomass of the ocean; and the possible extraction of glycerol for commercial purposes from certain algae (*Dunaliella*) growing in highly saline waters, such as those of the Dead and Red seas.

Pathogenic Microbes. The protozoan parasite that causes sleeping sickness in thousands of people and kills thousands of domesticated animals, mainly in Africa, was cultured for the first time. Progress was made in immunization against malaria.

The Ebola virus that in 1977 caused a severe human epidemic and claimed many lives in Sudan and Zaire was shown to be similar but not identical to the Marburg virus that ten years earlier had caused deaths in Uganda and Europe. Hope for chemotherapy of virus diseases came with the discovery that adenine arabinoside is useful in treating herpes infections.

Pseudorabies, an itching disease of swine, which reached almost epidemic proportions in 1977, may be brought under control for the first time by an improved vaccine.

The bark beetle causing Dutch elm disease can be destroyed in the laboratory by a fungus, but the practical aspects of field tests have not been worked out.

Petroleum Recovery. Microorganisms have been discovered that metabolize petroleum fractions and thereby help obliterate the harmful effects of oil spills. This and some other uses of microbes, proposed in 1977, may have great economic significance.

The recovery of petroleum products from oil shale is made difficult by carbonates in the shale which decrease permeability and hinder extraction of the oil. By applying certain bacteria (thiobacilli), which produce acids from shale components, the carbonates can be dissolved in the shale matrix, thus increasing porosity and facilitating the removal of oil products. The tar sands in Canada constitute the major secondary source of oil in the world, but there are obstacles to its extraction. A novel approach for obtaining hydrocarbons from such sands has been described. It makes use of certain microbes to adsorb and emulsify oil, so as to offer definite assistance in conventional processing of the tar into oil.

Patents on Microorganisms. Numerous patents have been issued in various countries on microorganisms or the processes they carry out to create such useful products as antibiotics, industrial chemicals, edible substances, or vaccines. Until 1977, however, international protection under such a patent was debatable. As important new microbial processes continue to be developed and microbial genetic engineering to gain significance, greater protection is clearly desirable. Consequently, on April 23, an international treaty, sponsored by the World Intellectual Property Organization, was ratified by the major countries. This treaty simplifies procedures for securing a patent in microbiology and provides greater defense against attempted infringements.

J. R. PORTER
Department of Microbiology
University of Iowa

After his victory in the May elections, Likud leader Menahem Begin, third from left, met with other Israeli politicians to discuss the formation of a new government.

UPI

MIDDLE EAST

The really significant developments in the Middle East in 1977 all took place in the last two months of the year. Earlier, a certain tentativeness in events had been apparent. The year ended with President Anwar el-Sadat riding the crest of a wave of popularity in Egypt. It had begun with riots and demonstrations (against price increases, later rescinded) that had made his tenure of power seem fragile. Israel acquired a new prime minister in June as the result of a startling general election upset in May, itself the outcome of a long chain of scandals and revelations.

U. S. Fumbling. The United States had a new administration, whose handling of the American role in the Middle East, so centrally significant in the time of Secretary of State Henry Kissinger, could hardly be said at the start to demonstrate expertise or even consistency. Thus, on March 7, welcoming Israeli Premier Itzhak Rabin to Washington, President Carter said Israel should have "defensible borders" (in this context, meaning retain all or most of the lands gained in 1967). On March 9, he partially reneged on this. The president then, on March 16, endorsed the incompatible idea of a Palestinian "homeland"—the first U. S. president to do so. Kissinger had worked four years, with Sadat's cooperation, to ease the USSR out of any major role in the Middle East; Carter did all he could to bring it back in, making an unprecedented joint U. S.-USSR statement (October 1) which urged Israel to recognize "the legitimate rights of the Palestinian people."

Libyan-Egyptian War. Relations between Qaddafi's Libya and Sadat's Egypt, already degenerating in 1976, erupted in the summer of 1977 when a curious little war broke out (July 21),

lasting a few days. There was a clash on the border, and some Egyptian bombing.

Progress in the Gulf Emirates. A happier picture was presented by another oil-rich area, the United Arab Emirates. They continued in 1977 to make spectacular economic progress, importing workers to man their industries and building programs. The total proven oil reserves of Abu Dhabi, Dubai, and Sharjah are about 4.23 billion (U. S.) tons—greater than those of the entire United States, including Alaska.

Arab-Israeli Relations. In the central matter of Arab-Israeli relations, most of 1977 passed in discreet fencing. A variety of public statements suggested that the Palestine Liberation Organization (PLO) might in some (unlikely) circumstances recognize the existence of Israel; or that Israeli Foreign Minister Moshe Dayan might be willing to agree to the presence of some Palestinians at the conference table in Geneva, provided they were not the PLO. But the interest of these fine-drawn distinctions faded when the unexpected event of Sadat's trip to Israel burst upon a surprised world (*see* Special Report, page 334).

Aftermath of Sadat Visit. The few remaining weeks of the year exhibited more concentrated diplomatic maneuvering in the Middle East than the whole of the rest of the year. The flurry of activity was due to the fact that what Egypt and Israel had done caught all other states and groups of the Middle East, as well as the United States and the Soviet Union, completely off balance. They were faced with new events that were uncomfortable because they did not fit their long-ingrained expectations. It was a period in which myths were dispersed and bland assumptions successfully challenged.

Reality v. Mythology. Among the myths most obviously shattered was the one of "Arab unity." This "unity," really no more than an ideological

In May, U. S. President Jimmy Carter met with Syrian President Hafez al-Assad, center, in Geneva, Switzerland, to elicit his views on Middle East peace prospects.

UPI

slogan expressing a velleity, probably originated in the days of President Nasser of Egypt; it fitted in with his ambitions for Egypt's regional hegemony in the Arab world. But in fact, Egypt itself is only marginally Arab. Many Egyptians have no wish to claim kinship with the Bedouin of the desert; before Nasser, few did. One result of Sadat's trip was the resurgence of simple Egyptian nationalism.

The Geneva Shibboleth. The second myth is that a separate peace between Israel and Egypt would be some kind of disaster. The corollary of that is the idea that the only satisfactory peace in the Middle East would be one of a comprehensive nature, brought about by a reconvened Geneva conference in which all interested parties participate. The Geneva conference met only once, in December 1973, when it adjourned after two days. It has never been clear why a reconvened conference, summoned without prior agreement on major issues, should be expected to achieve anything.

The United States, however, as co-chairman with the USSR of the Geneva conference, continued to treat its reconvening as unquestionably desirable. This perhaps was the reason for the fumbling in U. S. policy at the time of Sadat's trip. But apart from Morocco and Sudan, which signaled immediate support for Sadat, similar symptoms of disarray and resentment afflicted many states. Some, such as Jordan and Saudi Arabia, hestitated and temporized, while others retreated, like the USSR and the "rejectionist" states, into sterile opposition.

Conferences. Immediately after his Jerusalem visit, Sadat called for a follow-up meeting in Cairo. He issued eight invitations: to Israel, the United States, the Soviet Union, Syria, Jordan, Lebanon, the United Nations, and the PLO. Israel accepted immediately, as did the United States after some hesitation. The UN was will-

ing, and the Vatican said it would send an observer to the postponed opening on December 14. Syria, Jordan, Lebanon, and the PLO said they would not attend, and the Soviet Union also rejected participation.

An anti-Sadat counter-conference, called for December 1 in Tripoli by Col. Qaddafi, was attended by the "rejectionist front" of Syria, Algeria, Southern Yemen, and Iraq, plus the PLO. It denounced Sadat's moves toward Israel and voted to "freeze" relations with Egypt. Iraq quit the conference before the end on the ground the others were too moderate. Yasir Arafat and his mainline PLO appeared to yield to Palestinian extremists.

Sadat Responds. Sadat, basking in popularity in his homeland, responded vigorously. On December 5, he summarily broke diplomatic relations with Syria, Iraq, Libya, Algeria, and Southern Yemen; by December 8, he was calling his Arab foes "moronic dwarfs." He also ordered all consulates and other offices outside Cairo of the Soviet Union and its East-European satellites closed. In an interview he called into question how much the USSR wanted peace in the Middle East, pointing out that the USSR supplied arms to all the Tripoli states.

At year's end much was happening and there were real chances, at least, of substantial improvement if the Cairo conference did not entirely fail. Israel was in search of normalization of relations, including the exchange of ambassadors and the opening of borders to trade; Egypt sought substantial territorial concessions. Perhaps the most significant point was that the game was in the hands of the Middle East states themselves and no longer those of the superpowers, in further evidence of which Begin met Sadat in Egypt, Christmas Day.

ARTHUR CAMPBELL TURNER
University of California, Riverside

Sadat in Jerusalem

In international politics alleged novelties are ten a penny, but genuinely unprecedented happenings are quite rare. The visit of President Anwar el-Sadat of Egypt to Jerusalem on November 19–21, 1977, was, however, truly a unique occasion, a walk on untrod paths. Since Israel's foundation in 1948, no Arab state has communicated directly and officially with it. Even when negotiations have been necessary, they have occurred through the laborious device of intermediaries. Four wars between Israelis and Arabs have highlighted three decades of unremitting hostility. Thus, for the leader of Egypt to make a visit to Israel was a diplomatic innovation of Himalayan proportions.

Fast Tempo of Events. Not less surprising than the visit itself was the rapidity with which it came about. Although, during a trip to Rumania in August, Begin had mentioned to President Ceauşescu his readiness to meet any Arab leader anywhere, and Sadat was no doubt told of this during his own meeting with Ceauşescu two months later, the whole astonishing affair was really only ten days in the making.

The opening gambit occurred on November 9, when Sadat spoke to a new session of the Egyptian parliament. Toward the end of a long speech he said, to stress his desire for peace, that he "would go even to the home of the Israelis, to the Knesset, to discuss peace with them." This seemed at first a mere rhetorical flourish, but when repeated to visiting U. S. congressmen it began to assume the aspect of sincerity. Begin, on his side, told visiting French officials he was inviting Sadat to come to discuss a lasting peace. The two men were now nudging each other (in a way uncommon in the Middle East) into competitive demonstrations of peaceful intentions. Possibly the decisive moment occurred in twin television interviews with Walter Cronkite, in which Sadat declared his readiness to go to Jerusalem within a week and Begin said he could come "any time, any day."

In the absence of Israeli-Egyptian diplomatic links, the formal invitation from Begin to Sadat was conveyed through U. S. channels. Sadat accepted and pressed on with his plan, wading dauntlessly through political waters of increasing storminess. A visit to Damascus to secure the concurrence of Syria's President Assad did not succeed. On Sadat's return to Cairo, his foreign minister, Ismail Fahmy, resigned, and so, within hours, did Fahmy's replacement. Sadat named Butros Ghali acting foreign minister. Protests and anti-Sadat demonstrations erupted in many Arab countries.

Ironies. In Israel, the visit evoked a mood of wild euphoria. Sadat was given the ultimate red-carpet treatment amid every sign of great popular enthusiasm. He arrived on the evening of Saturday, November 19, greeted by a 21-gun salute, inspected a guard of honor, and shook hands with Premier Begin. The occasion was full of ironies. Among those with whom Sadat chatted amiably were Gen. Ariel Sharon, who crossed the Suez Canal in the 1973 war, and Foreign Minister Moshe Dayan, hero of the 1956 and 1967 wars.

On Sunday, Sadat worshipped at Al Aksa Mosque, then made a tour of other holy places, including the Dome of the Rock, the Church of the Holy Sepulchre, and Yad Vashem, the memorial to Jews killed in the holocaust.

Knesset Speeches. Sadat and Begin had luncheon in private and then proceeded to the Knesset. Their two speeches there were the centerpiece of the visit. The speeches were largely addressed to an audience other than that before the speakers. Sadat aimed at the Arab world, Begin at his home constituency.

Sadat spoke of breaking down the "psychological wall . . . that constitutes 70% of the problem." Perhaps the most interesting passage was that in which he accepted Israel's existence: "I proclaim to the whole world: we accept living with you in a just and lasting peace . . . Israel has become an established fact." But he adamantly restated Arab demands for total Israeli withdrawal from lands occupied in 1967. He also said that "peace cannot be realized without the Palestinians," but he did not specify the Palestine Liberation Organization.

Begin did not mention the Palestinians at all. He spoke eloquently of the need for security because of Jewish sufferings of the recent past. "We will never again put our people in jeopardy." He offered no territorial concessions. But he offered to open Israel's borders immediately to every kind of peaceable traffic with Egypt, and to normalize relations.

On Monday morning, Sadat talked with representatives of all Israel's political parties, among them his old adversary, Golda Meir. On Monday afternoon he flew home. In Cairo, his public reception was ecstatic. Whatever other Arab states might say, in Egypt the longing for peace was widespread and profound.

Assessments. The immediate aftermath of the Sadat visit brought confusion among Arab states, a welter of conference proposals, and a wide variety of assessments of the Egyptian's daring initiative. Commentators were unanimous only in their indecisiveness. But the opinion slowly crystallized that something great and important—a significant, undreamed-of breakthrough whose ultimate consequences were impossible to foresee—had been achieved.

ARTHUR CAMPBELL TURNER

British Prime Minister James Callaghan addresses a NATO foreign ministers' meeting.

MILITARY AFFAIRS

In 1977 the worldwide buildup in military forces continued virtually unabated. Despite discussions about the desirability of decreasing conventional arms shipments from the United States, the USSR, and some Western European countries to the developing nations of Asia, Africa, Latin America, and the Middle East, there was little evidence anything substantive was being accomplished. For example, the U. S. conventional arms sales abroad for the fiscal year were about $10 billion. The Soviet Union engaged in a $1 billion arms deal with Iraq.

Toward the end of the year the United Nations Security Council adopted a ban on arms sales to the Republic of South Africa in retaliation for the white government's crackdown on blacks. However, the effect of the arms embargo was likely to be minimized because of the extensive manufacture of arms by South Africa.

Although negotiators from the superpowers were in almost constant session during 1977, both the United States and the Soviet Union were poised by year's end to deploy significant new weapons systems should there be no new SALT agreement, and should NATO and the Warsaw Pact powers fail to agree on troop reductions in Europe. Thus, the somber possibility of heightened arms competition between Washington and Moscow dominated the arms scene in 1977.

The United States. After years of research and development, and the construction of three prototype models, President Carter decided against the production of the B–1 bomber. His decision appeared to be based on several factors. One was the cost of the proposed bomber force. Another was the belief that other delivery systems were available that seemed to be more reliable than the B–1 at substantially less cost. Before bowing to the president's decision, proponents of the B–1 had argued strenuously for the new plane to replace the 330 B–52 bombers currently constituting the backbone of the Strategic Air Command. The belief that the B–52's should be replaced stemmed from the fact that the newest models in the B–52 fleet were built in 1962.

Supporters of the B–1 also expressed fears that the decision not to build the new plane would lead to the reduction of the American strategic force posture from what is known as the triad mode of deployment to a duad. Currently, the triad comprises three separate strategic nuclear delivery systems, each of which is capable of independently wreaking havoc on the Soviet Union or other nations. The three triad components are the long range bombers such as the B–52's; submarine-launched ballistic missiles (SLBM's); and land-based intercontinental ballistic missiles (ICBM's). The logic for maintaining three separate means of retaliation relates to the insurance factor. For example, should the Soviet Union score a technological breakthrough that would negate one, or possibly two, of the American retaliatory systems, one would still remain unimpaired, and presumably deterrence of war would continue. Those favoring the B–1 believed that to let the bomber component of the triad gradually succumb to attrition and age would be running too high a risk that the Soviets could eventually blunt the missile delivery systems.

While some fretted over the President's decision not to build the B–1, others were unhappy with Carter because of his decision to produce and deploy another strategic nuclear weapon—the air-launched cruise missile (ALCM). This weapon is a type of hybrid between a pilotless plane and a winged missile. The characteristics which make the cruise missile particularly attractive are its low cost rela-

President Carter decided against going ahead with production of the B–1 bomber, a supersonic plane sought by the Air Force.

WIDE WORLD

tive to the B–1; its accuracy; and the capability of the cruise missile to operate at very low altitude by means of an elaborate computer system that senses the proximity of the craft to the ground. This last feature enables the cruise missile to elude radar (that operates on a line-of-sight principle) by flying close to the ground and only coming up over the horizon at the last minute.

According to Carter, the cruise missiles will be carried aboard the B–52 bombers, but they could also be designed to be launched from submarines and surface ships. The range of the cruise missiles is several hundred to several thousand miles, depending on design intent. Thus, B–52's may launch the cruise missiles far beyond the range of defensive fighter aircraft and defensive missiles. Presumably, this fact will substantially increase the useful life of the B–52 fleet.

In the autumn, Secretary of Defense Harold Brown announced his approval of development funds for a new intercontinental ballistic missile system known as the MX (missile experimental). Because of the potential cost of the system, variously estimated at $35 to $40 billion, and the fear that deployment would encourage the Soviet Union to step up its arms program, Brown's announcement triggered substantial controversy. Those who supported the initial $245 million for development were concerned about the alleged reduction in the survivability of the 1,000 fixed-base ICBM's in the American Minuteman force. The cause for this concern is the steady improvement in Soviet ICBM capability, particularly in terms of the large size of Soviet warheads, their increased accuracy, and the addition of multiple warheads to Soviet missile launchers.

Specifically, it is feared that the Soviet Union is developing what is known as a "first strike" capability, i.e., the capacity to fire first at the U. S. missiles and destroy many of them before they can be launched in retaliation. Defense

UPI

During 1977, the U. S. Congress enacted legislation authorizing the expenditure of $295 million for the continued development of the X-M 1 tank.

planners worry that their Soviet counterparts might have such confidence in the "first strike" ability of Soviet missiles to deter any U. S. response that the Kremlin might be led into adventuristic foreign activity. Because it would be difficult for a Soviet "first strike" to be launched against the MX system, proponents argued that the MX was necessary to maintain the viability of the U. S. land-based missile component of the triad concept.

Much of the Pentagon's interest in the MX system is based on the belief that the new missile will be essentially invulnerable to Soviet efforts to destroy it before launch. The invulnerable characteristic would derive from an unusual manner of deployment. The 300 MX missiles that have been proposed would be housed in tunnels between six and twelve miles (10 and 20 km) in length. The tunnels would be constructed of concrete and be buried six feet (1.8 meters) underground. The MX missiles in the tunnels would be moved randomly up and down the length of each tunnel to prevent precise targeting by Soviet planners. Should an emergency arise a hydraulic device would break through the tunnel and the covering ground and thrust the missile into an upright position from which it could be fired like any other ICBM.

The MX would be designed to carry up to 14 warheads. The Minuteman III carries three warheads. Presumably the MX warheads will be more accurate and more powerful than those currently deployed on the Minuteman missiles. Such an increase in capability constitutes one objection being made in the Congress against the MX development. The argument is that deployment of the MX might undermine attempts to put a ceiling on the arms competition because Moscow could feel so threatened by the new missile that compensatory arms acquisitions would be adopted by the Soviets. It is also contended that the Soviets might be worried that the MX would give a "first strike" advantage to the United States, a situation that would also require additional arming by the Soviet Union.

Still another controversy developed when news leaked out that the United States had developed what the press immediately termed the "neutron bomb." The name neutron bomb is misleading because the weapon is not a pure neutron device. It is instead a nuclear weapon that has been significantly modified. The modification causes less of the energy released in the nuclear explosion to occur in the form of thermal and blast effects, and residual radiation, and more of the energy released to occur in the form of instant radiation. Weapons so modified are properly called enhanced radiation weapons. Because instant radiation affects living things, but does not affect structures such as buildings and bridges, the new weapon is thought of as being primarily an antipersonnel device that kills within a small radius below its point of detonation.

The chief advantage claimed for such weapons is that they can more effectively be used against enemy troops in the field with less collateral damage to nearby structures, and with less residual radiation remaining to affect friendly troops or an indigenous population. By comparison, regular tactical nuclear weapons create more thermal and blast damage, and leave greater amounts of residual radiation, and thus such weapons are claimed to be inferior by proponents of enhanced radiation weapons.

Those who urged President Carter to order the production of the enhanced radiation weapon, and its deployment to the NATO countries of Western Europe, cited several reasons in support of their views. First was the contention that the 7,000 tactical nuclear weapons now deployed by the United States to Western Europe would be too destructive of property should they be used in the crowded and urbanized areas of West Germany, Belgium, the Netherlands, and France, where presumably an attack by the Soviet Union would be repulsed. Thus, it was argued that the deterrent value of currently deployed nuclear weapons is undercut by the fact the United States might be hesitant to use them. Second, advocates of enhanced radiation weapons contended that such weapons were needed to offset the numerical superiority, vis-à-vis NATO forces, of Soviet and Warsaw Pact forces in Eastern Europe.

Against these claims were arrayed counterarguments by those who opposed the future production and subsequent deployment to Europe of enhanced radiation weapons. Leading the opposition to authorization of money to produce the new weapon was Sen. Mark Hatfield (R-Oreg.), joined by Democratic Senators Edward Kennedy of Massachusetts, Gary Hart of Colorado, and Alan Cranston of California.

In midsummer the Senate voted 58 to 38 to reject Senator Hatfield's effort to cut out funding for enhanced radiation weapons from a public works bill. This legislative action left the final decision up to the president regarding deployment of the new weapon to U. S. forces stationed in Western Europe.

Those who oppose enhanced radiation weapons based much of their opposition on the contention that because such weapons would be more usable, they would in fact be more likely to be used in various types of future confrontations, thus leading to greater chances of small-scale nuclear wars escalating into all-out thermonuclear conflict. Some of those in opposition to the enhanced radiation weapons suggested that it is immoral to design a weapon to kill persons but to spare property.

In a move almost as controversial in some quarters as the weapons systems decisions, Carter pushed ahead with his plan to reduce the incremental strength of American ground forces stationed in South Korea. The predictable opposition to this proposal was that any reduction of American forces in that part of the world might invite military attack by the North Koreans. To this contention the Carter administration answered that sea and air forces in the Korean area would more than offset any withdrawn ground strength.

The Soviet Union. By Western accounts the Soviet Union was not idle in 1977 in regard to the development of new weapons systems. A new development that Secretary of Defense Brown described as "somewhat troubling" was the appearance of an antisatellite system. According to Brown the Soviets now possess the capability to destroy some American satellites as they orbit the earth. The defense secretary did not disclose exactly which U. S. satellites could be destroyed. The United States operates reconnaissance vehicles that gather information regarding Soviet military activities, as well as early warning, weather, navigational, and communications satellites. Brown said the United States does not currently possess an antisatellite capability, but that research is under way that might produce such a system.

Late in the year the Pentagon announced that the Soviet Union had begun production of a mobile missile designated the SS–16. Although it is obvious that a mobile ICBM would be more difficult to detect and subsequently destroy than a fixed-base ICBM, such a system would have the disadvantage of being less accurate than one fired from a fixed site. Therefore some in the American defense community wondered about the utility of the missile to the Soviet Union.

Given the American decision to deploy cruise missiles aboard B–52 bombers, it was not surprising to learn that the Soviet Union was constructing towers along the Russian borders several hundred feet high to house "down-looking" radar. It was assumed in the West that such installations were designed to give the radar greater time to detect and to track incoming cruise missiles programmed to follow ground-hugging paths to their targets.

Some U. S. defense officials voiced concern over a different form of Soviet activity—the continued construction of civil defense facilities such as shelters to provide protection against nuclear blast, thermal effects, and radiation. It appeared that the greatest effort was invested in protecting elites such as government officials and military leaders, with lesser efforts for key factory personnel. What bothered defense planners was the possibility that Soviet leaders might mistakenly come to believe their civil defense activity would enable the Soviet Union to survive a nuclear exchange with the United States, and thus the Soviet Union would no longer be deterred from war. Secretary Brown commented that it would be very difficult for the government of the Soviet Union to protect its peoples from the effects of an American nuclear attack.

ROBERT M. LAWRENCE
Colorado State University

MINING

The world's mining and mineral processing industry in 1977 generally set new record highs both in terms of quantity and value of output of most commodities. The quantitative highs of 1977 in many cases topped record highs set in 1974; 1975 output for most commodities was appreciably lower than 1974 levels, and in the case of a number of commodities, output in 1976 did not rise to the 1974 levels. Because of inflation and higher real production costs, the pattern of mineral commodity production value changes did not parallel that of the quantitative changes, there being only a slight value downturn in 1975, and continued significant gains following that slump.

Value of World Output. Total world crude mineral output (including fuels) value in 1977 was estimated at about (U. S.) $213 billion (in terms of constant 1973 dollars) compared with $203.3 billion for 1976, $193.2 billion for 1975, $194.9 billion for 1974, and $191.5 billion for 1973 (all previous published figures were revised). Detailed country-by-country results were not available for 1974–77, but almost assuredly the leading nations in 1973 retained their rankings in 1977: the United States and the USSR were in close contention for the position of world leader, each with about 18% of the total, followed by Saudi Arabia (about 6%), China (about 5%), Iran and Canada (each about 4.5%), Venezuela, West Germany, and Libya (each about 3%), and South Africa (about 2.5%).

From the viewpoint of commodities, crude oil clearly remained the leader, accounting for nearly half of the total, followed by anthracite and bituminous coal (with almost 20%), natural gas (about 7%), copper (about 6.5%), iron (about 4.5%), lignite coal and natural gas liquids (each about 2%), and zinc (about 1%).

U. S. Mineral Policy. The Carter administration moved promptly to propose a single agency to centralize U. S. government energy-oriented activities. A new cabinet-level department of energy was established on October 1. At the same time, the Congress was engaged in extensive debates regarding the comprehensive energy policy proposed by the administration. Aside from the energy program, the Carter team did not formulate a comprehensive policy aimed at ensuring supplies of other mineral raw materials for which U. S. domestic resources are inadequate to meet domestic demand. Some—such as manganese ore, chromite, cobalt, and natural diamond—are not produced at all, and others—such as bauxite, nickel, platinum, and fluorspar—are produced domestically in quantities less than U. S. industrial requirements.

Of some interest were continued unsuccessful international deliberations on ocean mining rights. The technology exists in developed nations—including the United States, the USSR, and Japan—to initiate mining of seafloor nodules containing manganese, copper, nickel, and cobalt, thereby improving the world reserve base for these commodities. However, developing nations now producing these commodities claim that such development might prove economically damaging to them. These developing nations fear a reduction in their income from minerals and metals sold to the developed nations. Continued international deadlock over the sharing of profits from offshore mining, however, may provoke the developed nations, the United States included, into taking unilateral action to initiate ocean mining.

Ferrous Ores and Metals. Preliminary and partial information suggests that world iron ore output was of the order of 900 million tons, very close to the 1976 level. Partial 1977 results, extrapolated to full year figures, give the following estimated output levels for the leading world producers (in million tons): USSR, 240; Australia, 100; Brazil, 95; United States, 78; China, 70; India, 50; France, 42; Sweden, 28; Canada, 20; Liberia, 20; Venezuela, 19.

Insufficient data exist to estimate 1977 output of principal ferroalloying metal ores—manganese, chrome, and tungsten. Among newsworthy events in the area of these commodities was the imposition of restrictions on U. S. imports of chromite from Rhodesia in March 1977 in response to that nation's racial policies and the passage in November of a UN Security Council resolution imposing a mandatory embargo on shipments of arms and related materiel to South Africa in retaliation for the country's repression of its black citizens.

World steel production in 1977 is estimated at about 690 million metric tons. Production was estimated as follows (in million metric tons): USSR, 146; United States, 120; Japan, 105; West Germany, 41; and China, 31.

Nonferrous Ores and Metals. It is expected that when complete 1977 worldwide production returns become available, most nonferrous metals will be shown to have achieved new production records, exceeding not only the output levels of 1975 and 1976, but also the 1974 levels that were historical highs for many commodities. All major metals—aluminum, copper, lead, nickel, and zinc—were expected to share in this growth. Mercury output was expected to remain about even with that of 1976, as producers endeavored to improve market conditions by reducing output so that accumulated stocks could decline.

Precious Metals. It is expected that final returns will show continued increases in world production of gold and silver in 1977. Gold output clearly remained below the record level of 50.6 million ounces set in 1969, but may prove to have exceeded 40 million ounces. Silver production was expected to reach 310 million ounces or more. The situation regarding platinum in 1977 remained clouded; world output in 1976 was estimated at about 6 million troy ounces, with the USSR and South Africa together accounting for over 90% of the total.

Fertilizer Materials. Preliminary data suggest that of the three major fertilizer materials (phosphate rock, potash, and nitrogen), only nitrogen registered a record production in 1977. Both phosphate rock and potash showed modest gains over 1976 output levels. In the case of phosphate rock, it is significant to note the downturn in production between 1975 and 1976 registered by the "phosphate islands" of the Pacific—Nauru and Christmas Island—and the sharp decline of output in Western Sahara (from nearly 2.8 million tons in 1975 to only 173,000 tons in 1976). The latter decline was the result of political changes and was sufficient to remove that area from the list of leading producers. In the case of potash, leading producers—such as Canada, West Germany, and France—suffered output declines between 1975 and 1976 and prospects for recovery in 1977 appeared poor.

The world output of nitrogen for the year ending June 30, 1976, totaled 43.9 million metric tons, including the following amounts from major producers: United States, 9.3 million; the USSR, 8.5 million; China, 3.3 million (estimated); Japan, 1.6 million; Poland and India, each 1.5 million; France, 1.4 million; and Rumania and West Germany, each 1.3 million. A level of about 44.7 million tons was expected for the year ending June 30, 1977.

Other Trends. The USSR remained in undisputed first place among world asbestos producers for the third consecutive year in 1977, despite second-ranked Canada's recovery from the major strike of 1975. Although definitive figures were not available, gains in output in 1977 were expected in Cyprus, Brazil, South Africa, and Australia, as well as in the USSR and Canada.

World cement output in 1977 was very close to the 1976 level of 730.7 million metric tons, with production on an increasing trend in the latter part of the year that compensated for disappointing results during the first quarter in many industrialized nations. World gypsum output in 1977 was expected to total about 62 million tons.

Data are insufficient to fix world natural diamond output for 1977. Political problems in major producing nations—including Zaire, South Africa, and Angola—made forecasting difficult. Output in the USSR presumably advanced. There were indications of production in China, but insufficient information was available to fix the level of output there for any year. The output of natural stones continued to be supplemented by the manufacture of diamonds in several nations—including the United States (output estimated at over 17 million carats), South Africa, Ireland, and the USSR.

World sulfur output in 1977 exceeded only slightly the 49.5 million ton level of 1976. *See also* Mineral Production Tables, pages 570–71.

CHARLES L. KIMBELL
U. S. Bureau of the Mines

Sen. Hubert H. Humphrey, a cancer victim, returns to the Capitol in October following a two-month absence.

UPI

MINNESOTA

Minnesota's four million residents continued to capitalize on the state's human and natural resources.

Politics. Counting among its natives the vice president, the secretary of agriculture, and two Supreme Court justices, the state was well represented on the national political scene. Perhaps Minnesota's best-known son, Sen. Hubert H. Humphrey, continued to play a national leadership role although now fighting a battle against terminal cancer. The Senate honored Humphrey with a 30-minute tribute in October.

Rudy Perpich, the state's first governor from its iron-rich northeast corner, governed state operations with a populist approach spiced by a down-home ethnic flair never before seen in the capital.

Economy. Unemployment remained at or below national levels. Ample rains graced state farmlands and many crops yielded record harvests. Although farmers borrowed record sums,

---
MINNESOTA · Information Highlights

Area: 84,068 square miles (217,736 km²).
Population (1976 est.): 3,965,000.
Chief Cities (1970 census): St. Paul, the capital, 309,-828; Minneapolis, 434,400.
Government (1977): *Chief Officers*—governor, Rudy Perpich (DFL); lt. gov., Alec G. Olson (DFL). *Legislature*—Senate, 67 members; House of Representatives, 134 members.
Education (1976–77): *Enrollment*—public elementary schools, 415,084 pupils; public secondary, 447,507; nonpublic, 100,200; colleges and universities, 176,-011 students. *Public school expenditures,* $1,793,-332,000 ($1,670 per pupil).
State Finances (fiscal year 1976): *Revenues,* $4,090,-202,000; *expenditures,* $3,840,302,000.
Personal Income (1976): $24,515,000; per capita, $6,183.
Labor Force (July 1977): *Nonagricultural wage and salary earners,* 1,571,800; *unemployed,* 89,500 (4.6% of total force).

their efforts promoted Minnesota to third rank in the production of food staple crops, such as corn, wheat, rye, oats, and flax.

In midsummer, 14,000 steelworkers struck mines and plants across the Iron Range, halting all iron production. Effects of the walkout soon spread beyond state lines.

Environment. Two state congressmen sparred at home and in Washington over uses of the million acre Boundary Waters Canoe Area on the Canadian border. The controversy over disposal of taconite wastes into Lake Superior by the Reserve Mining Co. stumbled through its ninth year in state and federal courts, but an end seemed near as Reserve began construction of a land waste dump. And in central Minnesota, irate farmers protested in their fields the construction of high-voltage power lines.

Legislature. During its 1977 session, the legislature passed an omnibus transportation bill that appropriated additional funds for highways, mass transit, and railroad subsidies; increased the state minimum wage, unemployment compensation payments, and the employer's tax rates; banned spray cans using chlorofluorocarbon propellants and the sale of milk in nonrefillable plastic containers; and established the Minnesota Department of Economic Security, encompassing the function of several departments.

Since the state has a wide variety of professional sports teams, the legislature authorized up to $60 million to construct a new stadium. A commission was appointed to decide the location of the facility. Bocce ball was declared the official state sport.

GLENN N. SANDVIK
"The Duluth News-Tribune & Herald"

MISSISSIPPI

Municipal elections, reapportionment, and a somewhat disappointing legislative session dominated Mississippi news in 1977.

Municipal Elections. Nearly all of the state's 288 municipalities held elections in June, and in many of these the balloting was the first since a federal court in 1975 rendered a decision requiring them to choose aldermen by wards rather than at large. Black mayors were elected in 15 municipalities, all of which had black populations in excess of 65%, and blacks also increased their numbers among aldermen. Of the larger municipalities, however, only Meridian, Greenville, and Vicksburg elected blacks to the governing board. Republicans won victories in 15 mayoral contests, but Jackson shifted to a Democratic mayor.

Reapportionment. In May, the U. S. Supreme Court ruled that the 1976 legislative redistricting plan fashioned by a three-judge panel of the Fifth U. S. Circuit Court of Appeals diluted black voting strength. In August, the panel invited the legislature, the U. S. Department of

------- MISSISSIPPI · Information Highlights -------

Area: 47,716 square miles (123,584 km²).
Population (1976 est.): 2,354,000.
Chief Cities (1970 census): Jackson, the capital, 153,-968; Biloxi, 48,486; Meridian, 45,083.
Government (1977): *Chief Officers*—governor, Cliff Finch (D); lt. gov., Evelyn Gandy (D). *Legislature*—Senate, 52 members; House of Representatives, 122 members.
Education (1976–77): *Enrollment*—public elementary schools, 282,393 pupils; public secondary, 227,816; nonpublic, 66,300; colleges and universities, 87,743 students. *Public school expenditures,* $549,000,000 ($1,013 per pupil).
State Finances (fiscal year 1976): *Revenues,* $1,836,-834,000; *expenditures,* $1,825,708,000.
Personal Income (1976): $10,663,000,000; per capita, $4,529.
Labor Force (July 1977): *Nonagricultural wage and salary earners,* 762,300; *unemployed,* 60,200 (6.1% of total force).

Justice, and attorneys for the plaintiffs in the case to submit reapportionment plans not later than October 29. Following August and October special sessions, a reluctant legislature filed a plan creating single-member districts which frequently splintered county lines. At year's end, however, this plan had not been ruled upon. A second, and less strict, plan was approved by the legislature in December and submitted to the Justice Department for review under the Federal Voting Rights Act of 1965.

Legislature. The 90-day regular session of the legislature produced a record-large balanced budget without increasing taxes, but few major new programs emerged. The overriding issue of property-tax reform was left unsettled by the legislators, and both government reorganization and revitalization of the sagging state highway program were assigned to interim joint committees for study. Among the significant measures that gained legislative approval in 1977 were regulation of strip mining, reform of the marijuana laws, and revision of the lobbying code.

Miscellany. Early 1977 was marked by record-cold weather that caused serious shortages of natural gas in some areas. President Jimmy Carter visited Mississippi in July, conducting a televised "town meeting" from Yazoo City. Progress continued on the Tennessee-Tombigbee Waterway.

DANA B. BRAMMER
University of Mississippi

MISSOURI

Weather continued to make news in Missouri in 1977. After the coldest winter in nearly a century, heat and drought characterized the early summer. To prove the adage that if Missouri weather is objectionable today, just wait for tomorrow, August ushered in a period of heavy rains which continued into the autumn. On September 12–13, more than 12 inches (30 cm) of rain in less than 24 hours turned Brush Creek, normally a trickle of water flowing south of Kansas City's famed Country Club

UPI
Workmen repair a Sedalia, Mo., home damaged by a tornado. Another home, foreground, was totally destroyed.

Plaza, into a raging torrent. It swept over the shopping center, a show place of the city, causing $30-million in damage and 25 deaths.

Legislation. The 79th General Assembly gave Missouri its first three-billion-dollar budget, but a stalemate over the location of a new state prison necessitated a special session. Then the legislators agreed to a medium security facility in the St. Louis area.

Despite that disagreement, the regular session produced significant legislation. One bill was an overhaul of the 142-year-old criminal code. Election laws were also revised for greater uniformity and efficiency. Under pressure from women's groups, a bill was adopted to limit defense lawyers' use of the previous sexual history of a rape victim, but the legislature once more failed to ratify the Equal Rights Amendment. Two other controversial measures, one providing for changes in the formula

------- MISSOURI · Information Highlights -------

Area: 69,686 square miles (180,487 km²).
Population (1976 est.): 4,778,000.
Chief Cities (1970 census): Jefferson City, the capital, 32,407; St. Louis, 622,236.
Government (1977): *Chief Officers*—governor, Joseph P. Teasdale (D); lt. gov., William C. Phelps (R). *General Assembly*—Senate, 34 members; House of Representatives, 163 members.
Education (1976–77): *Enrollment*—public elementary schools, 630,956 pupils; public secondary, 319,186; nonpublic, 141,200; colleges and universities, 205,-929 students. *Public school expenditures,* $1,246,-624,000.
State Finances (fiscal year 1976): *Revenues,* $2,894,-819,000; *expenditures,* $2,850,813,000.
Personal Income (1976): $28,494,000,000; per capita, $5,963.
Labor Force (July 1977): *Nonagricultural wage and salary earners,* 1,782,000; *unemployed,* 121,700 (5.6% of total force).

for public school aid and the other for adjustments in welfare benefits, were passed.

Governor's Troubles. The new governor, Joseph P. Teasdale, divided his efforts between legislative issues and some 120 appointments to state agencies. Senate confirmation of key appointees often proved as difficult to obtain as enactment of the governor's pet bills. During the gubernatorial campaign, Teasdale had charged that the Public Service Commission too often favored the utilities, but his efforts to force mass resignations and to place consumer advocate Alberta Slavin on the commission failed. "Senatorial courtesy" also blocked several other Teasdale appointments. His removal of James T. LePage as director of the Department of Revenue occasioned considerable criticism.

In July, Richard J. Rabbitt, speaker of the Missouri House of Representatives, 1973–1976, and representative since 1960, was convicted on 15 counts of extortion and mail fraud involving pay-offs from lobbyists. This was the first major scandal in Missouri politics since the Pendergast era of the 1920's and 1930's.

Unresolved in 1977 was that perennial controversy over the future of Lambert Field as St. Louis' major airport.

RUTH W. TOWNE
Northeast Missouri State University

MONTANA

The year opened with the announcement on January 5 of the purchase of the Anaconda Company, the third largest copper producer, by the Atlantic-Richfield Company (ARCO), the nation's eighth largest oil company.

The Legislative Session. The biennial session of the Legislative Assembly opened on January 3. Gov. Tom Judge urged restraint on expenditures in spite of a $52-million surplus. The unusually harmonious session was controlled by the Democrats in the House, 58 to 42, and in the evenly divided Senate, 25 to 25, because in such cases the presiding officer must be of the governor's party.

No landmark legislation was passed, but a

--- MONTANA · Information Highlights ---

Area: 147,138 square miles (381,087 km²).
Population (1976 est.): 753,000.
Chief Cities (1970 census): Helena, the capital, 22,557; Billings, 61,581; Great Falls, 60,091.
Government (1977): *Chief Officers*—governor, Thomas L. Judge (D); lt. gov., Ted Schwinden (D). *Legislature*—Senate, 50 members; House of Representatives, 100 members.
Education (1976–77): *Enrollment*—public elementary schools, 112,930 pupils; public secondary, 57,622; nonpublic, 8,800; colleges and universities, 29,812 students. *Public school expenditures*, $301,400,000 ($1,649 per pupil).
State Finances (fiscal year 1976): *Revenues*, $737,101,-000; *expenditures*, $687,758,000.
Personal Income (1976): $4,283,000,000; per capita, $5,689.
Labor Force (July 1976): *Nonagricultural wage and salary earners*, 256,700; *unemployed*, 20,300 (5.9% of total force).

tax relief measure for property owners, which the people had approved in November, was funded by $29,600,000. Taxes on livestock were reduced, and inheritance taxes were modified so that payments on such estates as large ranches would be easier to meet.

A proposed constitutional amendment would empower the legislature's Interim Finance Committee to control budget amendments. Another would raise the legal drinking age from 18 to 19. An energy office was created in the office of the lieutenant governor, and the governor was given "emergency powers in energy crisis situations." A new judicial district, the 19th, was created for Lincoln and Sanders counties. Newsmen were protected against demands that they reveal sources of information. Controversial HB 122, an 876-page measure proposing many changes in local government, was defeated.

Other Events. A two-month hearing on a Department of Natural Resources study of the municipal, industrial, agricultural, and recreational needs for the water in the Yellowstone River presented a future demand for several times more water than the river produces.

U. S. Sen. Lee Metcalf's announcement that he would not seek reelection in 1978 after 26 years in Congress brought an announcement of candidacy from the first district congressman, Democrat Max Baucus. Many candidates then announced for the Baucus House seat.

Other noteworthy events included a controversial International Woman's Year meeting in Helena, dominated by conservatives; Crow and Cheyenne Indian negotiations with coal companies for the extraction of enormous amounts of coal from their reservations; only one major forest fire—just south of Missoula—in a dry summer; and depressingly low agricultural prices for near-record production.

MERRILL G. BURLINGAME
Montana State University

MONTREAL

Like Expo '67, the '76 Olympics left Montreal an economically ill city. Available jobs have decreased by 15,000, despite the creation of 48,000 new jobs in Quebec province. Between July 1976 and July 1977, unemployment in the city jumped from 6.3 to 9.5%, which was only 1% less than the provincial average. This depression results from a combination of factors—economic stagnation throughout Canada, investors' fear of the governing Parti Québécois (according to some), post-Olympic slump, and high taxes which were raised even higher to pay for the Olympics. The federal government has declared Montreal a "designated area," making it eligible for special grants that could create about 25,000 new jobs in the next three years—provided that the grants materialize and verbose federal-provincial conflicts are put to rest.

An antique auto exhibit was held at La Place in the weather-protected Desjardins complex in Montreal early in the year. The center, built in 1976, contains office towers and a shopping mall.

UPI

Despite the opening of some facilities to the public, the main "white elephant"—the Olympic Stadium itself—is still the object of a study conducted by the Marsan committee (will it recommend that a $150-million roof be added?). It has allowed commercial sports, such as baseball and football, and mass entertainment, such as an Emerson, Lake and Palmer concert, to draw between 50,000 and 60,000 spectators. Meanwhile, another huge project, a Center for Congresses, remains shrouded in uncertainty. Such a center, according to the tourist industry, would restore Montreal to its former role of tourist metropolis, despite U. S. fiscal restrictions on national congresses held outside its borders.

If, in 1976, political analysts forecast a stiff fight between Mayor Jean Drapeau's Parti Civique and the RCM (Rassemblement des citoyens de Montréal) in the municipal elections scheduled for November 1978, a split in the RCM, between what have been labeled as the left and the center, leaves the opposition rather weak for the next challenge. By maintaining a low profile, Mayor Drapeau is riding the post-Olympic wave. The standing of the parties in City Hall is now: Parti Civique, 36 seats, RCM, 18, and 1 independent.

A thorough overhaul of the Urban Community of Montreal police force was started with the replacement of Director René Daigneault by H.-P. Vignola and Inspector André de Luca as his deputy. The top-heavy hierarchy has been streamlined, and more efficiency is expected of the 5,200-man force. Policemen have obtained a promise from the city to spend $141 million in the next 50 years for retired policemen, their widows, or orphans. In return, they have dropped their suit for $26 million. A new deal has been struck, and everybody, except the underworld, hopes the unified force will finally become efficient.

JEAN-PIERRE WALLOT
University of Montreal

MOROCCO

After five years of rule by decree, King Hassan II gambled on his huge popularity in 1977, and restored a Moroccan parliament overwhelmingly favorable to him. But Hassan's success with internal politics was eclipsed by the relentless war in the former Spanish Sahara that drained Morocco's morale and resources.

Spanish Sahara. The Algerian-backed Polisario Front insurgents, seeking autonomy for the territory annexed by Morocco and Mauritania in 1976, tied down more than a third of Morocco's 90,000-strong armed forces in about 15 fortified towns. Military spending increased by 50% to $733 million in 1977 and, with troop morale low, Hassan dispatched a handpicked force of 1,200 soldiers to Zaire to help beat back a force of invaders in Shaba province.

The first of some 1,200 Moroccan troops are dispatched to Zaire to help defeat a force invading the province of Shaba.

LIAISON AGENCY

Polisario losses in the Sahara were believed small, 5–10 monthly, while one estimate of the Moroccan death toll was 50 a month.

Compounding Morocco's difficulties was the need to bolster its weak partner in the annexation, Mauritania, which got the southern third of the territory ceded by Spain. Mauritania relied increasingly on Moroccan air and ground support following several daring raids by Polisario on the heavily garrisoned Mauritanian mining center of Zouerate. Morocco airlifted 600 troops to Zouerate in July to defend the town whose iron ore mines account for more than 70% of Mauritania's income.

Morocco had counted on the territory's economic resources to help finance its own growth, but the 1.7 billion tons of exceptionally pure phosphates at Bu Craa largely remained in the ground. Polisario attacks continued to close down the conveyor belt that carries phosphates to port and hampered Moroccan efforts to move the mineral, which is used in fertilizer, by truck.

Both the United Nations and the Organization of African Unity found the dispute too hot to handle. The UN issued contradictory resolutions, while the OAU postponed indefinitely a special summit on the war scheduled at its February conference in Togo. Morocco walked out of the opening session in Togo to protest the presence of a Polisario delegation. Both Prince Fahd of Saudi Arabia and President Léopold Senghor of Senegal tried to mediate between Morocco and Algeria, which supports the insurgents.

Politics. Riding the crest of a popular wave dating from the November 1975 march by 300,000 Moroccans into the Spanish Sahara, King Hassan restored parliamentary democracy as a "reward" to opposition parties that support his policy of defending the annexed territory at all costs. Independents who called themselves "unconditional monarchists" and backers of "Hassanism" won an absolute majority in the parliament, surpassing the old-guard conservative parties. All told, supporters of the king gained 187 of the 264 seats in the new Chamber of Representatives, while the opposition vote was badly split. Unlike previous attempts to form a parliament, the opposition parties took part in the elections, although they contended that restoring democracy was merely a cover for continued royal absolutism. The nationalist opposition, Istiqlal, won 45 seats, while the other main opposition, the Socialist Union of Popular Forces, captured only 16. Socialist Union leader Abderrahim Bouabid, whom Hassan brought into the cabinet along with the Istiqlal leader three months before the elections, claimed the vote was rigged and resigned.

Economy. The stagnating world price for phosphates, mainstay of the economy, and the increasing cost of paying for the war in the Sahara contributed to an economic downturn in 1977. But Morocco got a needed boost from the long-term multimillion dollar sale of 5 million tons of phosphate ore to the Soviet Union. The sale, which Moroccan officials said included a tacit Soviet pledge not to take sides between Morocco and Algeria in the Sahara dispute, angered Algeria and the Polisario Front. The 1977 budget of $4.9 billion earmarked about half for development spending, including an urgent program to develop the Sahara territory. Tourism slumped, unemployment remained a serious problem, and an inflation rate of nearly 20% more than neutralized late 1976 pay increases.

JOSEPH MARGOLIS
"African Update," African-American Institute

─── **MOROCCO · Information Highlights** ───

Official Name: Kingdom of Morocco.
Location: Northwest Africa.
Area: 172,413 square miles (446,550 km²).
Population (1977 est.): 18,300,000.
Chief Cities (1973 est.): Rabat, the capital, 385,000; Casablanca, 2,000,000; Marrakesh, 330,000; Fez, 322,000.
Government: *Head of state,* Hassan II, king (acceded 1961). *Head of government,* Ahmed Osman, premier (took office 1972).
Monetary Unit: Dirham (4.56 dirhams equal U. S.$1, Aug. 1977).
Manufacturing (major products): Processed foods, metals, textiles, wine, cement, leather goods, chemicals and pharmaceuticals.
Major Agricultural Products: Barley, wheat, citrus fruits, vegetables, sugar beets, almonds, tomatoes, grapes, sheep, wool.

Star Wars, starring Harrison Ford, right, Alec Guinness, and Mark Hamill, was generally proclaimed as the movie of the year and was expected to succeed *Jaws* as the box office champion.

MOTION PICTURES

After a long period in which male film stars dominated the screen, actresses began to retrieve their place of importance in films that stressed the role of women in relationships. Perhaps it was a result of new attention to the position of women in society; perhaps it was merely a swing of the pendulum. Whatever the reason, the "buddy" films were giving way to motion pictures featuring actresses.

The most dynamic impression was made by Diane Keaton, acknowledged increasingly as a major talent. She had already become known as the skillful and appealing leading lady in Woody Allen's comedies. Keaton conveyed poignancy as well as humor in *Annie Hall*, a popular film that illustrated Allen's artistic growth. She expanded her range dramatically with her tour de force in *Looking for Mr. Goodbar*, thereby earning recognition as a dramatic actress of high caliber.

Jane Fonda had one of the best dramatic roles of her career as the youthful Lillian Hellman in *Julia*, based on Hellman's reminiscence in *Pentimento* of her friendship with an anti-Nazi heroine in the 1930's. Vanessa Redgrave, although on screen less, made a memorable impact as Julia. Two extraordinary women's roles were played by Shelley Duvall and Sissy Spacek in Robert Altman's *3 Women*. Canadian actress Hollis McLaren had another of the year's choice parts as a schizophrenic in *Outrageous*, an unusual Canadian film. Kathleen Quinlan made

an auspicious starring debut as a schizophrenic in *I Never Promised You a Rose Garden*. Marsha Mason was *The Goodbye Girl*, a character enduring troubles with men and her stage career in a script by Neil Simon. Liv Ullmann, who received the New York Film Critics Circle's best actress award for *Face to Face*, was back in Ingmar Bergman's *The Serpent's Egg*, about the ominous conditions in Germany in the 1920's. Memories of the types of vehicles that existed for actresses in the 1930's and 1940's were stirred by *The Turning Point*, a backstage ballet drama fraught with frustrations and jealousies. Anne Bancroft played the dancer who went on to become a star, Shirley MacLaine her friend who gave up dancing for domesticity.

Geraldine Chaplin made contributions in three films, as a troubled, lonely woman in *Welcome to L. A.*, both the mother and her grown-up daughter in the reminiscence *Cria!* (Spanish), and a woman in love with a gigolo in *Roseland*. Lilia Skala, veteran actress and an Oscar nominee in 1963 for *Lilies of the Field*, was lauded for her portrayal in *Roseland* of an aging regular at New York's landmark ballroom. The greatest reception of an actress from France in some time was accorded Isabelle Huppert for her sensitive performance as the shy, pliable young woman in *The Lacemaker*. Märthe Keller was given a Hollywood buildup for *Black Sunday* and *Bobby Deerfield*. Lily Tomlin again demonstrated her magnetism in *The Late Show*.

Written by and starring Robby Benson, *One on One* was declared by some the *Rocky* of 1977.

The Men. Actors were not being neglected. As a result of the Academy Awards lavished upon *Rocky,* its author and star, Sylvester Stallone, loomed as an important new force and was being widely sought for assorted roles. Richard Dreyfuss had a dynamic part as the irrepressible actor in *The Goodbye Girl* and also starred in *Close Encounters of the Third Kind.* Henry Winkler, whose fame derived from playing Fonzie in *Happy Days* on television, starred effectively in *Heroes,* about a returning Vietnam veteran with problems. Although *Bobby Deerfield* was cooly received by critics, Al Pacino was generally praised for his acting. Richard Burton regained ground lost through some of the lesser films in which he has appeared by giving an electric performance in *Equus.* John Gielgud and Dirk Bogarde excelled in *Providence.* Craig Russell, who impersonates female stars on the nightclub circuit, used his act as a centerpiece for his lively, sensitive dramatic role as a female impersonator in *Outrageous.*

Among the most discussed male performances of the year were the acting efforts of ballet's famed stars, Rudolf Nureyev and Mikhail Baryshnikov. Nureyev fared questionably, being left on a limb by the excesses of director Ken Russell, whose *Valentino* starred Nureyev as the silent screen lover. Nureyev tried hard but won few admirers. It was different for Baryshnikov, who demonstrated a strong, promising screen presence both in acting and dancing.

Industry. On the surface, the most encouraging event for the film industry was the success of *Star Wars.* Although the film, which recaptured the aura of such old movie serials as *Buck Rogers* and *Flash Gordon,* had little buildup, it instantly attracted legions of admirers and repeat viewers. *Jaws* had won the box office film championship, but *Star Wars* was projected as the new winner when all of the national and international figures were in. This popularity whetted the appetite of producers eager for such bonanzas, of which *Rocky* was another pivotal example. While this offered encouragement to an industry often in the doldrums, it also worked against those hoping to make films of less universal appeal and profit potential.

Meanwhile, theater operators were continuing to feel a crunch. Complaints about shortage of product did not necessarily mean fewer films were available, but that there were fewer capable of packing the theaters. When a potential winner did come along, the distributors were demanding sky-high payments for making them available. Theater owners were seeking ways of at least remaining solvent if not reaping profits. An experiment was begun to see whether advertisements shown on screen might be an answer, or whether they would stir audience resentment to the detriment of the theaters.

Big budget films were risky despite previous successes. *A Bridge Too Far* ($25 million) appeared seriously overextended when the response did not match the enthusiasm of producer Joseph E. Levine. Likewise, despite the encouragement of Dino De Laurentiis, his *King Kong* ($2 million) disappointed and was quickly forgotten. Columbia had some $23 million on the line with *Close Encounters of the Third Kind,* directed by Steven Spielberg, who made *Jaws.* One of the biggest fiascos was William

FROM THE MOTION PICTURE ''THE LATE SHOW,''
COURTESY OF WARNER BROTHERS INC., COPYRIGHT © 1977

The year of the actress: Lily Tomlin was very funny as she tried to help detective Art Carney in *The Late Show*.

FROM THE MOTION PICTURE ''A PIECE OF THE ACTION,''
COURTESY OF WARNER BROTHERS INC., COPYRIGHT © 1977

Sidney Poitier and Bill Cosby are two criminals trapped into becoming social workers in *A Piece of the Action*.

Friedkin's $22 million remake of the French thriller *The Wages of Fear,* this time called *Sorcerer. Exorcist II, the Heretic* was such a pale sequel that its release was barely noticed.

Controversy. When *1900,* the latest feature of Bernardo Bertolucci (*Last Tango in Paris*), was released in Italy it was more than five hours long. Paramount, with a contract for its showing in the United States, wanted it cut to three and one-half hours. The producer, Alberto Grimaldi, obliged, and Bertolucci shouted foul, maintaining that his work was being destroyed. After much verbiage, acrimony, and international protest, a version running four hours and five minutes was agreed upon, premiered at the New York Film Festival, and then released to mixed reviews. Through a combination of Hollywood-style romanticism and Marxist-oriented politics, Bartolucci attempted to portray the dynamics of Italian class struggle in this century.

Salò, the last film made by Pier Paolo Pasolini before he was murdered, also stirred intense controversy, and was subjected to censorship in Europe. When shown unfettered at the New York Film Festival and then placed in release, it stood revealed as a serious if distasteful allegory about the brutality of authoritarianism. Pasolini, who adapted the Marquis de Sade's *120 Days of Sodom,* saw fascism in terms of an orgy of perversion and torture.

Gregory Peck complained that some of his strongest scenes in *MacArthur* were omitted to avoid building sentiment for the controversial general, depicted by Peck in the drama of war and politics. Peck succeeded in having some of the scenes restored, but the film, although in-

teresting for the history it covered, lacked sufficient fire to convey convincingly the turbulence of MacArthur's military and public life.

Mores. The gap widened between old filmmaking taboos and contemporary permissiveness. Those with an aversion to anything-goes language, frontal nudity, and explicit sex on screen were finding their sensibilities ignored. Cases in point were two sports-oriented comedies. *Slap Shot,* starring Paul Newman as a hockey player, had the kind of profanity that in other days would have been unthinkable for a major Hollywood film. *Semi-Tough* teamed Kris Kristofferson and Burt Reynolds as pro football players in love with the same woman (Jill Clayburgh), and all freely exercised new language prerogatives. In *Valentino,* Nureyev was seen frontally nude, and in *1900,* De Niro and Depardieu were exhibited with the same candor. Until recently male nudity was frowned upon, even while female nudity was permitted. The rating system has become much more lenient in accordance with the public's acceptance of change. What formerly would have been an X (under 17 banned) was now an R (under 17 admitted only with an adult) or even a PG (parental guidance suggested). Violence was increasingly a factor in determining the stringency of a rating.

Honors. In the Academy Awards competition, the five top honors were: best picture, *Rocky;* best direction, John Avildsen for *Rocky;* best actor, Peter Finch for *Network* (posthumously); best actress, Faye Dunaway for *Network;* best screenplay, Paddy Chayefsky for *Network.* The major surprise at the Oscar cere-

Agnès Varda directed Valerie Mairesse and Thérèse Liotard in *One Sings, the Other Doesn't,* the story of a lasting friendship between two young women.

Jane Fonda is Lillian Hellman and Vanessa Redgrave portrays the title role in *Julia,* which is based on a true story by Hellman.

20TH CENTURY-FOX

MOTION PICTURES OF 1977

Airport 1977. Director, Jerry Jameson; screenplay by Michael Scheff and David Spector. With Jack Lemmon, Brenda Vaccaro, Lee Grant, Joseph Cotton, Olivia de Havilland, James Stewart.

Annie Hall. Director, Woody Allen; written by Woody Allen and Marshall Brickman. With Woody Allen, Diane Keaton, Carol Kane, Paul Simon, Colleen Dewhurst.

Between the Lines. Director, John Micklin Silver; screenplay by Fred Barron. With John Heard, Lindsay Crouse, Jeff Goldblum.

Black and White in Color. Director, Jean-Jacques Annaud; screenplay, Annaud, Georges Conchon. With Jacques Spiesser, Jean Carnet, Jacques Dufilho, Catherine Rouvel.

Black Sunday. Director, John Frankenheimer; screenplay by Ernest Lehman, Kenneth Ross, Ivan Moffat; based on novel by Thomas Harris. With Robert Shaw, Bruce Dern, Märthe Keller, Fritz Weaver.

Bobby Deerfield. Director and producer, Sydney Pollack; based on novel by Erich Maria Remarque. With Al Pacino, Märthe Keller.

A Bridge Too Far. Director, Richard Attenborough; screenplay by William Goldman. With Robert Redford, Sean Connery, Michael Caine, Dirk Bogarde, Laurence Olivier, Liv Ullmann.

Close Encounters of the Third Kind. Director, Steven Spielberg; screenplay, Spielberg. With Richard Dreyfuss, François Truffaut, Teri Garr, Melinda Dillon.

Cria! Directed and written by Carlos Saura; produced by Elias Querejeta. With Geraldine Chaplin, Ana Torrent.

The Deep. Director, Peter Yates; screenplay by Peter Benchley and Tracy Keenan Wynn; based on Benchley's novel. With Robert Shaw, Jacqueline Bisset, Nick Nolte.

Equus. Director, Sidney Lumet; screenplay by Peter Shaffer, based on his play. With Richard Burton, Peter Firth.

Exorcist II. Director, John Boorman; screenplay by William Goodhart. With Linda Blair, Louise Fletcher, Richard Burton, Max von Sydow.

Fellini's Casanova. Director, Federico Fellini. With Donald Sutherland.

Fun With Dick and Jane. Director, Ted Kotcheff. With George Segal, Jane Fonda, Ed McMahon.

The Goodbye Girl. Director, Herbert Ross; screenplay by Neil Simon. With Richard Dreyfuss, Marsha Mason, Quinn Cummings.

Greased Lightning. Director, Michael Schultz. With Richard Pryor, Cleavon Little, Beau Bridges, Vincent Gardenia, Richard Havens, Julian Bond.

Handle With Care. Director, Jonathan Demme; screenplay by Paul Brickman. With Ann Wedgeworth, Candy Clark, Alix Elias.

Heroes. Director, Jeremy Paul Kagen; screenplay, James Carabatsos. With Henry Winkler, Sally Field.

I Never Promised You a Rose Garden. Director, Anthony Page; screenplay by Gavin Lambert and Lewis John Carlino; based on novel by Hannah Green. With Bibi Andersson, Kathleen Quinlan, Sylvia Sidney.

Julia. Director, Fred Zinnemann; screenplay, Alvin Sargent; based on story by Lillian Hellman. With Jane Fonda, Vanessa Redgrave, Jason Robards, Hal Holbrook, Maximilian Schell.

Kentucky Fried Movie. Director, John Landis; screenplay by Jerry Zucker, James Abrahams, David Zucker.

The Lacemaker. Director, Claude Goretta; screenplay, Goretta, Pascal Lainé. With Isabelle Huppert, Yves Beneyton.

The Last Remake of Beau Geste. Director, Marty Feldman. With Ann-Margaret, Marty Feldman, Michael York, Peter Ustinov, James Earl Jones.

The Late Show. Directed and written by Robert Benton. With Art Carney, Lily Tomlin.

Let Joy Reign Supreme. Director, Bertrand Tavernier; screenplay, Tavernier, Jean Aurenche. With Philippe Noiret, Jean Rochefort, Jean-Pierre Marielle.

Looking for Mr. Goodbar. Director, Richard Brooks; screenplay, Brooks; based on novel by Judith Rossner. With Diane Keaton, Richard Kiley, Tuesday Weld, William Atherton.

MacArthur. Director, Joseph Sargent; written by Hal Barwood and Matthew Robbins. With Gregory Peck, Ed Flanders, Dan O'Herlihy.

The Man Who Loved Women. Director, François Truffaut; screenplay, Truffaut, Michel Fermaud, Suzanne Schiffman. With Charles Denner, Brigitte Fossey, Nelly Borgeaud, Geneviève Fontanel, Leslie Caron.

Sophia Loren and Marcello Mastroianni star in the Carlo Ponti production, *A Special Day*. Ettore Scola was the director.

Mr. Klein. Director, Joseph Losey; script by Franco Solinas. With Alain Delon, Jeanne Moreau.

New York, New York. Director, Martin Scorsese; screenplay, Earl Mac Rauch, Mardik Martin. With Robert DeNiro, Liza Minnelli.

1900. Director, Bernardo Bertolucci; screenplay, Bertolucci, Franco Arcalli, Giuseppe Bertolucci. With Robert DeNiro, Gérard Depardieu, Dominique Sanda, Burt Lancaster, Sterling Hayden.

Oh, God! Director, Carl Reiner; screenplay by Larry Gelbart; based on novel by Avery Corman. With George Burns, John Denver, Teri Garr, Donald Pleasence.

One on One. Director, Lamont Johnson; written by Robby Benson and Jerry Segal. With Robby Benson, Annette O'Toole, Gail Strickland.

One Sings, the Other Doesn't. Directed and written by Agnès Varda. With Valerie Mairesse, Thérèse Liotard.

The Other Side of Midnight. Director, Charles Jarrott; based on novel by Sidney Sheldon. With Marie-France Pisier, Susan Sarandon, John Beck, Raf Vallone.

Outrageous. Directed and written by Richard Benner; screenplay by Richard Benner. With Craig Russell, Hollis McLaren.

A Piece of the Action. Director, Sidney Poitier; screenplay by Charles Blackwell. With Sidney Poitier, Bill Cosby, James Earl Jones.

Providence. Director, Alain Resnais; screenplay, David Mercer. With Dirk Bogarde, John Gielgud, David Warner, Ellen Burstyn.

Pumping Iron. Directors and producers, George Butler and Robert Fiore. With Arnold Schwartzenegger, Louis Ferrigno, Michael Katz, Ken Waller.

Rollercoaster. Director, James Goldstone; screenplay by Richard Levinson and William Link. With George Segal, Timothy Buttons, Susan Strasberg, Henry Fonda.

Roseland. Director, James Ivory. With Geraldine Chaplin, Joan Copeland, Don DeNatale, Helen Gallagher, Lou Jacobi.

Semi-Tough. Director, Michael Ritchie; screenplay, Walter Bernstein. With Burt Reynolds, Kris Kristofferson, Jill Clayburgh.

Short Eyes. Director, Robert M. Young; screenplay, Miguel Piñero. With José Pérez, Nathan George, Don Blakely, Shawn Elliott, Tito Goya.

Slap Shot. Director, George Roy Hill; written by Nancy Dowd. With Paul Newman, Lindsay Crouse.

Sorcerer. Director and producer, William Friedkin; screenplay, William Green; based on the novel *The Wages of Fear* by Georges Arnaud. With Roy Scheider, Bruno Cremer, Francisco Rabal.

A Special Day. Director, Ettore Scola; story and screenplay by Ruggero Maccari and Scola in collaboration with Mauzirio Costanzo. With Sophia Loren, Marcello Mastroianni.

The Spy Who Loved Me. Director, Lewis Gilbert; screenplay, Christopher Wood, Richard Maibaum; based on Ian Fleming novel. With Roger Moore, Barbara Bach, Curt Jürgens.

Star Wars. Written and directed by George Lucas. With Mark Hamil, Harrison Ford, Carrie Fisher, Peter Cushing, Alec Guinness.

Stroszek. Written and directed by Werner Herzog. With Bruno S., Eva Mattes, Clemens Scheitz.

That Obscure Object of Desire. Director, Luís Buñuel. With Fernando Rey, Carole Bouquet, Angela Molina.

Thieves. Director, John Berry; screenplay by Herb Gardner. With Marlo Thomas, Charles Grodin.

3 Women. Director, writer, and producer, Robert Altman. With Shelley Duvall, Sissy Spacek, Janice Rule, Robert Fortier.

The Turning Point. Director, Herbert Ross; screenplay, Arthur Laurents. With Anne Bancroft, Shirley MacLaine, Mikhail Baryshnikov, Leslie Browne.

Valentino. Director, Ken Russell. With Rudolf Nureyev, Leslie Caron, Michelle Phillips, Carol Kane.

Welcome to L. A. Directed and written by Alan Rudolph. With Keith Carradine, Geraldine Chaplin, Sissy Spacek.

Which Way is Up? Director, Michael Schultz; adapted from Lina Wertmüller's *The Seduction of Mimi*. With Richard Pryor.

You Light Up My Life. Produced, written, and directed by Joseph Brooks. With Didi Conn, Joe Silver, Melanie Mayron, Michael Zaslow.

mony was the victory in the best foreign language film category. There had been few doubts that the winner would be either Lina Wertmüller's *Seven Beauties* or Jean-Charles Tacchella's *Cousin Cousine*. The winner was a film few had heard of prior to screenings, *Black and White in Color,* an antiwar story in an Ivory Coast setting, directed by Jean-Jacques Annaud, who previously made documentaries and TV commercials.

The New York Film Critics gave its best picture honor to *All the President's Men,* as did the National Society of Film Critics. At the Cannes Film Festival, the top honor went to *Padre Padrone* (Italy), a drama made for television about a Sardinian shepherd who becomes self-educated and a novelist. The New York Film Society at Lincoln Center honored director Martin Scorsese for his work on the occasion of the release of *New York, New York,* which opened to sharply divided opinions. Scorsese is a prime example of the student filmmaker (New York University Film School) who rose to success in the commercial world.

Legacy. Some 50,000 films from many countries constitute the imposing legacy to cinema of Henri Langlois, who died at the age of 62 in Paris. Langlois earned a lofty place among film historians by founding the French Cinémathèque in Paris, and dedicatedly gathering and preserving films for viewing and study. Many of today's major filmmakers acknowledge the importance of the Cinémathèque to their education, enabling them to see the works of past directors and learn from their technique. The accomplishment of Langlois has inspired further efforts to preserve films, now recognized as an important art form. Since they were not regarded with such reverence in earlier days, and since films were on perishable stock, important works were lost. The American Film Institute has a program of tracking down films of value, preserving them, and when necessary, transferring them to durable stock.

WILLIAM WOLF, *Film Critic, "Cue"*

MOZAMBIQUE

In 1977, Mozambique pursued its previously established goals of institutionalizing a Marxist system, reordering society, and sustaining the campaign against white-ruled Rhodesia.

Politics. The outstanding political event occurred in February when the Frente de Libertacão de Moçambique (FRELIMO) held its third congress. FRELIMO declared itself a vanguard Marxist-Leninist party. This capped a long Marxist evolutionary path from formation in 1962, through a 10-year war (1964–1974), to sovereignty in 1975. President Samora Machel told the congress that "the creation of the party comes as a necessity for the development of the revolution." FRELIMO strives to destroy capitalism. Hospitals, schools, and law services were nationalized to provide equal treatment for all.

Economy. Of all FRELIMO priorities, economic development was foremost. The economy suffered severe disruption with the exodus of nearly all 200,000 Portuguese settlers who feared African rule and Marxism. The 1976 border closing with Rhodesia to underscore commitment to majority rule and to comply with UN sanctions has cost $385 million, offset by only $100 million in foreign aid. With technicians and capital lacking, Mozambique has received much aid from the Soviet bloc as well as Western socialist and capitalist countries. The impact of the aid has not been felt. Only tea has come near the 1973 peak crop production. The giant hydroelectric dam, Cabora Bassa on the Zambezi River, started only limited output in June. Full production is not expected until sometime in 1978.

Agriculture is emphasized as the base of development, with industrialization viewed as the dynamic factor. Plans and initial efforts in 1977 have been along collectivist patterns rather than those of private farms. Yet FRELIMO was cautious about taking over private firms.

Foreign Affairs. Cooperative economic projects were planned with Tanzania and Zambia. As one of the five "front-line" states, Mozambique allows use of its territory by Zimbabwe guerrillas, whose raids have brought retaliatory strikes from Rhodesia. FRELIMO reported 150 raids causing 1,432 deaths and $13 million in property damage in its appeal to the UN Security Council, which asked member states in June to give material assistance to Mozambique's defense. Communist and non-Communist states, including the United States, supported the resolution. So far, most military equipment and training cadres have come from the Soviet bloc and Cuba.

Internationally, Mozambique's relations have grown closer to the USSR and more distant from China. In March, Mozambique and the USSR signed a 20-year friendship and cooperation treaty during President Nikolai Podgorny's visit to Mozambique. Relations also became much warmer with Cuba, which now trains many Mozambicans.

THOMAS H. HENRIKSEN
State University of New York, Plattsburgh

───── **MOZAMBIQUE · Information Highlights** ─────

Official Name: People's Republic of Mozambique.
Location: East Africa.
Area: 302,328 square miles (783,029 km²).
Population (1977 est.): 9,500,000.
Chief City (1973 est.): Maputo, the capital, 383,775.
Government: *Head of state and government,* Samora Machel (took office June 1975). *Legislature* (unicameral)—People's Assembly.
Monetary Unit: Escudo (38.71 escudos equal U. S.$1, Apr. 1977).
Manufacturing (major products): Petroleum products, beer, cement.
Major Agricultural Products: Cashews, cotton, sugar, copra, tea.

MUSIC

There was double meaning in the symbolic gesture of Jan. 1, 1977, when samples of American music of over 200 years were placed in a time capsule in Washington, D. C. The U. S. A.'s bicentennial was over. Returned to its normal back position on the nation's programs in 1977, American-composed classical music was honored more in premieres than in the repeat performances essential for acceptance.

New Works. Among the few American composers substantially recognized was David Del Tredici. His *Final Alice,* widely praised, was performed by six major orchestras. The repeat performances were supported by the terms of the original National Endowment for the Arts' Bicentennial Commission. Among the notable major premieres were Elliott Carter's *A Symphony of Three Orchestras* (New York, February 17), Gene Gutche's *Perseus and Andromeda XX* (Cincinnati, February 25), Jacob Druckman's *Chiaroscura* (Cleveland, April 14), George Crumb's *Star Child* (New York, May 5), Sir Michael Tippett's Symphony No. 4 (Chicago, October 6), Andrew Imbrie's Flute Concerto (New York City, October 13), Michael Colgrass' *Déja Vu* (New York City, October 20), Toru Takemitsu's *A Flock Descends into the Pentagonal Garden* (San Francisco, November 30).

Richard Wernick, a 43-year-old music professor at the University of Pennsylvania, was awarded the Pulitzer Prize in music for his *Visions of Terror and Wonder* for mezzo soprano and orchestra. The work was first performed at the Aspen Music Festival in July 1976.

Most new music in concert remained the province of numerous specialized performing groups, including the Group for Contemporary Music, New York; Boston's Musica Viva; and the Contemporary Chamber Players, Chicago. From their performances, occasional larger works on symphony programs, new scores for ballet, film, and theater, a larger pattern could be discerned.

The long crisis in modern musical style showed increased signs of resolving and a clearer sense of direction. The polarity of the extremes was reduced.

Improvisatory, chance, and notational procedures were drawn upon as additional and useful, but not exclusive, ways to write. As composers worked with and incorporated idioms from every era into their music, the new eclecticism was more decisively affirmed. Meanwhile, those who persisted in pursuing the old extreme ideas, whether of the former avant-garde or of the reactionary conventionalism, became more isolated, academic, and repetitive.

There were other premieres and other repeats of new works, as well as echoes of bi-

MARIANNE BARCELLONA, PHOTOGRAPHER
COURTESY, NEW YORK PHILHARMONIC

At Avery Fisher Hall, the successful "Celebration of Black Composers" featured Leon Thompson conducting the New York Philharmonic and Irene Oliver as soloist.

centennial-year commissioning projects, but basically, the big budget orchestras retreated to conservatively hedged programs. The Minnesota Orchestra was selected in the major orchestras category for one of the 20 awards for service to contemporary music. Ironically, the Minnesota Orchestra was one of the least active in that sphere. Somewhat later, its conductor, Stanislav Skrowaczewski, resigned as of August 1979 to have more time to compose.

Orchestra Developments. The singular orchestra events included festivals commemorating the 150th anniversary of Beethoven's death, by the Cleveland Orchestra in Cleveland, New York, and Mexico City, under Loren Maazel, and by the Detroit Symphony under Antal Dorati (in conjunction with a Beethoven Congress, November 4–6). The New York Philharmonic presented three concerts and two recitals in "Celebration of Black Composers" from the past and present (August 30–September 2). This first such recognition by a major orchestra was gratifying overall and musically successful.

The mobility of orchestral conductors was high worldwide, notably so in the United States. Carlo Maria Giulini accepted the music direc-

The new Spoleto Festival U. S. A. presented Gian-Carlo Menotti's *The Consul* with, left to right, Sandra Walker, Marvellee Cariaga, Sylvia Davis, Alice Garrott.

BILL STRUTTS, PHOTOGRAPHER SPOLETO FESTIVAL U. S. A.

torship of the Los Angeles Philharmonic to begin in 1978, succeeding Zubin Mehta, who had followed Pierre Boulez as the New York Philharmonic's conductor. Boulez moved to the directorship of the major electronic music center, l'Institut de Recherche et de la Coordination Acoustique/Musique (IRCAM) in Paris.

Meanwhile, Antal Dorati took over the helm of the Detroit Symphony after he was unceremoniously replaced as the National Symphony's music director. Mstislav Rostropovich then became the "slava" (glory) of Washington, D. C. Others who began new tenures as music directors were Edo de Waart (San Francisco Symphony), John Nelson (Indianapolis Symphony), Leonard Slatkin (New Orleans Philharmonic), and Eduardo Mata (Dallas Symphony; Kurt Masur, new principal guest conductor).

In a classic example of the currently wide practice of multiple podium possession, Sir Georg Solti, musical director of the Chicago Symphony and the Royal Opera, Covent Garden, also became the London Philharmonic's principal conductor. Claudio Abbado, musical director of the La Scala Opera, Milan, was named to succeed Andre Previn in 1979 as the London Symphony Orchestra's conductor. Gennady Rozhdestvensky was appointed musical

director of the BBC Symphony. Rudolf Barshai, conductor of the Moscow Chamber Orchestra, emigrated to Israel.

Chamber Music and Recitals. Only a moderate level of activity, if not a further decline, was evident in chamber music and recitals. This medium flourished primarily in performances by major celebrities on tour, established groups (Chamber Music Society of Lincoln Center, the Theater Chamber Players of Washington, D. C., the St. Paul Chamber Orchestra with Dennis Russell Davies conducting), and definitely in the ubiquitous festivals. A significant and successful newcomer in that field was the Spoleto Festival U. S. A. in Charleston, S. C., May 25–June 5, Gian-Carlo Menotti's first U. S. version of his Festival of Two Worlds. Besides ambitious chamber, recital, and dance offerings, productions of Tchaikovsky's *Queen of Spades* and Menotti's *The Consul* were mounted.

Opera in the United States. In presenting two new works, the New York City Opera regained a certain leadership. Leon Kirchner's *Lily* (to Saul Bellow's novel *Henderson, the Rain King*) on April 14, drew contrasting critical responses.

The Voice of Ariadne, with its Scottish composer, Thea Musgrave, conducting its U. S. premiere on September 30 made a weak impression. Still lighter in weight, Nina Rota's *The Italian Straw Hat* opened the Santa Fe Opera's season, July 6–August 27.

Otherwise, U. S. professional companies were entirely retrospective, albeit with some interesting and rare revivals: Cavalli's *Giasone* (Clarion Concerts, New York City, January 3), Smetana's *Dalibor* (Opera Orchestra of New York, January 9), Glinka's *Ruslan and Lyudmila* (Opera Company of Boston, March 5), Viktor Ullmann's *The Emperor of Atlantis* (1944) on a triple bill with Holst's *Savitri* and Monteverdi's *The Combat* (San Francisco's Spring Opera Theater, April 21), Busoni's *Doktor Faust* (Wolf Trap Festival, August 5), Massenet's *Le Roi de Lahore* (Vancouver and Seattle, October).

Antal Dorati became conductor of the Detroit Symphony.

DETROIT SYMPHONY ORCHESTRA

The Metropolitan Opera added three unusual works to its repertoire: a stark production of Poulenc's *The Dialogues of the Carmelites* (with Régine Crespin and Shirley Verrett, February 5), Meyerbeer's *Le Prophète,* heavily criticized (Marilyn Horne and James McCracken), and Berg's *Lulu* (James Levine, conductor) in March.

A great impasse in union contract negotiations was surmounted at the eleventh hour, enabling the Met to open the 1977–78 season, its 93rd, with *Boris Godunov* (October 10).

The opera scene was given a lift via Public Broadcasting Service telecasts of four productions live from the Met, and one each, starring Beverly Sills, from the New York City Opera and San Diego Opera, and five productions originating in Vienna and La Scala Opera, Milan. In addition, the seasons of the Chicago Lyric Opera and the San Francisco Opera were heard by National Public Radio broadcasts in FM stereo. The Chicago season opened on September 23 with Donizetti's *L'Elisir d'Amore.*

Outstanding in San Francisco's season, ten operas in 61 performances, September 9–November 27, were Janacek's *Katya Kabanova* (with Elisabeth Soederstroem, Rafael Kubelik conducting) and Strauss' *Ariadne auf Naxos* (with Leontyne Price, her first Ariadne). Included were two Jean Pierre Ponnelle productions, Puccini's *Turandot* (with Montserrat Caballe and Luciano Pavarotti) and Mozart's *Idomeneo* (borrowed from Stuttgart, and also used for performances by the same cast in the Chicago Lyric's season).

International Opera. Typically, opera in Europe was more adventurous. In West Germany, there were Wolfgang Fortner's *That's Fine* (to a text by Beckett, April 24), and Hans Werner Henze's *Wir erreichen dem Fluss* (to an Edward Bond libretto, using three orchestras, Dennis Russell Davies conducting, Stuttgart). Friedrich Goldmann's *Opera Fantasy* and Udo Zimmermann's *Schuhuh und die fliegende Prinzessin* were featured in East Berlin's Sixth Music Biennial.

In England, Michael Tippett's fourth opera, *The Ice Break,* which deals with modern society in crisis, made the biggest impact of the operatic premieres (Royal Opera, Covent Garden, Colin Davis conducting, July 7). Other premieres were Thea Musgrave's *Mary, Queen of Scots* (Edinburgh Festival) and David Blake's *Toussaint* (English National Opera).

Unable to meet chorus and musicians' demands for overtime wages for operas of extraordinary length, the English National Opera cancelled three performances of *Toussaint* and the Royal Opera cut the first two acts of Berlioz' *Les Troyens* and cut and compressed Verdi's *Don Carlos* during September and October.

Government Support of the Arts. For the first time in the history of the National Endowment of the Arts, the U. S. Congress appropriated the full budget requested, $123.5 million for fiscal year 1978, $29.5 million more than for 1977. The 1969 NEA budget was a mere $8 million.

ROBERT COMMANDAY
Music Critic, "San Francisco Chronicle"

The Metropolitan Opera added to its repertoire Poulenc's *The Dialogues of the Carmelites,* with Régine Crespin as the prioress and Mignon Dunn as Mother Marie.

The sudden death of Elvis Presley led to a record-buying spurt of albums by the King of Rock 'n' Roll.

MUSIC, POPULAR

The United States had been drifting to the right politically since 1974 or 1975, and in 1977 popular music joined other aspects of popular culture in coloring in the mood behind this development. Like the runaway hit movies *Rocky* and *Star Wars,* the "new" music trends that emerged during 1977 made an obvious—probably reactionary—play for deliberate oversimplification.

Punk Rock. Trendy music had also edged this way since 1975, but Punk Rock, whose peddling of a hoodlum mystique may have peaked in 1977, took the theme further than had disco (a commercial success and a critical flop) or reggae (a critical success and a commercial flop) in the years before. Punk Rock actually was much more of a factor in England than in America, although New Jersey's Bruce Springsteen was seen as a father figure of the style. It started as a deliberate attempt to be primitive in the playing of rock and was delivered with the rationale that this was a rejection of the commercialization that had sapped rock's energy. Of course, it became institutionalized itself by America's inexorable commerce. Through it all there was debate about whether some of its practitioners, such as the Ramones, were primitive or simply inept; the bands that seemed likely to last longer than the fad, such as Springsteen's associates, Southside Johnny and the Asbury Jukes, were as clever as they were "primitive."

Broadway, Jazz, and Movies. In more polite circles, another version of the same thing was going on. Broadway had a new hit musical in

Annie, which seemed calculated to be as square as possible and was based on the old comic strip of the same nature, *Little Orphan Annie,* traditionally a repository of conservative slogans. Jazz continued its slow climb back into the public awareness. In style-setting cities such as Cambridge, Mass., jazz was booked in places that had booked mostly folk singers for a decade. However, it was not a particularly sophisticated kind of jazz that was catching the public's ear. Guitarist-singer George Benson's status grew, and Dexter Gordon, a sax stylist who had been living in Denmark since 1962, made a triumphant (at least in terms of publicity) "return" and an album recorded live in New York. More complex performers, such as Keith Jarrett (who recorded an album in which he played a 200-year-old giant German pipe organ), continued to have a specialized following.

The most publicized musical movie, starring Barbra Streisand and Kris Kristofferson, also squared with what might be called "the squaring of America." It was an allegedly "modernized" remake of *A Star is Born.*

Past Heroes, Country Music, Presley. And there were returns to action by heroes of the past, especially in album releases. Old Beatles' performances were released in "At the Hollywood Bowl" and "Live! at the Star Club in Hamburg, Germany 1962." Crosby, Stills and Nash reunited for an album, as did Stephen Stills and Neil Young, partners in the late Buffalo Springfield. Sly and the Family Stone were back with an album; so were the Hollies, Martha Reeves, Booker T and the MG's, Melanie, and José Feliciano.

In country music, the simplicity theme also beckoned, and attention focused on George Jones, an excellent veteran singer and maker of old-time "hard" country music. In that genre, of course, simplicity is *supposed* to be inherent but it has not always been.

But America's (if not the world's) largest single record-buying spurt did not have much to do with trends or the cultural-political ambience; it was pegged to an event—the death in August of Elvis Presley, the King of Rock 'n' Roll. It was one of the two milestones the music industry passed (the other was the 100th anniversary of Edison's phonograph), and it triggered a raid on record stores not merely for "Moody Blue," or Presley's latest album, but for every Presley album in stock.

Albums and Tours. Several of the most (critically and commercially) successful albums and tours did not have much to do with trends either but with the relationship of established performers and their established, and growing, audiences. There was a sort of subtheme to *some* of the work by these figures; Jimmy Buffett's "Changes in Latitude, Changes in Attitudes" and Jonathan Edwards' "Sailboat," for example, connected with a public mood to take time out and enjoy the summer. But such releases

Peter Frampton performed before a large crowd at New York's Madison Square Garden. His albums led the charts.

as Bonnie Raitt's "Sweet Forgiveness," Joni Mitchell's "Hejira," Linda Ronstadt's "Simple Dreams," James Taylor's "JT," Waylon Jennings' "Ol' Waylon," Joan Baez' "Gulf Winds," Emmylou Harris' "Luxury Liner," the Eagles' "Hotel California," Kate and Anna McGarrigle's "Dancer With Bruised Knees," and Jackson Browne's "The Pretender" showed those performers holding to their own various styles and elaborating upon their viewpoints.

The year's developments seemed to confirm the existence of a committed, dependable audience that a committed, dependable pop musician could earn a share of. Once the audience was won, the musician could continue to be deemed "relevant" as long as he or she tried to make reasonably honest music. In short, it seemed possible to be above the scramble for headlines about "the latest thing"—possible, but not easy to accomplish. The trend vendors, as usual, were in and out of favor for extra-musical reasons, demonstrating something about the mood of the moment but probably having little long-term effect on music itself.

NOEL COPPAGE
Contributing Editor, "Stereo Review"

NEBRASKA

Good crops but financial problems for farmers, a controversial school financing plan, a new criminal code, and higher taxes concerned Nebraskans in 1977.

Agriculture. Early 1977 was very dry, but late summer rain was above average, and the major crops were excellent. Estimated yield in bushels was: corn 648,000,000 (228,350,000 hl); grain sorghum 138,000,000 (48,630,000 hl); wheat 107,000,000 (37,700,000 hl); and soybeans 42,000,000 (14,800,000 hl). However, farmers, squeezed between low grain prices and high costs of supplies, were in serious trouble.

Education. Leadership of major universities changed as Ronald W. Roskens replaced D. B. Varner as president of the University of Nebraska. Roskens was replaced as chancellor of the University of Nebraska at Omaha by Del D. Weber.

Integration of Omaha public schools continued without serious incident. The most controversial educational issue in 1977 arose from legislation passed over Gov. J. James Exon's veto. It would have increased the $55-million state school aid, raised from sales and income taxes, by $20 million in 1977 and by an additional $20 million in each of the two following years. Opposition was immediate, and a referendum petition suspended the law, referring it to the voters in the 1978 general election.

Legislation and Taxes. The 90-day session of the 85th legislature also saw another gubernatorial veto of a controversial bill overridden on the last day. The law in question was the new 768-page criminal code, the first major revision in more than a century. After study and amendment by the 1978 legislature, the code is scheduled to go into effect.

Overall appropriations resulted in the first billion-dollar budget in Nebraska history. About one half of the total will come from the tax-supported General Fund. The legislature voted to raise the gasoline tax from 8.5¢ to 9.5¢ a gallon (2.2¢–2.5¢/l); provided exemption from personal property taxes for farm equipment and livestock and for business inventories; and imposed fees for entering state parks.

No legislation was passed on control of the state's water resources, increased irrigation, and proposed dam projects.

Anticipating revenue needs, the Board of Equalization raised income taxes from 17% to 18% of federal liability and sales taxes from 3% to 3½%.

ORVILLE H. ZABEL, *Creighton University*

--------- **NEBRASKA · Information Highlights** ---------

Area: 77,227 square miles (200,018 km²).
Population (1976 est.): 1,553,000.
Chief Cities (1970 census): Lincoln, the capital, 149,518; Omaha, 346,929; Grand Island, 31,269; Hastings, 23,580.
Government (1977): *Chief Officers*—governor, J. James Exon (D); lt. gov., Gerald T. Whelan (D). *Legislature* (unicameral)—49 members (nonpartisan).
Education (1976–77): *Enrollment*—public elementary schools, 164,125 pupils; public secondary, 147,899; nonpublic, 45,300; colleges and universities, 66,040 students. *Public school expenditures,* $476,850,000 ($1,457 per pupil).
State Finances (fiscal year 1976): *Revenues,* $1,006,-610,000; *expenditures,* $983,070,000.
Personal Income (1976): $9,450,000,000; per capita, $6,086.
Labor Force (July 1977): *Nonagricultural wage and salary earners,* 585,000; *unemployed,* 17,300 (2.3% of total force).

In May, South Moluccan terrorists seized control of a train and school and held 161 persons as hostages. Dutch troops freed the captives. The released persons were transported from the scene to a Groningen hospital by bus, right.

UPI

NETHERLANDS

The year of 1977 was by no means a dull one for the Dutch. In February, a wave of strikes and lockouts brought Rotterdam harbor and several industries to a standstill. On March 22—two months before parliamentary elections were to be held—the center-left cabinet of Joop den Uyl resigned. On May 23, South Moluccan terrorists seized control of a train and a school and held 161 persons as hostages. Parliamentary elections took place on May 25. Turnout (87.5%) was unusually high. The newly formed Christian Democratic Appeal (a federation of the Catholic and two Protestant parties) won 49 of 150 seats in the lower house—a gain of one over 1972. Socialists, led by the prime minister, gained 10 seats for a total of 53, while the opposition Liberals won 28 seats—6 more than in 1972. It was mid-December before a new government could be formed. Headed by Andreas van Agt, leader of the Christian Democrats, it included his party and the Liberals, with some conditional backing from four small rightist splinter parties.

The previous cabinet was a victim of pre-election maneuvers; despite serious disagreements it had stayed together for nearly four years. But looking to the elections, the Socialists made participation in a second center-left coalition conditional on the passage of four measures:

control of land speculation, codetermination in industry, sharing of excess profits, and control over investment. The cabinet resigned on the first one.

South Moluccans. For a time, South Moluccan terrorism overshadowed the elections. In a repetition of their December 1975 action, terrorists seized control of a train en route to Groningen and of an elementary school in the village of Bovensmilde. There were 54 passengers on board the train and 107 pupils and teachers in the school. The terrorists demanded release of their comrades, imprisoned for the earlier action, and a jet to fly out of the country. Dutch authorities refused to negotiate until the children were released. The terrorists complied four days later, but all attempts at negotiation failed. Dutch troops stormed the train and the school on June 11. Six terrorists and two hostages died. The remaining terrorists were tried and convicted in September.

During the trial in Assen, Dutch police came under sniper fire. A house-to-house search revealed weapons and plans for another siege. There are some 40,000 South Moluccans in the Netherlands, descendants of 5,000 refugees who came there after fighting with the Dutch in their struggle against Indonesian independence. The South Moluccans have resisted assimilation, clinging to a dream of an independent Republic of the South Moluccas. They want the Dutch government to put pressure on Indonesia for the freedom of their islands. That, however, is a totally unrealistic request.

The Economy. The economic outlook remained mixed. Although the rate of inflation was expected to drop below 7%, unemployment hovered close to 7%, and economic growth remained sluggish (3–4%). Since 1975, the government has been preoccupied with keeping the rate of increase in government expenditures to 1% of the national income. The public sector now absorbs 57% of the national income. Demands to maintain real incomes and stimulate the economy remain problematic.

STEVEN B. WOLINETZ
Memorial University of Newfoundland

NETHERLANDS · Information Highlights

Official Name: Kingdom of the Netherlands.
Location: Northwestern Europe.
Area: 15,770 square miles (40,844 km²).
Population (1977 est.): 13,900,000.
Chief Cities (1975 est.): Amsterdam, the capital, 758,-000; Rotterdam, 621,000; The Hague, 483,000.
Government: *Head of state*, Juliana, queen (acceded Sept. 1948). *Head of government*, Andreas van Agt, prime minister (took office Dec. 1977). *Legislature* —Staten General: First Chamber and Second Chamber.
Monetary Unit: Guilder (2.45 guilders equal U.S.$1, Aug. 1977).
Manufacturing (major products): Metals, processed foods, petroleum products, chemicals, textiles, machinery, electrical appliances, clothing.
Major Agricultural Products: Sugar beets, potatoes, wheat, barley, rye, oats, flax.

NEVADA

Nevada's tourist-based economy continued to prosper during 1977, and the construction of several large hotel-casinos in the Reno area appeared to presage an economic uplift in the northern part of the state to rival the post-World War II boom in Las Vegas.

Legislation. As in 1975, the most dramatic event of the biennial legislative session was the consideration of the ratification of the Equal Rights Amendment (ERA) to the U. S. Constitution. Invoking a seldom-used rule, which requires each senator to cast a "yea" or "nay" vote unless unanimous consent is granted to abstain, Lt. Gov. Robert E. Rose counted two abstentions as "nay" votes. The presiding officer then broke the resultant 10–10 tie by casting a constitutionally questionable vote in favor of ERA. The furor over Rose's actions was quieted somewhat when the Assembly reversed its 1975 position and defeated the controversial amendment, 25–14.

Another emotionally charged measure, legalizing prescription sales of the drugs Laetrile and Gerovital in Nevada, was enacted by the legislature after intensive pressure from the state's most powerful lobbyists. Other significant legislation included a tough "open meeting" law, with a possible loss of office as penalty for violation; an omnibus gaming law which tightened the state's control over the industry; a landlord-tenant law which spells out rights of tenants; and a measure to change the voting procedures of the Tahoe Regional Planning Agency. The enactment of the latter bill showed the considerable influence of Gov. Mike O'Callaghan. It can become effective only if also approved by the California Legislature.

Economy. Gambling and sales-tax revenues for the 1976–77 fiscal year increased by 12.3 and 17%, respectively, over the previous year. The construction of the 1,000-room MGM Grand Hotel and several other large hotel-casinos in Reno set off a speculative housing boom in the area. Statewide employment reached a record high of 310,000 in August.

Declaring that the granting of a gambling license was a "privilege" and not a right, the Nevada Supreme Court turned back a challenge to the state's tough control procedures. The U. S. Supreme Court refused an appeal on the grounds that a substantial federal question was not involved in the case.

Education. After serving 10 years as chancellor of the University of Nevada, Neil D. Humphrey resigned in August to accept the presidency of the University of Alaska.

DON W. DRIGGS, *University of Nevada, Reno*

NEW BRUNSWICK

The government responded to rising unemployment by boosting capital spending, but continued to emphasize the fighting of inflation. Saint John had a disastrous jail fire.

Budget. A three-stage reduction in personal income tax and a one percent reduction in corporate income tax for small businesses were announced in Finance Minister Lawrence Garvie's budget, presented to the legislature March 15. Total expenditures were forecast at a record $1.32 billion, up $154 million from the previous year. Revenue was estimated at $1.15 billion. Record capital expenditures of $179 million, up 19%, were projected. Civil service growth was limited.

Kickbacks. Premier Richard B. Hatfield announced March 11 a judicial inquiry to investigate "unprecedented allegations" by Liberal Opposition Leader Robert Higgins that the justice department interfered with a 1973 RCMP investigation of a kickback scheme on government business contracts. Chief Justice C. J. A. Hughes was named to conduct the inquiry.

Legislative. The legislature was terminated June 17 after a 16-week session. The session ended with the tabling of a white paper proposing a freedom-of-information act, and the approval of bills creating a provincial police commission and a series of tax changes.

Tragedy. Twenty-one prisoners were killed and 13 others injured June 21 when fire roared through the detention area of Saint John city hall. Most of the dead and injured were pris-

---

NEVADA • Information Highlights

Area: 110,540 square miles (286,299 km²).
Population (1976 est.): 610,000.
Chief Cities (1970 census): Carson City, the capital, 15,468; Las Vegas, 125,787; Reno, 72,863.
Government (1977): *Chief Officers*—governor, Michael O'Callaghan (D); lt. gov., Robert E. Rose (D). *Legislature*—Senate, 20 members; Assembly, 40 members.
Education (1976–77): *Enrollment*—public elementary schools, 72,838 pupils; public secondary, 68,953; nonpublic, 5,600; colleges and universities, 20,916 students. *Public school expenditures,* $212,600,000 ($1,309 per pupil).
State Finances (fiscal year 1976): *Revenues,* $689,035,-000; *expenditures,* $589,920,000.
Personal Income (1976): $4,368,000; per capita, $7,162.
Labor Force (June 1977): *Nonagricultural wage and salary earners,* 307,900; *unemployed,* 23,000 (7% of total force).

— NEW BRUNSWICK • Information Highlights —

Area: 28,354 square miles (73,437 km²).
Population (1976 census): 677,250.
Chief Cities (1976 census): Fredericton, the capital, 45,248; St. John, 85,956; Moncton, 55,934.
Government (1977): *Chief Officers*—lt. gov., Hedard Robichaud; premier, Richard B. Hatfield (Progressive Conservative); chief justice, Charles J. A. Hughes. *Legislature*—Legislative Assembly, 58 members.
Education (1976–77): *Enrollment*—public elementary and secondary schools, 162,700 pupils; private schools, 270; Indian (federal) schools, 860; post-secondary, 12,580 students. *Total expenditures,* $217,081,000.
Public Finance (1977–78): *Revenues,* $1,151,000,000; *expenditures,* $1,317,000,000.
Personal Income (average weekly salary, July 1977): $222.04
Unemployment Rate (August 1977, seasonally adjusted): 14.3%.
(All monetary figures are in Canadian dollars.)

oners transferred to the city lockup the previous week from a provincial jail after a series of fires in that facility damaged 20 cells.

Forestry. New Brunswick's annual spruce budworm spraying program covered about 4.5 million acres (1.8 million hectares), only half the area covered the previous year when half the province was sprayed. The 1976 program had generated charges that the spraying endangered health.

Francophone. It was announced June 13 that the federal government had agreed to help finance the establishment of a French-language law school at Moncton University.

JOHN BEST, *Chief, Canada World News*

NEW HAMPSHIRE

Environmental, fiscal, and political issues dominated New Hampshire news in 1977; the state received national attention during the large demonstration at the construction site of the Seabrook nuclear power plant. A battle over the state's operating and capital budgets opened at the beginning of the year, and in the political arena Gov. Meldrim Thomson (R) had trouble not only with the Democrats, but also with members of his own party.

Antinuclear Demonstration. The controversy over the construction of a nuclear power plant at Seabrook reached a climax on May 1, with a large demonstration that blocked access to the site. More than 1,400 of the 2,000 demonstrators were arrested and confined in several state armories pending arraignment and trial. Later, all were released on personal recognizance. The demonstrators received national attention because of the prominence they gave to the issues of nuclear safety and the impact of nuclear power on the environment. Court challenges of construction permits complicated the situation. Though construction is continuing, the future of the plant is still not free of uncertainty.

Budgetary Crisis. The state's fiscal crisis arose because revenue sources could not keep pace with inflation and increased demands for services. New Hampshire remains the only state without a general sales or income tax, and the governor has pledged to veto legislation implementing either. With a limited range of choices, the House and Senate were unable to agree on a budget by June 30, when the fiscal year ended. A continuing resolution carried the operation of state government through late October. After considerable debate, punctuated with some strong invective, the General Court passed a budget on October 20 and sent it to the governor. Thomson let it become law on October 27 without his signature, thereby ending the fiscal crisis. In mid-summer, the governor had vetoed the capital budget funding state construction projects, claiming it was too costly for the state. That matter awaited resolution.

Economy. Considering the problems confronting state government, the general health of the New Hampshire economy remained good, with unemployment hovering around 4%. The winter of 1976–77 was not unusually severe and brought no serious economic slowdown.

New Hampshire seems to be doing well, but many believe that the state has yet to face the challenges of the late 1970's.

WILLIAM L. TAYLOR, *Plymouth State College*

--- **NEW HAMPSHIRE • Information Highlights** ---

Area: 9,304 square miles (24,097 km²).

Population (1976 est.): 822,000.

Chief Cities (1970 census): Concord, the capital, 30,-022; Manchester, 87,754; Nashua, 55,820; Portsmouth, 25,717.

Government (1977): *Chief Officers*—governor, Meldrim Thomson, Jr. (R). *General Court*—Senate, 24 members; House of Representatives, 400 members.

Education (1976–77): *Enrollment*—public elementary schools, 105,035 pupils; public secondary, 70,461; nonpublic, 20,500; colleges and universities, 37,190 students. *Public school expenditures,* $223,232,000 ($1,180 per pupil).

State Finances (fiscal year 1976): *Revenues,* $589,-303,000; *expenditures,* $631,766,000.

Personal Income (1976): $4,942,000,000; per capita, $6,010.

Labor Force (June 1977): *Nonagricultural wage and salary earners,* 335,000; *unemployed,* 19,900 (4.9% of total force).

UPI

The construction of a nuclear power plant at Seabrook, N.H., caused extreme controversy and a major demonstration. Gov. Meldrim Thomson, Jr., personally thanked National Guardsmen called to the site for their assistance.

Brendan Byrne's reelection as governor of New Jersey was one of the major political comeback stories of recent years.

NEW JERSEY

The amazing political comeback of Gov. Brendan Byrne, who was reelected in November, was the major story in New Jersey in 1977.

The Election. Action began early among Democrats, because many candidates wished to take advantage of Byrne's apparent unpopularity arising from his sponsorship of a state income tax in 1976. Byrne himself was undecided on running and did not announce his candidacy until mid-April. By June 7, the date of the state primary election, nine other candidates were in the field.

Byrne's weakness was seen in the fact that two major elements in the Democratic party, the Hudson County organization and the AFL-CIO, initially threw their support to others. In the primary Byrne received about 30% of the vote, enough to defeat his many opponents. In the Republican primary, State Sen. Raymond Bateman defeated Assemblyman Thomas Kean.

The campaign between Byrne and Bateman developed into a referendum on the income tax. Byrne defended his record and Bateman announced he would let the tax expire in June 1978. Until early autumn Bateman held a commanding lead in public opinion polls, attracting much support from urban blue-collar workers resentful because the chief beneficiaries of Byrne's financial program seemed to be middle-class homeowners who worked outside the state. Bateman's position began to erode in late September, however, when he presented a detailed 11-point economic platform calling for spending freezes or an increase in the state sales tax that could replace the income tax without loss of revenue. Byrne launched an aggressive attack, saying the plan was unrealistic. Aided by massive television advertising, he moved ahead of Bateman in the last week of the campaign.

In the election, Byrne won by 300,000 votes, or 57%, a margin considerably larger than expected. He carried the Republican stronghold of Bergen County as well as blue-collar districts thought to be solid for Bateman. It was billed as the greatest political comeback in the history of the state and a clear victory for the income tax. The immediate expectation was that the issue had been laid to rest as a source of controversy in New Jersey, opening the way for consideration of other major problems facing the state. Byrne's strength was also demonstrated by the Democrats retaining control of both houses of the legislature, gaining seats in the Assembly but losing some in the Senate.

Atlantic City. Gov. Byrne on June 2 signed the Casino Control Act, regulating casino gambling in Atlantic City. The law permits licenses to be issued only to casinos connected with major hotels that have certain specified facilities. It provides for a system of regulation, licensing, and law enforcement administered by a five-member commission appointed by the governor. The law also specifies the number of hours casinos may remain open and lays down rules on credit and the serving of alcoholic beverages at gambling tables. The first casinos were expected to open for business in early 1978.

Drilling for Oil. The U. S. Court of Appeals on August 25 overturned a lower court ruling that had blocked exploratory oil drilling in tracts leased by the federal government off the New Jersey shore. The court declared itself satisfied that the U. S. Department of the Interior could handle any environmental hazards and "deal with them thoroughly."

HERMANN K. PLATT, *St. Peter's College*

NEW JERSEY • Information Highlights

Area: 7,836 square miles (20,295 km²).
Population (1976 est.): 7,336,000.
Chief Cities (1970 census): Trenton, the capital, 104,-638; Newark, 382,288; Jersey City, 260,545.
Government (1977): *Chief Officers*—governor, Brendan T. Byrne (D). *Legislature*—Senate, 40 members; General Assembly, 80 members.
Education (1976–77): *Enrollment*—public elementary schools, 890,400 pupils; public secondary, 536,600; nonpublic, 300,800; colleges and universities, 264,-655 students. *Public school expenditures*, $2,957,-000,000 ($1,909 per pupil).
State Finances (fiscal year 1976): *Revenues*, $5,739,-354,000; *expenditures*, $5,853,457,000.
Personal Income (1976): $54,152,000,000; per capita, $7,381.
Labor Force (July 1977): *Nonagricultural wage and salary earners*, 2,839,400; *unemployed*, 293,600 (8.7% of total force).

NASA's Louis Rosenblum dedicated the nation's first solar-powered weather station in Clines Corners, N. M.

——— NEW MEXICO · Information Highlights ———
Area: 121,666 square miles (315,115 km²).
Population (1976): 1,168,000.
Chief Cities (1970 census): Santa Fe, the capital, 41,-167; Albuquerque, 243,751; Las Cruces, 37,857; Roswell, 33,908.
Government (1977): *Chief Officers*—governor, Jerry Apodaca (D); lt. gov., Robert E. Ferguson (D). *Legislature*—Senate, 42 members; House of Representatives, 70 members.
Education (1976–77); *Enrollment*—public elementary schools, 143,871 pupils; public secondary, 140,848; nonpublic, 14,000; colleges and universities, 50,542 students. *Public school expenditures,* $448,908,000 ($1,287 per pupil).
State Finances (fiscal year 1976): *Revenues,* $1,244,-706,000; *expenditures,* $1,071,351,000.
Personal Income (1976): $6,217,000,000; per capita, $5,322.
Labor Force (July 1977): *Nonagricultural wage and salary earners,* 417,400; *unemployed,* 40,200 (8.1% of total force).

NEW MEXICO

Heavy demands were placed upon New Mexico in 1977 to supply the rest of the country with coal, natural gas, oil, and uranium. Many communities had to confront problems associated with rapid energy development.

In early summer, a disastrous forest fire destroyed 15,000 acres (6,000 ha) of timberland in the Jemez Mountains east of Santa Fe.

On October 4, David Rusk, a liberal Democrat and son of former U. S. Secretary of State Dean Rusk, was elected mayor of Albuquerque.

Indian Affairs. A growing controversy over "Indian sovereignty" developed as New Mexico's tribes sought to exclude the state from jurisdiction over reservation lands. Wendell Chino, chief of the 2,200-member Mescalero Apache tribe, spoke out against government attempts to impose taxes upon non-Indians doing business inside reservation boundaries. State Sen. I. M. Smalley of Deming responded by proposing an amendment to the New Mexico constitution outlawing Indian voting rights unless tribes recognized the sovereignty of the state.

At the first Pueblo Indian Convocation, held in Albuquerque on July 28–29, tribal leaders called upon their talented and well-educated young people, who are working in distant cities such as Los Angeles and Washington, D. C., to return and assume responsibility for developing village life. In many pueblos, Indians themselves are beginning to fill jobs relating to government services.

Pueblo Indian crafts received national attention when the Santa Fe office of the U. S. Postal Service on April 13 issued a handsome block of commemorative stamps depicting four samples of historic Pueblo pottery.

Education. In May, the University of New Mexico at Albuquerque released a detailed report, demonstrating its strong leadership in providing educational opportunities for minority students. It showed a percentage of Hispanic enrollment triple that of major universities in western and southwestern states with high proportions of Hispanic residents. Full-time enrollment of Indian students was more than 3%.

Energy. The Public Service Company of New Mexico and Union Oil Company announced a joint project to develop a $50-million experimental geothermal power plant in the Jemez Mountains. Against opposition from environmentalists, the U. S. Energy Research and Development Administration went forward with plans for a nuclear waste disposal site in Eddy County east of Carlsbad.

MARC SIMMONS
Author, "New Mexico, A History"

NEW YORK

During the longest session since 1911, the bicentennial legislature enacted a number of important and controversial bills amid a somewhat muffled split between the Democratic Assembly and the Republican Senate, as both parties began to prepare for the statewide elections in 1978. Most of Gov. Hugh Carey's program was enacted.

Crime. Reflecting community concerns, the legislature passed many bills relating to crime. One piece of legislation decriminalized the possession of small amounts of marijuana for personal use and reduced some penalties for sale. Also enacted was a bill providing a mandatory prison sentence for a felon convicted of a violent crime against anyone over 62 years of age or a handicapped person. Youthful offender treatment was denied to those aged 16 to 18 who commit such crimes. The State Liquor

Authority was empowered to revoke or suspend liquor licenses of bars featuring topless entertainers or waitresses. A bill to expand the death penalty to premeditated murder and murder committed during a felony in addition to that of police or correction personnel was vetoed by the governor.

Finance. The legislature approved a $11.5-billion (U. S.) budget, about $450 million higher than in 1976–77, and some $100 million larger than Gov. Carey requested. Included in the final passage was the expiration of a 2.5% personal income surcharge calculated to save taxpayers $120 million, and a tapered tax credit of $5–$50 for persons earning up to $30,000. This probably reflected a gain in the state's economy. The state had a per capita income of $7,019 (8th in the country), a rise of 8.2% over the previous year. Many cuts in welfare and medicaid expenditures proposed by Gov. Carey were approved, but the legislature refused to accept school-aid reductions and raised such assistance by $75 million. The balanced budget resulted in reduction of interest rates for the state—3.8% at the end of the year, compared to a 7% rate in 1976.

Weather. The year began with the state in the grip of a severe winter. On February 5, President Carter declared the city of Buffalo and nine surrounding counties a major disaster area. By that time, Buffalo had had a total snow-fall of 160 inches (406 cm) while 300–400 thousand workers had been laid off. Shortages of gas added to the crisis.

Miscellaneous. The Emergency Tenant Protection Act, covering rent stabilization, mainly in New York City, was extended for four years. An increase in weekly unemployment and disability payments was also enacted. These rose from $95 to $125 and from $95 to $215, respectively.

Elections. Noteworthy results in the fall elections were the defeat of a proposed state constitutional convention and a similar defeat of a $750-million bond issue meant to stimulate the state's economy. Equally noteworthy was the passage of a constitutional amendment providing for gubernatorial appointment of judges of the New York Court of Appeals. This probably foreshadowed a plan for the appointment of all state judicial posts.

LEO HERSHKOWITZ
Queens College, City University of New York

NEW YORK CITY

Events in the "Big Apple" continued to parallel those of past years. These centered on a recurrent financial crisis that defied permanent solution, and an array of social and energy-related occurrences. With major city offices once again open at the polls, candidates, of whom there were many, had a busy year.

Fiscal Crisis. New York managed to weather another year of deficit financing only with the aid of federal loans and the cooperation of municipal labor unions. The city faced bankruptcy at the beginning of the year, as city banks and the state-created Municipal Assistance Corporation were reluctant to make any further investments in city bonds. Mayor Abraham D. Beame angrily accused bankers of "holding

Helicopter service between New York's airports and midtown Manhattan was halted after a helicopter overturned on top of the Pan-Am Building, killing 5 persons.

UPI

NEW YORK • Information Highlights

Area: 49,576 square miles (128,402 km²).
Population (1976 est.): 18,084,000.
Chief Cities (1970 census): Albany, the capital, 115,-781; New York, 7,895,563; Buffalo, 462,768; Rochester, 296,233.
Government (1977): *Chief Officers*—governor, Hugh L. Carey (D); lt. gov., Mary Anne Krupsak (D). *Legislature*—Senate, 60 members; Assembly, 150 members.
Education (1976–77): *Enrollment*—public elementary schools, 1,706,000 pupils; public secondary, 1,672,-997; nonpublic, 705,600; colleges and universities, 990,196 students. *Public school expenditures,* $7,-824,200,000 ($2,096).
State Finances (fiscal year 1976): *Revenues,* $21,022,-373,000; *expenditures,* $21,027,229,000.
Personal Income (1976): $126,925,000,000; per capita, $7,019.
Labor Force (June 1977): *Nonagricultural wage and salary earners,* 6,817,500; *unemployed,* 640,700 (8.3% of total force).

a gun to our heads," and labor unions demanded a "firm commitment" on payback schemes from the banks. Creditors demanded strict fiscal control and a balanced budget before any new aid could be extended. On March 10, however, the Emergency Financial Control Board approved a plan to pay off a $983-million short-term debt, and the following day U. S. Treasury Secretary W. Michael Blumenthal released a $255-million short-term federal loan to be paid back by June 30, 1977. That date was later changed to some time after 1978.

The city was dealt another blow when the Securities and Exchange Commission released a report on August 26, charging the mayor, Comptroller Harrison J. Goldin, and a group of commercial banks with failure to warn investors in city securities of the imminent fiscal crisis. Both officials denied the charges, placing the blame on banks that had "secretly dumped" city securities. Moody's Investor's Service gave New York City bonds their lowest rating.

These economic difficulties were underscored

N. Y. C.'s new skyscraper, Citicorp Center, designed by Hugh Stubbins, is the world's eighth tallest structure.

by the growing loss of middle-class residents and a 10.2% unemployment rate, the highest in any major U. S. city. New York also had trouble holding on to large corporations, while failing to attract new businesses.

Politics. Rep. Edward I. Koch won the Democratic run-off primary for mayor on September 19, defeating N. Y. Secretary of State Mario M. Cuomo, Gov. Hugh M. Carey's choice, who had come in second on September 8. The other Democratic primary candidates were Bella Abzug, Mayor Abraham D. Beame, Herman Badillo, Percy Sutton, and Joel Harnett. Incumbent City Council President Paul O'Dwyer lost his bid for renomination to State Sen. Carol Bellamy.

After a heated campaign, Koch, promising strict austerity, defeated Cuomo, who ran on the Liberal party ticket, by a vote of 712,976 to 597,257. Republican Roy Goodman and Conservative Barry Farber finished far behind, with votes of 60,599 and 58,498, respectively. Goldin and Bellamy won their races easily.

Energy. A massive power failure throughout the city and Westchester County left 9 million people without electricity for up to 25 hours on July 13–14. It was the first major black-out affecting the city since 1965. LaGuardia and Kennedy airports were inoperative for eight hours, tunnels were closed, and traffic snarled while temperatures rose to the mid-90's. Although most citizens remained calm, there were looting and vandalism in some areas, leading to the arrest of 3,700 persons. Damage was especially serious in the black and Hispanic neighborhoods of Brooklyn and South Bronx.

Other Events. The crash of a New York airways helicopter on May 16 atop the 59-story Pam-Am Building caused the death of five persons and ended helicopter service from the building to major airports.

George H. Willig, a toy-designer and amateur mountain climber from Queens, scaled the 1,350-foot (410-m) South Tower of the World Trade Center on May 26. The city filed a $250,000 lawsuit, but dropped the action and fined Willig $1.10—a penny for each story climbed.

One of the most dramatic manhunts in the city's history came to an end on August 10, with the arrest of David R. Berkowitz, alias "Son of Sam." Between July 1976 and June 26, 1977, "Son of Sam" allegedly killed five persons and wounded six others. Traced through a parking ticket, the army veteran was the subject of tangled court proceedings to determine his mental ability to stand trial.

The New York Yankees returned the world championship to the city after defeating the Los Angeles Dodgers. The first such championship in 15 years brought rejoicing to the "Big Apple."
See also BIOGRAPHY: Koch, Edward I.

LEO HERSHKOWITZ
Queens College, City University of New York

NEW ZEALAND

With tough, orthodox economic policies, the New Zealand government strove to keep inflation under control, but unemployment rose and business confidence ebbed. The external value of the dollar dropped marginally.

The Economy. In public opinion polls, the economy was usually selected by more than half of those polled as the most important problem facing the country. The external deficit was somewhat reduced, but the deficit in nontrade invisible items soared 30% in a year to an all-time high. Massive overseas borrowing continued. The 1976 inflation of 15.6% was eclipsed by a record rise of 4.8% in the second quarter of 1977. A 6% general wage increase and 3.5% state servants salary hike were partly to blame.

The budget in July was coolly received and was generally termed "pepper pot" in its effects. Its prime emphasis was two-fold: first, tax concessions to low and single-income families, especially those with children; second, a forceful new energy policy, under which the government would enter the business of oil exploration. A new inflation-related savings bond was announced, and housing finance was eased. The budget failed to come to grips with the issue of a wage policy, and the leading daily newspaper dismissed it as a make-shift affair, almost painfully negative and neither coercive nor challenging. A supplementary budget in October lowered personal income tax by 5% and sought to widen employment prospects.

Early in the year the financial conglomerate Securitibank collapsed, with a deficiency of some $13 million, and as the year drew to a close, the incidence of business failures in New Zealand climbed alarmingly.

Foreign Affairs. Overseas visits by Prime Minister Robert Muldoon and cabinet ministers sought to expand trade opportunities. Muldoon toured parts of South East Asia and the Middle East and some EEC (European Economic Community) countries in March. At the Commonwealth Conference in London he dealt with the explosive issue of New Zealand's sporting contacts with South Africa by agreeing to urge sporting bodies not to compete against South

Sir Keith Holyoake, 73, was designated governor general of New Zealand. The appointment of the former prime minister was criticized by both parties as too political. Nevertheless, Sir Keith took office in October.

African teams. He sought to muffle the effects of some outspoken comments about President Carter's initial foreign policy, and made an official visit to Washington in November.

Domestic Events. Two parliamentary by-elections, one caused by the controversial appointment of former Prime Minister Sir Keith Holyoake as governor general, were held during the year. Neither seat changed hands, although there was some swing toward the opposition Labour party. This was not repeated at the triennial local elections in October, when Sir Dove-Myer Robinson was returned for an unprecedented sixth term as mayor of Auckland. Queen Elizabeth II and the Duke of Edinburgh visited the country in February on a silver jubilee tour.

The Royal Commission on Contraception, Sterilization, and Abortion reported against any liberalization of policy and favored the establishment of panels to adjudicate on requests for abortion.

In July, Prime Minister Muldoon was sued for defamation and $22,500 in damages by the leader of an antiracial discrimination group but won the jury's verdict. On October 1, a new 200-mile restricted fishing zone was introduced in some of the rich trawling grounds around New Zealand to combat the depletion of reserves by foreign trawlers.

G. W. A. BUSH, *The University of Auckland*

NEW ZEALAND • Information Highlights

Official Name: New Zealand.
Location: South Pacific Ocean.
Area: 103,736 square miles (268,675 km²).
Population (1977 est.): 3,200,000.
Chief Cities (1976 est.): Wellington, the capital, 350,-000; Auckland, 800,000; Christchurch, 325,000.
Government: *Head of state,* Elizabeth II, queen, represented by Sir Keith Holyoake, governor general (took office Oct. 1977). *Head of government,* Robert Muldoon, prime minister (took office Dec. 1975). *Legislature* (unicameral)—House of Representatives.
Monetary Unit: New Zealand dollar (1.03 N. Z. dollars equal U. S.$1, Aug. 1977).
Manufacturing (major products): Processed foods, meat, wood products, cement, fertilizers.
Major Agricultural Products: Wheat, potatoes, dairy products, sheep wool, forest products.

According to legend, St. Brendan crossed the Atlantic Ocean in a leather boat. Some 1,400 years later, four sailors reenacted the voyage, in 50 days, landing in Musgrave Harbor, Newfoundland, June 27.

UPI

NEWFOUNDLAND

Public issues in 1977 centered around three topics: employment, hydroelectricity, and the fishery.

Economy. The April budget announced the closing of a province-owned liner-board mill at Stephenville. The mill, taken over from Canadian Javelin in 1972, had a $55-million operating loss in 1977. About 650 jobs were affected. This closing, added to an earlier shutdown of the oil refinery at Come-by-Chance, drove up the unemployment rate to nearly 15% (the national average was 8%). In some industries in the province, this meant an unemployment rate of 30%.

Continuing disputes with Quebec over hydroelectric development, confirmed the view of Newfoundlanders that Quebec had control of resources that belonged to them. In April, 1976, Premier Moores had committed his government never to trade rights to five rivers, which rise in Newfoundland but flow through Quebec, for any offer by that province for extra power from Churchill Falls. Extra power at cost (0.35¢ per kwh) was needed to justify building a transmission line from Labrador to the island. When Quebec held to its selling price of 12.4–14.2¢, Premier Moores was forced to halt building of the tunnel. The federal government proved un-

---

— NEWFOUNDLAND · Information Highlights —

Area: 156,185 square miles (404,520 km²).
Population (1976 census): 557,725.
Chief Cities (1976 census): St. John's, the capital, 86,576; Corner Brook, 25,198.
Government (1977): *Chief Officers*—lt. gov., Gordon Winter; premier, F. D. Moores (Progressive Conservative). *Legislature*—Legislative Assembly, 51 members.
Education (1976–77): *Enrollment*—public elementary and secondary schools, 156,540; private schools, 340; post-secondary, 8,350 students.
Personal Income (average weekly salary, July 1977): $245.80.
Unemployment Rate (August 1977, seasonally adjusted): 15.9%.
(All monetary figures are in Canadian dollars.)

---

able to intervene, and Newfoundland turned to the courts. There the matter rests.

Both levels of government sought to improve Newfoundland fisheries. The federal government is trying to make sure that Canada's international allocation is well used; and the province increased spending on the fisheries from $15.7 million in 1976 to $23.7 million. Taxes were raised and expenditure restrained.

Politics. The aftermath of the 1975 provincial election continued into June 1977. Irregularities forced three by-elections in June 1976, and irregularities in one of these forced a second by-election in June 1977. In the meantime, Joseph Smallwood's Liberal Reform party rejoined the Liberals, and the final standings were: Progressive Conservatives, 31; Liberals, 19; Independents, 1. The Liberals replaced Edward Roberts as party leader with William Rowe.

SUSAN McCORQUODALE
Memorial University of Newfoundland

NIGERIA

Constitutional issues dominated Nigeria's domestic politics in 1977. The first steps toward the promised return to civilian government were taken by reorganizing local government and electing a Constituent Assembly.

Government Reforms. The federal military government, headed by Lt. Gen. Olusegun Obasanjo, completed the reform of lower administrative echelons as a prerequisite for the devolution of more power to civilians. In December 1976, the old divisional administration was replaced by a new uniform system of local government. All local councils are now elected, directly in the south and indirectly in the north.

The Constitutional Drafting Committee in October 1976 produced a draft constitution which called for a powerful central government, headed by a strong directly elected president. The military government urged public discussion of the proposals. During the first half of 1977, meetings were held for this purpose throughout Nigeria. In July the government issued a decree establishing a Constituent Assembly, and on August 31 the local government councils selected more than 200 members for the assembly. It will be responsible for a finished constitution by October 1978.

Economy. Nigeria's strength remains its petroleum which provides more than 90% of all export value. Early in the year, the government assumed direct management of more private oil holdings. Administration was also simplified by merging the Nigerian National Oil Company, which holds a 55% share in most fields, with the Ministry of Petroleum Resources. The quota on production, established after the peak year of 1974, was relaxed so that a projected 750 million barrels (101 million metric tons) could be produced in 1977; by July more than 403 million barrels (54.5 million tons) had been extracted. Contracts worth $260 million were made for the construction of oil depots in most major cities as a part of a nationwide distribution system to be completed in 1978. The government is also beginning to study ways of exploiting the huge natural gas reserves.

The negative aspects of Nigeria's dependence on petroleum are seen in the continued decrease of agricultural exports such as cocoa, oil palm products, and peanuts. The Marketing Board reported handling only 10,000 tons of peanuts in the 1976–77 economic year. Furthermore, influx of great amounts of capital has created high inflation. Although lower than the previous year, the inflation rate for 1976 was over 25%. The government continues to control wages, mandating only a 7% increase for 1977. The foreign trade surplus for 1976 was $2,368 million, which was 21% better than the previous year but less than half what the Third National Development Plan had projected. Government expenditure during the 1976–77 fiscal year was $8,685 million, which left a surplus in excess of $1,535 million. Major development projects include the improving of harbors, reconstructing roads, building three new airports, and continuing the development of water resources.

Foreign Affairs. Nigeria is one of the most important states in the 16-member Economic Community of West Africa (ECOWAS), which

UPI

Nigerian leader Obasanjo tells the UN of the need for total decolonization and the end of racism in Africa.

is modeled on the European Economic Community. In August, after a two-year study period, following ratification of the basic treaty, the community's secretariat was established at Lagos. ECOWAS planners must determine during the next 13 years how to equalize the tariffs of all member states. The military government supports ECOWAS, although it means the surrender of some sovereignty. ECOWAS will initially cost Nigeria both trade and compensation to less affluent members.

On January 15 the second World Black and African Festival of Arts and Culture (FESTAC) opened in Lagos (see pages 43–45). Later, at the meeting in Libreville, Gabon, of the Organization of African Unity, the Nigerian representatives became arbitrators in most of the disputes wracking that organization. Lt. Gen. Obasanjo in March offered to mediate between the factions in Zaire and later was asked by the Kenya government to help revive the defunct East African Community. Gen. Garba, Minister of External Affairs, has stated that Nigeria's good offices would be available to other African states. All Nigerian officials underscored their unequivocal opposition to the apartheid policies of South Africa and the Smith regime of Rhodesia. This is one of the reasons for the continuing coolness in Nigeria's relations with the United States and Britain. Britain's foreign secretary and the U. S. representative to the UN were both informed of this during their visits to Lagos, and Lt. Gen. Obasanjo, on his state visit to the United States in October, stressed this as a major difficulty in improving relations between the two nations.

HARRY A. GAILEY
San Jose State University

--------- **NIGERIA · Information Highlights** ---------

Official Name: Federal Republic of Nigeria.
Location: West Africa.
Area: 356,668 square miles (923,768 km²).
Population (1977 est.): 66,600,000.
Chief Cities (1976 est.): Lagos, the capital, 1,100,000; Ibadan, 850,000; Ogbomosho, 435,000; Kano, 400,000.
Government: *Head of state and government,* Lt. Gen. Olusegun Obasanjo (assumed power Feb. 1976).
Monetary Unit: Naira (0.65 naira equals U. S.$1, Aug. 1977).
Manufacturing (major products): Processed foods, cotton textiles, cement, petroleum products.
Major Agricultural Products: Groundnuts, palm kernels, cacao, rubber, cotton, sweet potatoes and yams, forest products.

The visitors gallery is jammed as the North Carolina Senate votes on ratification of the federal Equal Rights Amendment (ERA). Following the close vote, rejecting ratification, a group of ERA opponents rejoiced outside the legislature.

PHOTOS UPI

NORTH CAROLINA

Politics and the weather provided the headlines in North Carolina during 1977. Only on the weather was there unanimity.

Weather. The winter was the coldest and the summer the hottest on record. A severe drought damaged crops and led to strict water controls in several cities, notably Chapel Hill.

Politics. Gov. James B. Hunt, Jr., buoyed by the largest vote ever cast for a political candidate, cheered blacks and women by his early appointments, including Howard Lee, Sara Hodgkins, and Sarah Morrow, as members of his cabinet. Despite verbal sparring with Lt. Gov. James Green, Hunt won legislative approval of most of his priority requests. His major setback was the defeat of the Equal Rights Amendment. In a referendum, the people voted to amend the constitution to allow a governor to run for a second term and to require the legislature to adopt a balanced budget. Bond issues for roads and clean water were passed.

Economy. The state's economic conditions improved; unemployment dropped to the lowest rate since 1974, and General Fund tax collections increased by 14%. The budget for the new biennium was just under $8 billion (U. S.). The state minimum wage was raised to the federal level, and a bitter war of words continued between the J. P. Stevens Company and the Amalgamated Clothing and Textile Workers Union at the Roanoke Rapids plant.

Education and Culture. Dissatisfaction with the performance of the public schools was reflected in legislation requiring new testing programs and the appropriation of $50 million for an intensified reading program. Gov. Hunt's failure to reappoint Dallas Herring as chairman of the State Board of Education was unpopular, but the new appointee, David Bruton, appeared to echo Herring's emphasis on basic education. Construction began in Raleigh on the new Museum of Art; the North Carolina Symphony was well received in a concert in New York's Carnegie Hall; and Reed Gold Mine, the scene of the first documented discovery of gold in the United States, was made a state historic site.

Controversy. The 1972 conviction and sentencing of the "Wilmington Ten" for firebomb-

— **NORTH CAROLINA** • Information Highlights —

Area: 52,586 square miles (136,198 km²).
Population (1976 est.): 5,469,000.
Chief Cities (1970 census): Raleigh, the capital, 123,-793; Charlotte, 241,178; Greensboro, 144,076.
Government (1977): *Chief Officers—governor,* James B. Hunt, Jr. (D); lt. gov., James C. Green (D). *General Assembly*—Senate, 50 members; House of Representatives, 120 members.
Education (1976–77): *Enrollment*—public elementary schools, 825,381 pupils; public secondary, 365,935; nonpublic, 56,800; colleges and universities, 187,-155 students. *Public school expenditures,* $1,738,-623,000 ($1,137 per pupil).
State Finances (fiscal year 1976): *Revenues,* $3,874,-953,000; *expenditures,* $4,165,676,000.
Personal Income (1976): $29,821,000,000; per capita, $5,453.
Labor Force (July 1977): *Nonagricultural wage and salary earners,* 2,092,200; *unemployed,* 153,000 (5.7% of total force).

ings and conspiracy were challenged by civil rights groups, but Gov. Hunt refused to substitute executive authority for judicial.

North Carolinians in the News. President Carter appointed Juanita Kreps secretary of commerce, former Gov. Robert W. Scott federal co-chairman of the Appalachian Regional Commission, and Rep. H. M. Michaeux, Jr., the South's first black U. S. Attorney.

H. G. JONES, *University of North Carolina*

NORTH DAKOTA

The future of the Garrison Diversion irrigation and municipal water-supply project worried North Dakotans in 1977, and falling farm prices spread gloom across the state.

Water. President Carter listed the $600-million Garrison project, 20% completed, among water works he wanted terminated. But when Congress appropriated $18.6 million for Garrison in fiscal 1978, Carter agreed to partial funding. The National Audubon Society tried

North Dakota's Gov. Arthur Link (D) testifies before the Senate Environment and Public Works Committee.

UPI

to halt the project through federal court action and succeeded when an out-of-court agreement with the Department of the Interior curtailed further construction, pending an environmental impact study. The state then intervened in the Audubon suit, claiming that congressional action nullified the agreement with the Department of the Interior. North Dakota's future legal strategy is to convince federal agencies and courts that it has a contractual guarantee from the U. S. government that the project will be completed.

The International Joint Commission (IJC), however, delivered another blow to Garrison. It recommended that no part of the project affecting Canada by completed. That would reduce the area to be irrigated from 247,000 acres (100,000 ha) to 50,000 acres (20,000 ha). The IJC findings were based on a 1909 U. S.-Canadian treaty, forbidding pollution of any boundary waters by either country to the detriment of health and property in the other. The commission claimed that return flows from North Dakota into the province of Manitoba would be harmful to Canada, especially its fisheries. The IJC proposal eliminates municipal water-supply projects in the state's three major cities and in many smaller communities.

Agriculture. The year was disappointing to the state's major industry. The growing season began too dry and ended too wet, commodity prices fell to a six-year low, and production costs soared to an all-time high. The wheat harvest, cornerstone of the farm economy, was 20% below that of 1976. Much of the grain sprouted in the swath after heavy August and September rains and had to be sold for animal feed. The production of oats, barley, flax, sunflowers, potatoes, and sugar beets exceeded 1976 crops, but prices were down 30%. Livestock prices were as much as 10% lower than in 1976.

Legislature. A record 23-hour marathon in the state House of Representatives, equally divided between Republicans and Democrats fashioned a compromise agreement on coal severance taxes and ended a 67-day session—the longest in state history since 1889–90.

STAN CANN, *"The Forum," Fargo*

— **NORTH DAKOTA** • Information Highlights —

Area: 70,665 square miles (183,022 km²).
Population (1976 est.): 643,000.
Chief Cities (1970 census): Bismarck, the capital, 34,-703; Fargo, 53,365; Grand Forks, 39,008.
Government (1977): *Chief Officers*—governor, Arthur A. Link (D); lt. gov., Wayne G. Sanstead (D). *Legislative Assembly*—Senate, 50 members; House of Representatives, 100 members.
Education (1976–77): *Enrollment*—public elementary schools, 59,076 pupils; public secondary, 70,030; nonpublic, 12,400; colleges and universities, 26,641 students. Public school expenditures, $190,925,000 ($1,335 per pupil).
State Finances (fiscal year 1976): *Revenues,* $649,692,-000; *expenditures,* $575,856,000.
Personal Income (1976): $3,761,000,000; per capita, $5,846.
Labor Force (June 1977): *Nonagricultural wage and salary earners,* 226,700; *unemployed,* 11,900 (3.9% of total force).

NORTHWEST TERRITORIES

The decision not to lay a gas pipeline through the Mackenzie Valley to carry Alaskan North Slope gas to southern U. S. markets was the most important development in 1977.

Pipeline Decision. In May, Justice Thomas Berger, having held extensive public hearings, recommended a 10-year delay of a Mackenzie Valley pipeline to allow time for settlement of native land claims. He also stated that a route through the Yukon, along the Alaska Highway, was environmentally preferable. The Canadian government subsequently announced its support for the Yukon route, and so did U. S. President Carter. An agreement was reached between the two countries, supported by the Canadian Parliament and the U. S. Congress. (A third alternative, using cryogenic tankers to carry supercooled gas, had been discarded earlier.)

The economic implications for the Mackenzie Valley are enormous, especially in terms of employment. Economic planners have already shifted gears, emphasizing development of renewable resources, tourism, and other secondary industries.

Political Developments. Prime Minister Pierre Elliott Trudeau in August appointed Charles M. ("Bud") Drury, a former Liberal cabinet minister, as his special representative to study constitutional reform in the Northwest Territories. Drury began consultations with groups and individuals and will recommend the manner in which the territories should evolve toward responsible government.

Land Claims. The Métis Association of the Northwest Territories presented the federal government with a land claim proposal in 1977. Negotiations are continuing on this and earlier proposals received from the Inuit and Indian peoples of the territories.

Legislation. The major new law enacted in 1977 was an Education Ordinance which allows the formation of local educational authorities to give communities more control over the education of their children. The Council of the Northwest Territories voted a budget of more than $243 million.

ROSS M. HARVEY
Assistant Director of Information
Government of the Northwest Territories

─── **NORTHWEST TERRITORIES** · Information ───
Highlights

Area: 1,304,903 square miles (3,379,699 km²).
Population (1976 census): 42,609.
Chief City (1976 census): Yellowknife, the capital, 8,256.
Government (1977): *Chief Officer*—commissioner, Stuart M. Hodgson. *Legislature*—Territorial Council, 15 elected members.
Education (Sept. 1977): *Enrollment*—elementary and secondary schools, 12,711 pupils. *Public school expenditures* (1976–77), $37,761,400.
Public Finance (fiscal year 1976–77): *Revenues,* $217,-694,184; *expenditures,* $213,377,878.
Mining (1976 est.): *Production value,* $185,158,000.
(All monetary figures are in Canadian dollars.)

NORWAY

Thanks mainly to its offshore petroleum resources, Norway rode out continued recession in 1977 with high employment and moderate economic growth.

Rate of Growth. Government economists estimated that the gross national product in 1977 would be 4.3% higher than in 1976. This, however, was well below earlier estimates which foresaw 7% growth. The lower figure reflected the fact that petroleum output rose more slowly than anticipated, while industrial production rose hardly at all. Exports actually fell (in volume) by some 4%.

The optimistic earlier forecasts were based on the belief that the long-awaited world economic upturn would gather real strength in 1977. When that failed, the government was forced to continue financial aid to many key industries. This aid, running into hundreds of millions of dollars, took the form of loans, loan guarantees, and direct grants. Industries benefiting from it included shipping, shipbuilding, forest industries, and fisheries.

Wages and Prices. Though the government's policies succeeded in keeping unemployment well below 1% of the labor force, they had some undesirable side effects. Wages continued to rise, making Norwegian goods less competitive, both abroad and at home. International currency movements, particularly two successive devaluations of the Swedish krona, strengthened this trend. Each time Sweden devalued (by 6% in April and 10% in August), Norway followed only half-way. This gave Swedish goods a price advantage, both on the Norwegian market—Norway trades heavily with Sweden—and internationally where Sweden and Norway compete.

Trade Deficit. As exports dropped, imports rose, because high wages and full employment encouraged consumer spending. Imports of new cars, for instance, broke all records.

The widening trade gap helped push the payments deficit to record levels. Other factors contributing to the deficit were continuing heavy investment in ships and offshore petroleum and lower earnings by the merchant fleet—a result of the world shipping depression. By October,

─── **NORWAY** · Information Highlights ───

Official Name: Kingdom of Norway.
Location: Northern Europe.
Area: 125,181 square miles (324,219 km²).
Population (1977 est.): 4,000,000.
Chief Cities (1975 est.): Oslo, the capital, 465,000; Bergen, 214,000; Trondheim, 134,000.
Government: *Head of state,* Olav V. king (acceded Sept. 1957). *Head of government,* Odvar Nordli, prime minister (took office Jan. 1976). *Legislature*—Storting: Lagting and Odelsting.
Monetary Unit: Krone (5.46 kroner equal U. S.$1, Aug. 1977).
Manufacturing (major products): Metals, pulp and paper, chemicals, ships, fish products.
Major Agricultural Products: Potatoes, barley, apples, pears, dairy products, livestock.

Norway's Premier Odvar Nordli, right, and Minister of Finance Per Kleppe explicitly demonstrate the most recent devaluation of the krone.

UPI

the government was anticipating a payments deficit of $5 billion (U. S.) for 1977, compared with $3.9 billion in 1976.

Economic issues were much debated in campaigning for the September parliamentary elections. Opposition parties said the Labor government had carried too far its policy of borrowing abroad, against future oil income, to sustain the economy at home. After a narrow victory in the election, Labor introduced a restrictive budget designed to curb the growth in consumer demand. The budget also featured special measures to help Norwegian industry.

Oil Blow-Out. A major event in the oil industry was the blow-out of an oil well on the Ekofisk field in April. The blow-out, which took a week to get under control, was very costly. It also raised doubts about the wisdom of pushing ahead too rapidly with the exploitation of offshore oil resources. Plans to begin exploratory drilling in the fish-rich waters off northern Norway were temporarily shelved after the accident, and a decision on further concessions in the North Sea was postponed. The accident was found to be due to a combination of human error and inadequate administrative routines. (*See also* ENVIRONMENT.)

THOR GJESTER
Editor, "Økonomisk Revy," Oslo

NOVA SCOTIA

In 1977, Nova Scotians were preoccupied with rising unemployment and fuel costs and with tension caused by the possibility of Quebec's separation from Canada.

Legislation and Government. The government has decided to establish a Black Culture Centre to coordinate efforts to promote the heritage of black people in Nova Scotia. Similarly, the government has acted to reduce discrimination based on sex. A new advisory council on the status of women will advise the government on steps needed to reduce exploitation of women in the labor market and on how to improve their social status.

Another independent organization, the Provincial Grain Commission, has been promulgated to facilitate buying, selling, and storing provincial grain output. The commission will also administer a production incentive program to improve the quality and quantity of grain output in the province. The extension of the economic zone at sea to 200 miles has prompted the government to take additional measures to strengthen the fishing industry.

Canadian Unity. The task force on Canadian unity had its first public hearing in Halifax on Quebec's possible separation. Presentations to the task force stressed the importance of keeping Quebec in the Confederation and developing federal policies to reduce regional economic imbalances.

Economy. Nova Scotians have been experiencing increasing fuel prices, high unemployment, and rather a small improvement in their real income. Domestic electric power customers had to put up with a 47% hike in power rates. This coincided with an unemployment rate of nearly 11% (16% in the Cape Breton area).

Residential construction was down, and a moderate gain in capital spending of about 5% in constant dollars could barely sustain economic growth. Though export trade remained brisk, retail trade showed a sluggish increase of 4.6%.

R. P. SETH
Mount St. Vincent University, Halifax

---NOVA SCOTIA · Information Highlights---

Area: 21,425 square miles (55,490 km²).
Population (1976 census): 828,571.
Chief Cities (1976 census): Halifax, the capital, 117,882: Dartmouth, 65,341; Sydney, 30,645.
Government (1977): *Chief Officers*—lt. gov., Clarence Gosse; premier, Gerald A. Regan (Liberal); atty. gen. Leonard L. Pace (L); min. of educ., George M. Mitchell (L); chief justice, Ian M. McKeigan. *Legislature*—Legislative Assembly, 46 members.
Education (1974–75): *Enrollment:* public elementary and secondary schools, 201,360 pupils; private schools, 1,300; Indian, 750; post-secondary, 21,250 students. *Total expenditures,* $299,966,000.
Personal Income (average weekly salary, July 1977): $214.20.
Unemployment Rate (August 1977, seasonally adjusted): 10.3%.
(All monetary figures are in Canadian dollars.)

WIDE WORLD

ANTHONY EDEN (1897–1977)
The epitome of the traditional British diplomat

EDEN, (Robert) Anthony, 1st Earl of Avon

British diplomat and prime minister: b. near Bishop Auckland, County Durham, England, June 12, 1897; d. Wiltshire, England, Jan. 14, 1977.

Anthony Eden's life was a long, sometimes difficult struggle to reach the top of the British political tree: the prime ministership. When he did enter 10 Downing Street in April 1955, replacing Sir Winston Churchill, he had a world reputation as a skillful diplomat and negotiator and as a strong opponent of any kind of authoritarian government, left or right.

Yet when he left office early in 1957, broken in health and with his policies disavowed by the Labour opposition and by many members of his own Conservative Party, his effective political career was at an end.

The reason can be summed up in a single word: Suez. The Anglo-French adventure to seize the Suez Canal, which he saw as a great opportunity to defeat the authoritarianism of Egypt's President Nasser, was attacked violently by his own countrymen, although they were by no means unanimous in their opposition, by the United Nations, and, most important of all, in the United States by the Eisenhower administration.

His tragedy was that the action he led was one that would have been applauded 20 years before as a blow against authoritarian rule. But, in the changed postwar period, it was considered imprudent. So Eden had to go.

Of the event, Eden later said: "I am still unrepentant about Suez. People never look at what would have happened if we had done nothing. There is a parallel with the 30's. If you allow people to break agreements with impunity, the appetite grows to feed on such things.

"I don't see what we ought to have done. One cannot dodge. It is hard to act rather than dodge."

He was created Earl of Avon in 1961. He appeared periodically to speak in the House of Lords. He wrote three highly informative volumes of memoirs and numerous newspaper and magazine articles. But politically he was finished.

Career. Anthony Eden was one of the survivors of Britain's World War I generation. He fought throughout that war, was decorated, and never forgot its lessons. Yet he was flexible enough, when foreign secretary (1951–55), to support West German rearmament against the new authoritarian threat posed by the Soviet Union.

Eden first became a world figure in the troubled decade before World War II. As minister without portfolio for League of Nations affairs (1935) and later as foreign secretary (1935–38), he fought bitterly first for collective security against the mounting menace of Nazi Germany and then for British rearmament and an end to appeasement.

Handsome, debonair, and immaculately dressed, he appeared the epitome of the traditional British diplomat. But there was a tough North Country strain beneath the outer man. When Neville Chamberlain, then prime minister, went behind Eden's back early in 1938 to negotiate with the Italian dictator Benito Mussolini, Eden resigned.

Churchill's arrival in power in May 1940 brought Eden back as secretary of state for war and, finally, foreign secretary again (December 1940–45). He had served as dominions secretary from September 1939.

This was perhaps his greatest period. He negotiated with the Soviets, helped Churchill plan political strategy, was resolute in defense of democracy in Greece when Britain was short of everything but resolution and valor.

Although he seldom has been given credit for it, Eden was a consummate politician. His long years in office prove that. But he was also a statesman able to see beyond the immediate future and an Englishman prepared to place his country on the side of freedom. He bore defeat as he bore triumph with grace.

Personal Life. In 1922, Eden married Beatrice Helen Beckett, daughter of a banker and newspaper owner. Prior to their divorce in June 1950, the couple had two sons. One son was killed in World War II; the other inherited the earldom. Lord Avon was also survived by his widow, Clarissa Spencer-Churchill, Sir Winston's niece who married Eden in 1952.

DREW MIDDLETON

[1] Arranged chronologically by death date

CRAWFORD, Joan

American film star: b. San Antonio, Texas, March 23, 1908; d. N.Y.C., May 10, 1977.

Joan Crawford, one of Hollywood's greatest stars, personified filmdom's most glamorous era. Her prolific career spanned five decades.

Special Qualities. Crawford made more than 80 films but was most closely identified with so-called "women's pictures." Whether as a shop-girl or sophisticate, she was best as the fiercely determined, sometimes self-sacrificing woman who, although beset by catastrophic problems, would battle her way through a male-dominated world and emerge with dignity.

Renowned "women's director" George Cukor, who guided her in *The Women, Susan and God,* and *A Woman's Face,* wrote in *The New York Times* of May 22, 1977: "She was the perfect image of the movie star and, as such, largely the creation of her own indomitable will. She had, of course, very remarkable material to work with: a quick native intelligence, tremendous animal vitality, a lovely figure, and, above all, her face."

Started as Dancer. The actress was born Lucille Fay LeSueur in 1908. (Various sources list the year as 1906 or 1904.) Her parents, Thomas and Anna Johnson LeSueur, who nicknamed her Billie, were divorced when she was an infant. Billie's sporadic schooling included three months at Stephens College in Columbia, Mo. Determined to become a dancer, she paid for lessons by working as a salesperson and eventually became a chorine in Midwest nightclubs.

Her first important break came when Broadway producer J. J. Schubert asked her to come to New York to perform in the chorus of *Innocent Eyes.* After hours she danced at Harry Richman's speakeasy, and this in turn led to an M-G-M screen test and a $75 weekly contract. In January 1925, she arrived in Hollywood and soon was designated Joan Crawford. It took three years before her first major screen success in *Our Dancing Daughters* (1928). She also reaped publicity from her romance with Douglas Fairbanks, Jr., who became her first husband.

Ability to Adapt. Crawford was able to adjust to changing film patterns and early made the transition to talkies. Nevertheless, she felt M-G-M was not offering her opportunities for growth and moved to Warner Bros. in 1942. Just when her career was waning, *Mildred Pierce* (1945) earned her an Academy Award. In the 1950's she moved on to character parts commensurate with her maturity.

Crawford was also married to actors Franchot Tone and Phillip Terry, and then in 1955 to Alfred N. Steele, board chairman of the Pepsi-Cola Company. After his death in 1959, she was named a director of the firm.

WILLIAM WOLF

MAKARIOS III

Archbishop and president of Cyprus: b. Ano Panaya, near Paphos, Cyprus, Aug. 13, 1913; d. Nicosia, Aug. 3, 1977.

For almost three decades Makarios III was the charismatic leader of the Greek Cypriots, serving as their religious primate and president.

His Beatitude Archbishop Makarios III was the son of a shepherd named Charalambos Mouskos and was originally called Michael Christodoulos Mouskos. Later, in church service, he took the name Makarios, meaning "blessed." He was ordained a deacon in 1938 and a priest in 1946. From 1946 to 1948 he studied at Boston University's School of Theology, and during that time became pastor of the Greek Orthodox Church in Woburn, Mass. In 1948 he was chosen bishop of Kitium, and in 1950 he succeeded Makarios II as archbishop of the Greek Orthodox Church of Cyprus.

In his new position, Makarios challenged the status of Cyprus as a British crown colony by championing the cause of *enosis,* or union with Greece. He won the support of the Greek Cypriots who made up about 80% of the island's population; the Turkish Cypriots—about 18% of the islanders—were unalterably opposed. After an outbreak of pro-*enosis* civil disturbances in 1955, Makarios was deported to the Seychelles by the British in March 1956. He remained there for a year. In subsequent negotiations with Great Britain, Greece, and Turkey he dropped his call for *enosis* and accepted a complicated settlement which made Cyprus independent and gave the Turkish Cypriots a significant role in its government. Returning to the island in March 1959, Makarios was elected president in December and took office in August 1960. He was reelected in 1968 and 1973.

The delicate structure of government, including both Greek and Turkish Cypriots, collapsed in late 1963 when violence broke out. The Turkish Cypriots withdrew to their own enclaves, and the two segments were thus effectively split. The UN sent in a force to help keep the peace.

The gravest crisis of Makarios' career came in 1974, when the pro-*enosis* military government which then ruled Greece turned against him. On July 15, 1974, the Cypriot National Guard, which was under the command of Greek officers, attacked the archbishop's palace, and he barely escaped with his life. He fled abroad, and Nikos Giorgiades Sampson became president. The Turkish government, citing the need to protect the Turkish Cypriots, then invaded Cyprus and took over about 40% of the island. Makarios returned to Cyprus on Dec. 7, 1974, to resume the presidency.

Makarios suffered a heart attack on Palm Sunday 1977. Four months later he died.

GEORGE J. MARCOPOULOS

RCA

ELVIS PRESLEY (1935–1977)
The King of Rock 'n' Roll

PRESLEY, Elvis

U. S. singer: b. Tupelo, Miss., Jan. 8, 1935; d. Memphis, Tenn., Aug. 16, 1977.

Elvis Presley did not invent rock 'n' roll music, nor was he the first to perform it—indeed, through most of his 23 years as a public figure, he did not particularly concentrate on it —but he was the first person to personify the essence of the genre, a style of adolescent rebellion that started defining itself in the 1950's. He was, virtually throughout his career, almost universally known as "the King of Rock 'n' Roll." His hit songs included "Heartbreak Hotel," "Hound Dog," "All Shook Up," "Don't Be Cruel," "Love Me Tender," "Teddy Bear," and "Loving You."

Elvis Aron Presley was born in Tupelo, Miss., the only surviving child of Gladys and Vernon Presley. His twin brother, Jesse Garon, died at birth. "They say when one twin dies, the other grows up with all [his] qualities," Elvis was to say later, as if pondering the contradictory, dual nature of the legend that surrounded him half his lifetime. His father gave Elvis a $2.95 guitar when he was 12. The following year the family moved to Memphis, looking for economic opportunity, and there Elvis went through high school and on to a $35 a week job driving a truck. In the summer of 1953, he paid Sun Records $4 to use its facilities to make a recording for his mother's birthday present. Marion Keisker, secretary to Sun President Sam Phillips,

taped the session because she knew Phillips—at that time when the basic elements of rock 'n' roll were starting to coalesce—was looking for "a black sound inside a white boy." About a year later, Phillips acted on that discovery and the result included the release of "That's All Right," a regional hit and the start of the Elvis Presley legend.

A promoter known as Colonel Tom Parker landed Presley a national recording contract, leading promptly to "Heartbreak Hotel," first in a long string of million-selling recordings, and an appearance on *The Ed Sullivan Show*. Even though the television cameras prudently aimed above the waist—Presley's uninhibited, suggestive, hip-wriggling style being considered lewd by many in the late 1950's—everyone of every age got the message, which involved adolescents having their own music and their own spokesman, and the fact that adults did not approve, or even understand, was part of the attraction.

Yet Presley, uninhibited, rebellious, even sneering onstage, remained deferential to adult, established authority offstage. He was unabashedly "square" in some ways, religious, devoted to his mother, materialistic but generous; he developed a pattern of giving expensive gifts, including automobiles and even airplanes, to his friends—and sometimes to strangers. He submitted amiably to being drafted into the Army, having his famous (and symbolic) duck-tail haircut and sideburns shorn, and when he was discharged he "went Hollywood."

Guided by Parker, he continued to sell millions of records and eventually starred in 33 motion pictures, sometimes filming as many as three a year. At first some, such as *Jailhouse Rock*, paid homage to his role in expanding the adolescent consciousness and sense of identity, but the movies by and large were bland and cut to a formula. Presley eventually was to label them disdainfully "travelogues." Nevertheless, the sound-track from *Blue Hawaii* produced his best-selling album.

Presley and Priscilla Beaulieu, whom he had met in Germany when he was in the Army, were married in 1967. A daughter, Lisa Marie, was born on Feb. 1, 1968. The marriage ended in divorce in 1973.

Presley died at Graceland, his million-dollar Memphis mansion, of cardiac arrhythmia—a severely irregular heartbeat—brought about by "undetermined causes." Eighty thousand fans jammed the street outside Graceland prior to the funeral, so many sent flowers to the cemetery that Memphis ran out of flowers, and there was an immediate rush for Presley records, books about the star, and general Elvis memorabilia. Tributes to the dead King were mixed with speculation about his problems in handling success, but there was no doubt he would be remembered as a definite revolutionary force in American culture.

NOEL COPPAGE

STOKOWSKI, Leopold (Stokes)

Orchestral conductor: b. London, April 18, 1882; d. Nether Wallop, Hampshire, England, Sept. 13, 1977.

Leopold Stokowski was one of the greatest conductors of the century, famed for his innovative approaches, for popularizing classical music via films, radio, and recordings. His career, which spanned 70 years and included over 7,000 performances, ended five years before he could complete his last contract which would have had him recording until he was 100.

Life and Career. The child of a Polish father and a mother of Irish descent, Stokowski studied violin, piano, and organ, by 18 becoming a fellow in the Royal College of Organists (the highest rank). He was graduated from Queens College, Oxford, with a bachelor of music degree.

He began his American career in 1905 as organist of St. Bartholomew's Church, New York City, becoming conductor four years later of the Cincinnati Symphony. In 1911, he married the pianist Olga Samaroff (née Lucy Hickenlooper, San Antonio, Tex.), the first of his three marriages, each ending in divorce.

At his next post, conductor of the Philadelphia Orchestra (1912–36), his distinctive achievements began and the legend was founded. With his uncanny ear for sonority and color, he became the unchallenged master of the orchestral palette, making the Philadelphia Orchestra an unequaled virtuoso instrument.

Stokowski did everything he could to improve the sound, dispensing with uniform string section bowing, changing the traditional seating arrangement to a pattern adopted by orchestras everywhere, experimenting and pioneering in repertoire, recording, and film techniques.

His personal presence and magnetism were crucial to the legend. He had spotlights to create an aureole around his golden, later white, hair, and to pick out the deft play of his hands (he scorned use of the baton). The showman in him was strong; he used publicity masterfully, maintaining a deliberately provocative public image. The word "charisma" as applied to a conductor began in this century with him.

While noted colleagues were bent on preserving the scores' literal integrity, Stokowski went after the poetry in the music. His often vivid, overstated interpretations drew accusations of charlatanism from critics while capturing the popular imagination. Typical were his orchestral arrangements of Bach organ works and his touching up of other scores.

Stokowski challenged critics and Philadelphia audiences with new music, answering protests, even booing, with lectures from the podium and more new works. These included American premieres of Mahler's Eighth Symphony, Schönberg's "Gurrelieder," Berg's "Wozzeck," Charles Ives' Fourth Symphony. The three films he

COPYRIGHT © BETH BERGMAN 1977

LEOPOLD STOKOWSKI (1882–1977)
Among conductors, "charisma" began with him.

made in Hollywood with the Philadelphia Orchestra brought him world fame, climactically Walt Disney's *Fantasia* which took wild liberties with the classical music used.

Meanwhile, his public personal life continued flamboyantly. His marriage to Olga Samaroff (1911–23) produced one daughter. There were two daughters from his marriage (1926–37) to the heiress Evangeline Brewster Johnson (after which he was linked romantically to Greta Garbo) and two sons from his last marriage (1945–55) to Gloria Vanderbilt de Cicco.

He remained the Philadelphia Orchestra's co-conductor from 1936 to 1941, then conducted and recorded with major orchestras worldwide. He formed the All-American Youth Symphony in 1940, the New York City Symphony in 1944, was the Houston Symphony's music director (1955–61); he created and conducted, at no salary, the American Symphony in New York to train young musicians (1962–72).

His last performances were less vivid, his gestures more restricted but the incandescence remained. His mysterious comprehension of time, sonority, rhythm and musical shape, his modern, social outlook marked Stokowski a titan among conductors.

ROBERT COMMANDAY

CULVER PICTURES

BING CROSBY (1904–1977)
"An average guy who could carry a tune."

CROSBY, Harry Lillis (Bing)

Singer, recording artist, film and television star: b. Tacoma, Washington, May 2, 1904; d. Madrid, Spain, Oct. 14, 1977.

"I'm dreaming of a white Christmas . . . ." "Where the blue of the night meets the gold of the day, bu-bu-bu-boo . . . ." Bing Crosby's mellifluous voice was part of America's entertainment for fifty years. Sales of his recordings totaled some 400 million on 88 different labels throughout the world. His "White Christmas" alone sold 40 million copies. Few entertainers have reached a similar level of popularity.

Special Quality. The key to Crosby's appeal was his ability to stir affectionate feelings through his voice and his carefully nurtured public image. His easy-going, friendly, unassuming singing style never went out of fashion despite upheavals that brought to the fore singers such as Elvis Presley and the Beatles. He exuded charm as a screen and television personality, and his annual Christmas telecasts were like yule visits from an old family friend.

Harry Lillis Crosby allegedly acquired the name Bing through his fascination with a comic strip, "Bingville Bugle." He started toward a law career as a student at Gonzaga University in Spokane, but he began playing the drums in college and found that he could earn more money in spare time music jobs than as an assistant in a law firm. With fellow musician Al Rinker and singer Mildred Bailey (Rinker's sister), he formed a trio. Bandleader Paul Whiteman was impressed and hired them; he later fired them after growing impatient with Crosby's early casualness about his work.

Timing. The growth of radio was a fortuitous development for Crosby, who sang on the air for the first time in 1931. His crooning caught on with the public, and Crosby was to enjoy fame for the rest of his life. When he appeared at the Paramount Theater in New York in 1932, he remained for a record run of 20 weeks. By 1934 he was receiving 10,000 fan letters a month and 85 fan clubs existed internationally.

Crosby capitalized on the expanding recording industry, as well as contributed to its growth. The conversion of motion pictures to sound gave him another avenue. Crosby made his screen debut in 1930 with Paul Whiteman in *King of Jazz*. Mack Sennett signed him to appear in eight shorts for Paramount. Between 1930 and 1966, he made more than 60 motion pictures.

Academy Award. Crosby won an Oscar in 1944 for playing a priest in *Going My Way*, and an Oscar nomination in 1954 for his performance in *The Country Girl*. His broadest film acclaim resulted from the "road pictures" with Bob Hope and Dorothy Lamour. The first, *Road to Singapore* (1940), set the pattern for the free-form comedy adventures, including breezy jokes and haunting musical numbers. Before his death there were plans for a reprise, *The Road to the Fountain of Youth*.

Acquired Wealth. Crosby grew rich (estimates range from $40 to $70 million), and at various times, apart from his production company, had business interests as varied as a race track, the Pittsburgh Pirates and Detroit Tigers' baseball clubs, a television station, cattle ranches, real estate, a frozen orange juice company, and oil wells. He gave generously of his time for charity, often through exhibition golf matches with Hope, with whom he maintained a close friendship. His autobiography, *Call Me Lucky*, written with Pete Martin, was published in 1953 by Simon & Schuster.

After performing at the Palladium in London, where he had videotaped his 1977 Christmas show, he left for Madrid to relax. He was stricken with a fatal heart attack while playing golf.

The star is survived by his wife, the former Kathryn Grant; their two sons and a daughter; four sons from his marriage to singer Dixie Lee, who died of cancer in 1952; his brother, retired bandleader Bob Crosby; a sister, Mary Rose Pool; and 16 grandchildren. A Catholic, Crosby was accorded a requiem mass in Westwood, Calif., and was buried in Holy Cross Catholic Cemetery. At Christmas, Crosby's voice was present as usual.

WILLIAM WOLF

CHARLIE CHAPLIN (1889–1977)
"grand old man of comedy"

UPI

CHAPLIN, Sir Charles Spencer

British actor, motion-picture writer, producer, and director: b. London, England, April 16, 1889; d. Corsier-sur-Vevey, Switzerland, Dec. 25, 1977.

Charlie Chaplin, who almost single-handedly transformed the motion-picture medium into an art form, died peacefully at his home in Switzerland on Dec. 25, 1977. Following his death, Chaplin was hailed by many as the world's greatest filmmaker. Between 1914 and 1967, the comedian, who also wrote, produced, and directed motion pictures, appeared in more than 80 movies.

Commenting on his roles, early in his career, Chaplin said: "All my pictures are built around the idea of getting me into trouble and so giving me the chance to be desperately serious in my attempt to appear as a normal little gentleman. That is why no matter how desperate the predicament is, I am always very much in earnest about clutching my cane, straightening my derby hat and fixing my tie, even though I have just landed on my head."

Background. The son of music hall performers, Charles Spencer Chaplin was born on April 16, 1889, in London, where he grew up amid poverty. He began as a boy to perform in London music halls, became a successful vaudeville trouper, and in 1910 went with the Fred Karno troupe on a tour in the United States.

His performances there led to Hollywood film contracts, beginning with work for Mack Sennett's Keystone studios in 1913. During the next few years he appeared in scores of two-reel comedies, usually as the little vagabond who somehow manages to survive the adversities of life. After founding his own studio in 1918, he wrote, directed, produced, and acted in his own films, rarely deviating from his classic role.

Chaplin's full-length features include *The Kid* (1921), *The Gold Rush* (1925), *The Circus* (1928), and *City Lights* (1931). His last silent film was *Modern Times* (1936), a satire on industrial society, for which he also composed the musical score. In his poignant lampoon of Nazism, *The Great Dictator* (1940), Chaplin appeared in a dual role—as Hynkel, the dictator of Tomania, and as a Jewish barber. He was seen as a debonair French Bluebeard with an antiwar message in *Monsieur Verdoux* (1947), and as an aging vaudevillian in *Limelight* (1952).

Meanwhile, Chaplin's personal and political life came increasingly under fire. Although he was acquitted of Mann Act charges in 1944, a court ruled against him in a paternity suit in 1945. Admittedly a "citizen of the world" and a "peacemonger," he became the target of congressional committees because of his identification with liberal causes in the midst of the Cold War. While on a trip abroad in 1952, Chaplin, who had remained a British subject, was notified that his reentry into the United States would be challenged. Thereafter he made his home in Switzerland with his fourth wife, the former Oona O'Neill, daughter of Eugene O'Neill, and their children. Chaplin starred in his production *A King in New York* (1957), a sharp satire on contemporary America, and wrote and directed *A Countess From Hongkong* (1967). He published *My Autobiography* in 1964.

Chaplin made a triumphant return to the United States in April 1972, his first visit since he was barred in 1952. The welcome he received indicated that his popularity as the tragicomic "little tramp" of Hollywood's golden age had remained intact. During his four-day stay in New York City, he was presented with the Handel Medallion, the city's highest award for achievement in the arts, and was guest of honor at a "Salute to Charlie Chaplin," staged by the Film Society of Lincoln Center. During the Academy Award ceremonies in Hollywood that year, he was awarded a special honorary Oscar for "the incalculable effect he has had in making motion pictures the art form of this century."

He was knighted by Queen Elizabeth II in London in 1975. At the time, Sir Charles commented: "Life is a marvelous, a wonderful thing, but as you get on, you always think of moments past—and you always think of death."

Following a "completely private funeral," Sir Charles Spencer Chaplin was buried near his Swiss home.

HENRY S. SLOAN

The following is a selected list of more than 170 prominent persons who died in 1977. Articles on some major figures appear on the preceding pages.

Adrian of Cambridge, Edgar Douglas Adrian, 1st baron (87), British physiologist: b. London, Nov. 30, 1889; d. London, Aug. 4, 1977. One of the world's foremost physiologists, he shared the Nobel Prize for medicine in 1932 with Sir Charles Sherrington for discoveries about the mechanism of sense organs and motor nerve cells. Besides his outstanding work as a researcher and experimenter, he had another career as master of Trinity College, Cambridge, and chancellor of the university. He also served as president of the Royal Society (1950–55) and the British Association for the Advancement of Science (1954).

Ahmed, Fakhruddin Ali (71), president of India; a former minister of agriculture in Indira Gandhi's cabinet, he became president in 1974 and in 1975 declared the state of emergency under which the government seized near-dictatorial powers: d. New Delhi, Feb. 11.

Queen Alia of Jordan (28), third wife of King Hussein and the first to be named queen; born Alia Toukan, of a Jordanian family; educated in the West and said to have been thoroughly westernized: d. (in helicopter crash) near Tafileh, southern Jordan, Feb. 9.

Ames, Elizabeth (92), U. S. patron of artists; planned the artists' retreat of Yaddo, Saratoga Springs, N. Y., in 1924, and directed it for 45 years, nurturing many of the nation's creative artists: d. Saratoga Springs, March 28.

Anderson, Eddie ("Rochester") (71), U. S. comedian; best known as Jack Benny's skeptical manservant during 30 years of radio and TV broadcasting, he also appeared in several films and won acclaim for his performance in *Cabin in the Sky:* d. Los Angeles, Calif., Feb. 28.

Arvey, Jacob M. (81), U. S. political figure; Democratic boss of Chicago in the late 1940's, he was the predecessor of Mayor Richard Daley and started the political careers of such well-known personalities as Paul H. Douglas and Adlai Stevenson: d. Chicago, Ill., Aug. 25.

Ba Maw (80), Burmese statesman; was Burma's first prime minister (1937–39) and later became head of state in the Japanese puppet government (1943–45); fled to Japan, where he gave himself up in 1946, was imprisoned in Tokyo, then allowed to return to Burma in 1947: d. Rangoon, Burma, May 28.

Baden-Powell, Lady Olave (88), British organization official; the widow of Lord Baden-Powell, founder of the scout movement, she was the chief guide of the World association of Girl Guides and Girl Scouts: d. London, June 26.

Beel, Louis J. M. (74), former prime minister of the Netherlands; headed the Dutch government in 1946–48 and again in 1958–59: d. Utrecht, Netherlands, Feb. 11.

Ben-Ami, Jacob (86), U. S. actor; a founder and star performer of the Jewish Art Theater in New York, he drew critical acclaim both for his Yiddish and English productions: d. New York City, July 22.

Biayenda, Emile (50), Congolese cardinal; archbishop of Brazzaville from 1971, he was made cardinal in 1973: d. (kidnapped, murdered) Brazzaville, Congo, March 23.

Biberman, Abner (69), U. S. actor and director; a member of the New York Group Theater, who appeared in such productions as *Waiting for Lefty* and *Winterset,* he also had character roles in some 100 films; later turned director and worked on such television series as *Ben Casey, The Virginian,* and *Ironside:* d. San Diego, Calif., June 20.

Bibring, Grete Lehner (78), Austrian-born U. S. psychiatrist; a student and colleague of Sigmund Freud, she was director of psychiatric research at the Beth Israel Hospital, Boston, and professor (emeritus) of clinical psychiatry at Harvard University: d. Cambridge, Mass., Aug. 10.

Biggs, E. Power (70), British-born musician; a leading organist since the late 1930's who for 16 years (1942–58) broadcast weekly recitals over the CBS network and made countless recordings, he did more than anyone else to awaken interest in serious organ music: d. Boston, Mass., March 10.

Bijedić Džemal (60), Yugoslav prime minister; a member of the Communist Party Presidium, he had headed the government since July 1971: d. (in air crash) near Sarajevo, Jan. 18.

Bliven, Bruce Ormsby (87), U. S. journalist, editor, and author; joined *The New Republic* as managing editor in 1923 and was its editor from 1930 to 1953; became the intellectual godfather of the New Deal, whose liberal ideas he promulgated: d. Palo Alto, Calif., May 27.

Bodansky, Oskar (76), U. S. chemist and physician; was one of the first to use biochemistry for the detection of diseases, especially cancer: d. New York City, Aug. 21.

Bolton, Frances (91), former U. S. representative from Ohio; succeeded her late husband, Chester C. Bolton, in 1939 and served as Republican member of Congress until 1969: d. Lyndhurst, Ohio, March 9.

Borgonovo Pohl, Mauricio A. (37), foreign minister of El Salvador; a scion of one of the country's wealthiest families, he had held office for nearly five years when kidnapped on April 19: d. (found murdered) near San Salvador, May 10.

Boyd, Stephen (48), Irish-born screen actor; played a variety of hero and villain roles in Hollywood movies, but was best remembered as Charlton Heston's chariot-race opponent in *Ben-Hur:* d. Los Angeles, Calif., June 2.

Brauer, Richard D. (76), German-born U. S. mathematician; pioneered in the development of algebra with his "Brauer group" concept and also developed the theory of "modular representation": d. Belmont, Mass., April 17.

Braun, Wernher von (65), German-born physicist and rocket engineer: b. Wirsitz, East Prussia (now Poland), March 23, 1912; d. Alexandria, Va., June 16, 1976. He began to experiment with rockets at 18 and at 20 became the German army's top civilian rocket specialist. He developed the dreaded V-2 which ravaged England during the latter part of World War II. Captured by the Americans —along with 118 of his co-workers—in 1945, he was taken to the United States, where he worked first for the army and later for the National Aeronautics and Space Administration as director of the agency's space flight center in Huntsville, Ala. More than any other single man, he made possible the manned flight to the moon.

Brooks, Geraldine (52), U. S. actress; equally at home in stage, movie, and television roles, she had a second career as a nature photographer and in 1975 published a book of her pictures with essays by her husband, Budd Schulberg: d. Riverhead, N. Y., June 19.

Bruce, David K. E. (79), U. S. diplomat: b. Baltimore, Md., Feb. 12, 1898; d. Washington, D. C., Dec. 5, 1977. A man of great wit and charm, he was especially adept at cooling heated situations and served with distinction in numerous State Department posts and as ambassador to France (1949–52), West Germany (1957–61), and Great Britain (1961–69); was later called from retirement to head the U. S. delegation at the stalemated Paris peace talks with Vietnam, then went on to open the first U. S. "liaison" office in Communist China (1973); his last post was as chief U. S. delegate to NATO (1974–76).

Queen Alia of Jordan   **Eddie Anderson**   **Frances Bolton**   **Wernher von Braun**

PHOTOS UPI

Bryant, Alice Franklin (in her late 70's), U. S. antiwar activist; held by the Japanese for two and a half years during World War II, she thereafter campaigned against war, particularly the Vietnam conflict: d. Seattle, Wash., June 7.

Budker, Gersh Itskovich (59), Soviet physicist; head of the Siberian Institute of Nuclear Physics in Novosibirsk from 1957 and a winner of the Lenin Prize in 1967, he was considered one of the most innovative designers of high-energy physics experiments in the world: d. USSR (announced July 5).

Bunn, Alden (52), U. S. blues singer, better known as **Tarheel Slim**; was highly regarded by blues, rhythm-and-blues, and gospel lovers: d. New York City, Aug. 21.

Bustamante, Sir Alexander (93), first prime minister of independent Jamaica; a powerful labor leader with a somewhat adventurous background, he became the hero of Jamaica's struggle for sovereignty and led it to independence in 1962, serving as prime minister to 1967: d. Kingston, Jamaica, Aug. 6.

Cabot, Sebastian (59), English-born character actor; was best known as French, the gentleman's gentleman in the television series *Family Affair*: d. Victoria, B.C., Aug. 23.

Cain, James M. (85), U. S. writer; the hard-boiled author of 18 books—among them *The Postman Always Rings Twice* (1934), *Double Indemnity* (1936), *Serenade* (1937), and *Mildred Pierce* (1941)—he started out as a newspaperman and later wrote for *The American Mercury*, for Walter Lippmann (editorials), and for *The New Yorker*; sometimes described as "the poet of the pot-boiler," he also wrote for the screen, and three of his novels were made into successful movies: d. University Park, Md., Oct. 27.

Callas, Maria (53), U. S. opera singer: b. New York City, Dec. 3, 1923; d. Paris, France, Sept. 16, 1977. One of the outstanding sopranos of her time, she inspired the revival of the 19th-century bel canto opera and thereby exerted a unique influence on operatic repertories. While critics disputed about her vocal technique, she was universally acclaimed for her musicianship, her projection, intensity, and theatrical talents. She studied in Athens and made her debut in 1947 in Verona, Italy, soon going on to La Scala in Milan, and later to the Metropolitan Opera in New York. Surrounded by admirers and also by controversy, myth, disputes, and legal actions, she was seldom out of the limelight. She gave her last public recital in 1974.

Carr, John Dickson (70), U. S. writer; an acknowledged master of the mystery novel whose specialty was the locked-room murder, he wrote some 120 detective novels as well as hundreds of short stories and was twice winner of the "Edgar" award: d. Greenville, S. C., Feb. 27.

Chomsky, William (81), U. S. educator; one of the world's foremost Hebrew grammarians and father of linguist Noam Chomsky, he taught in Philadelphia for more than half a century: d. Philadelphia, Pa., July 19.

Churchill, Lady Clementine (92), widow of Sir Winston Churchill, Britain's World War II prime minister; was made life peeress as Baroness Spencer-Churchill of Chartwell in 1965: d. London, Dec. 12.

Clark, Tom C. (77), U. S. jurist: b. Dallas, Tex., Sept. 23, 1899; d. New York City, June 13, 1976. He joined the U. S. Department of Justice in 1937 and was head of the anti-trust and later criminal division before becoming attorney general in the Truman administration in 1945. Four years later President Truman appointed him to the U. S. Supreme Court, and he participated in most of the landmark decisions of the Warren years. He retired from the court in 1967, after his son, Ramsey, had become U. S. attorney general, to prevent the possibility of conflict. But he remained active until his death and was believed to be the only retired justice in history to have sat on all 11 circuits of the U. S. Court of Appeals.

Clouzot, Henri-Georges (69), French film director; a one-time assistant to director Anatole Litvak, he became a master of the suspense film; particularly remembered for *The Wages of Fear* (1952) and *Diabolique* (1954): d. Paris, Jan. 12.

Collins, Charles C. ("Chuck") (73), U. S. athlete and businessman; was best known as one of the "seven mules" on the unbeaten Notre Dame football team of 1924; later was coach, and business executive for a freight company: d. Ridgewood, N. J., April 14.

Conway, William (64), Irish cardinal; a recognized theological scholar, he was made archbishop of Armagh, Northern Ireland, in 1963 and cardinal two years later; served on a number of papal commissions: d. Armagh, April 18.

Corcoran, Fred (72), U. S. sports promoter; served 11 years as the Professional Golfers' Association's traveling tournament manager and three as its promotional director; helped form the Ladies Professional Golf Association; from 1954 was the impresario of the World Cup; also

Maria Callas   **Clementine Churchill**

was business representative of many sports stars: d. White Plains, N. Y., June 23.

Cotzias, George C. (58), Greek-born U. S. physician; an internationally prominent neurologist, he was best known for having developed the so-called L-Dopa therapy for Parkinson's disease, which has also proved effective against brain damage from manganese poisoning: d. New York City, June 13.

Crosland, Anthony (58), British foreign secretary; a Labour member of Parliament from Grimsby since 1959, he served in minor governmental posts before being appointed to the foreign office in April 1976; authored *The Nature of Socialism* (1956): d. Oxford, England, Feb. 19.

Dahlberg, Edward (76), U. S. writer and critic; known for his autobiographical works, including *Bottom Dogs*, *From Flushing to Calvary*, and *Can These Bones Live*, and for his distinctive bookish prose: d. Santa Barbara, Calif., Feb. 27.

Derry, Tibor (82), Hungarian writer; exiled and imprisoned before World War II for his opposition to right-wing rule, he won recognition after the war as one of Hungary's most prominent fiction writers, but soon drew fire as a critic of Communist bureaucracy and was considered a leading intellectual force behind the 1956 uprising; sentenced to nine years in prison, he was released in 1960: d. Budapest, Aug. 18.

Desmond, Paul (original name **Breitenfeld**) (52), U. S. musician; an alto saxophonist who played with the Dave Brubeck Quartet for 17 years, he elicited from his instrument a light, airy sound that provided a striking contrast to Brubeck's piano; one of his compositions, *Take Five*, became the quartet's best known selection: d. New York City, May 30.

Devine, Andy (71), U. S. film actor; best known as the squeaky-voiced, bumbling sidekick of cowboy heroes, he played in some 300 movies: d. Orange, Calif., Feb. 18.

Dodds, Gilbert L. ("Gil") (58), U. S. athlete and clergyman; nicknamed "The Flying Parson," he was considered the best American one-mile runner of his time; set a world indoor record of 4 min. 5.3 sec. in 1948: d. St. Charles, Ill., Feb. 3.

DuBois, Shirley Graham (69), U. S.-born writer and composer; author of an award-winning book on Frederick Douglass, *There Once Was a Slave*, and two operas, she married W. E. B. DuBois, the black civil rights leader, in 1951 and moved with him to Ghana in 1961; later lived in Cairo and elsewhere: d. Peking, China, March 27.

Eglevsky, André (60), Russian-born classical dancer who performed with the Ballet Russe de Monte Carlo and later with many U. S. companies; a stylist of distinction, he was particularly noted for the ease and smoothness of his pirouettes: d. Elmira, N. Y., Dec. 4.

Eiseley, Loren (69), U. S. anthropologist and author; a professor for some 40 years, he was widely known as a writer who "expressed the intellectual rigor and curiosity of a scientist with the eloquence and sensitivity of a poet"; his books included *The Immense Journey* (1957), *Darwin's Century* (1958), *The Firmament of Time* (1960), *The Unexpected Universe* (1969), *The Night Country* (1971), *All the Strange Hours*, an autobiography (1975), and *Another Kind of Autumn*, poetry (posthumous, 1977): d. Philadelphia, Pa., July 9.

Erhard, Ludwig (80), former chancellor of West Germany: b. Fürth, Bavaria, Feb. 4, 1897; d. Bonn, May 5, 1977. More than any other man, he was credited with having wrought the "economic miracle" of postwar Germany. In the early summer of 1945 he was chosen, because of his anti-Nazi reputation, to help figure out ways to get Bavarian factories back into operation. From the Bavarian Ministry of Economics, which he assumed in 1945, he planned the currency reform in the combined U. S. and British occupation zones, which took place in 1948. The success of his policies won him the Ministry of Economics in the new Federal Republic of Germany in 1949. He succeeded Konrad Adenauer in the chancellorship in 1963 and two years later led his party to a decisive victory in the Bundestag elections. A year later, however, he was replaced—the victim of party squabbles and a parliamentary crisis.

Faulkner, Brian (56), former premier of Northern Ireland; a Protestant member of the Stormont Parliament since he was 28, he was premier in 1971–72 and again in 1973–74; was made life peer as Baron Faulkner in January: d. (by accident) near Saintfield, Northern Ireland, March 3.

Fedin, Konstantin A. (85), Soviet writer; author of such novels as *First Joys, No Ordinary Summer, Brothers,* and *Rape of Europe,* he headed the board of the Soviet Union of Writers: d. Moscow, July 15.

Fieser, Louis F. (78), U. S. chemist; professor emeritus of organic chemistry at Harvard University, he was credited with such diverse achievements as the development of vitamin K, a blood-clotting agent, and the invention of combat napalm: d. Cambridge, Mass., July 25.

Finch, Peter (60), British actor; was best known for his work in films, including *The Detective* (1954), *The Nun's Story* (1959), *The Pumpkin Eater* (1964), *Sunday, Bloody Sunday* (1971), and *Network* (1976), for which he was awarded a posthumous Academy Award in 1977: d. Los Angeles, Calif., Jan. 14.

Fish, George W. (81), U. S. physician; a founder of the Squier Urology Clinic at the Columbia Presbyterian Medical Center, he developed new surgical techniques for treating complications in kidney ailments; served as model for the "Dr. Kildare" stories of film and TV fame: d. East Hampton, N. Y., Feb. 22.

Foley, Martha (80), U. S. editor and educator; after a journalistic career in the 1920's and 1930's, she began in 1941 editing annual anthologies of *The Best American Short Stories* and continued for 35 years; also taught courses on the short story at Columbia University from 1945 to 1966: d. Northampton, Mass., Sept. 5.

Foy, Brian (80), U. S. vaudeville performer and film producer; one of the celebrated "Seven Little Foys" in the early part of the century, he later went to Hollywood where he produced the first all-talking picture, *The Lights of New York* (1928) and the three-dimensional *House of Wax* (1953); for his low-budget "B" films he was sometimes nicknamed the "King of the B's": d. Los Angeles, Calif., April 20.

Fraser, Alexa Stirling (79), U. S. golfer; one of the biggest names in women's golf in her time, she was a three-time winner of the U. S. national championship (1916, 1919, and 1920) and a two-time winner of the Canadian championship: d. Ottawa, Ont., April 15.

Gabo, Naum (87), Russian-born sculptor; one of the masters of modern art, he was the father of the Constructivist movement and the author of its *Realistic Manifesto* in 1920; left his mark on the art of several countries before settling in the United States; he became a citizen in 1952: d. Waterbury, Conn., Aug. 23.

Garner, Erroll (55), U. S. jazz pianist and composer; a self-taught musician who could neither read nor write music, he was a master of the keyboard and composed such popular songs as *Misty* and *That's My Kick;* was the first jazz musician in 1959 to be booked by impresario Sol Hurok: d. Los Angeles, Calif., Jan. 2.

Garson, Stuart (78), Canadian political figure; served as premier of Manitoba from 1943 to 1948 and from 1948 to 1957 as a member of Parliament and Canada's minister of justice: d. Winnipeg, May 4.

Ginzburg, Yevgenia (71), Soviet author; was arrested in 1937, charged with links to terrorist groups, and spent 18 years in Stalin's labor camps; wrote *Into the Whirlwind* about life in the camps: d. Moscow, May 25.

Goldblatt, Harry (86), U. S. physician; a pioneer in research on blood pressure, he produced experimental hypertension, showing that blood flow from the kidneys played an important role in blood pressure elevation: d. Rochester, N. Y., Jan. 6.

Grauer, Benjamin Franklin ("Ben") (69), U. S. broadcaster; joining NBC as a radio announcer in 1930, he served

PHOTOS UPI

Ludwig Erhard   Peter Finch

variously as newsman, commentator, interviewer, actor, moderator, and program host in a career that spanned 43 years with the network: d. New York City, May 31.

Gries, Tom (54), U. S. screen writer and film director; was best known for *Will Penny,* an artistically successful western; had just finished filming *The Greatest,* the story of Muhammad Ali, starring the heavyweight champion himself: d. Pacific Palisades, Calif., Jan. 3.

Gropper, William (79), U. S. artist; was a frequent contributor of cartoons to leftist publications; often compared to Daumier, Chagall, or Grosz, his drawings and paintings were savagely critical of the powerful and the wealthy: d. Manhasset, N. Y., Jan. 6.

Habe, Hans (original name **Jean Bekessy**) (66), Budapest-born novelist and editor; wrote *A Thousand Shall Fall* (1941), a novel made into the film *The Cross of Lorraine,* about the betrayal of the French army in 1940 by its leaders; after the war he became editor in chief of the 18 U. S.-published newspapers in occupied Germany: d. Locarno, Switzerland, Sept. 29.

Hambro, Edvard Isak (65), Norwegian diplomat; a former president of the UN General Assembly (1970), he was Norwegian ambassador to France and a member of the Permanent Court of Arbitration in The Hague: d. Paris, Feb. 1.

Hamer, Fannie Lou (60), U. S. civil rights worker; a sharecropper on a Mississippi cotton plantation, she joined the civil rights activists in 1962, at the age of 45, and subsequently became one of the most respected and durable black leaders in the Deep South: d. Mound Bayou, Miss., March 14.

Harris, Stanley ("Bucky") (81), baseball player and manager; member of the Baseball Hall of Fame, he managed five major-league teams during a 29-year career, two of them to World Series victories (1929 and 1947): d. Bethesda, Md., Nov. 8.

Hawks, Howard (81), U. S. film director; a sophisticated professional, he made a long list of successful, fast-paced movies, including *Bringing Up Baby, To Have and Have Not, Sergeant York,* and *Gentlemen Prefer Blondes;* was awarded an honorary Academy Award for his work in 1975: d. Palm Springs, Calif., Dec. 26.

Helpern, Milton (75), U. S. physician; served 42 years (1931–73) with New York City's Medical Examiner's office, the last 20 as chief; was probably the most eminent U. S. expert on forensic medicine, earning a wide reputation as a medical detective; wrote (with three other physicians) *Legal Medicine, Pathology and Toxicology,* recognized as the definitive work on the subject: d. San Diego, Calif., April 22.

Hershey, Lewis Blaine (83), U. S. general: b. Steuben County, Ind., Sept. 12, 1893; d. Angola, Ind., May 20, 1977. He helped found the Selective Service System before World War II and directed it from 1941 to 1970. A good, strong-minded administrator, he became practically synonymous with the system and as such was increasingly despised and hated during the unpopular Korean and Vietnam wars. He retired in 1973, the oldest man on active duty.

Hobson, Julius W. (54), U. S. civil rights activist; an economist and statistician for the Social Security Administration, he was the most influential black activist in Washington, D. C., and was credited with many of the political and educational changes that transformed the city in the 1960's; his latest success was the establishment in 1974 of the first elected city council for 100 years: d. Washington, D. C., March 23.

Howe, Quincy (76), U. S. broadcast journalist; a book editor and erstwhile director of the American Civil Liberties Union, he began broadcasting news and comments, then a novelty, over WQXR in 1939, later joined CBS, and

Lewis Blaine Hershey

Ernie Lombardi

PHOTOS UPI

after World War II made the transition to television; established and edited *Atlas* magazine (1961–65) and wrote *A World History of Our Times* in 3 volumes: d. New York City, Feb. 17.

Hubbard, Robert Calvin ("Cal") (77), U. S. athlete; was elected to three halls of fame—two as a football player and one as an umpire for baseball—the only man so honored; was chief of umpires of the American League from 1953 to 1969: d. Gulfport, Fla., Oct. 17.

Hull, Henry (86), U. S. stage and screen actor; created the role of Jeeter Lester in *Tobacco Road* (1933), which had a record-breaking run on Broadway; appeared in more than 40 films: d. Cornwall, England, March 8.

Hutchins, Robert Maynard (78), U. S. educator: b. Brooklyn, N. Y., Jan. 17, 1899; d. Santa Barbara, Calif., May 14, 1977. One of the most innovative American academicians, he revolutionized the country's higher education with his concept that college students should be taught reasoning rather than vocational skills. Working his way through college, he was graduated from Yale in 1921 and two years later, at the age of 24, became secretary of that university. While on the job, he entered and was graduated from the Yale Law School, magna cum laude. At 28, he was appointed dean of the law school, a post he held for two years. He then became president of the University of Chicago, where he stayed until 1951, the last six years as chancellor rather than president. He later established the Center for the Study of Democratic Institutions at Santa Barbara, Calif.

Hyland, Diana (41), U. S. actress; was known to TV audiences as the mother of eight in the ABC series *Eight is Enough;* also appeared in *Peyton Place* and *Young Dr. Malone:* d. Los Angeles, Calif., March 27.

Ilyushin, Sergei Vladimirovich (82), Soviet aircraft designer; created more than 50 planes during his career, among them the IL-2 fighter-bomber of World War II and the 350-seat IL-86 airbus: d. Moscow (announced Feb. 9).

Isaac, Bobby (43), U. S. stock car racer; a winner of 37 Grand National races, he was the holder of the closed-court speed record for stock cars, set in 1970: d. Hickory, N. C., Aug. 13.

Johnson, Nunnally (79), U. S. screen writer, producer, and director; wrote the scripts for such films as *The Grapes of Wrath, Tobacco Road, The Keys of the Kingdom, The Desert Fox, The Man in the Gray Flannel Suit,* and *The Three Faces of Eve,* the last two of which he also directed: d. Los Angeles, Calif., March 25.

Jones, James (55), U. S. novelist: b. Robinson, Ill., Nov. 6, 1921; d. Southampton, N. Y., 1976. An enlisted man in the army from 1939 to 1944, he knew war and the military at first hand, and he wrote about them so convincingly that his first book, *From Here to Eternity* (1951), not only won him the National Book Award, but also world fame. Living in Paris, from 1958 to 1975, he published several other novels, among them *The Pistol* (1959), *The Thin Red Line* (1962), and *Go to the Widow-Maker* (1967), but never again commanded the critical acclaim that his first book had evoked.

Jumblat, Kemal (59), Lebanese Druse chief and political leader; a member of the Lebanese parliament from 1946 and chairman of the Progressive Socialist party which he founded in 1949, he led the alliance of leftists and Muslims in the Lebanese civil war and was a forceful proponent of change in the country's sectarian political system: d. (assassinated) near Beirut, March 16.

Kantor, MacKinlay (73), U. S. writer; the respected author of 43 books—novels, short fiction, and poetry—he won the Pulitzer Prize in 1956 for his *Andersonville,* the story of a Southern prison camp during the Civil War; another of his books was adapted to the screen in the highly successful film *The Best Years of Our Lives* (1946): d. Sarasota, Fla., Oct. 11.

Karp, Richard (74), Austrian-born U. S. conductor and opera executive; fled Europe for the United States in the 1930's and was director of the Pittsburgh Opera Company from 1942: d. Pittsburgh, Pa., Feb. 2.

Kaufman, Sue (50), U. S. novelist; was best known for *The Diary of a Mad Housewife* (1967), which was made into a successful movie; also wrote *Green Holly, The Headshrinker's Test,* and the short story collection *The Master and Other Stories:* d. New York City, June 25.

Keita, Modibo (61), former president of Mali; said to have been descended from the rulers of the medieval Mali empire, he became Mali's first president in 1960; was deposed by junior officers in 1968 and thereafter held in detention: d. Bamako, Mali, May 16.

Kennedy, J. Walter (64), basketball commissioner; under his chairmanship (1963–1975) of the National Basketball Association, the game came to rival baseball and football as one of the most popular professional sports: d. Stamford, Conn., June 26.

Khokhlov, Rem V. (51), Soviet physicist and educator; an expert on lasers, he was the rector, from 1973, of the University of Moscow: d. Moscow, Aug. 8.

Kleinschmidt, Edward E. (101), German-born U. S. inventor; a holder of some 120 patents, he was best known for the high-speed teletype machine he invented in 1914, then a major breakthrough in communications: d. Canaan, Conn., Aug. 9.

Langlois, Henri (62), French film historian; founded and directed the French Cinémathèque, a combined film museum and film bank containing some 50,000 films from all over the world: d. Paris, Jan. 12.

Laurence, William L. (89), U. S. journalist; a science reporter and editor of *The New York Times* for 34 years, he was the winner of two Pulitzer Prizes and was the only journalist to witness the first nuclear blast at Alamogordo, N. M., in 1945; later that year he flew as the sole reporter on the atomic bombing mission to Nagasaki: d. Majorca, Spain, March 19.

Leach, Maria (85), U. S. editor and folklorist; was best known as the editor of *The Dictionary of Folklore, Mythology and Legend,* which was published in two volumes in 1949–50 and reissued in 1972: d. Barrington, Nova Scotia, May 22.

Lee, Benjamin W. (42), Korean-born physicist; a former professor at the State University of New York at Stony Brook and the Institute for Advanced Studies at the University of Paris, he headed the theoretical group at the Fermi National Accelerator Laboratory in Batavia, Ill., from 1971; d. (in car crash) near Kewanee, Ill., June 16.

Levitt, Saul (66), U. S. playwright and novelist; was best known as author of *The Andersonville Trial:* d. New York City, Sept. 30.

Levy, David M. (84), U. S. child psychiatrist; originated the concept of "sibling rivalry" and was the first to use the Rorschach test in the United States: d. New York City, March 1.

Lieberson, Goddard (66), British-born U. S. business executive; a musician and composer, he joined the CBS-owned Columbia Records in 1939 as studio recording director and was instrumental in developing the 33-rpm long-playing record: d. New York City, May 29.

Litvinov, Ivy (87), English-born writer and widow of Maksim Litvinov, Soviet diplomat; taught English and edited a Russian-English dictionary in the USSR; returned to England in 1972: d. Hove, England, April 28.

Lombardi, Ernie (69), U. S. athlete; one of baseball's great catchers: d. Santa Cruz, Calif., Sept. 26.

Lombardo, Guy (75), U. S. bandleader; from 1929 on he led his Royal Canadians band in playing *Auld Lang Syne* on New Year's Eve. Playing "the sweetest music this side of heaven," his band was for years a fixture in the Roosevelt Hotel grill in New York: d. Houston, Tex., Nov. 5.

Lowell, Robert (60), U. S. poet: b. Boston, Mass., March 1, 1917; d. New York City, Sept. 12, 1977. By many regarded as the best English-language poet of his generation, he won the Pulitzer Prize in 1947 for the second of his 17 volumes of poetry, *Lord Weary's Castle,* and went on to capture such awards as the poetry prize of the American Academy of Arts and Letters, the Guinness Poetry Award, and the National Book Award. In May, 1977, he was given the National Medal for Literature. He was poetry consultant for the Library of Congress in 1947–48 and taught literature at Boston University, Harvard, and in England. His last volume, *Day by Day,* was published just a month before his death. He also wrote the dramatic trilogy *The Old Glory* on themes from American history.

Alfred Lunt   John L. McClellan   Groucho Marx   Zero Mostel

Lowman, Charles LeRoy (97), U. S. physician; a leading orthopedic surgeon, he founded Orthopedic Hospital in Los Angeles in 1909 and from then until 1972 held a weekly outpatient clinic for the city's children; until 1976 he also made frequent flights to Calexico, Mexico, to help at a free clinic for handicapped children: d. Los Angeles, Calif., April 17.

Lubin, Ernst (60), U. S. pianist, composer, and author; an enthusiast of piano duets, he wrote a book on the subject and also performed duets in Carnegie Hall and elsewhere: d. (murdered) New York City, March 15.

Lunt, Alfred (84), U. S. actor: b. Milwaukee, Wis., Aug. 19, 1892; d. Chicago, Ill., Aug. 3, 1977. The uncrowned king of American actors, he reigned over the U. S. stage for nearly 40 years with his British-born consort, Lynn Fontanne. He made his professional debut at 20 and five years later caught the eye of Booth Tarkington, who in 1919 wrote the leading role of *Clarence* specifically for him; it was a resounding success. At that time he also met Miss Fontanne, by then a noted actress of the comedy stage, and they were married in 1922. They appeared together for the first time in Ferenc Molnar's *The Guardsman* (1923), and rarely played separately after that. Their forte was sophisticated comedy, such as Noel Coward's *Design for Living*, yet they scored one of their greatest critical successes in a serious play, *The Visit* by Friedrich Dürrenmatt. Lunt also directed many of the plays in which he appeared and two opera productions for the Metropolitan Opera Company.

Lupescu, Magda (Princess Elena) (81), widow of King Carol of Rumania; a legendary beauty, she had been the king's companion for 22 years and commonly regarded as the real power behind his throne before marrying him in exile in 1947: d. Estoril, Portugal, June 29.

McClellan, John L. (81), U. S. senator from Arkansas; the second most senior member of the Senate, which he entered in 1943, and long-time chairman of the Permanent Investigations Committee, he earned national prominence for his inquiries into organized labor, organized crime, and overseas servicemen's clubs; later became chairman of the Appropriations Committee; was known as a foe of civil rights legislation and a staunch defender of military appropriations: d. Little Rock, Ark., Nov. 28.

McCulloch, Robert (65), U. S. industrialist; a millionaire oilman and chain-saw manufacturer, he became a celebrity when he bought the London Bridge and shipped it, stone by stone, for reconstruction in Arizona: d. Bel Air, Calif., Feb. 25.

Magallanes, Nicholas (54), Mexican-born ballet dancer; a principal dancer with the New York City Ballet from its inception, he excelled in dramatic portrayals such as the title role in George Balanchine's *Orpheus*, Rimbaud in Frederick Ashton's *Illuminations*, and the chief victim in Jerome Robbins' *The Cage*: d. North Merrick, N. Y., May 2.

Malcuzyński, Witold (62), Polish-born pianist; a pupil of Jan Paderewski, he first achieved notice by winning the international Chopin competition in Warsaw in 1937 and went on to become one of the leading interpreters of that composer; made his American debut in Carnegie Hall in 1942 and his last U. S. appearance in the same hall in May 1977: d. Palma, Majorca, July 17.

Mark, Julius (78), U. S. religious leader; a longtime national head of Reform Judaism, he served for 20 years as senior rabbi of Temple Emanu-El, largest Jewish congregation in the world, retiring in 1968: d. New York City, Sept. 7.

Markel, Lester (83), U. S. editor; headed the Sunday edition of *The New York Times* from 1923 to 1964 and was associate editor of the paper until 1968: d. New York City, Oct. 23.

Marriott, John (83), U. S. actor; a veteran of countless stage, film, and TV productions, he was best remembered for his portrayal of Joe Mott, the discredited black gambler in the first production of O'Neill's *The Iceman Cometh:* d. Queens, N. Y., April 5.

Marshall, S. L. A. (77), U. S. soldier-historian; one of the nation's foremost military historians, who chronicled the Spanish Civil War, World War II in both Europe and the Pacific, and the Korean and Vietnam wars, as well as conflicts in the Middle East and elsewhere; won critical acclaim for such books as *Pork Chop Hill* (also made into a successful movie) and *The River and the Gauntlet:* d. El Paso, Tex., Dec. 17.

Marx, Groucho (original name **Julius Henry Marx**) (86), U. S. comedian; b. New York City, Oct. 2, 1890; d. Los Angeles, Aug. 19, 1977. The third-oldest of the Marx brothers, he was to many the epitome of the zany world of comedy. Throughout their common career, beginning on the vaudeville stage before World War I and continuing in their films—*Horse Feathers, Duck Soup, A Night at the Opera, A Day at the Races, The Big Store, A Night in Casablanca, Love Happy,* and others—he was the centerpiece of the comedy, the master of the ad-lib, the champion of the insult. "I wouldn't belong to any club that would have me for a member," he said of himself. He later was the host of the highly successful *You Bet Your Life* television show (1947–62).

Marx, Milton ("Gummo") (84), U. S. vaudeville actor; one of the five famous Marx brothers, he became their agent and manager when they moved from the vaudeville stage to the Hollywood screen in 1933 and was never seen in their films: d. Palm Springs, Calif., April 21.

Massamba-Debat, Alphonse (56), former president of the Congo; a minister in the government of President Youlou (1961–63), he became president in 1963 but was ousted in a 1968 coup: d. (executed) Brazzaville, March 25.

Masterman, Sir John (86), British public official; deputy chief of British intelligence during World War II, he engineered and directed a network of double agents that practically controlled the German espionage system in Britain: d. London, June 6.

Miller, Harry W. (97), U. S. physician; a thyroid surgeon known as the "China Doctor" because of his missionary work in that country, he served as a physician to Chou En-lai and Madame Chiang Kai-shek; was also a pioneer in the field of nutrition: d. Riverside, Calif., Jan. 1.

Moran of Manton, Charles McMoran Wilson, 1st Baron (94), British physician, a distinguished author, and one of England's most prominent medical advisers; president of the Royal College of Physicians for a record nine years, he was Sir Winston Churchill's personal physician: d. Newton Valence, Hampshire, England, April 12.

Morgenstern, Oskar (75), German-born U. S. economist and educator; the coauthor, with John von Neumann, of *The Theory of Games and Economic Behavior*, he was one of the first to develop and apply the game theory as a tool of economic forecasting: d. Princeton, N. J., July 26.

Mostel, Zero (original name **Samuel Joel Mostel**) (62), U. S. stage and screen actor: b. Brooklyn, N. Y., Feb. 28, 1915; d. Philadelphia, Pa., Sept. 8, 1977. A versatile actor and mimic, who could make his audience cry with both laughter and sentiment, he began as a stand-up comic and went on to perform for all the media—radio, television, stage, and films. He was blacklisted during the McCarthy era, but was back on Broadway by 1958, scoring critical successes; his last movie part was that of a blacklisted actor in *The Front* (1976). He was remembered for his roles in *Ulysses in Nighttown* (1958), *Rhinoceros* (1961), and *A Funny Thing Happened on the Way to the Forum* (1963), but most of all for that of Tevye, the milkman, in *Fiddler on the Roof* (1964). An accomplished painter, he was also an art collector.

Mowrer, Edgar Ansel (84), U. S. journalist who won the Pulitzer Prize in 1933 for his dispatches on the rise of

Nazism; was chief of the Chicago *Daily News* Berlin bureau from 1923 to 1933, when he was expelled by the Nazis; expelled as well from Mussolini's Italy (1936) and Stalin's USSR (1937), he subsequently served as a Washington correspondent: d. Madeira, March 2.

Mueller, Erwin (65), German-born physicist; was the inventor in 1955 of the ion field microscope, through which he became the first person to see an atom; was elected to the National Academy of Sciences in 1975: d. Washington, D. C., May 17.

Musial, Joe (72), U. S. cartoonist; drew the "Katzenjammer Kids" from 1952 and was said to have been the ghost artist behind more top comic strips than any other cartoonist; initiated the use of comics as educational tool: d. Manhasset, N. Y., June 6.

Nabokov, Vladimir (78), Russian-born U. S. novelist: b. St. Petersburg (now Leningrad), April 23, 1899; d. Montreux, Switzerland, July 2, 1977. An undeniable force in modern world literature, he was by some regarded as a mere gifted artificer, while others saw in him a creative genius of the first rank. Son of a rich lawyer, he fled the Russian revolution with his family to Berlin in 1919. After graduation from Cambridge, England, in 1922, he earned a meager living in Berlin while also writing novels and stories in Russian. In 1939 he accepted an invitation to lecture on Slavic literature at Stanford University, Calif., and he thereafter remained in the United States for 20 years, becoming a U. S. citizen. Though writing all the while, it was only the publication of *Lolita* (1958) which catapulted him into literary prominence and gave him enough income to devote himself wholly to his writing. From 1959 on, he made his home in Switzerland. Among his other works written in English are *The Real Life of Sebastian Knight* (1941), *Bend Sinister* (1947), *Conclusive Evidence,* also known as *Speak Memory* (1951), *Pnin* (1957), *Pale Fire* (1962), and *Ada* (1969). He also made a controversial, annotated translation of Pushkin's *Eugene Onegin* (1963). Most of his earlier output was gradually translated into English after he became famous. Among those works are *Mary, King Queen Knave, The Great Deed, The Luzhin Defense, Despair,* and *Laughter in the Dark*. His great hobby was lepidopterology, the study of butterflies, and he worked for a time as an entomologist at Harvard. Of several species and subspecies of butterflies that he discovered, one was named after him—Nabokov's wood nymph.

Ngouabi, Marien (38), president of the Congo; a French-trained paratroop major, he came to power in a coup in 1968 and led the country to the left, establishing a "people's republic" with links to China, Cuba, and the Soviet Union: d. (assassinated) Brazzaville, March 18.

Nin, Anaïs (73), U. S. writer: b. Neuilly, France, Feb. 21, 1903; d. Los Angeles, Calif., Jan. 14, 1977. She was the author of several novels, among them *House of Incest* and *Winter of Artifice,* in which she typically conveyed the world of the psyche rather than external reality. Her best-known work, however, was the multivolume *Diary of Anaïs Nin.*

O'Brien, Robert David (60), U. S. athlete; was the only college football player ever to win the Heisman, Camp, and Maxwell awards all in the same year (1938): d. Fort Worth, Tex., Nov. 18.

O'Donnell, Kenneth P. (53), U. S. political figure; a personal friend of President John F. Kennedy, he served as his appointments secretary (1960–63) and later made two unsuccessful bids for the governorship of Massachusetts: d. Boston, Sept. 9.

Otero, Katherine Stinson (86), U. S. aviator, the fourth woman to qualify for a pilot's license (1912); known as "the flying schoolgirl," she appeared as a stunt pilot at air shows across the country, set several distance and endurance records, and later flew mail for the government: d. Santa Fe, N. Mex., July 8.

Patocka, Jan (69), Czech educator; a retired professor of philosophy, he was one of three spokesmen for the "Charter 77" human rights group in Czechoslovakia and had been repeatedly interrogated by the police and the Interior Ministry: d. Prague, March 13.

Payne, Virginia (66), U. S. actress; was best known as the voice of "Ma Perkins," a CBS radio soap opera that lasted from 1933 to 1960; also appeared in many stage roles: d. Cincinnati, Ohio, Feb. 10.

Pellicer, Carlos (77), Mexican poet and senator from the state of Tabasco; was praised as one of the most satisfying Mexican poets of this century: d. Mexico City, Feb. 16.

Pitts, Robert F. (68), U. S. physician; was internationally known for his studies of the kidney and nervous system, which led to standard therapies and procedures in hospitals throughout the world: d. Live Oak, Fla., June 6.

Powell, Clilan B. (83), U. S. physician and editor; was the first black appointed to the N. Y. State Athletic Commission and the first black physician to specialize in roentgenology; edited *The New York Amsterdam News* (1935–71): d. Briarcliff Manor, N. Y., Sept. 22.

Powers, Francis Gary, *see* Los Angeles, p. 311.

Powers, John R. (84), U. S. businessman; an aspiring actor, he founded what is believed to be the world's first modeling agency, thereby becoming the father of a billion-dollar industry: d. Glendale, Calif., July 19.

Printemps, Yvonne (82), French operetta singer; was long one of the most sparkling stars of the French musical theater: d. Paris, Jan. 18.

Prinze, Freddie (22), U. S. comedian; achieved stardom in one of the title roles of the television series *Chico and The Man:* d. (suicide) Los Angeles, Calif., Jan. 29.

Prío Socarrás, Carlos (74), former president of Cuba; an erstwhile labor minister, he became president in 1948 and was overthrown by Gen. Fulgencio Batista in 1952; initially supported Fidel Castro but later broke with him and became spokesman for the Miami Cuban exiles' community: d. (suicide) Miami Beach, Fla., April 5.

Radcliffe of Werneth, Cyril John Radcliffe, Viscount (78), British lawyer; one of Britain's most distinguished legal authorities, he was known as the "Great Investigator" for his leadership of official inquiries into sensitive national security issues; headed the commission that charted the division of India and Pakistan in 1947 and ten years later helped formulate a draft constitution for Cyprus: d. Warwick, England, April 2.

Rattigan, Sir Terence (66), British playwright; author of such London hits as *French Without Tears* (1936), *Love in Idleness* (1944; American title, *O Mistress Mine*), *The Winslow Boy* (1946), *The Browning Version* (1948), *The Sleeping Prince* (1953; film version, *The Prince and the Showgirl*), and *Separate Tables* (1955), he was one of Britain's most successful dramatists, but never did quite so well on Broadway, where critics looked askance at his "well-made plays"; his last, *Cause Célèbre,* starring Glynis Johns, opened in London in July: d. Hamilton, Bermuda, Nov. 30.

Ritchard, Cyril (79), Australian-born actor, singer, and director; a remarkably versatile performer whose career spanned half a century, he was at his best in musical comedy and was especially remembered as Captain Hook in *Peter Pan,* but also excelled in straight drama and as a director, both of theater and grand opera: d. Chicago, Ill., Dec. 18.

Roberts, Clifford (84), U. S. sports promoter; was the cofounder and for 43 years the chairman of the Masters golf tournament: d. (suicide) Augusta, Ga., Sept. 29.

Ross, Nellie Tayloe (101), former U. S. public official; the first woman to serve as governor of a state—Wyoming, 1925–27—she later was director of the U. S. Mint (1933–53): d. Washington, D. C., Dec. 19.

Rossellini, Roberto (71), Italian film director; the first and most prominent of the postwar neorealist film makers, he gained fame with the classic *Rome, Open City* (1945), which he followed with such antiwar films as *Paisan* (1946) and *Germany, Year Zero* (1948); had a celebrated illicit affair with and then married, Ingrid Bergman, who played in two of his films, *Stromboli* (1950) and *The Greatest Love,* and who bore him three children before they were divorced in 1957; made his last film in the old mode in 1959—*Generale Della Rovere,* starring Vittorio De Sica—and then concentrated on "educational" films, such as *The Rise of Louis XIV* (1966): d. Rome, June 3.

Anaïs Nin   **Freddie Prinze**

Ethel Waters

UPI

Rostand, Jean (83), French essayist and biologist; son of writer Edmond Rostand, he was a satirist who had a seat in the Académie française since 1959, while in his scientific career his work revolutionized the fields of parthenogenesis and artificial insemination: d. Saint-Cloud, France, Sept. 3.

Rupp, Adolph F. (76), U.S. basketball coach; during 42 years as head coach at the University of Kentucky led the Wildcats to 879 victories, the most ever by a college coach, and four national titles: d. Lexington, Ky., Dec. 10.

Saypol, Irving Howard (71), U.S. jurist; as U.S. attorney for the southern district of New York (1949–51), he zealously supervised the case against Alger Hiss and personally prosecuted Ethel and Julius Rosenberg; was elevated to the N.Y. State Supreme Court in 1951 and presided over some famous cases; indicted by a grand jury in 1976 on bribery and perjury charges that were later dismissed: d. New York City, June 30.

Schermerhorn, Willem (82), former prime minister of the Netherlands; a resistance leader during World War II, he headed the first Dutch postwar cabinet (1945–46) and was member of the Dutch parliament until 1963: d. Haarlem, Netherlands, March 10.

Schippers, Thomas (47), U.S. musician; music director of the Cincinnati Symphony since 1970, he was also a regular guest conductor in the world's great opera houses and at the Bayreuth Festival: d. New York City, Dec. 16.

Schlesinger, Elizabeth Bancroft (90), U.S. feminist and scholar, widow of historian Arthur M. Schlesinger, Sr.; a pre-World War I marching suffragette, she returned to her early interest after World War II, one of a few scholars to pioneer in the modern study of women's history: d. Williamsburg, Va., June 1.

Schuschnigg, Kurt (79), Austrian politician and academician; as chancellor of Austria, 1934–38, he succeeded Engelbert Dollfuss, whom Nazi extremists had assassinated, and was under constant pressure from Berlin to steer the country on a "German course"; having promised in early 1938 to place Nazis in his government, he defied Hitler by announcing a referendum on the future of the country and was forced to resign; Austria was annexed shortly after, and he emigrated to the United States, where he taught political science for 20 years, returning to Austria in 1967: d. near Innsbruck, Nov. 18.

Schuyler, George S. (82), U.S. author and journalist; a writer of scathing wit and perception, he was originally a socialist and a cofounder with A. Philip Randolph of the *Messenger Magazine*, but later turned more and more to the right, becoming, in the eyes of most blacks, a sheer reactionary; authored the novel *Black No More* in 1931: d. New York City, Aug. 31.

Serebryakov, Pavel (68), Soviet musician; a pianist of international renown, he was the rector of the Leningrad Conservatory and often represented the Soviet Union on juries of international music competitions: d. Leningrad, (announced) Aug. 18.

Shankar, Uday (76), Indian dancer, brother of the sitarist Ravi Shankar; starting his career as partner of Anna Pavlova, for whom he created two ballets on Hindu themes, he became the greatest popularizer in the West of Indian dance, to which he brought a renaissance in the form of modernization and synthesis of tradition; was considered "one of the greatest dancers of his epoch, East or West, in his own idiom ranking with Nijinsky . . .": d. Calcutta, India, Sept. 26.

Shor, Bernard ("Toots") (73), U.S. "saloonkeeper"; probably New York's most famous restaurant owner, he ran a succession of "watering spots" frequented by celebrities for more than 35 years: d. New York City, Jan. 23.

Soloviev, Yuri (36), Soviet ballet dancer; a member of the famous Kirov Ballet, he was one of a generation of superb male dancers that included Nureyev, Panov, and Baryshnikov: d. (suicide) near Leningrad, Jan. 16.

Soper, Fred L. (83), U.S. physician; a pioneer exponent of preventive medicine, he developed new techniques for the control and eradication of yellow fever, malaria, and other diseases during 22 years in Latin America for the Rockefeller Foundation; later headed the foundation's war-time typhus team in Europe and North Africa and served as director of the Pan American Health Organization: d. Wichita, Kansas, Feb. 9.

Staffa, Dino (72), Italian cardinal; a conservative whose career was mostly within the Vatican administration, he was made prefect of the Supreme Tribunal of the Apostolic Signatura, the highest court of the Roman Catholic Church, in 1967 and was elevated to the College of Cardinals shortly after: d. Rome, Aug. 7.

Sullivan, William C. (65), U.S. law enforcement officer; served 30 years with the FBI, becoming for a while the bureau's third-ranking official, but was forced to resign in 1971 because of his criticism of J. Edgar Hoover: d. (killed in a hunting accident) near Sugar Hill, N.H., Nov. 9.

Untermeyer, Louis (92), U.S. poet and anthologist; exerted considerable influence on American literature by his writings and lectures, but especially by his four-score-plus anthologies, many of which were long required reading on American campuses: d. Newton, Conn., Dec. 18.

Velasco Alvarado, Juan (67), Peruvian general and former president; came to power in a military coup in 1958 and carried out wide-ranging nationalizations within the Peruvian economy before being toppled in another coup in 1975: d. Lima, Peru, Dec. 24.

Waters, Ethel (80), U.S. singer and actress; b. Chester, Pa., Oct. 31, 1896; d. Chatsworth, Calif., Sept. 1, 1977. A woman of indomitable vitality, she worked her way up from utter poverty through night spot appearances to the Broadway stage, motion pictures, and television. She sang the *St. Louis Blues* in Philadelphia clubs when it was still brand new and popularized such songs as *Cabin in the Sky* and *Stormy Weather*. From Philadelphia she went to Harlem, where she was recruited for *Africana*, the first of her many Broadway shows, in 1927. She began her movie career in 1929 and appeared in nine films until 1959, among them *Cabin in the Sky*, *Pinky*, and *The Member of the Wedding*. On television she starred in the *Beulah* series in 1953 and appeared in *The Sound and the Fury* in 1955.

Weinberg, Sydney A. (67), U.S. inventor; helped develop techniques—such as the projection of X-ray motion pictures and cameras for taking color pictures inside the stomach—extending the use of photography as a diagnostic tool: d. Brighton, N.Y., March 29.

White, Katherine (84), U.S. editor; served as the first fiction editor of *The New Yorker* magazine and as such exerted incalculable influence on contemporary American literature; was coeditor, with her husband, E.B. White, of *A Subtreasury of American Humor* (1941): d. North Brooklin, Me., July 20.

Wilcox, Herbert (85), British film director and producer; one of Britain's foremost film makers, he was often embroiled in controversy over his films, which sometimes encountered crippling censorship, especially his portrayals of historical figures; won four Academy Awards during a 40-year career: d. London, May 15.

Willard, Charles F. (93), U.S. aviator; was the fourth American (after the Wright brothers and Glenn Curtiss) to fly an airplane and became the nation's first barnstorming pilot: d. Glendale, Calif., Feb. 1.

Woodham-Smith, Cecil (80), British historian; a one-time writer of light fiction, she later produced four biographical and historical works of exemplary scholarship—about Florence Nightingale, the charge of the Light Brigade, the Irish famine, and Queen Victoria: d. London, March 16.

Wrigley, Philip K. (82), U.S. industrialist; headed the world's largest chewing-gum company and was the owner of the Chicago Cubs baseball team: d. Elkhorn, Wis., April 12.

Yang Sen (in his 90's), Chinese general; was one of the last Chinese warlords who joined Chiang Kai-shek in 1926 and thereafter fought both Chinese Communist and Japanese invasion forces; served as governor of Kweichow province (1945–47) and mayor of Chungking (1948–49) before retreating to Taiwan where he was strategy adviser to the Chiang regime: d. Taipei, May 15.

Zuckmayer, Carl (80), German playwright; was best known for *The Captain of Köpenick*, a brilliant satire of German militarism, which has been described as one of the few great comedies in German literature; also wrote *The Devil's General* and the script for *The Blue Angel*, the film that launched Marlene Dietrich's movie career: d. Visp, Switzerland, Jan. 18.

OCEANIA

The island nations of the Pacific had a busy year in spite of subdued economic activity resulting from sluggish export returns and the lingering effects of earlier bouts of inflation.

The people of Commonwealth countries extended spontaneous welcomes to Queen Elizabeth II during her Silver Jubilee visit and showed a unified approach to international issues. In French-speaking territories, the quest for independence remained a background issue.

In the region's largest nation, Papua New Guinea (PNG), signs of factionalism persisted, especially in the Highlands, but Prime Minister Michael Somare's electoral victory consolidated his position. Matters related to the PNG border with Australia were left in abeyance, but tensions between PNG and Indonesia continued over demarcation of the border with West Irian and the drift eastward of small tribal groups. PNG rejected applications by the USSR and China to set up embassies in Port Moresby.

The British government announced an exgratia payment of U. S.$11 million to the 2,500 Banabans now living on Rabi Island, in Fiji, as a final settlement of Banaban claims. The Australian government increased aid to nine countries. Priority was to be accorded projects strengthening the islanders' sense of self-reliance. Australia undertook to provide at least $66 million in bilateral aid over three years, with Fiji receiving one third, Western Samoa a sixth, and lesser amounts going to Tonga, the Solomon Islands, New Hebrides, the Gilberts, Cook Islands, Niue, and Tuvalu. Regional projects will receive about $3.5 million.

Political Developments. Elections in PNG were the first since independence. Well before they were held, Governor General Sir John Guise resigned to reenter active politics. He was replaced by Sir Tore Lokoloko, a 48-year-old opposition member with nine-years' parliamentary experience. In the elections, Somare's Pangu Party retained power.

In Fiji's elections of March–April, the governing Alliance Party (predominantly Fijian) was reduced to 24 seats while the predominantly Indian National Federation Party, led by Siddiq Koya, secured 26, with the remaining two seats going to an Independent and a representative of the Fiji Nationalist Party who had been an Alliance member. Factionalism inhibited the NFP from forming a government, and Governor General Ratu Sir George Cakobau recommissioned Ratu Sir Kamisese Mara. For some months, Koya did not press a parliamentary challenge; an adverse vote in August resulted in a new election, which Mara won handsomely. Meanwhile eight dock leaders had been sentenced to prison for their part in waterfront strikes affecting the sugar industry.

Hammer DeRoburt's loss of the presidency of Nauru to political neophyte 31-year-old Bernard Dowiyogo came as a surprise. DeRoburt had been president from Jan. 1, 1968, when Nauru attained independence. The change came following the elections of December 1976.

Economic Change. The boom in coffee prices reached the village people of the Highlands of PNG, bringing some wealth and confusion. Lower copper prices cut the PNG government's returns from the Bougainville mining enterprise. New Caledonia's exports of nickel declined. In French Polynesia, there was concern about slow development of local agriculture and industry, declining French military expenditures in the area, and a slackening of the tourist trade.

Fiji's sugar industry was in the doldrums, and a tropical fruit preserving plant on the Cook Islands closed after 16 years.

Constitutional Developments. In the Anglo-French Condominium of New Hebrides, the New Hebrides Representatives Assembly was boycotted by the biggest party, the Vanuaaku Pati (formerly the National Party). It was an ineffectual move to force the exclusion of the six Chamber of Commerce representatives from the assembly.

A constitutional committee moved Tuvalu (formerly Ellice Islands) closer to independence within the Commonwealth. The Council of Ministers of the Solomon Islands took the view that there was no need to hasten independence.

Strains were apparent in U. S.-Micronesia relations, partly as a result of reports of CIA surveillance of Micronesia delegates to political status talks but also because of defiance by the Congress of Micronesia on the handling of the area's important tuna resources. Talks on the future of the UN-mandated Trust Territory of the Pacific were inconclusive. Meanwhile, the 4,000 people of Kosrae (southeast of Ponape) celebrated the island's new status as a District within the Trust Territory.

Softball was PNG's fastest-growing sport. Guam opened a greyhound racing track.

R. M. YOUNGER, *Australian Author*

OCEANIA · Information Highlights

Nation	Area (sq mi—km²)	Population (in millions)	Capital	Head of State and Government
Fiji	7,055 (18,272)	0.6	Suva	Ratu Sir George Cakobau, governor general Ratu Sir Kamisese Mara, prime minister
Nauru	8 (21)	.008	. . .	Bernard Dowiyogo, president
Papua New Guinea	178,260 (461,693)	2.9	Port Moresby	Sir Tore Lokoloko, governor general Michael Somare, prime minister
Tonga	270 (700)	.09	Nuku'alofa	Taufa'ahau Tupou IV, king Prince Tu'ipelehake, prime minister
Western Samoa	1,097 (2,841)	0.2	Apia	Malietoa Tanumafili II, head of state Tupuola Efi, prime minister

OCEANOGRAPHY

Although the International Decade of Ocean Exploration (IDOE) continues until 1980, many major projects were yielding significant results in 1977.

Physical Oceanography. The POLYMODE study involving physical oceanographers from the United States and the USSR includes two main efforts. The first is a statistical and geographical experiment that has continued since 1974. In this experiment, there is a sequence of moored instrument arrays that cover large areas of the North Atlantic. They are used to sample eddy characteristics in several different environments. This program has revealed that the intensity of eddy fields is variable from one region to another, with sudden changes in energy near the Gulf Stream. A second program concerns a smaller area in the central North Atlantic that is to be intensively surveyed by a major multinational effort in 1978.

The Ocean and Weather Patterns. The first global geophysical experiment (FGGE) for meteorological studies, which examines the interaction of atmospheric and oceanic phenomena, will be conducted during 1978 under the general direction of GARP (the Global Atmospheric Research Program). The experiment will be sponsored in the United States by the National Oceanographic and Atmospheric Agency (NOAA). In addition, several regional experiments have been developed within GARP, such as the monsoon experiment (MONEX) scheduled for 1979 to observe the seasonal winds of the Indian Ocean.

Joint Indian and Soviet expeditions in 1973 provided data and experience for the development of a program in 1977 for the Arabian Sea and the Bay of Bengal as a prelude to MONEX. One objective of the study is to increase our understanding of the beginning of the rainy season associated with the monsoons. Another objective is to develop a full description of the monsoon circulation, which is reflected in the ocean in the Somali current system and the upwellings of the Arabian Sea. The ultimate goal of MONEX will be to obtain data that will enable prediction of the monsoons. Virtually all countries of the Indian Ocean basin and South China Sea are participating, with significant contributions from the United States and the USSR.

GARP is also coordinating a program (NAMEX) to review the northwest African situation in which drought has aided the southward spread of the Sahara Desert. A program on the interaction of processes in high latitudes (POLEX) is also being planned, with participation by Australia, Canada, France, West Germany, Finland, Iceland, Japan, New Zealand, Norway, Sweden, the United States, and the USSR.

Chemistry of the Ocean. The chemistry of the ocean has been under investigation by the geochemical ocean sections program (GEOSECS). Data from earlier expeditions in the Atlantic and Pacific, which include information on radioactive and chemical pollutants, have now become available. Some 7,000 separate water samples were collected in the Atlantic Ocean alone at 110 stations from the Arctic to the Antarctic. Thirty-liter samples were collected at up to 50 depths in the water column. The Indian Ocean area will be similarly surveyed in 1978.

Tritium, a radioactive isotope of hydrogen, was measured in the GEOSECS survey. This isotope enters the ocean from the atmosphere, where it occurs as a result of nuclear weapons tests conducted in the 1950's and early 1960's. This testing created about 100 times the natural concentration of tritium. However, the surface concentration in the ocean is still only about one tritium atom for every billion billion ordinary hydrogen atoms. Nevertheless, the presence of tritium in ocean samples can be used to indicate the relative movement of the sampled water down from the surface. Measurements aid in identifying those areas of the ocean that are significantly influenced by surface processes within about a decade of their occurrence. Thus, using the data from GEOSECS and elsewhere, calculations have been made on the rates of exchange between the atmosphere and the different layers of the ocean. This is a valuable contribution to the understanding of ocean mechanics.

By analyzing the amount of helium in the water, an estimate of the tritium decay can be obtained. This can be used as a measure of rates of chemical change within the water mass, such as the oxygen utilization rate. These aspects of chemistry are interrelated to the effect of the wind-driven surface circulation and the eddy-controlled deeper circulation systems. GEOSECS data will be further analyzed to help us understand many aspects of the ocean. For instance, the distribution and recirculation of seawater properties, such as heat content, nutrient concentrations, and man-made contaminants of diverse kinds, affect all factors in the ocean.

Marine Geology. Since the ocean represents more than 70% of the surface of the globe, knowledge of the features of the seabed provides a major input to understanding geologic processes. Geological research on the sea floor continues to provide details that can be correlated with the major hypotheses of plate tectonics and sea-floor spreading.

The Deep Sea Drilling Program (DSDP), using the special drill ship *Glomar Challenger*, concentrated on various aspects of plate tectonics in 1977. One area that was examined was the oldest portion of the Atlantic Ocean floor near the continental margin of northwest Africa and the Canary Islands, representing crustal formations about 180 million years old. An area near Bermuda in which the crustal rock was thought to represent a period about 100 million years ago was studied. Near Bermuda, the crust was drilled to a total depth of 868 meters (2,847 ft) below the sea floor, penetrating about 544

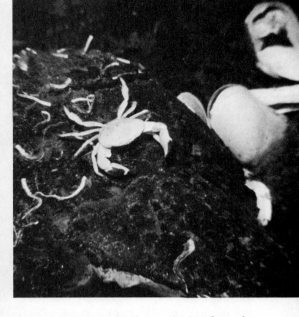

During 11 dives in 11 days, scientists from the submersible *Alvin* (*left*) examined the Galapagos Rift in the Pacific Ocean. Groups of animals similar to the crab, seaworms, and clams (*above*) showed the scientists where to focus their investigations.

PHOTOS WOODS HOLE OCEANOGRAPHIC INSTITUTION

meters (1,785 ft) of basaltic rock. Chemical studies of the core indicated differentiation of the magmatic source material into at least seven batches with different degrees of melting and recrystallization. Special studies were made of the rock magnetism and of acoustical transmission through the rock. There was evidence of five magnetic reversals in the rock from the core. Accumulation of such data is slowly building up the details that are needed for a full understanding of sea-floor spreading and differences in the upper mantle.

The Atlantic Ocean drilling marked the close of the first year of an International Phase of Ocean Drilling (IPOD).

The DSDP group was at work in the north central Pacific Ocean basin in the area of the Emperor Seamount chain. Drilling here is designed to test the hypothesis that the rate of motion of the Pacific plate has been constant for millions of years. Core material has shown that the submerged seamounts were once raised above the surface of the ocean. These seamounts and the Hawaiian Islands are thought to make up a single mountain range that was formed over the last 70 million years as the Pacific crustal plate moved north and then west over a stationary source of heat and molten lava. This source is now thought to be near the active volcanoes of Kilauea and Mauna Loa on the island of Hawaii, the youngest member of the extended seamount chain.

Research has also been centered on the mid-ocean rift valleys where spreading forces are now most active. The bathyscaphe *Trieste* continued explorations in 1977 in the Cayman trough of the Caribbean, surveyed earlier by the submersible *Alvin*. In the Pacific, examination of the Galapagos portion of the East Pacific rise (near the equator, off the coast of Peru) by surface vessels with special scanners identified a series of hot spots. About ten sites along the spreading axis of the Galapagos Rift were shown to contain water and gaseous emissions coming from the earth's mantle.

During 1977, *Alvin* descended to depths of 2,500 meters (8,200 ft) at these sites and observed numerous animal colonies clustered around vents where hot seawater erupts from the sea floor. A two-ton camera sled that could be towed directly over the sea floor and could take up to 3,000 color photographs per lowering was also used in the observations.

Pillow lavas similar to those seen in other rift areas were observed. The dense biological communities centered on the vents were a new feature, however. A preliminary hypothesis suggests that hydrogen sulfide in the magmatic emissions is used by bacteria that serve as a base for a unique food chain.

See also GEOLOGY.

DAVID A. MCGILL
Professor of Ocean Science
U. S. Coast Guard Academy

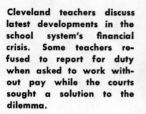

Cleveland teachers discuss latest developments in the school system's financial crisis. Some teachers refused to report for duty when asked to work without pay while the courts sought a solution to the dilemma.

UPI

OHIO

Weather, school problems, and an election in which voters were in a nay-saying mood dominated the state's headlines in 1977.

Election. Four state issues were voted down in the November balloting. A new state law permitting "instant" registration on election days was repealed. A constitutional amendment to ban leg-hold animal traps was defeated. Also rejected were two other amendments that would have permitted state and local government loans at low-interest rates for new housing for low and moderate income families and would have allowed the state a flexible debt ceiling. Ohio traditionally is held to a $750,000 debt limit.

Youth prevailed in the major mayoralty elections. In Toledo, Democrat Doug DeGood, a 30-year-old councilman, was elected chief executive. In Cleveland, Dennis J. Kucinich, 31-year-old clerk of the city's municipal court, won. Kucinich, a former councilman, edged another Democrat, Edward F. Feighan, 30, a state legislator, by 3,000 votes after they had nosed out the incumbent Republican, Ralph J. Perk, in the bi-partisan primary.

Schools. Financial problems kept more than 40 Ohio public school systems in turmoil. In October the Legislature was considering an emergency measure to let the systems borrow their way out of debt and remain open. U. S. District Judge Frank J. Battisti then ordered Cleveland schools to remain open even though the board of education said it had run out of money. The state lawmakers held off when the judge acted. The dilemma for the board members—of being in contempt of court if they closed classrooms, and of defying state laws if they did not—was resolved soon thereafter when the state decided not to order closing. By November the Cleveland system was being pressed by two banks to repay loans of $15 million. The Cleveland schools had begun "desegregation" steps in September, at Battisti's order, which resulted from an NAACP lawsuit.

Weather. In January records for unpleasantness were numerous and thousands of factory workers lost wages as fuel for heating and production dwindled drastically.

On Jan. 20, the state government declared an energy emergency for the Dayton area, where natural gas was especially short. Sixty-four other cities were placed on an energy alert. Schools were asked to close for 30 days. Businesses were called on to hold to a 40-hour week. In Cleveland temperatures stayed below freezing from Dec. 26, 1976, to Feb. 3, 1977.

Production. Ohio steeled itself for economic problems after a September announcement that Youngstown Sheet & Tube Co. would cut 5,000 employees at its Mahoning Valley plants. But Ford Motor Co. in December announced plans for a $500-million transmission plant near Cincinnati, which eventually would employ $3,500.

Population. Bureau of Census estimates, released in May, indicated that Ohio contained about 10,690,000 persons on July 1, 1976, compared with 10,735,000 a year earlier. The Ohio Development office listed these reasons for lower population: deterioration of inner areas of such cities as Cleveland and Cincinnati; some dispersal of industry; retirees' going to warmer climates; and heat shortages or high prices, causing some people to head south or west.

Prehistory. The discovery of Indian graves southeast of Huron has delayed construction of a right-of-way linking completed parts of the U. S. Route 2 east-west freeway.

JOHN F. HUTH, JR.
"The Plain Dealer," Cleveland

OHIO · Information Highlights

Area: 41,222 square miles (106,765 km²).
Population (1976 est.): 10,690,000.
Chief Cities (1970 census): Columbus, the capital, 540,025; Cleveland, 750,879; Cincinnati, 452,524.
Government (1977): *Chief Officers*—governor, James A. Rhodes (R); lt. gov., Richard F. Celeste (D). *General Assembly*—Senate, 33 members; House of Representatives, 99 members.
Education (1976–77): *Enrollment*—public elementary schools, 1,332,632 pupils; public secondary, 916,808; nonpublic, 284,100; colleges and universities, 367,776 students. *Public school expenditures,* $3,363,000,000 ($1,305 per pupil).
State Finances (fiscal year 1976): *Revenues,* $8,086,425,000; *expenditures,* $7,737,614,000.
Personal Income (1976): $68,541,000,000; per capita, $6,412.
Labor Force (July 1977): *Nonagricultural wage and salary earners,* 4,221,300; *unemployed,* 296,400 (6.2% of total force).

OKLAHOMA

Crime and punishment were much on the mind of Oklahomans in 1977. Just as the legislature had finished grappling with a novel method of execution for capital crimes, the brutal murder of three small girls seemed to point up the inadequacy of the death penalty as a deterrent.

Legislation. The legislature met in regular session from January 4 to June 8 and in a special session, June 13–17. Of some 1,000 measures introduced, more than 350 were enacted.

Among the most noteworthy bills passed during the regular session was one providing for execution by the injection of a lethal drug. Called more humane than other methods of execution by its proponents, it was the first such system to be enacted in the United States. In case the courts find the law unconstitutional, it contains a fall-back provision for death by electrocution. Another law permits the Department of Corrections to contract inmates of state prisons for public works. Compensation was set at the cost of the project, plus 10%. The state has been under pressure from a federal district court to reduce overcrowding in its facilities.

In the area of labor, the state's worker compensation laws were thoroughly revised. Changes were made in the organization of the industrial court and the adjudication of claims; eligibility for unemployment compensaton was also tightened. On the other hand, benefit levels were raised and contributions by employers increased. A separate bill raised the minimum wage in the state to $2.00.

Advocates of open government welcomed the enactment of a bill requiring public meetings to be held at places convenient to the general public and with an adequate advance notice of time and locale; voting is also to be public. A sunset law provides for the termination, modification, re-creation, or consolidation of 111 specified state agencies between 1978 and 1983. Any agency to be terminated under the law will have one year to wind up its affairs or prove to a legislative review committee its public need.

UPI

Oklahoma City's 26-story Biltmore Hotel is demolished by explosives. The site is part of a renewal project.

Laetrile Legalized. Those favoring the use of Laetrile, the controversial cancer drug, were heartened when U. S. District Court Judge Luther Bohanon decided that victims of terminal cancer could legally import the substance from Mexico. Initially ruling in favor of just one patient, Judge Bohanon later expanded his opinion, issuing a list of conditions governing the access of Laetrile in the state. They include a sworn statement from a physician attesting to "evidence of a rapidly progressing malignancy." There was a further stipulation that recognized forms of cancer treatment be administered as well. In June, the Oklahoma legislature voted to legalize the manufacture and sale of Laetrile, the eighth state legislature to do so.

Girl Scouts Slain. The state was shocked by the mid-June murder of three Girl Scouts, aged eight, nine, and ten, who were on a camping trip near Locust Grove in northwestern Oklahoma. About 100 other Girl Scouts and 40 attendants were in the camp at the time of the stranglings but apparently slept through them. At least one of the slain girls had been sexually molested.

A 1973 prison escapee who had been serving a sentence for kidnapping and rape was soon charged with the murders, but a posse of some 600 lawmen and local residents was unable to capture the suspect. A team of jungle-warfare veterans of the Vietnam war that tried to ambush the alleged killer was equally unsuccessful.

HALLBERG HALLMUNDSSON

OKLAHOMA • Information Highlights

Area: 69,919 square miles (181,090 km²).

Population (1976 est.): 2,766,000.

Chief Cities (1970 census): Oklahoma City, the capital, 368,856; Tulsa, 330,350; Lawton, 74,470; Norman, 52,117.

Government (1977): *Chief Officers*—governor, David L. Boren (D); lt. gov., George Nigh (D). *Legislature*—Senate, 48 members; House of Representatives, 101 members.

Education (1976–77): *Enrollment*—public elementary schools. 319.468 pupils; public secondary, 278,197; nonpublic (1976–77), 10.200; colleges and universities, 131,558 students. *Public school expenditures,* $792,000,000 ($1,195 per pupil).

State Finances (fiscal year 1976): *Revenues,* $2,032-489,000; *expenditures,* $1,968,534,000.

Personal Income (1976): $15,788,000,000; per capita, $5,707.

Labor Force (July 1977): *Nonagricultural wage and salary earners,* 974,000; *unemployed,* 52,500 (4.4% of total force).

OLDER AMERICANS

The financial needs of present and future retirees under Social Security vied with health and other service needs of all older persons for legislative priorities in 1977. National governmental leaders seemed somewhat more willing to consider liberalized provisions than in recent years, but commitments by the Carter administration and Congress to work for a balanced budget by 1981 meant that every proposal received severe scrutiny.

Inflation was somewhat reduced and was less than in most countries, but it still took a heavy toll on the spending capacity of people living on fixed incomes. The 5.9% cost-of-living increase in Social Security benefits that became effective on July 1 counteracted this somewhat. Still, pressure groups of the elderly were pushing hard for a special index that would more adequately represent the typical food, lodging, and medical-care expenditures of older people when benefits are to be adjusted.

The unusually cold weather in many parts of the country and the widespread increases in utility rates caused great hardship. Tragic incidents due to utilities being cut off for nonpayment of bills led to many improvised emergency provisions. However, the special problems incident to all such unusual demands on limited incomes remain an unresolved area in local and national planning.

System Deficit. The Social Security system operated at a deficit in 1977; at the same rate of payout the trust funds were headed for exhaustion by 1983. While there was loose talk about prospects that the whole system would collapse, the system was functioning essentially as intended.

On December 15, Congress passed and sent to the president a bill that was designed to end the deficits that were draining cash from the funds. The bill provides for a series of increases, starting in 1979, in Social Security taxes paid by more than 100 million employers, employees, and self-employed people. The bill will increase benefits for people 65 or older who continue to work by increasing the $3,000 maximum that they could earn in 1977 without loss of benefits, to $4,000 in 1978. Thereafter, the maximum will rise annually by $500, to the limit of $6,000 in 1982.

For beneficiaries under 65 the lower limits of the present law will continue to apply. The 1978 limit is $3,240. Blind persons who are collecting disability benefits will be allowed to earn income up to the new, higher limits for the elderly without loss of benefits. Acknowledging that this provision creates a favored category of disabled people, the conference report said that the criteria should not be applied to other types of disability.

Retirement. A healthy longevity leads many people to chafe at having to quit work at 65.

During the year important court decisions invalidated particular employer plans requiring retirement before 65. Among the proposals heard in Congress was one that would prohibit forced retirement before 70 except for incompetence, provided that workers *could* still retire at 65 with full Social Security benefits.

Enthusiasm was not universal. The *Wall Street Journal,* for instance, feared embarrassing court suits to prove worker incompetency; higher insurance rates for employers; and further impediments to young people trying to enter the labor market. At year's end, Congress had in conference a measure to provide some choices.

It is interesting to note that in other countries now having higher standard retirement ages, such as Norway, those seeking greater freedom of choice are for permitting voluntary retirement at earlier ages.

Income. For many older persons Social Security was inadequate for basic needs. More than two million aged persons were receiving Supplemental Security Income, and they and many others were eligible for food stamps. For them, elimination of the purchase requirement for stamps would be welcome, but welfare reform proposals, due for lengthy debate and modification in Congress, were sources of both hope and anxiety.

Services. Less publicized were proposals for better organized and expanded services to all older people, particularly under the Older Americans Act and Titles XIX and XX of the Social Security Act. These laws authorize a wide range of services such as day care, home health care, recreation, and counseling. The choice of services has been left largely to the states and local communities. Enough experience has now been gained to permit more effective federal leadership, while inflation demands increased appropriations. Cooperative planning between state and local officials, the Department of Health, Education, and Welfare (HEW), the Office of Management and Budget (OMB), and Congressional committees promises to produce positive legislation. The permanent status given to the Senate Committee on Aging in the face of efforts to terminate it was a sign of this direction. So were congressional moves toward authorizing a 1981 White House conference on aging.

New Developments. Several American developments attracted worldwide attention among persons concerned about the condition of older people. One was the passage of California's "Right to Die" law, which permits the removal of life-support equipment from certain terminally ill patients. Another was the introduction of rapid transit buses in Pennsylvania and Missouri that were equipped to accommodate wheel chairs. A third was the effort to improve the TV image of the elderly.

RALPH E. PUMPHREY
Washington University, St. Louis

ONTARIO

The key issues of 1977 in Ontario were the economic recession, the rights of the French-speaking minority, and the quest for majority government.

Minority Rights. The election in December 1976 of a Parti Québécois government in neighboring Quebec, with its latent threat to national unity, rekindled interest in the demands of Franco-Ontarians for the provision of education and basic governmental services in French. In March, Premier William G. Davis announced that more French-language health services would be available and an experimental program of court trials in French was initiated. In the fall, Atty. Gen. Roy McMurtry indicated that trials in French would be available in certain areas but a shortage of French-speaking lawyers and judges prevented wider implementation. The cabinet's intentions were tested by the refusal of a school board in Windsor to build a separate high school for French students. When the board proved unmoved by argument, Education Minister Thomas Wells introduced a bil requiring construction of the school. It passed supported by all parties in the legislature. In addition, financial incentives to school boards to increase French instruction for Anglophones were raised by $29 million to $64 million.

The Economy. Growing unemployment and budget deficits determined Treasurer Darcy McKeough's April budget, which raised cigarette taxes and car license fees and provided $98 million for job creation. As a conservation measure, the sales tax was removed from insulation materials, but a proposed 5¢ tax on snap-top cans, intended as an antipollution gesture, has been strongly opposed by the New Democratic party (NDP) as likely to increase unemployment.

In an attempt to balance the budget by 1981, the provincial civil service was frozen, its size actually cut, and the rate of increase in grants made to municipalities reduced. This means that many towns and cities will have to cut services or raise taxes next year.

UPI

Cindy Nicholas, the first woman to swim the English Channel both ways nonstop, is welcomed back to Ontario.

------ **ONTARIO · Information Highlights** ------

Area: 412,582 square miles (1,068,587 km²).
Population (1976 census): 8,264,465.
Chief Cities (1976 census): Toronto, the provincial capital, 633,318; Ottawa, the federal capital, 304,462.
Government (1976): *Chief Officers*—lt. gov., Pauline McGibbon; premier, William G. Davis (Progressive Conservative); atty. gen., Roy McMurtry; min. of educ., Thomas Wells; chief justice, Alexander Gale. *Legislature*—Legislative Assembly, 125 members.
Education (1976–77): *Enrollment*—public elementary and secondary schools, 1,979,700 pupils; private schools, 55,420; Indian (federal) schools, 7,380; post-secondary, 231,800 students. *Total expenditures*, $3,565,253,000.
Public Finance (1977–78 est.): *Revenues*, $12,621,000,-000; *expenditures*, $13,698,000,000.
Personal Income (average weekly salary, July 1977): $252.66.
Unemployment Rate (August 1977, seasonally adjusted): 7.0%.
(All monetary figures given in Canadian dollars.)

Provincial Election. Restrictions on a minority government were highlighted in April, when a bill extending rent controls was amended by the opposition to cut permitted rent increases from 8% to 6%. With his Conservative party standings high in the opinion polls, Premier Davis chose to treat the amendment as a defeat on a matter of confidence and called an election for July 9, hoping to win the majority that eluded him in 1975. Such hopes were dashed, however. The Conservatives gained six seats but remained five short of a majority. Final standings were: Progressive Conservatives, 58 (39% popular vote); Liberals, 34 (32%); and NDP, 33 (28%).

The Liberals, under their new leader, Dr. Stuart Smith, were expected to fare very badly, but they regained their former status as the official opposition from the NDP. Their program, denounced as simplistic by their opponents, struck a responsive, if conservative, chord by calling for guaranteed rights for Franco-Ontarians, tax and expenditure increases restricted to the level of federal Anti-Inflation Board guidelines, and the restoration to local municipalities of powers taken over by regional governments. The NDP was hurt by its platform on nationalization and the promise to raise the minimum hourly wage to $4. NDP leader Stephen Lewis announced that he would step down in February 1978.

PETER J. KING, *Carleton University*

OREGON

Long a leader in the area of environmental concerns, Oregon was the first state to enact a "bottle bill," requiring deposits on all beverage bottles and cans. In 1977, it became the first to prohibit sales of aerosol products using fluorocarbon propellents.

The legislature wrestled with the issue of field burning. Spokesmen for the perennial grass-seed industry contend that annual burning of the grass stubble after harvest is the only practical means to control pests and ensure yields. The grass-seed industry is important in the agricultural economy of the Willamette Valley, the most populous portion of the state. Gradual phase-out of field burning had been legislated during a previous session, yet the legislature passed a bill, later vetoed, postponing earlier target area units. A subsequent bill, limiting areas to be burned to 195,000 acres (79,000 ha), was signed by Governor Straub.

Nuclear power generation, long an issue among the state's environmentalists, came to the fore with the initiation of power generation at the Trojan plant near Rainier. The plant has been plagued by repeated system failures resulting in a number of shut-downs.

Drought. The state suffered its most severe drought since the early 1930's. Precipitation from Sept. 1, 1976, to June 30, 1977, amounted to only 46% of normal. Department of Agriculture estimates in July predicted $200 billion (U. S.) crop losses due to drought. Late summer rains mitigated these predictions, but Oregonians began preparing for a power curtailment during the winter of 1977–78 because of record low run-off in the Columbia basin.

Education. At the end of 1976, budget levies for a number of school districts had failed approval by the voters. One district was forced to close its schools for a time, but favorable verdicts in subsequent elections, many during 1977, permitted the reopening of closed schools, and precluded closure of others.

In October, the teachers of Baker school district went on strike. Schools remained open,

---

OREGON • Information Highlights

Area: 96,981 square miles (251,181 km²).
Population (1976 est.): 2,329,000.
Chief Cities (1970 census): Salem, the capital, 68,856; Portland, 380,555; Eugene, 78,389.
Government (1977): *Chief Officers*—governor, Robert W. Straub (D); secy. of state, Norma Paulus (R). *Legislative Assembly*—Senate, 30 members; House of Representatives, 60 members.
Education (1976–77): *Enrollment*—public elementary schools, 273,253 pupils; public secondary, 201,454; nonpublic, 24,100; colleges and universities, 112,-148 students. *Public school expenditures*, $792,000,-000 ($1,488 per pupil).
State Finances (fiscal year 1976): *Revenues*, $2,322,-644,000; *expenditures*, $2,161,043,000.
Personal Income (1976): $14,580,000,000; per capita, $6,261.
Labor Force (July 1977): *Nonagricultural wage and salary earners*, 904,700; *unemployed*, 87,500 (7.9% of total force).

---

however, by using substitute teachers, many of them from neighboring Idaho.

Other Events. Dutch elm disease, the scourge of residential streets and neighborhoods across the nation during the past two decades, has finally arrived in Portland. Five thousand trees are threatened.

The Oregon salmon industry suffered its worst season of recent years. Catches of Chinook salmon were particularly poor, coho catches somewhat better, but ground-fish catches set new records, as salmon fishermen turned to alternate species.

L. CARL BRANDHORST
Oregon College of Education

OTTAWA

As Canada's capital, Ottawa has had to face the local implications of the Parti Québécois victory in Quebec. One result is a reinforced determination by the federal government to boost its presence in Hull, on the Quebec side of the Ottawa River, by transferring government offices, with some 15,000 civil servants, across the river. This policy is strongly opposed by local politicians. Led by Mayor Lorry Greenberg, they argue that it will vacate more than 3 million square feet (280,000 m²) of commercial office space, imperiling the city's tax-base, and create severe commuter transportation problems. Federal employees, especially Anglophones, are unlikely to take up residence in Hull, owing to the political uncertainty and the new Quebec policy on language in education.

The long-awaited Mayo Report, commissioned by the provincial government, was published in March. It advocates sweeping changes in the structure of the capital region. Major proposals include the elimination of four municipalities, including the amalgamation of the exclusive village of Rockcliffe with the largely French-speaking town of Vanier, and the incorporation of parts of the city of Ottawa into neighboring townships; stronger powers for the regional government and direct election of regional councillors on a ward basis; the abolition of direct election of local mayors; the merger of all regional police forces; and the creation of one board of education responsible for overall administration, with four sub-boards beneath it: one English, one French, and two public ones. Despite general hostility to the proposals, the city council endorsed one of Dr. Mayo's suggestions: it voted to abolish the Ottawa Board of Control.

Renovation of the old By Ward market, a popular tourist attraction, was completed in the spring, part of the current program of restoring the older part of the city. In September Ottawa acquired an English-language morning newspaper after a lapse of many years, with the publication of the tabloid *Ottawa Today*.

PETER J. KING, *Carleton University*

PAKISTAN

Weakened by rioting, repression, and political separatist movements in 1976, the government of Prime Minister Zulfikar Ali Bhutto collapsed in 1977 and was superseded in a coup led by General Zia ul-Haq. At year's end General Zia ruled with uncertain authority. Bhutto, jailed but not silent, continued to strike out at his political foes.

Domestic Affairs. Bhutto took over Pakistan after the 1971 civil war. In his own words, he rebuilt Pakistan, but not without creating strains. Pakistan is beset by widespread language separatist movements. Whoever rules has widespread although usually disparate political opposition.

The crisis came in the spring of 1977, when parliamentary elections were held. Nine parties opposing Bhutto buried their ideological differences to form the Pakistan National Alliance. Opposition leaders insisted that the election would not be honest. The March 7 election gave a strong majority to Bhutto's Pakistan People's Party, but the opposition refused to accept the results. Their 36 members (out of 200) who had won were asked to refuse to take their seats. Demonstrations were held throughout Pakistan. Quickly, the situation went out of control. A national strike took place in late March. Bhutto was called on to resign. He arrested more than two dozen opposition leaders, made a demagogic appeal to the public, and established curfews and police control.

In April, Bhutto established martial law in Karachi, Lahore, and Hyderabad. But he also made concessions, particularly to extreme religious leaders, including alcoholic prohibition, and offered to hold new elections. These offers were rejected. By July about 350 people had been killed in rioting throughout the country. Bhutto announced on May 13 that he would hold a referendum to let the people decide whether he should continue in office.

Whether the opposition and Bhutto could have consummated some deal—they were making progress and had agreed to new elections—became moot after July 5, when Zia, the army chief of staff, mounted a coup and arrested government leaders, including Bhutto. Zia proclaimed his attachment to civilian government and promised new elections for October. One of the first acts (July 10) of the military ruler was the reimposition of traditional Islamic draconian punishments for theft and insulting the modesty of women. Radio and television were ostensibly freed of censorship in August, and several weeks later the press was also freed.

Bhutto, who had been freed on July 28 and who had taken to the political trail once again, was rearrested on Sept. 3 for allegedly ordering a political opponent murdered in 1974. On October 1, Zia canceled the elections and proclaimed indefinite martial law rule. Promising

UPI

Physically disabled citizens of Karachi join a rally of those seeking the overthrow of the Bhutto government.

to try Bhutto for murder and other crimes, Zia permitted Bhutto to argue his preliminary cases in court. At the end of October, Bhutto argued that the survival of democracy was at stake in Pakistan and that the government's case was a "spiteful personal vendetta."

Foreign Affairs. The crisis gave little time for foreign affairs. Bhutto claimed that the United States was supporting his opposition. In September, France reaffirmed its decision to sell a nuclear plant to Pakistan. Relations with India were tranquil. Whatever Bhutto's shortcomings, he had achieved a viable foreign policy. Its only current failing was a less than friendly relationship with the United States.

CARL LEIDEN
University of Texas, Austin

─────── **PAKISTAN · Information Highlights** ───────

Official Name: Islamic Republic of Pakistan.
Location: South Asia.
Area: 310,403 square miles (803,943 km²).
Population (1977 est.): 74,500,000.
Chief Cities (1974): Islamabad, the capital, 250,000; Karachi, 3,500,000; Lahore, 2,100,000.
Government: *Head of state,* Fazal Elahi Chaudhri, president (took office Aug. 1973). *Head of government,* Mohammed Zia ul-Haq (took office July 1977). *Legislature*—Parliament: Senate and National Assembly.
Monetary Unit: Rupee (9.93 rupees equal U. S.$1, Aug. 1977).
Manufacturing (major products): Textiles, processed foods, cement, petroleum products.
Major Agricultural Products: Wheat, cotton, rice, sugarcane, corn, millet, chickpeas, rapeseed, livestock.

PANAMA

After 13 years of negotiations, Panama concluded a canal treaty, as yet unratified by the United States, calling for gradual assumption by Panamanians of canal operations and defense before the year 2000. General Omar Torrijos and President Jimmy Carter signed the document in Washington on September 7. Another treaty was signed guaranteeing the permanent neutrality of the canal.

Terms of the Canal Treaties. The United States retained the right to defend the neutrality of the waterway permanently. American naval forces were granted permanent and unconditional access to the canal. For the rest of this century, the United States would have primary responsibility for protecting the channel. Panama would provide space to U. S. armed forces fulfilling the defense role.

Panama would receive over one half of the land in the Canal Zone immediately and would gain jurisdiction over that community in three years. Financially, Panama would receive an annuity of $10 million (up from $2.3 million) and up to $10 million from tolls, if traffic permitted. In official junkets related to the treaty matter, Torrijos visited countries on five continents in 1977.

Political Affairs. Torrijos accepted the resignation of Foreign Minister Aquilino Boyd on February 9. Boyd was replaced by Nicolas Gonzalez-Revilla. Changes at the Foreign Ministry followed a pattern of dismissal for potential challengers to Torrijos.

The canal question, coupled with a deteriorating economy and the diminishing popularity of Torrijos, led to an outpouring of opposition to official policies. Protesting provisions of the treaties that would leave American civilians and armed forces in Panama, up to 6,000 students entered the Canal Zone on June 6. Panamanian national guardsmen looked on during those demonstrations, but used clubs to disperse 200 students who, on June 27, carried their campaign to the foreign ministry and also the U. S. embassy in Panama.

Prior to the October ratification plebiscite in Panama, opponents of the treaties were allowed access to the press and held many rallies. Opposition centered on the continuation of a U. S. presence at the waterway and perpetual U. S. intervention rights. In the first political issue nationally debated during Torrijos' nine-year tenure, the pacts were approved by about 70% of the voters.

Economic Affairs. A 1977 recovery plan, calling for increased investment and reduced unemployment, failed to revive a flat economy. Lacking confidence in Torrijos and his economic policies, private investors did not provide development funds. The decline in domestic private investment coincided with a near exhaustion of funding possibilities elsewhere. Agriculture was expected to suffer from the extended dry season.

Despite this clouded picture, new development projects were announced. A $260 million hydroelectric project in Chiriqui province was partially funded with a $98 million loan from the Inter-American Development Bank. Its construction will create 2,500 jobs. Once completed, irrigated lands in the area will be opened to colonization schemes. Equipping the isthmus to transship Alaskan oil, the Northville Corporation planned a $42 million petroterminal at Puerto Armuelles, Chiriqui.

LARRY L. PIPPIN
University of the Pacific

——— **PANAMA · Information Highlights** ———

Official Name: Republic of Panama.
Location: On the isthmus of Panama, which links Central America and South America.
Area: 29,209 square miles (75,650 km²).
Population (1977 est.): 1,800,000.
Chief City (1975): Panama, the capital, 404,000.
Government: *Military junta*, led by Gen. Omar Torrijos Herrera (took power Oct. 1972). *Head of state*, Demetrio Lakas Bahas, president (took office Dec. 1969). *Legislature:* unicameral—People's Assembly.
Monetary Unit: Balboa (1 balboa equals U. S.$1, Aug. 1977).
Manufacturing (major products): Processed foods, petroleum products, textiles, wood products.
Major Agricultural Products: Bananas, vegetables, rice, forest products.

UPI

Gen. Omar Torrijos and President Jimmy Carter congratulate one another after they signed the Panama Canal treaties, September 7.

PARAGUAY

Paraguay continued to be characterized by various international groups as politically repressed and relatively undeveloped.

Domestic Politics. After 23 years of President Alfredo Stroessner's dictatorial rule, Paraguay prepared to elect him again in February 1978. Because the 1967 constitution specifically forbids the reelection of a president beyond two terms, it was necessary for him to remove that prohibition, an action obligingly carried out by a convention made up entirely of members of his own party. The opposition parties refused to send delegates.

The way thus seemed clear for Stroessner to win a new term, because the Electoral Commission refused to recognize the legality of the reunion of the opposition Liberal and Radical Liberal parties, which have been split for 15 years. Legality was conferred on the Radical Liberals, the minority wing. By October 1977, however, both parties were recognized on the condition that they run candidates and promise to participate in the election. Both promised to do so.

Repression. Political repression has become normal during Stroessner's long rule. In July, his regime carried out arrests aimed at silencing the *Movimiento Independiente,* a university-based group opposed to political ties with Brazil and to electoral irregularities. Amnesty International estimated that there are from 350 to 450 political prisoners in Paraguay.

The Inter-American Association for Freedom and Democracy asked the United Nations to investigate the plight of women political prisoners, some of whom have been in jail for 16 years. Eleven have since been released, as have three communists held for 19 years. The releases were attributed to Stroessner's perception that President Carter was serious about his support for human rights. The International League for Human Rights called attention in September to a new wave of "brutal repression."

Economic Developments. For years Paraguay has been the lowest consumer of electric power in Latin America. But Paraguay may become a high consumer, producer, and exporter of electricity. By 1986 the dams on the Acaray River will be producing 8,000,000 kilowatts annually, an increase in power of 200% in 30 years.

A good road from Asunción, the capital, to the Brazilian border has begun to transform the whole area. About 12,000 farmers are now living in several colonies, and many little industries, sugar mills, and oil extraction plants have sprung up in the region. About 70 towns in the interior have been or are being electrified.

Foreign Affairs. President Stroessner was in Washington in September for the signing of the Panama Canal treaties along with the other Latin American heads of state. Paraguay also sent representatives to the Latin American parliamentary meeting in the Netherlands Antilles.

LEO B. LOTT, *University of Montana*

PENNSYLVANIA

Generally, citizens of the commonwealth had a good year in 1977. Unemployment in many chronically depressed areas fell to the lowest levels in 6–10 years, while business, industrial, and agricultural output remained firm. But forces of nature and upheavals in state government periodically disturbed the largely untroubled picture.

Weather. Bitter, record-breaking cold, arriving with the new year, depleted natural gas supplies in Pennsylvania. It forced shutdowns at more than 300 industrial plants and idled some 265,000 workers before winter released its stranglehold. But nature's cruelest blow was struck at a historic target, Johnstown, where 2,300 lost their lives in the flood of 1889. On July 20, torrential rainfall sent mountain streams on a rampage, a dam crumbled, and a wall of water swept through the valley below. As the community struggled in the ensuing weeks to rebuild devastated homes and factories, damage estimates exceeded $200 million. Toward the end of the year, 76 were known to have died, one person had been declared dead, and 10 were listed as missing.

On February 24, a chartered plane crashed in a Harrisburg suburb, killing State Transportation Secretary William Sherlock, State Sen. Richard Frame, and seven others. Nine lives were lost in a mine accident at Tower City on March 1.

State Government. Criminal indictments and lesser charges of wrongdoing were leveled against a number of high administrative officials and members of the legislature. House Speaker Herbert Fineman was convicted of obstructing justice and sentenced to two years in prison for attempting to quash an investigation into bribery and sale of student admissions to professional schools. State Sen. Henri Cianfrani, chairman of the powerful Appropriations Committee, awaited trial following a 110-count federal indictment on charges of racketeering, mail fraud, income-tax evasion, and obstruction of justice. Another senator and a former house

─────── **PARAGUAY • Information Highlights** ───────

Official Name: Republic of Paraguay.
Location: Central South America.
Area: 157,047 square miles (406,752 km²).
Population (1977 est.): 2,800,000.
Chief City (1974 est.): Asunción, the capital, 400,000.
Government: *Head of state and government,* Gen. Alfredo Stroessner, president (took office Aug. 1954). *Legislature*—Congress: Senate and Chamber of Deputies.
Monetary Unit: Guarani (126 guaranies equal U.S.$1, Aug. 1977).
Manufacturing (major products): Meats, leather, wood products, quebracho extract, vegetable oil.
Major Agricultural Products: Cassava, bananas, tobacco, cotton, soybeans, oilseeds, citrus fruits, cattle, forest products.

Pennsylvania Gov. Milton Shapp, who reached age 65 in June, is presented with a senior citizen transit identification card.

UPI

member were also charged with Fineman and Cianfrani. State Adj. Gen. Harry J. Mier, Jr., resigned under fire and was fined $1,000 upon pleading guilty to making personal use of National Guard property.

In September, Gov. Milton J. Shapp fired Commonwealth Secretary C. DeLores Tucker, the highest-ranking black female state official in the nation, charging that she used her office as a "clearinghouse" to handle personal speaking engagements. The governor himself repaid some $300,000 which the Federal Election Commission charged the Shapp presidential campaign had illegally received in matching campaign funds in 1976. No accusations of wrongdoing were made against the governor personally.

An impasse over tax increases in the legislature left the state without a budget for 20 days. State workers went unpaid and welfare payments were cut off until a partial budget was adopted in mid-August. But the lawmakers continued to debate the funding level for colleges and universities and the question of additional taxation until late in the year.

Religion. A large delegation of Roman Catholics represented the commonwealth at the canonization in Rome on June 19 of a 19th-century bishop of Philadelphia, John Neumann.

RICHARD ELGIN
"The Patriot-News," Harrisburg

─── **PENNSYLVANIA • Information Highlights** ───

Area: 45,333 square miles (117,412 km²).
Population (1976 est.): 11,862,000.
Chief Cities (1970 census): Harrisburg, the capital, 68,-061; Philadelphia, 1,950,098; Pittsburgh, 520,117.
Government (1977): *Chief Officers*—governor, Milton J. Shapp (D); lt. gov., Ernest P. Kline (D). *General Assembly*—Senate, 50 members; House of Representatives, 203 members.
Education (1976–77): *Enrollment*—public elementary schools, 1,093,574 pupils; public secondary, 1,100,-099; nonpublic, 467,900; colleges and universities, 429,628 students. *Public school expenditures,* $4,526,300,000 ($1,730 per pupil).
State Finances (fiscal year 1976): *Revenues,* $10,596,-881,000; *expenditures,* $11,133,842,000.
Personal Income (1976): $76,385,000,000; per capita, $6,439.
Labor Force (July 1977): *Nonagricultural wage and salary earners,* 4,557,300; *unemployed,* 346,400 (6.7% of total force).

PERU

Peru's major events in 1977 involved the government of Gen. Francisco Morales Bermúdez, who announced plans to step down in 1980.

Civilian Rule Pledged. In a July 28 television address, Morales Bermúdez announced that a constituent assembly would be elected in 1978 to plan for a return to elected civilian government in 1980. After nine years in power, the military government indicated that Peru was facing an economic crisis that required austerity at home and financial help from abroad.

In January, the government took a series of measures aimed at generating support, including amnesty for various opposition political and labor leaders. A July 1976 ban on seven magazines was lifted. Gen. Luis Cisneros, the interior minister, announced on February 12 that municipal elections would be held in 1978. In May, Morales met with leaders of the APRA and Popular Christian parties to discuss the government's plans for the years 1977–1980 and Aprista demands for general elections by 1980.

Austerity Measures. Facing more than $500 million in foreign debts that had to be repaid in 1977, the government on June 10 promulgated measures drafted by Economy Minister Walter Piazza Tanguis. Prices were raised on fuel, food, and public transport in order to reduce imports and inflation. Demonstrations

─────── **PERU • Information Highlights** ───────

Official Name: Republic of Peru.
Location: West coast of South America.
Area: 496,223 square miles (1,285,216 km²).
Population (1977 est.): 16,600,000.
Chief City (1972 census): Lima, the capital, 3,350,000 (met. area).
Government: *Head of state,* Gen. Francisco Morales Bermúdez (took office August 1975). *Head of government,* Gen. Guillermo Arbulú Galliani, prime minister (took office July 1976).
Monetary Unit: Sol (79.89 soles equal U. S.$1, July 1977).
Manufacturing (major products): Processed foods, textiles, chemicals, metal products, automobiles, fish meal, oil.
Major Agricultural Products: Cotton, sugar, rice, coffee, sheep, potatoes.

and strikes broke out in June, followed by a 24-hour general strike in Lima on July 19. Police arrested more than 300 labor leaders affiliated with the Communist and Christian Democratic trade unions and the Confederation of Workers of the Peruvian Revolution, which normally supported the government. Only the Peruvian Workers Confederation, affiliated with the Aprista Party, did not strike. Juan Cardinal Landazurri Ricketts warned the government on July 26 not to try to solve the economic crisis with force.

Economy Minister Luis Barua Castañeda resigned on May 13 after the government refused to reduce subsidies to PetroPeru, the state oil company, and refused to continue devaluations of the sol. His successor, Piazza, resigned on July 6 because of cabinet refusal to accept devaluation of the sol to 90 to the dollar by the end of 1977 after it had reached a rate of 80 to the dollar in July. Military officers also refused to reduce overseas purchases of arms.

The government canceled anchovy fishing on May 6 after only 450,000 metric tons were caught—compared with a catch of 4 million tons in 1976. Some fisheries experts called for a ban on all anchovy fishing for at least two years so that stocks could recover. Peru stood to lose more than $300 million in 1977 as a result of the decline in fishmeal exports.

Peru hoped to reduce its daily oil imports of 50,000 barrels to 10,000 barrels a day by mid-1977. On May 25, a 530-mile (853-km) pipeline was opened over the Andes in northern Peru to the Pacific Ocean port of Bayovar. In January another producing region was discovered near Shiviyacu in the Amazon jungle.

Foreign Relations. During a March visit, Argentina's President Jorge Videla signed an agreement whereby Argentina would build a nuclear research plant in Peru. Relations with the United States improved with Mrs. Rosalynn Carter's visit in June. On July 15, Brazil and Peru signed agreements to expand trade and promote joint development of the Amazon River Basin.

NEALE J. PEARSON, *Texas Tech University*

PHILIPPINES

President Ferdinand E. Marcos marked the fifth anniversary of his establishment of martial law in September, claiming that the internal security conditions that prompted his resort to dictatorial rule continued.

Politics. The Geneva-based International Commission of Jurists, which had dispatched three missions to the Philippines since 1975, claimed that martial law was designed to "perpetuate the personal power" of President Marcos. Marcos, however, sought to combat this image, in August, by promising to hold local elections in 1978, lifting an overnight curfew, and releasing some 1,500 prisoners (most of them criminals, not political detainees).

Opposition to the Marcos regime persisted, as evidenced by Manila demonstrations in August and September. Thousands of students, workers, and clergymen participated in the marches, which were broken up by club-swinging police.

The most outspoken criticism of martial law came from a radical minority within the Roman Catholic Church. Led by Bishop Francisco Claver, 24 Catholic bishops attacked persisting "social injustices" under Marcos' government.

Marcos' oppressive rule was given publicity by the illegal flight, from detention, of political

UPI

Addressing the World Law Conference in Manila in August, Philippine President Ferdinand Marcos announces a partial relaxation of martial law restrictions.

foes Eugenio López, Jr., and Sergio Osmena 3d to the United States in search of asylum. In November, Benigno S. Aquino, a former senator and once Marcos' chief political opponent, was sentenced to death on charges of murder, subversion, and illegal possession of firearms. Marcos later ordered the trial reopened.

Insurgencies. The most serious rebel challenge to the Marcos government came from the renewed insurrection of the Moro National Liberation Front on the big island of Mindanao and the Sulu archipelago in the south. The cease-fire between the separatist Muslim insurgents and the Marcos regime deteriorated sharply in September and thereafter.

The cease-fire had been negotiated in December 1976 with a commission of the 42-member nation Islamic Conference (in which Libya, previously chief supplier of the Moros, played a major pacifying role). The Moro National Liberation Front boycotted an April referendum for a Muslim-ruled autonomous region in 13 southern provinces. An officially announced 97.93% of 3,019,140 voters cast their ballots against the plan.

Libya charged that the referendum violated the earlier agreement on ways to settle the Muslim problem, and a 17-member Islamic Conference delegation that subsequently visited the Philippines failed to find a new solution. The basic problem was that, while a majority of the Philippines' Muslim minority lives in the 13 provinces in question, Christians still form a majority in eight of these provinces. More than 20,000 have died in the fighting since 1972.

In the Philippines' other rebellion, that of the Communist "New Peoples Army" in northern and central Luzon island in the north, an expanded government army effectively held its own against the rebels. The Communists, who had numbered 3,000 when martial law was declared, increased their size to approximately 2,000 in 1977 after diminishing to about 1,000 in the intervening years.

Economy. The country's gross national product increased at a higher rate under Marcos' martial law than previously—averaging 6.8% annually between 1972 and 1977 (as compared with 5.5% during the preceding five years). The impact of this economic growth was largely negated, however, by inflation. Real wages in 1977 were less than in Marcos' first martial law years.

More important was the fact that there still was no promised redistribution of wealth. The highly publicized Marcos' land reform plan of the initial martial rule years had resulted by 1977 in only 1,800 former tenant farmers having deeds to their own land.

Foreign Affairs. The Philippines continued to seek identification as a third world country, but clearly based its foreign policy on close relations with the United States, Japan, and its four allies in the five-government Association of Southeast Asian Nations (ASEAN)—Indonesia, Malaysia, Singapore, and Thailand.

Stalled talks with Washington over the terms of continued U. S. use of Clark Air Force Base and Subic Bay naval facility resumed in September after nine months' delay. A near agreement was reported at year-end. Key points of disagreement concerned compensation to the Philippines and jurisdiction over crimes committed by Americans on the bases.

The USSR opened its first embassy in Manila following a 1976 agreement on the exchange of diplomatic representatives.

RICHARD BUTWELL
State University of New York College at Fredonia

Juan Ona is the new chargé d'affaires in Moscow as the Philippines and the USSR open diplomatic relations.

UPI

—— PHILIPPINES · Information Highlights ——

Official Name: Republic of the Philippines.
Location: Southeast Asia.
Area: 115,830 square miles (300,000 km²).
Population (1977 est.): 44,300,000.
Chief Cities (1975 est.): Manila, the capital, 1,459,000; Quezon City, 960,000; Cebu, 408,000.
Government: *Head of state,* Ferdinand E. Marcos, president (took office for 2d term Dec. 1969). *Head of government,* Marcos, prime minister (took office under new constitution Jan. 1973). *Legislature* (unicameral)—National Assembly.
Monetary Unit: Peso (7.40 pesos equal U. S.$1, Aug. 1977).
Manufacturing (major products): Petroleum products, processed foods, tobacco products, plywood and veneers, paper.
Major Agricultural Products: Rice, corn, coconuts, sugarcane, abaca, sweet potatoes, lumber.

Harry Callahan's image *Trees in Snow, Chicago, 1948* was part of a retrospective at the Museum of Modern Art.

PHOTOGRAPHY

In the eyes of the public and photographic manufacturers, in showplaces and in publications, photography was increasingly recognized in 1977 as one of the most popular means of communication in our time. Be it a complex camera with creative new options or an instant print vehicle, making the camera easy to use was the goal of manufacturers. And fast color films added punch to their efforts to make photography simple by enabling photographers to shoot under virtually any lighting condition.

New Equipment. Among manufacturers of single-lens reflex (SLR) 35mm cameras, the by-word was the compact body and an accompanying package of accessories, including new lens mounts, a motor winder, an electronic flash, and more advanced electronics overall. In the attempt by manufacturers to extend the 35mm market to the casual amateur, the SLRs were being made as simple to operate as a box camera. Some SLRs issued at moderate prices could become competitive with simpler cameras.

At the annual Photo Marketing Association (PMA) trade show in Chicago, the Pentax ME led the way as the smallest and lightest compact SLR, weighing in at 16.2 ounces (459 grams); its body measures 5-5/32 × 3-1/4 × 1-15/16 inches (131.0 × 82.6 × 49.2 mm). The FM was the contender offered by Nikon, which also exhibited a new line of auto-indexing (AI) lenses. Rollei and Mamiya also brought out compacts, as did Fuji, whose AZ–1 was the first camera with a 43–75mm zoom as a standard lens. Minolta brought out the XD-11, the first compact 35mm SLR camera with aperture and shutter priority automation and fully manual control.

Kodak introduced the Handle at $39.95, a lower priced version of the EK–4 and EK–6, Kodak's first instant print cameras, which were marketed in 1976. Polaroid's competitively priced answer was the One Step. Both cameras eject pictures when a handle is cranked and both are the first aim-and-shoot instants: the user does not have to make any focusing, aperture, or shutter adjustments because focus is fixed and shutter and aperture are automatic.

Polaroid also introduced another first, its instant movie system called Polavision: a super

The Museum of Modern Art also presented photos from the county courthouse project sponsored by Joseph E. Seagram & Sons, Inc. Included were Frank Gohlke's photo of the Hennepin County Courthouse in Minneapolis and Richard Pare's shot of the St. Louis City Courthouse (page 399).

8mm movie camera close to conventional appearance, a film cassette measuring 5¼ × 2¾ × ½ inches (133.3 × 69.9 × 12.7 mm), and a Polavision player for projecting up to three minutes of film. The cassette, once removed from the camera, must be placed in a viewer box where it takes 90 seconds to be processed and 30 seconds more to be rewound for showing. The film runs 2 minutes, 40 seconds.

Hasselblad marketed its first new 2¼ × 2¼ inch (57 × 57 mm) format SLR camera in a decade, the 2000FC, which can make use of focal-plane or spring-leaf shutters that come with Hasselblad lenses. And manufacturers continued to introduce more sophisticated 110-format pocket camera models.

In conventional super 8 movie equipment, the number of new sound and movie cameras, as well as projectors, was staggering. Every manufacturer offered expanded or changed lines that provided lighter weight and greater versatility for moviemakers. Several introduced pocket or mini movie cameras in modest price ranges. All had XL or low light filming capability. Chinon, only a year in the marketplace, introduced a new line of seven Trimweight budget super 8 sound cameras, and Sankyo Seiki's cameras incorporated an electro-automatic focusing system.

Among new lenses of interest were Nikon's Nikkor 200mm f/2, the fastest yet at that focal length, and Minolta's 500mm catadioptric, the world's smallest and lightest in that focal arena. To appeal to the increasing number of persons who make their own color prints, Beseler introduced the first color enlarger head to offer a condenser and diffusion light source, and Omega came out with a compact one-piece color analyzer to determine precise filtration and exposure.

The age of ASA 400 color-print photography was fully realized in 1977, with Kodak, Sakura, and 3M entering the high-speed color negative film market in 110 and 35mm format. Fujicolor 400, the first film available at that film speed, which had been officially introduced at the 1976 *photokina* trade show in Germany, was available for sale in 1977. Kodak introduced three new Ektachromes: 64 (daylight), 160 (tungsten), and 200 (daylight). Polaroid unveiled five new films for a variety of medical, scientific, and professional applications. Ilford offered Cibachrome RC and Kodak Ektachrome RC, type 2203, two new positive-to-positive color printing papers for photo-finishers.

Two companies followed the trend of switching from distribution through a U. S. sales agent to outright U. S. sales. Asahi Optical Co. products will be sold by Pentax Corp., and all other products distributed through their former agent, Honeywell, Inc., will be handled by Rollei. Olympus Optical Co. products will be sold through its wholly-owned U. S. sales firm, Olympus Camera Corp.; former agent Ponder & Best changed its name to Vivitar, Inc., and continues to market that company's line of photo products. GAF, oldest U. S. consumer photo firm, discontinued its line of film, paper, and cameras for the amateur market, citing adverse effects caused by Eastman Kodak's alleged monopolistic practices in the same sales arena, for which GAF was suing Kodak. Berkey and Pavelle also had suits pending against Kodak, as did Polaroid for patent infringements regarding the instant print process.

RICHARD PARE PHOTOGRAPHER
HENRY SINGLETON, WILLIAM RUMBOLD, AND OTHERS ARCHITECTS

According to the latest *Wolfman Report of the Photographic Industry in the United States,* the industry has recovered fully from the 1973–75 recession with the outlook for future growth optimistic. Canon, Kodak, and Minolta advertised on television and many manufacturers increased their advertising in general consumer magazines. *Time* recognized the new advertising trend with a special supplement in which the results of the magazine's first photo contest in its 53 years appeared. And many newspapers ran general interest photography supplements. "Picture Your World" was the name of the supplement organized by PMA, the most widely based trade organization in the industry, and marked the first joint venture by the industry as a whole.

Photography as Art. By 1977, photography had been accepted unquestionably as a major art form. While no major trend prevailed, a profusion of work representative of many styles and movements appeared in photo galleries and in other galleries previously restricted to painting.

As in the past, many of the more noteworthy shows were presented in New York. The Whitney Museum of American Art displayed "Unposed Portraits" by a half dozen "new-style" personal documentarians. The Carlton Gallery honored Helen Gee and the Limelight Gallery via the work of some photographers who showed during the 1950's in her gallery-within-a-coffeehouse, the first photo gallery to exist for any length of time. The Museum of Modern Art presented major retrospectives for Harry Callahan and Tina Modotti, and presented photos from the county courthouse project sponsored by Joseph E. Seagram & Sons, Inc., in which 23 photographers were assigned to different counties nationwide.

The Brooklyn Museum presented a major retrospective for sociologist-reformer Lewis Hine. The International Center of Photography exhibited the newspaper journalism pictures of Weegee (Arthur Fellig). The Metropolitan Museum of Art and the Marlborough Gallery displayed the platinum prints of Irving Penn.

Shows were given for master photographers Man Ray and Josef Sudek, both of whom had died in 1976. Two longtime workers in the medium had their first one-person shows in New York: Roy DeCarava (Negro chronicles in America) and Lilo Raymond (interiors and still lifes). William DeLappa displayed "The Portraits of Violet and Al," a staged fictional work accomplished with cameras and development processes of the 1950's to recreate the family snapshot album of that era. Ben Fernandez showed "Four Generations . . . The Odyssey of the Fernandez Family," a real family album of their journey from Spain to Puerto Rico to New York.

Thematic group shows grew in number: "Emerging Los Angeles Photographers," "Instants Extended: New Images on Polaroid Land Film," "Some Color Photographs" by 29 photographers, "Self Portraits," and "Rated-X." And at the National Portrait Gallery in Washington, D. C., photography was added to its exhibits for the first time.

New books showed Americans' continuing interest in the documentation of American history, people, and landscapes. *Disfarmer: The Heber Springs Portraits, 1939–46,* presented a local commercial photographer's documentation of the lives of the people in a small Arkansas town. Robert Adams' *denver* continued the trend toward landscape photography in man-made settings. *A Vision Shared: A Classic Portrait of America and Its People* (1935–43) included the work of 11 Federal Farm Security Administration photographers who photographed America during the Great Depression in the largest and most significant documentary ever done in the United States.

Women provided the subject matter in Eva Shaderowfsky's *Suburban Portraits,* a view of the lives of four women in a New Jersey suburb; in Susan Meiselas' *Carnival Strippers;* in Eric Kroll's *Sex Objects,* about women who work in massage parlors; and in Helmut Newton's *White Women,* which dealt with eroticism. Duane Michals' *Real Dreams* depicted fantasies and insights in predominantly "sequence" imagery, and Ben Maddow wrote *Faces: A Narrative History of the Portrait in Photography,* a comprehensive study.

While the heavy purchase of late 19th and early 20th century imagery continued in an increased number of auctions in New York City, living photographers produced a number of print portfolios for sale. They included 10 photographs taken by W. Eugene Smith from 1944 to 1972, color images by Stephen Shore, photographs of Mardi Gras by Charles Gatewood and George Gardner, and "Portfolio One" from Arizona State University.

In the photo press, *Popular Photography* celebrated its 40th birthday; and *Photograph*, a publication of critical reviews and interviews, celebrated its first. And in the general press, the subject of photography and fine images appeared more frequently. Susan Sontag wrote about "Photography Unlimited" in the *New York Review of Books*. *Rolling Stone* started a photography column. A new magazine, *Outside*, planned to run a nature portfolio in every issue, and *Nuestro* showed portfolios by photographers of Latin descent.

On the West Coast, a source book on photography in the San Francisco Bay area was made possible by a grant from the San Francisco Museum of Art. Margery Mann, one of the contributors to the book, died in 1977. A noted teacher, photographer, critic, and curator, she taught at the San Francisco Art Institute and wrote for *Aperture, Artforum, Camera 35*, and *Popular Photography*, among others. A close friend and biographer of Imogen Cunningham, she also organized a number of shows, including a historical survey of photographs by women.

BARBARA LOBRON
Writer, Editor, and Photographer

PENTAX CORP.

The new Pentax ME is an extremely small and light weight single-lens reflex 35mm camera. With its accessories, it is designed for the casual amateur.

PENTAX CORP.

PHYSICS

During 1977, rapid progress was made in such diverse fields of physics as superconductivity, synchrotron radiation sources, and controlled thermonuclear fusion.

Fractional Electric Charge. Some seventy years ago the U. S. physicist R. A. Millikan established that electric charge was quantized and the smallest unit was that of the electron. His classic experiment led him to conclude that the charge on many small oil droplets was always an integral multiple of the electron charge. In 1977 W. M. Fairbank and G. S. LaRue of Stanford University, reporting on a modern day version of the oil drop experiment, claimed that the charge equaled only about one third of an electron charge.

For perhaps half a century after Millikan's experiment, fractional electric charges were not even seriously considered. Then after the development of high energy physics, it was proposed that many of the "elementary" particles actually consisted of subparticles or quarks. Quarks were a very useful tool in interpreting the large numbers of particles in the nuclear "zoo," but they were never observed directly. Originally, only three kinds of quarks were proposed. Later, a fourth quark was considered with a new property, called charm. However, skepticism about charm remained until 1974. By a remarkable coincidence, groups of experimentalists, headed by S. C. C. Ting of MIT and B. Richter of Stanford Linear Accelerator Laboratory (SLAC), independently discovered a new particle—the psi particle. A whole series of related particles was discovered almost immediately. These results required that charm (and quarks in general) be taken seriously. Elementary particle physics was in an exceptionally active period, and Ting and Richter were awarded the 1976 Nobel Prize for Physics.

Problems with quarks remained. Why had no one ever observed a quark directly? Theorists set about creating models in which a quark could not exist separately and therefore could never be observed directly. Although some physicists considered this approach unrealistic, the models agreed with the experimental evidence.

In Millikan's experiment an oil drop was levitated in an electric field. The amount of charge on the drop determined how much electric field was needed to counteract the gravitational force. In the Stanford experiment small niobium balls were levitated in a magnetic field. The experiment was performed at $4.3°$ K, at which temperature niobium is superconducting. One ball was observed to have plus one third of the electron charge, while another ball had minus one third. However in this experiment, it is exceptionally difficult to guarantee that no spurious background exists. Critics were quick to question. If there were so many free quarks, why were all previous searches unsuccessful? Although the majority opinion is against the existence of free quarks, some physicists are convinced of the contrary.

Superheavy Elements. Evidence of primordial superheavy elements was presented by a group of physicists from several institutions in 1976. The elements were observed by bombarding small inclusions in a mineral sample and detecting the X-rays emitted. The X-ray energies agreed with those predicted for several superheavy elements, and the strongest confidence was in element 126. Since physicists had long predicted the existence of many more heavier elements than now exist in nature (elements 93–105 have been artificially created), the purported discovery created a tremendous flurry of activity.

Unfortunately the additional experimental results seem to be negative. An experiment at the Stanford Synchrotron Radiation Project by C. Sparks and S. Raman of Oak Ridge National Laboratory used an X-ray beam to excite X-ray transitions. None of the expected transitions was observed. This experiment may be definitive, since it does not have the drawbacks of the initial experiments. An alternative explanation of the original results was put forward by John Fox of Florida State University. According to Fox, when protons bombard cerium, one of the main elements in the mineral sample, a gamma ray is created with the same energy as the X-ray peak for element 126. This new gamma ray thus provides a simpler explanation for the unexpected peak in the spectrum than a superheavy element. The early interpretation is now generally discredited. Nevertheless, as 1977 ended, physicists still believed that superheavy elements exist, were continuing to hunt for them, and were attempting to create them.

Controlled Thermonuclear Fusion. One attractive alternative energy source is the process that fuels the stars: thermonuclear fusion. The raw materials for the process are virtually unlimited, but the practical problems in controlled fusion are monumental. The materials must be heated sufficiently for the fusion reaction to occur, and the reaction must be contained. The temperatures involved are in the 10 million to 100 million degrees Kelvin range.

Although most of the effort for the past generation has involved magnetic confinement, implosion schemes have become very popular in recent years. One approach has utilized lasers shining on a fuel pellet of deuterium and tritium (heavy isotopes of hydrogen). In 1977 a team of researchers at Los Alamos Scientific Laboratory announced that fusion reactions were achieved with gas lasers. Major efforts with different types of lasers were underway late in 1977 at Lawrence Livermore Laboratory. An alternative approach is to keep the implosion method, but use beams other than laser light. A group of scientists at Sandia Laboratories, Albuquerque, N. M., used electron beams to fuse deuterium nuclei. The signature of the fusion reaction was the emission of high energy neutrons. Other scientists argue that beams of light ions would be even more suitable. Which method ultimately succeeds depends in large part on the pattern of federal funding for magnetic versus implosion techniques and laser versus ion beams. It seems wise to remember that practical fusion reactors are at least a generation off.

Superconductivity. Some materials, when cooled to a very low temperature, lose all resistance to an electrical current. The transition from normal to superconducting behavior usually takes place at temperatures of a few degrees Kelvin. The goal is a superconductor that can be used at relatively high temperatures (30–40° K) so that liquid hydrogen rather than expensive liquid helium can be used as the coolant. The uses for such a superconductor are quite practical. Whatever the energy sources of the future, electricity will no doubt be generated and transmitted. In present day transmission of electricity there are enormous losses. Superconducting transmission wires could in principle prevent this great power loss.

In the search for higher temperature superconductors the thrust has changed from single elements to combinations of two materials (binary compounds) and then to combinations of three materials (ternary compounds). The record high for superconductivity is now about 23° K. Superconductivity often occurs in compounds whose components are not superconductors themselves. New results reported by B. Matthias of the University of California at San Diego and Bell Laboratories on compounds of rhodium, boron, and one of several rare earths are very surprising. Some of these compounds turn superconducting at a low temperature, and then, when cooled further, lose their superconductivity.

Synchrotron Radiation. Accelerated charged particles emit synchrotron radiation, certain properties of which make the radiation very useful to molecular biologists, solid-state physicists, and many others. Synchrotron radiation users have operated as secondary users at particle physics accelerators or at smaller installations. The growing interest in synchrotron radiation has led to a shortage of facilities. The new Department of Energy's Energy Research and Development Administration is asking for a major facility at Brookhaven National Laboratory, while the National Science Foundation seeks to expand facilities at Wisconsin and Stanford. In addition to many applications in solid-state physics (distances between nearest atoms can be measured to one ten-billionth of a centimeter in some materials), a new technique, called micro lithography, stirred excitement. In the fabrication of submicron integrated circuits the X-ray lithographic techniques could permit as much as 100 times more information per chip.

GARY MITCHELL, *Department of Physics*
North Carolina State University

Edward Gierek, Poland's Communist Party secretary, conferred with Pope Paul VI at the Vatican, December 1.

POLAND

In domestic affairs, 1977 was a year of mounting social and political tensions. The regime sought to maintain a precarious balance between widespread demands for more consumer goods and more freedom on the one hand and dwindling resources and threat of international bankruptcy on the other.

Political Unrest. There were no substantial changes in the leadership or organization of the ruling party, but constant unrest, break-downs in industrial discipline, and persistent rumors of mass outbreaks made its position precarious. In October, an opposition Polish publication, *Glos,* described the party's rule as "in decay."

Some of the more substantial, overt opposition came from intellectuals of the so-called Workers' Defense Committee, set up to defend persons prosecuted in connection with the previous year's food-price riots. In February, the government responded with a partial amnesty for those rioters who had indicated "repentance." Protesting intellectuals were denounced in the party press, but no arrests were reported. In March, however, homes of several students associated with the committee were raided, and arrests ensued. On March 27, the committee transformed itself into a larger and broader opposition group, the Movement for the Defense of Human and Civil Rights. It dedicated itself to working *within* the legal system to gain freedom of expression for all political groupings. By late July all of the remaining persons arrested in connection with the 1976 disturbances were set free. But tensions had been increased by reports in May that one of the detained students had died in custody, and the ensuing public protests led to several new arrests.

Economy. While industrial output continued to increase according to official reports, agriculture, affected by a 1976 drought, was in decline. Worker productivity appeared to be lagging; there were reports of illegal strikes and slow-

downs in mining and industrial establishments. Above all, imports continued to outpace exports by a substantial margin. The trade deficit rose by 25% over 1976, to nearly $500 million. Exports increased by 7.5% but only half as much as the government had planned, while imports were higher by 10.8%, instead of only 6%. Poland's debt to Western creditors exceeded $8 billion (U. S.) at the beginning of 1977, and on top of that the price of Soviet oil was raised in January. The government continued to subsidize basic food prices, but declining crops and increasing demands by consumers made the subsidies more difficult to maintain. Early in the year, the economic plan was revised, so as to increase food production and the stock of capital equipment for agriculture by diverting funds from investment in all the other sectors of the economy. Farmers were encouraged to give up to the state small inefficient farms in exchange for pensions at age 65, so as to "rationalize" and augment food output. Price increases were widely viewed in Poland as likely to provoke serious anti-government disturbances, reminiscent of December 1970 and June 1976.

U. S. President Jimmy Carter visited Poland on December 29–30.

ALEXANDER J. GROTH
University of California, Davis

POLAND · Information Highlights

Official Name: Polish People's Republic.
Location: Eastern Europe.
Area: 120,724 square miles (312,677 km²).
Population (1977 est.): 34,700,000.
Chief Cities (1975 est.): Warsaw, the capital, 1,410,-000; Łodz, 787,000; Cracow, 668,000.
Government: *Head of state,* Henryk Jabłonski, chairman of the Council of State (took office 1972). *Head of government,* Piotr Jaroszewicz, chairman of the Council of Ministers (1970). *First secretary of the United Polish Workers' party,* Edward Gierek 1970). *Legislature* (unicameral)—Sejm.
Monetary Unit: Zloty (3.30 zlotys equal U. S.$1, 1977).
Manufacturing (major products): Petroleum products, transport equipment, chemicals, machinery.
Major Agricultural Products: Rye, oats, potatoes, sugar beets, wheat, tobacco, livestock.

POLAR RESEARCH

Nearly 300 U. S. scientists traveled to the Antarctic during 1976–77 to conduct some 75 research projects in six disciplines. In the Arctic, major federally-supported research was conducted on outer continental shelf areas.

Antarctic. In March 1977, the nine nations active in year-round antarctic research were joined by Poland, which established its first permanent antarctic research outpost, Arctowski Station, on King George Island, west of the Antarctic Peninsula.

Glaciological and geophysical studies of the Ross Ice Shelf during the austral summer continued to reveal the physical characteristics and history of this region of floating ice, which is about the size of Texas. The planned U. S. drilling of a 25-cm (10-inch) hole through the shelf about 475 km (295 miles) from the open Ross Sea to permit access to the subshelf environment failed when the drill became stuck 330 m (1,083 feet) down, about 80% of the way through. Drilling will be reattempted in 1977–78. Instruments lowered through the completed hole may detect unique life forms that have evolved in an extremely cold, dark ocean environment isolated from the rest of the world for thousands of years.

A team of U. S. and Japanese geologists found 11 relatively large meteorites in the Transantarctic Mountains during 1976–77. The meteorites, some weighing 20 kg (44 pounds) or more, have been preserved in the antarctic ice sheet and brought to the surface by moving ice in regions of high ablation. Since 1973, Japanese researchers have found nearly a thousand whole or fragmented meteorites in Antarctica. These, plus the 11 new ones, account for nearly one third of all meteorites known to science.

Biomedical research at the U. S. McMurdo and Amundsen-Scott South Pole Stations during 1976–77 provided further evidence against the long-held belief that prolonged isolation, such as that experienced while wintering in Antarctica or traveling in space, results in a loss of immunity to common respiratory diseases. Results to date show no significant decrease in the count of white blood cells during isolation. Further research will seek to verify this preliminary finding.

Arctic. A five-year study of processes and resources of the Bering Sea shelf (called PROBES) began in May with observations of marine life and related physical and chemical forces off Alaska. These waters are productive fishing grounds, and the likelihood of submarine mineral deposits is substantial. The collected data will provide an ecological basis for managing living and mineral resources. In 1977, observations were made at 83 stations in the Bering Sea aboard the University of Alaska's research ship *Acona*. The data were used to construct models of the distribution, survival, and food-chain interactions of pollock eggs and larvae. Japanese and Soviet researchers are participating in the five-year project.

An environmental assessment of the outer continental shelf area of the Beaufort and Chukchi seas adjacent to Alaska continued in 1977. There were more than 30 projects with over 100 researchers from U. S. universities as well as state and federal agencies. The purpose of the study is to collect basic data on marine biology, chemistry, physical oceanography, meteorology, sea ice, and other disciplines in areas where oil and gas may be recovered.

The Coast Guard icebreaker *Polar Sea* began limited operation in January to train crews and prepare the ship for full service. Modifications were made on the ship's propellers, and commissioning was scheduled for early 1978, prior to deployment in arctic waters. The *Polar Star,* a sister ship, underwent repairs of its propellers, damaged in arctic ice trials in 1976. The repairs were delayed because of a plant strike, but the *Polar Star* was expected to support research in the Antarctic in 1977–78. The two icebreakers, the Coast Guard's newest, have computers for satellite navigation and processing oceanographic data, five scientific research laboratories, and accommodations for 10 scientists.

JERRY R. STRINGER *and* L. G. BLANCHARD
Polar Programs, National Science Foundation

U. S. COAST GUARD

The U. S. Coast Guard's new icebreaker "Polar Sea" initiated limited operations in January 1977. The "polar class" ships have two propulsion systems, diesel-electric and gas turbine.

POPULATION

The rate of global population growth peaked in the early 1970's and is now subsiding, according to Lester Brown, president of Worldwatch Institute. Most of the reduction has been due to lower birth rates in Western Europe, North America, and East Asia.

In East Asia the decline was influenced by the drop in the birth rate of the People's Republic of China from an estimated 32 to 19 per thousand over a five-year period.

With a few exceptions such as Barbados, the Bahamas, and Mauritius, little progress has been made in reducing fertility in Latin America or Africa. Because of the generally young populations of these regions, total births remain high even though births per woman began to decline. In Mexico, for example, 46% of the population is under 15 years of age. This country reversed its pronatalist policies in 1972 and set up more than 600 family planning clinics by 1976. Nevertheless, in 1977 Mexico still had a population that was doubling every 20 years.

United States Trends. In July 1977 the United States Bureau of the Census published new estimates of the nation's future population. If there were a net inflow of 400,000 legal immigrants each year, an average of 2.1 children per woman, and continuing decrease in deaths, the population would increase from 215 to 260 million in the next 23 years. Illegal immigration, an increasingly important element of population growth in the United States, is not included in the calculations because of the lack of reliable information on its size and rate of change.

The assumption that there are 2.1 children per woman is roughly in accord with current fertility expectations of young married women. The National Center for Health Statistics in 1977 reported that married women aged 18 to 24 expected to have an average of 2.3 children in their completed families. This figure, based on a 1973 national survey, compares with fertility expectations for married women in the same age category of 2.6 children in 1970 and of 3.1 in 1960. Because some women will never marry or have children, the average number of children for all women will be less than that for married women only.

The number of births per thousand persons for the 12-month period ending in May 1977 was 3% higher than the level for the same period a year earlier, 15.1 and 14.6, respectively. The number of deaths per thousand persons declined slightly from 9.0 to 8.7 for the same periods. Consequently, the amount of population growth due to the excess of births over deaths increased from 1.2 million additional persons for the year ending in May 1976 to 1.4 million persons for the same period the following year. There was one divorce recorded for every two marriages during the 12 months ending in May 1977.

Canadian Population Trends. In spite of a slightly higher surplus of births over deaths, the Canadian population grew at a slower rate in 1976 than in 1975 because of a decline in net immigration. There were 149,000 immigrants on balance in 1976 compared with 188,000 in 1975. The fastest growing province in 1976 was Alberta, which had a growth rate of 3.5%. The most slowly growing were Newfoundland and Nova Scotia, each with 0.7% growth rates.

ROBERT E. KENNEDY, JR.
University of Minnesota

PORTUGAL

In 1977 Portugal's first democratically chosen government in a half century sought to retain power through shifting alliances as economic conditions went from bad to worse.

Far from the mainstream of European trade and investment, the Portuguese economy deteriorated during the final decade of the Salazar-Caetano dictatorship, which was overthrown on April 25, 1974. After a brief period of moderate rule, radical officers ran the country for more than a year. They undertook haphazard reforms which chilled industrial and agricultural investment, prompting many skilled managers to flee the country. Too, the worldwide recession and sharp rise in fuel costs hit energy-starved Portugal harder than any other European nation. This stunning blow coincided with the decision of countries such as France to limit the entry of Portuguese workers, who had formerly sent hard currency back to their families. Meanwhile, approximately 500,000 overseas settlers poured into this Iberian nation following the violence that attended the freeing of Angola and Mozambique.

Upon his appointment in mid-1976, Prime Minister Mário Soares faced high unemployment, soaring prices, under-production, an absence of private investment, and a $1 billion trade deficit.

Soares' Program. To combat these conditions, Soares announced austerity measures in September 1976 and February 1977. These steps included a 15% devaluation of the escudo, a 15% limit on wage hikes, imposition of tough import controls, a major increase in the bank discount

——— PORTUGAL · Information Highlights ———

Official Name: Portuguese Republic.
Location: Southwestern Europe.
Area: 35,553 square miles (92,082 km²).
Population (1977 est.): 9,200,000.
Chief Cities (1974 est.): Lisbon, the capital, 775,000; Oporto, 312,000.
Government: *Head of state,* António Ramalho Eanes, president (took office July 1976). *Head of government,* Mário Soares (took office July 1976). *Legislature* (unicameral)—National Assembly.
Monetary Unit: Escudo (39.86 escudos equal U. S.$1, Aug. 1977).
Manufacturing (major products): Wine, canned fish, processed foods, textiles, ships.
Major Agricultural Products: Grapes, tomatoes, potatoes, wheat, figs, olives, forest products.

An "even better" friendship between Portugal and the United States was predicted following the April White House meeting of Prime Minister Mário Soares and President Carter.

UPI

rate, a boost in telephone and postal charges, and price controls on a "shopping basket" of foodstuffs. These steps convinced foreign lenders that Portugal was serious about tackling its economic problems. In April 1977, the International Monetary Fund made available $49 million to ease the balance of payments deficit. President Carter then took the lead in creating an 11-nation international consortium to furnish an additional $750 million.

In the wake of these reforms, tourism improved, Portuguese workers employed in foreign countries increased the remittances they sent back home, and the economy registered a modest growth in national income. Nonetheless, unemployment gripped 25% of the work force in 1977, and prices rose twice as fast as wages. Private investment remained extremely weak and Portugal imported more than 50% of its food. The upshot was that the balance of payments deficit exceeded that of 1976.

Governmental and Political Developments. Amid these difficulties, the 53-year-old Soares governed with a cabinet of Socialists, military officers, and technicians. Although his Socialist Party held only 107 seats in the 265-member legislative assembly, he rejected suggestions of an alliance with either the Social Democrats (73 legislative seats) and the Democratic Center Party (42) to his right or the Communists (4) to his left. A skilled politician, Soares sought the support of different parties, depending upon the votes needed to pass a given bill. Nevertheless, his government was brought down in early December by a combined vote of the Communists, Social Democrats, and the Democratic Center. At the end of the year, Soares was trying to form a new cabinet, the opposition parties having failed to agree on a successor.

A pact with the Communists would bring into power a secretive, highly disciplined, pro-Moscow party, thereby frightening already timid investors and increasing the flight of key personnel. On the other hand, an alliance with the centrist Popular Democrats or the more conservative Democratic Center Party might cause extremists within Soares' own party to defect.

As president, Eanes is both head of state and commander-in-chief of the armed forces. The 1976 Constitution accords him the right to declare a state of emergency and govern by decree. Short of that, he may dismiss the prime minister, dissolve the Legislative Assembly, and call new elections. Such a prospect is unappealing to Eanes and most civilian politicians because Portugal's voters are in a sullen mood and would likely turn out many incumbents.

Observers believe that the dissolution of parliament could spark renewed military intervention in the country's politics. By the end of 1977, a growing number of officers evinced doubts over the civilians' ability to achieve the reformist goals of the 1975 upheaval.

European Integration. Most Portuguese elites endorse their country's integration into Western Europe, a process that would halt if the military took power. In 1976, Portugal won admission to the Council of Europe. It has also assumed a greater role in NATO, and hopes for full Common Market membership.

GEORGE W. GRAYSON
College of William and Mary

Portugal's Foreign Minister José Manuel de Medeiros Ferreira addressed the UN General Assembly in September.

UPI

POSTAL SERVICE

U. S. Postal Service (USPS) revenues, relative to expenditures, continued to rise during 1977. An encouraging sign had come in the July–September 1976 transition period between the old and a new federal fiscal year, when revenues exceeded expenditures by $15 million. This was the first surplus during an official accounting period of the new corporation, which replaced the old Post Office Department in 1971.

FY 1977 Performance. For the next three months the USPS was again in the black, making $69.8 million. For FY 1977 (beginning Oct. 1, 1976) the deficit of $400 million was only one third that of FY 1976.

Behind this performance lay three developments. The volume of mail rose by more than 2 billion (U. S.) pieces, reaching a new high of 92 billion and ending the volume plateau of the early 1970's. Personnel declined 20,000 more, to 658,000 by July 1977, and productivity climbed very slightly.

Also of note was the nostalgic ending of the 113-year-old Railway Mail Service on June 30, 1977. The following October 9 saw the inauguration of "express mail" on a general basis, with guaranteed delivery time at an extra charge. But appointment of a new advisory Commission on Postal Service, authorized by Congress in 1976 and reporting on April 18, 1977, stressed the gravity of a six-year debate over the USPS record since 1971.

Major Accomplishments. Management development, impossible under the patronage-ridden Department, has resulted in thousands of promotions into and up through postmaster and other managerial ranks. Mechanization has enabled the service to remain a world leader in postal productivity. Efforts have been made to react to customer needs, and better salary and working conditions have attracted record numbers of employment applicants.

Financial Predictions. While forecasting an FY 1978 deficit of $554 million in an October 1977 report to his 11-person Board of Governors, Senior Assistant Postmaster General Francis X. Biglin estimated a surplus of $282 million for FY 1979. He expected the volume of mail to rise to nearly 100 billion pieces by 1981. In addition, the Postal Service has submitted a request for a rate increase to the Postal Rate Commission. If the request is approved, private letter writers would continue to pay a "citizen rate" of 13 cents, but business and other organizations would pay 16 cents.

If these new rates stayed in effect, Biglin saw, as a result of inflation and rising personnel costs, a deficit of $391 million for FY 1980 and $1.4 billion (a little above the average for recent years) for 1981.

Basic Problems. Personnel costs, deriving from the collective bargaining approach established by the 1971 act, formed 86% of total costs in FY 1976, with no reduction in sight. The top management structure can be seen as top-heavy and expensive. Mechanization has had less impact on productivity than expected. Other cost-cutting efforts have been delayed by the postal unions and congressional opposition.

Rising rates have been driving some publishers out of business. Over the last 25 years the competitive United Parcel Service and others have cut into the important parcel post mail, where the USPS has no monopoly, by as much as 60%. Since 1971 Congress has subsidized postal operations by $9.5 billion and the service itself has borrowed $3 billion.

The 1977 Commission Report. The Commission on Postal Service recommended no change in the basic USPS corporate structure. But it urged a moderate increase in the public service subsidy to 10% of expenses and asked Congress to change the law under which a recent federal court decision called for lower first-class rates, from which USPS gets over one half of its income. The commission supported reduction in delivery to five days a week and asked that the primary service objective be timeliness rather than fast or low-cost delivery. The USPS was strongly encouraged to decide in the immediate future whether it should get into the electronic communications business.

The Long-Run Problem. Most postal reform proposals assume improvement in the basic system now in operation. However, experts predict that messages of all kinds will soon be transmitted electronically. The messages now sent through postal channels constitute only one fifth of the total messages, the remainder going primarily by telephonic means.

The USPS, therefore, is facing a kind of water-shed technological dilemma, well expressed in the Commission's 1977 report: "The impact of electronic communications on postal volume has just begun. . . . Over the next decade, electronic communication is expected to capture a large part of business communications, causing letter mail volume to decline. If massive appropriations are made to the Postal Service to maintain the postal delivery system at current service levels, an archaic institution could be preserved without adequate social, political or economic justification."

The World Postal Scene. While all nations with high personnel costs, including most industrialized nations, are facing similar postal problems, the U. S. system stands out quite favorably in comparison. In productivity and low first-class rates, the United States is second only to Canada, which is more heavily subsidized. U. S. postal productivity is more than twice that of Australia, France, Japan, Italy, and Britain, and the 13-cent first class rate is much lower than the 18-cent average of industrialized nations.

PAUL P. VAN RIPER
Texas A&M University

PRINCE EDWARD ISLAND

The provincial government acted in 1977 to preserve land for agriculture and to keep rents down. The province got a new chief justice, and the Conservatives lost a seat in Parliament.

Agriculture. The provincial cabinet in August approved an agricultural land identification program designed to keep land in agricultural use in predominantly agrarian Prince Edward Island. Under new regulations, if a nonresident buys agricultural land in the province it must be used for agriculture.

Rents. Tenants will not face rent increases higher than 6% in 1978. Provincial Secretary Arthur MacDonald said rent increases would be limited to that percentage in places where the landlord pays for heating, and to 4% where the tenant pays.

Language. On July 27, Premier Alex Campbell rejected Quebec Premier René Lévesque's offer to negotiate language rights with the other Canadian provinces. While P. E. I. did not contemplate entering formal agreements with Quebec on language rights, Campbell reiterated that it will meet language requirements of French-speaking residents "as best we can."

Politics. The Liberals took the federal seat of Malpeque away from the Conservatives in a by-election May 24. Liberal Donald Wood's

PRINCE EDWARD ISLAND • Information Highlights

Area: 2,184 square miles (5,656 km²).
Population (1976 census): 118,229.
Chief Cities (1976 census): Charlottetown, the capital, 17,063; Summerside, 8,592.
Government (1977): *Chief Officers*—lt. gov., Gordon L. Bennett; premier, Alexander B. Campbell (Liberal); minister of justice, Alexander Campbell; chief justice, John Paton Nicholson. *Legislature*—Legislative Assembly, 32 members.
Education (1976–77): *Enrollment*—public elementary and secondary schools, 27,480 pupils; Indian (federal) schools, 50; post-secondary, 2,210. *Total expenditures,* $47,891,000.
Public Finance (1977–78 budget): *Revenues,* $234 million; *expenditures,* $240 million.
(All monetary figures given in Canadian dollars.)

success broke a 25-year Tory hold on the seat, made vacant when Angus MacLean resigned in 1976 to become provincial Conservative leader.

The Bench. John Paton Nicholson was named chief justice of the P. E. I. Supreme Court January 14. A justice of the high court since 1970, he replaced Chief Justice St. Clair Trainor who retired Dec. 8, 1976.

Budget. Finance Minister Bennett Campbell's budget, introduced March 30, provided for a $6 million deficit on expenditures of $240 million and revenues of $234 million. It called for a 53% increase in job-creation projects to combat unemployment.

Legislative. A 65-day legislative session was terminated May 14 after passage of 57 bills. Two of the bills paved the way for creation of a comprehensive grain-marketing system.

JOHN BEST, *Chief, Canada World News*

PRISONS

Despite changing details and a shift in headlines, the situation in the nation's prisons has remained basically the same over the past several years. For a while, public attention, galvanized by the dramatic execution of Gary Gilmore on Jan. 17, 1977, focused on capital punishment and, peripherally, on the hundreds of prisoners waiting on death rows. But the national system of criminal justice continued, as in years past, to allocate to the police approximately 75¢ out of every dollar spent, and less than 10¢ to "corrections." With almost 9¢ out of the 10¢ going for salaries and custodial expenses, there was little left for programs and projects which might positively alter the settings or the lives of the more than 400,000 inmates in U. S. federal, state, and local facilities. (*See also* CRIME.)

Capital Punishment. Prisoners on death rows, as of Jan. 1, 1977, were reported to number 444. Gilmore's death by firing squad shortly afterward ended a 10-year de facto moratorium on executions in the United States. It did not, as some had predicted, precipitate a rash of further

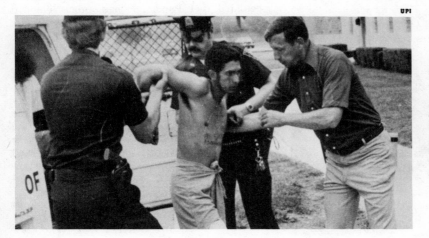

UPI

A prisoner, injured in a fire at the Federal Correction Institution in Danbury, Conn., is returned to the prison following hospital treatment. The blaze killed 5 persons and injured 68.

executions. In spite of a number of new death sentences, the total number of prisoners on death rows diminished because previous capital punishment laws in several states were declared unconstitutional by the courts. In June, a report, published by the National Coalition Against the Death Penalty, listed 370 prisoners in 19 states under sentence of death. Six states—Florida, Ohio, Georgia, Texas, Mississippi, and Arizona —accounted for 316 of the 370 condemned convicts. An equal number of blacks and whites was listed—178 of each—as well as 13 Hispanics and one American Indian. A number of state legislatures, including those of Illinois, North and South Carolina, Oklahoma, Tennessee, Texas, and Virginia, passed new laws, which in some cases provided for capital punishment for as many as 16 kinds of first-degree murder. The year closed, however, without further executions, and in spite of a growing trend toward longer sentences, most prisoners sentenced will eventually return to society.

Prison Deaths. Fires, apparently deliberately set, caused 47 prisoner deaths in two states. On June 26, 34 inmates and eight visitors died in the Maury County, Tenn., jail, as fumes from smoldering polyvinyl chloride and foam plastic spread through the ventilation system of the 13-year-old facility. The next day, Andrew J. Zinmer, 16, a runaway from a home for emotionally disturbed children, was charged with causing the blaze with a cigarette obtained from a visitor. On July 7, a fire broke out in the Danbury, Conn., Federal Correction Institution; here, five inmates were killed and 68 injured by intense heat and heavy smoke from burning fiberglass partitions. The 40-year-old facility has a planned capacity of 500 prisoners, but 839 were

To rehabilitate inmates and to educate children, a New York correctional center conducts a day-care program.

UPI

housed in it. A federal board of inquiry reported in September that the fire had been "humanly initiated," though it did not identify the responsible parties. The board found no deliberate dereliction or malfeasance, but recommended extensive improvements in fire safety and inspection procedures. On June 21, fire broke out in the padding of a maximum security cell in the police station at Saint John, New Brunswick, Canada, killing 20 of 27 prisoners.

In July, inmate clashes, racially oriented and gang supported, left three prisoners dead and four injured at the San Quentin prison in California. Since 1971, when George Jackson, the black radical prisoner and writer, was slain along with two other inmates and three guards, 38 convicts have been killed in this maximum-security facility. The violence in 1977 began in April, when a member of a black "Guerrilla Family" was put to death by a member of a white "Aryan Brotherhood." Although the gang structure at San Quentin is more intense and active than in other prisons, it does underline the significance of inmate power groups within many prison systems. By May, after another black and three white prisoners had been stabbed, most of the facility's 2,300 inmates were confined to their cells. In July, 45 inmates with ties to the various gangs were transferred to other institutions around the state, and a team of experts trained in settling prison conflicts was called in to help ease the tensions. Folsom Prison, Calif., locked its 1,900 prisoners in for a week in July after a black inmate was stabbed and racial clashes erupted.

On July 26, Vincent Papa, a major drug dealer who was serving a 22-year sentence and was under investigation in the theft of $70-million worth of heroin and cocaine held over from the so-called French Connection case in New York, was murdered in the federal penitentiary in Atlanta, Ga. Three home-made knives were found near the victim, who had been stabbed eight times as he walked down a ramp to an exercise yard. The motives and identities of the assailants remained a mystery, although officials speculated that Papa, 59, had either offended Mafia leaders serving time in the prison, or was under suspicion of being an informant.

Prisoners' Rights. On April 26, a special committee of the American Bar Association released a 239-page report on the legal rights of prisoners. The report recommended that, except where restrictions for security and safety were needed, prisoners be guaranteed the same legal rights as free citizens. On April 27, the U. S. Supreme Court ruled, 6–3, that states were obligated to provide inmates with adequate legal assistance "in the preparation and filing of meaningful legal papers." (*See also* LAW: *The Supreme Court.*)

DONALD GOODMAN
John Jay College of Criminal Justice
City University of New York

B. Williams, left; the chairman of Amnesty International; Nobel committee chairlady; M. Corrigan; and R. Yalow.

PRIZES AND AWARDS

NOBEL PRIZES

With the exception of the Nobel Peace Prize, which was given in Oslo, Norway, the 1977 Nobel Prizes were presented by King Carl XVI Gustaf in Stockholm, Sweden, on December 10. The recipients of the prizes, which were valued at an estimated $145,000 per category, were:

Chemistry: Ilya Prigogine, Free University of Brussels, for "his contributions to nonequilibrium thermodynamics, particularly the theory of dissipative structures."

Economics: Bertil Ohlin, former Swedish university professor and leader of the Swedish Liberal Party; James E. Meade, former professor, Cambridge University, for their "pathbreaking contributions to the theory of international trade and international capital movements."

Literature: Vicente Aleixandre, Spanish poet, for his "creative poetic writing, which, with roots in the traditions of Spanish lyric verse and in modern currents, illuminates man's condition in the cosmos and in present-day society."

Medicine or Physiology: Rosalyn S. Yalow, Veterans Administration Hospital, Bronx, N. Y.; Roger C. L. Guillemin, Salk Institute, La Jolla, Calif.; and Andrew V. Schally, Veterans Administration Hospital, New Orleans, and Tulane University, for discoveries that "have opened new vistas within biological and medical research far outside the border of their own spheres of interest."

Peace Prize (1977): Amnesty International, London, whose "efforts on behalf of defending human dignity against violence and subjugation have proved that the basis for peace in the world must be justice for all human beings." **(1976):** Mairead Corrigan and Betty Williams, Northern Ireland, for whose "initiative paved the way for the strong resistance against violence and misuse of power which was present in broad circles of the people."

Physics: Philip W. Anderson, Bell Telephone Laboratories, Murray Hill, N. J., and Princeton, N. J.; John H. Van Vleck, professor emeritus, Harvard University; and Sir Nevill F. Mott, Cambridge University, England, for work underlying the development of computer memories, office copying machines, and other devices of modern electronics.

ART

American Academy and Institute of Arts and Letters Awards
Arnold W. Brunner Prize in Architecture: Henry N. Cobb
Distinguished Service to the Arts: James Laughlin
Gold Medal for Sculpture: Isamu Noguchi
Charles E. Ives Awards: Charles Ives Society; Yale University Library

Marjorie Peabody Waite Award ($1,500): Kenzo Okada
Richard and Hinda Rosenthal Foundation Award to a younger painter ($2,000): Sigrid Burton

"Dance" Magazine Awards: Murray Louis; Natalia Makarova; Peter Martins

Ditson Conductor Award ($1,000): Eugene Ormandy

Avery Fisher Prizes ($2,500 each): André-Michel Schub; Richard Stoltzman

Andrew W. Mellon Prize for artists ($50,000): Pierre Alechinsky

National Academy of Recording Arts and Sciences Grammy Awards for excellence in phonograph records
Album of the year: *Songs in the Key of Life*, Stevie Wonder
Classical album of the year: *Beethoven: (The) Five Piano Concertos*, Artur Rubinstein and Daniel Barenboim, conducting the London Philharmonic
Country music song: *Broken Lady*, Larry Gatlin, writer
Jazz vocal performance: *Fitzgerald & Pass . . . Again*, Ella Fitzgerald
New artist: Starland Vocal Band
Record of the year: *This Masquerade*, George Benson
Song of the year: *I Write the Songs*, Bruce Johnston

Pulitzer Prize for music: Richard Wernick, *Visions of Terror and Wonder*

JOURNALISM

Maria Moors Cabot Prizes for "distinguished journalistic contributions to the advancement of inter-American understanding" ($1,000 each): Pedro J. Chamorro Cardenal, *La Presna*, Managua, Nicaragua; Jonathan Kandell, *The New York Times*

National Magazine Awards
Fiction, criticism, and belles lettres: *Mother Jones*
Public service: *Philadelphia*
Reporting excellence: *Audubon*
Service to the individual: *Harper's*
Specialized journalism: *Architectural Record*
Visual excellence: *Rolling Stone*

Overseas Press Club Awards
Book on foreign affairs: John Toland, *Adolph Hitler*
Business news reporting from abroad ($500) Alfred Zanker, *U. S. News & World Report*
Cartoon on foreign affairs: Warren King, *New York Daily News*
Daily newspaper or wire service reporting from abroad: Edward Cody, The Associated Press, Beirut, Lebanon
Daily newspaper or wire service interpretation of foreign affairs: Flora Lewis, Paris Bureau Chief, *The New York Times*
Magazine interpretation of foreign affairs: Tad Szulc, *The New Republic*
Magazine reporting from abroad: *Newsweek*
Photographic reporting from abroad: Robert W. Madden and W. E. Garrett, *National Geographic*

Radio interpretation of foreign news: CBS News, "The World Looks at America"

Radio spot news from abroad: ABC, coverage of the siege of the Palestinian refugee camp at Tell Zaatar; CBS, Lebanon civil-war coverage

Television interpretation of foreign affairs: NBC-TV News, "New World—Hard Choices"

Television spot news: Mike Lee, CBS News

Bob Considine Memorial Award ($1,000): Robin Wright, *The Christian Science Monitor*

Robert Capa Gold Medal: Catherine Leroy, *Time*

Madeline Dane Ross Award ($350): June Goodwin, *The Christian Science Monitor*

Pulitzer Prizes

Commentary: George F. Will, Washington Post Writers Group

Criticism: William McPherson, *The Washington Post*

Editorial cartooning: Paul Szep, *The Boston Globe*

Editorial writing: Norman F. Cardoza, Foster Church, Warren L. Lerude, *The Reno Evening Gazette* and *The Nevada State Journal*

Feature photography: Robin Hood, *The Chattanooga News-Free Press*

General local reporting: Margo Huston, *The Milwaukee Journal*

National reporting: Walter Mears, The Associated Press

Public service: *The Lufkin* (Tex.) *News*

Special local reporting: Acel Moore and Wendell Rawls, Jr., *The Philadelphia Inquirer*

Spot news photography: Stanley Foreman, *The Boston Herald-American*

Spot news reporting: Neal Ulevich, The Associated Press

LITERATURE

Academy of American Poets Awards

Copernicus Award ($10,000): Muriel Rukeyser

Edgar Allan Poe Award ($5,000): Stan Rice

Walt Whitman Award ($1,000): Lauren Shakely

American Academy and Institute of Arts and Letters Awards

American Academy in Rome Fellowship in Creative Writing ($7,180): Daniel M. Epstein

E. M. Forster Award ($5,000): David Cook

Gold Medal for the Novel: Saul Bellow

National Medal for Literature ($10,000): Robert Lowell

Richard and Hinda Rosenthal Foundation Award for Fiction ($2,000): Spencer Holst, *Spencer Holst Stories*

Morton Dauwen Zabel Award ($2,500): David Shapiro

American Library Association Awards see page 295

Bancroft Prizes for best books in American history or diplomacy ($4,000 each): Alan Dawley, *Class and Community, the Industrial Revolution in Lynn;* Barry W. Higman, *Slave Population and the Economy in Jamaica, 1807–1834*

Bollingen Prize in Poetry ($5,000): David Ignatow

Canada's Governor General's Literary Awards ($5,000 each): Marian Engel, *Bear;* André Major, *Les rescapés;* Joe Rosenblatt, *Top Soil;* Alphonse Piché, *Poèmes 1946–1968;* Carl Berger, The *Writing of Canadian History;* Fernand Ouellet, *Le Bas Canada 1791–1840*

Ernest Hemingway Foundation Award "for the best first novel by an American published during the previous year" ($6,000): Renata Adler, *Speedboat*

National Book Awards ($1,000 each)

Biography and autobiography: William A. Swanberg, *Norman Thomas: The Last Idealist*

Children's literature: Katherine W. Paterson, *The Master Puppeteer*

Contemporary thought: Bruno Bettelheim, *The Uses of Enchantment: The Meaning and Importance of Fairy Tales*

Fiction: Wallace E. Stegner, *The Spectator Bird*

History: Irving Howe, *The World of Our Fathers*

Poetry: Richard Eberhart, *Collected Poems: 1930–1976*

Translation: Li-li Ch'en, *Master Tung's Western Chamber Romance*

Special citation of merit: Alex Haley, *Roots*

Pulitzer Prizes

Biography: John E. Mack, *A Prince of Our Disorder*

Fiction: no award given

General nonfiction: William W. Warner, *Beautiful*

UPI

Tatum O'Neill presents Jason Robards with an Oscar for his supporting performance in *All the President's Men*.

Swimmers: Watermen, Crabs and the Chesapeake Bay

History: David M. Potter, *The Impending Crisis* (posthumously)

Poetry: James Merrill, *Divine Comedies*

Special award: Alex Haley, *Roots*

MOTION PICTURES

Academy of Motion Picture Arts and Sciences ("Oscar") Awards

Actor: Peter Finch, *Network* (posthumously)

Actress: Faye Dunaway, *Network*

Cinematography: Haskell Wexler, *Bound for Glory*

Director: John Avildsen, *Rocky*

Documentary Feature: *Harlan County, U.S.A.*

Film: *Rocky*

Foreign language film: *Black and White in Color*

Original dramatic score: Jerry Goldsmith, *The Omen*

Original screenplay: Paddy Chayefsky, *Network*

Original song score and adaptation: Leonard Rosenman, *Bound for Glory*

Screenplay based on material from another medium: William Goldman, *All the President's Men*

Song: *Evergreen*, Barbra Streisand

Supporting actor: Jason Robards, *All the President's Men*

Supporting actress: Beatrice Straight, *Network*

PUBLIC SERVICE

The Jefferson Awards of the American Institute for Public Service

Public service benefiting communities: Rev. Alfred Boeddekker, San Francisco; Jean Chaudhuri, Traditional Indian Alliance, Tucson; Leonard Cobb, Harborview Medical Center, Seattle; Olga Mele, Hartford, Conn.; Marjory Taylor, Marlborough-Westborough Mental Health Association, Massachusetts

Public service benefiting the disadvantaged: Howard Rusk, New York University Institute of Rehabilitation Medicine

Public service by a private citizen: Art Buchwald, columnist

Public service by an elected official: Mike Mansfield, U.S. ambassador to Japan; former Senate majority leader

Public service by an individual, 35 years of age or under: Max Cleland, administrator, U.S. Veterans Administration

Rockefeller Public Service Awards for contributions toward solving critical social problems ($10,000 each): King Hubert, former research geophysicist, U.S. Geological Survey; John W. Runyan, Jr., University of Tennessee College of Medicine; Howard Browley, Gas and Electric Corporation, Rochester, N.Y.; Julian H. Levi, Southeast Chicago Commission, and Arthur Brazier, Center for Community Change; Frieda R. Mitchell, United Communities for Child Care Development, and Sophia Bracy Harris, Federation of Community-Controlled Centers of Alabama

U. S. Presidential Medal of Freedom (presented by President Gerald Ford, Jan. 10, 1977): I. W. Abel, John Bardeen, Irving Berlin, Norman Borlaug, Omar N. Bradley, Arleigh Burke, Alexander Calder (posthumously), Bruce Catton, Joe DiMaggio, Ariel Durant, Will Durant, Arthur Fiedler, Henry J. Friendly, Lady Bird Johnson, Archibald MacLeish, James Albert Michener, Georgia O'Keeffe, Nelson A. Rockefeller, Norman Rockwell, Katherine Filene Shouse, Lowell Thomas, James D. Watson. (Presented by President Jimmy Carter, July 11): Martin Luther King, Jr. (posthumously), Jonas E. Salk

SCIENCE

Albert Lasker Awards
   Basic Medical Research Award ($15,000 shared): K. Sune D. Bergström, WHO Advisory Council on Medical Research; Bengt Samuelsson, Karolinska Institute; John R. Vane, Wellcome Research Laboratories, Beckenham, England
   Clinical Medical Research Award ($15,000 shared): Inge G. Edler, University Hospital, Lund, Sweden; C. Hellmuth Hertz, Lund Institute of Technology, Lund, Sweden

U. S. National Medals of Science: Roger Charles Lewis Guillemin, Salk Institute; Keith R. Porter, University of Colorado; Efraim Racker, Cornell University; Edward O. Wilson, Harvard University; Morris Cohen, MIT; Peter C. Goldmark, formerly of CBS; Erwin W. Mueller, Pennsylvania State University (posthumously); K. O. Friedricks, New York University; Hassler Whitney, Institute for Advanced Studies; Samuel A. Goudsmit, University of Nevada; Herbert S. Gutowsky, University of Illinois, Urbana; Frederick D. Rossini, Rice University; Verner E. Suomi, University of Wisconsin, Madison; Henry Taube, Stanford University; George E. Uhlenbeck, Rockefeller University

TELEVISION AND RADIO

Academy of Television Arts & Sciences (Emmy) Awards
   Actor—comedy series: Carroll O'Connor, *All in the Family* (CBS)
   Actor—drama series: James Garner, *The Rockford Files* (NBC)
   Actor—drama or comedy special: Ed Flanders, *Harry S. Truman: Plain Speaking*
   Actor—limited series: Christopher Plummer, *The Moneychangers* (NBC)
   Actor—single performance in a drama or comedy series: Louis Gossett, Jr., *Roots* (ABC)
   Actress—comedy series: Beatrice Arthur, *Maude* (CBS)
   Actress—drama series: Lindsay Wagner, *The Bionic Woman* (ABC)
   Actress—drama or comedy special: Sally Field, *Sybil* (NBC)
   Actress—limited series: Patty Duke Astin, *Captains and the Kings*
   Actress—single performance in a drama or comedy series: Beulah Bondi, "The Pony Cart," *The Waltons* (CBS)
   Children's special: *Ballet Shoes* Parts 1 & 2 (PBS)
   Classical program in the performing arts: *American Ballet Theater: Swan Lake, Live From Lincoln Center* (PBS)
   Comedy series: *The Mary Tyler Moore Show* (CBS)
   Comedy-variety or music series: *Van Dyke and Company* (NBC)
   Drama series: *Upstairs Downstairs* (PBS)
   Limited series: *Roots* (ABC)
   Program achievement: *The Tonight Show Starring Johnny Carson* (NBC)
   Special—drama or comedy: *Eleanor and Franklin: The White House Years* (ABC); *Sybil* (NBC)
   Supporting actor—comedy series: Gary Burghoff, *M*A*S*H*
   Supporting actor—drama series: Gary Frank, *Family*
   Supporting actress—comedy series: Mary Kay Place, *Mary Hartman, Mary Hartman* (syndicated)
   Supporting actress—dramatic series: Kristy McNichol, *Family* (ABC)

George Foster Peabody Awards for broadcasting
   Radio: Associated Press Radio, *The Garden Plot: Food as a Weapon;* South Carolina Educational Radio Network, *American Popular Song With Alec Wilder and Friends;* WGIR AM-FM, Manchester, N. H., *Flashback 1976*

   Television: ABC News, *Animals, Animals and Suddenly an Eagle;* ABC Sports, coverage of the Olympics; Charles Bathold, WHO, Des Moines; CBS News, *In Celebration of US;* CBS News, *Sixty Minutes;* Perry Como, Christmas show from Austria; *Eleanor and Franklin*, ABC; Jim Karayan and the League of Women Voters, Washington, *'76 Presidential Debates;* KCET-28, Los Angeles, *Visions;* KERA, Dallas, *A Thirst in the Garden;* Franklin McMahon, WBBM, Chicago, *Primary Colors;* Sy Pearlman, NBC, New York, *Weekends* "Sawyer Brothers"; Hughes Rudd and Bruce Morton, *The CBS Morning News;* *Sybil*, NBC; Tomorrow Entertainment Inc., New York, *Judge Horton and the Scottsboro Boys;* WETA, Washington, *In Performance at Wolf Trap;* WETA, Washington, and WNET, New York, *A Conversation With Jimmy Carter;* WLBT, Jackson, Miss., *Power Politics in Mississippi;* WNET, New York, *The Adams Chronicles*

THEATER

Antoinette Perry ("Tony") Awards
   Actor (drama): Al Pacino, *The Basic Training of Pavlo Hummel*
   Actor (musical): Barry Bostwick, *Robber Bridegroom*
   Actress (drama): Julie Harris, *The Belle of Amherst*
   Actress (musical): Dorothy Loudon, *Annie*
   Choreography: Peter Gennaro, *Annie*
   Costume design: Theoni V. Aldredge, *Annie;* Santo Loquasto, *The Cherry Orchard*
   Director (drama): Gordon Davidson, *The Shadow Box*
   Director (musical): Gene Saks, *I Love My Wife*
   Featured actor (drama): Jonathan Pryce, *Comedians*
   Featured actor (musical): Lenny Baker, *I Love My Wife*
   Featured actress (drama): Trazana Beverly, *For Colored Girls Who Have Considered Suicide/When the Rainbow is Enuf*
   Featured actress (musical): Dolores Hall, *Your Arms Too Short to Box With God*
   Most innovative production of a revival: *Porgy and Bess*
   Musical: *Annie*
   Play: *The Shadow Box*
   Score: Martin Charnin and Charles Strouse, *Annie*
   Special awards: Barry Manilow; Diana Ross; Lily Tomlin; Mark Taper Forum, Los Angeles; Equity Library Theater, New York City; National Theater of the Deaf
   Lawrence Langer Award for distinguished lifetime achievement in the theater: Cheryl Crawford

New York Drama Critics' Circle Theater Awards
   American play: *American Buffalo*
   Musical: *Annie*
   Play: *Otherwise Engaged*

Pulitzer Prize for drama: Michael Cristofer, *The Shadow Box*

At the Shubert Theater in June, Barry Bostwick, left, Dorothy Loudon, and Al Pacino received Tony Awards.

UPI

PHOTOS UPI

Australian publisher Rupert Murdoch bought the N. Y. *Post* and the New York Magazine Company. Protesting the purchase, *New York* magazine employees abandoned work (*right*).

PUBLISHING

Publishers experienced a profitable year in 1977 as advertising revenues reached new highs, circulation figures moved upward, and gross sales hit new peaks.

Book publishers and magazine and newspaper editors shared the year's newsworthy events, especially the capture of the "Son of Sam" (David Berkowitz) in Yonkers, New York, and the death of Elvis Presley in Memphis, Tenn.

Newsweek called Berkowitz' capture the "biggest crime story since Patty Hearst." As New York dailies published hundreds of thousands of extra copies, criticism followed. *Good Housekeeping* editor John Mack Carter called the *Post*'s "banner headlines of a type size that one hopes is the legal limit for a tabloid format." The competition recalled the Hearst-Pulitzer days, especially when three photographers and a reporter broke into Berkowitz' apartment.

Memorial supplements and extra press runs characterized Presley's death coverage. The Louisville *Courier-Journal* printed a special 16-page supplement, distributing nearly 7 million copies through some 20 dailies.

Both incidents inspired quickly-prepared books, and in the case of Elvis, a reprinting of earlier volumes. The K-Mart chain stores ordered 2,250,000 copies of *Elvis: What Happened?*, an account of the singer's life as told by three former employees before Presley's death.

Some serious problems faced publishers, such as higher postal rates and declining service, newsprint prices, the possible shortage of quality paper for books and magazines, and climbing labor costs.

Publishers urged more modernization of the Postal Service, a rollback to 1975 rates, and more volume discounts.

The new copyright law went into effect Jan. 1, 1978, providing longer protection for authors and, no doubt, creating problems that courts will have to decide.

Books. Lists of best sellers, as reported by the industry's bible, *Publishers Weekly,* revealed that a few authors dominated the 1977 fiction field. Leon Uris' *Trinity* led early in 1977, followed by Erich Segal's *Oliver's Story.* John Cheever's *Falconer* led until *The Thorn Birds,* by Colleen McCullough, took over in June. Others high on the list included Paul Erdman's *The Crash of '79,* Richard Bach's *Illusions: The Adventures of a Reluctant Messiah,* John MacDonald's *Condominium,* and J. R. R. Tolkien's *The Silmarillion.*

In nonfiction, Dr. Wayne W. Dyer's *Your Erroneous Zones* topped the list in April, remaining there for months. As 1976 ended, Alex Haley's *Roots* was the talk of the nation. Eventually, Gail Sheehy's *Passages: the Predictable Crises of Adult Life,* topped *Publishers Weekly* reports. *The Book of Lists,* by the Wallace family, led by fall. Robert Ringer's *Looking Out for #1* and James Herriot's *All Things Wise and Wonderful* were widely read.

Previous bestsellers topped the paperback list, with the Woodward-Bernstein work, *The Final Days,* an early leader before interest in Watergate declined. Others with high rankings included Harold Robbin's *The Lonely Lady;* Shere Hite's *The Hite Report: A Nationwide Study of Female Sexuality;* Jacqueline Susann's last book, *Dolores;* John Jake's *The Warriors* (part of the bicentennial series); Peter Benchley's *The Deep;* and Sheehy's *Passages.*

Kathleen A. Woodiwiss' *Shanna* long led the trade area, with Alex Comfort's *The Joy of Sex* and Sylvia Porter's *Money Book* selling well.

Alex Haley continued to experience success and problems with *Roots,* aided by television. Unprecedented hardback sales resulted in lawsuits, some against Haley, and one by Haley against his publisher over promotion practices.

The Association of American Publishers reported sales in 1976 topped $4.1 billion, up 8.7% over the previous year. Increases also were reported for early 1977. *U. S. News and World Report* noted that nearly $12 billion was spent in 1976 on newspapers, magazines, and books.

Booksellers complained about too many books to stock, and publishers complained about the necessity to sell sufficient copies for profit.

Some major publishers cut back on the number of their titles. John P. Dessauer, writing in *Publishers Weekly*, called for "careful choices, good judgment, and discrimination" in his plea for fewer titles.

Religious books continued to soar, inspired by Billy Graham, Norma Zimmer, Charles Colson, the Carter family, and others. Many reflected a "born again" philosophy.

Christian News Service reported more than 30 volumes belong to the "Millionaires' Club," led by Halley's *Bible Handbook* and Kenneth Taylor's *Reach Out* in the 4-million class. *The Living Bible* sold another two million copies and has passed 22 million. *The Good News Bible*, which entered the market in late 1976, has sold three million copies.

Paperbacks lured high bids, with Avon Books paying $1.9 million for Colleen McCullough's *The Thorn Birds*. Pocket Books paid nearly $1.6 million for Dorothy Ulnaks' *The Investigation*.

Magazines. Based on 1977 trends, the magazine industry visualized a more successful 1978. Consumer publications reported 1977 increases in circulation and advertisements, with specialty magazines up front.

TV Guide continued to dominate. For 1976, it received $157 million in ad revenue; for the first half of 1977, it reached $86 million, up 20% over the previous period. Time, Inc., a diversified concern that became the first billion-dollar publishing firm in 1976, expected still higher revenues in 1977–78.

In mid-1977 the circulation leaders were *TV Guide*, 19.8 million; *Reader's Digest*, 18.5; *National Geographic*, 9.6; *Family Circle*, 8.3; *Woman's Day*, 8.2; *Better Homes & Gardens*, 8; *McCall's*, 6.5; *Ladies' Home Journal*, 6; *Good Housekeeping*, 5; and *Playboy*, 4.9. *TV Guide* circulation, down as a result of selling its Canadian editions, was up in the United States. The *National Enquirer*, considered a magazine by some, topped 5 million.

In 1976 the ad revenue leaders were *TV Guide*, $156 million; *Time*, $131; *Newsweek*, $107; *Reader's Digest*, $80; *Sports Illustrated*, $78; *Business Week*, $67; *Better Homes & Gardens*. $56; *Family Circle*, $55; *Woman's Day*, $54; and *McCall's*, $47. In total advertising pages, *Business Week* continued its leadership, followed by *The New Yorker*, *TV Guide*, *Newsweek*, *Time*, *Sports Illustrated*, *People*, *Yachting*, *Forbes*, and *New York*.

The Media Industry Newsletter predicted that "it now looks as if the Postal Service could lose all magazine mailing at some future point, which is approaching rapidly as bureaucrats keep pulling new injunctions out of their drawers." More magazines are sold in food stores.

The magazine audience continued to be specialized; of some 600 new publications in the past two years, most were designed for limited audiences. *Quest/77* voiced the "new American optimism" and reached 300,000 by early 1978. *Human Nature*, set for early 1978, was designed "to bring to life everything important about the humanity inside us and around us."

Meanwhile, *People* and *Us* battled for the same market, and "the merchants of raunchiness," as *Time* called the skin magazines, had more problems. *Playboy*, losing circulation but gaining advertising, centered its operations in Los Angeles, chopping off losing branches. *Playboy* is now the most "conservative" of this group, with *Hustler*, having court problems, the "most raunchy."

Esquire was sold to Clay Felker, formerly with *New York*, Milton Glazer, a graphic artist, and the London-based Associated Newspapers Group, Ltd. *Forbes* celebrated its 60th anniversary. *Fortune* changed to 24 issues in 1978. And *Life* continued its Year in Review editions.

Newspapers. The future of newspapers involves the "greatest challenges and opportunities," according to Joe D. Smith, Jr., chairman of the American Newspaper Publishers Association (ANPA). He predicted the time would come "when changing interests and needs of our readers and advertisers" will be met. This will come about through advances in technology designed to halt the price hikes in newsprint, labor, and distribution.

Jerry W. Friedheim, ANPA general manager, predicted more "electronic newsrooms, high-speed communications, automated engravings, offset printing, plastic plates, and direct lithography." He warned that "we must be beholden to government neither for the right nor for the financial resources to publish."

Robert Toth, Los Angeles *Times* correspondent in Moscow, was questioned for several days by Soviet police.

UPI

"Within two decades, virtually all daily newspapers in America will be owned by perhaps fewer than two dozen major communications conglomerates," reported the Washington *Post*. During 1977 communications groups became bigger, acquiring more independent publications as well as other groups.

Such group growth alarmed Sen. Edward Kennedy, chairman of the Antitrust and Monopoly Committee. He found such takeover to be "intensely troubling in our democracy," yet noted that the "death of many big city papers has been offset by birth of many in suburbia."

Editor & Publisher reported 72 newspapers changed hands in 1976, and the trend continued through 1977. No deal topped the $300 million involved in Sam Newhouse's purchase of Booth Newspapers in Michigan, *Parade* magazine, and a group of suburban weeklies in Cleveland. Some Kansas City *Star* employees became overnight millionaires when that firm was sold to Capital Cities Communications, Inc. for $125 million. The Buffalo Evening News, Inc., became the property of the Blue Chip Stamps of California in a $33-million transaction. Gannett acquired Speidel Newspapers for some $170 million. Other papers added radio-television outlets, increasing diversification.

By mid-1977 some 167 groups owned 1,047 dailies, accounting for 71% of the circulation. Knight-Ridder led in daily circulation with 3,681,301. The Chicago Tribune Company led with a Sunday edition circulation total of 4,325,362, while Gannett led in total papers with 73 dailies.

In New York Rupert Murdoch bought the *Post* and *Village Voice* plus both *New York* and *New West* magazines. Murdoch made the *Post* more "provocative and lively" and circulation climbed.

Circulation for U. S. and Canadian newspapers climbed slightly in 1976–77. *Editor & Publisher* said there were six more dailies, up to 1,762, and 11 more Sunday papers, up to 650. Daily circulation topped 60,977,011, while Sunday circulation topped 51,565,334. Circulation for the 7,530 weeklies reached 39,000,000 in 1977, according to the National Newspaper Association.

Dailies spent more than a billion dollars to cover the news. Readers paid some of this, with 68% of the papers charging 15¢ a copy. In readership surveys New Yorkers learned that the *News* reached 36% of the adults; the *Times*, 13.6%; and the *Post*, 9.2%.

Publishers sought higher circulations for 1978 by recruiting more trained personnel and adding supplements, special sections, and target-market features. The goal is worthwhile: U. S. readers spent more than $4.2 billion for papers in 1976, while Canadian readers spent $315 million. Greater revenues were forecast for 1977 and 1978, with readers contributing an increasingly large share.

The weekly *National Enquirer* led the nation in circulation, reaching 5,700,000 with its report on Freddie Prinze's death.

Strikes have declined, with only 11 in 1976, and fewer in 1977. The Newspaper Guild and the International Typographical Union appear nearer to merger. The International Mailers Union, United Paperworkers International Union, and International Printing and Graphic Communications Union (pressmen) expressed an interest in an all-inclusive union of some 750,000 members.

The United Press International celebrated its 70th birthday in 1977. Founded by E. W. Scripps as United Press, it now serves 7,000 clients. The Associated Press began transmitting complete New York Stock Exchange tables in 3.5 minutes, using its automated systems to move 10,000 words per minute.

Legislators continued their disputes with the press, offering 98 new bills in the U. S. Congress by mid-1977 that could curb reporting. The Reporters Committee for Freedom of the Press alerted publishers to this hostility of federal legislators.

The Federal Trade Commission stunned the industry with charges of discrimination against advertisers by the commonly accepted practice of offering discounts based on volume. The Los Angeles *Times* became the test target. *Editor & Publisher* editorially noted that the government practices such discrimination in its postal rates.

Carl Bernstein claimed in *Rolling Stone* magazine that 400 American journalists had cooperated with the Central Intelligence Agency during the past 25 years. Bernstein called their use "among the most productive means of intelligence-gathering employed by the CIA, and (it) continues today."

Early in 1977 the industry was subjected to a Federal Appeals Court decision that sought to outlaw most ownership arrangements involving newspapers and radio or television stations. *Editor & Publisher* reported that 79 joint newspaper-television ownerships in 74 cites would be affected, as well as 167 paper-radio combinations.

The death of the *National Observer* was widely mourned. Founded in 1962 by Dow Jones & Co., the weekly reported losses of $16.2 million during its career. It had difficulty attracting advertisers to its mixed audience. Sam Newhouse closed the 157-year-old *Long Island Press*, putting nearly 700 persons out of work. As 1977 ended a new *Trib* was promised for New York, despite many legal obstacles.

The trend to offset printing continued, with more than 1,200 dailies using this process. Advertising revenues reached a new high of $11 billion in 1977, and more was expected in 1978. Investigative reporters convened in Phoenix to probe the bombing death of one of their colleagues, Don Bolles of the *Arizona Republic*.

WILLIAM H. TAFT
University of Missouri

Puerto Rico's Supreme Court Justice José Trias Monte administers oath of office to the Commonwealth's new governor, Carlos Romero Barceló, January 2.

UPI

PUERTO RICO

Drought and continued decline in economic activity characterized the conditions in Puerto Rico during 1977, the first year of the administration of Gov. Carlos Romero Barceló of the New Progressive Party.

Lack of Rain—Loss of Jobs. The southern coast, where sugarcane can be grown only with the support of an extensive irrigation system, and the southern and eastern slopes of the central mountain chain were the hardest hit by the lack of precipitation. The northern coast, more urbanized and less in need of rain, received somewhat more moisture but still below normal expectations. The island escaped the effects of any devastating tropical storms, which have been notably infrequent in the Caribbean in recent years.

As a result of the drought in the farming areas, the agricultural production of the island declined markedly in 1977. The harvest of tobacco, a minor crop, was cut by 30%, due primarily to the lack of rain in the eastern highlands. The decline in production was partly responsible for the closing of Puerto Rico's largest tobacco processing plant, which left some 600 laborers unemployed.

Sugar Turned Sour. Drought, strikes, and plummeting prices all contributed to a state of crisis in the sugar industry. The cane harvest yielded 45,000 tons less sugar than had been anticipated. The total sugar production fell from 308,000 tons in 1976 to only 260,000 tons in 1977; this is considerably less than one third of what Puerto Rico used to produce during peak years. The cost of sugar production on the island was estimated to be about 26 cents per pound (454 g), but the U. S. federal government's guaranteed market price was only 13.5 cents a pound. In the light of this situation, the Puerto Rican government announced a 12-year plan to phase down the production of sugar and diversify agricultural activities. As a first step in this new program, the government, which is the sole producer of sugar on the island, closed four mills, throwing 1,212 mill workers and 1,760 field hands out of their jobs. The justification for this drastic step was that the public corporation producing sugar would eventually cut its losses, which were $57.7 million in 1976 and $65.5 million in 1977. The number of mills in Puerto Rico has declined from 40 in 1943 to the seven that are still in operation for the 1978 harvest.

Unemployment at All-Time High. The industrial sector of the economy, though not affected by the drought (except as noted above), was not much better off than agriculture. Unemployment figures, which at the beginning of the year were at an all-time high of 21%, rose to 22.2% in June, before easing again to the original percentage; they remained steady through the rest of the year. Attempts to stimulate the industrial sector and bring new manufacturing plants to the island were not successful.

Figures at the close of the fiscal year indicated that only 196 projects, providing 11,247 jobs, had been developed, while at least 83 plants closed during the same period. In contrast, 288 plants with 23,452 new jobs had been opened during the previous fiscal year. Puerto Rico has a growing population, and the return migration from the mainland has surpassed the outmigration, so the industrial picture of the island was far from bright.

Politics. As could be expected, the adverse economic situation had its effect on politics. Polarization of the political scene has increased with the growing dependence on U. S. governmental subsidies. The assassination in September for avowed political reasons of a prominent stateside managerial lawyer had all the appearance of a beginning terrorist campaign.

THOMAS G. MATHEWS
Institute of Caribbean Studies
University of Puerto Rico

--- **PUERTO RICO · Information Highlights** ---

Area: 3,435 square miles (8,897 km²).
Population (1976 est.): 3,200,000.
Chief Cities (1975): San Juan, the capital, 471,400; Bayamon, 180,800; Ponce, 176,100; Carolina, 142,-700.
Government (1976): *Chief Officers*—governor, Carlos Romero Barceló (New Progressive Party); secretary of state, Reinaldo Paniagua. *Legislature*—Senate, 29 members; House of Representatives, 54 members.
Education (1976): *Enrollment*—total, 688,592—elementary, 475,979; secondary, 212,613.
Manufacturing (major products): Sugar, molasses, rum.
Major Agricultural Products: Sugarcane, coffee, coconuts, tobacco, pineapples.

QUEBEC

Quebec's and Canada's economies continued to deteriorate in 1977. There was a sharp drop of the dollar, and the unemployment rate in Quebec reached a record 11.4% in October. This was coupled with a jump of about 9% in the cost of living. Despite its claims that federal policies govern the economy, the Quebec government was prodded to action: stimuli were given to small and average companies creating new jobs, and new public and private investments of more than $500 million were promised through mid-1979. Long-term programs were also put into motion: restructuring of the "soft" manufacturing sectors (textiles, shoes, clothing, furniture) and better use of natural resources. Tourism needs a boost; Quebec has lost 5–6% of its visitors annually for five years, while record crowds of Quebeckers vacation in the United States. Despite some long strikes, however, the social climate improved. Unusual summit meetings among business, labor, and government were held in the summer, followed by sectorial mini-summits. That, along with Finance Minister Jacques Parizeau's conservative budget, Quebec Hydro's solid administration, and lowering of costs at James Bay may have accounted for Moody's "AA" quotation on Quebec bonds.

Legislation. During the first session of the National Assembly, 36 laws were approved, including one providing free medication and full pension for all 65 years old or more, and another providing "democratic financing" of political parties. Law 101, the most controversial bill, was approved after four and a half months of bitter debate. The aim of the law is to frenchify public life, business, and education in Quebec. A complete public school system is maintained, however, for English-speaking Quebeckers (but not for future immigrants). A frenchification program for companies doing business in Quebec must be approved and started by 1983, although exceptions are allowed. Defiance of the law is slowly crumbling, except on judicial grounds, as Quebec subventions are cut in the case of children illegally registered in English schools. Premier René Lévesque, however, has promised flexibility.

The bill to create a "no-fault" public-private automobile insurance system met some opposition. So did bill 45, devised to force unions to use secret ballots to vote on strikes and to prevent companies from using "scabs." The "referendum bill" produced regular clashes. Inspired in part by European precedents, it aims at establishing machinery for referendums and at regulating the costs and length of campaigns.

Referendum Issues. Pre-referendum campaigns started late in the year. No less than four federal task forces were engaged in gathering ammunition and organizing opposition to the sovereignty-association thesis. The Quebec government contended that the province has lost $4–8 billion (U. S.) to Ottawa since 1961, while the federal government asserted that Quebec has received $1.7 billion in surplus. Polls showed a minority of less than 20% for complete secession, but a large majority (⅔) for a new constitution. Meanwhile, federal-provincial clashes were numerous, especially in the fields of communications, immigration, housing, and urban affairs. Other skirmishes occurred after public disclosure of illegal and criminal acts by the RCMP (Royal Canadian Mounted Police), such as burglary, seizure of documents, spying on the Parti Québécois, and arson. The Quebec government stated its intention to submit RCMP activities in Quebec to its authority and created an investigation commission. The solicitor general of Canada called the commission's legality into question.

Lévesque in France. René Lévesque's visit to France and the lavish reception he received, gave international publicity to his sovereignty-association platform. Although France asserted it would not meddle in Quebec and Canadian affairs, it promised support for Quebec's decision, whatever it would be—a subtle international warning that Quebec had allies it could count on in case of need.

Leaders in Politics. While business, labor, and leftists were sharp-shooting at the PQ, the Union Nationale played a cautious waiting game. The Liberals finally bounced back from their defeat and were searching for a new leader. Gérard D. Lévesque, Raymond Garneau, Claude Castonguay, Jean-Paul L'Allier, and even federal Finance Minister Jean Chrétien were all considered probable runners. Claude Ryan, editor of *Le Devoir,* refused to jump in. Jean Lesage, however, was placed at the head of the Liberal committee preparing the battle against the sovereignty-association thesis. Thus, the old leader of the "Quiet Revolution" and author of *Masters in Our House* found himself fighting his former companion, René Lévesque, who used to struggle beside him for Quebec autonomy.

JEAN-PIERRE WALLOT, *University of Montreal*

QUEBEC • Information Highlights

Area: 594,860 square miles (1,540,687 km²).
Population (1976 census): 6,234,445.
Chief Cities (1976 census): Québec, the capital, 177,082; Montréal, 1,080,546; Laval, 246,243.
Government (1977): *Chief Officers*—lt. gov., Hughes Lapointe; premier, René Lévesque (Parti Québécois); min. of finance, Jacques Parizeau; min. of intergovernmental affairs, Claude Morin; chief justice, Lucien Tremblay. *Legislature*—Legislative Assembly, 110 members.
Education (1976–77): *Enrollment*—public elementary and secondary schools, 1,318,800 pupils; private schools, 105,170; Indian (federal) schools, 4,700; post-secondary, 201,600 students. *Total school expenditures,* $2,824,519,000.
Public Finance (1977–78): *Revenues,* $10,895,000,000; *expenditures,* $11,535,000,000.
Personal Income (average weekly salary, July 1977): $248.03.
Unemployment Rate (August 1977, seasonally adjusted): 10.2%.
(All monetary figures are in Canadian dollars.)

Quebeckers for independence demonstrate in Montreal against Prime Minister Trudeau's stance of Canadian "unity," which they consider nothing but a fraud.

QUEBEC—SPECIAL REPORT:

The Threat of Secession

For a while the shock of the Parti Québécois (PQ) victory in Quebec, on Nov. 15, 1976, was softened by the illusion that power would dilute the new government's faith in sovereignty. Despite warnings from Premier René Lévesque, it was well into 1977 before Canadian and U. S. public opinion began to take seriously the threat of Quebec's secession. Then, instead of trying to gain a better understanding of the drive for sovereignty, too many seemed to be gambling on the outcome of the projected referendum. In fact, the province of Quebec and the nation of Canada are heading into a period of uncertainty that may last a decade or more, for no referendum nor ballot can permanently solve the present nexus of problems.

Trends and Issues. While polls have contradicted each other, a consistent trend since the spring of 1977 indicates that a large minority to a slight majority of Quebeckers would support sovereignty if coupled with an economic association with Canada. Although the idea of independence is gaining, only one Quebecker in five favors a total break. Thus, the propaganda prior to the referendum and the question asked (for instance, a mandate to negotiate sovereignty with economic association) will bear directly on the outcome.

Serious obstacles face both separatists and federalists. For the latter, it is hard to explain why unemployment in Quebec has been more than 8% for years; why bilingual Francophones in Quebec (80% of the population) earn less than unilingual Anglophones in similar jobs with the same qualifications; why they are the lowest paid of all ethnic groups and occupy relatively few directorships and management jobs; why 360,000 Quebeckers have left their province in the last ten years to seek better opportunities (in English) elsewhere; why federal ministers balk at protecting Quebec jobs in textiles, shoes, clothing, and furniture; and why so few federal

programs of economic and regional expansion materialize in Quebec. The PQ, on the other hand, has to convince Quebec voters that Canada will negotiate an economic association, despite public refusals by the western provinces and Ontario; that U. S. investors will not shy off, even if the government shows few socialist tendencies; that the provincial premiers' refusal to negotiate reciprocity in the matter of language is not a typical example of the kind of negotiations ahead; that, at worst, independent Quebec could find allies and markets.

Historical Background. Outsiders can hardly understand the Quebec problem in the highly assimilative context of North America. Although Canada was conquered by the British in 1760 and thereafter colonized by them, large numbers of British immigrants did not establish themselves in Quebec prior to 1815–20. By then, French Canadians numbered more than 300,000 and their heavy majority, coupled with the U. S. threat, had brought them concessions insuring the maintenance of their language, civil laws, and religion. Even so, they tried a national and democratic revolution in 1837–38, but being poorly planned, it was easily crushed. The Union Act of 1840, designed to assimilate them, and Confederation, in 1867, ratified the reality of a provincialized people, escaping assimilation, yet unable to become a separate nation. The dream of a *nation canadienne* was then replaced by the struggle for survival, *la survivance,* though, occasionally, some alleged injustices would awaken short-lived separatist movements.

The Modern Movement. Modern organizations for sovereignty grew out of other forces and ideologies. Industrialization, urbanization, growing social-security measures, the Depression, and World War II all helped to breed a hardening resistance to federal invasion of provincial affairs. To Quebeckers, provincial autonomy was essential because it gave them the only govern-

Leader René Lévesque traveled widely in quest of his party's victory. Here he is seen with a local candidate.

ment controlled by a French-speaking majority. That control was used during the "Quiet Revolution" of the 1960's to modernize Quebec. Those busy years of self-government in action convinced Quebec intellectuals and politicians that they could be both modernist and nationalist. The ideology of catching up, embodied in intellectuals like Pierre Elliott Trudeau, was left behind in the surge of a new ideology of development and participation along more nationalist lines. More and more French-speaking Quebeckers came to look upon the provincial government as their only real one and as the ideal tool by which their economic, social, and cultural goals could be achieved. The majority saw in stronger autonomy and more effective use of the province a means to dynamize the "nation." Others reasoned that a minority people, in a "two-nations" federal state, could succeed in saving its culture only if it could connect it to actual economic, social, and political roots. To them, the most important issue was not what *distinguished* French Quebeckers from other nations—notably their "culture" in the narrow sense—but what could make them *similar* in one essential respect: sovereignty. No concession could dilute this issue, since the dynamism of the "nation" was tied to its degree of self-government.

The Choices. From small fragments, democratic forces for sovereignty coalesced around René Lévesque in 1968 to form the PQ. Its relatively swift rise in popular esteem (23%, 30%, and 41% of the vote in the elections of 1970, 1973, and 1976) was not independent of the fade-out of the autonomy ideal under premiers Jean-Jacques Bertrand and Robert Bourassa from 1968 to 1976. This political vacuum in more traditional Quebec nationalism, together with the apparent leadership since the mid-1960's of French Canadians in a centralizing federal government, led to a polarization that distorts Quebec–Ottawa politics and excludes compromises. More and more, Quebeckers are faced with a choice between a centralized federalism, basing its appeal on multiculturalism and dollars, and the sovereignty-association of the PQ, described as the only viable "middle-of-the-road" course.

A referendum is supposed to settle the "Quebec question" once and for all. This is highly improbable. A federalist victory, whatever may be the mixture of that federalism, would hardly prevent a severe blow to the civil consensus, because a third or more of the population is likely to reject the basic rules of the Canadian system. Moreover, it would not eliminate the fact that a majority of French-speaking Quebeckers feel that they constitute a nation, with its own territory, institutions, language, half-government, and past history. To them, Canada cannot simply be a mosaic of numerous peoples, more or less equal, in which Quebec is just one province like the nine others. To them, French Quebec is a *nation québécoise*. True, they are divided on the concrete form their nationalism should take, and the majority still seems to believe they can succeed in a decentralized federal system. But the discovery of being a majority and a nation in Quebec, though slow in coming, could not be obliterated by a vote against secession. Of course, a PQ victory in the referendum would put on the provincial government enormous pressure to obtain an economic association with Canada and to secure a high standard of living within a short time. Only protracted negotiations can be foreseen.

Contradiction in Search of a Solution. Thus, the struggle is not between "federalists" and "separatists," but rather between different conceptions of federalism, tactically allied for the occasion, and views of sovereignty that range from total secession to a very decentralized version of the Canadian confederation. The exacerbation of the conflict is due not only to the lack of autonomous Quebec leadership since 1968, but also to the real aspirations and needs of English Canada for more "national" policies, reduction of regional disparities, and stronger national unity and prosperity. The two necessities clash: English Canada's need for more "national government," French Quebec's need for more autonomy. This contradiction, acute since the end of World War II, cannot be solved in the present context of one province against nine others and a federal government. Public opinion throughout Canada, however, may impose some compromises; it seems to be more and more favoring decentralization. But at the present, the question asked of Quebeckers is how can their nation best develop—in a revamped but still functioning Canadian federation, or outside it as a sovereign nation? The answer is at best problematic, and its significance will hinge on results, not rhetoric.

JEAN-PIERRE WALLOT

The language of instruction is one of the hottest issues in Quebec. While French became the official language in August 1977, the province is still bilingual, and store ads as well as road signs are posted in French and English.

Federalists have a hard time explaining why the French in Quebec, some 80% of the population, always seem to get the short end of the stick, be it in housing or employment.

PHOTOS JEAN-PIERRE LAFFONT/SYGMA

RECORDED SOUND

The year 1977 marked two important anniversaries in the era of sound reproduction: the centennial of its real beginning, Thomas A. Edison's demonstration of the first working phonograph, and the fiftieth anniversary of the release of *The Jazz Singer,* a motion picture that is generally credited with ushering in the age of the "talking movie."

The Acoustic Era. Edison's machine, depicted with fair accuracy on a 1977 commemorative stamp issued by the U. S. Post Service, was entirely a mechanical contrivance, without benefit of any electronic amplification. But aside from that, it differed hardly at all in operating principle from today's phono recording and reproducing apparatus.

Like many precocious inventions, Edison's phonograph was also premature. In 1877 no one could have envisioned today's prosperous recording industry—least of all Edison who, ever the utilitarian, predicted a brilliant future for the phonograph as an office dictating machine, an educational tool, and a general purpose mechanical servant with a voice. He generally failed in promoting his invention for any of these applications. Briefly it enjoyed brisk popularity as a novelty item, usually at staged demonstrations for the public, but within a few years its appeal had foundered. Almost ten years later the phonograph was revived by modifications made to it by Charles S. Tainter and Chichester A. Bell (nephew of Alexander Graham Bell), who called their new machine the "graphophone." One of these modifications was the substitution of a wax-coated cardboard cylinder (and later a solid wax cylinder) for Edison's tinfoil-covered metal drum. Recordings could be conveniently taken off the machine and replaced, and even used on other machines with relative ease. Ultimately, Edison and the graphophone developers joined forces and prospered supplying recorded cylinders to coin-operated phonographs, which became extremely popular in amusement arcades and the "phonograph parlors" of the early 1890's.

In 1887, Emile Berliner applied for a patent on a disc-playing phonograph, the "gramophone." Berliner's scheme provided for the mass duplication of recorded discs—first in hard rubber and then in shellac—by a molding process (mass duplication of cylinders could not be so easily achieved). Berliner suggested a rotational speed for his records of about 70 revolutions per minute, anticipating the future 78-rpm standard.

RCA's Trademark

Edison's Invention (1877)

Wind-up Phonograph (1902)

For a time the cylinder and disc competed, but by 1913 the practical advantages of the latter had all but driven the former from the marketplace.

By 1920, the acoustic phonograph was approaching its theoretical limits of development, and the expiration of basic patents, protecting the U. S. recording giants—Victor and Columbia—from competition was bringing new ideas and innovators into the recording field. One of these was AT&T's Bell Laboratories, whose engineers applied some of the technologies of the vigorous new medium of radio—microphones and vacuum-tube amplifiers in particular—to create an all-electronic recording system employing an electromagnetic recording "head" to vibrate the recording stylus. This was demonstrated in 1924. By 1925 there was an all electronic phonograph

First Orthophonic Machine (1925)

RCA

RCA Victrola (1946–47)

RCA

Late in 1877, Thomas Alva Edison had his laboratories build the first cylindrical recording device (p. 420). Edison demonstrated his invention with his own rendition of "Mary Had a Little Lamb." By the early 1900's, the painting "His Master's Voice" (top, p. 420) had become the trademark of the new Victor Talking Machine Company. A few of the many recording machines developed during the 100 years are pictured here.

RCA

The 45-RPM Record Player (1949)

SONY

Stereo System (1977)

(electromagnetic pickup cartridge, vacuum-tube amplifier, and loudspeaker) available to complement it, the Brunswick "Panatrope."

In cooperation with General Electric, Brunswick also offered a novel type of microphone in which a small mirror, vibrated by sound, reflected light of varying intensities onto a photoelectric cell. It is of interest not because it contributed significantly to the development of the phonograph (it did not), but because it belongs to the then emerging technology of motion-picture sound.

Talking Movies. *The Jazz Singer* of 1927 was far from the first motion picture with sound accompaniment recorded specifically for it. In 1913 Edison, as always in the thick of things, made 19 "talking" motion pictures. He used a phonograph synchronized with the film, as did

The Jazz Singer's "Vitaphone" process. The first real "talkies" would come in 1929, with General Electric's perfected "Photophone" system, based on work done as early as 1903 by Eugen Lauste and on the subsequent efforts of Theodore Case and Lee De Forest in the earlier 1920's.

The Photophone process exposed the motion-picture film itself to a sound-modulated light source. When developed, the film had an optical sound "track" that could be played by another light source within the projector and a photoelectric sensor. Later, as magnetic tape recording matured, it was possible to apply magnetic stripes to the film to carry the sound track. This improved fidelity, and it also made more convenient the application of several stripes to the film for multichannel (stereo) sound tracks, as pioneered by Walt Disney's *Fantasia* in 1940, using multiple optical and then magnetic tracks. George Lucas' film *Star Wars,* released in 1977, has an optical sound track encoded by the Sansui QS four-channel matrix system and processed by the Dolby noise reduction system developed for cinema.

Stereo and the LP. Stereo—or sound recorded and reproduced through more than one acoustical perspective, in order to create a spatial illusion—stood apart from the mainstream of sound-recording activity through much of its history. Bell Laboratories pursued it in the course of general investigations into acoustics and hearing, and in 1933 astounded visitors to Chicago World's Fair who, simply by donning a pair of stereo earphones, were aurally transported into a closed room where a mannequin with microphones in its ear cavities was seated. Magnetic tape, which in 1949 began to replace disc recorders in studio recording sessions, brought stereo to the home listener in 1956. It had also, in 1948, spurred development of a new phonograph record, the LP, better suited to receive the content of studio master tapes.

The first successful long-playing (LP) record was developed at CBS by Peter Goldmark and William S. Bachman. It not only multiplied the four-minute playing time typical of 12-inch (3 cm) 78's by a factor of about six; it also conferred a much quieter record material (Vinylite), a potentially higher standard of fidelity, and superior pickup cartridges. Its introduction lent great impetus to the quest for "high fidelity," which was just beginning to gather itself into an industry at this time.

In 1948 the first stereo LP's were met by widespread consumer confusion, but they prevailed to become the standard for recorded music throughout the world. In 1969 reports of a new recording technique being investigated by Acoustic Research, a high-fidelity company, precipitated the music industry into four-channel or *quadraphonic* sound.

In very short order Peter Scheiber of Audiodata had suggested a way to record four channels of information on an LP, and T. Inoue of the Japan Victor Corporation had countered with another. Competing noncompatible systems battled in the marketplace until, today, although work continues, many believe the four-channel phenomenon has run its course.

An announcement from Japan, late in 1977, spoke of a new type of audio record, an 1,800-rpm flexible disc recorded by a photographic process and intended to be played by a scanning laser. A joint development of three Japanese companies (Mitsubishi, Teac, and Tokyo Denka), it adapts technology evolved in Europe and the United States for video recording. Perhaps this is the first hint that recording techniques established so long ago by Edison are soon to be superseded.

RALPH W. HODGES
Technical Editor, "Stereo Review"

SOME POPULAR RECORDINGS OF 1977

CLASSICAL

BACH: *Christmas Oratorio.* Ameling, Baker, Tear, Fischer-Dieskau; Ledger (Angel)
BEETHOVEN: *Piano Sonatas Nos. 1, 7.* Richter; Barenboim (Angel)
BRUCKNER: *Symphonies Nos. 7, 8.* Böhm (Deutsche Grammophon)
CHOPIN: *Piano Music.* Zimerman (Deutsche Grammophon)
CIMAROSA: *Il Matrimonio segreto (The Secret Marriage).* Auger, Varady, Hamari, Davies, Fischer-Dieskau; Barenboim (Deutsche Grammophon)
DELIBES: *Coppélia* (complete ballet). Mari (Angel)
DVOŘÁK: *Quartets.* Prague Quartet (Deutsche Grammophon)
ELGAR: *Concerto for Cello.* Du Pré; Barenboim (Columbia)
GIULIANI: *Concerto in A for Guitar.* Romero (Philips)
GRANADOS: *Goyescas.* De Larrocha (London)
HANDEL: *Oboe Sonatas.* Roseman, Brewer (Nonesuch)
HAYDN: *Symphonies Nos. 44, 49.* Barenboim (Deutsche Grammophon)
LISZT: *Transcendental Etudes.* Arrau (Philips)
MENDELSSOHN: *Octet in E flat for Strings:* Cleveland and Tokyo Quartets (RCA)
MOZART: *Quartet in F for Oboe.* Koch, Amadeus Quartet (Deutsche Grammophon)
MUSSORGSKY: *Boris Godounov.* Lukomska, Gedda, Talvela; Semkow (Angel)
SCHUBERT: *Symphony No. 8.* Karajan (Angel)
STRAUSS, R.: *Concerto in D for Violin.* Hoelscher; Kempe (Angel)
TCHAIKOVSKY: *Symphony No. 4.* Abbado (Deutsche Grammophon)
VERDI: *Requiem.* Price, Baker, Luchetti, Van Dam; Solti (RCA)

POPULAR

AEROSMITH: *Draw the Line* (Columbia)
THE BEATLES: *Love Songs* (Capitol)
THE BEE GEES: *Children of the World* (RSO)
JACKSON BROWNE: *Running on Empty* (Asylum)
SHAUN CASSIDY: *Shaun Cassidy* (Warner)
JUDY COLLINS: *So Early in the Spring* (Elektra)
CROSBY, STILLS & NASH: *CSN* (Atlantic)
THE EAGLES: *Hotel California* (Asylum)
EARTH, WIND & FIRE: *All 'n All* (Columbia)
FLEETWOOD MAC: *Rumours* (Warner Brothers)
PETER FRAMPTON: *I'm In You* (A & M)
EMMYLOU HARRIS: *Luxury Liner* (Warner Brothers)
HEART: *Little Queen* (Portrait)
KISS: *Kiss Alive II* (Casablanca)
JERRY LEE LEWIS: *Country Class* (Mercury)
LORETTA LYNN: *I Remember Patsy* (MCA)
BARRY MANILOW: *Live* (Arista)
RANDY NEWMAN: *Little Criminals* (Warner)
JONI MITCHELL: *Hejira* (Asylum)
HARRY NILSSON: *Knnillssonn* (RCA)
ELVIS PRESLEY: *Moody Blues* (RCA)
QUEEN: *News of the World* (Elektra)
LINDA RONSTADT: *Simple Dreams* (Asylum)
BARBRA STREISAND: *Superstar* (Columbia)
STEELY DAN: *Aja* (ABC)
ROD STEWART: *Foot Loose & Fancy* (Warner Brothers)
JAMES TAYLOR: *JT* (Columbia)
WINGS: *Over America* (Capitol)
NEIL YOUNG: *American Stars 'n' Bars* (Reprise)

JAZZ

COUNT BASIE, DIZZY GILLESPIE, ELLA FITZGERALD, OSCAR PETERSON, MILT JACKSON: *Montreux '77* (Pablo)
COUNT BASIE and HIS ORCHESTRA: *Prime Time* (Pablo)
MILES DAVIS: *Water Babies* (Columbia)
DUKE ELLINGTON: *Intimate* (Pablo)
DAVE FRISHBERG: *Getting Some Fun Out of Life* (Concord)
ELMO HOPE: *Last Sessions* (Inner City)
KEITH JARRETT: *Staircase* (ECM)
GERRY MULLIGAN: *New Sextet, Idol Gossip* (Chiaroscuro)
WEATHER REPORT: *Heavy* (Columbia)

MUSICALS, MOVIES, AND TELEVISION

ANNIE: original cast (Columbia)
NEW YORK, NEW YORK: soundtrack (United Artists)
ROOTS: music from the television series (A & M)
STAR WARS: soundtrack (20th Century)

Evangelist Ruth Stapleton, sister of President Carter, speaks from the pulpit at London's Westminster Abbey.

Survey

World Jewry is currently experiencing a renaissance. It is marked by a return to tradition and a search for sources of personal and social transformation. Fictional works by popular authors continue to reflect this interest; and Hasidism, a traditional spiritual and mystical movement, has drawn the attention of Jews and non-Jews. Its significance is attested to by the awarding of a doctorate by the Jewish Theological Seminary in New York City to Zen Buddhist student Jacob Yuroh Teshima for his comparative study of Zen and Hasidism.

Reform Judaism, most modernistic of Jewish denominations, published a new home prayer book, *Gates of the House.* Traditional elements have been restored, sexist language has been eliminated, and a new covenant of life ceremony for girls on the eighth day after birth has been included.

The General Secretariat of the Islamic World League took a united stand against the film *Mohammad, Messenger of God,* also entitled *The Message.* Exception was taken to the film's qualification of traditional teachings. The Black Muslim movement in the United States, under the leadership of Wallace D. Muhammad, underwent a period of "revival and restoration of pure Islam." No longer known as the Nation of Islam, it represents itself as the World Community of Islam in the West.

Yogi Bhajan, leader of the fast-growing 3HO (Happy, Healthy, Holy organization) cult, was in difficulty with Sikh officialdom. Sikhism opposes various characteristics of the Bhajan's cult, including the teaching of yoga and vegetarianism. The 3HO claims 250,000 followers and 110 ashrams (retreats) worldwide.

The credibility of the *Book of Mormon* was again questioned. Three experts tend to agree that the handwriting of portions of Joseph Smith's manuscript and that of Solomon Spalding, Congregational minister and novelist who died in 1876, are one and the same.

Evangelicalism is a form of Christianity which emphasizes individual response to the full-

Followers of Catholic traditionalist Archbishop Lefebvre conduct a "sign-up" desk in a Paris church.

ness of salvation offered in Jesus Christ. In recent decades it has experienced a resurgence of power not unlike the "second awakening" of the early 19th century. Its strength is difficult to measure because it encompasses masses of Christians in the so-called mainline Protestant denominations, as well as denominations which promote its program. Recently, the movement has shown increased interest in social ethics.

Traditionalist Archbishop Marcel Lefebvre continued his crusade for the old Latin Mass and against ecumenism and communism. During a successful U. S. tour, he consecrated a church in Texas, said Mass, and attended several rallies.

RICHARD E. WENTZ, *Arizona State University*

Protestantism

Among well over 200 Protestant and Orthodox denominations, plus Roman Catholicism and Judaism, no single U. S. church has ever been strong enough to even contemplate challenging the traditional constitutional position that religion and government must be separate. Consequently, there is little danger of a "church-state" ever developing in the United States. But at the opposite side of the argument, there remains some uncertainty as to how the government will ensure the right of religious groups to remain free and to exercise their beliefs. During 1977 considerable debate developed over what control, if any, the government should have over religious groups. The conflict ensued because of the definition of what is "religious."

Early in the year, for example, the U. S. Internal Revenue Service defined those organizations engaged in activities that are "exclusively religious." Such groups contrast with organizations that engage in activities that may also be carried out by secular groups. Colleges, hospitals, homes for the aged and young, are enterprises that could be secular or religious. The IRS ruled that when a church unit engages in an activity that can be duplicated by a secular unit, then that church unit must file a tax return, even if no tax is owed.

In effect, the U. S. government was defining for the public what it considers "religious." Church groups were angered at what they believed to be an interference in religious matters. The Lutheran Council in the USA accused the IRS of "an unwarranted intrusion into the affairs of the church." The first amendment to the U. S. Constitution protects the freedom of worship and religion, but present court battles suggest that it is still unclear just how "worship" and "religion" are to be defined in order to grant that freedom. It is also unclear whether the granting of a definition itself constitutes a violation of the first amendment.

Sun Myung Moon is a Korean evangelist and industrialist who has developed a large following in the United States, especially among the young. But when his Unification Church sought tax exempt status in New York State, it was denied on the grounds that Unification is not a church. In a related case, a California judge

---

RELIGION—SPECIAL REPORT: Women

The most controversial religious issue of 1977 had to do with the ordination of women to the priesthood.

Roman Catholicism. In January, the Vatican issued an 18-page statement designed to dampen the hopes of Roman Catholics who believed the church was moving toward sharing the priestly ministry with women. Since Vatican Council II, Catholics have heard an increasing number of voices that questioned whether church tradition should be upheld and women barred from administering the sacraments and thus sharing fully in the previously all-male ministry of the church. Almost no one expected a drastic immediate change in the centuries-old practice of restricting the priesthood to males, yet advocates of new roles for women, most of them in Europe and North America, believed that their arguments in favor of change were being heard.

The Vatican declaration from the Sacred Congregation for the Doctrine of Faith decisively countered those arguments, though it was not cited as "infallible and irrevocable." This meant that some day the church could change its view, and many felt that not too long after the pontificate of Paul VI leadership may edge toward change. The current statement, however, was

so emphatic that papal successors would have greater difficulty making an easy transition.

The statement cheered church conservatives but inspired criticism from many theologians who faulted the Vatican both for the process by which the Pope and his colleagues arrived at the statement and the arguments used. For example, the distinguished Canadian Jesuit David Stanley resigned from the Pontifical Biblical Commission because this high-level body in its official report to the Pope found no biblical commands against such ordination. The papal statement contended that women must be excluded because in the central act of the priesthood, celebrating the Eucharist or Mass, there must be a "natural resemblance" between the priest and Christ. Critics contended that on those terms Gentiles could not be ordained, because Jesus sent out only Jews for the ministry.

The Episcopal Church. In the same month, the Episcopal Church in the United States followed up on actions taken in September 1976 in General Convention and began to ordain women. Before that action, 11 women were "irregularly" ordained, but as of January over 30 were authorized to carry on sacramental ministry. The first of the new ordinations occurred in

permitted the parents of five young adults, aged 21–25, to "reprogram" their children after their conversion to the Unification Church. Some supporters of Moon argued that this was a violation of their freedom of religion, and the Americans United for Separation of Church and State charged that the ruling was "a major defeat for religious liberty." In a statement, the National Council of Churches of Christ, the official body of American Protestantism, said that the Unification Church "is not a Christian Church," for its teachings are incompatible with Christian belief.

A meeting in St. Louis, Mo., in September prepared the way for the possible creation of "The Anglican Church in North America," a group of Episcopalians who are dissatisfied with the present liberal trend of their church. More than 1,750 persons, including 350 clergymen, considered whether the Protestant Episcopal Church in the U.S.A. had lost touch with the traditional faith. Most of those in attendance considered themselves Anglo-Catholics, and were particularly bothered by the manner in which the Episcopal Church has begun to accept women for ordination as priests. The dissidents also objected to their denomination's involvement in such ecumenical bodies as the World Council of Churches and the Consultation on Church Union.

One of the year's most emotional issues was homosexuality. In a special election in Florida's Dade County, Anita Bryant, a well-known entertainer, employed biblical language in her opposi-

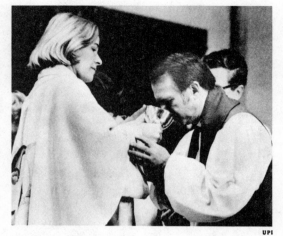

UPI

The Rev. Daphne W. P. Hawkes, a newly ordained Episcopal priest, distributes Holy Communion.

tion to an ordinance that had given persons of a homosexual preference the right to hold positions in public schools. The more liberal Protestant groups tended to support civil rights for homosexuals, but differed on whether or not to permit homosexuals to be ordained. Conservative groups, however, tended to agree with Ms. Bryant that homosexuality was a "sin," and based this assertion on biblical citations.

JAMES M. WALL
Editor, "The Christian Century"

Clergy

Indianapolis when Bishop Donal J. Davis ordained Jacqueline Means, a 40-year-old chaplain at a prison. One of the more celebrated rites involved 66-year-old black lawyer Pauli Murray.

With this action the Episcopal Church in the United States joined the Canadian Anglicans and others in including women. The Archbishop of Canterbury, F. Donald Coggan, a theological conservative, has gone on record as favoring the entrance of women to the priesthood, but the American Presiding Bishop John Maury Allin was reluctant to agree to the practice and offered his resignation to fellow bishops if they felt this would be in keeping.

In September, 1,500–2,000 dissidents against the action of General Convention the previous September met in St. Louis to discuss the possibility of schism and the formation of a new church in order to protest the change and other "modernizing" or "secularizing" adaptations. The Episcopal Church moved toward its deepest crisis in years.

Other Denominations. Curiously, these two widely-publicized events and trends drew attention away from the equally dramatic expansion in numbers of women ministering in other churches. World Lutheranism numbers almost

600 women in its ministry, and over 70 American denominations regularly ordain women. Certainly the trend is toward greater involvement of women, as a glance at United States seminary enrollment makes clear at once. The percentage of women preparing for the ministry in these professional schools has risen in just ten years from 3% to 40% and in four years alone there has been an increase from 1,077 to 3,025 in the Protestant schools. Almost two thirds of all people preparing for United Church of Christ ministry today are women, and over half of the ministerial students at Union Theological Seminary in New York City are women.

Achieving ordination does not spell the end of difficulties for women in churches which long ruled them out. In most mainline denominations there is some over supply of clergy, and all graduates have to vie for positions and often settle for small parishes for some years. In many cases women suffer in the competition, despite the fact that they win seminary honors and the majority of the parishioners are women. However, the changes of the 1970's have been so drastic that they cannot but have an effect on the churches that until now have held out.

MARTIN E. MARTY

UPI

A stained-glass window in a Philadelphia church recalls the work of John Neumann, canonized on June 19, 1977.

Roman Catholicism

Dominant themes in the Catholic Church throughout 1977 were the questions of human rights and world peace, with church-state confrontations over social injustice taking on particular significance in Third World nations.

Church unity and the authority of Pope Paul VI were directly challenged over the continuing implementation of Vatican II reforms by dissident French Archbishop Marcel Lefebvre (*see also* BIOGRAPHY), and by those seeking a greater role for women in the ministry. Problems in missionary areas included the slaying of priests, religious, and lay catechists.

Church-state clashes occurred in several Latin American nations, including Brazil, Argentina, Chile, Paraguay, El Salvador, Nicaragua, and Guatemala, as bishops became outspokenly critical of military regimes. Missionaries were murdered in Rhodesia and Central America; martial law was denounced by Catholic leaders in the Philippines; Congolese Cardinal Emile Biayenda was kidnapped and slain in a tribal feud; and church leaders in South Africa confronted the apartheid policy of the government on power-sharing with blacks and on the question of integrated church schools.

At about the same time, an international Anglican-Catholic commission issued a statement on authority which expressed a consensus that some kind of universal primacy be exercised by the bishop of Rome. A subsequent international report on Methodist-Catholic dialogue affirmed a common understanding on spirituality, salvation, the Eucharist, and the ministry.

In sporadic outbursts of dissent, a Canadian theologian, Father David Stanley, resigned from the Vatican Biblical Commission over the Vatican's handling of the women's ordination document; Memphis, Tenn., Bishop Carroll Dozier charged a high Vatican official with misrepresenting his two 1976 "reconciliation rites" for lapsed Catholics; and West Germany's bishops expressed strong dissatisfaction with Father Hans Kung's theological writings.

In May, the U. S. bishops revoked their excommunication sanction against Catholics who divorce and remarry outside the Church, and they asked the Vatican to allow the optional practice of Communion in the hand, which was later granted.

While Pope Paul was cementing relations with Eastern European nations by receiving Hungary's Communist Party chief, Janos Kadar, and naming a new Czechoslovak cardinal, Frantisek Tomasek, a group of 30 theologians meeting in the United States urged the planning of a Third Vatican Council.

A five-member commission of the Catholic Theological Society of America issued a controversial study on human sexuality which stressed the use of an informed conscience in making moral decisions rather than rigid church norms. Several bishops and theologians criticized the study as harmful to church teaching and authority. American bishops attending the canonization of John Cardinal Neumann, fourth bishop of Philadelphia, were told by Pope Paul to stand firm in the face of challenges to Church doctrine and authority.

Sharbel Makhlouf, a Lebanese hermit monk who died in 1898, became the first member of the Eastern rite to be canonized.

President Jimmy Carter named David Walters, a 60-year-old Miami lawyer, to be his personal representative to the Vatican.

So-called "pro-life" forces in the American church continued to put pressure on state and federal legislators to work for a human life amendment to the U. S. Constitution which would override the 1973 Supreme Court rulings permitting elective abortions.

Catholics were in the majority as some 50,000 charismatic Christians gathered in Kansas City, Mo., in July, for the first interreligious conference on the Charismatic Renewal. Emerging from the conference was a strong ecumenical witness to Christian unity.

Prior to the month-long Synod of Bishops in Rome, which reaffirmed the church's commitment to religious education, Pope Paul named Abbot-Primate Rembert Weakland of the Benedictine order to be archbishop of Milwaukee.

ROBERT L. JOHNSTON
Religious News Service

Members of the greater Washington Jewish community and their supporters hold a pro-Israel rally near the White House in October.

UPI

Judaism

The 1977 event of dominant interest to Jews was the change in the Israeli government which brought to power a nationalist party under the premiership of religious-tradition-oriented Menahem Begin. The change exercised an impact with ramifications for world Jewry.

Most importantly, the issue of Jewish identity, known as the "Who is a Jew" question, was revived as the government introduced a measure to invest the Orthodox rabbinate with exclusive power of definition. American leaders of Conservative and Reform Judaism, believing this development to be a threat to "Jewish pluralism," called for united action to counter it.

Israeli governmental action affecting other basic issues with socio-religious implications involved proposals to limit the existing abortion law, to prevent autopsies without family consent, to ban pornographic films, to prohibit the marketing of pork in Jewish population centers, and to introduce a program of traditional education into secular schools.

The most dramatic change was marked by the reevaluation of governmental policy toward Judea and Samaria, parts of Biblical Israel captured in the Six Day War. Based on a nationalist-religious conviction of the Jews' historic right to the region, settlement on several sites by the religious pioneer group Gush Emunim was legalized. The move stirred waves of response within Judaism. Jews everywhere watched with anticipation late-in-the-year developments, including the visit of the Egyptian president to Israel, holding out hope of peace.

Continued repressive policies against Jews living in the Soviet Union and restriction on emigration to Israel elicited worldwide protest. Mass arrest in Moscow of organizers of a symposium on Jewish culture prompted solidarity symposia by scholars in several U. S. cities, while in New York thousands rallied to protest the charge of treason against Jewish activist Anatoli Sharansky. An international coalition of women demonstrated for the rights of Soviet Jews at the opening of the European Security Conference in Belgrade.

Proliferation of neo-Nazi activities in Germany and Austria, anti-Semitic excesses in Argentina, Arab anti-Jewish propaganda in Mexico, and continued Arab terrorist attacks in Israel caused grave concern. Representatives of Arab Jews in Israel appealed to the president of Syria on behalf of 4,000 Jews living in Syria under severe restrictions.

The "good fence" between Israel and Lebanon, where a team of Israeli physicians and nurses treat Arab sick and wounded, remained a spark of hope for future possibility of peace.

See also ISRAEL; MIDDLE EAST.

LIVIA E. BITTON JACKSON, *Israel*
On leave, City University of New York

Orthodox Eastern Church

Plans for the convocation of a Great Council of all Orthodox bishops in the world continued under the leadership of the Patriarchate of Constantinople. The Church of Antioch, headed by Patriarch Elias IV, was appointed to prepare the agenda for dealing with the problem of the canonical unification of the various Orthodox National dioceses in Western Europe and America. The Patriarch visited the United States and Canada, meeting with Christian leaders and investigating the life and work of the Orthodox in these countries.

In May, a meeting was held in Geneva to discuss a date for celebrating Easter among the Orthodox and to seek a common date with non-Orthodox Christians for marking the feast.

In the USSR, Metropolitan Juvenaly replaced Metropolitan Nikodim as the head of the department of foreign affairs of the Moscow Patriarchate. The Russian church canonized Metropolitan Innocent of Moscow on October 6. The canonization of this famous 19th century missionary priest, John Veniaminov, who spent most of his life in Siberia and Alaska and is called Alaska's apostle of Orthodoxy, was done quietly and without the expected participation of bishops from the United States.

His Beatitude Elias IV, patriarch of the Church of Antioch, confers with President Carter in July.

In Africa, Bishop George Gathuna of Kenya officially charged the local Greek Metropolitan Frumentius with racism. In letters to the Patriarchate of Alexandria, under whose auspices the Nairobi cleric performs, and government leaders, Gathuna called for Frumentius' dismissal.

Orthodox church leaders continued to voice opposition to the ordination of women. However, at a world Congress of Orthodox Women in Rumania in July, delegates called for a greater participation of women in church life.

Metropolitan Ireney Bekish, the primate of the Orthodox Church in America, resigned, and Metropolitan John Martin succeeded the late Metropolitan Orestes P. Chornock as head of the Carpatho-Russian Orthodox Diocese. Archbishop Makarios of Cyprus died in August, leaving the divisions in the Cypriot Church caused by his political activity to survive him.

REV. THOMAS HOPKO
St. Vladimir's Orthodox Theological Seminary

Islam

Throughout 1977, Muslim governments and international organizations endeavored to promote harmony within the Islamic community, but divisive issues persisted. The Eighth Islamic Foreign Ministers Conference in Tripoli, Libya, attempted to settle the conflict between the Philippine government and the Moro National Liberation Front, which seeks autonomy for Muslim regions in the southern islands. Libya and Saudi Arabia had earlier failed to resolve this problem, and the conference did not effect a satisfactory solution. Saudi Arabia and the United Arab Emirates also tried to soothe disagreements among Pakistani Muslims, but political party concerns thwarted their efforts.

Signs of cooperation did appear, however. At the first international economic conference of Islamic countries in London, Karim Gaye of Senegal urged delegates to form a common market to attain a stronger voice in political and economic affairs. Further examples of Islamic cooperation included Saudi Arabia's $15-million contribution to the Islamic Solidarity Fund and its $10-million donation to support Islamic universities in Africa. Other countries added another $10 million to the Solidarity Fund.

Violence stemming from religious differences flared in Egypt in 1977, when demonstrators from conservative religious organizations charged the government with abandoning basic Islamic principles. The disturbances culminated in the assassination of a former cabinet minister and several bombing incidents in Cairo. Numerous people affiliated with right-wing religious groups were arrested.

KENNETH J. PERKINS
University of South Carolina

Far Eastern Religions

Kumbh Mela is the Hindu Jar Festival. The term "jar" harks back to a nectar which was involved in a cosmic struggle between gods and demons. The battle was fought at the point of confluence of the Jumna and Ganges rivers, where they also join with a mythical underground river, the Saraswati. Drops of nectar fell into the waters and return every twelve years to sweeten them. This is the occasion for pilgrimage and ritual bathing. In January 1977 the configuration of sun, moon, and stars was exactly as at the original creation, according to many Hindu holy men. Accordingly, that time was the holiest in all of history for bathing at the Sangam (sacred confluence). Millions of the Hindu faithful observed it.

In the Philippines the Moro National Liberation Front continued to struggle for control of 13 provinces which have been traditionally Muslim. Seventy percent of the population in the contested area is Christian as the result of recent immigration.

Gyalwa Karmapa XVI, second ranking holy man of Tibetan Buddhism, moved into headquarters in San Francisco. The popularity of Tibetan doctrines and teachings continues to grow. Its methods for increasing human response to the chain of compassion have become popular among intellectuals. It is difficult to judge the strength of the movement; however, Karmapa participated in consecration rites for a monastery in Kent, N. Y.

The restoration of a 9th century Buddhist temple in Borobudur, Indonesia, resulted in the discovery of the remains of four previous shrines. This made the location extremely important for Buddhist history and development.

RICHARD E. WENTZ

RHODE ISLAND

Nineteen seventy-seven saw problems at the state institutions take center stage. In August, Federal Judge Raymond J. Pettine ordered the state to close the maximum security building at the Adult Correctional Institution within twelve months, and make other reforms under his supervision. Gov. J. Joseph Garrahy, inaugurated in January, thus faced a new and acute crisis at the prison as well as related problems at the Ladd School for the retarded and elsewhere.

Environmental questions were in the news. The Federal Power Commission proposed a liquefied natural gas terminal for Narragansett Bay. The governor attacked this plan.

A tragic fire struck Providence College in December, killing seven young women students.

The Economy. A solid economic upturn continued during 1977. In June, a study showed that Rhode Island was recovering at a rate paralleling that of the national economy. In the past the state has lagged behind. In the early fall, manufacturing jobs were continuing to increase and projections indicated that this trend would continue.

Controversy over development of the abandoned Navy land was still in full swing four years after the pullout was announced, with environmental impact studies in progress.

Government. The 1977 session of the General Assembly began under new leadership. In the House major reforms were instituted to open up the legislative process.

It proved possible to balance the budget with no new taxes, and indeed to remove the sales tax on clothing. A new state scholarship system was instituted with more generous funding. Departments of Elderly Affairs and Environmental Management were created to consolidate services in those areas, and a comprehensive auto inspection system was set up.

Politics. Maneuvering for the 1978 election year began during 1977. Republican Mayor Vincent A. Cianci, Jr., of Providence was talking about running for governor, though he did not rule out a quest for reelection.

RHODE ISLAND · Information Highlights

Area: 1,214 square miles (3,144 km²).
Population (1976 est.): 927,000.
Chief Cities (1970 census): Providence, the capital, 179,116; Warwick, 83,694; Pawtucket, 76,984.
Government (1977): *Chief Officers*—governor, J. Joseph Garrahy (D); lt. gov., Thomas R. DiLuglio (D). *Assembly*—Senate, 50 members; House of Representatives, 100 members.
Education (1976–77): *Enrollment*—public elementary schools, 97,338 pupils; public secondary, 75,035; nonpublic, 32,300; colleges and universities, 61,716 students. *Public school expenditures,* $293,413,000 ($1,503 per pupil).
State Finances (fiscal year 1976): *Revenues,* $1,007,025,000; *expenditures,* $980,430,000.
Personal Income (1976): $5,866,000,000; per capita, $6,331.
Labor Force (July 1977): *Nonagricultural wage and salary earners,* 372,100; *unemployed,* 36,700 (8.3% of total force).

Democratic Senator Claiborne Pell is up for reelection in 1978 and began campaign preparations in 1977 by appointing his finance chairman. Rumors of primary challenges for his seat circulated, and several persons showed interest in the Democratic mayoralty nomination in Providence.

Tourism. Newport had another busy summer following the "Tall Ships" of 1976, highlighted by the America's Cup races. This further enhanced the city's effort to substitute tourist business for the lost naval bases.

ELMER E. CORNWELL, JR.
Brown University

RHODESIA

For Rhodesia, 1977 was another year of tension, insecurity, and bloody guerrilla warfare. The problem of how to achieve a negotiated transfer from the white minority government to a black majority one, as well as the question of which black leaders should rule the state, seemed no nearer to resolution. A second Anglo-American attempt to find a formula collapsed, in spite of eight months of meetings, shuttle diplomacy, international pressure, and fresh starts. Prime Minister Ian Smith returned to his own alternative plan for an internal settlement with the more moderate black leaders within the country. His public acceptance, on November 24, of universal adult suffrage was his most dramatic concession since the abortive Geneva talks began in 1976. The outcome of his proposals, like the test of their genuineness, could not be foreseen. Neither London nor Washington believes that a settlement can be achieved without inclusion of the loosely allied Patriotic Front leaders, Joshua Nkomo and Robert Mugabe, and their guerrilla forces. These two leaders condemned the latest Smith moves and anyone responding to them. Smith's plans centered on Bishop Abel Muzorewa, the Rev. Ndabaningi Sithole, and their organizations. At the end of November, both leaders agreed to enter preliminary talks. The Patriotic Front responded by reiterating its demands for a handover of power to the guerrilla forces.

The Anglo-American Plan. The demise of the 1976 Geneva conference was revealed on Jan. 24, 1977, when Ivor Richard, the British chairman, stated that Smith had rejected his latest proposals. The same day, Smith announced his intention of seeking an internal settlement with leaders of his own choosing. He promised the removal of much discriminatory legislation. He had, it appeared, not a transfer of government to blacks in mind, but a "broad-based" administration; he failed to attract either Bishop Muzorewa or the Rev. Sithole. On April 19, following an eight-day mission to the neighboring ("front-line") presidents, the nationalist leaders, and prime ministers Smith and Vorster (of South Africa), British Foreign Secretary

Trainees prepare to join the Selous Scouts, a Rhodesian military unit created in 1974 to specialize in combating guerrillas.

UPI

David Owen announced a new U. S.-British plan for a constitutional conference to be held in June or July. On May 6, he and U. S. Secretary of State Cyrus Vance both announced that instead of a full-scale conference a series of lower-level meetings would be held. A constitutional conference would be called only when sufficient agreement had been reached. The Anglo-American plan was presented to all the leaders involved between August 27 and September 1 and quickly ran into difficulties. Smith did not reject the plan outright, but took exception to the dismantling of government forces in favor of an international force, his own replacement by a British resident commissioner, and the absence of constitutional guarantees to whites in return for surrendering power. The Patriotic Front leaders demanded that their guerrilla forces supervise the transitional period, and refused to entertain special minority rights. Fresh from an overwhelming election victory on August 31, Smith said he would move swiftly on his own plan for an internal settlement. Such a plan would bypass Britain and the United States but above all the Patriotic Front, which in January had been recognized by the "front-line" presidents and the Organization of African Unity. When Britain's resident commissioner designate, Lord Carver, and the UN special representative, Gen. Prem Chand, arrived in October to try to arrange a cease-fire, the Anglo-American initiative had collapsed.

The War. The guerrilla war intensified, and civilian as well as military casualties increased. In August, it was reported that of 375 security personnel killed since 1973, 155 had been killed in 1977; of a total loss of 3,174 guerrilla fighters, 984 were killed during the same period. Three events especially claimed public attention. The first was the murder, on February 6, of four nuns and three priests at St. Paul's Mission, Musami, 70 miles (110 km) northeast of Salisbury. The second was the bombing of a large, crowded Salisbury store at midday, June 6, which killed 11 and wounded 76 more.

And on November 23–26, Rhodesian air and ground forces raided two camps inside Mozambique and claimed to have killed more than 1,200 guerrillas and taken much war materiel. In October, a third battalion of African Rifles was added to the counter-insurgency forces. The guerrilla forces within Rhodesia were commonly estimated at 3,000.

Domestic Affairs. Challenged by the defection of extremists in his party, who opposed his suggested reforms, and the loss of his two-thirds majority in Parliament, Prime Minister Smith, at the end of July, called for a general election on August 31. As a result, he won 90% of the white electorate's vote and all of the 50 white seats in Parliament. Clearly, the whites still regarded him as their best representative and rejected what was then known of the Anglo-American plan. In March, the U.S. Congress repealed the so-called Byrd Amendment which since 1971 had permitted U. S. companies to import chrome and ferro-chrome in violation of the UN sanctions against Rhodesia. The country continued to lose emigrants; those leaving were generally said to number more than 1,000 a month.

As the year closed, Bishop Muzorewa and the Rev. Sithole, claiming that the large majority of Africans supported them, not the Patriotic Front, stressed to the British foreign secretary that any settlement without them, and with the Front, was unthinkable.

R. B. BALLINGER
Rhode Island College

─── **RHODESIA · Information Highlights** ───

Official Name: Rhodesia.
Area: 150,803 square miles (390,580 km²).
Population (1977 est.): 6,800,000.
Chief Cities (1975 est.): Salisbury, the capital, 555,000; Bulawayo, 339,000.
Government: *Head of state,* John Wrathall, president (took office Dec. 1975). *Head of government,* Ian Smith, prime minister (took office 1964).
Monetary Unit: Rhodesian dollar (0.61 R. dollar equals U. S.$1, Dec. 1976).
Major Agricultural Products: Tobacco, sugar, tea, groundnuts, cotton, corn, millet, sorghum.

RUMANIA

Human and natural upheavals disturbed the normally placid Rumania in 1977.

Domestic Affairs. There were major changes in the party and governmental hierarchies, allegedly to improve coordination between them. Nicolae Ceauşescu, secretary general of the Rumanian Communist Party and president of the republic, appeared to gain in personal power. His wife, Elena, was appointed to the enlarged Permanent Bureau, the party's highest decision-making body. His brother-in-law, Gheorghe Petrescu, was appointed secretary of state for the machine-building industry. His son, Nicu, was elected head of the party's youth organization during 1976.

For the first time in many years, the tough Communist regime faced serious domestic challenge. As elsewhere in Eastern Europe, a number of political dissidents charged the government with violating the Helsinki Agreement on human rights, which Rumania had signed in 1975. In February, Paul Goma, a well-known writer and political critic, and nine other activists appealed publicly to the signatory powers, charging the Rumanian government with breaches of constitutional rights of assembly, speech, press, religion, and inviolability of the home, correspondence, and telephone communication. Ceauşescu denounced the group as "traitors," and in April Goma was arrested. In general, the Rumanian regime handled the situation with less harshness and greater success than the Soviet Union and other bloc members. Fewer critics were jailed. Instead, their employment was cut off and they were offered blanket permission to emigrate. In May, Goma himself was freed, as part of the general amnesty declared by Ceauşescu in honor of the 100th anniversary of Rumanian independence, May 9. By June 30, the regime felt secure enough to announce that henceforth government censorship of the media would become self-censorship.

More threatening were the mass demonstrations and strikes by tens of thousands of miners that began in August. Seizing government representatives as hostages, the strikers denounced

PHOTOS UPI

A major earthquake hit Rumania on March 4, centering on Bucharest (photos) and other industrial centers. Some 1,500 persons were reported dead, 11,000 were injured, and 80,000 were left homeless. Damage was estimated at $2 billion.

────── RUMANIA · Information Highlights ──────

Official Name: Socialist Republic of Rumania.
Location: Southeastern Europe.
Area: 91,700 square miles (237,500 km²).
Population (1977 est.): 21,700,000.
Chief Cities (1974 met. est.): Bucharest, the capital,
1,682,000; Constanta, 262,000; Ploieşti, 233,000.
Government: *Head of state,* Nicolae Ceauşescu, presi-
dent and secretary general of the Communist Party
(took office 1965). *Head of government,* Manea
Manescu, premier (took office March 1974). *Legisla-
ture* (unicameral)—Grand National Assembly.
Monetary Unit: Leu (4.96 lei equal U. S.$1, Nov. 1977).
Manufacturing (major products): Construction materials,
metal, chemicals, machinery, processed foods, textiles, petroleum products.
Major Agricultural Products: Corn, sugar beets, potatoes, wheat, rye, sunflower seeds.

the inadequacy of food, housing, consumer
goods, and pensions. Although Ceauşescu and
other high-ranking officials met with the protestors and promised improvement, unrest continued in the Jiu Valley to year-end, requiring
several thousand troops to be sent to the area.
Sympathetic repercussions were felt in factories
in Brasov and Bucharest.

Economy. In May, the Occidental Petroleum
Corporation completed negotiations to supply
Rumania with up to 27.3 million tons of coal
for its steel industry through 1987. The $2
billion deal was a breakthrough in East-West
trade and, with Rumania advancing $53 mil-
lion to help construct the mine in Virginia, the
first major investment by a socialist state in the
United States was completed. In February, the
World Bank approved a $60 million loan to
Rumania for an irrigation project, and in April
the Rumanians announced the discovery of oil
deposits of undetermined size off the Black Sea
coast.

Foreign Affairs. In July, in expressing support for the Spanish Communist Party's public
rejection of Soviet domination, the Rumanian
leadership reiterated its position that every communist party must be free to pursue its own
policies. While offering to mediate between
Arabs and Israelis, Ceauşescu continued to insist on the Israeli withdrawal from all occupied
Arab lands and the right of the Palestinians to
their own state and representation at any Geneva
conference on the Middle East.

JOSEPH F. ZACEK
State University of New York at Albany

SASKATCHEWAN

Resource Development. Saskatchewan's top
priority in 1977 was the exploration and development of oil and natural gas to prevent energy
shortage. Higher rates to consumers inhibited
waste of diminishing supplies.

The Potash Corporation of Saskatchewan
bought its third potash mine from West German
and French interests. It is located at Lanigan,
70 miles (113 km) southeast of Saskatoon.

Work progressed on the 300-Mw thermal
power plant, a coal-powered operation, on the
East Poplar River at Coronach, 2 miles (3 km)

north of the Montana border. A dam, creating
a 6-mile (9.5-km) reservoir to be used for cooling purposes, has been studied by an International Joint Commission, which ensures that at
least half the flow of the river will pass on to
the United States.

Agriculture. Prospects for a bumper wheat
crop of 420.4 million bushels (148.1 million hl)
were substantially degraded when wet weather
hampered the harvest and lowered yields in
northern Saskatchewan. For the first time in five
years, farmers were caught in a cost-price
squeeze, and the province was faced with a
slowdown of economic growth.

Farm costs have risen about 10% per year,
while the price of wheat dropped from approximately $5.50 to as low as $2.40 per bushel
(35 l) over a two-year period.

Elections. Three by-elections left the New
Democratic party still holding 29 seats in the
legislature, with a substantial victory in Pelly
constituency. The Liberals lost both Saskatoon-
Sutherland and Prince Albert-Duck Lake to the
Progressive Conservatives. The latter was a
Liberal stronghold, made vacant by former
Premier David Steuart's appointment to the
senate.

In June, Colin Thatcher, a legislator, quit
the provincial Liberal party to join the Progressive Conservatives. Son of the late Premier
Ross Thatcher, he was incensed by the control
the federal party wielded over Saskatchewan
Liberals. Both Progressive Conservatives and
Liberals now hold 11 seats, and Saskatchewan
is in the unique position of having no official
opposition party in the legislature.

Health Care. The first step in a 10-year,
province-wide hospital upgrading program began with the construction of new radiotherapy
facilities in the Cancer Clinic at Regina's Pasqua
Hospital. The $66-million program continues
with a major expansion at Regina General Hospital which will necessitate expropriation of 36
homes. Five new hospitals were opened in
rural areas, with more on the drawing board.

DOROTHY HAYDEN
Regina Public Library

────── SASKATCHEWAN · Information Highlights ──────

Area: 251,700 square miles (651,900 km²).
Population (1976 census): 921,323.
Chief Cities (1971 census): Regina, the capital, 149,-
593; Saskatoon, 133,750; Moose Jaw, 32,581.
Government (1977): *Chief Officers*—lt. gov., George
Porteous; premier, Allan Blakeney; atty. gen., Roy
Romanow; min. of culture and youth and min. of
educ., Ed Tchorzewski; chief justice, E. M. Culliton.
Legislature—Legislative Assembly, 60 members.
Education (1976–77): *Enrollment*—public elementary and
secondary schools, 216,050 pupils; private schools,
1,480; Indian (federal) schools, 5,910 students; post-
secondary, 16,960 students. *Total expenditures,*
$343,770,000.
Public Finance (1977–78 est.): *Revenues,* $1,410,300,000;
expenditures, $1,500,000,000.
Personal Income (average weekly salary, July 1977):
$240.86.
Unemployment Rate (August 1977, seasonally adjusted):
4.0%.
(All monetary figures are in Canadian dollars.)

In May, Saudi Arabia's Crown Prince Fahd was escorted in Washington by Secretary of State Vance.

UPI

SAUDI ARABIA

Shaping a new economy on the basis of immense oil revenues while maintaining existing conservative values continued to be Saudi Arabia's chief concern in 1977.

Finance and Economy. The $142,000,000,000 five-year development plan was readjusted in 1977 in order to make it more compatible with the economic structure of the country. Acute shortage of port facilities, housing, and skilled manpower forced planners to scale down the projected Jubail steel plant and to extend completion dates for the gas distribution system. Commodity price controls and subsidies for food were used to reduce the 30% annual inflation. The construction of ports, roads, housing, and an industrial infrastructure began to move from the planning to the execution stage.

Oil production and revenue continued to be high. In 1976 oil production averaged 8,000,000 barrels (1,080,000 metric tons) per day. In the first six months of 1977 it was 9,300,000 barrels (1,100,000 tons) despite the fire in a pumping station near Dhahran in May. Government revenue, obtained mostly from oil, was estimated to be $41,000,000,000 in 1977.

The United States bought twice as much oil from the Saudis in 1977 as in 1976. In return, it sold $4,000,000,000 worth of goods to Saudi Arabia.

About one third of the Saudi 1977 budget of $31,000,000,000 was spent on defense, but larger amounts were also earmarked for education than ever before. Saudi Arabia in 1977 became the third largest investor in International Monetary Fund reserves, with an equity of $5,000,-000,000. Estimates of government assets abroad ranged from $28,000,000,000 to $46,000,000,-000.

Foreign Affairs. In December 1976, Saudi Arabia announced that it opposed the decision of the Organization of Petroleum Exporting Countries (OPEC) to raise oil prices by 15%. Instead, Saudi Arabia increased its prices by only 5%. The split between the country and OPEC threatened in 1977 to break the agreement to maintain high prices for oil, since purchasers naturally pressed the Saudis to expand their sales. A visit by French President Valéry Giscard d'Estaing in January was highlighted by a Saudi agreement to sell France 30% more oil in 1977–79 than in the previous three years.

Saudi Arabia's moderation in oil was matched by its role as a mediator of Arab differences and a donor to Arab causes. A compromise in the Lebanese civil war had been engineered in Riyadh in 1976. In July 1977, Saudi Arabia pledged to pay for Egypt's armaments for the next five years. Loans were made to Lebanon, Yemen, and Djibouti and other African states.

In May, Crown Prince Fahd visited Washington, where he extolled the special relationship existing between the two countries, while deploring U. S. opposition to the Arab boycott of U. S. firms doing business with Israel. Saudi purchase of the 40% of Arabian American Oil Company stock still held by American oil companies had not been completed by the end of 1977.

Government. King Khalid was in London from February to April 1977 for medical treatment. Crown Prince Fahd ran the government in Khalid's absence. No major changes were made in the Saudi government during the year. The king maintained domestic stability while governing without a constitution, parliament, and political parties.

WILLIAM L. OCHSENWALD
Virginia Polytechnic Institute

───── **SAUDI ARABIA • Information Highlights** ─────

Official Name: Kingdom of Saudi Arabia.
Location: Arabian Peninsula in southwest Asia.
Area: 830,000 square miles (2,149,690 km²).
Population (1977 est.): 7,600,000.
Chief Cities (1976 est.): Riyadh, the capital, 667,000; Jidda, 561,000; Mecca, 367,000.
Government: *Head of state and government,* Khalid ibn Abd al-Aziz al-Saud, king (acceded March 1975).
Monetary Unit: Riyal (3.53 riyals equal U. S.$1, July 1977).
Manufacturing (major products): Petroleum products, cement, fertilizers, iron and steel.
Major Agricultural Products: Dates, vegetables, wheat.

SINGAPORE

Singapore continued its steady, though somewhat slowed, progress toward status as a developed nation. The People's Action Party (PAP) continued to provide firm leadership in 1977.

Economy. The 1977–78 budget was similar to the budget for fiscal 1976–77, but included a slightly larger deficit. Gross domestic product was up 7% in 1976 and about the same growth was predicted for 1977. Unemployment remained at the 4–5% level. Singapore's per capita gross national product has exceeded $1,000, thus threatening the removal of the republic from the "underdeveloped" rolls. Such an action would be costly to Singapore in the international marketplace. Long-term, the action may be inevitable in view of the government's prediction that per capita GNP (now $2,500) may exceed $3,000 during the next several years. Tight controls to combat inflation remained as the government held salary increases to a maximum of 6% until 1978.

Domestic Affairs. In snap elections held in December 1976, the PAP captured all 69 parliamentary seats. In these and two 1977 by-elections, opposition parties were able to take about 25% of the vote, but the opposition remains fragmented and no match for the incumbent party. Most opposition support comes from the upper middle class, the group that has benefited most from the economic growth. Singapore also continued numerous social innovations connected with increasing urbanization. Reclamation projects, mainly for housing, industry, and recreation, added 5.4% to the land.

Foreign Affairs. The prime ministers of Australia, New Zealand, and Japan met with leaders of the Association of Southeast Asian Nations during the ASEAN summit in August. Singapore seeks more trade, aid, technological help, and lower tariff barriers against its products. Few concrete accomplishments were recorded in these areas at the summit, though Japan pledged $450 million (versus $1 billion requested). Intra-ASEAN cooperation improved, and Singapore signed bilateral agreements with Thailand and the Philippines for 10% across-the-board reductions of tariffs.

Prime Minister Lee Kuan Yew met with President Carter in Washington in October.

Jo H. TILMAN and ROBERT O. TILMAN

SINGAPORE • Information Highlights

Official Name: Republic of Singapore.
Location: Southeast Asia.
Area: 244 square miles (632 km²).
Population (1977 est.): 2,300,000.
Chief City (1974 est.): Singapore, the capital, 1,327,-500.
Government: *Head of state,* Benjamin H. Sheares, president (took office Jan. 1971). *Head of government,* Lee Kuan Yew, prime minister (took office 1959). *Legislature* (unicameral)—Parliament.
Monetary Unit: Singapore dollar (2.45 S. dollars equal U. S.$1, Aug. 1977).
Manufacturing (major products): Petroleum products, steel, textiles, tires, wood products.

SOCIAL WELFARE

In 1977, state and local governments, Congress, and a new president were feeling their way toward workable social programs in keeping with long-proclaimed ideals. Early in the year extension and expansion of job programs, especially for youth, were debated hotly before the programs were passed. Later, reports validated complaints by minority leaders that most of the aid had bypassed their groups. Unemployment among white youths had dropped, but among blacks it remained as high as 40%. Efforts to pass the Humphrey–Hawkins bill to reduce unemployment to 3% won administration support, but its cost and inflationary tendencies suggested that a compromise would be necessary for congressional approval. Such legislation would, however, provide a framework within which the "workfare" aspects of welfare reform could be implemented.

Because of clashes between state and federal

During an October visit to Ottawa, Singapore's Prime Minister Lee Kuan Yew relaxes with Canada's Prime Minister Pierre Trudeau.

administrations over enforcement of quality control standards in public assistance, Medicaid, and social services, Congress postponed the effective date of one law and the Department of Health, Education, and Welfare (HEW) modified some of its regulations. Social services in particular presented difficulties. The need some people have for help with their personal problems and with finding opportunities to live full, satisfactory lives, is not eliminated just by improving income. Even the wealthy discover that inactivity after a busy life, inability to get out of the house, illness, loneliness, and fear can deprive life of its meaning. The possibility of paying for such help diminishes, of course, as income drops toward the lowest level, where food and shelter absorb so much that there is nothing left for even a bus fare to the doctor. In the past, churches and voluntary agencies served some of these needy, though in an uneven way.

As the federal government assumed more of the financial assistance burden, the states were propelled into providing day care centers for children and adults, "meals on wheels" for the homebound, educational and recreational activities, and other services in which they had little experience. They felt caught between the broad permissions in Title XX of the Social Security Act and rigid administrative regulations. Serious efforts are under way to bring more compatability into the workings of the programs. State and federal officials, working with congressional committee staffs, are developing new legislative and administrative guidelines for 1978 consideration.

Abortion Controversy. Aftershocks from the 1974 U.S. Supreme Court decision on abortion continued to trouble the political and social-welfare scenes. Opponents of abortion were scandalized by the huge number of women availing themselves of this alternative. In Washington, D.C., in 1976, abortions outnumbered live births. In Nassau county, N.Y., in 1975, one third of all pregnancies were so terminated.

In July the Supreme Court ruled that public hospitals need not perform free abortions on poor women and that states need not include abortions in their Medicaid programs. The entire HEW appropriation bill was held up for months while Congress aired opposing views. In December it agreed to permit federal funding of abortions in life-and-death cases; in cases where two doctors assert that the woman would suffer "severe and lasting damage" if she carried to term; and for all cases of rape.

As against the powerful "right to life" argument that abortion is murder, there was a rising tide of argument that these limitations were a form of discrimination against the poor since no limitations of access were put on those with money; that this would perpetuate and intensify the plight of the poor; and that in the long run the cost in dollars as well as human suffering

UPI

A pro-abortionist demonstrates at the Pennsylvania Capitol. Pro and anti abortion protests were common.

would be immense. The Supreme Court and President Carter took the position that this inequity was inevitable, but later President Carter announced that he would take steps to promote alternatives to abortion, and leaders of the Roman Catholic Church said they recognized the social consequences of their position and would undertake a campaign to secure the necessary social and economic supports for all children.

Welfare Legislation. Enactment of "welfare reform" legislation still proved difficult to accomplish. Unless the solutions to many aspects, dealt with separately, were compatible the "welfare mess" might be made worse. Involved were Aid to Families with Dependent Children (AFDC), Food Stamps, Supplemental Security Income (SSI), Social Security (OASDI), a jobs and training program for the unemployed and underemployed, social services, and national health insurance. The grand design would require at least two or three years to hammer out in Congress, but progress was being made.

Many Carter administration proposals appeared similar to ones put forward under Presidents Nixon and Ford, but there was greater recognition of federal responsibility to provide jobs as well as training for those unable to find work. Hence the "workfare" aspects of the Carter proposals include many more opportunities and incentives than the previous proposals. Recommendations for their quick implementation, however, were limited by administration and congressional commitments to avoid excessive inflation and to achieve a balanced budget by 1981.

Food Stamps. Originally introduced as a means of helping farmers dispose of their surpluses, food stamps are now clearly identified as one means of support for the poor, whether employed or not. During the 1975 recession more than 18 million persons were benefiting, about one of every 12 persons in the United States. Even so, the requirement that the user must buy a block of stamps before getting a "bonus" of more stamps prevented many who needed help the most from getting it. The complex administration, as well as fraud among contractors who sold the stamps, made for bad feelings.

In September the requirement for purchase of stamps was dropped from the law; only bonus stamps will now be distributed, automatically, to those eligible. As a test, a few able-bodied recipients will be required to earn their stamps by public service work. It is estimated that these changes will bring in 3 million new recipients while more stringent eligibility requirements will cut off 1.5 million "working poor." Recipients are thus expected to again approach 18 million in 1978.

SOCIAL SECURITY

Modifications in the social security law were being prepared. Despite sensational reports that it was about to collapse, the system was functioning essentially as intended, and Congress was performing its intended responsibility of periodic review and adjustment.

The largest income support program in the world, the system, in February 1977, was paying cash benefits to 21 million retired and 4.7 million disabled persons and their dependents, as well as to 7.5 million survivors of deceased workers. This total, an increase of 900,000 in a year, represents one of every six persons in the United States. Cash benefits now amount to more than $80 billion per year. Separate trust funds for the retirement, disability, and health sections of the system are small in relation to the total program and are intended only to smooth out short-term fluctuations in income and outlay. Tax payments from workers and employers, deposited in the trust funds, had been expected to match the benefits paid out. But the health fund had been supplemented from general revenues, the disability fund was nearly depleted, and at the 1977 rate of payout, the basic retirement fund would have been gone by 1983.

Two major factors have contributed to the depletion of the funds.

1. Recession-caused unemployment forced many to retire early, while the number paying into the fund was greatly reduced.

2. Inflation caused Congress to provide cost-of-living increases both on existing benefit payments and on the basic benefit scales. This put immediate and long-term pressures on the funds. At the same time, with higher wages, new retirees had increasingly higher earnings records and higher benefit levels—a "coupling effect" that could only become more serious. The steady increase in the life span means that many more beneficiaries can be expected in the future. At the same time, reduced birth rates in recent years mean that about the year 2025 there will be a period when fewer workers will be obliged to support many more retirees.

The Search for Increased Funding. To provide funds Congress considered such proposals as:

Increasing taxes on both workers and employers (a Ford recommendation opposed by Carter as placing too heavy burdens on business and low-income workers);

Increasing the earnings on which both workers and employers pay taxes;

Requiring employers to pay taxes on their entire payrolls;

Using general revenue funds to replace part of the Social Security taxes lost due to high unemployment (recommended by Carter); and

Requiring all federal, state, and local governmental employees to be covered.

The 1977 Social Security Act. On December 15, Congress approved, with votes of 56–21 in the Senate and 189–163 in the House, and sent to the president a Social Security financing bill. The measure, which the president signed on December 20, raises benefits for pensioners over 65 who continue to work, but its main purpose is to end the deficits that have drained the Social Security trust funds.

By a law already on the books, the payroll tax rate paid by both employers and employees was to rise on Jan. 1, 1978, from 5.85% to 6.05% of the taxable wage base. The new legislation will raise the rate in 1979, 1981, 1982, 1985, 1986, and 1990, to the level of 7.65%. (When first collected in 1937, the tax was 1%.)

The taxable wage base, which in 1977 was $16,500, is to rise to $17,700 in January 1978, to $22,900 in January 1979, to $25,900 in January 1980, and to $29,700 in 1981. Thereafter, it would rise in line with wage inflation. Assuming an inflation of 5.75% a year, the projection is for a wage base of $42,600 by 1987. At that level, the maximum tax payable would be $3,046, up from the 1977 maximum of $965.

For people on Social Security pensions who worked in 1977, any under age 72 lost 50% of each dollar they earned above the limit of $3,000. Under the provisions of the new bill anyone 65 and over may earn up to the limit of

Appearing before the Senate Finance Committee, HEW Secretary Joseph Califano explains the administration's proposals regarding the Social Security system to Maine Sen. Wm. Hathaway.

UPI

$4,000 in 1978 without losing benefits, up to $4,500 in 1979, up to $5,000 in 1980, up to $5,500 in 1981, and up to $6,000 in 1982. In 1982 the exemption age will drop to 70 years.

The new Act ends an error in the 1972 Social Security bill, whereby the initial benefits were adjusted for inflation twice: once for wage inflation and once for price inflation. Henceforth, the calculation of initial benefits will be adjusted for wage inflation. Thereafter, benefits will be adjusted once a year, as at the present time, for price inflation.

Among the most discussed questions is that concerned with automatic retirement at age 65. At year's end Congress had in conference a measure that would provide greater choice.

Reconsidering the Benefits. Despite repeated extensions of OASDI coverage, some people, because of age or nonparticipation in covered employment, are still not entitled to benefits. Furthermore, many former low-income workers receive inadequate benefits. Originally, the states were supposed to help such persons under federally supported programs. In practice, such help varied excessively and in 1972, at President Nixon's suggestion, Congress created the federal SSI program, which still required much state supplementation. Federal and state administrative problems have plagued the program from the start.

Meantime, the other federal-state assistance program, AFDC, has been criticized from all sides. Suggestions by President Nixon for its federalization failed of passage because compromise between a Republican president and a Democratically controlled Congress was frustrated by a bipartisan struggle between liberals who wanted the plan to provide more, and conservatives who wanted less. President Carter's 1977 welfare reform proposals are sufficiently similar to Nixon's original ones that it will be interesting to see how the same general political lineup in Congress deals with them.

The complicated, interlocking proposals include:

1. Replacing SSI, AFDC, and Food Stamps with comprehensive federal income supports to assure everybody a basic minimum income;

2. Transitional state supplementation up to a federally determined poverty line;

3. Inclusion of the "working poor" with decreasing benefits up to maximum allowable earnings determined by size of family;

4. Employment training programs locally designed in relation to job opportunities;

5. Classification of recipients according to their capacity to work—those unable to work would receive a standard allowance; those able to work and not in training would receive lesser assistance unless unable to secure private or public employment for at least six weeks; persons needed to care either for children under 7 or for older or disabled persons would be excused from the work requirement; mothers with children 7 to 13 would be expected to work part time, or full time if suitable day care facilities were available;

6. An extensive public employment program along the lines of the Humphrey-Hawkins bill, including financial incentives to participants to move to private employment when available.

This ambitious program is potentially very expensive, with some offsetting savings in unemployment insurance, public assistance, food stamps, and costs of the present complicated administration. Also, revenues can be anticipated from taxes on earnings and on the larger volume of business generated. Such fiscal benefits would be delayed. Both to facilitate a smooth transition and to avoid the shock to the budget and the economy any immediate shift would cause, the administration proposes that the new program be introduced gradually. Congressional leaders promise to pass at least some of the basic legislation during 1978.

RALPH E. PUMPHREY, *Washington University*

Prime Minister B. J. Vorster met with U. S. Vice President Walter Mondale in Vienna in May. They did not see eye to eye on South Africa's future direction.

UPI

SOUTH AFRICA

At the close of 1976 it was apparent that South Africa could expect neither to realize the early promise of its détente initiatives in Southern Africa nor to isolate its domestic policies from international pressures for change.

The events of 1977 confirmed both judgments. The external pressures on the Republic —especially from the Western powers—mounted dramatically; so did the white population's resentment of them. The government was forced to abandon at least its immediate plans for Namibia (South West Africa). And as the year ended, it faced an unprecedented Security Council ban at the UN. This mandatory arms ban was a direct response to the government's measures to silence its black opponents and their sympathizers. Not since the Sharpeville crisis and its aftermath had the government taken such drastic steps, or met with such widespread condemnation.

Tensions and Protests. The urban unrest and violence, which first erupted in the Soweto riots of June 1976, continued intermittently throughout 1977. On February 9, a demonstration by some 6,000 Soweto students was dispersed without bloodshed by the police. On April 27, thousands of young blacks in Soweto protested rent increases; three were wounded and 47 arrested. The sense of challenge and crisis was especially marked in June over the commemoration by blacks of the 1976 protests. On June 16, nine were wounded when the police used birdshot. On June 23, almost the entire student population of Soweto marched in a demonstration there. The same day, hundreds marched in Johannesburg, singing freedom songs, giving black power salutes and carrying placards which read "Thou shalt not kill students" and "Bantu education is for the education of slavery," be-

fore they were dispersed. The same week the president of the Chamber of Mines called for change to meet the "grave issues [which] face the country." But black unrest and white anxiety found its gravest and most violent expression over the mysterious death of the "black consciousness" leader Stephen Biko, on September 12, while in police custody. Contradictory government versions of his death, strong suspicions of foul play, the fact that 20 blacks had died in police custody since 1976, and the refusal to appoint a judicial commission of inquiry created a major political crisis. His funeral was attended by thousands of blacks and diplomats from 13 western nations. It led in the days that followed to further demonstrations, violence, and arrests. The Johannesburg *Star* reported that, across the country, nearly 200,000 students were boycotting classes or had been shut out of schools. In Soweto, 500 out of 750 teachers resigned in support of the students. On October 19, the government declared unlawful and banned 18 organizations, closed the black daily and weekend newspapers *The World* and *Weekend World*, detaining their editor and a

─── SOUTH AFRICA · Information Highlights ───

Official Name: Republic of South Africa.
Location: Southern tip of Africa.
Area: 471,444 square miles (1,221,040 km²).
Population (1977 est.): 26,100,000.
Chief Cities (1970 census): Pretoria, the administrative capital, 543,950; Cape Town, the legislative capital, 691,296; Johannesburg, 642,967; Durban, 495,458.
Government: *Head of state,* Nicolaas D. Diederichs, president (took office April 1975). *Head of government,* B. Johannes Vorster, prime minister (took office 1966). *Legislature*—Parliament: Senate and House of Assembly.
Monetary Unit: Rand (0.87 rand equals U. S.$1, Aug. 1977).
Manufacturing (major products): Textiles, iron and steel, chemicals, fertilizers, assembled automobiles, metals.
Major Agricultural Products: Sugarcane, tobacco, corn, fruits, wheat, dairy products, sheep, wool.

number of black leaders, along with editor Donald Woods of the East London *Daily Despatch*. Woods was then "banned." So was the director of the Christian Institute; authorities said they endangered law and order. (Woods made his escape to Lesotho on New Year's Eve.) On November 10, some 600 blacks were arrested after a police raid on a township near Pretoria. The inquest on Biko's death began November 14. Relentless cross-examination of police witnesses by the senior counsel representing his family gave the proceedings the air of a trial. However, the magistrate exonerated the police.

Foreign Affairs. Prime Minister B. J. Vorster had meetings with the British Foreign Secretary David Owen in Cape Town, April 13, and U. S. Vice President Walter Mondale in Vienna, May 19–20, regarding his government's policies. But public attention focused largely on the hardening of the U. S. stand on apartheid and the future of Namibia. Relations between the two countries grew more strained during the year, despite Vorster's agreement to cooperate with the United States and Britain in their new Rhodesia plan. Ambassador Young's reference, on April 14, to the Nationalist government as illegitimate and Mondale's definition of the system he urged on Vorster in place of apartheid as "one man, one vote" sent shock waves through the country. These still reverberated in the campaign for the general election in November. The new foreign minister, "Pik" Botha, stated that the United States was "at present a greater threat to South Africa than Russia." Vorster, defending the October crackdown, declared U. S. reaction "totally irrelevant." Earlier, he had told an American audience in Johannesburg that the rift was not of his making, but the present U. S. administration was seeking to impose a one-man, one-vote black majority rule, which could only destroy South Africa.

Opposition leaders also deplored the U. S. stance. In talks beginning April 27 the U. S., British, French, Canadian, and West German ambassadors informed Vorster that his plans for Namibia would not be internationally recognized or supported by their countries. On May 17, in a television interview, President Carter warned that unless South Africa moved to end white rule in Namibia it would face strong UN action. As a result of this pressure the government abandoned its plan to install an interim government for Namibia in July and hold ethnically based elections. It was not Namibia, however, but the October arrests and bans which led the UN Security Council to a unanimous arms embargo against South Africa. This was a compromise acceptable only after the United States, Britain, and France had vetoed proposals for far-reaching economic sanctions.

Domestic Affairs. The $10-billion (U. S.) budget provided for increases (over 1976) of 21.3% on defense, 15% on police, and 52% on black education. The concern with security was also reflected in the extension of compulsory military training from 12 to 24 months, and in tightened exchange controls. On November 10, it was announced that an extra $290 million would be spent over the next three years on non-white housing.

On September 20, Vorster surprised the country by calling for a general election on November 30. As expected, he increased his already overwhelming majority, capturing some 70% of the vote. The demise of the official opposition, the United Party, was one reason Vorster gave for his action. Another was his new constitutional plan for an executive president, presiding over a mixed council of cabinet ministers drawn from separate Coloured and Indian parliaments, as well as the existing one.

R. B. BALLINGER, *Rhode Island College*

UPI

Foreign Minister R. F. ("Pik") Botha declared at the UN in June that South Africa would resist all pressures to change its racial policies and would "go it alone" if necessary.

SOUTH CAROLINA

The year 1977 was an interesting one in South Carolina. The first Spoleto Festival was successfully held in Charleston, and so was the Miss Universe Pageant.

Government. The state government ended the year with a surplus, thus reversing the recession that began in 1974. Among significant legislation enacted were laws restoring the death penalty, establishing a coastal-zone management plan, fixing a minimum financial support for all school districts, adding judges to the family court system, licensing day-care centers, and strengthening the laws on child abuse. A constitutional amendment, classifying property for taxation, was also passed.

Education. A state-supported program to equalize school-district finances was approved, but the districts continued to stress their need for financial independence from county councils. Vocational training and programs for all special-type education were expanded in order to reduce the number of high school dropouts. The State Educational Association also voted to require a certain minimum performance before granting a high school diploma.

The University of South Carolina opened its medical school in the autumn; 24 students were enrolled. Together with the College of Charleston and Winthrop College, the university also approved cooperative graduate programs in public administration.

Economy. Despite drought, which induced President Carter to declare the state a disaster area, there was an abundance of fresh peaches. But production of other major crops was seriously curtailed. Several major new industrial establishments were announced, foremost among them an aluminum reduction plant.

Environment. The Congaree Swamp area of virgin forests was preserved by action of the federal government. Large areas were added to the state park system, and a major park is being developed around the city of Columbia.

ROBERT H. STOUDEMIRE
University of South Carolina

SOUTH DAKOTA

Legislation. The legislature voted the expenditure of $155,627,999 into general appropriations for the fiscal year 1977–78. This sum will fund state agencies and public services; provide $1.75 million for local and rural water systems; pay $100,000 higher educational expenses for students whose families have suffered from the drought; bring emergency relief to drought-stricken counties; enhance retirement systems for state employees; and supply $100,000 for post-graduate education of physicians willing to practice family medicine.

Partisan tension persisted throughout the 45-day session between Gov. Richard Kneip (D) and the Republicans, who control both houses of the legislature. As a result, Governor Kneip failed to propose a graduated income tax for the first time since he became governor and vetoed 30 bills, but saw 16 of the vetoes overridden by his partisan adversaries. The most significant laws to come out of the session revised state budgeting procedures, set up a special committee to review the operation of the Department of Commerce and Consumer Affairs, and raised the annual salaries of the governor and other constitutional officials to more competitive levels.

Economy. Ample rainfall brought significant improvement in the state's economy for the first time since 1974. Crop yields for major staples rose sharply. Prices of cattle, corn, and grain increased slightly. Average personal income went up by more than 8%, total employment increased by approximately 15,000, and tourist industries flourished.

Higher Education. Solutions were sought to budgetary deficiencies that have placed South Dakota academic salaries among the lowest in the nation. Legislators acknowledged the problem and committed nearly $50 million to higher education, but the annual salary increases from this amount came to only $250. Union advocates called for political action.

HERBERT T. HOOVER
University of South Dakota

— SOUTH CAROLINA · Information Highlights —

Area: 31,055 square miles (80,432 km²).
Population (1976 est.): 2,848,000.
Chief Cities (1970 census): Columbia, the capital, 113,-542; Charleston, 66,945; Greenville, 61,436.
Government (1977): *Chief Officers*—governor, James B. Edwards (R); lt. gov., W. Brantley Harvey, Jr. (D). *General Assembly*—Senate, 46 members; House of Representatives, 124 members.
Education (1976–77): *Enrollment*—public elementary schools, 373,804 pupils; public secondary, 246,907; nonpublic, 49,400; colleges and universities, 121,265 students. *Public school expenditures,* $782,500,000 ($1,132 per pupil).
State Finances (fiscal year 1976): *Revenues,* $2,162,-617,000; *expenditures,* $2,265,776,000.
Personal Income (1976): $14,662,000,000; per capita, $5,147.
Labor Force (June 1977): *Nonagricultural wage and salary earners,* 1,095,200; *unemployed,* 73,200 (5.6% of total force).

— SOUTH DAKOTA · Information Highlights —

Area: 77,047 square miles (199,552 km²).
Population (1976 est.): 686,000.
Chief Cities (1970 census): Pierre, the capital, 9,699; Sioux Falls, 72,488; Rapid City, 43,836.
Government (1977): *Chief Officers*—governor, Richard F. Kneip (D); lt. gov., Harvey Wollman (D). *Legislature*—Senate, 35 members; House of Representatives, 70 members.
Education (1976–77): *Enrollment*—public elementary schools, 97,296 pupils; public secondary, 50,784; nonpublic, 14,800; colleges and universities, 29,359 students. *Public school expenditures,* $210,059,000 ($1,215 per pupil).
State Finances (fiscal year 1976): *Revenues,* $496,264,-000; *expenditures,* $492,032,000.
Personal Income (1976): $3,512,000,000; per capita, $5,120.
Labor Force (July 1977): *Nonagricultural wage and salary earners,* 230,900; *unemployed,* 11,800 (3.4% of total force).

SPACE EXPLORATION

The successful completion of the atmospheric test of the United States' new Space Shuttle, Enterprise, was one of the highlights of space activity in 1977. The pace of exploration of the outer planets of the solar system was increased with the launch of Voyager 1 and 2 by the United States. The Soviet Union continued its active manned space program with the launch of one Salyut space laboratory and three Soyuz manned spacecraft.

MANNED SPACE FLIGHT

Soyuz 24. On February 7, Soyuz 24 was launched from the Baikonur Cosmodrome with flight commander Col. Viktor Gorbatko and flight engineer Yuri Glaskov on board. The Soyuz performed several maneuvers before docking on February 8 with the Salyut 5 space station, which had been in orbit since June 22, 1976. After a night of rest in the Soyuz spacecraft, the cosmonauts entered the space station, which was in a low 178 x 138 mile (287 x 222 km) orbit, to begin their planned research program. The primary purpose of this mission was apparently to obtain high resolution photographs of the earth's surface and to conduct studies of crystal growth.

Eighteen days after launch, Soyuz 24 was successfully recovered 22 miles (36 km) northeast of the town of Arkalyk in Kazakhstan. The day after the cosmonauts returned to earth, a recovery capsule loaded with flight data was automatically ejected from Salyut 5 and recovered by the Soviets.

The Salyut 5 space station was left in an automatic mode by the cosmonauts and continued to carry out scientific and technical experiments while maintaining the desired environment. Salyut 5 reentered the earth's atmosphere over the Pacific Ocean where it burned up on August 8. The Soviets reported that during its life about 300 experiments were conducted.

Salyut 6. A new Soviet space station, Salyut 6, was launched on September 29 from Baikonur Cosmodrome into a 171 x 136 mile (275 x 219 km) orbit. On October 7 the Soviet space station was maneuvered into a 219 x 209 mile (352 x 336 km) orbit to await the arrival of a Soyuz spacecraft.

Soyuz 25–26. In October the USSR launched Soyuz 25 from the same pad that launched the first Sputnik 20 years before. Cosmonauts Vladimir Kovalenok and Valeriy Ryumin carried a copy of the new Soviet constitution adopted to mark in November the 60th anniversary of communist rule in Russia. However, the Soyuz 25/Salyut 6 rendezvous failed at a point in the flight where the Soviet cosmonauts normally switch from an automatic rendezvous to manual

With Vladimir Kovalenok, below left, and Valeriy Ryumin aboard, the USSR launched Soyuz 25, above, on Oct. 9. A docking failure forced the return, Oct. 11.

PHOTOS UPI

control to maneuver the Soyuz the last 298 feet (91 m) before docking. The inability of the Soyuz to dock with Salyut 6 dictated an immediate return to earth for the Soyuz crew because of very limited power on the Soyuz spacecraft. The planned long-duration flight lasted only two days. On December 10 Soyuz 26 was launched with Cosmonauts Yuri Romanenko and Georgi Grechko aboard. Although the docking unit faltered again, the cosmonauts succeeded in entering Salyut 6 on December 11.

PLANETARY PROBES

Voyager. The United States launched Voyager 2 and 1 on August 20 and September 5, respectively, on a decade-long odyssey that could take them to as many as 15 major bodies of the outer solar system. Making measurements and taking closeup pictures of Jupiter, Saturn, and their many moons, and perhaps of the planet Uranus, the Voyagers are designed to return information that could shed new light on the origin and early history of the solar system, including our own planet earth.

Voyager 2 was launched first and Voyager 1 second because Voyager 1 was to fly a faster trajectory than its companion and reach Jupiter in March 1979, four months before Voyager 2. Voyager 1 was planned to reach Saturn in November 1980, about nine months ahead of its sister spacecraft.

After completing their planetary missions, the two spacecraft should continue outward from the solar system and penetrate interstellar space.

Each 1,819-pound (825 kg) spacecraft uses 11 instruments including the spacecraft radio to study the planets, their satellites, the rings of Saturn, the magnetic regions surrounding the planets, and interplanetary space. The Voyagers carry wide-angle and narrow-angle television cameras, cosmic ray detectors, infrared spectrometers and radiometers, low-energy charged-particle detectors, magnetometers, photopolarimeters, planetary radioastronomy receivers, plasma and plasma wave instruments, and ultraviolet spectrometers.

The closest approach of either spacecraft will be about 173,000 miles (278,000 km) from Jupiter and 86,000 miles (138,000 km) from Saturn. During these encounter periods, the

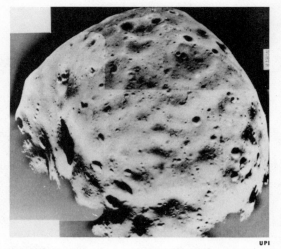
UPI

'The Viking Orbiter flew within 300 miles (480 km) of Mars and photographed its asteroid-size moon, Phobos.

A Titan rocket blasts Voyager I, scheduled to return information regarding the solar system, into space.
UPI

television cameras may provide pictures of these two giant planets with greater resolution than has ever been achieved before. The cameras also should take the first high resolution closeup photos of the Galilean satellites of Jupiter; Titan, the major satellite of Saturn; and Saturn's rings.

Other Voyager instruments will study the atmosphere of the planets and their satellites; their magnetosphere; the relationships between these regions and the solar wind that streams through interplanetary space; and the radio signals from Jupiter, which emits the strongest radio noise in the sky except for that of the sun.

An option is being maintained to send Voyager 2 to the planet Uranus, 20 times farther from the sun than earth. Encounter, which would occur in January 1986, would permit the first closeup examination of the recently discovered rings of Uranus.

Viking. The two U. S. Viking spacecraft that began their exploration of Mars in mid-1976 continued making scientific measurements in 1977 after a two-month shutdown from mid-November 1976 to mid-January 1977 when the communications link between Mars and earth was temporarily lost due to solar conjunction.

The data received from the Viking lander still did not produce firm evidence that life in any form exists on Mars. However, the data do not rule out the possibility of biological activity.

The Viking 1 orbiter provided the first closeup picture of Phobos, the larger of the two moons of Mars, during February 1977. The photographs revealed that the small moon, which is only 13 miles (21 km) across, is irregular in shape, with a heavily pitted surface.

During 1977 the Viking spacecraft also observed two global dust storms indicating that such events are more frequent than previously thought. Particles from these storms remained suspended for weeks after the winds died down because of the lack of rain to clear the air.

Another interesting event observed by the Viking 2 lander in September 1977 was revealed in a photograph of the Martian surface that showed patches of white around the base of rocks near the spacecraft. It is believed that these white areas are frost, made up of perhaps frozen carbon dioxide or "dry ice."

EARTH SATELLITES

Research Satellites. The French/Matra–Signe–3 spacecraft was launched by the USSR from Kapustin Ya on June 17. The 262-pound (119 kg) spacecraft was designed to collect gamma ray, X-ray, and solar ultraviolet data. The Soviet Union launched Cosmos 936 into orbit on August 3 carrying biological experiments from the USSR, United States, France, Czechoslovakia, East Germany, Hungary, Rumania, Bulgaria, and Poland. The biological laboratory, carrying live plants, fruit flies, and white rats, conducted experiments to understand the effects of weightlessness on living organisms. Such research is an essential prelude to making space travel easier for human beings.

Cosmos 936 carried a centrifuge device for keeping ten specially bred laboratory rats in conditions approximating earth gravity while 20 more rats traveled in conditions of weightlessness. The health of both sets of rats was monitored from earth. The Cosmos 936 flight also tested the effect of cosmic radiation on the heredity and metabolic processes of plants and animals. After 21 days in space, Cosmos 936 was successfully recovered on August 23.

The United States launched the High Energy Astronomy Observatory (HEAO–1) on August 12 to survey and map X-ray sources throughout the celestial sphere and also measure low energy gamma-ray flux. HEAO–1, at 7,000 pounds (3,175 kg) the heaviest unmanned earth orbiting satellite ever launched, carried a new generation of experiments that dwarfed earlier rocket and satellite experiments. Scientists expect that these experiments will discover hundreds or perhaps thousands of new sources of X-ray radiation, and that totally new phenomena and classes of sources will be found. The celestial gamma ray and cosmic ray data will also be measured with unprecedented detail in the hope that their origins may be better understood.

On September 22 the USSR launched Prognoz–6 from Baikonur Cosmodrome for the study of cosmic rays and solar flux. The 2,006-pound (910 kg) satellite carried instruments provided by the USSR and France.

Intercosmos 17 was launched by the Soviet Union on September 24 from Plesetsk to continue the series of space research activities between the USSR and Hungary, Rumania, and Czechoslovakia.

On October 22 the United States launched ISEE A & B on a single launch vehicle to study solar-terrestrial relationships. This international

UPI

With the launch of PALAPA 2, to assist PALAPA 1, Indonesia established a satellite communications network.

cooperative project between NASA in the United States and the European Space Agency (ESA) was designed to investigate the detailed structure of the boundaries between the earth's magnetosphere and interplanetary space, to investigate the fluctuations in the solar wind, and the relations between these fluctuations and changes in the magnetosphere boundaries. The 723-pound (328 kg) ISEE–A spacecraft was designed and built by the United States and the 348-pound (158 kg) ISEE–B spacecraft was designed and built by the ESA.

The Japanese launched two spacecraft into orbit, bringing the total Japanese spacecraft launched to 10. The 295-pound (134 kg) TANSEI–2 engineering spacecraft was launched February 19 from the Uchinoura Space Center to verify the performance of an improved launch vehicle. The 287-pound (130 kg) KIKU–2 (ETS–2) engineering spacecraft was launched February 23 and placed in a synchronous orbit at 130° E longitude. KIKU-2, Japan's first attempt to launch a synchronous satellite, is designed to pave the way for future Japanese meteorological and communications spacecraft.

Communications Satellites. In 1977 the communications satellites continue to represent the largest number of satellites for any particular class with 12 launches.

The USSR launched 8 domestic communications satellites in 1977. Three were of the Molniya 1 class (Molniya 1–36, 1–37, and 1–38 on March 24, June 24, and August 30); one was of the Molniya 2 class (Molniya 2–17 on February 11); two were of the Molniya 3 class (Molniya 3–7 on April 28 and 3–8 on October 28); one was the third geostationary communications satellite, RADUGA–3, launched on July 23; and one was the EKRAN–2, a television communications spacecraft placed in synchronous orbit at 97° E longitude.

The space shuttle: the orbiter Enterprise, perched on top of a modified Boeing 747, begins its test flight.

Indonesia established a domestic satellite communications network when the 1,268-pound (575 kg) satellite, PALAPA 2, was launched by the United States on March 10. PALAPA 2 joins PALAPA 1, launched on July 8, 1976, to provide improved communication services throughout Indonesia's 3,000-odd inhabited islands. Each satellite can handle 5,000 telephone calls or 12 television channels at once.

An Italian experimental communications satellite, SIRIO–I, was launched by the United States on August 25 and placed in a synchronous orbit over the west coast of Africa at 15° W longitude. The principle experiment on SIRIO is designed to study super-high frequency radio transmission problems.

One satellite, INTELSAT IVA–F4, was launched on May 26 by the United States to maintain global communications satellites.

A Japanese experimental satellite, CS, was launched by the United States on December 14 and placed in a synchronous orbit to test the relay of communication and television signals among the Japanese islands.

Weather Satellites. The USSR launched four weather satellites in its Meteor series on January 6, April 5, June 29 and December 14. The United States launched three geostationary meteorological satellites: the U. S. GOES–2 on June 16, the Japanese satellite GMS (Himawai I) on July 14, and the ESA Meteosat on November 22. In addition to providing meteorological data for each of their countries, these three satellites will be part of a comprehensive worldwide meteorological observation program (the First Global Atmospheric Research Program Experiment) which begins in late 1978.

ADVANCES IN SPACE TECHNOLOGY

Space Shuttle. The development of the U. S. Space Shuttle made excellent progress in 1977. The flight test phase of the orbiter was completed ahead of schedule Other significant accomplishments include the successful firing of the first solid rocket motor, delivery of the first external fuel tank, and a long-duration firing of the main engine.

The test flight of the orbiter Enterprise began in February with the orbiter perched on top of a modified Boeing 747. The combined load of 293 tons (289 metric tons)—72 (70) of them in the 122 foot-long (32 m) Enterprise— not only rose smoothly from the runway but also maneuvered gracefully throughout its first two-hour, five-minute flight. With Fitzhugh Fulton, Jr., at the controls, the coupled craft was put through a series of maneuvers to test its low-speed performance and handling qualities before making a smooth landing at Edwards Air Force Base in California. Four additional captive/unmanned flights were made during February and March to evaluate the coupled craft's stability and control characteristics and to evaluate the performance and procedures to be used for releasing the Enterprise from its parent 747.

The captive/manned flight phase was conducted during June and July. These three flights with all orbiter systems powered and the orbiter manned by two astronauts, verified crew procedures and integrated systems operations in preparation for the free-flight phase.

On August 12, the first separation and free flight of the Enterprise was completed successfully. The combined 747/orbiter took off from a paved runway at NASA's Dryden Flight Research Center, Edwards, Calif. The landing was made on a 7-mile (11 km) strip on Rogers Dry Lake, an unpaved but hard and smooth expanse of baked earth where there was ample margin for aiming errors. Takeoff came on schedule with Fitzhugh L. Fulton, Jr., and Thomas C. McMurtry, NASA test pilots, at the controls of the 747. For 48 minutes the combined craft flew over the desert while Fred W. Haise, Jr., and C. Gordon Fullerton checked all the orbiter's systems.

The external fuel tank, 154 feet (46.2 m) long, is the largest component of the space shuttle.

As the time approached for the Shuttle to separate, Fulton brought the 747's engines up to full thrust and pitched down to a slight glide. At this point, Enterprise pilot Haise initiated separation by firing a series of explosive bolts at an altitude of 24,000 feet (7,300 m). Haise banked the orbiter to the left while Fulton steered the 747 to the right and several hundred feet below for a clean separation. As the Enterprise descended, at about 20,000 feet (6,000 m), the astronauts practiced leveling the vehicle out for a landing just to make sure at a relatively safe altitude that they understood how well the orbiter responded to their manipulation of the control flaps, elevons, rudder, and speed brakes. The Enterprise was maneuvered through two 90° turns and then its nose was pointed downward toward the salt and clay flatbeds, where it glided into a landing after a flight of five minutes. It was a major milestone in NASA's project to develop the first space plane.

With the successful completion of five additional tests during the months of September, October, and November, the Enterprise's free-flight test program was completed and preparations were made to modify the craft for use in ground vibration testing before its reconfiguration for future orbital flights.

The timetable for the Space Shuttle program calls for the second orbiter, a replica of the prototype Enterprise, to make its first flight into orbit in March 1979 from Cape Kennedy. It will be propelled at launch by two mammoth rockets strapped to its sides and a huge fuel tank clamped to its belly. The rockets will be parachuted after launch from a height of 25 miles (40 km) back into the sea to be reused, while the fuel tanks will be jettisoned at 140 miles (225 km) to disintegrate in the atmosphere. Once in orbit, the craft will be able to sustain a mission of up to 30 days before its engine picks it out of orbit for the swift glide back to earth. Current plans call for building five of the orbiters, each capable of about 100 round trips into space.

To obtain pilots for the Space Shuttle in the early 1980's, NASA requested that interested individuals submit applications. More than 8,000 applications were received. From this list, NASA experts planned to select about 15 pilots and 17 mission specialists who will assist in the operation of each flight.

Spacelab. Important progress in the development of the Spacelab, which will be situated in the cargo bay of the Space Shuttle, has been made by the European Space Agency. Detailed design activity is nearing completion with more than half of the subsystem critical design review having been successfully accomplished. The rest will be completed in time for the overall critical design review scheduled for early 1978. Manufacturing of the first flight unit was begun.

Spacelab, which will first be flown in 1980, is an orbital facility that provides a pressurized shirt-sleeves laboratory for scientists to conduct research in space. It is a reusable system that is transported to and from orbit in the cargo bay of the Space Shuttle orbiter and remains there throughout the flight. The spacelab is regarded as a short-stay space station that can remain in orbit for up to 30 days, with a normal mission duration of seven days. In orbit, the experiments carried by Spacelab are operated by a team of up to four payload specialists (men or women) who normally work in the laboratory, but spend their off-duty time in the orbiter cabin.

Spacelab users will be drawn from the various disciplines of science and technology. Investigations have shown that at least the following fields are likely to obtain benefits from the utilization of Spacelab: high-energy astrophysics; ultraviolet, optical, infrared, and X-ray stellar, planetary, and solar astronomy; atmospheric, ionospheric, and magnetospheric physics; life sciences, including biology, biomedics, and behavior; remote earth sensing meteorology, land-use planning, resources and pollution control; material science (including crystal growth, pure metals and alloys, and composite material) and fluid physics; processing and manufacturing in space; and communication and navigation. It is foreseen that Spacelab will play a major role in the various development phases of these disciplines, which include research, instrument development, experimental processes, and operational programs.

PITT G. THOME
National Aeronautics
and Space Administration

In May, campaign workers in Madrid prepare for Spain's first democratic elections in four decades.

UPI

SPAIN

The ascent to power of King Juan Carlos de Borbon after the death of Francisco Franco in 1975 has ushered in a new era in Spanish history. Memories of the 36-year military-imposed dictatorship are fading as democratic institutions take root in this Iberian nation of 38 million passionate people.

General Election. On June 15, 1977, Spanish voters went to the polls in the first general election in four decades. Although sporadic violence marred the campaign, about 80% of Spain's eligible voters cast ballots as 6,000 candidates, representing 156 parties, contested 350 seats in the Congress of Deputies and 207 in the Senate.

The Union of the Democratic Center (UCD), a hybrid center-left coalition headed by Prime Minister Adolfo Suárez González, emerged as the dominant political force. It captured 165 seats in congress and 107 in the senate. The social-democratic Spanish Socialist Workers Party garnered 118 congressional and 107 senate seats, while the Communists won 20 places in the lower house and 12 in the upper chamber.

After the election, King Juan Carlos, who enjoys great popularity, asked Adolfo Suárez González to continue as prime minister. Composed overwhelmingly of UCD members, the new cabinet swore to give "loyalty to the king, respect for individual rights and strict observance of the law."

Regionalism and Terrorism. One of the new government's first acts was to commit itself to greater autonomy for Catalonia, the northeast portion of Spain that embraces Barcelona. Josep Tarradellas, the president-in-exile of the Generalitat, the region's pre-Franco government, returned to Spain. Meanwhile, the 48 deputies and 16 senators elected from Catalonia met in the Barcelona Parliament building to vote for regional autonomy, amnesty for political prisoners, and legalization of all political parties.

On June 19 most of the congressmen and senators from the three Basque provinces met in Guernica. They also urged autonomy for their region, which was beset by agitation on behalf of political prisoners during the campaign. On May 18 terrorists, believed to be members of the ETA separatist group, murdered a policeman, apparently in retaliation for the deaths of six pro-amnesty demonstrators.

Exuding confidence after the election, the Suárez government legalized three fringe organizations that had been denied a role in the election process: the rightist Carlist Party, the Spanish Workers Party, and the Maoist-oriented Revolutionary Workers Organization.

Despite the rapid liberalization of Spain's political system—a process grudgingly accepted by the conservative military—extremists continue to commit random acts of violence. The "storm troopers" of the ETA have specialized in kidnapping and assaults on motorists. The anti-fascist GRAPO and FRAP have attracted attention for kidnapping and bombings. One of GRAPO's bombs exploded in the American cultural center on May 17, just hours before Vice President Walter Mondale arrived in Madrid for a goodwill visit.

Though of minor significance, ultraright Francoists struck back at the leftists. Their organizations include the Apostolic Anti-Communist Alliance and the Guerrillas of Christ the King.

The Economy. Terrorism notwithstanding, the Suárez regime is in control of the country. Its major challenge is to steady and stimulate the economy of a nation afflicted by a 25% increase in energy imports, a 20% boost in prices, a 6% unemployment rate, and rampant tax evasion.

The government published an austerity program in midyear. It devalued the peseta 25%

on July 12, increased the discount rate to 8%, clamped additional controls on basic foodstuffs, and advanced tax reforms. These measures include added levies on luxuries, a larger inheritance tax, and a progressive tax on the affluent. Meanwhile, more public spending was announced for highway and home construction to generate jobs for 800,000 people.

To gain backing on the economic front, the moderate prime minister has invited support from a variety of groups, including the recently legalized Spanish Communist Party (PCE). Led by its secretary-general, Santiago Carrillo, the PCE is regarded as moderate. Though relatively small in size, it enjoys a significant following in the Worker's Commissions found in key industries. The socialist General Workers' Union has also supported Suárez on many measures, but the anarcho-syndicalist National Workers' Confederation opposes not only the austerity plan but the government itself.

Most Spanish economists believe that the long-term interests of their nation lie with joining the European Common Market. An application for membership will be made in 1978.

Foreign Affairs. The Madrid regime continues to enjoy close relations with the United States. However, in 1977 it also announced diplomatic ties with seven Eastern bloc countries, including the Soviet Union with which relations have been strained since the 1936–39 Spanish civil war in which Moscow aided the losing Republicans. To avoid antagonizing the Arab states, Spain acts as if Israel did not exist.

Although the leftist parties are chary about the step, Spain will probably enter NATO as a part of its integration into Western Europe. Lifting its blockade of British-controlled Gibraltar is an obvious prerequisite to affiliation with the military alliance.

Spain, which surrounds this vital citadel, wants recognition of its sovereignty over Gibraltar. In return for this, Suárez promises political autonomy and economic benefits for

UPI

Ending a three-day visit to Venezuela, Spain's King Juan Carlos bids good-bye to President Carlos Andrés Pérez.

Gibraltar, as well as permission for a British or NATO base in this gateway to the Mediterranean. While effusive about democracy in Iberia, Dr. David Owen, the British foreign minister, failed to pursue these proposals during a September 1977 visit to Madrid.

The Gibraltar question and devotion to the 39-year-old monarch are two of the few things on which most Spanish leaders agree. Still in doubt are (1) the political orientation of Suárez's own political party, many of whose members once worked for the Franco regime, (2) the role of the now dominant king vis-à-vis the new parliament, and (3) the proper balance between central authority and regional autonomy.

The Spanish will attempt to resolve these issues as they move to galvanize a strong but drifting economy, while seeking greater involvement in continental affairs.

GEORGE W. GRAYSON
College of William and Mary

Dolores Ibarruri ("La Pasionaria"), Spain's Communist Party president, returns to Madrid after a long exile.

UPI

SPAIN · Information Highlights

Official Name: Spanish State.
Location: Iberian Peninsula in southwestern Europe.
Area: 194,897 square miles (504,782 km²).
Population (1977 est.): 36,500,000.
Chief Cities (1975): Madrid, the capital, 3,500,000; Barcelona, 2,000,000; Valencia, 700,000.
Government: *Head of state,* Juan Carlos I, king (took office Nov. 1975). *Head of government,* Adolfo Suárez González, prime minister (took office July 1976). *Legislature*—Cortes: Senate and Congress of Deputies.
Monetary Unit: Peseta (84.51 pesetas equal U. S.$1, Aug. 1977).
Manufacturing (major products): Iron and steel, electrical machinery, automobiles, textiles, chemicals, ships, processed foods, leather.
Major Agricultural Products: Wheat, rye, barley, corn, citrus fruits, vegetables, almonds, olives, potatoes, forest products, sheep.

SPORTS

Finances in Pro Sports

In the last decade professional sports have become a national phenomenon, growing so fast that many observers are asking: Can pro sports survive the current financial demands on them?

The Athletes. The economic well-being of pro athletes has never been greater. The players are represented by unions, business agents, and lawyers. They negotiate multiyear, multimillion dollar contracts, and strong pensions. Ten years ago a handful of athletes made over $100,000 a year. Today's superstars earn from $300,000 to $500,000 annually. Muhammad Ali, the world's heavyweight boxing champion, has earned $5 million for just one bout. Pelé, the Brazilian soccer star, got a package deal of $7 million in 1975 from Warner Communications, a conglomerate, to play for and represent their team, the New York Cosmos. Björn Borg, the Swedish Wimbledon champion who earns $350,000 a year in purses, reaps much more as a client of a management group. It negotiates advertising commercials for his brand of sneakers, his car, breakfast cereal, the airline he travels on, and even the sweatband he wears on his forehead. In 1977, Steve Cauthen, a 17-year-old jockey in his first year of competition, earned more than $500,000. He became the first jockey to ride winners of more than $5 million in racing purses.

Free Agents. In 1976, baseball's stringent "reserve clause," tying players exclusively to one team, was relaxed. The new regulation meant that during 1976–77 anyone could play out his option without a signed contract, then be free to sign a contract with any team for the best offer. Thereafter, the player would need six years of league service before becoming a free agent. All other major team sports adopted similar codes. George Steinbrenner, the owner of the New York Yankees, spent millions to get free agents. He signed Reggie Jackson to a five-year, $2.9 million contract. In fact, the Yankees had 11 players whose salary exceeded $100,000 a year. Their payroll for 1977 was over $3.5 million, but they won the World Series.

Television. The most influential force affecting the finances of pro sports has been television. The telecasting of major team events enriches the clubs and leagues by hundreds of millions of dollars. In an historic, record-breaking commitment in 1977, the National Football League (NFL) negotiated a four-year, $576-million pact with the three major networks to broadcast its games.

The Owners. Businessmen often favor sports as a way to invest profitably and to diversify their enterprises. They keep a watchful eye on expansion opportunities in areas with good market demographics. They enjoy prestige and status by being associated with pro athletes who form an elitist group, similar to entertainment stars.

Government in Sports. Municipal and state governments have vested interests in expansion and franchise shifts. Many costly new stadium complexes are built with government funds. Favorable rental and tax benefits induce teams to settle in prime-market cities. For example, 26 of the 28 NFL teams play in city, county, or state-built facilities. The benefits such facilities offer cities include new jobs, funds for the local economy, and civic pride. The loss of a team is equally a blow to economic life and prestige. Clubs in untenable financial situations seek to do better in a new location. Lawsuits often accompany franchise shifts. Some cities have sued to block team departures.

Fans and Attendance. All signs indicate that the fans are ready to turn out in paying droves for sports events. In 1977, a record 39.5 million saw the 26 baseball teams in action, compared with 16 million in 1951 when there were 16 teams. In 1976, the 28-team NFL drew 11.5 million, compared with 2 million in 1951, when there were 12 teams. In other major team sports the trend was similar.

Expansion. The possibilities of more expansion, although diminished, still exist. Baseball had new teams in Seattle and Toronto in 1977. The North American Soccer League added teams in Detroit and Memphis for 1978, lifting its total to 21. On the other hand, the World Hockey Association, troubled by financial problems, sought a merger with its more affluent rival, the National Hockey League, and was turned down. Poor attendance forced the New York Nets of the National Basketball Association to shift from Long Island to New Jersey in 1977.

Conclusion. Player salaries are bound to level off. Despite high costs, some owners will continue to spend large sums to improve their teams. Others will hold the line. Some citizens groups are questioning the wisdom of subsidizing sports teams at a time when public services and other needs are going unheeded. Fans, in general, appear willing to pay higher ticket prices and other rising costs. In 1977, baseball ticket prices were raised by 16 teams, a record. When will the bubble burst? It seems certain that the pro sports business will undergo many, and expensive, changes, but on the evidence to date it is a pretty safe bet that the ballooning costs will not diminish the appeal of pro sports for the sports-minded American public.

GEORGE DE GREGORIO
Sports Department, "The New York Times"

A. J. Foyt (above) won the Indianapolis 500 for a record fourth time. Janet Guthrie was the first woman to start the race. She finished in the 29th position.

AUTO RACING

The legendary A. J. Foyt added an exclamation mark to a brilliant racing career by becoming the first man to win the Indianapolis 500-mile (800-km) race four times. The 42-year-old Texan also won the California "200" and the San Jovite to run his all-time record number of United States Auto Club championship victories to 59.

Foyt collected $252,278 from the $1 million purse.

Janet Guthrie became the first woman to start the world famed "500." Janet was the 18th fastest qualifier in the 33-car field, but early engine problems forced her to retire. She was awarded the 29th position.

The Pocono and Ontario 50-mile (80-km) races, the other two races in USAC Triple Crown, were captured by Tom Sneva and Al Unser. Sneva, who also finished second in the Indy, went on to capture the 1977 USAC driving title.

Niki Lauda, returning from a fiery crash at Nuerburgring, West Germany, won the world championship for the second time in three years. However, the talk of the Grand Prix Circuit was Mario Andretti of the United States. Mario won four Formula One events, but mechanical malfunctions kept him from taking the prestigious title to the United States.

Andretti, who was born in Italy, also achieved the dream of a lifetime by winning the Grand Prix of Italy at Monza.

Donnie Allison captured the Daytona "500," showpiece of the National Association for Stock Car Racing (NASCAR). And Frenchman Patrick Tambay led the Can-Am series.

ROBERT J. COLLINS
Sports Editor, "The Indianapolis Star"

AUTO RACING

World Champion: Niki Lauda, Austria
USAC: Tom Sneva, U. S.
Can-Am: Patrick Tambay, France
NASCAR: Cale Yarborough, U. S.

Major Race Winners
Indianapolis 500: A. J. Foyt, U. S.
Pocono 500: Tom Sneva
Ontario 500: Al Unser, U. S.
Daytona 500: Donnie Allison, U. S.
Long Beach Grand Prix: Mario Andretti, U. S.
U. S. Grand Prix: James Hunt, Great Britain

Grand Prix for Formula One Cars, 1977
Argentinian: Jody Scheckter, South Africa
Brazilian: Carlos Reuttemann, Switzerland
South African: Niki Lauda
Long Beach: Mario Andretti
Spanish: Mario Andretti
Monte Carlo: Jody Scheckter
Belgian: Gunnar Nilsson, Sweden
Swedish: Jacques Lafitte, France
French: Mario Andretti
British: James Hunt
West German: Niki Lauda
Austrian: Alan Jones, Australia
Dutch: Niki Lauda
Italian: Mario Andretti
United States: James Hunt
Japanese: James Hunt

The Year
in Sports

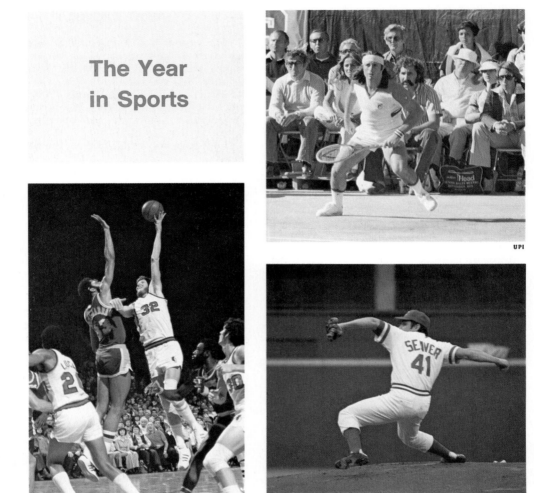

HANK DELESPINASSE, "SPORTS ILLUSTRATED" © TIME INC.

UPI

Guillermo Vilas won the U. S. Open men's tennis championship, defeating Jimmy Connors; Bill Walton (32) led the Portland Trail Blazers to their first NBA title; and in the year's most discussed baseball trade, Tom Seaver, New York Mets' superstar, became a member of the Cincinnati Reds.

JERRY LIEBMAN

Before extremely large crowds, Pelé and his New York Cosmos captured the North American Soccer League championship.

Ballooning is a sure-fire focus of attention. The National Hot Air Balloon Championships were held in Indianola, Iowa. The U. S. yacht *Courageous* defeated *Australia*, 4–0, to retain the America's Cup.

UPI

Seattle Slew became the first undefeated horse to take the Triple Crown.

UPI

New Zealand's John Walker won the 1,500 meter race at the U.S. Olympic Invitational track meet in New York in February.

UPI

For the benefit of Montreal fans, Canadien stars Yvan Cournoyer and Serge Savard parade with "their" Stanley Cup.

BASEBALL

The New York Yankees, after a season of turmoil and travail, completed the 1977 baseball season in sweet triumph.

The Yankees, spending lavishly to sign free-agent stars Reggie Jackson and Don Gullett, were expected to make a shambles of the American League Eastern Division race. However, for half the season, they seemed more concerned with internal squabbling than winning games. Manager Billy Martin feuded with owner George Steinbrenner and with Jackson, the slugging outfielder who was given a five-year, $2.9 million contract to join the Yankees. Jackson and Thurman Munson, the standout catcher, were at odds. Players wanted to be traded. Players sulked. Players wanted Martin fired.

The Yankees were dubbed "the best team money could buy" as well as "a traveling dock fight." At one point during the World Series, Jackson said Martin deserved the Nobel Peace Prize for managing the team. Ultimately, the Yankees overcame all their strife to win the World Series—their 21st world championship, but their first since 1962.

New Yorkers gave the Yankees a ticker-tape parade after they defeated the Los Angeles Dodgers, four games to two, in the fall classic. And the final game, an 8–4 victory in Yankee Stadium, proved to be a memorable event. The outspoken Jackson, who seemed to be in the eye of every Yankee storm, became the toast of New York by slamming three home runs. The homers, which drove in five runs, were hit in three successive at-bats, each on the first pitch. The last was a colossal wallop over Yankee Stadium's center-field fence.

In the 73 previous World Series, only Babe Ruth had hit three homers in one game; the Sultan of Swat did it twice, in 1926 and 1928, both times in St. Louis. But not even the Yankee legend had hit three in successive at-bats. And no one, until Jackson, had clouted five homers in one World Series.

The Yankees, by winning 40 of their last 53 games, fought off the Boston Red Sox and the Baltimore Orioles in the division race. In a league championship series rematch, the Yankees again defeated the Kansas City Royals. It was the Yankees' 31st AL pennant.

Division Races. In the National League, the Dodgers won the Western Division title easily under first-year manager Tommy Lasorda, unseating the two-time defending world champion Cincinnati Reds. The Philadelphia Phillies also breezed in the Eastern Division. In the play-off, the Dodgers surprised the experts by downing the Phillies, three games to one.

This was a season of a livelier baseball and home runs flew at a rapid pace. George Foster of the Cincinnati Reds became the first player in 12 years to reach the 50-homer mark; he hit 52 and batted in 149 runs.

BASEBALL

Professional—Major Leagues

AMERICAN LEAGUE
(Final Standings, 1977)

Eastern Division	W	L	Pct.	Western Division	W	L	Pct.
New York....	100	62	.617	Kansas City...	102	60	.630
Baltimore.....	97	64	.602	Texas........	94	68	.580
Boston.......	97	64	.602	Chicago......	90	72	.556
Detroit.......	74	88	.457	Minnesota....	84	77	.522
Cleveland.....	71	90	.441	California.....	74	88	.457
Milwaukee...	67	95	.414	Seattle.......	64	98	.395
Toronto......	54	107	.335	Oakland......	63	98	.391

NATIONAL LEAGUE
(Final Standings, 1977)

Eastern Division	W	L	Pct.	Western Division	W	L	Pct.
Philadelphia..	101	61	.623	Los Angeles...	98	64	.605
Pittsburgh....	96	66	.593	Cincinnati....	88	74	.543
St. Louis.....	83	79	.512	Houston......	81	81	.500
Chicago......	81	81	.500	San Francisco	75	87	.463
Montreal.....	75	87	.463	San Diego....	69	93	.426
New York....	64	98	.395	Atlanta.......	61	101	.377

Play-offs—American League: New York defeated Kansas City, 3 games to 2; National League: Los Angeles defeated Philadelphia, 3 games to 1.

World Series—New York defeated Los Angeles, 4 games to 2. First Game (Yankee Stadium, New York, Oct. 11): New York 4, Los Angeles 3; second game (Yankee Stadium, Oct. 12): Los Angeles 6, New York 1; third game (Dodger Stadium, Los Angeles, Oct. 14): New York 5, Los Angeles 3; fourth game (Dodger Stadium, Oct. 15): New York 4, Los Angeles 2; fifth game (Dodger Stadium, Oct. 16): Los Angeles 10, New York 4; sixth game (Yankee Stadium, Oct. 18): New York 8, Los Angeles 4. Total attendance: 337,708. Most valuable player: Reggie Jackson.

All-Star Game (Yankee Stadium, New York, July 19): National League 7, American League 5.

Most Valuable Players—American League: Rod Carew, Minnesota; National League: George Foster, Cincinnati.

Cy Young Memorial Awards (outstanding pitchers)—American League: Sparky Lyle, New York; National League: Steve Carlton, Philadelphia.

Rookie of the Year—American League: Eddie Murray, Baltimore; National League: Andre Dawson, Montreal.

Leading Hitters—(Percentage) American: Rod Carew, Minnesota, .388; National: Dave Parker, Pittsburgh, .338. (Runs Batted In) American: Larry Hisle, Minnesota, 119; National: George Foster, Cincinnati, 149. (Home Runs) American: Jim Rice, Boston, 39; National League: Foster, 52. (Runs) American League: Carew 128; National League: Foster 124.

Leading Pitchers—(Earned run average) American League: Frank Tanana, California, 2.54; National League: John Candelaria, Pittsburgh, 2.34. (Victories) American (3 tied at 20): Dave Goltz, Minnesota; Jim Palmer, Baltimore; Dennis Leonard, Kansas City; National: Steve Carlton, Philadelphia, 23. (Strikeouts) American: Nolan Ryan, California, 341; National: Phil Niekro, Atlanta, 262. (Shutouts) American: Tanana, 7; National: Tom Seaver, Cincinnati, 7.

No-Hit Games Pitched: Jim Colborn, Kansas City Royals v. Texas Rangers; Dennis Eckersley, Cleveland Indians v. California Angels.

Hall of Fame Inductees—Ernie Banks, Al Lopez, Joe Sewell, Amos Rusie, Pop Lloyd, Martin Dihigo.

Professional—Minor Leagues, Class AAA

American Association (play-offs): Denver Bears
International League (governor's cup): Charleston Charlies
Pacific Coast League: Phoenix Giants
Mexican League: Nuevo Laredo Tecolotes

Amateur—NCAA

Class I: Arizona State

On Aug. 29 in San Diego, Lou Brock of the St. Louis Cardinals stole the 893rd base of his career, surpassing Ty Cobb's record.

There were other significant achievements. Rod Carew of the Minnesota Twins hit .388, highest major league average in 20 years. Lou Brock of the St. Louis Cardinals reached 900 stolen bases for his career, breaking Ty Cobb's record of 892. Dave Parker of the Pittsburgh Pirates batted .338 to lead the NL.

Steve Carlton won 23 games for the Phillies. The Pirates' John Candelaria won 20 and lost 5, and led the NL with an earned-run average of 2.34. Yankees reliever Sparky Lyle won 13 games, saved 26 others, and had a 2.17 ERA. Nolan Ryan of the California Angels registered 341 strikeouts, a record fifth time that Ryan went over the 300 mark in strikeouts.

The Unusual and Changes. It was a season of strange events, as well. In spring training, Lenny Randle of the Texas Rangers beat up his manager, Frank Lucchesi, after losing his second-base job. Atlanta Braves owner Ted Turner declared himself manager of the team but, after one game, was sent back into the stands by a league directive. The Rangers, who fired Lucchesi, hired Eddie Stanky from the college ranks but, after managing one game, Stanky said he missed his family and resigned. An electricity blackout in New York City left 22,000 fans at Shea Stadium sitting in the darkness singing "White Christmas."

Many top players changed teams. The new right of free-agency, negotiated by the Players' Association, enabled such standouts as Jackson, Gullett, Gary Matthews, Gene Tenace, Rollie Fingers, Bill Campbell, Wayne Garland, and Dave Cash to join different clubs and become millionaires via multiyear contracts. The Angels were the biggest spenders, giving more than $5 million to three players—Bobby Grich, Don Baylor, and Joe Rudi—but the club fell a notch in the standings.

On June 15, the trading deadline, the New York Mets dealt premier pitcher Tom Seaver, who was unhappy with management, to the Reds. Seaver wound up with a 21–6 record but he was not enough to bring the Reds a pennant.

The usual turnover in managers claimed Frank Robinson, first black pilot in the majors. He was fired by the Cleveland Indians.

There was expansion as the American League added the Toronto Blue Jays and the Seattle Mariners. The American League thus had 14 clubs; the National League remained at 12.

Sadaharu Oh, 37-year-old first baseman with the Tokyo Yomiuri Giants, hit the 756th home-run of his career, surpassing Hank Aaron's record of 755. However, commissioner Bowie Kuhn announced that Aaron's mark would continue to be recognized in the United States.

Philip K. Wrigley, the 82-year-old chewing-gum magnate who owned the Chicago Cubs for 43 years, died on April 12.

BOB BROEG
Sports Editor
"St. Louis Post-Dispatch"

The big question of the baseball season: Would Rod Carew hit .400? The Minnesota star fell 12 points short.

UPI

BASKETBALL

Since its development early in the century, basketball has been considered the perfect game for teaching the concept of teamwork. So, it seemed incongruous that the favored Philadelphia 76ers failed to win the professional basketball championship because of a lack of teamwork. On the college level, Marquette University won the NCAA crown, and women's basketball rose to new heights of popularity.

THE PROFESSIONAL SEASON

Led by George McGinnis, voted the most valuable player of the 76ers, Julius (Doctor J.) Erving, who was purchased from the New York Nets for $3 million at the start of the season, and Doug Collins, the Philadelphia team won the first two games of the championship series with the Portland Trail Blazers at Philadelphia. But with Bill Walton and Maurice Lucas setting the pace in a team effort, the Blazers overshadowed the individualistic achievements of the 76er stars and romped to victory in the next four games. Only the sixth and concluding contest was really close, 109–107.

Walton, after a couple of ineffective seasons because of injuries and other complications, had finally developed into the fine pro player he was

expected to be after he led UCLA to the NCAA championship in 1973 and was graduated in 1974. The 6-foot, 11-inch (210 cm) center was outstanding in his playmaking and rebounding as well as in scoring, and was the unanimous choice for most valuable in the play-offs. Lucas aided Walton in rebounding and in feeding Bob Gross and Dave Twardzik. Jack Ramsay, the coach who built the club on the concept of team play, said: "They are talented and they are willing to play together." This was in contrast to the 76ers, who failed, at times, to run basic patterns and to play defense.

The final series was the culmination of the National Basketball Association's first season with 22 teams, including 4 from the former American Basketball Association. Two of those teams, the Denver Nuggets and the San Antonio Spurs, proved strong challengers to the NBA's established powers. In fact, Denver, in winning the Midwest Division of the Western Conference, led all clubs in home attendance with 703,133 admissions.

The Los Angeles Lakers, paced by Kareem Abdul-Jabbar who was again voted the league's most valuable player, won the Pacific Division with the league's best mark, 53 won and 29 lost. In the Eastern Conference, Philadelphia took Atlantic Division honors and Houston triumphed in the Central Division.

In the Eastern semifinals, Houston eliminated Washington, 4 games to 2, but Philadelphia had to go all out to get past Boston, 4–3. Then in the conference final the 76ers were again extended to beat Houston, 4–2. Meanwhile, in the West, Portland defeated Denver, 4–2, and then routed the Lakers in 4 straight games after Los Angeles had beaten the Golden State Warriors, 4–3.

The league came to the aid of its four new teams, Denver, San Antonio, the Indiana Pacers, and the Nets who plan to move to New Jersey. The owners voted to wait until 1980 for payments of $200,000 due from each in June 1977.

THE COLLEGE SEASON

Marquette University's basketball team celebrated a last hurrah and a first hurrah at the same time in 1977. The last hurrah was a final salute to Al McGuire, the Warriors' coach, who retired at season's end after 20 years of college coaching, the last 13 at Marquette. The first hurrah was complete victory for the first time in the NCAA basketball tournament The Warriors staved off defeat, twice by one swish of the ball through the basket, through the five brackets of the play-offs. In the closing seconds of the final, with victory assured, Al McGuire, the tough and temperamental guy from New York, sat on the bench in full view of a TV audience of 40 million with his head in his hands, weeping.

In that final, Marquette defeated North Carolina, 67–59, playing with patience after losing a 12-point halftime lead. North Carolina, paced

RICHARD LEE

Led by Lucy Harris (15), Delta State won the Intercollegiate Athletics for Women title for the third consecutive year. Women's basketball gained in popularity.

head's jump shot at the buzzer, 51–49. Whitehead took a long pass from Butch Lee, which bounced off the upstretched hands of Cedric (Cornbread) Maxwell, Charlotte's 6-foot, 8-inch (203 cm) star center.

The surprising team from Charlotte had achieved the biggest upset in its previous game by subduing top-ranked Michigan, 75–68. Meanwhile, North Carolina (at Chapel Hill) had eliminated three of the top-ranked teams—Notre Dame, 79–77; Kentucky, 79–72; and Nevada-Las Vegas, 84–83.

Michigan had regained the top ranking just before the start of the play-offs when the University of San Francisco lost at Notre Dame, 93–82. The Dons had won all 29 of their previous games and had been voted the top team for eight weeks. Michigan, the runner-up to Indiana for the championship in 1976, had been designated Number 1 at the start of the season until beaten by Providence late in December. Meanwhile, Indiana's 33-game winning streak was shattered, December 1, by Toledo, 59–57.

San Francisco did not last long in the play-off. The Dons were run over by Nevada-Las Vegas, 121–95, in the first round, and the Runnin' Rebels eliminated Utah, 88–83, and surprising Idaho State, 107–90. Idaho State had ousted UCLA, 76–75.

Women's Tournament. Delta State of Cleveland, Miss., captured the Association of Intercollegiate Athletics for Women title for the third straight year. The Lady Statesmen, led by Lucy Harris, who was drafted by the New Orleans Jazz of the NBA, defeated Louisiana State, 68–55, in the final. Tennessee took third place by defeating Immaculata, 91–71. Delta had ousted Tennessee, 62–58, and LSU had stopped Immaculata, 74–68, in the semifinals.

BILL BRADDOCK, *"The New York Times"*

by ailing Phil Ford and John Kuester, who had led the Tar Heels through the semifinal when Ford was sidelined by an elbow injury, could not consistently break Marquette's sagging defense. North Carolina's famed four-corner offense resulted in more than one score for Marquette.

Marquette actually had more trouble getting into the play-offs than it had staying in them. The Warriors had a 21–7 won-lost record when selected as an at-large team, just after losing to Michigan by a point for their third straight loss. They eliminated Cincinnati, 66–61, in their first test and then nipped Kansas State, 67–66, converting a free throw after a K-State basket was disallowed and a foul charged in the final seconds. In the regional final, Marquette downed Wake Forest, 82–68. The semifinal matchup was with the new power, North Carolina at Charlotte. Marquette won on Jerome White-

---

COLLEGE BASKETBALL

Conference Champions

Atlantic Coast: North Carolina
Big Eight: Kansas State
Big Sky: Idaho State
Big Ten: Michigan
East Coast—Eastern Division: Hofstra; Western Division: Lafayette
Eastern Independent—Eastern Division: Rutgers; Western Division: West Virginia
Ivy League: Princeton
Metro-7: Louisville
Mid-American: Miami, Ohio
Missouri Valley: Southern Illinois
Ohio Valley: Austin Peay
Pacific-8: UCLA
Pacific Coast Athletic: Long Beach State
Southeastern: Kentucky and Tennessee
Southern: Virginia Military
Southwest: Arkansas
Sun Belt: North Carolina, Charlotte
West Coast Athletic: San Francisco
Western Athletic: Utah

Tournaments

NCAA: Marquette
NIT: St. Bonaventure
NCAA Division II: Tennessee, Chattanooga
NCAA Division III: Wittenberg

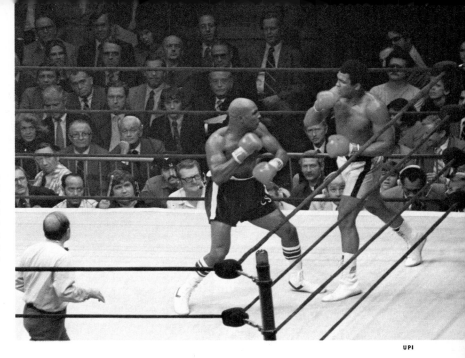

Before a sellout crowd in New York City's Madison Square Garden, Sept. 29, Muhammad Ali retained his heavyweight crown by scoring a unanimous decision over Earnie Shavers. The fight was one of Ali's toughest.

BOXING

Boxing's most illustrious figure, Muhammad Ali, continued to dominate the sport. In two title defenses, the 35-year-old champion retained his crown. Ringside observers, however, were saying it was time for him to retire. Still, in his title defense against Earnie Shavers, Ali's appeal led to an estimated 70 million TV viewers to watch the heavyweight fight.

Champions. Carlos Monzon of Argentina, the middleweight champion, retired after outpointing Rodrigo Valdes of Colombia at Monte Carlo on July 30. Monzon held the World Boxing Association (WBA) crown from 1970. He became the sole champion by taking the World Boxing Council (WBC) title from Valdes in 1976. Monzon's record listed 89 victories, 3 losses, and 9 draws. Valdes gained the title by outpointing Benny Briscoe of Philadelphia in November.

Fifteen champions retained their titles and six new titleholders were crowned. In the light heavyweight class, John Conteh of England, the WBC champion since 1974, stopped Ken Hutchins of Kalamazoo, Mich., in the third round in London on March 5. When Conteh failed to defend against the No. 1 contender, Miguel Cuello of Argentina, he was stripped of his title on May 18. On May 21, Cuello gained the title by knocking out Jesse Burnett of Los Angeles at 2:49 of the ninth round.

Ali. Alfredo Evangelista, a Spaniard with a lackluster record, stayed 15 rounds with Ali in the champion's first defense of the year on May 16 at Landover, Md. Ali, who trained only slightly for the bout, gave a dull performance. The press and a national TV audience considered the bout a fiasco. Ali was criticized for being matched against so inept an opponent. However, the champion's second defense, on September 29, against Earnie Shavers, an Ohioan with an impressive knockout record, proved to be one of Ali's toughest fights. Ali gained a unanimous decision and there were no knockdowns. Shavers repeatedly hurt and staggered Ali with solid rights to the head. The champion withstood Shavers' late-round barrage and slugged toe-to-toe with the challenger in the final minute. Ali's share of the purse, plus ancillary benefits, exceeded $3 million.

GEORGE DE GREGORIO

BOXING

World Professional Champions
(Year of achieving title in parentheses)

Junior Flyweight—Yoko Gushiken, Japan (1976), World Boxing Association (WBA); Luis Estaba, Venezuela (1975), World Boxing Council (WBC).
Flyweight—Guty Espadas, Mexico (1976), WBA; Miguel Canto, Mexico (1975), WBC.
Bantamweight—Jorge Lujan, Panama (1977), WBA; Carlos Zarate, Mexico (1976), WBC.
Junior Featherweight—Wilfredo Gomez, Puerto Rico (1977), WBC.
Featherweight—Rafael Ortega, Panama (1977), WBA; Danny Lopez, Los Angeles (1976), WBC.
Junior Lightweight—Sammy Serrano, Puerto Rico (1976), WBA; Alfredo Escalera, Puerto Rico (1975), WBC.
Lightweight—Roberto Duran, Panama (1972), WBA; Esteban de Jesus, Puerto Rico (1976), WBC.
Junior Welterweight—Antonio Cervantes, Colombia (1977), WBA; Seansak Muangsurin, Thailand (1976), WBC.
Welterweight—José Cuevas, Mexico (1976), WBA; Carlos Palomino, Westminster, Calif. (1976), WBC.
Middleweight—Rodrigo Valdes, Colombia (1977)
Light Heavyweight—Victor Galindez, Argentina (1974), WBA; Miguel Cuello, Argentina (1977), WBC.
Heavyweight—Muhammad Ali, Chicago (1964 and 1974).

National AAU Champions
(Winston-Salem, N.C., May 3–7)

106 Pounds—Israel Acosta, Milwaukee, Wis.
112 Pounds—Jerome Coffee, Nashville, Tenn.
119 Pounds—Rocky Lockridge, Tacoma, Wash.
125 Pounds—Johnny Bumphus, Tacoma, Wash.
132 Pounds—Anthony Fletcher, Philadelphia, Pa.
139 Pounds—Thomas Hearns, Detroit, Mich.
147 Pounds—Mike McCallum, Nashville, Tenn.
156 Pounds—Clinton Jackson, Nashville, Tenn.
165 Pounds—Jerome Bennett, United States Air Force.
178 Pounds—Larry Strogen, Shreveport, La.
Heavyweight—Greg Page, Louisville, Ky.
Team—Southeastern AAU (15 points).

FOOTBALL

Following a series of upsets in the annual Bowl games, the Irish of Notre Dame were ranked as the No. 1 college football team in the nation. They were followed by Alabama and Arkansas. The University of Texas, No. 1 at the end of the regular season, was voted the No. 4 spot in the Associated Press sportswriters' poll and No. 5 in the United Press International coaches' poll. On the professional level, Denver and Dallas clashed in the 1978 Super Bowl game.

THE PROFESSIONAL SEASON

The Super Bowl XII opponents were a study in contrast: the perennial also-rans, the Denver Broncos, who had already made an entry in the National Football League record book by being the first team to reach the ultimate game in their first venture into the play-offs, and the consistently successful Dallas Cowboys, who were post-season contenders for the 11th time in 12 years and who had gone to the Super Bowl on three previous occasions.

Craig Morton personified the Broncos' frustration at having failed in the first 17 years of their existence to qualify for title consideration. The Denver quarterback had been traded by the Cowboys after nine and a half years of mostly warming the bench and two and a half miserable seasons with the New York Giants. In his first deal as the Broncos' new head coach, Red Miller rescued Morton.

In comparison the Cowboys had a charismatic leader in Roger Staubach. He had beaten out Morton, groomed to be Don Meredith's successor, for the quarterback post. Equally im-

UPI

Denver quarterback Craig Morton asks Bronco fans for quiet as he leads his team to AFC championship.

portant, coach Tom Landry, with a talent-rich squad, was able gradually to blend Tony Dorsett into his multifaceted offense. The 1976 Heisman Trophy winner was a part-time player for the first nine games before he became a starter at running back. And yet Dorsett finished the regular season as the eighth rookie in NFL annals to rush for more than 1,000 yards (1,007).

Super Bowl XII was widely expected to be a defensive struggle, but eight Denver turnovers

---

PROFESSIONAL FOOTBALL

NATIONAL FOOTBALL LEAGUE

Final Standings

AMERICAN CONFERENCE
Eastern Division

	W	L	T	Pct.	For	Agst.
Baltimore	10	4	0	.714	295	221
Miami	10	4	0	.714	313	197
New England	9	5	0	.643	278	217
Jets	3	11	0	.214	191	300
Buffalo	3	11	0	.214	160	313

Central Division

	W	L	T	Pct.	For	Agst.
Pittsburgh	9	5	0	.643	283	243
Cincinnati	8	6	0	.571	238	235
Houston	8	6	0	.571	299	230
Cleveland	6	8	0	.429	269	267

Western Division

	W	L	T	Pct.	For	Agst.
Denver	12	2	0	.857	274	148
Oakland*	11	3	0	.786	351	230
San Diego	7	7	0	.500	222	205
Seattle	5	9	0	.357	282	373
Kansas City	2	12	0	.143	225	349

* Clinched play-off berth

Play-offs
Oakland 37, Baltimore 31
Denver 34, Pittsburgh 21
Championship
Denver 20, Oakland 17

NATIONAL CONFERENCE
Eastern Division

	W	L	T	Pct.	For	Agst.
Dallas	12	2	0	.857	345	212
Washington	9	5	0	.643	196	189
St. Louis	7	7	0	.500	272	287
Giants	5	9	0	.357	181	265
Philadelphia	5	9	0	.357	220	207

Central Division

	W	L	T	Pct.	For	Agst.
Minnesota	9	5	0	.643	231	227
Chicago*	9	5	0	.643	255	253
Detroit	6	8	0	.429	299	252
Green Bay	4	10	0	.286	134	219
Tampa Bay	2	12	0	.143	103	223

Western Division

	W	L	T	Pct.	For	Agst.
Los Angeles	10	4	0	.714	302	146
Atlanta	7	7	0	.500	179	129
San Francisco	5	9	0	.357	220	260
New Orleans	3	11	0	.214	232	336

Play-offs
Dallas 37, Chicago 7
Minnesota 14, Los Angeles 7
Championship
Dallas 23, Minnesota 6

Super Bowl: Dallas 27, Denver 10

UPI

Tony Dorset, Dallas' prize rookie, runs for a score as the Cowboys defeat Chicago in play-off action.

have the same won-lost records. That situation existed in the American Conference's Eastern Division when the Baltimore Colts and the Miami Dolphins ended the season with 10–4 marks. Since the teams had split in their two meetings, the Colts gained the nod because they had a better intraconference record (9–3) than the Dolphins (8–4).

The most remarkable individual performance of the season was achieved by Walter Payton of the Chicago Bears. A third-year pro, he rushed for 275 yards against the Vikings to surpass O. J. Simpson's single-game record by two yards. The Buffalo Bills' star had set the previous mark only the year before. Payton finished with 1,852 yards to become the third highest rusher in an NFL season. Simpson established the standard in 1973 when he ran for 2,003 yards. Jim Brown of the Cleveland Browns holds second place with 1,863 yards, gained in 1963.

In Canada's 65th annual Grey Cup, the Montreal Alouettes of the Eastern Conference routed the Edmonton Eskimos, the Western Conference champions, 41–6.

THE COLLEGE SEASON

The University of Texas, with a new head coach, Fred Akers, was ignored in all the 1977 preseason rankings and was considered likely to finish fourth in the Southwest Conference. But the Longhorns, proving as difficult to stop as a cattle stampede, powered their way undefeated through an 11-game regular season, captured the league championship, and won a berth in the Cotton Bowl.

Chief mechanic in the Longhorns' offense was Earl Campbell, a strong 6-foot (183-cm), 220-pound (100-kg) senior running back and pass-catcher, who collected a bushel of rushing records and earned for himself the coveted Heisman Trophy as the outstanding player of the year. Other swift assets in the Texas offensive machine were the Johnny Joneses: Johnny (Lam) Jones, a receiver with Olympic speed, and Johnny (Ham) Jones, a muscular running back. In addition, the Longhorns survived injuries to their first three quarterbacks that would have put any other team out of commission. Another key contributor to Texas' finest season was Russell Erxleben, a talented punter and place-kicker. So unyielding were the Longhorns' defenders, led by Brad Shearer, that they did not allow a touchdown on a rush until late in the season.

All that stood in the way of the Longhorns' perfect season were the Irish of Notre Dame. Their matchup in the Cotton Bowl was the most attractive of the bowl extravaganzas. With a record marred only by a 20–13 upset defeat at the hands of Mississippi in its second game, Notre Dame conquered ten foes, most of them impressively. The Irish partisans were quick to note that Notre Dame's schedule was more difficult than the Longhorns'. The Irish attack was

and two Dallas scoring strikes in the second half made it a one-sided, 27–10, affair for the Cowboys. Morton was intercepted four times and finally was replaced by Norris Weese midway in the third period. Four fumbles were lost by the Broncos and two by the Cowboys, testifying to the aggressive play by the defensive units.

In their conference championship victories, the contrast between the Broncos and the Cowboys was again present.

Although they had the benefit of "Broncomania" in the form of their frenzied fans in Mile High Stadium, the Broncos needed an official's controversial call to help them beat the defending Super Bowl champion Oakland Raiders, 20–17, for the American Conference title.

Rob Lytle, a Denver running back, fumbled at the Oakland 2-yard line and Mike McCoy recovered for the Raiders. But the referee ruled the play had stopped before the fumble and the Broncos retained possession. Jon Keyworth plunged over on the next play for a 14–3 Denver lead in the third period. An interception by Bob Swenson, a linebacker, set up what proved to be the winning touchdown for Denver in the fourth quarter as Morton passed 7 yards to Haven Moses two plays later.

At Dallas, the Cowboys grasped National Conference honors from the Minnesota Vikings with considerably greater ease. With Ed (Too Tall) Jones and Harvey Martin most prominent in the Dallas defense, the Vikings were held to two field goals. The Cowboys were in command all the way for a 23–6 victory.

Receiving considerable attention and criticism was the complicated NFL formula for determining a division champion when two teams

Following Notre Dame's win over Texas in the Cotton Bowl (*right*) coach Dan Devine relays word that the Irish are No. 1.

PHOTOS UPI

sparked by Joe Montana at quarterback and Vagas Ferguson at running back.

In the biggest of three major bowl upsets, the Irish decisively defeated Texas, 38–10. The Longhorns committed six turnovers that coach Dan Devine's troops capitalized on for their one-sided triumph. Ferguson scored three touchdowns as the mammoth Irish offensive linemen outmuscled the lighter Texas defenders.

The annual prize of a trip to the Rose Bowl by the Big Ten Conference champion again was determined by the outcome of the Michigan-Ohio State struggle. Michigan prevailed this time by a score of 13–6 in its Ann Arbor backyard, a result that so incensed Ohio State coach Woody Hayes that he struck a television cameraman on the sideline late in the fourth quarter. The Wolverines' opponent in the oldest bowl classic was Washington, which emerged on top in the Pacific Eight race. Washington was also a surprise victor, defeating Michigan 27–20, for the Wolverines' fourth loss in their last four

Rose Bowl visits. A fourth-quarter comeback by Michigan was nearly successful.

Oklahoma, which seldom misses a bowl appearance, went to the Orange Bowl as the Big Eight representative after trouncing Nebraska, 38–7. The only blemish on its record was a 13–6 loss to the Longhorns. Arkansas, under its new coach, Lou Holtz, the former coach of the New York Jets, wrapped up a 10–1 season and met the Sooners at Miami. In another stunner, the Razorbacks walloped Oklahoma, favored by 18 points, 31–6.

Coach Bear Bryant produced another typical powerhouse at Alabama (10–1) and received another ticket to the Sugar Bowl. Ohio State's consolation after losing to Michigan was to meet Jeff Rutledge & Company at New Orleans. But it was small consolation for the Buckeyes, who were trounced, 35–6. Alabama proved to be the only favorite in four major bowl games to live up to expectations.

LUD DUROSKA, *"The New York Times"*

COLLEGE FOOTBALL

Intercollegiate and Conference Champions

Heisman Trophy—Earl Campbell, Texas
Eastern (Lambert Trophy)—Penn State
Eastern Small College—Lambert Bowl: Westminster; Lambert Cup: Leigh
Atlantic Coast—North Carolina
Big Eight—Oklahoma
Big Sky—Boise State
Big Ten—Michigan, Ohio State (tied)
Ivy League—Yale
Mid-American—Miami
Missouri Valley—West Texas State
Ohio Valley—Austin Peay
Pacific-8—Washington
Southeastern—Alabama
Southern—Tennessee (Chattanooga), VMI (tied)
Southland—Louisiana Tech
Southwest—University of Texas
Western Athletic—Arizona State, Brigham Young (tied)
Yankee—Massachusetts

NCAA Championships

Division II—Leigh
Division III—Widener

NAIA Championships

Division I—Abilene Christian
Division II—Westminster

Major Bowl Games

Independence Bowl (Shreveport, La., Dec. 17)—Louisiana Tech 21, University of Louisville 14
Liberty Bowl (Memphis, Dec. 19)—Nebraska 21, North Carolina 17
Hall of Fame Bowl (Birmingham, Ala., Dec. 22)—Maryland 17, Minnesota 7
Tangerine Bowl (Orlando, Fla., Dec. 23)—Florida State 40, Texas Tech 17
Fiesta Bowl (Tempe, Ariz., Dec. 25)—Penn State 42, Arizona State 30
Gator Bowl (Jacksonville, Fla., Dec. 30)—Pittsburgh 34, Clemson 3
Astro-Bluebonnet Bowl (Houston, Dec. 31)—Southern California 47, Texas A & M 28
Peach Bowl (Atlanta, Dec. 31)—North Carolina State 24, Iowa State 14
Sun Bowl (El Paso, Tex., Dec. 31)—Stanford 24, Louisiana State 14
Cotton Bowl (Dallas, Jan. 2)—Notre Dame 38, University of Texas 10
Orange Bowl (Miami, Jan. 2)—Arkansas 31, Oklahoma 6
Rose Bowl (Pasadena, Calif., Jan. 2)—University of Washington 27, Michigan 20
Sugar Bowl (New Orleans, Jan. 2)—Alabama 35, Ohio State 6

GOLF

The 1977 Professional Golfers Association season will go down as the year of Tom Watson, who highlighted his sensational campaign with a pair of victories over Jack Nicklaus in the Masters and British Open. But crowding Watson for attention were the comeback of young Lanny Wadkins and a pair of individual assaults on par by Al Geiberger and Hale Irwin.

Watson, 28, was already a two-time winner going into the Masters. Tied with Nicklaus at the end of 14 holes in the final round, he rolled in a 20-foot birdie putt on 17 while Nicklaus was bogeying 18 to decide the issue.

Three months later the two met again in one of golf's classic confrontations over the Ailsa Course, Turnberry, Scotland. After identical rounds of 68-70-65, Nicklaus pulled three strokes ahead at the end of four holes on the final day. But Watson battled back to tie with a 60-foot birdie putt on 15, then birdied 17 and 18 for another 65 and a one-stroke victory, his second British Open triumph.

Hubert Green survived a telephoned death threat and a fast finish by Lou Graham to win the U. S. Open in Tulsa. Surrounded by police the last four holes, he played them in even par and wrapped up his first major title with a two-under-par 278, one better than Graham.

The week before, Geiberger had stunned the golf world with a 13-under-par 59 in the Danny

AL SATTERWHITE "SPORTS ILLUSTRATED" © TIME INC.

Lanny Wadkins scores a sudden death play-off victory over Gene Littler at the PGA Championship in August.

Thomas Memphis Classic, the first official PGA tournament score in the 50s. Late in August, Irwin bombarded hallowed Pinehurst No. 2, long rated by *Golf Digest* magazine as one of the country's top ten courses, with a 20-under-par 264 to win the Colgate Hall of Fame Classic.

Wadkins, once the tour's brightest young star until a gall bladder illness plunged him into a three-year slump, regained the headlines with a play-off victory over Gene Littler in the PGA. Wadkins, 27, followed this with a spectacular 13-under-par 267 at Firestone C. C. to win the World Series of Golf and its $100,000 prize.

Watson, who won three other events to go with his two major victories, topped the money list with $310,653 and won the Vardon Trophy with a 70.32 scoring average. Nicklaus, winner of three tournaments, was next with $284,509, followed by Wadkins with $244,882.

Judy Rankin again led the money-winners on the Ladies Professional Golfers Association tour with $122,890. She also won the Vare Trophy for low scoring average with 72.16. JoAnne Carner was second with $113,711 and three tournament victories.

Debbie Austin, who had not won in nine years on tour, jumped out with five victories in 1977 and earned, along with Bruce Lietzke, *Golf Digest*'s Most Improved Player Award. Hollis Stacy, another nonwinner heretofore, took home three titles, including the U. S. Open.

LARRY DENNIS, *"Golf Digest"*

GOLF

Men's Individual Champions

U. S. Open—Hubert Green (278)
British Open—Tom Watson (268)
Masters—Tom Watson (276)
PGA Championship—Lanny Wadkins (282)
World Series of Golf—Lanny Wadkins (267)
Tournament Players Championship—Mark Hayes (289)
Canadian Open—Lee Trevino (280)
Mony Tournament of Champions—Jack Nicklaus (281)

PGA Tournament Winners

Phoenix Open—Jerry Pate (277)
Joe Garagiola-Tucson Open—Bruce Lietzke (275)
Bing Crosby National Pro-Am—Tom Watson (273)
Andy Williams-San Diego Open—Tom Watson (269)
Hawaiian Open—Bruce Lietzke (273)
Bob Hope Desert Classic—Rik Massengale (337)
Glen Campbell-Los Angeles Open—Tom Purtzer (273)
Jackie Gleason Inverary Classic—Jack Nicklaus (275)
Florida Citrus Open—Gary Koch (274)
Doral-Eastern Open—Andy Bean (277)
Houston Open—Gene Littler (276)
Byron Nelson Classic—Ray Floyd (276)
Kemper Open—Tom Weiskopf (277)
Danny Thomas Memphis Classic—Al Geiberger (273)
Sammy Davis, Jr.-Greater Hartford Open—Bill Kratzert (265)
Colgate Hall of Fame Classic—Hale Irwin (264)
Buick Open—Bobby Cole (271)
Pensacola Open—Leonard Thompson (268)

Pro Team

Ryder Cup—United States 12½, Great Britain-Ireland 7½
World Cup—Spain

Amateur Team

Walker Cup—United States 16, Great Britain-Ireland 8

Men's Individual Amateur Champions

U. S. Amateur—John Fought
British Amateur—Peter McEvoy
U. S. Public Links—Jerry Vidovic

Women's Individual Pro Champions

U. S. Open—Hollis Stacy (292)
LPGA Championship—Chako Higuchi (279)

Women's Individual Amateur Champion

U. S. Amateur—Beth Daniel

UPI

In an eight-team tournament in Vienna, Czechoslovakia (white jerseys) retained its world championship title.

HOCKEY

The Canadian Province of Québec pulled off an unprecedented "double" in 1977 when the Montreal Canadiens won the Stanley Cup and the Québec Nordiques captured their first Avco Cup, but the year's most coveted title was again claimed by Czechoslovakia's national team.

NHL. The biggest problem the Montreal Canadiens faced heading into the 1976–77 season was what they possibly could do to improve upon their Stanley Cup-winning performance of 1975–76. After all, they had set a league record with 58 victories and then won 12 of 13 play-off games, including a four-game sweep of the defending champion Philadelphia Flyers.

Yet the Canadiens, encountering additional pressure as reigning champions, proved to be even stronger by going through 94 games—80 regular season and 14 in the play-offs—with only 10 losses, 2 fewer than they had lost in 93 games the year before. Their 60 victories broke their regular-season record and, although beaten twice in 14 play-offs, they again captured the cup by winning four straight games in the final round. This time they beat the Boston Bruins by scores of 7–3, 3–0, 4–2, and 2–1.

The Canadiens, who trailed by a goal only once in their best-of-seven series against Boston, assured their 18th Stanley Cup of the modern era—they had won it twice prior to the formation of the NHL—when Jacques Lemaire took a perfect feed from behind the net by Guy Lafleur to beat goaltender Gerry Cheevers in the fifth

minute of overtime in the final game. It solidified Lafleur's selection as winner of the Conn Smythe Trophy as the most valuable player in the play-offs, during which he scored 26 points —one shy of the record.

Lafleur simply never let up after registering 136 points—56 goals and 80 assists—during the regular season en route to the league scoring championship. He also broke the record by scoring at least one point in his final 28 games, a mark he can extend in the 1977–78 campaign. But the Canadiens also benefited from a 60-goal season, plus eight more in the play-offs, by Steve Shutt, who finished with 105 points over the 80 games.

The defensive muscle was provided by Guy Lapointe, Larry Robinson, and Serge Savard, all veteran defensemen, and by the Canadiens' checking line. But the Canadiens had even more defensive punch, getting a Vezina Trophy-winning performance from goaltenders Ken Dryden and backup Michel (Bunny) Larocque who allowed only 171 goals over the 4,800-minute regular season. Dryden was also sensational in the play-offs.

NHL records set by the Canadiens included fewest losses (8), longest unbeaten streak at home (34 games, which may be extended in the 1977–78 season), fewest losses at home (1), most road victories (27), and most points in the standings (132).

In the play-offs, the Canadiens actually faced their most difficult challenge against the New York Islanders who lost the best-of-seven semifinals, four games to two. Previously, the Canadiens had swept the St. Louis Blues in four straight while the Islanders did the same to the Buffalo Sabres. Meanwhile, the Bruins had eliminated the Los Angeles Kings in six games and then won four straight over the Flyers—the first two games in overtime.

World Championship. Czechoslovakia successfully defended its title in an eight-team international tournament staged in Vienna, Austria. Undoubtedly the series will be remembered best because of the controversial play of Canada which had returned to competition after several years' absence.

Canada's violence, particularly during an 11–1 drubbing by the Soviet Union the first time they met, was bitterly criticized, especially in the European press.

The Czechs won seven and tied one of their eight games to finish with 15 total points, one better than both Sweden and the Soviet Union, which finished second and third, respectively, because of Sweden's goal-scoring edge in their head-to-head meetings. Canada, which finished 6–3–1, was the only other team in the medal round while Finland, the United States, West Germany, and Rumania finished in that order in the consolation standings.

Vladimir Petrov of the Soviet Union captured the tournament scoring championship with 21 points, including seven goals; his teammate Boris Mikhailov was runner-up with 19. Petrov earned a berth on the all-star team, along with teammates Valeri Vasiliyev, a defenseman, and Helmut Balderis, a forward. Others selected were defenseman Frantisek Pospisil and forward Vladimir Martinec of Czechoslovakia and goaltender Göran Högosta of Sweden.

WHA. The Québec Nordiques captured the World Hockey Association championship by defeating the Winnipeg Jets, 8–2, in the seventh game of their best-of-seven final series for the Avco World Trophy. The Nordiques prevented the Jets from winning it two years in a row.

Serge Bernier was an almost-unanimous selection as MVP of the play-offs for racking up 14 goals and 22 assists for 36 points, a record. His 14 goals tied a record set earlier in the play-offs by teammate Réal Cloutier and his 22 assists also constituted a record.

Québec and Houston had won the division championships earlier but the Aeros, with Gordie Howe and sons Mark and Marty, were eliminated by the Jets in the play-offs. Later, the Howes were traded to the New England Whalers, the aftermath of the Aeros' financial dilemma. It was a bad year all around for WHA teams with Minnesota, despite its winning record, dropping out of the league in January and several other franchises in serious trouble. Attempts to merge the NHL and the WHA were unsuccessful.

ED CONRAD

Sports Department, "The Gazette," Montréal

HOCKEY

National Hockey League
(Final Standings, 1976–77)

Campbell Conference

Patrick Division	W	L	T	Pts.	Goals For	Goals Against
Philadelphia	48	16	16	112	323	213
N. Y. Islanders	47	21	12	106	288	193
Atlanta	34	34	12	80	264	265
N. Y. Rangers	29	37	14	72	272	310
Smythe Division						
St. Louis	32	39	9	73	239	276
Minnesota	23	39	18	64	240	310
Chicago	26	43	11	63	240	298
Vancouver	25	42	13	63	235	294
Colorado	20	46	14	54	226	307

Wales Conference

Norris Division	W	L	T	Pts.	Goals For	Goals Against
Montreal	60	8	12	132	387	171
Los Angeles	34	31	15	83	271	241
Pittsburgh	34	33	13	81	240	252
Washington	24	42	14	62	221	307
Detroit	16	55	9	41	183	309
Adams Division						
Boston	49	23	8	106	312	240
Buffalo	48	24	8	104	301	220
Toronto	33	32	15	81	301	285
Cleveland	25	42	13	63	240	292

Stanley Cup: Montréal Canadiens

All-Star Game: Wales Conference 4, Campbell Conference 3

Individual Honors

Hart Trophy (most valuable): Guy Lafleur, Montréal Canadiens
Ross Trophy (leading scorer): Lafleur
Norris Trophy (best defenseman): Larry Robinson, Montréal Canadiens
Lady Bing Trophy (sportsmanship): Marcel Dionne, Los Angeles Kings
Vezina Trophy (goalie, shared): Ken Dryden and Michel Larocque, Montréal Canadiens
Calder Trophy (rookie of the year): Willi Plett, Atlanta Flyers
Conn Smythe Trophy (most valuable in play-offs): Lafleur
Coach of the Year: Scotty Bowman, Montréal Canadiens

World Hockey Association

Eastern Division	W	L	T	Pts.	Goals For	Goals Against
Quebec	47	31	3	97	353	295
Cincinnati	39	37	5	83	354	303
Indianapolis	36	37	8	80	276	305
New England	35	40	6	76	275	290
Birmingham	31	46	4	66	289	309
Western Division						
Houston	50	24	6	106	320	241
Winnipeg	46	32	2	94	366	291
San Diego	40	37	4	84	284	283
Edmonton	34	43	4	72	243	304
Calgary	31	43	7	69	252	296
Phoenix	28	48	4	60	281	383

Avco Cup: Québec Nordiques

Individual Honors

Scorer: Réal Cloutier, Québec Nordiques
Most Valuable Player: Robbie Ftorek, Phoenix Roadrunners
Most Valuable Player in Play-offs: Serge Bernier, Québec Nordiques
Most Sportsmanlike: Dave Keon, New England Whalers
Rookie of the Year: George Lyle, New England Whalers
Defenseman of the Year: Ron Plumb, Cincinnati Stingers
Goalies: Ron Grahame and Wayne Rutledge, Houston Aeros

World Cup

Final Standings

1. Czechoslovakia	4. Canada	7. West Germany
2. Sweden	5. Finland	8. Rumania
3. Soviet Union	6. United States	

Intercollegiate Champions

NCAA: Wisconsin

HORSE RACING

Steve Cauthen, a young jockey, and Triple Crown champion Seattle Slew, who was chosen Horse of the Year, created the major 1977 news in horse racing.

Cauthen, who turned 17 on May 1, had a sensational year. The Walton, Ky., jockey rode horses which earned a record $6.1 million in purses, shattering the former mark of $4,709,-500. Moreover, he led the country in victories, with a total of 487.

Forego, a 7-year-old gelding, who had won the Horse of the Year title the three previous seasons, finished second in the balloting. His wins included the Metropolitan and Woodward handicaps, in each of which he carried 133 pounds (60.3 kg), and the Nassau County Handicap (136 pounds–61.7 kg). Though his overall record for the year—four victories in seven starts and earnings of $268,740—was not so impressive as in each of his three previous seasons, it still was one to be proud of.

Forego increased his career earnings to $1,923,957, second only to Kelso ($1,977,896) on the all-time money list.

Seattle Slew became the first unbeaten horse to win the Kentucky Derby, Preakness, and Belmont—the three races that make up the Triple Crown. In his first start after capturing the Triple Crown, he went down to defeat, finishing a distant fourth in the Swaps Stakes. It

UPI

Steve Cauthen, a 17-year-old jockey from Walton, Ky., won some 400 races and over $6 million in purses.

turned out to be Seattle Slew's last race of a most exciting year.

Affirmed finished ahead of Alydar in four of their six meetings and ruled as champion among 2-year-old colts and geldings. Johnny D. won the Washington, D. C., International and the Turf Classic to capture the grass horse title.

Harness Racing. Green Speed won the Hambletonian in straight heats, his time of 1:55⅗ in each heat tying the all-age trotting record for the mile. The time also was a world record for a 3-year-old trotter.

Quarter Horses. Hot Idea sprinted the 440 yards (402 m) in 21.75 seconds to capture the first prize of $330,000 in the All American Quarter Horse at Ruidoso Downs.

JIM BOLUS
Sports Department
"The Courier-Journal," Louisville, Ky.

HORSE RACING

Major U. S. Thoroughbred Races

Belmont Stakes: Seattle Slew, $181,800 (value of race)
Brooklyn Handicap: Great Contractor, $111,100
Champagne Stakes: Alydar, $134,000
Coaching Club American Oaks: Our Mims, $109,800
Hollywood Gold Cup: Crystal Water, $350,000
Hollywood Invitational: Vigors, $200,000
Jockey Club Gold Cup: On the Sly, $346,800
Kentucky Derby: Seattle Slew, $267,200
Laurel Futurity: Affirmed, $144,650
Man o' War Stakes: Majestic Light, $113,100
Marlboro Cup: Proud Birdie, $279,600
Metropolitan Handicap: Forego, $114,400
Preakness Stakes: Seattle Slew, $191,100
Santa Anita Handicap: Crystal Water, $273,550
Spinster Stakes: Cum Laude Laurie, $84,575
Suburban Handicap: Quiet Little Table, $106,400
Swaps Stakes: J. O. Tobin, $316,400
Turf Classic: Johnny D., $200,000
Washington, D.C., International: Johnny D., $200,000
Woodward Handicap: Forego, $175,000

Major U. S. Harness Races

Cane Pace: Jade Prince, $286,500
Dexter Cup: Cold Comfort, $166,656
Fox Stake: Say Hello, $100,000
Hambletonian: Green Speed, $284,131
Kentucky Futurity: Texas, $100,000
Little Brown Jug: Governor Skipper, $150,000
Meadowlands Pace: Escort, $425,000
Messenger Stake: Governor Skipper, $159,155
Roosevelt International: Delfo, $200,000
Woodrow Wilson Pace: No No Yankee, $280,000
Yonkers Trot: Green Speed, $239,000

SOCCER

May 1977 was the month in which Franz Beckenbauer, captain of West Germany's 1974 World Cup winning team and Europe's soccer player of the year, left Bayern Munich to join the New York Cosmos. He was still only 31. It was the first major signing of a major player by a North American Soccer League club. The fabled Brazilian, Pelé, who retired at the end of the season, had been in retirement when the Cosmos signed him in 1974. A crowd of over 45,000 watched Beckenbauer's first Cosmos game in Tampa Bay, Florida.

With Beckenbauer and Pelé, the Cosmos went on to capture the league championship.

Throughout the season, NASL clubs drew increasingly large crowds, attesting to the new popularity of soccer in the United States. In fact, the televised title game was seen nationally and in ten other countries.

Elsewhere, the emphasis was on qualifying for World Cup soccer, the competition finals scheduled for Argentina in June 1978. Brazil, under Coutinho, a former Army captain, was developing a powerful side with a fine midfield, led by Roberto Rivelino.

For the first time since 1968, and for only the second time ever, Liverpool took the European Champions' Cup. The team defeated the fancied West Germany's Borussia Mönchengladbach in the final in Rome, 3–1. Kevin Keegan was a star for Liverpool, but soon afterward signed for the West German Hamburg club for a reported $175,000 a year.

Even without Beckenbauer, the West Germans were a superb team, beating Argentina in Buenos Aires. In their ensuing games against England and Scotland, the Argentinians showed a worrying recrudescence of the violence that marred their play in the 1966 World Cup. Earlier, the new young manager of Argentina, Cesar Luis Menotti, had promised a return to more elegant soccer.

Tactically, total football—versatility, adventure, and attack—still prevailed. The West German national team played it. So did the brilliant Dutch, who humiliated England, 2–0, at Wembley in February. The Dutch still had the world's best forward in superb Johan Cruyff.

BRIAN GLANVILLE, *"Sunday Times,"* London

SWIMMING

Twenty-two-year-old Joe Bottom of the United States broke the oldest swimming record when he swam the 100-meter butterfly in 54.18 seconds at East Berlin on August 27, erasing the standard set by Mark Spitz in the 1972 Olympics.

The U. S.-East German meet was a highlight of the season. American men won 13 of 15 events and lowered three world records. Bottom also swam on the world-record-breaking 400 freestyle relay (indoor) team that was timed at 3:21.11. Brian Goodell, from Mission Viejo, Calif., bettered his world 400 freestyle mark with 3:51.56. He also won Amateur Athletic Union (AAU) titles in the 400 and 1,500 and was named swimmer of the year.

The East German women took 12 of 14 events, but two U. S. teen-agers did well. Tracy Caulkins, 14, won the 200 butterfly in 2:12.43 and Alice Browne, 15, beat Petra Thumer, the world-record holder, in the 800 freestyle with 8:36.62, an American record.

Ulrike Tauber took the 200 individual medley in a world record 2:15.85 and Christiane Knacke, 15, clipped .35 seconds from the world 100 butterfly mark set by Kornelia Ender. Her time was 59.78 seconds.

SWIMMING

Men's U. S. Long-Course Champions

100-Meter Freestyle: Jonty Skinner, South Africa
200-Meter Freestyle: James Montgomery, Madison, Wis.
400-Meter Freestyle: Brian Goodell, Mission Viejo, Calif.
1,500-Meter Freestyle: Brian Goodell
100-Meter Backstroke: Mark Tonelli, Australia
200-Meter Backstroke: Peter Rocca, Orinda, Calif.
100-Meter Breaststroke: Rick Hofstetter, McKeesport, Pa.
200-Meter Breaststroke: Rob Long, Wayne, Pa.
100-Meter Butterfly: Greg Jagenburg, Drexel Hill, Pa.
200-Meter Butterfly: Mike Bruner, Los Altos, Calif.
200-Meter Ind. Medley: Scott Spann, Greenville, S.C.
400-Meter Ind. Medley: Jesse Vassallo, Mission Viejo, Calif.
400-Meter Freestyle Relay: Beach Swim Club, Long Beach, Calif. (Andy Veris, Jack Babashoff, Rick DeMont, Bruce Furniss)
400-Meter Medley Relay: Cummins Engine Swim Club, Bloomington, Ind. (Romulo Arantes, Rick Hofstetter, A. Schaefer Henry, James Montgomery)
800-Meter Freestyle Relay: Beach S.C., Long Beach, Calif. (Andy Veris, Bruce Furniss, Rick DeMont, Tim Shaw)
Team: Beach S.C., Long Beach, Calif.

Women's U. S. Long-Course Champions

100-Meter Freestyle: Wendy Boglioli, Ocean, N.J.
200-Meter Freestyle: Gail Amundrud, Ottawa, Ont.
400-Meter Freestyle: Rebecca Perrott, New Zealand
1,500-Meter Freestyle: Alice Browne, Corona Del Mar, Calif.
100-Meter Backstroke: Linda Jezek, Los Altos, Calif.
200-Meter Backstroke: Linda Jezek
100-Meter Breaststroke: Robin Corsiglia, Beaconsfield, Quebec
200-Meter Breaststroke: Kathy Treible, Brookfield, Wis.
100-Meter Butterfly: Wendy Boglioli
200-Meter Butterfly: Nancy Hogshead, Nashville, Tenn.
200-Meter Ind. Medley: Tracy Caulkins, Nashville, Tenn.
400-Meter Ind. Medley: Tracy Caulkins
400-Meter Freestyle Relay: Central Jersey, Milltown, N.J. (Wendy Boglioli, Corrinna Weinkofsky, Judi Jaeger, Dana Morton)
400-Meter Medley Relay: Nashville (Tenn.) Swim Club (Joan Pennington, Tracy Caulkins, Karinne Miller, Amy Caulkins)
800-Meter Freestyle Relay: Mission Viejo (Calif.) Nadadores (Tracey Wickham, Kim Black, Valerie Lee, Jennifer Hooker)
Team: Mission Viejo (Calif.) Nadadores

Earlier in August at the European championships in Jönköping, Sweden, Gerald Moerken of West Germany set a world mark of 1:02.86 in the 100 breaststroke. Petra Thumer broke her 400 freestyle record of 4:09.89 with 4:08.91. At Montreal on August 4, Graham Smith of Canada set a world mark of 2:05.31 in the 200 individual medley.

In the AAU long-course championships at Mission Viejo, one world mark and eight American records fell to women. Alice Browne of Corona Del Mar, Calif., completed the 1,500 freestyle in 16:24.60, clipping nine seconds from the previous world record held by Jennifer Turrall of Australia.

GEORGE DE GREGORIO

TENNIS

The year 1977 showed that the world of tennis will never again be a quiet or demure spectacle. No sooner did the sport's wild political wars cool down than the players themselves proved to be totally unpredictable.

Based on the form of the previous three years, Chris Evert and Jimmy Connors were supposed to rule tennis unchallenged for the next ten years. If, at the beginning of the season, someone had predicted that Evert would not reach the Wimbledon finals and Connors would drop to third in the world rankings, the soothsayer would have had his license taken away. But both happened.

The President's Commission on Olympic Sports

Baron Pierre de Coubertin, founder of the modern Olympic Games said: "The most important thing [in the Olympic Games] is not to win but to take part, just as the most important thing in life is not the triumph but the struggle. The essential thing is not to have conquered but to have fought well."

The United States has had some outstanding triumphs in sport competitions and its athletes have fought well, but concerns about its athletic achievements have been continual. President John F. Kennedy stated that "We are under-exercised as a nation; we look instead of play; we ride instead of walk. Our existence deprives us of the minimum of physical activity essential for healthy living. And the remedy, in my judgment, lies in one direction—that is, developing programs for broad participation in exercise by all of our young men and women, all of our boys and girls."

What could the U. S. amateur sports program accomplish with better organization and management, increased funding, and the elimination of many ongoing disputes? With better resources, increased finances, and organizational harmony, could the U. S. teams performing in the Olympics and other international competitions more nearly realize their potential; and would individual sports participation increase?

To seek answers to some of these questions, President Gerald R. Ford in June 1975 signed an executive order establishing the President's Commission on Olympic Sports. The commission was directed to study the U. S. Olympic Committee and other amateur sports organizations as they relate to the effectiveness of the U. S. effort in international and Olympic competition. Based on these studies, recommendations for an improved structure were to be made to the president with suggested actions for constructive change. The commission was headed by Gerald B. Zornow, chairman of the board of directors of Eastman Kodak Company, and consisted of 13 other members appointed by President Ford, including several former Olympic stars, 4 senators named by the president pro tempore of the Senate, and 4 Congressmen chosen by the House speaker. The objectives of the commission were to define and eliminate the barriers that limit the opportunity of U. S. athletes to develop their skills in every Olympic sport.

Findings and Recommendations. The commission, which issued its report on Jan. 13, 1977, found that no truly effective system exists for amateur athletics in the United States. Rather, there are numerous organizations that function independently in amateur sports. Individually, many, if not all, of these organizations are capable of meeting their own organizational goals and to some degree of meeting the needs of athletes who participate in their programs.

The commission's recommendations included establishing a central sports organization. The organization's primary purpose would be to enable the athletic groups to combine for the advancement of American sporting achievement and the encouragement of greater participation. The organization would be directed to achieve a truly unified sports system. It would settle organizational disputes concerning the right to be the recognized national governing body in a sport; induce all organizations with significant national programs in a sport to belong to the national governing body so that their activities could be coordinated; guarantee an athlete's right to compete; finance amateur sports more effectively; and introduce a central policymaking forum to identify U. S. sports problems and effect solutions. Of course, all of this is to be accomplished by building on the existing system and taking into account the views of the American public, the president, Congress, and the existing international and domestic sports organizations.

The commission, through detailed study of each of the 30 Olympic sports, urged that the development of national training centers and sports institutes be considered. Priority must be given to coordinating development programs through all levels of each sport. The club system must be strengthened in order to mesh with school sports programs. National teams in appropriate sports must be started. More sports should be introduced in the schools. Finally, high, clear standards should be developed for certification as coaches, judges, and officials.

Under the central sports organization, the commission proposed the establishment of the following committees: a sports medicine committee to serve as a national forum and clearing house for research, clinical application, information, and education; a handicapped in sports committee to ease sport opportunities for this significant segment of the American populace; and women in sports. Well-structured programs for women, access to facilities, and proper female representation in the decision-making and policymaking processes were areas investigated by the latter committee. Despite recent improvements, opportunities for women in sports still fall short of what is wanted and needed.

Amateur sports must become better organized, managed, and funded if the United States wishes to broaden participation and perform better in international competition. Implementation of the commission's recommendations would work toward the accomplishment of these goals.

RAFER JOHNSON

At 14, Tracy Austin became the youngest player in modern tennis to reach the U. S. Open's quarter finals.

UPI

In a stunning reversal, Britain's Virginia Wade beat Evert and Betty Stove in successive rounds to capture Wimbledon. It was fitting that Wade do so on the occasion of her Queen's Jubilee Celebration. Björn Borg won the men's title at Wimbledon for the second straight year, defeating Jimmy Connors in a thrilling five-set final. That Connors failed to take part in the tournament's center court jubilee ceremony perhaps forecast his frustration in being overshadowed by Borg and Guillermo Vilas.

Vilas, a husky Argentine, set a modern record for endurance by winning seven straight clay court titles (French Open, Washington, Louisville, Orange, Westchester, U. S. Open) which included a victory string of 40 matches. Vilas then won two Davis Cup singles matches and four more in a minor French event before defaulting to Ilie Nastase and his controversial "spaghetti" strung racquet. The International Tennis Federation, in one of its more obscure rulings, promptly banned use of the "spaghetti" stringing technique. Heretofore, there had been no limitation on the size, shape, or weight of a tennis racquet.

If Vilas' victory streak is not considered interrupted by the marred Nastase triumph, the Argentine continued undefeated through three round robin tournaments in South America and three full draws in Paris, Caracas, and Buenos Aires. Based on this record of 11 straight championships and 83 wins of 84 played, Vilas deserved consideration as the world's number one player for 1977. No other player won two Grand Slam events (French Open, U. S. Open) and no one came close to his record number of points in the yearlong Colgate Grand Prix which earned the pampas hero an additional $300,000 as top prize in the bonus pool.

Chris Evert's reign as the world's best woman player was threatened but not so severely as Connors'. Chris won the Virginia Slims, Family Circle, Colgate, and U. S. Open titles. The Australian and French championships went to other women uncontested. Only Wimbledon flawed her record, but it is a major blemish to the purists, who treasure the All England Cham-

pionships as emblematic of world supremacy in tennis. Yet if Vilas' record on clay is impressive, Evert's statistics on the same surface are fantasy. Stretching over six years, Ms. Evert is undefeated on clay for 23 tournaments, involving 113 matches. Evert's late season triumphs over Wade in the Colgate final and Wightman Cup must have convinced all but emotionalists that the "ice maiden" was still number one.

The women produced some contrasts in the age spectrum highlighted by 34-year-old Billie Jean King's comeback with tournament wins at the end of 1977. At 14, Tracy Austin became the youngest person in modern tennis to reach the quarter finals at Forest Hills. John McEnroe, 18, became the youngest man ever to reach the Wimbledon semifinals.

In 1977—Queen Elizabeth's silver jubilee and the 100th anniversary of Wimbledon—Britain's Virginia Wade appropriately captured the tournament's women's singles crown.

UPI

TENNIS

Major Team Competitions

Davis Cup: Australia 3-1.
Federation Cup: United States defeated Great Britain, 7-0.
Stevens Cup: United States defeated Australia, 3-0 in final.
World Team Tennis: New York Apples.

Major Tournaments

U.S. Open—Men's Singles: Guillermo Vilas, Argentina; women's singles: *Chris Evert; men's doubles: Bob Hewitt, South Africa, and Frew McMillan, South Africa; women's doubles: Martina Navratilova and Betty Stove, Netherlands; men's 35 singles: Martin Riessen; junior men's singles: Van Winitsky; junior women's singles: Claudia Casabianca, Argentina; hall of fame doubles: Fred Stolle, Australia, and Lew Hoad, Australia.

U.S. Clay Court Championship—Men's Singles: Manuel Orantes, Spain; women's singles: Laura Du Pont; men's doubles: Patricio Cornejo, Chile, and Jaime Fillol, Chile; women's doubles: Linky Boshoff and Llana Kloss, South Africa.

U.S. National Indoors—Men's Singles: Björn Borg, Sweden; men's doubles: Sherwood Stewart and Fred McNair.

National Amateur Clay Courts—Men's Singles: Bruce Foxworth; women's singles: Sheila McInerney; men's doubles: Gary Plock and John Rast; women's doubles: Barbara Hallquist and Sheila McInerney.

National Men's 35 Clay Court Championship—Men's Singles: Cliff Drysdale, South Africa; men's doubles: Bob Carmichael and Cliff Drysdale, South Africa.

USTA Women's Clay Court Championships—Women's Senior Singles: Nancy Reed; doubles: Charlene Grafton and Nancy Reed; women's 50 singles: June Gay; doubles: June Gay and Bunny Vosters; women's 60 singles: Dodo Cheney; doubles: Sheila Evans and Edna Maynard.

National Junior—Singles: Van Winitsky; doubles: Van Winitsky and Robert Van'tHof.

National Girls 18—Singles: Tracy Austin; doubles: Lea Antonopolis and Kathy Jordan.

Other U. S. Championships

NCAA Division I—Singles: Matt Mitchell; doubles: Bruce Manson and Chris Lewis; team: Stanford.

NCAA Division II—Singles: Juan Farrow; doubles: Curt Sadler and Jeff Williams; team: University of California, Irvine.

NAIA—Singles: Gordon Jones; doubles: Gordon Jones and Jim Twigg; team: Flagler College.

Women's Intercollegiate Championship—Singles: Barbara Hallquist, USC; doubles: Nancy Yeargin and Nicole Marois; team: USC.

Professional Championships

U.S. Pro Championships—Men's Singles: Manuel Orantes, Spain; men's doubles: Stan Smith and Bob Lutz.

World Championship Tennis Tour—Men's Singles: Jimmy Connors; men's doubles: Vijay Amritraj, India, and Dick Stockton.

Virginia Slims Tour—Final: Chris Evert.

* Except as noted, players are from the U.S.

Other Countries

Wimbledon—Men's Singles: Björn Borg, Sweden; women's singles: Virginia Wade, Britain; men's doubles: Ross Case and Geoff Masters, Australia; women's doubles: Helen Gourlay Cawley, Australia, and Jo Ann Russell; junior boys: Van Winitsky; junior girls: Lea Antonopolis.

Australian Open—Men's Singles: Roscoe Tanner; women's singles: Kerry Reid, Australia; men's doubles: Arthur Ashe and Tony Roche, Australia.

French Open—Men's Singles: Guillermo Vilas, Argentina; women's singles: Mima Jausovec, Yugoslavia; men's doubles: Brian Gottfried and Raul Ramirez, Mexico; women's doubles: Regina Marsikova, Czechoslovakia, and Pam Teeguarden.

Italian Open—Men's Singles: Vitas Gerulaitis; women's singles: Janet Newberry; men's doubles: Brian Gottfried and Raul Ramirez, Mexico; women's doubles: Brigitte Cuypers and Marise Kruger, South Africa.

Canadian Open—Men's Singles: Jeff Borowiak; women's singles: Regina Marsikova, Czechoslovakia; men's doubles: Bob Hewitt, South Africa, and Raul Ramirez, Mexico; women's doubles: Linky Boshoff and Llana Kloss, South Africa.

LEADING MONEY WINNERS IN 1977

Virginia Slims

Chris Evert	$174,500	Betty Stove	$ 49,800
Martina Navratilova	148,775	Margaret Court	33,612
Sue Barker	117,400	Kristien Shaw	30,275
Rosemary Casals	60,200	*Mima Jausovec	29,725
Virginia Wade	55,000	François Durr	22,450

* Retains amateur status

Men's Overall Season Earnings
(includes Colgate Grand Prix)

Jimmy Connors	$822,656	Brian Gottfried	$292,988
Guillermo Vilas	725,985	Vitas Gerulaitis	258,272
Björn Borg	340,348	Wojtek Fibak	204,839
Ilie Nastase	306,956	Eddie Dibbs	202,535
Dick Stockton	295,606	Roscoe Tanner	196,268

World Championship Tennis

Jimmy Connors	$308,123	Eddie Dibbs	$136,500
Dick Stockton	236,049	Andriano Panatta	130,750
Ilie Nastase	228,000	Wojtek Fibak	123,278
Vitas Gerulaitis	144,500	Cliff Drysdale	60,942

(Includes prize money earned in Shakey's Tournaments of Champions)

Women's Overall Season Earnings

Chris Evert	$503,134	Sue Barker	$187,548
Martina Navratilova	300,317	Kerry Reid	151,346
Virginia Wade	258,746	R. Casals	126,193
Betty Stove	229,162	D. Fromholtz	106,410
Billie Jean King	193,194	Wendy Turnbull	98,568

The controversy over transsexual Renee Richards simmered quietly beneath the surface. She participated only in minor satellite tournaments until a New York State judge ruled that she be allowed to play in the U. S. Open. Then, she lost speedily in the first round.

World Team Tennis continued to consolidate. The ten teams will drop to nine unless a replacement can be found for the itinerant Soviets, who had no home base and produced no spectator bonanza. No team made a profit, although every owner will show a gain based upon the increased value of his franchise. Overall, spectator response and hopes were higher in 1977. . . . Some positive steps were taken to implement a code of discipline. A point penalty system was imposed for the first time at Forest Hills and Ilie Nastase was banned from the 1978 Davis Cup for alleged obscene conduct during his match against Britain. . . . After 54 years, the U. S. Open was planning to move from the West Side Tennis Club to a $6 million renovated stadium in Flushing Meadows, N. Y.

EUGENE L. SCOTT, *Publisher, "Tennis Week"*

TRACK AND FIELD

In a non-Olympic year, runners took center stage from field-event performers. Seven world records fell to runners, while only one field mark tumbled. A new event, the World Cup, stirred interest on the international track and field scene.

Alberto Juantoreno of Cuba, the gold medalist in the 400- and 800-meter runs in the 1976 Olympics, excited the track world with his head-to-head encounters with Mike Boit of Kenya. Their first confrontation took place in August at Zurich, Switzerland, in the 800. Earlier that month, Juantoreno had bettered his world mark with a time of 1:43.43 at the World University Games in Sofia, Bulgaria. In Zurich, Juantoreno withstood a challenge by Boit at the 200-meter mark and went on to win by one second at 1:43.64. In a rematch in the World Cup meet on September 2 in Düsseldorf, West Germany, Boit led with 70 meters to go, but the Cuban, known for his stamina, overtook him to win with 1:44 to Boit's 1:44.1. In the 400 Juan-

UPI

At the European Athletic Cup Final, East Germany's Karin Rossley set a record in the 400-meter hurdles.

Another Cuban, Alejandro Casanas, reduced Rod Milburn's five-year-old world mark (13.24) in the 110-meter hurdles by .03 at the World University Games. In the 400-meter hurdles, Edwin Moses of the United States bettered (47.45) his previous world standard (47.64) in the national Amateur Athletic Union outdoor meet in Los Angeles on June 11. The world 800 relay mark tumbled to Arizona State (1:21.4) at Philadelphia on April 30. Dick Quax of New Zealand (13:12.9) broke the 5,000 world record and Samson Kimombwa of Kenya (27:30.5) shattered the 10,000 mark.

The Soviet Union's Vladimir Yashchenko high jumped 7 feet 7¾ inches on July 3 at Richmond, Va., to best Dwight Stones' world mark of 7–7¼.

GEORGE DE GREGORIO

toreno, claiming a faulty start, won a protest after finishing third in the race. The event was rerun and the tall athlete from Cuba won easily in 45.35.

East Germany defeated the United States, 127–120, for the title in the World Cup, which limited entries to eight in each event. Maxie Parks of Los Angeles collapsed while leading on the last leg of the 1,600-meter relay, the last event. The United States won the 400-meter relay with a world record 38.03.

YACHTING

The 126-year-old America's Cup dominated the sailing scene in 1976.

America's Cup. For the 23rd time, the United States successfully defended the "auld mug," despite the strongest challenge in history. Ted Turner, the feisty and outspoken Atlanta TV executive, defended the cup as skipper of the 12-meter *Courageous.* The 1974 defender yacht beat the 12-meter *Australia,* 4–0, in a best four out of seven series which began on September 13 off Newport, R. I. *Australia,* with Noel Robins as skipper, had defeated three other foreign challengers in summer-long trials to select a challenger. But *France I* from Hyères, France, *Sverige* from Göteborg, Sweden, and *Gretel II* from Sydney, Australia, were no match for the Aussie boat from Perth. On the U. S. side, *Courageous* and its crew surfaced as the clear choice against contenders *Independence,* sponsored by the King's Point Fund, and *Enterprise,* backed by the Fort Schuyler Foundation. The final match-race series was held in a record six days.

Other Races. The Admiral's Cup races, sailed off Cowes, England, July 28–August 6, brought together teams from 19 nations. The cup remained in British hands, with teams from Hong Kong and the United States finishing in the top three. The 1977 Congressional Cup races, sponsored by the Long Beach Club in March, pitted 10 crews against each other in a series of windward-leeward courses. Many of the same skippers who would appear later in the America's Cup trials sailed in the California series. And Ted Turner, first in the America's Cup, was also first in the Congressional Cup. Other America's Cup skippers were Ted Hood, who finished fourth; Pelle Petterson and Noel Robins, who tied for sixth place; and Lowell North, who finished ninth.

See also BIOGRAPHY: Turner, Robert Edward, 3d; Yachting, page 471.

BARBARA LLOYD, *"The Newport News"*

TRACK AND FIELD

Men's U. S. Outdoor Champions

100-Meter Dash: Don Quarrie, Los Angeles
200-Meter Dash: Derald Harris, Los Medanos J.C.
400-Meter Dash: Robert Taylor, Philadelphia Pioneers
800-Meter Run: Mark Belger, Philadelphia Pioneers
1,500-Meter Run: Steve Scott, Irvine, Calif.
5,000-Meter Run: Marty Liquori, Florida A.A.
10,000-Meter Run: Frank Shorter, Colorado T.C., Boulder
3,000-Meter Steeplechase: James Munyala, Philadelphia Pioneers
110-Meter Hurdles: James Owens, Los Angeles, and Charles Foster, Philadelphia Pioneers
400-Meter Hurdles: Edwin Moses, Atlanta, Ga.
5,000-Meter Walk: Todd Scully, Long Branch, N.J.
Pole Vault: Mike Tully, Long Beach, Calif.
High Jump: Dwight Stones, Desert Oasis T.C.
Long Jump: Arnie Robinson, Los Angeles
Triple Jump: Milan Tiff, Los Angeles
Hammer Throw: Emmitt Berry, Los Angeles
Javelin: Bruce Kennedy, San José, Calif.
Discus: Mac Wilkins, Portland, Ore.
Shotput: Terry Albritton, U. of Hawaii

Women's U. S. Outdoor Champions

100-Meter Dash: Evelyn Ashford, Los Angeles
200-Meter Dash: Evelyn Ashford
400-Meter Dash: Sharon Dabney, Clippers T.C.
800-Meter Run: Sue Latter, Michigan State
1,500-Meter Run: Francie Larrieu Lutz, Long Beach, Calif.
3,000-Meter Run: Jan Merrill, Waterford, Conn.
10,000-Meter Run: Peg Neppel, Iowa State
100-Meter Hurdles: Patty Van Wolvelaere, Los Angeles
400-Meter Hurdles: Mary Ayres, Prairie View T.C.
Javelin: Kathy Schmidt, Los Angeles
Shotput: Maren Seidler, Chicago, Ill.
Discus: Jane Haist, Canada
Long Jump: Jodi Anderson, Los Angeles
High Jump: Joni Huntley, Sheridan, Ore.

SPORTS SUMMARIES

ARCHERY—World: men: Richard McKinney, Muncie, Ind.; women: Luann Ryon, Riverside, Calif.; team: United States. **National Archery Association:** men: amateur: Richard McKinney; crossbow: Rolfe Smith; women: amateur: Luann Ryon; crossbow: Carol Pelose, Greenbelt, Md.

BADMINTON—World: singles: men: Fleming Delfs, Denmark; women: Lene Koppen, Denmark; doubles: men: Tjun-Tjun and Johan Wahjudi, Indonesia; women: Etsuko Toganoo and Emilo Ueno, Japan; mixed: Steen Skovgaard and Lene Koppen, Denmark.

BOWLING—American Bowling Congress—Regular Division: singles: Frank Gadaleto, Lansing, Mich. (738): doubles: Bob and Walt Roy, Glenwood Springs, Colo. (1,318): all-events: Bud Debenham, Los Angeles (2,117); team: Rendel's GMC, Joliet, Ill. (3,075). Classic Division: singles: Mickey Higham, Kansas City, Mo. (801): doubles: tie between Frank Werman and Randy Neal, Los Angeles (1,337) and Kevin Gannon, Long Beach, Calif., and Don Bell, Santa Maria, Calif. (1,337); all-events: Dick Ritger, River Falls, Wis. (1,964); team: Columbia 300 Bowling Balls, San Antonio, Tex. (3,122). Booster Division: team: Greater Richmond B. A. Capitals, Richmond, Va. (2,846); Masters: Earl Anthony, Tacoma, Wash. **Women's International Bowling Congress—**Open Division: singles: Akiko Yamaga, Tokyo, Japan (714); doubles: Ozella Houston and Dorothy Jackson, Detroit (1,234); all-events: Akiko Yamaga (1,895); team: Allgauer's Fireside Restaurant, Chicago (2,818).

CANOEING—Flatwater: kayak: men: 500 and 1,000 meters: Steve Kelly, New York: 10,000 meters: Brent Turner, St. Charles, Ill.; women: 500 and 5,000 meters: Ann Turner, St. Charles, Ill. Canadian (canoe): 500, 1,000, and 10,000 meters: Roland Muhlen, Cincinnati. Long distance races (13 miles): kayak: men: Brent Turner; women: Ann Turner; canoe: Ray Effinger, New York.

CHESS—U. S. Championships: men: Walter Browne, Berkeley, Calif.; open: Leonid Shamkovich, New York; national open: Jayne Sunye, Brazil; women's open: Ruth Orton, Fayetteville, Ark.

CROSS-COUNTRY—AAU (10,000 meters): Nick Rose, England (30:14.3); team: Colorado Track Club, Boulder; **NCAA** Division I (10,000 meters): Henry Rono, Washington State; Division II (10,000 meters): Mike Bollman, North Dakota (30:08.7); team: Eastern Illinois; Division III (8,000 meters): Dale Kramer, Carleton (25:44); team: Occidental (149); **NAIA** (5 miles): Garry Henry, Pembroke State (24:11); team: Adams State, Colo. (102). **IC4A** (5 miles): John Flora, Northeastern (24:17); team: Massachusetts (123). **Women:** AAU (3 miles): Jan Merrill, New London, Conn. (16:54.4); team: Iowa State (129); Collegiate (AIAW, 3 miles): Kathy Mills, Penn State (16:50.2); team: Iowa State (92). **World:** men: Leon Scholts, Belgium (37:45); Junior (4¾ miles): Tom Hunt, San Diego, Calif. (23.15.4).

CURLING—World: Sweden; **United States:** men: Hibbing, Minn. (Bruce Roberts, skip); women: Westchester (N. Y.) Wicks (Mrs. Margaret Smith, skip).

CYCLING—World: amateur: men: road: Claudio Corti, Italy; sprint: Hans-Jürgen Gesche, East Germany; time trial: Lothar Thoms, East Germany; pursuit: Norbert P. Durpisch, East Germany; motor-paced: Gaby Minnebo, Netherlands; points race: Constant Tourne, Belgium; tandem: Vladimir Vackae and Miroslav Vymazal, Czechoslovakia. Women: road: Josiane Bost, France; sprint: Galina Tsareva, USSR; pursuit: Vera Kuznetsova, USSR. Professional: road: Francesco Moser, Italy; sprint: Koichi Nakano, Japan; pursuit: Gregor Braun, West Germany; motor-paced: Cees Stam, Netherlands.

DOG SHOWS—Westminster (New York): Best: Ch. Dersade Bobby's Girl, Sealyham terrier, owned by Dorothy Wymer, Churchtown, Pa. (3,029 dogs entered). **International** (Chicago): Best: Ch. Rimskittle Bartered Bride, white standard poodle, owned by Mrs. Margaret Durney, Moraga, Calif.

FENCING—World: foil: Aleksandr Romanvok, USSR; saber: Paul Gerevich, Hungary; épée: Johan Harmenberg, Sweden; women's foil: Valentina Siderova, USSR. **United States:** foil: Mike Marx, Portland, Ore.: team: New York Athletic Club; épée: Leonid Derbinskiy, New York University; team: New York A. C.; saber: Tom Losonczy, New York A. C.; team: Fencers Club, New York; women's foil: Sheila Armstrong, Jersey City, N. J.

GYMNASTICS—AAU: men: all-around: Koji Saito, Toledo, Ohio; floor exercise: Saito; vault: Guy Spann, Arizona State; pommel horse: Robert McHatti, Minnesota University; still rings: Victor Randazzo, New York A. C.; horizontal bar: Gene Whelan, New York A. C.; parallel bars: Whelan; team: New York A. C. Women: all-around: Stephanie Willim, Silver Spring, Md.; floor exercise, vault, uneven parallel bars, and balance beam: Stephanie Willim; team: Philadelphia Freedoms. **NCAA:** Division I: all-around: Kurt Thomas, Indiana State; floor exercise: Ron Galimore, Louisiana State; vault: Steve Wejmar, Washington; pommel horse: Chuck Walter, New Mexico; still rings: Doug Wood, Iowa State; horizontal bar: John Hart, UCLA; parallel bars: Thomas; team: tie between Indiana State and Oklahoma. **Women's Collegiate (AIAW):** all-around: Ann Carr, Penn State; floor exercise: Connie

Jo Israel, Clarion State; vault: Karilyn Burdick, Cal State-Fullerton; uneven bars: Cheryl Diamond, Southwest Missouri; balance beam: Jeanie Beagle, Louisiana State; team: Clarion State (Pa.).

HANDBALL—United States Handball Association 4-wall: singles: open: Naty Alvarado, Pomona, Calif.; masters: Jim Faulk, Dallas; golden masters: Jack Briscoe, St. Louis; doubles: open: Skip McDowell and Matt Kelly, Long Beach, Calif.; masters: Burt Durkin and Jack Stebbin, Milwaukee; one-wall: singles: Al Torres, New York; doubles: Torres and Artie Reyer, New York.

HORSE SHOWS—American Horse Show Association Equitation Medals: hunter seat: Elizabeth Sheehan, Plymouth, Mass.; saddle seat: Carol Reams, Ashland, Ky.; stock seat: Doug Evertz, Santa Ana, Calif.; Dressage Awards: champion, 1st level: Chrysos, owned by Susan Rotson, Oakland, Calif.; 2d level: Whozit, Holly Essex, Midland, Tex.; 3d level: Pinchbeck Lord Peter, Linda Oliver, Great Falls, Va.; 4th level: Adagio, Deann Cramer, Webberville, Mich.

ICE SKATING, FIGURE—World: men: Vladimir Kovelov, USSR; women: Linda Fratianne, Northridge, Calif.; pairs: Irina Rodnina and Aleksandr Zaitsev, USSR; dance: Irina Moiseyeva and Andrei Minenkov, USSR; **United States:** men: Charles Tickner, Littleton, Colo.; women: Linda Fratianne; pairs: Tai Babilonia, Mission Hills, Calif., and Randy Gardner, Los Angeles; dance: Judi Genovese, Vernon, Conn., and Kent Weigle, West Hartford, Conn.

ICE SKATING, SPEED—World: men's all-around: Eric Heiden, Madison, Wis.; women's all-around: Vera Bryndzey, USSR. Sprints: men's all-around: Eric Heiden; women's all-around: Sylvia Burka, Winnipeg, Manitoba. **United States:** National Outdoor: men's all-around: Jim Chapin, St. Louis; women's all-around: Liz Crowe, St. Louis; National Indoor: men's all-around: Jack Mortell, Wilmette, Ill.; women's all-around: Celeste Chlapaty, Skokie, Ill.

LACROSSE—NCAA: Division I: Cornell; Division II: Hobart; Club: Mount Washington L. C., Baltimore.

MOTORBOAT RACING—World: offshore: Betty Cook, Newport Beach, Calif.; **United States:** offshore: Joel Halpern, Bronxville, N. Y.; unlimited hydroplanes: Atlas Van Lines, owned and driven by Bill Muncey, La Mesa, Calif.; distance races: Swift Hurricane Classic: Preston Henn, Pompano Beach, Fla.; Bacardi Cup: Henn; Stroh's Grand National: Sandy Satullo, Fairview Park, Ohio; Benihana Grand Prix: Halpern, Betty Cook, and Bob Nordskog, Van Nuys, Calif.; hydroplane races: President's Cup: Atlas Van Lines, Muncey; Gar Wood Trophy: Atlas Van Lines; Gold Cup: Atlas Van Lines.

MOTORCYCLE RACING—Grand National Championship (Camel pro series): Jay Springsteen, Lapeer, Mich.; moto-cross champions: 125 cc: tie between Broc Glover, El Cajon, Calif., and Danny LaPorte, Yucca Valley, Calif.; 250 cc: Tony DiStefano, Morrisville, Pa.; 500 cc: Marty Smith, San Diego.

PADDLEBALL—United States: Steve Keeley, San Diego.

PARACHUTING—United States: men: overall: Jim Hayhurst, U. S. Army, Fort Bragg; style: tie between Hayhurst and Royal Hatch, Raeford, N. C.; accuracy: Jack Brake, Salt Lake City: women: overall, style, and accuracy: Perry Hicks, Raeford, N. C.

POLO—National Championships: open: Retama, Wichita Falls, Tex.; Gold Cup (18–22 goals): Lone Oak, Dallas; America Cup (16 goals): Boca Raton, Fla.; Continental Cup (14 goals): Milwaukee; Copper Cup (10 goals): Mallet Hill, Cochranville, Pa.; Butler Handicap: San Antonio, Tex. Collegiate (indoor): Xavier of Ohio.

RACQUETBALL—Amateur: singles: men: Jerry Zuckerman, St. Louis; women: Karen Walton, San Clemente, Calif.; doubles: men: Dave Charlson and Roger Sanders, San Diego; women: Jan Pasternak, Houston, Tex., and Linda Siau, Riverside, Calif.

RODEO—Professional Rodeo Cowboys Association Champions: all-around: Tom Ferguson, Miami, Okla.; saddle bronc riding: Bobby Berger, Norman, Okla.; bareback bronc riding: Joe Alexander, Cora, Wyo.; bull riding: Don Gay, Mesquite, Tex.; steer wrestling: Larry Ferguson, Miami, Okla.; calf roping: Roy D. Cooper, Durant, Okla.; team roping: Jerald Camarillo, Oakdale, Calif.; women's barrel racing: Jimmy Gibbs, Valley Mills, Tex.

ROLLER SKATING—World: singles: men: Thomas Neider, West Germany; women: Natalie Dunn, Bakersfield, Calif.; pairs: Karen Mejia and Ray Chappatta, Melrose Park, Ill; dance: Fleurette Arseneault and Dan Littel, East Meadows, N. Y. **United States:** singles: men: Dean Maynard, San Diego; women: Robbie Coleman, Memphis.

ROWING—World: men: singles: Joachim Dreiske, East Germany; doubles: Chris Baillieu and Mike Hart, Britain; eights: East Germany; women: singles: Christine Shieblich, East Germany; East Germany won all six finals. **United States:** men: heavyweight: singles, ¼-mile: Jim Dietz, New York A. C.: singles: Sean Drea, Undine Barge Club, Philadelphia; pairs: Bud Ibbotson and Tom Wafenpaugh, College B. C., Philadelphia; pairs with coxswains: University of Pennsylvania; eights: University of Pennsylvania. **Intercollegiate I. R. A.:** varsity: Cornell. **Dad Vail Regatta:** eights and overall: Coast Guard Academy; **Eastern Sprints:** heavyweight: varsity: Harvard; second var-

Linda Fratianne won the world's figure skating competition; Eric Heiden captured the all-around speed skating crown.

sity: Penn; freshmen: Penn; lightweight: varsity: Harvard; second varsity: Harvard; freshmen: Yale; team: Rowe Cup (heavyweight): Penn, 39 points; Jope Cup (lightweight): Harvard; women: heavyweight: eights: Yale; fours: Penn; lightweight: eights: Radcliffe; novice eights: Wisconsin. **Western Sprints:** eights: varsity: British Columbia; junior varsity: Orange Coast; freshmen: Orange Coast; lightweight: UCLA; fours: varsity: Orange Coast; freshmen: Long Beach State; lightweight: British Columbia. **Dual Regattas:** Harvard defeated Yale; Oxford defeated Cambridge. **British Royal Henley:** diamond sculls: Tim Crooks, Leander Club, London: double sculls: M. J. Hart and C. L. Baillieu, Leander, London; silver goblets (pairs): Visitors' Plate: University of Washington; Wyfold Cup (fours): City Orient R. C., London: Prince Philip Cup (fours with coxswains): Garda B. C., Dublin: Ladies Plate (eights): Trinity College, Dublin; Thames Cup (eights): London R. C.; Princess Elizabeth Cup (schoolboy eights): Ridley College, St. Catharines, Ontario; Grand Challenge Cup (eights): University of Washington.

SHOOTING—Trapshooting: Grand American, Vandalia, Ohio, Handicap: men: James Edwards, Fairfield, Ohio (19½ yds.) 99; women: Mildred Paxton, Charleston, W. Va. (19 yds.) 97; junior: Guy Schwichtenberg, Lester Prairie, Minn. (18½ yds.) 95, in shootoff with Dean Weiland, Colgate, Wis. (18½ yds.) 95; veterans: Verne R. Harkins, Desoto, Iowa (20½ yds.) 95; senior: George Tony, Indianapolis (18½ yds.) 96; doubles: men: Philip Wright, Hudson, N. H. 99; women: Lou Anne Munson, Howard Lake, Minn. 92. **National Skeet Shooting Association Champions:** men: John Shima, San Antonio, Tex. (548); women: Conni Place, Pompano Beach, Fla. (544); junior: Todd Bender, Fountain Valley, Calif. (538); junior women: Catherine Hamburg, N. Y. (374); veteran: Tom San Filipo, Fairfield, Calif. (528); senior: K. E. Pletcher, Bellevue, Neb. (533).

SKIING—World Cup: overall: men: Ingemar Stenmark, Sweden; women: Lise-Marie Morerod, Switzerland. **Nations Cup:** overall: Austria. **United States Champions:** alpine: men: slalom: Cary Adgate, Boyne City, Mich.; giant slalom: Phil Mahre, White Pass, Wash.; downhill not held; women: slalom: Christin Cooper, Sun Valley, Idaho; giant slalom: Becky Dorsey, Wenham, Mass.; nordic: jumping: class A: Jim Denney, Duluth, Minn.; junior: Jeff Denney, Duluth; cross-country: men: 15 kilometers: Stan Dunklee, Brattleboro, Vt.; 30 kilometers: Tim Caldwell, Putney, Vt.; 50 kilometers: Stan Dunklee; women: 7.5 kilometers, 20 kilometers: Shirley Firth, Banff, Alberta; 10 kilometers: Sharon Firth, Banff, combined: cross-country: Jim Galanes, Brattleboro, Vt.; jumping: Walter Malmquist, Post Mills, Vt.; combined: Galanes.

SOFTBALL—U. S. Amateur Softball Association: men: fast pitch: Billard Barbell, Reading, Pa.; slow pitch: Nelson Painting, Oklahoma City; 16-inch slow pitch: Republic Bank Bobcats, Chicago; industrial slow pitch: Armco Triangles, Middletown, Ohio; national church slow pitch: Hickory Hammock Baptist Church, Milton, Fla.; modified pitch: Clinica, Miami, Fla.; class A fast pitch: Sawaia, Miami, Ariz.; class A slow pitch: Higgins Cycle, Greensboro, N. C.; women: fast pitch: Raybestos Brakettes, Stratford, Conn.; slow pitch: Fox Valley Lassies, St. Charles, Ill. **Collegiate:** University of Northern Iowa.

SQUASH RACQUETS—U. S. Squash Racquets Association: singles: Thomas E. Page, Philadelphia; veterans singles: Les Harding, Toronto; senior singles: Henri Salaun, Boston; doubles: Les Harding and Peter Hall, Hamilton, Ont.; veterans doubles: Thomas Jones, New York, and John Swann, Toronto; senior doubles: Eric Wiffen and Gordon Guyatt, Toronto; collegiate singles: Michael Desaulniers, Harvard. **U. S. Women's Squash Racquets Association:** singles: Gretchen Spruance; Wilmington, Del.; senior sing'es: Marigold Edwards, Pittsburgh; doubles: Mrs. F. A. C. Vosters, Wilmington, Del., and Gretchen Spruance; collegiate singles: Gail Ramsay, Penn State.

British Open: men: Geoffrey Hunt, Britain; women: Heather McKay, Canada.

TABLE TENNIS—World: men: singles: Mitsuru Kohno, Japan; doubles: Li Chen-shih and Liang Ke-liang, China; women: singles: Pak Yung Sun, North Korea; doubles: Pak Yong Ok, North Korea, and Liang Ke-liang, China; mixed doubles: Jacques Secretin and Claude Bergeret, France; men's team (Swathling Cup): China; women's team (Corillon Cup): China. **United States:** men: singles: Jochen Weiss, West Germany; senior singles (over 40): Bernie Bukiet, Hollywood, Calif.; women: singles: In Sock Bhushan, Columbus, Ohio; seniors: Dorothy Taschner, Mundelein, Ill.

VOLLEYBALL—U. S. Volleyball Association: men's open: Chuck's Steak House, Santa Barbara, Calif.; women's open: South Bay Spoilers, Hermosa Beach, Calif.; senior: Sir Dal Rae-Nick's, Beverly Hills, Calif. **AAU:** men: Maccabi Union, Los Angeles; women: Nick's Fish Market, Santa Monica, Calif. **Collegiate:** NCAA: University of Southern California. **Professional: International Volleyball Association:** Orange County Stars.

WATER SKIING—World: men: overall: Mike Hazelwood, Britain; slalom: Bob LaPoint, Castro Valley, Calif.; tricks: Carlos Suárez, Venezuela; jumping: Mike Suyderhoud, Petaluma, Calif.; women: overall: Cindy Todd, Pierson, Fla.; slalom: Cindy Todd; tricks: Maria Carrasco, Venezuela; jumping: Linda Giddens, Eastman, Ga.

WEIGHT LIFTING—AAU: 114½ pounds: Curt White, Charleston, Ill. (413¼ pounds total); 123½: Patrick Omori, Honolulu (463); 132¼: Phil Sanderson, Billings, Mont. (540¼); 148¾: James Benjamin, Columbus, Ohio (562½); 165¼: David Reigle, York, Pa. (639¼); 181¾: Robert Napier, Richardson, Tex. (710¾); 198¼: Phil Grippaldi, York, Pa. (744); 220¼: Mark Cameron, York, Pa. (749¼); 242½: Ray Blaha, Garfield Heights, Ohio (743¾); superheavyweight: Sam Walker, Dallas, Tex. (777¼).

WRESTLING—World: 105.5 pounds: Anatoli Beloglazov, USSR; 114.5: Yuji Takada, Japan; 125.5: Tadashi Sasaki, Japan; 136.5: Vladimir Uymin, USSR; 149.5: Pavel Pinigin, USSR; 163: Stanley Dziedzic, Lansing, Mich.; 180.5: Adolph Seger, West Germany; 198: Anatoli Propopchuk, USSR; 220: Aslanbek Bisultanov, USSR; unlimited: Soslan Andiev, USSR. **United States: AAU:** freestyle: 105.5: Bill Rosado, Bakersfield, Calif.; 114.5: Kayoto Shimizu, Japan; 125.5: Aikiro Yamati, Japan; 136.5: Jim Humphrey, Bakersfield; 149.5: Chuck Yagla, Ames, Iowa; 163.1: Stan Dziedzic; 180.5: Mark Lieberman, New York A. C.; 198: Ben Peterson, Comstock, Wis.; 220: Harold Smith, Toledo, Ohio; unlimited: Greg Wojciechowski, Toledo; outstanding wrestler: Yamati; team champion: New York A. C. **Greco-Roman:** 105.5: James Howard, U. S. Marines; 114.5: Enrique Jiménez, Mexico; 125.5: Brian Gust, Minnesota W. C.; 136.5: Hachiro Oichi, New York; 149.5: David Schultz, San Francisco Peninsula W. C.; 163: Abdul Raheem Ali, Minnesota W. C.; 180.5: Dan Chandler, Minnesota W. C.; 198: William Bragg, Oregon W. C.; 220: Brad Rheingans, Minnesota W. C.; heavyweight: Bob Walker, Athletes in Action; team: Minnesota W. C.

YACHTING—U. S. Yacht Racing Union: Mallory Cup (men): Marvin Beckmann, Houston, Tex.; Adams Cup (women): Cindy Stieffel, Waveland, Mo.; O'Day. Trophy (men's single-handed): Dave Chapin, Springfield, Ill.; Mertz Trophy (women's single-handed): Poppy Truman, Berkeley, Calif.; Adams Memorial Trophy (women's double-handed): Jan C. O'Malley and Pat O'Malley, Mantoloking, N. J.; Prince of Wales Bowl (club): Coronado (Calif.) Y. C., Ed Trevelyan, skipper; National Sea Explorers: Chris Friend (Richard Ashman, crew), New Orleans. **Distance Races:** Annapolis to Newport, R. I. (475 miles—760 km): overall: *Jack Knife* (Class III), Jack Greenberg, Miami, Fla.; TransPacific (Los Angeles to Honolulu): overall: *Merlin*, Bill Lee, Santa Cruz, Calif.

Compiled by BILL BRADDOCK

SRI LANKA

In 1977, for the sixth time since 1956, the government in power was voted out in a general election. The year was also characterized by an unusual degree of violence and by continuing economic difficulties.

Pre-Election. As the year began, the country was nearly paralyzed by nationwide strikes, which had started in mid-December 1976. On January 5 an emergency was proclaimed, and on the following day the government ordered the striking employees back to work. Press censorship was imposed, and troops were called out. By means of such tough measures the strikes were ended.

The dominant Sri Lanka Freedom Party (SLFP), headed by Prime Minister Sirimavo Bandaranaike, faced a growing crisis because of internal tensions and increasing difficulties with its ally, the pro-Moscow Communist party. On February 22, the Communists ended their coalition with the SLFP.

On February 10, Prime Minister Bandaranaike prorogued the National State Assembly for three months, and six days later she lifted the national emergency that had been in effect since 1971. On May 18, the parliament was dissolved, and general elections were announced for July 21.

The Elections. Nine political parties were recognized by the commissioner of elections, but only four were of any importance: the ruling SLFP; the United National party (UNP), the main opposition party; the United Left Front (ULF), formed before the elections were called by the Trotskyite Lanka Sama Samaj party, the Communist party, and two other leftist parties; and the Tamil United Liberation Front (TULF), a coalition of all the main Tamil parties, which advocated a separate Tamil state.

The campaign was marred by frequent outbursts of violence, but the polling on July 21, with a turnout of more than 80% of the 6.73 million eligible voters, was peaceful. The election result was a crushing defeat for the SLFP, whose seats in the National State Assembly were reduced from 84 to 8. The UNP, which had held only 19, won 139 of the 168 seats. The TULF won 17 seats (increasing its representation by 7), and the ULF, whose major constituents had held 22 seats, failed to win a single one.

Post-Election. On July 23, a new UNP government, headed by J. R. Jayewardene, a 71-year-old veteran, was sworn in. It was greeted by a wave of violence in various parts of the country, curbed temporarily by the imposition of local curfews and other emergency measures. Another more serious wave of violence began in mid-August. This was directed mainly against the Tamils and led to the migration of several thousand Tamil residents of Colombo and vicinity to the Tamil areas in the north.

Keeping an election pledge, the new government changed the political system from a parliamentary to a French-style presidential system. Under the new arrangement, Jayewardene was scheduled to give up the prime ministership and become president in 1978.

The Economy. The country continued to be plagued with inflation running as high as 30–40% and an unemployment rate of 15–20% (even higher among the young). The devaluation of the rupee by some 20% in March led to a reduction in the price of some commodities. Later, the new government liberalized the import and distribution of essential goods and reduced the price of flour and bread. The value of tea exports, the main foreign exchange earner, fell by about $40 million.

NORMAN D. PALMER
University of Pennsylvania

SRI LANKA · Information Highlights

Official Name: Republic of Sri Lanka.
Location: Island off the southeastern coast of India.
Area: 25,332 square miles (65,610 km²).
Population (1977 est.): 14,100,000.
Chief City (1973 est.): Colombo, the capital, 890,000.
Government: *Head of state,* William Gopallawa, president (took office May 1972). *Head of government,* Junius R. Jayewardene, prime minister (took office July 1977). *Legislature* (unicameral)—National State Assembly
Monetary Unit: Rupee (7.34 rupees equal U. S.$1, Aug. 1977).
Manufacturing (major products): Milled rice, chemicals.
Major Agricultural Products: Tea, rubber, coconuts.

Following victory in Sri Lanka's elections, J. R. Jayewardene, left, of the United National party is officially appointed prime minister by President Wm. Gopallawa.

STAMP COLLECTING

The year of Lindbergh and Rubens, as it must be called, 1977 also had a record number of international stamp shows.

In early 1975, aviation enthusiasts of Long Island, whence "Lindy" took off for the first successful nonstop flight across the Atlantic to Paris, petitioned the Postal Service for a stamp to commemorate the golden jubilee of that epochal flight. Though turned down time and again for a variety of specious reasons, they succeeded in having the stamp approved and issued on May 20. It depicts the *Spirit of St. Louis* but neither portrays nor names Charles A. Lindbergh. The attractive stamp was extremely popular; some four million first-day covers were serviced—the largest number since the moon-landing commemorative of 1969. The anniversary of the flight was also observed by hundreds of stamps from about 80 other countries.

Also universally commemorated by stamps was the 400th anniversary of the birth of Peter Paul Rubens, the Flemish master artist.

While International Philatelic Federation statutes call for only one international stamp competition a year, there were eight in 1977, all remarkably successful: in Holland, Uruguay, San Marino, Spain, Puerto Rico, Switzerland (for juniors' entries only), Berlin, and the Philippines (for aero-philatelic collections).

The stamp market continued to show its strength by the climb of prices for popular classic issues to incredibly high levels at both private and public auctions in all the world's philatelic centers. By contrast, many of the more recent specimens from countries that habitually issue gaudy pictorials, primarily for sale to uninformed beginners and inexperienced topical collectors, did not do well. The new standard stamp catalogue either did not increase list quotations or reduced them since 1976.

In the United States, the Postal Service initiated a nationwide program to introduce and promote stamp collecting in schools. The American Philatelic Society also embarked on a campaign to encourage youngsters to set out on the path of collecting stamps for enjoyment.

ERNEST A. KEHR, *Stamp News Bureau*

SELECTED U. S. COMMEMORATIVE STAMPS, 1977

Subject	Denomination	Date
Battle of Princeton	13¢	Jan. 7
Sound Recording	13¢	March 23
Pueblo Pottery	4 x 13¢	April 13
Spirit of St. Louis	13¢	May 20
Colorado Statehood	13¢	May 21
American Butterflies	4 x 13¢	June 6
Lafayette	13¢	June 13
Civilian Skills	4 x 13¢	July 4
Peace Bridge	13¢	Aug. 4
Battle of Oriskany	13¢	Aug. 6
Alta, Calif., Settlement	13¢	Sept. 9
Articles of Confederation	13¢	Sept. 30
Talking Pictures Jubilee	13¢	Oct. 6
Burgoyne's Surrender	13¢	Oct. 7
Energy Conservation	2 x 13¢	Oct. 20
Christmas	2 x 13¢	Oct. 21
Petition for Redress	2 x 10¢	Nov. 4 and 17

STOCKS AND BONDS

After two years of advance, the securities markets turned downward in 1977. In fact, 1977 could be characterized as a year of disappointment and unrealized expectation. The year began on a note of optimism and promise —a new U. S. president, a recovering economy, a generally positive tone to the securities markets. Both the Dow Jones Industrials and the Standard & Poor's 400 indexes entered the year at close to record levels. But time passed and the optimism turned to malaise, which, in turn, fueled fairly significant weakness in both stock and, to a lesser extent, bond prices. Paradoxically, the decline occurred despite both a reasonably sound economic backdrop and rising corporate earnings and dividends. At year-end, the Dow Jones Industrials and the Standard & Poor's 400 indexes had posted declines of 17.3% and 12.3%, respectively. The bond market was not immune to the negative tone of investor psychology. Concern over the Federal Reserve Board's ability to control the money supply, coupled with rising interest rates, sent bond prices lower.

Stock Prices. The stock market entered 1977 on a positive note. Stock prices had registered a marked improvement in the last two months of 1976, reflecting positive investor reaction to the then President-elect Jimmy Carter's initial actions and appointments. This salutary environment carried into the initial two weeks of January, as the new president unveiled his economic program which was aimed at job creation through selective public works, and bolstering consumer spending through fiscal means, including a permanent tax cut and a tax rebate. However, stock prices turned downward in mid-January following the November–December increase. The sell-off began in large-capitalization stocks, many of which had led to the market's 1975–76 advance.

Stock prices continued to wane through February and March, although there were sporadic rallies. Concern over inflation and interest rates did much to dampen investor enthusiasm. The disagreement between Federal Reserve Board Chairman Arthur Burns and President Carter on the merits of the president's economic stimulus program did nothing to allay investor worries.

In mid-April, the administration's withdrawal of the proposed $50 tax rebate gave the market a psychological lift and stocks moved higher. Reports that the economy had registered better-than-expected progress in the first quarter of 1977 after the fourth-quarter-of-1976 lull also helped to spark some buying. However, the rebound quickly ran out of steam and the decline in stock prices resumed.

During the summer months, the stock market made several rally attempts but each rally ran out of momentum. Crosscurrents included concern over the growth of money supply and rising interest rates, and reservations about the administration's energy program on the one hand, and continued strength in the economy, on the other. At the end of July, stocks registered a sharp, three-day decline, which set the stage for further lackluster markets in the fall. The sell-off reflected growing concern over the probable slowing of economic growth, nervousness over a sharp drop of the value of the dollar against certain foreign currencies, and a dramatic bulge in the money supply. While rallies appeared from time to time in the fall, the stock market continued to have difficulty finding a toehold. Interest rates continued to rise, and each fresh investor hope proved short-lived.

Signs that the administration might be settling down to accomplish specific economic objectives helped to arrest the market's slide at the end of the year. The initial reaction to the proposed $25 million tax reduction program was essentially positive, as was the business community's view of the appointment of G. William Miller as chairman of the Federal Reserve Board. Burns had been highly regarded by the financial community as a symbol of conservatism and a leader in the movement to control inflation.

The stock market's performance in 1977 was an interesting phenomenon. While the popular averages—the Dow and the S&P 400—posted fair-sized losses, the broader universe of stocks presented a far less dreary picture. In fact, two indexes, the American Stock Exchange Index and the NASDAQ composite of over-the-counter stocks were actually up, scoring respective gains of 16.4% and 7.3%. Several observations can be drawn from this disparity in performance. The stocks contained in the Dow and the S&P 400 are representative of the large-capitalization stocks in which investors sought refuge during the 1967–74 period of "shocks" to the economic, political, and social system. Helped along by the impact of ERISA (Employee Retirement Income Security Act) and other factors, these stocks became over-owned. In subsequent years, some investment funds began to flow out of these stocks and a look for alternatives began. The equity alternative seemed to be "values" among the second- and third-tier situations. In 1977, a new wrinkle appeared—substantial earnings disappointments for companies contained in the popular averages, most notably, the Dow. The earnings short-falls led to rather hefty sell-offs in the specific stocks affected and this, in turn, had a well-documented adverse impact on the performance of the popular averages. Since corporate earnings and dividends generally fared well in 1977, however, one should not be surprised to see that some of the broader-based market averages actually posted gains in 1976. Another observation—if one looks at three market indicators, the Dow, the S&P 400, and the NYSE Composite—the stock market as a whole had not performed well for ten years. At the end of 1977, all three averages (the Dow, the S&P 400, and the NYSE Composite) were below their 1966 levels. The actual declines were 8.3%,

0.8%, and 11.2%, respectively. Of course, this is before factoring in the impact of inflation, on the one hand, and dividends, on the other. But as a rough cut, the statistics do not inspire confidence. Because of the events of the past decade, investors may have become much more knowledgeable, cautious, and conservative in their approach. This is reflected in such trends as the rise in popularity of fixed income instruments (where, incidentally, yields have, on average, doubled between 1967 and 1977), the move toward diversifying into the less traditional areas of investment (art, antiques, land, real estate), and an increasingly selective approach toward the equity market. The attitude is also transmitted in the way investors view the ongoing events of the world and the nation. For example, one factor that impeded market action in 1977 was the perception by investors that the Carter administration did not have a good grip on the problems of economic policy.

Two other areas deserve mention in a discussion of stock market activity in 1977. First, some of the most visible moves in stock prices reflected the spate of merger, acquisition, and tender offer activity. This caused the stocks of the companies involved to become volatile—rising and falling on talk of bids, counterbids, and withdrawals of offers. Second, gold stocks were noticeably strong performers. This reflected the substantial rise in the price of gold.

Earnings and Dividends. For most companies, earnings continued to rise in 1977. In terms of Standard & Poor's industrial-stock price index, net income (partly estimated) jumped to $11.74 a share, up from $10.64 in 1976. Dividends trended higher, averaging $5.04 (indicated) a share on Standard & Poor's 400-index, up from $4.20 in 1976. These stocks sold in a range of 11.4–8.9 times partly estimated earnings and had a return of 4.99%–3.71% (indicated) in 1977. This compares with a 1976 multiple range of 14.0–11.1 and a yield range of 3.89%–3.25%.

Volume. Trading on the New York Stock Exchange was moderately under 1976's record of 5,360,116,438 shares; 1977 volume was 5,273,767,151 shares.

Bond Prices. Bond prices eased fairly steadily during 1977, following the dramatic rally of 1976. The decline was fueled by rising interest rates and concern over inflation. Yields on highest-grade industrials rose steadily, from a low of 7.83% in the week of Jan. 5, 1977 to a high of 8.32% in the final week of 1977. This compares with a low of 7.82% and a high of 8.47% in 1976. Bond prices move inversely to their yields; in other words, bond prices drop as yields rise. Each one-hundredth of a percent is called a "basis point." An increase in yield of this magnitude, roughly 50 basis points, means that bond prices declined on average around 6%–7%.

CAROLYN J. COLE, *Vice President*
Paine, Webber, Jackson & Curtis, Inc.

Hua Kuo-feng, China's Communist Party chairman, welcomed Sudan's President Numeiry to Peking in June.

UPI

SUDAN

Sudan focused on building up its infrastructure in 1977, laying the groundwork for a huge project using Arab oil money and Western know-how to tap the food-supplying potential of Africa's largest country. With this economic breakthrough on the horizon, President Jaafar al-Numeiry moved to stabilize his rule by welcoming home his most implacable enemy.

Development. Emphasis in the first phase of the U. S. $5.7 billion six-year project launched in the spring was on infrastructure—better communications and roads to link cities within Sudan and Sudan with the rest of the world, and an oil pipeline connecting Port Sudan on the Red Sea with Khartoum.

In March, on the fifth anniversary of the ending of the civil war between the Arab north and the African south, Numeiry opened in Juba, the south's capital, a TV station and telephone-telex complex, linking Juba and Khartoum by earth satellite. Four of a planned 14 satellite stations have been completed. A 508-mile (820-km) oil pipeline connecting Port Sudan with Khartoum was finished after a year-long delay caused by leaks. Constantly clogged Port Sudan, which handles 95% of the country's import and export traffic, will get relief with a new port, planned at Suakin.

The world's biggest sugar complex, built in 20 months by Lonrho, was completed in 1977.

The British conglomerate was dropped as manager because of cost overruns from a projected $150 million to an actual price tag of over $500 million. The Kenana sugar complex, located in the fertile triangle between the White and the Blue Nile, will eventually include Sudan's second largest electricity generator, fueled by sugarcane by-products.

Politics. Pressure from the conservative Arab states of Saudi Arabia and Kuwait, which are largely financing the huge agribusiness development of Sudan as a breadbasket for the Arab world, apparently was behind Numeiry's surprise reconciliation with former Prime Minister Sadik al-Mahdi. The exiled leader of the conservative Islamic Mahdist sect had several times joined forces with other groups in attempts to overthrow Numeiry. The bloodiest attempt occurred in July 1976, when hundreds were killed in the fighting and reprisals.

Mahdi returned home from London in October to a tumultuous hero's welcome. Only a year before he had been sentenced to death in absentia for his nearly successful coup. Numeiry issued a general amnesty for political prisoners, freeing about 1,000 detainees.

Foreign Affairs. With U. S. businessmen checking into the new Kuwaiti-built Hilton Hotel in Khartoum, Sudan drew closer to the United States. The Carter administration approved the sale of six military transport planes to Sudan, which wants to buy about $500 million worth of weapons from the West in the next few years. The thaw in relations with Washington followed the expulsion in May of 90 Soviet military advisers. Numeiry accused the Soviets and Libya of backing abortive coups against him, and charged Ethiopia with supporting a failed mutiny by air defense units in the south in February.

Warm ties with Egypt were accentuated in October by a symbolic week-long joint session of the Egyptian and Sudanese parliaments in Cairo. Eventually, the two neighbors hope to merge.

JOSEPH MARGOLIS
"African Update," African-American Institute

SUDAN · Information Highlights

Official Name: Democratic Republic of Sudan.
Location: Northeast Africa.
Area: 967,497 square miles (2,505,813 km²).
Population (1977 est.): 16,300,000.
Chief Cities (1973 est.): Khartoum, the capital, 322,-000; Omdurman, 305,000.
Government: *Head of state*, Gen. Jaafar Mohammed al-Numeiry, president (took office Oct. 1971). *Legislature* (unicameral)—People's Assembly.
Monetary Unit: Pound (0.35 pound equals U. S.$1, Aug. 1977).
Manufacturing (major products): Vegetable oil, processed foods, textiles, shoes, pharmaceuticals.
Major Agricultural Products: Cotton, oilseeds, gum arabic, sorghum, sesame seeds, groundnuts, wheat, livestock.

SWEDEN

Lagging industrial production and government efforts to revitalize the economy preoccupied the Swedes in 1977.

Economy. In April, Sweden devalued the krona by 6%, then left the "snake," the West European currency cooperation, and in August devalued again by 10% in an effort to increase lagging exports by some 8–9% in 1978. The payroll tax was cut by 50%. Other government measures aimed at buoying the economy were a raise of the value-added tax by 3%, restrictions on less essential building, cutbacks in the government's budget, a rise in municipal consumption, and the holding back of local taxes. Later steps will include complete abolishment of the payroll tax, a wage-saving system, and increasing the supply of capital for industry. Restructuring of shipyards, steel mills, and textile factories, the industries hardest hit by the recession, will proceed. The negative trade balance totaled some $7.4 billion (U. S.) by 1977, forcing more foreign borrowings. By the end of the year, Sweden was shouldering a record total of nearly $7 billion in foreign debts, an increase of almost 150% over the previous year.

Industry. Industrial production continued its downward trend, and productivity was further reduced by growing absenteeism, making sick leaves much higher in Sweden—400,000 workers a day, or 10% of the entire work force—than in any other industrialized country. Labor costs have risen since 1974 by a record 65%, while output has increased only 6%. As a result, exports slumped appreciably, and investment dropped. Unemployment continued its increase, standing at more than 2% by the end of the year. A proposed merger of Sweden's two auto manufacturers, Volvo and SAAB, was called off after protracted negotiations.

Domestic Politics. The neo-Stalinist, faithful-to-Moscow faction of the parliamentary Communist party, broke out of the party with nearly 40% of the members. This means that the Communists might lose representation in parliament, and without them, the Social-Democrats would need a landslide to regain the government power which was lost to the present "bourgeois" party coalition in the 1976 general election.

The Royal Family. The first child of King Carl XVI Gustaf and Queen Silvia, a daughter, was born July 14. The princess was christened Victoria Ingrid Alice Désirée on September 27. The king and queen paid a state visit to West Germany on October 25–31 at the invitation of federal President Walter Scheel. The queen was born a commoner, the daughter of a West German business executive.

General Events. Uppsala University, the oldest in Sweden and all Scandinavia, celebrated its 500th anniversary by organizing an international church history conference with the theme "The Church in A Changing Society." Some 225 delegates from 26 countries attended. Festivities culminated September 28–30, when 102 honorary degrees were conferred. Among the honored was social anthropologist Margaret Mead. Net immigration to Sweden during the first half of 1977 numbered 12,400 persons, more than twice as high a figure as for the same period in 1976. Some of the principal export industries put up more than $2 million to build and enter a 12-meter yacht, *Sverige,* in the America's Cup races in Newport, R. I. The Swedish entry lost in the final trials to Australia's chief challenger, *Australia.*

MAC LINDAHL
Harvard University

SWEDEN • Information Highlights

Official Name: Kingdom of Sweden.
Location: Northern Europe.
Area: 173,649 square miles (449,750 km²).
Population (1977 est.): 8,200,000.
Chief Cities (1974 est.): Stockholm, the capital, 671,000; Göteborg, 446,000; Malmö, 247,000.
Government: *Head of State,* Carl XVI Gustaf, king (acceded Sept. 1973). *Head of government,* Thorbjörn Fälldin, prime minister (took office Oct. 1976). *Legislature* (unicameral)—Riksdag.
Monetary Unit: Krona (4.85 kronor equal U. S.$1, Aug. 1977).
Manufacturing (major products): Pulp and paper, iron and steel, machinery and equipment, ships.
Major Agricultural Products: Oats, sugar beets, potatoes, wheat, livestock, forest products.

Princess Victoria Ingrid Alice Désirée, the first child of King Carl XVI Gustaf and Queen Silvia, is baptized in the Stockholm palace chapel.

SWITZERLAND

Two major scandals, one military, the other fiscal, rocked Switzerland in 1977. On June 17, Brig. Gen. Jean-Louis Jeanmaire, former head of the Swiss air defense system, was convicted of long-term spying for the Soviet Union and sentenced to 18 years' imprisonment. During the spring and summer, several banking scandals emerged. The most shocking involved three officers of the Swiss Credit Bank who had made $880 million in unauthorized loans, $400 million of which proved unrecoverable. These events prompted new regulations, imposing greater restrictions on the acceptance and use of funds deposited in secret accounts.

Referenda Decisions. On March 13, Swiss voters rejected a proposal to limit foreign residents to 12.5% of the total population. They approved a law requiring popular ratification of treaties involving mutual defense and membership in international organizations. As a result, the government decided not to file for membership in the UN, since it was unlikely the citizenry would approve.

On June 12, the substitution of a value-added tax for the present sales tax was defeated, despite support from the government and all but the Socialist trade unions.

So often were the Swiss called to the polls in 1977 that on September 25 they voted to increase the number of signatures needed on initiative petitions from 50,000 to 100,000 for constitutional changes, and from 35,000 to 50,000 for legislative acts.

Women's Rights. The Swiss Supreme Court ruled on October 13 that women in government employ should receive the same pay as men for equal work. On September 25, in a national referendum, voters rejected a bill to allow elective abortions during the first 12 weeks of pregnancy. With that defeat, a June 1977 law, allowing abortions for other than medical reasons only when certified by a social worker as necessary in order to spare the mother "grave distress," automatically went into effect.

Economy. Exports in the first half of 1977 were up $1,036,000,000 (14.8%) over the same period in 1976. However, imports rose $1,509,000,000 (21.8%).

PAUL C. HELMREICH, *Wheaton College, Mass.*

──── SWITZERLAND · Information Highlights ────

Official Name: Swiss Confederation.
Location: Central Europe.
Area: 15,941 square miles (41,288 km²).
Population (1977 est.): 6,200,000.
Chief Cities (1975 est.): Bern, the capital, 153,000; Zurich, 396,000; Basel, 196,000.
Government: *Head of state,* Kurt, Furgler, president (took office Jan. 1977). *Legislature*—Federal Assembly: Council of States and National Council.
Monetary Unit: Franc (2.40 francs equal U. S.$1, Aug. 1977).
Manufacturing (major products): Machinery, chemicals, textiles, watches, clocks, clock parts.
Major Agricultural Products: Potatoes, sugar beets, wheat, barley, dairy products, forest products.

SYRIA

A boycott of national elections in August shook Syrian President Hafez al-Assad's preoccupation with events in southern Lebanon and compelled him to focus more attention on Syria's sagging economy and the serious public disaffection for his regime's domestic and foreign policies. In foreign affairs, Assad's consistently pessimistic view that peace in the Middle East could not be achieved in 1977 was confirmed on the eve of Egyptian President Anwar el-Sadat's historic trip to Israel in late November: Assad publicly condemned Sadat's mission, thus driving a wedge between Syria and its former ally.

Middle East Conflict. Following meetings on November 16–17, Assad and Sadat, who together had launched the October 1973 Arab-Israeli War, announced that they could not agree on Sadat's scheduled November 19–21 visit to Israel. In the Syrian president's view, Sadat's trip seriously undermined the unity of the Arab position on negotiations with Israel. It was reported that, despite Sadat's assurances and prior agreements to the contrary, Assad feared that the Egyptian president would conclude another bilateral agreement with the Israelis and further compromise Arab insistence on full Israeli withdrawal from the occupied territories and recognition of the rights of the Palestinians.

Syria's violent media reaction, Assad's public displeasure, and the ultimate December 5 break in Syrian-Egyptian relations over Sadat's initiative were consistent with earlier positions. On January 24, Assad had noted that an overall settlement was not in sight and in February reiterated his conviction that neither 1977 nor 1978 would be the "year of peace." Assad maintained an uncompromising position on the Palestinian issue: following April meetings between Foreign Minister Abdel Halim Khaddam and U. S. officials in Washington and his own May 8–9 meeting with President Carter in Geneva, Assad did not retreat from his conviction that the Palestinians should have their own state on the occupied West Bank.

In the year-long negotiations on the U. S. initiative to reconvene the Geneva Peace Conference, Assad did not take a flexible position. On August 4, he killed a joint U. S.-Egyptian proposal for the foreign ministers of Syria, Jordan, Egypt, and Israel to form a "working group" to ease differences prior to going to Geneva. A week later, he again sank a U. S. proposal for Arab-Israeli "proximity" talks during the September UN General Assembly meetings, stating that there should be no bargaining with the rights of the Palestinians. Earlier in the month, Foreign Minister Khaddam had unsuccessfully proposed to an Arab League foreign ministers' meeting in Cairo that the Arabs should campaign to oust Israel from the UN because of its settlement activities on the West Bank.

UPI

Upon arrival in Moscow, Syria's President Hafez al-Assad joins Soviet President Leonid Brezhnev in reviewing the guard of honor.

Lebanon. For most of the year, Assad was preoccupied with his search for a settlement to end the Lebanese civil war. Although there had been a formal cease-fire in effect since October 1976, incessant fighting between the Syrian-backed Palestinians and the Israeli-backed Christians near the Israeli border had frustrated the Syrian president. Foreign Minister Khaddam was sent to Lebanon to smooth over the February 1–15 crisis, when Syrian troops advanced to within 9 miles (14.5 km) of the Israeli border, and was instrumental in negotiating the July Shtura agreement on the future of Palestinian-Lebanese relations. A subsequent outbreak of fighting, believed to have been incited by the Israelis, delayed the implementation of the Shtura accords until the latter half of September.

Internal Politics. Although the Arab oil-producing states had pledged more than $570 million to Syria for 1977–78 in March, most of the aid was for military purposes and, therefore, of little help to the depressed economy.

Charges that corruption and financial mismanagement within the Assad government were responsible for most of Syria's domestic woes reached serious proportions in August and September. Not only did the government-run press make allegations, but the president himself also became the subject of personal denunciations.

Much of the trouble focused on the dominant political position of members of Assad's own Alawite religious sect, particularly because 75% of the population are members of orthodox Sunni Islam. A series of unexplained bombings and political assassinations culminated in the boycott of the August 1 elections for the Syrian Ba'athist National Council. When less than 5% of the electorate voted, Assad, in a gesture to restore public confidence in his selflessness and to set an example for his government, donated all of his personal properties to the state.

F. NICHOLAS WILLARD
Georgetown University

─────── **SYRIA · Information Highlights** ───────

Official Name: Syrian Arab Republic.
Location: Southwest Asia.
Area: 71,498 square miles (185,180 km²).
Population (1977 est.): 7,800,000.
Chief Cities (1974): Damascus, the capital, 835,000; Aleppo, 500,000; Homs, 164,000.
Government: *Head of state,* Lt. Gen. Hafez al-Assad, president (took office March 1971). *Head of government,* Abdel Rahman Khleifawi, prime minister (took office Aug. 1976). *Legislature* (unicameral)—People's Council.
Monetary Unit: Pound (3.95 pounds equal U. S.$1, Aug. 1977).
Manufacturing (major products): Petroleum products, textiles, cement, glass, soap.
Major Agricultural Products: Wheat, barley, sugar beets.

TANZANIA

Tanzania's two political parties, the Tanganyika African National Union and Zanzibar's Afro-Shirazi Party, merged in February 1977 to form the Chama Cha Mapinduzi, or single Revolutionary Party. This was the main political event in a year that saw some heart-searching about Tanzania's socialist experiment.

Internal Affairs. The union of the two parties was accomplished on February 5, the tenth anniversary of the declaration that set Tanzania on its socialist course. In a frank assessment of that experiment, President Julius K. Nyerere concluded that Tanzania was neither socialist nor self-reliant, and that the goal of making it so was not even in sight. In a forthright statement Nyerere wrote: "The nature of exploitation has changed but it has not been altogether eliminated. There are still great inequalities between citizens. Our democracy is imperfect. A life of poverty is still the experience of the majority of our citizens."

Among the successes of the past 10 years, he listed the "reasonably good progress" toward providing the country's 14 million people with basic health, education, and transportation. He also mentioned the resettlement of virtually all of Tanzania's people into 7,684 villages in the program of "villagization."

International Affairs. Nyerere became the first black African leader to make a state visit to President Carter's White House. As chairman of the leaders of the front-line states confronting Rhodesia, he discussed southern Africa with the U. S. president at their August meeting. "A good deal of progress" was said to be made.

Tanzania closed its border with Kenya in February after blaming Kenya for scuttling the East Africa Airways Corporation, which had been jointly administered by the two countries along with Uganda. The border remained closed toward the end of the year, hampering tourism, particularly in Tanzania. As a result, the East African Community, a trading association established by Tanzania, Kenya, and Uganda, finally collapsed. The dream of East African unity had ended, at least for the time being.

JAMES PRINGLE

TANZANIA · Information Highlights

Official Name: United Republic of Tanzania.
Location: East Africa.
Area: 364,899 square miles (945,087 km²).
Population (1977 est.): 16,000,000.
Chief City (1974 est.): Dar es Salaam, the capital, 300,000.
Government: *Head of state,* Julius K. Nyerere, president (took office 1964). *Chief Minister,* Rashidi Kawawa, premier (took office 1972). *Legislature* (unicameral) —National Assembly.
Monetary Unit: Shilling (8.33 shillings equal U. S.$1, Aug. 1977).
Manufacturing (major products): Textiles, cement, petroleum products, refined sugar, aluminum.
Major Agricultural Products: Cloves, sisal, cotton, coffee, oilseeds, groundnuts, tea, tobacco, sugarcane.

TAXATION

There was spreading realization in 1977 that current growth rates were not rapid enough to prevent a gradual increase in unemployment in most countries. Inflation continued at high rates. Many governments thus considered tax changes to alleviate these problems and the attendant threat to rising living standards.

Congressional Action. In response to President Carter's proposals for tax changes to move the U. S. economy closer to full employment, Congress enacted the Tax Reduction and Simplification Act of 1977, which cut taxes by $2.8 billion in fiscal year 1977 and $17.7 billion in 1978. The major reduction was in the form of an increase in the standard deduction for most taxpayers. Flat deductions of $2,200 for single persons and $3,200 for married couples filing jointly will supplant the previous minimum low-income allowance and percentage standard deduction. The act also extended several provisions of the law that were due to expire at the end of 1977, including the $35 general credit for each taxpayer and dependent, the earned income credit for the working poor with children, and the lower tax rates on the first $50,000 of corporate taxable income. The law also established a new jobs credit of up to $2,000 for each net new employee hired by an employer in 1977 or 1978.

In October the president announced he would further delay his general tax reduction and revision proposals until Congress completed action on his energy and social security bills.

On December 15, House and Senate conferees approved a compromise social security financing bill that will raise the payroll tax rate and the taxable base, starting in 1979, above the increases scheduled under previous law. The maximum tax on the employer and employee each will rise gradually from $965 in 1977 to an estimated $3,046 in 1987. The maximum tax in 1978, which is scheduled to rise to $1,071, will not be affected. Congress rejected two financing proposals put forth by the president. The first would have moved some of the burden of the social security tax to general revenues in times of high unemployment. The other proposal would have abandoned the principle of equal contributions by employers and employees by removing the ceiling on the wage base on which employers pay the tax, while retaining a ceiling, though higher than now, on the employee tax base.

Congress also considered many tax changes that were included in Carter's national energy plan. These included higher taxes on consumer and business use of energy, with the amounts to be rebated on a per capita basis; and new tax incentives for energy conservation.

State and Local Revenues. State and local governments collected $10 billion more in tax and other general revenues than they spent in fiscal year 1977. Tax receipts in 1977 were $174 billion, an increase of $19 billion or 12% over 1976. The dollar increase was the largest ever recorded in a single year, and the percentage gain was the highest since 1972. Federal grants to state and local governments continued to advance rapidly, reaching $70 billion in fiscal 1977 for an increase of $11 billion over 1976.

New 1977 state laws will have only a nominal effect on tax revenues, raising them by less than half a billion dollars annually. Sixteen state legislatures increased the rate of one or more major taxes. One half of the new revenues raised by the 1977 tax laws will come from higher excise taxes on cigarettes, gasoline, and alcoholic beverages.

As the states continued to grapple with problems of school financing, the financing plans were struck down in two additional states. The state supreme court declared that Connecticut's system was unconstitutional because it relies too heavily on local property taxes. Residents of Maine voted to repeal the state school finance plan enacted in 1973 and based on a uniform statewide property tax. The state tax had replaced local taxes and required wealthier districts to help support the less affluent. In the last six years 24 states have adopted tax laws designed to smooth out inequities in school financing programs, and others are in the process of doing so.

Supreme Court Decisions. The two major corporate cases considered by the U. S. Supreme Court dealt with technical issues of defining the income of insurance companies for federal tax purposes. In *U. S.* v. *Consumer Life Insurance Co.* the issue was how unearned premium reserves should be treated for tax purposes. In *Commissioner of Internal Revenue* v. *Standard Life & Accident Insurance Co.,* the question concerned the treatment for income tax purposes of the portion of the unpaid premiums that state law requires a company to add to its reserves. In both cases the court deferred to long-standing practices approved by the various state regulatory authorities, and in favor of the companies.

In *Commissioner of Internal Revenue* v. *Robert J. Kowalski,* the court ruled that cash meal allowances paid by New Jersey to its state troopers are includable in income for federal tax purposes. The policeman had claimed that such payments qualify for the legal exclusion provided for meals furnished for the convenience of the employer. The decision may have repercussions elsewhere, because 15 states pay cash meal allowances to some 10,000 policemen.

The court also made a decision on where the government's power to collect taxes ends and the taxpayer's right to privacy begins. In *GM Leasing Corp.* v. *U. S.* the court ruled that the Internal Revenue Service's forcible entry into a corporation's business premises to seize records in satisfaction of a tax claim violated the company's constitutional right to privacy. Upheld by the court, however, was the service's right to seize property from open areas to satisfy a valid tax claim.

In its major decision in the area of state taxation, the court overturned a 1951 Supreme Court decision, *Spector Motor Service* v. *O'Connor,* which had held that a state tax on the privilege of doing business is *per se* unconstitutional when applied to interstate commerce. In *Complete Auto Transit Co. Inc.* v. *Brady, Chairman, Mississippi State Tax Commission,* the court upheld the right of the state to impose an occupational sales tax on the privilege of doing business in the state, if the activity has a substantial nexus with the taxing state, is fairly apportioned, does not discriminate against interstate commerce, and is fairly related to the services provided by the state. The tax in the case was imposed by Mississippi on transportation within the state of motor vehicles assembled out of state, and shipped by rail to Jackson, where they are later loaded on trucks of a Michigan auto corporation for delivery to the in-state dealers.

Canada. The 1977 spring budget eased Canada's taxes on dividends and capital gains, raised the employment expense deduction, and extended the investment tax credit for three years. The personal income tax structure was adjusted for inflation, under provisions of previous law.

Other Countries. Britain moved to reduce the burden of income taxes by cutting the basic rate from 35% to 34%, increasing personal allowances, and introducing the automatic indexing of personal tax allowances for inflation beginning in 1978–79. Consumer taxes were increased as part of an effort to restore the balance between taxes on income and taxes on consumption.

In France, personal income taxes were adjusted for inflation, with greater relief in the lower brackets; and motor vehicle duty rates and the taxes on petroleum products and tobacco were increased. West Germany approved a modest tax package of measures to spur the economy, including tax cuts for individuals and businesses. Sweden increased its value-added tax rates and introduced a temporary 15% levy on certain building construction activities. Ireland enacted sharp reductions in the rates of both corporate and personal income taxes.

Spain imposed a new net worth tax for individuals and an additional 5% tax on individuals with higher incomes. In Australia, the individual income tax structure was adjusted to offset the rise in inflation, but the corporate income tax rate was raised from 42½ to 46%. Japan provided no business tax incentives to improve its sagging growth rate nor any individual tax cuts, but relied instead on higher government spending.

ELSIE M. WATTERS
Tax Foundation

TELECOMMUNICATIONS

The ongoing fight by American Telephone & Telegraph Co. (AT&T) and its allies in the telephone industry to retain their monopoly position over U. S. telephone services took several significant turns during the year.

New Proposal. In September, AT&T and independent telephone companies reversed their long-standing opposition to services provided by interconnect companies and said they would formally accept the idea of competition in the sale of such terminal equipment as the basic telephone instrument, switchboards, and other devices used at the subscriber's end of the telephone network. Under the proposal, contained in a memorandum to the Senate and House Communications Subcommittees, subscribers would be free to purchase extension phones and other terminal equipment from outside sources. The policy switch is viewed as an effort by AT&T and independent companies to salvage some control over their market in the face of adverse court rulings and congressional calls for change.

Specifically, the memorandum proposed that Congress write into law the requirement that a telephone company provide its single-line customers—a category that accounts for more than two thirds of all telephone users, including nearly all home subscribers—with a "telephone-company-owned and maintained instrument." Under this so-called "primary instrument concept," the subscriber then would be free to pur-

chase other telephone equipment from competing sources.

Legislative Action. The so-called "Bell Bill," or Consumer Communications Reform Act, introduced in 1976, is dormant in the U. S. Senate. In the House, however, the legislation, which would bar competition from present telephone and future network communications services and transfer jurisdiction over telephone terminals to state agencies, was broadened to include the entire Communications Act of 1934.

At the same time, a major effort was begun by the House Communications Subcommittee to rewrite the Communications Act. The subcommittee began by holding panel discussions on broadcasting issues, including industry supervision, spectrum, the First Amendment, ownership, and industry structure. The subcommittee then asked for suggestions from other industry segments. It is expected to spend most of its time dealing with material submitted by AT&T and independent telephone companies.

Court Ruling. Further complicating AT&T's position, a federal appeals court found that the company might not be entitled to its existing monopoly of long-distance telephone service unless it demonstrated that its rights to link phone customers were in "the public interest." So far, the court's opinion affects only one relatively small Bell System competitor, MCI Telecommunications Corp. Essentially, the court ruled that MCI may offer a type of long-distance service known as Execunet in competition with AT&T. In the broadest view, the court's decision would open every aspect of AT&T's current monopoly to challenge. The full impact of the ruling is not clear, but several specialized carriers are following the Execunet situation very closely.

Against this background, Congress is expected to begin shaping legislation which could lead to basic changes in federal communications law.

Other Developments. Most of the functions performed by the White House Office of Telecommunications Policy were assigned to the Department of Commerce, to be headed by a newly created assistant secretary for communications and information. At the same time, the Office of Management and Budget, which is part of the Executive Office, will, according to a White House announcement, "take responsibility for federal telecommunications procurement and management policy and arbitration of interagency disputes about frequency allocation."

Having previously deferred AT&T's expansion of Dataphone Digital Service (DDS) for data communications users, due to "low earnings and failure of AT&T to retain actual investment and expense data," the Federal Communications Commission gave AT&T permission to expand its current authorized DDS network by 40 cities (to a total of 64) and to provide the new Dataphone Switched Digital Service in 27 cities.

RONALD A. SCHNEIDERMAN
"Consumer Electronics Daily"

TELEPHONES IN MAJOR COUNTRIES

Country	Telephones Jan. 1, 1976	% increase from 1975	No. per 100 population
Argentina	2,469,250	4.0	9.66
Australia	5,266,843	5.3	39.01
Austria	2,132,758	7.4	28.13
Belgium	2,776,882	4.1	28.34
Brazil	3,371,284	27.1	3.08
Bulgaria	777,127	8.2	8.90
Canada	13,142,235	5.5	57.15
China, Nationalist	1,117,989	24.1	6.92
Colombia	1,285,670	8.4	5.45
Czechoslovakia	2,614,761	5.4	17.62
Denmark	2,316,208	6.1	44.97
Egypt[1]	503,200	6.7	1.37
Finland	1,833,993	9.2	38.89
France	13,833,346	11.5	26.2
Germany, East	2,570,113	4.9	15.23
Germany, West	19,602,606	4.5	31.7
Greece	2,008,522	7.9	22.12
Hong Kong	1,033,735	4.6	23.6
Hungary	1,048,090	3.4	9.91
India	1,816,901	7.5	0.30
Iran	688,396	11.4	2.00
Israel	796,348	8.3	22.8
Italy	14,495,677	5.8	25.88
Japan	45,514,709	8.6	40.47
Mexico	2,914,531	14.5	4.76
Netherlands, The	5,047,117	7.7	36.75
New Zealand	1,570,784	5.1	50.18
Norway	1,406,995	3.8	35.03
Poland	2,577,636	7.4	7.54
Portugal	1,065,974	5.4	12.3
Rumania[1]	1,076,566	21.5	5.10
South Africa	2,072,131	7.0	8.1
Spain	7,835,970	11.3	21.98
Sweden	5,422,795	4.7	66.07
Switzerland	3,912,971	3.2	61.09
Turkey	1,011,790	12.4	2.52
United Kingdom	21,035,602	3.4	37.51
USSR	16,949,000	7.4	6.63
United States	149,011,000	3.5	69.49
Venezuela	649,603	17.2	5.34
Yugoslavia	1,301,219	13.9	6.06

[1] 1975   Source: AT&T

TELEVISION AND RADIO

The ratings race, the networks' frantic pursuit of the number one position in terms of audience, dominated television broadcasting throughout the year and led to changes not only in programming, but in sports and news coverage, and management. Prestige seemed to be the dominant concern—not, as in the past, earnings —for all three networks were essentially sold out. The intensity of the ratings race had been forecast in 1976 when ABC, in a stunning reversal of form, had charged to the front from its usual lowly third position. The year 1977 became catchup time for the two senior networks.

Ratings and *Roots*. ABC got off to an astonishing start in January, daring to show the 12-hour dramatization of Alex Haley's book, *Roots,* on eight consecutive nights. The gamble paid off, setting many new records. *Roots* week gave ABC an unprecedented 35.5 national Nielsen rating, about ten points higher than any network had ever achieved in a single week; some 80 million people, the largest audience ever for any single TV event, watched all or part of the final episode; the 16 top-rated shows of the week were all ABC shows, with the seven episodes of *Roots* as the top seven shows. Television had never seen the like of this record and, it seems reasonable to say, television will never be quite the same again.

ABC's domination continued, aided by the success of three of the four programs it introduced in the "second (January) season," and the unmatched ability to find the right time slots for almost all of its shows. Of the dozen or so new programs from NBC and CBS, only three immediately achieved the share of audience considered essential for survival.

In late summer, with the "new (September) season" close at hand, all three networks indulged in an unusual degree of what the industry calls "stunting," beginning with heavy (sometimes burdensome) doses of on-air promotions for their new programs. Stunting continued into the two prime-time weeks of September 5–17. In those two weeks, as the newsweekly *Broadcasting* pointed out, in a space of 40 hours the networks presented an average of 35 hours each of specials and premieres. Against ABC's highly-touted *Washington: Behind Closed Doors,* played on six consecutive nights from September 6 through 11, NBC and CBS threw first-run movies, important specials, and one- and two-hour versions of returning old half-hour and hour favorites, such as *M*A*S*H* and *Hawaii Five-O. Closed Doors,* as things turned out, was not another *Roots,* but when the initial two-week period of the new season was ended, ABC had a comfortable 3-point rating lead over its nearer competitor. A different measure of ABC's success was that during the year it was able to in-

crease its station affiliations from 182 to 195, thereby greatly increasing its potential audience.

To meet the ABC challenge both CBS and NBC made extensive changes in top management, while at the same time changing operational structures to correspond to the ABC pattern, with Entertainment, Sports, and News becoming separate divisions. Each division is under its own head and each head answers to the network president.

News. Over the years, news programming, once carried as the prestige part of a network's offerings, has grown to become big business. During most of these years, the CBS *Evening News with Walter Cronkite* has enjoyed the number one position, with NBC's *Nightly News* pressing closely, and ABC's *Evening News* lagging well behind. The 1976 addition of Barbara Walters as co-anchor with Harry Reasoner did little to raise ratings and so, in the spring of 1977, ABC made a dramatic bid for eventual supremacy. The network appointed the innovative Roone Arledge president of the news division as of June 1, in addition to his presidency of ABC Sports. The network also allocated the money for a greatly expanded news staff. In the fall, NBC moved David Brinkley to Washington, as permanent anchor there for the news of the nation's capital, and created new sets for both the *NBC Nightly News* and the *Today* show, banishing the familiar desks. In neither of the sets did the participants seem comfortable.

Sports. Jockeying by the networks for the U. S. rights to televise the 1980 summer Olympics in Moscow had been intense through the

A cartoonist view of the David Frost–Richard Nixon interviews. The former president emphasized his past defense.

The "new season" began in September with much "stunting" (on-air promotion). *The Betty White Show*, starring favorites from the *Mary Tyler Moore* show—Betty White and Georgia Engel—received much initial attention.

late months of 1976. It came to an end in February, when NBC signed an agreement with the Soviet Olympic Committee. According to many observers, the estimated cost of $125 million will go much higher by the time of the event. In October, the House Communications Subcommittee, as a part of its investigation into the relationship between the networks and sports, questioned executives of all three networks on the kind of pressures brought to bear by the Soviet Union to secure shows favorable to the USSR on American television, and on what the Soviets might demand once the games were under way. That Congressional investigation and a Federal Communications Commission investigation of "winner-take-all" tennis matches on CBS occurred because the networks had become promoters, rather than simply broadcasters, of a goodly number of sports events. Boxing, for instance, returned to TV in a big way. Two events were noteworthy. ABC had to suspend its *United States Boxing Championships,* for which the network had put up $1.5 million in prize money, in mid-term, because of allegations of kickbacks and rigged records and matches. NBC's broadcast of the Muhammad Ali–Earnie Shavers heavyweight title fight on September 29 drew over half the available audience in its time period.

Federal Communications Commission (FCC). There were changes at the FCC. Chairman Richard E. Wiley resigned to make way for a Democrat, Charles D. Ferris, formerly general counsel to Rep. Thomas P. O'Neill. The FCC chairmanship thus returned to Democratic hands for the first time since 1966. Tyrone Brown, a Washington attorney, was appointed to fill the seat formerly held by Benjamin L. Hooks. These appointments brought the commission back to its traditional posture, in which four of the seven members are of the party in the White House.

During the year, Wiley's FCC (he left office in October, when the new appointments were confirmed) faced court reversals of its decisions and rules regarding such matters as media cross-ownership, the family-viewing concept, the "indecency" of a George Carlin comedy record broadcast by WBAI (FM), and pay cable siphoning of movies and sports from broadcasting. The FCC appealed most of these reversals. It was heartened by an opinion of a three-judge panel of the Court of Appeals in Washington. The opinion upheld the FCC's decision that, in the words of *Broadcasting,* "a policy statement and reliance on broadcaster self-regulation were an appropriate response, at least for the time being, to problems in children's programming and advertising." The original questions had been raised by ACT (Action for Children's Television) three years before.

As Wiley left the FCC, there was widespread favorable comment on his tenure as chairman. His energy and efficiency, his conservatism, in that he worked for as little regulation as possible, his resistance to FCC involvement in program decisions, and his careful regard for broadcasters' First Amendment rights were particularly emphasized.

Citizen's Groups. The clamor for a greater voice in television's affairs seemed at times deafening. Citizen's groups concerned themselves with minority rights in employment and station ownership, children's programs and advertising, the stereotyping of the elderly in programs, sex and violence. Violence in programs was found to have been slightly subdued in the new season, and there was only one new police show, NBC's inept *CHiPs.* The National Association of Broadcasters, after tussling with the sex and violence problem for several months, decided in September against writing into the TV code any specific prohibitions. Instead, it passed a code amendment leaving it to the licensee to decide what should or should not be seen on a station.

As for sex, along came *Soap*. ABC announced it, with fanfares, in the spring, as a daring satire of the sexiness of daytime serials. Promptly and predictably, several religious groups damned it, in some cases without having screened it. ABC made some minor changes in the program, but put it on the air in the new season, against *One Day At A Time*. The critics found it witless and heavy-handed, but early ratings showed it drawing at least a third of the audience.

Public Television. Continuing tension between the Corporation for Public Television and the Public Broadcasting Service occasioned ferment in public television. The unrest was also produced by attacks by Congressional and citizen's groups on PTV's record in minority employment, by questions of its increasing dependence on program funding by commercial corporations, and by its extensive use of British program imports.

Two significant steps were taken to help solve some of these problems. In June, the Carnegie Corporation announced the formation of a Carnegie Commission on the Future of Public Broadcasting, headed by Columbia University president William McGill. The commission was given an initial grant of $1 million and was expected to complete its work in about 18 months. In October, President Carter sent to Congress a bill intended to clarify the issue of the governing authority in public broadcasting, strengthen the system's independence, provide more and surer funding under a new five-year plan, and repeal the statutory ban on editorializing by public broadcasting stations.

CTW, formerly the Children's Television Workshop, famous for *Sesame Street* and *The Electric Company,* moved into adult programming with an eight-week, nine-hour mini-series, *The Best of Families*. The series, effectively combining drama and American social history of the 1880 to 1900 period, had a production cost of $6 million. As an example of PBS's money problems, it took CTW three years to raise the funding, from foundations and corporations.

Television and Congress. In April, the House Communications Subcommittee, under chairman Lionel Van Deerlin (D-Calif.), dug into its projected "rewrite" of the communications act. Beginning with some 850 pages of "option papers" by its staff, the project considered all the ways in which telecommunications might be restructured. During the remainder of the year, informal sessions and formal hearings were held and staff papers prepared on such subjects as TV violence, broadcasting's structure and practices, minority ownership, and public television.

TELEVISION STATIONS AND SETS [1]

Country	Stations	Sets [2]
Albania	1	3,500
Algeria (Low-power: 60)	23	440,000
Angola	1	NA
Argentina (Low-power: 44)	33	4,700,000
Australia (Low-power: 120)	128	4,532,000
Austria (Low-power: 302)	297	1,988,000
Bahamas	2	30,000
Bahrain	1	60,000
Bangladesh	5	28,000
Barbados	1	40,000
Belgium (Low-power: 12)	19	2,646,000
Bolivia	1	100,000
Brazil (Low-power: 15)	74	15,000,000
Brunei	2	18,500
Bulgaria (Low-power: 185)	13	1,530,000
Cambodia	2	30,000
Canada	850	8,500,000
Central African Empire	1	100
Chad	1	NA
Chile (Low-power: 37)	43	1,200,000
China (Low-power: 8)	40	3,400,000
Colombia (Low-power: 42)	18	1,600,000
Congo	1	2,500
Costa Rica (Low-power: 5)	4	250,000
Cuba (Low-power: 13)	25	700,000
Cyprus (Low-power: 3)	2	82,000
Czechoslovakia (Low-power: 878)	55	3,901,500
Denmark (Low-power: 22)	30	1,850,000
Djibouti	1	3,000
Dominican Republic	8	305,000
Ecuador	10	250,000
Egypt	22	1,301,000
El Salvador	5	109,300
Equatorial Guinea	1	500
Ethiopia	3	30,000
Finland	104	1,795,713
France (Low-power: 2,092)	225	14,694,000
Gabon	2	5,000
Germany, E.	28	5,170,000
Germany, W. (Low-power: 3,034)	185	20,500,000
Ghana (Low-power: 8)	4	40,000
Greece (Low-power: 40)	20	1,075,000
Guatemala (Low-power: 9)	3	150,000
Haiti	3	13,000
Honduras	7	47,000
Hong Kong (Low-power: 22)	5	862,000
Hungary	33	2,540,000
Iceland (Low-power: 68)	9	57,000
India	9	400,000
Indonesia (Low-power: 16)	38	542,440
Iran (Low-power: 38)	17	2,018,000
Iraq	7	500,000
Ireland	31	703,000
Israel (Low-power: 25)	11	475,000
Italy (Low-power: 1,254)	94	12,660,000
Ivory Coast (Low-power: 3)	10	205,000
Jamaica	11	120,000
Japan (Low-power: 7,122)	213	27,000,000
Jordan (Low-power: 5)	6	171,000
Kenya	5	55,000
Korea, S. (Low-power: 24)	12	2,900,000
Kuwait	3	130,000
Lebanon	8	500,000
Liberia (Low-power: 4)	1	10,000
Libyan Arab Republic	11	160,000
Luxembourg (Low-power: 1)	1	86,500
Madagascar (Low-power: 3)	2	8,200
Malaysia (Low-power: 3)	32	564,000
Malta	1	76,000
Mauritius (Low-power:3)	1	67,100
Mexico (Low-power: 72)	80	5,480,000
Mongolia	1	2,000
Morocco (Low-power: 3)	20	522,900
Netherlands	20	5,286,150
New Zealand	32	816,175
Nicaragua (Low-power: 1)	2	72,200
Niger	2	244
Nigeria (Low-power: 2)	9	300,000
Norway (Low-power: 688)	100	1,088,200
Oman (Low-power: 6)	2	30,000
Pakistan	15	450,000
Panama	12	228,000
Paraguay	1	52,000
Peru (Low-power: 9)	12	750,000
Philippines	23	650,000
Poland (Low-power: 80)	50	5,695,300
Portugal (Low-power: 39)	14	1,100,000
Qatar	2	35,000
Rhodesia	2	67,600
Rumania (Low-power: 180)	25	3,030,000
Saudi Arabia	8	300,000
Senegal	1	1,700
Sierra Leone	1	8,000
Singapore	2	360,000
South Africa (Low-power: 19)	18	780,000
Spain (Low-power: 772)	51	7,425,000
Sudan	2	90,000
Surinam (Low-power: 1)	1	33,000
Sweden (Low-power: 90)	266	4,510,500
Switzerland	93	1,821,000
Syria	8	315,800
Tanzania	2	7,152
Thailand (Low-power: 11)	9	720,000
Trinidad & Tobago	3	125,000
Tunisia	9	250,000
Turkey	51	1,800,000
Uganda	6	65,000
United Arab Emirates	4	92,000
United Kingdom (Low-power: 318)	333	18,000,000
United States	974	139,400,000
Upper Volta	1	7,700
Uruguay	18	350,000
USSR (Low-power: 698)	167	50,000,000
Venezuela	31	1,460,000
Vietnam	1	500,000
Yemen (Low-power: 2)	3	30,000
Yugoslavia (Low-power: 335)	62	3,345,000
Zaire	2	7,500
Zambia	3	22,000

[1] As of mid-1977. [2] Includes black and white and color sets. Source: *Television Factbook,* 1978 Edition.

In honor of the inauguration of Jimmy Carter, a gala entertainment was held at the John F. Kennedy Center in Washington. Some of the nation's top stars, from all fields, performed. Leonard Bernstein conducted the National Symphony. The program was telecast live.

PHOTOS CBS

"INAUGURAL EVE SPECIAL"

The "New Spirit" concert also featured Shirley MacLaine, and Mike Nichols and Elaine May in a skit about the first Jewish president.

Cable. The Supreme Court's refusal to hear an appeal on a lower court's overturning of the FCC's rules against pay cable's siphoning of movies and sports events from on-air broadcasting essentially transferred the problem to Congress. House Communications Subcommittee chairman Van Deerlin said the matter would be considered in connection with the review of the communications act, but would likely not lead to legislation until after the draft of a new communications bill.

Pay cable's largest operation, Home Box Office, broke into the black, showing a profit for the first time in its nearly five-year history. The House Communications Subcommittee was sympathetic to regular cable television's major desire, the end of restrictions on its use of distant signals.

In June the FCC launched an inquiry into the economic relationship between broadcasting and cable TV. Hard facts rather than "intuition" were sought as guides for future policy.

In Florida, a 15-year-old boy was tried on a first degree murder charge. The defense claimed insanity, owing to "involuntary, subliminal television intoxication." There is irony in the fact that this trial was locally televised, as part of a year-long test. The jury rejected the unusual defense and found the boy guilty.

Beginning in March, the level of television viewing dropped by about 3% and remained down through the year. No one quite knew why.

RADIO

Commercial radio, both AM and FM, enjoyed a 10–12% increase in business during the year. The prices paid for station acquisition also indicated radio's healthy economy. A record sale figure of over $4 million was paid by Cox Broadcasting for WWSH (FM) Washington.

The FCC's oldest case came close to an end. Involving KOB (AM) Albuquerque, N. M., and WABC (AM) New York City, the case dates to 1941. In October 1977, the U. S. Court of Appeals in Washington affirmed the FCC judgment supporting WABC's right to operate as the Class 1-A station on the shared 770 khz frequency, with 50 kw power day and night, and free of interference from the Albuquerque station. KOB, claiming that the decision robs it of 100,000 listeners at night, could appeal to the Supreme Court.

Radio's ubiquitous mix of music, information, and commercials was ameliorated when producer-director-supersalesman Himan Brown put his *General Mills Adventure Theater* into production. Starting in February, on 218 radio stations, it joined another Brown production, *CBS Mystery Theater,* as the only new drama.

In July, R. Peter Straus, president of WMCA (AM) New York, was appointed director of the Voice of America.

Miscellany. As CBS celebrated its 50th anniversary, William S. Paley, its founder and major force, resigned as chief executive officer. He turned the post over to CBS president John D. Backe. Paley, 75, made it clear that as chairman he would remain active in CBS affairs.

NBC agreed to a consent decree requiring the network to disburse about $2 million in back pay, salary equalizations, and training programs for many of its women employees.

JOHN M. GUNN
Formerly, Professor of Radio-TV-Film
State University of New York at Albany

In Miami, Fla., defense lawyers failed to convince a jury that TV violence led a 15-year-old boy to commit murder.

UPI

MAJOR U. S. TELEVISION PROGRAMS

The Amazing Howard Hughes—A two-part television movie based on the known facts in the life of the reclusive American billionaire; with Tommy Lee Jones and Ed Flanders. CBS, April 13–14.

The Battle Over Panama—A special in-depth news documentary, giving the background and all-sided arguments on "the most divisive foreign-policy issue since Vietnam"; with Bill Moyers. CBS, Nov. 1.

The Best of Families—An eight-episode dramatic series about America, and particularly New York City, in the last 20 years of the 19th century; hosted by John Houseman. PBS, beginning Oct. 27.

Bing—A musical special, taped in March, celebrating Bing Crosby's 50th year in show business; with the singer himself, Bob Hope, Paul Anka, Pearl Bailey, Joe Bushkin, Rosemary Clooney, and the Crosby family. CBS, Oct. 24.

La Bohème—Live telecast of Puccini's opera from the Metropolitan Opera House in New York City; hosted by Tony Randall; with Renata Scotto, Luciano Pavarotti, Maralin Niska; conductor, James Levine. PBS, March 15.

The CIA's Secret Army—A special two-hour report looking into the overt and covert activities of anti-Castro Cuban terrorists, originally recruited by the CIA and based in Miami, Fla.; with Bill Moyers. CBS, June 10.

Dickens of London—A 10-part dramatic series about the life and times of Charles Dickens, as remembered by him on his last American tour; hosted by Alistair Cooke; with Roy Dotrice, Simon Bell, and others. PBS, beginning Aug. 28.

The 11th Annual Country Music Association Awards—Presentations with music, on a live telecast from the Grand Ole Opry in Nashville, Tenn.; hosted by Johnny Cash; with June Carter Cash, Chet Atkins, Roy Clark, Mac Davis, Loretta Lynn, and many others. CBS, Oct. 10.

Elton John: In Concert—Highlights from a concert given by the rock performer in Edinburgh, Scotland in 1976. ABC, Feb. 3.

Emily, Emily—A Hallmark Hall of Fame presentation about a 19-year-old retardate who learns to function in the everyday world; with John Forsythe, Karen Grassle, James Farentino. NBC, Feb. 7.

Fidel Castro Speaks—An hour-long, wide-ranging interview with the Cuban president, providing glimpses into his philosophy and personal feelings; conducted by Barbara Walters. ABC, June 9.

Die Fledermaus—A telecast, via satellite, from the Royal Opera House at Covent Garden, London, with Tony Randall as host; conductor, Zubin Mehta. NEW, Dec. 31.

The Gathering—Movie made for television about a dying man who attempts to reunite his estranged family for his last Christmas; with Edward Asner and Maureen Stapleton. ABC, Dec. 4.

Giselle—Live telecast of the American Ballet Theatre's performance in the Metropolitan Opera House in New York City; hosted by Dick Cavett; starring Natalia Makarova as Giselle, Mikhail Baryshnikov as Albrecht, and Martine van Hamel as Myrta. PBS, June 2.

Hard Times—A four-part dramatization of Charles Dickens' novel about the impact of the industrial revolution on the human spirit; with Jacqueline Tong, Timothy West, and Rosalie Crutchley. PBS, beginning May 11.

Highlights of the Russian Dance Festival—A showcase featuring leading Soviet dancers, musicians, and pantomimists under the direction of Igor Moiseyev; hosted by Orson Welles. NBC, July 7.

The Hunchback of Notre Dame—A new television version, made by the BBC, of Victor Hugo's popular novel set in 15th-century Paris; with Warren Clarke, Terrence Bayler, Kenneth Haigh, David Rintoul. NBC, July 18.

I, Claudius—A 13-episode dramatization of Robert Graves' novels of intrigue, murder, and corruption in imperial Rome; hosted by Alistair Cooke; with Derek Jacobi, Brian Blessed, and others. PBS, beginning Nov. 6.

Inaugural Eve Gala Performance—Entertainers and other celebrities paying tribute to Jimmy Carter and Walter Mondale on the eve of the inauguration; with Hank Aaron, Muhammad Ali, Leonard Bernstein, Bette Davis, James Dickey, Elaine May, Paul Newman, Freddie Prinze, Beverly Sills, John Wayne, and others. CBS, Jan. 19.

Italian Fascism: Seen Through Its Own Eyes—A Scandinavian compilation of propaganda films made in Italy during the 20-year reign of Benito Mussolini. NET, Aug. 6.

Jesus of Nazareth—Franco Zeffirelli's two-part production for television of the life of Christ, written by Anthony Burgess; with Robert Powell in the title role and starring Lord Laurence Olivier, Sir Ralph Richardson, Michael York, Anne Bancroft, and others. NBC, April 3, 10.

BETH BERGMAN, NEW YORK CITY OPERA

Live opera performances, including Beverly Sills in Manon, **were seen on the TV screen for the first time. Masterpiece Theatre presented** Dickens of London **in ten episodes.**

PUBLIC BROADCASTING SERVICE

Just an Old Sweet Song—A made-for-TV movie about an urban black family that leaves its home in Detroit for a visit to the South; with Cicely Tyson, Robert Hooks, Beah Richards, Tia Rance. CBS, Aug. 25.

The Last Hurrah—A Hallmark Hall of Fame presentation of the familiar story of big-city power politics; with Carroll O'Connor, Burgess Meredith. NBC, Nov. 16.

The Mysteries of the Great Pyramid—An hour-long documentary, presenting the history, legends, and speculation surrounding the pyramid of Cheops; narrated by Omar Sharif. CBS, April 20.

The Nixon Interviews with David Frost—A series of five 90-minute conversations with the former president in which he speaks out about the events of his presidency, including Watergate. NEW, May 4, 12, 19, 25, and Sept. 3.

The Nutcracker—A presentation of the ballet by the corps of the Bolshoi Theater in Moscow; with Betty Ford as narrator and host. NBC, Dec. 18.

The Pallisers—A 22-part dramatic series based on Anthony Trollope's novels of Victorian England's upper crust; hosted by Sir John Gielgud; with Susan Hampshire and Philip Latham. PBS, beginning Jan. 31.

The Paul Simon Special—Musical variety show and a get-together with Art Garfunkel; guests, Chevy Chase, the Jesse Dixon Singers, Charles Grodin, Lily Tomlin. NBC, Dec. 8.

The People vs. Inez Garcia—Dramatic production based on the records of a real trial of a woman who admittedly killed a man who helped rape her; with Silvana Gallardo and Robert Loggia. NET, May 25.

Poldark—A 16-episode dramatization of a tetralogy by Winston Graham, set in Cornwall, England, during the last years of the 18th century; hosted by Alistair Cooke; with Robin Ellis and Angharad Rees. PBS, beginning May 8.

The Queen's Silver Jubilee Gala at Covent Garden—Selections from performances celebrating Queen Elizabeth II's 25-year reign, featuring the Royal Ballet and Royal Opera; with Rudolf Nureyev, Margot Fonteyn, and others. PBS, May 31.

Raid on Entebbe—Television movie about the daring Israeli rescue mission in Uganda on July 3–4, 1976; with an all-star cast, including Peter Finch, Martin Balsam, Charles Bronson, Horst Bucholz, Sylvia Sidney, Jack Warden, and Yaphet Kotto. NBC, Jan. 9.

Rigoletto—Verdi's opera telecast live from the Metropolitan Opera House in New York City; hosted by Tony Randall; with Ilena Cotrubas, Isola Jones, Cornell MacNeil, Placido Domingo; conductor, James Levine. PBS, Nov. 7.

Rock Follies—A five-part satirical comedy about three budding English actresses who make it by forming their own rock 'n' roll group. PBS, March 7–11.

Roots—An eight-episode (12-hour) dramatization of Alex Haley's book about the origin and progression toward freedom of a black American family; with LeVar Burton, Cicely Tyson, Leslie Uggams, Ben Vereen, Burl Ives, John Amos, Edward Asner, Lloyd Bridges, Lorne Greene, and many others. ABC, Jan. 23–30.

Scenes From a Marriage—Ingmar Bergman's six-part study, made for television, of love and marriage in modern society; starring Liv Ullmann and Erland Josephson; introduced by Liv Ullmann. PBS, beginning March 6.

Seventh Avenue—A three-part dramatization of a novel by Norman Bogner about the seamy side of New York's garment district; with Steven Keats, Alan King, Herschel Bernardi, Jane Seymour, Eli Wallach, and others. NBC, Feb. 10, 17, 24.

The Stars Salute America's Greatest Movies—The American Film Institute's 10th anniversary gala, celebrating the 10 best films as determined by a ballot of AFI members; host, Charlton Heston; guests, Lauren Bacall, Olivia de Havilland, Henry Fonda, Sidney Poitier, Rod Steiger, James Stewart, Lily Tomlin, Cicely Tyson, Michael York, and others. CBS, Nov. 21.

Tell Me My Name—A television movie about an adopted girl of 19, who seeks out her natural mother, and the consequences to the mother and her family; with Barbara Barrie, Arthur Hill, Valerie Mahaffey. CBS, Dec. 20.

The Trial of Lee Harvey Oswald—A two-part dramatization of what might have happened if President Kennedy's alleged assassin had stood trial; with John Pleshette, Ben Gazzara, Lorne Greene. ABC, Sept. 30, Oct. 2.

Tut: the Boy King—An hour-long exploration of the treasures of gold, alabaster, and precious stones from King Tutankhamen's 3,000-year-old tomb; narrated by Orson Welles. NBC, July 27.

The Volga—A National Geographic special, presenting a view of Russia and its people rarely seen by Americans. NET, March 8.

Washington: Behind Closed Doors—A six-part dramatization based on John Ehrlichman's novel, The Company, about a paranoid president and his cynical, corrupt administration; with Jason Robards, Cliff Robertson, Stephanie Powers, Robert Vaughn, Barry Nelson, Lois Nettleton, Andy Griffith, and John Houseman. ABC, Sept. 6–11.

"Roots"

Roots was more than the hit of the 1976–77 television season, it was a social and cultural phenomenon and a milestone in television history, marking turning points in the medium both for form and subject matter. For an eight-day period, from Sunday, Jan. 23, to Sunday, Jan. 30, 1977, nearly half the United States was absorbed in the 12-hour dramatization of Alex Haley's fictionalized account of his family's history as black Americans. The story spanned a 200-year period from the capture and enslavement of Kunta Kinte, Haley's forebear in The Gambia, Africa, to the abolition of slavery after the U. S. Civil War.

Although its subject was slavery from the black point of view and its cast predominantly black, *Roots* drew the largest cumulative and per-episode audiences ever for an entertainment program. ABC-TV and David L. Wolper Productions had acquired the television rights to the book two years before its publication by Doubleday. The program was televised when the book had reached the top of the best-seller lists, a fact that contributed greatly to the attention the series received. The popularity of *Roots* was taken as evidence of how far the United States had come in terms of race relations.

LeVar Burton portrayed Kunta Kinte in the successful TV version of Alex Haley's "Roots."

UPI

Until the 1970's, blacks had been infrequent on TV screens. According to the industry's conventional wisdom of the 1950's and 1960's, blacks would not attract either a mass audience or advertising support and would cause Southern stations to defect from the network line-up. Largely, those suppositions were based on NBC's unsuccessful experience in 1957 with a weekly variety hour that starred Nat (King) Cole.

A score of years later, none of the ABC stations rejected *Roots,* though some Southern broadcasters conceded that five years earlier the program's effect in their communities might have been explosive. The mayors of 30 cities proclaimed the broadcast week "Roots Week," and more than 250 colleges and universities offered, or proposed to offer later, courses based on the work. The show sparked few disturbances, none of them serious, in the cities that were capitals of the civil rights turmoil of the 1960's. The Ku Klux Klan did, however, appeal to the Federal Communications Commission, without success, for time to express an opposing view under the Fairness Doctrine.

The eight episodes of *Roots* averaged a 44.9 Nielsen rating and a 66% share of audience, far surpassing the averages for any previous program series. Growing night by night, the audience reached a peak for the final two-hour episode, which drew 51.5% of all TV households in the United States, or a total of 36,380,000 households. That exceeded by 2.4 million homes the previous record for an entertainment program, established two months earlier by the movie *Gone With the Wind* on NBC. Nielsen estimated that 130 million different viewers, in approximately 85% of the TV households in the United States, saw all or part of the series.

Heading the large cast of *Roots* were LeVar Burton, Ben Vereen, John Amos, Maya Angelou, Cicely Tyson, Edward Asner, Harry Rhodes, and Robert Reed. David Wolper served as executive producer and Stan Margulies as producer. The scripts were written by William Blinn, Ernest Kinoy, James Lee, and Max Cohen. The original music was by Quincy Jones.

That ABC had not expected *Roots* to hit the jackpot was indicated by the fact that the episodes played just before the February "sweep" weeks, a rating period crucial to local stations and during which the networks offer what they believe to be their strongest shows.

Among its other effects, *Roots* spurred a lively syndication sale for a British Broadcasting Corporation series, *The Fight Against Slavery,* and it opened the way to television's presentation of serialized novels on consecutive nights instead of consecutive weeks.

LES BROWN

UPI

Flanked by Tennessee's correction and safety commissioners, Gov. Ray Blanton reports on James Earl Ray's prison escape. Ladder used is in the foreground.

TENNESSEE

Legislation. Significant legislative developments in 1977 included a sizable increase in the state budget for general services, particularly education, and a new death-penalty statute for major crimes. The increase in appropriations for higher education during the biennium exceeded 30%, a figure larger than that of any of the eight surrounding states. The death-penalty measure, vetoed by Gov. Ray Blanton, was passed over his objections.

Politics. By late autumn, rumors of gubernatorial candidates for the 1978 election began to surface. Lamar Alexander, defeated in 1974, was the first Republican to announce officially. House Speaker Ned McWhorter and banker Jake Butcher received considerable publicity as possible Democratic candidates. A revision of the prohibition against immediate succession by incumbent chief executives was under consideration by a constitutional convention.

The Courts. In a landmark decision in August, the state Supreme Court ruled unconstitutional a 1969 statute which had allowed some lenders to charge interest rates in effect considerably above the 10% limit prescribed in the state constitution. Many of the lending agencies ceased all personal lending operations. The archaic 10% interest limit was also under review by the constitutional convention. In another

landmark case, the U. S. District Court at Nashville ordered a merger of the University of Tennessee at Nashville with Tennessee State University, a predominantly black institution. The decision was appealed.

Economy. Gains in labor and farm incomes have brightened the economic outlook in the state. In the past few years soybeans have replaced corn, cotton, and tobacco as the state's leading cash crop. Larger plantings in 1977 resulted in a harvest of about 50 million bushels (17.6 million hl), an increase of nearly 25% over 1976. Farm-land values have risen more than 20% since 1975.

While the national unemployment rate exceeded 8%, that in Tennessee was at a three-year low of less than 6%. Nashville had the lowest rate among the four major cities.

Education. Although preliminary estimates indicated that the state's population was up more than 7% since 1970, enrollment in public schools, community colleges, and universities leveled off. Dr. Emmett Fields became president of Vanderbilt University, and Dr. Walter J. Leonard assumed the presidency of Fisk University.

Legislators and taxpayers alike expressed alarm at a Department of Education report which indicated that nearly one fourth of the state's high school graduates are awarded diplomas without having learned basic skills in mathematics and English. Board members proposed a proficiency test, which students would have to complete before receiving a diploma, and scheduled public hearings on the matter.

Names in the News. Country-music star Ronnie Milsap won the prestigious Entertainer-of-the-Year award, and Henning native Alex Haley won both fame and fortune with his *Roots,* which was awarded a special National Book Award. Tennesseans who died during the year included Elvis Presley, king of rock and roll music (see special obituary, p. 372); James Stokley, poet and writer; Irving Wolfe, composer; and Jesse Ely Wills, a leader in the Fugitive poetry movement of the 1920's.

ROBERT E. CORLEW
Middle Tennessee State University

―――― **TENNESSEE · Information Highlights** ――――

Area: 42,244 square miles (109,412 km²).
Population (1976 est.): 4,214,000.
Chief Cities (1970 census): Nashville, the capital, 447,-877; Memphis, 623,530; Knoxville, 174,587.
Government (1977): *Chief Officers*—governor, Ray Blanton (D). *General Assembly*—Senate, 33 members; House of Representatives, 99 members.
Education (1976–77): *Enrollment*—public elementary schools, 541,776 pupils; public secondary, 300,198; nonpublic, 44,700; colleges and universities, 169,-050 students. *Public school expenditures,* $1,143,-529,000 ($1,083 per pupil).
State Finances (fiscal year 1976): *Revenues,* $2,643,-189,000; *expenditures,* $2,807,698,000.
Personal Income (1976): $22,606,000,000; per capita, $5,364.
Labor Force (July 1977): *Nonagricultural wage and salary earners,* 1,643,800; *unemployed,* 108,700 (5.7% of total force).

TEXAS

Politics continued to play a large part in Texan life, but other issues also demanded the citizens' attention.

Political Developments. Although Jimmy Carter narrowly carried the state in 1976, his energy program quickly ran into opposition in Texas. Leading figures in the oil and gas industry indicated their hostility to any price-fixing schemes and insisted that incentives must be provided to encourage further exploration and development. Former Governor John Connally, secretary of the Treasury under President Nixon, was blunt in his criticism of Carter's energy package. Now a Republican, Connally also assailed other aspects of the Carter legislative program. In foreign affairs, polls clearly revealed that the great majority of Texans favored retention of the Panama Canal and opposed any change in its present status.

Gov. Dolph Briscoe announced that he would seek a third term in 1978. Preston Smith, who held that office from 1969 to 1973, but was later discredited in a Houston real-estate scandal, and Ben Barnes, former "boy wonder" of Texas politics, hurt by that same scandal, indicated they might run. Lt. Gov. William P. Hobby and Attorney General John Hill are also likely candidates.

Nationally, Sen. John Tower indicated he would seek reelection, while Congressman Robert Krueger of New Braunfels promised to challenge him for the seat. Sen. Lloyd Bentsen, unsuccessful Democratic presidential aspirant in 1976, concentrated on national questions. Increasingly, Bentsen sought a solution to the sensitive problem of illegal Mexican aliens crossing the Rio Grande and seeking work in Texas.

Civil Rights. The state was rocked by two trials involving alleged police brutality against Mexican-Americans. A San Antonio sheriff, Frank Hayes, was accused of murdering a prisoner in his custody. Acquitted in state court, he was later convicted on a federal civil rights count and sentenced to 50 years in prison.

An even more sensational case occurred in Houston, where two city policemen were indicted for beating insensible a Mexican-American veteran, Joe Campos Torres, and then throwing him into Buffalo Bayou to drown. Accused of murder, the officers obtained a change of venue, and the trial was moved to Huntsville. The two were then found guilty of the lesser charge of "negligent criminal homicide." They were sentenced to one year in prison and a minimum fine, but the sentence was suspended and the officers placed on probation. Mexican-American spokesmen were outraged and appealed to U. S. Attorney General Griffin Bell for federal intervention on a civil-rights basis.

Education and the Arts. The University of Texas sustained its ranking among the nation's most prestigious state universities, particularly on the graduate level. A member of its Chemistry Department was awarded a Nobel Prize in that field in 1977. Because of their proximity to major NASA facilities, Rice University and the University of Houston increased their participation in space-related research activities.

Houston and Dallas, boasting well-known symphony orchestras, art museums, and ballet companies, have emerged as major cultural centers. However, the Kimball Museum in Fort Worth remained the state's most beautiful art center, attracting famous international exhibitions. See also HOUSTON.

STANLEY E. SIEGEL
University of Houston

Texas farmers, driving heavy machinery, form a caravan to protest low farm prices. Traffic snarls resulted.

UPI

--------- **TEXAS · Information Highlights** ---------

Area: 267,338 square miles (692,405 km²).
Population (1976 est.): 12,487,000.
Chief Cities (1970 census): Austin, the capital, 251,808; Houston, 1,232,802; Dallas, 844,401.
Government (1977): *Chief Officers*—governor, Dolph Briscoe (D); lt. gov., William P. Hobby (D). *Legislature*—Senate, 31 members; House of Representatives, 150 members.
Education (1976–77): *Enrollment*—public elementary schools, 1,522,381 pupils; public secondary, 1,300,373; nonpublic, 135,300; colleges and universities, 550,002 students. *Public school expenditures,* $3,502,136,000 ($1,075 per pupil).
State Finances (fiscal year 1976): *Revenues,* $7,942,919,000; *expenditures,* $7,386,147,000.
Personal Income (1976): $77,436,000,000; per capita, $6,201.
Labor Force (June 1977): *Nonagricultural wage and salary earners,* 4,853,000; *unemployed,* 313,700 (5.4% of total force).

In July, Thanin Kraivichien, right, and an aide, inspect a Thai-Cambodian border area, scene of a heavy clash. The prime minister was later dismissed for delaying Thailand's return to democracy.

UPI

THAILAND

It was a confused year of military rule, coups, and attempted coups. A new military government appeared strong at year-end.

Domestic Affairs. A military junta took over in October 1976 when it toppled a three-year old Thai civilian government. Martial law continued in force thereafter, although a civilian government, led by Thanin Kraivichien, had been appointed. Thanin's government gradually grew more independent of the military junta and also more oppressive.

In putting Thanin in power in late 1976 the junta had promised a quick return to normal democratic government. Thanin eventually came up with a 12-year plan for the return to democratic institutions. This was viewed as too long by the junta. Relations between the junta and Thanin continued to deteriorate. In October 1977, the junta demanded a showdown with Thanin, then turned out his government. Since there was no constitutional provision for his ouster, it can be termed another coup but it was bloodless and was organized by the ruling military group. Retired Admiral Sa-ngad Chaloryu, chairman of the junta, promised elections promptly, perhaps in 1978. His equal in the junta and perhaps the center of power in Thailand, Kriangsak Chamanand, took over as premier.

─────── **THAILAND · Information Highlights** ───────

Official Name: Kingdom of Thailand.
Location: Southeast Asia.
Area: 198,456 square miles (514,000 km²).
Population (1977 est.): 44,400,000.
Chief Cities (1975 est.): Bangkok, the capital, 4,000,000; Chiang Mai, 100,000.
Government: *Head of state,* Bhumibol Adulyadej, king (acceded June 1946). *Head of government,* Kriangsak Chamanand, premier (took office Nov. 1977). *Chairman of the Administrative Reform Council,* Sangad Chaloryu. *Legislature*—National Assembly: Senate and House of Representatives (suspended Oct. 1976).
Monetary Unit: Baht (20.40 baht equal U.S.$1, Aug. 1977).
Manufacturing (major products): Processed foods, textiles, clothing.
Major Agricultural Products: Rice, rubber, tapioca, corn, tobacco, fruits, sugarcane, kenaf and jute.

In the spring the political situation had become incredibly complicated. Former exiled military strongmen, notably Thanom Kittikachorn, were back in Thailand and allegedly were gathering support against the junta. Still another military group, led by Gen. Chalard Hiranyasira, attempted a coup in March. It fizzled out but only after the death of Gen. Arun Thavathasin, commander of an army division and a close and popular friend of King Bhumibol Adulyadej. The five coup leaders were at first promised exile in return for releasing two senior military hostages but later were ordered to trial. In fact no trial was ever held. General Chalard was simply executed—partly in retaliation for the death of General Arun—and his other four companions were imprisoned for "life."

Thailand, accustomed to coups and sudden government changes, took the year's developments calmly. There were still insurgents in the outer reaches. A bomb was thrown at the king and queen in September but they were not hurt.

In January the crown prince of Thailand, Vajiralongkorn, was married to his first cousin, Somsawali Kittiyakorn.

Foreign Affairs. Thailand and Cambodia disputed over their common border much of the year. There were several violent exchanges involving troops. For example, 30 Thais were killed in a raid in January and nearly 30 more died in two raids in August. Accusations and threats were exchanged, and the dispute persisted.

In May, Vietnam, Laos, and Thailand agreed to continue with their plan to develop the water resources of the Mekong River. Thailand cooperated with Malaysia in a large-scale military effort to stamp out the communist insurgents along the Thai-Malaysia border.

On June 30th, the Southeast Asia Treaty Organization (SEATO), with Thailand as one of its principal members, dissolved itself. The building that had been SEATO headquarters became part of Thailand's foreign ministry. Relations with the United States were generally good.

CARL LEIDEN
The University of Texas, Austin

THEATER

Mandy Patinkin, Patricia Elliot, and Lawrence Luckinbill star in *The Shadow Box*, winner of a Tony Award and Pulitzer Prize as the year's best play.

In the American theater, 1977 proved to be a year of unparalleled success for new dramatists. The annual best-play awards serve as a convenient index by which to gauge the extent of the newcomers' reception. The New York Drama Critics Circle gave its prize for the best new American play to *American Buffalo* by 29-year-old David Mamet, whose previous reputation rested mainly on a double bill which had been well received off Broadway. Both the Tony Award for the best nonmusical play on Broadway and the Pulitzer Prize were won by 31-year-old Michael Cristofer, an actor, for *The Shadow Box*. Other new writers who made notable impressions on New York audiences during the year were Albert Innaurato, John Bishop, and D. J. Coburn. Waiting in the wings with a frequently staged regional success which has now been scheduled for Broadway was yet another young newcomer, Christopher Durang. In view of the fact that the first half of 1977 completed the season in which Preston Jones and Ntozake Shange made their exciting Broadway debuts, it was possible to be persuaded that a dramatic renaissance was under way.

New Writing Talent. Perhaps the presence of new native talent helped to shorten the list of successful foreign visitors. Except for two vet-

eran British authors, Tom Stoppard and Simon Gray, the foreign dramatists who won the most attention were new arrivals on the New York stage—David Rudkin and Trevor Griffiths, both British, and Roberto Athayde, a Brazilian. Also, the regional theaters discovered a foreign dramatist for whom New York would obviously not have to wait very long, István Orkény, a Hungarian.

Little was heard from our veteran American dramatists. William Gibson made a late, spectacular appearance with a play of current history, *Golda* (about the former Israeli Prime Minister, Golda Meir), but new works by Tennessee Williams and Paul Zindel quickly made their passage through Broadway without inspiring much enthusiasm. New plays by Arthur Miller and Edward Albee were staged in regional theaters, but no one found any reason to expect their prompt arrival in New York. Even David Rabe was in danger of being taken for another inactive veteran of the theater, since this young dramatist, like George Bernard Shaw and Eugene O'Neill, was represented only by a revival.

American Buffalo helped to confirm Mamet's position as the most promising of the new arrivals. In this comedy two inept conspirators and one equally inept young apprentice plan to rob a coin collector but are foiled by circumstance and their own incompetence. Their hopeless bumblings give new proof of Mamet's mastery of dialogue and of our urban idiom. Two more plays by Mamet won praise at regional theaters—*The Water Engine,* about the invention and suppression of an engine that runs on water instead of gasoline (at the St. Nicholas Theater of Chicago, to which Mamet is closely linked), and *Reunion,* in which a father and daughter meet after a long separation (at New Haven's Yale Repertory Theater). Mamet's *A Life in the Theater* was seen early in the year at the Goodman Theater of Chicago; in the fall it won a favorable reception off Broadway. In this hilarious one-act play, an older actor and a younger one exchange revealing chitchat about the theater and enact typical scenes from a large repertoire, usually with the embarrassing results that haunt an actor's nightmares. Ellis Rabb was alarmingly persuasive as the older actor. Once again Mamet had demonstrated his particular talent for one-to-one conversations.

While Mamet found his fun in the speech patterns of his inarticulate characters, Cristofer and Innaurato expended their energy in winning sympathy for ordinary, plainspoken folk, but their own truest sympathies seemed to lie elsewhere, with those who were not so typical—the bisexual intellectual of Cristofer's *The Shadow Box* and the sexually ambiguous college boy of Innaurato's *Gemini. The Shadow Box,* which journeyed over the well traveled road from New Haven's Long Wharf Theater to Broadway, earnestly examined three people facing death in the company of their families and/or friends at a special rest home for the dying. *Gemini,* which moved from off Broadway's Circle Repertory to one of Broadway's smaller theaters, provided a vigorous, rather jolly portrait of urban low life but placed at center stage the troubled son of a hearty proletarian father and two of his carefree college classmates. Another play by Innaurato, *The Transfiguration of Benno Blimpie,* in one act and performed off Broadway, strenuously interpreted the sorrows of a phenomenally fat boy but was meritorious mainly as a vehicle for James Coco's remarkable acting in the title role. John Bishop's presentation of the lives of commonplace people in *The Way Back Down* had no special pleading but only a certain vivid honesty to its account of a middle-aged racing car driver who revisits the home town he abandoned long before and briefly considers settling in for a humdrum life without the excitement of racing.

Coburn and Durang showed special skill at comedy. In Coburn's *The Gin Game,* a vehicle for delightful performances by Jessica Tandy and Hume Cronyn (and also a transfer from the Long Wharf to Broadway), two inmates of a home for the aged play countless games of gin rummy. The continual victories of the woman, who is new to the game, bring out the worst in both players. Durang's *A History of the American Film,* which was staged in Hartford, Washington, and Los Angeles, viewed American life through film stereotypes. The same author's *The Vietnamization of New Jersey* satirized plays about Vietnam veterans and parodied Rabe's *Sticks and Bones* in particular.

Williams' new play, *Vieux Carré,* set in a New Orleans rooming house, showed us a tyran-

In D. L. Coburn's *The Gin Game,* Jessica Tandy and Hume Cronyn are residents of a home for the aged who play countless games of gin rummy. Mike Nichols directed.

ZOE DOMINIC

nical landlady, a tubercular poet, and an intelligent young woman obsessively linked to a dumb, sexual athlete; somehow Williams failed to make it seem new. In *Ladies at the Alamo,* Zindel explored rivalries in the management of a regional theater and at least succeeded in drawing lively performances from Estelle Parsons and Eileen Heckart.

Stoppard's double bill, *Dirty Linen* and *New-Found-Land,* most of it consisting of an engaging satirical treatment of sex scandals in British political life, had a short run. Gray's *Otherwise Engaged,* in which Tom Courtenay imparted more human sympathy to the leading role than his cooler predecessors in London had done, won a longer run for its comic portrait of a publisher who presides over others' misfortunes as well as his own. Griffiths' *Comedians,* another British importation, painted a grimly earnest portrait of a school for comedians whose instructor urges his charges to be socially responsible. Neither the instructor nor his pupils seemed so talented a stand-up performer as Estelle Parsons in the first Brazilian play to be widely performed around the world, Roberto Athayde's *Miss Margarida's Way,* in which Miss Parsons was a tyrannical, sex-obsessed school teacher and the theater audience was her eighth-grade class. Miss Margarida was so mad in the first act that she had nowhere to go in the second, but Miss Parsons was nevertheless tremendous in the part. A Swedish play, Per Olov Enquist's *The Night of the Tribades*, an interesting portrait of the great Swedish dramatist August Strindberg and two of the women in his life, got an encouraging reception when it was acted at Princeton early in the year by an able American cast, but foreign stars were imported for the Broadway production, with disastrous results. Eileen Atkins gave a fine cutting edge to the character of a lesbian interloper, but Max von Sydow and Bibi Andersson indicated they were uncertain of themselves as Strindberg and his first wife.

Revivals, Papp, the "Times." Broadway revivals were made possible chiefly by the availability of stars. Unfortunately, Shaw's *Caesar and Cleopatra* had the wrong stars, Rex Harrison and Elizabeth Ashley, who seemed not inclined to buckle down and seriously play their parts. On the other hand, Liv Ullmann imparted a badly needed vitality to the title role of *Anna Christie,* one of O'Neill's more dated dramas. The highlight of the year for the Circle in the Square's Broadway theater was its animated production of Molière's *Tartuffe,* with John Wood playing the title character as a scrawny, pop-eyed religious enthusiast. At Lincoln Center, a young Rumanian director, Andrei Serban, provided bold new interpretations of Chekhov's *The Cherry Orchard* and Aeschylus' *Agamemnon.* He was more successful with the former, which had the benefit of a moving performance by Irene Worth as the mistress of the house.

The Cherry Orchard had broader comic effects than usual and a variety of symbolic, pictorial motifs. In *Agamemnon,* the leading roles were doubled and the chorus was unusually insistent.

Encouraged by the favorable reception of his *Threepenny Opera* and his *Cherry Orchard,* Joseph Papp, the impresario of the New York Shakespeare Festival of Central Park, the Public Theater, and the Vivian Beaumont Theater of Lincoln Center, announced that the Vivian Beaumont would be dedicated to innovative reinterpretations of classic plays. In a newspaper interview he disclosed his plans for completely rearranging the cavernous auditorium of the Beaumont. Soon after came the Tony Awards, to which a new category had been added, chiefly to accommodate *Threepenny Opera* and *The Cherry Orchard*—"the most innovative production of a classic." To the surprise of a great many, this award went to neither of the Papp productions but to *Porgy and Bess.* A few days later Papp publicized a decision he said he had reached long before: he quit Lincoln Center, explaining that the amount of money lost there even by successful productions was excessive. He would now concentrate his activity at the Public and do his innovative classics there. *Miss Margarida's Way* subsequently became the first of the new Public shows to graduate to Broadway. Central Park, for the first time since Papp began his theatrical activity there had no free Shakespeare in the summer; instead, *Threepenny Opera* and *Agamemnon* were brought over from the Beaumont. (It was, in general, a bad summer for Shakespeare in New York and vicinity. Financial difficulties caused the Shakespeare theater at Stratford, Conn., to cancel its season.)

Papp was not the only theatrical titan whose situation was altered in 1977. As the year began, the two most powerful figures in the New York theater were Joseph Papp and Clive Barnes, the critic of drama and dance for *The New York Times.* It is a truism that the play reviewer of the *Times,* whoever he is, is the most powerful critical voice in America. In the spring, the *Times* announced that, because he had had too much to do, Barnes would confine himself to dance criticism; his successor as drama critic would be Richard Eder, the second-string film critic, who had spent most of his working life as a foreign correspondent. Barnes joined the New York *Post* as drama critic.

Musicals. Broadway had two big musical hits in the course of the year, *Annie,* a triumph of 1930's nostalgia suggested by the comic strip *Little Orphan Annie,* which featured a doggedly cheerful child, and *The Act,* a personal triumph for Liza Minnelli who managed, by the force of her personality and her singing, to divert attention from an unusually turgid book about a formerly successful Hollywood star who is reduced to presenting an act at a Las Vegas night club. *I Love My Wife,* which had to do with

ROBERT C. RAGSDALE

Teresa Wright, right, starred in the Hartford Stage Company's production of *All the Way Home*. During the Stratford (Ontario) Festival's 25th annual season, William Hutt and Margaret Tyzack were featured in *Ghosts*, under the direction of Arif Hasnain.

PHOTOGRAPH BY LANNY NAGLER, HARTFORD STAGE COMPANY

two married couples who contemplate experiments in wife-swapping but do not carry them out, owed its more modest success primarily to the inspired comic antics of Lenny Baker. *Side by Side by Sondheim,* a sprightly concert of Stephen Sondheim's songs, was, surprisingly, an importation from London. Another pleasant, low-keyed entertainment was offered by two performers who sang their own material in *A Party with Comden and Green.* Two well received musical revivals gave clear evidence of their authenticity by starring their original leading men, Yul Brynner in *The King and I* and Richard Kiley in *Man of La Mancha.* The Chelsea Theater Center staged an ancient musical by Bertolt Brecht and Kurt Weill, *Happy End,* which is notable for its haunting songs and its farcical plot, about Chicago gangsters and the Salvation Army. This diverting show briefly continued its life on Broadway.

Off Broadway most of the best work was done by the permanent organizations. The Brooklyn Academy of Music established its own BAM Theater Company, under the leadership of British Frank Dunlop, who directed Langdon

Mitchell's *The New York Idea,* an American comedy of 1906, and Chekhov's *Three Sisters. The New York Idea,* in which Blythe Danner and Rosemary Harris appeared, surely never looked better. Dunlop's stars were again dazzling in *Three Sisters,* but Miss Harris, Ellen Burstyn, and Tovah Feldshuh were incongruous sisters.

Public Theater. The Public Theater's most admired production was David Rudkin's *Ashes* (which had transferred from the Manhattan Theater Club), a British play about a young married couple who are frustrated first in their efforts to conceive a child and then in their efforts to adopt one. Moving performances by Brian Murray and especially Roberta Maxwell gave this play new elements of pathos and irony that it seemed not to have when it was staged in London. Also at the Public, two new plays by John Guare, *Marco Polo Sings a Solo* and *Landscape of the Body,* proved controversial but added little to Guare's reputation. The American Place Theater's two principal successes were Ronald Ribman's *Cold Storage,* about two patients in wheelchairs contemplating death, and Jules Feiffer's *Hold Me!,* a revue based on Feiffer's cartoons. A Broadway production of *Cold Storage* was planned for the 1977–78 season, but *Hold Me!* went on to an immediate extension in a commercial run off Broadway. Without the benefit of high-powered institutional support, Elizabeth Swados (who provided the musical scores for *The Cherry Orchard* and *Agamemnon* at Lincoln Center) conceived, composed, and directed a highly original off Broadway revue, *Nightclub Cantata*.

Regional. Apart from plays already mentioned, the most noteworthy success of the year in the regional theaters was a Hungarian comedy, István Orkény's *Catsplay*, about a woman in her sixties who refuses to act her age. Both at Washington's Arena Stage and at the Guthrie Theater of Minneapolis, Helen Burns acted the leading role with the fullest realization of its comic and tragic potentialities. Edward Albee's double bill, *Counting the Ways* and *Listening,* two austere and stylized conversation pieces, were presented in Hartford. Arthur Miller's *The Archbishop's Ceiling,* a moderately interesting play about a harried East European writer, had a run at Washington's Eisenhower Theater in the Kennedy Center. At Yale, Andrei Serban directed Strindberg's *The Ghost Sonata,* and, on this occasion, Serban's inventiveness seemed well suited to Strindberg's experimental play.

Perhaps the most striking news about the regional theaters had to do with their future plans. After representatives of seven American theaters visited the Soviet Union in May, the Alley Theater of Houston, the American Conservatory Theater of San Francisco, and the Guthrie of Minneapolis, arranged for visiting Soviet directors to stage plays for them in 1978.

The Stratford Festival of Ontario celebrated its 25th anniversary with productions that starred three British visitors, Maggie Smith, Brian Bedford, and Margaret Tyzack. *A Midsummer Night's Dream, Richard III,* and Molnar's *The Guardsman,* all of them directed by Robin Phillips, were exceptionally well received.

In London, critical interest was drawn most of all by the activities of the permanent theaters. The National Theatre won praise for Jonson's *Volpone* with Paul Scofield in the lead and John Gielgud in a supporting role and for a touching presentation of an Austrian play of more than forty years ago, Odon von Horvath's *Tales from the Vienna Woods.* At the Aldwych Theatre in London, the Royal Shakespeare Company exhibited a stunning new play about the growth of native fascism in England, David Edgar's *Destiny.*

On the continent there was probably no more theatrical or more provocative production than the Moscow Taganka Theater's dramatization of Mikhail Bulgakov's satirical novel *The Master and Margarita,* which drew the wrath of *Pravda* but kept running nevertheless.

HENRY POPKIN
State University of New York at Buffalo

BROADWAY OPENINGS OF 1977

PLAYS

Agamemnon, by Aeschylus, partly in the original Greek and partly in Edith Hamilton's translation; directed by Andrei Serban; May 18–June 19.

An Almost Perfect Person, by Judith Ross; directed by Zoe Caldwell; with Colleen Dewhurst; October 27–.

American Buffalo, by David Mamet; directed by Ulu Grosbard; with Robert Duvall; February 16–June 11.

Anna Christie, by Eugene O'Neill; directed by José Quintero; with Liv Ullmann; April 14–July 30.

A Touch of the Poet, by Eugene O'Neill; directed by José Quintero; with Jason Robards, Geraldine Fitz-Gerald, and Milo O'Shea; Dec. 28–.

The Basic Training of Pavlo Hummel, by David Rabe; directed by David Wheeler; with Al Pacino; April 24–July 1, July 19–September 3.

Bully, by Jerome Alden; directed by Peter H. Hunt; with James Whitmore; November 1–5.

Caesar and Cloepatra, by George Bernard Shaw; directed by Ellis Rabb; with Rex Harrison and Elizabeth Ashley; February 24–March 5.

Chapter Two, by Neil Simon; directed by Herbert Ross; with Judd Hirsch; December 4–.

Cold Storage, by Ronald Ribman; directed by Frank Corsaro; with Martin Balsam and Len Cariou; December 29–.

The Cherry Orchard, by Anton Chekhov, translated by Jean-Claude van Itallie; directed by Andrei Serban; with Irene Worth; February 17–April 10.

Dirty Linen & New-Found-Land, by Tom Stoppard; directed by Ed Berman; January 11–May 28.

Dracula, by Hamilton Deane and John L. Balderston; directed by Dennis Rosa; with Frank Langella; October 20–.

Gemini, by Albert Innaurato; directed by Peter Mark Schifter; May 21–.

The Gin Game, by D. L. Coburn; directed by Mike Nichols; with Jessica Tandy and Hume Cronyn; October 6–.

Golda, by William Gibson; directed by Arthur Penn; with Anne Bancroft; November 14–.

The Importance of Being Earnest, by Oscar Wilde; directed by Stephen Porter; June 16–August 28.

Ladies at the Alamo, by Paul Zindel; directed by Frank Perry; with Estelle Parsons, Eileen Heckart, and Rosemary Murphy; April 7–23.

Mark Twain Tonight!, based on the writings of Mark Twain; with Hal Holbrook; March 15–26.

The Merchant, by Arnold Wesker; directed by John Dexter; with John Clements, Roberta Maxwell, and Joseph Leon; November 16–18.

Miss Margarida's Way, written and directed by Roberto Athayde; with Estelle Parsons; Sept. 16–Jan. 1.

Mummenschanz, Swiss pantomime; March 30–.

The Night of the Tribades, by Per Olov Enquist, translated by Ross Shideler; directed by Michael Kahn; with Max von Sydow, Bibi Andersson, and Eileen Atkins; October 13–22.

Otherwise Engaged, by Simon Gray; directed by Harold Pinter; with Tom Courtenay; February 2–October 30.

Romeo and Juliet, by William Shakespeare; directed by Theodore Mann; with Paul Rudd and Pamela Payton-Wright; March 17–May 22.

PHOTOS MARTHA SWOPE

Frank Langella has the lead in Broadway's *Dracula*. In *Annie*, one of the season's most popular musicals, Andrea McArdle is Annie, Sandy is her pal, the dog, and Reid Shelton portrays Oliver Warbucks.

Saint Joan, by George Bernard Shaw; directed by John Clark; with Lynn Redgrave; December 15–.

The Shadow Box, by Michael Cristofer; directed by Gordon Davidson; March 31–December 31.

Some of My Best Friends, by Stanley Hart; directed by Harold Prince; with Ted Knight; October 25–29.

Something Old, Something New, by Henry Denker; directed by Robert H. Livingston; with Molly Picon; January 1.

Tartuffe, by Molière, translated by Richard Wilbur; directed by Stephen Porter; with John Wood, Tammy Grimes, Mildred Dunnock, and Patricia Elliott; September 25–November 20.

The Trip Back Down, by John Bishop; directed by Terry Schreiber; with John Cullum; January 4–March 5.

Unexpected Guests, by Jordan Crittenden; directed by Charles Grodin; March 2–6.

Vieux Carré, by Tennessee Williams; directed by Arthur Allan Seidelman; with Sylvia Sidney; May 11–15.

MUSICALS

The Act, book by George Furth, music by John Kander, lyrics by Fred Ebb; choreography by Ron Lewis; directed by Martin Scorsese; with Liza Minnelli and Barry Nelson; October 29–.

Annie, book by Thomas Meehan, music by Charles Strouse, lyrics by Martin Charnin; directed by Martin Charnin; April 21–.

Hair, book and lyrics by Gerome Ragni and James Rado, music by Galt MacDermot; directed by Tom O'Horgan; August 4–November 5.

Happy End, book and lyrics by Bertolt Brecht (adapted by Michael Feingold), music by Kurt Weill; directed by Robert Kalfin; musical staging by Patricia Birch; with Meryl Streep; May 7–July 10.

I Love My Wife, based on a play by Luis Rego, book and lyrics by Michael Stewart, music by Cy Coleman; directed by Gene Saks; with Lenny Baker; April 17–.

Jesus Christ Superstar, music by Andrew Lloyd Webber; lyrics by Tim Rice; conceived by Tom O'Horgan; November 23–,

Ipi-Tombi, in South African black tribal languages, conceived by Bertha Egnos, music by Bertha Egnos; devised by Bertha Egnos; January 12–February 13.

The King and I, based on *Anna and the King of Siam,* by Margaret Landon, book and lyrics by Oscar Hammerstein II, music by Richard Rodgers; directed by Yuriko; with Yul Brynner and Constance Towers; May 2–.

Man of La Mancha, book by Dale Wasserman, music by Mitch Leigh, lyrics by Joe Darion, suggested by the life and works of Cervantes; directed by Albert Marre; with Richard Kiley; September 15–December 31.

A Party with Betty Comden and Adolph Green; February 10–April 30.

Piaf . . . a Remembrance, by David Cohen; directed by Lee Rachman; February 14–March 5.

Side by Side by Sondheim, revue with lyrics by Stephen Sondheim, music by Stephen Sondheim, Leonard Bernstein, Mary Rodgers, Richard Rodgers, and Julie Styne; directed by Ned Sherrin; April 18–.

TOKYO

Despite continuing financial difficulties, the capital of Japan, once known as the world's most polluted city, has made some progress in improving its environment. In the fiscal year ending March 31, 1977, for instance, the city succeeded in reducing the amount of wastes pouring from plants into Tokyo Bay by some 13%. Now, on a fine Sunday, 100,000 anglers enjoy fishing in the bay, and Mt. Fuji, the snow-capped symbol of Japan, is seen more frequently.

Flight to Suburbia. The population of the city proper, believed to be the world's third largest, after Shanghai and Buenos Aires, keeps shrinking as people move out to the suburbs and surrounding prefectures. The population in 1977 was estimated to be 8.5 million—down 1.3% from the previous year.

Fiscal Woes. Snowballing expenditures and declining corporate-tax revenues keep Tokyo poised on the verge of bankruptcy. An annual shortfall of $1 billion (U. S.) is expected in the fiscal year ending in March 1978. Despite criticisms that he has spent too much on welfare, Gov. Ryokichi Minobe in 1977 announced a

Condominiums, selling from $46,000 to $55,000 for a small, three-bedroom unit, are completed in Tokyo.

UPI

three-year, $32-billion fiscal plan, placing even more emphasis on welfare, medicaid, and anti-earthquake measures. Moreover, in a heated "fiscal war" with the central government, the governor again declared his determination to regain for the city more sources of taxation and more independence to issue deficit-covering bonds.

Cost of Living. Life in Tokyo is still more expensive than anywhere else in the world, and prices continued to rise in 1977. Telegram charges doubled. Cabbage went up 82%. Phone bills increased an average 68%. Bus fares rose one third. Even so, the inflation rate is somewhat slower than before.

Safe City. The rate of violent crime remained at a level low rate. Congestion and cost notwithstanding, Tokyo is a safe place to be.

HIROTAKA YOSHIZAKI
"The New York Times," Tokyo

TORONTO

The year 1977 was an eventful one in Metropolitan Toronto. Some of the issues and problems had their origins in previous years. For instance, a few more racially motivated attacks took place in the city's subway system, increasing the concern over such incidents that had begun in 1976. Also, Toronto's continuing battle against the proliferation of pornography and sex shops on a section of Yonge Street, the city's main north-south thoroughfare, grew in intensity, especially after the homosexual assault and murder of a 12-year-old shoeshine boy in the area. On a different level, the Robarts Commission, established in 1975 to analyze the difficulties of the city's two-tiered government, published its controversial report. It recommended considerable modification of the administrative system to make it more efficient and more accessible to the public. The commission also advocated several boundary changes between city boroughs.

Development. In February the first portion of the $250-million Eaton Centre was opened—a massive downtown retail complex of more than 150 stores. And, in the fall, the $30-million, pyramid-shaped Metro Central Reference Library was ready for use.

Education. The University of Toronto celebrated its 150th anniversary in 1977, and on June 15 the new Faculty Association signed its first contract with the administration. The problems facing the city's school system continued throughout the year. In April, the Toronto Board of Education released 150 teachers because of financial cutbacks and declining enrollment.

Events. In May the worst fire in more than 70 years occurred in the downtown area. A 12-hour bank siege in July ended with the safe release of 11 hostages and the voluntary surrender of the lone gunman who had held them.

E. JARVIS
University of Western Ontario

UPI

Following court suits, the Concorde supersonic jetliner landed in New York for the first time, Oct. 19.

TRANSPORTATION

Survey

Transportation activities in general experienced growth and progress in 1977, but the year was also punctuated by airline disasters and oil spillages.

Airlines. Airline travel increased, with 4 million Americans taking advantage of Advanced Booking Charter and One Stop Tour Charters. The increase in charter business in 1977 was projected to be greater than 40%, as compared with the overall growth of the airline industry of 6%. A new entry in the North Atlantic market is the British Laker Airways, whose Skytrain, a relatively inexpensive, no-frills transatlantic air shuttle service between New York and London, began operating in October 1977. After a series of legal suits and 16 months of testing at Washington's Dulles Airport, the Concorde supersonic jetliners, flown by British Airways and Air France, began landing at New York's JFK International Airport in October 1977.

Railroads. For most American railroads, 1977 was a year of continued recovery from the dismal business of 1975. The midyear estimate of 1977 rail traffic called for 823 billion ton-miles of freight service by year-end, a substantial increase over the 754 billion ton-miles of 1975. New freight car orders topped an estimated 55,000 in 1977 as compared with 36,000 new orders in 1976.

President Carter's plan to place more emphasis on coal in the United States' energy scheme gave a shot of optimism to the rail industry. The additional coal could result in an estimated 3% annual increase in rail traffic by 1985, with orders for more coal-hauling equipment likely to begin by 1978 or 1979.

Shipping. As of July 1, 1977, exactly 700 ships were active in the privately owned sector of the U. S. merchant marine, totaling 17.5 million deadweight tons. This represented a decrease of 8 ships but an increase of 883,000 deadweight tons over July 1, 1976.

Pipelines. After a four-year delay and additional costs of $3.2 billion, oil began flowing from Prudhoe Bay through the 799-mile (1,280 km) Alaskan pipeline in June 1977. The pipeline reached a capacity of 1.2 million barrels per day, about 10% of U. S. domestic oil consumption. In its first month of operation, however, the pipeline was plagued by several major mishaps, including an explosion that demolished pump station no. 8, which resulted in shutdowns for a total of 13 days. In mid-September, an agreement between Canada and the United States was announced to build a trans-Canadian pipeline to carry natural gas from Alaska's North Slope (Prudhoe Bay) to the 48 states.

Mass Transit. Encouraged by a recent trend of gradual increases in transit ridership in U. S. cities, the DOT continued its large scale financial support of local transit operators. Through 1976, DOT had spent almost $6 billion in grants for capital improvements, funds which have made possible the purchase of roughly 30,000 buses, 2,500 rapid transit cars, 1,500 commuter rail cars, and 2,300 vehicles devoted solely to transportation for elderly and handicapped persons.

Mopeds. Enthusiasm for motor/pedal bikes (mopeds) surfaced in 1977. With one-cylinder engines and top speeds of 17 to 30 mph (27–48 km/h), mopeds can travel 120 to 200 miles (192–320 km) on a gallon of gasoline. By late 1977, mopeds were permitted in 27 states. Prices ranged from $300 to $600.

THEODORE H. POISTER
The Pennsylvania State University

Aviation

Economic recovery of U. S. airlines, begun in 1976, continued through mid-1977 with only a few hiccups.

Profits. During the first half of 1977, the industry as a whole was up about 12% in profit over the same period of 1976, to about $140 million. The final figures for 1976 had shown that all of the major trunklines made a profit with the exception of Trans World, which ended the year $21.6 million in the red. The 1976 profitability champions were Delta ($81.5 million), Eastern ($45.8 million), American ($44.5 million), and Northwest ($43.2 million).

Traffic. In comparison with 1976, boardings showed continued growth but the 4–5% increase over the first half of 1976 was smaller than the 10% jump in the first half of 1976 over the like period of 1975.

Fares. Fewer increases were sought in 1977 as traffic growth brought relative prosperity. On the other side of the coin, there were relatively few lower-fare innovations. An exception was the beginning of Freddie Laker's Skytrain, a no-frills, first-come, first-served operation between New York to London. The fare was $135 to London, £59 to New York, with meals that can be purchased at moderate cost. British Airways, Pan American, and Trans World quickly responded with budget fares of their own, $280 round trip but with the possibility of advance reservations. This competition could lead to a permanent reduction of fares on this route. Domestically, American put in a bid for a "Super Saver" fare between New York and California

Federal Aviation Administration technicians monitor noise levels during maiden flight of Concorde to New York.

UPI

of $227 round trip, a cut of almost $200 from the standard economy fare.

Concorde. The long battle by British Airways and Air France to obtain landing rights in New York City for this supersonic commercial transport appeared successful in late October. Federal District and Appeals courts ruled that the Port Authority of New York and New Jersey, which operates Kennedy Airport, had been discriminatory in keeping the new aircraft out. The Concorde's backers scored points when one of the aircraft arrived for proving flights, and did not trigger the noise-monitoring equipment during several takeoffs. Anti-Concorde groups, mostly from communities around Kennedy, were not placated. They are upset by all jet noise, and Concorde has served as a focus for their anger. In another development, the federal government decided, on the basis of 16 months of Concorde trial flights to Washington's Dulles Airport, to permit Concorde flights to 13 other U. S. airports, if the airlines so decide. To avoid sonic booms, the Concorde would have to fly at less than the speed of sound over land areas.

Regulatory Reform. Pushed by the former Ford administration and over the objections of most airlines, the issue of regulatory reform gained ground in 1977. Specifically, the issue won the support of a mixed group of laissez-faire capitalists and consumer advocates. Airlines have long been regulated by the Civil Aeronautics Board, which awards routes and sets fares. The reformers would allow liberalized entry of new airlines on most routes and latitude in establishing fares—with the assumption that increased competition will reduce fares. A regulatory-reform bill, sponsored by Sens. Edward M. Kennedy (D-Mass.) and Howard Cannon (D-Nev.), ran into snags in late summer in the Senate.

Most airlines are very concerned about this issue, which could change radically the environment in which they operate. They say that their most lucrative routes on which competition presently is restricted to a few carriers—New York-Los Angeles, for example—subsidize less traveled routes; that if increased competition cuts down their business on the heavy routes, they may not be able to serve the smaller cities. Also, according to the airlines, reform could reduce the willingness of lenders to help finance fleet renewal and could drive some of the weaker carriers into merger or bankruptcy.

Safety. After an excellent safety record in 1976—45 fatalities, the lowest since 1954—U. S. airlines had two severe accidents in 1977. In March, a Pan American 747 and a Dutch KLM 747 collided in fog on the runway at Tenerife Airport in the Canary Islands. This was much the worst disaster in aviation history, with nearly 600 dead on the two jumbo jets. A Southern Airways DC-9 crashed less than a month later near Atlanta, Ga., after flying through a hail-

(Continued on page 502)

The Lindbergh Anniversary

The solo nonstop flight from Long Island to Paris by Charles Augustus Lindbergh, Jr., fifty years ago captured the public imagination in 1927 perhaps even more than the first moon landing by U. S. astronauts in 1969. Dubbed the "Lone Eagle" by the press, the 25-year-old Lindbergh took off in his gasoline-heavy, modified Ryan Airlines, Inc., M-1 Brougham monoplane, the *Spirit of St. Louis,* from Roosevelt Field on May 20, 1927, at 7:52 AM and landed at Paris' Le Bourget Airport 33 hours, 32 minutes later.

It is not clear that the publicity-shy Brig. Gen. Lindbergh would have enjoyed the festivities that marked the golden anniversary of his historic flight. He never considered himself a hero—indeed, about 75 persons before him had flown across the Atlantic—but he is credited in the public's mind with being the pioneer.

Celebrations. The 1977 commemoration began with a flight at 7:52 AM on May 20 of one of the four surviving sister ships of the *Spirit of St. Louis.* James Pyle, a 63-year-old aviator, flew the airplane from Grumman Field on Long Island. This Ryan Brougham, used in the film *Spirit of St. Louis,* was displayed two weeks later at the Paris Air Show. Lindbergh's first airplane, a Curtiss JN-4 "Jennie," restored by the Long Island Early Fliers, was displayed at the Roosevelt Field shopping center. The original *Spirit,* still bearing the registration number NX-211, is the property of the Smithsonian Institution in Washington, D. C., and is in the new National Air and Space Museum.

On Long Island, Reeve Lindbergh Brown, the aviator's youngest child, was the honored guest at a ceremony at Eisenhower Park where Deputy Postmaster General William Bolger dedicated a new 13-cent Lindbergh commemorative stamp. Anne Morrow Lindbergh, Lindbergh's widow and a well-known author, christened a Boeing 747 *Clipper Lindbergh* for Pan American World Airways at New York's Kennedy Airport; Lindbergh had been a consultant for the airline. Mrs. Lindbergh also spoke at a fund-raising dinner for the benefit of the Lindbergh Memorial Fund, which sponsors conservationist activities. "Charles Lindbergh never turned his back on his profession, on aviation or science, or the miracles of technology," she told the guests. "But he felt strongly that we must find a balance between our inventions and the environment from which these inventions had grown. He spent the last 20 years of his life working to protect our earth and its resources . . . ."

Fourteen members of the Ryan team that built the *Spirit of St. Louis* were honored at a dinner in San Diego, where Lindbergh had obtained some of his financial backing for the

Anne Morrow Lindbergh inspects a reproduction of her late husband's famous plane, "Spirit of St. Louis."

flight. In St. Louis, where Lindbergh obtained the bulk of his financing, there were a parade and dinner. Another sister ship of *Spirit,* belonging to a St. Louis historical society, was flown that day. At Hana, Hawaii, where Lindbergh lived and is buried, there was a commemorative reading from his published works. Lindbergh's boyhood home in Minnesota was dedicated on May 21 as a national historical monument.

In a statement, President Carter said:

"This year marks the fiftieth anniversary of the historical transatlantic flight of Charles A. Lindbergh. In his solo journey from New York to Paris on May 20, 1927, America's 'Lone Eagle' inaugurated a new age in aviation and a new era of international flight.

"Celebrated around the world, this momentous event established Lindbergh as one of our country's most heroic figures. It symbolized the continuing devotion of our people to the exploration of new frontiers and demonstrated what can be accomplished when innovative and promising technology is guided by a courageous and determined man.

"Linking two continents, the 33½-hour flight of the *Spirit of St. Louis* was a landmark in aviation history. It initiated the rise to world leadership of the United States aviation industry. It pioneered international air travel that has helped to bring nations and peoples together and was the critical first step in our subsequent brilliant history of space discovery . . . ."

WARREN WETMORE

storm, killing 62 of the passengers on board and 8 persons on the ground.

New Aircraft. The configurations of three new aircraft designs—the McDonnell Douglas DC-X-200 and the Boeing 7N7 and 7X7—remained uncertain for most of 1977. Manufacturers hoped to have the designs finalized by the end of the year. These will be medium-range aircraft carrying 180–200 passengers, but there was disagreement among the large airlines—whose orders are required for the programs to get under way—on size, range, and number of engines, two or three. The new aircraft will be required to accommodate the traffic expansion foreseen for the 1980's and possibly to replace some of the older aircraft, especially those which would have difficulty in meeting more stringent noise standards. Another point in favor of new aircraft is that they will consume substantially less fuel per seat-mile flown than most current aircraft. The airlines are estimated to need $5–9 billion in financing for new flying equipment through 1984.

WARREN C. WETMORE
Aviation Weekly and Space Technology

Highways

The severe cold and snow of the first months of 1977 left local and state governments in the United States with $218-billion worth of needed repairs to bridges and highways. These costs put a new strain on the budgets of many states that were already experiencing difficulties in financing their highway programs. To complement the long-standing federal support for new highway construction, some states are trying to persuade the federal government to allocate federal money for road and bridge repairs. The roads are estimated to be deteriorating 50%

A 50-passenger, battery-powered bus, used in England since 1974, was seen at a Chicago vehicle exposition.

UPI

faster than they can be repaired and at least 40,000 bridges in the U. S. federal aid highway system are critically deficient.

USSR. The highway system in Russia is in much worse shape. Although only 1.5% of the population own automobiles (compared with nearly 50% in the United States), automobile production has jumped from 350,000 cars in 1970 to 1.25 million in 1976, and the road network is poorly equipped to handle the increased traffic. Roughly 90% of the 860,000 miles (1,384,000 km) of Soviet highways are unpaved. During the spring thaws 70% of the roads are impassable.

The Auto Business. In the United States, federal standards for minimum gasoline mileage took effect in September. The cars in each manufacturer's fleet of 1978-model cars were required to average 18 miles (29 km) per gallon. Gradually, the minimum will increase until 1985, when the minimum will be 27.5 miles (44.3 km) per gallon.

Although smaller cars are more fuel efficient, big car sales have experienced a boom, with a substantial increase in market share in 1976 and a further increase during 1977. While American compacts and subcompacts have decreased in sales, foreign import sales increased dramatically, expanding their estimated share of the market from 13.8% in 1976 to 18.2% in 1977. Japanese models accounted for much of this increase. On the other hand the familiar Volkswagen Beetle slumped substantially in sales and was taken off the U. S. market.

Safety. U. S. highways are reported to be safer in 1976 than in any other recent year, with accidents down 17% from 1973. The decrease has been attributed to the 55 miles (88.5 km) per hour national speed limit. Early in 1977, former Secretary of Transportation William Coleman persuaded General Motors, Ford, Mercedes, and Volkswagen to begin a 500,000-car demonstration program of airbags and automatic seat belts, beginning in 1979. Airbags are to become mandatory by 1984. It has also been found that while small cars are more fuel-efficient, big cars are apparently safer. Over 10% of subcompact car drivers who filed accident reports also filed medical-injury claims, compared with 5.7% for drivers in full-size cars.

THEODORE H. POISTER

Mass Transit

In general, 1977 saw increased emphasis on assistance for the elderly and handicapped. Beginning in October the Urban Mass Transportation Administration (UMTA) stopped awarding grants for capital or operating purposes to metropolitan areas whose transportation improvement programs do not include specialized projects for this population.

The priority on serving the elderly and handicapped is also reflected in the "interim" specifications for the advance-design bus developed

Rail highlights included: the running of a steam-powered train to mark the 150th birthday of the Baltimore and Ohio and the testing of a new Soviet high-speed train.

by UMTA, which provide for full wheelchair accessibility. Issuance of final specifications has been held up to give further consideration to standards for emission control, product liability, noise abatement, the so-called "kneeling feature" designed to alleviate problems of the elderly in boarding and alighting from buses, and wheelchair loading platforms.

U. S. Cities. The total number of passengers on urban transit systems was expected to increase in 1977, continuing the modest annual increases that began in 1973. The performance of the Bay Area Rapid Transit System in the San Francisco area, however, has generally been disappointing. While the system's operating costs have been about five times the amounts originally forecast, usage is only about 50% of forecast.

In contrast, some 33,000 riders per day, three times the expected number, are using the 5.7 mile (9.2 km) Phase I of the Washington Metrorail project (METRO). In July, METRO's Phase II was inaugurated when service began on a 11.9-mile (19.2 km) line serving 18 new stations. A further expansion, an additional 5.7-mile (9.2 km) line to Silver Spring, Md., was planned for November 1977. Eventually, METRO will serve 86 stations on 98 miles (158 km) of rail.

In Chicago, 11 people were killed and 180 were injured when one commuter train crashed into the rear of another and fell 20 feet (9 m) below the tracks.

Other Countries. Many cities are relying on transit systems to help cope with traffic congestion, particularly in downtown areas. In Paris, inexpensive monthly commuting tickets for bus, subway, and train are being used, along with exclusive bus lanes, to lure commuters to transit. Other cities using reserved or priority bus lanes include Lima, Peru, and Toronto, Canada, where 70% of all trips to the city center are made by mass transit.

In Sydney, Australia, free bus service has been introduced in the downtown shopping area but has not yet generated the anticipated response. In Rome, Italy, the low 6¢ fares have not persuaded many commuters to leave their automobiles at home.

THEODORE H. POISTER

Railroads

There are 50-odd Class I railroads in the United States (Class I designates a railroad with at least $10 million in annual revenues), and a large number of them, all freight-haulers, were moderately prosperous in 1977. But taken as a whole, the U. S. railroad industry presented to the public a picture of deepening crisis. This was largely due to the fact that the two carriers that occupy the most visible parts of the railroad spectrum—the National Railroad Passenger Corp. (Amtrak) and the Consolidated Rail Corp. (Conrail)—experienced unexpected setbacks during the year.

Amtrak. Faced with growing losses, Amtrak ran into what amounted to a taxpayer revolt. Congress turned down Amtrak's request for $534 million in operating subsidies for fiscal 1978 and instead offered $488 million. This caused Amtrak to announce substantial service cutbacks, including the withdrawal of 22 trains in the Northeast Corridor. The resulting outcry led Congress to give Amtrak an additional $8 million to delay the cutbacks temporarily; at the same time, Amtrak was ordered to take a new look at its national network of about 275 trains (compared to the approximately 20,000 intercity trains that plied the rails 50 years ago), with a view to cutting off some of the biggest losers.

Conrail. Unlike Amtrak, Conrail is a private corporation, formed by congressional mandate from the ruins of half a dozen bankrupt carriers; but like Amtrak, Conrail is federally funded, the difference being that Amtrak's funds are grants, while Conrail's funds are, in effect, loans. Congress originally authorized $2.1 billion (U. S.) in financial assistance to Conrail; but a number of adverse developments in 1977 —including a harsh winter that cost the carrier an estimated $100 million—made it likely that additional government investment in Conrail would be needed.

Rates. Even with Conrail's losses figured in, the freight railroads, as a group, managed to show a small profit, though increases in labor and operating costs outpaced gains in revenue. Late in the year, the railroads asked the Interstate Commerce Commission (ICC) for a 5% across-the-board freight-rate increase, estimated to yield nearly $1 billion in additional annual revenues. The Council on Wage and Price Stability, opposing the increase, pointed out that railroad rates had increased by 80% during the 1970–1976 period, compared to an increase of only 56% in the cost-of-living index. The council conceded, however, that during the same period railroad labor costs had increased 83%, the price of fuel tripled, and the cost of other materials gone up by 85%.

Labor. Labor-management relations took a turn for the worse when the railroads filed notices with the labor organizations, demanding important changes in operating work rules and in the basis of pay for freight-train crews. The railroads estimated that these changes would save around $1 billion a year. The president of the United Transportation Union responded with a demand that Congress look into the desirability of nationalizing the railroads.

Mergers. The Southern Railway and the Missouri Pacific Railroad broke off merger talks after failing to agree on financial terms. The Burlington Northern and the Frisco railroads did agree on terms and announced that they would seek ICC authority to merge. In the year's other major merger activity, the Norfolk & Western Railway and the Chessie System (the Chesapeake & Ohio and the Baltimore & Ohio railroads) applied to the ICC for authority to acquire joint control of the Detroit, Toledo & Ironton.

Capital Outlays. Expenditures in 1977 for railroad capital improvements were estimated at $2.8 billion, compared to $2.4 billion in 1976. Orders were placed for approximately 60,000 new freight cars, compared to 36,000 in 1976. President Carter's energy plan, calling for more reliance on coal as an energy source, was viewed as a long-range gain by the railroads, which get 29% of their total freight tonnage from coal mines. Many of the new cars ordered in 1977 were open-tops suitable for the hauling of coal.

LUTHER S. MILLER, *Editor, "Railway Age"*

Ships and Shipping

Container shipping on the Atlantic and Gulf coasts of the United States was halted on October 1 due to a strike by longshoremen. A new three-year agreement, ending the walkout, was reached in mid-November. The strike had a major effect on the shipping industry, including imports expected for Christmas sale.

On Dec. 15, 1976, the Liberian-registered oil tanker *Argo Merchant* went aground off Nantucket Island, Mass., and dumped 7.3 million gallons (27.6 million liters) of oil into the sea. By mid-January, there were nine more tanker accidents in the news, five of which involved major oil losses. Of the five ships which wrecked, leaked, or blew up in December 1976, four were licensed under the Liberian flag. U. S. maritime chiefs led a wave of popular disdain for the lax Liberian standards for licensing ships and captains.

Many of the older and questionable tankers make their oil deliveries to the East coast and Gulf ports of the United States, because the harbors there are generally too shallow for the newer supertankers. With approximately 30,000 oil tanker arrivals annually, the U. S. Coast Guard estimates that 86 tanker groundings a year can be expected. This fact, along with the accidental destruction of 19 tankers in 1976 (almost double the 1975 toll) and the worldwide loss of 200,000 tons of oil in the first nine months of 1976 alone, prompted President Carter to initiate action that would require 30% of all U. S. imported oil to be carried by American ships. This measure pleased U. S. maritime officials, as high labor costs had nearly priced U. S. tankers out of the market.

The Great Lakes fleet (168 ships) suffered from drought-induced low water levels. All of the Great Lakes were expected to peak in 1977 at least 1.5 feet (.45 m) below their most recent highs. Grounding incidents increased, and dredging operations were delayed for reasons of environmental protection.

Environmental protection was also the issue that has kept the U. S. tuna fleet holed up in California harbors in late 1976 and early 1977. The tuna fleet waited while the U. S. Congress debated over the number of porpoises that tuna fishermen should be allowed to kill—porpoise schools swim above schools of tuna and often get tangled in tuna nets. The rest of the U. S. fishing industry was given a boost when a bill extending U. S. fishing rights to 200 miles offshore went into effect.

In Europe, progress continued on an inland waterway. France gave high priority to the acquisition of land for a new canal intended to connect the Rhône and Rhine rivers by 1987. Construction went forward on a West German canal that by 1985 will connect the Danube river to the Main, a tributary of the Rhine.

THEODORE H. POISTER

American passengers from the luxury liner *Daphne* visit the construction site of new government buildings in Havana. Once a favorite tourist spot, Cuba was reopened to Americans on a limited basis during 1977.

UPI

TRAVEL

For both the travel industry and the traveler, 1977 was a year of happy statistics.

The worldwide recession finally ended as far as travel was concerned, and domestic and international travelers took to the road in record numbers, producing record profits. For the first time, but hopefully not the last, more money went for travel than for armaments in 1977. The United States was the leader in world tourism income in 1977, followed by France, West Germany, Austria, Spain, Great Britain, and Italy.

Travelers around the world spent an estimated $360 billion during the year, some $60 billion more than went for arms purchases in the same period. The $360-billion figure represents about 6% of the gross world product.

U. S. travelers alone spent about $120 billion on domestic and international tourism, compared with some $98 billion spent by the government for national defense.

Domestic travel, less affected by the recession than international travel, remained strong. But areas that had relied heavily on their Bicentennial connection continued to suffer from "Bicentennial backlash." The public, apparently surfeited with history, avoided once popular attractions such as colonial Williamsburg and Plimoth Plantation, which reported attendance drops of 15% to 20%.

International travel was up about 15% as Americans headed abroad again with their old enthusiasm. Europe was the most popular destination, with Britain definitely the lead attraction.

The American traveler's world expanded a little in 1977. The U. S. government removed restrictions (of dubious legality and largely ignored) on travel to Cuba, Vietnam, and North Korea. In the case of Cuba, a symbolic gesture was followed up by practical acts of détente, including an exchange of liaison missions.

Travel has now become so important that in 1977 the U. S. Census Bureau undertook a $2.2 million study of American travel patterns—the most comprehensive tourism survey a nation has ever conducted.

Travel to Britain. With pomp, ceremony, and panache, the British observed Queen Elizabeth II's 25th anniversary on the throne. Despite generally rainy weather, the Silver Jubilee was an occasion of national rejoicing marked by bonfires, parades, and pageants at which visitors and natives happily mingled. Britain played host to a record 11 million visitors, an increase of approximately 25% over 1976.

Travel to Cuba. In May the Carras Line cruise ship *Daphne* put in at Havana, the first cruise ship from a U. S. port to do so since 1959. The event marked the return of Cuba to the international tourist scene and Havana's reemergence as a cruise port. Although there is considerable interest in Cuba, tourism from the United States remained a trickle, consisting mainly of the curious and the politically minded.

Middle East Travel. Peace was a key travel element, notably in the Middle East. Tourism to both Israel and Jordan was up nearly 50%, while travelers even began trickling back to battered Lebanon.

UPI

Freddie Laker has some fun prior to the first Skytrain walk-on service to New York from London for $105.

Cruise Ships. Although cruise ships undoubtedly welcome the addition of Havana to their lists of possible ports of call, they are doing all right without it. About a million Americans are expected to take a cruise during the 1977–78 season, roughly double the number a decade ago. The latest addition to the North American fleet is the Cunard *Princess,* which reached Florida in November. The 536-foot-long (163-meter) *Princess* carries 750 passengers and is typical of the modern breed of medium-sized liners, which are much more economical to operate than the superships like the QE2.

Air Travel. Air travel also registered substantial gains in 1977, stimulated by the continuing popularity of "alphabet fares," such as the OTC (one-stop tour charter) and ABC (advance booking charter). There also was a proliferation domestically of discount fares such as the "Super Savers," which offered savings of up to 44% on transcontinental air tickets purchased at least 30 days in advance.

The Super Savers and similar fares, designed to encourage advance booking and flight during off-peak hours, were immediately popular with the public. Surveys indicated that better than

25% of all passengers flying within the United States were using discount tickets. Despite some grumbling from airlines about low profitability, discount fares seemed to be luring new travelers into the skyways and are probably here to stay.

On the international air scene, competition was simultaneously restricted and expanded. The United States and Britain concluded a new agreement restricting carrier capacity between the two countries and, with the exception of the New York–London route, allowing only one British and one American carrier to operate between United States and British destinations.

But 1977 also was the year they finally unleashed Freddie Laker and his Skytrain. An ebullient entrepreneur who built Laker Airways into one of Britain's leading charter operators, Laker battled for six years for the right to operate a no-frills, low-priced, shuttle-type air service across the Atlantic.

The Skytrain concept was vigorously opposed by members of the International Air Transport Association (IATA), the rate-setting cartel to which most major airlines belong. It also was regarded with suspicion by aeronautical authorities within both the United States and British governments. The public was for it, however, and Laker has become something of a hero to air service consumers.

The first Laker Skytrain took off from New York on September 26, filled to capacity. Some passengers had waited more than two days to ensure that they would get a seat. Skytrain tickets are sold on a first-come, first-served basis, and the price—$240 roundtrip—does not include meals. Skytrain's rockbottom price, coupled with limited amenities, attracted mainly travelers with more time than money—young backpackers in most cases.

The IATA carriers obviously feared Laker and responded with their own low-priced fares, admittedly aimed at Skytrain. They included a super APEX (advance purchase excursion) of $290 and bargain and standby fares of $256, the last two available only between New York and London.

The APEX tickets must be purchased 45 days in advance, with a minimum stay of 14 days and a maximum of 45. Bargain tickets can be purchased in advance, with the passenger selecting the week he wants to fly, and the airline assigning the flight. Standby passengers take their chances, showing up at the airport on the day they want to fly.

Although aimed at Laker, these discount fares are also expected to hurt charter airlines. The charter industry, which has been growing rapidly in recent years, branded the new fares "predatory" and began lobbying to prevent their spread to other routes.

See also GREAT BRITAIN; TRANSPORTATION.

WILLIAM A. DAVIS
Travel Editor
"The Boston Globe"

Tunisia's capital of Tunis was host to a November meeting of the Arab League foreign ministers. The conference considered the issue of Arab unity.

UPI

TUNISIA

Tunisia's mixed economy, emphasizing foreign investment and export industry, was dealt a blow in 1977 by European Common Market protectionism and the recession in Europe. Economic troubles may have been behind ailing President-for-life Habib Bourguiba's political liberalization swing. Beleaguered by persistent dissent, Bourguiba gave his official blessing to a moderate opposition grouping.

Economy. While practically self-sufficient in food production, Tunisia concentrated on expanding its light industry sector, particularly textile manufacturing directed mainly at the Common Market. An ambitious program, initiated in the early 1970's, gives generous tax benefits and exemptions from import duties to all businesses set up for export only. Based on foreign investment, the new five-year plan that got under way in 1977 projected a quadrupling of production and the creation of 20,000 jobs annually, including 7,000 in the export industries.

But in June the Common Market suddenly cut back on the amount of North African imports allowed into Europe. About 5,000 of the 28,000 textile employees in job-starved Tunisia faced unemployment. Low European prices for the country's foreign exchange-earning phosphates and olive oil also hurt the economy.

Industrial and agricultural workers got a 33% boost in their basic incomes to an average of just under $100 a month. At the same time, prices, including gasoline, cooking fuel, cigarettes, wine, and spices, went up. Such staples as cereals, breads, sugar, milk, and butter were kept at low prices by government subsidies.

Domestic Events. The Bourguiba regime attacked the problem of persistent dissent in two ways. In March, 23 Ben Salahists, members of a clandestine left-wing organization that includes prominent educators, were arrested, accused of opposing national unity and distributing subversive tracts. Led by an exiled former minister of finance, Ahmad Ben Salah, the group has links to the Popular Unity Movement, which published a five-point program alleging, among other things, that the regime imprisoned and tortured its political opponents.

Two months after the police crackdown, the regime officially recognized, for the first time since the constitution was initiated in 1959, an opposition political grouping, the Tunisian League for Human Rights. Made up of teachers, professional people, civil servants, and trade unionists espousing all shades of opinion, the league pressed the government for increased civil liberties. The group, which had petitioned for recognition for over a year, specifically called for independence of the judiciary, a free press, and freedom from arbitrary arrest, imprisonment, and torture.

Foreign Affairs. Tunisia and neighboring Libya defused a long-standing dispute over offshore oil rights by referring the matter for arbitration by the International Court of Justice in the Hague. The quarrel flared when an oil drilling ship belonging to an American company, under contract to Libya, began drilling in a part of the Mediterranean claimed by both Tunisia and Libya. The U. S. drilling ship had replaced an Italian rig that was ordered to leave by the Tunisians. Ties with Italy remained strong. The Italian state fuel agency signed a pact with Tunis to build a gas pipeline from Algeria through Tunisia and across the Mediterranean to Italy.

JOSEPH MARGOLIS
"African Update"
African-American Institute

─────── **TUNISIA · Information Highlights** ───────

Official Name: Republic of Tunisia.
Location: North Africa.
Area: 63,170 square miles (163,610 km²).
Population (1977 est.): 6,000,000.
Chief City (1972 est.): Tunis, the capital, 750,000.
Government: *Head of state,* Habib Bourguiba, president (took office 1957). *Chief minister,* Hedi Nouira, premier (took office Nov. 1970). *Legislature* (unicameral)—National Assembly.
Monetary Unit: Dinar (0.42 dinar equals U. S.$1, Aug. 1977).
Manufacturing (major products): Processed foods, wines, petroleum products, olive oil, pulp and wood products.
Major Agricultural Products: Wheat, olives, vegetables, grapes, citrus fruits, forest products.

TURKEY

Turkey continued to face serious problems in 1977. Prime Minister Süleyman Demirel announced wide-ranging measures to stimulate the economy, curb inflation (about 20%), and reduce unemployment (about 2,000,000). Recession in Europe threatened an unwelcome homecoming of many of the 1,000,000 workers abroad. Nevertheless, Turkey's GNP (gross national product) growth rate of 7.2% in 1976 was impressive, and some 200 projects valued at $10 billion (U. S.) were to be open to foreign investment. The lira was devalued by 8% on March 2. A large foreign trade deficit continued.

Politics. Whatever the achievements of the Demirel government, violence remained the order of the day. Since March 1975, some 130 people have been killed in student riots.

Elections were held on June 5. The Republican People's party of former Prime Minister Bulent Ecevit had been expected to win decisively, but the elections brought no clear-cut decision. Capturing only 214 seats in the National Assembly, the party was 13 short of majority. Ecevit tried to form a government, but gave up on July 4, and Demirel, backed by 189 seats, once more came to power. His cabinet, however, lasted only as long as the year; it was brought down on December 31. Bulent Ecevit was then again asked to form a new government.

Economic Assistance. From 1954 to 1976, Turkey received from Communist countries grants and credits totaling $1,410,000,000, of which $1,180,000,000 came from the USSR. At the end of 1977, Turkey was discussing Communist participation in $2,200,000,000 worth of economic agreements, and the country held the fourth place among recipients of Soviet aid. A protocol of December 1976 authorized studies of projects with a cost of $1,200,000,000, half of which Moscow had agreed in principle to furnish. Under the protocol, the capacity of the Iskenderun steel complex was to be enlarged from 1,000,000 to 4,000,000 tons annually.

In August, Turkey and Libya signed an agreement on construction of seven new industrial projects in Turkey at a cost of $842,000,000. Turkey, Iran, and Pakistan signed a treaty on March 12, pledging economic and cultural cooperation and looking toward the establishment of a free trade area.

Relations with NATO. Turkey and Greece, NATO allies of the United States, continued at odds, if not in actual conflict, over Cyprus and the continental shelf in the eastern Mediterranean and Aegean seas. The United States was much interested in finding a solution because of the shattering impact of the Greco-Turkish tension on NATO, and, pending a solution, it embargoed shipments of arms to Turkey. Gen. Alexander Haig, supreme commander of NATO forces in Europe, urged Congress on March 1 to end the embargo. President Carter backed arms assistance to Turkey, in return for which Turkey would reopen certain bases for the United States. The program involved $1,000,000,000 in aid over a four-year period, and a similar offer was made to Greece. But Congress refused to go along until resolution had been found to the Cyprus problem. The president indicated that he would ask Congress to relax the embargo to permit the sale of $175,000,000 in military equipment. On May 11, Prime Minister Demirel told the NATO council in London that Turkey would have to restrict its NATO contribution if the United States arms embargo continued.

HARRY N. HOWARD
The American University, Washington, D. C.

TURKEY · Information Highlights

Official Name: Republic of Turkey.
Location: Southeastern Europe and southwestern Asia.
Area: 301,381 square miles (780,576 km²).
Population (1977 est.): 41,900,000.
Chief Cities (1974 est.): Ankara, the capital, 1,522,000; Istanbul, 2,487,000; Izmir, 619,000.
Government: *Head of state,* Fahri Korutürk, president (took office April 1973). *Head of government,* Süleyman Demirel, prime minister (took office March 1975). *Legislature*—Grand National Assembly: Senate and National Assembly.
Monetary Unit: Lira (17.68 liras equal U. S.$1, Aug. 1977).
Manufacturing (major products): Textiles, petroleum products, cement, iron and steel, fertilizers, processed foods.
Major Agricultural Products: Raisins, wheat, cotton, rye, sugar beets, barley, fruit, tobacco, hazelnuts, sheep, cattle.

UPI

In Istanbul in September, Turkey's Prime Minister Süleyman Demirel opens the Tenth World Energy Conference, attended by some 4,000 delegates from over 70 nations.

Uganda's President Idi Amin, left, confers with his Foreign Minister Juma Oris during opening session of the Organization of African Unity meeting in July.

UPI

UGANDA

Uganda continued in 1977 to be a pariah in world affairs under the tyrannical rule of President Idi Amin (*see also* BIOGRAPHY). There were again widespread abuse of human rights, arbitrary killings, and even massacre in Uganda. Amin awarded himself the "Highest Order of the Conqueror of the British Empire."

Domestic Affairs. A fresh purge of Lango and Acholi tribesmen, whom Amin apparently saw as a threat to his power, began early in 1977. The killings began after the discovery of an alleged plot to kill Amin by troops from these tribes brought to Kampala to celebrate the sixth anniversary of Amin's seizure of power. In February, Archbishop Janani Luwum, Uganda's leading Anglican churchman, died in suspicious circumstances, and there was a new worldwide wave of revulsion against the Amin regime.

Late in February Amin precipitated the first international crisis of Jimmy Carter's presidency when he ordered approximately 200 Americans residing in Uganda to meet him in Kampala. Amin finally backed down, possibly because the United States nuclear-powered aircraft carrier *Enterprise* was standing by off the Kenya coast.

Amin's first hoax of the year was perpetrated in June after Britain had banned him from entering the country to attend the Commonwealth Conference. Amin announced he was flying there anyway, and Uganda Radio variously reported him to be circling in his plane over Ireland, France, and Germany before it turned out to be a bluff.

In late June the second hoax came after an apparent assassination attempt near Entebbe on the shores of Lake Victoria. While a new purge began, Amin disappeared and Ugandan spokesmen, contacted from Nairobi, said the president was missing and that "any one finding him should contact Uganda." Before long, the dictator surfaced again, having been on a honeymoon, he said, with his latest wife, Sarah. In midyear also, Health Minister Henry Kyemba became the latest government minister to defect, detailing the terror of life in Uganda.

In July, Amin turned up in Libreville, Gabon, for the annual meeting of the Organization of African Unity (OAU). He appeared fit and well, belying reports he had been wounded in the latest attempt on his life. There was no specific condemnation of human rights abuses in Uganda at the OAU session.

In September, Amin perpetrated his third hoax. Aides claimed the president was in a coma after a minor operation on his neck performed by Soviet doctors. At the time 12 of Amin's political opponents were awaiting execution in Kampala on charges of plotting against the regime. Several Arab states asked Amin to show clemency and not to execute the men during Ramadan. The "coma" was a convenient excuse to ignore this plea, and the executions went ahead in a brutal ceremony in central Kampala. It seemed likely that Amin, a Muslim himself, would lose some of his defenders in the Arab world as a result of the executions. Later in September, Amin banned all but four of the Christian churches operating in Uganda.

Economy. Because of mismanagement, vast stores of coffee were being held in Uganda when coffee prices hit the roof. Thus, the completely stagnant Ugandan economy had a windfall, and coffee was being airfreighted out of the country toward the end of the year. The income from coffee and tea staved off disaster. The bulk of the population lives at subsistence levels, with high inflation and a shortage of everyday goods.

JAMES PRINGLE

UGANDA · Information Highlights

Official Name: Republic of Uganda.
Location: East Africa.
Area: 91,134 square miles (236,036 km²).
Population (1977 est.): 12,400,000.
Chief City (1976 est.): Kampala, the capital, 410,000.
Government: *Head of state and government.* Gen. Idi Amin, president (assumed power Feb. 1971). *Legislature* (unicameral)—National Assembly (dissolved Feb. 1971).
Monetary Unit: Shilling (8.31 shillings equal U. S.$1, May 1977).
Manufacturing (major products): Processed agricultural products, steel, textiles.
Major Agricultural Products: Coffee, tea, millet, cotton, sisal, tobacco, sweet potatoes, cassava.

USSR

The adoption of a new Soviet constitution and Leonid Brezhnev's promotion to the USSR presidency accompanied 1977 ceremonies celebrating the 60th anniversary of Communist rule in Russia. But Soviet governmental policies at home and abroad experienced the usual mixture of successes and failures. Though industrial and armament production rose to new heights, bad weather lowered the cereal crops, necessitating Soviet purchase of 15 million metric tons of foreign (mostly American) grain. U. S. President Carter's open sympathy for Soviet dissident liberals and his proposal for drastic arms reduction surprised and annoyed the Soviet government, which rejected fast disarmament and accused the United States of conducting psychological warfare. No SALT II (Strategic Arms Limitation Talks II) treaty was concluded in 1977, but the United States and the USSR agreed to an informal extension of the SALT I pact, which expired on October 3.

Africa presented problems during the year. Both Somalia and the Sudan expelled all Soviet advisers, and Guinea forbade long-range Soviet reconnaissance planes to continue using Guinean airports.

FOREIGN AFFAIRS

United States. Much U. S.-USSR friction occurred throughout 1977. Early in the year the U. S. State Department warned the Soviet government not to silence the Russian dissident physicist Andrei Sakharov and protested against the Soviet arrest of another dissident, Aleksandr Ginzburg. During February, the USSR expelled a U. S. reporter of the Associated Press, George Krimsky, for alleged espionage and the United States in retaliation expelled Vladimir I. Alek-

seyev, a Soviet Tass correspondent in Washington. In March, the Soviet press accused two officers of the U. S. embassy in Moscow of bribing USSR dissidents to supply Soviet defense data to the U. S. Central Intelligence Agency (CIA). In late spring, the U. S. government seized a Soviet trawler for excessive fishing within the U. S. 200-mile economic zone, and forced the ship to pay a $250,000 fine. In the autumn, a bomb exploded near the Washington office of Aeroflot, the Soviet airline, but caused no injuries; it was apparently planted by anti-Castro Cubans. The U. S. government protested in October that the Soviet secret police (KGB) in Tbilisi, capital of the Georgian S. S. R., asked Constantine Warvariv, a U. S. delegate to UNESCO (UN Educational, Scientific, and Cultural Organization), to become a Soviet spy, threatening to expose him as a World War II Nazi mass murderer if he refused. Warvariv did refuse, noting that he had been a prisoner of the Nazis, but the Soviet press still accused him of wartime killings.

In August, a fire caused by defective wiring damaged the upper floors of the U. S. embassy in Moscow, but Soviet firemen did not steal any embassy files or secret equipment. SALT II negotiations resumed in March, when the United States offered a modification of the U. S.-USSR Vladivostok agreement, by which each side would reduce its total number of intercontinental bombers, intercontinental rockets, and submarine missiles from 2,400 to 2,000 or 1,800, and multiple-warhead missiles from 1,320 to 1,200 or 1,100; no missile modernizing would be permitted.

The United States offer did not mention the cruise missile under development in the United States, and the USSR rejected this offer as an attempt to weaken Soviet strategic parity with the United States.

President Leonid Brezhnev and U. S. Ambassador Malcolm Toon review the mid-1977 status of Soviet-U. S. relations.

UPI

Ending two days of talks in France, June 22, President Brezhnev and French President Valéry Giscard d'Estaing sign six documents of mutual understanding and cooperation.

UPI

In April, the USSR protested against the increase in appropriations for Radio Liberty and Radio Free Europe, two official U. S. radio stations broadcasting uncensored news into Communist Eastern Europe and the USSR.

Despite such frictions, a U. S.-USSR treaty was concluded in May for cooperation in space science and space medicine, and in compiling data from rocket flights to other planets and the moon. Both superpowers also signed a UN convention outlawing use of military or other hostile techniques for altering the environment.

In September, while SALT II negotiations continued, the United States and the USSR agreed to an informal extension of the 1972 SALT I pact, expiring on October 3, which limited total strategic missiles, submarine missiles, and missile submarines. Shortly thereafter, Soviet Foreign Minister Andrei Gromyko asked the UN to prevent U. S. production of the so-called "neutron bomb."

Europe. Soviet relations with most European nations were harmonious in 1977. The USSR concluded economic cooperation and technical-aid treaties with Finland, trade and economic cooperation pacts with France, and an agreement with Great Britain on the prevention of accidental nuclear war. When Rumania suffered a severe earthquake during March, the USSR immediately sent medical supplies and began aiding Rumanian urban reconstruction. During the year, the Soviet Union rendered technical aid to Greece, Iceland, and Portugal, and exchanged such aid with Finland, Bulgaria, Czechoslovakia, East Germany, Hungary, Poland, Rumania, and Yugoslavia. For the first time since the late 1930's, Spain established diplomatic relations with the USSR in 1977.

Some unpleasant incidents occurred during the year. Among them were the expulsion of a Soviet UNESCO official from France for industrial espionage, and Norway's expulsion of three Soviet trade officials, an embassy secretary, a chauffeur, and a Tass newsman for spying. So-

viet citizens, fleeing from their homeland, hijacked an Aeroflot passenger plane to Sweden in May and another to Finland in July.

Middle East. Soviet policy relating to the Middle East was more active in the economic than the political sphere. The USSR concluded pacts of economic cooperation, technical aid, and aircraft hijacking prevention with Turkey, a 12-year technical-aid treaty with Afghanistan, and technical-aid, telecommunications, and trade agreements with India, which received a new $200-million Soviet credit. USSR technical aid was also rendered to Bangladesh, Iran, Iraq, Jordan, Kuwait, Nepal, Pakistan, Southern Yemen, Sri Lanka, Syria, and Yemen. The Palestine Liberation Organization (PLO) announced that it was receiving Soviet arms.

The weak Soviet political influence in the Middle East was strengthened in early autumn by U. S.-USSR agreement to convene a Geneva conference of Israel and Arab representatives, including Palestinians, which would attempt to achieve Middle East peace by inducing Israel to return occupied Arab territory, creating a Palestinian state, and guaranteeing Israeli security. When Egyptian President Anwar el-Sadat visited Israel in late November in a personal attempt to promote peace negotiations, the Soviet press voiced displeasure and accused him of disrupting Arab unity.

Far East. Soviet activity in the Far East during 1977 was more economic than political. In January, the USSR aided the Philippine economy by purchasing 600,000 tons of Philippine sugar. During the spring, a trade pact was concluded with North Korea, and trade and fisheries treaties with Japan. Soviet technical aid was rendered to Burma, Laos, Malaysia, Mongolia, North Korea, Singapore, Thailand, and Vietnam.

In February, Japan protested the new Soviet 200-mile coastal fishing zone, which included waters around the four southern Kuril Islands under USSR control but claimed by Japan. Later, the Japanese Communist party asked its

PHOTOS UPI

Moscovites read newspaper articles telling of the adoption of a new Soviet constitution. Later, Vasili Kuznetsov thanked the Supreme Soviet for naming him first vice president, a post created by the new constitution.

Soviet counterpart to return all the Kuril Islands to Japan; the USSR party angrily refused.

Sino-Soviet relations slightly improved, although the USSR protested to the Peking government that China's anti-Soviet propaganda was endangering world peace. In October, after eight years of negotiation, the two countries agreed upon new navigation rules for the Amur and Ussuri rivers on their joint border.

Africa. Trying to expand Soviet influence in Africa, the USSR in 1977 concluded trade and technical-aid treaties with Tanzania, a 20-year nonaggression pact with Mozambique, trade and cultural exchange agreements with Tunisia, technical-aid and cultural exchange treaties with Ethiopia, and an agreement with Angola to form a joint commission for economic cooperation. All together, the USSR rendered technical aid to 27 African countries, of which more than 18 were also receiving Soviet arms. In addition, the USSR openly admitted that it was arming black guerrillas fighting the white governments of Rhodesia and South Africa.

Despite this widespread aid, Soviet setbacks occurred in Africa throughout 1977. In the spring, the USSR sympathized with rebels in the former Katanga province of Zaire; the government, however, suppressed the rebellion with aid from the United States, China, two West European, and three North African countries. In May, the Sudan expelled all 90 of its Soviet military advisers and closed the military department of the Soviet embassy to lessen USSR local influence. In the fall, Guinea stopped Soviet long-range reconnaissance flights from Guinean airports over the South Atlantic Ocean.

Angered by USSR support of Ethiopia in the undeclared Somali-Ethiopian war, Somalia on November 13 expelled all of its 3,000 Soviet advisers, barred further USSR use of two Somali naval bases, and renounced the 1974 Soviet-Somali treaty of friendship.

Latin America. The Soviet Union in 1977 rendered technical aid to Communist Cuba and to Argentina, Brazil, Colombia, Mexico, Peru, Trinidad, and Venezuela. Cuba received the largest share, about $2.5-million worth per day; as a result, it owed the USSR more than $5 billion (U. S.). In the autumn, Argentina seized eight Soviet fishing vessels for fishing within the 200-mile Argentine coastal limit. When one Soviet ship tried to flee, it was damaged by Argentine naval gunfire.

Canada. In September, Canada seized two Soviet trawlers for violating the 200-mile fishing limit along the Canadian Pacific coast. Earlier in the year, the Canadian government deported a Soviet exchange physicist, Lev G. Khvostantsev, on charges of espionage.

SPACE AND DEFENSE

Space Program. By March 1977, the USSR had launched 1,113 space satellites since the first Soviet sputnik went aloft in 1957. Of this total, 121 were orbited in 1976 alone.

On Feb. 7, 1977, spaceship Soyuz 24 was lofted with a two-man crew. After docking with the Salyut 5 orbital research station, the Soyuz 24 returned safely to earth on February 25. The unmanned Salyut 6 space station was successfully launched on September 29. A Soyuz 25 spaceship, with a two-man crew, was lofted on October 9, tried but failed to dock with Salyut 6, then returned to earth on October 11. Another attempt in December succeeded.

During June and October, the USSR made two successful tests of a new unprecedented hunter-killer satellite, which was able to intercept low-flying Soviet target satellites.

Armed Forces. In 1977, the Soviet armed forces totaled about 4,400,000 men. Their equipment was numerically first in the world in terms of tanks, intercontinental ballistic missiles, submarine-based and medium-range missiles, medium-range bombers, and submarines. But Soviet armament lagged behind the United States in terms of aircraft carriers, long-range bombers, tactical nuclear weapons, and total nuclear warheads.

Warsaw Pact land maneuvers by combined Soviet, Czechoslovakian, and Hungarian troops were conducted in Czechoslovakia and Hungary in March, and 27,000 Soviet troops maneuvered near the Polish border in July.

In January, Gen. Nikolai V. Ogarkov, a missile specialist, was appointed chief of the General Staff of the Soviet Armed Forces, replacing Viktor G. Kulikov, a tank expert, who became commander of the Warsaw Pact forces.

By 1977, 90 million Soviet citizens had passed the ready-for-labor-and-defense tests of militarized sport, and the Civil Defense Society achieved a membership of 80 million.

GOVERNMENT AND POLITICS

After a nationwide discussion, a new USSR constitution was adopted on October 7, replacing the Stalin constitution of 1936. No shifts of power were made between the various governmental bodies, but the terms of the USSR, union republic, and autonomous republic soviets (legislatures) were changed from four to five years, and those of lower soviets from two to two and a half, while the term of the USSR prosecutor general was reduced from seven to five years. The office of the first vice president was created within the USSR Supreme Soviet Presidium (collective presidency). The new constitution describes Soviet foreign policy as a combination of peace and world revolution, and clearly states that the Communist party governs the USSR. Otherwise, it is a longer and more detailed version of the old document.

The most important personnel change of 1977 occurred during May–June, when Nikolai V. Podgorny was removed from the party Politburo and from the USSR presidency, sent into retirement, and replaced as president by Leonid Brezhnev, who retained his other position of Communist party secretary general. Thus, Brezhnev became Soviet chief of state and definitely the top leader of the USSR.

In October, Konstantin U. Chernenko, a party secretary, was made a candidate member of the powerful party Politburo, a status also achieved by Vasili V. Kuznetsov, who was immediately promoted from deputy foreign minister to first vice president of the USSR.

The Soviet Communist party had 15.9 million members in 1977 and the Komsomol (Young Communist League) 36 million.

Dissidents. The government continued to imprison some dissidents and exile others. Among the prominent 1977 exiles were the mathematician Valentin F. Turchin and the humorist Feliks Kandel-Kamov. Meanwhile, many Jews seeking to emigrate were dismissed from their jobs and sometimes imprisoned.

Crime. The Soviet press admitted that alcoholism was a nationwide problem, causing much petty crime. The most common crimes were listed as hooliganism, embezzlement, extortion, theft of state property, minority nationalism, and religious fanaticism.

UPI

A Russian fishing trawler photographed from the deck of a U. S. vessel. Both the Soviet Union and the United States extended their national protected fishing areas to 200 miles offshore during the year.

CULTURE

The Soviet Union boasted that it had one third of the world's newspaper circulation, published one seventh of the world's books, and was served by one third of the world's doctors. Literacy is almost universal, but two fifths of all Soviet adults have no more than grade-school education.

ECONOMY

Industry. Soviet industrial production increased by about 5.8% in 1977, compared to 4.8% in 1976. The USSR in 1977 was first in the world in the output of iron, steel, coal, petroleum, cement, chemical fertilizers, locomotives, and shoes. But factory mechanization was poor; according to official accounts, 35% of industrial work was still being performed by manual labor.

Agriculture. Because of bad weather, the 1977 grain harvest was only 194 million metric tons, 19 million tons below plan and 30 million tons less than in 1976. In the fall, the USSR purchased 15 million tons of foreign grain, mostly from the United States.

Transport and Trade. Soviet railways carried half of the world's rail freight, and the USSR merchant marine was sixth in size. On March 1, the USSR established a 200-mile fishing zone off its Arctic and Pacific coasts. In August, the *Arktika*, a new Soviet atomic icebreaker, broke through heavy ice to become the world's first ship to reach the North Pole. Aeroflot, the Soviet state airline, began regular flights to the Cape Verde Islands, Ethiopia, Madagascar, Zaire, Zambia, and Mexico.

The USSR in 1977 was the world's largest exporter of raw materials, especially iron and timber. Exported oil was the chief earner of foreign currency; in January, the price of Soviet oil was raised by 22.5% for Communist Eastern Europe. Yet the USSR had accumulated a debt of $17 billion to Western nations.

ELLSWORTH RAYMOND
New York University

USSR · Information Highlights

Official Name: Union of Soviet Socialist Republics.
Area: 8,649,412 square miles (22,402,000 km²).
Population (1977 est.): 259,000,000.
Chief Cities (1975 est.): Moscow, the capital, 7,635,-000; Leningrad, 4,300,000; Kiev, 1,947,000.
Government: *Head of state,* Leonid I. Brezhnev, president (took office June 1977). *Head of government,* Aleksei N. Kosygin, premier (took office Oct. 1964). *Secretary general of the Communist party,* Leonid I. Brezhnev (took office 1964). *Legislature*—Supreme Soviet: Soviet of the Union, Soviet of Nationalities.
Monetary Unit: Ruble (0.75 ruble equals U. S.$1, 1977).
Manufacturing (major products): Steel, cement, chemical fertilizer, machine tools, electric power.
Major Agricultural Products: Grain, sugar beets, sunflower seeds, potatoes, cotton.

Red Square, Moscow, remains a center of Soviet life as well as a major tourist attraction.

UPI

Jimmy Carter delivered his first foreign policy address as president before the United Nations in March.

UNITED NATIONS

It became apparent in 1977 that efforts to find a solution to the world's economic problems and, in so doing, create a new socio-economic order, were destined to play an ever increasing part in the activities of the United Nations. The tendency had shown itself in much sharper terms during 1975 and 1976, but there was a growing realization on the part of the poor nations that the problems they faced were not so simple to solve as appeared on the surface, though various potent economic weapons were at their disposal. The industrial powers in turn seemed to have come to a better understanding of their own responsibility in making economic arrangements that would provide stability both for themselves and the primary producers upon whom their own economies depended. The world, perhaps for the first time in history, seemed to be groping toward economic interdependence on a broad scale. But progress was slow and, to many countries, unsatisfactory, as the final session, May 30–June 2, of the Paris Conference on International Economic Cooperation proved. It was described in a draft resolution before the reconvened session of the 31st General Assembly as failing "to reach agreements which could contribute" to the new order.

The political problems before the UN in 1977 were little changed. They centered on the Middle East and southern Africa, and, to a lesser extent, on Cyprus.

The United States announced its withdrawal from the International Labor Organization, to take effect on November 5. The decision, due to the politicization and domination of the organization by the Communist and Arab blocs, was foreshadowed two years earlier, when the Ford administration filed notice of withdrawal.

The principal activities of the United Nations in its 32nd year are summarized below under the following headings: General Assembly; Security Council; Economic and Social Council; Trusteeship and Decolonization; and Legal Activities.

GENERAL ASSEMBLY

The 31st session of the General Assembly reconvened on Sept. 13, 1977, for a discussion of the results of the Paris Conference on International Economic Cooperation. A draft resolution was submitted by the so-called Group of 77. Regretting that the conference had made no progress in solving the problems, the resolution itself failed to reach a consensus.

The 32nd session opened on September 20 and elected Lazar Mojsov of Yugoslavia as president. Djibouti and Vietnam were admitted as members, bringing the total membership to 149. The main point made by Mojsov in his inaugural address was that the establishment of a new international economic order had become indispensable. The General Assembly adopted an agenda of 128 items and then embarked on an overall review of world affairs.

A debate on Namibia, which followed, culminated in a series of eight resolutions, adopted in the week of November 6–12. The main resolution, passed by a vote of 117 to 0, with 24 abstentions, reiterated that "any independence talks regarding Namibia must be between the representatives of the South West Africa People's Organization (SWAPO) and South Africa under the auspices of the UN." The assembly also declared South Africa liable for reparations for damage caused by its illegal occupation of Namibia, condemned and rejected the South African decision to annex Walvis Bay, and called for sanctions against the republic.

Turning to the situation in South Africa itself in the first half of November, the assembly called on all countries to end ownership by their nationals of business enterprises in South Africa.

A resolution denouncing Israeli settlements on the occupied West Bank of the Jordan and calling for a halt to any action which would result in changing the legal status, geographic nature, or demographic composition of Arab territories occupied since 1967, including Jerusalem, was approved by a vote of 131 to 1 (Israel), with 7 abstentions, on October 28.

The assembly debate on the Middle East, which took place toward the end of November, was as acrimonious as usual. The visit by President Anwar el-Sadat of Egypt to Israel on November 19–21 caused a split in Arab unity, which manifested itself in the assembly, particularly on November 21, when the Egyptian representative walked out because of the harsh criticism of the visit made by the Syrian representative. The debate concluded with the passage of a Syrian-inspired resolution, calling on Israel to end its occupation of Arab territories, and for the resumption of the Geneva conference, with the participation of the Palestine Liberation Organization. The vote, on November 25, was 102 to 4 (the United States, Canada, El Salvador, and Israel), with 29 abstentions.

Prompted by the hijacking of a Lufthansa airliner and the appearance before it of Derry Pearce, president of the International Federation of Air Pilots' Associations, the assembly's Special Political Committee approved a draft resolution advocating stronger measures against hijacking. The resolution was endorsed by the assembly itself on November 3 without a vote.

Other matters that came before the assembly and its various committees included increased aid to Vietnam, disarmament, Cyprus, the Western Sahara, East Timor, and the future political position of the island of Mayotte in relation to the Comoran archipelago.

UPI

Chen Chu, China's new ambassador to the UN, presents his credentials to UN Secretary General Kurt Waldheim.

SECURITY COUNCIL

The complex problems of southern Africa dominated the Security Council's discussions in 1977. Though the Middle East appeared on its agenda from time to time, the council was unable to promote a settlement.

Southern Africa. Rhodesian aggression against Botswana was condemned by a vote of 13 to 0 in a resolution on January 14; the United States and the United Kingdom abstained. Another resolution, on May 25, approved aid programs for Botswana and Lesotho. Two resolutions, concerning aggression by mercenaries against Benin, were passed on February 8 and April 14. After debating a complaint by Mozambique that it had been invaded by Rhodesian forces, the council, on June 30, requested all states to assist Mozambique in strengthening its defenses.

A United Kingdom proposal, approved by the council on September 29 by a vote of 13 to 0 (the USSR abstained, and China did not participate), requested the secretary general to appoint a representative to consult with the British resident commissioner-designate in Rhodesia and all other parties concerned regarding transition to majority rule. Lt. Gen. D. Prem Chand of India was appointed.

Consideration of the situation in South Africa culminated, on March 30, in four resolutions. Should South Africa fail to comply with the council's previous resolutions, they proposed a strengthening of the arms embargo, a halt to all investments in South Africa, and action under all relevant sections of the UN charter. Developments in South Africa itself led to a request, on October 20, from Mahmoud Mestiri of Tunisia that the council should meet again on the problem. Two weeks of discussions ended on November 4, with the unanimous passage of a resolution imposing a world-wide mandatory ban on the shipment of arms and related materiel to South Africa—the first time such a measure had been applied to a member state. Earlier in the discussion, an African resolution calling for an end to repression and apartheid, had also passed unanimously, but three other drafts, which would have imposed economic and other sanctions, were vetoed by the United States, France, and the United Kingdom. Canada and West Germany had also voted against them.

Middle East. The Middle East situation was discussed by the council during March 25–28 at the request of Egypt. The council had before it a report from the secretary general, which concluded that the problem was intractable. No action was taken, and the council adjourned to a date to be set after consultation among the members. On October 27, the council met to consider the recommendations of the Committee on Palestinian Rights, already endorsed by the assembly. The report recommended the return of displaced Palestinians, the withdrawal by Israel from occupied territories, and the establishment of an independent Palestinian state.

Cyprus. Cyprus appeared briefly on the council's agenda on April 30, when the secretary general reported on the intercommunal talks held in Vienna from March 31 to April 7. Formal meetings of the council in early September, on a complaint by Cyprus of Turkish moves to colonize part of Famagusta, gave way to informal contacts and consultations. A resolution, calling on the parties concerned to refrain from all unilateral actions that might affect the solution of the problem, emerged from these consultations on September 15.

ECONOMIC AND SOCIAL COUNCIL

The Economic and Social Council held its organizing session for 1977 on January 11–14. It decided to refer to its Commission on Human Rights the question of "the consequences for the enjoyment of human rights by the oppressed peoples of southern Africa of the use by France, the United Kingdom, and the United States of their veto power in the Security Council." Meeting again from April 12 to May 13, the council adopted a number of resolutions aimed at combating the evils of apartheid, including a recommendation that the General Assembly proclaim 1978 International Anti-Apartheid Year. During a session held at Geneva from July 6 to August 4, the council called for increased assistance to the so-called front-line states of Africa and urged intensive efforts to bring about a new economic order.

Two new bodies, established after the International Covenant on Civil and Political Rights came into force on March 23, 1976, met for the first time in 1977. The International Rights Committee met March 21 to April 1 and the Human Rights Committee during August 4–31.

A recommendation that the importance of population policies should be taken into account by the General Assembly was made by the Population Commission, which met during January 10–21. It also established a group of experts to make proposals on the first review of the World Population Plan of Action in 1979.

The first UN Water Conference was held at Mar del Plata, Argentina, during March 14–25, and a preparatory committee, meeting during January 10–17, agreed on a draft agenda for a Conference on Technical Cooperation Among Developing Countries in March or April 1978.

TRUSTEESHIP AND DECOLONIZATION

Conditions in the Trust Territory of the Pacific Islands (Micronesia), administered by the United States, were considered by the Trusteeship Council on June 6–23. The council noted with satisfaction the U. S. view that the islands should be a single governmental unit and welcomed the U. S. intention to find, in conjunction with the Micronesians, a mutually satisfactory basis for the termination of the Trusteeship Agreement by 1981.

The Special Committee of 24 met on January 12 and reelected Salim A. Salim of Tanzania as chairman for the sixth time in succession. Its substantive work began on February 25, with a discussion of Namibia, which was highly critical of South African policy. In a consensus on March 14, the committee denounced South Africa's continued illegal occupation of Namibia. Rhodesia was the subject of the committee's discussions from April 19 to May 2, but no action was taken. At a series of meetings in July and August, the committee condemned both the activities of foreign financial interests in Rhodesia and military arrangements in colonial territories. It made a number of recommendations on the remaining non-self-governing territories, but deferred consideration of Puerto Rico, East Timor, and the Western Sahara to a later date.

LEGAL ACTIVITIES

On June 10, Libya and Tunisia agreed to submit their dispute over the Gulf of Gabès, which both claim, to the International Court of Justice. The court took no immediate action.

The Commission on International Trade Law, meeting from May 23 to June 17, approved a draft convention on the rights and duties of buyers and sellers under international contracts.

A new composite text, covering all aspects discussed since the conference began in 1973, was compiled by the sixth session of the UN Conference on the Law of the Sea, held in New York from May 23 to July 15.

RICHARD E. WEBB
Formerly, British Information Service, N. Y. C.

ORGANIZATION OF THE UNITED NATIONS

THE SECRETARIAT

Secretary General: Kurt Waldheim (until Dec. 31, 1981)

THE GENERAL ASSEMBLY (1977)

President: Lazar Mojsov (Yugoslavia). The 149 member nations were as follows:

Afghanistan	German Democratic	Nigeria
Albania	Republic	Norway
Algeria	Germany, Federal	Oman
Angola	Republic of	Pakistan
Argentina	Ghana	Panama
Australia	Greece	Papua-New Guinea
Austria	Grenada	Paraguay
Bahamas	Guatemala	Peru
Bahrain	Guinea	Philippines
Bangladesh	Guinea-Bissau	Poland
Barbados	Guyana	Portugal
Belgium	Haiti	Qatar
Belorussian SSR	Honduras	Rumania
Benin	Hungary	Rwanda
Bhutan	Iceland	São Tomé and
Bolivia	India	Príncipe
Botswana	Indonesia	Saudi Arabia
Brazil	Iran	Senegal
Bulgaria	Iraq	Seychelles
Burma	Ireland	Sierra Leone
Burundi	Israel	Singapore
Cambodia	Italy	Somalia
Cameroon	Ivory Coast	South Africa
Canada	Jamaica	Spain
Cape Verde	Japan	Sri Lanka (Ceylon)
Central African	Jordan	Sudan
Empire	Kenya	Surinam
Chad	Kuwait	Swaziland
Chile	Laos	Sweden
China, People's	Lebanon	Syria
Republic of	Lesotho	Tanzania
Colombia	Liberia	Thailand
Comoros	Libya	Togo
Congo	Luxembourg	Trinidad and Tobago
Costa Rica	Madagascar	Tunisia
Cuba	Malawi	Turkey
Cyprus	Malaysia	Uganda
Czechoslovakia	Maldives	Ukrainian SSR
Denmark	Mali	USSR
Djibouti	Malta	United Arab Emirates
Dominican Republic	Mauritania	United Kingdom
Ecuador	Mauritius	United States
Egypt	Mexico	Upper Volta
El Salvador	Mongolia	Uruguay
Equatorial Guinea	Morocco	Venezuela
Ethiopia	Mozambique	Vietnam
Fiji	Nepal	Western Samoa
Finland	Netherlands	Yemen
France	New Zealand	Yemen, Democratic
Gabon	Nicaragua	Yugoslavia
Gambia	Niger	Zaire
		Zambia

COMMITTEES

General: Composed of 25 members as follows: The General Assembly president; the 17 General Assembly vice presidents (heads of delegations or their deputies of China, Cyprus, Democratic Yemen, Denmark, Ecuador, France, Gabon, Guatemala, Indonesia, Lesotho, Madagascar, Netherlands, Peru, Sierra Leone, USSR, United Kingdom, United States); and the chairmen of the following main committees, which are composed of all 149 member countries:

First (Political and Security): Frank E. Boaten (Ghana)

Special Political: Bernhard Neugebauer (German Democratic Republic)

Second (Economic and Financial): Peter Jankowitsch (Austria)

Third (Social, Humanitarian and Cultural): Lucille Mair (Jamaica)

Fourth (Trust and Non-Self-Governing Territories): Mowaffak Allaf (Syria)

Fifth (Administrative and Budgetary): Morteza Talieh (Iran)

Sixth (Legal): Enrique Gaviria (Colombia)

THE SECURITY COUNCIL

Membership ends on December 31 of the year noted; asterisks indicate permanent membership.

Bolivia (1979)	Germany, Fed.	Nigeria (1979)
Canada (1978)	Rep. of (1978)	USSR*
China*	India (1978)	United Kingdom*
Czechoslovakia (1979)	Kuwait (1979)	United States*
France*	Mauritius (1978)	Venezuela (1978)
Gabon (1979)		

Military Staff Committee: Representatives of chief of staffs of permanent members.

Disarmament Commission: Representatives of all UN members.

THE ECONOMIC AND SOCIAL COUNCIL

President: Donald O. Mills (Jamaica). Membership ends on December 31 of the year noted.

Afghanistan (1978)	Iran (1979)	Sweden (1980)
Algeria (1978)	Iraq (1979)	Syria (1979)
Argentina (1980)	Italy (1979)	Tanzania (1980)
Austria (1978)	Jamaica (1979)	Togo (1978)
Bangladesh (1978)	Japan (1980)	Trinidad and
Bolivia (1978)	Lesotho (1980)	Tobago (1980)
Brazil (1978)	Malaysia (1978)	Tunisia (1978)
Cameroon (1980)	Malta (1980)	Uganda (1978)
Central African	Mauritania (1979)	Ukrainian SSR
Empire (1980)	Mexico (1979)	(1979)
China (1980)	Netherlands (1979)	USSR (1980)
Colombia (1979)	New Zealand (1979)	United Arab
Cuba (1978)	Nigeria (1978)	Emirates (1980)
Finland (1980)	Philippines (1979)	United Kingdom
France (1978)	Poland (1979)	(1980)
Germany, Federal	Portugal (1978)	United States
Republic of (1978)	Rumania (1979)	(1979)
Greece (1978)	Rwanda (1979)	Upper Volta (1979)
Hungary (1980)	Somalia (1979)	Venezuela (1978)
India (1980)	Sudan (1979)	Yugoslavia (1978)

THE TRUSTEESHIP COUNCIL

President: Robin A. C. Byatt (United Kingdom)

Australia[1]	France[2]	United Kingdom[2]
China[2]	USSR[2]	United States[1]

[1] Administers Trust Territory. [2] Permanent member of Security Council not administering Trust Territory.

THE INTERNATIONAL COURT OF JUSTICE

Membership ends on February 5 of the year noted.

President: Eduardo Jiménez de Aréchaga (Uruguay, 1979)
Vice President: Nagendra Singh (India, 1982)

Isaac Forster (Senegal, 1982)	Federico de Castro (Spain, 1979)
André Gros (France, 1982)	Platon Morozov (USSR, 1979)
Taslim Olawale Elias (Nigeria, 1985)	Manfred Lachs (Poland, 1985)
Herman Mosler (Federal Republic of Germany, 1985)	Sir Humphrey Waldock (United Kingdom, 1981)
Shigeru Oda (Japan, 1985)	José María Ruda (Argentina, 1982)
Salah El Dine Tarazi (Syria, 1985)	Hardy C. Dillard (U. S., 1979)
Louis Ignacio-Pinto (Benin, 1979)	

SPECIALIZED AGENCIES

Food and Agriculture Organization (FAO); Intergovernmental Maritime Consultative Organization (IMCO); International Atomic Energy Agency (IAEA); International Bank for Reconstruction and Development (World Bank, IBRD); International Civil Aviation Organization (ICAO); International Development Association (IDA); International Finance Corporation (IFC); International Labor Organization (ILO); International Monetary Fund (IMF); International Telecommunication Union (ITU); United Nations Educational, Scientific and Cultural Organization (UNESCO); Universal Postal Union (UPU); United Nations International Children's Emergency Fund (UNICEF); World Health Organization (WHO); World Meteorological Organization (WMO).

UNITED STATES

President Jimmy Carter confers with his predecessor, Gerald Ford, in the Oval Office.

UPI

Domestic Affairs

In his inaugural address on January 20, President Jimmy Carter promised his fellow countrymen "a new beginning" in their government, and his induction into office pointed up the fact that a time of change and transition was at hand. The Democratic Party had returned to the White House after eight years of Republican rule. Moreover, the former Georgia governor was the first citizen of a Deep South state to be elected president since the Civil War.

After the political scandals and economic difficulties of the recent past, Americans were ready for a fresh start in Washington. But as the events of 1977 demonstrated, many of the old problems remained to plague the country. The energy crisis had become chronic. Crime and financial burdens deepened the malaise of the cities. Inflation and unemployment threatened the health of the economy. Despite the brave rhetoric of the new president, as the year ended the remedies for most of the nation's ills still waited to be developed sometime in the future.

The Presidency. "We have learned that more is not necessarily better, that even our great nation has its recognized limits. . . ." These words from Carter's inaugural address reflected the recognition, which shaped the first year of his presidency, that the thrust for change implicit in his campaign for the White House, had to be tempered by restraint.

There were several reasons for caution. Carter's victory over Gerald Ford had been relatively narrow and he needed to strengthen and broaden his base of support. Moreover, though the political climate had improved under the Ford presidency, the legacy of Watergate lingered on in a pervasive public skepticism. In a confidential memorandum prepared for the new president, which became public during the year, one of his advisers, Patrick Caddell, warned: "Americans have no real expectations that government is willing or able to solve most of the country's major problems." Before he could successfully carry out sweeping actions to deal with national problems, Caddell advised, the new president first had to build the confidence and trust of the people.

The early days of the Carter presidency thus were heavily infused with symbolism, steps taken to humanize the image of the so-called Imperial Presidency, and to demonstrate the new chief executive's personal concern for the citizenry. It began on Inauguration Day when the president, instead of riding in a limousine, walked with his family the 1.5 miles (2.4 km) from the Capitol to the White House. A bitter cold wave gave Carter an opportunity to identify himself with the hardships of average Americans. With natural gas fuels in short supply in many areas, the president ordered the White House thermostats turned down.

On January 31, in his first post-inaugural speech to the nation, he appeared before a glowing fire in the White House library, dressed informally in a gray cardigan sweater, to warn that "the energy crisis is permanent." At the same time the president reiterated his intention to carry out his campaign promises. Indeed President Carter had already begun to keep them, as he pointed out. On January 21, in one of his first official acts as president, Carter had

519

At noon Jan. 20, 1977, Jimmy Carter, former governor of Georgia, was sworn in as the 39th president of the United States. Chief Justice Warren E. Burger administered the oath as Mrs. Carter held the Bible. Moments earlier, Walter F. Mondale of Minnesota had taken the oath as the nation's 41st vice president.

THE CARTER-MONDALE INAUGURATION — JAN. 20, 1977

"For myself and for our nation, I want to thank my predecessor for all he has done to heal our land.

"In this outward and physical ceremony, we attest once again to the inner and spiritual strength of our nation. . . .

"This inauguration ceremony marks a new beginning, a new dedication within our government, a new spirit among us all. A president may sense and proclaim that new spirit, but only a people can provide it. . . ."

President Jimmy Carter
Inaugural Address

President and Mrs. Carter share the dance floor at an inaugural "party."

Following the inaugural ceremony at the Capitol, the new president and members of his family walked down Pennsylvania Avenue to the White House. At the executive mansion, the first family, other dignitaries, and guests watched the inaugural parade for three hours from a reviewing stand, which was heated by solar energy.

ALL PHOTOS UPI

House Speaker Thomas P. O'Neill presides at the opening of the 95th Congress.

granted a pardon to almost all Vietnam-era draft evaders.

Carter followed up the success of his fireside chat with other efforts at mass communication. On March 5 he took part in a two-hour radio call-in show, answering questions from 42 listeners around the country on a variety of issues for an estimated audience of 24 million. On March 16, in his first full-scale trip as president, he responded to questions from local citizens at a simulated town meeting in Clinton, Mass., while millions watched on television. On July 21 he made a similar appearance in Yazoo City, Miss., before a crowd packed in a high school gym.

Within the White House, Carter sought to strip away some of the pomp and perquisites of office. He put an end to limousine service for his top aides, had television sets removed from many White House offices, and discouraged the playing of the traditional presidential fanfare, "Hail to the Chief."

Many Americans found these gestures refreshing and reassuring, but some complained that the new president stressed style rather than substance and worried that the symbolism was intended as a substitute for action. But they did not have to wait long for action, or at least attempts at action. Early in his presidency, Carter made clear that dealing with the energy problem would be his top priority for the year. On March 1 he asked Congress to create a new department of energy. On April 18, in a nationally televised address, he described the energy problem as "unprecedented in our history," and, borrowing a phrase from William James, called efforts to find a solution "the moral equivalent of war." On April 20 he outlined his

program before a joint session of Congress. To achieve conservation, the "cornerstone" of his program, he proposed increasing the price of crude oil, through higher taxes, and of newly discovered natural gas, and he called for an excise tax on gas-guzzling cars and a standby gasoline tax. To ease the economic burden and encourage conservation he asked for a package of tax rebates and credits.

Carter also sought to revive the struggling economy. On January 27 he outlined a two-year, $31.2-billion economic stimulus package including public service jobs, public works programs, and a $50 rebate for each taxpayer and dependent. The controversial rebate was the centerpiece of the program, and the president at first defended it vigorously. But as the unemployment rate dropped and concern about inflation mounted, misgivings about the rebate increased within the administration. (The unemployment rate, which had been 7.9% of the work force in December, dropped to 7% in April. At year's end it was 6.4%. The consumer price index had risen an average of 5.8% in 1976. The annual rate for 1977 was 5.3%.) On April 14 the president announced he was scrapping the rebate idea. Although this decision was approved by many businessmen, it left unsatisfied many liberals who felt that the president was not acting vigorously enough to help the jobless and was paying too little attention in general to the plight of the poor and the blacks in the cities.

Anxiety about these problems was heightened by the widespread looting and vandalism that followed a power blackout in New York City on July 13 and 14. On July 24, in a speech to an Urban League conference in Washington,

UPI

Sen. Ted Stevens (R-Alaska) listens as Senate Minority Leader Howard Baker of Tennessee addresses newsmen.

League President Vernon Jordan accused the Carter administration of not keeping its commitments to black supporters. In an address to the league Carter responded by saying he had "no apologies" for his policies; then he personally told Jordan that criticism of the administration was "damaging to the hopes and aspirations of poor people."

Amid protests from liberals and blacks over his reaction to Jordan's criticism, Carter forged ahead with his own plans for improving the condition of the poor. On August 6 he unveiled a sweeping program for reform of the welfare system. Existing welfare programs would be scrapped, government efforts to find and create jobs for the poor would be expanded, and more flexible income-support programs for low-income families would be created.

For a time, however, such presidential initiatives were overshadowed by the public furor over the president's longtime friend and close adviser, Bert Lance, director of the Office of Management and Budget. Attention focused on Lance's conduct of his financial affairs before he joined the federal government when he sought the waiver of a requirement, imposed at his confirmation, that he sell a large block of bank stock to avoid a possible conflict of interest. The Senate Government Affairs Committee at first appeared ready to grant the waiver. But investigations by reporters and government agencies disclosed substantial overdrafts and other irregularities in Lance's record as a banker in Georgia. Carter sought to rebut the resultant criticism. "Bert, I'm proud of you," he told the budget director on August 18 at a press conference. But critics pressed the charge that Lance's behavior was inconsistent with the high ethical standards that Carter had set for public servants during the campaign. On September 21, after bitter Senate hearings had been carried on national television, Lance resigned. He denied any wrongdoing, and Carter proclaimed his continued faith in his integrity.

In the wake of the Lance affair, Carter's standing in the polls dropped and he appeared to have been damaged politically. No one doubted that he could eventually recover. But critics contended that the president's handling of the affair pointed up significant weaknesses within the White House: Carter's tendency to depend for advice on a small circle of Georgians and his refusal to appoint a chief of staff. Hamilton Jordan, who had managed Carter's campaign, continued as his chief political adviser and Vice President Walter Mondale was frequently consulted on substantive matters, more so apparently than past vice presidents. But neither Jordan nor Mondale had the authority for overall staff coordination.

The Congress. Like the White House, the Congress started the year under new management. In the House, Rep. Thomas P. O'Neill (D-Mass.) was chosen speaker, succeeding retired Rep. Carl Albert (D-Okla.). Rep. Jim Wright (D-Tex.) took over the majority lead-

UPI

Before a joint session of Congress in April, President Carter presented his national energy program.

er's post. In the Senate, Robert C. Byrd (D-W. Va.) became majority leader, succeeding Mike Mansfield (D-Mont.). Sen. Alan Cranston (D-Calif.) repalced Byrd as majority whip.

Although the same party controlled both houses of Congress and the presidency for the first time since 1968, the executive and the legislative branches did not often work in harmony. Some congressmen blamed the White House, complaining about the failure of presidential aides to consult with or inform them on matters of mutual concern. And presidential efforts to cut funding for federally supported water resource projects and dams irritated many congressmen.

Another factor contributing to the lack of cooperation was that Congress was heavily involved in its own internal problems. One was pay raises for members of Congress, as well as for federal judges and top officials of the executive branch. Supporters of the increases pointed out that Congress had had only a 5% boost since 1969. The raises, which went into effect February 20 after moves that might have blocked them were defeated, increased congressional salaries to $57,500 from $44,600.

Partly to offset public criticism of the raises, both houses acted to impose stricter controls on the financial activities of their members. On March 2 the House adopted a new ethics code requiring disclosure of all income and gifts totaling more than $100 and limiting outside earnings to 15% of a member's salary, or $8,625. The Senate imposed similar restrictions.

Further incentives to develop new codes were allegations first heard in 1976 that congressmen, mostly House members, had accepted gifts from South Korean lobbyists in return for promises to give favorable treatment to legislation helpful to the South Korean government. More charges were aired in 1977 and the press began to refer to the scandal as "Koreagate." The charges started a Justice Department in-

Walter Mondale is welcomed home from a foreign trip by the president and Mrs. Mondale. The vice president became an integral part of the Carter administration.

vestigation as well as congressional inquiries. The central figure among the lobbyists was Tongsun Park, a Korean businessman and prominent personality on the Washington social scene in the 1970's, who allegedly had given money and gifts to various congressmen to promote his own interests and those of his government.

Some observers complained that the Congress was not sufficiently diligent in looking into these charges; this criticism came to a head on July 15 when Philip Lacovara, former member of the Watergate prosecutor's staff, resigned as special counsel to the House Committee on Standards of Official Conduct. He complained that committee Chairman John J. Flynt, Jr. (D-Ga.), was not vigorous enough in conducting the investigation. To head off further criticism, Leon A. Jaworski, former chief Watergate prosecutor, was retained on July 20

A good and an open relationship with the press is a stated objective of the Carter team. Jody Powell, 33-year-old Georgian and long-time Carter associate, serves as White House press secretary.

to replace Lacovara. A special agreement with House Speaker O'Neill guaranteed Jaworski broad independence.

Meanwhile, President Carter responded to similar criticism, mostly from Republicans, of the Justice Department investigation. On July 18, he rejected demands that he appoint a special prosecutor to head the investigation into the charges, which evidently involved mostly Democrats. He said the Justice Department was making "substantial progress" and that he had ordered Attorney General Griffin Bell "to vigorously pursue the matter."

On September 6, Bell made public a 36-count indictment of Park, charging that he had given illegal campaign contributions or other gifts to about 25 present and former members of Congress. And Bell said he would ask President Carter to renew diplomatic efforts to have Park, who was in Seoul, return to the United States. On September 27 a second Korean-born businessman, Hancho C. Kim, was indicted on charges of collaboration with the Korean Central Intelligence Agency to influence members of Congress improperly. And on October 14, Richard T. Hanna, a former Democratic Representative from California, was indicted on charges of mail fraud and bribery. Hanna was accused of trying to persuade the government of South Korea to make Tongsun Park the agent for Korean purchases of U. S. rice, in return for which Park had allegedly promised to give some of the proceeds to Hanna.

The House Committee on Standards continued its inquiries; public hearings were expected early in 1978. The Senate ethics committee disclosed plans to question all 100 senators and 50 former senators about their possible connection with South Korean officials and agents. But the Justice Department investigation in the case was hindered by Park's absence. On November 4 President Carter publicly complained that the South Korean government had failed to persuade Park to return to the United States and said his absence was "impeding the course of justice." An agreement between Park and the Justice Department was worked out late in the year.

On broader national issues, the attempt to forge a national energy policy held center stage in the first session of the 95th Congress. Carter's proposal for a new Department of Energy to implement his program won approval from both houses and was signed into law. The House of Representatives gave its approval to most of the Carter program, but the president's proposals ran into tougher sledding in the Senate. In November, while Congress recessed, the differing House and Senate versions of the legislation were submitted for compromise, but Congress adjourned before agreement was reached.

Another thorny issue that required compromise was the effort to put the social security system on a sound financial basis. Both houses agreed that a social security tax rate increase was needed, but the Senate supported a measure that would require employers to pay more than their workers. The final agreement provided for a $227 billion payroll tax increase over the next decades, with employers and employees continuing to make equal contributions.

Even before the November recess Congress had taken significant action in response to the president's proposals for economic stimulus. It tripled, from $2 billion to $6 billion, the authorization for federal grants for local public works. It appropriated $7.9 billion to increase public service jobs under the Comprehensive Employment and Training Act, created about 200,000 new jobs, and provided for a $34 billion tax cut over the next three years. The labor force also got a boost from a new minimum wage law.

Congress passed a four-year farm and food law that adjusted price supports, increased the limit on payments to individual farmers, and established an on-farm grain reserve program. It also eliminated the requirement that persons eligible for food stamps pay the government a certain amount of cash before they could receive the stamp benefits.

Major environmental action included extending the deadlines on new auto emission standards until 1980 and giving those industries that were converting to coal from oil or natural gas until 1980 to comply with clean air standards. A new strip mining law provided for a state-federal program to regulate surface mining of coal and banned mining on developed farmlands of alluvial valley floors.

The president vetoed a rabbit meat inspection bill. He also rejected a bill authorizing $80 million for a nuclear breeder reactor on the Clinch River in Tennessee. The president said that the reactor, fueled by plutonium, would

With Clark Clifford at his side, Bert Lance prepares to testify before Senate Government Affairs Committee.

UPI

UPI

Leon A. Jaworski heads an investigation into charges that some congressmen accepted gifts from Korean lobbyists.

hurt the administration's efforts to curb the spread of nuclear weapons technology.

Central Intelligence Agency. The CIA, the center of considerable controversy in recent years, continued to be a subject of scrutiny and concern in 1977. On February 18 *The Washington Post* disclosed that the CIA had paid millions of dollars to King Hussein of Jordan since 1957. The *Post* also reported that President Carter had ordered a halt to the payments after he had learned of them. The White House refused to comment except to say that the president had initiated a comprehensive review of all intelligence activities to ensure that they were "proper."

Carter, in remarks to State Department employees on February 24, defended the need for secrecy in intelligence on grounds that intelligence sources would be reluctant to provide information if they feared they would be exposed. He said that his review of intelligence activities had not produced any examples of illegality in the previous six or eight months.

Public anxiety about the agency's present activities was heightened by disclosures of its past involvements. Early in August it was revealed that the CIA had sponsored a $25 million program of mind control experiments at universities, prisons, and hospitals. The experiments, from 1950 to 1973, used drugs, hypnosis, and behavior control devices to develop psychological techniques that could be used against enemy agents.

The dilemma posed by the operation of an agency for espionage and covert activities in a country governed by the rule of law was dramatically illustrated by the case of Richard Helms, former director of the CIA. The case grew out of Helms' testimony in 1973 before a Senate committee looking into the CIA's involvement in Chilean domestic politics. Helms told the committee that the CIA had not sought to block the election of Chilean President Salvatore Allende, when in fact, it was later disclosed, the agency had given money to Allende's opponents.

The Justice Department was reluctant to punish Helms severely because of his claim that his testimony was dictated by the need to protect national security. Under a compromise agreement reached after plea bargaining, Helms was permitted on November 4 to plead no contest to two misdemeanor charges that he had failed to testify "fully, completely, and accurately" before a Senate committee. Federal District Judge Barrington D. Park accepted the plea and gave Helms a suspended sentence of two years in jail. But he fined him $2,000 and told him: "You now stand before this court in disgrace and shame."

Civil Rights. Battles over civil rights were waged in several arenas. The long struggle for school desegregation won another victory on June 27 when the Supreme Court ruled in a Dayton, Ohio, case that federal judges have the power to order citywide busing when the impact of school segregation had been citywide.

Efforts to make up for the harm done by previous segregation stirred increased debate. Attention focused on a suit brought before the Supreme Court by Allan Bakke, a white, 37-year-old former Marine, against the University of California at Davis. Bakke contended that he had been twice denied admission to the university's medical school because he was white, while less qualified members of minority groups had been admitted under a special admissions program for the "disadvantaged." In a "friend of the court" brief filed September 19 the Justice Department contended that professional schools should be free to give minority applicants special consideration, but stopped short of endorsing explicit racial quotas.

Supporters of a constitutional amendment granting equal rights to women were disappointed by the failure to get additional states to ratify the proposal. Only one state has ratified since March 1975 and three of the 35 states that have ratified have tried to rescind their action.

ROBERT SHOGAN
Washington Bureau, "Los Angeles Times"

—— **UNITED STATES · Information Highlights** ——

Official Name: United States of America.
Area: 3,615,123 square miles (9,363,169 km²).
Population (1977 est.): 216,700,000.
Chief Cities (1970 census): Washington, D. C., the capital, 756,510; New York, 7,895,563; Chicago, 3,-369,359; Los Angeles, 2,816,061; Philadelphia, 1,-950,098.
Government: *Head of state and government,* Jimmy Carter, president (took office Jan. 1977). *Legislature* —Congress: Senate and House of Representatives.
Monetary Unit: Dollar.
Manufacturing (major products): Motor vehicles, aircraft, ships and railroad equipment, industrial machinery, processed foods, chemicals, electrical equipment and supplies, fabricated metals.
Major Agricultural Products: Wheat, rye, corn, barley, oats, soybeans, tobacco, cotton, sorghum.

THE U.S. ECONOMY

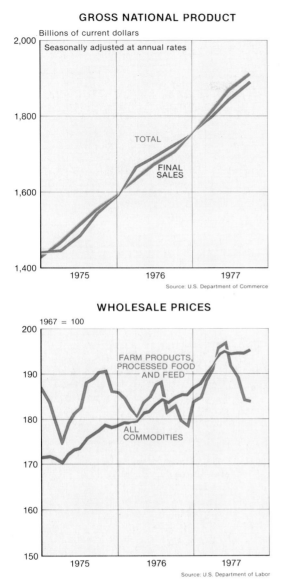

GROSS NATIONAL PRODUCT

Billions of current dollars

Seasonally adjusted at annual rates

TOTAL

FINAL SALES

2,000 — 1,800 — 1,600 — 1,400

1975   1976   1977

Source: U.S. Department of Commerce

WHOLESALE PRICES

1967 = 100

FARM PRODUCTS, PROCESSED FOOD AND FEED

ALL COMMODITIES

200 — 190 — 180 — 170 — 160 — 150

1975   1976   1977

Source: U.S. Department of Labor

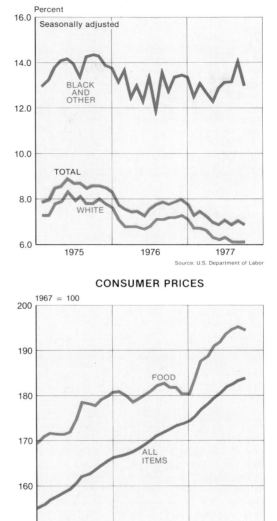

UNEMPLOYMENT RATE

Percent

Seasonally adjusted

BLACK AND OTHER

TOTAL

WHITE

16.0 — 14.0 — 12.0 — 10.0 — 8.0 — 6.0

1975   1976   1977

Source: U.S. Department of Labor

CONSUMER PRICES

1967 = 100

FOOD

ALL ITEMS

200 — 190 — 180 — 170 — 160 — 150

1975   1976   1977

Source: U.S. Department of Labor

THE ECONOMY

During 1977 the U. S. economy was characterized by a continuation of the expansion that had begun in the early months of 1975, and that was only briefly interrupted toward the end of 1976 and early 1977, in large part due to the devastating winter season. A steady flow of new orders to manufacturers sustained a relatively high level of industrial activity through most of the year so that corporate profits improved considerably.

As usually happens, consumers provided the major impetus to the economic advance, particularly as they continued to spend heavily for big-ticket items such as cars and houses. Although the employment situation improved somewhat, a steady rise in the nation's labor force kept the unemployment rate at levels generally considered unacceptable.

Some headway was made in the fight against inflation, but the basic forces responsible for the recent price spiral still appeared largely intact, contributing to lingering fears and uncertainties regarding the price situation in the years to come.

While business activity moved forward at a historically acceptable pace, some problem areas persisted in the economy. In addition to inflation and unemployment, less than desirable business spending for expansion of production facilities and a record U. S. trade deficit that contributed to the deterioration of the dollar in international markets in 1977 were the major blurred spots in an otherwise cheerful economic picture.

John G. Heimann officially takes over as comptroller of the currency (administrator of national banks). Treasury Secretary W. Michael Blumenthal administers the oath; Mrs. Heimann holds the Bible.

UPI

The Nation's Total Output. The accelerating pace of the business advance in the first quarter of 1977 was reflected in the robust growth of the Gross National Product (GNP), and total output passed the $1.9 trillion mark in the third quarter. In real terms, the GNP rose to more than $1.3 trillion in the first quarter of 1977, equal to an annual rate of over 7%. During the second quarter the increase in the GNP moderated a bit to just over 6% and was further diminished to a shade below 5% in the third period. The degree of slowdown in the pace of growth, however, turned out to have been much less severe than had been previously feared by many.

Improved consumer attitudes were evident throughout most of the year as individuals loosened their purse strings and showed a willingness to assume still heavier debt burdens, as well as to dip into their savings, in order to maintain a high level of expenditures. Total spending during the first three quarters of 1977 rose by nearly 11% from 1976, surpassing the $1.2 trillion mark for the first time. Outlays for durables, nondurables, and services all rose at respectable rates.

Gross private domestic investment contributed heavily to the economic upturn, rising by more than 21% in the first three quarters of the year when compared with a year earlier. But much of the rise was due to the generally bright residential housing picture, and outlays for non-farm residential housing units surged by nearly 36%. Business outlays for plant and equipment continued to disappoint, although the rate of advance, at nearly 14% in the first three quarters of 1977 versus the like 1976 period, was considerably above that of 1976. Indications were that outlays might firm up further in 1978 and sustain the economic expansion.

The ongoing business recovery was spurred by heavy business investment in inventories, and stocks were built up at an increasingly rapid pace as the year wore on.

Toward the end of 1977 it began to be evident that the federal spending shortfalls experienced during the year would soon end. In the first quarter of the year federal outlays rose by some 11% over the comparable 1976 period, about twice the rate of increase during all of 1976. At the same time, state and local expenditures advanced by over 7%, about the same as they had done the year before.

In the closing months of the year federal spending began to run ahead of earlier projections and, with expectations for a relatively high level of state and local spending, it became clear that overall government spending would continue as one basic source of stimulation in the economy.

Industrial Activity. Industrial production continued along a generally rising path and any interruptions that occurred in this trend were minor. As measured by the Federal Reserve Board's index, output rose over 5% between January and October of 1977 to 139.1 (FRB index, 1967 = 100), and stood nearly 7% above the year-earlier level. Generally brisk activity throughout a broad spectrum of U. S. industry contributed to the advance, but production of consumer durables and business equipment led the advance. The former, sparked by robust automobile demand, was nearly 14% higher in October when compared with the year-earlier month and business equipment output was nearly 12% higher.

During the year the output of finished and intermediate products ran comfortably ahead of materials production, suggesting that a relatively favorable balance in the production stream was in effect as demands were satisfied and no serious inventory gluts occurred.

The Employment Scene. In spite of generally firm business activity throughout the year, the problem of high unemployment again proved sticky. Although many new jobs were created because of improved business conditions, the number of people who entered the labor market as active job seekers also increased. As a result the unemployment rate was not dented sufficiently, making this one of the areas of greater concern in the economy.

The total number of unemployed as a percent of the civilian labor force was still hovering dangerously close to the 7% area through the third quarter. That is not to say that progress did not occur. In October the jobless rate at 6.9% was down from a 1977 high of 7.5% in February and a strong burst of employment late in the year reduced the December rate to 6.4%.

Price Developments. The fact that the price spiral became subdued at a time when business activity was expanding was a favorable development. As measured by the government's implicit price deflator, which uses 1972 as the base year, the increase in prices diminished to an annual rate of less than 5% in the third quarter of 1977, compared with a 6% average during the first half, 5.3% in 1976, and close to 10% in the two years previous. The Labor Department's index of consumer prices (1967 = 100) tells much the same story. In October the index was some 7% above the year-earlier month, but most of the increase took place in the earlier months of the year. Between July and October prices rose at an annual rate of only 4% or so.

The rise in wholesale prices already began to slow markedly before midyear, dropping to an annual increase of less than 2% between May and November 1977. However, the small advance here was largely due to falling food prices, which plunged at a yearly pace of more than 10%.

Industrial commodity prices—a more meaningful indicator of basic inflationary pressures in the economy because they are prone to be more permanent, once enacted, and less susceptible to supply/demand-induced gyrations—continued to advance at more than a 5% rate. While some relief in this area was noted toward the end of the year, the evidence that inflationary pressures were finally subsiding in a more fundamental sense was far from conclusive.

In addition, inflation worries were kept alive by the realization that both fiscal and Federal Reserve monetary policies continued to be basically stimulative.

Stocks and Bonds. The financial markets were largely characterized by the sensitive manner in which they reacted to technical and fundamental developments. Stock prices began a downspin at the year's beginning that persisted through the end of February. The decline moderated thereafter, and bottomed out in early June, at which time a modest advance began that lasted through the closing weeks of July. Between July and October a sharp drop carried equity prices below the previous low for the year. By November, prices were again rising.

The credit markets experienced their share of gyrations, but for the year as a whole a rather mixed pattern emerged. Short-term interest rates proceeded in a sharp uptrend through most of the year, with 90-day Treasury bill rates, for example, rising by as much as 180 basis points. Longer-term yields, on the other hand, traced a relatively flat trend for most of 1977, and began to show signs of increasing only in the latter months of the year. Large short-term credit demands by consumers and business were an important factor in the markets.

The credit markets were influenced by the attempts of the Federal Reserve to limit money-supply growth within what it considered acceptable limits and by the continued heavy borrowing by the federal and state and local governments. Corporate activity in the credit markets was below that of 1976, but was still too large to be classified as light. The persistence of the business recovery as the year came to a close strengthened prospects for relatively heavy credit demands during 1978, and further tightening efforts by the central bank.

The Administration's Energy Program. After Carter's campaign pledges of 1976 to enact serious, viable energy policies for the nation, 1977 witnessed the beginning of executive-legislative struggles to create such a program. The presidential transition early in the year slowed formulation of a definite proposal to Congress until April.

The president designated James R. Schlesinger as the secretary of the new Department of Energy, and Congress confirmed his nomination. Schlesinger spent the rest of the year lobbying for the administration's proposal. The House of Representatives passed the proposal relatively intact. However, the Senate version was considerably different and by year-end a compromise energy policy was still being developed.

The importance of the plan to administer energy and the nation's industrial dependence on sustained availability of affordable fuel supplies cannot be overemphasized. In recognition of this fact, all sectors of the economy reacted in response to the various proposals. Uncertainty in the business community and in the markets for private capital was obvious, even though the nation's economy remained strong. The future impact of energy regulation on supply, profitability, and growth rates remained clear in the minds of consumers and business planners alike. Appropriately, the president made this proposal the primary executive effort during his first year in office and based most subsequent proposals on the importance of enacting an effective energy policy.

The Outlook. Business closed 1977 on an optimistic note and robust attitudes were largely dominant. Although many problems remained unresolved, the hope was that at least some of them would be moved closer to resolution in 1978. Much would depend, of course, on the final shape of the energy and tax programs.

See also BANKING; CONSUMERISM; ENERGY; INTERNATIONAL TRADE AND FINANCE; TAXATION.

JACKSON PHILLIPS, *Executive Vice President Moody's Investors Service, Inc.*

FOREIGN AFFAIRS

In its first year, the Carter administration attempted to change both American foreign policy and procedure. Characterized by a sense of motion, self-confidence, and optimism, if not impatience, the new administration paid less tribute to national interest and propagated the virtues of accommodation, open diplomacy, and moral principles as a substitute for what it called *Realpolitik*.

From the very outset, emissaries were dispatched in many directions, and attention was addressed simultaneously to an array of international problems. Most major functional and regional issues antedated the new administration, however, so that innovation was more concerned with priorities, emphasis, tempo, and style.

The president assumed personal control but worked closely with an inner team consisting of Vice President Walter Mondale, National Security Adviser Zbigniew Brzezinski, and Secretary of State Cyrus Vance—his "Friday Breakfast Club"—supported by a secondary foursome prised of Defense Secretary Harold Brown, Arms Control Director Paul Warnke, CIA Director Stansfield Turner, and Ambassador Andrew Young.

General Policy. President Carter defined American goals as striving for peace, controlling the weaponry of war, building a more cooperative and just international economic system, and advancing the cause of human rights, dignity, and well-being of all people.

In a major foreign-policy address in May, he said that the world today is "a new world that calls for a new American foreign policy." He declared that the U. S. can have a policy that is democratic, is based on fundamental values, uses power and influence for humane purposes, and "is designed to serve mankind." It can also have a foreign policy "that the American people both support and . . . know about and understand," he said.

Spelling out his objectives in the UN General Assembly, the president said: "Unless we establish a code of international behavior in which the resort to violence becomes increasingly irrelevant to the pursuit of national interests, we will crush the world's dreams for human development and the full flowering of human freedom." Concluding, he added, "We can see a world at peace. We can work for a world without want. We can build a global community dedicated to these purposes and to human dignity." Coalescing the vision, creativity, and ideas of many nations, he said, is the responsibility not only of the United States but of the entire world.

Conduct of Diplomacy. With the addition of Djibouti (formerly Afars and Issas), the community of nations increased to 157. The United States accredited 141 diplomatic missions, including the special missions to China and Cuba,

and maintained some 127 consular offices.

President Carter went to Europe in May to address the NATO Council and meet with the leaders of the Western industrialized powers. He embarked on his second trip abroad, visiting seven countries in Europe, Asia, and Africa, after Christmas. Other summiteers included Vice President Mondale (2 trips), Ambassador Young (7 trips), and the First Lady (who visited 7 Latin American countries). Secretary Vance made 10 trips abroad, primarily to negotiate with the Soviet government on disarmament, deal with the Middle East crisis, and consult with China. The president received approximately 50 foreign leaders in Washington.

The United States is a member of most of the 100 multipartite intergovernmental organizations and during 1977 sent delegations to 900 sessions of these agencies and international conferences. At the beginning of the year, the country was party to some 6,240 treaties and agreements, and during 1977 the government signed approximately 20 new treaties and nearly 500 executive agreements.

Human Rights. President Carter championed human rights as the hallmark of American foreign relations. Policy statements were replete with references to human dignity, fundamental freedoms, mistreatment of peoples, and shared values. The president recommended strengthening of UN and inter-American human rights machinery. He signed the Inter-American Convention on Human Rights, and decided to submit the UN Human Rights Covenants (1966) to the Senate for approval. The United States also withheld assistance from states that failed to meet legislated human rights standards, and expanded its refugee and asylum programs.

The purposes of improving human rights throughout the world were clear, but implementation of policy was difficult and conflicted with the basic principle of nonintervention. Results, therefore, were mixed. Whereas oppressed peoples welcomed the initiative, U. S. relations with their governments were strained. The net result was a combination of articulated goals, raised expectations, and application primarily in relations with normally friendly states or those in which little change could be expected.

Arms Proliferation and Control. President Carter espoused severe restrictions or even a freeze on new generations of nuclear weapons, substantial reduction of strategic arms, exploration of the possibility of total cessation of nuclear testing, and negotiation of arrangements to halt nuclear proliferation.

The Strategic Arms Limitation Talks (SALT) with the Soviet government came to a standstill because of weaponry advances on both sides. The United States also miscalculated Soviet reaction to the human rights campaign and to sweeping arms reduction proposals publicized without prior consultation with the Soviets. Discussions proceeded at three levels—ministerial meetings,

President Carter and aide Zbigniew Brzezinski exchanged ideas with the USSR through Ambassador Anatoli Dobrynin.

Geneva talks, and ambassadorial exchanges. Portions of SALT I (1972) expired in October, and negotiations accelerated in the autumn. New treaties restricting underground nuclear tests and peaceful nuclear explosions (in both cases limiting them to 150 kilotons) were signed to supplement the 1963 Limited Test Ban Treaty and to curb nuclear arms proliferation.

Addressing the UN in October, the president declared the United States willing to reduce nuclear weapons, on a reciprocal basis, by 10, 20, or even 50%. "Then we will work for further reductions to a world truly free of nuclear weapons." Negotiations were held with the USSR and the United Kingdom for a comprehensive ban on nuclear explosions, and a move was initiated to outlaw chemical weapons.

To cope with nuclear proliferation, the United States reemphasized the need for agreement to prevent the export of nuclear fuel and technology that may be used to produce weapons. "By genuine cooperation," the president said, "we can make certain that this terrible club expands no further." He signed Protocol I to the Treaty of Tlatelolco (1967)—establishing a Latin American nuclear-free zone.

North-South Dialogue, Trade, and Aid. Concluding 18 months of discussion, the Conference on International Economic Cooperation (CIEC), in a joint communiqué of the 27 participating countries reported general agreement on a number of issues in the fields of energy, raw materials, development, and financial resources. These negotiations transmuted the confrontation of previous years into a more useful discussion within a single forum.

Subsequent negotiations were transferred to several international agencies, such as the UN Conference on Trade and Development (UNCTAD) for a common fund to support commodity agreements; the International Monetary Fund and International Bank for development assistance, supplementary credit facilities, and

general capital expansion; and other agencies for multilateral trade and agricultural assistance.

To counter erosion of consensus for a more open international trading system, President Carter rejected pressures for restrictive quotas on certain imports and opted rather to negotiate marketing agreements and to provide aid to American producers. These actions enabled him to assume leadership at the London summit in May in support of a free world trading system. Supplementing its bilateral assistance programs, the United States also made a substantial contribution to the International Development Association for soft loans to the poorest countries, and supported replenishment of the International Finance Corporation to encourage private contributions to the development process.

United Nations System. The Carter administration adopted a somewhat more conciliatory tone and posture in the UN. But it expressed concern over such growing problems as politicization of debate, creeping diffusion of power, structural and functional growth and management complexity, and membership proliferation.

The United States voted for the admission of Vietnam and Djibouti, raising UN membership to 149. It also increased its support of the UN Development Program (UNDP) and joined in establishing an International Fund for Agricultural Development. The country has been active in all of the UN specialized agencies, contributing approximately $400 to $500 million annually to their budgets (about 25%).

However, because of certain irresponsible actions in UNESCO (UN Educational, Scientific, and Cultural Organization), the U. S. continued to withhold a portion of its contributions, and following the required two-year notice, in November terminated its membership in the International Labor Organization.

Terrorism and Hijacking. International terrorism, involving more than 200 incidents per year, has become a political weapon, not only of terrorists but also of the countries that spawn them or give them sanctuary. In the United States, the Office of Combating Terrorism monitors the problem. Methods devised to cope with it include extensive intelligence surveillance, physical security of U. S. officials and installations, and planned crisis-management procedures.

The United States also cooperated with other governments in various ways—negotiating three hijacking conventions (adhered to by 70 countries), inducing the International Civil Aviation Organization to adopt technical security standards to prevent aviation crimes, negotiating separate conventions to prevent and punish crimes against internationally protected persons such as diplomats, and negotiating direct bilateral arrangements to control or discourage terrorist activities.

Law of the Sea. The United States participated actively in the 6th session of the UN Law of the Sea Conference. Meeting in New York, it produced an "Informal Composite Negotiating Text" of a comprehensive treaty to govern the use of the oceans and their resources, consisting of more than 300 articles and 7 annexes.

Broad agreement has been reached on a 12-mile territorial sea, transit through straits, and the rights of coastal states to resources in a 200-mile exclusive economic zone. Some progress was made on issues relating to international security and freedom of navigation in the economic zone. Less success was achieved on the international regime to administer deep seabed mining. The United States held the proposals on the seabed to be unacceptable and expressed objection to the way they were prepared. Other unsettled issues of concern to the United States include jurisdiction and research in the economic zone.

Western Hemisphere. President Carter declared the inter-American challenge to be not

reaffirmation of the principles of the Organization of American States (OAS) Charter, "but to find ways to make them a reality." The United States wants to reform the OAS to render it more dynamic and effective—by streamlining structure, employing more informal consultation, and changing the budgetary system to reduce the U. S. contribution from 66 to 49%. Diplomatic relations with Cuba, severed in 1961, were resumed on September 1 by the exchange of "interest sections" and consular officers.

After 13 years of negotiation, the United States in September signed a new canal treaty with Panama. It provides for U. S. operation of the Panama Canal to the end of 1999, the immediate termination of the Canal Zone, a managed phasing down of U. S. employees, and compensation to Panama amounting to an estimated $50 million per year. A second treaty, also open to accession by other countries, provides for the permanent neutralization of the canal. President Carter and the Panamanian chief executive met in Washington and issued a statement on the right of the United States to intervene to guarantee canal security. The Panamanian people approved the treaty in a plebiscite by a 2–1 margin. Considerable opposition to the treaty emerged in the United States; the Senate had not approved it by year-end.

Europe. In May, President Carter assured NATO allies that the North Atlantic alliance remains the heart of U. S. European policy. Supplementing collective deterrent strength, he said, a long-term defense program needs to be established, and cooperation in development and procurement of equipment must be improved. The president joined the British, French, and West German leaders in reaffirming support for free Berlin.

Although the new administration revived the term "détente," U. S.-Soviet relations made few major advances. Under the 1975 Helsinki agree-

No longer opposed to Vietnamese membership in the UN, the United States in May opened negotiations with Vietnam in Paris on the eventual normalization of relations between the two countries.

UPI

Secretary of State Cyrus Vance met with Chairman Hua Kuo-feng in Peking in August. Deputy Premier Teng Hsiao-p'ing termed the visit a setback for Sino-U. S. relations.

ment on Security and Cooperation in Europe, the United States attacked the East European countries for dereliction with regard to human rights, notification of Warsaw Pact maneuvers, economic reporting ("Basket 2"), and cooperation for the freer flow of people and information ("Basket 3").

Mideast and Africa. The United States exerted major effort to restore momentum to the stalled Kissinger diplomacy in the Middle East, to unfreeze the positions of the Arab and Israeli governments, and coax them to the Geneva conference table. Although the president initially insisted on "substantial" accommodation before convening the conference, this position was moderated. Most of the year was devoted to negotiating on substantive and procedural matters.

The central issues remained unchanged— Arab acceptance of Israel as an independent country, secure and acceptable borders, disposition of the territories occupied in 1967, the fate of the Palestinians, and their role in negotiations. In Washington, the president met with the leaders of Egypt, Jordan, Saudi Arabia, Syria, and Israel, and Secretary Vance conferred with them in their capitals. The new administration reiterated U. S. commitment to the security of Israel, maintaining that a peace settlement cannot be imposed from the outside.

In southern Africa, the United States continued to support a negotiated arrangement for an independent Namibia (South West Africa) without Cuban or other foreign intervention. It also continued to work closely with the British on a negotiable formula for resolving the conflict in Rhodesia. But joint proposals for transition from white to black majority rule in 1978, with a British administrator supervising free elections and an interim UN security force, were declared unacceptable by Rhodesia.

South Africa remains ostracized by the UN and much of the world community. The United States has voluntarily banned arms sales to the country since 1963. Responding to a government crackdown on black dissident leaders, the UN Security Council in November unanimously voted a mandatory global arms and military technology embargo of South Africa. The UN resolution constituted a compromise between comprehensive economic sanctions and a more limited arms embargo supported by the United States and other Western powers.

Asia. In June, Secretary Vance announced that "the United States is and will remain an Asian and Pacific power" and that "constructive dialogue" with the People's Republic of China is continuing. The United States, under the Shanghai agreement of 1972, is seeking to move toward full normalization of relations, without jeopardizing the security of the people of Taiwan. The United States also reiterated existing policies of preserving a balanced and flexible military posture in the Western Pacific. It declared that mutual security treaties with Japan, South Korea, the Philippines, and other allies were a cornerstone of peace in the area, and proposed normalizing relations with Vietnam.

The United States announced its decision to withdraw its 33,000 ground troops, on a phased basis, from Korea by 1982, while retaining its naval, air, and other supportive forces intact and assisting Korea to increase its defense capability. By agreement with other members, the moribund Southeast Asia Treaty Organization (SEATO) was disestablished on June 30, although the Southeast Asia Collective Defense Treaty (Manila Pact) of 1954 remained in effect. Meanwhile, the United States worked to strengthen economic ties with members of ASEAN (Association of Southeast Asian Nations). The Soviet Union agreed with the United States in October to freeze their military positions at existing levels in the Indian Ocean as a first step toward removing all outside forces from the area.

ELMER PLISCHKE, *University of Maryland*

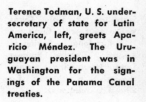

Terence Todman, U. S. under-secretary of state for Latin America, left, greets Aparicio Méndez. The Uruguayan president was in Washington for the signings of the Panama Canal treaties.

UPI

URUGUAY

Continuing political repression and economic crisis marked 1977 in Uruguay. Both were complicated by tensions in foreign relations.

Repressive Measures. The independence of the judiciary was destroyed on July 1, when President Aparicio Méndez signed Institutional Act No. 8. The decree put appointments of all judges, previously named by the Supreme Court, in the hands of the president and the Council of State. It also put all judges "on probation" for four years. In August, the president announced that his successor would be elected in 1981. However, all leaders of existing political parties would be barred, and one candidate would be named by the Council of State.

Large numbers of political prisoners remained in jail. A petition to the Supreme Court by relatives of 5,000 of these went unanswered, and more prisoners were rounded up, including teachers, doctors, and union leaders. Protests, however, became outspoken. The Blanco and Colorado parties announced support for U. S. President Carter's human-rights policy, and Colorado leader Jorge Batlle urged the two major parties to "act together." Military opposition was shown by the April 20 decision of the Council of State to dismiss all officers whose ideas were not "coherent" with those of the military commanders.

Economy. The economic situation remained grave. In July, representatives of landholders announced that agriculture and grazing were "stagnant" and asked for government aid. It was denied. Inflation continued at a rate of 5–10% a month, while wage increases lagged behind. In September, the International Monetary Fund extended a $29-million loan.

Foreign Affairs. The bad human-rights situation created many foreign problems. In February, U. S. Secretary of State Cyrus Vance announced that aid to Uruguay would be severely curtailed for this reason, whereupon President Méndez withdrew all requests for U. S. aid. Robert White, U. S. ambassador to the Organization of American States (OAS) told a cultural meeting in Montevideo that culture could not flourish without the rights of association, freedom of expression, and protection against arbitrary arrest. He was denounced by Uruguayan officials.

The most serious international crisis occurred in July. The arrest of a reporter of the Mexican newspaper *Excelsior* brought protests from UN Secretary General Kurt Waldheim and OAS Secretary General Alejandro Orfila. When the government finally released the reporter, it promptly arrested another *Excelsior* representative; this time protests were ignored.

ROBERT J. ALEXANDER, *Rutgers University*

UTAH

Criminal justice and drought were major concerns in Utah during 1977.

Crime. Gary Mark Gilmore died before a firing squad at the Utah State Prison on Monday, Jan. 17, 1977, at 8:07 AM.

Thus the first execution in the United States in 10 years, and the first in Utah in nearly 17 years, took place amidst frantic efforts by opponents of capital punishment to stay the execution. Gary Gilmore had been convicted of the murder of Bernie Jenkins Bushnell of Provo.

The case had a bizarre ending. At the last minute (7 hours prior to the execution), a reprieve in the form of a temporary restraining order was issued by Chief Judge Willis W. Ritter of the U. S. District Court for Utah in response to a class action suit by the American Civil Liberties Union. Utah Attorney General

---

—— URUGUAY • Information Highlights ——

Official Name: Eastern Republic of Uruguay.
Location: Southeastern coast of South America.
Area: 68,536 square miles (177,508 km²).
Population (1977 est.): 2,800,000.
Chief City (1975 census): Montevideo, the capital, 1,230,000.
Government: *Head of state and government,* Aparicio Méndez, president (took office Sept. 1976). *Legislature*—General Assembly (suspended June 1973).
Monetary Unit: Peso (4.76 pesos equal U. S.$1, July 1977).
Manufacturing (major products): Meat products, textiles, construction and building materials, beverages, chemicals.
Major Agricultural Products: Wheat, corn, rice, livestock, wool.

UTAH • Information Highlights

Area: 84,916 square miles (219,932 km²).
Population (1976 est.): 1,228,000.
Chief Cities (1970 census): Salt Lake City, the capital, 175,885; Ogden, 69,478; Provo, 53,131.
Government (1977): *Chief Officers*—governor, Scott M. Matheson (D); secy. of state, David S. Monson (R). *Legislature*—Senate, 29 members; House of Representatives, 75 members.
Education (1976–77): *Enrollment*—public elementary schools, 168,428 pupils; public secondary, 146,043; nonpublic, 3,900; colleges and universities, 74,295 students. *Public school expenditures*, $484,543,000 ($1,168 per pupil).
State Finances (fiscal year 1976): *Revenues*, $1,118,-467,000; *expenditures*, $1,072,396,000.
Personal Income (1976): $6,570,000,000; per capita, $5,350.
Labor Force (July 1977): *Nonagricultural wage and salary earners*, 478,000; *unemployed*, 25,400 (4.7% of total force).

Robert B. Hansen immediately prepared an appeal, which was flown to Denver and delivered to the 10th Circuit Court of Appeals. The appellate court overruled Judge Ritter's order. The court's decision was delivered to the Utah State Prison at 7:42 AM, and the execution proceeded. All of this took place in the face of much publicized statements by Gilmore that he wanted to die. In fact, he twice attempted suicide after an earlier stay of execution.

The execution of Gilmore represented a defeat for those seeking to abolish capital punishment. Their attempts began when the U. S. Supreme Court ruled that death is not necessarily cruel and unusual punishment for murder.

A waitress wears a T-shirt carrying the new health warning required at Utah's liquor-selling establishments.

UPI

Drought. Utah was plagued by severe drought conditions in 1977—a result of the unusually dry winter of 1976–77. This focused everybody's attention on the problem of water scarcity, which must be faced by a population in a semi-arid region. The entire economy of the state is dependent upon adequate water supply.

A state water plan has been in existence since 1961 and is kept current by the Utah Division of Water Resources. The Central Utah Reclamation Project, which was designed to allow the state to use its entitlement to water from the Colorado River system, came under attack by President Jimmy Carter earlier in the year. But strong protests from Gov. Scott Matheson and the Utah congressional delegation resulted in reversal of President Carter's position.

It is clear, however, that even with this project, the supply of water for use in Utah is limited. Another dry winter, or a succession of dry winters, could turn this year's problem into a critical situation, if not an outright disaster.

LORENZO K. KIMBALL, *University of Utah*

VENEZUELA

Referred to as a "haven of democratic safety in our times" by *Hemisphérica,* and praised by Andrew Young, U. S. ambassador to the United Nations, as a real democracy, Venezuela in 1977 was in fact one of two surviving democratic systems in South America.

Domestic Politics. Party rivalry intensified as the parties began to choose their nominees for the presidential election in December 1978. Acción Democrática, the majority party of the president, became the first Venezuelan party ever to hold a direct primary. Of those who voted, 65% backed Luis Pinerua Ordaz, who was supported by former President Betancourt. He is favored to win the presidency in 1978.

President Carlos Andrés Pérez' prestige was damaged when his party failed to nominate his choice. The president, in trouble with his party for other reasons, aroused opposition when he let it be known he expected to be active in party politics after his term expires. Two left-wing parties nominated candidates, as did the Communist party. One independent is in the race.

In an unusual move, the cabinet resigned en masse in January, thus giving the president a free hand to reorganize his administration and to incorporate the five new ministries authorized by Congress. There are now 22 portfolios. Another cabinet reshuffling took place seven months later.

Auditor's Report. The auditor general, in his annual message to Congress in April, criticized the government for corruption and inefficiency and accused it of poor management, inadequate planning, fiscal irregularities, and delays in accounting. In July the president responded by announcing a series of austerity measures that he said were necessary if the government was to meet the health, housing, and employment needs of a population of 16 million in 1985. His measures were denounced by Fedecameras, the powerful business organization, which objected most to his proposal to limit industrial profits to 30% of a company's investment. Early in the year the president served notice that he would push a comprehensive tax reform bill through Congress.

Food Shortages. Drought in some areas and too much rain in others caused a drop in agricultural production, resulting in food shortages in most urban areas. Housewives demonstrated in protest against empty supermarkets. The government began massive importation of food.

Crime. The government blamed a rise in violence and kidnapping and guerrilla activity in rural areas on ordinary criminal elements and not on a resurgent guerrilla movement.

Economic Developments. Venezuela's per capita income in 1976 was $2,500, the highest in Latin America. The gross national product grew by 11% in 1976. Monetary reserves in April 1977 were $8.5 billion and the unit of currency, the bolivar, has become one of the hard currencies of the world. The 1977 budget was set at $8.33 billion (U.S.), up from $7.7 billion in 1976.

In spite of its vast revenues from oil, the government ended 1976 with a budget deficit of $1.7 billion. Inflation and uncontrolled government were cited as reasons. In September, the price of Venezuelan crude oil was raised by 16 cents a barrel. The government set up a $69.7 million credit line to help its Latin neighbors meet OPEC prices. The government called its nationalized oil industry a "successful business" and said it would invest $800 million in the industry in 1977. It will also spend $1 billion over the next 15 years to construct 2,500 miles (4,000 km) of railroads.

Foreign Affairs. President Pérez was one of seven Latin presidents to sign a letter to President Carter supporting Panama's claims to its territory. The Venezuelan president paid a state visit to Washington in late June and made a speech denouncing military dictatorships in Latin America. He attended the September signing of the Panama Canal treaties in Washington along with 26 other heads of state. In December 1976 he visited eight European countries and in May seven oil-producing countries. The latter was an unsuccessful bid to resolve oil price disputes. In June he was host to Mrs. Carter. He welcomed Argentine President Jorge Videla to Caracas in May. This visit was denounced by students and journalists because of human rights violations in Argentina.

President Pérez was named in the U.S. press as one of many heads of state who had received CIA money. President Carter apologized for the allegation. The dispute with Colombia over ownership of waters in the Gulf of Venezuela is stalemated because Venezuelan political parties refuse to back the government's proposals. The president said he will not negotiate further until he has their support.

LEO B. LOTT, *University of Montana*

------ **VENEZUELA · Information Highlights** ------

Official Name: Republic of Venezuela.
Location: Northwestern South America.
Area: 352,143 square miles (912,050 km²).
Population (1977 est.): 12,700,000.
Chief Cities (1974): Caracas, the capital, 2,400,000; Maracaibo, 900,000; Barquisimeto, 350,000.
Government: *Head of state and government,* Carlos Andrés Pérez, president (took office March 1974). *Legislature*—Congress: Senate and Chamber of Deputies.
Monetary Unit: Bolivar (4.29 bolivares equal U.S.$1, Aug. 1977).
Manufacturing (major products): Processed foods, paper and paperboard, petroleum products, beverages, metal products, furniture, clothing.
Major Agricultural Products: Coffee, cacao, bananas, sugarcane, cotton, rice, corn, dairy products.

UPI

Venezuela's First Lady, left, Spain's King Juan Carlos, President Carlos Andrés Pérez, and Queen Sofia listen to their national anthems at Bolivar Plaza, Caracas. The royal couple visited Venezuela and five Central American nations to strengthen Spain's ties in the area.

VERMONT

Vermont celebrated the bicentennial of its Declaration of Independence from New York and Great Britain and the adoption of its first constitution in 1977. Special license plates were authorized to commemorate the 14 years, 1777–1791, during which Vermont was an independent republic.

Administration. Gov. Richard A. Snelling (R) set a business-like tone, stressing cost-cutting, tight executive authority, and economic development in preference to the state's traditional emphasis on environmental controls. Chittenden County (Burlington) was one of the fastest growing areas in the nation, and prosperity lifted state tax receipts; the treasury registered a surplus of $21 million for fiscal 1976. Despite its substantial growth, Vermont remained one of only two states with no city large enough to establish a Standard Metropolitan Statistical Area.

The relationship between state and church was strained when Sister Elizabeth Candon, a Democrat and a Catholic nun appointed human services secretary by Gov. Snelling, was criticized by the bishop of the Burlington Diocese for her support of state funding of abortions. The bishop strongly implied Sister Elizabeth would be disciplined by the church if that support continued. Gov. Snelling intervened to secure a truce.

Legislature. The legislature startled the Vermont public in January by resolving the undecided lieutenant-governor election in favor of second-ranking T. Garry Buckley (R), instead of front-runner John Alden (D).

The legislature enacted a ban on phosphate detergents, a requirement for legislative approval of any nuclear-waste storage, and a state authority to reappraise property tax, combined with a land-use tax abatement program. Other significant measures were the repeal of the sales tax on home-heating fuel and the enactment of a state lottery.

Education. News of higher education continued to headline the resignation and appoint-

ment of presidents. The chancellor of the Vermont State Colleges resigned after serving for little more than a year, and a new president for Goddard College was appointed amid controversy over the selection process.

Secondary and elementary educators expressed doubts about the effectiveness of the federal special education program. The Miller formula for apportioning state aid to education, which is based on community property, was also attacked. In a number of instances it was discarded, and funds were allocated on a straight per pupil basis.

SAMUEL B. HAND *and* ROBERT V. DANIELS
University of Vermont

VIETNAM

Vietnam's first year as a reunited country was a generally successful one diplomatically —with its government admitted to the United Nations and Western-supported international lending agencies beginning to aid it. But it was a difficult year economically with a smaller rice harvest than ordinarily—for the third straight year.

Politics. The northern Communists' strategy for the domination of the formerly independent south became more apparent during the year. Despite the formal reunification of the former North and South Vietnam in July 1976, the Hanoi-based government continued to treat the south as a virtually conquered country. This was partly accomplished by moving in northerners and moving out southerners from the main cities. Vietnamese from the southern part of the country continued to be given only token participation in the post-reunification central government, while hitherto southern political organization passed out of existence. The National Libera-

U. S. State Department and Vietnam officials agree on the release of 22 Americans killed in the Vietnam war.

UPI

VERMONT • Information Highlights

Area: 9,609 square miles (24,887 km²).
Population (1976 est.): 476,000.
Chief Cities (1970 census): Montpelier, the capital, 8,609; Burlington, 38,633; Rutland, 19,293; Bennington, 14,586.
Government (1977): *Chief Officers*—governor, Richard A. Snelling (R); lt. gov., T. Garry Buckley (R). General Assembly—Senate, 30 members; House of Representatives, 150 members.
Education (1976–77): *Enrollment*—public elementary schools, 62,330 pupils; public secondary, 42,026; nonpublic, 9,800; colleges and universities, 27,977 students. *Public school expenditures,* $165,707,000 ($1,390 per pupil).
State Finances (fiscal year 1976): *Revenues,* $537,515,000; *expenditures,* $530,955,000.
Personal Income (1976): $2,577,000,000; per capita, $5,411.
Labor Force (July 1977): *Nonagricultural wage and salary earners,* 177,300; *unemployed,* 15,200 (6.8% of total force).

Foreign Minister Nguyen Duy Trinh represents the new UN member, Vietnam, at the General Assembly opening in September.

UPI

tion Front, spearhead of the opposition to the U. S.-aided Thieu regime in the 1960's, was formally terminated in 1977. Tens of thousands of northerners had been moved to the south—as school teachers, security chiefs, and tax collectors, and other functionaries. More than 100,000 former supporters of the former anti-Communist southern regime were still reportedly detained in "re-education centers," many of them in the north.

Some 700,000 former inhabitants of Ho Chi Minh City, the renamed Saigon, had been evacuated to "new economic zones"—designed to boost agricultural production as well as to break up the onetime Saigon middle class. According to the Hanoi regime itself, another 700,000 were still to be moved out of the city. This caused much fear and discontent.

The reunification of the country would not be complete, according to the central government, until the full "socialist transformation" of the south—which one official predicted would be accomplished by 1980. According to the government's announced plan, a total of 10 million northerners would also ultimately be "resettled" in the south, but no timetable for such a massive population movement was given.

Economy. For the third straight year the Vietnamese rice harvest fell short of expectations. Estimated production for the year was 12 million tons of rice paddy and one million tons of subsidiary crops—one million tons of rice less than 1976 and three million below the state target. More important, the 1977 rice crop was a full 20% below the usual level.

A devastating typhoon and drought (when there should have been rain)—combined with an unusually cold winter, questionable agricul-

tural policies, bad management thereof, and peasant resistance to the government's farm policy—were important factors in the rice and other commodity shortfall. The resulting food shortage necessitated smaller ration allocations. The basic rice allotment was cut 10% in the spring and the Vietnamese were required to take one third of their "rice ration" in wheat flour, sweet potatoes, and manioc (tapioca). The large-scale movement of rice north from the once rich southern rice basket also contributed to discontent in the south and the feeling of exploitation by the northerners. The monthly rice ration at year's-end was 28 to 46 pounds (12.7–19.9 kg) a month—the allotment varying with a person's work assignment.

As a result of the food shortage there was an increase in reported cases of malnutrition (although not of starvation) and a sharper work production decline due to reduced human energy levels. The country's modest amount of foreign exchange had to be used for food imports instead of tools and machinery.

VIETNAM · Information Highlights

Official Name: Socialist Republic of Vietnam.
Location: Southeast Asia.
Area: 128,402 square miles (332,560 km²).
Population (1977 est.): 47,300,000.
Chief Cities (1976 est.): Hanoi, the capital, 1,443,500; Ho Chi Minh City, 3,460,500; Haiphong, 1,191,000; Da Nang, 500,000.
Government: *Head of state,* Ton Duc Thang, president (took office 1969). *Head of government,* Pham Van Dong, premier (took office 1954). *First secretary of Communist Party,* Le Duan. *Legislature* (unicameral) —National Assembly.
Monetary Unit: Dong (2.42 dong equal U. S.$1, Nov. 1977).
Manufacturing (major products): Processed foods, cement, textiles, chemicals, rubber products.
Major Agricultural Products: Rice, sugarcane, tea, sweet potatoes, cassava, rubber, corn, fruits.

Foreign Affairs. A record 105 member governments cosponsored Vietnam's application to join the United Nations, which was successfully passed at the opening session of the 32nd General Assembly in September. Hanoi became the UN's 149th member capital.

No less important was acceptance of, and aid to, Vietnam on the part of key UN specialized agencies. In January, the International Monetary Fund also made its first loan ($35 million) to Hanoi to help cover an unexpected shortfall of foreign exchange to finance imports. The same month, the World Bank sent its first mission to Vietnam.

Vietnam was less successful, however, in pursuit of trade and aid relations with the United States. Hanoi made reconstruction assistance and a start of commercial ties (banned by the U. S. Congress) a precondition for the exchange of diplomatic representatives; Washington insisted that the establishment of embassies must precede economic cooperation. President Carter met briefly with Vietnam's ambassador to the UN in September, and indications were that differences between the two governments were lessening.

Hanoi's closest ally remained the USSR, but Vietnam also drew closer to neighboring Laos, pulling it more intimately into its orbit by major military, economic, and border pacts signed in July. Relations with China remained correct but cool, while there was actual fighting along Vietnam's border with fellow Indochinese Communist country Kampuchea (Cambodia). The Hanoi government pursued closer ties with the Western European countries—especially France. Premier Pham Van Dong visited France in April, his first trip to a Western land since the end of the Vietnam War.

See also ASIA.

RICHARD BUTWELL
State University of New York at Fredonia

VIRGIN ISLANDS, U. S.

On March 31, 1977, Virgin Islanders celebrated the 60th anniversary of the transfer of sovereignty from Denmark to the United States. Almost all observers would agree that while the association of the islands with the United States has had its difficult moments, the relationship has never been the cause of serious protestations. Even the sporadic acts of violence in recent years, particularly on the island of St. Croix, have been either personal or racial rather than directly political in nature. Two perhaps related events of 1977 highlighted the political aspect of the responsibility for the Virgin Islands that the United States undertook in 1917.

In April, a four-member UN commission visited the islands to hold public hearings and generally explore, by questioning officials, the nature of the political and social conditions of the islanders. The U. S. government presented

UPI
A black market still exists in Vietnam as the nation suffers a shortage of food and other consumer items.

no opposition to the visit and asked local authorities to give all cooperation necessary for the success of the probe. The commission, whose report was published later in the year, found that while they had expressed no sympathy for independence, the Virgin Islanders should have an opportunity to decide their political destiny in a referendum to be held at some time in the near future.

In May, the U. S. Congress enacted a law permitting the people of the Virgin Islands to draw up their own constitution. The islanders had prepared a constitution without authorization on two previous occasions, in 1964 and 1971, but the latter draft was rejected in a referendum in 1972. After some delay, elections were held in September to choose 60 delegates (from 173 candidates) to a constitutional convention in October. A shadow was cast over the process when the public failed to respond to the electoral call. The turnout of slightly less than 30% (6,914 out of 23,748) of the eligible voters lent support to the argument that the convention should have been postponed until after the 1978 election of a governor of the islands.

Convinced that Gov. Cyril King has very little chance of being reelected, various prominent politicians, including the incumbent resident commissioner for the Virgin Islands in Congress, have expressed interest in running for the post. Evidence of the governor's lack of political strength may be gleaned from the fact that the only member of his party elected to the 15-seat legislature quit the party (Independent Citizens' Movement) in 1977, choosing rather to identify himself as an independent.

THOMAS G. MATHEWS
University of Puerto Rico

Virginia's newly elected governor, John Dalton, and his wife, Eddy, arrive at election headquarters. The Republican defeated Henry Howell of Norfolk.

UPI

VIRGINIA

For Virginia in 1977 the most important news was the election of Lt. Gov. John Dalton to the governor's chair. Dalton defeated perennial candidate Henry Howell of Norfolk.

The Campaign. The two Democratic aspirants, Howell and Attorney General Andrew Miller, announced their candidacies early in 1976. Howell, making his third try for the office, received his customary support from labor unions, blacks, and teachers. He surprised the pundits by defeating Miller in the primary.

The Republicans nominated their statewide slate at a convention in Roanoke. Dalton, a resident of Radford, used to represent the mountain brand of moderate Virginia Republicanism. However, during the 1970's he veered to the right in an attempt to attract conservative Democrats into the party.

While maintaining his liberal gadfly image as advocate of the little man and consumer against the utility/corporate establishment, Howell moderated positions on certain issues, declining, for example, to push repeal of the state's right-to-work law. Dalton stressed fiscal responsibility and industrial progress. The clearest difference between the two candidates was probably Howell's advocacy of, and Dalton's opposition to, collective bargaining for state employees.

In the November election, voters elected Dalton over Howell by a 4 to 3 margin. Democrat Charles Robb, son-in-law of ex-President Lyndon Johnson, was elected lieutenant governor, and Republican State Senator Marshall Coleman was elected attorney general. In races for the House of Delegates, Republicans picked up five seats, making the breakdown there 75 Democrats, 22 Republicans, and three independents.

Voters approved bonds totaling $125 million for higher education, correctional and mental health institutions, parks, and ports. This was the second time in a decade that Virginia had resorted to bonded indebtedness.

Legislative Session. The state's stringent financial situation was revealed when the House of Delegates passed an appropriations bill leaving no room for pay increases for state employees. At Gov. Godwin's urging, the State Senate devised an involved scheme of transferring monies and expediting tax collections which made available funds for a 4.8% salary increment.

The Assembly also restored the death penalty for first-degree murder; allowed local governments to tax land on the basis of agricultural use rather than market value; extended the moratorium against city annexation suits for 10 years; reduced the average number of students in public school classrooms; began a program of statewide testing of students; made state loans available for installation of home solar energy devices; and gave the governor greater powers to appoint and remove members of state boards and commissions. The Assembly once again declined to ratify the proposed equal rights amendment.

Weather. The state endured bitter cold in January. Gov. Godwin rationed supplies of natural gas, which forced some manufacturing establishments to close temporarily. A combination of cold, snow, and limited fuel resulted in extensive closings of public schools. Conversely, the state suffered through an abnormally hot summer. Crops in all sections except the far southwest were severely damaged by drought.

WILLIAM LARSEN, *Radford College*

VIRGINIA · Information Highlights

Area: 40,817 square miles (105,716 km²).
Population (1976 est.): 5,032,000.
Chief Cities (1970 census): Richmond, the capital, 249,430; Norfolk, 307,951; Virginia Beach, 172,106.
Government (1977): *Chief Officers*—governor, Mills E. Godwin, Jr. (R); lt. gov., John N. Dalton (R). *General Assembly*—Senate, 40 members; House of Delegates, 100 members.
Education (1976–77): *Enrollment*—public elementary schools, 659,233 pupils; public secondary, 441,490; nonpublic, 89,800; colleges and universities, 220,231 students. *Public school expenditures,* $1,660,867,000 ($1,272 per pupil).
State Finances (fiscal year 1976): *Revenues,* $3,648,728,000; *expenditures,* $3,551,768,000.
Personal Income (1976): $31,908,000,000; per capita, $6,341.
Labor Force (July 1977): *Nonagricultural wage and salary earners,* 1,921,300; *unemployed,* 130,000 (5.4% of total force).

WASHINGTON

The state's longest legislative session in history—164 days—did not produce a hoped-for tax reform to be submitted to the voters, but it did enact bills to create a department of transportation, define basic education, establish limits on special levies for schools, and carry out pension reform.

The basic education issue arose in January, when Thurston County Superior Court Judge Robert Doran held that the practice of using special levies as a major money source for common schools was unconstitutional and directed the legislature to find a more equitable funding procedure. The state's constitution obligates the legislature to fund "basic education," but basic education was not defined. The new law outlines subjects to be taught and establishes teacher-pupil ratios.

Lawmakers had wrestled for years with pension reform proposals, but always met strong opposition from politically powerful public-employee unions. One part of the pension reform package raised the normal retirement age of teachers and most other public employees from 60 to 65; that of police and firefighters was raised from 50 to 58.

Voters' Preferences. In its waning moments, the legislature passed an increase of the variable-rate gasoline tax. Public reaction was immediate. Sufficient petition signatures were gathered to certify an initiative to roll back the tax. The law was abrogated in the November elections. Voters had also been hopeful the legislature would remove the sales tax on food, and when it did not, they promptly certified initiative to remove the tax. Gov. Dixy Lee Ray and legislators argued against the initiative, threatening cuts of state services. Nevertheless, the voters repealed the tax.

The solidly Democratic Seventh Congressional District chose Jack Cunningham (R) over Marvin Durning (D) in a by-election to replace former Rep. Brock Adams. The latter vacated the seat when he took office as U. S. secretary of transportation in January.

UPI

Dixy Lee Ray, former AEC chairman and one of the nation's two women governors, enters her office.

Battle Between Judges. The 1954 decision by U. S. District Judge George Boldt to grant treaty Indians the right to catch 50% of the salmon returning to traditional off-reservation Indian fishing grounds continued to cause trouble. Washington State Supreme Court Justice Charles T. Wright in October ordered the director of the Washington State Department of Fisheries to disobey a previous order by Judge Boldt to allocate the salmon between Indians and non-Indian commercial fishermen. Judge Wright ruled that the department could not discriminate between Indians and non-Indian fishermen in establishing regulations, even though it was acting under federal court orders. Judge Boldt then issued a restraining order, thus limiting the department's authority to make rules affecting Indian fishing rights.

Oil Shipments. The first tanker load of Alaskan North Slope oil was delivered to Cherry Point, near Bellingham, in August, but the event was overshadowed by the continuing controversy as to whether Alaskan oil should be delivered to Washington ports and transshipped across the state. The debate was partially settled when Congress amended and President Carter signed the Marine Mammal Protection Act to prohibit delivery of oil in Washington ports east of Port Angeles on the Strait of Juan de Fuca, thus keeping oil tankers out of Puget Sound.

WARREN W. ETCHESON
University of Washington

WASHINGTON · Information Highlights

Area: 68,192 square miles (176,617 km²).
Population (1976 est.): 3,612,000.
Chief Cities (1970 census): Olympia, the capital, 23,-111; Seattle, 530,831; Spokane, 170,516; Tacoma, 154,581.
Government (1977): *Chief Officers*—governor, Dixy Lee Ray (D); lt. gov., John A. Cherberg (D). *Legislature* —Senate, 49 members; House of Representatives, 98 members.
Education (1976–77): *Enrollment*—public elementary schools, 395,749 pupils; public secondary, 384,981; nonpublic, 44,500; colleges and universities, 173,165 students. *Public school expenditures,* $1,338,549,000 ($1,583 per pupil).
State Finances (fiscal year 1976): *Revenues,* $3,976,-086,000; *expenditures,* $3,638,718,000.
Personal Income (1976): $24,569,000,000; per capita, $6,802.
Labor Force (June 1977): *Nonagricultural wage and salary earners,* 1,343,500; *unemployed,* 119,400 (7.1% of total force).

WASHINGTON, D. C.

The U. S. capital provided the setting for the inauguration of President Jimmy Carter on January 20. The new president and his wife then set a historic precedent by walking the length of the parade route from the Capitol to the White House. The inaugural period included seven parties, fireworks, dances, recitals, exhibits, concerts, and prayer meetings.

Government. As the city entered its third year of home rule, Sterling Tucker was selected council chairman. Wilhelmina J. Rolark joined the council, along with five others reelected to second terms in November 1976.

Julius Hobson, Sr., 54, died of cancer in March. Among his many achievements as a local civil rights activist was the termination of the track system in the city's public schools. Hilda Mason, member of the Statehood party founded by Hobson, was appointed by the party leaders to fill his at-large council seat. Mason, a former school-board member, subsequently won the seat in a special election held to fill the remaining 18 months of the term.

Albert P. Russo was appointed director of the Department of Human Resources. He replaced Joseph P. Yeldell, who became general assistant to Mayor Walter Washington after being cleared of accusations of abusing the agency's leasing and hiring authority.

Crime. Twelve Hanafi Muslims (a mostly black Islamic sect), engaged in a holy war, invaded the international headquarters of B'nai B'rith, the Islamic Center, and the District Building on March 9. The takeover, led by Hamaas Abdul Khaalis, was an effort to compel federal authorities to turn over to him five Black Muslims convicted of murdering seven Hanafi women and children in 1973, and to stop the showing in America of a film about the Prophet Muhammad, considered by Hanafis to be sacrilegious. During the siege, which lasted more than 38 hours, some 150 people were held hostage and a 24-year-old radio reporter was fatally shot; a city councilman was among those seriously wounded and crippled at the three sites. All 12 invaders were convicted of conspiracy and multiple counts of armed kidnapping by a jury of ten women and two men. Three, including Khaalis, were also convicted of second-degree murder and assault with intent to kill. Khaalis, 55, was sentenced to serve 41–123 years in prison. Abdul Muzikar, 22, who fired the gun that killed one man and wounded two others, received a sentence of 78 years to life. Other sentences ranged from 24 to 132 years.

Education. The University of the District of Columbia, created by the merger of the city's three public schools, The Washington Technical Institute, D. C. Teachers College, and Federal City College, officially began operating on August 1. Lisle C. Carpenter, Jr., became the first president of the university. A 51-year-old lawyer, he had formerly presided over the Atlanta University Center, having had prior governmental and academic experience.

Transportation. The Metro subway became a genuine regional rapid-transit system on July 1, when the new Blue Line opened; it links 18 stations on a 12-mile (19-km) route between the National Airport in Virginia and the Robert F. Kennedy Stadium area in the District of Columbia. The system intersects the existing Red Line and now includes 24 stations. Riders must purchase a fare card, a magnetically encoded ticket, from a vending machine and feed it into computers at both ends of their train trip. The fare is based on the distance traveled.

MORRIS J. LEVITT, *Howard University*

UPI

In March, a group of Hanafi Muslim gunmen shot their way into the District Building (city hall), Washington, and held hostages there for two days.

WEST VIRGINIA

Cold weather, floods, and coal strikes monopolized West Virginians' attention in 1977.

Calamitous Winter. Record low temperatures, heavy snows, and energy shortages combined to make the winter months a time of hardship and concern. Thaw-fed reservoirs emptied more slowly than expected in March, briefly stilling fears of flooding. But on April 3–4, heavy rains brought the worst floods in history to 10 southern counties, as the Tug, New, Guyandotte, and Greenbrier rivers overflowed, destroying 2,000 housing units and seriously damaging 8,000 others. Almost 650 businesses were severely crippled or wiped out. As if that were not enough, frost persisted well into the second week in June, threatening the fruit and cattle industries.

The Legislature. Until early April, the legislature appeared to be headed for completion of business in regulation (60 days) time for the first time in many years. But it had to schedule a special session and leave the 1977–78 budget unfinished as flood relief suddenly became a major unanticipated priority.

The extraordinary session began early in May. Although only 11 days were actually needed, recesses extended it to June 22, when it finally adjourned. Emergency flood funds were an important portion of an $840-million approved budget, which was held under earlier billion-dollar estimates primarily because of an austerity demand by Gov. John D. (Jay) Rockefeller, IV. The first Democratic chief executive in eight years, Rockefeller faced unexpected reductions in revenues caused by the energy crunch and flood damage, as well as renewed wildcat strikes in the coal industry.

Overall, Rockefeller fared well with his program in the legislature, gaining approval of sweeping health and mine-safety reorganization bills, economic development plans, slightly tougher strip-mine reclamation measures, stronger laws providing access to public records, and an ambitious secondary-road improvement program.

UPI

Gov. Jay Rockefeller joins National Guardsmen in inspecting snowbound roads in Preston County, W. Va.

He lost his major campaign objective, repeal of the 3% sales tax on food; the legislature reasoned that the loss of revenue would be impractical in a year of no new taxes and of natural disasters.

Economic Outlook. The state's economic picture grew still dimmer toward the year's end. The announcement in October of projected layoffs and factory closings by the state's steel producers fed the gloom. By the end of the month, all "economic indicators" were turning downward. Subsequently, spokesmen for both bituminous coal mine owners and union workmen predicted a prolonged strike. The miners insisted on an unlimited right to strike, and the owners were equally firm in their opposition to wildcat shutdowns which have plagued the industry since the present pact was signed in 1974. Since no agreement had been reached by December 6, when a new contract was due to be signed, the United Mine Workers' traditional policy of "no contract, no work" was applied. The state girded for a long stoppage and the accompanying loss of revenue. The miners had walked out repeatedly during the year, protesting conditions of secondary roads they had to travel to get to the mines; local policies dealing with seniority and related issues; and especially their reduced hospital and medical benefits, caused at least in part by the decreased flow of money into welfare funds as a result of the strikes themselves.

DONOVAN H. BOND
West Virginia University

WEST VIRGINIA · Information Highlights

Area: 24,181 square miles (62,629 km²).

Population (1976 est.): 1,821,000.

Chief Cities (1970 census): Charleston, the capital, 71,505; Huntington, 74,315; Wheeling, 48,188.

Government (1976): *Chief Officers*—governor, John D. Rockefeller, IV (D); secy. of state, A. James Manchin (D). *Legislature*—Senate, 34 members; House of Delegates, 100 members.

Education (1976–77): *Enrollment*—public elementary schools, 233,880 pupils; public secondary, 170,891; nonpublic, 12,700; colleges and universities, 70,378 students. *Public school expenditures*, $561,918,000 ($1,127 per pupil).

State Finances (fiscal year 1976): *Revenues*, $1,771,748,000; *expenditures*, $1,726,426,000.

Personal Income (1976): $9,941,000,000; per capita, $5,460.

Labor Force (June 1977): *Nonagricultural wage and salary earners*, 618,700; *unemployed*, 40,500 (5.8% of total force).

WISCONSIN

A transition in the governor's office and major action in the legislature highlighted the year in Wisconsin.

Executive Transition. Although a Carter administration appointment had been rumored for Gov. Patrick J. Lucey, it came as somewhat of a surprise when he was named ambassador to Mexico. He had not had previous connections with the country or its people. But after he left in July, there was a scramble for state positions in the resultant new political alignment. During his six and a half years in office, Gov. Lucey's Democratic party had become dominant, and camps formed for a fierce primary in 1978. Lt. Gov. Martin Schreiber, who became acting governor, appeared to have the lead but was expected to face major opposition from David Carley, a businessman who had run for governor before. And Gov. Lucey's departure led some Republicans to believe that they would also have a chance. Although the election would not take place until November 1978, the campaign had begun.

Legislative Action. With a two-to-one majority in both houses, Democrats laid the groundwork for the 1978 campaign in two legislative sessions in 1977, most notably with a tax cut for the poor and the elderly. And the budget for the biennium did not call for any tax increases for anyone. There were other major legislative actions, however. A campaign finance law will offer state tax funds to help pay for election campaigns. A no-fault divorce law substitutes "irretrievable breakdown of marriage" for all existing grounds for divorce. The right to privacy was ensured in another law. Some municipal employees, including school teachers, were given a limited right to strike. On the final day of the fall session, however, legislators may have lost some of their voter support when they gave themselves a pay raise that will total 10.5% over two years.

Lake Pollution. For years, pollution of Lake Michigan has been a matter of debate among Wisconsin, Illinois, and Michigan. On July 29, a federal judge in Chicago, John F. Grady, issued an order that will have long-range effects not only on the lake but on metropolitan Milwaukee taxpayers. The judge ruled in favor of Illinois and Michigan, which contended that pollution from the Milwaukee metropolitan sewerage district was endangering the health of Illinois residents. Milwaukee officials estimated that the cost of building the necessary facilities to correct the problem would be $845 million. Acting Gov. Schreiber asked the federal government to help pay the cost.

Milwaukee Integration. While an appeal of a federal judge's desegregation order struggled through the courts, Milwaukee schools began their second year of integration under the order. In the fall, it was estimated that two thirds of the city's 152 schools had a black population of 25–50%, thus meeting the court's requirements. Nevertheless, it was clear that most of the integration was accomplished by the busing of blacks into white schools, and black groups tried to rally support for what they called two-way integration.

Economy. Wisconsin's farm income rose slightly in 1977 over the previous year. Total employment increased substantially, reaching well over two million persons. The greatest relative gain was in manufacturing employment. Unemployment fell from about 5.5% to 4.7%. The population continued its gradual growth, and there was a net in-migration into the state.

PAUL SALSINI, *"The Milwaukee Journal"*

Following victory in a recall election, Moria Krueger, 33, became the first woman judge in Dane County, Wis.

UPI

WISCONSIN • Information Highlights

Area: 56,154 square miles (145,439 km²).
Population (1976 est.): 4,609,000.
Chief Cities (1970 census): Madison, the capital, 172,-007; Milwaukee, 717,372; Racine, 95,162.
Government (1977): *Chief Officers*—acting governor, Martin J. Schreiber (D). *Legislature*—Senate, 33 members; Assembly, 99 members.
Education (1976–77): *Enrollment*—public elementary schools, 522,600 pupils; public secondary, 422,737; nonpublic, 189,400; colleges and universities, 179,-444 students. *Public school expenditures,* $1,601,-287,000 ($1,635 per pupil).
State Finances (fiscal year 1976): *Revenues,* $4,400,-184,000; *expenditures,* $4,190,261,000.
Personal Income (1976): $28,190,000,000; per capita, $6,117.
Labor Force (July 1977): *Nonagricultural wage and salary earners,* 1,790,300; *unemployed,* 107,400 (4.7% of total force).

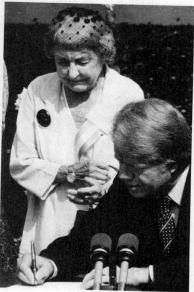

PHOTOS UPI

As paraders supported ERA, suffragette Hazel Hunkins Hallinan watched the President proclaim Women's Equality Day.

WOMEN

A slow forward movement of women's concerns could be detected in 1977. The emphasis, however, was definitely on "slow."

Snail's Pace of Progress. In *A Room of One's Own,* a volume of essays on women, published in 1929, Virginia Woolf described her experience in a library. "I went to the shelf where the histories stand," she wrote, "I looked up 'women,' found 'wife-beating.' "

Wife-beating is still easy to find, and not only in libraries. In the United States, it is most common in isolated areas, such as parts of impoverished, rural Appalachia—though several "battered-spouse" measures, considered necessary, were among the highlights of the legislature's session in "progressive" New York. But in the more remote communities of the country the women's movement has made hardly a dent in age-old attitudes, and women are still expected to be totally subservient to their husbands. In fact, a study by two professors at Marshall University, Huntington, W. Va., found that the economic status of women in that state has not perceptibly changed in 30 years.

Not that progress has been that much quicker in the heart of the nation. At the end of 200 years of U. S. history only three women had ever been picked to serve as heads of government departments. And even when President Jimmy Carter in 1977 included two more in his cabinet (Secretary of Commerce Juanita Kreps and Secretary of Housing and Urban Development Patricia Roberts Harris), his choice showed a shrewd sense of economy: Mrs. Harris is also a black. It looked like a case of killing two birds with one stone.

Several other women were named for lesser, yet important posts in the new administration, among them Eleanor Holmes Norton, who became chairman of the Equal Employment Opportunity Commission, Margaret Costanza, assistant to the president, Bette B. Anderson, undersecretary of the Treasury, Eula Bingham, assistant secretary of labor, and Carol T. Foreman, assistant secretary of agriculture.

Equal Rights Amendment. Aside from his appointments of women, President Carter aided the women's cause by declaring his strong support for the Equal Rights Amendment (ERA). Both he and Mrs. Carter, in fact, lobbied for the amendment. Vice President Walter Mondale also made calls to state legislators on behalf of ERA.

Despite such illustrious support and intense activity by women's organizations, ERA did not do well in 1977. The year began on a promising enough note: Indiana, a state which twice before had rejected the amendment, finally ratified it on January 18, becoming the 35th state to do so and the first in two years. The rest of the year, however, saw one setback after another. The Virginia Senate rejected it on January 27, and the North Carolina Senate followed suit on March 1. It died without a vote in the Oklahoma legislature on March 15, and the same day it was defeated for the second time in the Missouri Senate. It was also voted down in the Nevada Assembly and the Florida Senate and tabled in the Georgia Senate, although the attempt to pass it was couched in terms of honoring Rosalynn Carter. The Illinois General Assembly rejected it on June 6, as it has done each year since it was first passed by Congress.

In addition, three states that previously had approved ERA—Idaho, Nebraska, and Tennessee—voted to rescind their ratification. But the women's movement contends that those decisions will almost certainly be voided, since there is a precedent to support the view that Congress alone has the authority to decide whether a state legislature may reverse its approval of a constitutional amendment. Still, a legal battle is likely if ERA is passed by a narrow margin by March 22, 1979, the deadline for national ratification.

It had been the hope of those who sponsored a birthday salute on Jan. 11, 1977, to Dr. Alice Paul, the original drafter of ERA in 1923, that she might live to see it ratified, but that was not to be. Dr. Paul died on July 9 at age 92.

Conservative Backlash. There seems to be little doubt that it is opposition among certain women's groups, rather than male recalcitrance, which is holding up the amendment, and in some cases it has created divisions in nationwide organizations. Thus, after the national board of directors of the Girl Scouts of America endorsed ERA in late January, troop 47 in Chelsea, Mich., resigned from the main body in protest to being used as "political pawns."

Such backlash, blamed mainly on political rightists, was one of the principal themes of a convention in San Jose, Calif., of the National Women's Political Caucus. The three-day meeting, held in September, warned against growing opposition to ERA by such conservative elements as business interests, right-wing Republicans, the Mormon Church, and the Ku Klux Klan. Some delegates, however, placed the responsibility partly on women themselves, suggesting that they might have spread their efforts too thinly by simultaneously expending energy on other causes, such as abortion. Mildred Jeffrey of Detroit was elected to chair the caucus until 1979. In April, Eleanor Smeal had been elected president, for a term of 2½ years, of the National Organization for Women (NOW). She became the first head of the organization to be paid a salary.

A National Women's Conference in observance of the International Women's Year was held in Houston, Texas, in November. The sometimes stormy meeting prepared recommendations for President Carter and Congress on dismantling barriers to the equality of women.

Politics. Some barriers did fall in 1977, but since it was an off-election year, little could be expected on the political front. Yet the trend in some municipal elections, such as those of New York City, seemed to be toward women candidates—provided they sought less than the top spots. Thus, Bella Abzug lost her primary bid for the mayoralty, while another woman, State Senator Carol Bellamy, was elected president of the City Council and seven women were chosen for judgeships.

Perhaps the most spectacular victory over sexism, however, was scored in a rare judicial recall election in Madison, Wis., where Judge Archie Simonson of Dane County was soundly defeated by his female challenger, Moira Krueger. The recall grew out of the judge's remark from the bench, widely reported, that a teen-age defendant in a rape case had been reacting "normally" to the existing climate of sexual permissiveness and provocative women's clothing by participating in the crime.

International Developments. If women's progress in the United States has not been exceedingly swift, it has been still slower in some other parts of the world. In the principality of Liechtenstein, for example, women cast their ballots for the first time on April 17, electing justices of the peace in Vaduz, the capital. This was achieved under a 1976 law, which left it to communal assemblies to grant them suffrage in local affairs; they still do not have a voice on the national level. Swiss women, it may be recalled, were given the vote only a few years ago.

Even in such countries as West Germany, where the right to vote is long established and the constitution includes an equal-rights clause ("All persons shall be equal before the law; men and women shall have equal rights"), women's equality with men is still mainly on paper. Economically, they are an underprivileged class, earning an average 70% of a man's salary for the same work. Educationally, they are held back by a reactionary mentality among too many parents, who still think schooling for their daughters is a luxury. There are two women in Helmut Schmidt's cabinet, both in minor posts, but on the whole German women take little part in politics.

Half-way around the world, in tradition-bound Japan, the story is remarkably similar. While Japanese women have begun to break out of the time-honored mold, the pace is painfully slow. The country's laws prescribe equal pay for equal work, but the opportunity for equality, except in the lowliest positions, rarely presents itself. Nearly half of all Japanese women work outside the home, but it is estimated that less than 1% hold executive-level jobs. Only 25 of the 760 Diet seats are occupied by women.

The only two women in the world who were in top government positions, Prime Ministers Indira Gandhi of India and Sirimavo Bandaranaike of Sri Lanka, went down to crushing defeat in elections during 1977. In Europe, Antoinette Spaak, daughter of the late Paul-Henri Spaak, became the first woman to lead a Belgian political party. She was elected head of the Front Démocratique des Francophones on June 15.

MAY NEWMAN HALLMUNDSSON
Pace University

WYOMING

Energy-related issues continued to affect the social, political, economic, and physical environment in Wyoming during 1977.

The Legislature. Meeting in regular session, the state legislature devoted considerable effort to an increase in the mineral severance taxes on coal and trona. In addition a formula for redistribution and use of increased mineral royalties from federal lands was adopted. A capital construction plan and financing, including development of water resources, was completed. The Wyoming legislature also passed a new institutional health services act, rewrote the death penalty act, and revised the adoption code.

Politics and Investigations. Important political news in 1977 centered on the high-ranking incumbents who would not seek reelection in 1978. U. S. Senator Cliff Hansen (Rep.) had decided to retire after two Senate terms and one term as governor. Five-term congressman Teno Roncalio (Dem.) announced his decision not to run again. There was considerable speculation that Democratic Governor Ed Herschler would not seek a second term.

A district judge in Cheyenne, Joseph Maier, impaneled a grand jury on November 21 after studying a report by Lawrence Yonkee, a special investigator appointed by the Wyoming Supreme Court at the request of Governor Herschler. Although the scope of the grand jury investigation was not clear, it was possible that misconduct in several state institutions might emerge. The state director of criminal investigation, who was dismissed in May, charged that the state attorney general was involved in a cover-up of criminal activity in these institutions. The CBS television program "60 Minutes" aired these problems on October 30.

Another "60 Minutes" program and the Denver *Post* investigated evidence of prostitution, gambling, drugs, and payoffs in Rock Springs, Wyo. Problems encountered in this community seemed to implicate important state and local officials.

Economic Issues. Drought conditions plagued the state. Low prices for farm goods and high costs created problems. Plans to increase grazing fees for users of Forest Service and Bureau of Land Management lands were announced by the secretaries of agriculture and interior. The Carter administration also released a water policy statement that many westerners felt was an attempt to usurp state water rights.

JOHN B. RICHARD
The University of Wyoming

YUGOSLAVIA

Celebrations of President Tito's 85th birthday in May assumed exceptional proportions and reflected a higher degree of political stability than in previous years. Still, the problem of political prisoners in jails, and the resurgence of official attacks against Serbian and Croatian nationalists, indicated the potential for political and ethnic confrontations. A rift between Tito and his wife Jovanka, officially acknowledged in October, also apparently had political significance. A book published in September by Tito's heir-apparent, Edvard Kardelj, was considered a key ideological document and a platform for the 1978 congress of the League of Communists of Yugoslavia.

Džemal Bijedić, Yugoslav prime minister, died in a plane accident on January 18. He was replaced, on March 15, by Veselin Djuranović, former president of the central committee of the League of Communists of Montenegro.

In February a group of 92 prominent intellectuals addressed a letter of solidarity to the initiators of the Czechoslovak "Charter 77" (a manifesto requesting the Czechoslovak government to respect human rights).

Economy. Official expectations that 1977 would represent a turning point in eliminating

President Tito bids farewell to Džemal Bijedić, who is about to leave for Libya. En route, the prime minister and his wife, center, were killed in a plane crash.

President Tito welcomes Arthur Goldberg, head of the U. S. delegation to the European security conference, to Yugoslavia. Belgrade served as host city for the meeting.

UPI

basic deficiencies of the Yugoslav economy were largely unmet. On the positive side, the industrial production for the first eight months of 1977 increased by 10.9% in comparison with the same period in 1976. It was also a good harvest year. The wheat crop totaled 5.6 million tons, slightly less than last year, while the corn harvest reached 9.5 million tons, 4% higher than in 1976.

On the negative side, the rate of inflation in September was 14.5% higher than a year ago. Most disquieting, however, was the unexpectedly large trade deficit. In comparison with the first eight months of 1976, exports were up by 5.9%, while imports increased by 37%. The foreign trade deficit amounted to 37.2 billion dinars ($2,066 million). Unemployment rose to 720,000 in May.

On May 20, the United States approved the export license for key components of an electricity generating nuclear reactor in Dalmatia.

Foreign Relations. As in 1976 Yugoslav diplomacy was essentially conducted through Tito's extensive foreign travels. In January he visited Libya and Egypt. Between August 16 and 24 he paid an official visit to the Soviet Union, having long discussions with Leonid Brezhnev.

A communiqué following their talks stressed the "common aims of building socialism and communism" as well as common views on many internal issues (support of African national liberation movements, the Israeli withdrawal from occupied Arab territories, and further disarmament. measures). It also endorsed Yugoslav concepts of independence and noninterference, omitted any mention of the controversial issue of Eurocommunism, and remained silent on Yugoslav-Soviet economic relations.

Tito proceeded to North Korea (August 24–30) where he and President Kim Il Sung signed an appeal for the withdrawal of all foreign troops from South Korea. Next, Tito went for nine days to mainland China, his first visit to the country whose earlier Maoist regime denounced his "revisionism." He received an enthusiastic official welcome and conferred with Chinese leaders. The Chinese press agency asserted that the Chinese and the Yugoslav people are united in opposing hegemonism—an allusion to the Soviet Union. In October, Tito visited France, Portugal, and Algeria.

Yugoslav-U. S. official relations improved. Vice President Walter Mondale visited Yugoslavia and met with Tito. Despite the latter's criticism of President Carter's human rights policy, Mondale declared that relations between the two countries "are on the finest possible basis." A cordial welcome was given to Kardelj when he visited the United States in September. He was received by President Carter.

The 1975 Helsinki conference on European security and cooperation had a 1977 follow-up in Belgrade. Representatives of 33 European states, the United States, and Canada met for a preparatory phase of the conference from June 15 until August 5. The main session, with the task of assessing implementation of the Helsinki agreements, opened on October 4.

MILORAD M. DRACHKOVITCH
Stanford University

YUGOSLAVIA • Information Highlights

Official Name: Socialist Federal Republic of Yugoslavia.
Location: Southeastern Europe.
Area: 98,766 square miles (255,804 km²).
Population (1977 est.): 21,800,000.
Chief Cities (1974 est.): Belgrade, the capital, 845,000; Zagreb, 602,000; Skopje, 389,000.
Government: *Head of state,* Tito (Josip Broz), president (took office 1953). *Head of government,* Veselin Djuranović, prime minister (took office March 1977), *Legislature*—Federal Assembly: Federal Chamber and Chamber of Republics and Provinces.
Monetary Unit: Dinar (18.20 dinars equal U. S.$1, June 1977).
Manufacturing (major products): Iron and steel, processed foods, chemicals; machinery, textiles.
Major Agricultural Products: Corn, wheat, fruits, potatoes, sugar beets, forest products, livestock.

YUKON

A major U. S.–Canadian energy agreement, developments in transportation corridors, moves toward more autonomy in government, and native land claims were major issues in the Yukon during 1977.

Government and Politics. Two key figures of the Yukon Territorial Government (YTG) resigned. Merv Miller and Peter Gillespie, both federal appointees, stepped down from the YTG Executive Committee (cabinet) and in so doing established for the first time a majority of elected members in the cabinet. One position was left vacant, while Yukon resident Douglas Bell was appointed deputy commissioner. The Legislative Assembly voted to increase its membership from 12 to 16 in order to have more native participation in government.

Indian Land Claims. A significant step toward an agreement on native land claims was taken when labor-style negotiations between the Council for Yukon Indians (CYI) and the federal government were abandoned and a more cooperative process was adopted. Land-claims talks were adjourned during the summer but resumed in the fall. The CYI enlarged its negotiating team from two members to 12—one for each native community.

Economy. A U. S.–Canadian agreement to build a natural-gas pipeline from Alaska across the Yukon to the lower 48 states marked the beginning of the biggest single development in Yukon history. Construction is planned for 1981. The pipeline agreement was the central issue in 1977. Major developments in highway construction also moved ahead. Agreement was reached to pave a major portion of the Alaska Highway that runs through Yukon. The United States agreed to pay the full cost of the project. Another road link, between the Yukon capital of Whitehorse and the Alaskan port of Skagway, neared completion in 1977. In the north, the Dempster Highway crossed the Arctic Circle, the first public road in America to stretch that far north.

The year 1977 was strike-free in the mining industry, and steps were taken toward developing further mineral deposits. A large aluminum smelter is being considered, along with further hydro projects.

ANDREW HUME
"The Whitehorse Star"

--------- YUKON • Information Highlights ---------

Area: 207,076 square miles (536,327 km²).
Population (1976 census): 21,836.
Chief City (1976 census): Whitehorse, the capital, 13,-311.
Government (1977): *Chief Officers*—commissioner, James Smith; deputy commissioner, Douglas Bell. *Legislature*—Territorial Council, 16 members.
Education (1976–77): *Enrollment*—public elementary and secondary schools, 4,990 pupils.
Personal Income (1974): $259,000,000; $4,544 per person.

ZAIRE

The year 1977 saw the strongest challenge to President Mobutu Sese Seko since he took power in a military coup in 1965. Faced with an invasion in the copper-rich southern Shaba region (formerly Katanga), there seemed a danger that Zaire itself might split apart. However, Mobutu took charge of the counteroffensive. Against all predictions, he emerged with a strengthened leadership position after the invaders had been driven back into Angola.

Domestic Events. The invasion by a ragtag army of about 2,000 Katangese gendarmes, who reentered the country after some ten years of exile in Angola, occurred in March. It followed a threat, little heeded at the time, made by former Vice Premier Antoine Gizenga the previous year that he would return to Zaire to lead an armed struggle against the Mobutu regime. The rebels, possibly trained by Angolan-based Cubans and armed by the Soviet Union, made quick initial inroads. Riding on bicycles, they quickly outflanked troops of Zaire's underpaid, demoralized army of 30,000, which then fled the battlefield. The rebels occupied several towns like Mutshatsha and Dilolo and at one stage appeared to threaten Kolwezi, the headquarters of the state-owned Gecamines Copper Co.

The fighting was an echo of the chaos and dissolution of the early 1960's. In fact, the invaders had previously fought the central government of the Congo, as Zaire was then known, under the leadership of Moise Tshombe, the late leader of secessionist Katanga. The local population welcomed the new invaders, who were largely of the same tribal grouping as themselves. The Zairian army, whose troops largely came from other parts of the vast territory, were unpopular locally.

Alarmed by the rapid advance of the rebels, Mobutu turned to the West for assistance. The response of the United States was lukewarm, and from the Americans the Zairian leader received only limited amounts of "nonlethal" military aid. However, French President Valéry Giscard d'Estaing moved boldly to assist, sending in aircraft to ferry equipment as well as a limited number of advisers. Help also came from China, West Germany, and Belgium, which was anxious to preserve its still considerable interests in its former colony. Uganda's President Idi Amin also put in a well-publicized appearance and promised to send paratroopers, including his latest wife "Suicide" Sarah, but none showed up. But the crucial help came in early April when Morocco's King Hassan II, whose army is fighting guerrillas in the former colony of Spanish Sahara, decided to send 3,000 troops with their equipment. These well-trained Moroccan forces turned the tide.

Dismayed by the bumbling of his own generals, Mobutu took personal command of the forces in the battle zone, although actual combat itself was slight. Some bizarre and typically Zairian elements intruded—for instance, the Zairian government ordered Coca-Cola from the United States for its troops, and pygmies were dispatched to the war zone. Armed with bows and arrows, the little people could not adjust to the tall elephant grass of southern Shaba and were soon withdrawn. The Katangese began withdrawing, and the civilian population went with them. Reporters who accompanied the advancing Zairian troops, whose spirits had been buoyed by their Moroccan allies, found only empty villages. By late in the year, the plight of these refugees, who had crossed into Angola, had grown serious. By mid-May the war was all but over with the capture of the border town of Dilolo by the joint Zaire-Moroccan forces.

After the successful conclusion of the invasion, Mobutu's position in Zaire, which had appeared to be eroding because of near bankruptcy, inflation, and continuing poverty, was much strengthened. In early July, Mobutu sacked his cabinet and personally took over control of the army. He also fired or retired about 50 generals and other high-ranking officers. One victim was Foreign Minister Nguzu Karl-I-Bond, who in August was charged with high treason for allegedly having had advance warning of the invasion and not having passed on this knowledge to Mobutu. Karl-I-Bond, who had sometimes been mentioned as a possible successor to Mobutu, was found guilty and sentenced to death, but this sentence was later commuted.

Economy. Shaba provides most of Zaire's exports, but the copper and mineral output were not affected by the fighting. Zaire, however, still faced enormous economic problems, with sagging commodity prices and rising petroleum costs coupled with its continued massive import of foodstuffs. Meanwhile, inflation continued to run at an annual rate of 80%, causing serious dissatisfaction among the long-suffering public. In order to try to limit inflation, Zaire announced in midyear it would give no wage increases in the public sector. This order affected about 100,000 workers.

Meanwhile, one third of Zaire's foreign exchange was going toward repayments of foreign debt. Zaire owes $3 billion in foreign debts, including $500 million in commercial bank loans. Coffee, not copper, was given a chance of saving the situation. Zaire's crop in 1977 was estimated at 80,000 metric tons, which was valued at more than $500 million.

JAMES PRINGLE

ZAIRE • Information Highlights

Official Name: Republic of Zaire.
Location: Central equatorial Africa.
Area: 905,565 square miles (2,345,409 km²).
Population (1977 est.): 26,300,000.
Chief Cities (1974 est.): Kinshasa, the capital, 2,008,-000; Kananga, 601,000.
Government: *Head of state and government,* Mobutu Sese Seko, president (took office Nov. 1965). *Legislature* (unicameral)—National Legislative Council.
Monetary Unit: Zaire (0.86 zaire equals U. S.$1, June 1977).
Manufacturing (major products): Processed foods, clothing, textiles, soap.
Major Agricultural Products: Palm oil and kernels, coffee, rubber, tea, cacao, groundnuts, bananas, cassava.

UPI

President Mobutu Sese Seko waves a sculptured stick to acknowledge applause during an April rally, held to show support for the Zairian leader in his conflict with Katangan insurgents.

The Bronx (N. Y.) Zoo's new Wild Asia exhibit, emphasizing the natural environment of the animals, opened in August. Visitors tour the area by monorail.

ZOOLOGY

Paleozoology. The fossil record has long been interpreted to include periods during which wholesale extinctions were common throughout the world. One of these periods is the Triassic-Jurassic juncture, when many four-legged animals were thought to have become extinct within a short time. Drs. Paul E. Olsen of Yale University and Peter M. Galton of the University of Bridgeport, Conn., have convincingly shown (*Science,* Sept. 2, 1977) that the idea of these so-called periods of world-wide extinction stems from misinterpretation of the time scale of fossil records. The actual disappearances occurred gradually over a long period of time and coincided with the gradual replacement by more advanced groups.

The oldest known fossil reptile, from Upper Pennsylvanian deposits in Kansas, was described in detail by Dr. Robert R. Reisz of the University of Toronto, Canada. Dr. Reisz showed that primitive reptiles existed several million years earlier than generally thought. This fossil, known as *Petrolaosaurus kansenis,* represents the most primitive reptile known.

Origin of Domestic Dogs. The origin of the various breeds of domestic dogs has been the topic of much past speculation. The origin of the various New World dogs remains particularly obscure. Stanley J. Olsen (University of Arizona) and John W. Olsen (University of California, Berkeley) now have proposed (*Science,* Aug. 5, 1977) that the ancestor of all New World dogs was the Chinese wolf. They report that remains of tamed wolves have been found in association with early mammoth-hunting man in North America. The Olsens speculate that the smallest subspecies of wolf (*Canis lupus chanco* of China) is the probable ancestor of North American primitive domestic dogs. They also think that Eskimos may have tamed various *Canis lupus lycaon* of northwestern North America and interbred them with other dogs to develop the "husky" breed.

Evolution. Dr. O. Cuellar of the Department of Biology at the University of Utah has proposed a new evolutionary-ecological pattern of some animals. Many examples of species that normally reproduce sexually (including lizards, grasshoppers, and other invertebrates) appear to survive only in disclimax communities, that is, communities in which the ecological stability has been disturbed, such as some ecotonal areas subject to major multiannual variations in species present: areas often burned out by fires, beaches, and islands. In such situations parthenogenetic populations have survival advantages for two reasons: (1) since only females are produced, the rate of increase is double that of related sexually reproducing species, and (2) one individual can establish a new colony (*Science,* Aug. 26, 1977).

Mutualism is a relationship between two species that exist in nature due to interactions between the two. Stanley A. Temple of the University of Wisconsin at Madison has reported (*Science,* Aug. 26, 1977) on the probability of such a relation between a plant and the extinct dodo bird on Mauritius in the Indian Ocean. As a result of the extermination of the dodo, some three centuries ago, a large monoecious tree, restricted to the same island, is now almost extinct. In the past, this tree was quite common and often harvested for lumber. By 1973, only 13 trees, each estimated to be more than 300 years old, remained. Even though many seeds were produced, none germinated, either in nature or in nurseries. The reason appears to be a thick coating over the seed. Professor Temple speculates that the extinct dodo fed on the seeds, whose covering the bird's well-developed gizzard and digestive enzymes reduced to the point that made germination possible. A thinner covering probably would have resulted in seed destruction by the gizzard.

Habitat Selection. American elk are known as forest dwellers which, in regions of heavy snow, move into adjacent nonforested areas only during the winter months. There they avoid deep snow and feed on low shrubs. W. H. Rickard and associates of Battelle Laboratories at Richland, Wash., have shown that large nonforested areas not grazed by domestic animals and little disturbed by human proximity are inhabited by elk even during the summer. Apparently, the movement to forests was a mechanism for reducing competition with other large herbivores.

Populations. Cycles in lemming populations have been known for centuries and studied in detail for the past 50 years. Many variations in population density have been recorded and diverse environmental evidence accumulated. Norman C. Negus and Patricia J. Berger of the University of Utah have demonstrated—in the laboratory as well as in the field—that related rodents fed a supplement of fresh green grass (wheatgrass) will become reproductively active even in the winter. They have also shown that initiation of reproduction is more dependent on vegetative growth than on temperature.

Buffalo Populations. A new book by A. R. E. Sinclair, *The African Buffalo, A Study of Resource Limitation of Populations* (University of Chicago Press, 1977), presents as its central theme the regulation of population density as a density-dependent mechanism. Sinclair concludes that where sufficient drinking water is interspersed with grasses and herbs, populations reach dominant proportions in terms of total biomass of the ecosystem. In other words, there is more weight per unit area of water buffalo than any other kind of animal. Such situations still exist in a few parts of East Africa. This is reminiscent of the past populations of the American bison on the Great Plains.

Fish Culture. As human populations increase, so does the demand for proteins. More and more, the natural populations of marine and fresh-water fish are being depleted. Dr. A. H. Weatherley and B. M. G. Cogger of the University of Toronto, Canada, have summarized the current status of fish culture, that is, actual "cultivation" of fish by man. In brief, much remains to be discovered on how to develop economically profitable, high-intensity production systems. The few current attempts are generally hampered by high costs. As a result, they are not competitive with chicken or beef-raising operations (*Science,* July 29, 1977).

Rare and Endangered Species. Whaling has reduced the stock of some whales to the point that zoologists consider the species in danger of extinction. John Walsh (*Science,* Aug. 26, 1977) reports on the difficulties of international attempts to enforce a moratorium on bowhead hunting. This whale plays a central role in Eskimo life, being important as a food source as well as in native culture. Any efforts by international groups are therefore viewed by Canadian, Alaskan, and Siberian Eskimos as destructive of their normal way of life. This and similar situations raise the question of relative importance. Should primitive societies be forced to change basic patterns of life to conform to the desires of some minority preservation-minded group?

E. LENDELL COCKRUM, *University of Arizona*

PHOTOS UPI

Zoologists and other animal lovers welcomed a klipspringer antelope, born at the St. Louis Zoo, and a polar bear cub, born to Princess Snowball at a Chicago zoo.

STATISTICAL AND TABULAR DATA

AMBASSADORS AND ENVOYS[1]

Countries	From U.S.	To U.S.	Countries	From U.S.	To U.S.
AFGHANISTAN	Theodore Eliot, Jr.	Abdul Wahid Karim	LUXEMBOURG	James G. Lowenstein[3]	Adrien Meisch
ALGERIA	U. S. Haynes, Jr.[3]	Abdelaziz Maoui	MALAGASY REP.	(Vacant)	Norbert Rakoto malala[2]
ARGENTINA	Raul H. Castro	Jorge A. A. Espil	MALAWI	Robert A. Stevenson	Jacob T. X. Muwamba
AUSTRALIA	Philip H. Alston, Jr.	Alan Philip Renouf	MALAYSIA	Robert H. Miller[3]	Zain Azraai
AUSTRIA	Milton A. Wolf[3]	Karl Herbert Schober	MALDIVE IS.	W. Howard Wriggins[3]	(Vacant)
BAHAMAS	William B. Schwartz, Jr.	Livingston B. Johnson	MALI	Patricia M. Byrne	Ibrahima Sima
BAHRAIN	Wat T. Cluverius, IV	Abdulaziz A. Buali	MALTA	Lowell Bruce Laingen	Victor Gauci[2]
BANGLADESH	David T. Schneider[3]	Mustafizur R. Siddiqi	MAURITANIA	E. Gregory Kryza	Mohamed Nassim Kochman
BARBADOS	Frank V. Ortiz[3]	Oliver H. Jackman			
BELGIUM	Anne C. Chambers[3]	Willy Van Cauwenberg	MAURITIUS	Robert V. Keeley	Pierre G. G. Balancy
BENIN	(Vacant)	Thomas Setondji Boya	MEXICO	Patrick J. Lucey	Hugo B. Margain
BOLIVIA	Paul H. Boeker[3]	Alberto Crespo	MOROCCO	Robert Anderson	Ali Bengelloun
BOTSWANA	Donald R. Norland	Bias Mookodi	MOZAMBIQUE	Willard A. De Pree	(Vacant)
BRAZIL	John Hugh Crimmins	João B. Pinheiro	NAURU	Philip H. Alston, Jr.[3]	(Vacant)
BULGARIA	Raymond L. Garthoff[3]	Lubomir D. Popov	NEPAL	Lester E. Edmond[3]	Padma Bahadur Khatri
BURMA	Maurice D. Bean[3]	U Tin Lat	NETHERLANDS	Robert J. McCloskey	A. R. Tammenoms Bakker
BURUNDI	Thomas J. Corcoran[3]	Laurent Nzeyimana			
CAMEROON	Mabel M. Smythe[3]	Benoit Bindzi	NEW ZEALAND	Armistead Selden, Jr.	Lloyd White
CANADA	Thomas O. Enders	Peter M. Towe	NICARAGUA	Mauricio Solaun[3]	G. Sevilla-Sacasa
CAPE VERDE	Edward Marks[3]	Raul Querido Varela	NIGER	Charles A. James	Andre Wright
CENTRAL AFR.			NIGERIA	Donald B. Easum	Olujimi Jolaoso
EMP.	Anthony Quainton	Christophe Maidou	NORWAY	Louis A. Lerner[3]	S. Christian Sommerfelt
CHAD	William G. Bradford	Pierre T. Gaba	OMAN	William D. Wolle	Farid M. A. al-Hinai
CHILE	George W. Landau[3]	Jorge Cauas	PAKISTAN	Arthur W. Hummel, Jr.	Sahabzada Yaqub-Khan
CHINA (Rep. of)	Leonard Unger	James C. H. Shen	PANAMA	William J. Jorden	Gabriel Lewis
COLOMBIA	Diego C. Asencio[3]	Virgilio Barco	PAPUA NEW		
COSTA RICA	Marvin Weissman[3]	Rodolfo Silva	GUINEA	Mary S. Olmsted	Paulias Nguna Matane
CYPRUS	William Crawford, Jr.	Nicos G. Dimitriou	PARAGUAY	Robert E. White[3]	Mario L. Escobar
CZECHOSLOVAKIA	Thomas R. Byrne	Jaromir Johanes	PERU	Harry W. Shlaudeman[3]	Carlos Garcia-Bedoya
DENMARK	John Gunther Dean	Otto R. Borch	PHILIPPINES	David D. Newsom[3]	Eduardo Z. Romualdez
DOMINICAN REP.	Robert A. Hurwitch	Horacio Vicioso-Soto	POLAND	Richard T. Davies	Witold Trampczynski
ECUADOR	Richard Bloomfield	Gustavo Y. Borja	PORTUGAL	Frank C. Carlucci	João Hall Themido
EGYPT	Hermann F. Eilts	Ashraf A. Ghorbal	QATAR	Andrew I. Killgore	Abdullah Saleh Al-Mana
EL SALVADOR	(Vacant)	F. Bertrand Galindo	RUMANIA	O. Rudolph Aggrey[3]	Nicolae M. Nicolae
ETHIOPIA	(Vacant)	Getachew Tadesse[2]	RWANDA	T. Frank Crigler	Bonaventure Ubalijoro
FIJI	Armistead Selden, Jr.	Berenado Vunibobo	SÃO TOMÉ AND		
FINLAND	Rozanne L. Ridgway[3]	Leo Tuominen	PRÍNCIPE	Andrew L. Steigman	(Vacant)
FRANCE	Arthur A. Hartman[3]	J. Kosciusko-Morizet	SAUDI ARABIA	John C. West	Ali Abdallah Alireza
GABON	Andrew L. Steigman	Rene Kombila	SENEGAL	Herman J. Cohen[3]	André Coulbary
GAMBIA, The	Herman J. Cohen[3]	(Vacant)	SEYCHELLES	Wilbert J. Le Melle[3]	(Vacant)
GERMANY (E)	David B. Bolen	Rolf Sieber	SIERRA LEONE	John A. Linehan[3]	Philip J. Palmer
GERMANY (W)	Walter Stoessel, Jr.	Berndt von Staden	SINGAPORE	John H. Holdridge	Punch Coomaraswamy
GHANA	Robert P. Smith	Samuel Ernest Quarm	SOMALIA	John L. Loughran	Abdullahi Ahmed Addou
GREAT BRITAIN	Kingman Brewster, Jr.	Peter Jay	SOUTH AFRICA	William G. Bowdler	Donald Bell Sole
GREECE	William E. Schaufele, Jr.[3]		SPAIN	Wells Stabler	Juan José Rovira
		M. D. Alexandrakis	SRI LANKA	W. Howard Wriggins[3]	Neville Kanakaratne
GRENADA	Frank V. Ortiz, Jr.[3]	Marie J. McIntyre	SUDAN	Donald C. Bergus[3]	Omer Salih Eissa
GUATEMALA	Davis Eugene Boster	Abundio Maldonado	SURINAM	J. Owen Zurhellen, Jr.	(Vacant)
GUINEA	Oliver S. Crosby	Ibrahima Camara	SWAZILAND	Donald R. Norland	Simon Musa Kunene
GUINEA-BISSAU	Edward Marks[3]	G. V. V. Fernandes	SWEDEN	R. O. Kennedy-Minott	Count Wilhelm Wacht-meister
GUYANA	John R. Burke[3]	Laurence E. Mann			
HAITI	William B. Jones	Georges Salomon	SWITZERLAND	Marvin L. Warner	Raymond Probst
HONDURAS	Mari-Luci Jaramillo[3]	Roberto Lazarus	SYRIA	Richard W. Murphy	Sabah Kabbani
HUNGARY	Philip M. Kaiser[3]	Ferenc Esztergalyos	TANZANIA	James W. Spain	Paul L. Bomani
ICELAND	James J. Blake	Hans G. Andersen	THAILAND	Charles Whitehouse	Arun Panupong
INDIA	Robert F. Goheen	N. A. Palkhivala	TOGO	Ronald D. Palmer	Messanvi Kokou Kekeh
INDONESIA	Edward E. Masters	Roesmin Nurjadin	TONGA	Armistead Selden, Jr.	(Vacant)
IRAN	William H. Sullivan[3]	Ardeshir Zahedi	TRINIDAD AND		
IRELAND	William V. Shannon	John G. Molloy	TOBAGO	Richard K. Fox, Jr.[3]	Victor C. McIntyre
ISRAEL	Samuel W. Lewis[3]	Simcha Dinitz	TUNISIA	Edward W. Mulcahy	Ali Hedda
ITALY	Richard N. Gardner	Roberto Gaja	TURKEY	Ronald I. Spiers[3]	Melih Esenbel
IVORY COAST	Monteagle Stearns	Timothée N'Guetta Ahoua	UGANDA	(Vacant)	Mahmud Musa[2]
			USSR	Malcolm Toon	Anatoliy F. Dobrynin
JAMAICA	Frederick Irving[3]	Alfred A. Rattray	UNITED ARAB		
JAPAN	Michael J. Mansfield	Fumihiko Togo	EMIRATES	François M. Dickman	Hamad A. R. Al Madfa
JORDAN	Thomas R. Pickering	Abdullah Salah	UPPER VOLTA	Pierre R. Graham	Télésphore Yaguibou
KENYA	Wilbert J. Le Melle[3]	John P. Mbogua	URUGUAY	Lawrence A. Pezzullo[3]	José Perez Caldas
KOREA (S)	Richard L. Sneider	Yong Shik Kim	VENEZUELA	Viron P. Vaky	Ignacio Iribarren
KUWAIT	Frank E. Maestrone	Khalid M. Jaffar	WESTERN SAMOA	Armistead Selden, Jr.	(Vacant)
LAOS	(Vacant)	Somphong Vanitsaveth[2]	YEMEN	Thomas J. Scotes	Y. M. Al-Mutawakel
LEBANON	Richard B. Parker	Najati Kabbani	YUGOSLAVIA	Lawrence S. Eagle-burger[3]	Dimce Belovski
LESOTHO	Donald R. Norland	Thabo R. Makeka			
LIBERIA	W. Beverly Carter, Jr.	Francis A. W. Dennis	ZAIRE	Walter L. Cutler	Kasongo Mutuale
LIBYA	(Vacant)	Shaban F. Gashut[2]	ZAMBIA	Stephen Low	Putteho M. Ngonda

[1] As of December 1977
[2] Chargé d'affaires
[3] Nominated but not confirmed by Congress

THE UNITED STATES BUDGET

Prior to leaving office, President Gerald R. Ford presented his administration's budget for fiscal year 1978 to Congress. Total receipts and expenditures were estimated at $393 billion and $440 billion respectively. Later, the Carter administration submitted its revisions of the Ford budget to Congress. The Carter budget (*below*) rejected Ford proposals "that would have needlessly added to the burden on the elderly and those who depend upon medicare, medicaid, and food programs," and also rejected "further financial strain on state and local government."

Description (*millions of dollars*)	1976 actual	TQ[1] actual	1977 estimate	1978 estimate
Receipts by source:				
Individual income taxes	131,603	38,801	148,917	179,222
Corporation income taxes	41,409	8,460	57,182	61,645
Social insurance taxes and contributions	92,714	25,760	108,006	123,814
Excise taxes	16,963	4,473	17,939	18,581
Estate and gift taxes	5,216	1,455	5,909	5,835
Custom duties	4,074	1,212	4,720	5,286
Miscellaneous receipts	8,026	1,612	6,704	7,241
Total budget receipts	300,005	81,773	349,377	401,624
Outlays by function:				
National defense[2]	89,996	22,518	100,075	111,947
International affairs	5,067	1,997	6,926	7,847
General science, space, and technology	4,370	1,161	4,461	4,737
Natural resources, environment, and energy	11,282	3,324	17,139	20,504
Agriculture	2,502	584	2,899	2,333
Commerce and transportation	17,248	4,700	15,769	20,093
Community and regional development	5,300	1,530	7,989	9,976
Education, training, employment, and social services	18,167	5,013	22,199	26,473
Health	33,448	8,720	39,505	44,485
Income security	127,406	32,796	141,573	146,549
Veterans benefits and services	18,432	3,962	18,388	19,143
Law enforcement and justice	3,320	859	3,705	3,862
General government	2,927	878	3,754	3,941
Revenue sharing and general purpose fiscal assistance	7,119	2,024	9,853	9,707
Interest	34,589	7,246	38,248	41,785
Allowances[3]	....	....	....	2,651
Undistributed offsetting receipts	−14,704	−2,567	−15,067	−16,660
Total budget outlays	336,466	94,746	417,417	459,373[4]
Budget deficit (−)	−66,461	−12,973	−68,040	−57,749

[1] The fiscal year now runs from October 1 through September 30; for the period July 1, 1976, to Sept. 30, 1976, a three-month "transition quarter" (TQ) was established. [2] Includes allowances for civilian and military pay raises for Department of Defense. [3] Includes allowances for civilian agency pay raises and contingencies. [4] In September, Congress voted final approval of a $458.3 billion expenditure budget.
Source: *Fiscal Year 1978 Budget Revisions, February 1977*

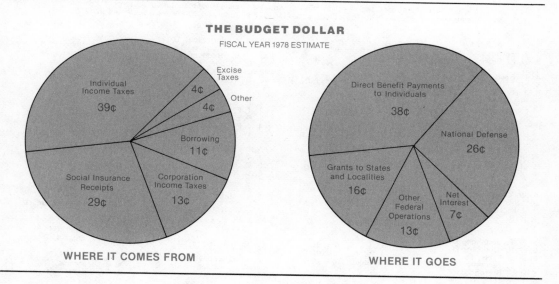

THE BUDGET DOLLAR
FISCAL YEAR 1978 ESTIMATE

Individual Income Taxes 39¢ · Excise Taxes 4¢ · Other 4¢ · Borrowing 11¢ · Corporation Income Taxes 13¢ · Social Insurance Receipts 29¢

WHERE IT COMES FROM

Direct Benefit Payments to Individuals 38¢ · National Defense 26¢ · Grants to States and Localities 16¢ · Other Federal Operations 13¢ · Net Interest 7¢

WHERE IT GOES

UNITED STATES: 95TH CONGRESS

SENATE MEMBERSHIP

(As of January 1978: 62 Democrats, 38 Republicans)

Letters after senators' names refer to party affiliation—D for Democrat, R for Republican. Single asterisk (*) denotes term expiring in January 1979; double asterisk (**), term expiring in January 1981; triple asterisk (***), term expiring in January 1983; (1) ran as independent; (2) filled vacancy; (3) died January 1978.

ALABAMA
*J. J. Sparkman, D
**J. B. Allen, D

ALASKA
*T. Stevens, R
**M. Gravel, D

ARIZONA
**B. Goldwater, R
***D. DeConcini, D

ARKANSAS
**D. Bumpers, D
*K. Hodges, Jr., D (2)

CALIFORNIA
**A. Cranston, D
***S. I. Hayakawa, R

COLORADO
*F. K. Haskell, D
**G. Hart, D

CONNECTICUT
**A. A. Ribicoff, D
***L. P. Weicker, Jr., R

DELAWARE
***W. V. Roth, Jr., R
*J. R. Biden, Jr., D

FLORIDA
***L. M. Chiles, Jr., D
**R. B. Stone, D

GEORGIA
**H. E. Talmadge, D
*S. Nunn, D

HAWAII
**D. K. Inouye, D
***S. M. Matsunaga, D

IDAHO
**F. Church, D
*J. A. McClure, R

ILLINOIS
*C. H. Percy, R
**A. E. Stevenson, D

INDIANA
**B. Bayh, D
***R. G. Lugar, R

IOWA
*D. Clark, D
**J. C. Culver, D

KANSAS
*J. B. Pearson, R
**R. J. Dole, R

KENTUCKY
*W. Huddleston, D
**W. H. Ford, D

LOUISIANA
*R. B. Long, D
*J. B. Johnston, D

MAINE
***E. S. Muskie, D
*W. D. Hathaway, D

MARYLAND
**C. M. Mathias, Jr., R
***P. S. Sarbanes, D

MASSACHUSETTS
***E. M. Kennedy, D
*E. W. Brooke, R

MICHIGAN
*R. P. Griffin, R
***D. W. Riegle, Jr., D

MINNESOTA
***H. H. Humphrey, D (3)
*W. R. Anderson, D

MISSISSIPPI
*J. O. Eastland, D
***J. C. Stennis, D

MISSOURI
**T. F. Eagleton, D
***J. C. Danforth, R

MONTANA
*L. Metcalf, D (3)
***J. Melcher, D

NEBRASKA
*C. T. Curtis, R
***E. Zorinsky, D

NEVADA
***H. W. Cannon, D
**P. Laxalt, R

NEW HAMPSHIRE
*T. J. McIntyre, D
**J. A. Durkin, D

NEW JERSEY
*C. P. Case, R
***H. A. Williams, Jr., D

NEW MEXICO
*P. V. Domenici, R
***H. Schmitt, R

NEW YORK
**J. K. Javits, R
***D. P. Moynihan, D

NORTH CAROLINA
*J. Helms, R
**R. B. Morgan, D

NORTH DAKOTA
**M. R. Young, R
***Q. N. Burdick, D

OHIO
**J. H. Glenn, Jr., D
***H. M. Metzenbaum, D

OKLAHOMA
**H. L. Bellmon, R
*D. F. Bartlett, R

OREGON
*M. O. Hatfield, R
**B. Packwood, R

PENNSYLVANIA
**R. S. Schweiker, R
***H. J. Heinz, III, R

RHODE ISLAND
*C. Pell, D
***J. H. Chafee, R

SOUTH CAROLINA
*S. Thurmond, R
**E. F. Hollings, D

SOUTH DAKOTA
**G. S. McGovern, D
*J. G. Abourezk, D

TENNESSEE
*H. H. Baker, Jr., R
***J. Sasser, D

TEXAS
*J. G. Tower, R
***L. M. Bentsen, D

UTAH
**J. Garn, R
***O. Hatch, R

VERMONT
***R. T. Stafford, R
**P. J. Leahy, D

VIRGINIA
***H. F. Byrd, Jr., D (1)
*W. L. Scott, R

WASHINGTON
**W. G. Magnuson, D
***H. M. Jackson, D

WEST VIRGINIA
*J. Randolph, D
***R. C. Byrd, D

WISCONSIN
***W. Proxmire, D
**G. Nelson, D

WYOMING
*C. P. Hansen, R
***M. Wallop, R

HOUSE MEMBERSHIP

(As of January 1978: 287 Democrats, 146 Republicans, 2 vacant)

"At-L." In place of Congressional district number means "representative at large." *Indicates elected Nov. 2, 1976; **Elected in special 1977 election; all others were reelected in 1976.

ALABAMA
1. J. Edwards, R
2. W. L. Dickinson, R
3. W. Nichols, D
4. T. Bevill, D
5. *R. Flippo, D
6. J. H. Buchanan, Jr., R
7. W. Flowers, D

ALASKA
At-L. D. Young, R

ARIZONA
1. J. J. Rhodes, R
2. M. K. Udall, D
3. *B. Stump, D
4. *E. Rudd, R

ARKANSAS
1. W. V. Alexander, Jr., D
2. *J. G. Tucker, Jr., D
3. J. P. Hammerschmidt, R
4. R. H. Thornton, Jr., D

CALIFORNIA
1. H. T. Johnson, D
2. D. H. Clausen, R
3. J. E. Moss, D
4. R. L. Leggett, D
5. J. L. Burton, D
6. P. Burton, D
7. G. Miller, D
8. R. V. Dellums, D
9. F. H. Stark, Jr., D
10. D. Edwards, D
11. L. J. Ryan, D
12. P. N. McCloskey, Jr., R
13. N. Y. Mineta, D
14. J. J. McFall, D
15. B. F. Sisk, D
16. *L. E. Panetta, D
17. J. Krebs, D
18. W. M. Ketchum, R
19. R. J. Lagomarsino, R
20. B. M. Goldwater, Jr., R
21. J. C. Corman, D
22. C. J. Moorhead, R
23. *A. C. Beilenson, D
24. H. A. Waxman, D
25. E. Roybal, D
26. J. H. Rousselot, R
27. *R. K. Dornan, R
28. Y. B. Burke, D
29. A. F. Hawkins, D
30. G. E. Danielson, D
31. C. H. Wilson, D
32. G. M. Anderson, D
33. D. M. Clawson, R
34. M. W. Hannaford, D
35. J. Lloyd, D
36. G. E. Brown, Jr., D
37. S. N. Pettis, R
38. J. M. Patterson, D
39. C. E. Wiggins, R
40. *R. E. Badham, R
41. B. Wilson, R
42. L. Van Deerlin, D
43. C. W. Burgener, R

COLORADO
1. P. Schroeder, D
2. T. E. Wirth, D
3. F. E. Evans, D
4. J. P. Johnson, R
5. W. L. Armstrong, R

CONNECTICUT
1. W. R. Cotter, D
2. C. J. Dodd, D
3. R. N. Giaimo, D
4. S. B. McKinney, R
5. R. A. Sarasin, R
6. T. Moffett, D

DELAWARE
At-L. *T. B. Evans, Jr., R

FLORIDA
1. R. L. F. Sikes, D
2. D. Fuqua, D
3. C. E. Bennett, D
4. W. V. Chappell, Jr., D
5. R. Kelly, R
6. C. W. Young, R
7. S. M. Gibbons, D
8. *A. P. Ireland, D
9. L. Frey, Jr., R
10. L. A. Bafalis, R
11. P. G. Rogers, D
12. J. H. Burke, R
13. W. Lehman, D
14. C. D. Pepper, D
15. D. B. Fascell, D

GEORGIA
1. R. B. Ginn, D
2. M. D. Mathis, D
3. J. Brinkley, D
4. E. H. Levitas, D
5. **W. F. Fowler, Jr., D
6. J. J. Flynt, Jr., D
7. L. P. McDonald, D
8. *B. L. Evans, D
9. E. L. Jenkins, D
10. D. D. Barnard, Jr., D

HAWAII
1. *C. Heftel, D
2. *D. K. Akaka, D

IDAHO
1. S. D. Symms, R
2. G. V. Hansen, R

ILLINOIS

1. R. H. Metcalfe, D
2. M. F. Murphy, D
3. M. A. Russo, D
4. E. J. Derwinski, R
5. J. G. Fary, D
6. H. J. Hyde, R
7. C. Collins, D
8. D. Rostenkowski, D
9. S. R. Yates, D
10. A. J. Mikva, D
11. F. Annunzio, D
12. P. M. Crane, R
13. R. McClory, R
14. J. N. Erlenborn, R
15. *T. J. Corcoran, R
16. J. B. Anderson, R
17. G. M. O'Brien, R
18. R. H. Michel, R
19. T. Railsback, R
20. P. Findley, R
21. E. R. Madigan, R
22. G. E. Shipley, D
23. C. M. Price, D
24. P. Simon, D

INDIANA

1. *A. Benjamin, Jr., D
2. F. J. Fithian, D
3. J. Brademas, D
4. *D. Quayle, R
5. E. H. Hillis, R
6. D. W. Evans, D
7. J. T. Myers, R
8. *D. L. Cornwell, D
9. L. H. Hamilton, D
10. P. R. Sharp, D
11. A. Jacobs, Jr., D

IOWA

1. *J. A. S. Leach, R
2. M. T. Blouin, D
3. C. E. Grassley, R
4. N. Smith, D
5. T. R. Harkin, D
6. B. W. Bedell, D

KANSAS

1. K. G. Sebelius, R
2. M. E. Keys, D
3. L. Winn, Jr., R
4. *D. Glickman, D
5. J. Skubitz, R

KENTUCKY

1. C. Hubbard, Jr., D
2. W. H. Natcher, D
3. R. L. Mazzoli, D
4. G. Snyder, R
5. T. L. Carter, R
6. J. B. Breckinridge, D
7. C. D. Perkins, D

LOUISIANA

1. **R. L. Livingston, Jr., R
2. C. C. Boggs, D
3. D. C. Treen, R
4. J. D. Waggonner, Jr., D
5. *J. Huckaby, R
6. W. H. Moore, R
7. J. B. Breaux, D
8. G. W. Long, D

MAINE

1. D. F. Emery, R
2. W. S. Cohen, R

MARYLAND

1. R. E. Bauman, R
2. C. D. Long, D
3. *B. A. Mikulski, D
4. M. S. Holt, R
5. G. N. Spellman, D
6. G. E. Byron, D
7. P. J. Mitchell, D
8. *N. I. Steers, Jr., R

MASSACHUSETTS

1. S. O. Conte, R
2. E. P. Boland, D
3. J. D. Early, D
4. R. F. Drinan, D
5. P. Tsongas, D
6. M. J. Harrington, D
7. *E. J. Markey, D
8. T. P. O'Neill, Jr., D
9. J. J. Moakley, D
10. M. M. Heckler, R
11. J. A. Burke, D
12. G. E. Studds, D

MICHIGAN

1. J. Conyers, Jr., D
2. *C. D. Pursell, R
3. G. Brown, R

4. *D. A. Stockman, R
5. *H. S. Sawyer, R
6. M. R. Carr, D
7. *D. E. Kildee, D
8. B. Traxler, D
9. G. A. Vander Jagt, R
10. E. A. Cederberg, R
11. P. E. Ruppe, R
12. *D. E. Bonior, D
13. C. C. Diggs, Jr., D
14. L. N. Nedzi, D
15. W. D. Ford, D
16. J. D. Dingell, D
17. W. M. Brodhead, D
18. J. J. Blanchard, D
19. W. S. Broomfield, R

MINNESOTA

1. A. H. Quie, R
2. T. M. Hagedorn, R
3. B. Frenzel, R
4. *B. F. Vento, D
5. D. M. Fraser, D
6. R. M. Nolan, D
7. **A. Stangeland, R
8. J. L. Oberstar, D

MISSISSIPPI

1. J. L. Whitten, D
2. D. R. Bowen, D
3. G. V. Montgomery, D
4. T. Cochran, R
5. T. Lott, R

MISSOURI

1. W. L. Clay, D
2. *R. A. Young, D
3. *R. A. Gephardt, D
4. *I. Skelton, D
5. R. Bolling, D
6. *E. T. Coleman, R
7. G. Taylor, R
8. R. H. Ichord, D
9. *H. L. Volkmer, D
10. B. D. Burlison, D

MONTANA

1. M. Baucus, D
2. *R. Marlenee, R

NEBRASKA

1. C. Thone, R
2. *J. J. Cavanaugh, D
3. V. Smith, R

NEVADA

At-L. J. D. Santini, D

NEW HAMPSHIRE

1. N. E. D'Amours, D
2. J. C. Cleveland, R

NEW JERSEY

1. J. J. Florio, D
2. W. J. Hughes, D
3. J. J. Howard, D
4. F. Thompson, Jr., D
5. M. Fenwick, R
6. E. B. Forsythe, R
7. A. Maguire, D
8. R. A. Roe, D
9. *H. C. Hollenbeck, R
10. P. W. Rodino, Jr., D
11. J. G. Minish, D
12. M. J. Rinaldo, R
13. H. S. Meyner, D
14. *J. A. Le Fante, D
15. E. J. Patten, D

NEW MEXICO

1. M. Lujan, Jr., R
2. H. Runnels, D

NEW YORK

1. O. G. Pike, D
2. T. J. Downey, D
3. J. A. Ambro, D
4. N. F. Lent, R
5. J. W. Wydler, R
6. L. L. Wolff, D
7. J. P. Addabbo, D
8. B. S. Rosenthal, D
9. J. J. Delaney, D
10. M. Biaggi, D
11. J. H. Scheuer, D
12. S. A. Chisholm, D
13. S. J. Solarz, D
14. F. W. Richmond, D
15. L. C. Zeferetti, D
16. E. Holtzman, D
17. J. M. Murphy, D
18. Vacant
19. C. B. Rangel, D
20. *T. Weiss, D
21. Vacant

22. J. B. Bingham, D
23. *B. F. Caputo, R
24. R. L. Ottinger, D
25. H. Fish, Jr., R
26. B. A. Gilman, R
27. M. F. McHugh, D
28. S. S. Stratton, D
29. E. W. Pattison, D
30. R. C. McEwen, R
31. D. J. Mitchell, R
32. J. M. Hanley, D
33. W. F. Walsh, R
34. F. Horton, R
35. B. B. Conable, Jr., R
36. J. J. LaFalce, D
37. H. J. Nowak, D
38. J. Kemp, R
39. S. N. Lundine, D

NORTH CAROLINA

1. W. B. Jones, D
2. L. H. Fountain, D
3. *C. O. Whitley, Sr., D
4. I. F. Andrews, D
5. S. L. Neal, D
6. L. R. Preyer, D
7. C. Rose, D
8. W. G. Hefner, D
9. J. G. Martin, R
10. J. T. Broyhill, R
11. *L. Gudger, D

NORTH DAKOTA

At-L. M. Andrews, R

OHIO

1. W. D. Gradison, Jr., R
2. *T. A. Luken, D
3. C. W. Whalen, Jr., R
4. T. Guyer, R
5. D. L. Latta, R
6. W. H. Harsha, R
7. C. J. Brown, R
8. T. N. Kindness, R
9. T. L. Ashley, D
10. C. E. Miller, R
11. J. W. Stanton, R
12. S. L. Devine, R
13. *D. J. Pease, D
14. J. F. Seiberling, D
15. C. P. Wylie, R
16. R. Regula, R
17. J. M. Ashbrook, R
18. *D. Applegate, D
19. C. J. Carney, D
20. *M. R. Oakar, D
21. L. Stokes, D
22. C. A. Vanik, D
23. R. M. Mottl, D

OKLAHOMA

1. J. R. Jones, D
2. T. Risenhoover, D
3. W. W. Watkins, D
4. T. Steed, D
5. *M. Edwards, R
6. G. English, D

OREGON

1. L. AuCoin, D
2. A. Ullman, D
3. R. B. Duncan, D
4. J. Weaver, D

PENNSYLVANIA

1. *M. Myers, D
2. R. N. C. Nix, D
3. *R. F. Lederer, D
4. J. Eilberg, D
5. R. T. Schulze, R
6. G. Yatron, D
7. R. W. Edgar, D
8. *P. H. Kostmayer, D
9. B. Shuster, R
10. J. M. McDade, R
11. D. J. Flood, D
12. J. P. Murtha, D
13. L. Coughlin, R
14. W. S. Moorhead, D
15. F. B. Rooney, D
16. *R. S. Walker, R
17. *A. E. Ertel, D
18. *D. Walgren, D
19. W. F. Goodling, R
20. J. M. Gaydos, D
21. J. H. Dent, D
22. *A. J. Murphy, D
23. *J. S. Ammerman, D
24. *M. L. Marks, R
25. G. A. Myers, R

RHODE ISLAND

1. F. J. St Germain, D
2. E. P. Beard, D

SOUTH CAROLINA

1. M. J. Davis, D
2. F. D. Spence, R
3. B. C. Derrick, Jr., D
4. J. R. Mann, D
5. K. Holland, D
6. J. W. Jenrette, Jr., D

SOUTH DAKOTA

1. L. Pressler, R
2. J. Abdnor, R

TENNESSEE

1. J. H. Quillen, R
2. J. J. Duncan, R
3. M. L. Lloyd, D
4. *A. Gore, Jr., D
5. C. R. Allen, D
6. R. L. Beard, Jr., R
7. E. Jones, D
8. H. Ford, D

TEXAS

1. S. B. Hall, Jr., D
2. C. Wilson, D
3. J. M. Collins, R
4. R. Roberts, D
5. *J. A. Mattox, D
6. O. E. Teague, D
7. B. Archer, R
8. B. Eckhardt, D
9. J. Brooks, D
10. J. J. Pickle, D
11. W. R. Poage, D
12. *C. Wright, Jr., D
13. J. E. Hightower, D
14. J. Young, D
15. E. de la Garza, D
16. R. C. White, D
17. O. Burleson, D
18. B. C. Jordan, D
19. G. H. Mahon, D
20. H. B. Gonzalez, D
21. R. C. Krueger, D
22. *B. Gammage, D
23. A. Kazen, Jr., D
24. D. Milford, D

UTAH

1. G. McKay, D
2. *D. D. Marriott, R

VERMONT

At-L. J. M. Jeffords, R

VIRGINIA

1. *P. S. Trible, Jr., R
2. G. W. Whitehurst, R
3. D. E. Satterfield, III, D
4. R. W. Daniel, Jr., R
5. D. Daniel, D
6. M. C. Butler, R
7. J. K. Robinson, R
8. H. E. Harris, II, D
9. W. C. Wampler, R
10. J. L. Fisher, D

WASHINGTON

1. J. M. Pritchard, R
2. L. Meeds, D
3. D. L. Bonker, D
4. M. McCormack, D
5. T. S. Foley, D
6. *N. D. Dicks, D
7. **J. Cunningham, R

WEST VIRGINIA

1. R. H. Mollohan, D
2. H. O. Staggers, D
3. J. Slack, D
4. *N. J. Rahall, D

WISCONSIN

1. L. Aspin, D
2. R. W. Kastenmeier, D
3. A. J. Baldus, D
4. C. J. Zablocki, D
5. H. S. Reuss, D
6. W. A. Steiger, R
7. D. R. Obey, D
8. R. J. Cornell, D
9. R. W. Kasten, Jr., R

WYOMING

At-L. T. Roncalio, D

PUERTO RICO

Resident Commissioner
*B. Corrada

DISTRICT OF COLUMBIA

Delegate
W. E. Fauntroy, D

557

THE UNITED STATES GOVERNMENT

President: Jimmy Carter
Vice President: Walter F. Mondale

EXECUTIVE OFFICE OF THE PRESIDENT

The White House Office
Assistant to the President for National Security Affairs: Zbigniew Brzezinski
Assistant to the President for Public Liaison: Margaret Costanza
Assistant to the President for Domestic Affairs and Policy: Stuart E. Eizenstat
Assistant to the President: Hamilton Jordan
Counsel to the President: Robert J. Lipshutz
Assistant to the President for Congressional Liaison: Frank B. Moore
Assistant to the President for Reorganization: Richard A. Pettigrew
Press Secretary to the President: Joseph (Jody) L. Powell
Secretary to the Cabinet and Assistant to the President for Intergovernmental Affairs: Jack H. Watson, Jr.

Office of Management and Budget
Director: James T. McIntyre, Jr.*

Council of Economic Advisers
Chairman: Charles L. Schultze
Member: Lyle E. Gramley
Member: William D. Nordhaus

Central Intelligence Agency
Director: Stansfield Turner

Office of Special Representative for Trade Negotiations
Special Representative: Robert S. Strauss

Council on Environmental Quality
Chairman: Charles H. Warren
Member: James Gustave Speth
Member: Marion Edey

Office of Telecommunications Policy
Director: William J. Thaler, acting

Office of Drug Abuse Policy
Director: Peter G. Bourne

Office of Science and Technology Policy
Director: Frank Press

OFFICE OF THE VICE PRESIDENT

Chief of Staff: Richard Moe
Counsel to the Vice President and Deputy Chief of Staff: Michael S. Berman
Press Secretary: Albert Eisele

THE CABINET

Department of Agriculture
Secretary: Bob Bergland
Deputy Secretary: John C. White[1]

Department of Commerce
Secretary: Juanita M. Kreps
Undersecretary: Sidney L. Harman
National Oceanic and Atmospheric Administration, Administrator: Robert M. White
Assistant Secretary for Maritime Affairs: Robert J. Blackwell
Bureau of the Census, Director: Manuel D. Plotkin
Assistant Secretary for Tourism: Fabian Chavez, Jr.
National Bureau of Standards, Director: Ernest Ambler*
Commissioner of Patents and Trademarks: C. Marshall Dann

Department of Defense
Secretary: Harold Brown
Deputy Secretary: Charles W. Duncan, Jr.
Director of Defense Research and Engineering: William J. Perry
Joint Chiefs of Staff
  Chairman: Gen. George S. Brown, USAF
  Chief of Staff, U. S. Army: Gen. Bernard W. Rogers, USA
  Chief of Naval Operations: Adm. James L. Holloway III, USN
  Chief of Staff, U. S. Air Force: Gen. David C. Jones, USAF
Secretary of the Air Force: John Stetson
Secretary of the Army: Clifford L. Alexander, Jr.
Secretary of the Navy: W. Graham Claytor, Jr.
Commandant of the Marine Corps: Gen. Louis Wilson, USMC

Department of Energy
Secretary: James R. Schlesinger
Deputy Secretary: John F. O'Leary
Office of Energy Research, Director: John M. Deutch

Department of Health, Education, and Welfare
Secretary: Joseph A. Califano, Jr.
Undersecretary: Hale Champion
Office for Civil Rights, Director: David Tatel
Office of Equal Employment Opportunity, Director: Samuel M. Hoston
Administration on Aging, Commissioner: Robert C. Benedict*
Assistant Secretary for Human Development: Arabella Martinez
Assistant Secretary for Education: Mary Berry
Commissioner of Education: Ernest L. Boyer
Assistant Secretary for Health: James F. Dickson III, M.D., acting
Alcohol, Drug Abuse, and Mental Health Administration, Administrator: Gerald L. Klerman
Center for Disease Control, Director: William H. Foege, M.D.
Commissioner of Food and Drugs: Donald Kennedy
Health Resources Administration, Administrator: vacant
National Institutes of Health, Director: Donald S. Fredrickson
Health Care Financing Administration, Administrator: Don I. Wortman, acting
Commissioner of Social Security: James B. Cardwell
Office of Child Support Enforcement, Director: James B. Caldwell

Department of Housing and Urban Development
Secretary: Patricia Roberts Harris
Undersecretary: Jay Janis
Assistant Secretary for Housing—Federal Housing Commissioner: Lawrence P. Simons
Assistant Secretary for Fair Housing and Equal Opportunity: Chester C. McGuire, Jr.

Department of the Interior
Secretary: Cecil D. Andrus
Undersecretary: James A. Joseph
Solicitor: Leo M. Krulitz
Commissioner of Indian Affairs: Forrest J. Gerard
United States Fish and Wildlife Service, Director: Lynn A. Greenwalt
National Park Service, Director: Gary E. Everhardt
Bureau of Mines, Director: vacant
Geological Survey, Director: Vincent E. McKelvey

Department of Justice
Attorney General: Griffin B. Bell
Deputy Attorney General: Benjamin R. Civiletti*
Solicitor General: Wade H. McCree, Jr.
Assistant Attorney General, Antitrust Division: Donald I. Baker
Assistant Attorney General, Civil Division: Barbara A. Babcock
Assistant Attorney General, Civil Rights Division: Drew S. Days III

Federal Bureau of Investigation, Director: Clarence M. Kelley[2]

Drug Enforcement Administration, Administrator: Peter B. Bensinger

Immigration and Naturalization Service Commissioner: Leonard F. Chapman, Jr.

Bureau of Prisons, Director: Norman A. Carlson

Department of Labor

Secretary: F. Ray Marshall

Undersecretary: Robert J. Brown

Solicitor: Carin A. Clauss

Deputy Undersecretary for International Affairs: Howard D. Samuel

Assistant Secretary for Policy, Evaluation, and Research: Arnold H. Packer

Assistant Secretary for Administration and Management: Fred G. Clark

Assistant Secretary for Employment and Training: Ernest G. Green

Assistant Secretary for Labor-Management Relations: Francis X. Burkhardt

Assistant Secretary for Employment Standards: Donald E. Elisburg

Assistant Secretary for Occupational Safety and Health: Eula Bingham

Commissioner of Labor Statistics: Julius Shiskin

Department of State

Secretary: Cyrus R. Vance

Chief of Protocol: Evan S. Dobelle

Ambassador at Large: Ellsworth Bunker

Ambassador at Large: Elliott L. Richardson

Deputy Secretary: Warren M. Christopher

Undersecretary for Political Affairs: Philip C. Habib

Undersecretary for Economic Affairs: Richard N. Cooper

Undersecretary for Security Assistance: Lucy Wilson Benson

Assistant Secretary for African Affairs: William E. Schaufele, Jr.

Assistant Secretary for East Asian and Pacific Affairs: Richard C. Holbrooke

Assistant Secretary for European Affairs: Arthur A. Hartman

Assistant Secretary for Inter-American Affairs and U.S. Coordinator, Alliance for Progress: Terence A. Todman

Assistant Secretary for Near Eastern and South Asian Affairs: Alfred L. Atherton, Jr.

Assistant Secretary for Public Affairs: Hodding Carter III

Permanent Representative to the Organization of American States: Gale W. McGee

Agency for International Development, Administrator: John J. Gilligan

United Nations Representative: Andrew Young

Department of Transportation

Secretary: Brock Adams

Deputy Secretary: Alan A. Butchman

Coast Guard Commandant: Adm. Owen W. Siler, USCG

Federal Aviation Administration, Administrator: Langhorne M. Bond

Federal Highway Administration, Administrator: William M. Cox

Federal Railroad Administration, Administrator: vacant

National Highway Traffic Safety Administration, Administrator: Joan B. Claybrooke

Urban Mass Transportation Administration, Administrator: Charles F. Bingman, acting

Saint Lawrence Seaway Development Corporation, Administrator: David W. Oberlin

Department of Treasury

Secretary: W. Michael Blumenthal

Deputy Secretary: Robert Carswell

Undersecretary for Monetary Affairs: Anthony M. Solomon

Undersecretary: Bette B. Anderson

Treasurer of the United States: Azie Taylor Morton

Bureau of Alcohol, Tobacco and Firearms, Director: Rex D. Davis

Comptroller of the Currency: John A. Heimann

Commissioner of Customs: Vernon D. Acree

Bureau of Engraving and Printing, Director: James A. Conlon

Internal Revenue Service, Commissioner: Jerome Kurtz

Bureau of the Mint, Director: Stella B. Hackel*

Bureau of the Public Debt, Commissioner: H. J. Hintgen

U. S. Secret Service, Director: H. Stuart Knight

INDEPENDENT AGENCIES

ACTION: Sam Brown, director

Peace Corps: Carolyn R. Payton, director

American Battle Monuments Commission, Chairman: Gen. Mark W. Clark, USA (Ret.)

Appalachian Regional Commission, Federal cochairman: Donald W. Whitehead

Civil Aeronautics Board: John E. Robson, chairman

Commission on Civil Rights: Arthur S. Flemming, chairman

Consumer Product Safety Commission: S. John Byington, chairman

Environmental Protection Agency: Douglas M. Costle, administrator

Equal Employment Opportunity Commission: Eleanor Holmes Norton, commissioner

Export-Import Bank: John L. Moore, president and chairman

Farm Credit Board: E. Riddell Lage, chairman

Federal Communications Commission: Richard E. Wiley, chairman

Federal Deposit Insurance Corporation: Robert E. Barnett, chairman, board of directors

Federal Election Commission: Vernon W. Thomson, chairman

Federal Home Loan Bank Board: Robert H. McKinney, chairman

Federal Maritime Commission: Richard J. Daschbach, chairman

Federal Mediation and Conciliation Service: Wayne L. Horvitz, national director

Federal Power Commission: Charles B. Curtis, chairman

Federal Reserve System: G. William Miller,* chairman

Federal Trade Commission: Michael Pertschuk, chairman

Foreign Claims Settlement Commission: J. Raymond Bell, chairman

General Services Administration: Joel (Jay) W. Solomon, administrator

Federal Preparedness Agency: Dalimil Kybal, acting director

Automated Data and Telecommunications Service: Warren E. Burton, acting commissioner

Public Buildings Service: Thomas L. Peyton, Jr., acting commissioner

National Archives and Records Service: James B. Rhoads, archivist of the United States

Indian Claims Commission: Jerome K. Kuykendall, chairman

Interstate Commerce Commission: George M. Stafford, chairman

National Aeronautics and Space Administration: Robert Alan Frosch, administrator

National Foundation on the Arts and Humanities

National Endowment for the Arts: Livingston Biddle, Jr.

National Endowment for the Humanities: Joseph Duffey

National Labor Relations Board: John H. Fanning, chairman

National Science Foundation: Richard C. Atkinson, director

Postal Rate Commission: Alvin H. Gandal,* chairman

Securities and Exchange Commission: Harold M. Williams, chairman

Selective Service System: Byron V. Pepitone, director

Small Business Administration: A. Vernon Weaver, Jr., administrator

Tennessee Valley Authority: Aubrey J. Wagner, chairman

U. S. Arms Control and Disarmament Agency: Paul C. Warnke, director

U. S. Civil Service Commission: Alan K. Campbell, chairman

U. S. Information Agency: John E. Reinhardt, director

U. S. Postal Service: Benjamin F. Bailar, postmaster general

Veterans Administration: Max Cleland, administrator

As of Jan. 1, 1978   *Nominated but not confirmed   [1] Named chairman, Democratic National Committee   [2] To resign

Sources: *U. S. Government Manual; Weekly Compilations of Presidential Documents*

UNITED STATES:

Major Legislation Enacted in 1977

SUBJECT	PURPOSE
Natural gas	Gives emergency powers to the president and Federal Power Commission to distribute natural gas where needed in a gas emergency. Signed February 2. Public Law 95-2.
Reorganization of executive branch	Empowers the president to reorganize and streamline the executive branch to ensure maximum efficiency. Signed April 6. Public Law 95-17.
Drought relief	Provides direct grants and loans for locally-designed water projects, and some emergency loans to farmers, ranchers. Signed April 7. Public Law 95-18.
Interest rates	Extends the authority to regulate interest rates paid by depository institutions. Signed April 19. Public Law 95-22.
Public works employment	Provides $4 billion immediate funding for state and local projects, the jobs to be in the private sector. Signed May 13. Public Law 95-28.
Economic stimulus	Provides more than $20 billion in general revenue sharing funds to get people back to work who are difficult to employ. Signed May 13. Public Law 95-29.
Tax simplification and reduction	Simplifies the income tax codes, provides greater equity, and reduces taxes. Signed May 23. Public Law 95-30.
Eleanor Roosevelt home	Makes Val-Kill, Eleanor Roosevelt's home in Hyde Park, New York, a national historic site. Signed May 26. Public Law 85-32.
Kennedy library	Accepts the gift of land for the creation of the John Fitzgerald Kennedy library on Columbia Point in Boston Harbor. Signed May 26. Public Law 95-34.
Conservation	Increases funds to $900 million per year for 1978, 1979, to aid in national parks acquisitions. Signed June 11. Public Law 95-42.
Water sharing	Establishes the framework for a new Westlands Water District to assure equitable prices for water and enforce acreage limitations. Signed June 16. Public Law 95-46.
Foreign boycotts	Amends the export administration to end the divisive effects of foreign boycotts aimed at Jewish Americans. Signed June 22. Public Law 95-52.
Food and agriculture	Ties target prices to production costs; provides a simple food stamp system; eliminates acreage allotments; and provides for an adequate food reserve under farmers' control. Signed September 29. Public Law 95-113.
Juvenile delinquency	Draws a sharp distinction between serious and not serious crime and encourages the deinstitutionalization of the nonserious. Signed October 3. Public Law 95-115.
Veterans discharges	Provides uniform standards for review and upgrading of less-than-honorable discharges and for determining the veterans' benefits. Signed October 8. Public Law 95-126.
Housing, community development	Makes $12.4 billion available for community block grant programs, and prohibits redlining depressed areas. Signed October 12. Public Law 95-128.
Health care fraud	Imposes heavier penalties for anyone convicted of false claims or taking kickbacks. Requires everyone with 5% ownership in a health-providing company to reveal their identities. Signed October 25. Public Law 95-142.
Prisoner exchange	Implements the process whereby Americans in Mexican or Canadian jails, or Mexicans and Canadians in American jails, can go back home to serve out their terms. Signed October 28. Public Law 95-144.
Minimum wage	Raises the minimum wage on Jan. 1, 1978 to $2.65 per hour. Signed November 1. Public Law 95-151.
Wildlife preservation	Authorizes the completion of Tinicum National Environmental Center, near Philadelphia, for the preservation of wildlife. Signed November 4. Public Law 95-152.
Ocean dumping	Ends the dumping of sewage sludge in the Atlantic Ocean as of December 1981. Signed November 4. Public Law 95-153.
Mariana Islands	Creates a district court, establishes the Commonwealth of the Northern Mariana Islands in political union with the U. S. Signed November 8. Public Law 95-157.
Alcan pipeline	Possibly the greatest single engineering project ever, the pipeline from Alaska through Canada to the 48 States will make possible the delivery of 3.6 billion cubic feet of gas daily. Signed November 8. Public Law 95-158.
Mine safety	Extends to other miners the same health and safety standards coal miners have. Signed November 9. Public Law 95-164.
Jobs, health, education	Expands the Job Corps by 14,000; increases by 400,000 the college students receiving grants; provides funds to immunize all children against dangerous communicable diseases. Signed December 9. Public Law 95-205.
Rural health clinics	Requires that Medicare, Medicaid programs pay for services of physician assistants and nurse practitioners in clinics in rural areas that are without adequate care. Signed December 13. Public Law 95-210.
Social security	Revamps the social security system. (See page 436.) Signed December 20. Public Law 95-216.

POPULATION
Vital Statistics of Selected Countries

	Estimated population mid-1977	Birthrate per 1,000 population	Deathrate per 1,000 population	Infant mortality per 1,000	Life ex-pectancy at birth	Urban popula-tion (%)	Population projection to yr. 2000
World	4,083,000,000	30	12	103	62	59	6,182,000,000
Afghanistan	20,000,000	43	21	182	40	15	36,100,000
Albania	2,500,000	33	8	87	67	34	4,100,000
Algeria	17,800,000	48	15	142	53	52	36,500,000
Angola	6,300,000	47	24	203	38	18	11,700,000
Argentina	26,100,000	23	9	59	68	80	32,900,000
Australia	13,900,000	17	8	16	71	86	19,600,000
Austria	7,500,000	12	13	21	71	52	8,100,000
Bangladesh	83,300,000	47	20	132	47	9	154,900,000
Belgium	9,900,000	12	12	16	71	87	10,700,000
Bolivia	4,800,000	44	18	108	47	34	8,700,000
Brazil	112,000,000	37	9	82	61	59	205,000,000
Bulgaria	8,800,000	17	10	23	71	59	9,900,000
Burma	31,800,000	40	16	126	50	22	53,300,000
Cambodia	8,000,000	47	19	127	45	12	14,700,000
Canada	23,500,000	16	7	15	73	76	31,600,000
Chad	4,200,000	44	24	160	38	14	6,900,000
Chile	11,000,000	24	8	77	63	76	15,800,000
China, mainland	850,000,000	27	10	—	62	24	1,126,000,000
Colombia	25,200,000	33	9	97	61	64	47,100,000
Congo	1,400,000	45	21	180	44	40	2,700,000
Cuba	9,600,000	22	6	29	70	60	14,900,000
	15,000,000	20	12	21	71	67	16,900,000
Denmark	5,100,000	14	10	12	74	80	5,400,000
Ecuador	7,500,000	42	10	78	60	41	14,700,000
Egypt	38,900,000	36	12	116	52	45	63,900,000
El Salvador	4,300,000	40	8	58	58	39	8,600,000
Ethiopia	29,400,000	43	18	181	42	12	53,800,000
Finland	4,800,000	14	9	10	71	58	4,800,000
France	53,400,000	14	11	12	72	70	61,700,000
Gabon	530,000	32	22	178	41	32	700,000
Germany, East	16,700,000	11	14	16	71	75	17,700,000
Germany, West	61,200,000	10	12	20	71	88	65,500,000
Ghana	10,400,000	47	20	156	48	31	21,100,000
Greece	9,100,000	16	9	24	72	65	9,800,000
Guatemala	6,400,000	43	12	80	53	34	12,200,000
Guinea	4,700,000	47	23	175	41	20	8,500,000
Haiti	5,300,000	36	16	150	50	20	7,900,000
Honduras	3,300,000	49	15	117	54	31	6,900,000
Hungary	10,700,000	18	12	33	70	50	11,100,000
Iceland	225,000	21	7	11	74	86	300,000
India	662,700,000	34	13	122	50	21	1,023,700,000
Indonesia	136,900,000	38	14	137	48	18	226,900,000
Iran	34,800,000	44	16	139	51	44	66,100,000
Iraq	11,800,000	44	11	99	53	64	24,300,000
Ireland	3,200,000	22	11	17	71	52	4,000,000
Israel	3,600,000	28	7	22	72	82	5,500,000
Italy	56,500,000	15	10	21	72	53	61,900,000
Japan	114,200,000	17	6	10	74	72	133,400,000
Kenya	14,400,000	49	16	119	50	10	31,500,000
Lebanon	2,800,000	40	10	59	64	60	5,600,000
Lesotho	1,100,000	39	20	114	46	3	1,800,000
Libya	2,700,000	48	9	130	55	30	5,200,000
Madagascar	7,900,000	50	21	102	44	14	16,400,000
Malawi	5,300,000	48	24	142	43	10	9,900,000
Malaysia	12,600,000	35	7	75	63	27	21,600,000
Mali	5,900,000	50	26	188	38	13	11,000,000
Mexico	64,400,000	42	7	66	63	62	134,600,000
Morocco	18,300,000	48	16	130	53	38	35,500,000
Nepal	13,200,000	43	20	169	44	4	23,200,000
Netherlands	13,900,000	13	8	11	74	77	16,100,000
New Zealand	3,200,000	18	8	16	72	81	4,400,000
Nicaragua	2,300,000	48	14	123	53	49	4,800,000
Nigeria	66,600,000	49	23	180	41	18	134,900,000
Norway	4,000,000	14	10	11	74	45	4,500,000
Pakistan	74,500,000	44	15	121	51	26	145,500,000
Panama	1,800,000	31	5	40	66	50	3,200,000
Paraguay	2,800,000	40	9	65	62	37	5,300,000
Peru	16,600,000	41	12	110	56	55	31,200,000
Philippines	44,300,000	35	8	74	58	32	83,700,000
Poland	34,700,000	19	9	25	70	54	40,200,000
Portugal	9,200,000	20	11	38	69	26	10,400,000
Rumania	21,700,000	20	9	35	69	43	25,900,000
Saudi Arabia	7,600,000	50	20	152	45	21	14,800,000
South Africa	26,100,000	40	15	117	52	48	51,200,000
Spain	36,500,000	18	8	14	72	61	45,400,000
Sweden	8,200,000	13	11	8	75	81	9,200,000
Syria	7,800,000	45	15	93	57	46	16,000,000
Tanzania	16,000,000	47	22	162	44	7	33,100,000
Thailand	44,400,000	35	11	89	58	13	84,600,000
Tunisia	6,000,000	34	11	125	55	47	10,800,000
Turkey	41,900,000	39	12	119	57	43	72,400,000
Uganda	12,400,000	43	16	160	50	7	24,700,000
USSR	259,000,000	18	9	28	69	60	314,000,000
United Kingdom	56,000,000	12	12	16	72	78	61,900,000
United States	216,700,000	15	9	16	72	74	262,500,000
Uruguay	2,800,000	21	10	45	70	81	3,400,000
Venezuela	12,700,000	37	6	49	65	74	23,200,000
Vietnam	47,300,000	42	40	—	50	22	78,900,000
Yemen	5,600,000	50	21	152	45	9	11,000,000
Yugoslavia	21,800,000	18	9	40	68	39	25,700,000
Zaire	26,300,000	45	20	160	44	26	50,500,000
Zambia	5,200,000	50	19	160	46	36	11,300,000

Source: "1977 World Population Data Sheet of the Population Reference Bureau, Inc."

CANADIAN CENSUS

Growth of the population of Canada,

Census year	Population No.	Increase during intercensal period		Average annual rate of population growth %
		No.	%	
1851	2,436,297			
1861	3,229,633	793,336	32.6	2.9
1871	3,689,257	459,624	14.2	1.3
1881	4,324,810	635,553	17.2	1.6
1891	4,833,239	508,429	11.8	1.1
1901	5,371,315	538,076	11.1	1.1
1911	7,206,643	1,835,328	34.2	3.0
1921	8,787,949	1,581,306	21.9	2.0
1931	10,376,786	1,588,837	18.1	1.7
1941	11,506,655	1,129,869	10.9	1.0
1951[1]	14,009,429	2,502,774	21.8	1.7
1961	18,238,247	4,228,818	30.2	2.7
1971	21,568,311	3,330,064	18.3	1.7
1976	22,992,604	1,424,293	6.6	—

[1] 1951 Census figures include Newfoundland for the first time. Excluding Newfoundland the increase would have been 2,141,358 or 18.6%.

	1971	1976		1971	1976
Alberta	1,627,874	1,838,037	Nova Scotia	788,960	828,571
British Columbia	2,184,621	2,466,608	Ontario	7,703,106	8,264,465
Manitoba	988,247	1,021,506	Prince Edward Island	111,641	118,229
New Brunswick	634,557	677,250	Quebec	6,027,764	6,234,445
Newfoundland	522,104	557,725	Saskatchewan	926,242	921,323
Northwest Territories	34,807	42,609	Yukon Territory	18,388	21,836

1976 POPULATION OF CITIES, TOWNS, AND VILLAGES

Ajax, Ont.	20,774	Chateauguay, Que.	36,329	Granby, Que.	37,132
Alma, Que.	25,638	Chatham, N.B.	7,601	Grand Falls, N.B.	6,223
Amherst, N.S.	10,263	Chatham, Ont.	38,685	Grand Falls, Nfld.	8,729
Amherstburg, Ont.	5,566	Chibougamau, Que.	10,536	Grand' Mère, Que.	15,999
Amos, Que.	9,213	Chicoutimi, Que.	57,737	Grande Prairie, Alta.	17,626
Ancaster, Ont.	14,255	Chilliwack, B.C.	8,634	Gravenhurst, Ont.	7,986
Ancienne-Lorette, Que.	11,694	Coaticook, Que.	6,392	Greenfield Park, Que.	18,430
Anjou, Que.	36,596	Cobourg, Ont.	11,421	Grimsby, Ont.	15,567
Antigonish, N.S.	5,442	Comox, B.C.	5,359	Guelph, Ont.	67,538
Arnprior, Ont.	6,111	Conception Bay South, Nfld.	9,743	Haldimand, Ont.	16,375
Arthabaska, Que.	5,907	Corner Brook, Nfld.	25,198	Halifax, N.S.	117,882
Asbestos, Que.	9,075	Cornwall, Ont.	46,121	Halton Hills, Ont.	34,477
Aurora, Ont.	14,249	Côte-St.-Luc, Que.	25,721	Hamilton, Ont.	312,003
Aylmer, Ont.	5,125	Courtenay, B.C.	7,733	Hampstead, Que.	7,562
Aylmer, Que.	25,714	Cowansville, Que.	11,902	Hanover, Ont.	5,691
Baie-Comeau, Que.	11,911	Cranbrook, B.C.	13,510	Happy Valley-Goose Bay, Nfld.	8,075
Barrie, Ont.	34,389	Dalhousie, N.B.	5,640	Hauterive, Que.	14,724
Bathurst, N.B.	16,301	Dartmouth, N.S.	65,361	Hawkesbury, Ont.	9,789
Beaconsfield, Que.	20,417	Dauphin, Man.	9,109	Hearst, Ont.	5,195
Beauharnois, Que.	7,665	Dawson Creek, B.C.	10,528	Hinton, Alta.	6,731
Beauport, Que.	55,339	Deep River, Ont.	5,565	Hull, Que.	61,039
Bécancour, Que.	9,043	Deux-Montagnes, Que.	8,957	Huntsville, Ont.	11,123
Belleville, Ont.	35,311	Dolbeau, Que.	8,451	Iberville, Que.	8,897
Beloeil, Que.	15,913	Dollard-des-Ormeaux, Que.	36,837	Île-Perrot, Que.	5,272
Blainville, Que.	12,517	Donnacona, Que.	5,800	Ingersoll, Ont.	8,198
Boisbriand, Que.	10,132	Dorion, Que.	5,843	Iroquois Falls, Ont.	6,887
Boucherville, Que.	25,530	Dorval, Que.	19,131	Joliette, Que.	18,118
Bracebridge, Ont.	8,428	Drumheller, Alta.	6,154	Jonquière, Que.	60,691
Bradford, Ont.	5,080	Drummondville, Que.	29,286	Kamloops, B.C.	58,311
Brampton, Ont.	103,459	Drummondville-Sud, Que.	9,420	Kapuskasing, Ont.	12,676
Brandon, Man.	34,901	Dryden, Ont.	6,799	Kelowna, B.C.	51,955
Brantford, Ont.	66,950	Dundas, Ont.	19,179	Kenora, Ont.	10,565
Bridgewater, N.S.	6,010	Dunnville, Ont.	11,642	Kentville, N.S.	5,056
Brockville, Ont.	19,903	Edmonton, Alta.	461,361	Kimberley, B.C.	7,111
Brooks, Alta.	6,339	Edmundston, N.B.	12,710	Kingston, Ont.	56,032
Brossard, Que.	37,641	Elliot Lake, Ont.	8,849	Kirkland, Que.	7,476
Buckingham, Que.	14,328	Espanola, Ont.	5,926	Kirkland Lake, Ont.	13,567
Burlington, Ont.	104,314	Essex, Ont.	5,577	Kitchener, Ont.	131,870
Caledon, Ont.	22,434	Estevan, Sask.	8,847	La Baie, Que.	20,116
Calgary, Alta.	469,917	Farnham, Que.	6,476	La Prairie, Que.	9,173
Cambridge, Ont.	72,383	Fergus, Ont.	6,001	La Tuque, Que.	12,067
Campbellton, N.B.	9,282	Flin Flon, Man. & Sask.	8,560	Lac-Mégantic, Que.	6,457
Camrose, Alta.	10,104	Fort Erie, Ont.	24,031	Lachine, Que.	41,503
Candiac, Que.	7,166	Fort Frances, Ont.	9,325	Lahute, Que.	11,928
Cap-de-la-Madeleine, Que.	32,126	Fort McMurray, Alta.	15,424	Langley, B.C.	10,123
Carbonear, Nfld.	5,026	Fort St. John, B.C.	8,947	Lasalle, Que.	76,713
Carleton Place, Ont.	5,256	Fort Saskatchewan, Alta.	8,304	Laval, Que.	246,243
Castlegar, B.C.	6,255	Fredericton, N.B.	45,248	Lauzon, Que.	12,663
Chambly, Que.	11,815	Gananoque, Ont.	5,103	Leamington, Ont.	11,169
Channel-Port aux Basques, Nfld.	6,187	Gandes, Nfld.	9,301	Leduc, Alta.	8,576
Charlesbourg, Que.	63,147	Gaspé, Que.	16,842	Lemoyne, Que.	7,202
Charlottetown, P.E.I.	17,063	Gatineau, Que.	73,479	Lethbridge, Alta.	46,752
Charny, Que.	6,461	Glace Bay, N.S.	21,836	Levis, Que.	17,819
		Goderich, Ont.	7,385	Lincoln, Ont.	14,460

Lindsay, Ont.	13,062	
Listowel, Ont.	5,126	
Lloydminster, Alta. & Sask.	10,311	
London, Ont.	240,392	
Longueuil, Que.	122,429	
Loretteville, Que.	14,767	
Lorraine, Que.	5,388	
Magog, Que.	13,290	
Malartic, Que.	5,092	
Maniwaki, Que.	5,969	
Markham, Ont.	56,206	
Marystown, Nfld.	5,915	
Mascouche, Que.	14,266	
Matane, Que.	12,726	
Medicine Hat, Alta.	32,811	
Melfort, Sask.	5,141	
Melville, Sask.	5,149	
Merritt, B.C.	5,680	
Midland, Ont.	11,568	
Milton, Ont.	20,756	
Mirabel, Que.	13,486	
Mississauga, Ont.	250,017	
Mistassini, Que.	5,473	
Moncton, N.B.	55,934	
Mont-Joli, Que.	6,508	
Mont-Laurier, Que.	8,565	
Mont-Royal, Que.	20,514	
Mont-St.-Hilaire, Que.	7,688	
Montmagny, Que.	12,326	
Montreal, Que.	1,080,546	
Montreal-Nord, Que.	97,250	
Montreal-Ouest, Que.	5,980	
Moose Jaw, Sask.	32,581	
Mount Pearl, Nfld.	10,193	
Nanaimo, B.C.	40,336	
Nanticoke, Ont.	19,489	
Nelson, B.C.	9,235	
New Glasgow, N.S.	10,672	
New Liskeard, Ont.	5,601	
New Waterford, N.S.	9,223	
New Westminster, B.C.	38,393	
Newcastle, N.B.	6,423	
Newcastle, Ont.	31,928	
Newmarket, Ont.	24,795	
Niagara Falls, Ont.	69,423	
Niagara-on-the-Lake, Ont.	12,485	
Nickel Centre, Ont.	13,157	
Noranda, Que.	9,809	
North Battleford, Sask.	13,158	
North Bay, Ont.	51,639	
North Sydney, N.S.	8,319	
North Vancouver, B.C.	31,934	
Oakville, Ont.	68,950	
Onaping Falls, Ont.	6,776	
Orangeville, Ont.	12,021	
Orillia, Ont.	24,412	
Oromocto, N.B.	10,276	
Oshawa, Ont.	107,023	
Ottawa, Ont.	304,462	
Outremont, Que.	27,089	
Owen Sound, Ont.	19,525	
Parry Sound, Ont.	5,501	
Pelham, Ont.	10,071	
Pembroke, Ont.	14,927	
Penetanguishene, Ont.	5,460	
Penticton, B.C.	21,344	
Percé, Que.	5,198	
Perth, Ont.	5,675	
Petawawa, Ont.	5,815	
Peterborough, Ont.	59,683	
Pickering, Ont.	27,879	
Pierrefonds, Que.	35,402	
Pincourt, Que.	7,892	
Plessisville, Que.	7,238	
Pointe-aux-Trembles, Que.	35,618	
Pointe-Claire, Que.	25,917	
Port Alberni, B.C.	19,585	
Port-Cartier, Que.	8,139	
Port Colborne, Ont.	20,536	
Port Coquitlam, B.C.	23,926	
Port Elgin, Ont.	5,069	
Port Hope, Ont.	9,788	
Port Moody, B.C.	11,649	
Portage la Prairie, Man.	12,555	
Prince Albert, Sask.	28,631	
Prince George, B.C.	59,929	
Prince Rupert, B.C.	14,754	
Québec, Que.	177,082	
Quesnel, B.C.	7,637	
Rayside-Balfour, Ont.	16,035	
Red Deer, Alta.	32,184	
Regina, Sask.	149,593	
Renfrew, Ont.	8,617	
Repentigny, Que.	26,698	
Richmond Hill, Ont.	34,716	
Rimouski, Que.	27,897	
Riverview, N.B.	14,177	
Rivière-du-Loup, Que.	13,103	
Roberval, Que.	8,543	
Rosemère, Que.	7,112	
Rouyn, Que.	17,678	
Roxboro, Que.	7,106	
Sackville, N.B.	5,755	
St. Albert, Alta.	24,129	
St.-Antoine, Que.	6,872	
St.-Basile-le-Grand, Que.	5,843	
St.-Bruno-de-Montarville, Que.	21,272	
St. Catharines, Ont.	123,351	
St.-Constant, Que.	7,659	
St.-Eustache, Que.	21,248	
St.-Georges, Que.	8,605	
St.-Georges-Ouest, Que.	6,478	
St.-Hubert, Que.	49,706	
St.-Hyacinthe, Que.	37,500	
St.-Jean, Que.	34,363	
St.-Jérôme, Que.	25,175	
St. John, N.B.	85,956	
St. John's, Nfld.	86,576	
St.-Lambert, Que.	20,318	
St.-Laurent, Que.	64,404	
St.-Léonard, Que.	78,452	
St.-Luc, Que.	7,103	
St.-Paul-l'Ermite, Que.	6,107	
St.-Pierre, Que.	6,039	
St.-Romuald-d'Etchemin, Que.	9,160	
St. Thomas, Ont.	27,206	
Ste.-Agathe-des-Monts, Que.	5,435	
Ste.-Anne-des-Monts, Que.	5,945	
Ste.-Catherine, Que.	5,036	
Ste.-Foy, Que.	71,237	
Ste.-Julie, Que.	8,666	
Ste.-Thérèse	17,479	
Sarnia, Ont.	55,576	
Saskatoon, Sask.	133,750	
Sault Ste. Marie, Ont.	81,048	
Selkirk, Man.	9,862	
Sept-Îles, Que.	30,617	
Shawinigan, Que.	24,921	
Shawinigan-Sud, Que.	11,155	
Sherbrooke, Que.	76,804	
Sherwood, P.E.I.	5,602	
Sidney, B.C.	6,732	
Sillery, Que.	13,580	
Simcoe, Ont.	14,189	
Smiths Falls, Ont.	9,279	
Sorel, Que.	19,666	
Springhill, N.S.	5,220	
Spruce Grove, Alta.	6,907	
Steinbach, Man.	5,979	
Stellarton, N.S.	5,366	
Stephenville, Nfld.	10,284	
Stoney Creek, Ont.	30,294	
Stratford, Ont.	25,657	
Sturgeon Falls, Ont.	6,400	
Sudbury, Ont.	97,604	
Summerside, P.E.I.	8,592	
Swift Current, Sask.	14,264	
Sydney, N.S.	30,645	
Sydney Mines, N.S.	8,965	
Taber, Alta.	5,296	
Tecumseh, Ont.	5,326	
Terrebonne, Que.	11,204	
The Pas, Man.	6,602	
Thetford Mines, Que.	20,784	
Thompson, Man.	17,291	
Thorold, Ont.	14,944	
Thunder Bay, Ont.	111,476	
Tillsonburg, Ont.	9,404	
Timmins, Ont.	44,747	
Toronto, Ont.	633,318	
Met. area	2,124,291	
Tracy, Que.	12,284	
Trail, B.C.	9,976	
Trenton, Ont.	15,465	
Trois-Rivières, Que.	52,518	
Trois-Rivières Ouest, Que.	10,564	
Truro, N.S.	12,840	
Val-Belair, Que.	10,716	
Val-d'Or, Que.	19,915	
Valley East, Ont.	19,591	
Valleyfield (Salaberry-de-), Que.	29,716	
Vancouver, B.C.	410,188	
Vanier, Ont.	19,812	
Vanier, Que.	10,683	
Varennes, Que.	6,469	
Vaudreuil, Que.	5,630	
Vaughan, Ont.	17,782	
Verdun, Que.	68,013	
Vernon, B.C.	17,546	
Victoria, B.C.	62,551	
Victoriaville, Que.	21,825	
Walden, Ont.	10,453	
Wallaceburg, Ont.	11,132	
Waterloo, Ont.	46,623	
Westmount, Que.	22,153	
Wetaskiwin, Alta.	6,754	
Weyburn, Sask.	8,892	
Whitby, Ont.	28,173	
Whitchurch-Stouffville, Ont.	12,884	
White Rock, B.C.	12,497	
Whitehorse, Yukon	13,311	
Williams Lake, B.C.	6,199	
Windsor, Nfld.	6,349	
Windsor, Ont.	196,526	
Windsor, Que.	5,637	
Winnipeg, Man.	560,874	
Woodstock, Ont.	26,779	
Yarmouth, N.S.	7,801	
Yellowknife, N.W.T.	8,256	
Yorkton, Sask.	14,119	

Projected population of Canada up to 2001

Year	Population as at June 1 '000	Annual rate of population growth %	Distribution by age			
			0-19 %	20-44 %	45-64 %	65+ %
1971	21,568.3	...	39.4	33.9	18.6	8.1
1976	23,086.1	1.4	36.1	36.4	18.9	8.6
1981	25,311.5	1.8	34.3	38.6	18.1	9.0
1986	27,810.9	1.9	33.9	39.6	17.2	9.3
1991	30,177.6	1.6	34.9	38.1	17.2	9.8
1996	32,347.1	1.4	35.6	36.2	18.3	9.9
2001	34,611.4	1.3	34.6	35.4	20.2	9.8

Projection assumptions: total fertility will change from 2.19 children in 1971 to 2.60 by 1985 and then remain constant through 2001; net migration gain of 100,000 per year; and expectation of life at birth will increase gradually to 70.2 years for males and 78.4 for females by 1986 and then remain constant through 2001.

	1971	1976		1971	1976
Australian Capital Territory	144,100	197,600	South Australia	1,173,700	1,244,800
New South Wales	4,601,200	4,777,100	Tasmania	390,400	402,900
Northern Territory	86,400	97,100	Victoria	3,502,400	3,647,000
Queensland	1,827,100	2,037,200	Western Australia	1,030,500	1,144,900

	1971	1976
National Total	12,755,600	13,548,500

	Males	Females	Total		Males	Females	Total
Adelaide, S.A.	421,154	436,042	857,196	Kurri Kurri-Weston, N.S.W.	6,021	6,122	12,143
Albany, W.A.	6,745	6,951	13,696	Kwinana-New Town, W.A.	5,538	5,443	10,981
Albury-Wodonga, N.S.W.				Launceston, Tas.	30,713	32,671	63,386
and Vic.	22,713	22,854	45,567	Leeton, N.S.W.	3,319	3,312	6,631
Alice Springs, N. Terr.	7,284	6,865	14,149	Lismore, N.S.W.	10,628	11,454	22,082
Ararat, Vic.	4,206	4,082	8,288	Lithgow, N.S.W.	6,327	6,376	12,703
Armidale, N.S.W.	9,760	9,951	19,711	Mackay, Qld.	15,723	15,799	31,522
Ayr, Qld.	4,392	4,214	8,606	Maitland, N.S.W.	18,060	17,970	36,030
Bairnsdale, Vic.	4,450	4,680	9,130	Mandurah, W.A.	3,523	3,527	7,050
Ballarat, Vic.	29,421	31,316	60,737	Mareeba, Qld.	2,842	2,934	5,776
Ballina, N.S.W.	3,597	3,726	7,323	Maroochydore-Mooloolaba,			
Bathurst, N.S.W.	9,206	9,383	18,589	Qld.	5,096	5,187	10,283
Bendigo, Vic.	24,208	25,961	50,169	Maryborough, Qld.	10,076	10,594	20,670
Benulla, Vic.	4,030	4,270	8,300	Maryborough, Vic.	3,659	3,910	7,569
Bowen, Qld.	3,472	3,235	6,707	Melbourne, Vic.	1,224,626	1,254,796	2,479,422
Bowral, N.S.W.	3,161	3,122	6,283	Melton, Vic.	6,093	5,929	12,022
Brisbane, Qld.	439,904	453,083	892,987	Mildura, Vic.	6,936	7,481	14,417
Brisbane Water, N.S.W.	26,488	28,331	54,819	Moe-Yallourn, Vic.	9,498	9,306	18,804
Broken Hill, N.S.W.	13,888	13,759	27,647	Mount Gambier, S.A.	9,623	9,669	19,292
Budgewei Lake, N.S.W.	7,782	7,966	15,748	Mount Isa, Qld.	13,428	11,949	25,377
Bunbury, W.A.	9,686	9,827	19,513	Moree, N.S.W.	4,712	4,647	9,359
Bundaberg, Qld.	15,416	15,773	31,189	Morwell, Vic.	8,292	7,802	16,094
Burnie-Somerset, Tas.	9,536	9,579	19,115	Mudgee, N.S.W.	2,759	2,965	5,724
Busselton, W.A.	2,749	2,801	5,550	Murray Bridge, S.A.	4,337	4,403	8,740
Cairns, Qld.	19,685	19,620	39,305	Murwillumbah, N.S.W.	3,499	3,795	7,294
Caloundra, Qld.	5,124	5,478	10,602	Muswellbrook, N.S.W.	3,935	3,870	7,805
Camden, N.S.W.	3,800	3,844	7,644	Nambour, Qld.	3,611	3,824	7,435
Canberra, A.C.T.	98,336	96,181	194,517	Narrabri, N.S.W.	3,569	3,382	6,951
Canberra, N.S.W.	9,557	8,981	18,538	Nelson Bay, N.S.W.	2,686	2,690	5,376
Carnarvon, W.A.	2,713	2,628	5,341	New Norfolk, Tas.	3,379	3,300	6,679
Casino, N.S.W.	4,564	4,892	9,456	Newcastle, N.S.W.	124,335	126,797	251,132
Castlemaine, Vic.	3,715	3,868	7,583	Northam, W.A.	3,483	3,383	6,866
Cessnock-Bellbird, N.S.W.	7,877	8,379	16,256	Nowra-Bomaderry, N.S.W.	7,802	7,694	15,496
Charters Towers, Qld.	4,262	3,652	7,914	Ocean Grove-Barwan			
Coffs Harbour, N.S.W.	6,053	6,144	12,197	Heads, Vic.	2,634	2,751	5,385
Colac, Vic.	5,080	5,351	10,431	Orange, N.S.W.	12,882	13,372	26,254
Collie, W.A.	3,456	3,315	6,771	Parkas, N.S.W.	4,352	4,553	8,905
Cooma, N.S.W.	3,716	3,637	7,353	Perth, W.A.	360,307	370,968	731,275
Cootamundra, N.S.W.	3,099	3,285	6,384	Port Augusta, S.A.	6,794	6,298	13,092
Cowra, N.S.W.	3,780	3,954	7,734	Port Hedland, W.A.	6,483	4,661	11,144
Crafers, S.A.	3,262	3,338	6,600	Port Lincoln, S.A.	5,065	5,207	10,272
Cranbourne, Vic.	2,593	2,569	5,162	Port Macquarie, N.S.W.	6,473	6,889	13,362
Dalby, Qld.	4,342	4,655	8,997	Port Pirie, S.A.	7,427	7,578	15,005
Darwin, N. Terr.	22,676	18,698	41,374	Portland, Vic.	4,105	4,193	8,298
Denilinquin, N.S.W.	3,392	3,473	6,865	Raymond Terrace, N.S.W.	3,540	3,449	6,989
Devonport, Tas.	9,414	9,985	19,399	Richmond-Windsor, N.S.W.	6,897	6,543	13,440
Dubbo, N.S.W.	9,958	10,191	20,149	Rockhampton, Qld.	24,633	25,499	50,132
Echuca-Moama, Vic.	3,801	4,072	7,873	Rockingham, W.A.	8,948	8,745	17,693
Esperance, W.A.	2,694	2,568	5,262	Roma, Qld.	2,978	2,920	5,898
Forbes, N.S.W.	3,912	3,842	7,754	Sale, Vic.	6,120	5,991	12,111
Forster-Tuncurry, N.S.W.	3,071	3,124	6,195	Seymour, Vic.	3,162	3,078	6,240
Gawler, S.A.	4,244	4,352	8,596	Shepparton-Mooroopna,			
Geelong, Vic.	60,677	61,403	122,080	Vic.	12,689	13,159	25,848
George Town, Tas.	2,727	2,569	5,296	Singleton, N.S.W.	3,895	4,022	7,917
Geraldton, W.A.	9,622	9,151	18,773	Stawell, Vic.	2,990	3,160	6,150
Gladstone, Qld.	9,713	8,878	18,591	Sunbury, Vic.	4,331	3,912	8,243
Glen Innes, N.S.W.	2,874	3,079	5,953	Swan Hill, Vic.	3,900	3,957	7,857
Gold Coast, N.S.W.				Sydney, N.S.W.	1,362,696	1,402,344	2,765,040
and Qld.	51,036	54,741	105,777	Tamworth, N.S.W.	13,283	13,990	27,273
Goulburn, N.S.W.	10,992	10,743	21,735	Taree, N.S.W.	6,515	6,925	13,440
Grafton, N.S.W.	8,057	8,459	16,516	Terrigal-Wamberel, N.S.W.	3,608	3,845	7,453
Griffith, N.S.W.	5,957	5,973	11,930	Tewantin-Noosa, Qld.	2,882	2,952	5,834
Gunnedah, N.S.W.	4,337	4,352	8,689	The Entrance, N.S.W.	9,713	10,394	20,107
Gympie, Qld.	5,449	5,756	11,205	Toowoomba, Qld.	31,013	32,943	63,956
Hamilton, Vic.	4,674	4,830	9,504	Townsville, Qld.	40,474	38,179	78,653
Hervey Bay, Qld.	4,495	4,655	9,150	Traralgon, Vic.	7,608	7,481	15,089
Hobart, Tas.	64,521	67,003	131,524	Tumut, N.S.W.	2,777	2,792	5,569
Horsham, Vic.	5,609	6,038	11,647	Ulverstone, Tas.	4,173	4,620	8,793
Ingham, Qld.	2,978	2,890	5,868	Wagga Wagga, N.S.W.	15,946	17,038	32,984
Innisfail, Qld.	4,075	3,858	7,933	Wangaratta, Vic.	7,868	8,289	16,157
Inverell, N.S.W.	4,547	4,885	9,432	Warragul, Vic.	3,628	3,814	7,442
Kalgoorlie-Boulder, W.A.	9,896	9,145	19,041	Warrnambool, Vic.	9,828	10,367	20,195
Katoomba-Wentworth				Warwick, Qld.	4,398	4,771	9,169
Falls, N.S.W.	5,742	6,559	12,301	Wellington, N.S.W.	2,603	2,792	5,395
Kempsey, N.S.W.	4,355	4,526	8,881	Whyalla, S.A.	17,389	16,037	33,426
Kiama, N.S.W.	3,038	3,095	6,133	Wollongong, N.S.W.	100,639	96,488	197,127
Kingaroy, Qld.	2,453	2,635	5,088	Yeppoon, Qld.	2,749	2,826	5,575
Kingston, Tas.	3,134	3,125	6,259	Young, N.S.W.	3,174	3,285	6,459

ECONOMIC INDEXES

The International Monetary Fund (IMF) issued its *Annual Report* in September 1977. In an opening comment on the world economic scene, the *Report* noted:

"Economic and financial conditions in many parts of the world were distinctly better at mid-1977 than they had been one or two years earlier. Nevertheless, most Fund member countries were still attempting to restore order to their economies in the wake of the major disturbances of the 1973–75 period: a rapid upsurge of prices and costs, the severe and prolonged recession, and the international oil crisis.

"Because of these disturbances, the international economic scene in 1977 is described in the *Report* as still unsatisfactory by past standards. Economic growth rates are generally subnormal in a setting of high unemployment, excess plant capacity, and lagging investment. Inflation is also a widespread problem, and in several countries it is coupled with weakness of the external position. In many countries, in addition, economic officials had to deal with inflationary expectations, a lack of business and consumer confidence, and significant distortions in the structure of the national economy."

Name & Region	Consumer Price Index—1976 1970 = 100 All items	Food	Wholesale Price Index—1976 1970 = 100	Industrial Production Index—1976 1970 = 100	Unemployment Rate %—1976	Foreign Trade 1976—Million U.S. Dollars Imports	Exports	Estimated GNP 1976—Million U.S. Dollars	GNP Per Capita—1975 U.S. Dollars
AFGHANISTAN	121.6					350[1]	223[1]	1,300	130
ALBANIA								1,100[6]	600
ALGERIA	128.0[1]	141.5[1]				5,312	5,061	14,500	780
ANGOLA						625[6]	1,227[6]		680
ANTIGUA	205.0	243.7							
ARGENTINA	6,539.0	6,632.4	7,770	122		3,033	3,916	52,100	1,590
AUSTRALIA	184.9	173.0	166.2[3]	114	4.4	11,084	12,868	100,700	5,640
AUSTRIA	152.6	144.4	143.4	125	2.0	11,523	8,507	39,800	4,720
BAHAMAS	137.0[8]	143.8[8]				3,560	2,879		2,600
BAHRAIN						1,664	1,346	1,600	2,440
BANGLADESH	252.1[9]	241.7[9]				874[1]	303[1]	5,300[18]	110
BARBADOS	246.4	273.7				237	104		1,260
BELGIUM	163.2	159.6	147.2	119	8.6	35,368[2]	32,847[2]	66,500	6,070
BENIN						150[1]	46[1]	425	140
BHUTAN									70
BOLIVIA	266.8	292.5				558[1]	513	2,500	320
BOTSWANA	171.2	166.2							330
BRAZIL	254.3[8]	267.1[8]	372.1			13,622	10,128	131,000	1,010
BRUNEI						269[1]	1,023[1]	382	
BULGARIA				164		5,626	5,382	21,100	2,040
BURMA	285.4	299.7				170[1]	158[1]	2,700[1]	110
BURUNDI	163.6	171.2				58	55		100
CAMBODIA	1,819.9[6]	2,277.7[6]				101[8]	10[8]	1,500[19]	70
CAMEROON	181.8	191.3				609	511	1,700	270
CANADA	153.2	168.0	178.8	128	7.2	37,910	38,128	175,300	6,650
CAPE VERDE	225.4[6]	246.2[6]							470
CEN. AFR. EMP.	169.8	172.1	151.9[1]			69[1]	47[1]	302	230
CHAD	152.9	144.6				92[6]	37[6]	330[18]	120
CHILE	86,565	112,040	258,663	82[15]	15.0[1]	1,911[6]	1,661[1]	9,000	760
CHINA								309,000	350
CHINA (TAIWAN)								16,100[1]	890
COLOMBIA	280.8	328.6	353.7			1,572	1,694	15,200	550
CONGO	156.9	158.0				164[1]	178[1]	600	500
COSTA RICA	196.2	191.6	242.3			774	584	1,125[17]	910
CUBA						3,883[1]	3,680		800
CYPRUS	148.5	163.5			7.1	430	257	807[17]	1,180
CZECHOSLOVAKIA	101.6	100.8		146		9,706	9,035	45,700	3,710
DENMARK	169.8	181.0	174.8	114[15]	10.0	12,419	9,113	34,200	6,920
DOMINICA	215.4	213.1							
DOM. REP.	173.3[12]	168.9[12]	164.9			764	716	4,000	720
ECUADOR	208.1	244.7				1,010	1,122	4,700	550
EGYPT	147.3	174.0	141.9			3,808	1,522	12,900	310
EL SALVADOR	161.7	164.8	208.2	128[1,15]		705	721	1,800	450
EQ. GUINEA									320
ETHIOPIA	152.9	159.6				353	278	2,900[1]	100

Name & Region	Consumer Price Index—1976 1970 = 100 All items	Food	Wholesale Price Index—1976 1970 = 100	Industrial Production Index—1976 1970 = 100	Unemployment Rate %—1976	Foreign Trade 1976—Million U.S. Dollars Imports	Exports	Estimated GNP 1976—Million U.S. Dollars	GNP Per Capita—1975 U.S. Dollars
FIJI	186.3	196.2				262	130		920
FINLAND	201.7	208.8	210.4	125	4.0	7,393	6,342	32,400	5,100
FRANCE	166.9	172.3	159.3[4]	123		64,404	55,817	353,200	5,760
FRENCH GUYANA	176.1	174.6				86	4		
GABON	158.2[1,12]		164.4[1]			471[1]	898	1,710	2,240
GAMBIA	192.9	217.9				74	35		190
GERMANY, E.				145		13,196	11,361	48,000	4,230
GERMANY, W.	140.8	136.8	140.8	114	4.6	87,784	102,032	449,100	6,610
GHANA	351.5	414.1	234.4[1]			821[1]	760[1]	3,600[6]	460
GIBRALTAR	211.1	251.7				38	3		
GREECE	202.4	215.4	226.1	166		6,013	2,543	22,760	2,360
GUADELOUPE	180.7	188.6				318	90		1,240
GUATEMALA	110.7[10]	109.6[10]	176.4			808	760	4,200	650
GUINEA								410[18]	130
GUINEA-BISSAU									390
GUYANA	157.6	192.3				363	269	478	560
HAITI	200.1	213.2				121[1]	79[1]	1,100	180
HONDURAS	142.3	154.0				453	392	1,100	350
HONG KONG	112.0[11]	107.0[11]				8,882	8,526		1,720
HUNGARY	120.3	120.9		141		5,529	4,934	23,100	2,480
ICELAND	403.9	459.9				470	404	763[6]	5,620
INDIA	160.9	156.0	176.8	132		5,515	5,424	89,700[1]	150
INDONESIA	292.2	337.5	286.3			5,673	8,547	29,200[1]	180
IRAN	174.8	172.1	154.2[1]			12,894	23,385	56,800[1,16]	1,440
IRAQ	149.5	152.8	147.5			3,461	8,840	14,200	1,280
IRELAND	219.9	226.9	231.0	129	12.3	4,192	3,313	8,100	2,420
ISRAEL	387.6	401.5	405.1	144	3.6	4,052	2,310	12,600	3,580
ITALY	199.8	201.6	236.4	122	3.7	43,428	36,969	161,600	2,940
IVORY COAST	162.0	159.8				1,296	1,620	2,400	500
JAMAICA	214.1	230.7			22.4	913	633		1,290
JAPAN	188.4	195.9	165.4	125	2.0	64,799	67,225	567,000	4,460
JORDAN	192.4	266.5				1,023	206	1,300	460
KENYA	163.3[8]	158.9[8]				941	656	2,800[1]	220
KOREA, N.								8,900	430
KOREA, S.	234.8	274.0	266.8	357	3.9	8,774	7,716	18,400[1]	550
KUWAIT	139.6	165.1				3,233	9,847	12,600	11,510
LAOS	457.3[1]	544.9[1]				65[6]	5[17]	211[18]	70
LEBANON	125.5[6]	142.7[6]				1,224[9]	497[9]	3,700[6]	1,070
LESOTHO	145.4[9]	149.4[9]							180
LIBERIA	178.6	171.4				399	476	436[18]	410
LIBYA	129.6	95.9				3,950	8,401	12,200[1]	5,080
LUXEMBOURG	155.6	160.9		100				2,420[16]	6,050
MADAGASCAR	163.9	176.3				235[1]	289[1]	1,400	200
MALAWI	163.8	175.7				205	148	640	150
MALAYSIA	145.9[7]	162.0[7]		164		4,245	5,707	8,600	720
MALI		181.5[1]				150	97	375[18]	90
MALTA	133.7	137.2[1]				421	229		1,220
MARTINIQUE	184.3	181.4				385	124		1,540
MAURITANIA	140.4[6]	153.8[6]				180	178	290	310
MAURITIUS	177.7[1]	189.0[1]				350	265		580
MEXICO	204.3	207.9	204.6	142		6,030	3,298	93,200	1,190
MONGOLIA								2,800[6]	700
MOROCCO	117.1[13]	118.6[13]	167.7	142		2,618	1,262	7,850	470
MOZAMBIQUE	171.6	187.9				417[1]	202[1]	2,000[18]	310
NEPAL	159.8[1]	153.7[1]						1,000[18]	110
NETHERLANDS	164.6	152.5	146.0[5]	125	5.5	39,574	40,167	85,100	5,590
NETH. ANTILLES	163.5	219.4				2,827[1]	2,442		1,590
NEW ZEALAND	190.2	185.8	200.3			3,254	2,795	12,560[20]	4,680
NICARAGUA	110.6[13]	109.0[13]				532	542	1,800	720
NIGER	178.2	201.3				92[1]	85[1]	489[18]	130
NIGERIA	226.7	268.4				8,199	10,567	24,300[1]	310
NORWAY	163.2	167.1	163.0	137	1.3	11,109	7,917	31,100	6,540

Name & Region	Consumer Price Index—1976 1970 = 100 All items	Food	Wholesale Price Index—1976 1970 = 100	Industrial Production Index—1976 1970 = 100	Unemployment Rate %—1976	Foreign Trade 1976—Million U.S. Dollars Imports	Exports	Estimated GNP 1976—Million U.S. Dollars	GNP Per Capita—1975 U.S. Dollars
OMAN									2,070
PAKISTAN	212.4[12]	221.6[12]	243.4	120[1,15]		2,134	1,144	10,100[1]	140
PANAMA	144.8	156.2	202.4			838	227	1,650[6]	1,060
PAPUA N.G.	168.4[12]	174.0[12]				430	573		450
PARAGUAY	180.5	199.7				220	179	1,700	570
PERU	241.8	263.2				2,183	1,365	10,700	810
PHILIPPINES	234.6[1]	253.3[1]	252.1[1]	141	4.0[6]	3,950	2,443	16,500	370
POLAND	118.1	117.8		181		13,867	11,017	68,100	2,910
PORTUGAL	244.2	263.8	208.0	138		4,317	1,820	15,800	1,610
PUERTO RICO	153.3	173.3			19.6				2,300
QATAR								425[1]	8,320
REUNION	180.0	187.9				450	94		1,550
RHODESIA	143.0	143.6		129				3,400	540
RUMANIA						5,342[1]	5,341[1]	45,300	1,300
RWANDA	150.0[6]	151.0[6]				103	81	233[18]	90
SAMOA, W.	142.7[9]	149.0[9]				29	7		320
SAUDI ARABIA						11,759	36,119	37,200[1]	3,010
SENEGAL	193.0	214.2		156		576[1]	461[1]	1,200[6]	370
SEYCHELLES	278.8	142.5[13]						31[6]	520
SIERRA LEONE	176.3	195.4				156	112	600[6]	200
SINGAPORE	123.1[9]	119.3[9]		185[15]		9,070	6,585	6,500[1]	2,510
SOMALIA	165.4	182.9				155[1]	85	300[17]	100
SOUTH AFRICA	174.1[14]	184.0[14]	204.0	124[15]		6,751	4,776	31,700	1,320
SPAIN	207.9	210.5	191.0	152		17,463	8,727	101,700	2,700
SRI LANKA	145.2	148.0				548	527	2,800	150
SUDAN	210.8	201.2				980	554	2,800[6]	290
SURINAM	162.9	173.5				262[1]	277[1]		1,180
SWAZILAND	165.8	169.0							470
SWEDEN	161.7	168.8	176.0	114	1.2	19,334	18,440	76,500	7,880
SWITZERLAND	147.3	139.3	132.2	98		14,774	14,845	58,900	8,050
SYRIA	195.1	197.7	191.1			1,986	1,066	4,700[1,16]	660
TANZANIA	200.6	226.5	184.7			570	459	1,900[6]	170
THAILAND	159.6	172.8				3,280[1]	2,331[1]	14,700[1]	350
TOGO	177.2	198.7				174[1]	126[1]	605	270
TONGA	177.6	187.6							
TRIN. & TOB.	204.6	226.1			15.3[6]	1,976	2,210		1,900
TUNISIA	135.8	141.5	154.2	137		1,529	789	4,800[1]	760
TURKEY	251.7	277.2	272.5			4,993	1,960	40,200	860
UGANDA	434.2	490.4				80	360	2,000[6]	250
USSR	99.7	100.9		150		38,108	37,169	656,837	2,620
UN. ARAB EM.								8,500	10,480
UN. KINGDOM	214.9	247.3	299.1[3]	102	5.8	55,986	46,271	224,500	3,840
USA	146.6	157.4	165.7	122	7.7	128,872	113,323	1,692,400	7,060
UPPER VOLTA						151[1]	44[1]	504	90
URUGUAY	2,085.6	2,128.3	2,281			599	536	3,500	1,330
VENEZUELA	142.0	164.3	162.6	88[1]		5,327[1]	9,149	32,500	2,220
YEMEN						413	8	830[17]	210
YEMEN, S.						312[1]	187[1]	500[18]	240
YUGOSLAVIA	271.0	278.3	242.0	153	11.4	7,367	4,878	30,200[1,16]	1,480
ZAIRE	232.0[1]	260.6[1]				827	930	3,500[6]	150
ZAMBIA	168.5	177.1	126.9[1]	115[1]		937[1]	810[1]	2,500[6]	540

[1] 1975. [2] Includes Luxembourg. [3] Includes basic materials only. [4] Includes domestic goods only. [5] Includes consumer goods only. [6] 1974. [7] Includes the mainland only. [8] 1972 = 100. [9] 1973 = 100. [10] 1975 = 100. [11] 1973–74 = 100. [12] 1971 = 100. [13] 1974 = 100. [14] White population only. [15] Includes manufacturing only. [16] Gross domestic product. [17] 1973. [18] 1972. [19] 1971. [20] 1977.

Sources: "Monthly Bulletin of Statistics," United Nations.
"The Military Balance 1977–1978," The International Institute for Strategic Studies.
"World Population Data Sheet, 1977," Population Reference Bureau, Washington, D.C.

AGRICULTURAL PRODUCTION: SELECTED COUNTRIES (1975)

(in thousand metric tons)

	Coffee	Cotton	Eggs	Maize	Milk[1]	Potatoes	Rice	Soybeans	Wheat
AFGHANISTAN	...	50	16	780	572	...	450	...	2,800
ALBANIA	...	7	4	220	271	...	17	...	300
ALGERIA	...	...	14	...	633	575	2	...	1,848
ANGOLA	69	11	3	450	138	...	20	...	10
ARGENTINA	...	160	192	7,700	5,671	1,349	351	485	8,570
AUSTRALIA	...	33	192	133	6,698	742	388	74	11,980
AUSTRIA	...	...	88	981	3,190	1,579	...	...	945
BANGLADESH	...	1	25	2	1,362	880	19,143	...	117
BELGIUM[2]	...	...	221	38	3,869	1,306	...	...	724
BOLIVIA	15	22	15	305	...	834	127	12	62
BRAZIL	1,228	517	504	16,354	7,211	1,669	7,538	9,892	1,788
BULGARIA	...	11	102	2,822	1,803	318	68	80	2,771
BURMA	1	16	70	62	387	...	9,221	14	64
CAMEROON	87	19	6	350	...	...	20	...	...
CANADA	...	...	305	3,645	8,025	2,754	...	367	17,078
CHAD	...	63	3	10	155	...	37	...	...
CHILE	...	...	61	329	995	738	76	...	1,002
CHINA	5	2,385	3,630	33,138	5,418	40,040	116,267	12,062	41,003
COLOMBIA	540	125	135	800	2,838	1,120	1,614	105	57
COSTA RICA	79	...	19	92	265	...	159	...	...
CUBA	25	...	83	125	600	88	420	...	...
CZECHOSLOVAKIA	...	...	225	843	5,726	3,565	...	...	4,202
DENMARK	...	...	75	...	4,918	661	...	...	520
DOM. REP.	55	...	12	55	281	...	239	...	...
ECUADOR	76	11	24	280	790	499	348	12	65
EGYPT	...	382	69	2,781	1,888	720	2,423	...	2,033
EL SALVADOR	193	78	25	439	...	...	61	...	...
ETHIOPIA	174	18	69	1,470	618	170	...	...	734
FINLAND	...	...	76	...	3,066	680	...	...	622
FRANCE	...	...	763	8,163	29,704	7,228	48	...	15,041
GERMANY, E	...	...	278	2	8,126	7,673	...	...	2,736
GERMANY, W.	...	...	893	531	21,627	10,853	...	...	7,014
GREECE	...	131	103	468	1,625	895	104	...	2,140
GUATEMALA	129	105	32	683	310	...	33	...	45
HONDURAS	50	5	18	339	180	...	29	...	...
HUNGARY	...	...	223	7,215	2,035	1,600	69	...	4,007
INDIA	93	1,193	83	7,036	25,677	6,225	74,186	...	24,104
INDONESIA	162	2	66	2,638	43	180	22,570	563	...
IRAN	...	165	110	40	2,083	570	1,615	70	5,483
IRAQ	...	15	15	23	682	...	61	...	845
IRELAND	...	...	41	...	4,260	992	...	...	207
ISRAEL	...	49	90	15	658	163	...	...	243
ITALY	...	1	636	5,326	9,759	2,943	1,009	...	9,610
IVORY COAST	258	24	4	129	...	...	467	...	...
JAPAN	...	...	1,786	11	4,963	3,261	17,097	126	241
KENYA	66	5	18	1,600	811	220	32	...	158
KOREA, NORTH	...	3	70	2,100	...	1,200	3,700	290	150
KOREA, SOUTH	...	3	151	60	...	675	6,485	320	97
MADAGASCAR	88	10	10	118	...	116	1,844	...	...
MALAWI	...	6	9	1,000	28	...	32	...	...
MALAYSIA	5	...	104	24	26	...	2,013	...	...
MALI	...	24	5	71	109	...	120	...	...
MEXICO	214	206	410	8,459	5,183	693	510	699	2,798
MOROCCO	...	7	58	371	519	200	29	...	1,575
MOZAMBIQUE	...	33	9	250	70	...	101	...	...
NEPAL	...	...	13	784	683	308	2,582	...	331
NETHERLANDS	...	...	326	6	10,221	5,003	...	...	528
NEW ZEALAND	...	...	54	205	6,014	206	...	...	203
NICARAGUA	48	123	17	192	...	...	89	...	...
NIGERIA	3	46	107	1,000	297	...	368	65	...
NORWAY	...	...	38	...	1,832	435	...	...	48
PAKISTAN	...	514	37	802	5,771	289	3,926	...	7,673
PANAMA	5	...	12	65	73	...	185	...	...
PARAGUAY	9	33	17	301	121	...	45	216	18
PERU	59	59	50	625	975	1,870	537	1	143
PHILIPPINES	62	...	160	2,697	...	...	6,217	6	...
POLAND	...	...	449	79	16,429	46,429	...	...	5,207
PORTUGAL	...	...	45	506	815	1,047	133	...	611
RHODESIA	...	43	8	1,400	253	...	...	...	85
RUMANIA	...	...	249	9,241	4,579	2,716	69	213	4,862
SENEGAL	...	14	6	42	106	...	130	...	...
SOUTH AFRICA	...	44	154	9,140	2,440	719	...	20	1,792
SPAIN	...	43	574	1,792	5,674	5,338	379	14	4,302
SRI LANKA	9	...	17	27	250	...	1,154	...	...
SUDAN	...	229	19	55	1,986	...	7	...	269
SWEDEN	...	...	109	...	3,170	837	...	...	1,481
SWITZERLAND	...	...	40	139	3,396	960	...	...	345
SYRIA	...	142	33	32	566	125	...	...	1,550
TANZANIA	55	42	20	1,354	696	79	430	...	56
THAILAND	...	11	134	3,023	...	...	15,300	114	...
TURKEY	...	480	130	1,200	...	2,490	240	7	14,830
UGANDA	213	35	13	523	330	...	16	5	...
USSR	...	2,648	3,176	7,328	90,800	88,703	2,009	780	66,224
UN. KINGDOM	...	...	799	...	13,937	4,551	...	...	4,488
USA	1	1,807	3,797	147,251	52,371	14,512	5,805	42,079	58,102
URUGUAY	...	...	17	157	742	121	193	17	456
VENEZUELA	65	31	96	653	1,224	152	363	...	...
VIETNAM	8	3	108	320	...	...	12,000	30	...
YEMEN	5	10	3	107	236	...	...	...	78
YUGOSLAVIA	...	2	180	9,389	3,802	2,394	37	30	4,405
ZAIRE	64	9	16	420	27	47	189	2	...

Source: *UN Statistical Yearbook 1976.* **Note.** Some of the figures are provisional or estimates.
[1] Total production from all sources, including cows, buffaloes, sheep, and goats. [2] Includes Luxembourg.

INDUSTRIAL PRODUCTION: SELECTED COUNTRIES (1975)

	Beer (in thousand hecto-liters)	Cotton yarn (in thousand metric tons)	Crude steel (in thousand metric tons)	Electricity (in million kilowatt hours)	Gasoline (in thousand metric tons)	Motor vehicles (in thousands)	News-print (in thousand metric tons)	Nitrogen fertilizer[7] (in thousand metric tons)	Sugar (in thousand metric tons)
AFGHANISTAN	...	1[2]	...	748	...	...	...	39	10
ALBANIA	144[1]	...	...	1,800	100	...	...	36	18
ALGERIA	705[1]	8[1]	181[2]	3,744	797	6[2,4]	...	61	18
ANGOLA	1,196[1]	3[1]	...	1,305	70	1[2,4]	...	...	18
ARGENTINA	3,943	89	1,465	31,985	3,851	227	6	...	30
AUSTRALIA	19,573	24	8,063	73,932	9,232	361	196	18	1,367
AUSTRIA	7,757	16	4,066	35,205	1,491	3	147	180	2,930
BANGLADESH	...	41	76	1,378	44	...	...	237	523
BELGIUM	13,797	44	11,584	48,307	4,603	864[4]	77[6]	610[6]	800
BOLIVIA	563[2]	1[2]	...	1,000	339	...	...	...	213
BRAZIL	22,238	60	8,306	78,068	10,472	905	128	160	6,299
BULGARIA	4,516	79	2,265	27,789	1,670	21	...	673	215
BURMA	30	8	...	773	178	...	...	47	82
CANADA	20,402	78[2]	13,025	284,482	26,065	1,424	6,966	916	120
CHILE	833	23[1]	457	8,732	884	8[4]	120	116	219
CHINA	...	...	29,000	...	...	...	998	3,300	4,000
COLOMBIA	7,649[1]	22[1]	264	14,100	2,325	30[4]	...	100	970
COSTA RICA	...	...	...	1,536	59	...	...	30	205
CUBA	2,111	...	298	6,150	935	...	...	82	6,427
CZECHOSLOVAKIA	22,628	129	14,323	59,464	1,432	211	77	525	780
DENMARK	8,881	2	559	17,551	1,483	2[4]	...	80	410
DOM. REP.	445	1[2]	...	1,632	322	...	...	...	1,170
ECUADOR	889[2]	...	...	1,290	668	...	...	...	292
EGYPT	293[2]	181	348	10,421	1,267	11[2,4]	...	151	537
EL SALVADOR	386	6[2]	...	1,068	115	1[2,4]	...	5	244
ETHIOPIA	422	12[1]	...	665	69	...	...	...	135
FINLAND	2,706[2]	15[2]	1,618	25,258	1,393	23[2]	992	202	88
FRANCE	22,660	232	21,528	195,965	16,549	3,298	238	1,354	2,712
GERMANY, E.	20,400	59	6,480	87,245	2,933	197	96	539	683
GERMANY, W.	88,426	192	40,414	323,208	16,970	3,191	486	1,259	2,571
GHANA	500	...	...	4,050	253	...	...	...	8
GREECE	1,286	70[2]	612	15,151	852	6[2,4]	...	289	308
GUATEMALA	526	...	...	1,100	209	...	...	5	384
HONDURAS	317[2]	...	...	480	84	...	...	...	75
HUNGARY	6,619	61	3,673	20,465	1,128	77[5]	...	453	335
ICELAND	26	...	...	2,319	...	...	...	9	...
INDIA	583	989	7,884	88,240	1,222	70	52	1,508	5,048
INDONESIA	492	54[1]	...	3,345	1,812	76[2,4]	...	208	1,000
IRAN	...	...	...	15,000	3,581	108[2,4]	...	126	606
IRAQ	123[2]	2[2]	...	3,400	650	...	...	24	21
IRELAND	5,050[2]	4	82	7,730	378	6[2,4]	...	100	197[1]
ISRAEL	355	24	130	9,712	914	6[4]	...	45	30
ITALY	6,493	200	21,568	151,834	14,080	1,459	243	1,000	1,429
IVORY COAST	680	6	...	860	200	5[4]	...	5	...
JAMAICA	663	...	...	2,331	209	...	...	3	366
JAPAN	38,966	460	102,313	501,297	21,395	6,948	2,160	1,557	459
KENYA	1,538	...	...	971	363	...	...	...	174
KOREA, SOUTH	1,773	134	2,010	20,800	491	37[4]	155	541	...
LEBANON	...	5[1]	...	1,850	512	...	...	1	10
LUXEMBOURG	803	...	4,625	1,483	...	...	...	...	...
MADAGASCAR	212	...	...	335	125	...	...	...	121
MALAYSIA	...	...	...	5,847	30	48[4]	...	34	59
MEXICO	19,684	158	5,196	43,779	7,900	362	29	581	2,724
MOROCCO	254	...	1	2,950	368	30[4]	...	19	268
MOZAMBIQUE	808[2]	4[2]	...	717	120	...	...	3	260
NETHERLANDS	12,430	30	4,822	57,594	6,574	86[5]	134	1,153	924
NEW ZEALAND	4,210	...	...	21,336	1,226	80[4]	219	...	...
NIGERIA	2,968	5	...	3,211	535	12[4]	...	...	40
NORWAY	1,869[2]	2	919	77,564	906	...	435	356	...
PAKISTAN	29	351	...	9,350	305	...	...	317	540
PANAMA	423	...	...	1,879[3]	342	...	...	...	130
PARAGUAY	253[2]	24[2]	...	510	67	...	...	...	70
PERU	...	...	443	8,300	1,529	34[4]	...	35	964
PHILIPPINES	...	36	...	12,359	1,887	48[4]	...	57	2,672
POLAND	12,901	212	14,574	97,168	2,387	249	83	1,533	1,847
PORTUGAL	3,143	96	386	10,728	755	71[4]	1	203	13
RHODESIA	...	...	350	6,131	...	...	...	65	257
RUMANIA	7,449	145	9,549	53,720	3,445	107	44	1,292	583
SAUDI ARABIA	...	...	...	1,988	4,790	...	...	100	...
SENEGAL	113[2]	...	...	389	120	...	...	9	...
SOUTH AFRICA	5,496	41	6,580	74,914	3,758	311[4]	210	300	1,968
SPAIN	16,620	138	11,115	92,385	4,803	813	104	825	800
SRI LANKA	32[2]	6[2]	...	1,149	88	...	...	...	20
SUDAN	93[2]	...	...	350	114	...	...	...	139
SWEDEN	4,386[2]	7	5,613	92,543	1,528	370	1,182	169	278
TANZANIA	589	...	...	636	106	...	...	4	112
THAILAND	613	...	...	7,910	706	16[4]	...	4	1,216
TRIN. & TOB.	246	...	...	1,214	1,664	8[4]	...	58	163
TUNISIA	309	9[1]	129	1,346	132	2[4]	...	...	5
TURKEY	1,527	...	1,457	15,569	2,046	105[4]	...	172	758
UGANDA	389	...	8	830	...	...	...	...	27
USSR	57,100	1,573	141,328	1,049,825	...	1,966	1,334	8,465	8,200
UN. KINGDOM	64,565	125	20,198	302,557	13,956	1,649	319	1,055	725
USA	185,257	1,142	105,817	2,175,525	281,477	8,987	3,120	9,262[8]	5,680
VENEZUELA	...	...	1,075	21,179	4,701	...	...	50	535
YUGOSLAVIA	8,454	107	2,916	40,040	1,745	225[5]	79	358	500
ZAIRE	5,723[2]	...	...	3,440	128	...	...	...	62
ZAMBIA	2,670[1]	...	...	6,191	173	5[1,4]	...	6	95

[1] 1973. [2] 1974. [3] Includes the Canal Zone. [4] Assembly only. [5] Production and assembly. [6] Includes Luxembourg. [7] 1975–76. [8] Excludes sodium nitrate; includes data for Puerto Rico.
Source: *UN Statistical Yearbook 1976.*

Aluminum, smelter (thousand metric tons)

	1975	1976
United States	3,519	3,857
USSRe	1,530	1,600
Japan	1,013	919
West Germany	678	697
Canada	887	626
Norway	595	608
France	383	385
United Kingdom	308	335
Netherlands	261	256
Australia	214	232
Spain	212	214
India	167	212
Italy	190	206
Chinae	160	200
Rumania	204	200
Yugoslavia	168	198
Other countriesa	1,619	1,752
Total	12,108	12,497

Antimony, mineb (metric tons)

	1975	1976
Bolivia	11,917	15,307
Chinae	12,000	12,000
South Africa	15,924	10,786
USSRe	7,500	7,700
Turkey	3,638	4,328
Thailand	3,133	3,671
Mexico	3,137	2,546
Canada	1,830	1,990
Yugoslavia	2,183	e1,915
Australia	1,923	1,649
Morocco	1,052	1,415
Guatemala	856	1,120
Italy	1,010	1,015
Czechoslovakiae	750	750
Other countriesa	2,996	3,368
Total	69,849	69,560

Asbestosc (thousand metric tons)

	1975	1976
USSRe	1,900	2,290
Canada	1,056	1,549
South Africa	355	370
Italy	147	165
Rhodesiae	165	165
Chinae	150	150
United States	89	104
Brazil	74	e75
Swaziland	41	42
Cyprus	35	35
Other countriesa	135	110
Total	4,147	5,055

Baritec (thousand metric tons)

	1975	1976
United States	1,196	1,120
USSRe	350	400
Peru	e230	331
Ireland	295	323
Chinae	250	280
Mexico	300	270
West Germany	247	262
India	175	186
Italy	213	179
Thailand	258	151
Morocco	120	131
North Koreae	120	120
Rumaniae	116	116
Greece	105	61
Other countriesa	850	869
Total	4,825	4,799

Bauxitec (thousand metric tons)

	1975	1976
Australia	20,958	24,085
Guinea	9,140	10,848
Jamaica	11,571	10,306
USSRe,d	6,470	6,620
Surinam	4,928	4,565
Hungary	2,889	2,918
Greece	3,244	2,747
France	2,563	2,330
Guyana	e3,250	2,106
Yugoslavia	2,306	2,033
United States	1,801	1,989
India	1,273	1,436
Chinae	970	1,100
Brazil	969	e1,000
Indonesia	993	940
Other countriesa	4,472	4,839
Total	77,797	79,862

Cementc (million metric tons)

	1975	1976
USSR	122.0	124.0
Japan	65.5	68.7
United States	63.3	61.4
Italy	34.2	36.3
Chinae	30.0	35.0
West Germany	33.5	34.0
France	29.2	29.0
Spain	24.0	25.3
Poland	18.6	19.8
India	16.2	18.5
Brazil	16.7	17.9
United Kingdom	16.9	15.8
Mexico	11.6	12.5
Turkey	10.7	12.3

Cementc (cont'd) (million metric tons)

	1975	1976
South Korea	10.1	11.9
East Germany	10.7	11.3
Other countriesa	182.1	197.0
Total	695.4	730.7

Chromitec (thousand metric tons)

	1975	1976
South Africa	2,075	2,409
USSRe	2,080	2,120
Albaniae	779	795
Turkeye	670	740
Rhodesiae	590	610
Philippines	520	428
Finland	332	414
India	499	401
Brazil	173	e170
Iran	175	e160
Other countriesa	340	364
Total	8,233	8,611

Coal, all gradesf (million metric tons)

	1975	1976
USSR	701	712
United States	594	609
Chinae	470	480
East Germany	247	247
West Germany	216	224
Poland	211	209
United Kingdom	129	124
Czechoslovakia	115	118
Australia	95	106
India	98	105
South Africa	68	75
North Koreae	40	41
Yugoslavia	35	37
Rumania	27	27
France	26	26
Canada	25	25
Hungary	25	25
Bulgaria	28	25
Greece	18	22
Other countriesa	114	116
Total	3,282	3,353

Copper, mineb (thousand metric tons)

	1975	1976
United States	1,282	1,457
Chile	828	1,005
USSRe	765	800
Canada	734	747
Zambia	677	709
Zaire	496	445
Polande	235	270
Philippines	226	232
Australia	219	217
Peru	179	201
South Africa	179	197
Papua New Guinea	172	176
Yugoslavia	115	120
Chinae	100	100
Mexico	78	89
Japan	85	81
Indonesia	64	68
Other countriesa	524	541
Total	6,958	7,455

Diamond (thousand carats)

	1975	1976
Zaire	12,810	11,821
USSRe	9,700	9,900
South Africa	7,295	7,022
Botswana	2,397	2,361
Ghana	2,328	2,283
South West Africa	1,747	1,694
Sierra Leonee	1,500	1,500
Venezuela	1,060	833
Angola	460	660
Tanzania	448	e450
Other countriesa	1,363	1,202
Total	41,108	39,726

Fluorsparg (thousand metric tons)

	1975	1976
Mexico	1,089	897
USSRe	475	490
Chinae	350	350
France	500	350
Spain	372	306
Mongoliae	302	300
Italy	231	210
South Africa	203	200
United Kingdom	231	e200
Thailand	244	195
United States	127	163
Other countriesa	649	666
Total	4,773	4,327

Gas, natural, marketed productionh (billion cubic feet)

	1975	1976
United States	20,109	19,952
USSR	10,206	11,336
Netherlands	3,208	3,436
Canada	3,090	3,067
Chinae	1,400	1,600
United Kingdom	1,274	1,316
Rumania	1,132	1,054
Iran	771	794
West Germany	639	658
Mexico	584	578
Italy	514	552

Gas, natural (cont'd), marketed productionh (billion cubic feet)

	1975	1976
Libya	383	e390
Other countriesa	4,163	4,619
Total	47,473	49,352

Gold, mineb (thousand troy ounces)

	1975	1976
South Africa	22,938	22,936
USSRe	7,500	7,700
Canada	1,654	1,686
Papua New Guinea	611	1,229
United States	1,052	1,048
Rhodesiae	800	800
Ghana	524	532
Philippines	502	501
Australia	527	498
Dominican Republic	195	414
Colombia	309	298
Spain	125	e270
Brazil	172	183
Yugoslavia	178	177
Other countriesa	1,589	1,611
Total	38,676	39,883

Graphitec (thousand metric tons)

	1975	1976
USSRe	90.0	90.0
North Koreae	75.0	75.0
Mexico	60.8	e62.0
Chinae	50.0	50.0
South Korea	47.2	e50.0
Austria	30.6	e32.5
India	18.9	e20.0
Madagascar	17.8	e18.0
West Germany	13.6	e14.0
Other countriesa	34.3	40.0
Total	438.2	451.5

Gypsumc (thousand metric tons)

	1975	1976
United States	9,751	11,980
USSRe	6,900	7,100
France	5,814	5,850
Canada	5,189	5,135
Spain	4,220	e4,200
United Kingdom	3,479	4,000
Italye	3,500	3,500
West Germany	2,297	2,535
Iran	2,450	2,500
Mexico	1,256	1,414
Polande	1,200	1,260
Australia	949	e940
India	810	711
Austria	770	662
Other countriesa	8,436	10,795
Total	57,021	60,082

Iron Orec (million metric tons)

	1975	1976
USSR	232.8	239.0
Australia	97.7	93.2
Brazil	89.9	e91.8
United States	80.1	81.3
Chinae	65.0	65.0
Canada	46.9	57.0
France	49.6	45.2
India	41.3	43.0
Sweden	30.9	30.5
Liberia	27.2	18.8
Venezuela	24.8	e18.2
South Africa	12.3	15.7
Chile	10.0	10.4
Mauritania	8.7	9.7
North Koreae	9.4	9.5
Spain	7.6	7.6
Other countriesa	73.4	79.9
Total	907.6	897.6

Iron, steel ingots (million metric tons)

	1975	1976
USSR	141.0	145.0
United States	105.8	116.3
Japan	102.3	107.4
West Germany	40.4	42.4
Chinae	29.0	29.0
Italy	21.8	23.3
France	21.5	23.2
United Kingdom	20.2	22.3
Poland	15.0	15.6
Czechoslovakia	14.3	14.7
Canada	13.0	13.1
Belgium	11.6	12.1
Rumania	9.4	10.7
India	7.9	9.1
Brazil	8.3	9.1
Australia	7.8	7.8
South Africa	6.5	7.1
East Germany	6.4	6.7
Netherlands	4.8	5.2
Sweden	5.6	5.1
Mexico	5.3	5.1
Luxembourg	4.6	4.6
Other countriesa	43.9	45.7
Total	646.4	680.6

Lead, smelter (thousand metric tons)

	1975	1976
United States	577	592
USSRe	480	500
Australia	311	343
Japan	194	219

Lead, smelter (cont'd) (thousand metric tons)

	1975	1976
Mexico	173	190
Canada	172	e175
France	135	159
Yugoslavia	126	111
Bulgaria	112	110
Belgium	106	104
West Germany	92	101
China^e	100	100
Poland	76	81
North Korea^e	80	80
Spain	73	76
Peru	71	74
Italy	33	45
Other countries^a	403	380
Total	3,314	3,440

Magnesium (thousand metric tons)

	1975	1976
United States^e	105.0	115.0
USSR^e	60.0	63.0
Norway	38.3	38.8
Japan	8.5	11.2
France	7.5	8.0
Italy	6.3	e6.9
Canada	3.8	5.9
China^e	1.0	1.0
Total	230.4	249.8

Manganese Ore^c (thousand metric tons)

	1975	1976
USSR	8,459	8,500
South Africa	5,769	5,452
Brazil	2,156	e2,200
Australia	1,555	2,154
Gabon	2,217	2,152
India	1,531	1,689
China	1,000	1,000
Mexico	428	423
Ghana	403	312
Hungary	182	175
Zaire	309	157
Other countries^a	556	507
Total	24,565	24,784

Mercury^b (76-pound flasks)

	1975	1976
USSR^e	55,000	56,000
Spain	44,010	44,000
Algeria	28,000	31,000
China^e	26,000	26,000
United States	7,366	23,133
Italy	31,677	22,278
Mexico	14,214	15,026
Yugoslavia	16,941	12,503
Czechoslovakia^e	6,000	6,000
Turkey	5,421	4,445
Other countries^a	17,800	3,602
Total	252,429	243,987

Molybdenum, mine^b (metric tons)

	1975	1976
United States	47,704	51,948
Canada	14,415	13,027
Chile	9,091	10,899
USSR^e	9,060	9,350
China^e	1,500	1,500
Other countries^a	1,035	886
Total	82,805	87,610

Nickel, mine^b (thousand metric tons)

	1975	1976
Canada	242.2	262.5
USSR^e	132.0	140.0
New Caledonia	133.1	106.6
Australia	75.8	83.1
Cuba	36.6	37.0
Greece	28.1	27.6
Dominican Republic	26.9	24.4
South Africa	20.8	22.4
Philippines	9.5	18.8
Indonesia	19.2	e17.8
Rhodesia^e	10.0	15.0
United States	17.3	14.9
Botswana	16.6	12.6
Other countries^a	20.7	21.7
Total	788.8	804.4

Petroleum, crude (million barrels)

	1975	1976
USSR	3,609	3,822
Saudi Arabia	2,583	3,140
United States	3,052	2,972
Iran	1,953	2,168
Venezuela	856	840
Iraq	826	835
Kuwait	762	786
Nigeria	652	756
United Arab Emirates	618	711
Libya	551	704
China^e	572	646
Indonesia	477	550
Canada	521	489
Algeria	351	384

Petroleum, crude (cont'd) (million barrels)

	1975	1976
Mexico	294	327
Qatar	159	182
Australia	150	153
Argentina	144	146
Oman	125	134
Rumania	109	e109
Other countries^a	1,134	1,286
Total	19,498	21,140

Phosphate Rock^c (thousand metric tons)

	1975	1976
United States	44,285	44,146
USSR	24,120	24,230
Morocco	13,548	15,293
China^e	3,400	3,750
Tunisia	3,488	3,294
Togo	1,161	2,009
Senegal	1,801	1,799
South Africa	1,646	1,702
Jordan	1,112	1,702
Vietnam^e	1,400	1,500
Christmas Island	1,391	1,033
Nauru	1,534	755
Israel	429	613
Other countries^a	8,066	5,110
Total	107,381	106,936

Potash (thousand metric tons of K$_2$O equivalent)

	1975	1976
USSR	7,900	8,500
Canada	5,436	4,996
East Germany	3,019	e3,100
United States	2,269	2,305
West Germany	2,223	2,036
France	2,085	1,738
Other countries^a	2,093	2,127
Total	25,025	24,802

Pyrite^c (thousand metric tons)

	1975	1976
USSR^e	7,900	8,100
Spain	2,735	2,349
China^e	2,000	2,000
Japan	1,097	958
Rumania^e	870	870
Italy	962	850
South Africa	651	845
Finland	718	674
United States	635	762
North Korea^e	500	700
Greece^e	500	500
West Germany	492	e490
Yugoslavia	399	440
Portugal	462	416
Sweden	414	404
Norway	475	368
Other countries^e	1,816	1,682
Total	22,626	22,408

Salt^c (million metric tons)

	1975	1976
United States	37.25	40.11
China^e	29.94	30.00
USSR	13.70	14.00
West Germany	9.32	e10.00
United Kingdom	7.78	7.90
India	3.33	4.48
France	5.54	6.42
Canada	5.16	5.75
Poland	5.11	5.47
Australia	5.06	5.35
Mexico	5.35	4.59
Rumania	3.83	4.21
Italy	4.41	4.01
Netherlands	2.69	3.03
East Germany	2.43	e2.40
Other countries^a	23.97	31.55
Total	164.87	179.27

Silver, mine^b (million troy ounces)

	1975	1976
USSR	43.00	44.00
Mexico	38.03	42.64
Canada	39.70	40.89
Peru	37.53	35.58
United States	34.94	34.33
Australia	23.45	25.10
Japan	8.73	9.30
Poland^e	7.40	8.00
Chile	6.26	7.29
Bolivia	5.47	5.09
Sweden	4.52	e4.70
Yugoslavia	5.41	4.63
Spain	3.45	3.11
Honduras	3.80	2.96
South Africa	3.08	2.82
Other countries^a	33.11	34.46
Total	297.88	304.90

Sulfur, all forms^i (thousand metric tons)

	1975	1976
United States	11,440	10,877
USSR^e	8,200	8,400
Canada	7,547	7,415
Poland	5,054	5,181
Japan	2,420	2,647
Mexico	2,255	2,230
France	1,921	1,996
Spain	1,423	e1,210
China^e	1,150	1,200
Italy	838	e840
Finland	878	775
West Germany	736	750
Iraq	790	675
Iran	507	399
Other countries^a	4,764	4,871
Total	49,923	49,466

Tin, mine^b (thousand metric tons)

	1975	1976
Malaysia	64.4	63.4
USSR^e	30.0	31.0
Bolivia	25.6	29.8
Indonesia	24.4	22.2
Thailand	16.4	20.5
China^e	22.0	20.0
Australia	9.1	10.4
Brazil	5.0	5.9
Zaire	4.6	4.0
Other countries^a	19.5	18.6
Total	221.0	225.8

Titanium Materials^c,j (thousand metric tons)

	1975	1976
Ilmenite		
Australia	1,030	1,002
Norway	527	767
United States	651	592
Malaysia	112	180
Finland	123	123
Other countries^a	150	142
Total ilmenite	2,593	2,806
Rutile		
Australia	344	395
Other countries^a	7	5
Total rutile	351	400
Titaniferous slag		
Canada	750	823
Japan	4	3
Total titaniferous slag	754	826

Tungsten, mine^b (metric tons)

	1975	1976
China^e	9,000	9,000
USSR^e	7,800	8,000
Bolivia	2,568	3,039
United States	2,490	2,662
South Korea	2,403	2,565
Australia	1,933	2,440
North Korea^e	2,150	2,150
Thailand	1,637	1,896
Canada	1,172	e1,600
Portugal	1,424	1,276
Brazil	1,132	e1,200
Other countries^a	4,485	5,881
Total	38,194	41,709

Uranium Oxide (U$_3$O$_8$)^b,j (metric tons)

	1975	1976
United States	10,523	11,521
Canada	5,518	6,058
South Africa	2,934	3,254
France	2,041	2,138
Niger	1,651	1,722
Gabon	1,097	1,085
Other countries^a	434	1,525
Total	24,198	27,303

Zinc, smelter (thousand metric tons)

	1975	1976
Japan	702	742
USSR	690	720
Canada	427	473
United States	397	453
West Germany	295	305
Australia	193	243
Poland	243	240
Belgium	218	235
France	181	233
Italy	180	191
Mexico	154	171
Spain	135	161
North Korea^e	140	138
Netherlands	124	126
Finland	110	111
Yugoslavia	98	105
China^e	100	100
Bulgaria	92	e92
South Africa	26	27
Other countries^a	569	561
Total	5,074	5,427

---

a Estimated in part. b Content of ore. c Gross weight. d Includes calculated bauxite equivalent of estimated output of aluminum ores other than bauxite (nepheline concentrates and alunite ores). e Estimate. f Includes anthracitic, bituminous, and lignitic coal (including that coal classified in Europe as "brown coal"). g Marketable gross weight. h Marketed production (includes gas sold or used by producers; excludes gas reinjected to reservoirs and gas flared or vented to atmosphere which has no economic value and which does not represent a part of world energy consumption). i Includes: (1) Frasch-process sulfur, (2) elemental sulfur mined by conventional methods, (3) by-product recovered elemental sulfur, and (4) recovered sulfur content of pyrite and other sulfide ores. j Excludes output (if any) by Albania, Bulgaria, China, Czechoslovakia, East Germany, Hungary, North Korea, Mongolia, Poland, Rumania, the USSR, and Vietnam. Compiled by Charles L. Kimbell, U.S. Bureau of Mines.

EDUCATION: SELECTED COUNTRIES

	Year	Primary (in thousands) Students	Teachers	Secondary (in thousands) Students	Teachers	Higher (in thousands) Students	Teachers	Expenditures % of GNP	% of total publ. exp.
ALGERIA	1975	2,641	65	502	...	30.1[2]	2.9[2]	6.5[2]	19.7[2]
ARGENTINA	1975	3,579	196	1,243	162	498[1]	42[1]	4[1]	18.8[1]
AUSTRALIA	1974	1,779	73.7	1,059	68.6	253	18.5	6.4	15.8
AUSTRIA	1974	513	61.8	905	...	84.1	10.5	5.3	8.5
BAHRAIN	1974	40.4	...	16.8	...	0.7	0.07	3.4	9.5
BOTSWANA	1975	116.3	3.5	14.3	0.9	0.3[1]	0.03[1]		15.6[1]
BULGARIA	1974	979	47.7	369	26.5	127	10.8	5.3	8.6
BURUNDI	1974	135	4.2	12.4	...	0.5	0.1	2.3[2]	20.5[2]
CANADA	1974	2,617	...	2,629	...	707	44.5	7.6	...
CEN. AFR. EMP.	1974	216	3.1	18.8	0.4	0.3	...	3.3[2]	18.6[2]
CHAD	1974	208	...	13.6	0.4	0.5	0.1		10
CHILE	1975	2,299	65.8	449	29.6	150	11.4	3.8[1]	...
COLOMBIA	1974	3,792	115	1,284	66.3	149	17.7	3.3[2]	21.2[2]
CONGO	1974	307	5.1	88	2.1	3	0.2		18.2[5]
CUBA	1974	1,923	78.5	453	35.3	68.5	5.7	9.3	...
CYPRUS	1974	56.6	2.1	51.1	2.3	0.6	0.08	3.7	13.1
CZECHOSLOVAKIA	1974	1,884	96.1	405	24.6	144	21.2	4.5	6.8
ECUADOR	1975	1,267	32.3	380	23.5	57.7[3]	...	3.2[4]	19.8[4]
EGYPT	1974	4,146	104	1,983	69.5	408	19.1	5.8[2]	17.6[2]
EL SALVADOR	1974	723	15.4	44.7	...	26.1	2	3.6[2]	28.4[2]
FINLAND	1973	393	21.3	517	35.4	71.5[1]	4.4[1]	6.1[1]	16.5[1]
FRANCE	1975	4,605	...	5,026	...	772[1]	...	4.7[1]	24.1[1]
GAMBIA	1975	24.6	0.9	6.6	0.4	...	...	3.7[2]	14.5[2]
GERMANY, E.	1975	2,579	159	461	...	307[1]	33.6[1]	5.6[1]	7.6[1]
GERMANY, W.	1975	6,425	...	5,464	...	841	...	4.1[2]	14[2]
GHANA	1974	1,051	35.3	532	22.8	8	...		19.7
GUINEA-BISS.	1975	55.5	2.4	3	0.2	...	...	1.2[3]	10[3]
HONDURAS	1975	461	13	...	...	10.4[1]	0.6[1]	3.3[1]	21.7[1]
HUNGARY	1974	1,040	65.7	385	22.3	103	11.6	4.6	6.1
ICELAND	1974	26.9	1.4	25	2.4	2.7	0.5	4.8[4]	14.5[4]
INDIA	1975	66,000	2,560	24,900	...	2,230[1]	...	...	28.4
INDONESIA	1975	14,280	...	2,565	...	240[3]	...	2.4[1]	12.7[1]
IRAN	1974	4,119	135	1,990	69.4	135	12.3	3.8	12.2
IRAQ	1974	1,524	57.6	480	18.4	78.8	3.3	4.3	11.5
IRELAND	1974	402	13.4	273	20.9	37.9	4.1	5.9	12
ISRAEL	1974	523	...	168	...	75.3	14	6.7[2]	7.4[2]
ITALY	1973	4,969	246	4,415	...	929[1]	42.6[1]	5.2[1]	13.8[1]
IVORY COAST	1974	641	14.4	104	4.6	6.2	0.4	5.9	33.9
JAMAICA	1974	434	11	130	4.6	8.4[2]	0.6[2]	7.1	23
JAPAN	1974	10,089	406	9,037	504	2,156	18.4	4.3[3]	19.5[3]
JORDAN	1974	372	10.4	143	6.7	9.3	0.6	3.6	8.3
KENYA	1975	2,881	86.1	227	9.2	11.4[1]	...	5.9[1]	20.5[1]
KOREA, SOUTH	1975	5,599	108	3,176	83.8	297	15.3	4.1[1]	14.2[1]
KUWAIT	1974	102	5.7	97.7	8.7	5.8	0.5	2.6	14.7
LESOTHO	1975	222	4.2	16.5	0.7	0.6[1]	0.07[1]	4.4[4]	18.4[4]
LIBYA	1974	523	22.8	130	9.9	12	0.8		12.2
MALAWI	1974	612	10.5	17.1	0.9	1.2	0.2	2.4	13.4
MALI	1974	276	7.9	11.3	...	2.4	0.3	4.4[3]	...
MAURITIUS	1975	151	...	65.8	...	1.3[1]	0.2[1]	3.1[1]	9.9[1]
MEXICO	1975	11,571	254	2,617	151	453[1]	34.9[1]	3.2[1]	21.1[1]
MONGOLIA	1974	128	4.1	176	7.4	8.9[3]	...		18.1[3]
MOROCCO	1975	1,548	37.2	476	20.1	34.1[1]	1.9[1]	5.3[2]	20.5[2]
NEPAL	1974	401	19.9	237	...	21.8	1.8		10.5[5]
NETHERLANDS	1974	1,448	52.5	1,210	...	265	...	7.9[2]	26.6[2]
NEW ZEALAND	1975	393	21.2	365	12.1	66.7[1]	4.4[1]	5.6[1]	17[1]
NIGER	1974	121	3	12.3	0.6	0.4	0.05	2[3]	14.8[3]
NORWAY	1974	387	39.5	340	...	64.6	...	7	15.1
OMAN	1974	48.6	2	0.7	0.1	...	...	2.1	...
PAKISTAN	1974	5,166	123	1,795	96.9	112[2]	5.1[2]	2.3[5]	5.2[5]
PANAMA	1975	337	...	126	...	24.3[1]	1[1]	5.9[1]	25.5[1]
PAPUA N.G.	1975	238	7.8	40.8	2	5.6[2]	...	6.8[4]	20.4[4]
PERU	1975	2,971	76.7	1,009	40.4	180	...	4.2[1]	21.7[1]
POLAND	1975	4,310	...	1,441	...	522[1]	46.1[1]	3.7[1]	9[1]
PORTUGAL	1974	933	34.6	668	49.1	59.9[2]	4.2[2]	2.1[2]	12.5[2]
RUMANIA	1974	2,890	140	802	42.9	153	13.9		6.6
RWANDA	1974	387	7.9	11.2	...	1	0.2	2.7[2]	24.8[2]
SAUDI ARABIA	1974	626	30	179	12.6	19.8	1.8		8.2
SIERRA LEONE	1974	190	6	47.6	1.6	1.7[2]	0.3[2]	3.5[2]	19.1[2]
SINGAPORE	1974	338	11	180	7.9	18.2	1.8	2.7	9
SPAIN	1975	3,653	...	2,918[1]	...	453[1]	28.5[1]	1.7[1]	11[1]
SRI LANKA	1974	1,368	...	1,064	...	14.6	1.9	2.7	10
SUDAN	1974	1,131	28.7	256	11.8	22.2	1.3	8	14.8
SWAZILAND	1975	89.5	2.4	16.2	0.7	1.1	0.2		10.3
SWEDEN	1974	705	43	532	54.7	129	...	7.5	13.9
TANZANIA	1975	1,592	29.8	63.2	3.2	3.1	0.4	3.8[4]	15[4]
THAILAND	1975	6,685	...	954	...	75.4[1]	10[1]	2.6[1]	18.2[1]
TOGO	1975	363	6.1	64.6	1.6	2.4	0.2		21.9
TUNISIA	1975	933	23.3	184	8.8	17.5[3]	1.4[3]		26.4[1]
TURKEY	1974	5,355	159	1,517[2]	57.2[2]	219	13.8	5.6[3]	...
UGANDA	1974	941	27.6	79.4	3.3	5.6	0.6	3.6[3]	16.4[3]
USSR	1974	38,375	2,415	10,414	...	4,751	...	7.6	13.6
USA	1974	27,141	1,331	19,981	1,083	10,224	633	6.6	18.9
UPPER VOLTA	1974	134	2.8	15.8	0.7	0.8	0.1		19.1
URUGUAY	1975	331[1]	14.4[1]	...	...	32.6	2.3		...
VENEZUELA	1975	1,990[1]	63.2[1]	631[1]	35.7[1]	214	15.8	5.3[2]	21.8[2]
YEMEN	1974	233	5.8	18	1	1	0.06		6.3
YEMEN, SOUTH	1974	197	6.5	39.7	1.7	0.9	0.09	3.5[4]	...
YUGOSLAVIA	1974	2,867	128	828	23.1	360	...	6	...

Source: *UN Statistical Yearbook 1976.*
Note. The figures for the secondary level include teacher-training as well as general and vocational education.
[1] 1974. [2] 1973. [3] 1972. [4] 1971. [5] 1975.

HEALTH: SELECTED COUNTRIES

	Year	Hospitals	Total beds	Population per bed	Year	Physicians	Population per physician	Dentists	Nursing personnel
AUSTRIA	1974	327	86,746	87	1974	15,168	498	1,522	25,383
BAHRAIN	1974	11	981	248	1974	178	1,348	20	699
BANGLADESH	1972	...	10,310	6,946	1973	7,663	9,345	...	...
BARBADOS	1974	13	2,130	114	1974	160	1,500	16	584
BELGIUM	1974	479	87,164	112	1974	17,272	566	2,153	...
BENIN	1974	54	3,667	826	1974	84	36,071	8	941
BOTSWANA	1975	21	2,074	332	1974	63	10,476	5	460
BRAZIL	1973	4,431	382,952	266	1972	48,726	2,025	27,553	24,315
BULGARIA	1974	...	73,315	118	1974	18,238	476	3,594	31,890
BURMA	1972	385	24,074	1,199	1973	4,280	6,906	146	4,199
BURUNDI	1972	136	4,221	806	1973	74	48,649	3	444
CANADA	1973	1,386	207,699	106	1974	37,277	603	8,487	...
CEN. AFR. EMP.	1972	52	3,161	522	1973	59	27,097	1	729
CHAD	1974	45	3,464	1,140	1974	89	44,382	2	565
CHILE	1974	295	37,208	279	1974	4,306	...	1,406	22,276
COLOMBIA	1974	795	44,928	533	1973	10,625	2,184	3,150	12,114
CONGO	1972	110	5,541	177	1973	162	6,173	10	1,572
COSTA RICA	1974	45	7,388	260	1974	1,213	...	...	3,016
CUBA	1974	324	38,954	233	1968	7,000	1,153	...	12,023
CYPRUS[1]	1974	124	3,169	164	1974	557	...	180	1,327
CZECHOSLOVAKIA	1974	416	148,432	99	1974	33,996	432	6,227	85,992
DOM. REP.	1973	339	12,618	351	1973	2,374	1,866	516	3,332
EGYPT	1973	1,444	76,611	464	1974	7,495	...	2,083	8,241
EL SALVADOR	1973	74	6,997	552	1973	950	4,063	345	3,379
FINLAND	1974	719	70,301	67	1974	6,234	752	3,151	36,218
FRANCE	1973	...	534,023	98	1974	77,143	681	25,069	281,531
GERMANY, E.	1974	584	184,214	92	1974	30,798	557	7,600	...
GERMANY, W.	1974	3,483	716,530	87	1974	120,260	516	31,613	222,932
GHANA	1973	243	13,461	694	1974	856	11,227	44	11,011
GREECE	1974	725	56,885	158	1974	17,942	499	5,283	13,800
GUYANA	1973	43	3,987	190	1974	237	3,249	22	...
HAITI	1973	60	3,868	1,344	1974	346	...	96	813
HONDURAS	1974	38	4,717	622	1974	874	3,352	179	1,736
HUNGARY	1974	...	87,251	120	1974	22,835	459	3,093	...
INDONESIA	1973	1,371	88,086	1,415	1974	7,027	18,863	1,900	14,784
IRAN	1974	535	49,194	650	1973	11,373	2,752	1,846	14,973
IRAQ	1974	178	22,346	482	1974	4,545	2,369	631	249
IRELAND	1974	224	34,019	91	1971	3,565	836	659	19,284
ISRAEL	1974	87	19,317	171	1973	9,143	351	1,789	...
ITALY	1972	2,189	575,162	95	1973	109,166	502	...	...
JAMAICA	1974	34	7,780	257	1974	570	3,509	107	3,674
JAPAN	1972	38,175	1,364,327	78	1973	124,684	868	39,486	316,803
JORDAN	1974	27	1,986	937	1974	763	2,438	123	1,831
KOREA, SOUTH	1974	175	22,089	1,515	1974	13,013	2,571	2,286	13,294
LAOS	1974	39	3,232	1,008	1974	151	21,589	16	936
LESOTHO	1974	107	2,114	482	1974	50	20,400	3	53
LIBYA	1974	55	9,741	240	1974	2,063	1,139	136	6,924
LUXEMBOURG	1974	27	3,906	88	1974	368	978	113	1,223
MADAGASCAR	1973	834	19,781	403	1973	687	...	80	2,226
MALAYSIA	1974[2]	305	40,124	...	1974	1,556	...	378	8,010
MAURITIUS	1974	35	3,209	271	1974	235	...	14	971
MONGOLIA	1974	396	13,648	103	1974	2,604	538	116	5,052
MOROCCO	1974	144	23,056	732	1974	1,223	13,802	114	...
NEPAL	1974	55	1,858	6,630	1974	338	36,450	8	335
NETHERLANDS	1973	600	136,216	99	1974	20,200	670	4,110	45,800
NEW ZEALAND	1973	...	31,959	93	1972	3,426	846	1,006	19,094
NICARAGUA	1974	59	4,627	450	1974	1,214	1,713	300	2,735
NIGER	1973	...	2,935	1,526	1974	109	41,101	6	833
NIGERIA	1972	...	42,101	1,378	1973	2,343	25,463	103	9,567
NORWAY	1974	848	54,676	73	1974	6,590	605	3,667	26,500
PAKISTAN	1974	4,234	36,417	1,871	1974	17,194	...	597	6,010
PANAMA	1974	55	5,808	281	1974	1,313	1,234	210	3,395
PARAGUAY	1972	134	3,875	677	1974	1,370	1,875	540	2,157
POLAND	1974	1,315	261,012	129	1974	56,949	592	15,656	124,649
PORTUGAL	1974	581	53,454	163	1974	10,312	851	...	10,749
QATAR	1973	...	661	130	1974	96	938	7	247
RHODESIA	1974	253	19,285	316	1973	1,035	5,700	162	5,092
RUMANIA	1974	...	191,910	110	1973	25,870	805	5,289	36,419
RWANDA	1974	182	6,142	671	1974	77	53,506	2	359
SENEGAL	1974	42	5,722	754	1974	281	14,092	29	2,245
SINGAPORE	1974	17	8,178	271	1974	1,586	1,400	422	5,751
SOUTH AFRICA	1973	788	156,245	152	1973	12,060	2,016	1,767	53,835
SPAIN	1973	1,285	180,547	193	1973	51,743	673	3,613	...
SRI LANKA	1973	456	39,732	333	1972	3,251	4,007	280	6,458
SUDAN	1974	137	15,792	1,097	1974	1,400	12,371	149	11,160
SURINAM	1974	16	2,288	180	1974	202	2,030	15	476
SWAZILAND	1973	33	1,719	269	1974	54	8,888	6	485
SWEDEN	1973	720	123,996	66	1973	12,610	645	7,000	55,580
SYRIA	1974	98	6,753	1,054	1973	2,371	2,905	561	2,632
THAILAND	1973	615	51,435	774	1973	4,662	...	596	9,184
TOGO	1972	26	3,075	680	1973	100	21,200	5	731
TRIN. & TOB.	1972	28	4,804	218	1974	494	2,157	62	1,679
TURKEY	1974	799	83,693	463	1974	20,868	1,834	4,750	25,120
UGANDA	1974	241	15,723	710	1974	540	20,685	19	1,627
USSR	1974	24,627	2,933,000	86	1974	697,400	363	101,600	1,185,500
UN. KINGDOM	1974[2]	...	500,650	...	1974[2]	75,141	...	16,385	214,633
USA	1974	7,370	1,418,939	149	1973	338,111	622	107,320	1,349,000
UPPER VOLTA	1971	148	4,675	1,174	1974	99	59,595	9	1,306
VENEZUELA	1974	355	34,263	339	1973	13,017	866	3,093	24,205
YEMEN	1972	37	4,200	1,443	1974	245	26,449	11	568
YUGOSLAVIA	1973	261	124,367	169	1974	24,920	849	4,793	46,860
ZAIRE	1973	...	72,090	327	1973	818	28,802	22	9,285

Source: *UN Statistical Yearbook 1976.*
[1] Data refer to Greek population only.   [2] Partly based on 1973 figures.

MILITARY STRENGTH

NUCLEAR DELIVERY VEHICLES: COMPARATIVE STRENGTHS AND CHARACTERISTICS

(A) United States and Soviet Union

I Missiles and Artillery

	Category[1]	UNITED STATES Type	Range (mi)[2]	Warhead yield range[3]	First deploy-ment	Number deployed (7/77)	SOVIET UNION Type[4]	Range (mi)	Warhead yield range[3]	First deploy-ment	Number deployed (7/77)
Land-based	ICBM	Titan II	7,000	5–10 MT	1962	54	SS-7 Saddler	6,900	5 MT	1961	} 109
		Minuteman II	7,000	1–2 MT	1966	450	SS-8 Sasin	6,900	5 MT	1963	
		Minuteman III	7,500	3 × 170 KT	1970	550	SS-9 Scarp	7,500	18–25 MT or 3 × 5 MT[5]	1965	238
							SS-11 Sego	6,500	1–2 MT or 3 × KT[6]	1966	840
							SS-13 Savage[7]	5,000	1 MT	1968	60
							SS-17	6,500	4 × KT or 1 × 5 MT[8]	1975	40
							SS-18	7,500	15–25 MT or 8 × MT[9]	1975	50
							SS-19	6,500	6 × KT or 1 × 5 MT[8]	1975	140
	M/IRBM						SS-4 Sandal	1,200	1 MT	1959	500
							SS-5 Skean	2,300	1 MT	1961	100
							SS-20	3,000	3 × KT[10]	1977	(20)
	SRBM	Pershing[11]	450	high KT	1962	108[12]	SS-1b Scud A[11]	50	KT	1957	
		Lance[11]	70	low KT	1972	36[12]	SS-1c Scud B[11]	185	KT	1965	} (750)
		Honest John[11]	25	KT	1953	n.a.	SS-12 Scaleboard	500	MT	1969	
							FROG 7[11]	10–45	KT	1957–65	(450)
	LRCM						SS-N-3 Shaddock	450	KT	1962	(100)
Sea-based	SLBM	Polaris A3	2,880	3 × 200 KT	1964	160	SS-N-4 Sark	350	1–2 MT	1961	27
		Poseidon C3	2,880	10 × 50 KT[13]	1971	496	SS-N-5 Serb	750	1–2 MT	1964	54
							SS-N-6 Sawfly[14]	1,750	1–2 MT or 3 × KT[15]	1969	544
							SS-N-8[16]	4,800	1–2 MT	1972	284
	SLCM						SS-N-3 Shaddock[17]	450	KT	1962	324
Air-launched	ALCM	Hound Dog	600	KT	1961	(400)	AS-3 Kangaroo	400	KT	1961	n.a.
							AS-4 Kitchen	450	KT	1962	(800)
	ALBM	SRAM	150	KT	1972	1,500					
Artillery	Self-propelled	M-110 203mm how[11]	10	KT	1962	200[12]					
		M-109 155mm how[11]	10	2KT	1964	300[12]					
	Towed	M-115 203mm how[11]	10	KT	1950s	n.a.	M-55 203mm gun/how[11]	18	KT	1950s	n.a.

II Aircraft[19]

Category[19]	UNITED STATES Type	Range (mi)[20]	Speed (Mach no.)	First deploy-ment	Number deployed (7/77)	SOVIET UNION Type[21]	Range (mi)[20]	Speed (Mach no.)	First deploy-ment	Number deployed (7/77)
Long-range bombers	B-52D	11,500	0.95	1956	} 373[22]	Tu-95 Bear	8,000	0.78	1956	100
	B-52G-H	12,500	0.95	1959		Mya-4 Bison	6,000	0.87	1956	35[23]
Medium-range bombers	FB-111A	3,800	2.5	1969	68	Tu-16 Badger	4,000	0.8	1955	740[24]
						Tu-? Backfire B	5,500	2.5	1974	65[24]
Land-based strike (incl. short-range bombers)	F-105D	2,100	2.25	1960		Il-28 Beagle	2,500	0.8	1950	
	F-4C-J	2,300	2.4	1962	(350)[12]	Su-7 Fitter A	900	1.7	1959	
	F-111A/E	3,800	2.2/2.5	1967		Tu-22 Blinder	1,400	1.5	1962	
	A-7D	3,400	0.9	1968		MiG-21 Fishbed J/K/L	1,150	2.2	1970	} (1,000)[12]
						MiG-27 Flogger D	1,800	2.5	1971	
						Su-17-20 Fitter C	1,100	1.6	1974	
						Su-19 Fencer A	1,800	2.3	1974	
Carrier-based strike	A-4	2,055	0.9	1956						
	A-6A	3,225	0.9	1963	(200)[12]					
	A-7A/B/E	3,400	0.9	1966						
	F-4	2,000	2.4	1962						

[1] ICBM range = 4,000+ statute miles; IRBM range = 1,500–4,000 miles; MRBM range = 500–1,500 miles; SRBM range = under 500 miles; LRCM range = over 350 miles.

[2] Statute miles (1 mi = 1.61 km). Operational range depends upon the payload carried; use of maximum payload may reduce missile range by up to 25%.

[3] Estimated maxima; warhead yields vary greatly. KT (kiloton) range = less than 1 MT (megaton).

[4] Numerical designations of Soviet missiles (e.g. SS-9) are of US origin; names (e.g. Scarp) are of NATO origin.

[5] The SS-9 exists in three operational modes; 18- or 25-MT single-warhead and 3 MRV of 4–5 MT each.

[6] A 3-MRV version of the SS-11 has replaced some of the single-warhead systems.

[7] A solid-fuel replacement for the SS-13, the SS-X-16, which has about twice the throw-weight and may also be deployed in a land-mobile mode, is undergoing tests.

[8] The SS-17 and SS-19 have begun deployment in modified SS-11 silos. Operational missiles are equipped with MIRV, but single-warhead versions have been tested.

[9] The SS-18, a follow-on to the SS-9, has been tested in two single-warhead and 5–8-MIRV versions.

[10] The SS-20 has been tested at longer ranges with a single, lower-yield warhead.

[11] Dual-capable (able to deliver conventional or nuclear warheads). Conventional warheads for US Lance and Pershing under development. Though shown in the table, it is uncertain whether Soviet 203mm artillery is nuclear-capable.

[12] Figures for systems in Europe only.

[13] Poseidon can carry up to 14 RV (reentry vehicle) over a reduced range.

[14] A solid propellant replacement for the SS-N-6, the SS-NX-17, has been tested and is thought to be capable of deploying MIRV.

[15] The SS-N-6 has been tested with new single warhead (MT range) and with 3 MRV.

[16] A 3-warhead MIRV replacement for the SS-N-8, the SS-NX-18, has been tested.

[17] A longer-range version of the SS-N-3, the SS-X-12, is reportedly under development.

[18] All aircraft are dual-capable, but some in the strike aircraft categories are not presently configured for the nuclear role.

[19] Long-range bomber = maximum range 6,000+ miles; medium-range bomber = maximum range 3,500–6,000 miles, primarily designed for bombing missions. Backfire is classified as a medium-range bomber on the basis of reported range characteristics.

[20] Theoretical maximum range in statute miles, with internal fuel only, at optimum altitude and speed. Ranges of strike aircraft assume no weapons load. Especially in the case of strike aircraft, therefore, range falls sharply for flights at higher speeds, lower altitude or with full weapons load.

[21] Names of Soviet aircraft (e.g. Bear) are of NATO origin.

[22] Excluding aircraft in storage or reserve.

[23] Excluding approximately 45 Mya-4 configured as tankers.

[24] Including aircraft in the Naval Air Force (some 280 Tu-16 and 30 Backfire) but excluding Tu-16 tankers.

III US–Soviet Strategic Balance: Static Measurements[1]

		Deliverable warheads[2]	Equivalent megatonnage[3]	Missile throw-weight (million lb)[4]	Bomber payload (million lb)[4]
USA	ICBM	2,154	1,460	2.2	
	SLBM	5,120	830	1.1	
	Long-range bombers	4,056	4,400		
	Totals	11,330	6,690	3.3	22.8
USSR	ICBM	2,647	2,950	7.8	
	SLBM	909	860	1.3	
	Long-range bombers	270	780		
	Totals	3,826	4,590	9.1	4.7

(B) Other NATO and Warsaw Pact Countries

IV Missiles and Artillery

	Category[5]	NATO (excluding USA) Type[6]	Operated by[7]	Range (mi)[8]	First deployment	Number deployed (7/77)	WARSAW PACT (excluding USSR) Type[9]	Operated by	Range (mi)[8]	First deployment	Number deployed (7/77)
Land-based missiles	IRBM SRBM	SSBS S-2	FR	1,875	1971	18					
		Sergeant[10]	GE	85	1962	20	SS-1b Scud A[11]	All	50	1957	(130)
		Pershing[10]	GE	450	1962	72	SS-1c Scud B[11]	All	185	1965	
		Lance	BR, GE, IT	70	1976	(44)					
		Pluton	FR	75	1974	24					
		Honest John[12]		25	1953	(112)	FROG 3–7[11]	All	10–45	1957–65	(200)
SLBM	SLBM	Polaris A3	BR	2,880	1967	64					
		MSBS M-1	FR	1,550	1972	32					
		MSBS M-2	FR	1,900	1974	16					
		MSBS M-20	FR	3,000	1977	16					
Artillery	SP	M-110 203mm how[13]		10	1962	n.a.					
		M-109 155mm how[14]		10	1964	n.a.					
	Towed	M-115 203mm how[13]		10	1950s	n.a.					

V Aircraft[15]

Category[16]	NATO (excluding USA) Type[17]	Operated by[7]	Range (mi)[18]	Speed (Mach no.)[19]	First deployment	Deployed (7/77)	WARSAW PACT (excluding USSR) Type[20]	Operated by[21]	Range (mi)[18]	Speed (Mach no.)[19]	First deployment	Deployed (7/77)
Medium-range bombers	Vulcan B2	BR	4,000	0.95	1960	50	Il-28 Beagle[23]	PO	2,500	0.81	1950	n.a.[24]
Strike aircraft (incl. short-range bombers)[25]	F-104[22]	11	1,300	2.2	1958	n.a.[24]	Su-7 Fitter A[23]	CZ, HY, PO	900	1.7	1959	n.a.[24]
	F-4	BR, GE	1,600	2.4	1962	n.a.[24]						
	Buccaneer	BR	2,300	0.95	1962	70	Su-20 Fitter C[23]	PO	1,100	1.6	1974	n.a.[24]
	Mirage IVA	FR	2,000	2.2	1964	50						
	Jaguar	BR, FR	1,000	1.1	1973 / 1974	72 / 120						

[1] These are estimates of static strategic capability derived from Tables I and II. These measurements are useful in comparing force size, but provide limited information about force effectiveness. More elaborate dynamic presentations of the balance can be used to portray effectiveness, but this requires the enumeration of factors not shown here, such as accuracy and defensive capability.

[2] This measures the number of targets each side can attack. Only separately-targetable delivery vehicles are included in missile totals. Bomber totals assume both stand-off missile and gravity bomb deployment.

[3] Equivalent megatonnage (EMT) measures damage to unprotected area targets. Assuming that a warhead falls within the boundary of the target area, the EMT of a specific weapon is expressed as the two-thirds power of its explosive yield, or $Y^{2/3}$. Totals assume maximum yield values shown in Tables I and II.

[4] Neither missile throw-weight nor bomber payload provides a measure of destructive power, but both give some indication of the capacity of a given system to be exploited for different purposes. An ICBM, for example, can be used to deliver a small number of larger-yield warheads (to maximize EMT) or a larger number of smaller warheads (to maximize target coverage). The same is true for bombers, but calculations are complicated by the range versatility of aircraft and the large choice of weapons they can carry. Because bomber payload is a less precise indicator of potential military capacity than missile throw-weight, the table gives separate estimates for missiles and bombers.

[5] IRBM range 1,500–4,000 miles; SRBM range under 500 miles.

[6] All NATO vehicles are of American origin, with the exception of the SSBS IRBM, MSBS SLBM and Pluton, which are of French origin.

[7] BR = Britain, FR = France, GE = Germany, IT = Italy.

[8] Statute miles (1 mi = 1.61 km). Use of maximum payload may reduce range by up to 25%.

[9] All Warsaw Pact vehicles are of Soviet origin. Numerical designations (e.g., SS-Ib) are of American origin, names (Scud A, FROG) of NATO origin.

[10] These SRBM are operated by Germany but the nuclear warheads for them are in American custody. Sergeant is dual-capable.

[11] These dual-capable systems are operated by the countries shown, but nuclear warheads for them are in Soviet custody.

[12] Honest John is dual-capable and is operated by Belgium, Germany, Greece, the Netherlands, and Turkey, but the nuclear warheads are in American custody.

[13] The 203mm (8-in.) howitze is dual-capable. It is operated by Belgium, Britain, Denmark, Germany, Greece, Italy, the Netherlands, and Turkey, but the nuclear warheads are in American custody. There are no nuclear warheads on Danish soil.

[14] The 155mm how. is primarily a conventional artillery weapon but is dual-capable. It is operated by Belgium, Britain, Canada, Denmark, Germany, Greece, Italy, the Netherlands, Norway, and Turkey, but in very few cases is it likely to have a nuclear role, certainly not in the case of Canada. Any nuclear warheads would be in American custody, none of them being held on either Danish or Norwegian soil.

[15] All aircraft listed are dual-capable but many would be more likely to carry conventional than nuclear weapons.

[16] Medium-range bomber = maximum range 3,500–6,000 miles, primarily designed for bombing missions.

[17] Vulcan and Buccaneer are of British origin; F-104 and F-4 are of American origin; Mirage is of French origin; Jaguar is Anglo-French.

[18] Theoretical maximum range in statute miles, with internal fuel only, at optimum altitude and speed. Ranges for strike aircraft assume no weapons load. Especially in the case of strike aircraft, therefore, range falls sharply for flights at lower altitude, at higher speed or with full weapons load (e.g., combat radius of F-104, at operational height and speed, with typical weapons load, is approximately 420 miles).

[19] Mach 1 = speed of sound.

[20] Warsaw Pact aircraft are of Soviet origin; the names listed (e.g., Beagle) are of NATO origin.

[21] CZ = Czechoslovakia, HY = Hungary, PO = Poland.

[22] The dual-capable F-104 is operated by Belgium, Canada, Denmark, Germany, Greece, Italy, the Netherlands, Norway, and Turkey, but the Canadian aircraft no longer have a nuclear role. The nuclear warheads are held in American custody.

[23] Nuclear warheads for these dual-capable aircraft are held in Soviet custody.

[24] The absence of figures here reflects the uncertainty as to how many of these dual-capable aircraft actually have a nuclear role.

[25] Certain other aircraft, such as the Mirage III, may also be capable of carrying tactical nuclear weapons.

Source: "The Military Balance 1977–1978," The International Institute for Strategic Studies.

FOREIGN AID: SELECTED COUNTRIES

	Aid received (1973–75 annual averages in millions of U.S. dollars)				Aid given (1975) (in millions of U.S. dollars)			
	Bi-lateral	Multi-lateral	Total	Total per capita (in U.S. $)	Official	Private	Total	% of GNP
AFGHANISTAN	265	15	280	...	...	...	...	...
ALGERIA	265	18	283	...	...	...	...	...
ARGENTINA	299	26	325	...	...	...	...	...
AUSTRALIA	...	...	...	...	515	53	568	0.72
AUSTRIA	...	...	...	...	89	51	140	0.42
BANGLADESH	545	159	704	...	...	...	...	...
BELGIUM	...	...	...	...	410	400	810	1.2
BENIN	20	17	37	12.19	...	...	...	...
BOLIVIA	32	20	52	...	...	...	...	...
BOTSWANA	33	7	40	60.58	...	...	...	...
BRAZIL	157	52	209	...	...	...	...	...
BULGARIA	...	...	...	...	17	...	17	0.08
BURMA	64	12	76	2.51	...	...	...	...
BURUNDI	20	15	35	9.55	...	...	...	...
CAMBODIA	186	3	189	...	...	...	...	...
CAMEROON	77	25	102	...	...	...	...	...
CANADA	...	...	...	...	1,021	925	1,946	1.06
CEN. AFR. EMP.	22	16	38	22.19	...	...	...	...
CHAD	53	24	77	...	...	...	...	...
CHILE	56	17	73	...	...	...	...	...
CHINA	...	...	...	...	272	...	272	...
COLOMBIA	90	33	123	...	...	...	...	...
CONGO	30	15	45	...	...	...	...	...
CZECHOSLOVAKIA	...	...	...	...	168	...	168	0.4
DENMARK	...	...	...	...	210	22	232	0.6
ECUADOR	23	27	50	7.14	...	...	...	...
EGYPT	278	67	345	...	...	...	...	...
ETHIOPIA	69	36	105	3.81	...	...	...	...
FINLAND	...	...	...	...	54	18	72	0.3
FRANCE	...	...	...	...	2,448	1,209	3,657	1.0
GABON	26	7	33	62.87	...	...	...	...
GERMANY, E.	...	...	...	...	277	...	277	0.6
GERMANY, W.	...	...	...	...	1,596	2,429	4,025	0.9
GHANA	77	11	88	...	...	...	...	...
HONDURAS	18	12	30	10.24	...	...	...	...
HUNGARY	...	...	...	...	151	...	151	...
INDIA	792	483	1,275	...	...	...	...	...
INDONESIA	561	125	686	...	...	...	...	...
IRAN	161	8	169	...	...	...	...	...
IRAQ	152	7	159	...	...	...	...	...
ISRAEL	256	1	257	76.35	...	...	...	...
ITALY	...	...	...	...	360	1,269	1,629	0.9
IVORY COAST	58	23	81	16.98	...	...	...	...
JAPAN	...	...	...	...	2,549	356	2,905	0.6
JORDAN	104	19	123	...	...	...	...	...
KENYA	94	19	113	8.70	...	...	...	...
KOREA, SOUTH	232	26	258	7.72	...	...	...	...
LAOS	63	4	67	...	...	...	...	...
MALAWI	33	11	44	9.07	...	...	...	...
MALAYSIA	64	7	71	6.05	...	...	...	...
MEXICO	31	47	78	...	...	...	...	...
MOROCCO	110	19	129	7.60	...	...	...	...
NEPAL	51	12	63	...	...	...	...	...
NETHERLANDS	...	...	...	...	600	574	1,174	1.4
NEW ZEALAND	...	...	...	...	73	2	75	0.6
NICARAGUA	22	18	40	19.39	...	...	...	...
NIGERIA	73	16	89	1.46	...	...	...	...
NORWAY	...	...	...	...	185	85	270	1.0
PAKISTAN	369	71	440	...	...	...	...	...
PANAMA	18	10	28	17.44	...	...	...	...
PAPUA N.G.	249	5	254	96.01	...	...	...	...
PARAGUAY	13	19	32	12.43	...	...	...	...
PERU	63	20	83	5.47	...	...	...	...
PHILIPPINES	169	19	188	4.55	...	...	...	...
POLAND	...	...	...	...	54	...	54	0.08
RUMANIA	...	...	...	...	465	...	465	1.1
RWANDA	37	18	55	13.32	...	...	...	...
SENEGAL	81	39	120	...	...	...	...	...
SOMALIA	38	29	67	...	...	...	...	...
SRI LANKA	98	26	124	...	...	...	...	...
SUDAN	82	41	123	...	...	...	...	...
SURINAM	38	5	43	106.18	...	...	...	...
SWEDEN	...	...	...	...	565	136	701	1.0
SWITZERLAND	...	...	...	...	99	253	352	0.6
SYRIA	393	12	405	...	...	...	...	...
TANZANIA	182	25	207	...	...	...	...	...
THAILAND	64	8	72	1.76	...	...	...	...
TOGO	22	13	35	15.83	...	...	...	...
TUNISIA	137	23	160	...	...	...	...	...
TURKEY	289	...	289	...	...	...	...	...
USSR	...	...	...	...	1,642	...	1,642	0.3
UN. KINGDOM	...	...	...	...	885	1,380	2,265	1.0
USA	...	...	...	...	4,742	10,942	15,684	1.0
UPPER VOLTA	83	32	115	...	...	...	...	...
ZAIRE	178	33	211	...	...	...	...	...
ZAMBIA	74	7	81	...	...	...	...	...

Source: Based on data in the *UN Statistical Yearbook 1976* and *The Military Balance 1976–77* (The International Institute for Strategic Studies).

Note. Bilateral aid is that which is granted directly by one country to another, while multilateral aid is channeled through institutions, such as the World Bank, financial entities of the European Community, or agencies and programs of the United Nations.

SOCIETIES AND ORGANIZATIONS

This article lists some of the most noteworthy associations, societies, foundations, and trusts of the United States and Canada. The information has been verified by the organization concerned.

Academy of Motion Picture Arts & Sciences. Membership: 3,900. Executive director, James M. Roberts. Headquarters: 8949 Wilshire Blvd., Beverly Hills, Calif. 90211.

Alcoholics Anonymous (The General Service Board of A. A., Inc.). Membership: over 1,000,000 in more than 28,000 affiliated groups. Chairman, John L. Norris, M. D. Headquarters: 468 Park Ave. S., New York, N. Y. Mailing Address: Box 459, Grand Central Station, New York, N. Y. 10017.

American Academy and Institute of Arts and Letters. Membership: 250. Executive director, Margaret M. Mills. Headquarters: 633 West 155th St., New York, N. Y. 10032.

American Academy of Political and Social Science. Membership: 17,500, including 7,000 libraries. Annual meeting: Philadelphia, Pa., April 1978. President, Marvin E. Wolfgang. Headquarters: 3937 Chestnut St., Philadelphia, Pa. 19104.

American Anthropological Association. Membership: 10,268. President, Richard Adams; executive director, Edward J. Lehman. Headquarters: 1703 New Hampshire Ave. NW, Washington, D. C. 20009.

American Association for the Advancement of Science. Membership: 122,000 and 291 affiliated groups. Meeting: Washington, D. C. Feb. 12–17, 1978. President: Emilio Q. Daddario; executive officer, William D. Carey. Headquarters: 1515 Massachusetts Ave. NW, Washington, D. C. 20005.

American Association of Museums. Membership: 6,000. Annual meeting, Kansas City, Mo., May 28–June 2, 1978. Director, Dr. Richard McLanathan. Headquarters: 1055 Thomas Jefferson St., Suite 428, Washington, D. C. 20007.

American Association of University Professors. Membership: 79,559. President, Peter O. Steiner. Headquarters: One Dupont Circle NW, Washington, D. C. 20036.

American Association of University Women. Membership: 190,000. President, Dr. Marjorie Bell Chambers; general director, Dr. Helen B. Wolfe. Headquarters: 2401 Virginia Ave. NW, Washington, D. C. 20037.

American Astronomical Society. Membership: 3,400. Meetings, 1978: Austin, Tex., Jan. 8–11; Madison, Wis., June 24–28. President, E. M. Burbidge; executive officer, H. M. Gurin. Address: 211 FitzRandolph Rd., Princeton, N. J. 08540.

American Automobile Association. Membership: 18,500,000 in 928 affiliated groups. President, James B. Creal. Headquarters: 8111 Gatehouse Rd., Falls Church, Va. 22042.

American Bankers Association. Membership: 13,382. President, W. Liddon McPeters. Headquarters: 1120 Connecticut Ave. NW, Washington, D. C. 20036.

American Bar Association. Membership: 217,137. President, William B. Spann, Jr.; secretary, Herbert D. Sledd; executive director, Bert H. Early. Headquarters: 1155 East 60th St., Chicago, Ill. 60637.

American Bible Society. 1976 Scripture distribution: 209,748,451 copies. Annual meeting: New York, N. Y., May 11, 1978. President, Edmund F. Wagner. Headquarters: 1865 Broadway, New York, N. Y. 10023.

American Booksellers Association, Inc. Membership: 5,100. National convention: Atlanta, Ga., May 27–30, 1978. President, Robert D. Hale; executive director, G. Roysce Smith. Headquarters: 122 East 42nd St., New York, N. Y. 10017.

American Cancer Society, Inc. Membership: 194 voting members; 58 charter divisions. President, R. Lee Clark, M. D. Headquarters: 777 Third Ave., New York, N. Y. 10017.

American Chemical Society. Membership: 110,000. National meetings, 1978: Anaheim, Calif., March 12–17; Miami Beach, Fla., Sept. 10–15. President, Anna J. Harrison; executive director, Raymond P. Mariella. Headquarters: 1155 16th St. NW, Washington, D. C. 20036.

American Civil Liberties Union. Membership: 250,000. Executive director, Aryeh Neier; board chairman, Norman Dorsen. Headquarters: 22 East 40th St., New York, N. Y. 10016.

American Council of Learned Societies. Membership: 42 professional societies concerned with the humanities and the humanistic aspects of the social sciences. President, R. M. Lumiansky; vice president, Gordon B. Turner. Headquarters: 345 East 46th St., New York, N. Y. 10017.

American Council on Education. Membership: 1,271 colleges and universities, 109 associated organizations, 53 affiliates, 60 constituent organizations, and 5 international affiliates. Annual meeting: Washington, D. C., Oct. 11–13, 1978. President, Jack W. Peltason. Headquarters: One Dupont Circle NW, Washington, D. C. 20036.

American Dental Association. Membership: 127,000. President, Frank F. Shuler, D. D. S.; president-elect, Frank P. Bowyer, Jr., D. D. S.; executive director, C. Gordon Watson, D. D. S. Headquarters: 211 E. Chicago Ave., Chicago, Ill., 60611.

American Economic Association. Membership: 17,900 and 6,600 subscribers. Annual meeting: Chicago, Ill., Aug. 29–31, 1978. President, Jacob Marschak. Headquarters: 1313 21st Ave. S., Nashville, Tenn. 37212.

American Farm Bureau Federation. Membership: 2,676,259 families. Annual meeting: January. President, Allan Grant. Headquarters: 225 Touhy Ave., Park Ridge, Ill. 60068.

American Geographical Society. Fellows and subscribers: 10,000. President, Richard H. Nolte; director, Sarah K. Myers. Headquarters: Broadway at 156th St., New York, N. Y. 10032.

American Geophysical Union. Membership: 12,000 individuals and 32 organizations. Meetings, 1978: Miami, Fla., April 17–21 and San Francisco, Calif., Dec. 4–8. President, Arthur E. Maxwell; executive director, A. F. Spilhaus, Jr. Headquarters: 1909 K St. NW, Washington, D. C. 20006.

American Heart Association. Membership: 140,000 in 55 affiliates, 125 chapters and about 1,000 local subdivisions. President, W. Gerald Austen, M. D. Headquarters: 7320 Greenville Avenue, Dallas, Tex. 75231.

American Historical Association. Membership: 15,000. President, Charles Gibson; executive director, Mack Thompson. Headquarters: 400 A St. SE, Washington, D. C. 20003.

American Horticultural Society. Membership: 35,000 individuals, 400 organizations, institutions, and commercial establishments. National congress: Nashville, Tenn., October 1978. President, Dr. Henry M. Cathey. Headquarters: Mt. Vernon, Va. 22121.

American Hospital Association. Membership: 25,594 persons; 6,496 institutions. Annual meeting: Washington, D. C., Jan. 29–Feb. 1, 1978; convention: Anaheim, Calif., Sept. 11–14, 1978. Chairman of the board of trustees, John M. Stagl; president, John Alexander McMahon. Headquarters: 840 North Lake Shore Drive, Chicago, Ill. 60611.

American Hotel and Motel Association. Membership: 6,500. Annual convention, Seattle, Wash., Oct. 24–27, 1978. Executive vice president, Robert L. Richards. Headquarters: 888 Seventh Ave., New York, N. Y. 10019.

American Institute of Aeronautics and Astronautics. Membership: 22,500, plus 4,000 student members. Executive secretary, James J. Hartford. Headquarters: 1290 Avenue of the Americas, New York, N. Y. 10019.

American Institute of Architects. Membership: 26,000. President, Elmer E. Botsai, FAIA. Headquarters: 1735 New York Ave. NW, Washington, D. C. 20006.

American Institute of Biological Sciences. Membership: 11,000, with 41 adherent societies and 12 affiliate organizations. Annual meeting: Athens, Ga., Aug. 20–25, 1978. President, George A. Gries; executive director, Richard Trumbull. Headquarters: 1401 Wilson Blvd., Arlington, Va. 22209.

American Institute of Certified Public Accountants. Membership: 130,000. Annual meeting: San Francisco, Calif., Oct. 22–24, 1978. Chairman of the board, Stanley J. Scott; president, Wallace E. Olson. Headquarters: 1211 Avenue of the Americas, New York, N. Y. 10036.

American Institute of Chemical Engineers. Membership: 37,729. President, A. S. West; executive director, F. J. Van Antwerpen. Headquarters: 345 East 47th St., New York, N. Y. 10017.

American Institute of Graphic Arts. Membership: 2,000. President, Massimo Vignelli; executive director, Flora Finn Gross. Headquarters: 1059 Third Ave., New York, N. Y. 10021.

American Institute of Mining, Metallurgical and Petroleum Engineers, Inc. Membership: 59,373. Annual meeting: Denver, Colo., Feb. 26–March 2, 1978. President, H. Arthur Nedom; executive director, Joe B. Alford. Headquarters: 345 East 47th St., New York, N. Y. 10017.

American Legion, The. Membership: 2,700,000. Headquarters: 700 N. Pennsylvania St., Indianapolis, Ind. 46206.

American Library Association. Membership 30,000. Semiannual conventions, 1978: Chicago, Ill., Jan. 22–28 and June 25–July 1. Executive director: Robert Wedgeworth. Headquarters: 50 E. Huron St., Chicago, Ill. 60611.

American Lung Association. Membership: 175 affiliated groups. Annual meeting: Boston, Mass., May 1978. President, Robert Douglas. Headquarters: 1740 Broadway, New York, N. Y. 10019.

American Management Associations. Membership: 60,000. Chairman of the board, Lee S. Bickmore; president and chief executive officer, James L. Hayes. Headquarters: 135 West 50th St., New York, N. Y. 10020.

American Mathematical Society. Membership: 16,403. President, R. H. Bing; secretary, Everett Pitcher. Headquarters: P. O. Box 6248, Providence, R. I. 02940.

American Medical Association. Membership: 185,000. President, John H. Budd, M. D.; executive vice president, James H. Sammons, M. D. Headquarters: 535 N. Dearborn St., Chicago, Ill. 60610.

American Meteorological Society. Membership: 9,000, including 113 corporate members. President, Dr. Werner A. Baum; executive director, Dr. Kenneth C. Spengler. Headquarters: 45 Beacon St., Boston, Mass. 02108.

American National Red Cross. Membership: 30,044,842 in 3,135 chapters. National convention: Hartford, Conn., May 14–17, 1978. Chairman, Frank Stanton; president, George M. Esley. Headquarters: 17th and D Sts. NW, Washington, D. C. 20006.

American Newspaper Publishers Association. Membership: 1,175. Annual convention: Montreal, Quebec, May 6–11, 1978. Chairman and president, Joe D. Smith, Jr. Headquarters: 11600 Sunrise Valley Drive, Reston, Va. 22091. Mail Address: P. O. Box 17407, Dulles International Airport, Washington, D. C. 20041.

American Nurses' Association. Membership: 200,000 in 53 state and territorial associations. National convention: Honolulu, June 11–16, 1978. President, Anne Zimmerman. Headquarters: 2420 Pershing Road, Kansas City, Mo. 64108.

American Physical Society. Membership: 29,000 American and foreign. Annual meeting: San Francisco, Calif., Jan. 23–26, 1978. President, George E. Pake; executive secretary, W. W. Havens, Jr. Headquarters: 335 East 45th St., New York, N. Y. 10017.

American Psychiatric Association. Membership: 23,688; 71 district branches. Annual meeting: Atlanta, Ga., May 8–12, 1978. President, Jack Weinberg, M. D. Headquarters: 1700 18th St. NW, Washington, D. C. 20009.

American Psychological Association. Membership: 45,000. Annual meeting: Toronto, Ont., 1978. President, Theodore H. Blau. Headquarters: 1200 17th St. NW, Washington, D. C. 20036.

American Society of Civil Engineers. Membership: 75,000. President, William R. Gibbs. Headquarters: 345 East 47th St., New York, N. Y. 10017.

American Society of Composers, Authors, and Publishers. Membership: 18,000 composers and authors; 5,500 publishers. President, Stanley Adams; secretary, Morton Gould. Headquarters: One Lincoln Plaza, New York, N. Y. 10023.

American Society of Mechanical Engineers. Membership: 84,000. President, S. Peter Kezios. Headquarters: 345 East 47th St., New York, N. Y. 10017.

American Society of Newspaper Editors. Membership: 800. National convention: Washington, D. C., April 9–13, 1978. President, Eugene C. Patterson. Headquarters: Box 551, 1350 Sullivan Trail, Easton, Pa. 18042.

American Sociological Association. Membership: 14,000. Annual meeting: San Francisco, Calif., Sept. 4–8, 1978. President, Amos H. Hawley. Headquarters: 1722 N St. NW, Washington, D. C. 20036.

American Statistical Association. Membership: 11,582. President, Leslie Kish; secretary, Fred C. Leone. Headquarters: 806 15th St. NW, Washington, D. C. 20005.

American Youth Hostels, Inc. Membership: 65,000; 31 councils in the United States. President, Dick Leary. Headquarters: National Campus, Delaplane, Va. 22025.

Archaeological Institute of America. Membership: 6,500; subscribers 24,000. President, Robert H. Dyson, Jr. Headquarters: 260 W. Broadway, New York, N. Y. 10013.

Arthritis Foundation, The. Membership: 73 chapters. Annual meeting: New York, June 2–3, 1978. Chairman, H M Poole, Jr.; president, Clifford M. Clarke. Headquarters: 3400 Peachtree Rd., NE, Atlanta, Ga. 30326.

Association of American Publishers. Membership: approximately 320. Annual meeting: spring 1978. Chairman of the board, Harold T. Miller; president, Townsend W. Hoopes; senior vice president, Austin J. McCaffrey. Addresses: One Park Avenue, New York, N. Y. 10016 and 1707 L St. NW, Washington, D. C. 20036.

Association of Junior Leagues, Inc. Membership: 234 member Leagues in U. S., Canada, and Mexico. Annual conference: Kansas City, Mo., May 7–11, 1978. President, Mrs. Susan R. Greene. Headquarters: 825 Third Avenue, New York, N. Y. 10022.

Benevolent and Protective Order of Elks. Membership: 1,623,092 in 2,214 Lodges. Grand exalted ruler, Willis C. McDonald; grand secretary, Homer Huhn, Jr. Headquarters: 2750 Lake View Ave., Chicago, Ill. 60614.

Big Brothers / Big Sisters of America. Membership: more than 357 local agencies. Annual convention, Washington, D. C., June 20–24, 1978. Executive vice president, L. P. Reade. Headquarters: 220 Suburban Station Bldg., Philadelphia, Pa. 19103.

B'nai B'rith. Membership: 500,000 in about 4,000 men's, women's, and youth units. President, David M. Blumberg; executive vice president, Dr. Daniel Thursz. Headquarters: 1640 Rhode Island Ave. NW, Washington, D. C. 20036.

Boys' Clubs of America. Membership: 1,071,000 in 1,077 clubs. National conference: New York City, May 7–11, 1978. President, John L. Burns; national director, William R. Bricker. Headquarters: 771 First Ave., New York, N. Y. 10017.

Boy Scouts of America. Membership: 4,884,082 boys and leaders in 420 Scouting councils. Biennial meeting: Phoenix, Ariz., May 17–19, 1978. President, Downing Jenks; chief Scout executive, Harvey L. Price. National office: North Brunswick, N. J. 08902.

Camp Fire Girls, Inc. Membership: 500,000 in over 35,000 communities. President, Mrs. Jack S. Burk; national executive director, Dr. Hester Turner. Headquarters: 4601 Madison Avenue, Kansas City, Mo. 64112.

Canadian Library Association. Membership: 3,569 persons, 973 institutions, 4,502 personnel. Annual conference: Edmonton, Alta. Executive director: Paul Kitchen. Headquarters: 151 Sparks St., Ottawa, Ont. K1P 5E3.

Canadian Medical Association. Membership: 30,000. Annual meeting: Winnipeg, June 19–24, 1978. President, Dr. R. Gourdeau. Headquarters: 1867 Alta Vista Drive, Ottawa, Ont. K1G 0G8.

Chamber of Commerce of the United States of America. Membership about 4,000 trade associations and local and state chambers, more than 57,000 business members. President, Richard L. Lesher; chairman of the board, William K. Eastham. Headquarters: 1615 H St. NW, Washington, D. C. 20062.

Common Cause. Membership: 275,000. Chairwoman: Nan Waterman. Headquarters: 2030 M St. NW, Washington, D. C. 20036.

Consumers Union of U. S. Executive director: Rhoda H. Karpatkin. Headquarters: 256 Washington St., Mount Vernon, N. Y. 10550.

Council of Better Business Bureaus. Membership: 1,000. Headquarters: 1150 17th St. NW, Washington, D. C. 20036.

Council on Foreign Relations, Inc. Membership: 1,750. Annual meeting: New York, N. Y., Nov. 22, 1978. President, Winston Lord. Headquarters: 58 East 68th St., New York, N. Y. 10021.

Daughters of the American Revolution (National Society). Membership: 205,789 in 3,082 chapters. Continental congress: Washington, D. C., April 17–21, 1978. President general, Mrs. George Upham Baylies. Headquarters: 1776 D St. NW, Washington, D. C. 20006.

Foreign Policy Association. Chairman, Carter L. Burgess. Headquarters: 345 E. 46th St., New York, N. Y. 10017.

Freemasonry, Ancient Accepted Scottish Rite of (Northern Masonic Jurisdiction): Supreme Council, 33°. Membership: 513,355 in 380 affiliated groups. Sovereign grand commander, Stanley F. Maxwell. Headquarters: 33 Marrett Road, Lexington, Mass. 02173.

Freemasonry, Ancient and Accepted Scottish Rite of (Southern Jurisdiction): Supreme Council, 33°. Membership: 650,000 in 217 affiliated groups. Sovereign grand commander, Henry C. Clausen. Headquarters: 1733 16th St. NW, Washington, D. C. 20009.

Future Farmers of America. Membership: 509,735 in 50 state associations. National advisor, H. N. Hunsicker; executive secretary, Coleman Harris. Headquarters: Box 15160, Alexandria, Va. 22309.

Gamblers Anonymous. Membership: 6,500. National executive secretary, James J. Zeysing. Headquarters: 2705¼ W. Eighth St., Los Angeles, Calif. 90005.

Garden Club of America, The. Membership: over 13,000 in 182 member clubs. Annual meeting: Birmingham, Ala., April 3–6, 1978. President, Mrs. Benjamin M. Belcher. Headquarters: 598 Madison Avenue, New York, N. Y. 10022.

General Federation of Women's Clubs. Membership: 10,000,000 in 14,000 U. S. organizations and 36 abroad. National convention: Phoenix, Ariz., June 4–10, 1978. President, Mrs. Harry Wagner, Jr. Headquarters: 1734 N St. NW, Washington, D. C. 20036.

Geological Society of America. Membership: 13,000. Annual meeting: Toronto, Ont., Oct. 23–26, 1978. President, Peter T. Flawn; executive director, John C. Frye. Headquarters: 3300 Penrose Place, Boulder, Colo. 80301.

Girl Scouts of the U.S.A. Membership: 3,160,000. National president, Dr. Gloria D. Scott; national executive director, Frances R. Hesselbein. Headquarters: 830 Third Avenue, New York, N.Y. 10022.

Humane Society of the United States. Annual convention: Dearborn, Mich., Oct. 12–15, 1978. President, John A. Hoyt. Headquarters: 2100 L St. NW, Washington, D.C. 20037.

Institute of Electrical and Electronics Engineers, Inc. Membership: 180,000. President, Robert M. Saunders. Headquarters: 345 East 47th St., New York, N.Y. 10017.

Jewish War Veterans of the U.S.A. Membership: 100,000 in 750 units. National commander, Dr. Robert Shor. Headquarters: 1712 New Hampshire Ave. NW, Washington, D.C. 20009.

Kiwanis International. Membership: 283,000 in 7,000 clubs in U.S. and abroad. President, Stanley E. Schneider. Headquarters: 101 East Erie St., Chicago, Ill. 60611.

Knights of Columbus. Membership: 1,235,000. Supreme knight, Virgil C. Dechant. Headquarters: Columbus Plaza, New Haven, Conn. 06507.

Knights of Pythias, Supreme Lodge. Membership: 151,065 in 1,406 subordinate lodges. Supreme chancellor, Victor C. Jorgensen. Office: 47 N. Grant St., Stockton, Calif. 95202.

League of Women Voters of the U.S. Membership: 137,-000. President, Ruth C. Clusen. Headquarters: 1730 M St. NW, Washington, D.C. 20036.

Lions International. Membership: 1,200,000 in 31,000 clubs in 149 countries and areas. Annual convention: Tokyo, Japan, June 1978. President, Joseph M. McLoughlin. Headquarters: 300 22nd Street, Oak Brook, Ill. 60521.

Modern Language Association of America. Membership: 30,000. President, Edith Kern; executive director, William D. Schaefer. Headquarters: 62 Fifth Ave., New York, N.Y. 10011.

National Academy of Sciences. Membership: approx. 1,200. Annual meeting: Washington, D.C., April 24–26, 1978. President, Philip Handler. Headquarters: 2101 Constitution Ave. NW, Washington, D.C. 20418.

National Association for Mental Health, Inc. Membership: 1,000 state and local organizations. Executive director, Brian O'Connell. Headquarters: 1800 North Kent St., Rosslyn Station, Arlington, Va. 22209.

National Association for the Advancement of Colored People. Membership: 450,000 in 1,700 units. National convention: Portland, Ore., July 3–7, 1978. President, W. Montague Cobb, M.D.; board chairman, Margaret Bush Wilson; executive director, Benjamin L. Hooks. Headquarters: 1790 Broadway, New York, N.Y. 10019.

National Association of Manufacturers. Membership: 13,-000. President, Heath Larry. Headquarters: 1776 F St. NW, Washington, D.C. 20006.

National Audubon Society. Membership: 370,000. President, Dr. Elvis J. Stahr; senior vice president, Paul M. Howard, Jr. Headquarters: 950 Third Ave., New York, N.Y. 10022.

National Conference of Christians and Jews, Inc. Membership: 70 regional offices. President, Dr. David Hyatt. Headquarters: 43 West 57th St., New York, N.Y. 10019.

National Council of the Churches of Christ in the U.S.A. Membership: 30 Protestant, Anglican, and Orthodox denominations. President, Dr. William P. Thompson; general secretary, Dr. Claire Randall. Headquarters: 475 Riverside Dr., New York, N.Y. 10027.

National Council on the Aging. Membership: 3,200. Executive director, Jack Ossofsky. Headquarters: 1828 L St. NW, Washington, D.C. 20036.

National Easter Seal Society for Crippled Children and Adults. Membership: 52 state and territorial societies. President, Dr. Lamar Soutter. Headquarters: 2023 W. Ogden Ave., Chicago, Ill. 60612.

National Education Association of the U.S. Membership: 1,800,000 with units in every state, and 12,000 local affiliates. Annual meeting: Dallas, Tex., July 2–7, 1978. President, John Ryor. Headquarters: 1201 16th St. NW, Washington, D.C. 20036.

National Federation of Business and Professional Women's Clubs, Inc. Membership: 170,000 in 3,800 clubs. President, Piilani Desha. Headquarters: 2012 Massachusetts Ave. NW, Washington, D.C. 20036.

National Federation of Independent Business, Inc. Membership: 542,000. President, Wilson S. Johnson. Headquarters: 150 West 20th Ave., San Mateo, Calif. 94403.

National Federation of Music Clubs. Membership: 500,000 in 4,300 clubs and 12 national affiliates. Biennial convention: Portland, Ore., April 1979. President, Mrs. Frank A. Vought. Headquarters: 310 S. Michigan Ave., Chicago, Ill. 60604.

National Foundation—March of Dimes, The. Membership: 1,600 chapters. President, Joseph F. Nee. Headquarters: 1275 Mamaroneck Ave., White Plains, N.Y. 10605.

National Organization for Women (NOW). Membership: 700 local groups. President, Eleanor Smeal. Headquarters: 425 13th St., Suite 1048, Washington, D.C. 20004.

National PTA (National Parent-Teacher Association). Membership: 6,403,854 in 30,574 local units. National convention: Atlanta, Ga., June 11–14, 1978. President, Mrs. Grace Baisinger. Headquarters: 700 North Rush St., Chicago, Ill. 60611.

National Safety Council. Membership: 15,000. National Safety Congress and Exposition: Chicago, Ill., Oct. 2–5, 1978. President, Vincent L. Tofany. Headquarters: 444 N. Michigan Ave., Chicago, Ill. 60611.

National Urban League, Inc. Executive director, Vernon E. Jordan, Jr. Headquarters: 500 East 62nd St., New York, N.Y. 10021.

National Woman's Christian Temperance Union. Membership: about 250,000 in 6,000 local unions. National convention: Atlanta, Ga., Aug. 24–28, 1978. President, Mrs. Herman Stanley. Headquarters: 1730 Chicago Ave., Evanston, Ill. 60201.

Parents Without Partners. Membership: 130,000. National convention: San Francisco, Calif., July 12–15, 1978. Executive director, George B. Williams. Headquarters: 7910 Woodmont Ave., Suite 1000, Washington, D.C. 20014.

Phi Beta Kappa. Membership: 275,000. Secretary, Kenneth Greene. Headquarters: 1811 Q St. NW, Washington, D.C. 20009.

Planned Parenthood Federation of America, Inc. (Planned Parenthood–World Population). Chairman of the Federation, Mrs. Julian M. Marshall. Headquarters: 810 Seventh Ave., New York, N.Y. 10019.

Photographic Society of America. Membership: 18,700. Executive secretary, Charles E. Morris. Headquarters: 2005 Walnut St., Philadelphia, Pa. 19103.

Rotary International. Membership: 809,250 in 17,325 clubs functioning in 152 countries. International convention: Tokyo, Japan, May 14–18, 1978. General secretary, Harry A. Stewart. Headquarters: 1600 Ridge Ave., Evanston, Ill. 60201.

Salvation Army. Membership: 384,817. National commander: Paul S. Kaiser. Headquarters: 120 W. 14th St., New York, N.Y. 10011.

Special Libraries Association. Membership: 10,000. Annual conference: Atlanta, Ga., June 1978. President, Shirley Echelman; executive director, F. E. McKenna. Headquarters: 235 Park Ave. S., New York, N.Y. 10003.

United Dairy Industry Association (including American Dairy Association). Membership: 340,000. Annual convention, Dearborn, Mich., March 19–23, 1978. Executive vice president, Alden R. Grimes. Headquarters: 6300 N. River Rd., Rosemont, Ill. 60018.

United States Jaycees, The. Membership: 347,334 in 8,590 affiliated groups. Annual meeting: Atlantic City, N.J., June 1978. President, Bob Rushton. Headquarters: P.O. Box 7, Tulsa, Okla. 74102.

United Way of America. Chairman of the Board of Governors, John W. Hanley. Headquarters: 801 N. Fairfax St., Alexandria, Va. 22314.

Veterans of Foreign Wars of the United States. Membership: V.F.W. and Auxiliary: 2,412,600. Commander-in-Chief, Dr. John Wasylik. Headquarters: V.F.W. Building, Broadway at 34th St., Kansas City, Mo. 64111.

World Council of Churches (U.S. Conference). Membership: 28 churches or denominations in U.S. Moderator, Robert J. Marshall. Headquarters: 475 Riverside Dr., New York, N.Y. 10027.

Young Men's Christian Associations (National Council). Membership: 8,900,000 in 1,786 organizations. National board chairman, William E. Schneider. Headquarters: 291 Broadway, New York, N.Y. 10007.

Young Women's Christian Association of the U.S.A. Members and participants: approx. 2,400,000. President, Elizabeth Steel Genné; executive director, Sara-Alyce P. Wright. Headquarters: 600 Lexington Ave., New York, N.Y. 10022.

Zionist Organization of America. Membership: 120,000 in 600 districts. 81st National convention: Washington, D.C., Sept. 6–10, 1978. President, Dr. Joseph P. Sternstein; national executive director, Leon Ilutovich. Headquarters: ZOA House, 4 East 34th St., New York, N.Y. 10016.

MAJOR UNIVERSITIES AND COLLEGES, U.S. AND CANADA

Note: Symbols and abbreviations that follow the name of each school listed are as follows: Level of Instruction—(1) senior college granting bachelor's and/or first professional degree; (2) senior college granting master's and/or second professional degree; (3) college or university offering a doctoral program. Student Body—All colleges and universities are co-educational unless indicated: (M) men only; (W) women only; (S) separate colleges for men and women. Control—(Pub.) district, municipal, state, or federal; (Pvt.) proprietary, corporation, or church. Enrollment statistics for U.S. universities and colleges are for the 1976–77 academic year; Canadian statistics are for the 1974–75 academic year.

Name and Location	Level	Control	Enrollment
Abilene Christian University, Abilene, Tex...	2	Pvt.	4,486
Acadia University, Wolfville, Nova Scotia....	2	Pvt.	2,589
Adams State College, Alamosa, Colo.........	2	Pub.	2,825
Adelphi University, Garden City, N.Y.......	3	Pvt.	10,246
Adrian College, Adrian, Mich..............	1	Pvt.	1,044
Akron, The University of, Akron, Ohio......	3	Pub.	21,757
Alabama, University of, in Birmingham, Ala..	3	Pub.	11,641
Alabama, University of, in Huntsville, Ala...	3	Pub.	3,692
Alabama, University of, in University, Ala....	3	Pub.	16,916
Alabama Agricultural and Mechanical University, Normal, Ala.	2	Pub.	4,520
Alabama State University, Montgomery, Ala.	2	Pub.	3,567
Alaska, University of, Northern Region, Fairbanks, Alaska..................	3	Pub.	4,331
Alaska, University of, South Central Region, Anchorage, Alaska................	2	Pub.	7,026
Alaska Methodist University, Anchorage....	2	Pvt.	504
Albany State College, Albany, Ga.........	1	Pub.	2,096
Alberta, The University of, Edmonton.....	3	Pub.	18,978
Albion College, Albion, Mich.............	1	Pvt.	1,774
Albright College, Reading, Pa.............	1	Pvt.	1,485
Albuquerque, University of, Albuquerque, N. Mex...................	1	Pvt.	3,000
Alcorn State University, Lorman, Miss.......	1	Pub.	3,091
Alderson-Broaddus College, Philippi, W. Va..	1	Pvt.	891
Alfred University, Alfred, N.Y.............	3	Pvt.	1,737
Allegheny College, Meadville, Pa..........	2	Pvt.	1,966
Alma College, Alma, Mich................	1	Pvt.	1,139
Alverno College, Milwaukee, Wis..........	1	Pvt.	833
American International College, Springfield, Mass....................	2	Pvt.	2,319
American University, Washington, D.C......	3	Pvt.	13,594
Amherst College, Amherst, Mass..........	2	Pvt.	1,320
Ana G. Méndez Educational Foundation, Rio Piedras, P.R................	1	Pvt.	5,397
Anderson College, Anderson, Ind..........	1	Pvt.	1,911
Andrews University, Berrien Springs, Mich...	3	Pvt.	2,655
Angelo State College, San Angelo, Tex......	2	Pub.	4,721
Antioch College, Yellow Springs, Ohio......	2	Pvt.	4,531
Appalachian State University, Boone, N.C....	2	Pub.	10,208
Aquinas College, Grand Rapids, Mich.......	2	Pvt.	1,706
Arizona, University of, Tucson, Ariz.......	3	Pub.	29,149
Arizona State University, Tempe, Ariz.......	3	Pub.	37,395
Arkansas, University of, Fayetteville, Ark....	3	Pub.	14,037
Arkansas, University of, Little Rock.........	2	Pub.	8,435
Arkansas, University of, Pine Bluff, Ark.....	1	Pub.	2,599
Arkansas Polytechnic College, Russellville...	1	Pub.	2,266
Arkansas State University, State University..	2	Pub.	7,191
Armstrong State College, Savannah, Ga......	2	Pub.	3,827
Art Center College of Design, Pasadena, Calif................	2	Pvt.	1,140
Art Institute of Chicago, Schools of the, Chicago, Ill................	2	Pvt.	1,658
Asbury College, Wilmore, Ky.............	1	Pvt.	1,225
Ashland College, Ashland, Ohio............	1	Pvt.	2,130
Assumption College, Worcester, Mass.......	2	Pvt.	1,852
Athens College, Athens, Ala..............	1	Pvt.	862
Atlanta University, Atlanta, Ga............	3	Pvt.	1,090
Atlantic Christian College, Wilson, N.C......	1	Pvt.	1,648
Auburn University, Auburn, Ala............	3	Pub.	17,044
Auburn University at Montgomery, Ala......	2	Pub.	3,797
Augsburg College, Minneapolis, Minn.......	1	Pvt.	1,762
Augusta College, Augusta, Ga.............	2	Pub.	4,100
Augustana College, Rock Island, Ill........	2	Pvt.	2,357
Augustana College, Sioux Falls, S. Dak.....	2	Pvt.	2,243
Aurora College, Aurora, Ill................	1	Pvt.	918

Name and Location	Level	Control	Enrollment
Austin College, Sherman, Tex.............	2	Pvt.	1,214
Austin Peay State University, Clarksville, Tenn..................	2	Pub.	4,167
Averett College, Danville, Va..............	1	Pvt.	1,097
Avila College, Kansas City, Mo............	1	Pvt.	1,694
Azusa Pacific College, Azusa, Calif.........	2	Pvt.	1,697
Babson College, Babson Park, Mass.........	2	Pvt.	2,634
Baker University, Baldwin City, Kans.......	1	Pvt.	876
Baldwin-Wallace College, Berea, Ohio......	2	Pvt.	3,039
Ball State University, Muncie, Ind.........	3	Pub.	18,369
Baltimore, University of, Baltimore, Md.....	2	Pub.	5,706
Bank Street College of Education, N.Y.C.....	2	Pvt.	1,416
Baptist College at Charleston, S.C..........	1	Pvt.	2,540
Bard College, Annandale-on-Hudson, N.Y...	1	Pvt.	641
Barry College, Miami, Fla.................	2	Pvt.	1,523
Bates College, Lewiston, Me..............	1	Pvt.	1,286
Bayamón Central University, Bayamón, P.R..	1	Pvt.	1,534
Baylor University, Waco, Tex..............	3	Pvt.	8,756
Beaver College, Glenside, Pa..............	2	Pvt.	1,338
Bellarmine College, Louisville, Ky.........	1	Pvt.	1,561
Belmont College, Nashville, Tenn..........	1	Pvt.	1,114
Beloit College, Beloit, Wis...............	2	Pvt.	1,516
Bemidji State College, Bemidji, Minn.......	2	Pub.	5,465
Benedict College, Columbia, S.C...........	1	Pvt.	1,626
Benedictine College, Atchison, Kans.......	1	Pvt.	979
Bentley College, Waltham, Mass...........	2	Pvt.	4,765
Berea College, Berea, Ky.................	1	Pvt.	1,504
Berklee College of Music, Boston, Mass.....	1	Pvt.	2,236
Berry College, Mount Berry, Ga............	2	Pvt.	1,692
Bethany College, Bethany, W. Va..........	1	Pvt.	1,177
Bethany Nazarene College, Bethany, Okla...	2	Pvt.	1,208
Bethel College, St. Paul, Minn............	1	Pvt.	1,623
Bethune-Cookman College, Daytona Beach..	1	Pvt.	1,520
Biola College, La Mirada, Calif............	2	Pvt.	2,605
Birmingham-Southern College, Birmingham, Ala................	1	Pvt.	727
Biscayne College, Miami, Fla..............	1	Pvt.	1,710
Bishop College, Dallas, Tex...............	1	Pvt.	1,861
Black Hills State College, Spearfish, S. Dak..	2	Pub.	2,342
Bloomfield College, Bloomfield, N.J........	1	Pvt.	1,714
Bloomsburg State College, Bloomsburg, Pa...	2	Pub.	5,962
Bluefield State College, Bluefield, W. Va.....	1	Pub.	1,328
Boise State University, Boise, Idaho........	2	Pub.	10,245
Boston College, Chestnut Hill, Mass........	3	Pvt.	13,544
Boston State College, Boston, Mass........	2	Pub.	11,230
Boston University, Boston, Mass...........	3	Pvt.	29,292
Bowdoin College, Brunswick, Me...........	2	Pvt.	1,348
Bowie State College, Bowie, Md...........	2	Pub.	2,851
Bowling Green State University, Bowling Green, Ohio................	3	Pub.	16,263
Bradley University, Peoria, Ill.............	2	Pvt.	4,893
Brandeis University, Waltham, Mass........	3	Pvt.	3,537
Brandon University, Brandon, Manitoba.....	1	Pvt.	959
Brescia College, Owensboro, Ky...........	1	Pvt.	928
Briar Cliff College, Sioux City, Iowa........	1	Pvt.	900
Bridgeport, University of, Bridgeport, Conn...	2	Pvt.	7,293
Bridgewater College, Bridgewater, Va.......	1	Pvt.	796
Bridgewater State College, Bridgewater, Mass................	2	Pub.	8,170
Brigham Young University, Provo, Utah.....	3	Pvt.	27,218
Hawaii Campus, Laie, Oahu........	1	Pvt.	1,068
British Columbia, University of, Vancouver ..	3	Pub.	19,151
Brock University, St. Catharines, Ont........	2	Pub.	2,291
Brown University, Providence, R.I..........	3	Pvt.	6,766
Bryant College, Smithfield, R.I............	2	Pvt.	4,856

Name and Location	Level	Control	Enrollment
Bryn Mawr College, Bryn Mawr, Pa........	3	Pvt.	1,592
Bucknell University, Lewisburg, Pa.........	2	Pvt.	3,248
Buena Vista College, Storm Lake, Iowa......	1	Pvt.	874
Butler University, Indianapolis, Ind.........	2	Pvt.	4,282
Caldwell College, Caldwell, N.J. (W)........	1	Pvt.	790
Calgary, University of, Calgary, Alberta.....	3	Pub.	9,449
California, University of:			
Berkeley..............................	3	Pub.	35,439
Davis................................	3	Pub.	17,784
Irvine................................	3	Pub.	12,706
Los Angeles..........................	3	Pub.	39,009
Riverside.............................	3	Pub.	6,054
San Diego............................	3	Pub.	10,119
San Francisco........................	3	Pub.	3,182
Santa Barbara........................	3	Pub.	15,607
Santa Cruz...........................	3	Pub.	10,105
California College of Arts & Crafts, Oakland..	2	Pvt.	1,132
California Institute of Technology, Pasadena.	3	Pvt.	1,597
California Institute of the Arts, Valencia....	2	Pvt.	697
California Lutheran College, Thousand Oaks	2	Pvt.	2,234
California Polytechnic State University, San Luis Obispo, Calif......................	2	Pub.	15,537
California State College, Bakersfield, Calif...	2	Pub.	3,481
California State College, Dominguez Hills...	2	Pub.	7,733
California State College, San Bernardino....	2	Pub.	4,223
California State College, Sonoma, Calif.....	2	Pub.	9,004
California State College, Stanislaus, Calif....	2	Pub.	3,483
California State College, California, Pa.....	2	Pub.	5,163
California State Polytechnic College, Pomona, Calif......................	2	Pub.	13,005
California State University, Chico, Calif.....	2	Pub.	14,020
California State University, Fresno, Calif.....	2	Pub.	17,042
California State University, Fullerton, Calif...	2	Pub.	22,269
California State University, Hayward, Calif...	2	Pub.	13,122
California State University, Long Beach.....	2	Pub.	34,427
California State University, Los Angeles.....	2	Pub.	25,962
California State University, Northridge, Calif.	2	Pub.	28,735
California State University, Sacramento.....	2	Pub.	22,565
Calumet College, East Chicago, Ind.........	1	Pvt.	1,625
Calvin College, Grand Rapids, Mich.........	2	Pvt.	3,674
Cameron University, Lawton, Okla..........	1	Pub.	5,193
Campbell College, Buies Creek, N.C.........	1	Pvt.	1,724
Campbellsville College, Campbellsville, Ky...	1	Pvt.	711
Canisius College, Buffalo, N.Y..............	2	Pvt.	4,274
Capital University, Columbus, Ohio.........	2	Pvt.	2,667
Cardinal Stritch College, Milwaukee, Wis....	2	Pvt.	1,292
Carleton College, Northfield, Minn.........	1	Pvt.	1,725
Carleton University, Ottawa, Ont...........	3	Pvt.	8,444
Carlow College, Pittsburgh, Pa.............	1	Pvt.	983
Carnegie-Mellon University, Pittsburgh, Pa..	3	Pvt.	4,842
Carroll College, Helena, Mont..............	1	Pvt.	1,397
Carroll College, Waukesha, Wis............	1	Pvt.	1,255
Carson-Newman College, Jefferson City, Tenn................................	1	Pvt.	1,559
Carthage College, Kenosha, Wis............	2	Pvt.	1,651
Case Western Reserve University, Cleveland	3	Pvt.	8,688
Castleton State College, Castleton, Vt.......	1	Pub.	1,836
Catawba College, Salisbury, N.C............	1	Pvt.	1,020
Catholic University of America, Washington .	3	Pvt.	7,258
Catholic University of Puerto Rico, Ponce...	2	Pvt.	9,687
Cedar Crest College, Allentown, Pa. (W)...	1	Pvt.	709
Centenary College of Louisiana, Shreveport..	1	Pvt.	820
Central Arkansas, University of, Conway, Ark...................................	2	Pub.	4,740
Central College, Pella, Iowa...............	1	Pvt.	1,186
Central Connecticut State College, New Britain, Conn........................	2	Pub.	13,471
Central Methodist College, Fayette, Mo.....	1	Pvt.	697
Central Michigan University, Mt. Pleasant, Mich.................................	2	Pub.	17,565
Central Missouri State University, Warrensburg, Mo.....................	2	Pub.	9,041
Central State University, Wilberforce, Ohio..	1	Pub.	2,335
Central State University, Edmond, Okla.....	2	Pub.	12,736
Central Washington State College, Ellensburg, Wash....................	2	Pub.	7,536
Chadron State College, Chadron, Nebr.......	2	Pub.	2,024
Chaminade College of Honolulu, Hawaii.....	2	Pvt.	2,521
Chapman College, Orange, Calif............	2	Pvt.	5,751
Charleston, College of, Charleston, S.C......	2	Pub.	5,359
Chestnut Hill College, Philadelphia, Pa. (W).	1	Pvt.	829
Cheyney State College, Cheyney, Pa........	1	Pub.	2,720
Chicago, University of, Chicago, Ill..........	3	Pvt.	9,480
Chicago State University, Chicago, Ill........	2	Pub.	6,615
Christian Brothers College, Memphis, Tenn..	1	Pvt.	872
Christopher Newport College, Newport News, Va...................................	1	Pub.	2,988
Cincinnati, University of, Cincinnati, Ohio...	3	Pub.	34,885
Citadel, The, Charleston, S.C..............	2	Pub.	3,352
Claflin College, Orangeburg, S.C............	1	Pvt.	923
Claremont Men's College, Claremont, Calif. (M)................................	1	Pvt.	866
Clarion State College, Clarion, Pa...........	2	Pub.	4,885
Clark College, Atlanta, Ga.................	1	Pvt.	1,660
Clark University, Worcester, Mass..........	3	Pvt.	2,983
Clarkson College of Technology, Potsdam, N.Y.................................	3	Pvt.	2,976
Clemson University, Clemson, S.C..........	3	Pub.	11,213
Cleveland Institute of Art, Cleveland, Ohio...	1	Pvt.	830
Cleveland State University, Cleveland, Ohio.	3	Pub.	16,974
Coe College, Cedar Rapids, Iowa..........	1	Pvt.	1,213
Colby College, Waterville, Me.............	2	Pvt.	1,636
Colgate University, Hamilton, N.Y..........	2	Pvt.	2,514
Colorado, University of, Boulder, Colo.......	3	Pub.	21,618
Colorado Springs.....................	2	Pub.	3,288
Denver.............................	2	Pub.	8,097
Colorado College, Colorado Springs, Colo...	2	Pvt.	1,882
Colorado School of Mines, Golden, Colo.....	3	Pub.	2,204
Colorado State University, Fort Collins, Colo.	3	Pub.	16,809
Colorado Women's College, Denver (W).....	1	Pvt.	637
Columbia College, Columbia, Mo...........	1	Pvt.	4,980
Columbia College, Columbia, S.C...........	1	Pvt.	868
Columbia Union College, Takoma Park, Md..	1	Pvt.	933
Columbia University, New York, N.Y........	3	Pvt.	15,460
Barnard College, New York (W).........	1	Pvt.	1,926
Teachers College, New York...........	3	Pvt.	5,785
Columbus College, Columbus, Ga...........	1	Pub.	5,322
Concord College, Athens, W. Va...........	1	Pub.	1,781
Concordia College, Moorhead, Minn........	1	Pvt.	2,570
Concordia Teachers College, River Forest, Ill.	2	Pvt.	1,189
Concordia Teachers College, Seward, Nebr...	2	Pvt.	1,149
Concordia University, Montreal............	2	Pvt.	9,407
Connecticut, University of, Storrs, Conn.....	3	Pub.	23,277
Connecticut College, New London, Conn.....	2	Pvt.	2,033
Converse College, Spartanburg, S.C.........	2	Pvt.	822
Cooper Union, New York, N.Y..............	2	Pvt.	915
Coppin State College, Baltimore, Md........	2	Pub.	2,897
Cornell College, Mount Vernon, Iowa.......	1	Pvt.	905
Cornell University, Ithaca, N.Y.............	3	Pvt.	17,295
Creighton University, Omaha, Nebr.........	3	Pvt.	4,745
Cumberland College, Williamsburg, Ky......	1	Pvt.	1,751
Curry College, Milton, Mass...............	1	Pvt.	901
Dakota State College, Madison, S. Dak......	1	Pub.	870
Dalhousie University, Halifax, Nova Scotia ..	3	Pvt.	6,343
Dallas, University of, Dallas, Tex...........	3	Pvt.	1,708
Dallas Baptist College, Dallas, Tex..........	1	Pvt.	1,266
Dartmouth College, Hanover, N.H..........	3	Pvt.	4,026
David Lipscomb College, Nashville, Tenn....	1	Pvt.	2,188
Davidson College, Davidson, N.C...........	1	Pvt.	1,278
Davis and Elkins College, Elkins, W. Va.....	1	Pvt.	862
Dayton, University of, Dayton, Ohio........	3	Pvt.	8,370
Defiance College, Defiance, Ohio...........	1	Pvt.	816
Delaware, University of, Newark, Del.......	3	Pub.	19,080
Delaware State College, Dover, Del.........	1	Pub.	1,833
Delaware Valley College of Science & Agriculture, Doylestown, Pa...........	1	Pvt.	1,435
Delta State College, Cleveland, Miss........	2	Pub.	3,452
Denison University, Granville, Ohio........	1	Pvt.	2,235
Denver, University of, Denver, Colo........	3	Pvt.	7,762
DePaul University, Chicago, Ill.............	3	Pvt.	10,915
DePauw University, Greencastle, Ind.......	2	Pvt.	2,396
Detroit, University of, Detroit, Mich........	3	Pvt.	8,054

Name and Location	Level	Control	Enroll-ment	Name and Location	Level	Control	Enroll-ment
Detroit Institute of Technology, Detroit......	1	Pvt.	1,539	Florida Institute of Technology, Melbourne..	2	Pvt.	2,826
Dickinson College, Carlisle, Pa............	1	Pvt.	1,660	Florida Memorial College, Opa Locka, Fla...	1	Pvt.	590
Dickinson State College, Dickinson, N. Dak..	1	Pub.	1,000	Florida Southern College, Lakeland, Fla....	1	Pvt.	1,548
Dillard University, New Orleans, La........	1	Pvt.	1,212	Florida State University, Tallahassee, Fla....	3	Pub.	22,381
District of Columbia Teachers College,				Florida Technological University, Orlando..	2	Pub.	10,940
Washington, D.C....................	1	Pub.	1,542	Fordham University, New York, N.Y........	3	Pvt.	14,243
Dominican College of San Rafael, San Rafael,				Fort Hays Kansas State College, Hays, Kans.	2	Pub.	5,141
Calif.....................	2	Pvt.	901	Fort Lewis College, Durango, Colo.........	1	Pub.	2,853
Dordt College, Sioux Center, Iowa..........	1	Pvt.	976	Fort Valley State College, Fort Valley, Ga....	2	Pub.	1,931
Dowling College, Oakdale, N.Y.............	2	Pvt.	1,854	Framingham State College, Framingham,			
Drake University, Des Moines, Iowa........	3	Pvt.	6,524	Mass.............................	2	Pub.	4,917
Drew University, Madison, N.J.............	3	Pvt.	2,048	Francis Marion College, Florence, S.C.......	1	Pub.	2,681
Drexel University, Philadelphia, Pa.........	3	Pvt.	9,082	Franklin & Marshall College, Lancaster, Pa..	1	Pvt.	2,862
Drury College, Springfield, Mo............	2	Pvt.	2,504	Franklin Pierce College, Rindge, N.H.......	1	Pvt.	775
Dubuque, University of, Dubuque, Iowa.....	1	Pvt.	980	Friends University, Wichita, Kans..........	1	Pvt.	876
Duke University, Durham, N.C. (incl. Trinity				Frostburg State College, Frostburg, Md......	2	Pub.	3,691
College & Women's College) (S)	3	Pvt.	9,165	Furman University, Greenville, S.C.........	2	Pvt.	2,585
Duquesne University, Pittsburgh, Pa........	3	Pvt.	7,795				
D'Youville College, Buffalo, N.Y............	1	Pvt.	1,101	Gallaudet College, Washington, D.C........	2	Pvt.	1,039
				Gannon College, Erie, Pa.................	2	Pvt.	3,455
Earlham College, Richmond, Ind...........	2	Pvt.	1,290	Gardner-Webb College, Boiling Springs, N.C.	1	Pvt.	1,402
East Carolina University, Greenville, N.C....	2	Pub.	13,580	General Motors Institute, Flint, Mich.......	1	Pvt.	2,447
East Central Oklahoma State University,				Geneva College, Beaver Falls, Pa..........	1	Pvt.	1,445
Ada, Okla..........................	2	Pub.	3,212	George Mason University, Fairfax, Va.......	2	Pub.	8,022
East Stroudsburg State College, East				George Peabody College for Teachers,			
Stroudsburg, Pa......................	2	Pub.	3,940	Nashville, Tenn....................	3	Pvt.	1,851
East Tennessee State University, Johnson				George Washington University, Washington.	3	Pvt.	22,120
City, Tenn..........................	3	Pub.	10,288	George Williams College, Downers Grove, Ill.	2	Pvt.	1,717
East Texas Baptist College, Marshall, Tex....	1	Pvt.	777	Georgetown College, Georgetown, Ky.......	2	Pvt.	1,062
East Texas State University, Commerce, Tex.	3	Pub.	9,981	Georgetown University, Washington, D.C....	3	Pvt.	11,043
Eastern Connecticut State College,				Georgia, University of, Athens, Ga.........	3	Pub.	23,008
Willimantic, Conn....................	2	Pub.	2,902	Georgia College, Milledgeville, Ga.........	2	Pub.	3,770
Eastern Illinois University, Charleston, Ill....	2	Pub.	9,879	Georgia Institute of Technology, Atlanta, Ga.	3	Pub.	8,870
Eastern Kentucky University, Richmond, Ky.	2	Pub.	13,430	Southern Technical Institute, Marietta...	1	Pub.	2,078
Eastern Mennonite College, Harrisonburg,				Georgia Southern College, Statesboro, Ga...	2	Pub.	6,222
Va................................	1	Pvt.	1,025	Georgia Southwestern College, Americus...	1	Pub.	2,635
Eastern Michigan University, Ypsilanti......	2	Pub.	18,931	Georgia State University, Atlanta, Ga.......	3	Pub.	20,290
Eastern Montana College, Billings, Mont....	2	Pub.	3,414	Gettysburg College, Gettysburg, Pa........	1	Pvt.	1,974
Eastern Nazarene College, Wollaston, Mass.	2	Pvt.	815	Glassboro State College, Glassboro, N.J....	2	Pub.	11,790
Eastern New Mexico University, Portales....	2	Pub.	4,225	Glenville State College, Glenville, W. Va.....	1	Pub.	1,514
Eastern Oregon State College, La Grande....	2	Pub.	1,484	Goddard College, Plainfield, Vt............	2	Pvt.	1,652
Eastern Washington State College, Cheney,				Golden Gate University, San Francisco, Calif.	2	Pvt.	9,100
Wash..............................	2	Pub.	7,185	Gonzaga University, Spokane, Wash........	2	Pvt.	3,046
Eckerd College, St. Petersburg, Fla........	1	Pvt.	845	Gordon College, Wenham, Mass...........	1	Pvt.	1,029
Edgecliff College, Edgecliff, Ohio...........	1	Pvt.	929	Goshen College, Goshen, Ind.............	1	Pvt.	1,265
Edinboro State College, Edinboro, Pa.......	2	Pub.	7,041	Goucher College, Baltimore, Md...........	2	Pvt.	943
Elizabeth City State University, Elizabeth				Graceland College, Lamoni, Iowa..........	1	Pvt.	1,451
City, N.C..........................	1	Pub.	1,629	Grambling State University, Grambling, La..	1	Pub.	3,958
Elizabethtown College, Elizabethtown, Pa...	1	Pvt.	2,041	Grand Canyon College, Phoenix, Ariz.......	1	Pvt.	1,201
Elmhurst College, Elmhurst, Ill............	1	Pvt.	2,552	Grand Valley State College, Allendale, Mich.	2	Pub.	7,340
Elmira College, Elmira, N.Y...............	2	Pvt.	3,320	Great Falls, College of, Great Falls, Mont....	1	Pvt.	1,203
Elon College, Elon College, N.C...........	1	Pvt.	2,210	Greenville College, Greenville, Ill..........	1	Pvt.	848
Embry-Riddle Aeronautical University,				Grinnell College, Grinnell, Iowa...........	1	Pvt.	1,150
Daytona Beach, Fla....................	1	Pvt.	2,927	Grove City College, Grove City, Pa.........	1	Pvt.	2,169
Emerson College, Boston, Mass...........	2	Pvt.	1,435	Guam, University of, Agana, Guam.........	2	Pub.	3,800
Emmanuel College, Boston, Mass..........	2	Pvt.	1,288	Guelph, University of, Guelph, Ont........	3	Pub.	9,381
Emory and Henry College, Emory, Va.......	1	Pvt.	818	Guilford College, Greensboro, N.C.........	1	Pvt.	1,664
Emory University, Atlanta, Ga.............	3	Pvt.	7,161	Gustavus Adolphus College, St. Peter, Minn.	1	Pvt.	2,098
Emporia Kansas State College, Emporia,				Gwynedd-Mercy College, Gwynedd Valley,			
Kans..............................	2	Pub.	6,511	Pa................................	1	Pvt.	917
Evangel College, Springfield, Mo...........	1	Pvt.	1,133				
Evansville, University of, Evansville, Ind.....	2	Pvt.	5,169	Hamilton College, Clinton, N.Y. (M)........	1	Pvt.	996
				Hamline University, St. Paul, Minn........	1	Pvt.	1,186
Fairfield University, Fairfield, Conn........	2	Pvt.	5,107	Hampden-Sydney College,			
Fairleigh Dickinson University, Rutherford,				Hampden-Sydney, Va. (M).............	1	Pvt.	803
Teaneck, Madison, N.J................	3	Pvt.	18,925	Hampton Institute, Hampton, Va...........	2	Pvt.	2,867
Fairmont State College, Fairmont, W. Va.....	1	Pub.	5,072	Hanover College, Hanover, Ind............	1	Pvt.	993
Fayetteville State University, Fayetteville,				Hardin-Simmons University, Abilene, Tex....	2	Pvt.	1,772
N.C...............................	1	Pub.	2,002	Harding College, Searcy, Ark.............	2	Pvt.	2,601
Ferris State College, Big Rapids, Mich.......	2	Pub.	9,460	Harris Teachers College, St. Louis, Mo......	1	Pub.	889
Findlay College, Findlay, Ohio............	1	Pvt.	958	Hartford, University of, West Hartford,			
Fisk University, Nashville, Tenn...........	2	Pvt.	1,424	Conn..............................	3	Pvt.	8,975
Fitchburg State College, Fitchburg, Mass....	2	Pub.	7,408	Hartwick College, Oneonta, N.Y...........	1	Pvt.	1,734
Florida, University of, Gainesville, Fla.......	3	Pub.	28,830	Harvard University, Cambridge, Mass.......	3	Pvt.	20,498
Florida Agricultural & Mechanical				Hastings College, Hastings, Nebr..........	1	Pvt.	684
University, Tallahassee, Fla.............	2	Pub.	5,290	Hawaii, University of, at Hilo.............	1	Pub.	3,078
Florida Atlantic University, Boca Raton, Fla..	3	Pub.	7,266	at Manoa.......................	3	Pub.	20,961

Name and Location	Level	Control	Enrollment
Heidelberg College, Tiffin, Ohio	1	Pvt.	1,107
Henderson State College, Arkadelphia, Ark..	2	Pub.	3,642
Hendrix College, Conway, Ark.	1	Pvt.	1,028
High Point College, High Point, N.C.	1	Pvt.	1,132
Hillsdale College, Hillsdale, Mich.	1	Pvt.	1,070
Hiram College, Hiram, Ohio.	1	Pvt.	1,184
Hobart & William Smith Colleges, Geneva, N.Y. (S)	1	Pvt.	1,797
Hofstra University, Hempstead, L.I., N.Y.	3	Pvt.	10,699
Hollins College, Hollins College, Va.	2	Pvt.	1,033
Holy Cross, College of the, Worcester, Mass.	2	Pvt.	2,680
Holy Family College, Philadelphia, Pa.	1	Pvt.	946
Holy Names College, Oakland, Calif.	2	Pvt.	698
Hope College, Holland, Mich.	1	Pvt.	2,275
Houghton College, Houghton, N.Y.	1	Pvt.	1,275
Houston, University of, Houston, Tex.	3	Pub.	34,419
Houston Baptist University, Houston, Tex.	1	Pvt.	1,520
Howard Payne College, Brownwood, Tex.	1	Pvt.	1,550
Howard University, Washington, D.C.	3	Pvt.	9,455
Humboldt State University, Arcata, Calif.	2	Pub.	7,651
Idaho, College of, Caldwell, Idaho.	2	Pvt.	881
Idaho, University of, Moscow, Idaho	3	Pub.	8,170
Idaho State University, Pocatello, Idaho	2	Pub.	7,344
Illinois, University of, Urbana & Chicago, Ill..	3	Pub.	57,583
Illinois at the Medical Center, University of, Chicago, Ill.	3	Pub.	4,054
Illinois Benedictine College, Lisle, Ill.	1	Pvt.	1,301
Illinois College, Jacksonville Ill.	1	Pvt.	798
Illinois Institute of Technology, Chicago, Ill.	3	Pvt.	6,530
Illinois State University, Normal, Ill.	3	Pub.	20,834
Illinois Wesleyan University, Bloomington	2	Pvt.	1,679
Immaculata College, Immaculata, Pa. (W)	1	Pvt.	1,218
Incarnate Word College, San Antonio, Tex.	2	Pvt.	1,440
Indiana Central University, Indianapolis, Ind.	2	Pvt.	2,887
Indiana State University, Terre Haute, Ind.	3	Pub.	10,987
Indiana University, Bloomington, Ind.	3	Pub.	32,651
Indiana University Regional Campuses			
Fort Wayne	2	Pub.	4,986
Kokomo	1	Pub.	2,637
Northwest at Gary	2	Pub.	4,929
Purdue at Indianapolis	2	Pub.	20,225
South Bend	2	Pub.	5,903
Southeast at New Albany	2	Pub.	3,842
Indiana University of Pennsylvania, Indiana, Pa.	3	Pub.	10,395
Insurance, College of, New York, N.Y.	2	Pvt.	1,559
Inter American University of Puerto Rico, San Germán, P.R.	2	Pvt.	16,657
Iona College, New Rochelle, N.Y.	2	Pvt.	4,908
Iowa, University of, Iowa City, Iowa	3	Pub.	23,036
Iowa State University of Science and Technology, Ames, Iowa	3	Pub.	21,751
Iowa Wesleyan College, Mount Pleasant	1	Pvt.	631
Ithaca College, Ithaca, N.Y.	2	Pvt.	4,606
Jackson State University, Jackson, Miss.	2	Pub.	7,718
Jacksonville State University, Jacksonville, Ala.	2	Pub.	6,461
Jacksonville University, Jacksonville, Fla.	2	Pvt.	2,308
Jersey City State College, Jersey City, N.J.	2	Pub.	11,285
John Carroll University, Cleveland, Ohio	2	Pvt.	3,624
Johns Hopkins University, Baltimore, Md.	3	Pvt.	10,111
Johnson C. Smith University, Charlotte, N.C.	1	Pvt.	1,377
Johnson State College, Johnson, Vt.	1	Pub.	1,313
Juilliard School, The, New York, N.Y.	3	Pvt.	1,199
Juniata College, Huntingdon, Pa.	1	Pvt.	1,067
Kalamazoo College, Kalamazoo, Mich.	1	Pvt.	1,497
Kansas, University of, Lawrence, Kans.	3	Pub.	22,194
Kansas State College of Pittsburg, Kans.	2	Pub.	5,688
Kansas State University, Manhattan, Kans.	3	Pub.	17,901
Kean College of New Jersey, Union, N.J.	2	Pub.	14,103
Kearney State College, Kearney, Nebr.	2	Pub.	5,322
Keene State College, Keene, N.H.	2	Pub.	3,105
Kent State University, Kent, Ohio.	3	Pub.	20,057
Kentucky, University of, Lexington, Ky.	3	Pub.	22,154
Kentucky State University, Frankfort, Ky.	2	Pub.	2,246
Kentucky Wesleyan College, Owensboro, Ky.	1	Pvt.	708
Kenyon College, Gambier, Ohio.	1	Pvt.	1,459
King's College, Wilkes-Barre, Pa.	1	Pvt.	2,292
Knox College, Galesburg, Ill.	1	Pvt.	1,150
Knoxville College, Knoxville, Tenn.	1	Pvt.	978
Kutztown State College, Kutztown, Pa.	2	Pub.	5,506
Lafayette College, Easton, Pa.	1	Pvt.	2,308
Lake Erie College, Painesville, Ohio.	1	Pvt.	902
Lake Forest College, Lake Forest, Ill.	1	Pvt.	1,080
Lake Superior State College, Sault Ste. Marie, Mich.	1	Pub.	2,371
Lakehead University, Port Arthur, Ont.	2	Pvt.	2,388
Lamar University, Beaumont, Tex.	2	Pub.	12,723
Lambuth College, Jackson, Tenn.	1	Pvt.	870
Lander College, Greenwood, S.C.	1	Pvt.	1,661
Langston University, Langston, Okla.	1	Pub.	1,155
La Salle College, Philadelphia, Pa.	2	Pvt.	5,995
Laurentian University of Sudbury, Sudbury, Ont.	2	Pub.	2,693
Laval University, Quebec, Que.	3	Pvt.	13,074
La Verne College, La Verne, Calif.	3	Pvt.	2,210
Lawrence Institute of Technology, Southfield, Mich.	1	Pvt.	4,413
Lawrence University, Appleton, Wis.	1	Pvt.	1,309
Lebanon Valley College, Annville, Pa.	1	Pvt.	1,394
Lee College, Cleveland, Tenn.	1	Pvt.	1,187
Lehigh University, Bethlehem, Pa.	3	Pvt.	6,251
Le Moyne College, Syracuse, N.Y.	1	Pvt.	1,918
Lenoir Rhyne College, Hickory, N.C.	1	Pvt.	1,285
Lesley College, Cambridge, Mass.	2	Pvt.	2,222
Lethbridge, The University of, Lethbridge, Alberta.	1	Pub.	1,154
Lewis & Clark College, Portland, Oreg.	2	Pvt.	2,979
Lewis-Clark State College, Lewiston, Idaho..	1	Pub.	1,641
Lewis University, Lockport, Ill.	2	Pvt.	3,271
Lincoln University, Jefferson City, Mo.	2	Pub.	2,413
Lincoln University, Lincoln University, Pa.	1	Pvt.	1,178
Linfield College, McMinnville, Oreg.	2	Pvt.	1,092
Livingston University, Livingston, Ala.	2	Pub.	1,444
Livingstone College, Salisbury, N.C.	1	Pvt.	857
Lock Haven State College, Lock Haven, Pa.	1	Pub.	2,436
Loma Linda University, Loma Linda, Calif.	3	Pvt.	4,396
Long Island University, Greenvale, N.Y. (incl. Brooklyn Center; Brooklyn College of Pharmacy; C.W. Post & Southampton campuses, Long Island, N.Y.)	3	Pvt.	24,000
Longwood College, Farmville, Va.	2	Pub.	2,212
Loras College, Dubuque, Iowa	2	Pvt.	1,566
Loretto Heights College, Denver, Colo.	1	Pvt.	780
Louisiana College, Pineville, La.	1	Pvt.	1,096
Louisiana State University at Shreveport, Shreveport, La.	3	Pub.	3,161
Louisiana State University & Agricultural Mechanical College System, Baton Rouge and New Orleans, La.	3	Pub.	25,617
Louisiana Tech University, Ruston, La.	3	Pub.	8,811
Louisville, University of, Louisville, Ky.	3	Pub.	15,436
Lowell, University of, Lowell, Mass.	3	Pub.	11,636
Loyola College, Baltimore, Md.	2	Pvt.	4,646
Loyola Marymount University, Los Angeles..	2	Pvt.	5,698
Loyola University, Chicago, Ill.	3	Pvt.	13,003
Loyola University, New Orleans, La.	2	Pvt.	4,615
Lubbock Christian College, Lubbock, Tex.	1	Pvt.	1,128
Luther College, Decorah, Iowa.	1	Pvt.	1,846
Lycoming College, Williamsport, Pa.	1	Pvt.	1,367
Lynchburg College, Lynchburg, Va.	2	Pvt.	2,133
Lyndon State College, Lyndonville, Vt.	1	Pub.	984
Macalester College, St. Paul, Minn.	2	Pvt.	1,676
Madonna College, Livonia, Mich.	1	Pvt.	1,782
McGill University, Montreal, Que.	3	Pvt.	15,156
McMaster University, Hamilton, Ont.	3	Pvt.	9,234
MacMurray College, Jacksonville, Ill.	1	Pvt.	746
McMurry College, Abilene, Tex.	1	Pvt.	1,330
McNeese State University, Lake Charles, La.	2	Pub.	5,997

Name and Location	Level	Control	Enroll- ment	Name and Location	Level	Control	Enroll- ment
Madison College, Harrisonburg, Va.........	2	Pub.	7,844	Mississippi University for Women, Columbus, Miss. (W)..................	2	Pub.	2,986
Maine, University of, at Farmington........	1	Pub.	2,117				
Maine, University of, at Orono............	3	Pub.	11,204	Mississippi Valley State University, Itta Bena, Miss...........................	1	Pub.	3,042
Maine, University of, at Portland-Gorham...	3	Pub.	9,169				
Maine, University of, at Presque Isle........	1	Pub.	1,414	Missouri, University of:			
Manchester College, North Manchester, Ind.	1	Pvt.	1,160	Columbia........................	3	Pub.	23,750
Manhattan College, Bronx, N.Y.	2	Pvt.	4,436	Kansas City......................	3	Pub.	11,215
Manhattan School of Music, New York, N.Y.	3	Pvt.	942	Rolla............................	3	Pub.	4,434
Manhattanville College, Purchase, N.Y.....	2	Pvt.	1,816	St. Louis........................	3	Pub.	11,937
Manitoba, University of, Winnipeg, Man.....	3	Pub.	14,136	Missouri Southern State College, Joplin, Mo.	1	Pub.	3,530
Mankato State University, Mankato, Minn...	2	Pub.	13,275	Missouri Western State College, St. Joseph..	1	Pub.	3,675
Mansfield State College, Mansfield, Pa......	2	Pub.	2,253	Molloy College, Rockville Center, N.Y.......	1	Pvt.	1,225
Marian College, Indianapolis, Ind...........	1	Pvt.	801	Moncton, University of, Moncton, N.B......	2	Pvt.	3,080
Marietta College, Marietta, Ohio............	2	Pvt.	1,807	Monmouth College, Monmouth, Ill..........	1	Pvt.	694
Marion College, Marion, Ind...............	1	Pvt.	834	Monmouth College, West Long Branch, N.J..	2	Pvt.	3,955
Marist College, Poughkeepsie, N.Y.........	2	Pvt.	2,170	Montana, University of, Missoula, Mont.....	3	Pub.	8,760
Marquette University, Milwaukee, Wis.....	3	Pvt.	10,320	Montana College of Mineral Science and Technology, Butte, Mont..............	2	Pub.	1,027
Mars Hill College, Mars Hill, N.C.........	1	Pvt.	1,688				
Marshall University, Huntington, W. Va.....	2	Pub.	10,834	Montana State University, Bozeman, Mont...	3	Pub.	8,938
Mary Hardin-Baylor College, Belton, Tex....	1	Pvt.	1,098	Montclair State College, Upper Montclair, N.J................................	2	Pub.	15,646
Marycrest College, Davenport, Iowa........	2	Pvt.	935				
Marygrove College, Detroit, Mich..........	2	Pvt.	871	Montevallo, University of, Montevallo, Ala...	2	Pub.	3,825
Maryland, University of, at Baltimore.......	3	Pub.	4,632	Montreal, University of, Montreal, Que......	3	Pvt.	14,999
Baltimore County, Catonsville...........	3	Pub.	5,631	Loyola College, Montreal, Que...........	1	Pvt.	4,000
at College Park....................	3	Pub.	35,890	Moorhead State University, Moorhead, Minn.............................	2	Pub.	5,396
Eastern Shore, Princess Anne...........	1	Pub.	1,103				
University College, College Park........	3	Pub.	11,901	Moravian College, Bethlehem, Pa...........	1	Pvt.	1,677
Maryland Institute, College of Art, Baltimore	2	Pvt.	1,108	Morehead State University, Morehead, Ky...	2	Pub.	7,139
Marymount College, Tarrytown, N.Y........	1	Pvt.	859	Morehouse College, Atlanta, Ga. (M).......	1	Pvt.	1,365
Marymount Manhattan College, N.Y.C......	1	Pvt.	2,493	Morgan State University, Baltimore, Md.....	2	Pub.	6,361
Mary Washington College, Fredericksburg, Va...................................	1	Pub.	2,126	Morningside College, Sioux City, Iowa......	2	Pvt.	1,547
				Morris Brown College, Atlanta, Ga.........	1	Pvt.	1,525
Marywood College, Scranton, Pa...........	2	Pvt.	2,843	Morris Harvey College, Charleston, W. Va...	1	Pvt.	2,134
Massachusetts, University of, Amherst......	3	Pub.	25,884	Mount Allison University, Sackville, N.B.....	2	Pvt.	1,405
Massachusetts, University of, Boston, Mass..	2	Pub.	7,473	Mount Holyoke College, South Hadley, Mass. (W)........................	2	Pvt.	1,964
Massachusetts College of Art, Boston, Mass..	2	Pub.	1,614				
Massachusetts Institute of Technology, Cambridge, Mass.....................	3	Pvt.	8,474	Mount Mary College, Milwaukee, Wis. (W)..	1	Pvt.	1,088
				Mount St. Joseph-on-the-Ohio, College of, Mt. St. Joseph, Ohio.................	1	Pvt.	894
Memorial University of Newfoundland, St. John's, Nfld.......................	3	Pub.	5,987				
				Mount St. Mary's College, Los Angeles, Calif.	2	Pvt.	1,077
Memphis State University, Memphis, Tenn..	3	Pub.	22,326	Mount St. Mary's College, Emmitsburg, Md.	2	Pvt.	1,383
Mercer University, Macon, Ga.............	2	Pvt.	2,192	Mount St. Vincent, College of, Bronx, N.Y...	1	Pvt.	1,106
Mercy College, Dobbs Ferry, N.Y..........	1	Pvt.	4,283	Mount St. Vincent University, Halifax, Nova Scotia (W)......................	2	Pvt.	1,179
Mercy College of Detroit, Detroit, Mich......	1	Pvt.	2,140				
Mercyhurst College, Erie, Pa..............	1	Pvt.	1,464	Mount Union College, Alliance, Ohio........	1	Pvt.	1,127
Meredith College, Raleigh, N.C. (W).......	1	Pvt.	1,505	Muhlenberg College, Allentown, Pa.........	1	Pvt.	1,911
Merrimack College, North Andover, Mass...	1	Pvt.	2,743	Mundelein College, Chicago, Ill............	2	Pvt.	1,333
Messiah College, Grantham, Pa............	1	Pvt.	1,037	Murray State University, Murray, Ky........	2	Pub.	8,238
Metropolitan State College, Denver, Colo....	1	Pub.	12,197	Muskingum College, New Concord, Ohio....	1	Pvt.	1,033
Miami, University of, Coral Gables, Fla......	3	Pvt.	14,801				
Miami University, Oxford, Ohio............	3	Pub.	14,642	National College of Education, Evanston, Ill..	2	Pvt.	3,403
Michigan, University of, Ann Arbor, Mich....	3	Pub.	37,505	Naval Postgraduate School, Monterey, Calif..	3	Pub.	1,020
Dearborn Campus.....................	1	Pub.	4,858	Nazareth College of Rochester, N.Y........	2	Pvt.	2,588
Flint...............................	1	Pub.	3,474	Nebraska, University of, Lincoln, Nebr.......	3	Pub.	22,380
Michigan State University, East Lansing....	3	Pub.	48,488	Nebraska, University of, at Omaha, Nebr....	2	Pub.	15,049
Michigan Technological University, Houghton, Mich......................	3	Pub.	5,958	Nebraska Wesleyan University, Lincoln.....	1	Pvt.	1,169
				Nevada, University of, Las Vegas...........	2	Pub.	7,808
Middle Tennessee State University, Murfreesboro, Tenn..................	3	Pub.	10,514	Reno............................	3	Pub.	8,166
				New Brunswick, University of, Fredericton..	3	Pub.	6,016
Middlebury College, Middlebury, Vt........	3	Pvt.	1,917	New England College, Henniker, N.H.......	1	Pvt.	1,584
Midwestern State University, Wichita Falls, Tex.................................	2	Pub.	4,586	New Hampshire, University of, Durham.....	3	Pub.	12,033
				New Haven, University of, West Haven, Conn.............................	2	Pvt.	6,453
Miles College, Birmingham, Ala............	1	Pvt.	1,245				
Millersville State College, Millersville, Pa....	2	Pub.	6,258	New Jersey Institute of Technology, Newark.	3	Pub.	5,605
Millikin University, Decatur, Ill............	1	Pvt.	1,646	New Mexico, University of, Albuquerque....	3	Pub.	21,690
Mills College, Oakland, Calif..............	2	Pvt.	1,018	New Mexico Highlands University, Las Vegas, N. Mex......................	2	Pub.	2,099
Millsaps College, Jackson, Miss...........	1	Pvt.	955				
Milwaukee School of Engineering, Milwaukee, Wis......................	2	Pvt.	2,131	New Mexico Institute of Mining & Technology, Socorro, N. Mex...........	3	Pub.	916
				New Mexico State University, Las Cruces...	3	Pub.	10,848
Minnesota, University of, Minneapolis......	3	Pub.	64,365	New Rochelle, College of, New Rochelle, N.Y...............................	2	Pvt.	2,975
Duluth..............................	2	Pub.	7,925				
Morris..............................	1	Pub.	1,680	New School for Social Research, N.Y.C......	3	Pvt.	19,687
Minot State College, Minot, N. Dak........	2	Pub.	2,206	New York, City University of, New York:			
Mississippi, University of, University, Miss..	3	Pub.	10,747	Bernard M. Baruch College, New York...	2	Pub.	17,043
Mississippi College, Clinton, Miss.........	2	Pvt.	2,977	Brooklyn College, Brooklyn.............	2	Pub.	34,639
Mississippi State University, Mississippi State, Miss.........................	3	Pub.	13,072	City College, New York................	2	Pub.	21,050

Name and Location	Level	Control	Enrollment
New York, City University of (Con't.)			
Graduate School and University Center, New York	3	Pub.	2,900
Herbert H. Lehman College, Bronx	2	Pub.	15,570
Hunter College, New York	2	Pub.	24,500
John Jay College of Criminal Justice, New York	2	Pub.	9,900
Queens College, Flushing	2	Pub.	28,750
Richmond College, Staten Island	2	Pub.	14,930
York College, Flushing	1	Pub.	6,000
New York, Polytechnic Institute of, Brooklyn, N.Y.	3	Pvt.	4,606
New York, State University of:			
College of Environmental Science and Forestry, Syracuse	3	Pub.	2,491
Downstate Medical Center, Brooklyn	3	Pub.	1,468
Maritime College, Bronx	2	Pub.	1,004
State University College at Brockport	2	Pub.	11,696
State University College at Buffalo	2	Pub.	12,604
State University College at Cortland	2	Pub.	6,075
State University College at Fredonia	2	Pub.	5,233
State University College at Geneseo	2	Pub.	6,214
State University College at New Paltz	2	Pub.	8,892
State University College at Oneonta	2	Pub.	6,264
State University College at Oswego	2	Pub.	9,730
State University College at Plattsburgh	2	Pub.	6,720
State University College at Potsdam	2	Pub.	5,021
State University at Albany	3	Pub.	15,447
State University at Binghamton	3	Pub.	9,695
State University at Buffalo	3	Pub.	24,505
State University at Stony Brook	3	Pub.	14,849
Upstate Medical Center, Syracuse	3	Pub.	1,006
New York Institute of Technology, Old Westbury, L.I., N.Y.	2	Pvt.	16,550
New York University, New York, N.Y.	3	Pvt.	28,597
Newberry College, Newberry, S.C.	1	Pvt.	856
Niagara University, Niagara University, N.Y.	2	Pvt.	3,838
Nicholls State University, Thibodaux, La.	2	Pub.	6,410
Norfolk State College, Norfolk, Va.	1	Pub.	6,783
North Adams State College, North Adams, Mass.	2	Pub.	2,869
North Alabama, University of, Florence, Ala.	2	Pub.	4,817
North Carolina, University of:			
Asheville	1	Pub.	1,394
Chapel Hill	3	Pub.	20,615
Charlotte	2	Pub.	7,570
Greensboro	3	Pub.	9,459
Wilmington	1	Pub.	3,209
North Carolina State University at Raleigh	3	Pub.	17,580
North Carolina Agricultural and Technical State University, Greensboro, N.C.	2	Pub.	5,345
North Carolina Central University, Durham	2	Pub.	4,730
North Central College, Naperville, Ill.	1	Pvt.	970
North Dakota, University of, Grand Forks	3	Pub.	8,632
North Dakota State University, Fargo	3	Pub.	7,906
North Georgia College, Dahlonega, Ga.	1	Pub.	1,779
North Park College, Chicago, Ill.	1	Pvt.	1,366
North Texas State University, Denton, Tex.	3	Pub.	16,717
Northeast Louisiana University, Monroe, La.	3	Pub.	9,718
Northeast Missouri State University, Kirksville, Mo.	2	Pub.	5,760
Northeastern Illinois University, Chicago, Ill.	2	Pub.	10,179
Northeastern Oklahoma State University, Tahlequah, Okla.	2	Pub.	6,128
Northeastern University, Boston, Mass.	3	Pvt.	35,970
Northern Arizona University, Flagstaff, Ariz.	3	Pub.	10,956
Northern Colorado, University of, Greeley, Colo.	3	Pub.	10,829
Northern Illinois University, De Kalb, Ill.	3	Pub.	24,964
Northern Iowa, University of, Cedar Falls, Iowa	2	Pub.	9,905
Northern Michigan University, Marquette, Mich.	2	Pub.	9,353
Northern Montana College, Havre, Mont.	1	Pub.	1,152
Northern State College, Aberdeen, S. Dak.	2	Pub.	2,369
Northrop University, Inglewood, Calif.	2	Pvt.	1,337
Northwest Missouri State College, Maryville, Mo.	2	Pub.	4,505
Northwest Nazarene College, Nampa, Idaho.	1	Pvt.	1,088
Northwestern Oklahoma State University, Alva, Okla.	2	Pub.	1,873
Northwestern State University of Louisiana, Natchitoches, La.	3	Pub.	6,598
Northwestern University, Evanston, Ill.	3	Pvt.	15,412
Norwich University, Northfield, Vt.	3	Pvt.	1,233
Notre Dame of Maryland, College of, Baltimore.	1	Pvt.	838
Notre Dame, College of, Belmont, Calif.	2	Pvt.	990
Notre Dame, University of, Notre Dame, Ind.	3	Pvt.	8,669
Nova University, Fort Lauderdale, Fla.	3	Pvt.	3,308
Oakland University, Rochester, Mich.	3	Pub.	10,565
Oberlin College, Oberlin, Ohio.	2	Pvt.	2,859
Occidental College, Los Angeles, Calif.	2	Pvt.	1,759
Oglethorpe College, Atlanta, Ga.	1	Pvt.	900
Ohio Dominican College, Columbus, Ohio.	1	Pvt.	1,010
Ohio Northern University, Ada, Ohio.	1	Pvt.	2,751
Ohio State University, Columbus, Ohio.	3	Pub.	50,095
Ohio University, Athens, Ohio.	3	Pub.	12,630
Ohio Wesleyan University, Delaware, Ohio.	1	Pvt.	2,249
Oklahoma, University of, Norman, Okla.	3	Pub.	23,995
Oklahoma Baptist University, Shawnee.	1	Pvt.	1,818
Oklahoma Christian College, Oklahoma City.	1	Pvt.	1,323
Oklahoma City University, Oklahoma City.	2	Pvt.	2,750
Oklahoma Panhandle State College, Goodwell, Okla.	1	Pub.	1,148
Oklahoma State University, Stillwater, Okla.	3	Pub.	21,033
Old Dominion University, Norfolk, Va.	2	Pub.	13,231
Olivet Nazarene College, Kankakee, Ill.	2	Pvt.	1,853
Oral Roberts University, Tulsa, Okla.	2	Pvt.	2,739
Oregon, University of, Eugene, Oreg.	3	Pub.	17,343
Oregon College of Education, Monmouth.	2	Pub.	3,370
Oregon Institute of Technology, Klamath Falls, Oreg.	1	Pub.	2,309
Oregon State University, Corvallis, Oreg.	3	Pub.	17,199
Ottawa, University of, Ottawa, Ont.	3	Pvt.	9,936
Otterbein College, Westerville, Ohio.	1	Pvt.	1,291
Ouachita Baptist University, Arkadelphia, Ark.	2	Pvt.	1,652
Our Lady of the Lake University, San Antonio, Tex.	2	Pvt.	1,802
Ozarks, School of the, Point Lookout, Mo.	1	Pvt.	1,160
Pace University, New York, N.Y.	3	Pvt.	8,642
Pleasantville and White Plains, N.Y.	3	Pvt.	5,130
Pacific, University of the, Stockton, Calif.	3	Pvt.	6,050
Pacific Lutheran University, Tacoma, Wash.	2	Pvt.	3,428
Pacific Union College, Angwin, Calif.	2	Pvt.	2,299
Pacific University, Forest Grove, Oreg.	2	Pvt.	1,062
Pan American University, Edinburg, Tex.	1	Pub.	8,235
Parks College of Aeronautical Technology, Cahokia, Ill.	1	Pvt.	767
Pembroke State University, Pembroke, N.C.	1	Pub.	2,183
Pennsylvania, University of, Philadelphia.	3	Pvt.	20,380
Pennsylvania State University, University Park, Abington, Allentown, Altoona, Chester, Dubois, Dunmore, Erie, Hazleton, Hershey, King of Prussia, McKeesport, Media, Middletown, Monaca, Mont Alto, New Kensington, Reading, Schuylkill Haven, Sharon, Uniontown, Wilkes-Barre and York, Pa.	3	Pub.	67,852
Pepperdine University, Malibu and Los Angeles, Calif.	2	Pvt.	9,099
Pfeiffer College, Misenheimer, N.C.	1	Pvt.	1,036
Philadelphia College of Art, Philadelphia, Pa.	2	Pvt.	1,525
Philadelphia College of Pharmacy & Science, Philadelphia, Pa.	3	Pvt.	1,087
Philadelphia College of Textiles & Science, Philadelphia, Pa.	2	Pvt.	2,118
Phillips University, Enid, Okla.	2	Pvt.	1,356

Name and Location	Level	Control	Enroll-ment
Pittsburgh, University of, Pittsburgh, Bradford, Greensburg, Johnstown, and Titusville, Pa.	3	Pvt.	34,949
Pitzer College, Claremont, Calif.	1	Pvt.	817
Plymouth State College, Plymouth, N.H.	2	Pub.	3,018
Point Loma College, San Diego, Calif.	2	Pvt.	1,605
Point Park College, Pittsburgh, Pa.	1	Pvt.	1,675
Pomona College, Claremont, Calif.	1	Pvt.	1,298
Portland, University of, Portland, Oreg.	2	Pvt.	2,222
Portland State University, Portland, Oreg.	3	Pub.	15,255
Prairie View Agricultural & Mechanical College, Prairie View, Tex.	2	Pub.	5,332
Pratt Institute, Brooklyn, N.Y.	2	Pvt.	4,565
Presbyterian College, Clinton, S.C.	1	Pvt.	850
Prince Edward Island, University of, Charlottetown, P.E.I.	1	Pub.	1,343
Princeton University, Princeton, N.J.	3	Pvt.	5,975
Principia College, Elsah, Ill.	1	Pvt.	892
Providence College, Providence, R.I.	3	Pvt.	5,515
Puerto Rico, University of, P.R.	3	Pub.	38,983
Puget Sound, University of, Tacoma, Wash.	2	Pvt.	5,017
Purdue University, Lafayette, Ind.	3	Pub.	29,335
Calumet at Hammond	2	Pub.	6,715
Fort Wayne	2	Pub.	5,420
Quebec, University of, Quebec, Que.	3	Pub.	10,080
Queen's University at Kingston, Ont.	3	Pvt.	9,590
Quincy College, Quincy, Ill.	1	Pvt.	1,251
Quinnipiac College, Hamden, Conn.	2	Pvt.	3,317
Radford College, Radford, Va.	2	Pub.	4,961
Randolph-Macon College, Ashland, Va.	1	Pvt.	811
Randolph-Macon Woman's College, Lynchburg, Va. (W)	1	Pvt.	730
Redlands, University of, Redlands, Calif.	2	Pvt.	2,852
Reed College, Portland, Oreg.	2	Pvt.	1,181
Regina, University of, Regina, Sask.	3	Pub.	3,638
Regis College, Denver, Colo.	1	Pvt.	1,094
Regis College, Weston, Mass. (W)	1	Pvt.	853
Rensselaer Polytechnic Institute, Troy, N.Y.	3	Pvt.	4,967
Rhode Island, University of, Kingston, R.I.	3	Pub.	16,527
Rhode Island College, Providence, R.I.	2	Pub.	7,728
Rhode Island School of Design, Providence	2	Pvt.	1,452
Rice University, Houston, Tex.	3	Pvt.	3,648
Richmond, University of, Richmond, Va.	2	Pvt.	4,226
Rider College, Trenton, N.J.	2	Pvt.	6,017
Ripon College, Ripon, Wis.	1	Pvt.	917
Rivier College, Nashua, N.H.	2	Pvt.	1,589
Roanoke College, Salem, Va.	1	Pvt.	1,176
Robert Morris College, Coraopolis, Pa.	1	Pvt.	3,804
Rochester, University of, Rochester, N.Y.	3	Pvt.	8,179
Rochester Institute of Technology, Rochester, N.Y.	2	Pvt.	12,201
Rockford College, Rockford, Ill.	2	Pvt.	1,203
Rockhurst College, Kansas City, Mo.	1	Pvt.	3,007
Roger Williams College, Bristol, R.I.	1	Pvt.	1,850
Rollins College, Winter Park, Fla.	2	Pvt.	4,230
Roosevelt University, Chicago, Ill.	2	Pvt.	7,628
Rosary College, River Forest, Ill.	2	Pvt.	1,286
Rosary Hill College, Buffalo, N.Y.	1	Pvt.	1,209
Rose-Hulman Institute of Technology, Terre Haute, Ind. (M)	2	Pvt.	1,049
Russell Sage College, Troy, N.Y.	2	Pvt.	4,229
Rutgers University, New Brunswick, Newark, Camden, N.J.	3	Pub.	46,300
Ryerson Polytechnical Institute, Toronto	1	Pvt.	8,672
Sacred Heart, College of the, Santurce, P.R. (W)	1	Pvt.	3,322
Sacred Heart University, Bridgeport, Conn.	1	Pvt.	2,477
Saginaw Valley State College, University Center, Mich.	2	Pub.	3,209
St. Ambrose College, Davenport, Iowa	1	Pvt.	1,454
St. Andrews Presbyterian College, Laurinburg, N.C.	1	Pvt.	544
St. Anselm's College, Manchester, N.H.	1	Pvt.	1,894
St. Augustine's College, Raleigh, N.C.	1	Pvt.	1,529

Name and Location	Level	Control	Enroll-ment
St. Benedict, College of, St. Joseph, Minn. (W)	1	Pvt.	1,597
St. Bonaventure University, St. Bonaventure, N.Y.	3	Pvt.	2,546
St. Catherine, College of, St. Paul, Minn. (W)	1	Pvt.	1,829
St. Cloud State University, St. Cloud, Minn.	2	Pub.	10,758
St. Edward's University, Austin, Tex.	2	Pvt.	1,645
St. Francis, College of, Joliet, Ill.	1	Pvt.	1,676
St. Francis College, Fort Wayne, Ind.	2	Pvt.	1,211
St. Francis College, Brooklyn, N.Y.	1	Pvt.	3,288
St. Francis College, Loretto, Pa.	2	Pvt.	1,661
St. Francis Xavier University, Antigonish, Nova Scotia	2	Pvt.	2,133
St. John Fisher College, Rochester, N.Y.	1	Pvt.	1,782
St. John's University, Collegeville, Minn. (M)	2	Pvt.	1,837
St. John's University, Jamaica and Staten Island, N.Y.	3	Pvt.	14,759
St. Joseph College, West Hartford, Conn.	2	Pvt.	1,027
St. Joseph's College, Rensselaer, Ind.	2	Pvt.	1,091
St. Joseph's College, Philadelphia, Pa.	2	Pvt.	5,716
St. Lawrence University, Canton, N.Y.	2	Pvt.	2,601
St. Leo College, St. Leo, Fla.	1	Pvt.	945
St. Louis University, St. Louis, Mo.	3	Pvt.	8,785
St. Mary's College, Moraga, Calif.	2	Pvt.	1,175
St. Mary's College, Notre Dame, Ind. (W)	1	Pvt.	1,680
St. Mary's College, Winona, Minn.	2	Pvt.	1,160
St. Mary's College of Maryland, St. Mary's City, Md.	1	Pub.	1,248
St. Mary's Dominican College, New Orleans, La.	1	Pvt.	731
St. Mary's University, Halifax, N.S.	2	Pub.	2,331
St. Mary's University, San Antonio, Tex.	2	Pvt.	3,376
St. Michael's College, Winooski, Vt.	2	Pvt.	1,700
St. Norbert College, De Pere, Wis.	1	Pvt.	1,461
St. Olaf College, Northfield, Minn.	1	Pvt.	2,875
St. Peter's College, Jersey City, N.J.	1	Pvt.	4,586
St. Rose, College of, Albany, N.Y.	2	Pvt.	2,020
St. Scholastica, College of, Duluth, Minn.	2	Pvt.	1,215
St. Teresa, College of, Winona, Minn.	1	Pvt.	1,133
St. Thomas, College of, St. Paul, Minn.	2	Pvt.	3,206
St. Thomas, University of, Houston, Tex.	2	Pvt.	1,733
St. Vincent College, Latrobe, Pa. (M)	2	Pvt.	988
St. Xavier College, Chicago, Ill.	2	Pvt.	1,449
Salem College, Salem, W. Va.	1	Pvt.	922
Salem State College, Salem, Mass.	2	Pub.	8,434
Salisbury State College, Salisbury, Md.	2	Pub.	3,840
Salve Regina—The Newport College, R.I.	2	Pvt.	1,730
Sam Houston State University, Huntsville, Tex.	2	Pub.	10,460
Samford University, Birmingham, Ala.	2	Pvt.	3,656
San Diego, University of, San Diego, Calif.	2	Pvt.	2,852
San Diego State University, San Diego, Calif.	3	Pub.	34,835
San Francisco, University of, San Francisco	3	Pvt.	6,422
San Francisco Art Institute, San Francisco	2	Pvt.	945
San Francisco State University, San Francisco, Calif.	3	Pub.	25,485
San Jose State University, San Jose, Calif.	2	Pub.	31,783
Santa Clara, University of, Santa Clara, Calif.	3	Pvt.	7,010
Santa Fe, College of, Santa Fe, N. Mex.	1	Pvt.	1,235
Sarah Lawrence College, Bronxville, N.Y.	2	Pvt.	1,056
Saskatchewan, University of, Saskatoon	3	Pub.	8,908
Savannah State College, Savannah, Ga.	1	Pub.	2,855
Science and Arts of Oklahoma, University of, Chickasha, Okla.	1	Pub.	1,230
Scranton, University of, Scranton, Pa.	2	Pvt.	4,124
Seattle Pacific College, Seattle, Wash.	2	Pvt.	2,250
Seattle University, Seattle, Wash.	2	Pvt.	3,445
Seton Hall University, South Orange, N.J.	3	Pvt.	9,902
Seton Hill College, Greensburg, Pa. (W)	1	Pvt.	837
Shaw University, Raleigh, N.C.	1	Pvt.	1,555
Shepherd College, Shepherdstown, W. Va.	1	Pub.	2,049
Sherbrooke, University of, Sherbrooke, Que.	3	Pvt.	4,949
Shippensburg State College, Shippensburg, Pa.	2	Pub.	5,760
Siena College, Loudonville, N.Y.	1	Pvt.	2,351
Simmons College, Boston, Mass.	3	Pvt.	2,625
Simon Fraser University, Burnaby, B.C.	3	Pub.	5,305

Name and Location	Level	Control	Enrollment
Simpson College, Indianola, Iowa...........	1	Pvt.	871
Sioux Falls College, Sioux Falls, S. Dak......	1	Pvt.	715
Skidmore College, Saratoga Springs, N.Y....	1	Pvt.	2,431
Slippery Rock State College, Slippery Rock, Pa...................................	2	Pub.	6,350
Smith College, Northampton, Mass...........	3	Pvt.	2,559
South, University of the, Sewanee, Tenn.....	2	Pvt.	1,122
South Alabama, University of, Mobile, Ala...	2	Pub.	6,719
South Carolina, Medical University of, Charleston, S.C.........................	3	Pub.	1,868
South Carolina, University of, Columbia, S.C.	3	Pub.	23,101
South Carolina State College, Orangeburg...	2	Pub.	3,519
South Dakota, University of, Vermillion.....	3	Pub.	7,000
Springfield, S. Dak....................	1	Pub.	805
South Dakota School of Mines & Technology, Rapid City, S. Dak.....................	3	Pub.	1,609
South Dakota State University, Brookings...	3	Pub.	6,930
South Florida, University of, Tampa, Fla.....	3	Pub.	23,232
Southeast Missouri State University, Cape Girardeau, Mo.......................	2	Pub.	7,936
Southeastern Louisiana University, Hammond, La........................	2	Pub.	7,071
Southeastern Massachusetts University, North Darmouth, Mass.................	2	Pub.	4,962
Southeastern Oklahoma State University, Durant, Okla......................	2	Pub.	4,410
Southern Arkansas University, Magnolia, Ark...............................	2	Pub.	1,970
Southern Baptist Theological Seminary, Louisville, Ky.......................	3	Pvt.	1,817
Southern California, University of, Los Angeles, Calif.......................	3	Pvt.	26,100
Southern Colorado, University of, Pueblo...	2	Pub.	6,572
Southern Connecticut State College, New Haven, Conn........................	2	Pub.	12,605
Southern Illinois University, Carbondale, Ill..	3	Pub.	21,214
Southern Illinois University, Edwardsville, Ill.	2	Pub.	13,607
Southern Methodist University, Dallas, Tex..	3	Pvt.	9,643
Southern Missionary College, Collegedale, Tenn...............................	1	Pvt.	1,710
Southern Mississippi, University of, University, Miss.....................	3	Pub.	11,462
Southern Oregon State College, Ashland, Oreg................................	2	Pub.	4,494
Southern University and Agricultural and Mechanical College, Baton Rouge, La....	2	Pub.	9,515
Southern Utah State College, Cedar City, Utah................................	1	Pub.	1,883
Southwest Baptist College, Bolivar, Mo......	1	Pvt.	1,430
Southwest Missouri State University, Springfield, Mo......................	2	Pub.	11,992
Southwest Texas State University, San Marcos, Tex........................	2	Pub.	13,354
Southwestern at Memphis, Tenn..........	1	Pvt.	1,102
Southwestern Baptist Theological Seminary, Fort Worth, Tex.....................	3	Pvt.	2,892
Southwestern Louisiana, University of, Lafayette, La......................	3	Pub.	12,351
Southwestern Oklahoma State University, Weatherford, Okla..................	2	Pub.	4,961
Southwestern University, Georgetown, Tex..	1	Pvt.	927
Spalding College, Louisville, Ky...........	2	Pvt.	1,086
Spelman College, Atlanta, Ga. (W)..........	1	Pvt.	1,244
Spring Hill College, Mobile, Ala...........	1	Pvt.	868
Springfield College, Springfield, Mass.......	3	Pvt.	2,842
Stanford University, Stanford, Calif........	3	Pvt.	12,684
Steed College, Johnson City, Tenn..........	1	Pvt.	2,167
Stephen F. Austin State University, Nacogdoches, Tex.....................	2	Pub.	11,414
Stephens College, Columbia, Mo...........	1	Pvt.	1,991
Stetson University, DeLand, Fla..........	2	Pvt.	2,718
Steubenville, College of, Steubenville, Ohio..	1	Pvt.	908
Stevens Institute of Technology, Hoboken, N.J.................................	3	Pvt.	2,156
Stonehill College, North Easton, Mass.......	1	Pvt.	2,264
Strayer College, Washington, D.C...........	1	Pvt.	1,694
Suffolk University, Boston, Mass...........	3	Pvt.	6,559

Name and Location	Level	Control	Enrollment
Sul Ross State College, Alpine, Tex........	2	Pub.	2,730
Susquehanna University, Selinsgrove, Pa....	1	Pvt.	1,591
Swarthmore College, Swarthmore, Pa.......	2	Pvt.	1,245
Sweet Briar College, Sweet Briar, Va. (W)...	1	Pvt.	657
Syracuse University, Syracuse, N.Y........	3	Pvt.	21,067
Tampa, University of, Tampa, Fla...........	1	Pvt.	1,968
Tarleton State College, Stephenville, Tex....	1	Pub.	3,103
Taylor University, Upland, Ind.............	1	Pvt.	1,462
Temple University, Philadelphia, Pa.........	3	Pvt.	34,950
Tennessee, University of, System:			
Chattanooga........................	2	Pub.	5,808
Knoxville...........................	3	Pub.	29,999
Martin.............................	2	Pub.	5,188
Health Sciences, Memphis.............	3	Pub.	2,088
Nashville..........................	2	Pub.	5,493
Tennessee State University, Nashville, Tenn.	2	Pub.	5,686
Tennessee Technological University, Cookeville, Tenn......................	2	Pub.	6,968
Texas, University of, System:			
Arlington..........................	3	Pub.	16,309
Austin.............................	3	Pub.	45,429
El Paso............................	2	Pub.	13,614
Texas Agricultural & Mechanical University, College Station, Tex..................	3	Pub.	24,915
Texas Arts and Industries University, Kingsville, Tex......................	2	Pub.	7,641
Texas Christian University, Fort Worth, Tex.	3	Pvt.	6,018
Texas Lutheran College, Seguin, Tex........	1	Pvt.	1,182
Texas Southern University, Houston, Tex....	2	Pub.	8,194
Texas Tech University, Lubbock, Tex.......	3	Pub.	22,580
Texas Wesleyan College, Fort Worth, Tex....	1	Pvt.	1,884
Texas Woman's University, Denton, Tex.....	3	Pub.	8,055
Thiel College, Greenville, Pa..............	1	Pvt.	1,084
Thomas Jefferson University, Philadelphia..	3	Pvt.	1,710
Thomas More College, Fort Mitchell, Ky.....	1	Pvt.	1,352
Toledo, University of, Toledo, Ohio.........	3	Pub.	17,030
Toronto, University of, Toronto, Ont........	3	Pub.	30,593
Tougaloo College, Tougaloo, Miss...........	1	Pvt.	788
Towson State College, Towson, Md........	2	Pub.	13,693
Transylvania University, Lexington, Ky......	1	Pvt.	722
Trent University, Peterborough, Ont........	2	Pvt.	2,004
Trenton State College, Trenton, N.J........	2	Pub.	12,339
Trevecca Nazarene College, Nashville, Tenn.	1	Pvt.	856
Trinity College, Deerfield, Ill..............	1	Pvt.	874
Trinity College, Hartford, Conn..........	2	Pvt.	2,002
Trinity College, Washington, D.C...........	2	Pvt.	949
Trinity University, San Antonio, Tex.......	2	Pvt.	3,546
Tri-State University, Angola, Ind...........	1	Pvt.	1,262
Troy State University, Troy, Ala...........	2	Pub.	3,965
Tufts University, Medford, Mass...........	3	Pvt.	6,232
Tulane University, New Orleans, La........	3	Pvt.	9,113
Tulsa, University of, Tulsa, Okla...........	3	Pvt.	6,540
Tuskegee Institute, Tuskegee Institute, Ala..	2	Pvt.	3,507
Union College, Barbourville, Ky...........	2	Pvt.	1,040
Union College, Lincoln, Nebr.............	1	Pvt.	882
Union College, Schenectady, N.Y..........	3	Pvt.	3,163
Union University, Jackson, Tenn...........	1	Pvt.	972
United States Air Force Academy, Colorado Springs, Colo.......................	1	Pub.	4,574
United States Coast Guard Academy, New London, Conn.......................	1	Pub.	1,134
United States International University (including California Western Campus, Elliott Campus, and School of Performing Arts), San Diego, Calif................	3	Pvt.	2,573
United States Merchant Marine Academy, Kings Point, N.Y.....................	1	Pub.	1,007
United States Military Academy, West Point, N.Y................................	1	Pub.	4,232
United States Naval Academy, Annapolis, Md.................................	1	Pub.	4,345
Upsala College, East Orange, N.J..........	1	Pvt.	1,705
Ursinus College, Collegeville, Pa...........	1	Pvt.	1,794
Utah, University of, Salt Lake City, Utah.....	3	Pub.	23,978
Utah State University, Logan, Utah........	3	Pub.	11,052

Name and Location	Level	Control	Enroll-ment
Valdosta State College, Valdosta, Ga........	2	Pub.	5,219
Valley State College, Valley City, N. Dak.....	1	Pub.	861
Valparaiso University, Valparaiso, Ind.......	2	Pvt.	4,319
Vanderbilt University, Nashville, Tenn......	3	Pvt.	6,981
Vassar College, Poughkeepsie, N.Y.........	2	Pvt.	2,314
Vermont, University of, Burlington, Vt......	3	Pub.	10,368
Victoria, University of, Victoria, B.C.........	3	Pvt.	5,215
Villanova University, Villanova, Pa..........	3	Pvt.	9,612
Virgin Islands, College of the, St. Thomas, V.I..	2	Pub.	2,079
Virginia, University of, Charlottesville, Va....	3	Pub.	25,678
Virginia Commonwealth University, Richmond, Va..........................	3	Pub.	17,982
Virginia Military Institute, Lexington, Va. (M).......................................	1	Pub.	1,244
Virginia Polytechnic Institute and State University, Blacksburg, Va.................	3	Pub.	20,570
Virginia State College, Petersburg, Va.......	2	Pub.	4,472
Virginia Union University, Richmond, Va.....	1	Pvt.	1,357
Wabash College, Crawfordsville, Ind. (M)...	1	Pvt.	842
Wagner College, Staten Island, N.Y.........	2	Pvt.	2,694
Wake Forest University, Winston-Salem, N.C......................................	3	Pvt.	4,442
Walla Walla College, College Place, Wash....	2	Pvt.	1,959
Walsh College, Canton, Ohio..............	1	Pvt.	704
Wartburg College, Waverly, Iowa...........	1	Pvt.	1,202
Washburn University of Topeka, Kans.......	2	Pub.	5,569
Washington, University of, Seattle, Wash....	3	Pub.	35,972
Washington and Jefferson College, Washington, Pa.........................	2	Pvt.	1,194
Washington and Lee University, Lexington, Va. (M).................................	1	Pvt.	1,597
Washington College, Chesterton, Md........	2	Pvt.	921
Washington State University, Pullman, Wash......................................	3	Pub.	16,337
Washington University, St. Louis, Mo.......	3	Pvt.	11,359
Waterloo, University of, Waterloo, Ont......	3	Pvt.	12,970
Wayland Baptist College, Plainview, Tex.....	1	Pvt.	1,083
Wayne State College, Wayne, Nebr.........	2	Pub.	2,099
Wayne State University, Detroit, Mich......	3	Pub.	38,074
Waynesburg College, Waynesburg, Pa.......	1	Pvt.	802
Weber State College, Ogden, Utah..........	1	Pub.	9,458
Webster College, St. Louis, Mo............	2	Pvt.	3,607
Wellesley College, Wellesley, Mass.........	2	Pvt.	2,045
Wesleyan University, Middletown, Conn.....	3	Pvt.	2,448
West Chester State College, West Chester, Pa.....................................	2	Pub.	9,295
West Coast University, Los Angeles, Calif....	2	Pvt.	891
West Florida, University of, Pensacola, Fla...	2	Pub.	5,250
West Georgia College, Carrollton, Ga.......	2	Pub.	5,683
West Liberty State College, West Liberty, W. Va.....................................	1	Pub.	2,680
West Texas State University, Canyon, Tex...	2	Pub.	6,701
West Virginia College of Graduate Studies, Institute, W. Va......................	2	Pub.	2,647
West Virginia Institute of Technology, Montgomery, W. Va....................	1	Pub.	3,042
West Virginia State College, Institute, W. Va.	1	Pub.	3,941
West Virginia University, Morgantown, W. Va.....................................	3	Pub.	20,007
West Virginia Wesleyan College, Buckhannon, W. Va.....................	1	Pvt.	1,800
Western Carolina University, Cullowhee, N.C......................................	2	Pub.	6,912
Western Connecticut State College, Danbury, Conn...................................	2	Pub.	5,248
Western Illinois University, Macomb, Ill.....	2	Pub.	15,357
Western Kentucky University, Bowling Green, Ky..............................	2	Pub.	13,040
Western Maryland College, Westminster, Md.......................................	2	Pvt.	2,351
Western Michigan University, Kalamazoo, Mich....................................	3	Pub.	23,238
Western Montana College, Dillon, Mont.....	2	Pub.	759
Western New England College, Springfield, Mass....................................	2	Pvt.	3,902

Name and Location	Level	Control	Enroll-ment
Western New Mexico University, Silver City, N. Mex.................................	2	Pub.	1,830
Western Ontario, The University of, London, Ont......................................	3	Pvt.	15,153
Western State College of Colorado, Gunnison, Colo.......................	2	Pub.	3,291
Western Washington State College, Bellingham, Wash.......................	2	Pub.	9,198
Westfield State College, Westfield, Mass....	2	Pub.	4,463
Westmar College, Le Mars, Iowa...........	1	Pvt.	721
Westminster College, Fulton, Mo...........	1	Pvt.	780
Westminster College, New Wilmington, Pa...	1	Pvt.	1,884
Westminster College, Salt Lake City, Utah...	1	Pvt.	1,052
Westmont College, Santa Barbara, Calif.....	1	Pvt.	892
Wheaton College, Wheaton, Ill.............	2	Pvt.	2,220
Wheaton College, Norton, Mass. (W).......	1	Pvt.	1,182
Wheelock College, Boston, Mass...........	2	Pvt.	846
Whitman College, Walla Walla, Wash.......	1	Pvt.	1,106
Whittier College, Whittier, Calif............	2	Pvt.	1,594
Whitworth College, Spokane, Wash.........	2	Pvt.	1,800
Wichita State University, Wichita, Kans.....	3	Pub.	15,714
Widener College, Chester, Pa..............	3	Pvt.	3,231
Wilberforce University, Wilberforce, Ohio...	1	Pvt.	1,265
Wilfrid Laurier University, Waterloo, Ont...	2	Pvt.	2,658
Wilkes College, Wilkes-Barre, Pa...........	2	Pvt.	2,812
Willamette University, Salem, Oreg.........	2	Pvt.	1,724
William and Mary, College of, Williamsburg, Va.....................................	3	Pub.	6,200
William Carey College, Hattiesburg, Miss....	2	Pvt.	1,481
William Jewell College, Liberty, Mo.........	1	Pvt.	1,621
William Paterson College of New Jersey, Wayne, N.J.............................	2	Pub.	14,499
William Penn College, Oskaloosa, Iowa.....	1	Pvt.	650
William Woods College, Fulton, Mo. (W)....	1	Pvt.	1,357
Williams College, Williamstown, Mass......	2	Pvt.	1,932
Wilmington College, Wilmington, Ohio......	1	Pvt.	723
Windham College, Putney, Vt..............	1	Pvt.	609
Windsor, University of, Windsor, Ont.......	3	Pvt.	6,001
Winnipeg, The University of, Winnipeg, Man.	2	Pvt.	2,599
Winona State College, Winona, Minn........	2	Pub.	4,847
Winston-Salem State University, Winston-Salem, N.C......................	1	Pub.	2,073
Winthrop College, Rock Hill, S.C...........	2	Pub.	3,957
Wisconsin, University of :			
Eau Claire, Wis.........................	2	Pub.	9,920
Green Bay, Wis..........................	2	Pub.	3,874
Kenosha................................	1	Pub.	5,404
La Crosse, Wis..........................	2	Pub.	7,734
Madison, Wis...........................	3	Pub.	38,603
Milwaukee, Wis.........................	3	Pub.	24,691
Oshkosh, Wis...........................	2	Pub.	10,239
Platteville, Wis..........................	2	Pub.	4,285
River Falls, Wis.........................	2	Pub.	4,433
Stevens Point, Wis......................	2	Pub.	8,220
Stout, Wis..............................	2	Pub.	5,609
Superior, Wis...........................	2	Pub.	2,610
Whitewater, Wis.........................	2	Pub.	8,727
Wittenberg University, Springfield, Ohio....	2	Pvt.	2,788
Wofford College, Spartanburg, S.C..........	1	Pvt.	979
Woodbury University, Los Angeles, Calif.....	2	Pvt.	1,419
Wooster, College of, Wooster, Ohio.........	1	Pvt.	1,876
Worcester Polytechnic Institute, Worcester, Mass..................................	3	Pvt.	2,831
Worcester State College, Worcester, Mass...	2	Pub.	5,652
Wright State University, Dayton, Ohio......	2	Pub.	13,723
Wyoming, University of, Laramie, Wyo......	3	Pub.	8,316
Xavier University, Cincinnati, Ohio.........	2	Pvt.	6,265
Xavier University of Louisiana, New Orleans, La....................................	2	Pvt.	1,765
Yale University, New Haven, Conn..........	3	Pvt.	9,734
Yeshiva University, New York, N.Y.........	3	Pvt.	3,328
York College of Pennsylvania, York, Pa......	1	Pvt.	3,211
York University, Downview, Ont...........	3	Pub.	11,561
Youngstown State University, Youngstown, Ohio..................................	2	Pub.	15,573

CONTRIBUTORS

ADRIAN, CHARLES R., Professor of Political Science, University of California, Riverside; Coauthor, *Governing Urban America:* BIOGRAPHY—*Rose Bird;* CALIFORNIA; LOS ANGELES

ALEXANDER, ROBERT J., Professor of Economics, Rutgers University: ECUADOR; GUYANA; URUGUAY

ALLER, LAWRENCE H., Professor of Astronomy, University of California, Los Angeles; Author, *Atoms, Stars, and Nebulae:* ASTRONOMY

AMBRE, AGO, Economist, Bureau of Economic Analysis, U. S. Department of Commerce: INDUSTRIAL REVIEW

AYERS, H. BRANDT, Editor and Publisher, *The Anniston Star,* Alabama; Juror, 1978 Pulitzer Prizes (Journalism): COMING OF AGE—*The Post-Adolescent U. S. South*

BALLINGER, RONALD B., Professor of History, Rhode Island College: RHODESIA; SOUTH AFRICA

BANKS, RONALD F., Professor of History, University of Maine, Orono: MAINE

BARKOVICH, BARBARA, California Public Utilities Commission: ENERGY

BECK, KAY, School of Urban Life, Georgia State University: GEORGIA

BERGEN, DANIEL P., Professor, Graduate Library School, University of Rhode Island: LIBRARIES

BEST, JOHN, Chief, *Canada World News,* Ottawa: NEW BRUNSWICK; PRINCE EDWARD ISLAND

BISSELL, RICHARD E., Visiting Professor, Temple University; Research Associate, Foreign Policy Research Institute; Author, *Apartheid and International Organizations:* AFRICA

BLANCHARD, LLOYD G., Editor, Polar Information Service, Division of Polar Programs, National Science Foundation: POLAR RESEARCH

BÖDVARSSON, HAUKUR, Coeditor, *News From Iceland:* ICELAND

BOLUS, JIM, Sportswriter, *The Courier-Journal,* Louisville, Ky.; Author, *Run for the Roses:* SPORTS—*Horse Racing*

BOND, DONOVAN H., Professor of Journalism, West Virginia University: WEST VIRGINIA

BOULAY, HARVEY, Assistant Professor of Political Science, Boston University: BOSTON; MASSACHUSETTS

BOVEY, JOHN A., Provincial Archivist of Manitoba: MANITOBA

BOWERS, Q. DAVID, Vice President, Professional Numismatists Guild; Columnist, *Coin World;* Author, *Collecting Rare Coins for Profit:* COIN COLLECTING

BRADDOCK, BILL, Sports Department, *The New York Times:* SPORTS—*Basketball, Sports Summaries*

BRAMMER, DANA B., Director, Bureau of Governmental Research, University of Mississippi: MISSISSIPPI

BRANDHORST, L. CARL, Associate Professor of Geography, Oregon College of Education: OREGON

BREWERTON, DAVID, Editor, *Policy Holder Insurance Journal,* London: LONDON

BRODIN, PIERRE E., Director of Studies, Lycée Français de New York: LITERATURE—*French*

BROEG, ROBERT, Sports Editor, *St. Louis Post-Dispatch:* BIOGRAPHY—*Rod Carew;* SPORTS—*Baseball*

BROWN, LES, Television Correspondent, *The New York Times;* Author, *Television: The Business Behind the Box, Electric Media,* and *The New York Times Encyclopedia of Television:* TELEVISION—"*Roots*"

BURKS, ARDATH W., Professor of Political Science, Rutgers University: BIOGRAPHY—*Takeo Fukuda;* JAPAN

BURLINGAME, MERRILL G., Professor of History, Montana State University; Author, *The Montana Frontier;* Coauthor, *A History of Montana:* MONTANA

BUSH, G. W. A., Senior Lecturer in Political Science, University of Auckland: NEW ZEALAND

BUTWELL, RICHARD, Dean for Arts and Sciences and Professor of Political Science, State University of New York College at Fredonia; Author, *Southeast Asia Today and Tomorrow* and *Indonesia:* ASIA; BURMA; CAMBODIA; LAOS; PHILIPPINES; VIETNAM

CAIRNS, JOHN C., Professor of History, University of Toronto: FRANCE

CAMMACK, PAUL, St. Antony's College, Oxford: BOLIVIA

CANN, STANLEY, Consultant, *The Forum,* Fargo: NORTH DAKOTA

CHALMERS, J. W., Faculty of Education, University of Alberta: ALBERTA

CHARLTON, LINDA, Reporter, Washington Bureau, *The New York Times:* BIOGRAPHY—*Rosalynn Carter;* LAW—*The Federal Papers Issue*

CHRISTOL, CARL Q., Professor of International Law and Chairman, Department of Political Science, University of Southern California: HUMAN RIGHTS

COCKRUM, E. LENDELL, Professor, Department of Ecology and Evolutionary Biology, University of Arizona: ZOOLOGY

COHEN, SIDNEY, Clinical Professor of Psychiatry, Neuropsychiatric Institute, University of California, Los Angeles; Author, *The Beyond Within: The LSD Story* and *The Drug Dilemma:* DRUG ADDICTION AND ABUSE

COLE, CAROLYN J., Vice President, Paine, Webber, Jackson & Curtis, Inc.: STOCKS AND BONDS

COLLINS, ROBERT J., Sports Editor, *The Indianapolis Star;* Author, *The Best of Bob Collins;* Coauthor, *What's It Like Out There?:* SPORTS—*Auto Racing*

COMMANDAY, ROBERT, Music and Dance Critic, *San Francisco Chronicle:* MUSIC; OBITUARIES—*Leopold Stokowski*

CONRAD, ED, Sports Department, *The Gazette,* Montreal; Author, *Humor in Hockey:* SPORTS—*Ice Hockey*

COPPAGE, NOEL, Contributing Editor, *Stereo Review:* MUSIC, POPULAR; OBITUARIES—*Elvis Presley*

CORLEW, ROBERT E., Chairman, Department of History, Middle Tennessee State University: TENNESSEE

CORNWELL, ELMER E., JR., Professor of Political Science, Brown University: RHODE ISLAND

CRAIG, PAUL P., Director, Energy and Resources Council, University of California; Associate, Workshop on Alternative Energy Strategies: ENERGY

CUNNINGHAM, PEGGY, Staff Reporter, *Baltimore News-American:* MARYLAND

CURTIS, L. PERRY, JR., Professor of History, Brown University: IRELAND

DANIELS, ROBERT V., Professor of History, University of Vermont: VERMONT

DARBY, JOSEPH W., III, Reporter, *The Times-Picayune,* New Orleans: LOUISIANA

DAVIS, WILLIAM A., Travel Editor, *The Boston Globe:* TRAVEL

DE GREGORIO, GEORGE, Sports Department, *The New York Times:* SPORTS—*Finances in Pro Sport, Boxing, Swimming, Track*

DELZELL, CHARLES F., Professor of History, Vanderbilt University; Editor, *The Future of History:* ITALY

DENNIS, LARRY, Associate Editor, *Golf Digest;* Coauthor, *One Move to Better Golf* and *Shape Your Swing the Modern Way:* SPORTS—*Golf*

DILLIN, JOHN, Staff Correspondent, Washington Bureau, *The Christian Science Monitor:* BIOGRAPHY—*Stansfield Turner*

DOBLER, CLIFFORD, Former Professor of Business Law, University of Idaho: IDAHO

DOLAN, PAUL, Professor of Political Science, University of Delaware; Author, *Government and Administration of Delaware:* DELAWARE

DORPALEN, ANDREAS, Professor of History, The Ohio State University: GERMANY

DORWIN, JOHN T., Senior Archaeologist, Soil Systems, Inc.: ARCHAEOLOGY—*The Americas*

DRACHKOVITCH, MILORAD M., Senior Fellow, The Hoover Institution, Stanford University; Author, *U. S. Aid to Yugoslavia and Poland:* YUGOSLAVIA

DREYFUSS, JOHN, Architecture and Design Writer, *Los Angeles Times:* ARCHITECTURE

DRIGGS, DON W., Professor of Political Science, University of Nevada, Reno: NEVADA

DUFF, ERNEST A., Professor of Political Science, Randolph-Macon Woman's College; Author, *Agrarian Reform in Colombia* and *Violence and Repression in Latin America:* COLOMBIA

DUNNE, JOSEPH A., MSGR., President and Executive Director, National Council on Compulsive Gambling, Inc.: GAMBLING—*A Losing Proposition*

DUROSKA, LUD, Sports Department, *The New York Times;* Author, *Football Rules in Pictures, Great Pro Quarterbacks,* and *Tennis for Beginners:* SPORTS—*Football*

DURRENCE, J. LARRY, Chairman, Department of History and Political Science, Florida Southern College: FLORIDA

EHRENHALT, ALAN, Political Editor, *Congressional Quarterly:* BIOGRAPHY—*Robert Byrd, Thomas P. O'Neill, John Rhodes*

ELGIN, RICHARD, State Desk, *The Patriot-News,* Harrisburg: PENNSYLVANIA

ELKINS, ANN, Senior Editor, Special Publications and Special Editions, Former Fashion Director, *Good Housekeeping Magazine:* FASHION

ENSTAD, ROBERT H., Reporter, *Chicago Tribune:* BIOGRAPHY—*Michael Bilandic;* CHICAGO; ILLINOIS

ETCHESON, WARREN W., Associate Dean, Graduate School of Business Administration, University of Washington: WASHINGTON

EWEGEN, ROBERT D., Staff Writer, *The Denver Post:* COLORADO

FISHER, PAUL, Director, Freedom of Information Center, University of Missouri: CENSORSHIP

FOLEJEWSKI, ZBIGNIEW, Professor and Chairman, Department of Slavic Studies and Modern Languages, University of Ottawa: LITERATURE—*Soviet*

FRIIS, ERIK J., Editor and Publisher, *The Scandinavian-American Bulletin;* Author, *The American-Scandinavian Foundation, 1910–1960: A Brief History;* Editor, *The Scandinavian Presence in North America:* DENMARK; FINLAND

GAILEY, HARRY A., Professor of History and Coordinator of African Studies, San Jose State University, Calif.: NIGERIA

GARFIELD, ROBERT, Assistant Professor of History and Co-director, Afro-American Studies Program, DePaul University, Chicago: DJIBOUTI; GHANA; KENYA

GEIS, GILBERT, Professor, Program in Social Ecology, University of California, Irvine; Author, *Man, Crime, and Society:* CRIME

GJESTER, THOR, Editor, *Okonomisk Revy,* Oslo: NORWAY

GLANVILLE, BRIAN, Association Football Correspondent, *Sunday Times,* London; Author, *History of the Soccer World Cup:* SPORTS—*Soccer*

GOODMAN, DONALD, John Jay College of Criminal Justice, City University of New York: PRISONS

GORDON, MAYNARD M., Editor, *Motor News Analysis* and *The Imported Car Reports:* AUTOMOBILES

GOUGH, BARRY M., Associate Professor of History, Wilfrid Laurier University; Author, *The Royal Navy and the Northwest Coast, To the Arctic and Pacific with Beechey* and *Canada:* CANADA—*National and International Affairs*

GRAYSON, GEORGE W., Professor of Government, College of William and Mary: PORTUGAL; SPAIN

GROTH, ALEXANDER J., Professor of Political Science, University of California, Davis; Author, *People's Poland;* Coauthor, *Contemporary Politics: Europe:* POLAND

GRUBERG, MARTIN, Professor of Political Science, University of Wisconsin, Oshkosh; Author, *Women in American Politics:* CIVIL LIBERTIES AND CIVIL RIGHTS

GUNN, JOHN M., Former Professor of Radio-TV-Film, State University of New York at Albany: TELEVISION AND RADIO

HALLMUNDSSON, MAY NEWMAN, Adjunct Associate Professor, Pace University: WOMEN

HAND, SAMUEL B., Professor of History, University of Vermont: VERMONT

HARVEY, ROSS M., Assistant Director of Information, Government of the Northwest Territories: NORTHWEST TERRITORIES

HAYDEN, DOROTHY, Head, Prairie History Room, Regina Public Library: SASKATCHEWAN

HAYES, KIRBY M., Professor of Food Science and Nutrition, University of Massachusetts: FOOD; MEDICINE AND HEALTH—*U. S. Food Laws*

HELMREICH, ERNST C., Thomas B. Reed Professor of History and Political Science, Bowdoin College, Bowdoin, Me.: AUSTRIA

HELMREICH, JONATHAN E., Dean of Instruction, Allegheny College, Meadville, Pa.; Author, *Belgium and Europe: A Study in Small Power Diplomacy:* LUXEMBOURG

HELMREICH, PAUL C., Professor of History, Wheaton College, Norton, Mass.; Author, *From Paris to Sèvres: The Partition of the Ottoman Empire at the Peace Conference of 1919–1920:* SWITZERLAND

HELMS, ANDREA R. C., Associate Professor of Political Science, University of Alaska: ALASKA

HENRIKSEN, THOMAS H., Associate Professor, Department of History, State University College, Plattsburgh, N. Y.; Author, *Mozambique: A History;* Member, Editorial Board, *African Studies Review:* ANGOLA; MOZAMBIQUE

HERBERT, WALTER B., Consultant on Canadian Cultural Matters; Fellow of the Royal Society of Arts: CANADA—*Cultural Affairs*

HERSHKOWITZ, LEO, Professor of History, Queens College, City University of New York; Author, *Tweed's New York: Another Look:* BIOGRAPHY—*Edward Koch;* NEW YORK; NEW YORK CITY

HODGES, RALPH W., Technical Editor, *Stereo Review:* RECORDED SOUND

HOGGART, SIMON, Political Correspondent, *The Guardian,* Manchester: BIOGRAPHY—*David Owen;* GREAT BRITAIN

HOOVER, HERBERT T., Professor of History, University of South Dakota; Author, *The Practice of Oral History:* SOUTH DAKOTA

HOPKO, THOMAS, REV., St. Vladimir's Orthodox Theological Seminary: RELIGION—*Orthodox Eastern Church*

HOPSON, JANET L., Contributing Editor, *Science News:* BIOCHEMISTRY

HOTTELET, RICHARD C., United Nations Correspondent, CBS News: THE THIRD WORLD

HOWARD, HARRY N., Board of Governors, Middle East Institute; Author, *Turkey, the Straits, and U. S. Policy:* TURKEY

HULTEN, PONTUS, Director, Musée national d'art moderne, Centre Georges Pompidou: ART—*The Georges Pompidou Center*

HUME, ANDREW, Former Reporter, *The Whitehorse Star:* YUKON TERRITORY

HUTH, JOHN F., JR., Reporter-Column Editor, *The Plain Dealer,* Cleveland: OHIO

JACKSON, LIVIA E. BITTON, Associate Professor, Department of Classical and Oriental Languages, Herbert H. Lehman College, City University of New York: RELIGION—*Judaism*

JACOBSON, JON L., Professor of Law and Director, Ocean Resources Law Program, University of Oregon; Coauthor, *The Future of International Fisheries Management:* LAW—*International*

JAFFE, HERMAN J., Department of Anthropology, Brooklyn College, City University of New York: ANTHROPOLOGY

JARVIS, ERIC, Department of History, University of Western Ontario: TORONTO

JEWELL, MALCOLM E., Professor of Political Science, University of Kentucky; Editor, *Legislative Studies Quarterly;* Author, *Legislative Representation in the Contemporary South;* Coauthor, *Kentucky Politics:* KENTUCKY

JOHNSON, RAFER, Former Olympic Decathlon Champion; Member, The President's Commission on Olympic Sports: SPORTS—*The President's Commission on Olympic Sports*

JOHNSTON, ROBERT L., Staff Writer and Editor, Religious News Service: BIOGRAPHY—*Marcel Lefebvre;* RELIGION—*Roman Catholicism*

JOHNSTONE, J. K., Professor of English, University of Saskatchewan; Fellow of the Royal Society of Literature; Author, *The Bloomsbury Group: A Study of E. M. Forster, Lytton Strachey, Virginia Woolf, and Their Circle:* LITERATURE—*English*

JONES, H. G., Curator, North Carolina Collection, University of North Carolina; Author, *For History's Sake* and *The Records of a Nation:* NORTH CAROLINA

KARNES, THOMAS L., Professor of History, Arizona State University; Author, *Failure of Union: Central America, 1824–1960* and *Latin American Policy of the United States:* CENTRAL AMERICA

KARSKI, JAN, Professor of Government, Georgetown University; Author, *Story of a Secret State:* BULGARIA; HUNGARY

KEHR, ERNEST A., Stamp News Bureau; Author, *The Romance of Stamp Collecting:* STAMP COLLECTING

KELLER, EUGENIA, Senior Editor, *Chemistry* Magazine: CHEMISTRY

KENNEDY, ROBERT E., JR., Associate Professor, Department of Sociology, University of Minnesota; Author, *The Irish: Emigration, Marriage and Fertility:* POPULATION

KIMBALL, LORENZO K., Professor of Political Science, University of Utah; Author, *The Changing Pattern of Political Power in Iraq:* UTAH

KIMBELL, CHARLES L., Supervisory Physical Scientist, United States Bureau of Mines: MINING

KING, PETER J., Associate Professor of History, Carleton University: ONTARIO; OTTAWA

KISSELGOFF, ANNA, Chief Dance Critic, *The New York Times:* DANCE

KOLLEGGER, JAMES G., President, Environmental Information Center, Inc.: ENVIRONMENT

KOSAKI, RICHARD H., Professor of Political Science, University of Hawaii: HAWAII

KRESS, JACK M., Professor of Criminal Justice, State University of New York at Albany; Author, *Sentencing Guidelines: Structuring Judicial Discretion* and *Introduction to Criminal Law:* CRIME—*Capital Punishment*

LAI, CHUEN-YAN DAVID, Associate Professor of Geography, University of Victoria, B. C.: HONG KONG

LANDSBERG, H. E., Professor Emeritus, Institute for Physical Science and Technology, University of Maryland: METEOROLOGY

LARSEN, WILLIAM, Professor of History, Radford College; Author, *Montague of Virginia, The Making of a Southern Progressive:* VIRGINIA

LAURENT, PIERRE-HENRI, Department of History, Tufts University, Medford, Mass.: BELGIUM

LAWRENCE, ROBERT M., Professor, Department of Political Science, Colorado State University; Author, *Arms Control and Disarmament: Practice and Promise;* Coeditor, *Nuclear Proliferation: Phase II:* ARMS CONTROL AND DISARMAMENT; MILITARY FORCES

LEE, STEWART M., Professor and Chairman, Department of Economics and Business Administration, Geneva College, Beaver Falls, Pa.; Coauthor, *Economics for Consumers:* CONSUMERISM

LEIDEN, CARL, Professor of Government, University of Texas at Austin: BANGLADESH; EGYPT; PAKISTAN; THAILAND

LEVEN, CHARLES L., Chairman, Department of Economics, and Director, Institute for Urban and Regional Studies, Washington University, St. Louis: THE CITIES—*A Continuing Crisis*

LEVIN, RUBEN, Editor, *Labor* Newspaper: LABOR

LEVITT, MORRIS J., Professor, Graduate Department of Political Science, Howard University; Coauthor, *State and Local Government and Politics:* WASHINGTON, D. C.

LEWIS, FLORA, European Diplomatic Correspondent and Chief, Paris Bureau, *The New York Times;* Winner of the Overseas Press Club Award, 1977; EUROPE—*The EEC at Twenty*

LINDAHL, MAC, Harvard University: SWEDEN

LLOYD, BARBARA M., Staff Reporter, *Newport Daily News:* BIOGRAPHY—*Robert E. Turner;* SPORTS—*Yachting*

LOBRON, BARBARA, Writer, Editor, Photographer; Cofounder and Contributing Editor, *Photograph* Magazine: PHOTOGRAPHY

LOTT, LEO B., Professor of Political Science, University of Montana; Author, *Venezuela and Paraguay: Political Modernity and Tradition in Conflict:* PARAGUAY; VENEZUELA

MABRY, DONALD J., Associate Professor of History, Mississippi State University; Author, *Mexico's Acción Nacional: A Catholic Alternative to Revolution:* MEXICO

MACAULAY, NEILL, Professor of History, University of Florida; Author, *The Prestes Column* and *A Rebel in Cuba:* BRAZIL; LATIN AMERICA

McCORQUODALE, SUSAN, Associate Professor, Department of Political Science, Memorial University of Newfoundland: NEWFOUNDLAND

McDOUGALL, EDGAR J., JR., Lecturer in Finance, University of Connecticut; Member, Center for Real Estate and Urban Economic Studies: HOUSING

McGILL, DAVID A., Professor of Ocean Science, U. S. Coast Guard Academy: OCEANOGRAPHY

MARCOPOULOS, GEORGE J., Associate Professor of History, Tufts University, Medford, Mass.: CYPRUS; GREECE; OBITUARIES—*Makarios III*

MARGOLIS, JOSEPH, *African Update,* African-American Institute: ALGERIA; MOROCCO; SUDAN; TUNISIA

MARTY, MARTIN E., Professor of Modern Church History, The Divinity School, University of Chicago; Author, *Righteous Empire: The Protestant Experience in America:* RELIGION—*Women Clergy*

MATHEWS, THOMAS G., Research Professor, Institute of Caribbean Studies, University of Puerto Rico: CARIBBEAN; PUERTO RICO; VIRGIN ISLANDS, U. S.

MATTHEWS, JOHN R., JR., Professor of Economics, College of William and Mary: INTERNATIONAL TRADE AND FINANCE

MEYER, EDWARD H., President and Chairman of the Board, Grey Advertising Inc.: ADVERTISING

MIDDLETON, DREW, Military Editor, *The New York Times:* OBITUARIES—*Anthony Eden*

MILLER, LUTHER S., Editor, *Railway Age:* TRANSPORTATION—*Railroads*

MITCHELL, GARY, Professor of Physics, North Carolina State University at Raleigh: PHYSICS

MODEL, PETER, Associate Professor, The Rockefeller University: GENETICS

NADLER, PAUL, Professor of Business Administration, Rutgers University; Author, *Commercial Banking in the Economy* and *Paul Nadler Writes About Banking:* BANKING

NEILL, R. F., Associate Professor of Economics, Carleton University, Ont.: CANADA—*The Economy*

NEWSOM, DONALD W., Professor and Head, Department of Horticulture, Louisiana State University: BOTANY; GARDENING AND HORTICULTURE

NIENABER, JEANNE, Assistant Professor, Department of Political Science, University of Arizona; Coauthor, *The Budgeting and Evaluation of Federal Recreation Programs:* ARIZONA

NOLAN, WILLIAM C., Associate Professor of Political Science, Southern Arkansas University: ARKANSAS

NORRIS, DAVID, London Journalist: ART—*The New Museum of London;* GREAT BRITAIN—*Queen Elizabeth's Silver Jubilee*

OCHSENWALD, WILLIAM L., Department of History, Virginia Polytechnic Institute; Coeditor, *Nationalism in a Non-National State:* SAUDI ARABIA

PALMER, NORMAN D., Professor of Political Science and South Asian Studies, University of Pennsylvania; Author, *Elections and Political Development: The South Asian Experience:* BIOGRAPHY—*Morarji Desai;* INDIA; SRI LANKA

PANO, NICHOLAS C., Associate Professor of History, Western Illinois University: ALBANIA

PARKER, FRANKLIN, Benedum Professor of Education, West Virginia University; Author, *Who Controls the Schools?* and *What Can We Learn From the Schools of China?;* Coeditor, series on *American Dissertations on Foreign Education: A Bibliography with Abstracts:* EDUCATION

PEARCE, JOHN B., Director, Environmental Assessment Division, Sandy Hook Marine Laboratory, National Oceanic and Atmospheric Administration: MARINE BIOLOGY

PEARSON, NEALE J., Associate Professor of Political Science, Texas Tech University: CHILE; PERU

PERKINS, KENNETH J., Assistant Professor of History, University of South Carolina: LIBYA; RELIGION—*Islam*

PHILLIPS, CHARLES F., JR., Professor of Economics, Washington and Lee University; Member, Commission on the Review of the National Policy Toward Gambling; Author, *The Economics of Regulation:* GAMBLING—*A Review of an Inherent Principle*

PHILLIPS, JACKSON, Executive Vice President, Moody's Investors Service, Inc.: UNITED STATES—*The Economy*

PIPPIN, LARRY L., Professor of Political Science, Elbert Covell College, University of the Pacific; Author, *The Remón Era:* ARGENTINA; PANAMA

PLATT, HERMANN K., Professor of History, St. Peter's College, Jersey City: NEW JERSEY

PLISCHKE, ELMER, Professor of Government and Politics, University of Maryland; Author, *Conduct of American Diplomacy* and *Microstates in World Affairs: Policy Problems and Options:* UNITED STATES—*Foreign Affairs*

POISTER, THEODORE H., Assistant Professor, Institute of Public Administration, and Research Associate, Pennsylvania Transportation Institute, Pennsylvania State University; Author, *Public Program Analysis: Applied Research Methods:* TRANSPORTATION—*Survey, Highways, Mass Transit, Shipping*

POLK, IRWIN J., Director of Children's Allergy Service, St. Luke's Hospital, New York City; Free-lance Medical Writer: MEDICINE AND HEALTH

POPKIN, HENRY, Professor of English, State University of New York at Buffalo: THEATER

PORTER, J. R., Professor, Department of Microbiology, College of Medicine, University of Iowa: MICROBIOLOGY

POULLADA, LEON B., Professor of Political Science, Northern Arizona University; Author, *Reform and Rebellion in Afghanistan:* AFGHANISTAN

PRINGLE, JAMES, Journalist, African Affairs: BIOGRAPHY—*Idi Amin;* TANZANIA; UGANDA; ZAIRE

PRITCHETT, C. HERMAN, Professor of Political Science, University of California, Santa Barbara: LAW—*The Supreme Court*

PUMPHREY, RALPH E., Professor of Social Work, Washington University, St. Louis; Coeditor, *The Heritage of American Social Work:* OLDER AMERICANS; SOCIAL WELFARE

QUIRK, WILLIAM H., North American Editor, *Construction Industry International* Magazine: ENGINEERING, CIVIL

RAGUSA, ISA, Research Art Historian, Department of Art and Archaeology, Princeton University: ART

RAYMOND, ELLSWORTH L., Professor of Politics, New York University; Author, *Soviet Economic Progress* and *The Soviet State:* UNION OF SOVIET SOCIALIST REPUBLICS

RICARD, FRANÇOIS, Associate Professor, Department of French Language and Literature, McGill University: LITERATURE—*Canadian: Quebec*

RICHARD, JOHN B., Department of Political Science, University of Wyoming; Author, *Government and Politics of Wyoming:* WYOMING

RICHMOND, ROBERT W., State Archivist, Kansas State Historical Society; Author, *Kansas: A Land of Contrasts:* KANSAS

RODRIGUEZ, ALFRED, Professor, Department of Modern and Classical Languages, University of New Mexico: LITERATURE—*Spanish* and *Spanish-American*

ROSE, ERNST, Professor Emeritus, New York University; Author, *A History of German Literature:* LITERATURE—*German*

ROSENBERG, SIMON W., Staff Dentist, Harvard Street Neighborhood Health Center, Dorchester, Mass.; Associate Visiting Dentist, Boston City Hospital: DENTISTRY—*A Vaccine Against Tooth Decay*

ROSS, RUSSELL M., Professor of Political Science, University of Iowa; Author, *Iowa Government and Administration:* IOWA

ROWLETT, RALPH M., Professor of Anthropology, University of Missouri, Columbia; Coauthor, *Neolithic Levels on the Titelberg:* ARCHAEOLOGY—*The Old World*

RUFF, NORMAN J., Assistant Professor of Political Science, University of Victoria, B. C.: BRITISH COLUMBIA

SAKURAI, EMIKO, Professor, Department of East Asian Languages, University of Hawaii: LITERATURE—*Japanese*

SALSINI, PAUL, State Editor, *The Milwaukee Journal:* WISCONSIN

SANDVIK, GLENN N., Reporter, *Duluth News-Tribune & Herald:* MINNESOTA

SAVAGE, DAVID, Lecturer, Department of English, Simon Fraser University, B. C.: LITERATURE—*Canadian: English*

SCHNEIDERMAN, RONALD A., Editor, *Consumer Electronics Daily:* TELECOMMUNICATIONS

SCHWAB, PETER, Associate Professor of Political Science, State University of New York, College at Purchase; Author, *Decision-Making in Ethiopia:* ETHIOPIA

SCOTT, EUGENE L., Publisher, *Tennis Week;* Author, *Tennis: Game of Motion* and *Racquetball: A Cult:* SPORTS—*Tennis*

SETH, R. P., Associate Professor, Mount Saint Vincent University, Halifax: NOVA SCOTIA

SHINN, RINN-SUP, Senior Research Scientist, Foreign Area Studies, The American University, Washington, D. C.; Coauthor, *Area Handbook for North Korea* and *Area Handbook for South Korea:* KOREA

SHOGAN, ROBERT, National Political Correspondent, Washington Bureau, *Los Angeles Times;* Author, *A Question of Judgment* and *Promises to Keep:* ELECTIONS—*United States;* UNITED STATES—*Domestic Affairs*

SIEGEL, STANLEY E., Professor of History, University of Houston; Author, *A Political History of the Texas Republic, 1836–1845:* HOUSTON; TEXAS

SIMMONS, MARC, Author, *New Mexico: A Bicentennial History* and *Spanish Government in New Mexico:* NEW MEXICO

SLOAN, HENRY, Associate Editor, *Current Biography:* BIOGRAPHY—*Rainer W. Fassbinder, David Frost, Alex Haley, Benjamin L. Hooks, Frank Press, Sylvester Stallone, Lily Tomlin;* OBITUARIES—Sir Charles Spencer ("Charlie") Chaplin

STERN, JEROME H., Associate Professor of English, Florida State University: LITERATURE—*American*

STOKES, W. LEE, Professor, Department of Geology and Geophysics, University of Utah; Author, *Essentials of Earth History* and *Introduction to Geology:* GEOLOGY

STOUDEMIRE, ROBERT H., Professor of Government and International Studies, University of South Carolina: SOUTH CAROLINA

STRINGER, JERRY R., Information Officer, Polar Information Service, Division of Polar Programs, National Science Foundation: POLAR RESEARCH

SYLVESTER, LORNA LUTES, Associate Editor, *Indiana Magazine of History,* Indiana University: INDIANA

TABORSKY, EDWARD, Professor of Government, University of Texas at Austin; Author, *Communism in Czechoslovakia, 1948–1960* and *Communist Penetration of the Third World:* CZECHOSLOVAKIA

TAFT, WILLIAM H., Professor of Journalism and Director of Graduate Studies, University of Missouri; Author, *American Journalism History:* PUBLISHING

TAN, CHESTER C., Professor of History, New York University; Author, *The Boxer Catastrophe* and *Chinese Political Thought in the 20th Century:* CHINA

TAYLOR, WILLIAM L., Associate Professor of History, Plymouth State College: NEW HAMPSHIRE

THEISEN, CHARLES W., Staff Writer, *The Detroit News:* MICHIGAN

THOMAS, JAMES D., Professor of Political Science, Bureau of Public Administration, The University of Alabama: ALABAMA

THOME, PITT G., Director, Weather, Climate and Environmental Quality Programs, Office of Application, National Aeronautics and Space Administration: SPACE EXPLORATION

TILMAN, JO H., Writer on Southeast Asia: MALAYSIA; SINGAPORE

TILMAN, ROBERT O., Professor of Political Science and Dean of the School of Liberal Arts, North Carolina State University; Author, *Man, State and Society in Contemporary Southeast Asia:* INDONESIA; MALAYSIA; SINGAPORE

TOWNE, CHARLES L., Former Associate Editor, *The Hartford Courant:* CONNECTICUT

TOWNE, RUTH W., Professor of History, Northeast Missouri State University; Author, *A Winner Never Quits: The Life and Times of Walter Harrington Kyle:* MISSOURI

TURNER, ARTHUR CAMPBELL, Professor of Political Science, University of California, Riverside: BIOGRAPHY—*Menahem Begin;* IRAN; IRAQ; ISRAEL; MIDDLE EAST

VALESIO, PAOLO, Professor of Italian, Yale University; Author, *Between Italian and French: The Fine Semantics of Active Versus Passive:* LITERATURE—*Italian*

VAN RIPER, PAUL P., Professor and Head, Department of Political Science, Texas A&M University; Author, *History of the United States Civil Service, The American Federal Executive,* and *Handbook of Practical Politics:* POSTAL SERVICE

VOLSKY, GEORGE, Center for Advanced International Studies, University of Miami: CUBA

WALL, JAMES M., Editor, *The Christian Century,* and President, The Christian Century Foundation; Author, *Church and Cinema* and *Three European Directors:* RELIGION—*Protestantism*

WALLOT, JEAN-PIERRE, Vice-Dean Academic, Faculty of Arts and Sciences, University of Montreal; Author, *Un Québec qui bougeait:* BIOGRAPHY—*René Lévesque;* MONTREAL; QUEBEC

WATTERS, ELSIE M., Director of Research, The Tax Foundation: TAXATION

WEBB, RICHARD E., Former Director, Reference and Library Division, British Information Services, New York: BIOGRAPHY—*Andrew Young;* UNITED NATIONS

WEEKS, JEANNE G., Member, American Society of Interior Designers; Coauthor, *Fabrics for Interiors:* INTERIOR DESIGN

WENTZ, RICHARD E., Chairman, Religious Studies Department, Arizona State University: RELIGION—*Survey, Far Eastern Religions*

WESTERN, JOE, Administrative Assistant and Press Secretary to U. S. Rep. Margaret M. Heckler, a member, U. S. House Agriculture Committee; formerly, Senior Editor, *The National Observer:* AGRICULTURE

WETMORE, WARREN C., Engineering Editor, *Aviation Week & Space Technology:* TRANSPORTATION—*Aviation, The Lindbergh Anniversary*

WILLARD, F. NICHOLAS, Department of History, Georgetown University: JORDAN; LEBANON; SYRIA

WILLIAMS, DENNIS A., Associate Editor, *Newsweek:* ETHNIC GROUPS

WILLIS, F. ROY, Professor of History, University of California, Davis; Author, *Europe in the Global Age* and *Italy Chooses Europe:* EUROPE

WIRTZ, WILLARD, Chairman, National Manpower Institute; Formerly, U. S. Secretary of Labor: LABOR—*Forced Retirement*

WOLF, WILLIAM, Film Critic, *Cue* Magazine; Lecturer, New York University; Author, *The Landmark Films* and *The Marx Brothers:* MOTION PICTURES; OBITUARIES—*Joan Crawford, Bing Crosby*

WOLINETZ, STEVEN B., Associate Professor of Political Science, Memorial University of Newfoundland; Author, *Party Realignment in the Netherlands:* NETHERLANDS

WOLMAN, M. GORDON, Professor of Geography, The Johns Hopkins University: WATER

WOODS, GEORGE A., Children's Books Editor, *The New York Times;* Author, *Vibrations* and *Catch a Killer:* LITERATURE—*Children's*

YANG, WINSTON L. Y., Professor of Chinese Studies, Seton Hall University, N. J.; Author, *Mao Tsung-kang:* BIOGRAPHY—*Teng Hsiao-p'ing*

YOSHIZAKI, HIROTAKA, Staff Reporter, Tokyo Bureau, *The New York Times:* TOKYO

YOUNG, ANDREW, U. S. Ambassador to the United Nations: FESTAC '77

YOUNGER, R. M., Author, *Australia and the Australians; Australia's Great River;* and *Australia! Australia! March to Nationhood:* AUSTRALIA; OCEANIA

ZABEL, ORVILLE H., Professor of History, Creighton University, Omaha: NEBRASKA

ZACEK, JOSEPH F., Professor of History, State University of New York at Albany: RUMANIA

INDEX

Main article headings appear in this index as bold-faced capitals; subjects within articles appear as lower-case entries. Both the general references and the subentries should be consulted for maximum usefulness of this index. Illustrations are indexed herein. Cross references are to the entries in this index.

A

AAMC: *see* Association of American Medical Colleges
ABC: *see* American Broadcasting Company
Abortions 156, 196, 290, 435
  Switzerland 477
Abu Dhabi 332
Academy Awards (films) 410
ACCIDENTS AND DISASTERS 68
  Earthquakes 220
  Transportation 500, 502, 504
Acheampong, Ignatius K. (Ghanaian gen., pol.) 227
Acholi (Afr. people) 509
Acid Protease Enzymes (biochem.) 114
Acrylonitrile (chem.) 147
Addiction, Drug: *see* Drug Addiction and Abuse
Addis Ababa, Eth. 54
Admiral's Cup Races 469
Adonis (asteroid) 105
Adrian, Edgar Douglas (Eng. physiol.) 376
ADVERTISING 69
  Lawyers' Fees 289
  Magazines 413
  Newspapers 414
Afars and Issas, French Territory of the: *see* Djibouti
AFDC: *see* Aid to Families with Dependent Children
Affirmative Action Programs (U.S.) 198
  Bakke Case 134, 178, 179
AFGHANISTAN 70
  Statistical Data 561 fol.
AFRICA 71
  Agriculture 79
  Anthropology 85
  Archaeology 87
  Cuba 166
  FESTAC '77 43
  France 217
  Third World 29, 31
  USSR 512
  United Nations 516
  United States 533
Afro-Americans: *see* Negroes, American
Age Discrimination in Employment Act (U.S.) 198
Aged: *see* Older Americans
Agency Shop (labor) 290
Agricultural Marketing Service (U.S.) 322
AGRICULTURE 77, 568
  American Agriculture Movement 159
  Chemicals 147
  Congress, U.S. 525
  Irrigation 54, 55
  Plant Genetics 129
  Prices 257
  World Food Supply 211
  See also specific crops; and articles on countries, provinces, and states
Agriculture, Department of (U.S.) 322, 558
Ahmed, Fakhruddin Ali (Indian pres.) 376
Aid to Families with Dependent Children (AFDC) 437
Air-Launched Cruise Missile 335, 336
Air Pollution 194
  Ozone Layer 147
Air Transportation 499, 500, 506
  Accidents 68
  Hijacking 224

Lindbergh Anniversary 501
  Meteorology 323
  SST Flights 196
Airbags, Automobile 161
Aircraft Industry 249
Airplane Crashes 68
Airplanes 335, 502
ALABAMA 80
  Shakespeare Festival 42
Alabama, University of 460
ALASKA 81
  Natural Gas 188
  Wilderness Preservation 197
Alaska, University of 81
Alaska Pipeline: *see* Trans-Alaska Pipeline System
Alaskan Wilderness Bill (U.S.) 81
ALBANIA 82
  Statistical Data 561 fol.
ALBERTA, prov., Can. 82
  Population 404
Alcan Gas Pipeline 81, 196, 499
ALCM: *see* Air-Launched Cruise Missile
Alcohol (bev.):
  Fetal Damage 320
Aleixandre, Vicente (Sp. poet) 309, 409
  Illus. 310
Aleutians, isls., Alas. 221
ALGERIA 83
  Egypt 182
  Statistical Data 561 fol.
  Illus. 35
Ali, Muhammad (Amer. Athl.) 448, 457
Alia (Jor. q.) 376
All Handicapped Children Act (U.S.) 178
All the President's Men (film) 350
Allahabad, India:
  Illus. 245
Alonso, Alicia (Cuban dancer) 169
  Illus. 171
Aluminum 570
Alves, Nito (Ang. pol.) 84
Alvin (submersible vessel) 385
  Illus. 385
Ambassadors, List of 554
Amchitka Island, Alas. 221
American Academy and Institute of Arts and Letters 297, 409, 410
American Academy of Poets 297
American Agriculture Movement 159
American Ballet Theater 172
American Broadcasting Company 482, 483
American Buffalo, play (Mamet) 492
American Convention on Human Rights 25
American Federation of Teachers 179
American Institute of Architects Research Corp. 90
American Library Association 300
American Literature 297
  Publishing 412
American Motors Corporation 109, 110
American Numismatic Association 158
American Numismatic Society 158
American Telephone & Telegraph Company 481
America's Cup Races 469
AMIN DADA, Idi (Ugandan pres.) 115, 509
Amino Acids (biochem.) 175

Amite County, Miss. 178
Amnesty International 92, 144, 291, 409
Amouzegar, Jamshid (Iran. premier) 263
Amtrak (National Railroad Passenger Corp.) 503
Amygdalin (drug) 320
Anaconda Company 342
Anchovy (fish) 395
Anderson, Eddie (Amer. act.) 376
Anderson, Philip W. (Amer. sci.) 409
Andreotti, Giulio (It. premier) 268
  Illus. 201
Andretti, Mario (Amer. auto racer) 449
Andrew (Brit. pr.) 228
Anglican Church in North America 425
Anglican Churches 426
  South Africa 181
  See also Episcopal Church
ANGOLA 72, 84
  Cuba 166
  Statistical Data 561 fol.
Animal and Plant Health Inspection Service (U.S.) 322
Animal Feed 330
Animals: *see* Livestock; Zoology
Anne (Brit. prin.) 228
Annie (musical) 354
  Illus. 497
Annie Hall (film) 345
Anniston Shakespeare Festival, Ala. 42
Antarctica 403
  Australia 107
ANTHROPOLOGY 85
Antigua 565
Antimony 570
Antiques, Prices of 96
Antisatellite System 338
Anti-Semitism:
  Argentina 92
Anti-Trust Laws 290
Antokolsky, Pavel (Sov. poet) 309
Apartheid 517
Apparel: *see* Clothing Industry; Fashion
Aquin, Hubert (Can. writ.) 303
Aquino, Benigno S. (Philipp. pol.) 396
Ara-A (drug) 319
Arab-Israeli Conflict 332
  Egypt 182
  Jordan 275
  Lebanon 293
  Libya 296
  Sadat's Visit to Jerusalem 334
  Syria 477
  Third World 31
  USSR 511
  United Nations 516, 517
  United States 533
Arab League 293
  Illus. 507
Archaeostronomy 85
ARCHAEOLOGY 85
  Borobudur, Indon. 428
Archery 470
ARCHITECTURE 89
  Prizes and Awards 409
Arctic 403
ARGENTINA 92, 285, 286
  Automobiles 109
  Bridges 192
  Chile 149
  Labor 283
  Literature 310
  Statistical Data 561 fol.
  Telephones 481
  USSR 512
Argo Merchant (ship) 504
ARIZONA 93, 193

ARKANSAS 94
Arkansas, University of 460
Arktika (Sov. icebreaker) 514
ARMS CONTROL AND DISARMAMENT 95
  SALT Negotiations 510, 511
  United States 530
Arms Sales 335
  Africa 72
  Austria to Syria 108
  South African Embargo 517, 533
  Turkish Embargo 508
ART 96
  Canada 142
  Prizes and Awards 409
Art Galleries: *see* Museums and Galleries
Artificial Sweeteners 147, 161, 213, 322
Aruba, isl., Carib. 144
Arvey, Jacob M. (Amer. pol.) 376
Asbestos 399, 570
ASEAN: *see* Association of Southeast Asian Nations
ASIA 103
  Agriculture 79
  Food 211
  Third World 31
  USSR 511
  United States 533
Askew, Reubin (Fla. gov.) 210
  Illus. 37
Assad, Hafez al- (Syr. pres.) 477, 478
  Illus. 333
Association of American Medical Colleges 179
Association of American Publishers 297
Association of Southeast Asian Nations 103, 272
Associations List of 577
Asteroids (astron.) 105
Astronauts (Cosmonauts) 441
ASTRONOMY 105
  Space Exploration 442
Atmosphere 323, 324
  Ozone Layer 147, 195
Atlanta, Ga.:
  Illus. 36
Atlantic City, N.J. 359
  Illus. 64
Atlantic-Richfield Company 342
Atomic Weapons: *see* Nuclear Weapons
Atwood, Margaret (Can. writ.) 303
Auctions, Art 96
Austin, Tracy (Amer. athl.) 467
AUSTRALIA 106
  Agriculture 79
  Automobiles 109
  Earthquake 221
  Indonesia 248
  Mining 339
  Oceania 383
  Population 564
  Statistical Data 561 fol.
  Taxation 480
  Telephones 481
AUSTRIA 108
  Automobiles 109
  Kolnbrein Dam 193
  Literature 307
  Statistical Data 561 fol.
  Telephones 481
Auto Racing 449
Automobile License Plates 289
AUTOMOBILES 109, 502, 569
  Airbags and Seat Belts 161
  Cities, Decline of 47
  Emission Standards 194, 525
  Gasoline-Mileage Standards 191
  Industrial Review 249
  Korea 254